THE 1991 ELIAS BASEBALL ANALYST

SEYMOUR SIWOFF, STEVE HIRDT,
TOM HIRDT & PETER HIRDT

A FIRESIDE BOOK • Published by Simon & Schuster
New York London Toronto Sydney Tokyo Singapore

FIRESIDE
Simon & Schuster Building
Rockefeller Center
1230 Avenue of the Americas
New York, New York 10020

Designed by Bonni Leon
Manufactured in the United States of America

10 9 8 7 6 5 4 3 2 1

ISBN 0-671-73325-7

CONTENTS

I—INTRODUCTION ix

II—TEAM SECTION 1

American League
Baltimore Orioles 3
Boston Red Sox 7
California Angels 11
Chicago White Sox 15
Cleveland Indians 19
Detroit Tigers 23
Kansas City Royals 27
Milwaukee Brewers 31
Minnesota Twins 35
New York Yankees 39
Oakland Athletics 43
Seattle Mariners 47
Texas Rangers 51
Toronto Blue Jays 55

National League
Atlanta Braves 59
Chicago Cubs 63
Cincinnati Reds 67
Houston Astros 71
Los Angeles Dodgers 75
Montreal Expos 79
New York Mets 83
Philadelphia Phillies 87
Pittsburgh Pirates 91
St. Louis Cardinals 95
San Diego Padres 99
San Francisco Giants 103

III—BATTER SECTION 107

American League Batters 109
National League Batters 193

IV—PITCHER SECTION 259

American League Pitchers 261
National League Pitchers 317

V—RANKINGS SECTION 365

Batting Rankings 366
Pitching Rankings 380

VI—SINGLE SEASON AND CAREER LEADERS 393

Batting Leaders 394
Pitching Leaders 402

VII—BALLPARKS 409

American League 411
National League 414
Ballpark Effects 416

VIII—THE 1961 YANKEES 421

ACKNOWLEDGMENTS

In recognition of the invaluable assistance provided by so many of our colleagues, the authors would like to thank the following:

The rest of the Elias Sports Bureau staff: Rocky Avakian, John Carson, Jay Chesler, John Chymczuk, Keung Hui, Frank Labombarda, John Labombarda, Santo Labombarda, Chris Lasch, Bob Rosen, Alex Stern, Christopher Thorn, Gil Traub, and Bob Waterman. Chris Thorn and Chris Lasch have done some truly remarkable work with our computers, without which so much of the research contained in this book would have been impossible. The Labombarda brothers, Bob Waterman, Alex Stern, and John Chymczuk repeatedly provided painstaking research on a moment's notice, and at all hours of the day and night, throughout the production process.

Our agent, Nat Sobel, Craig Holden, and the rest of the staff.

At Americomp, Jim Bristol.

At Simon & Schuster: Charlie and Farley, Gypsy da Silva, Suzanne Donahue, Stuart Gottesman, Bonni Leon, Tim McGuire, Eve Metz, Jay Schweitzer, George Turianski, and our editor, Jeff Neuman. It's been a pleasure to work once again with Jeff after a three-year hiatus. No one outside Elias has had a greater impact on the *Analyst* than Jeff Neuman. He helped us shape the original concept seven years ago and greatly influenced the new format in this seventh edition. Jeff has proven to us again how indispensable a truly great editor can be.

INTRODUCTION

Six years ago, the first edition of *The Elias Baseball Analyst* reflected our guess as to what it was about baseball that fans would want to know but couldn't find elsewhere. We came up with a format that let us address major issues for all teams and players, provided a table of previously unavailable statistics for each player to identify his strengths and weaknesses, and included several sections of rankings to add perspective to those statistics.

In later editions we added other features, like the Ballparks Section and Batter-Pitcher Matchups. But the format of the book remained essentially the same, and for a very simple reason: based on your response, it was apparent that you liked it that way. Well, the bad news is that this year's *Analyst* has undergone a major overhaul. The good news is that our seventh edition is by far the best in the series and one that we know you will savor.

First, you will notice that the front half of the book—the team section—has been redesigned, creating room for longer essays on key issues facing each club. But that enhancement is minor compared with those in the Batter and Pitcher Sections, where the comments on each player have tripled in length, and there is a section of miscellaneous statistics that introduces many new items, such as directional hitting, base running tendencies, and fielding statistics for batters, and detailed relief pitching statistics and opponents' base stealing for pitchers.

For those readers frustrated to find only a single individual opponent whom each player loves and hates to face in past editions, as many as six opponents are now listed. We have also provided a new breakdown in the statistics grid for each batter, showing his performance against ground-ball and fly-ball pitchers (or, for pitchers, against ground- and fly-ball hitters). As usual, we've tried to include in the actual player comments a blend of the illuminating, the surprising, the bizarre, and—of course—the downright quirky. (Be honest—where else would you discover that Pete Incaviglia is about to pass Lou Gehrig on the all-time strikeout list, although in about one-third the number of games?)

Due to the overwhelming response to our historical section on the 1969 Mets two years ago, we have reprised the concept with a detailed look at Roger Maris's home-run record and the 1961 Yankees. (If our New York chauvinism is showing a little, bear with us; the material is fascinating.) You'll be amazed at some of our findings, especially with regard to Maris's assault on Babe Ruth's mark, as we use contemporary tools to analyze the events of 30 years ago in the kind of detail that wasn't possible back then. Think of it as our version of an archaeological dig.

We have also restored the Rankings Section to its original full length, although the categories have been changed to include those that are most frequently used. (Goodbye, Top and Bottom 20 in Opponents' Home Run Percentage with the Bases Empty; hello, full listing—from top to bottom—in Batting Average with 2 Outs and Runners on Base.)

Our thanks to all of you who took the time to let us know how to improve the *Analyst*. We hope you find the new-and-improved model to your liking.

TEAM SECTION

The Team Section consists of comments and statistics for each of the twenty-six major-league teams. The examples here are taken from the 1990 season.

The first of three tables that follow the essay for each team is the Won-Lost Record by Starting Position chart. This chart lists, for each player on a team, the team's won-lost record in games started by that player at each position, and in the leadoff and cleanup spots in the batting order. In addition, the number of games started by each player against left-handed and right-handed pitchers is listed. The players are listed alphabetically.

WON-LOST RECORD BY STARTING POSITION

Baltimore Orioles	C	1B	2B	3B	SS	LF	CF	RF	DH	P	Leadoff	Cleanup	Starts vs. LH	Starts vs. RH	Total Starts
Jay Aldrich	-	-	-	-	-	-	-	-	-	-	-	-	-	-	-
Brady Anderson	-	-	-	-	-	17-18	11-8	0-1	4-1	-	10-11	-	11	49	32-28
Jeff Ballard	-	-	-	-	-	-	-	-	-	6-11	-	-	5	12	6-11
Jose Bautista	-	-	-	-	-	-	-	-	-	-	-	-	-	-	-
Juan Bell	-	-	-	-	-	-	-	-	-	-	-	-	-	-	-

Below this chart are the team's batting and pitching totals in a variety of categories and breakdowns. These breakdowns are explained in the introductory text to the Batter Section (see page 107) and the Pitcher Section (see page 259). To see how each team stacks up against the overall totals for its league, compare its totals to the league stat summaries on the next page.

American League

	AB	H	2B	3B	HR	RBI	BB	SO	BA	SA	OBA
Season	76800	19900	3559	460	1796	9154	7631	12689	.259	.388	.327
vs. Left-Handers	23970	6365	1158	143	607	2980	2427	3965	.266	.402	.333
vs. Right-Handers	52830	13535	2401	317	1189	6174	5204	8724	.256	.381	.325
vs. Ground-Ballers	34352	9087	1551	190	712	4152	3275	5265	.265	.383	.330
vs. Fly-Ballers	42448	10813	2008	270	1084	5002	4356	7424	.255	.391	.325
Home Games	37453	9844	1817	247	896	4620	3918	6133	.263	.396	.334
Road Games	39347	10056	1742	213	900	4534	3713	6556	.256	.379	.321
Grass Fields	54657	14031	2431	298	1309	6478	5542	9165	.257	.384	.326
Artificial Turf	22143	5869	1128	162	487	2676	2089	3524	.265	.397	.330
April	8916	2279	423	48	220	1075	919	1450	.256	.388	.327
May	13085	3351	603	78	335	1560	1272	2150	.256	.391	.323
June	13363	3524	656	79	327	1589	1288	2245	.264	.398	.329
July	13485	3516	628	83	335	1646	1340	2178	.261	.394	.329
August	13568	3535	603	85	291	1617	1321	2201	.261	.382	.327
Sept./Oct.	14383	3695	646	87	288	1667	1491	2465	.257	.374	.329
Leading Off Inn.	18533	4686	861	101	446	446	1595	2947	.253	.382	.316
Bases Empty	43327	10957	2008	244	1043	1043	3941	7215	.253	.383	.319
Runners On	33473	8943	1551	216	753	8111	3690	5474	.267	.394	.338
Runners/Scor. Pos.	19135	4957	873	134	405	7077	2623	3377	.259	.382	.342
Runners On/2 Out	14190	3563	599	99	314	3218	1698	2428	.251	.374	.335
Scor. Pos./2 Out	9151	2232	383	64	187	2819	1284	1636	.244	.361	.342
Late-Inning Pressure	11053	2738	445	60	227	1181	1192	2077	.248	.360	.322
Leading Off	2760	634	107	6	54	54	263	514	.230	.332	.300
Runners On	4723	1216	182	33	100	1054	591	873	.257	.373	.338
Runners/Scor. Pos.	2718	663	106	19	55	923	455	545	.244	.358	.348

RUNS BATTED IN	From 1B	From 2B	From 3B	Scoring Position
Percentage	4.8%	18.1%	41.3%	26.4%

Miscellaneous statistics: Ground outs-to-air outs ratio: 1.11. Leaders in batter comments are based on 200 plate appearances. . . . Grounded into 1844 double plays in 16,402 opportunities (one per 8.9). Leaders are based on 40 opportunities. . . . Drove in 2433 of 4382 runners from third base with less than two outs (56%). Leaders are based on 15 opportunities. . . . Base running: Advanced from first base to third on 1429 of 4130 outfield singles (35%); scored from second on 1690 of 2311 (73%). Leaders are based on 10 opportunities. . . . Assists per nine innings: first basemen, 0.72; second basemen, 3.08; shortstops, 3.04; third basemen, 2.00. Putouts per nine innings: left fielders, 2.11; center fielders, 2.70; right fielders, 2.16. Leaders are based on 500 innings played. . . . Opposing base stealers: 1503-for-2286 (66%). Leaders are based on 50 attempts.

National League

	AB	H	2B	3B	HR	RBI	BB	SO	BA	SA	OBA
Season	65968	16917	2967	405	1521	7650	6221	11164	.256	.383	.321
vs. Left-Handers	24400	6290	1141	145	574	2835	2269	3945	.258	.387	.321
vs. Right-Handers	41568	10627	1826	260	947	4815	3952	7219	.256	.380	.321
vs. Ground-Ballers	33161	8635	1470	194	706	3840	3019	5418	.260	.380	.323
vs. Fly-Ballers	32807	8282	1497	211	815	3810	3202	5746	.252	.385	.319
Home Games	32226	8350	1443	201	746	3862	3148	5294	.259	.386	.326
Road Games	33742	8567	1524	204	775	3788	3073	5870	.254	.380	.317
Grass Fields	33375	8758	1439	180	860	4076	3026	5713	.262	.394	.324
Artificial Turf	32593	8159	1528	225	661	3574	3195	5451	.250	.372	.318
April	7681	1942	322	41	161	847	734	1311	.253	.368	.319
May	10950	2897	504	66	278	1332	998	1822	.265	.399	.327
June	11522	3015	527	79	299	1424	1137	1969	.262	.399	.329
July	11161	2820	495	68	249	1298	1036	1910	.253	.376	.316
August	11851	3047	529	71	247	1285	1070	1953	.257	.376	.320
Sept./Oct.	12803	3196	590	80	287	1464	1246	2199	.250	.375	.317
Leading Off Inn.	16078	4127	714	93	409	409	1288	2542	.257	.389	.315
Bases Empty	37910	9436	1667	213	898	898	3163	6474	.249	.375	.310
Runners On	28058	7481	1300	192	623	6752	3058	4690	.267	.393	.336
Runners/Scor. Pos.	16655	4274	751	115	358	5907	2321	3071	.257	.380	.341
Runners On/2 Out	12123	2964	519	80	233	2635	1545	2233	.244	.358	.334
Scor. Pos./2 Out	8085	1900	345	54	152	2347	1270	1581	.235	.347	.343
Late-Inning Pressure	9966	2524	387	49	205	1058	1072	1793	.253	.364	.327
Leading Off	2511	644	98	11	63	63	229	424	.256	.380	.323
Runners On	4267	1091	165	21	71	924	546	773	.256	.354	.338
Runners/Scor. Pos.	2525	619	87	14	44	821	441	496	.245	.343	.351

RUNS BATTED IN	From 1B	From 2B	From 3B	Scoring Position
Percentage	5.1%	17.3%	40.2%	25.5%

Miscellaneous statistics: Ground outs-to-air outs ratio: 1.09. Leaders in batter comments are based on 200 plate appearances. . . . Grounded into 1233 double plays in 13,227 opportunities (one per 8.9). Leaders are based on 40 opportunities. . . . Drove in 2015 of 3659 runners from third base with less than two outs (55%). Leaders are based on 15 opportunities. . . . Base running: Advanced from first base to third on 1198 of 3364 outfield singles (36%); scored from second on 1324 of 1891 (70%). Leaders are based on 10 opportunities. . . . Assists per nine innings: first basemen, 0.75; second basemen, 2.92; shortstops, 2.91; third basemen, 1.96. Putouts per nine innings: left fielders, 2.13; center fielders, 2.69; right fielders, 2.14. Leaders are based on 500 innings played. . . . Opposing base stealers: 1787-for-2514 (71%). Leaders are based on 50 attempts.

American League

	W-L	ERA	AB	H	HR	BB	SO	BA	SA	OBA
Season	1133-1133	3.91	76800	19900	1796	7631	12689	.259	.388	.327
vs. Left-Handers			30234	7883	591	3165	4425	.261	.378	.331
vs. Right-Handers			46566	12017	1205	4466	8264	.258	.394	.325
vs. Ground-Ballers			36082	9379	583	3389	5535	.260	.366	.324
vs. Fly-Ballers			40718	10521	1213	4242	7154	.258	.407	.330
Home Games	604-529	3.74	39347	10056	900	3713	6556	.256	.379	.321
Road Games	529-604	4.08	37453	9844	896	3918	6133	.263	.396	.334
Grass Fields	809-809	3.87	54657	14031	1309	5542	9165	.257	.384	.326
Artificial Turf	324-324	3.99	22143	5869	487	2089	3524	.265	.397	.330
April	132-132	3.90	8916	2279	220	919	1450	.256	.388	.327
May	193-193	3.92	13085	3351	335	1272	2150	.256	.391	.323
June	196-196	3.94	13363	3524	327	1288	2245	.264	.398	.329
July	197-197	3.95	13485	3516	335	1340	2178	.261	.394	.329
August	200-200	3.92	13568	3535	291	1321	2201	.261	.382	.327
Sept./Oct.	215-215	3.81	14383	3695	288	1491	2465	.257	.374	.329
Leading Off Inn.			18533	4686	446	1595	2947	.253	.382	.316
Bases Empty			43327	10957	1043	3941	7215	.253	.383	.319
Runners On			33473	8943	753	3690	5474	.267	.394	.338
Runners/Scor. Pos.			19135	4957	405	2623	3377	.259	.382	.342
Runners On/2 Out			14190	3563	314	1698	2428	.251	.374	.335
Scor. Pos./2 Out			9151	2232	187	1284	1636	.244	.361	.342
Late-Inning Pressure			11053	2738	227	1192	2077	.248	.360	.322
Leading Off			2760	634	54	263	514	.230	.332	.300
Runners On			4723	1216	100	591	873	.257	.373	.338
Runners/Scor. Pos.			2718	663	55	455	545	.244	.358	.348
First 9 Batters			39143	10016	856	4165	7087	.256	.378	.329
Second 9 Batters			20308	5300	496	1828	3076	.261	.393	.324
All Batters Thereafter			17349	4584	444	1638	2526	.264	.403	.329

Miscellaneous statistics: Ground outs-to-air outs ratio: 1.11. Leaders in pitcher comments are based on 400 batters faced. . . . Grounded into 1844 double plays in 16,402 opportunities (one per 8.9). Leaders are based on 100 innings pitched. . . . Allowed 2494 first-inning runs in 4532 starts (4.49 ERA). . . . Batting support: 4.30 runs per start. . . . Stranded 4574 inherited runners, allowed 2444 to score (65%). Leaders are based on 25 inherited runners. . . . Opposing base stealers: 1503-for-2286 (66%). Leaders are based on 10 attempts.

National League

	W-L	ERA	AB	H	HR	BB	SO	BA	SA	OBA
Season	972-972	3.79	65968	16917	1521	6221	11164	.256	.383	.321
vs. Left-Handers			28956	7607	610	3127	4720	.263	.385	.335
vs. Right-Handers			37012	9310	911	3094	6444	.252	.381	.311
vs. Ground-Ballers			30521	7647	424	2657	5477	.251	.348	.312
vs. Fly-Ballers			35447	9270	1097	3564	5687	.262	.413	.329
Home Games	527-445	3.63	33742	8567	775	3073	5870	.254	.380	.317
Road Games	445-527	3.96	32226	8350	746	3148	5294	.259	.386	.326
Grass Fields	486-486	3.99	33375	8758	860	3026	5713	.262	.394	.324
Artificial Turf	486-486	3.59	32593	8159	661	3195	5451	.250	.372	.318
April	114-114	3.66	7681	1942	161	734	1311	.253	.368	.319
May	160-160	3.92	10950	2897	278	998	1822	.265	.399	.327
June	168-168	4.10	11522	3015	299	1137	1969	.262	.399	.329
July	166-166	3.76	11161	2820	249	1036	1910	.253	.376	.316
August	173-173	3.57	11851	3047	247	1070	1953	.257	.376	.320
Sept./Oct.	191-191	3.72	12803	3196	287	1246	2199	.250	.375	.317
Leading Off Inn.			16078	4127	409	1288	2542	.257	.389	.315
Bases Empty			37910	9436	898	3163	6474	.249	.375	.310
Runners On			28058	7481	623	3058	4690	.267	.393	.336
Runners/Scor. Pos.			16655	4274	358	2321	3071	.257	.380	.341
Runners On/2 Out			12123	2964	233	1545	2233	.244	.358	.334
Scor. Pos./2 Out			8085	1900	152	1270	1581	.235	.347	.343
Late-Inning Pressure			9966	2524	205	1072	1793	.253	.364	.327
Leading Off			2511	644	63	229	424	.256	.380	.323
Runners On			4267	1091	71	546	773	.256	.354	.338
Runners/Scor. Pos.			2525	619	44	441	496	.245	.343	.351
First 9 Batters			34987	8768	753	3511	6550	.251	.369	.320
Second 9 Batters			16573	4274	377	1487	2663	.258	.387	.320
All Batters Thereafter			14408	3875	391	1223	1951	.269	.412	.327

Miscellaneous statistics: Ground outs-to-air outs ratio: 1.09. Leaders in pitcher comments are based on 400 batters faced. . . . Grounded into 1233 double plays in 13,227 opportunities (one per 8.9). Leaders are based on 100 innings pitched. . . . Allowed 2208 first-inning runs in 3888 starts (4.66 ERA). . . . Batting support: 4.20 runs per start. . . . Stranded 3122 inherited runners, allowed 1674 to score (65%). Leaders are based on 25 inherited runners. . . . Opposing base stealers: 1787-for-2514 (71%). Leaders are based on 10 attempts.

BALTIMORE ORIOLES

- **Cleaning up their biggest flaw.**
- **How well does power travel?**

Maybe it was the extra air traffic over the Northeast corridor. Or perhaps there was some infighting between Dancer and Prancer that led to a longer-than-expected trip. It could be that after all these years, he's just getting senile. Whatever the reason, Santa was a tad late getting to Baltimore this past winter—about sixteen days late, to be exact. But when he finally arrived, the jolly old elf brought Orioles fans exactly what they had asked for: a proven cleanup hitter and legitimate 30-home-run threat who could take over the role left vacant since Eddie Murray was traded two years earlier. And so, on January 10, the Orioles acquired Glenn Davis.

Rarely has an offseason acquisition so suitably addressed a team's primary weakness. Nine American League teams finished with better won-lost records than the Orioles last season, primarily because they finished 11th in the league in scoring with an average of only 4.16 runs per game. But it wasn't for lack of baserunners that the Orioles didn't score; buoyed by a major league–leading total of 660 walks, the Orioles' on-base average was a respectable .330, sixth in the league. The problem was getting those runners home: Baltimore stranded 7.64 baserunners per game, the highest rate in the league.

You don't have to look far to determine where the shortfall of runs occurred. It was in the number-four hole, emphasis on *hole*, in the Orioles' batting order. You know that enthusiastic "Oh!" with which Baltimore fans greet the final verse of the national anthem? It could also describe the production of the cleanup hitters.

The popular baseball thinking is that the players batting in the first two lineup positions are table-setters, and that the cleanup hitter is the guy who is supposed to drive them in. For once, we're not going to show anything here to challenge that conventional wisdom; leadoff hitters do score the most runs in the majors (with second-place hitters ranking second), and cleanup hitters do drive in the most runs. Below are the averages of runs scored and runs batted in per team, broken down by lineup position, in the major leagues last season:

	American League Runs	American League RBI	National League Runs	National League RBI
1st	97.5	59.4	106.8	54.8
2d	87.9	71.3	96.8	69.2
3d	84.9	88.5	88.5	90.7
4th	83.3	99.6	89.3	105.6
5th	80.9	79.0	78.0	91.8
6th	72.6	70.1	65.5	70.9
7th	64.4	72.5	61.5	63.0
8th	64.6	60.8	54.1	53.1
9th	60.1	52.6	40.6	31.6

On average, American League cleanup hitters had 11 more runs batted in than players in the next-highest A.L. lineup slot, while National League cleanup hitters had 15 more RBIs. Fourteen major-league teams got 100 or more runs batted in from their cleanup hitters, compared to only ten 100-RBI contributions from all the other lineup slots combined. (The breakdown of the latter: the Cubs had 103 RBIs from their number-two spot; the Dodgers, Royals, A's, Rangers, and Blue Jays got 100 or more RBIs from the three-hole; the Pirates, Padres, and Giants reached triple figures from their fifth-place hitters, and the Mets had 100 RBIs from the number-six hitters.)

Baltimore manager Frank Robinson tried six different players in the cleanup spot last season. Mickey Tettleton had 71 starts there, followed in frequency by Sam Horn (35), Cal Ripken (19), Joe Orsulak (16), Randy Milligan (13), and Ron Kittle (seven). That might have been the worst casting since Katharine Hepburn tested for the role of Scarlett O'Hara. The Orioles and the Yankees were the only teams in the majors to have as many as five players with 10 or more starts batting cleanup. (In 1960, it was a compliment to be keeping statistical company with the Yankees; in 1990, to paraphrase Robert Preston, it meant you had trouble with a capital "T" that rhymes with "P" that stands for "power.")

The Orioles' cleanup hitters won the Triple Crown last year—for poor performance, that is, and not only in their own league but in the major leagues as a whole. They had the lowest batting average, the fewest home runs, and the fewest runs batted in among each team's number-four hitters. They also had the lowest slugging average, the fewest hits, and the fewest extra-base hits in the majors. OK, we exaggerate; they were actually *tied* for the fewest extra-base hits with Montreal. The details:

Lowest Batting Average		Lowest Slugging Average	
Orioles	.222	**Orioles**	.369
Yankees	.237	Mariners	.398
Padres	.239	Expos	.404
Fewest Hits		**Fewest Extra-Base Hits**	
Orioles	128	**Orioles**	50
Padres	145	Expos	50
Athletics	148	Blue Jays	52
Fewest Home Runs		**Fewest Runs Batted In**	
Orioles	16	**Orioles**	78
Expos	17	Yankees	79
Three teams	18	Indians	91

The only category in which their cleanup hitters ranked high was the one that comes as a mixed blessing: walks. Baltimore's cleanup hitters walked 116 times, the most in the majors, but there's a school of baseball thought that says that cleanup hitters should hit, not walk; a cleanup hitter, who should be the hitter in the lineup capable of producing the most runs, shouldn't pass that responsibility to the next guy in the lineup unnecessarily. But Baltimore's cleanup hitters succeeded in turning the run-producing spot in the batting order into a table-setting position. They came to bat 210 times with runners in scoring position and drew 47 walks. Meanwhile, when they weren't walking, Baltimore's number-four hitters batted only .219 with runners in scoring position, another major-league low. And as suggested by the team's 11th-place standing in runs and their LOB leadership, this left a critical void in the offense.

But there seem to be happier days ahead. In Davis, the Orioles now have the quintessential cleanup hitter. In the four seasons in the majors in which he has had at least 500 at-bats, he has averaged more than 30 home runs and 95 runs batted in. Last year, he was leading the National League with 19 home runs when he suffered an injured rib cage in mid-June. Even though he eventually spent more than two months on the disabled list, he finished the season with 22 home runs and 64 RBIs in only 327 at-bats, an average of one homer every 14.9 at-bats. For good reason, Davis hasn't been penciled into a starting lineup anywhere but the cleanup spot since July 3, 1988, 315 starts ago.

For a home-run hitter, a move from the Astrodome to Baltimore's Memorial Stadium means going from the worst home-run park in the majors to one of the best. As shown in the rankings in the Ballparks Section on page 416, the Astrodome has retarded home-run production by more than 33 percent over the past five seasons, while Memorial Stadium has helped home runs by nearly 11 percent. Some quick math indicates that Davis might have about 30 more home runs to his credit had he played his entire career to this point in Baltimore rather than in Houston.

Last season, Davis's home-run breakdown was extreme, which serves to underscore the point. He hit only four homers in 175 at-bats in the Dome, but had 18 in 152 at-bats in other National League parks. Among players with at least 10 road homers in a season, that's the highest road home-run rate in the 16 years we've been keeping the statistic. The top five:

	Road Games		
	AB	HR	AB/HR
Glenn Davis, 1990	152	18	8.44
Mark McGwire, 1987	279	28	9.96
Mike Schmidt, 1979	289	29	9.97
George Foster, 1977	319	31	10.29
Reggie Jackson, 1980	258	25	10.32

Because of injuries, Davis played in only 43 of the Astros' 81 road games, so we'll never know if he could have challenged the all-time records for road home runs, but he clearly had a shot at them: Babe Ruth hit 32 away from his House in 1927, and Foster's 31 in 1977 stands as the National League standard.

Now let's get to the issue of changing uniforms. Do home-run hitters who have been traded or who left their teams through free agency flourish or flounder in their first season in a new city?

There have been 125 players in major-league history who started seasons with new teams following years in which they hit 20 or more home runs. The list starts with Ruth himself, who was dealt by the Red Sox to the Yankees after belting a major-league record 29 home runs in the 1919 season. The most recent 20-homer hitters to make an offseason move were Joe Carter, Nick Esasky, and Dave Parker, each of whom changed teams after the 1989 season.

Only 29 of the 125 players hit more home runs in the succeeding season than they had the year before. Here's the breakdown, both with regard to the year-to-year change in total home runs and the change in home runs per at-bat:

	Increased	Same	Decreased
Total HRs	29 (23%)	5 (4%)	91 (73%)
HR Rate	37 (30%)	0	88 (70%)

But of course Davis is not just changing teams, he is changing leagues as well. Different hitting backgrounds, different teammates, different hotels, and, most importantly, different opposing pitchers. (For a further look at just who owns the advantage when a particular hitter faces a particular pitcher for the first time, see the Astros essay on page 71.) Going back to our group of 125 home-run hitters who changed teams, we extracted the 49 of them who had changed leagues as well as teams following a 20-home-run season. As measured by total home runs and home-run rate, we found the number of players making a successful transition to the new league to be reduced on both counts:

	Increased	Same	Decreased
Total HRs	7 (14%)	2 (4%)	40 (82%)
HR Rate	12 (24%)	0	37 (76%)

Here are the seven players who hit 20 or more home runs in a season and then, after moving to the other league between seasons, increased that total the next year:

Willie Kirkland	1960 Giants (21)	1961 Indians (27)
Frank Robinson	1965 Reds (33)	1966 Orioles (49)
Dick Allen	1971 Dodgers (23)	1972 White Sox (37)
Reggie Smith	1973 Red Sox (21)	1974 Cardinals (23)
Bobby Bonds	1974 Giants (21)	1975 Yankees (32)
Richie Zisk	1976 Pirates (21)	1977 White Sox (30)
Kirk Gibson	1987 Tigers (24)	1988 Dodgers (25)

Because of his two months on the disabled list, Davis's total of 22 home runs last season was artificially low, so he might indeed join this list in 1991. But whether Davis makes the list or not is not the point of this exercise; the point is to show that a change of leagues has a negative effect on home-run hitters, and that this effect must be taken into account when projecting how many homers Davis might hit this summer. One further caution: The last time that the Orioles traded for an Astros first baseman was in 1975, when Lee May did the Houston-to-Baltimore thing. May, like Davis, was a proven home-run hitter; he had seven consecutive 20-home-run seasons under his belt. But in his first season in the American League, May's home-run production fell from 24 homers in 556 at-bats with Houston in 1974 to 20 in 580 at-bats with Baltimore in 1975.

Will the change-of-league effect again be strong enough to offset the change-of-ballpark effect in Davis's case? Stay tuned.

What does the arrival of Davis do to Randy Milligan, who hit 20 home runs last season? Most likely, one of them will wind up as the DH, an abbreviation that came to mean "doesn't hit" in Baltimore last summer. Orioles designated hitters batted only .211, an average that takes its place on the list of the worst team batting averages by designated hitters since that fiendish rule was established in 1973:

Texas, 1988	.197
Oakland, 1987	.203
Minnesota, 1981	.208
Seattle, 1985	.211
Baltimore, 1990	.211

A look at who was responsible for the Orioles' weak DH showing reveals a couple of familiar suspects. Although Frank Robinson wrote in every name but his own in the DH spot—the Orioles started a league-high 15 players in that role—the assignment went most frequently to Sam Horn (59 starts) and Mickey Tettleton (39 starts), the two guys who also contributed to the team's poor production in the cleanup position.

With one key trade, the Orioles seem to have properly remedied the weaknesses in last year's offense. Given the vagaries of baseball economics, however, the question now becomes, "For how long?" If the team is successful in getting Davis's signature on a long-term contract, Robinson will be able to get his lineup cards mass-produced with the names of Davis and Ripken already in place. And one day, when the Orioles are leading the league in runs, he might even have trouble remembering the days when his cleanup hitters were the worst in the league. Maybe.

WON-LOST RECORD BY STARTING POSITION

Baltimore Orioles	C	1B	2B	3B	SS	LF	CF	RF	DH	P	Leadoff	Cleanup	Starts vs. LH	Starts vs. RH	Total Starts
Jay Aldrich	-	-	-	-	-	-	-	-	-	-	-	-	-	-	-
Brady Anderson	-	-	-	-	-	17-18	11-8	0-1	4-1	-	10-11	-	11	49	32-28
Jeff Ballard	-	-	-	-	-	-	-	-	-	6-11	-	-	5	12	6-11
Jose Bautista	-	-	-	-	-	-	-	-	-	-	-	-	-	-	-
Juan Bell	-	-	-	-	-	-	-	-	-	-	-	-	-	-	-
Danny H. Boone	-	-	-	-	-	-	-	-	-	0-1	-	-	-	1	0-1
Phil Bradley	-	-	-	-	-	34-34	-	-	-	-	30-28	-	25	43	34-34
Marty Brown	-	-	-	0-1	-	-	-	-	0-2	-	-	-	2	1	0-3
Mike Devereaux	-	-	-	-	-	-	42-51	-	0-1	-	5-6	-	47	47	42-52
Steve Finley	-	-	-	-	-	3-5	17-20	31-34	-	-	29-29	-	21	89	51-59
Dave Gallagher	-	-	-	-	-	4-8	0-2	1-0	-	-	1-8	-	13	2	5-10
Leo Gomez	-	-	-	9-3	-	-	-	-	-	-	-	-	5	7	9-3
Rene Gonzales	-	-	11-14	2-1	-	-	-	-	-	-	-	-	10	18	13-15
Pete Harnisch	-	-	-	-	-	-	-	-	-	14-17	-	-	11	20	14-17
Kevin Hickey	-	-	-	-	-	-	-	-	-	-	-	-	-	-	-
Chris Hoiles	5-1	2-4	-	-	-	-	-	-	2-4	-	-	-	10	8	9-9
Brian Holton	-	-	-	-	-	-	-	-	-	-	-	-	-	-	-
Sam Horn	-	5-4	-	-	-	-	-	-	31-28	-	-	17-18	-	68	36-32
Tim Hulett	-	-	3-8	13-10	-	-	-	-	2-2	-	-	-	15	23	18-20
Stan Jefferson	-	-	-	-	-	-	-	1-4	-	-	0-1	-	4	1	1-4
Dave W. Johnson	-	-	-	-	-	-	-	-	-	16-13	-	-	13	16	16-13
Ron Kittle	-	0-2	-	-	-	-	-	-	4-6	-	-	2-5	9	3	4-8
Brad Komminsk	-	-	-	-	-	0-1	6-4	7-9	-	-	-	-	23	4	13-14
Ben McDonald	-	-	-	-	-	-	-	-	-	10-5	-	-	4	11	10-5
Jeff McKnight	-	7-5	1-2	-	-	1-2	-	0-2	-	-	-	-	10	10	9-11
Bob Melvin	32-38	-	-	-	-	-	-	-	1-3	-	-	-	51	23	33-41
Jose Mesa	-	-	-	-	-	-	-	-	-	5-2	-	-	3	4	5-2
Bob Milacki	-	-	-	-	-	-	-	-	-	11-13	-	-	9	15	11-13
Randy Milligan	-	47-49	-	-	-	-	-	-	4-5	-	-	6-7	36	69	51-54
John Mitchell	-	-	-	-	-	-	-	-	-	8-9	-	-	6	11	8-9
Donell Nixon	-	-	-	-	-	2-2	-	-	1-1	-	1-2	-	4	2	3-3
Gregg Olson	-	-	-	-	-	-	-	-	-	-	-	-	-	-	-
Joe Orsulak	-	-	-	-	-	15-15	-	35-35	2-2	-	-	9-7	16	88	52-52
Joe W. Price	-	-	-	-	-	-	-	-	-	-	-	-	-	-	-
Billy Ripken	-	-	61-61	-	-	-	-	-	-	-	-	-	43	79	61-61
Cal Ripken	-	-	-	-	76-85	-	-	-	-	-	-	9-10	56	105	76-85
Curt Schilling	-	-	-	-	-	-	-	-	-	-	-	-	-	-	-
David Segui	-	14-18	-	-	-	-	-	-	1-3	-	-	-	10	26	15-21
Texas Mike Smith	-	-	-	-	-	-	-	-	-	-	-	-	-	-	-
Dorn Taylor	-	-	-	-	-	-	-	-	-	-	-	-	-	-	-
Anthony Telford	-	-	-	-	-	-	-	-	-	4-4	-	-	2	6	4-4
Mickey Tettleton	39-46	1-3	-	-	-	-	-	1-0	19-20	-	-	33-38	38	91	60-69
Jay Tibbs	-	-	-	-	-	-	-	-	-	2-8	-	-	2	8	2-8
Greg Walker	-	-	-	-	-	-	-	-	4-6	-	-	-	-	10	4-6
Mickey Weston	-	-	-	-	-	-	-	-	-	0-2	-	-	1	1	0-2
Mark Williamson	-	-	-	-	-	-	-	-	-	-	-	-	-	-	-
Craig Worthington	-	-	-	52-70	-	-	-	-	1-1	-	-	-	45	79	53-71

TEAM TOTALS: BATTING

	AB	H	2B	3B	HR	RBI	BB	SO	BA	SA	OBA
Season	5410	1328	234	22	132	623	660	962	.245	.370	.330
vs. Left-Handers	1717	416	82	6	47	187	193	285	.242	.379	.318
vs. Right-Handers	3693	912	152	16	85	436	467	677	.247	.366	.335
vs. Ground-Ballers	2428	597	110	7	44	277	282	419	.246	.351	.328
vs. Fly-Ballers	2982	731	124	15	88	346	378	543	.245	.385	.331
Home Games	2610	613	113	12	74	300	333	495	.235	.372	.322
Road Games	2800	715	121	10	58	323	327	467	.255	.368	.337
Grass Fields	4545	1108	192	19	110	518	557	820	.244	.367	.328
Artificial Turf	865	220	42	3	22	105	103	142	.254	.386	.337
April	686	161	25	4	11	72	101	141	.235	.331	.333
May	902	212	47	5	22	115	115	152	.235	.371	.329
June	968	260	43	3	26	114	120	160	.269	.400	.351
July	946	243	38	5	32	128	124	165	.257	.409	.344
August	893	209	33	4	16	91	103	160	.234	.334	.314
Sept./Oct.	1015	243	48	1	25	103	97	184	.239	.363	.307
Leading Off Inn.	1301	313	59	4	37	37	138	210	.241	.377	.319
Bases Empty	3023	727	139	9	90	90	328	511	.240	.382	.319
Runners On	2387	601	95	13	42	533	332	451	.252	.355	.343
Runners/Scor. Pos.	1359	330	53	7	28	484	232	269	.243	.354	.350
Runners On/2 Out	1029	252	45	7	20	226	168	196	.245	.361	.355
Scor. Pos./2 Out	681	158	25	3	16	206	120	129	.232	.348	.351
Late-Inning Pressure	850	202	27	2	28	94	115	148	.238	.373	.329
Leading Off	214	41	4	0	8	8	29	25	.192	.322	.294
Runners On	350	84	6	2	7	73	54	73	.240	.329	.338
Runners/Scor. Pos.	176	44	4	1	4	66	39	38	.250	.352	.374

RUNS BATTED IN	From 1B	From 2B	From 3B	Scoring Position
Totals	74/1804	193/1086	224/600	417/1686
Percentage	4.1%	17.8%	37.3%	24.7%

TEAM TOTALS: PITCHING

	W-L	ERA	AB	H	HR	BB	SO	BA	SA	OBA
Season	76-85	4.04	5479	1445	161	537	776	.264	.409	.328
vs. Left-Handers			2558	693	66	267	340	.271	.412	.338
vs. Right-Handers			2921	752	95	270	436	.257	.407	.320
vs. Ground-Ballers			2573	663	55	229	347	.258	.380	.317
vs. Fly-Ballers			2906	782	106	308	429	.269	.435	.338
Home Games	40-40	3.80	2788	706	82	263	415	.253	.391	.317
Road Games	36-45	4.28	2691	739	79	274	361	.275	.428	.340
Grass Fields	65-71	3.95	4630	1203	139	461	676	.260	.405	.326
Artificial Turf	11-14	4.53	849	242	22	76	100	.285	.433	.342
April	9-11	3.92	695	173	21	74	86	.249	.386	.322
May	12-15	4.16	910	243	28	86	127	.267	.411	.330
June	13-15	3.72	959	261	26	89	134	.272	.423	.332
July	17-11	3.88	944	241	29	79	151	.255	.410	.311
August	9-18	4.70	918	253	35	104	138	.276	.453	.347
Sept./Oct.	16-15	3.87	1053	274	22	105	140	.260	.371	.325
Leading Off Inn.			1314	340	42	119	167	.259	.412	.323
Bases Empty			3124	804	85	290	446	.257	.399	.322
Runners On			2355	641	76	247	330	.272	.423	.336
Runners/Scor. Pos.			1333	339	39	180	212	.254	.396	.332
Runners On/2 Out			989	242	24	128	172	.245	.373	.334
Scor. Pos./2 Out			637	153	13	95	117	.240	.361	.339
Late-Inning Pressure			785	203	22	94	135	.259	.387	.336
Leading Off			196	46	3	23	29	.235	.301	.318
Runners On			333	94	14	48	63	.282	.456	.367
Runners/Scor. Pos.			204	51	10	38	46	.250	.446	.359
First 9 Batters			2911	744	75	295	491	.256	.387	.323
Second 9 Batters			1424	386	43	127	167	.271	.427	.329
All Batters Thereafter			1144	315	43	115	118	.275	.443	.342

BOSTON RED SOX

- **Hub fans—bid curse adieu!**
- **Pitching pays, even in Fenway.**

For Red Sox fans who spent the winter eating fistfuls of Prozac to ease the ache of a four-game sweep by Oakland in the League Championship Series, we have two words: Grow up. Enough about the "Curse of the Bambino," and the never-ending litany of could've-beens. Feeling sorry for yourself because you've had to endure a World Series loss and two Championship Series sweeps in the past five years? There are a few thousand Indians fans we'd like to introduce to you.

The results haven't always been as hoped for, but over the years few teams have provided their fans with as many late-season and postseason thrills as the Red Sox have. Last season was no exception—a September-plus that began with Boston basking in the glory of three consecutive shutout victories over the Blue Jays in Toronto (the first time since 1962 that Boston had pitched three shutouts in a row), and ended with a nail-biting showdown and ultimate victory over the Jays that provided some of the most entertaining baseball we've seen. In retrospect, Boston's near collapse in mid-September only heightened the final-week drama. But, oh, the whining that oozed from despairing Sox fans during that time. You'd have thought they'd spent the season watching the Patriots.

Five days after its triple triumph in Toronto, Boston started the month of September with a lead of 6½ games, a significant cushion for this reason: Since divisional play began, only one team had blown a lead that large during September. Of course, the comfort of history had a cutting edge: The team that blew that six-and-a-half-game lead was the Red Sox—to the hated Yankees, no less, in 1978. So when the Blue Jays caught Boston on September 18, erasing the first five months of the season and creating a two-week pennant race, the outcry was sadly predictable: Red Sox fans bemoaned their team's lack of character. They cited as evidence demoralizing losses in the 1986 and 1988 postseasons and a pattern of blowing division leads after the All-Star break. The five second-half division leads blown by Boston over an 11-year period:

Year	Largest Lead	Latest Lead	Champion
1972	1.5 games (Sept. 30)	Oct. 1	Detroit
1974	7 games (Aug. 23)	Sept. 8	Baltimore
1977	3.5 games (Aug. 18)	Aug. 22	New York
1978	10.5 games (July 8)	Oct. 1	New York
1982	5 games (June 29)	Aug. 2	Milwaukee

Let's get real. Even among those seasons, the Red Sox twice played well enough throughout the second half to win their division (40–29 and 46–26 after the All-Star breaks in 1972 and 1977, respectively), only to lose to better teams. More to the point, Boston has now led the A.L. East at some point after the All-Star break in three of the past eight seasons, and has won the division title every time. Not bad for a supposedly gutless team.

Sure, Boston's seven-game loss to the Mets in the 1986 Series was frustrating after winning the first two games in New York; it was downright agonizing after being within a strike of the championship. But it was also respectable, given that the 1986 Mets posted the decade's best record in the National League—as did the 1975 Reds during the 1970s and the 1967 Cardinals during the 1960s before defeating Boston in their two prior Series appearances. Bad timing, sure, but hardly a mystical event, or a symptom of a team without character. (And Sox fans conveniently forgot that the gutless '86 team itself rallied from match point—one strike from elimination against California in the A.L.C.S.) Similarly, two playoff sweeps in three years at the hands of Oakland hardly represents an embarrassment, given that the A's, at least before visiting Cincinnati, were acclaimed as one of the best teams of our generation.

But, for the sake of argument, what if those failures of the past 20 years did constitute a lack of character? The 1990 Red Sox bore surprisingly little resemblance to the team whose fortunes trickled through Bill Buckner's legs only four Octobers earlier, let alone to the dinosaurs of the 1970s. Because several highly visible players have spent their entire major-league careers in Boston, it's easy to see no further than Dwight Evans, Wade Boggs, Roger Clemens, Mike Greenwell, and Marty Barrett. But no other Red Sox players were on the postseason roster in both 1986 and 1990. Beantown loyalists may find it difficult to exorcise the ghosts of past failures, but the Red Sox players who lost to Oakland last fall deserve the right to create their own history, for better or worse. Why malign Jody Reed, Carlos Quintana, and Dana Kiecker for the failures of predecessors like Rick Burleson, George Scott, and Bob Stanley?

On balance, we think Boston's head-to-head victory over Toronto for the A.L. East title in the season's final days should more than compensate for a quick playoff loss to a dominant Oakland team. It's interesting to note that only eight of the 84 races during the 21 years of divisional play were decided by the margin of the season series between the first- and second-place teams. One was the 1990 A.L. East race, decided by Boston's 10–3 margin over the team it had to beat, Toronto. That's hardly the mark of a team that can't win the big one.

So it's hard to feel much sympathy for those who perpetuate the myth that it's the uniform, and not the players wearing it, that defines Boston's history of futility—at least as they perceive it. Twenty years of exciting baseball is in no way futility, no matter which way the ball bounces in the final frame. Boston fans' inability to appreciate that fact may be the Bambino's real curse.

Think of the Red Sox, and you think offense. As Boston's personnel changed over the past half century, its profile remained constant. From the time Ted Williams made his major-league debut in 1939, the Red Sox ranked in the top half of the American League in scoring 44 times in 50 years. Williams begat Yaz, and Yaz begat Rice, and Rice begat Greenwell. But regardless of its cast of characters, Boston could always light up the scoreboard. Unfortunately, so could its opponents. During that same 50-year period, Boston ranked in the bottom half of the A.L. in runs allowed 37 times.

Over the past few years, several changes became apparent. The influence of former Red Sox hitting instructor Walt Hriniak manifested itself in higher batting averages and lower home-run and strikeout rates. In fact, in 1989 Boston became the first team in this century to lead the majors in batting average for a third consecutive season; last season, the Sox made it four in a row, the longest streak since Adam first hit fungoes to Eve. For the first three years of that streak, the exchange of power for batting-average points had a positive effect—Boston ranked fourth in the American League in scoring in 1987, and led the league in 1988 and 1989. But last year, with Nick Esasky gone and Dwight Evans nearing retirement, Boston hit only 106 home runs to rank 12th among the 14 A.L. teams (its lowest standing since a 9th-place finish in a 10-team league in 1961). That precipitated a sharp decline in scoring: The Red Sox averaged 4.3 runs per game, to rank seventh in the American League. But in a reversal of roles, for only the second time in the past 35 years Boston ranked higher in pitching than in hitting. Red Sox opponents scored 4.1 per game, the 4th-lowest rate in the league.

Of course, a large part of Boston's perennially high ranks in scoring and low ranks in pitching has been Fenway Park. From 1982 through 1990, Fenway Park inflated scoring by 9 percent compared to other American League stadiums. Had the Red Sox played their home games, for example, in the Oakland Coliseum, they certainly would have ranked lower in scoring throughout the years, regardless of their personnel. So what does that say about the 1990 team, which ranked only 7th in the league in scoring even with the aid of Fenway? We thought you'd never ask.

Last season, Boston ranked three slots better in pitching than hitting, its greatest disparity in that direction since 1936. That gap would have been far wider had Boston played in almost any other ballpark. To express those ranks in a way that cancels the effect of Fenway Park, we have resurrected the concept of park-neutral statistics, last seen in the sixth edition of *The Baseball Encyclopedia*.

Obviously, the reason that Fenway Park skews Red Sox statistics to such an extent is that Boston plays half its games there, or more than ten times as many as in any other A.L. stadium. To consider only road-game statistics would overcompensate for the problem; Boston would be penalized because it doesn't play *any* road games at Fenway Park. Park-neutral statistics include a small slice of a team's home games along with its road-game statistics to approximate a schedule that is divided equally among all stadiums.

The following table shows how Boston ranked in both batting (runs per game) and pitching (runs allowed per game) over the past nine seasons, both by the conventional measure and by park-neutral statistics. As expected, the park-neutral statistics indicate that the Red Sox's offense hasn't been nearly as potent as it seemed throughout the period—that over the past 10 years, Boston's offense and defense were often comparable, despite the Fenway-induced illusion that its offense was perennially better. And for the 1990 season, Boston's offense was among the league's worst, made only cosmetically acceptable by the Fenway illusion:

Conventional	**1981**	**1982**	**1983**	**1984**	**1985**	**1986**	**1987**	**1988**	**1989**	**1990**
Batting	1	6	7	2	3	3	4	1	1	7
Pitching	13	8	10	12	7	4	11	7	10	4

Park-Neutral	**1981**	**1982**	**1983**	**1984**	**1985**	**1986**	**1987**	**1988**	**1989**	**1990**
Batting	3	10	9	4	4	3	5	6	5	12
Pitching	12	3	9	6	5	3	12	5	11	5

Somewhat obscured in that maze of numbers is a trend of enormous importance for the Red Sox: The team has performed far better when its pitching is at least as good as its hitting. That applies not only to the past 10 years, but throughout a 24-year survey that includes the Red Sox's five most recent championship teams. The following table shows where Boston ranked in the A.L. in runs scored ("B") and runs allowed ("P"), adjusted to neutralize the Fenway Park scoring bias, and where the Red Sox finished in the standings ("S"):

Year	**B**	**P**	**S**	**Year**	**B**	**P**	**S**	**Year**	**B**	**P**	**S**	**Year**	**B**	**P**	**S**
1967	3	2	1	1973	5	2	2	1979	6	4	3	1985	4	5	5
1968	2	8	4	1974	6	3	3	1980	6	4	4	1986	3	3	1
1969	4	9	3	1975	3	3	1	1981	3	12	5	1987	5	12	5
1970	4	5	3	1976	6	4	3	1982	10	3	3	1988	6	5	1
1971	7	7	3	1977	6	2	2	1983	9	9	6	1989	5	11	3
1972	3	11	2	1978	3	3	2	1984	4	6	4	1990	12	5	1

When Boston's pitchers ranked at least as high as its hitters, the team finished significantly higher in the standings than when the opposite was true:

	Total	Position in Standings 1st	2d	3d	4th	5th	6th
Batting ranks higher	9	0	1	3	2	3	0
Batting & pitching equal	5	2	1	1	0	0	1
Pitching ranks higher	10	3	2	4	1	0	0

Boston won five division or league titles over the past 24 years, but none in the nine seasons in which its pitching ranked lower than its hitting after adjusting for the park factor. The Red Sox finished first or second only once in nine hitting-dominant seasons, but in eight of 15 other years.

That's the good news: Boston has fashioned a pitching-dominant team, a profile that has a successful track record at Fenway Park. On the other hand, that dominance is the product of another kind of illusion, attributable as much to the team's low ranking in batting as to its high ranking in pitching. Additionally, considering the tenuous nature of last season's staff, the Sox may actually find it easier to rebuild their offense than to coax comparable seasons from last year's collection of overachieving pitchers, especially with Mike Boddicker vacating the number-two starter spot. Greg Harris, Dana Kiecker, and Jeff Gray all contributed far more than even the most optimistic Sox watchers might have hoped for. Can they do it again? Ask us in October. But one thing's for sure: Even at their best, Kiecker and Harris aren't Hurst and the Can. Boston's free-agent additions, Matt Young and Danny Darwin—an 18-game loser and a 35-year-old coming off a career year—may be extensions of the puzzle, not solutions to it. And the questions surrounding Roger Clemens's sore shoulder and erratic behavior late last season created doubts throughout the winter.

Having lost Nick Esasky and Dwight Evans in consecutive seasons, the Red Sox will try to restore punch to their offense with the newly acquired Jack Clark and a pair of promising but untested rookies, Mo Vaughn and Phil Plantier. Equally essential will be a major contribution from a healthy Mike Greenwell. (A peek at his performance over the last three months of 1990 on page 136 should soothe the worn nerves of many Red Sox fans.)

The A.L. East won't remain without a dominant team forever. For the last several years, while the division was generally considered Toronto's to win or lose, the Red Sox have managed three division titles—thanks largely to their strong pitching staffs. Now, with the rest of the division apparently mired in mediocrity, Boston may have had a chance to become the team to step forward—or, like Curly in that old Three Stooges skit, at least to hold its ground while the others stepped back. But while Toronto has made bold steps toward solving what they saw as their major weaknesses, the Sox are headed back in the direction of the bashing teams of decades past, which produced homers by the bushelful but only a trickle of championships.

WON-LOST RECORD BY STARTING POSITION

Boston Red Sox	C	1B	2B	3B	SS	LF	CF	RF	DH	P	Leadoff	Cleanup	Starts vs. LH	Starts vs. RH	Total Starts
Larry Andersen	-	-	-	-	-	-	-	-	-	-	-	-	-	-	-
Marty Barrett	-	-	22-24	-	-	-	-	-	-	-	1-0	-	14	32	22-24
Mike Boddicker	-	-	-	-	-	-	-	-	-	22-12	-	-	15	19	22-12
Wade Boggs	-	-	-	83-69	-	-	-	-	1-2	-	48-42	-	50	105	84-71
Tom Bolton	-	-	-	-	-	-	-	-	-	9-7	-	-	2	14	9-7
Tom Brunansky	-	-	-	-	-	-	-	63-55	3-2	-	-	34-31	41	82	66-57
Bill Buckner	-	3-5	-	-	-	-	-	-	-	-	-	-	-	8	3-5
Ellis Burks	-	-	-	-	-	-	82-61	-	2-4	-	1-1	39-31	51	98	84-65
Roger Clemens	-	-	-	-	-	-	-	-	-	22-9	-	-	6	25	22-9
Scott Cooper	-	-	-	-	-	-	-	-	-	-	-	-	-	-	-
John Dopson	-	-	-	-	-	-	-	-	-	3-1	-	-	-	4	3-1
Dwight Evans	-	-	-	-	-	-	-	-	68-53	-	-	8-6	44	77	68-53
Wes Gardner	-	-	-	-	-	-	-	-	-	3-6	-	-	3	6	3-6
Rich Gedman	2-4	-	-	-	-	-	-	-	-	-	-	-	-	6	2-4
Jeff Gray	-	-	-	-	-	-	-	-	-	-	-	-	-	-	-
Mike Greenwell	-	-	-	-	-	86-71	-	-	-	-	-	6-4	48	109	86-71
Greg A. Harris	-	-	-	-	-	-	-	-	-	15-15	-	-	11	19	15-15
Danny Heep	-	3-1	-	-	-	-	-	3-5	2-2	-	-	1-0	-	16	8-8
Joe Hesketh	-	-	-	-	-	-	-	-	-	0-2	-	-	1	1	0-2
Eric Hetzel	-	-	-	-	-	-	-	-	-	2-6	-	-	5	3	2-6
Daryl Irvine	-	-	-	-	-	-	-	-	-	-	-	-	-	-	-
Dana Kiecker	-	-	-	-	-	-	-	-	-	12-13	-	-	9	16	12-13
Randy Kutcher	-	-	0-3	4-2	-	-	3-2	4-4	-	-	-	-	7	15	11-11
Dennis Lamp	-	-	-	-	-	-	-	-	-	0-1	-	-	-	1	0-1
Rick Lancellotti	-	2-0	-	-	-	-	-	-	-	-	-	-	-	2	2-0
John Leister	-	-	-	-	-	-	-	-	-	0-1	-	-	-	1	0-1
Mike Marshall	-	2-5	-	-	-	-	-	5-3	8-6	-	-	-	8	21	15-14
John Marzano	14-9	-	-	-	-	-	-	-	-	-	-	-	9	14	14-9
Rob Murphy	-	-	-	-	-	-	-	-	-	-	-	-	-	-	-
Tim Naehring	-	-	-	1-3	9-10	-	-	-	-	-	0-2	-	9	14	10-13
Jim Pankovits	-	-	-	-	-	-	-	-	-	-	-	-	-	-	-
Tony Pena	72-61	-	-	-	-	-	-	-	-	-	-	-	44	89	72-61
Phil Plantier	-	-	-	-	-	-	-	-	1-2	-	-	-	-	3	1-2
Carlos Quintana	-	73-60	-	-	-	-	-	0-1	-	-	-	0-1	52	82	73-61
Jeff Reardon	-	-	-	-	-	-	-	-	-	-	-	-	-	-	-
Jerry Reed	-	-	-	-	-	-	-	-	-	-	-	-	-	-	-
Jody Reed	-	-	66-47	-	18-20	-	-	-	0-1	-	37-29	-	48	104	84-68
Luis Rivera	-	-	-	-	61-44	-	-	-	-	-	1-0	-	35	70	61-44
Billy Jo Robidoux	-	5-3	-	-	-	-	-	-	2-2	-	-	-	-	12	7-5
Mike Rochford	-	-	-	-	-	-	-	-	-	0-1	-	-	1	-	0-1
Kevin Romine	-	-	-	-	-	2-3	3-11	13-6	1-0	-	-	0-1	17	22	19-20
Lee Smith	-	-	-	-	-	-	-	-	-	-	-	-	-	-	-
Jeff Stone	-	-	-	-	-	-	-	-	-	-	-	-	-	-	-

TEAM TOTALS: BATTING

	AB	H	2B	3B	HR	RBI	BB	SO	BA	SA	OBA
Season	5516	1502	298	31	106	660	598	795	.272	.395	.344
vs. Left-Handers	1772	496	99	11	32	223	178	258	.280	.402	.346
vs. Right-Handers	3744	1006	199	20	74	437	420	537	.269	.392	.343
vs. Ground-Ballers	2343	680	117	11	35	306	241	309	.290	.394	.358
vs. Fly-Ballers	3173	822	181	20	71	354	357	486	.259	.396	.334
Home Games	2723	794	174	15	61	373	306	397	.292	.434	.364
Road Games	2793	708	124	16	45	287	292	398	.253	.358	.324
Grass Fields	4690	1314	267	28	96	596	530	663	.280	.410	.354
Artificial Turf	826	188	31	3	10	64	68	132	.228	.309	.287
April	639	173	32	0	13	74	81	83	.271	.382	.354
May	881	224	45	6	14	91	94	128	.254	.367	.328
June	968	279	59	8	19	125	111	121	.288	.425	.360
July	983	266	62	5	16	105	97	152	.271	.393	.336
August	1002	285	41	4	23	140	107	146	.284	.402	.355
Sept./Oct.	1043	275	59	8	21	125	108	165	.264	.396	.332
Leading Off Inn.	1302	330	67	4	28	28	127	182	.253	.376	.324
Bases Empty	2948	789	158	15	63	63	305	434	.268	.396	.340
Runners On	2568	713	140	16	43	597	293	361	.278	.395	.349
Runners/Scor. Pos.	1438	390	71	11	27	541	213	226	.271	.392	.358
Runners On/2 Out	1088	297	60	6	19	252	121	170	.273	.392	.347
Scor. Pos./2 Out	687	180	30	5	14	230	100	118	.262	.381	.358
Late-Inning Pressure	819	237	39	7	13	92	93	135	.289	.402	.362
Leading Off	200	46	10	0	3	3	21	36	.230	.325	.309
Runners On	382	111	20	5	6	85	45	64	.291	.416	.362
Runners/Scor. Pos.	188	52	7	2	4	74	38	32	.277	.399	.389

RUNS BATTED IN	From 1B	From 2B	From 3B	Scoring Position
Totals	69/1928	208/1149	277/666	485/1815
Percentage	3.6%	18.1%	41.6%	26.7%

TEAM TOTALS: PITCHING

	W-L	ERA	AB	H	HR	BB	SO	BA	SA	OBA
Season	88-74	3.72	5517	1439	92	519	997	.261	.370	.327
vs. Left-Handers			2590	685	36	247	381	.264	.364	.329
vs. Right-Handers			2927	754	56	272	616	.258	.375	.325
vs. Ground-Ballers			2620	656	30	210	434	.250	.339	.309
vs. Fly-Ballers			2897	783	62	309	563	.270	.398	.343
Home Games	51-30	3.54	2825	743	44	241	514	.263	.367	.324
Road Games	37-44	3.91	2692	696	48	278	483	.259	.373	.330
Grass Fields	77-61	3.79	4721	1236	83	444	867	.262	.371	.328
Artificial Turf	11-13	3.29	796	203	9	75	130	.255	.364	.321
April	11-8	3.75	646	159	8	64	124	.246	.345	.320
May	12-14	3.98	868	230	20	81	142	.265	.392	.330
June	20-9	3.36	996	251	17	70	187	.252	.369	.301
July	12-17	4.25	985	283	14	101	157	.287	.407	.356
August	19-9	2.74	966	234	14	91	192	.242	.329	.310
Sept./Oct.	14-17	4.25	1056	282	19	112	195	.267	.371	.340
Leading Off Inn.			1334	333	26	107	218	.250	.364	.308
Bases Empty			3055	758	56	264	536	.248	.361	.311
Runners On			2462	681	36	255	461	.277	.381	.345
Runners/Scor. Pos.			1470	408	19	181	305	.278	.375	.353
Runners On/2 Out			1007	235	11	123	202	.233	.319	.325
Scor. Pos./2 Out			683	161	7	96	139	.236	.313	.337
Late-Inning Pressure			902	227	21	89	168	.252	.377	.322
Leading Off			230	60	5	14	40	.261	.370	.309
Runners On			380	102	9	47	66	.268	.400	.350
Runners/Scor. Pos.			226	63	4	33	44	.279	.389	.370
First 9 Batters			2826	763	54	293	537	.270	.390	.340
Second 9 Batters			1428	345	19	109	264	.242	.336	.298
All Batters Thereafter			1263	331	19	117	196	.262	.364	.329

CALIFORNIA ANGELS

- **The way of their errors.**
- **thirtyeverything.**

The California Angels began their 30th season in the American League with high hopes—well, as high as your hopes can be when you're in the same division with the reigning world champions coming off the most decisive World Series sweep in history. Still, the 1989 Angels, in their first season under Doug Rader, had finished with a 91–71 record and had pressed the best team in baseball hard into September. They trailed Oakland by only two and one-half games with 10 games to play, but then tailed off at the end and finished in third place, eight games behind.

In looking to 1990, Rader seemed to own an excess of the one commodity that everyone else wanted: starting pitching. The Angels had cut their runs allowed by 25 percent from 1988 to 1989, the 10th-largest trimming in the history of the league. Bert Blyleven, Chuck Finley, and Kirk McCaskill all had ERAs below 3.00 in 1989, the first time that any American League team had three regular starters below the Big Three-(point)-Oh since the DH rule was introduced in 1973. They also had another pair of left-handers who made opposing managers drool: Jim Abbott, who went 12–12 in 1989 after jumping from the University of Michigan to the Olympics to the majors, and Mark Langston, the top prize in the previous winter's free agent beauty pageant. They had so much starting pitching that veteran Mike Witt, who had thrown at least 220 innings for the Angels for six straight seasons, started the 1990 season in the bullpen and would be traded to the Yankees in May.

Every regular starter for the '89 team that challenged the Athletics was returning in 1990: Lance Parrish, Wally Joyner, Johnny Ray, Jack Howell, Dick Schofield, Chili Davis, Devon White, Claudell Washington, and Brian Downing. They were a good defensive group, made better with the addition of Dante Bichette, who would make 88 starts in the outfield. Bichette started the season as if he would surpass Magic Johnson's Southland record for assists; he had five in his first six games and had accumulated nine assists to go with four home runs just a month into the season.

So things were looking up, and after Langston and Witt pitched a combined no-hitter against Seattle in the Angels' third game of the season, the sky seemed to be the limit. But the limit turned out to be sea level; the Halos finished with a record of 80–82, and continued their strange inability to put two consistent seasons together. They have finished above the .500 mark 10 times in their history, but on only two of those occasions did they finish above .500 again the following season.

The pitching and defense, supposed strengths, turned sour. Far from a beauty, Langston couldn't have won Mr. Congeniality after finishing 10–17 with a 4.40 ERA. And two of his rotationmates, Abbott (4.51) and Blyleven (5.24), had even higher ERAs than Langston. Despite an All-Star season from Finley (18–9, 2.40), the Angels allowed 128 more runs than they had the previous season. No other team in the American League saw its runs allowed jump by even 90 runs.

In contrast with the starting pitchers, four of whom had at least 29 starts (the other, Blyleven, had 23), the position players were constantly in a state of flux. Injuries, position changes, and unfulfilled expectations led to season-long changes in the starting lineup. Only two Angels hitters (Lance Parrish, 523, and Devon White, 503) accumulated the 502 plate appearances necessary to qualify for the batting title, the fewest such players on any team in the major leagues.

Another factor in the large increase in runs allowed was a strange malady contracted by the team collectively: the inability to catch baseballs cleanly and to throw them accurately. The scientific term is *baseballus butterfingus*, known in layman's language as Angels' Disease. Non-Californians have long warned that there would be a day of reckoning for the perfect climate and hedonistic lifestyle enjoyed by residents of Orange County. But no one expected that years of eating avocado, kiwifruit, and sun-dried tofu would manifest itself in such an unusual manner.

In 1989, the Angels committed only 96 errors, the second-lowest total in the league. Last season that number zoomed to 142, the second-highest in the league. In a season in which the 13 other American League teams committed 124 fewer errors than they had the previous year—a reduction of nearly 10 errors per team—and in which no other team's increase in errors reached double figures, the Angels' total increased by 46:

	1989	**1990**	**Diff.**
Oakland	129	87	−42
Toronto	127	86	−41
Chicago	151	124	−27
Seattle	143	130	−13
Milwaukee	155	149	− 6
Minnesota	107	101	− 6
Boston	127	123	− 4
Texas	136	133	− 3
Cleveland	118	117	− 1
Detroit	130	131	+ 1
New York	122	126	+ 4
Baltimore	87	93	+ 6
Kansas City	114	122	+ 8
California	96	142	+46

In the past 13 years, only one other major league team had a year-to-year error increase that large.

And who do you think it was? Right: from 1982 to 1983, the Angels increased their error total from 108 to 154, an identical increase of 46 errors.

Baseball's microbiologists feel that the Angels' performance in 1990, almost universally regarded as shabby and uninspired, may actually lead us a long way toward understanding the disease that carries their name. We know now, for instance, that it is likely to strike the Angels every seven years, and that it hits Southern California teams much more ferociously than teams in other parts of the country: The last non-Angels error increase of such magnitude was in 1977, when the San Diego Padres went from 141 to 189.

As we also learn from the following breakdown of errors, some positions are much more susceptible to the disease than others:

	1989 Angels	1990 Angels	1990 A.L. Avg.
Pitchers	14	16	14.1
Catchers	9	8	9.8
First Basemen	6	9	11.7
Second Basemen	16	14	13.4
Third Basemen	16	34	26.1
Shortstops	17	34	21.4
Left Fielders	6	13	7.8
Center Fielders	5	11	6.6
Right Fielders	7	3	7.9

The only 30/30 Club the Angels qualified for was for errors by the left side of the infield. No other team last season reached 30 errors at each of those positions. The 1990 error totals for the Angels' third basemen and shortstops:

1989 Third Basemen

	Innings	Errors
Howell	1210	11
Hoffman	137.1	2
Rose	80	2
Anderson	27	1

1990 Third Basemen

	Innings	Errors
Howell	817	17
Schu	271	8
Hill	137	5
Anderson	127	3
Coachman	76	1
Rose	26	0

1989 Shortstops

	Innings	Errors
Schofield	774.2	7
Anderson	563.1	9
Hoffman	115.1	1
Disarcina	1	0

1990 Shortstops

	Innings	Errors
Schofield	865.1	17
Anderson	233	5
Hill	158.1	3
Disarcina	125	4
McLemore	61.1	4
Howell	11	1

Over the past 50 years, with the strike seasons of 1972 and 1981 excluded, only one other team had as large a one-year increase in errors by its left-side infielders. That team, the Milwaukee Brewers of 1975, was coming off a season in which its third baseman, Don Money, had set an all-time major league record with only five errors in 157 games. In 1975, when Money committed 14 errors and shortstop Robin Yount's total rose from 19 to 44, the Brewers' left-side total jumped from 36 to 78.

What makes the Angels an unlikely team to commit so many errors is that Anaheim Stadium, we kid you not, is a difficult park in which to make errors. As you know, for a number of years we've ranked stadiums by various kinds of influence they have on the game. For example, over the past five years, Wrigley Field was the best park for scoring runs, the Kingdome was the best for hitting home runs, and Tiger Stadium had the worst effect on batting averages. Well, Anaheim Stadium's claim to fame (O.K., we might have a warped sense of what constitutes fame) is that it ranks first among the major leagues' 16 grass fields in holding down errors.

From 1986 through 1990, there were 5.2 percent more errors committed in Angels' road games than in their home games, the largest such difference for any team that plays its home games on a grass field. (Five other stadiums have produced lower error rates, but all of them artificially surfaced. See page 419.) With most of these stadium effects, the stadium's contours or environment provide obvious causes for the statistical results. In this case, however, we don't know whether to congratulate the Anaheim Stadium groundskeepers or official scorer Ed Munson. Maybe the field is smoother, or maybe Munson sees as hits plays that most other American League scorers regard as errors. Whatever, take our word for it, Anaheim Stadium is a hard place to make errors in. If Frank Taveras had only known!

If the Angels looked a little gray around the edges to you last season, you were right. The franchise that turns 30 this season put on the field a collection of position players who, when averaged out, were as old as the franchise is. Ray was 33, Parrish turned 34 in June, Dave Winfield reached 39 the day the season ended (remarkably, Winfield's date of birth is *still* the day Bobby Thomson hit that home run) and Downing hit 40 a week later.

To determine the average age of a team's position players (including the DH), we note the age of each player as of July 1, and weight them according to total plate appearances. As a whole, the average age of major league position players last season was 28.94 years. Five teams had average ages over 30, including the Angels, who finished as the third-oldest at 30.34. The two teams whose position players, on average, were older than the Angels are the Tigers (31.09) and the Dodgers (30.58).

The Angels have been down this road before. The free agents that Gene Autry has lured out west over the past decade have contributed to nine of the last 10 Angels teams averaging out to 30 or older. The 1982 and 1985 teams (the former a division winner, the latter a near miss) rank as the second- and third-oldest teams in major league history (excluding pitchers), behind only the world champion Tigers of 1945:

	Avg. Age*	W–L	Finish
1945 Detroit	33.24	88–65	1st
1985 California	32.95	90–72	2nd
1982 California	32.94	93–69	1st
1983 Philadelphia	32.80	90–72	1st
1944 Detroit	32.73	88–66	2nd

*Excluding pitchers

The old teams on this list were very successful. But whoever scripted last year's baseball season wasn't listening. Of the seven teams with the oldest position players in 1990, only the Dodgers finished with a record of .500 or better. Those seven teams averaged 77 wins; the seven teams with the youngest lineups, including National League division winners Cincinnati and Pittsburgh, averaged 85 wins.

The two Tigers teams on that list had their options restricted by the war; in 1946, the team's average age was down to 30.90. The '83 Phillies took bold steps to arrest the aging process, letting Pete Rose and Joe Morgan leave and reducing their average age in 1984 to 28.98. But the Angels teams listed above were content to tread water against the flow of time; in both cases, their average age the next year was over 32.

During the past offseason, the Angels may have finally moved to stop the graying. No, they didn't stock the clubhouse with Grecian Formula 16; they acquired 25-year-old second baseman Luis Sojo and 23-year-old outfielder Junior Felix in a trade with the Blue Jays. These two loom as likely, younger replacements for Johnny Ray, who started 96 games last season and has been released, and for Devon White, who made 113 starts at age 27 and was sent to Toronto in the same deal.

So to summarize: The Angels turn 30 this season. Their third basemen and shortstops each committed more than 30 errors. And their position players averaged 30 years of age. As they used to say in the newspaper biz:

-30-

WON-LOST RECORD BY STARTING POSITION

California Angels	C	1B	2B	3B	SS	LF	CF	RF	DH	P	Leadoff	Cleanup	Starts vs. LH	Starts vs. RH	Total Starts
Jim Abbott	-	-	-	-	-	-	-	-	-	12-21	-	-	7	26	12-21
Kent Anderson	-	-	1-2	10-4	11-17	-	-	-	-	-	1-0	-	20	25	22-23
Scott Bailes	-	-	-	-	-	-	-	-	-	-	-	-	-	-	-
Dante Bichette	-	-	-	-	-	18-18	6-9	15-20	-	-	-	1-1	43	43	39-47
Bert Blyleven	-	-	-	-	-	-	-	-	-	11-12	-	-	6	17	11-12
Mark Clear	-	-	-	-	-	-	-	-	-	-	-	-	-	-	-
Pete Coachman	-	-	0-1	4-5	-	-	-	-	1-0	-	-	-	3	8	5-6
Sherman Corbett	-	-	-	-	-	-	-	-	-	-	-	-	-	-	-
Chili Davis	-	-	-	-	-	26-20	-	2-4	29-30	-	-	21-28	32	79	57-54
Gary Disarcina	-	-	2-0	-	9-4	-	-	-	-	-	-	-	3	12	11-4
Brian Downing	-	-	-	-	-	-	-	-	40-47	-	15-17	1-1	37	50	40-47
Mark Eichhorn	-	-	-	-	-	-	-	-	-	-	-	-	-	-	-
Mike Fetters	-	-	-	-	-	-	-	-	-	2-0	-	-	1	1	2-0
Chuck Finley	-	-	-	-	-	-	-	-	-	22-10	-	-	10	22	22-10
Willie Fraser	-	-	-	-	-	-	-	-	-	-	-	-	-	-	-
Joe Grahe	-	-	-	-	-	-	-	-	-	4-4	-	-	2	6	4-4
Bryan Harvey	-	-	-	-	-	-	-	-	-	-	-	-	-	-	-
Donnie Hill	-	3-0	28-25	8-7	7-11	-	-	-	-	-	-	-	24	65	46-43
Jack Howell	-	-	-	39-51	-	-	-	-	-	-	-	-	15	75	39-51
Wally Joyner	-	40-42	-	-	-	-	-	-	-	-	-	10-6	27	55	40-42
Mark Langston	-	-	-	-	-	-	-	-	-	13-20	-	-	12	21	13-20
Scott Lewis	-	-	-	-	-	-	-	-	-	1-1	-	-		2	1-1
Kirk McCaskill	-	-	-	-	-	-	-	-	-	15-14	-	-	10	19	15-14
Bob McClure	-	-	-	-	-	-	-	-	-	-	-	-	-	-	-
Mark McLemore	-	-	4-2	-	3-3	-	-	-	-	-	2-0	-	4	8	7-5
Greg Minton	-	-	-	-	-	-	-	-	-	-	-	-	-	-	-
John Orton	10-13	-	-	-	-	-	-	-	-	-	-	-	5	18	10-13
Lance Parrish	64-61	1-2	-	-	-	-	-	-	0-1	-	-	6-9	39	90	65-64
Luis Polonia	-	-	-	-	-	29-39	5-7	-	8-2	-	39-46	-	7	83	42-48
Johnny Ray	-	-	44-51	-	-	-	-	-	0-1	-	-	-	27	69	44-52
Jeff Richardson	-	-	-	-	-	-	-	-	-	-	-	-	-	-	-
Bob Rose	-	-	1-0	1-2	-	-	-	-	-	-	-	-	3	1	2-2
Dick Schofield	-	-	-	-	50-47	-	-	-	-	-	6-5	-	28	69	50-47
Bill Schroeder	6-7	2-1	-	-	-	-	-	-	-	-	-	-	7	9	8-8
Rick Schu	-	4-4	0-1	18-13	-	1-0	-	-	-	-	-	-	25	16	23-18
Lee Stevens	-	30-33	-	-	-	-	-	-	-	-	-	2-3	11	52	30-33
Ron Tingley	0-1	-	-	-	-	-	-	-	-	-	-	-		1	0-1
Max Venable	-	-	-	-	-	6-5	10-12	5-2	-	-	6-3	-	1	39	21-19
Claudell Washington	-	-	-	-	-	-	-	4-5	-	-	0-1	-	1	8	4-5
Devon White	-	-	-	-	-	-	59-54	-	-	-	11-10	-	34	79	59-54
Dave Winfield	-	-	-	-	-	-	-	54-51	2-1	-	-	39-34	36	72	56-52
Mike Witt	-	-	-	-	-	-	-	-	-	-	-	-	-	-	-
Cliff Young	-	-	-	-	-	-	-	-	-	-	-	-	-	-	-

TEAM TOTALS: BATTING

	AB	H	2B	3B	HR	RBI	BB	SO	BA	SA	OBA
Season	5570	1448	237	27	147	646	566	1000	.260	.391	.329
vs. Left-Handers	1616	437	64	7	44	207	171	279	.270	.400	.341
vs. Right-Handers	3954	1011	173	20	103	439	395	721	.256	.388	.324
vs. Ground-Ballers	2419	632	103	8	62	287	236	420	.261	.387	.328
vs. Fly-Ballers	3151	816	134	19	85	359	330	580	.259	.394	.330
Home Games	2718	722	108	11	89	336	286	466	.266	.412	.336
Road Games	2852	726	129	16	58	310	280	534	.255	.372	.322
Grass Fields	4731	1223	195	21	130	548	482	834	.259	.391	.328
Artificial Turf	839	225	42	6	17	98	84	166	.268	.393	.336
April	657	150	34	0	15	55	62	124	.228	.349	.297
May	1009	267	50	5	30	122	87	149	.265	.413	.324
June	935	224	39	3	32	104	110	172	.240	.390	.322
July	986	257	32	6	26	104	88	182	.261	.384	.320
August	955	266	37	6	22	132	109	184	.279	.399	.355
Sept./Oct.	1028	284	45	7	22	129	110	189	.276	.398	.345
Leading Off Inn.	1339	342	58	10	34	34	121	233	.255	.390	.319
Bases Empty	3146	821	139	16	82	82	290	552	.261	.394	.326
Runners On	2424	627	98	11	65	564	276	448	.259	.389	.332
Runners/Scor. Pos.	1320	329	51	9	36	493	182	266	.249	.383	.333
Runners On/2 Out	1043	246	34	4	35	230	121	207	.236	.377	.320
Scor. Pos./2 Out	630	142	23	4	23	203	84	143	.225	.384	.321
Late-Inning Pressure	890	219	32	4	22	91	97	169	.246	.365	.321
Leading Off	224	52	9	0	4	4	17	44	.232	.326	.289
Runners On	382	91	14	3	11	80	54	73	.238	.377	.329
Runners/Scor. Pos.	212	51	9	1	7	69	39	48	.241	.392	.352

RUNS BATTED IN	From 1B	From 2B	From 3B	Scoring Position
Totals	78/1844	177/1021	244/617	421/1638
Percentage	4.2%	17.3%	39.5%	25.7%

TEAM TOTALS: PITCHING

	W-L	ERA	AB	H	HR	BB	SO	BA	SA	OBA
Season	80-82	3.79	5548	1482	106	544	944	.267	.379	.334
vs. Left-Handers			1754	482	33	172	257	.275	.385	.342
vs. Right-Handers			3794	1000	73	372	687	.264	.376	.331
vs. Ground-Ballers			2568	682	34	231	429	.266	.360	.328
vs. Fly-Ballers			2980	800	72	313	515	.268	.395	.340
Home Games	42-39	3.61	2859	770	55	247	476	.269	.378	.328
Road Games	38-43	3.99	2689	712	51	297	468	.265	.380	.340
Grass Fields	70-68	3.65	4757	1263	88	452	835	.266	.371	.331
Artificial Turf	10-14	4.68	791	219	18	92	109	.277	.429	.354
April	8-11	3.27	644	167	12	78	99	.259	.373	.341
May	15-14	3.73	997	254	13	102	178	.255	.358	.323
June	15-13	3.38	939	252	20	82	170	.268	.384	.329
July	12-16	4.67	993	276	24	89	141	.278	.410	.341
August	16-12	3.95	968	268	17	97	171	.277	.371	.343
Sept./Oct.	14-16	3.60	1007	265	20	96	185	.263	.376	.330
Leading Off Inn.			1325	335	26	125	217	.253	.355	.321
Bases Empty			3070	798	66	275	521	.260	.375	.324
Runners On			2478	684	40	269	423	.276	.385	.346
Runners/Scor. Pos.			1395	375	22	192	243	.269	.381	.352
Runners On/2 Out			1039	285	25	129	180	.274	.408	.360
Scor. Pos./2 Out			666	183	15	99	110	.275	.408	.377
Late-Inning Pressure			817	201	13	85	174	.246	.334	.317
Leading Off			198	45	2	25	47	.227	.318	.314
Runners On			360	100	3	36	72	.278	.344	.340
Runners/Scor. Pos.			218	60	1	25	43	.275	.321	.341
First 9 Batters			2680	716	54	275	494	.267	.376	.336
Second 9 Batters			1471	362	23	132	233	.246	.343	.312
All Batters Thereafter			1397	404	29	137	217	.289	.424	.354

CHICAGO WHITE SOX

- **The best young team in baseball?**
- **One last look at old Comiskey.**

The Best Young Team in Baseball. Every year, it seems, a half dozen teams stake claim to that title. Often it designates nothing more than a team of underachieving veterans that has purged its roster after a slow start; the ensuing rookie-induced euphoria then masks deeper problems and clouds its fans' judgment about the team's future. To cite one example, a respectable second half fueled by Kevin Maas, Oscar Azocar, and Jim Leyritz gave the 1990 Yankees a clear case of rookie hysteria. The "Best Young Team" mantle became more a Halloween disguise than a cloak of honor.

Sometimes, a team with a productive young lineup appears to be the BYTiB, but an elderly pitching staff renders it worthless. Keep your eye on the Texas Rangers. Unless they can successfully replace Nolan Ryan and Charlie Hough in the rotation over the next few years, the heart of Texas's offense—including Ruben Sierra, Rafael Palmeiro, and Julio Franco, all still in their 20s—could be fighting middle-age bulge by the time its pitching staff is championship-ready.

Only once every few years does a young team suddenly assert itself as a likely winner for years to come. The 1990 Chicago White Sox, who won 94 games with the youngest team in the majors, was one of those rare teams. As a result, it's possible that within the next five years, the White Sox will be considered among the best teams, maybe even *the* best, in baseball. The evidence provided by one key indicator suggests that even the formidable specter of the Oakland A's—whose two best hitters are still in their mid-20s, and whose four first-round 1990 draft choices could blossom during that time—may not be enough to hold off these new-look White Sox.

What could make reputedly reasonable and right-thinking men (though sportswriters we admittedly are) challenge the certainty of Oakland's ongoing and impending dynasty? Here are the facts: Last season, Chicago had the youngest team in the majors with an average age of 26 years, 9 months, and posted a 94–88 record. Over the past 20 years, only five other teams won as many as 90 games with an average age under 27 years:

					Next 5 Seasons: Record & Titles						
Year	Team	W	L	Pct.	W	L	Pct.	Rank	Div.	Lg.	WS
1970	Reds	102	60	.630	479	323	.597	1	3	2	2
1971	Athletics	101	60	.627	462	340	.576	2	4	3	3
1972	Reds	95	59	.617	495	315	.611	1	3	2	2
1978	Brewers	93	69	.574	425	331	.562	2	1	1	0
1984	Mets	90	72	.556	485	323	.600	1	2	1	1

The table needs little elaboration, but let's spell it out for effect: Each of those teams became big winners immediately thereafter. Most proceeded to establish mini-dynasties. Three compiled the best record in the majors over the next five seasons; the other two had the second-best five-year marks. During those 25 seasons (the next five years for each of five teams), they accounted for 11 division titles, eight league championships, and six World Series titles—and that's even without double-counting the 1973 and 1975 Reds, who represented the aftershock from two teams listed above.

A roll call of the major contributors age 25 and under on those teams will show their abundance of young talent:

Cincinnati, 1970: Johnny Bench, Bernie Carbo, Dave Concepcion, Bobby Tolan, Gary Nolan, and Wayne Simpson.

Oakland, 1971: Dave Duncan, Reggie Jackson, Joe Rudi, Rick Monday, Vida Blue, Rollie Fingers, and Catfish Hunter.

Cincinnati, 1972: Johnny Bench (getting older, but still under 25), Dave Concepcion, Cesar Geronimo, Pedro Borbon, Ross Grimsley, Don Gullett, Gary Nolan, and Wayne Simpson.

Milwaukee, 1978: Sixto Lezcano, Paul Molitor, Charlie Moore, Robin Yount, Jerry Augustine, Lary Sorensen, and Bill Travers.

New York, 1984: Wally Backman, Mike Fitzgerald, Darryl Strawberry, Ron Darling, Sid Fernandez, and Dwight Gooden.

Twenty years from now, how will those names compare with Chicago's current under-25 group, including Sammy Sosa, Frank Thomas, Robin Ventura, Alex Fernandez, Jack McDowell, and Melido Perez, among others? Of course, anyone old enough to remember *The Godfather* without roman numerals will recall that those teams all commanded greater respect than the 1990 White Sox, even at similar developmental stages. After all, Chicago's 1990 season was an unexpected about-face for a franchise that only one year earlier had appeared to be in trouble. So a reasonable question on rebuttal would be: To what extent should Chicago's optimism be tempered by the knowledge that 1990 was a true breakthrough season, one in which the team snapped a streak of four consecutive losing years?

Looking back a little further, we found that seven more teams matched the criteria described above (a winning percentage equal to 90 wins over a 162-game schedule, and an average age of less than 27 years) during the 1960s. The Baltimore Orioles, who qualified in both 1966 and 1968, became a dominant team. But the others were hardly in the class of the Reds, A's, or Orioles of the early 1970s: the 1960 Orioles (.554 over the next five years), the 1962

Twins (.559), the 1964 Phillies (.486), the 1967 Red Sox (.535), and the 1969 Mets (.501).

Over the past 30 years, then, 12 teams qualified both by age and performance. Six were coming off winning seasons or off a single losing season. The other six came off streaks of losing years: the 1960 Orioles (2 consecutive losing seasons), 1962 Twins (8), 1967 Red Sox (8), 1969 Mets (7), 1978 Brewers (8), and 1984 Mets (7). Over the next five years, teams from the former group won five more games per season than the teams coming off losing streaks. That may not sound like a lot, especially when you consider that even teams from the less successful group won an average of 89 games per year. But the number of titles won by each group illustrates that the difference between 89 wins and 94 wins is often the difference between first and second place: Teams coming off losing streaks accounted for only three division titles and one World Series victory, compared to 17 and eight by the other teams.

Is this bad news for the White Sox? Not necessarily. The team has already demonstrated its ability to rebound from a dismal recent past to an unprecedented degree: Last year it became the first team in major-league history to play .600 or better at the All-Star break after finishing in last place a year earlier. And despite coming off four consecutive losing seasons prior to their 1990 breakthrough, Chicago shares another characteristic with many of the more successful teams mentioned above: Chicago ranked second in the American League in ERA last season. None of the 12 successful young teams led their leagues in ERA, but among the five that ranked second were the fledgings that grew into the three dominant teams of the 1970s: the 1968 Orioles, the 1970 Reds, and the 1971 A's. (Also included were the 1960 O's and the 1969 Mets.)

So the prognosis for the White Sox through the first half of the 1990s is encouraging. The rapid development of their first-round draft picks from each of the four most recent drafts (Jack McDowell, Robin Ventura, Alex Fernandez, and Frank Thomas) promises a broad base of young talent from which to grow. And if the excellence of its young pitching staff proves to be the dominant trait, and its streak of prior losing seasons the recessive one, Chicago could become the winningest team of the early 1990s. At worst, the Sox should still play consistently winning baseball over the next few years, and probably win a division title or two. Now all they'll need is a catchy nickname. Let's see . . . How about the "Big White Machine"?

Ouch!

Of course, the success of Chicago's young pitching staff last season was due in large part to the team's oldest component, Carlton Fisk. He was an indispensable part of the offense, batting .285 while leading the team with 18 home runs, but Fisk's greatest contribution may have been his influence on Chicago's starting rotation, which included Alex Fernandez, Greg Hibbard, Eric King, Jack McDowell, and Melido Perez—all 25 or younger on opening day. Along with occasional starter Adam Peterson, they gave the 1990 White Sox the youngest starting staff in the American League since 1981, when the White Sox sprouted a rotation that included Britt Burns, Richard Dotson, and Steve Trout, among others. To help mold that earlier staff, Chicago signed a veteran catcher, a 32-year-old backstop named Fisk, who helped them post the 4th-best ERA in the American League that year.

Nine years later, Fisk and his protégés did even better, compiling a 3.61 ERA that ranked second in the American League—a marked improvement from their 11th-place finish in 1989. The improved pitching was almost solely responsible for Chicago's turnaround; the White Sox actually scored fewer runs in 1990 than they did a year earlier, when they won 25 fewer games and finished last in the A.L. West. (That was the greatest single-season improvement by an American League team whose scoring decreased since 1903.)

How important was Fisk to the success of Chicago's staff? A survey of the past 30 years indicates that without a veteran signal caller, few young pitching staffs have flown successfully on their own.

Since 1960, there have been 41 teams with pitching staffs that averaged less than 26 years of age. Only eight of those teams ranked among the top three in their leagues in ERA. The average age of the regular catchers on those eight teams was 29.5 years, compared to 25.9 years for the regulars on the 33 other teams. A breakdown of where those teams ranked in ERA, classified according to the age of their regular catchers:

Team Rank in ERA	Age 28 Or Younger	Age 29 Or Older
Top half of league	6	7
Bottom half of league	24	4

The trend is also apparent when examined from another direction. Since 1960, the average age of regular catchers on the 62 league leaders in ERA was 29.2 years. That's a year and a half older than the average of regular catchers on all other teams, a margin that would occur by chance roughly one time in every 400. During the 1980s, only one team (the 1982 Dodgers with 23-year-old Mike Scioscia) led its league with a catcher aged 25 or younger—a segment that accounted for nearly 20 percent of all regular catchers. Half the league leaders had catchers at least 30 years old (30-year-olds accounted for 41 percent of the regulars). So the pattern is clear: Young pitching staffs rarely succeed, except under the guidance of a veteran catcher. And few pitching staffs of any age excel with a young receiver calling signals.

When Comiskey Park opened on July 1, 1910, Jack Johnson was preparing to defend his heavyweight title against ex-champ Jim Jeffries. Roald Amundsen of Norway and Robert Scott of Great Britain had just set off on a race to become the first man to reach the South Pole. And the hot "forbidden dance" of the moment wasn't the lambada, but the tango. So on longevity alone, Comiskey's closing merits noting.

The demolition of Comiskey Park represents one more desecration by the wrecker's ball of the dwindling number of stadiums built during a golden era of ballpark construction that lasted from 1909 to 1915. During that period, 13 new stadiums were built, providing homes for 14 of the 16 major-league teams. (The Giants and Yankees shared the "new" Polo Grounds.) By 1916, only two teams were playing their home games in parks that were more than seven years old. (The Cardinals didn't abandon Robison Field to share Sportsman's Park with the Browns until 1920, and the Phillies played in Baker Bowl until 1938.)

The catalyst for such turnover was the emergence of steel and concrete as viable building materials, replacing wood, the material of choice in the 19th century. The new stadiums, along with the years they opened:

Year	Stadium	City
1909	Shibe Park	Philadelphia (A's)
1909	Sportsman's Park	St. Louis (Browns)
1909	Forbes Field	Pittsburgh
1910	League Park	Cleveland
1910	White Sox Park	Chicago (White Sox)
1911	Griffith Stadium	Washington, D.C.
1911	Polo Grounds	New York (Giants, Yankees)
1912	Crosley Field	Cincinnati
1912	Fenway Park	Boston
1912	Navin Field	Detroit
1913	Ebbets Field	Brooklyn
1914	*Wrigley Field	Chicago (Cubs)
1915	Braves Field	Boston

* Built as Weeghman Park for the Federal League's Chicago Whales. The Cubs started playing there in 1916.

You'll note that Comiskey Park was known as White Sox Park from its opening until 1913 (and again from 1963 through 1975). The name of Navin Field was changed to Briggs Stadium in 1938, and to the current Tiger Stadium in 1976. Only three of those stadiums are still in use today: Tiger Stadium, Fenway Park, and Wrigley Field.

Incidentally, in its final season Comiskey had a few interesting events of statistical significance. On July 3, Carlton Fisk passed Bill Melton as the all-time stadium home-run record holder, when he hit his 91st there. Charlie Comiskey once said that he wanted a ballpark in which batters had to earn their home runs, and he wasn't kidding: No player reached the 100 mark. Fisk will go to his grave as the all-time leader there with 94.

Also of note: The White Sox were the only team in either league to score in every home game last season. It marked the first time in 81 years of baseball at Comiskey Park that the White Sox weren't shut out there at least once. And the last.

It's not that we can't appreciate the majesty of Wrigley Field's sunlit, ivy-covered walls on a crisp autumn day. (Yes, we were actually there in October a few times.) But any baseball fan who relished the smells of nearly a century's worth of spilled beers, fresh-baked waffles (it was waffles, wasn't it?), or grilled sausages—depending on which entrance he used—must mourn the passing of another of those really fine baseball places.

WON-LOST RECORD BY STARTING POSITION

Chicago White Sox	C	1B	2B	3B	SS	LF	CF	RF	DH	P	Leadoff	Cleanup	Starts vs. LH	Starts vs. RH	Total Starts
Daryl Boston	-	-	-	-	-	-	-	-	-	-	-	-	-	-	-
Phil Bradley	-	-	-	-	-	9-4	7-5	1-3	2-4	-	11-8	-	19	16	19-16
Ivan Calderon	-	-	-	-	-	74-55	-	-	16-11	-	12-6	0-1	64	92	90-66
Wayne Edwards	-	-	-	-	-	-	-	-	-	3-2	-	-	3	2	3-2
Alex Fernandez	-	-	-	-	-	-	-	-	-	6-7	-	-	8	5	6-7
Carlton Fisk	60-52	-	-	-	-	-	-	-	9-3	-	-	4-5	54	70	69-55
Scott Fletcher	-	-	82-65	-	-	-	-	-	-	-	-	-	60	87	82-65
Dave Gallagher	-	-	-	-	-	-	13-6	1-0	-	-	-	-	19	1	14-6
Craig Grebeck	-	-	3-0	17-10	5-5	-	-	-	-	-	-	-	34	6	25-15
Ozzie Guillen	-	-	-	-	89-63	-	-	-	-	-	-	-	57	95	89-63
Greg Hibbard	-	-	-	-	-	-	-	-	-	18-15	-	-	11	22	18-15
Shawn Hillegas	-	-	-	-	-	-	-	-	-	-	-	-	-	-	-
John Hudek	-	-	-	-	-	-	-	-	-	-	-	-	-	-	-
Lance Johnson	-	-	-	-	-	-	73-56	-	-	-	32-30	-	36	93	73-56
Barry Jones	-	-	-	-	-	-	-	-	-	-	-	-	-	-	-
Ron Karkovice	34-16	-	-	-	-	-	-	-	-	-	-	-	19	31	34-16
Eric King	-	-	-	-	-	-	-	-	-	18-7	-	-	12	13	18-7
Ron Kittle	-	15-9	-	-	-	-	-	-	32-19	-	-	29-14	34	41	47-28
Jerry Kutzler	-	-	-	-	-	-	-	-	-	5-2	-	-	2	5	5-2
Bill Long	-	-	-	-	-	-	-	-	-	-	-	-	-	-	-
Steve Lyons	-	8-6	9-3	-	-	0-1	1-1	-	-	-	-	-	3	26	18-11
Carlos Martinez	-	44-28	-	-	-	-	-	-	0-1	-	-	-	43	30	44-29
Rod McCray	-	-	-	-	-	-	-	-	-	-	-	-	-	-	-
Jack McDowell	-	-	-	-	-	-	-	-	-	19-14	-	-	14	19	19-14
Donn Pall	-	-	-	-	-	-	-	-	-	-	-	-	-	-	-
Dan Pasqua	-	-	-	-	-	11-8	-	12-8	26-25	-	-	42-37	4	86	49-41
Ken Patterson	-	-	-	-	-	-	-	-	-	-	-	-	-	-	-
Melido Perez	-	-	-	-	-	-	-	-	-	20-15	-	-	11	24	20-15
Adam Peterson	-	-	-	-	-	-	-	-	-	5-6	-	-	4	7	5-6
Scott Radinsky	-	-	-	-	-	-	-	-	-	-	-	-	-	-	-
Steve Rosenberg	-	-	-	-	-	-	-	-	-	-	-	-	-	-	-
Jose Segura	-	-	-	-	-	-	-	-	-	-	-	-	-	-	-
Sammy Sosa	-	-	-	-	-	-	-	80-57	-	-	39-24	-	65	72	80-57
Matt Stark	-	-	-	-	-	-	-	-	3-2	-	-	1-0	5	-	3-2
Bobby Thigpen	-	-	-	-	-	-	-	-	-	-	-	-	-	-	-
Frank Thomas	-	27-24	-	-	-	-	-	-	5-3	-	-	17-11	27	32	32-27
Robin Ventura	-	-	-	77-58	-	-	-	-	-	-	-	-	42	93	77-58
Greg Walker	-	0-1	-	-	-	-	-	-	1-0	-	-	1-0	-	2	1-1
Jerry Willard	-	-	-	-	-	-	-	-	-	-	-	-	-	-	-

TEAM TOTALS: BATTING

	AB	H	2B	3B	HR	RBI	BB	SO	BA	SA	OBA
Season	5402	1393	251	44	106	637	478	903	.258	.379	.320
vs. Left-Handers	1990	528	90	16	48	238	191	341	.265	.399	.330
vs. Right-Handers	3412	865	161	28	58	399	287	562	.254	.368	.314
vs. Ground-Ballers	2378	634	127	12	36	283	204	356	.267	.376	.326
vs. Fly-Ballers	3024	759	124	32	70	354	274	547	.251	.383	.315
Home Games	2629	703	133	30	41	316	252	433	.267	.388	.333
Road Games	2773	690	118	14	65	321	226	470	.249	.372	.307
Grass Fields	4500	1172	215	40	86	537	398	751	.260	.383	.322
Artificial Turf	902	221	36	4	20	100	80	152	.245	.360	.309
April	526	133	25	6	9	66	49	105	.253	.375	.317
May	939	244	37	6	23	110	101	159	.260	.386	.332
June	911	246	44	8	22	98	61	152	.270	.408	.318
July	937	243	48	9	14	112	70	129	.259	.375	.313
August	1042	250	50	11	19	127	91	161	.240	.364	.303
Sept./Oct.	1047	277	47	4	19	124	106	197	.265	.372	.335
Leading Off Inn.	1336	330	62	8	28	28	99	217	.247	.368	.302
Bases Empty	3148	769	135	20	63	63	257	535	.244	.360	.305
Runners On	2254	624	116	24	43	574	221	368	.277	.407	.339
Runners/Scor. Pos.	1330	369	69	16	26	511	166	236	.277	.412	.351
Runners On/2 Out	978	253	43	10	19	227	90	154	.259	.381	.326
Scor. Pos./2 Out	646	166	29	6	12	203	69	104	.257	.376	.332
Late-Inning Pressure	709	168	29	5	10	76	78	142	.237	.334	.314
Leading Off	185	46	8	1	1	1	19	30	.249	.319	.319
Runners On	286	75	11	3	5	71	45	60	.262	.374	.364
Runners/Scor. Pos.	187	47	8	3	3	66	39	46	.251	.374	.380

RUNS BATTED IN	From 1B	From 2B	From 3B	Scoring Position
Totals	78/1506	205/1020	248/594	453/1614
Percentage	5.2%	20.1%	41.8%	28.1%

TEAM TOTALS: PITCHING

	W-L	ERA	AB	H	HR	BB	SO	BA	SA	OBA
Season	94-68	3.61	5388	1313	106	548	914	.244	.358	.316
vs. Left-Handers			2178	540	40	220	361	.248	.365	.316
vs. Right-Handers			3210	773	66	328	553	.241	.354	.315
vs. Ground-Ballers			2511	640	31	257	388	.255	.351	.325
vs. Fly-Ballers			2877	673	75	291	526	.234	.365	.307
Home Games	49-31	3.53	2731	655	53	262	462	.240	.348	.309
Road Games	45-37	3.68	2657	658	53	286	452	.248	.369	.322
Grass Fields	81-54	3.51	4499	1077	91	460	781	.239	.353	.313
Artificial Turf	13-14	4.10	889	236	15	88	133	.265	.384	.330
April	10-6	3.30	520	109	14	51	93	.210	.329	.284
May	18-10	3.08	911	195	18	94	177	.214	.341	.289
June	17-10	2.93	912	217	18	95	159	.238	.337	.313
July	13-14	4.55	961	255	24	88	165	.265	.399	.329
August	17-15	4.01	1056	281	16	99	160	.266	.374	.330
Sept./Oct.	19-13	3.60	1028	256	16	121	160	.249	.354	.330
Leading Off Inn.			1325	308	25	117	213	.232	.340	.300
Bases Empty			3118	733	66	291	531	.235	.351	.305
Runners On			2270	580	40	257	383	.256	.369	.329
Runners/Scor. Pos.			1245	311	21	180	218	.250	.374	.337
Runners On/2 Out			959	224	20	103	155	.234	.351	.311
Scor. Pos./2 Out			596	134	12	82	94	.225	.352	.322
Late-Inning Pressure			911	205	14	121	174	.225	.326	.318
Leading Off			226	53	5	30	40	.235	.341	.332
Runners On			396	84	7	59	73	.212	.308	.310
Runners/Scor. Pos.			214	46	4	48	41	.215	.332	.349
First 9 Batters			2833	682	44	306	514	.241	.342	.316
Second 9 Batters			1424	378	39	124	229	.265	.406	.327
All Batters Thereafter			1131	253	23	118	171	.224	.340	.300

CLEVELAND INDIANS

- **Can you bring an offense up to speed?**
- **56 HR = 5 R?**

The more things change, the more they stay the same. Herewith, case number 1,637,822.

Twenty-three years ago, Hank Peters, starting his third season in Cleveland at the right hand of general manager Gabe Paul, struggled to help rebuild the Indians as the frustration of their fans mounted. The memory of Cleveland's last American title in 1954 had faded. And despite a sudden end a few years earlier to the Yankees' decades-long dynasty, the Tribe had just endured its eighth consecutive season without anything resembling a pennant race. The Indians hadn't come within 15 games of the league title since 1959.

Further complicating the situation was the age of the team. Only one American League team had an older lineup in 1967—the Tigers, and by a margin of just four days per player. Rocky Colavito had already been pawned the previous July at age 33. Now Paul and Peters had to confront the realities of a lineup built around the fading power of three of Rocco's contemporaries, Leon Wagner, Chuck Hinton, and Lee Maye. Their plan for the winter of '67 was to restructure the team around several young and talented starters: Sam McDowell, Luis Tiant, Steve Hargan, and Sonny Siebert. According to published reports, Cleveland's wish list was topped by several proven but still young National League run producers, most coming off disappointing seasons (ages as of November 1967):

Age	Player	Team	G	HR	RBI	BA
28	Johnny Callison	Phil.	149	14	64	.261
28	Rico Carty	Atl.	134	15	64	.255
28	Tommy Davis	N.Y.	154	16	73	.302
26	Willie Stargell	Pitt.	134	20	73	.271

An entire generation of Indians fans can only fantasize about how the acquisition of Stargell might have reshaped their baseball memories. By late November, the inability to acquire a solid RBI man prompted the Indians to a take a totally different approach. They would forsake the home run and exploit the stolen base, creating an on-field image more like that of their new manager, Alvin Dark, than that of the man he replaced, Joe Adcock. Within eight days, Paul swung two major deals. First, he traded power-hitting first baseman Fred Whitfield and a young reliever named George Culver to Cincinnati for outfielder Tommy Harper, who ranked third in the National League with a total of 111 steals over the previous four seasons; only Lou Brock (232) and Maury Wills (214) outstole Harper. Then Cleveland unloaded Hinton, the aging one-time base-stealing threat, for California center fielder Jose Cardenal, who ranked second in the A.L. with 37 stolen bases as a rookie in 1965.

Those two moves immediately turned a relatively powerful but ponderous and aging team into one built around youth, speed, and an outfield fast enough to prompt its new manager, Alvin Dark, to defend the team's failure to acquire an established run producer. "What's wrong with having three guys," asked Dark, "who can play center field in the same outfield? They'll certainly improve our defense and make our pitching better." (The third outfielder to whom Dark referred, incidentally, was Vic Davalillo.) Defensive coverage became a more important issue when Cleveland decided to move its outfield fences slightly further out, hoping to exploit the speed of its outfielders and reduce the effect of their loss of power.

To enhance its speed-based offense further, Cleveland promoted rookie second baseman Dave Nelson, who eventually stole 23 bases in 88 games. The team stole 115 bases, 40 more than in 1967, with Cardenal and Nelson accounting for more than half. But not everything went as planned. Harper was a bust, batting .217 for the season, and was lost to Seattle in the expansion draft shortly thereafter. The absence of power proved to be a greater liability than expected, prompting a desperate and damaging mid-season trade in which Cleveland dealt Davalillo, a productive hitter with a .278 career batting average, to the Angels for a still young but washed-up ex-phenom named Jimmie Hall. The offense fell from sixth in the league to eighth (though their runs-allowed total improved from sixth to third in the league, and the team rose from eighth to third in the standings). The ultimate verdict on Cleveland's plan is best illustrated by the fact that both Cardenal and Harper were gone within two years of their arrival, Harper made available in the expansion draft, Cardenal traded to St. Louis for Vada Pinson a year later.

It's been said that those who ignore history are doomed to repeat it. Well, nearly a quarter-century later, Hank Peters, now general manager of the Indians, has not only ignored his own history but has boldly defied it. This past winter, Peters and the Indians decided once again to forsake home-run power and to rebuild their team around youth and speed. Despite an eighth-place ranking in the American League with 110 home runs last season, the Indians chose not to pursue their individual leader, Candy Maldonado, who became a free agent after the 1990 season. Then Cleveland traded Cory Snyder to the White Sox for Eric King and Shawn Hillegas; Snyder and Brook Jacoby were second on the Indians in homers. Those are pretty bold decisions: No team had lost their two leading home-run hitters during the same offseason since the California Angels traded both Joe Rudi and Jason Thompson prior to the start of the 1981 season.

Cleveland's plan to accentuate speed and deemphasize power was prompted in large part by last season's arrival of outfielder Alex Cole. Cole batted .300 and stole 40 bases—the most ever by an Indians rookie—despite playing only 63 games. Cleveland hopes to flank Cole in the outfield this season with veteran Mitch Webster and prospect Turner Ward, an unintended tribute, perhaps, to Alvin Dark's three center fielders of 1968. (Both Webster and Ward stole 22 bases last season, for Cleveland and Colorado Springs, respectively.)

Can it work? Anything is possible. Will it work? Probably not. There have been 42 teams in major league history that stole at least 25 more bases than in the previous season while hitting at least 25 fewer home runs. Only eight increased their scoring, compared to 33 that failed to match their previous season's run production. (The 1978 Detroit Tigers scored exactly the same the number of runs as in 1977, despite the shift of balance from power to speed.) On average, those teams scored about one-third of a run per game less than before, a decrease that translates into more than 50 lost runs over the course of 162 games. Was the improvement on defense enough to offset this? No—the presumably better fielding represented by the additional speed meant an average decrease of just 0.19 runs per game, or 30 runs over the course of a season. On balance, this shift has been a loser.

But even given the futile history of such moves, several mitigating factors help to vindicate Cleveland's decision. For starters, well, the Indians need them badly. Bud Black is gone. John Farrell may return from offseason surgery before the end of the season; then again he may not. And Greg Swindell proved to be eminently hittable last season, allowing 245 hits (only one fewer than league leader Jim Abbott) while compiling a 4.40 ERA. So the acquisition of King and Hillegas for Snyder addresses the team's most serious weakness by dealing from its only strength, outfield depth.

More importantly, Cleveland's transformation to a running team isn't based on theory or current vogue, but rather on personnel. This isn't George Steinbrenner suddenly lusting for team speed and impulsively retooling his lineup with trades for Ken Griffey and Dave Collins that undermined the profile of his successful teams. The presence of Cole alone for a full season with the Indians should mean an increase of roughly 25 to 50 stolen bases. Should Ward win a starting position, Cleveland could conceivably double last season's stolen-base total (107). That's significant because among the group of 42 teams described earlier, those that added at least 50 steals tended to suffer less on the scoreboard than those with increases in the 25 to 50 range.

Twelve of those 42 teams increased their stolen bases by 50 or more, the 1968 Indians among them. Four actually increased their scoring, while eight declined; the average decrease was approximately one run per seven games, or the equivalent of 22 runs per 162:

Years	Team	HR	SB	R/G Yr.1	R/G Yr.2	Diff.
1979–80	Montreal	143–114	121–237	4.38	4.28	−0.10
1979–80	San Diego	93–67	100–239	3.75	3.63	−0.12
1975–76	Kansas City	118–65	155–218	4.38	4.40	+0.02
1975–76	Minnesota	121–81	81–146	4.55	4.59	+0.03
1975–76	Oakland	151–113	183–341	4.68	4.26	−0.42
1975–76	Pittsburgh	138–110	49–130	4.42	4.37	−0.05
1974–75	California	95–55	119–220	3.79	3.90	+0.11
1973–74	Philadelphia	134–95	51–115	3.96	4.17	+0.21
1971–72	Wash./Texas	86–56	68–126	3.38	2.99	−0.38
1967–68	Cleveland	131–75	53–115	3.45	3.19	−0.27
1965–66	Chi. White Sox	125–87	50–153	3.99	3.52	−0.47
1964–65	Kansas City	166–110	34–110	3.81	3.61	−0.20

Peters and Indians manager John McNamara probably wouldn't have instituted such a dramatic change to the team's character without confidence in its ability to approach or exceed the 200-steal level. And while it must be noted that no exchange of power for speed has ever produced a significantly stronger offensive team, the figures above suggest that such a sizable increase in steals might offset the loss of power from the bats of Maldonado and Snyder. After all, Candy and Cory may have ranked 1–2 in homers, but their combined total was still below that of either Jose Canseco or Mark McGwire by himself. It's an unfortunate irony that the millions wasted on Keith Hernandez a year ago could have paid for Maldonado's return, allowing for the infusion of speed without so great a sacrifice of power. Nevertheless, playing the difficult hand they've been dealt, the Indians have chosen an unlikely but ultimately reasonable course of action.

Cleveland announced another change to be implemented for the 1991 season in response to the team's power shortage, and it too represented a back-to-the-future approach. The Cleveland Stadium outfield fences will be moved further from home plate, in an effort to deny Indians opponents via geography what the home team has denied itself through personnel decisions.

Last season, the Indians hit 53 fewer home runs than they allowed, the largest deficit in the majors since 1987. (Cleveland hit 110 home runs, its opponents hit 163.) John McNamara noted during the offseason that despite the home-run deficit, his team was outscored by only five runs. He expressed confidence that the addition of 15 feet or so to the power alleys and center field would reduce the deficit enough to tip the run-scoring scales in Cleveland's favor.

The new distances may cost Cleveland's opponents more home runs than the Indians themselves lose.

But narrowing the home-run gap alone may not be enough to produce a scoring surplus for the Tribe; the incongruous scoring pattern that McNamara cited occurred because his pitchers allowed a large majority of their opponents' home runs with no one on base. Cleveland allowed the most home runs in the American League, but five teams allowed more than the Indians with runners on. The following tables contrast Cleveland's largesse with runners on and with the bases empty:

Runners On		**Bases Empty**	
Baltimore	76	**Cleveland**	107
Detroit	69	Baltimore	85
New York	64	Detroit	85
Toronto	63	New York	80
Minnesota	62	Toronto	80
Cleveland	56	Seattle	74
Kansas City	53	Minnesota	72
Oakland	51	Oakland	72
Milwaukee	50	Milwaukee	71
Texas	47	California	66
Seattle	46	Chicago	66
California	40	Texas	66
Chicago	40	Kansas City	63
Boston	36	Boston	56

The close correspondence between the order of teams in those lists—the Indians notwithstanding—suggests that Cleveland represents a statistical anomaly, a random event unlikely to recur. But since pitchers can alter their pitch selection with runners on base, we must consider the possibility—no matter how unlikely—that certain teams can limit their gopher balls to the most opportune times over a period of several years. And Cleveland happened to allow significantly fewer home runs with runners on than with the bases empty in 1989 as well: 69 with the bases empty (eighth-most in the A.L.), compared to 38 with runners on (tied for fewest in the league).

Still, during the 15 years that we've tracked home runs according to whether or not there were runners on base, only six other teams have ranked five positions better with runners on than with the bases empty in consecutive seasons. If such a trait were truly the result of strategy or talent, we should have seen many more such instances. Incidentally, only one of those six teams continued the pattern for a third consecutive season: the Texas Rangers, from 1976 through 1978. So it seems almost certain that Cleveland has been extraordinarily lucky with regard to the timing of the home runs its pitchers have allowed.

Well, whatever they're doing, the Indians had better keep it up, because they've got a lot to lose. A look at other teams outhomered by similar margins indicates how much is at stake. Over the previous 40 years, 27 teams allowed between 50 and 59 home runs more than they themselves hit. Only five outscored their opponents, one broke even, and 21 were outscored. The average deficit was 134 runs. (Of course, even if Cleveland's pitchers can't maintain their superiority in runners-on situations, the addition of Eric King to the rotation ought to curb the number of home runs allowed, bases empty or otherwise.) So even as the Indians put their new speed-oriented team on a field tailored to exploit that speed and minimize their lack of power, it could be the ability of their pitchers to continue to limit opposing two- and three-run homers that will determine how competitive they will be this season.

WON-LOST RECORD BY STARTING POSITION

Cleveland Indians	C	1B	2B	3B	SS	LF	CF	RF	DH	P	Leadoff	Cleanup	Starts vs. LH	Starts vs. RH	Total Starts
Beau Allred	-	-	-	-	-	-	2-1	0-1	-	-	-	-	-	4	2-2
Sandy Alomar Jr.	57-61	-	-	-	-	-	-	-	-	-	-	1-2	37	81	57-61
Carlos Baerga	-	-	4-4	21-24	6-7	-	-	-	-	-	1-2	-	23	43	31-35
Kevin Bearse	-	-	-	-	-	-	-	-	-	0-3	-	-	1	2	0-3
Albert Belle	-	-	-	-	-	-	-	-	5-1	-	-	-	2	4	5-1
Bud Black	-	-	-	-	-	-	-	-	-	13-16	-	-	13	16	13-16
Tom Brookens	-	1-0	9-9	15-4	1-0	-	-	-	-	-	-	-	28	11	26-13
Jerry Browne	-	-	63-71	-	-	-	-	-	-	-	36-37	-	41	93	63-71
Tom Candiotti	-	-	-	-	-	-	-	-	-	17-13	-	-	10	20	17-13
Alex Cole	-	-	-	-	-	-	25-32	-	-	-	25-32	-	12	45	25-32
John Farrell	-	-	-	-	-	-	-	-	-	9-8	-	-	7	10	9-8
Felix Fermin	-	-	-	-	65-75	-	-	-	-	-	-	-	47	93	65-75
Mauro Gozzo	-	-	-	-	-	-	-	-	-	-	-	-	-	-	-
Cecilio Guante	-	-	-	-	-	-	-	-	-	0-1	-	-	-	1	0-1
Keith Hernandez	-	15-24	-	-	-	-	-	-	-	-	-	-	8	31	15-24
Brook Jacoby	-	36-26	-	36-54	-	-	-	-	-	-	-	-	50	102	72-80
Chris James	-	-	-	-	-	6-5	-	1-0	56-65	-	-	2-1	50	83	63-70
Dion James	-	9-20	-	-	-	8-12	3-5	-	3-6	-	1-3	-	-	66	23-43
Stan Jefferson	-	-	-	-	-	10-8	5-4	-	-	-	6-4	-	4	23	15-12
Doug Jones	-	-	-	-	-	-	-	-	-	-	-	-	-	-	-
Jeff Kaiser	-	-	-	-	-	-	-	-	-	-	-	-	-	-	-
Candy Maldonado	-	-	-	-	-	41-55	-	20-18	12-8	-	-	61-68	53	101	73-81
Jeffery Manto	-	10-8	-	3-1	-	-	-	-	-	-	-	-	11	11	13-9
Mark McLemore	-	-	1-1	1-0	-	-	-	-	-	-	-	-	1	2	2-1
Charles Nagy	-	-	-	-	-	-	-	-	-	2-6	-	-	5	3	2-6
Rod Nichols	-	-	-	-	-	-	-	-	-	0-2	-	-	-	2	0-2
Al Nipper	-	-	-	-	-	-	-	-	-	2-3	-	-	2	3	2-3
Steven Olin	-	-	-	-	-	-	-	-	-	1-0	-	-	1	-	1-0
Jesse Orosco	-	-	-	-	-	-	-	-	-	-	-	-	-	-	-
Ken Phelps	-	5-6	-	-	-	-	-	-	1-5	-	-	0-1	-	17	6-11
Rafael Santana	-	-	-	-	2-2	-	-	-	-	-	-	-	1	3	2-2
Rudy Seanez	-	-	-	-	-	-	-	-	-	-	-	-	-	-	-
Jeff Shaw	-	-	-	-	-	-	-	-	-	4-5	-	-	1	8	4-5
Joel Skinner	20-24	-	-	-	-	-	-	-	-	-	-	-	17	27	20-24
Cory Snyder	-	-	-	-	3-1	-	-	50-61	-	-	-	13-13	45	70	53-62
Steve Springer	-	-	-	1-2	-	-	-	-	-	-	-	-	2	1	1-2
Greg Swindell	-	-	-	-	-	-	-	-	-	20-14	-	-	7	27	20-14
Efrain Valdez	-	-	-	-	-	-	-	-	-	-	-	-	-	-	-
Sergio Valdez	-	-	-	-	-	-	-	-	-	7-6	-	-	3	10	7-6
Mike Walker	-	-	-	-	-	-	-	-	-	2-8	-	-	4	6	2-8
Colby Ward	-	-	-	-	-	-	-	-	-	-	-	-	-	-	-
Turner Ward	-	-	-	-	-	-	-	6-5	-	-	-	-	2	9	6-5
Mitch Webster	-	1-1	-	-	-	12-5	42-43	-	-	-	8-7	-	52	52	55-49
Kevin Wickander	-	-	-	-	-	-	-	-	-	-	-	-	-	-	-

TEAM TOTALS: BATTING

	AB	H	2B	3B	HR	RBI	BB	SO	BA	SA	OBA
Season	5485	1465	266	41	110	675	458	836	.267	.391	.324
vs. Left-Handers	1626	463	69	10	36	216	150	228	.285	.406	.345
vs. Right-Handers	3859	1002	197	31	74	459	308	608	.260	.384	.314
vs. Ground-Ballers	2722	755	137	20	48	365	227	379	.277	.395	.333
vs. Fly-Ballers	2763	710	129	21	62	310	231	457	.257	.386	.314
Home Games	2655	725	129	19	52	332	247	403	.273	.395	.335
Road Games	2830	740	137	22	58	343	211	433	.261	.387	.313
Grass Fields	4600	1238	219	34	92	565	392	699	.269	.392	.326
Artificial Turf	885	227	47	7	18	110	66	137	.256	.386	.310
April	598	155	23	6	17	73	32	82	.259	.403	.299
May	908	220	33	7	18	100	60	169	.242	.354	.291
June	976	267	51	9	22	120	90	143	.274	.412	.333
July	994	248	44	7	13	91	91	140	.249	.347	.313
August	954	270	50	4	22	144	83	142	.283	.413	.341
Sept./Oct.	1055	305	65	8	18	147	102	160	.289	.417	.351
Leading Off Inn.	1317	332	52	8	23	23	104	215	.252	.356	.313
Bases Empty	3114	783	140	26	66	66	238	485	.251	.377	.309
Runners On	2371	682	126	15	44	609	220	351	.288	.409	.342
Runners/Scor. Pos.	1377	383	69	7	23	538	160	212	.278	.389	.341
Runners On/2 Out	1001	274	51	5	19	254	102	151	.274	.392	.342
Scor. Pos./2 Out	654	180	33	3	11	225	77	95	.275	.385	.352
Late-Inning Pressure	782	190	35	4	14	80	74	152	.243	.352	.309
Leading Off	199	40	9	0	3	3	14	48	.201	.291	.257
Runners On	308	79	20	1	3	69	40	55	.256	.357	.341
Runners/Scor. Pos.	183	50	11	0	2	63	31	34	.273	.366	.376

RUNS BATTED IN	From 1B	From 2B	From 3B	Scoring Position
Totals	84/1679	205/1055	276/623	481/1678
Percentage	5.0%	19.4%	44.3%	28.7%

TEAM TOTALS: PITCHING

	W-L	ERA	AB	H	HR	BB	SO	BA	SA	OBA
Season	77-85	4.26	5526	1491	163	518	860	.270	.417	.334
vs. Left-Handers			2095	557	52	216	274	.266	.390	.336
vs. Right-Handers			3431	934	111	302	586	.272	.433	.333
vs. Ground-Ballers			2574	690	39	218	372	.268	.366	.327
vs. Fly-Ballers			2952	801	124	300	488	.271	.462	.340
Home Games	41-40	4.27	2831	764	86	246	430	.270	.413	.329
Road Games	36-45	4.25	2695	727	77	272	430	.270	.422	.339
Grass Fields	65-72	4.24	4674	1247	140	425	738	.267	.412	.330
Artificial Turf	12-13	4.39	852	244	23	93	122	.286	.442	.358
April	9-9	4.44	598	161	16	49	89	.269	.426	.329
May	13-14	3.71	906	240	26	78	121	.265	.412	.323
June	14-14	4.93	979	264	39	115	149	.270	.447	.347
July	11-19	4.09	994	246	29	101	158	.247	.378	.320
August	12-16	4.73	990	286	28	97	160	.289	.430	.355
Sept./Oct.	18-13	3.78	1059	294	25	78	183	.278	.413	.328
Leading Off Inn.			1326	350	41	99	187	.264	.430	.318
Bases Empty			3127	823	107	265	492	.263	.427	.325
Runners On			2399	668	56	253	368	.278	.405	.345
Runners/Scor. Pos.			1388	378	26	178	243	.272	.385	.349
Runners On/2 Out			1041	279	21	128	179	.268	.383	.353
Scor. Pos./2 Out			677	180	12	94	126	.266	.375	.360
Late-Inning Pressure			675	166	13	68	115	.246	.348	.316
Leading Off			165	46	4	20	26	.279	.418	.357
Runners On			302	72	7	32	57	.238	.341	.313
Runners/Scor. Pos.			171	37	4	25	36	.216	.310	.315
First 9 Batters			2786	707	72	282	497	.254	.389	.324
Second 9 Batters			1470	423	49	140	198	.288	.447	.351
All Batters Thereafter			1270	361	42	96	165	.284	.444	.337

DETROIT TIGERS

- **The fifty file.**
- **The longest-running show on dirt.**

When Cecil Fielder launched home run number 50 into Yankee Stadium's left field upper deck last October, he became only the 11th player in major league history to reach that mark. The list of others who reached the 50 mark is impressive: George Foster, Jimmie Foxx, Hank Greenberg, Ralph Kiner, Mickey Mantle, Roger Maris, Willie Mays, Johnny Mize, Babe Ruth, and Hack Wilson. But even those illustrious names don't convey the enormity of Fielder's achievement nearly as well as the list of those who approached the 50 mark and fell short. The career highs of all 54 players who hit 40 or more home runs in a season, but never as many as 50:

49 — Andre Dawson, Lou Gehrig, Harmon Killebrew, Ted Kluszewski, Mark McGwire, and Frank Robinson.

48 — Frank Howard, Dave Kingman, Mike Schmidt, and Willie Stargell.

47 — Hank Aaron, Ernie Banks, George Bell, Reggie Jackson, Eddie Mathews, and Kevin Mitchell.

46 — Orlando Cepeda, Joe DiMaggio, Jim Gentile, and Jim Rice.

45 — Johnny Bench, Rocky Colavito, Willie McCovey, and Gorman Thomas.

44 — Dale Murphy and Carl Yastrzemski.

43 — Tony Armas, Davey Johnson, Chuck Klein, Al Rosen, Duke Snider, and Ted Williams.

42 — Jose Canseco, Gil Hodges, Rogers Hornsby, Mel Ott, Roy Sievers, Dick Stuart, Hal Trosky, Billy Williams, and Gus Zernial.

41 — Jeff Burroughs, Roy Campanella, Norm Cash, Darrell Evans, Ben Oglivie, Hank Sauer, and Cy Williams.

40 — Dick Allen, Jesse Barfield, Tony Perez, Rico Petrocelli, Wally Post, and Ryne Sandberg.

Fielder's 51 home runs last season were two more than either Killebrew or Gehrig hit in his best year; four more than the highest total ever compiled by Reggie Jackson, Ernie Banks, or the all-time career leader, Hank Aaron; and six more than Willie McCovey's best-ever season. That must have made for a pretty satisfying off-season for Cecil, don't you think?

How likely was Fielder to hit 50 home runs last season? Well, you asked for it (no, come to think of it, we asked for it), so here's our favorite freak-show statistic of the season: Fielder now holds the career record for most home runs after returning from Japanese baseball, a record he broke on *May 15*. (The previous high of 13 belongs to Bobby Jones—none of them a grand slam.)

But those who considered Fielder's performance a fluke apparently didn't realize that several seasons ago he was the reason that Fred McGriff was platooned by the Blue Jays. Back in 1987, Fielder hit 14 home runs in only 175 at-bats, the fourth-highest rate in the American League. But nothing in Fielder's past approached the average performance of other players on the brink of a 50-homer season—nothing, that is, except for his 38 home runs for the Hanshin Tigers of Japan's Central League in 1989. The following table lists the statistics for the year *prior* to every 50-homer season in baseball history. No one hit fewer than 22 homers in those seasons, and 13 of 17 hit 30 or more. Their average pre-50 performance included 38 home runs, 122 RBIs, and a .313 batting average:

Year	Player	G	AB	R	H	2B	3B	HR	RBI	BB	BA
1919	Babe Ruth	130	432	103	139	34	12	29	114	101	.322
1920	Babe Ruth	142	458	158	172	36	9	54	137	148	.376
1926	Babe Ruth	152	495	139	184	30	5	47	145	144	.372
1927	Babe Ruth	151	540	158	192	29	8	60	164	138	.356
1929	Hack Wilson	150	574	135	198	30	5	39	159	78	.345
1931	Jimmie Foxx	139	515	93	150	32	10	30	120	73	.291
1937	Jimmie Foxx	150	569	111	162	24	6	36	127	99	.285
1937	Hank Greenberg	154	594	137	200	49	14	40	183	102	.337
1946	Ralph Kiner	144	502	63	124	17	3	23	81	74	.247
1946	Johnny Mize	101	377	70	127	18	3	22	70	62	.337
1948	Ralph Kiner	156	555	104	147	19	5	40	123	112	.265
1954	Willie Mays	151	565	119	195	33	13	41	110	66	.345
1955	Mickey Mantle	147	517	121	158	25	11	37	99	113	.306
1960	Mickey Mantle	153	527	119	145	17	6	40	94	111	.275
1960	Roger Maris	136	499	98	141	18	7	39	112	70	.283
1964	Willie Mays	157	578	121	171	21	9	47	111	82	.296
1976	George Foster	144	562	86	172	21	9	29	121	52	.306

Of course, even that bare-bones analysis begs the question of what those players did in the seasons *after* hitting 50 home runs. Well, eight of those 17 seasons were followed by 40-plus years, and the only player to hit fewer than 30 home runs a year later was Wilson (who reputedly drank himself out of baseball within four years). Despite Wilson's poor performance in 1931, the group average for the following season was 39 home runs, 115 RBIs, and a .310 batting average. If you're Cecil Fielder, you take that season—no questions asked.

Records are made to be broken, and so too, we suppose, are quasi-records. So it was with a quirky curiosity that we watched Fielder's walk and strikeout totals swell along with his home-run count last summer. By the end of the season, Fielder had drawn 90 walks, struck out 182 times, and been hit by five pitches—a total of 277 plate appearances in which he failed to put the ball in play, the fifth-highest in major league history.

And Fielder wasn't the only player to crack the all-time top 10 in whatever it is that's called last season. His new teammate Mickey Tettleton, playing for Baltimore, accumulated 271 plate appearances without putting the ball in play.

But wait—there's more! Rob Deer, who also joined Detroit during the offseason—you'd better sit down for this one—also appears in the top 10, with a total of 277 PAWOPBIPs in 1987. (All right, we admit it lacks the ring of Charles Osgood's snappy *POSSLQ*.) The 10 highest single-season totals in major league history:

Year	Player	BB	SO	HP	Total
1969	Jimmy Wynn	148	142	3	293
1975	Mike Schmidt	101	180	4	285
1983	Mike Schmidt	128	148	3	279
1989	Jack Clark	132	145	1	278
1987	**Rob Deer**	86	186	5	277
1990	**Cecil Fielder**	90	182	5	277
1969	Bobby Bonds	77	189	10	276
1979	Gorman Thomas	98	175	2	275
1987	Jack Clark	136	139	0	275
1990	**Mickey Tettleton**	106	160	5	271

Mickey Mantle is fond of pointing out that between his 1734 walks and his 1710 strikeouts, he spent the equivalent of six full seasons at the plate without putting a ball in play. We're not sure why, but it appears that the Tigers are hell-bent on doing the same over the course of a single summer in Detroit.

The convergence of Fielder, Tettleton, and Deer at the corner of Michigan and Trumbull this summer ought to produce two noteworthy statistical skews, one obvious, the other not so. Last season, they combined for 489 strikeouts; spread across the continent as they were, no climatic changes were attributed to them with any degree of certainty. This summer, however, they should substantially cool the immediate Tiger Stadium area as they take a run at the 23-year-old major league mark of 1203 strikeouts, set by the 1968 New York Mets. The highest single-season totals in major league history:

Year	Team	SO
1968	New York Mets	1203
1970	San Diego Padres	1164
1986	Philadelphia Phillies	1154
1986	Seattle Mariners	1148
1969	San Diego Padres	1143
1969	Philadelphia Phillies	1130
1965	New York Mets	1129
1965	Washington Senators	1125
1964	Washington Senators	1124
1987	Philadelphia Phillies	1109

Only one team in history has produced three players with as many as 120 strikeouts in the same season: the 1986 Seattle Mariners, with Jim Presley (172), Danny Tartabull (157), and Phil Bradley (134). Before the 1991 season ends, the Tigers trio could make those guys look like the Alou brothers.

Detroit could also send plateward the fly-ball-hittingest lineup in the 17 years that we have compiled those figures. Last season, only one American League team had a greater tendency toward fly balls than the Tigers. The ground outs-to-air outs ratios of all 26 major league teams:

American League		National League	
Milwaukee	0.99	New York	0.85
Detroit	1.00	Pittsburgh	0.99
Oakland	1.05	Atlanta	1.00
Seattle	1.07	Philadelphia	1.07
Cleveland	1.08	San Diego	1.07
New York	1.09	San Francisco	1.09
Baltimore	1.11	Cincinnati	1.13
Chicago	1.12	Chicago	1.13
Boston	1.15	Houston	1.14
California	1.15	Los Angeles	1.19
Toronto	1.16	Montreal	1.21
Kansas City	1.17	St. Louis	1.24
Texas	1.18		
Minnesota	1.21		

The 1990 Mets were by far the most prolific fly-ball hitters assembled since we've been keeping track. The previous low average during that period was 0.90, by the 1985 Tigers. But the addition of Deer, whose 0.44 mark was the lowest in the majors last season, and Tettleton (0.96), along with a full season from sophomore Travis Fryman (0.93), could lower Detroit's figure to a similar level.

Now, if just one manager would rearrange his starting rotation to stack a deck of fly-ball pitchers against the Tigers, exploiting that skew, he would automatically become the *Elias Baseball Analyst* Manager of the Year for 1991. But we are realistic; most managers don't like to be told that there's something to be learned from the calculations of a bunch of guys who "never played the game." So if no one heeds this notice, we'll simply have to reinstitute in next year's edition our campaign of education for stubborn skippers regarding this underutilized trend.

The legend of Trammell and Whitaker continues. They hooked up at Montgomery in the Southern League in 1977, made their major league debuts together later that season in the second game of a doubleheader on September 9, 1977 (Tito Fuentes and Tom Veryzer started the first game), and have become fixtures there over the 13 seasons since then. That's the longest streak ever by a second baseman and shortstop by a wide margin. The following table shows that only 13 other pairs manned those positions together for even half that long:

Second Baseman	Shortstop	Team	Years
Lou Whitaker	**Alan Trammell**	Tigers	13 (1978–90)
Glenn Beckert	Don Kessinger	Cubs	9 (1965–73)
Davey Lopes	Bill Russell	Dodgers	9 (1973–81)
Cupid Childs	Ed McKean	Spiders	8 (1891–98)
Bobby Lowe	Herman Long	Beaneaters	8 (1893–1900)
Johnny Evers	Joe Tinker	Cubs	8 (1903–10)

Second Baseman	Shortstop	Team	Years
Charlie Gehringer	Billy Rogell	Tigers	8 (1931–38)
Joe Morgan	Dave Concepcion	Reds	8 (1972–79)
Otto Knabe	Mickey Doolan	Phillies	7 (1907–13)
Ralph Young	Donie Bush	Tigers	7 (1915–21)
Jackie Hayes	Luke Appling	White Sox	7 (1932–38)
Billy Herman	Billy Jurges	Cubs	7 (1932–38)
Nellie Fox	Luis Aparicio	White Sox	7 (1956–62)
Bill Mazeroski	Dick Groat	Pirates	7 (1956–62)

Although the margin between their batting averages has been stretched to 14 points over the past four seasons—during which time Trammell has outhit Whitaker .304 to .257—their career statistics remain remarkably similar:

Player	G	AB	R	H	2B	3B	HR	RBI	BB	SO	SB	BA
Trammell	1835	6702	1009	1929	329	50	152	810	707	712	199	.288
Whitaker	1827	6693	1040	1831	301	60	167	781	876	874	124	.274

Remarkably similar. So similar, in fact, that we began to wonder whether any two other players in major league history with such long careers matched to as great a degree. (If only computers could be used for good instead of evil!) And so, after long hours of pointless computation, we present our Patty and Cathy Lane Awards to John Mayberry and Andre Thornton. Their career statistics appear below; sorry, we've forgotten which is which:

G	AB	R	H	2B	3B	HR	RBI	BB	SO	SB	BA
1620	5447	881	1379	211	19	255	879	881	810	20	.253
1565	5291	792	1342	244	22	253	895	876	851	48	.254

Are Whittell and Tramaker at least the most similar *teammates* ever? Almost certainly. But if you're driven to browse through your *Baseball Encyclopedia* in pursuit of a definite answer, check out Roy White; it looks to us as if he's even more similar to Whitaker at this point than Trammell is!

WON-LOST RECORD BY STARTING POSITION

Detroit Tigers	C	1B	2B	3B	SS	LF	CF	RF	DH	P	Leadoff	Cleanup	Starts vs. LH	Starts vs. RH	Total Starts
Scott Aldred	-	-	-	-	-	-	-	-	-	1-2	-	-	1	2	1-2
Dave Bergman	-	11-12	-	-	-	-	-	-	14-16	-	-	1-1	-	53	25-28
Darnell Coles	-	-	-	2-4	-	1-0	-	2-1	9-8	-	-	-	23	4	14-13
Milton Cuyler	-	-	-	-	-	-	9-8	-	-	-	0-1	-	5	12	9-8
Brian DuBois	-	-	-	-	-	-	-	-	-	5-6	-	-	7	4	5-6
Cecil Fielder	-	68-71	-	-	-	-	-	-	7-8	-	-	54-61	49	105	75-79
Travis Fryman	-	-	-	25-20	7-7	-	-	-	-	-	-	-	24	35	32-27
Paul Gibson	-	-	-	-	-	-	-	-	-	-	-	-	-	-	-
Jerry Don Gleaton	-	-	-	-	-	-	-	-	-	-	-	-	-	-	-
Mike Heath	47-52	-	-	-	-	-	-	-	2-0	-	-	-	46	55	49-52
Mike Henneman	-	-	-	-	-	-	-	-	-	-	-	-	-	-	-
Tracy Jones	-	-	-	-	-	6-13	-	-	7-4	-	-	-	21	9	13-17
Matt Kinzer	-	-	-	-	-	-	-	-	-	-	-	-	-	-	-
Chet Lemon	-	-	-	-	-	-	1-1	43-43	1-1	-	-	-	40	50	45-45
Jim Lindeman	-	-	-	-	-	-	-	-	3-3	-	-	1-1	6	-	3-3
Urbano Lugo	-	-	-	-	-	-	-	-	-	0-1	-	-	-	1	0-1
Scott Lusader	-	-	-	-	-	1-0	1-1	12-10	-	-	-	-	1	24	14-11
Lance McCullers	-	-	-	-	-	-	-	-	-	1-0	-	-	1	-	1-0
Jack Morris	-	-	-	-	-	-	-	-	-	16-20	-	-	11	25	16-20
Lloyd Moseby	-	-	-	-	-	7-5	47-50	-	3-1	-	-	8-6	23	90	57-56
Matt Nokes	4-11	-	-	-	-	-	-	-	10-11	-	-	3-3	-	36	14-22
Randy Nosek	-	-	-	-	-	-	-	-	-	1-1	-	-	1	1	1-1
Edwin Nunez	-	-	-	-	-	-	-	-	-	-	-	-	-	-	-
Johnny Paredes	-	-	1-1	-	-	-	-	-	-	-	-	-	2	-	1-1
Clay Parker	-	-	-	-	-	-	-	-	-	0-1	-	-	1	-	0-1
Dan Petry	-	-	-	-	-	-	-	-	-	14-9	-	-	7	16	14-9
Tony Phillips	-	-	24-19	42-47	5-3	2-0	-	0-1	0-4	-	49-50	-	46	101	73-74
Kevin Ritz	-	-	-	-	-	-	-	-	-	0-4	-	-	1	3	0-4
Jeff M. Robinson	-	-	-	-	-	-	-	-	-	15-12	-	-	5	22	15-12
Ed Romero	-	-	-	10-12	-	-	-	-	-	-	-	-	15	7	10-12
Rich Rowland	3-1	-	-	-	-	-	-	-	1-1	-	-	-	4	2	4-2
Mark Salas	25-19	-	-	-	-	-	-	-	-	-	-	-	3	41	25-19
Mike Schwabe	-	-	-	-	-	-	-	-	-	-	-	-	-	-	-
Steve Searcy	-	-	-	-	-	-	-	-	-	4-8	-	-	4	8	4-8
Larry Sheets	-	-	-	-	-	24-23	-	7-12	18-20	-	-	5-5	-	104	49-55
John Shelby	-	-	-	-	-	6-6	17-15	6-6	-	-	1-0	-	16	40	29-27
Frank Tanana	-	-	-	-	-	-	-	-	-	14-15	-	-	6	23	14-15
Walt Terrell	-	-	-	-	-	-	-	-	-	8-4	-	-	4	8	8-4
Alan Trammell	-	-	-	-	67-73	-	-	-	1-2	-	-	-	45	98	68-75
Steve Wapnick	-	-	-	-	-	-	-	-	-	-	-	-	-	-	-
Gary Ward	-	-	-	-	-	31-36	-	4-6	3-4	-	-	7-6	42	42	38-46
Lou Whitaker	-	-	54-63	-	-	-	-	-	-	-	29-32	-	13	104	54-63
Ken Williams	-	-	-	-	-	1-0	4-8	5-4	-	-	-	-	17	5	10-12

TEAM TOTALS: BATTING

	AB	H	2B	3B	HR	RBI	BB	SO	BA	SA	OBA
Season	5479	1418	241	32	172	714	634	952	.259	.409	.337
vs. Left-Handers	1780	451	78	10	63	221	200	303	.253	.415	.330
vs. Right-Handers	3699	967	163	22	109	493	434	649	.261	.406	.341
vs. Ground-Ballers	2481	650	99	14	71	314	259	401	.262	.399	.334
vs. Fly-Ballers	2998	768	142	18	101	400	375	551	.256	.417	.340
Home Games	2628	676	109	15	92	355	332	473	.257	.415	.343
Road Games	2851	742	132	17	80	359	302	479	.260	.403	.332
Grass Fields	4635	1183	201	25	145	609	543	804	.255	.403	.335
Artificial Turf	844	235	40	7	27	105	91	148	.278	.438	.348
April	691	188	31	7	14	85	72	97	.272	.398	.344
May	986	256	43	5	39	122	100	161	.260	.432	.332
June	918	220	27	1	31	117	108	160	.240	.373	.318
July	946	248	43	8	32	139	136	174	.262	.426	.356
August	962	279	61	7	31	140	118	176	.290	.465	.369
Sept./Oct.	976	227	36	4	25	111	100	184	.233	.355	.304
Leading Off Inn.	1308	347	63	8	33	33	115	199	.265	.401	.330
Bases Empty	3032	793	142	17	93	93	326	508	.262	.412	.337
Runners On	2447	625	99	15	79	621	308	444	.255	.405	.338
Runners/Scor. Pos.	1374	339	55	11	45	534	214	273	.247	.401	.344
Runners On/2 Out	1015	236	33	7	36	250	136	193	.233	.385	.329
Scor. Pos./2 Out	634	148	22	4	20	211	101	125	.233	.375	.345
Late-Inning Pressure	670	155	29	2	12	71	102	134	.231	.334	.338
Leading Off	158	45	4	0	2	2	20	23	.285	.348	.376
Runners On	329	72	13	2	6	65	53	73	.219	.325	.332
Runners/Scor. Pos.	203	41	9	2	5	63	39	54	.202	.340	.339

RUNS BATTED IN	From 1B	From 2B	From 3B	Scoring Position
Totals	96/1834	190/1079	256/618	446/1697
Percentage	5.2%	17.6%	41.4%	26.3%

TEAM TOTALS: PITCHING

	W-L	ERA	AB	H	HR	BB	SO	BA	SA	OBA
Season	79-83	4.39	5409	1401	154	661	856	.259	.403	.341
vs. Left-Handers			1958	517	42	252	260	.264	.382	.349
vs. Right-Handers			3451	884	112	409	596	.256	.416	.337
vs. Ground-Ballers			2559	651	52	307	373	.254	.373	.337
vs. Fly-Ballers			2850	750	102	354	483	.263	.431	.346
Home Games	39-42	4.56	2738	692	75	330	445	.253	.393	.335
Road Games	40-41	4.20	2671	709	79	331	411	.265	.414	.348
Grass Fields	67-71	4.29	4635	1198	129	567	767	.258	.397	.341
Artificial Turf	12-12	4.93	774	203	25	94	89	.262	.441	.346
April	8-12	5.02	686	204	14	93	98	.297	.437	.384
May	12-17	4.27	965	243	34	109	155	.252	.415	.330
June	16-12	3.95	919	228	28	119	154	.248	.403	.334
July	13-15	5.07	962	245	26	113	153	.255	.402	.332
August	14-13	5.36	947	271	31	104	121	.286	.440	.359
Sept./Oct.	16-14	2.92	930	210	21	123	175	.226	.331	.321
Leading Off Inn.			1289	347	37	139	198	.269	.418	.343
Bases Empty			2975	771	85	329	476	.259	.404	.338
Runners On			2434	630	69	332	380	.259	.402	.345
Runners/Scor. Pos.			1434	348	45	249	246	.243	.386	.349
Runners On/2 Out			1010	243	32	154	155	.241	.378	.344
Scor. Pos./2 Out			683	153	24	116	113	.224	.367	.342
Late-Inning Pressure			721	186	17	87	111	.258	.372	.340
Leading Off			176	39	4	20	30	.222	.347	.305
Runners On			316	82	6	40	46	.259	.361	.342
Runners/Scor. Pos.			177	40	5	33	30	.226	.350	.346
First 9 Batters			2745	674	64	371	470	.246	.372	.337
Second 9 Batters			1506	414	57	169	213	.275	.448	.351
All Batters Thereafter			1158	313	33	121	173	.270	.421	.340

KANSAS CITY ROYALS

- **Are the Royals ready to bounce back?**
- **Down deep, they're shallow.**

Title this essay "When Bad Things Happen to Good Teams." It was a tough way to spend the summer of 1990, but Royals fans can take consolation from the fact that their team provided us with an opportunity to examine two of our favorite team trends: First, what happens to previously strong teams that suffer disastrous seasons? And second, do teams that right themselves after horrendous starts do better in the next season than teams with similar season-long records without noteworthy peaks and valleys?

A review of the facts: Kansas City won 92 games in 1989, finishing the season only seven games behind Oakland. During the offseason, the Royals signed N.L. Cy Young Award winner Mark Davis, Oakland's 19-game-winner Storm Davis, and (for comic relief) veteran starter Richard Dotson. Then came the lockout, a shortened spring training, and faster than you could say "Bruce Dal Canton" Kansas City found itself last in the A.L. West. It took Kansas City only 15 games to fall as far behind Oakland as they had finished the previous season. But just when it appeared the wheels were about to come off, Kansas City righted itself. For two months, the Royals did no better than to fall no further behind the pack, but they won 50 of their final 100 games to pass Minnesota and escape the division basement. What would have seemed an utter disaster in April had become a gritty accomplishment by October.

At first glance, it would appear that the trends of teams that had suffered declines like Kansas City's should be irrelevant to the Royals. After all, their hopes for another 180-degree turn in 1991 hinge primarily on the health of Bret Saberhagen and Mark Gubicza (both injured last season) and a rebound by Mark Davis. But a wave of injuries is often the cause of a plunge like Kansas City's; among teams that took similar dives in the recent past, the 1988 St. Louis Cardinals lost three pitchers to injury (Danny Cox, Greg Mathews, and Joe Magrane); so did the 1987 California Angels (John Candelaria, Kirk McCaskill, and Donnie Moore); and the 1986 Los Angeles Dodgers lost one starting pitcher (Jerry Reuss) and their best everyday player (Pedro Guerrero). Kansas City's current situation is neither unique nor atypical.

From 1900 through 1988, 42 teams played at least 10 games below the .500 mark after compiling records at least 15 games above .500 a year earlier. (Two were disqualified because the now scorned 1981 season was involved.) The teams in that group include those listed above, as well as the 1987 Astros and the 1986 Royals. The following table indicates how they performed in the seasons after the fall, divided into five categories: Complete Rebounds (a record equal to or better than the team's mark in its winning season); Moderate Rebounds (better than .500, but below the previous winning record); .500 Records; Slight Rebounds (below .500, but no worse than the previous season's mark); and Further Declines:

Next Season	Teams	Most Recent Teams
Complete Rebounds	5	1954 Giants, 1945 Senators
Moderate Rebounds	11	1989 Cardinals, 1988 Astros
.500 Records	4	1984 Angels, 1972 Rangers
Slight Rebounds	15	1980 Giants, 1979 White Sox
Further Declines	7	1959 Cardinals, 1933 Giants

The good news: 80 percent of those teams at least equaled their records of the previous season, and nearly half regained the .500 level. The bad news: The kind of rebound that Kansas City would need to contend in the now powerful A.L. West (that is, winning at least as many games as in 1989) hasn't occurred in either league since 1954, when the New York Giants won a shocking World Series victory over Cleveland after finishing fifth a year earlier. Of course, unless there's a comeback in the works that we haven't heard about, the Royals can't anticipate the return of Willie Mays to fuel their recovery. Then again, the Giants didn't benefit from the return to form of even a single pitcher injured in 1953.

But while 12 of the 42 teams either equaled their winning records of two years earlier or failed to surpass their losing records of the previous season, neither of those events has occurred since 1959; the last 15 teams to qualify all fell somewhere between those two extremes. And that obviously won't be good enough to win a division title in 1991. Could the effective return of Saberhagen, Gubicza, and Davis overcome that trend? Absolutely. But that's probably what Cardinals fans said about Cox, Mathews, and Magrane in 1988.

As we mentioned earlier, Kansas City staggered out of the gate in 1990, finishing the season 11 games below .500 despite winning 50 of its last 100 games. If the Royals were a racehorse, we would be tempted to disregard that last race entirely—throw it out because the horse broke slowly. That approach has some validity for baseball teams as well.

From 1900 through 1988, there were 116 teams that finished a season between 10 and 15 games blow the .500 mark. Of those, 37 built at least half of that season-long deficit within their first 30 games. The 1990 Royals are an example:

	W	L	+/−
First 30 games	10	20	−10
All other games	65	66	−1

The teams that started slowly had a greater tendency to improve the next season than did the other group, which had similar overall records but no pronounced early-season slump. The next table shows how many teams from each group reached various levels of competence a year later:

	Slow Starts	Other Teams
Teams in group	37	79
Improved next season	25 (68%)	44 (56%)
.500 or better	20 (54%)	31 (39%)
.550 or better	11 (30%)	10 (13%)
.600 or better	3 (8%)	4 (5%)

Although significant differences occurred in all but the last category, the widest divergence was at the .550 to .600 level. Teams that righted themselves after slow starts were roughly three times as likely to rebound to that level than were the other teams—an encouraging conclusion for the Royals.

The questionable status of Saberhagen, Gubicza, and Mark Davis is the most important issue to face the Royals this season, but it surely won't be their only obstacle. For years, Kansas City's lineup has grown older as the team waited for its organization to produce another generation of Bretts, Whites, and Wilsons. From 1981 through 1986, the best rookies to emerge from the Royals system were nothing more than role players: Don Slaught, Pat Sheridan, and Mike Kingery. A glimmer of optimism arose in 1987, when Kansas City's farm system snapped a long slump and launched two outstanding rookies, Bo Jackson and Kevin Seitzer. But since 1987 the talent flow has again dried up, producing only catcher Mike Macfarlane and wannabe starters Terry Shumpert and Brian McRae.

This season the Royals will finally be unable to escape the consequences for the organization's barren decade. Five players who accounted for a total of 365 starts last season are gone, and to make matters worse the Royals received nothing in return for any of those players. Pat Tabler was sold to the Mets in August, and the four others all became free agents after the end of the 1990 season: Bob Boone, Gerald Perry, Frank White, and Willie Wilson.

The fact that the Royals have nothing to show for players who started that many games says a lot about the weakness of their lineup last season, so we won't pretend that their absences will have a disastrous impact on this season's starting lineup (unless they are once again hit hard by injuries, that is). Terry Shumpert had won the second base spot from Frank White early last season, but was injured shortly thereafter. The emergence of Brian McRae in center field and the acquisition of Kirk Gibson as insurance will allow Bo Jackson to return to left field, Jim Eisenreich to play right, and Danny Tartabull to play his natural position, designated hitter. (Incidentally, numerophiles are urged to compare McRae's rookie season statistics to those of Mel Ott and Barry Larkin.) The continued development of Macfarlane behind the plate fills another void. But even if the Royals remain healthy, their bench is certain to suffer; no team can simply absorb the loss of 365 starts without replenishing its roster with reliable talent. Other than pitchers Mike Boddicker and Dan Schatzeder, Gibson was the only noteworthy player added to Kansas City's roster during the offseason, and Gibson himself played only 160 games over the past two seasons.

Even Kansas City's best-case scenario may leave the team with a bench of little more than Gibson or McRae, utility infielder Steve Jeltz, perennial prospects like Rey Palacios, Bill Pecota, and Gary Thurman, and a spring training discovery or two, raising these questions: How much has any team ever extracted from its regular starters, and how successful were the teams whose benches contributed the least?

First-tier players—and by that we mean those among the nine most frequent batters on each American League team (eight in the National League)—accounted for 75 percent of all plate appearances in the A.L. last season. The Boston Red Sox received the greatest contribution from their regular nine (5272 of the team's 6234 PAs, or 85 percent), and only one other team had an average higher than 80 percent: Toronto (80.4%). (The highest N.L. average was 71 percent by the San Diego Padres. The league average was only 68 percent, considerably lower since only eight players are included among the regulars, thereby including one PA for the second-tier group on every pass through the batting order, making 89 percent the highest possible figure.) On average, the American League "extras" drove in 186 runs per team.

The "Water from a Stone" award goes to the 1978 Red Sox, whose nine most frequent batters accumulated 89 percent of the team's plate appearances, a 20th-century high. The most productive lineup—or perhaps more accurately, the least productive bench— belonged to the Red Sox once again, in 1984, who drew the highest percentage of RBIs from its primary group: 708 of 810, or 87 percent.

Now, if the Red Sox know something about maximizing the contribution of their best players—and it certainly appears that they do—maybe they'd be so kind as to impart that wisdom to John Wathan and his Royals staff. Not only will the information be greatly appreciated, but let's face it—if you were Red Sox manager Joe Morgan, wouldn't you do whatever you could to help any team in the A.L. West dethrone the defending champs?

George Brett received tremendous publicity last season for winning the American League batting title—not because it was his third, not because it was 14 years since he won his first, and not because he was 37 years old, all of which should have added luster to the accomplishment. Brett earned more publicity for two other reasons: first, for becoming the first player ever to win batting titles in three different decades; and second, for sitting out the final game to maximize his chances of winning the championship.

Before the matter fades entirely from the public consciousness, we'd like to make clear what we think about it. To win batting titles 14 years apart represents nearly unprecedented longevity of excellence (see Brett's player comments on page 116)—even Ty Cobb's batting championships spanned only 13 years (though he did win 12 titles during that time). The fact that Brett's titles spanned three decades is nothing more than an accident of timing, like Jim Bunning's 100 wins in two leagues. Was that any more of an accomplishment than winning an equal number of games all in the same league, or for the same team? Of course not. It means only that Bunning was traded at about the midpoint of a long and fine career. *Nothing more.* Same for Frank Robinson's MVP awards in both leagues. The only difference between his and Ted Williams's two MVP awards (or Johnny Bench's, or Robin Yount's, or Willie Mays's, and so on) is that Robinson's team, the Reds, concluded in the winter of '65 (wrongly, as it turned out) that his value on the market exceeded his value on the field. The accomplishment is important; the arbitrary division that makes it unique isn't.

Jim Kaat has a marvelous term for such nonsense. He refers to his own status as a four-decade player—a distinction sought by some others with the urgency of a quest for world peace—as "conterfeit trivia." We love that phrase because it implies what has become true of so much of the stat-trivia that abounds today: It is intended to distort the facts rather than to illuminate them—*the antithesis of what statistical analysis should provide.*

As for Brett declining to start the final game of the season in order to protect his lead over Rickey Henderson, what can we say? Invariably, comparisons have been drawn between him and Ted Williams in 1941. (For a new slant on that great old story, see the Houston Astros essay.) But the explosion of interest in statistical achievements during the 49 years since then (particularly over the past decade) hasn't been without a price. Broadcasters, writers, and fans have become so fascinated by statistics that players have naturally come to place the same emphasis on them.

Williams recently said that he played those final games and took those final swings in the autumn of '41 because not to do so "wouldn't have been honest." Let's hope that we haven't reached the point in our society where the quality of basic honesty has been devalued; let's hope that even 50 years later, Williams would have competed down to the last out of the final game. He recognized in some way that a .400 average was supposed to be the measure of an accomplishment, not a goal in itself. Williams's goal wasn't to hit .400, it was to be a .400 hitter. Brett, and all those like him—he's been more the rule than the exception in this, alas—may have led their leagues in batting average, but can we really call them batting *champions*?

WON-LOST RECORD BY STARTING POSITION

Kansas City Royals	C	1B	2B	3B	SS	LF	CF	RF	DH	P	Leadoff	Cleanup	Starts vs. LH	Starts vs. RH	Total Starts
Kevin Appier	-	-	-	-	-	-	-	-	-	13-11	-	-	6	18	13-11
Luis Aquino	-	-	-	-	-	-	-	-	-	2-1	-	-	-	3	2-1
Jay Baller	-	-	-	-	-	-	-	-	-	-	-	-	-	-	-
Sean Berry	-	-	-	3-5	-	-	-	-	-	-	-	-	4	4	3-5
Bob Boone	19-21	-	-	-	-	-	-	-	-	-	-	-	11	29	19-21
George Brett	-	50-50	-	-	-	0-2	-	4-3	10-21	-	-	11-11	39	101	64-76
Jim M. Campbell	-	-	-	-	-	-	-	-	-	2-0	-	-	1	1	2-0
Chris Codiroli	-	-	-	-	-	-	-	-	-	0-2	-	-	1	1	0-2
Jeff Conine	-	2-3	-	-	-	-	-	-	-	-	-	-	3	2	2-3
Steve Crawford	-	-	-	-	-	-	-	-	-	-	-	-	-	-	-
Mark Davis	-	-	-	-	-	-	-	-	-	1-2	-	-	1	2	1-2
Storm Davis	-	-	-	-	-	-	-	-	-	10-10	-	-	8	12	10-10
Rich Dotson	-	-	-	-	-	-	-	-	-	3-4	-	-	3	4	3-4
Jim Eisenreich	-	-	-	-	-	27-30	6-9	23-29	0-2	-	1-0	1-3	32	94	56-70
Luis Encarnacion	-	-	-	-	-	-	-	-	-	-	-	-	-	-	-
Steve Farr	-	-	-	-	-	-	-	-	-	5-1	-	-	4	2	5-1
Pete Filson	-	-	-	-	-	-	-	-	-	1-6	-	-	-	7	1-6
Tom Gordon	-	-	-	-	-	-	-	-	-	15-17	-	-	9	23	15-17
Mark Gubicza	-	-	-	-	-	-	-	-	-	7-9	-	-	5	11	7-9
Bo Jackson	-	-	-	-	-	14-22	32-29	-	1-9	-	0-1	31-44	39	68	47-60
Steve Jeltz	-	-	4-11	-	5-8	-	-	-	-	-	-	-	9	19	9-19
Mike MacFarlane	51-52	-	-	-	-	-	-	-	3-2	-	-	-	41	67	54-54
Carlos Maldonado	-	-	-	-	-	-	-	-	-	-	-	-	-	-	-
Brent Mayne	1-3	-	-	-	-	-	-	-	-	-	-	-	-	4	1-3
Andy McGaffigan	-	-	-	-	-	-	-	-	-	6-5	-	-	4	7	6-5
Brian McRae	-	-	-	-	-	-	22-21	-	-	-	4-6	-	19	24	22-21
Larry McWilliams	-	-	-	-	-	-	-	-	-	-	-	-	-	-	-
Jeff Montgomery	-	-	-	-	-	-	-	-	-	-	-	-	-	-	-
Russ Morman	-	2-0	-	-	-	4-4	-	-	1-0	-	-	-	5	6	7-4
Rey Palacios	4-10	-	-	-	-	-	-	-	-	-	-	-	5	9	4-10
Bill Pecota	-	0-1	21-18	2-3	7-11	2-1	-	-	-	-	1-5	-	30	36	32-34
Gerald Perry	-	19-30	-	-	-	-	-	-	32-36	-	4-9	1-2	19	98	51-66
Bret Saberhagen	-	-	-	-	-	-	-	-	-	8-12	-	-	6	14	8-12
Israel Sanchez	-	-	-	-	-	-	-	-	-	-	-	-	-	-	-
Jeff Schulz	-	-	-	-	-	3-3	-	4-6	-	-	-	-	-	16	7-9
Kevin Seitzer	-	-	3-4	69-77	-	-	-	-	-	-	59-56	-	51	102	72-81
Terry Shumpert	-	-	11-14	-	-	-	-	-	-	-	1-0	-	6	19	11-14
Daryl Smith	-	-	-	-	-	-	-	-	-	0-1	-	-	-	1	0-1
Kurt Stillwell	-	-	-	-	63-67	-	-	-	-	-	-	-	30	100	63-67
Mel Stottlemyre, Jr.	-	-	-	-	-	-	-	-	-	0-2	-	-	1	1	0-2
Pat Tabler	-	2-2	-	1-1	-	3-5	-	13-13	9-2	-	-	-	25	26	28-23
Danny Tartabull	-	-	-	-	-	-	-	25-27	18-14	-	-	31-26	34	50	43-41
Gary Thurman	-	-	-	-	-	0-2	1-0	6-7	-	-	5-5	-	9	7	7-9
Hector Wagner	-	-	-	-	-	-	-	-	-	2-3	-	-	3	2	2-3
Frank White	-	-	36-39	-	-	-	-	-	-	-	-	-	30	45	36-39
Willie Wilson	-	-	-	-	-	22-17	14-27	0-1	1-0	-	0-4	-	27	55	37-45

TEAM TOTALS: BATTING

	AB	H	2B	3B	HR	RBI	BB	SO	BA	SA	OBA
Season	5488	1465	316	44	100	660	498	879	.267	.395	.328
vs. Left-Handers	1861	504	114	18	35	226	167	293	.271	.408	.330
vs. Right-Handers	3627	961	202	26	65	434	331	586	.265	.389	.327
vs. Ground-Ballers	2476	690	139	15	40	290	212	363	.279	.395	.337
vs. Fly-Ballers	3012	775	177	29	60	370	286	516	.257	.395	.321
Home Games	2707	752	168	30	42	346	245	400	.278	.409	.337
Road Games	2781	713	148	14	58	314	253	479	.256	.382	.319
Grass Fields	2092	534	104	9	43	235	198	358	.255	.375	.321
Artificial Turf	3396	931	212	35	57	425	300	521	.274	.408	.333
April	607	157	31	3	7	61	51	96	.259	.354	.318
May	985	268	52	9	14	115	87	167	.272	.386	.330
June	922	244	54	6	15	104	84	166	.265	.385	.326
July	1008	282	74	12	24	153	102	149	.280	.448	.343
August	964	263	46	7	23	127	85	137	.273	.407	.329
Sept./Oct.	1002	251	59	7	17	100	89	164	.250	.374	.317
Leading Off Inn.	1323	333	85	5	26	26	94	216	.252	.382	.305
Bases Empty	3048	773	175	25	57	57	253	497	.254	.384	.314
Runners On	2440	692	141	19	43	603	245	382	.284	.410	.345
Runners/Scor. Pos.	1480	387	83	12	25	541	198	253	.261	.384	.342
Runners On/2 Out	1022	278	47	8	20	240	125	177	.272	.392	.356
Scor. Pos./2 Out	685	174	33	5	10	209	108	124	.254	.361	.360
Late-Inning Pressure	793	200	32	5	20	83	68	146	.252	.381	.312
Leading Off	200	38	7	1	8	8	12	38	.190	.355	.239
Runners On	329	94	11	0	8	71	35	63	.286	.392	.353
Runners/Scor. Pos.	206	49	8	0	4	62	32	42	.238	.335	.339

RUNS BATTED IN	From 1B	From 2B	From 3B	Scoring Position
Totals	83/1663	211/1151	266/641	477/1792
Percentage	5.0%	18.3%	41.5%	26.6%

TEAM TOTALS: PITCHING

	W-L	ERA	AB	H	HR	BB	SO	BA	SA	OBA
Season	75-86	3.93	5492	1449	116	560	1006	.264	.386	.335
vs. Left-Handers			2424	656	52	306	395	.271	.393	.354
vs. Right-Handers			3068	793	64	254	611	.258	.380	.319
vs. Ground-Ballers			2550	668	43	254	425	.262	.365	.331
vs. Fly-Ballers			2942	781	73	306	581	.265	.403	.338
Home Games	45-36	3.58	2846	737	46	252	521	.259	.367	.321
Road Games	30-50	4.32	2646	712	70	308	485	.269	.406	.349
Grass Fields	22-39	4.49	2013	555	58	228	373	.276	.422	.352
Artificial Turf	53-47	3.61	3479	894	58	332	633	.257	.364	.324
April	6-12	4.50	618	168	13	68	124	.272	.398	.348
May	14-14	4.06	986	259	22	106	192	.263	.384	.337
June	11-16	3.14	883	217	17	73	184	.246	.364	.306
July	17-12	4.12	994	267	29	113	163	.269	.415	.345
August	17-12	3.22	986	253	13	78	154	.257	.356	.313
Sept./Oct.	10-20	4.69	1025	285	22	122	189	.278	.398	.357
Leading Off Inn.			1290	334	32	120	235	.259	.398	.329
Bases Empty			2962	772	63	275	537	.261	.386	.329
Runners On			2530	677	53	285	469	.268	.385	.341
Runners/Scor. Pos.			1471	370	34	209	297	.252	.376	.342
Runners On/2 Out			1086	295	29	126	201	.272	.408	.353
Scor. Pos./2 Out			715	185	19	100	136	.259	.394	.357
Late-Inning Pressure			701	189	16	76	157	.270	.388	.346
Leading Off			164	32	3	13	38	.195	.287	.267
Runners On			320	88	10	49	79	.275	.409	.373
Runners/Scor. Pos.			188	48	6	39	54	.255	.378	.386
First 9 Batters			2839	744	63	342	573	.262	.382	.345
Second 9 Batters			1478	364	25	116	236	.246	.352	.303
All Batters Thereafter			1175	341	28	102	197	.290	.437	.347

MILWAUKEE BREWERS

- **A tribute to a long-running triad.**
- **If you've got your health, you're not in Milwaukee.**

Remember the mid-1970s, when Americans hustled across dance floors, otherwise sane men wore leisure suits, and *Rocky* was accorded a place alongside *Casablanca* and *All About Eve* as an Academy Award–winning film? An era of impoverished judgment or what? Baseball's own contribution to the madness came in the wake of the McNally and Messersmith ruling, with the abolition of the reserve clause granting free agency to players after their sixth year of service. That development was viewed by most baseball traditionalists as the end of modern civilization. "Destruction of the balance of power" and "The rich get richer" became rallying cries for those who were certain that a few wealthy teams in large media markets would turn the World Series into their own private celebration. Few of us questioned the logic, although by 1975, 10 of the first 20 division winners had already successfully defended their titles; and over the last 50 years prior to divisional play, 48 of 100 pennant winners returned to the Series within two years. That was competitive balance?

Baseball's emancipation proclamation in 1975 hardly eliminated competitive balance; the 15 years since Peter Seitz freed the slaves have produced parity to an unprecedented degree. Over the past 10 years, every National League team and all but three American League teams have won a division title. Now, does anyone recall what it was that we found so damned attractive about watching the Yankees maul the Dodgers, Giants, or Cardinals every October?

Contrary to appearances, this isn't going to be a treatise on parity. But it's time to take a fresh look at another fear that arose when players were granted the same rights as most other American workers. Greedy players, it was said, would sell themselves to the highest bidders—isn't that what was once referred to as the Great American Way?—uprooting families, leaving friends, and in the process destroying another great baseball tradition: the career team player.

If he'd had the opportunity to leave for more money, would Stan Musial have played his entire career for the Cardinals? For a better shot at a World Series ring, would Ernie Banks have forsaken the Windy City for Pinstripes? Courted by rich and seductive owners, would Al Kaline, Carl Yastrzemski, and Brooks Robinson have become career-long symbols of the Tigers, Red Sox, and Orioles? Remember to ask those questions once inside the pearly gates (along with "Why is there always room for Jell-O?"), because no one in this galaxy has the answer. But after 15 years of less-restricted player movement, it appears true that players aren't as likely to spend long periods of their careers with a single team as they used to be.

A total of 1188 players in major-league history have played at least 1200 games or pitched at least 1800 innings. Of those, 322 (27 percent) had played for only one team by the end of the season in which they reached those levels. (Those levels are significant because contemporary players are certain to have attained six-year free-agent eligibility before reaching them.) And as the following table shows, players who attained those levels since the abolition of the reserve clause in 1976 were less likely to have played their entire major-league careers to that point with one team than at any time since the 19th century. The years listed below are those in which players reached the qualification levels (1200 games or 1800 innings):

	1800s	1900–19	1920–39	1940–59	1960–75	1976–90
Total players	107	167	207	185	232	290
With one team	17	41	53	64	83	64
Percentage	16	25	26	35	36	22

Some of the last examples of that dying breed still flourish in Milwaukee, where Robin Yount, Paul Molitor, and Jim Gantner have completed 13 consecutive seasons together in the only major-league uniforms they've ever worn (metaphorically, we hope). They are only the fifth trio of teammates in major-league history to have reached the 1500-game mark without playing for another team. The others:

- Dodgers, 1957–58: Carl Furillo, Gil Hodges, and Pee Wee Reese. Duke Snider joined them in 1958.
- Giants, 1970: Jim Davenport, Willie Mays, and Willie McCovey.
- Cubs, 1970–71: Ernie Banks, Ron Santo, and Billy Williams.
- Royals, 1988–90: George Brett, Frank White, and Willie Wilson.

Yount, Molitor, and Gantner have all had opportunities to leave the city and the team, and under quite favorable conditions. Molitor was granted free agency following the 1987 season, when he batted .353, hit in 39 consecutive games, and led the league in runs despite playing only 118 games. Yount became a free agent after winning the MVP award in 1989. Gantner had two chances to leave, the first after playing 155 games in 1988, then again following last season, when he opted to negotiate a new contract with Milwaukee without even testing the waters. Apparently, the freedom to leave also means the freedom to choose to stay.

But as we mentioned earlier, those players are exceptional. Over the last decade, fewer players spent long segments of their careers with their original team than at any time in this century. On the other hand, long-term team commitments may not become entirely extinct; the nomadic trend that began when the reserve clause was abolished has ebbed. The following table shows the number of players with at least 1500 games played at the end of each season since 1975. Note that the percentage of those players who had played for only one team appears to have bottomed out in the early- to mid-1980s, and risen since then:

Year	Total	One Team	Year	Total	One Team
1975	36	10 (28%)	1983	50	5 (10%)
1976	40	13 (33%)	1984	58	6 (10%)
1977	33	8 (24%)	1985	62	8 (13%)
1978	35	9 (26%)	1986	60	8 (13%)
1979	36	6 (17%)	1987	54	9 (17%)
1980	41	8 (20%)	1988	48	12 (25%)
1981	42	9 (21%)	1989	38	10 (26%)
1982	49	6 (12%)	1990	38	10 (26%)

Unfortunately, among those 10 players who finished the 1990 season with 1500 or more games and who had spent their entire major-league careers with the same team, three were cut loose within weeks of the season's end. Kansas City released Frank White and Willie Wilson, and Boston chose not to re-sign Dwight Evans. The thought of Evans playing in another uniform strikes us as particularly incongruous; only six players in major-league history played as many games as Evans and wore the same jersey throughout. Career leaders:

Carl Yastrzemski, Red Sox	3308	Luke Appling, White Sox	2422
Stan Musial, Cardinals	3026	Mike Schmidt, Phillies	2404
Brooks Robinson, Orioles	2896	Mickey Mantle, Yankees	2401
Al Kaline, Tigers	2834	Willie Stargell, Pirates	2360
Mel Ott, Giants	2732	Frank White, Royals	2324
Ernie Banks, Cubs	2528	Charlie Gehringer, Tigers	2323
Dwight Evans, Red Sox	2505	Ted Williams, Red Sox	2292
Dave Concepcion, Reds	2488	George Brett, Royals	2279
Robin Yount, Brewers	2449	Cap Anson, Chicago (N.L.)	2276
Roberto Clemente, Pirates	2433	Bill Russell, Dodgers	2181

To re-pose an earlier question: Might Musial, Banks, or Yastrzemski have forsaken their single-team identities in today's freer environment? Maybe not; they were anomalies for any era. The phenomenon of great players spending their entire careers with one team—which many assume was part of baseball since Alexander Cartwright first donned knickers—only became prevalent after World War II. Prior to the 1970s, only 21 players in major-league history had retired with as many as 1500 games played, all for a single club. That total grew by 12 during the 1970s, and by seven more in the 1980s. It may be that the increase in the number of players brought about by expansion alone is the best safeguard against the extinction of one-team players. But whatever the cause, the extent of the phenomenon—40 players in 115 years—has been seriously overstated by sportswriters prematurely decrying its death.

Presumably, most teams sit down each October to identify the areas in which they need to improve. Some need to beef up the offense; others have to fortify their starting rotations or their bullpens. A team's most pressing need might be related to chemistry: a veteran player on a young team, or an infusion of prospects on an aging one. Speed and defense are also important considerations. While teams often bemoan the number of injuries they incur during a season, it's easy to understand why few teams if any cite health and conditioning as essential offseason considerations.

But a look at the amount of time spent on the disabled list by each team's players over the past three seasons suggests that there's a lot more to injuries than just bad luck. Teams that were plagued by injuries in one season are likely to be hit badly again a year later. The lists of the top three teams in each league in this unfortunate category for each of the past three seasons illustrate the point. Only nine different teams accounted for the 18 slots. And the numbers involved are so large as to suggest that teams with chronic injury problems have as much to gain by shortening their disabled lists as they do by adding another home-run hitter or regular starting pitcher:

American	1988	American	1989	American	1990
Brewers	699	**Brewers**	1067	Mariners	800
Yankees	696	Yankees	819	Angels	774
Angels	612	Orioles	809	**Brewers**	627
National	**1988**	**National**	**1989**	**National**	**1990**
Cardinals	1006	Giants	849	Giants	927
Giants	721	Cardinals	817	Phillies	887
Phillies	496	Phillies	761	Dodgers	763

Clearly, one of the teams that needs to take a look at this pattern is Milwaukee. Brewers players have spent a total of 2393 days, or approximately 13 man-seasons, on the disabled list over the past three years. That's the highest total in the American League, and more than 60 percent higher than the major-league average. Lest you draw the conclusion that a few players with chronic injuries, like Juan Nieves and Bill Wegman, were responsible for Milwaukee's enormous total, think about this: 16 different Brewers players spent at least 60 days on the disabled list over the past three seasons. And that roster of often-injured players represents equal opportunity—batters and pitchers, young and old, one-timers and repeaters:

Player	Total	1988	1989	1990
Juan Nieves	303	63	182	58
Bill Wegman	262	17	123	122
Dale Sveum	182	0	182	0
Dave Stapleton	141	141	0	0
Mike Birkbeck	133	0	90	43
Paul Mirabella	132	15	117	0
Tom Filer	128	0	35	93
Mark Clear	115	115	0	0
Jim Gantner	113	0	47	66
Greg Brock	104	46	58	0
Glenn Braggs	93	93	0	0
Bryan Clutterbuck	86	0	86	0
Chris Bosio	78	0	0	78
Paul Molitor	72	0	11	61
Steve Stanicek	66	66	0	0
Mike Felder	63	63	0	0

No other team had more than 13 players who accumulated as many as 60 DL days from 1988 through 1990. And keep in mind that Milwaukee had 11 other players who spent at least 15 but fewer than 60 days on the disabled list during that same period. Those additional players even include several younger Brewers who didn't spend the entire three-year period in the majors (Gary Sheffield, Billy Spiers, and Greg Vaughn). The Brewers, we are told, were sufficiently concerned about the problem—especially with regard to their pitching staff—that they sought advice last season from Dick Such, pitching coach of the Twins. They went to the right doctor: Over the past two seasons, Minnesota's starting pitchers spent a total of 50 days on the disabled list.

Of course, Milwaukee's not alone. Two National League teams accumulated even more DL time over the past three seasons than the Brewers: San Francisco (2497 days) and St. Louis (2395). For those teams, a relatively injury-free season should constitute a prominent goal for the coming season. And while such goals are rarely stated in the free-agent-fed mania of the offseason, at least one player had the right idea, and, characteristically, a colorful way of expressing it: "My goals for the coming season? To hit .300, steal 50 bases, and remain injury-prone." Who says Mickey Rivers didn't know what he was talking about?

WON-LOST RECORD BY STARTING POSITION

Milwaukee Brewers	C	1B	2B	3B	SS	LF	CF	RF	DH	P	Leadoff	Cleanup	Starts vs. LH	Starts vs. RH	Total Starts
Don August	-	-	-	-	-	-	-	-	-	-	-	-	-	-	-
Bill Bates	-	-	4-5	-	-	-	-	-	-	-	1-1	-	-	9	4-5
Mike Birkbeck	-	-	-	-	-	-	-	-	-	-	-	-	-	-	-
Chris Bosio	-	-	-	-	-	-	-	-	-	5-15	-	-	4	16	5-15
Glenn Braggs	-	-	-	-	-	4-8	-	10-9	1-0	-	-	-	14	18	15-17
Greg Brock	-	44-56	-	-	-	-	-	-	-	-	-	-	15	85	44-56
Kevin D. Brown	-	-	-	-	-	-	-	-	-	1-2	-	-	1	2	1-2
George Canale	-	2-3	-	-	-	-	-	-	-	-	-	-	1	4	2-3
Mike Capel	-	-	-	-	-	-	-	-	-	-	-	-	-	-	-
Chuck Crim	-	-	-	-	-	-	-	-	-	-	-	-	-	-	-
Rob Deer	-	8-8	-	-	-	-	-	49-54	-	-	-	4-1	44	75	57-62
Edgar Diaz	-	-	0-7	1-1	31-26	-	-	-	-	-	-	-	33	33	32-34
Tom Edens	-	-	-	-	-	-	-	-	-	4-2	-	-	4	2	4-2
Narciso Elvira	-	-	-	-	-	-	-	-	-	-	-	-	-	-	-
Mike Felder	-	-	-	-	-	8-13	2-3	12-14	-	-	13-18	-	18	34	22-30
Tom Filer	-	-	-	-	-	-	-	-	-	2-2	-	-	-	4	2-2
Tony Fossas	-	-	-	-	-	-	-	-	-	-	-	-	-	-	-
Terry Francona	-	-	-	-	-	-	-	-	-	-	-	-	-	-	-
Jim Gantner	-	-	39-37	1-8	-	-	-	-	-	-	10-12	-	19	66	40-45
Darryl Hamilton	-	-	-	-	-	13-13	-	3-11	-	-	0-2	-	-	40	16-24
Ted Higuera	-	-	-	-	-	-	-	-	-	12-15	-	-	3	24	12-15
Mark Knudson	-	-	-	-	-	-	-	-	-	14-13	-	-	9	18	14-13
Bill Krueger	-	-	-	-	-	-	-	-	-	7-10	-	-	6	11	7-10
Mark Lee	-	-	-	-	-	-	-	-	-	-	-	-	-	-	-
Julio Machado	-	-	-	-	-	-	-	-	-	-	-	-	-	-	-
Tim McIntosh	0-1	-	-	-	-	-	-	-	-	-	-	-	1	-	0-1
Paul Mirabella	-	-	-	-	-	-	-	-	-	0-2	-	-	1	1	0-2
Paul Molitor	-	19-17	24-36	2-0	-	-	-	-	1-3	-	43-48	-	31	71	46-56
Jaime Navarro	-	-	-	-	-	-	-	-	-	12-10	-	-	6	16	12-10
Juan Nieves	-	-	-	-	-	-	-	-	-	-	-	-	-	-	-
Charlie O'Brien	20-22	-	-	-	-	-	-	-	-	-	-	-	26	16	20-22
Dave Parker	-	1-2	-	-	-	-	-	-	69-84	-	-	67-84	41	115	70-86
Dan Plesac	-	-	-	-	-	-	-	-	-	-	-	-	-	-	-
Gus Polidor	-	-	-	-	-	-	-	-	-	-	-	-	-	-	-
Dennis Powell	-	-	-	-	-	-	-	-	-	0-7	-	-	1	6	0-7
Ron Robinson	-	-	-	-	-	-	-	-	-	14-8	-	-	8	14	14-8
Bob Sebra	-	-	-	-	-	-	-	-	-	-	-	-	-	-	-
Gary Sheffield	-	-	-	58-67	-	-	-	-	-	-	7-3	-	37	88	58-67
Bill Spiers	-	-	-	-	43-61	-	-	-	-	-	0-4	-	18	86	43-61
B.J. Surhoff	54-65	-	-	3-4	-	-	-	-	-	-	-	-	20	106	57-69
Dale Sveum	-	0-2	7-3	9-8	0-1	-	-	-	-	-	-	-	16	14	16-14
Greg Vaughn	-	-	-	-	-	49-54	-	-	2-1	-	-	-	34	72	51-55
Randy Veres	-	-	-	-	-	-	-	-	-	-	-	-	-	-	-
Bill Wegman	-	-	-	-	-	-	-	-	-	3-2	-	-	3	2	3-2
Robin Yount	-	-	-	-	-	-	72-85	-	1-0	-	-	3-3	46	112	73-85

TEAM TOTALS: BATTING

	AB	H	2B	3B	HR	RBI	BB	SO	BA	SA	OBA
Season	5503	1408	247	36	128	680	519	821	.256	.384	.320
vs. Left-Handers	1579	405	79	10	49	202	153	257	.256	.412	.320
vs. Right-Handers	3924	1003	168	26	79	478	366	564	.256	.372	.320
vs. Ground-Ballers	2443	647	110	14	55	330	238	329	.265	.389	.330
vs. Fly-Ballers	3060	761	137	22	73	350	281	492	.249	.379	.312
Home Games	2657	663	119	17	60	331	262	397	.250	.375	.317
Road Games	2846	745	128	19	68	349	257	424	.262	.392	.323
Grass Fields	4658	1177	214	29	110	579	446	697	.253	.382	.318
Artificial Turf	845	231	33	7	18	101	73	124	.273	.393	.330
April	593	152	37	3	11	95	65	94	.256	.384	.334
May	878	214	36	5	18	101	93	149	.244	.358	.315
June	996	277	65	5	27	132	91	139	.278	.435	.337
July	971	249	35	5	27	131	97	148	.256	.386	.324
August	1016	265	32	10	25	113	82	140	.261	.386	.315
Sept./Oct.	1049	251	42	8	20	108	91	151	.239	.352	.300
Leading Off Inn.	1356	355	57	11	37	37	93	170	.262	.402	.310
Bases Empty	3157	781	136	21	72	72	256	469	.247	.372	.308
Runners On	2346	627	111	15	56	608	263	352	.267	.399	.336
Runners/Scor. Pos.	1383	358	70	11	30	534	201	228	.259	.390	.341
Runners On/2 Out	991	238	38	8	21	215	129	147	.240	.358	.329
Scor. Pos./2 Out	669	153	29	6	14	193	107	103	.229	.353	.338
Late-Inning Pressure	705	162	25	1	10	76	68	118	.230	.311	.299
Leading Off	173	42	6	0	4	4	16	24	.243	.347	.307
Runners On	303	73	9	1	5	71	37	49	.241	.327	.317
Runners/Scor. Pos.	192	46	4	1	2	62	33	30	.240	.302	.340

RUNS BATTED IN	From 1B	From 2B	From 3B	Scoring Position
Totals	76/1639	208/1092	268/609	476/1701
Percentage	4.6%	19.0%	44.0%	28.0%

TEAM TOTALS: PITCHING

	W-L	ERA	AB	H	HR	BB	SO	BA	SA	OBA
Season	74-88	4.08	5663	1558	121	469	771	.275	.399	.331
vs. Left-Handers			2177	577	32	167	258	.265	.362	.317
vs. Right-Handers			3486	981	89	302	513	.281	.422	.340
vs. Ground-Ballers			2775	772	39	206	353	.278	.382	.329
vs. Fly-Ballers			2888	786	82	263	418	.272	.415	.333
Home Games	39-42	3.96	2873	766	59	227	401	.267	.383	.321
Road Games	35-46	4.20	2790	792	62	242	370	.284	.416	.342
Grass Fields	63-75	4.07	4842	1320	108	405	657	.273	.397	.330
Artificial Turf	11-13	4.14	821	238	13	64	114	.290	.413	.341
April	12-6	2.87	606	145	9	59	86	.239	.333	.311
May	11-15	4.53	927	269	29	62	121	.290	.446	.332
June	10-19	5.27	1022	308	27	104	128	.301	.442	.364
July	12-15	3.41	980	261	21	75	150	.266	.390	.322
August	16-14	3.95	1025	266	18	71	140	.260	.367	.308
Sept./Oct.	13-19	4.05	1103	309	17	98	146	.280	.393	.340
Leading Off Inn.			1350	367	21	94	178	.272	.384	.322
Bases Empty			3096	838	71	229	429	.271	.401	.325
Runners On			2567	720	50	240	342	.280	.396	.338
Runners/Scor. Pos.			1447	395	25	171	212	.273	.377	.340
Runners On/2 Out			1100	299	19	109	156	.272	.385	.340
Scor. Pos./2 Out			695	181	12	83	108	.260	.371	.341
Late-Inning Pressure			786	207	13	66	130	.263	.368	.322
Leading Off			192	50	1	15	32	.260	.333	.321
Runners On			353	99	5	30	58	.280	.380	.336
Runners/Scor. Pos.			201	56	3	20	31	.279	.383	.339
First 9 Batters			2906	799	56	272	414	.275	.392	.338
Second 9 Batters			1529	429	39	102	213	.281	.413	.325
All Batters Thereafter			1228	330	26	95	144	.269	.397	.321

MINNESOTA TWINS

- **The best-hitting catcher in the league.**
- **The reasoned fall of Allan Anderson.**

Imagine you're watching a tennis match. First look left; now look right. *Pfwopp* . . . left. *Pfwopp* . . . right. *Pfwopp* . . . left. *Pfwumpf* (the distinctive sound of a topspin lob) . . . right. *Pfoowh* . . . left. *Thormp* (a winner) . . . right. Congratulations! You're duly certified to root for the Minnesota Twins.

Last season, the Twins compiled a losing record in April, a winning mark in May, and then continued to alternate between records above and below the .500 mark through August. By that time, it was apparent that it was going to take more than the Twin Cities cha-cha to compete with Oakland, and the Twins continued losing through September. A look at Minnesota's record by month:

April	May	June	July	August	Sept./Oct.
7–12	21–7	7–21	15–14	9–19	15–15

There have been 17 teams in this century who seesawed through an entire season with alternate winning and losing months, so in that regard the 1990 Twins were hardly unique. But notice their records in May and June. Minnesota was only the second team since 1900 to win three-quarters of its games in one month and lose three-quarters the next. The first, you may recall, was the 1987 Milwaukee Brewers, who opened the season with a 13-game winning streak (finishing the month of April with an 18–3 mark), but lost 11 straight in May (going 6–18 for the month). Minnesota's reversal had nothing to do with home stands and road trips; the Twins played two more games at the Metrodome than on the road during May, four more at home than on the road in June.

At a time when the ability to crunch numbers *ad infinitum* fosters the notion that all baseball statistics have explanations waiting to be discovered, the Twins' 1990 season provides a humbling but delightful antidote. Random events sometimes conspire to produce deliciously incongruous results. This is a classic example.

The team's dramatic turnaround in June was led by the utter collapse of its offense. Minnesota topped the American League in scoring with an average of 5.3 runs per game in May, then ranked last with a 3.1 run average in June. The Twins also fell from first to last in batting average from May to June (.295 to .238). Often, a collapse like that is attributable to injuries or to changes in the lineup. But in Minnesota's case, the lineup in June was about as similar as could be to the lineup in May: 929 of a possible 1004 plate appearances were made by the same players. The only noteworthy change was the increased playing time given Gene Larkin in right field at Randy Bush's expense.

Only two regular starters had higher batting averages in June than in May. The following table shows how pervasive this team-wide slump was. Right field and the DH slot were divided among many players. Larkin, who batted nearly 100 times in both months, spent time at both positions, and has been included as a floater:

Pos.	Player	May	June	Diff.
C	Brian Harper	.337 (28-for-83)	.286 (22-for-77)	−.052
1B	Kent Hrbek	.293 (29-for-99)	.200 (17-for-85)	−.093
2B	Fred Manrique	.253 (20-for-79)	.257 (18-for-70)	+.004
SS	Greg Gagne	.205 (15-for-73)	.222 (18-for-81)	+.017
3B	Gary Gaetti	.258 (25-for-97)	.227 (22-for-97)	−.031
LF	Dan Gladden	.313 (36-for-115)	.248 (25-for-101)	−.066
CF	Kirby Puckett	.382 (39-for-102)	.242 (24-for-99)	−.140
DH/RF	Gene Larkin	.310 (26-for-84)	.190 (16-for-84)	−.119

Last winter, that intrepid agnostic Roger Angell wrote in *The New Yorker* that he hadn't yet completed the lab work for his "radical theorem" that there exists somewhere a baseball statistic that cannot be explained. Consider this our first contribution to his research.

Now for our second contribution: the strange case of the Minnesota Twins' catchers. Baseball statistics are uncanny in their ability to tell stories. As Bill James wrote, "Baseball statistics have acquired the powers of language. . . . [They] can narrate stories of promise and frustration, of opportunities taken and opportunities missed, can tell of speed and grace, of wasted talent and determination overcoming misfortune." Don't believe it? Take a long look at the following:

Year	G	AB	R	H	2B	3B	HR	RBI	BB	SB	BA
1979	1	2	0	0	0	0	0	0	0	0	.000
1981	4	11	1	3	0	0	0	1	0	1	.273
1982	27	44	5	11	2	0	2	4	2	0	.250
1983	134	324	27	77	9	1	7	32	6	1	.238
1984	86	203	10	47	7	0	2	22	10	1	.232
1985	66	124	9	34	6	0	1	13	5	1	.274
1986	68	146	13	42	7	0	0	17	12	0	.288
1987	86	209	17	56	9	1	1	25	15	0	.268
1988	109	284	23	82	17	1	5	38	19	1	.289
Totals	581	1347	105	352	57	3	18	152	69	5	.261

What did you see? A player of promise whose reward for some fine play at the double-A level was a September promotion at an early age—too early perhaps. A few years later, a squandered chance to win a starting role, followed by several seasons of adequate part-time play. A useful utility player, one who never fulfilled his potential. The logical extension: a career of pinch-hitting and day-game starts after night games. That might be good for three-quarters of a million per in today's market, but when we look at those numbers, we see players whose careers never blossomed: Biff Pocoroba, Scott Bradley, Mike Fitzgerald, and so on.

Then lightning struck. This profile above isn't fictional, of course; it represents the combined career performance of Brian Harper and Junior Ortiz, Minnesota's catching platoon. According to the cliché, truth can be stranger than fiction, and here's an example. Over the past two seasons, Harper and Ortiz accumulated nearly as many at-bats as in the previous 10 years combined, and batted .295 in the process:

Year	G	AB	R	H	2B	3B	HR	RBI	BB	SB	BA
1989	217	615	59	175	30	1	9	79	33	4	.285
1990	205	649	79	198	49	4	6	72	31	3	.305
2-Year	422	1264	138	373	79	5	15	151	64	7	.295
Career	1003	2611	243	725	136	8	33	303	133	12	.278

Only one player who caught at least 100 games batted .290 or better last season. That player was Harper, who happened to be the only player to do so in 1989 as well—a remarkable achievement for a player who took more than 10 years just to reach the 400-game mark. Ortiz has never had as many as 250 at-bats in any of his nine seasons in the majors. He began the 1990 season by extending his streak of hitless at-bats to 34—a streak that ran from August 23, 1989, until April 28, 1990. From that point on, he batted .358. Combined with Harper's .294 mark, Minnesota's catchers hit .302 for the season.

Those figures are noteworthy not only for the career turnarounds of the players involved, but also for the punch they provided Minnesota from a position that's grown soft throughout the majors in recent years. Compare the production of Minnesota's catchers to the league average last season:

Catchers	AB	R	H	2B	3B	HR	RBI	BB	SB	BA	SA	OBA
Minnesota	596	70	180	44	4	5	63	24	3	.302	.414	.335
A.L. Avg.	567	64	147	26	2	13	68	49	4	.260	.379	.321

Of course, it wasn't always like that. Look back 10 or 15 years: Johnny Bench, Thurman Munson, Ted Simmons, Gary Carter, and Carlton Fisk at the highest level; Darrell Porter, Brian Downing, and Bob Boone close behind. Catchers like Jim Sundberg, Steve Yeager, John Stearns, and Butch Wynegar—All-Star contenders by today's standards—were all but guaranteed a three-day, midseason vacation each year. But even in that era, few teams received the batting support from their catchers that Harper and Ortiz provided last season. Over the previous 25 years, only two American League teams' catchers had higher batting averages: the 1977 Red Sox (mostly Carlton Fisk) and the 1987 Brewers (B.J. Surhoff and Bill Schroeder).

Those glory days may return; major-league rosters currently abound with promising young catchers: Sandy Alomar, Craig Biggio, Pat Borders, Joe Girardi, Joe Oliver, Benito Santiago, and Surhoff, among them. But for now, the most productive catcher in baseball may be a pair of journeymen playing for a team whose offense has been almost totally identified with home-grown All-Stars like Kirby Puckett, Kent Hrbek, and Gary Gaetti. During the 1990 season, when all three of their high-profile teammates fell short of their career averages, Brian Harper and Junior Ortiz helped keep the wheels from falling off Minnesota's sputtering offense.

We'd like a show of hands on this one: Was anyone out there surprised at the sudden deterioration of Allan Anderson? All right, that gentleman in St. Paul can put his hand down now.

With the departure of Frank Viola and Bert Blyleven, Anderson inherited the top spot in the Twins' rotation based on his total of 33 wins over the two previous seasons. He earned Minnesota's opening-day assignment in 1990, but it was all downhill thereafter. But a look at his three full seasons with Minnesota indicates that the decline started not in 1990, but a year earlier. He managed to win 17 games in 1989 in spite of an ERA increase of more than one run per nine innings over his league-leading 1988 average:

Year	W	L	Pct.	IP	H	ERA
1988	16	9	.640	202.1	199	2.45
1989	17	10	.630	196.2	214	3.80
1990	7	18	.280	188.2	214	4.53

Now, it isn't every season that a pitcher loses 350 points in winning percentage over 25 decisions—except maybe on Saturn, where a single orbit of the sun takes 29 earth years, so that the baseball season lasts almost as long as our own NBA season. The last pitcher to decline so sharply was Dave McNally in 1972. Consecutive ERA increases of this magnitude for pitchers working so many innings aren't exactly everyday occurrences, either—every 1800 days or so is more like it, considering the last was by Scott McGregor in 1984–85. So why, then, did Anderson's decline make so much sense?

The answer is simple, and should be devoured by fantasy-league owners like potato chips at the draft table: ERA increases are twice as likely for pitchers who allowed more than a hit an inning than by those who allowed less than that. From 1969 through 1989 (with the exclusion of the 1980 and 1981 seasons), nearly 1600 pitchers qualified for the major-league ERA title. The following table shows the tendency of their ERAs to rise or fall according to their hits-to-inning ratios (that is, above or below one hit per inning):

Hits per Inning	Pitchers	ERA Increase	ERA Decrease
More than one	513	259 (50.5%)	254 (49.5%)
One or less	1064	354 (33.3%)	710 (66.7%)

These figures explain Anderson's decline. Notice above that even when he led the American League in ERA in 1988, he allowed nearly a hit per inning. He crossed that line in 1989, and continued the progression a year later.

Pitchers are traditionally evaluated in terms of their won-lost records and their ERAs. But the reliability of wins and losses as a gauge of career performance is exceeded by its uncertainty for a single season. The table above indicates that even a pitcher's earned run average, often considered the best single-season measure, can be undermined by his "hitability"—at least as a leading indicator for the following year.

At one time, we were proud of the role we had played in trying to stamp out—forever, we hoped—the Metrodome's nickname, "Homerdome," a characterization that should have lasted about as long as it took to turn the air-conditioning on. (The Metrodome was a true homerdome for all of one sticky, sweaty season.) So it saddens us to report that writers, broadcasters, and players have been backsliding across this great country, reviving the term that informed baseball fans love to hate.

A quick check of the Metrodome entry in this edition's Ballparks section (page 412) reveals that nothing has changed since last year. Apparently the a.c. is still on, because the Metrodome has effected only a modest 4-percent increase in home runs over the past five years. So we'll be as blunt about this as we can: Unless sales of Right Guard deodorant to Twins season ticket holders triple, assume that the Metrodome still isn't the home-run park that a few influential boobs would have you believe.

Now, we're going to publish some new related research. Harsh as this may seem, if you're among those who still use the name "Homerdome," forget it. Go read the Yankees essay. You are being left back. The following is for enlightened fans only.

As you probably know, the basis for the data in the Ballparks section is a comparison between the rate of home runs hit—both for and against the Twins—in their home games and the rate in their road games. We are now in a position to take that method a step further, to break down those figures between left- and right-handed hitters, to show which stadiums have a strong skew, favoring hitters of one type or the other. And the results are another Metrodome surprise: Not only isn't it a Homerdome, it isn't even a Leftydome.

Perceptive readers of earlier *Analysts* quickly spotted the difference between the home and road home-run rates of left-handed hitter Kent Hrbek and right-hander Tom Brunansky (during his years with the Twins). For the years 1982 through 1986, Hrbek hit six more home runs at the Metrodome (61) than on the road (55); Brunansky hit 12 more on the road (71) than at home (59). Additionally, the asymmetry of the ballpark favors left-handers: 343 feet down the left-field line, 327 to right; 385 to left-center, 367 to right-center. So it appeared that the stadium should at least be a homerdome for left-handed hitters. But over the past two seasons, at least, that hasn't been the case. At-bats per home run for 1989 and 1990:

	Metrodome	Road Games	Diff.
Left-handed hitters	45.04	45.01	-0.1%
Right-handed hitters	47.55	44.29	-6.9%

Over the past two seasons, the Metrodome has actually decreased home runs by 2.9 percent overall. That decrease was attributable solely to its effect on right-handed hitters. So left-handers have had an edge over righties at the Metrodome, at least for the last two years, in that they weren't hurt by it; on the other hand, they didn't have an advantage at the Metrodome as opposed to a typical American League ballpark. (For a look at a surprisingly similar topic, see the 1961 Yankees essay.)

That last sound was another myth crashing.

WON-LOST RECORD BY STARTING POSITION

Minnesota Twins	C	1B	2B	3B	SS	LF	CF	RF	DH	P	Leadoff	Cleanup	Starts vs. LH	Starts vs. RH	Total Starts
Paul Abbott	-	-	-	-	-	-	-	-	-	1-6	-	-	3	4	1-6
Rick Aguilera	-	-	-	-	-	-	-	-	-	-	-	-	-	-	-
Allan Anderson	-	-	-	-	-	-	-	-	-	12-19	-	-	9	22	12-19
Doug Baker	-	-	-	-	-	-	-	-	-	-	-	-	-	-	-
Juan Berenguer	-	-	-	-	-	-	-	-	-	-	-	-	-	-	-
Randy Bush	-	1-0	-	-	-	1-0	-	13-13	9-15	-	-	2-2	-	52	24-28
John Candelaria	-	-	-	-	-	-	-	-	-	0-1	-	-	-	1	0-1
Larry Casian	-	-	-	-	-	-	-	-	-	1-2	-	-	1	2	1-2
Carmen Castillo	-	-	-	-	-	1-0	-	3-6	9-14	-	-	-	32	1	13-20
Tim Drummond	-	-	-	-	-	-	-	-	-	1-3	-	-	-	4	1-3
Jim Dwyer	-	-	-	-	-	-	-	-	6-9	-	-	-	-	15	6-9
Scott Erickson	-	-	-	-	-	-	-	-	-	12-5	-	-	4	13	12-5
Gary Gaetti	-	0-1	-	70-80	-	-	-	-	-	-	-	29-30	44	107	70-81
Greg Gagne	-	-	-	-	53-68	-	-	-	-	-	-	-	40	81	53-68
Richard Garces	-	-	-	-	-	-	-	-	-	-	-	-	-	-	-
Dan Gladden	-	-	-	-	-	58-69	-	-	0-1	-	55-62	-	40	88	58-70
Mark Guthrie	-	-	-	-	-	-	-	-	-	11-10	-	-	3	18	11-10
Chip Hale	-	-	1-0	-	-	-	-	-	-	-	-	-	-	1	1-0
Brian Harper	48-67	1-1	-	-	-	-	-	-	7-4	-	-	2-1	42	86	56-72
Kent Hrbek	-	51-66	-	-	-	-	-	-	13-6	-	-	40-50	30	106	64-72
Gene Larkin	-	14-12	-	-	-	-	-	21-23	16-26	-	-	1-5	33	79	51-61
Tim Laudner	-	-	-	-	-	-	-	-	-	-	-	-	-	-	-
Terry Leach	-	-	-	-	-	-	-	-	-	-	-	-	-	-	-
Scott Leius	-	-	-	-	4-4	-	-	-	-	-	-	-	6	2	4-4
Nelson Liriano	-	-	16-31	-	-	-	-	-	-	-	1-7	-	10	37	16-31
Shane Mack	-	-	-	-	-	3-8	14-21	17-19	-	-	5-7	-	42	40	34-48
Fred Manrique	-	-	31-29	-	-	-	-	-	-	-	-	-	11	49	31-29
John Moses	-	-	-	-	-	5-5	3-2	8-11	-	-	0-3	-	-	34	16-18
Pedro Munoz	-	-	-	-	-	1-1	-	11-8	0-1	-	6-4	-	7	15	12-10
Al Newman	-	-	26-28	4-8	17-16	0-1	-	-	-	-	7-5	-	34	66	47-53
Junior Ortiz	25-20	-	-	-	-	-	-	-	1-1	-	-	-	15	32	26-21
Kirby Puckett	-	-	-	-	-	5-4	57-65	1-8	3-1	-	-	-	45	99	66-78
Jack Savage	-	-	-	-	-	-	-	-	-	-	-	-	-	-	-
Roy Smith	-	-	-	-	-	-	-	-	-	9-14	-	-	9	14	9-14
Paul Sorrento	-	7-8	-	-	-	-	-	-	10-10	-	-	-	-	35	17-18
Kevin Tapani	-	-	-	-	-	-	-	-	-	13-15	-	-	12	16	13-15
Gary Wayne	-	-	-	-	-	-	-	-	-	-	-	-	-	-	-
Lenny Webster	1-1	-	-	-	-	-	-	-	-	-	-	-	1	1	1-1
David West	-	-	-	-	-	-	-	-	-	14-13	-	-	7	20	14-13
Rich Yett	-	-	-	-	-	-	-	-	-	-	-	-	-	-	-

TEAM TOTALS: BATTING

	AB	H	2B	3B	HR	RBI	BB	SO	BA	SA	OBA
Season	5499	1458	281	39	100	625	445	749	.265	.385	.324
vs. Left-Handers	1612	453	93	9	27	194	141	226	.281	.400	.342
vs. Right-Handers	3887	1005	188	30	73	431	304	523	.259	.379	.316
vs. Ground-Ballers	2357	624	116	17	31	258	187	286	.265	.368	.322
vs. Fly-Ballers	3142	834	165	22	69	367	258	463	.265	.398	.325
Home Games	2692	760	159	25	46	348	226	344	.282	.411	.340
Road Games	2807	698	122	14	54	277	219	405	.249	.360	.308
Grass Fields	2141	532	88	11	42	204	170	293	.248	.359	.308
Artificial Turf	3358	926	193	28	58	421	275	456	.276	.402	.333
April	643	171	41	3	15	83	71	75	.266	.409	.344
May	965	285	60	7	28	138	68	122	.295	.459	.343
June	924	220	43	6	13	84	64	149	.238	.340	.289
July	1007	283	58	6	19	118	93	124	.281	.407	.348
August	952	241	39	7	16	102	67	134	.253	.359	.306
Sept./Oct.	1008	258	40	10	9	100	82	145	.256	.342	.315
Leading Off Inn.	1344	365	71	12	24	24	94	165	.272	.396	.322
Bases Empty	3126	813	163	22	52	52	216	429	.260	.376	.314
Runners On	2373	645	118	17	48	573	229	320	.272	.397	.335
Runners/Scor. Pos.	1354	355	65	9	25	493	161	206	.262	.379	.336
Runners On/2 Out	982	244	41	6	18	201	96	141	.248	.357	.320
Scor. Pos./2 Out	636	154	26	3	12	177	65	99	.242	.349	.318
Late-Inning Pressure	771	191	28	6	9	70	71	121	.248	.335	.313
Leading Off	191	47	9	0	3	3	18	29	.246	.340	.311
Runners On	341	84	8	4	6	67	32	55	.246	.346	.305
Runners/Scor. Pos.	188	47	6	1	2	55	18	30	.250	.324	.305

RUNS BATTED IN	From 1B	From 2B	From 3B	Scoring Position
Totals	86/1692	171/1046	268/586	439/1632
Percentage	5.1%	16.3%	45.7%	26.9%

TEAM TOTALS: PITCHING

	W-L	ERA	AB	H	HR	BB	SO	BA	SA	OBA
Season	74-88	4.12	5531	1509	134	489	872	.273	.408	.332
vs. Left-Handers			1923	543	35	197	279	.282	.406	.348
vs. Right-Handers			3608	966	99	292	593	.268	.410	.324
vs. Ground-Ballers			2575	708	40	221	370	.275	.387	.333
vs. Fly-Ballers			2956	801	94	268	502	.271	.427	.332
Home Games	41-40	4.22	2840	780	69	237	461	.275	.417	.332
Road Games	33-48	4.03	2691	729	65	252	411	.271	.399	.332
Grass Fields	26-36	3.73	2050	545	47	190	330	.266	.383	.328
Artificial Turf	48-52	4.36	3481	964	87	299	542	.277	.423	.335
April	7-12	3.86	637	168	17	51	97	.264	.416	.318
May	21-7	4.14	958	250	31	73	159	.261	.410	.313
June	7-21	5.10	988	299	24	81	165	.303	.455	.355
July	15-14	3.47	1012	271	28	83	166	.268	.402	.326
August	9-19	4.83	937	263	17	105	136	.281	.414	.352
Sept./Oct.	15-15	3.39	999	258	17	96	149	.258	.356	.325
Leading Off Inn.			1344	347	33	86	219	.258	.402	.307
Bases Empty			3139	827	72	260	497	.263	.394	.322
Runners On			2392	682	62	229	375	.285	.427	.345
Runners/Scor. Pos.			1394	388	29	163	226	.278	.407	.345
Runners On/2 Out			1019	277	30	103	163	.272	.421	.343
Scor. Pos./2 Out			642	168	17	82	105	.262	.396	.347
Late-Inning Pressure			706	193	16	69	133	.273	.397	.341
Leading Off			174	41	3	14	34	.236	.345	.296
Runners On			320	87	6	34	60	.272	.391	.344
Runners/Scor. Pos.			180	52	4	26	38	.289	.439	.376
First 9 Batters			2908	758	63	267	527	.261	.382	.324
Second 9 Batters			1504	429	41	131	202	.285	.437	.342
All Batters Thereafter			1119	322	30	91	143	.288	.438	.342

NEW YORK YANKEES

- **A record-tying plunge.**
- **Is there reason for hope?**

Five years ago, it was as easy to foresee the impending fall of the Yankees as it normally is when a team wins 97 games and just misses a trip to the League Championship Series. Which is to say, unless you happen to be Jeane Dixon, it was impossible. The Yankees of 1985 were the highest-scoring team in either league, and the potential of its young lineup appeared to be limitless. Rickey Henderson and Don Mattingly were coming off their first full season together, and they seemed made for each other, leading the majors in runs and RBIs, respectively. Veterans Dave Winfield (105 runs, 114 RBIs) and Ron Guidry (22–6) gave no indication of slowing with age. Dave Righetti had a second consecutive productive season following his conversion from starter to stopper. And the development of several other young players from within the Yankees system, including Bobby Meacham, Mike Pagliarulo, and Dan Pasqua, suggested a promising future.

The Yankees were an ocean liner, steaming along at what an accident report might call "a high rate of speed." The crash was severe—the word *titanic* comes to mind. New York's record has declined in each of the five seasons since then, equaling the longest such streak in major-league history:

Base Year	Team	Base Year	Base+1	Base+2	Base+3	Base+4	Base+5
1900	Brooklyn Dodgers	82–54 .603	79–57 .581	75–63 .543	70–66 .515	56–97 .366	48–104 .316
1931	Philadelphia A's	107–45 .703	94–60 .610	79–72 .523	68–82 .453	58–91 .389	53–100 .346
1937	Chicago Cubs	93–61 .603	89–63 .585	84–70 .545	75–79 .487	70–84 .454	68–86 .441
1983	Baltimore Orioles	98–64 .605	85–77 .525	83–78 .516	73–89 .451	67–95 .414	54–107 .335
1985	**New York Yankees**	97–64 .602	90–72 .556	89–73 .549	85–76 .528	74–87 .460	67–95 .414

As with any wreck of such proportions, three questions are immediately raised: (1) How did it happen? (2) How bad is the damage? (3) What happens next?

The reasons for the wreck of the U.S.S. *Steinbrenner* are numerous but can be boiled down to a single, simple cause: bad decisions on player personnel, both in the team's philosophical approach to the issue and its individual player judgments. There are three primary sources of player acquisition: the minor-league system, trades, and the free-agent market. The Yankees struck out on three pitches.

Every baseball fan old enough to have a dog-eared Farrah poster in his attic will recall the flourish with which George Steinbrenner dove into the booming free-agent market of the mid-1970s. Steinbrenner immediately understood the value of these newly available mercenaries, and he was unequaled in his determination to buy them. But Steinbrenner's vision, undeniably a key ingredient in New York's three consecutive league championships from 1976 through 1978, was myopic.

The Yankees' signing of Dave Winfield in 1980, for all its value on a competitive level, sent an unmistakable message to every rival general manager: Tie up the best of your players before you lose them. The Yankees dominated the game of free-agent bingo throughout its brief run, but by the early 1980s, the pool of talent available in the free-agent marketplace began to dry up. Following the 1976, 1977, and 1978 regular seasons, 24 free agents were available coming off seasons in which they had reached one of the following thresholds: 80 runs or 80 RBIs for batters, 15 wins or 15 saves for pitchers. That total shrank to only 13 over the next three offseasons as premium players stopped shifting teams. The free agents reaching those levels:

1976: Sal Bando, Don Baylor, Dave Cash, Bobby Grich,Reggie Jackson, Gary Matthews, and Joe Rudi; Bill Campbell, Rollie Fingers, and Wayne Garland.

1977: Lyman Bostock, Oscar Gamble, Larry Hisle, Dave Kingman, and Richie Zisk; Goose Gossage and Mike Torrez.

1978: Rico Carty, Darrell Evans, and Pete Rose; Larry Gura, Tommy John, Mike Marshall, and Jim Slaton.

1979: Willie Horton; Nolan Ryan, Don Stanhouse, and Rick Wise.

1980: Ron LeFlore and Dave Winfield; Dan Spillner and Tug McGraw.

1981: Reggie Jackson and Jerry Remy; John Denny, Ed Farmer, and Ron Guidry. (50 runs or RBIs; 10 wins or saves)

By 1981, the Yankees faced another obstacle to building with free agents: a backlash against Steinbrenner and the carnival atmosphere that accompanied the team. The symbolic birth of the backlash was the departure of Reggie Jackson for California following the 1981 season. Although the Yankees still signed more than their share of free agents in succeeding seasons, they could no longer assume the best players would be theirs.

Nor did the Yankees take the steps necessary to reduce their reliance on that market: strengthening their own system and pursuing desirable players from other teams on the traditional trade market.

One startling fact summarizes the bankruptcy of New York's player-development system over the past 20 years: From the emergence of Thurman Munson in 1969 until that of Don Mattingly 13 years later, the Yankees didn't bring a single position player to the major leagues who would ultimately play 400 games for them. By comparison, the other 19 established clubs through that period produced an average of eight such players apiece; no other team produced fewer than four. But during that time, the Yankees' system produced not a single position player and only two pitchers—albeit great ones, Ron Guidry and Dave Righetti—who made a lasting positive impact on the team.

It has become fashionable to place much of the blame for the failure of New York's farm system on the draft choices forfeited by signing lesser free agents during that period. That blame is misplaced. Among the free agents signed in lieu of those picks were Dave Winfield, Jack Clark, and Steve Sax. And while it's impossible to say whom the Yankees would have chosen had they retained a full slate of first-round picks, there were no Clarks or Saxes among the players chosen in the slots that New York forfeited: Terry Francona (1980), Frank Castro (1981), Scott Jones (1982), Joel Davis (1983), Joey Cora (1985), Terry Carr (1986), Bill Haselman (1987), John Ericks (1988), and Kiki Jones (1989). (The Yankees retained their first-round pick in 1984, and wasted it on UCLA pitcher Jeff Pries, who never made it past Double A and was out of pro ball by 1988.)

What about trades? Well, as the veteran free-agent pool dried up, the Yankees made a long series of stopgap deals, pillaging their farm system to trade for the kinds of players no longer otherwise available. Jerry Mumphrey, Ken Griffey, Doyle Alexander, Shane Rawley, Roy Smalley, John Montefusco, and Toby Harrah came over, while the Yankees were surrendering prospects like Ruppert Jones (acquired for Bobby Brown), Willie McGee, Pat Tabler, Greg Gagne, Otis Nixon, Tim Lollar, Gene Nelson, and Dennis Rasmussen. This not only weakened the player-development leg of the tripod, but revealed a fundamental disregard for how the Yankees of the mid-seventies were put together.

It was the deals made by Gabe Paul that really laid the groundwork for the pennants won by "the best team money could buy." Even in 1976, when the only free agent to have joined the Yankees was Catfish Hunter, just two players who had spent their entire careers with the Yankees had as many as 100 at-bats: Roy White and Thurman Munson. Over the previous five years, Paul had orchestrated a number of trades in which the Yankees unloaded their extraneous and often aging parts for younger players of promise: a package of underachieving prospects for Graig Nettles; Fritz Peterson and some middle relievers for Chris Chambliss; Bobby Bonds for Mickey Rivers and Ed Figueroa; Doc Medich for Willie Randolph (and Dock Ellis and Ken Brett); Oscar Gamble for Bucky Dent (a deal in which the Yankees reluctantly tossed in a lower-level prospect named LaMarr Hoyt). The glory years of the 1970s were made possible by enormous success in all three areas—player development, free-agent acquisition, and trades. But when one leg of the tripod weakens, as when the free-agent pool evaporated, the strain on the other two increases. The Yankees found themselves on the wrong end of the deals they'd once been built with, and the house came crashing down. New York's recent collapse was made inevitable by the interrelated breakdown of all three parts.

How bad were the 1990 Yankees, who finished with the worst record in the American League? The pitching was poor: New York ranked 12th in the American League in ERA. The offense was even worse: The Yankees ranked last in scoring, with an average of 3.7 runs per game. And on closer examination, that offense—a term used against the advice of our attorneys—was even worse than it appears on first glance. The Yankees had the league's lowest batting average (.240), which isn't unusual for its lowest-scoring team; in 8 of the previous 14 seasons, the lowest batting and lowest scoring teams in the American League were one and the same. But normally, even those teams have other components—walks and extra-base hits—that compensate to some degree. Not in this case: The Yankees also ranked last in both those categories, to become only the second A.L. team in the past 45 years to trail the league in batting average, walks, and extra-base hits. (The other was the 1969 California Angels.)

New York's hitters did rank second in the league in one category, however. Unfortunately, it was strikeouts: Yankees batters struck out over 1000 times—1027 to be precise—for only the second time in the history of the franchise.

Under such demoralizing circumstances, it was easy for Yankees fans to get caught up in the hysteria that surrounded the emergence of several previously unheralded rookies. Deion Sanders had glowed with neon publicity, but by the end of the season Kevin Maas, Oscar Azocar, and Jim Leyritz had become the first three Yankees rookie teammates in nearly 50 years to compile at least 200 at-bats each. Their development (particularly that of Maas, whose accomplishments are detailed on page 153), combined with that of Roberto Kelly and Bob Geren in the two previous seasons, gave Yankees fans some hope.

The emergence of those rookies may have been more a symptom of the disease than a potential cure. As we pointed out in the Chicago White Sox essay, the sudden appearance of so many rookies often signals nothing more than a team's midseason surrender. Desperate times call for desperate measures;

or, to quote Bob Dylan, when you got nothing, you got nothing to lose. Realizing the futility of playing veterans like Claudell Washington, Wayne Tolleson, and Rick Cerone—the list could go on and on—the Yankees conducted spring training in August. And despite the euphoria that accompanied Kevin Maas's unprecedented home-run binge, they produced little else of value.

What would you think about a rookie who played a full season, batting .253 with 10 home runs and 44 RBIs? How would it color your overall impression if that rookie batted just .206 with two home runs during September and October? That was the combined output of Azocar and Leyritz; hardly something to get excited over. Of course, Maas made a splash so spectacular that if he continues on that pace, it won't matter if anyone else is in the pool. The rookie with the most comparable statistics was Dick Stuart (in 1958), who went on to hit 228 home runs—a total the Yankees should gladly accept from Maas, no questions asked. (Those who witnessed some of Maas's antics as he impersonated a first baseman last season surely recognized the similarities in the field as well.)

Year	Player	G	AB	R	H	2B	3B	HR	RBI	BB	SO	BA
1958	Dick Stuart	67	254	38	68	12	5	16	48	11	75	.268
1990	Kevin Maas	79	254	42	64	9	0	21	41	43	76	.252

If Maas takes the Stuart track, it would restore some needed respect to New York's shattered lineup. And if Don Mattingly returns from a half-season on the disabled list to his old form, the middle of the Yankees' batting order might even be sound. And if Steve Sax rebounds from an off season, if Roberto Kelly and Jesse Barfield duplicate their strong 1990 efforts, and if Bob Geren and Alvaro Espinoza prove that 1990 and not 1989 was the fluke, the Yankees could suddenly reemerge as a solid team in a division without a strong incumbent. Right. And if Phil Rizzuto suddenly discovers the fountain of youth, he'll return to play shortstop for the Yankees. The fact is that for the Yankees to contend for the A.L. East title anytime soon, almost everything has to fall perfectly into place. Life just doesn't work that way.

For example: As recently as a year ago, it appeared that New York had begun to put its disorganized house in order. Sax, Espinoza, Kelly, and Geren provided previously missing strength up the middle. The addition of Pascual Perez and Tim Leary was intended to bolster a starting rotation that already stood to improve through the emergence of at least one more pitcher from a cadre of promising contenders (Chuck Cary, Greg Cadaret, Eric Plunk, and Clay Parker among them). The promise of 1989 gave way to the disappointment of 1990 as only one of the 10 players mentioned above (Kelly) fulfilled the team's hopes.

But all this distracts us from an indisputable abstract reality: The Yankees have declined for five consecutive seasons. No team, no matter how bad, has taken even one more step down that futile road. The Yankees have reached the limit as we know it, and the only reasonable question is: How far will they bounce back? As we've pointed out, it would take a miracle for the Yankees to rebound into contention in the A.L. East. But sometimes, when you least expect it, things change totally and unbelievably. Two years ago, how many New Yorkers could have envisioned the decline of its three most publicized icons: Ed, Donald, and George?

WON-LOST RECORD BY STARTING POSITION

New York Yankees	C	1B	2B	3B	SS	LF	CF	RF	DH	P	Leadoff	Cleanup	Starts vs. LH	Starts vs. RH	Total Starts
Steve Adkins	-	-	-	-	-	-	-	-	-	2-3	-	-	1	4	2-3
Oscar Azocar	-	-	-	-	-	20-18	-	7-4	-	-	-	-	13	36	27-22
Steve Balboni	-	8-12	-	-	-	-	-	-	21-23	-	-	24-24	54	10	29-35
Jesse Barfield	-	-	-	-	-	-	2-1	54-79	-	-	-	3-7	54	82	56-80
Mike Blowers	-	-	-	16-26	-	-	-	-	0-1	-	-	-	18	25	16-27
Greg Cadaret	-	-	-	-	-	-	-	-	-	2-4	-	-	2	4	2-4
Chuck Cary	-	-	-	-	-	-	-	-	-	11-16	-	-	8	19	11-16
Rick Cerone	10-19	-	-	-	-	-	-	-	2-3	-	-	-	15	19	12-22
Brian Dorsett	2-3	-	-	-	-	-	-	-	4-1	-	-	-	5	5	6-4
Dave Eiland	-	-	-	-	-	-	-	-	-	2-3	-	-	3	2	2-3
Alvaro Espinoza	-	-	-	-	54-87	-	-	-	-	-	-	-	52	89	54-87
Bob Geren	37-44	-	-	-	-	-	-	-	-	-	-	-	40	41	37-44
Lee Guetterman	-	-	-	-	-	-	-	-	-	-	-	-	-	-	-
John Habyan	-	-	-	-	-	-	-	-	-	-	-	-	-	-	-
Mel Hall	-	-	-	-	-	12-24	-	4-8	17-28	-	-	23-43	9	84	33-60
Andy Hawkins	-	-	-	-	-	-	-	-	-	10-16	-	-	12	14	10-16
Jimmy Jones	-	-	-	-	-	-	-	-	-	4-3	-	-	3	4	4-3
Roberto Kelly	-	-	-	-	-	6-5	59-85	-	-	-	43-50	-	55	100	65-90
Dave LaPoint	-	-	-	-	-	-	-	-	-	13-14	-	-	10	17	13-14
Tim Leary	-	-	-	-	-	-	-	-	-	11-20	-	-	9	22	11-20
Mark Leiter	-	-	-	-	-	-	-	-	-	2-1	-	-	1	2	2-1
Jim Leyritz	4-6	-	-	31-36	-	3-5	-	0-1	-	-	-	-	35	51	38-48
Kevin Maas	-	25-28	-	-	-	-	-	-	5-12	-	-	6-9	13	57	30-40
Don Mattingly	-	34-55	-	-	-	-	-	-	3-6	-	-	3-6	30	68	37-61
Lance McCullers	-	-	-	-	-	-	-	-	-	-	-	-	-	-	-
Hensley Meulens	-	-	-	-	-	10-12	-	-	-	-	-	-	11	11	10-12
Alan Mills	-	-	-	-	-	-	-	-	-	-	-	-	-	-	-
Rich Monteleone	-	-	-	-	-	-	-	-	-	-	-	-	-	-	-
Matt Nokes	14-23	-	-	-	-	-	-	1-0	11-14	-	-	6-5	-	63	26-37
Clay Parker	-	-	-	-	-	-	-	-	-	1-1	-	-	-	2	1-1
Pascual Perez	-	-	-	-	-	-	-	-	-	1-2	-	-	1	2	1-2
Eric Plunk	-	-	-	-	-	-	-	-	-	-	-	-	-	-	-
Luis Polonia	-	-	-	-	-	-	-	-	1-3	-	-	-	-	4	1-3
Dave Righetti	-	-	-	-	-	-	-	-	-	-	-	-	-	-	-
Jeff D. Robinson	-	-	-	-	-	-	-	-	-	2-2	-	-	2	2	2-2
Deion Sanders	-	-	-	-	-	5-15	6-9	-	-	-	6-12	-	5	30	11-24
Steve Sax	-	-	66-88	-	-	-	-	-	-	-	18-32	-	54	100	66-88
Wayne Tolleson	-	-	0-6	-	10-3	-	-	-	-	-	-	-	1	18	10-9
Randy Velarde	-	-	1-0	20-33	3-5	1-2	-	-	-	-	-	-	22	43	25-40
Jim Walewander	-	-	0-1	-	-	-	-	-	-	-	-	-	-	1	0-1
Claudell Washington	-	-	-	-	-	5-10	-	1-3	-	-	0-1	-	-	19	6-13
Dave Winfield	-	-	-	-	-	5-4	-	-	3-4	-	-	2-1	9	7	8-8
Mike Witt	-	-	-	-	-	-	-	-	-	6-10	-	-	3	13	6-10

TEAM TOTALS: BATTING

	AB	H	2B	3B	HR	RBI	BB	SO	BA	SA	OBA
Season	5483	1322	208	19	147	561	427	1027	.241	.366	.300
vs. Left-Handers	1645	412	67	5	49	172	161	321	.250	.387	.321
vs. Right-Handers	3838	910	141	14	98	389	266	706	.237	.358	.292
vs. Ground-Ballers	2394	570	81	10	58	234	172	408	.238	.353	.293
vs. Fly-Ballers	3089	752	127	9	89	327	255	619	.243	.377	.306
Home Games	2710	666	122	11	64	277	214	486	.246	.370	.304
Road Games	2773	656	86	8	83	284	213	541	.237	.363	.297
Grass Fields	4587	1087	176	17	118	461	360	858	.237	.360	.297
Artificial Turf	896	235	32	2	29	100	67	169	.262	.400	.320
April	557	145	24	2	13	56	37	105	.260	.381	.308
May	917	213	34	5	22	102	63	175	.232	.352	.286
June	979	250	37	4	23	97	58	165	.255	.372	.297
July	983	244	36	2	34	104	90	186	.248	.393	.316
August	1017	232	38	3	30	94	79	189	.228	.360	.289
Sept./Oct.	1030	238	39	3	25	108	100	207	.231	.348	.308
Leading Off Inn.	1364	311	59	4	44	44	85	264	.228	.374	.279
Bases Empty	3288	775	126	9	94	94	229	644	.236	.365	.292
Runners On	2195	547	82	10	53	467	198	383	.249	.368	.313
Runners/Scor. Pos.	1237	290	43	7	26	394	136	229	.234	.344	.309
Runners On/2 Out	946	228	37	5	18	192	94	176	.241	.348	.314
Scor. Pos./2 Out	605	139	24	4	10	166	65	122	.230	.332	.310
Late-Inning Pressure	932	217	35	4	26	90	87	200	.233	.363	.301
Leading Off	237	55	12	0	3	3	18	55	.232	.321	.289
Runners On	375	89	13	2	10	74	35	71	.237	.363	.304
Runners/Scor. Pos.	227	44	3	2	5	60	27	50	.194	.291	.280

RUNS BATTED IN	From 1B	From 2B	From 3B	Scoring Position
Totals	68/1579	148/981	198/510	346/1491
Percentage	4.3%	15.1%	38.8%	23.2%

TEAM TOTALS: PITCHING

	W-L	ERA	AB	H	HR	BB	SO	BA	SA	OBA
Season	67-95	4.21	5475	1430	144	618	909	.261	.405	.336
vs. Left-Handers			2052	546	43	244	294	.266	.390	.344
vs. Right-Handers			3423	884	101	374	615	.258	.414	.332
vs. Ground-Ballers			2609	694	45	276	402	.266	.382	.336
vs. Fly-Ballers			2866	736	99	342	507	.257	.426	.337
Home Games	37-44	3.88	2827	704	78	315	482	.249	.386	.325
Road Games	30-51	4.58	2648	726	66	303	427	.274	.425	.349
Grass Fields	56-81	4.10	4617	1190	123	535	780	.258	.398	.335
Artificial Turf	11-14	4.86	858	240	21	83	129	.280	.442	.342
April	7-10	4.14	568	151	21	59	106	.266	.428	.336
May	10-17	3.76	916	240	20	91	160	.262	.392	.329
June	11-17	4.33	960	270	27	106	141	.281	.440	.352
July	12-17	4.05	975	258	23	108	130	.265	.398	.337
August	16-14	4.15	1012	258	27	126	176	.255	.383	.339
Sept./Oct.	11-20	4.75	1044	253	26	128	196	.242	.400	.325
Leading Off Inn.			1315	346	37	125	208	.263	.407	.331
Bases Empty			3068	811	80	322	494	.264	.410	.337
Runners On			2407	619	64	296	415	.257	.399	.335
Runners/Scor. Pos.			1369	347	38	216	253	.253	.402	.349
Runners On/2 Out			1014	244	24	122	172	.241	.368	.325
Scor. Pos./2 Out			653	161	12	94	111	.247	.364	.345
Late-Inning Pressure			800	198	20	115	117	.248	.379	.344
Leading Off			197	42	6	23	23	.213	.325	.299
Runners On			360	86	10	57	62	.239	.383	.342
Runners/Scor. Pos.			208	38	5	49	41	.183	.317	.337
First 9 Batters			2842	752	73	333	524	.265	.405	.341
Second 9 Batters			1446	368	34	141	226	.254	.392	.322
All Batters Thereafter			1187	310	37	144	159	.261	.421	.342

OAKLAND ATHLETICS

- **Should we have been shocked?**
- **The foulest of parks.**

Pity the poor Oakland A's. So misunderstood. First, they were expected to face enormous obstacles en route to a third consecutive title. They won the race handily. Next, they were expected to face sterner opposition in the 1990 American League Championship Series than when they rolled over the same team two years earlier. But Oakland inflicted an even worse beating on the Red Sox than in 1988. So finally, most of the civilized world prepared for another sweep in the World Series. Cincinnati complied by slapping the A's silly in four straight.

Certainly, those who thought Oakland would struggle in the regular season greatly overstated the case. Gone from the 1989 championship roster were 19-game winner Storm Davis, regular DH Dave Parker, and all-around goodfellow Tony Phillips. But those A's won 99 games despite having three of the best players in baseball available for only partial seasons: Dennis Eckersley and Jose Canseco (who spent 45 and 101 days on the disabled list, respectively), and Rickey Henderson, who didn't rejoin the team until the Yankees unloaded him in late June. From those three players alone, *perhaps the three most valuable players in the American League,* Oakland stood to gain more than a full season's worth of service. That gain from three irreplaceable players would surely offset the loss of three players Oakland could and did replace: Scott Sanderson in for Davis; Ken Phelps in for Parker (which looked better on paper than on the Oakland Coliseum turf); and Mike Gallego in for Phillips. In truth, the A's looked even stronger last spring than they had a year earlier. And so they were, winning 103 games.

Anyone who took the time to compare Oakland's 1990 lineup to the players who beat Boston two years earlier, particularly following the acquisition of Harold Baines and Willie McGee in late August, could have foreseen that the A.L.C.S. massacre would be worse than that of 1988. During the two years between their playoff meetings with Boston the A's made the following changes: Rickey Henderson for Stan Javier; McGee for Luis Polonia; Baines for Dave Parker; Willie Randolph for Glenn Hubbard; Mike Moore and Scott Sanderson for Storm Davis and Eric Cadaret (or was it Greg Plunk?). Let's call Baines for Parker a wash. The rest is a blowout.

However, all of that just made Cincinnati's World Series sweep even more shocking. Two years ago, after Oakland lost a five-game series to Los Angeles, we showed that even a mediocre team—by World Series standards—has about one chance in three of defeating a dominant Oakland-like opponent in the Series. We took all games played from 1900 through 1988 between teams with winning percentages similar to those of the '88 A's and Dodgers. The Dodgers look-alikes won approximately 44 percent. (A margin of two wins in either direction was needed to qualify.) At that rate, the Dodgers had approximately a 36 percent chance to win the 1988 Series—roughly two-to-one odds, hardly an earth-shaking event. (That was saved for the '89 Series.)

The corresponding figures for the clones of the 1990 Series teams were only slightly different. Teams with winning percentages within two wins of Oakland's 1990 record compiled a .589 winning percentage in regular-season play against teams within two wins of Cincinnati's 91–71 mark. That gave the Reds a 31 percent chance of winning the World Series.

What made this Series result shocking, of course, wasn't merely the fact that Cincinnati beat Oakland; but even those willing to concede that the Reds belonged on the same field as the A's—a stretch for many of us at the time—never envisioned a four-game sweep. The theoretical odds of 34-to-one, based on the figures above, were supported by the results of those games: there were 57 four-game series between won-lost clones of the A's and Reds, and only two were swept by the inferior teams. (Surprisingly, only five were swept by the better team.)

Getting back to reality for a moment, those odds were misleading for a number of reasons. First and foremost, Jose Canseco had become a liability both at bat and in the field. From August 3 until the end of the season, Canseco hit three home runs (tying Jay Bell and Luis Rivera, among others, for 105th place in the majors during that period). Walt Weiss missed the entire Series. And a deep five-man rotation, one of Oakland's regular-season strengths, has little value in a best-of-seven series; Scott Sanderson and Curt Young became afterthoughts. Across the field, the converse was true: Cincinnati's rotation was top-heavy and shallow, especially after All-Star Game starter Jack Armstrong went south at mid-season, but for the World Series Tom Browning and Jose Rijo were joined by a healthy Danny Jackson, turning a liability into an asset. Those three starters and the Nasty Boys (Rob Dibble, Randy Myers, and Norm Charlton), who accounted for only 60 percent of Cincinnati's pitching during the season, pitched all but $4\frac{2}{3}$ of the 37 innings against Oakland. (Ah, hindsight—ain't it great!)

So maybe even a Cincinnati sweep shouldn't have been a head-spinning, knocked-off-your-chair, eyes-to-the-sky stunner. After all, it was closer to 30-to-one than to 30,000-to-one. Had a similar four-game sweep occurred during the regular season, it would have melted into the fabric of a six-month schedule. But given the heightened attention on the World Series, the little surprises that punctuate a season of baseball are elevated to a higher status. Good plays seem great, mental mistakes become disastrous tactical errors, and surprise victories become shocking upsets.

When Willie McGee signed a contract with the San Francisco Giants last December, it appeared that Oakland had merely rented his services for the 1990 stretch run and postseason. For two months' worth of Willie McGee, Oakland paid the Cardinals Felix Jose—an ultimately extraneous deal for them that had little effect on the A.L. West race, the playoffs, or the World Series, and which could therefore be considered a poor deal. But a crucial element in Oakland's acquisition of McGee was the draft choice the A's will now receive as compensation for losing McGee through free agency.

This wasn't the first time last season that Oakland's appetite for amateur draft choices drew attention. Oakland had four first-round selections in the June 1990 draft: their own standard pick, and three supplementary selections for having lost Parker, Davis, and Phillips as free agents. For Oakland, the lure of additional first-round draft choices may have played a part in decisions not to pursue those players; all made substantial contributions, but all were eminently replaceable.

The idea that baseball's best team for the last few years, and probably the next few years as well, was already stockpiling for the second half of the decade was daunting for the rest of baseball. Owners across the country decried this whole notion of compensation for lost free agents. (Whose dumb idea was that, anyhow?) This uproar might have been justified if this were the NFL, where even low first-round choices almost inevitably become starters within a few years. But the baseball draft becomes a crapshoot long before the end of the first round.

To illustrate that point, let's look at the draft of five years ago. The first six picks all played in the majors last season; in selection order, they were Jeff King, Greg Swindell, Matt Williams, Kevin Brown, Kent Mercker, and Gary Sheffield. But of the remaining 20 first-round picks, only two made even mediocre contributions at the major-league level in 1990: Scott Scudder (17th selection) and Lee Stevens (22). The profile of the first round in the 1985 draft was nearly identical. Seven of the first 11 picks were substantial contributors in 1990: B.J. Surhoff (1), Will Clark (2), Bobby Witt (3), Barry Larkin (4), Bobby Bonds (6), Pete Incaviglia (8), and Walt Weiss (11). But among lower first-round picks, the success rate was one in three, with 10 never-weres more than compensating for Willie Fraser (15), Brian McRae (17), Joe Magrane (18), Gregg Jefferies (20), and Rafael Palmeiro (22).

The drafts from 1980 through 1984 also illustrate the river of reliability that cuts through the first round, separating likely major leaguers from hopeful wanna-bes. Only 14 of 50 top-10 selections (28%) in those seasons have reached one of the following thresholds in any season to date: 75 runs scored or 75 RBIs for batters, 10 wins or 15 saves for pitchers. That's a pretty poor success rate, but it's nearly double the rate for lower first-round picks: 14 for 80 (18%).

So where are all the current major leaguers coming from? The answer shows how questionable the value of a first-round pick truly is. Among the 370 players who attained any of those thresholds over the past five seasons, only 81 (22%) were first-round selections in the June free-agent draft. (The first-round group includes representatives of every draft from 1971 through 1988, with the curious exception of 1975.)

Let's grant that Todd Van Poppel, coaxed into an A's jersey after being selected 14th overall, was a legitimate number-one selection who slipped to that point only because he was considered unsignable. Still, the highest of Oakland's three other first-round picks, pitcher Don Peters, was the 26th pick overall. Two other pitchers, David Zancanaro and Kirk Dressendorfer, were made with supplemental first-round selections, going 34th and 36th respectively. Given the track record of past drafts, Oakland will be extremely fortunate to fill even two spots in its rotation from among them. And for a team whose pitching staff is already the oldest in the majors, that might be not only too little but also too late.

The Oakland Coliseum is the toughest major-league ballpark to score runs in. That's not a statement about Dave Stewart or Dennis Eckersley; put any group of pitchers to work in the Coliseum and they will probably allow fewer runs there than anywhere else. Other stadiums have well-earned reputations as pitchers' parks—the Astrodome and Dodger Stadium are examples. But no ballpark suppresses scoring to the extent that the Oakland Coliseum does.

A look through the Ballparks section of this book reveals why it's so tough to score runs at the Coliseum. Some parks inhibit home runs, others reduce batting averages, and still others limit the number of hits that go for extra bases. But very few curb all three to a significant degree. How many? To paraphrase an old Monty Python line, less than two. Over the past five years, only the Oakland Coliseum has reduced home runs, batting averages, and extra-base hit rates by at least five percent.

The most obvious factors in home-run rates are the heights of and distances to outfield fences. A quick glance at page 419 is all that's necessary to show that artificial turf is about the only factor in turning singles into doubles and triples; nine of the 10 stadiums with synthetic grass inflate extra-base hit rates, while 12 of the 14 grass fields deflate them.

But what about batting average? Since the Lord first said, "Let there be grass. And by the way, if you're going to insist on playing baseball indoors, you're on your own, babe," artificial turf has been considered an inflationary factor on batting averages. Nope. Once again, check the Ballparks section: Plastic grass increases extra-base hit rates and stolen-base percentages, but has much less impact on batting averages.

However, one of the stadium factors that has a discernible effect on batting averages is the amount of foul territory. And that's certainly true of Oakland Coliseum: As expected, there were more foul outs there last season than at any other park in either league. Notice in the following table the strong relationship between the number of foul outs and a stadium's tendency to decrease batting averages (five-year trends are listed where possible):

Stadium	FO	Effect	Stadium	FO	Effect
Oakland Coliseum	207	−6.2%	Busch Stadium	150	+0.9%
Candlestick Park	202	−2.2%	Royals Stadium	147	+2.4%
Dodger Stadium	201	−1.7%	Memorial Stadium	144	−2.7%
Tiger Stadium	190	−6.7%	Comiskey Park	141	+0.6%
Atlanta Stadium	175	+5.3%	Olympic Stadium	137	+0.5%
County Stadium	174	−0.4%	Three Rivers Stadium	129	−2.9%
Skydome	171	−1.9%	Wrigley Field	128	+7.0%
Veterans Stadium	168	+0.6%	Anaheim Stadium	124	−2.2%
Shea Stadium	166	−5.0%	Riverfront Stadium	122	+3.3%
San Diego Stadium	160	−4.2%	Cleveland Stadium	121	+1.8%
Kingdome	158	+0.9%	Yankee Stadium	118	+0.4%
Metrodome	154	+3.9%	Arlington Stadium	116	+2.7%
Astrodome	152	−1.8%	Fenway Park	110	+6.6%

Also of interest (especially to those of us whose minds are slightly warped) was the shape of the distribution of foul outs at several of the parks. It was surprising to see Yankee Stadium, with so much foul territory behind home plate, rank so low overall. And in fact, only three stadiums produced more foul outs to catchers last season (Dodger Stadium, Tiger Stadium, and the Astrodome). The Oakland Coliseum had a somewhat standard shape. The following table describes a typical distribution. Contrast that to the Coliseum, and the stadiums with the most unusual patterns (notable oddities are in bold):

Stadium	P	C	1B	2B	3B	SS	LF	RF
Major league average	14	944	1308	83	1046	108	264	197
	0.4%	24%	33%	2%	26%	3%	7%	5%
Oakland Coliseum	3	41	71	7	50	2	19	14
	1 %	20%	34%	3%	24%	1%	9%	7%
Comiskey Park	1	34	36	1	35	4	**24**	6
	1 %	24%	26%	1%	25%	3%	**17%**	4%
Yankee Stadium	0	**45**	34	2	24	4	2	7
	0 %	**38%**	29%	2%	20%	3%	2%	6%
Dodger Stadium	0	**65**	50	3	57	5	13	8
	0 %	**32%**	25%	1%	28%	2%	6%	4%
San Diego Stadium	0	32	52	3	38	3	**16**	**16**
	0 %	20%	33%	2%	24%	2%	**10%**	**10%**

That's right, not even Devon White was able to snare a foul ball from centerfield.

It's somewhat surprising that none of the three players who fouled out more than 25 times last season played his home games in the leading parks. The individual leaders were Joe Carter (34), Chris Sabo (33), and Cal Ripken (29). They were followed by Matt Williams (25), Rob Deer (24), Gregg Jefferies (24), and Ryne Sandberg (24). Rickey Henderson was the A's leader, among three other players tied for 8th with 23 foul outs. The others were Gary Gaetti, Ron Gant, and Robby Thompson.

The numbers above imply that no stadium should be considered a hitters' or pitchers' park simply for its foul out tendencies; no hitter can claim to be terribly victimized by the size of his home field's foul territory. The difference between the most extreme stadiums is still only about one for both teams per game, to be divided among roughly 70 at-bats. And even the player most penalized by foul outs last season, White Sox catcher Ron Karkovice, lost only 19 batting average points based on his total of 13 foul outs in 183 at-bats. Take away those outs and his batting average would increase from .246 to .265, the largest such increase in the majors (minimum: 100 ABs). Our special achievement award here goes to Chris Gwynn of the Dodgers, who played in 101 games (141 at-bats) without fouling out last season. This still leaves him, however, 944 games shy of Wilt Chamberlain's record.

WON-LOST RECORD BY STARTING POSITION

Oakland Athletics	C	1B	2B	3B	SS	LF	CF	RF	DH	P	Leadoff	Cleanup	Starts vs. LH	Starts vs. RH	Total Starts
Troy Afenir	1-1	-	-	-	-	-	-	-	-	-	-	-	2	-	1-1
Harold Baines	-	-	-	-	-	-	-	-	17-10	-	-	16-9	-	27	17-10
Joseph Bitker	-	-	-	-	-	-	-	-	-	-	-	-	-	-	-
Lance Blankenship	-	-	5-4	10-8	-	1-2	-	9-1	-	-	1-1	-	20	20	25-15
Mike Bordick	-	-	-	-	0-1	-	-	-	-	-	-	-	-	1	0-1
Todd Burns	-	-	-	-	-	-	-	-	-	1-1	-	-	-	2	1-1
Jose Canseco	-	-	-	-	-	-	-	53-34	27-14	-	-	-	37	91	80-48
Ozzie Canseco	-	-	-	-	-	0-1	-	1-0	1-1	-	-	-	4	-	2-2
Steve Chitren	-	-	-	-	-	-	-	-	-	-	-	-	-	-	-
Jim Corsi	-	-	-	-	-	-	-	-	-	-	-	-	-	-	-
Dennis Eckersley	-	-	-	-	-	-	-	-	-	-	-	-	-	-	-
Mike Gallego	-	-	50-23	10-7	22-11	-	-	-	-	-	-	-	42	81	82-41
Reggie Harris	-	-	-	-	-	-	-	-	-	1-0	-	-	-	1	1-0
Ron Hassey	40-17	-	-	-	-	-	-	-	7-4	-	-	1-5	9	59	47-21
Scott Hemond	-	-	-	2-1	-	-	-	-	-	-	0-1	-	2	1	2-1
Dave Henderson	-	-	-	-	-	1-0	71-36	2-2	3-1	-	-	15-7	38	78	77-39
Rickey Henderson	-	-	-	-	-	77-41	-	-	8-6	-	85-47	-	39	93	85-47
Rick Honeycutt	-	-	-	-	-	-	-	-	-	-	-	-	-	-	-
Steve Howard	-	-	-	-	-	1-0	-	3-4	3-3	-	-	-	8	6	7-7
Dann Howitt	-	3-0	-	-	-	-	-	2-0	-	-	-	-	-	5	5-0
Stan Javier	-	-	-	-	-	-	1-2	-	1-0	-	0-1	-	1	3	2-2
Doug Jennings	-	1-2	-	-	-	13-5	-	5-5	3-3	-	5-4	-	-	37	22-15
Felix Jose	-	-	-	-	-	10-10	8-10	28-13	3-2	-	1-1	-	15	69	49-35
Joe Klink	-	-	-	-	-	-	-	-	-	-	-	-	-	-	-
Carney Lansford	-	1-1	-	80-43	-	-	-	-	2-3	-	6-4	-	35	95	83-47
Darren Lewis	-	-	-	-	-	-	4-3	-	-	-	-	-	2	5	4-3
Willie McGee	-	-	-	-	-	-	19-8	-	-	-	3-0	-	5	22	19-8
Mark McGwire	-	95-55	-	-	-	-	-	-	-	-	-	65-32	44	106	95-55
Mike Moore	-	-	-	-	-	-	-	-	-	15-18	-	-	8	25	15-18
Gene Nelson	-	-	-	-	-	-	-	-	-	-	-	-	-	-	-
Mike Norris	-	-	-	-	-	-	-	-	-	-	-	-	-	-	-
Dave Otto	-	-	-	-	-	-	-	-	-	-	-	-	-	-	-
Ken Phelps	-	3-0	-	-	-	-	-	-	9-5	-	-	4-2	-	17	12-5
Jamie Quirk	15-11	0-1	-	1-0	-	-	-	-	-	-	-	-	6	22	16-12
Willie Randolph	-	-	48-32	-	-	-	-	-	4-1	-	1-0	-	25	60	52-33
Scott Sanderson	-	-	-	-	-	-	-	-	-	19-15	-	-	10	24	19-15
Terry Steinbach	47-30	-	-	-	-	-	-	-	15-6	-	-	2-4	32	66	62-36
Dave Stewart	-	-	-	-	-	-	-	-	-	25-11	-	-	12	24	25-11
Walter Weiss	-	-	-	-	81-47	-	-	-	-	-	1-0	-	30	98	81-47
Bob Welch	-	-	-	-	-	-	-	-	-	29-6	-	-	8	27	29-6
Curt Young	-	-	-	-	-	-	-	-	-	13-8	-	-	6	15	13-8

TEAM TOTALS: BATTING

	AB	H	2B	3B	HR	RBI	BB	SO	BA	SA	OBA
Season	5433	1379	209	22	164	693	651	992	.254	.391	.336
vs. Left-Handers	1397	387	62	7	49	206	152	231	.277	.437	.349
vs. Right-Handers	4036	992	147	15	115	487	499	761	.246	.375	.332
vs. Ground-Ballers	2823	747	112	13	82	377	321	454	.265	.401	.343
vs. Fly-Ballers	2610	632	97	9	82	316	330	538	.242	.380	.328
Home Games	2612	646	82	7	69	305	329	483	.247	.363	.334
Road Games	2821	733	127	15	95	388	322	509	.260	.417	.338
Grass Fields	4570	1148	158	15	140	568	564	828	.251	.384	.336
Artificial Turf	863	231	51	7	24	125	87	164	.268	.426	.336
April	666	168	28	2	27	89	84	109	.252	.422	.336
May	886	230	34	4	32	118	109	129	.260	.415	.342
June	916	225	46	5	26	109	90	195	.246	.392	.315
July	1038	269	37	3	39	134	97	190	.259	.413	.326
August	897	227	28	1	19	105	100	149	.253	.350	.330
Sept./Oct.	1030	260	36	7	21	138	171	220	.252	.362	.363
Leading Off Inn.	1280	311	50	5	37	37	158	215	.243	.377	.328
Bases Empty	3030	750	129	11	95	95	356	553	.248	.391	.330
Runners On	2403	629	80	11	69	598	295	439	.262	.390	.343
Runners/Scor. Pos.	1355	340	45	5	25	493	208	281	.251	.347	.347
Runners On/2 Out	1022	250	28	5	27	237	147	195	.245	.361	.345
Scor. Pos./2 Out	645	147	15	3	6	186	114	140	.228	.288	.351
Late-Inning Pressure	600	156	24	4	11	75	86	137	.260	.368	.355
Leading Off	144	31	5	0	2	2	23	36	.215	.292	.331
Runners On	280	81	9	3	7	71	31	53	.289	.418	.359
Runners/Scor. Pos.	150	46	6	1	4	62	28	31	.307	.440	.412

RUNS BATTED IN	From 1B	From 2B	From 3B	Scoring Position
Totals	90/1800	205/1073	234/597	439/1670
Percentage	5.0%	19.1%	39.2%	26.3%

TEAM TOTALS: PITCHING

	W-L	ERA	AB	H	HR	BB	SO	BA	SA	OBA
Season	103-59	3.18	5409	1287	123	494	831	.238	.362	.302
vs. Left-Handers			2493	580	50	237	345	.233	.352	.299
vs. Right-Handers			2916	707	73	257	486	.242	.371	.305
vs. Ground-Ballers			2482	599	51	217	364	.241	.361	.302
vs. Fly-Ballers			2927	688	72	277	467	.235	.363	.303
Home Games	51-30	2.56	2723	605	52	244	427	.222	.330	.287
Road Games	52-29	3.82	2686	682	71	250	404	.254	.394	.318
Grass Fields	87-50	2.99	4571	1065	103	425	716	.233	.354	.299
Artificial Turf	16-9	4.27	838	222	20	69	115	.265	.405	.323
April	14-5	3.34	656	154	16	62	71	.235	.357	.303
May	18-9	2.43	884	197	18	60	138	.223	.331	.273
June	15-12	3.49	902	225	22	85	140	.249	.377	.314
July	17-14	3.40	1033	260	22	94	157	.252	.376	.314
August	18-9	3.25	902	209	24	95	158	.232	.373	.306
Sept./Oct.	21-10	3.16	1032	242	21	98	167	.234	.356	.301
Leading Off Inn.			1356	333	28	97	206	.246	.363	.298
Bases Empty			3211	750	72	268	512	.234	.356	.296
Runners On			2198	537	51	226	319	.244	.371	.311
Runners/Scor. Pos.			1217	290	28	149	186	.238	.370	.313
Runners On/2 Out			958	220	18	105	142	.230	.339	.308
Scor. Pos./2 Out			599	131	11	76	103	.219	.334	.310
Late-Inning Pressure			819	160	13	60	178	.195	.278	.251
Leading Off			217	48	6	16	47	.221	.346	.275
Runners On			309	57	3	21	50	.184	.239	.235
Runners/Scor. Pos.			162	26	0	12	24	.160	.191	.217
First 9 Batters			2665	630	55	250	459	.236	.352	.303
Second 9 Batters			1417	351	36	125	192	.248	.380	.308
All Batters Thereafter			1327	306	32	119	180	.231	.362	.295

SEATTLE MARINERS

- **Heresy on leadoff walks.**
- **Fathers and sons, for the record.**

Like most baseball fans, you are probably unaware that George Bernard Shaw was a devoted follower of our national pastime. It's a little known fact that his classic, "He who can, does. He who cannot, teaches," was actually said of Mariners pitching coach Mike Paul. (We don't know whom Shaw had in mind when he added, "And he who cannot teach, teaches gym." Pete Rose?)

Paul was a marginal major league pitcher, who spent all or parts of seven different seasons in the majors but never posted a winning record. But as a teacher, Paul has apparently made his mark on Seattle's pitching staff with a somewhat unconventional philosophy. Perhaps the most distinctive trait of Paul's students is their reluctance to give an opposing leadoff hitter a fat pitch, even if that means walking him.

Whoa, kemo sabe! Walk the *leadoff* hitter? There are well-respected pitching mentors—George Bamberger comes to mind—who would lose their lunches at the mere thought of putting a leadoff hitter on base without making him earn his way there, a graphic echo of Frankie Frisch's often quoted sentiment (especially often quoted if you live within cable range of Ralph Kiner), "Oh, those bases on balls!" But Seattle pitchers defied the notion that a leadoff walk is a walk on the wild side, passing one leadoff hitter for every 10 they faced last season. Walk rates to opposing leadoff hitters by each American League team:

Team	Inns.	Leadoff BB	Rate	Team	Inns.	Leadoff BB	Rate
Minnesota	1439	86	16.7	Baltimore	1439	119	12.1
Milwaukee	1450	94	15.4	Kansas City	1425	120	11.9
Toronto	1458	96	15.2	California	1457	125	11.7
Oakland	1458	97	15.0	New York	1449	125	11.6
Cleveland	1431	99	14.5	Texas	1449	126	11.5
Boston	1447	107	13.5	Detroit	1434	139	10.3
Chicago	1453	117	12.4	**Seattle**	1448	145	10.0

Most baseball fans intuitively understand the importance of keeping the leadoff batter off base. Even so, many are surprised to discover how crucial the outcome of each inning's first confrontation is: Teams are *more than three times* as likely to score when the leadoff batter reaches base than they are when he makes out. The following table shows that disparity. "Scores" indicates the number of innings in which a team scored, not the number of runs it scored in those innings:

Leadoff Batter	American League Innings	American League Scores	National League Innings	National League Scores
Reaches base	4,991	2,681 (54%)	4,364	2,270 (52%)
Makes out	13,651	2,075 (15%)	11,786	1,801 (15%)

These figures would seem to undermine Seattle's approach. But there's a more basic question underlying the Mariners' philosophy. No one *wants* to walk the leadoff batter, but at what cost does a pitcher avoid it? Would Frisch, Bamberger, and their colleagues and disciples prefer a batting-practice approach, with pitchers laying fat, motionless fastballs over the plate to leadoff batters as the price for ensuring a walk-free environment? Or, to turn the question around, what did Seattle get in return for its pitchers' willingness to walk leadoff batters?

As the first table above shows, Seattle walked opposing leadoff hitters in a league-high total of 145 innings. The other leadoff hitters batted only .222 against the Mariners, the lowest average in the league: in all other at-bats, the Mariners staff allowed a .250 average, to rank third in the league. The following table contrasts the performance of Mariners opponents based on whether or not the batter was leading off. Seattle ranked higher in leadoff situations than otherwise in every category listed below, with the noteworthy exception of bases on balls—an exception that we think fueled an otherwise across-the-board improvement:

Category	Leadoff Hitters	Other At-Bats
Batting average	.222 (1st)	.250 (3d)
Slugging average	.328 (1st)	.369 (3d)
Singles	211 (1st)	744 (5th)
Extra-base hits	77 (1st)	287 (2d)
Bases on balls	145 (14th)	461 (11th)

Incidentally, the horror with which leadoff walks are regarded requires us to emphasize this common-sense fact: Teams are no more likely to score in innings in which the leadoff batter walks than they are when he reaches first base by other means. Despite the mythic risk of walking the leadoff batter, it's no more costly than allowing, say, a leadoff single. Last season, American League teams scored in 682 of the 1595 innings in which they drew leadoff walks (42.8%), compared to 1541 of 3511 other innings in which the leadoff batters reached first base but no further (43.9%), an insignificant difference.

Tim McCarver has appropriately called baseball a game of firsts: first pitch, first strike, first batter, first out. Since each inning's leadoff batter has such an enormous effect on his team's scoring chances, opposing pitchers ought to minimize that batter's chances of reaching base—via walk *or hit*. Those two aren't always mutually exclusive: Minnesota last season issued the fewest leadoff walks in the league, and reduced their opponents' batting average substantially in leadoff situations as well. But Seattle proved that a league-high total of leadoff walks doesn't spell disaster if that total is merely the residue of a cautious approach. While most teams preached against leadoff walks, the Mariners were more concerned with a larger issue: keeping the leadoff batter off base.

Seattle's streak of losing seasons—a streak that encompasses all 14 years of the franchise's history—finally gets its fling at immortality this season. One more losing record and Seattle will equal the longest streak in American League history. And should the Mariners match that mark, they, like a game-show contestant, will earn a shot in 1992 at the grand prize—the longest streak in major league history.

That may surprise some of you. Although we expect that no one lost a mortgage payment to Vegas bookies on Seattle's World Series chances, neither have the Mariners been an annual disaster. If the major leagues were divided into divisions according to the quality of the teams, like European soccer leagues, Seattle would certainly have earned a perennial spot in the fourth division. But they would have fielded a competitive fourth division team throughout the past five years, and would probably have earned promotion to the third division based on last season's encouraging performance. (All right—what we're trying to say is, they're not the Braves.)

Nevertheless, Seattle's current streak of 14 consecutive losing seasons is now the fourth longest in the entire history of major league baseball. But the following table shows that their record during the streak has been considerably better than that of almost any other team with a comparable streak:

Team	Streak/Years	W	L	Pct.
Phil. Phillies	16 (1933–48)	888	1554	.364
Boston Red Sox	15 (1919–33)	881	1398	.387
Phil./K.C. A's	15 (1953–67)	939	1422	.398
Phil. Phillies	14 (1918–31)	786	1310	.375
Seattle Mariners	14 (1977–90)	937	1275	.424
Philadelphia A's	13 (1934–46)	736	1245	.372
St. Louis Browns	12 (1930–41)	715	1122	.389
Washington Senators	11 (1901–11)	610	1009	.377
Boston Braves	11 (1903–13)	597	1062	.360
Brooklyn Dodgers	11 (1904–14)	669	1003	.400
Cincinnati Reds	11 (1945–55)	747	945	.441
Browns/Orioles	11 (1946–56)	645	1048	.381

How can a team that good—relatively speaking, of course—be bad for so long? It may have something to do with an odd pair of traits: Seattle's organization has been unusually productive during the 1980s, but the team has traded away more talent than any other team during that time. As demonstrated in last year's *Analyst,* players who spent their rookie seasons with the Mariners accounted for 500 more hits, drove in 200 more runs, and scored 250 more runs during the 1989 season than those produced by any other team in the majors. The reemergence of Cecil Fielder helped to boost Toronto past the Mariners on those lists in 1990, but Seattle still ranked no worse than third in any of the categories.

And of course, Seattle didn't limit its philanthropy to position players. From 1983 through 1989, four different pitchers who made their major league debuts with Seattle had seasons of 15 or more wins: Bud Black, Mark Langston, Mike Moore, and Shane Rawley. Only two had such seasons for Seattle, and by 1989 all were pitching elsewhere.

The constant supply of new talent has certainly kept Seattle from folding altogether. But the Mariners' costly little habit of sending their potential stars elsewhere has certainly contributed to the team's long streak of futility. Does anyone think that a lineup including Ken Griffey Jr., Alvin Davis, Harold Reynolds, Edgar Martinez, and Dave Valle, augmented by dearly departed Ivan Calderon, Dave Henderson, Danny Tartabull, and Spike Owen, couldn't win 81 games—especially if supported by a starting rotation of Langston, Moore, Black, Randy Johnson and Erik Hanson? (If you don't agree, write the Kingdome to claim your prize: automatic membership in the Omar Vizquel Fan Club.)

The new regime in Seattle, led by general manager Woody Woodward, seems keenly aware of the need to retain the team's young talent. Griffey and Martinez are likely to become the Kingdome fixtures that only Reynolds and Davis are now (and that Tartabull and Calderon, among others, should have become). Hanson and Johnson appear ready to blossom as legitimate stars. In fact, the acquisition of Johnson in the Mark Langston trade two years ago set the standard by which all other such trades will evermore be measured. Backed into a corner when Langston announced that he would not return to Seattle in 1990, Woodward nevertheless engineered a favorable deal for three of Montreal's hottest pitching prospects. Johnson has since become as valuable a pitcher as Langston himself.

Things are already improving. Like a thoroughbred that shows promise by contending to the top of the stretch before fading, Seattle showed signs of awakening last summer. The Mariners remained above the .500 mark later in the season than ever before (60–59 through games of August 17), and their 57–52 mark on August 5 marked the first time in franchise history that Seattle had stood five games over the .500 mark at any point in the season. Of course, the Mariners were unable to keep up with the mighty A's and the semi-mighty White Sox, and they ultimately couldn't even maintain their own modest pace. But if Seattle continues to produce an abundance of talent, not only will the Mariners' streak of losing seasons be brought to an abrupt end, but Oakland and Chicago might not be the only contenders in a division that has grown top-heavy.

What a country! Where else could a 40-year-old ballplayer, apparently washed up after being cut loose by a championship team-to-be, wind up in an even more desirable spot, sitting alongside his son in the Mariners dugout? The old man bats nearly .400 with his boy watching, and senior and junior hit back-to-back home runs as an encore. Only in America!

With the elder Griffey now set to return to Seattle for another season (.377 hitters can be somewhat difficult to find), the hottest barroom question in town this summer may be whether the Griffeys are the greatest father and son combination in major league history. To us, it appears that they are currently running behind Bobby and Barry Bonds, by virtue of the lead that Bobby built over Ken, Sr.:

Fathers	G	AB	R	H	2B	3B	HR	RBI	BB	SB	BA
Bonds	1849	7043	1258	1886	302	66	332	1024	914	461	.268
Griffey	2067	7144	1119	2119	357	77	151	850	706	200	.297

Despite Griffey's 31-point edge in batting average, this battle goes to the Bondses. Griffey's 233-hit advantage is nearly offset by his 208-walk shortfall, which reduces his margin in on-base average to a mere five points (.358 to .353). That advantage crumbles quickly under the weight of Bonds's massive edge in both home runs and stolen bases—he amassed more than twice as many as Griffey. Bonds also produced 150 more runs (a half-run is counted for each run scored or driven in).

Without disputing the enormous potential of Griffey, Jr., it won't be easy for him to keep pace with the accomplishments of Barry Bonds, the incumbent National League MVP. Nevertheless, it will be interesting to follow the progress of both the Griffeys and the Bondses as they, along with two different sets of Alomars, eclipse the achievements of many of the other fine father and son pairs throughout major league history, like the Bells, the Boones, and the Willses. Toward that end, our "Father and Son Record Book" (our roster of families uses those listed in *Total Baseball*):

Games: 4146, Gus and Buddy Bell; 3637, Ray and Bob Boone; 2973, Yogi and Dale Berra; 2958, Eddie Collins, Sr. and Jr.; 2905, Bob and Terry Kennedy; 2854, George and Dick Sisler; 2773, Maury and Bump Wills; 2631, Jim and Mike Hegan; 2566, Bobby and Barry Bonds; 2525, Roy Smalley, Sr. and Jr.

Runs: 2016, the Bells; 1859, the Collinses; 1726, the Bondses; 1586, George and Dick Sisler; 1539, the Willses; 1451, Jim and Queenie (some nicknames you don't want to ask about) O'Rourke; 1411, the Berras; 1361, H. Earl and Earl D. Averill; 1324, the Boones; 1298, George and Dave Sisler.

Hits: 4337, the Bells; 3532, George and Dick Sisler; 3377, the Collinses; 3098, the Boones; 2941, the Willses; 2837, George and Dave Sisler; 2753, the Berras; 2574, the Bondses; 2449, the Kennedys; 2418, the Griffeys.

Home Runs: 449, the Bondses; 407, the Bells and the Berras; 282, the Averills; 257, Dolf and Doug Camilli; 256, the Boones; 228, Hal Trosky, Sr. and Jr.; 224, the Smalleys; 189, the Griffeys; 173, the Kennedys; 155, George and Dick Sisler and Mike and Tom Tresh.

RBIs: 2048, the Bells; 1708, the Berras; 1563, the Boones; 1535, George and Dick Sisler; 1361, the Bondses; 1324, the Averills; 1315, the Collinses; 1180, George and Dave Sisler; 1129, the Kennedys; 1030, the Camillis.

Stolen Bases: 782, the Willses; 747, the Collinses; 630, the Bondses (we're going with the traditional figure here for Bobby, not the Miller Lite total); 381, George and Dick Sisler; 375, George and Dave Sisler; 317, Sandy and Roberto Alomar; 232, the Griffeys; 231, Sandy Alomar, Sr. and Jr.; 193, Julian and Stan Javier; 181, those madcap O'Rourkes.

WON-LOST RECORD BY STARTING POSITION

Seattle Mariners	C	1B	2B	3B	SS	LF	CF	RF	DH	P	Leadoff	Cleanup	Starts vs. LH	Starts vs. RH	Total Starts
Scott Bankhead	-	-	-	-	-	-	-	-	-	1-3	-	-	1	3	1-3
Scott Bradley	25-25	-	-	1-1	-	-	-	-	1-4	-	-	-	3	54	27-30
Mickey Brantley	-	-	-	-	-	-	-	-	-	-	-	-	-	-	-
Greg Briley	-	-	-	-	-	13-17	-	22-37	-	-	0-1	-	3	86	35-54
Mike Brumley	-	-	-	1-1	18-21	-	-	-	-	-	-	-	6	35	19-22
Jay Buhner	-	-	-	-	-	-	0-1	16-18	4-5	-	-	0-1	15	29	20-24
Dave Burba	-	-	-	-	-	-	-	-	-	-	-	-	-	-	-
Bryan Clark	-	-	-	-	-	-	-	-	-	-	-	-	-	-	-
Dave Cochrane	-	0-1	-	1-0	-	-	-	-	-	-	-	-	-	2	1-1
Darnell Coles	-	2-0	-	1-5	-	-	-	11-6	-	-	-	-	11	14	14-11
Keith Comstock	-	-	-	-	-	-	-	-	-	-	-	-	-	-	-
Henry Cotto	-	-	-	-	-	12-11	5-6	27-19	-	-	1-0	1-1	48	32	44-36
Alvin Davis	-	24-27	-	-	-	-	-	-	36-51	-	-	23-34	35	103	60-78
Rich Delucia	-	-	-	-	-	-	-	-	-	1-4	-	-	2	3	1-4
Mario Diaz	-	-	-	-	-	-	-	-	-	-	-	-	-	-	-
Gary Eave	-	-	-	-	-	-	-	-	-	1-4	-	-	-	5	1-4
Mike Gardiner	-	-	-	-	-	-	-	-	-	0-3	-	-	-	3	0-3
Brian Giles	-	-	1-1	-	14-14	-	-	-	-	-	-	-	16	14	15-15
Ken Griffey Jr.	-	-	-	-	-	-	72-78	-	1-1	-	-	1-1	42	110	73-79
Ken Griffey Sr.	-	-	-	-	-	8-11	-	-	-	-	-	-	-	19	8-11
Erik Hanson	-	-	-	-	-	-	-	-	-	18-15	-	-	16	17	18-15
Gene Harris	-	-	-	-	-	-	-	-	-	-	-	-	-	-	-
Brian Holman	-	-	-	-	-	-	-	-	-	15-13	-	-	9	19	15-13
Mike Jackson	-	-	-	-	-	-	-	-	-	-	-	-	-	-	-
Randy Johnson	-	-	-	-	-	-	-	-	-	19-14	-	-	10	23	19-14
Tracy Jones	-	-	-	-	-	10-7	-	-	3-1	-	-	1-1	9	12	13-8
Brent Knackert	-	-	-	-	-	-	-	-	-	1-1	-	-	-	2	1-1
Jeffrey Leonard	-	-	-	-	-	32-36	-	1-5	27-20	-	-	51-47	41	80	60-61
Vance Lovelace	-	-	-	-	-	-	-	-	-	-	-	-	-	-	-
Edgar Martinez	-	-	-	66-73	-	-	-	-	2-0	-	-	-	44	97	68-73
Tino Martinez	-	6-13	-	-	-	-	-	-	-	-	-	-	3	16	6-13
Scott Medvin	-	-	-	-	-	-	-	-	-	-	-	-	-	-	-
Jose Melendez	-	-	-	-	-	-	-	-	-	-	-	-	-	-	-
Pete M. O'Brien	-	45-44	-	-	-	2-3	-	-	3-3	-	-	-	33	67	50-50
Dennis Powell	-	-	-	-	-	-	-	-	-	-	-	-	-	-	-
Jerry Reed	-	-	-	-	-	-	-	-	-	-	-	-	-	-	-
Harold Reynolds	-	-	76-84	-	-	-	-	-	-	-	76-84	-	48	112	76-84
Jeff Schaefer	-	-	-	7-5	10-7	-	-	-	-	-	-	-	6	23	17-12
Mike Schooler	-	-	-	-	-	-	-	-	-	-	-	-	-	-	-
Matt Sinatro	6-8	-	-	-	-	-	-	-	-	-	-	-	10	4	6-8
Russ Swan	-	-	-	-	-	-	-	-	-	4-4	-	-	2	6	4-4
Bill Swift	-	-	-	-	-	-	-	-	-	5-3	-	-	2	6	5-3
Dave Valle	46-52	-	-	-	-	-	-	-	-	-	-	-	35	63	46-52
Omar Vizquel	-	-	-	-	35-43	-	-	-	-	-	-	-	24	54	35-43
Matt Young	-	-	-	-	-	-	-	-	-	12-21	-	-	6	27	12-21
Clint Zavaras	-	-	-	-	-	-	-	-	-	-	-	-	-	-	-

TEAM TOTALS: BATTING

	AB	H	2B	3B	HR	RBI	BB	SO	BA	SA	OBA
Season	5474	1419	251	26	107	610	596	749	.259	.373	.333
vs. Left-Handers	1797	479	84	8	38	235	189	254	.267	.386	.336
vs. Right-Handers	3677	940	167	18	69	375	407	495	.256	.367	.332
vs. Ground-Ballers	2076	553	89	15	42	235	234	302	.266	.384	.344
vs. Fly-Ballers	3398	866	162	11	65	375	362	447	.255	.366	.327
Home Games	2666	682	136	11	49	297	324	355	.256	.370	.338
Road Games	2808	737	115	15	58	313	272	394	.262	.376	.328
Grass Fields	2153	566	87	11	43	242	216	288	.263	.373	.330
Artificial Turf	3321	853	164	15	64	368	380	461	.257	.373	.335
April	675	163	31	3	17	72	52	70	.241	.372	.297
May	1003	282	42	8	26	126	98	136	.281	.417	.344
June	938	246	50	4	13	103	111	158	.262	.366	.341
July	899	229	38	1	17	107	94	120	.255	.356	.326
August	947	221	47	5	15	77	111	131	.233	.341	.316
Sept./Oct.	1012	278	43	5	19	125	130	134	.275	.383	.361
Leading Off Inn.	1305	328	62	5	22	22	136	153	.251	.357	.326
Bases Empty	3039	787	146	15	56	56	313	421	.259	.372	.332
Runners On	2435	632	105	11	51	554	283	328	.260	.375	.336
Runners/Scor. Pos.	1381	361	58	6	28	483	190	205	.261	.373	.346
Runners On/2 Out	1034	246	41	8	19	225	140	151	.238	.348	.334
Scor. Pos./2 Out	675	167	27	5	13	203	99	105	.247	.360	.350
Late-Inning Pressure	821	203	36	5	14	92	89	133	.247	.354	.325
Leading Off	204	45	8	0	2	2	19	27	.221	.289	.293
Runners On	351	90	16	3	9	87	44	58	.256	.396	.342
Runners/Scor. Pos.	203	47	8	2	6	75	28	38	.232	.379	.325

RUNS BATTED IN	From 1B	From 2B	From 3B	Scoring Position
Totals	84/1835	182/1127	237/577	419/1704
Percentage	4.6%	16.1%	41.1%	24.6%

TEAM TOTALS: PITCHING

	W-L	ERA	AB	H	HR	BB	SO	BA	SA	OBA
Season	77-85	3.69	5420	1319	120	606	1064	.243	.359	.321
vs. Left-Handers			1925	480	32	200	326	.249	.353	.319
vs. Right-Handers			3495	839	88	406	738	.240	.363	.322
vs. Ground-Ballers			2582	632	41	283	466	.245	.338	.321
vs. Fly-Ballers			2838	687	79	323	598	.242	.379	.322
Home Games	38-43	3.48	2778	673	60	322	519	.242	.356	.322
Road Games	39-42	3.92	2642	646	60	284	545	.245	.363	.321
Grass Fields	30-32	3.97	2028	492	49	233	435	.243	.359	.323
Artificial Turf	47-53	3.53	3392	827	71	373	629	.244	.359	.320
April	8-12	4.04	672	168	21	82	145	.250	.394	.331
May	15-14	3.96	991	244	22	120	188	.246	.366	.333
June	16-12	3.41	922	213	19	89	198	.231	.338	.301
July	15-12	3.46	881	204	19	102	158	.232	.345	.311
August	10-18	3.11	929	214	20	97	187	.230	.335	.304
Sept./Oct.	13-17	4.23	1025	276	19	116	188	.269	.383	.346
Leading Off Inn.			1298	288	27	145	249	.222	.328	.302
Bases Empty			3051	708	74	312	598	.232	.346	.307
Runners On			2369	611	46	294	466	.258	.376	.339
Runners/Scor. Pos.			1362	329	25	195	279	.242	.355	.332
Runners On/2 Out			970	219	19	130	215	.226	.326	.325
Scor. Pos./2 Out			649	139	13	91	149	.214	.314	.319
Late-Inning Pressure			820	204	17	97	167	.249	.356	.328
Leading Off			212	44	3	17	46	.208	.278	.270
Runners On			327	95	6	54	63	.291	.407	.385
Runners/Scor. Pos.			179	46	4	44	27	.257	.363	.393
First 9 Batters			2660	650	55	305	520	.244	.359	.324
Second 9 Batters			1351	334	30	157	244	.247	.362	.329
All Batters Thereafter			1409	335	35	144	300	.238	.358	.309

TEXAS RANGERS

- **The one-run winner's blues.**
- **Does anyone still doubt Ryan's Cooperstown credentials?**

Now that reruns of the George Reeves "Superman" series have resurfaced, some of you may have seen the episode in which an old psychic named Madame Salena correctly forecasts a number of suicides by prominent citizens of Metropolis. She reveals the identity of each successive victim at a series of private studio gatherings, raising a curtain to expose their life-sized figures in wax. You can imagine the commotion the night that a six-foot wax figure of Perry White was unveiled. Great Caesar's ghost! But that's a story for another time.

Our favorite part is the funereal monologue that Madame provides at each unveiling, especially the line that begins, "It . . . is . . . my . . . unhappy . . . duty . . ." We are reminded of that pronouncement each season when noting the team that had the best record in one-run games. As our regular readers know, that's a nearly foolproof indicator of a team about to fall. Now it is our unhappy duty to note that the Texas Rangers had a record of 37–22 in one-run games last season. For that reason, one of the surest bets for the 1991 season is that the Rangers will fail to reach last season's total of 83 wins.

The following table lists past winners of the Madame Salena Unhappy Duty Award, the teams in each season with the best records in one-run games according to games above the .500 mark. Only four of the 22 teams improved their records a year later. Half declined by at least 10 wins. The average drop was eight wins. The roster:

		1-Run		Overall Mark			Next Season		
Year	Team	W	L	W	L	Pct.	W	L	Pct.
1989	California Angels	33	21	91	71	.562	80	82	.494
1989	San Diego Padres	30	18	89	73	.549	75	87	.463
1988	Oakland Athletics	30	17	104	58	.642	99	63	.611
1987	Montreal Expos	28	14	91	71	.562	81	81	.500
1986	Boston Red Sox	24	10	95	66	.590	78	84	.481
1985	California Angels	30	13	90	72	.555	92	70	.567
1984	Detroit Tigers	25	11	104	58	.641	84	77	.521
1983	Chicago White Sox	28	17	99	63	.611	74	88	.456
1982	St. Louis Cardinals	35	22	92	70	.567	79	83	.487
1981	Baltimore Orioles	21	7	59	46	.561	94	68	.580
1980	Kansas City Royals	29	12	97	65	.598	50	53	.485
1979	Baltimore Orioles	32	20	102	57	.641	100	62	.617
1978	Cincinnati Reds	33	19	92	69	.571	90	71	.559
1977	Kansas City Royals	31	13	102	60	.629	92	70	.567
1976	Minnesota Twins	24	15	85	77	.524	84	77	.521
1975	St. Louis Cardinals	29	14	82	80	.506	72	90	.444
1974	San Diego Padres	31	16	60	102	.370	71	91	.438
1973	Cleveland Indians	25	16	71	91	.438	77	85	.475
1972	New York Mets	33	15	83	73	.532	82	79	.509
1971	Oakland Athletics	30	16	101	60	.627	93	62	.600
1970	Baltimore Orioles	40	15	108	54	.666	101	57	.639
1969	New York Mets	41	23	100	62	.617	83	79	.512

Many of our readers have had trouble understanding why we would attach a negative connotation to teams with good records in one-run games. Conventional wisdom holds that such teams win close games either because of an outstanding bullpen or through sheer determination. We haven't yet been able to measure the will-to-win factor (though we're fairly certain it will be found less crucial than such items as, say, team speed), but the example of the 1990 Red Sox strongly suggests that one-run wins don't necessarily imply a strong bullpen. The Red Sox had the 2d-best record in the league in one-run games last year, despite a bullpen that ranked dead last in ERA. But rather than discuss what one-run wins don't indicate, let's state categorically what they do imply: plain old luck.

Luck is rarely a factor in a blowout. The closer the outcome, the greater the chance that the result will hinge on a bad bounce, a gust of wind, or a broken-bat double down the line. Games decided by a single run are those most often determined by luck. Here's the statistical proof—a table of games played from 1969 through 1990, classified according to the margin of victory, and then divided into those won by the team with the better record for that season and those won by the worse team. At every step of the way, the larger the margin, the greater the chance that the better team won the game. Games between teams with the same records weren't included:

Margin	Better Team Wins	Worse Team Wins
1 run	7517 (55%)	6090 (45%)
2 runs	4605 (56%)	3647 (44%)
3 runs	3741 (58%)	2724 (42%)
4 runs	2881 (59%)	1989 (41%)
5 runs	2081 (60%)	1373 (40%)
6 runs	1468 (61%)	924 (39%)
7 runs	976 (62%)	600 (38%)
8 & up	1882 (64%)	1041 (36%)

Once you accept the premise that one-run games are the ones most likely to be determined by luck, it's logical that teams with good records in one-run games in one season would be unlikely to repeat that performance the next. The extent to which that's true is illustrated by a comparison of records in one-run games between 1989 and 1990:

1989	W	L	Pct.	1990	W	L	Pct.
Oakland	29	18	.617	Texas	37	22	.627
California	33	21	.611	Boston	31	22	.585
Kansas City	24	19	.558	Chicago	30	22	.577
Minnesota	25	20	.556	Oakland	23	18	.561
Toronto	25	22	.532	Minnesota	21	19	.525
Baltimore	18	16	.529	California	23	21	.523
Texas	20	18	.526	Detroit	22	22	.500
Cleveland	25	28	.472	Toronto	24	27	.471
New York	19	22	.463	Kansas City	21	26	.447
Milwaukee	17	20	.459	New York	23	29	.442
Seattle	23	28	.451	Baltimore	22	28	.440
Chicago	19	26	.422	Milwaukee	18	23	.439
Detroit	19	26	.422	Seattle	20	28	.417
Boston	13	25	.342	Cleveland	16	24	.400

There's a statistical test named after its inventor, a man named Pearson, to measure the similarity between two sets of numbers. On that similarity scale from 0 to 100 (where zero represents likeness on nothing more than a random basis, and one hundred represents an exact match), the records of American League teams in one-run games for 1989 and 1990 scores a one. That's 1 out of 100—virtually no similarity at all. By comparison, even in a season in which the White Sox rose from last place to second, a comparison of records in games decided by two runs or more scored 36 out of 100. In other words, what little year-to-year correspondence existed was attributable entirely to games decided by more than one run. More to the point for Texas, there's no reason to believe that a team lucky enough to compile a great record in one-run games in any season should even approach that mark again a year later. And that's why the Rangers will be hard-pressed to stay above the .500 mark in 1991.

Not too many years ago, there was considerable doubt as to whether Nolan Ryan belonged in the Hall of Fame. To some, Ryan will always remain an enigma—a pitcher whose parts seemed to equal more than the whole, with a résumé dotted by exclamation points, but with too many walks and too few wins.

In fact, Ryan's winning percentage is the second lowest among the 37 pitchers with 250 or more career wins. But defenders point out that Ryan often pitched for losing teams, reducing the chance that he'd put together the string of 20-win seasons that would have quieted even his most vocal critics. And when he pitched for some good Angels teams in the early 1970s, Ryan won 62 games over his most productive three-year period. Eventually, the discussion required a comparison of Ryan's record to that of the teams for which he played. Anyone who bothered to check the record found that Ryan usually outperformed his teammates—14 times in the 21 seasons in which he had at least 15 decisions—and often by a wide margin. The following table shows the five years in which Ryan's winning percentage was at least 100 points higher than that of his teammates:

Year	Team	Ryan		Teammates	
1974	California	22–16	.579	46–72	.390
1975	California	14–12	.538	58–75	.436
1981	Houston	11–5	.688	50–38	.568
1982	Houston	16–12	.571	61–69	.469
1989	Texas	16–10	.615	67–63	.515

By now, Ryan hardly needs our help polishing his Hall of Fame credentials. The past few seasons have guaranteed his eventual place in Cooperstown. The only remaining question seems to be whether it should take more than one ballot. Let's take a look, using the difference between a pitcher's performance and that of his teammates as our main tool.

To determine the career-long winning percentage of a pitcher's teammates, the contribution of any one season should be proportionate to the number of decisions he had that year. For instance, Ryan had only nine decisions for the 1969 Mets, who won 100 games; it would be unreasonable for that team to account for as large a slice of the total pie as, say, the 1974 Angels (see table above), for whom Ryan had a career-high 38 decisions.

The following table shows the pitchers with the biggest margins between their own winning percentages and those of their teammates. It includes all seasons from 1893 on, to coincide with the rule placing the pitching rubber 60 feet, six inches from home plate. Pitchers needed 200 decisions to qualify:

Pitcher	W	L	Pct.	Team	Diff.
Grover Alexander	373	208	.642	.498	.144
Walter Johnson	416	279	.599	.460	.138
Clark Griffith	223	134	.625	.490	.135
Amos Rusie	136	72	.654	.530	.124
Jesse Tannehill	197	116	.629	.507	.123
Lefty Grove	300	140	.682	.561	.121
Tom Seaver	311	205	.603	.484	.119
Noodles Hahn	129	92	.584	.466	.118
Cy Young	439	275	.615	.500	.114
Nap Rucker	134	134	.500	.387	.113

Since three active pitchers with more than 100 career decisions have even better marks than Alexander's, we've also printed a list of near-qualifiers, with between 100 and 199 decisions. John Tudor was a near miss (he ranked 11th with a .110 differential):

Pitcher	W	L	Pct.	Team	Diff.
Roger Clemens	116	51	.695	.500	.194
Dwight Gooden	119	46	.721	.568	.153
Russ Ford	98	71	.580	.432	.148
Ted Higuera	89	54	.622	.475	.148
Bert Cunningham	81	79	.506	.370	.137
Gene Packard	86	67	.562	.426	.136
Al Maul	62	55	.530	.399	.130
J.R. Richard	107	71	.601	.474	.127
Orel Hershiser	99	65	.604	.486	.118
Tom Seaton	94	64	.595	.480	.115

Lots of great pitchers, but where's Nolan Ryan? As it turns out, Ryan did pitch for predominantly losing teams, but their records weren't nearly poor enough to place Ryan's .526 winning percentage in the class of those listed above. In fact, Ryan out-performed his teammates by a margin of only .036, which ranked 23d among the 29 pitchers with at least 250 wins during the period under study. The tables above show that Walter Johnson, Noodles Hahn, and Russ Ford all had winning percentages at least 20 points higher than Ryan's, and teammates whose marks were more than 20 points lower than Ryan's. On the other hand, some renowned pitchers—including Hall of Famers Red Ruffing and Waite Hoyt—actually under-performed their teammates over the course of their careers. Among the others: Bob Friend, Doyle Alexander, and Ken Holtzman.

That doesn't mean that Ruffing, Hoyt, and the others weren't good or even great pitchers. It is worth noting, however, that both Ruffing and Hoyt are marginal Hall of Famers in the sense that Hoyt wasn't elected until 31 years after his retirement (and then by the somnolent veterans committee), while Ruffing was elected not only in his final season of eligibility by the baseball writers, but in a runoff after no player gained 75 percent in the basic election. Still, the figures above demonstrate two shortcomings of the system: First, it determines a pitcher's value by matching his performance against a standard that is too high. Second, it discounts the value of longevity.

Think about that in regard to Ryan. Every time he steps to the mound, isn't Ryan more likely to win than most other pitchers? Until that's no longer true, he has value—not beyond that of his rotation-mates, but beyond whoever would replace Ryan if he wasn't available. A question that more accurately assesses Ryan's career-long value: How many games has Ryan won beyond the number that a replacement pitcher might have won? That addresses both problems of the standard of comparison and the length of his career, since the longer he pitches well, the longer his career-long value will increase.

Let's assume that a typical replacement pitcher would have a .400 winning percentage. (Since pitchers with even .450 marks hold down fourth spots in rotations throughout both leagues, a replacement pitcher had to be significantly lower. Thus, our admittedly arbitrary .400 estimate. Anyway, whether we chose .375 or .425 wouldn't have changed the results significantly.) We won't bore you with the details of how we computed the number of games a .400 pitcher would have won, given the same number of opportunities as Ryan and for the same teams. But briefly, the relevant factors are the number of decisions times the .400 winning percentage after it has been adjusted for the teammates' winning percentage. (Remember, that .400 mark presumes that he pitches for a .500 team.)

After those laborious computations, we estimated that a .400 pitcher substituting for Ryan throughout his career would have won 224 games—78 fewer wins than Ryan's actual total. Only 14 pitchers since 1893 have compiled margins greater than Ryan's. The top 20:

Pitcher	Act.	Sub.	Diff.	Pitcher	Act.	Sub.	Diff.
Walter Johnson	416	252	164	Robin Roberts	286	200	86
Cy Young	439	286	153	Eddie Plank	327	242	85
Grover Alexander	373	231	142	Gaylord Perry	314	232	82
Christy Mathewson	373	257	116	Ferguson Jenkins	284	204	80
Tom Seaver	311	198	113	**Nolan Ryan**	302	224	78
Warren Spahn	363	258	105	Bob Feller	266	188	78
Phil Niekro	318	220	98	Juan Marichal	243	167	76
Lefty Grove	300	202	98	Don Sutton	324	250	74
Steve Carlton	329	236	93	Bob Gibson	251	177	74
Ted Lyons	260	169	91	Red Faber	254	180	74

Doesn't this list, as opposed to the previous ones, more closely match your opinion about the best pitchers of all time? On that basis alone, it merits attention. Does it weigh longevity a little too heavily? Or is Phil Niekro really one of the 10 most valuable pitchers of all time? His record is impressive: a better won-lost mark than that of his teammates in 15 of 17 seasons from 1966 through 1982. And for pitchers, longevity is in itself an accomplishment. That's a key distinction between hitters and pitchers. No pitcher could ever be part of a sham equivalent to that of a washed-up Pete Rose taking the field day after day in pursuit of a purely selfish goal; the negative feedback would be too obvious and immediate. No one gave Niekro, Sutton, or Ryan for that matter a spot that they didn't earn by virtue of their superiority to the other pitchers available. That superiority constitutes value.

And that's the true value of surveys such as the ones above—to provide a fresh perspective that encourages us to scrape the crust off years-old opinions. But as with so much about Ryan, you can use them to argue either side. Choose one study or the other—the difference between a pitcher's winning percentage and that of his teammates, or his accumulated value beyond replacement level—depending on whether you're looking to bury or praise him. We'd select the latter. But then again, breaking one of the most significant career pitching records by a mere 50 percent (so far) was enough for us. For pitchers, strikeouts are often a measure of batters' collective inability to hit them. And throughout the entire history of major-league baseball, no one's ever been tougher to hit than Nolan Ryan.

WON-LOST RECORD BY STARTING POSITION

Texas Rangers	C	1B	2B	3B	SS	LF	CF	RF	DH	P	Leadoff	Cleanup	Starts vs. LH	Starts vs. RH	Total Starts
Gerald Alexander	-	-	-	-	-	-	-	-	-	2-0	-	-	-	2	2-0
Brad Arnsberg	-	-	-	-	-	-	-	-	-	-	-	-	-	-	-
Harold Baines	-	-	-	-	-	-	-	1-1	44-42	-	-	0-6	16	72	45-43
John Barfield	-	-	-	-	-	-	-	-	-	-	-	-	-	-	-
Kevin Belcher	-	-	-	-	-	-	1-2	-	-	-	1-1	-	2	1	1-2
Joseph Bitker	-	-	-	-	-	-	-	-	-	-	-	-	-	-	-
Brian Bohanon	-	-	-	-	-	-	-	-	-	0-6	-	-	-	6	0-6
Thad Bosley	-	-	-	-	-	3-0	-	-	-	-	-	-	-	3	3-0
J. Kevin Brown	-	-	-	-	-	-	-	-	-	15-11	-	-	7	19	15-11
Steve Buechele	-	-	1-0	40-39	-	-	-	-	-	-	-	-	30	50	41-39
Scott Chiamparino	-	-	-	-	-	-	-	-	-	3-3	-	-	3	3	3-3
Scott Coolbaugh	-	-	-	29-27	-	-	-	-	-	-	-	-	16	40	29-27
Jack Daugherty	-	7-6	-	-	-	16-15	-	1-1	10-9	-	0-1	-	15	50	34-31
Cecil Espy	-	-	-	-	-	-	5-9	0-2	-	-	2-5	-	4	12	5-11
Julio Franco	-	-	76-76	-	-	-	-	-	2-0	-	0-4	0-1	52	102	78-76
Juan Gonzalez	-	-	-	-	-	-	7-4	1-2	5-3	-	-	-	7	15	13-9
Gary Green	-	-	-	-	16-15	-	-	-	-	-	-	-	16	15	16-15
Jose Guzman	-	-	-	-	-	-	-	-	-	-	-	-	-	-	-
Bill Haselman	-	-	-	-	-	-	-	-	1-2	-	-	-	3	-	1-2
John Hoover	-	-	-	-	-	-	-	-	-	-	-	-	-	-	-
Charlie Hough	-	-	-	-	-	-	-	-	-	15-17	-	-	12	20	15-17
Jeff Huson	-	-	2-3	6-4	44-45	-	-	-	-	-	31-27	-	7	97	52-52
Pete Incaviglia	-	-	-	-	-	61-63	9-6	-	-	-	-	3-3	51	88	70-69
Mike Jeffcoat	-	-	-	-	-	-	-	-	-	5-7	-	-	5	7	5-7
Chad Kreuter	4-4	-	-	-	-	-	-	-	-	-	-	-	7	1	4-4
Jeff Kunkel	-	-	4-0	5-7	23-19	-	-	-	-	-	2-1	-	40	18	32-26
Ramon Manon	-	-	-	-	-	-	-	-	-	-	-	-	-	-	-
Craig McMurtry	-	-	-	-	-	-	-	-	-	1-2	-	-	1	2	1-2
Gary Mielke	-	-	-	-	-	-	-	-	-	-	-	-	-	-	-
Jamie Moyer	-	-	-	-	-	-	-	-	-	2-8	-	-	5	5	2-8
Rafael Palmeiro	-	73-72	-	-	-	-	-	-	1-4	-	-	-	42	108	74-76
Geno Petralli	49-49	-	-	1-0	-	-	-	-	-	-	-	-	-	99	50-49
Gary Pettis	-	-	-	-	-	-	61-58	-	-	-	47-40	-	44	75	61-58
Kevin Reimer	-	-	-	-	-	3-0	-	0-3	8-3	-	-	-	-	17	11-6
Kenny Rogers	-	-	-	-	-	-	-	-	-	1-2	-	-	1	2	1-2
Jeff Russell	-	-	-	-	-	-	-	-	-	-	-	-	-	-	-
John Russell	8-8	2-0	-	-	-	0-1	-	-	4-7	-	-	-	25	5	14-16
Nolan Ryan	-	-	-	-	-	-	-	-	-	18-12	-	-	9	21	18-12
Ruben Sierra	-	-	-	-	-	-	-	80-70	3-4	-	-	80-69	53	104	83-74
Mike Stanley	22-18	1-1	-	2-2	-	-	-	-	5-5	-	-	-	47	9	30-26
Bobby Witt	-	-	-	-	-	-	-	-	-	21-11	-	-	10	22	21-11

TEAM TOTALS: BATTING

	AB	H	2B	3B	HR	RBI	BB	SO	BA	SA	OBA
Season	5469	1416	257	27	110	641	575	1054	.259	.376	.331
vs. Left-Handers	1734	469	87	6	32	214	199	337	.270	.383	.345
vs. Right-Handers	3735	947	170	21	78	427	376	717	.254	.373	.324
vs. Ground-Ballers	2477	626	100	12	44	268	236	448	.253	.356	.320
vs. Fly-Ballers	2992	790	157	15	66	373	339	606	.264	.393	.339
Home Games	2706	718	135	15	64	337	296	532	.265	.397	.341
Road Games	2763	698	122	12	46	304	279	522	.253	.355	.321
Grass Fields	4550	1174	210	20	98	545	482	887	.258	.378	.331
Artificial Turf	919	242	47	7	12	96	93	167	.263	.369	.332
April	671	162	31	4	20	89	83	159	.241	.389	.328
May	884	207	43	1	15	82	94	173	.234	.336	.308
June	1012	290	45	7	21	127	91	185	.287	.407	.348
July	891	241	51	4	21	125	92	159	.270	.407	.336
August	976	259	46	5	12	100	101	181	.265	.360	.336
Sept./Oct.	1035	257	41	6	21	118	114	197	.248	.360	.324
Leading Off Inn.	1323	328	56	5	32	32	121	282	.248	.370	.315
Bases Empty	3069	765	138	10	60	60	290	610	.249	.359	.318
Runners On	2400	651	119	17	50	581	285	444	.271	.397	.347
Runners/Scor. Pos.	1357	351	69	8	21	493	195	260	.259	.368	.346
Runners On/2 Out	1018	264	54	11	17	229	124	201	.259	.384	.345
Scor. Pos./2 Out	655	156	34	7	8	195	96	125	.238	.348	.343
Late-Inning Pressure	830	218	40	2	22	89	89	180	.263	.395	.334
Leading Off	205	56	10	1	9	9	24	54	.273	.463	.349
Runners On	356	99	17	1	7	74	48	62	.278	.390	.361
Runners/Scor. Pos.	193	48	12	1	2	62	39	35	.249	.352	.370

RUNS BATTED IN	From 1B	From 2B	From 3B	Scoring Position
Totals	96/1768	199/1071	236/570	435/1641
Percentage	5.4%	18.6%	41.4%	26.5%

TEAM TOTALS: PITCHING

	W-L	ERA	AB	H	HR	BB	SO	BA	SA	OBA
Season	83-79	3.83	5419	1343	113	623	997	.248	.370	.327
vs. Left-Handers			2128	505	35	248	382	.237	.347	.318
vs. Right-Handers			3291	838	78	375	615	.255	.385	.333
vs. Ground-Ballers			2517	633	38	283	430	.251	.356	.327
vs. Fly-Ballers			2902	710	75	340	567	.245	.382	.327
Home Games	47-35	3.61	2814	700	59	310	548	.249	.369	.326
Road Games	36-44	4.07	2605	643	54	313	449	.247	.371	.329
Grass Fields	72-64	3.75	4558	1116	97	529	854	.245	.367	.325
Artificial Turf	11-15	4.27	861	227	16	94	143	.264	.386	.339
April	11-9	3.89	668	166	17	76	117	.249	.383	.327
May	8-19	5.18	908	240	23	121	137	.264	.411	.356
June	16-13	3.82	994	247	23	97	195	.248	.371	.315
July	17-9	3.49	881	216	23	118	186	.245	.376	.333
August	14-15	3.47	945	230	12	94	152	.243	.346	.312
Sept./Oct.	17-14	3.27	1023	244	15	117	210	.239	.340	.322
Leading Off Inn.			1314	305	32	126	239	.232	.353	.303
Bases Empty			3098	740	66	319	607	.239	.360	.314
Runners On			2321	603	47	304	390	.260	.383	.344
Runners/Scor. Pos.			1355	345	26	220	254	.255	.365	.352
Runners On/2 Out			1020	251	18	143	179	.246	.363	.343
Scor. Pos./2 Out			658	163	11	108	123	.248	.350	.360
Late-Inning Pressure			806	200	12	99	152	.248	.371	.329
Leading Off			204	41	4	19	41	.201	.309	.269
Runners On			333	86	5	57	54	.258	.396	.361
Runners/Scor. Pos.			214	58	4	43	44	.271	.439	.384
First 9 Batters			2599	653	55	324	500	.251	.376	.336
Second 9 Batters			1392	344	25	147	264	.247	.356	.323
All Batters Thereafter			1428	346	33	152	233	.242	.371	.316

TORONTO BLUE JAYS

- **Toronto turns over, even before the trades.**
- **Leadoff woes.**

They're baa-aack . . .

Four years ago, the Toronto Blue Jays gave us the most precipitous final-week fold in the history of major-league baseball. Last season, they gave an encore performance and brought down the house in Boston. Trailing the Red Sox by as much as six-and-a-half games in early September, the Jays won 12 of their next 14 to assume the division lead on the 19th. But as Red Sox fans from Pawtucket to Bangor bemoaned their own team's lack of character, the Blue Jays performed their best Greg Louganis impression.

Back in 1987, when Toronto blew a lead of three-and-a-half games with seven to play, it represented the largest margin ever to evaporate that late in a season. They were the first team since the 1972 Red Sox to blow a lead of more than one game with as few as seven games remaining. Last season, the Blue Jays did it again. In both cases, they were eliminated on the final day of the regular season, on national television. Is it any wonder Toronto became the butt of jokes about fish bones and noxious fumes?

Think about that for a moment: 208 teams in this century have led their division or league by more than a game with six games or less remaining (even without including our favorite anomaly, 1981). Only six of those teams managed to lose the race. And the Blue Jays have done it twice in the last four years. (The others: the 1972 Red Sox, the 1962 Dodgers, the 1949 Cardinals, and the 1934 Giants.)

So logically, one would conclude that Toronto has an affinity for that fruit first made famous in the Garden of Eden, right? Regular readers of the *Analyst* are familiar with our affinity for contrarian viewpoints, and this will be no exception. Start with the obvious but essential fact that teams can blow leads only in tight races. Now consider that during the era of divisional play, not only are there twice as many races, but the margins have tended to be narrower than before. The following table shows the number of races decided by three games or less, before and after the switch to divisional play:

Years	Races	Margin	Close Races
1901–68	136	7.00	47 (34.6%)
1969–90	84	6.39	33 (39.3%)

From 1901 through 1968, an average of nearly seven races every 10 years were decided by three games or less. Since the leagues were split into divisions in 1969, that average has increased to 16 races per 10 years. That represents a 127 percent increase in what you might call blowable leads, for lack of a better term. And the Blue Jays may simply have been a random victim of this increase.

Keep in mind that Toronto hasn't been the only team whose character has been maligned in recent years for a failure to win more titles. Three of the four winningest teams of the past five seasons—the Blue Jays, Red Sox, and Mets—have been repeatedly tarred despite six division titles among them. And the mighty A's themselves may be one more postseason-series loss from becoming baseball's version of the Dallas Cowboys of the 1970s—a team more taunted for high-profile losses than praised for a decade of more numerous but less significant triumphs.

The margin between good baseball teams and great baseball teams has grown historically slim over the past decade. Every season, a handful of losers from the year before has made runs at division titles, while many of the previous season's contenders fell to pieces. Under those conditions, the few teams that have remained perennially competitive deserve praise on that basis alone. Instead, they have become symbols of futility and failure. Pure nonsense.

That having been said, we're not sure whether what follows is good news or bad. But even before Pat Gillick turned his roster inside out in a matter of days at baseball's December meetings, Toronto had positioned itself for several more runs at the title throughout the early 1990s. The Blue Jays lineup, which scored a league-high average of 4.7 runs per game, was the youngest in the majors last season.

That may be somewhat surprising, considering that Toronto's roster had been relatively stable over the past four years. Because Toronto's moves had been primarily intramural, with most of the changes coming from within the organization, Gillick had been widely criticized by the trade-happy media. Well it's a reasonable assumption that no one will be calling him "Stand Pat" in the foreseeable future. The trade that sent Fred McGriff and Tony Fernandez to the Padres for Joe Carter and Roberto Alomar dwarfed two prior moves in which the Jays added free agent Ken Dayley and then Devon White and Willie Fraser (in a trade for Junior Felix and Luis Sojo).

These moves, widely perceived as a wholesale policy change, were simply the final stroke—albeit a grand one—in a long and underpublicized process. True, over the previous five offseasons Toronto had made only one trade, and that was for a pitcher coming off an injury-filled season in which he won a single game (Craig McMurtry). But anyone who thinks the Blue Jays of 1990—even before the deals—were essentially the same team that fell apart during the final week of the 1987 season hasn't spent enough time looking north of the border.

During that time, Toronto reshaped its offense not with bold, newsmaking strokes but with more subtle nips and tucks that were noted only on the agate pages. The result was a lineup that was both younger and more potent—an unusual combination. The following table shows how much each American League team altered its lineup from 1987 to 1990, and its average age in each of those seasons. The degree of change is measured by the percentage of common plate appearances between 1987 and 1990:

Team	Change	1987	1990	Age Diff.
New York	89.1%	30.17	28.60	−1.56
Baltimore	83.6%	30.64	27.99	−2.65
Cleveland	82.1%	27.74	27.89	+0.15
Seattle	70.3%	27.40	28.40	+1.01
Chicago	67.8%	28.10	28.21	+0.11
Texas	67.3%	26.75	27.77	+1.02
California	65.2%	29.90	30.34	+0.44
Detroit	64.0%	31.60	31.09	−0.51
Oakland	61.7%	28.01	29.84	+1.83
Toronto	60.4%	28.20	27.30	−0.89
Boston	58.1%	29.39	29.50	+0.11
Kansas City	51.4%	29.75	30.19	+0.44
Milwaukee	45.2%	28.11	30.14	+2.02
Minnesota	42.0%	28.02	29.92	+1.89

There's a strong correlation between how much a team changed its personnel and how much it reduced its average age. The two teams that aged most were also the most static: Milwaukee and Minnesota. The only teams to slice more than a year off their averages were those with the greatest turnover: Baltimore and New York. And they were the only teams to reduce their age from 1987 to 1990 by more than the Blue Jays did, despite the fact that Toronto's roster remained relatively stable during that period. The Blue Jays consistently made roster moves from within the organization, substituting young players for old: Pat Borders and Greg Myers for Ernie Whitt; Fred McGriff for Willie Upshaw; Kelly Gruber for Garth Iorg; Junior Felix for Jesse Barfield; Glenallen Hill for Rick Leach; and John Olerud for Rance Mulliniks. Only the addition of Mookie Wilson (who replaced Lloyd Moseby) for the 1989 stretch run violated that rule.

The Blue Jays were able to accomplish this quiet remodeling by developing one of the most productive systems in baseball. The following table estimates the productivity of each team's system by assigning every player's statistics for the 1990 season to the team with which he made his major-league debut. The teams are ranked by runs produced (runs plus RBIs divided by two), and the figure represents the sum of the nine top players assigned to each team. For the Blue Jays, they were Cecil Fielder, Kelly Gruber, Fred McGriff, George Bell, Tony Fernandez, Jesse Barfield, Junior Felix, Lloyd Moseby, and Mitch Webster. Team by team:

American League		National League	
Toronto	721	New York	685
Oakland	599	San Francisco	586
Seattle	593	Cincinnati	584
Boston	576	San Diego	582
Chicago	499	Atlanta	572
Detroit	479	Chicago	561
Milwaukee	465	Montreal	547
Minnesota	463	Los Angeles	543
California	433	Pittsburgh	529
Texas	431	St. Louis	523
Kansas City	424	Philadelphia	514
Cleveland	410	Houston	303
New York	401		
Baltimore	399		

As a result of all their internal maneuvering, the 1990 Blue Jays became the first team since the 1963 Minnesota Twins to lead its league in scoring despite having the league's youngest lineup. (In fact, not once during the 1980s did the team with the youngest lineup in the American League rank as high as fourth in scoring.) The last National League team to do so was the 1958 San Francisco Giants. The success of both of those teams throughout the 1960s illustrates the significance of that low-age/high-scoring parlay. To underline that point, consider this fact: Only seven teams compiled records of .500 or better in the 1980s with their league's youngest lineup. All seven won division titles within the next three years:

Year	Team	W–L	Next Title	Best Young Hitters
1980	Braves	81–80	1982	Bob Horner and Dale Murphy
1982	Padres	81–81	1984	Terry Kennedy and Garry Templeton
1983	Padres	81–81	1984	Tony Gwynn and Alan Wiggins
1984	Twins	81–81	1987	Tom Brunansky, Gary Gaetti, Kent Hrbek, and Kirby Puckett
1985	Dodgers	95–67	1988	Mike Marshall and Steve Sax
1986	Giants	83–79	1987	Chris Brown, Will Clark, and Rob Thompson
1988	Pirates	85–75	1990	Barry Bonds and Bobby Bonilla

Only time will tell whether John Olerud or Glenallen Hill will follow the fast track of Murphy, Gwynn, Puckett, and Bonds. But it's truly ironic that in a single bold move, Gillick has erased a reputation that, even if well earned, should never have implied incompetence. We'd even suggest that his reluctance to pull the big-trade trigger for several seasons allowed the Jays to create a foundation of young players strong enough to make the San Diego trade possible. Would any GM have had the nerve to trade a player with the MVP potential of Fred McGriff—regardless of the return—without a John Olerud ready to step into his crater-like footsteps? How many other teams could state categorically, as Toronto did, that the strength of its lineup allows them to hand center field over to a player like Devon White, whose defensive abilities—extraordinary though they are—weren't enough to keep him in the Angels lineup? (The wisdom of such a statement, categorical or not, is an open question.)

And finally, whatever ghosts of the past haunted the Blue Jays clubhouse at the Skydome are now gone. Toronto's pool of young talent is so impressive, and the removal for better or worse of Fernandez and McGriff so decisive and final, that it's no longer relevant to discuss the Blue Jays as the reincarnation of the underachieving Expos of 10 years earlier. Any resemblance between the Blue Jays of the past and the current version, faint as it had grown prior to last winter, has now been eradicated.

The importance of scoring first has been well documented since we published the first edition of the *Analyst* six years ago. Every season, approximately two out of three games are won by the team that strikes first. (Last year, the figures were 68 percent in the American League, 66 percent in the National League.) That's particularly significant because first-inning scoring is an element that most teams can regulate, regardless of the strength of their offense in general. Even a low-scoring team can increase its first-inning output by batting a player with a high on-base average in the leadoff position. The following tables reveal that for 1990, only a random correspondence existed between a team's overall scoring and its first-inning total. There was a strong relationship, however, between first-inning scoring and a single, narrowly focused element of a team's offense—its on-base average from the leadoff position:

Overall	Runs	1st Inning	Runs	Leadoff	OBA
Toronto	767	Oakland	127	Oakland	.412
Detroit	750	Minnesota	97	Boston	.381
Oakland	733	Chicago	93	Detroit	.355
Cleveland	732	Kansas City	93	California	.348
Milwaukee	732	Seattle	93	Milwaukee	.333
Kansas City	707	Detroit	92	Seattle	.332
Boston	699	Boston	90	Baltimore	.330
California	690	Baltimore	86	Minnesota	.330
Chicago	682	Texas	86	Cleveland	.329
Texas	676	Milwaukee	85	Kansas City	.323
Baltimore	669	California	82	New York	.314
Minnesota	666	Cleveland	81	**Toronto**	.306
Seattle	640	**Toronto**	75	Texas	.295
New York	603	New York	72	Chicago	.288

Toronto provided a noteworthy example of the first-inning trend last season. The Blue Jays led the American League with an average of 4.7 runs per game, but only one A.L. team scored fewer runs in the first inning. That unusual pattern can be blamed on the team's leadoff hitters, who had the third-lowest on-base average in the league. Even a middle of the order that included Kelly Gruber, George Bell, and Fred McGriff couldn't compensate in the first inning for the failures of Toronto's leadoff batters.

(Incidentally, 1990 was an anomaly only for the complete absence of relationship between overall and first-inning scoring. Over the past three years, that relationship is discernible, though small. The correlation between leadoff OBA and first-inning scoring was significant in all three seasons.)

On closer examination, Toronto's first-inning problems were most prevalent in the 53 games in which Mookie Wilson batted leadoff. Like many teams, Toronto tried to load the top of its order with speed, in this case sacrificing on-base average. As a penalty, the Blue Jays scored only 13 first-inning runs in those games, or an average of 0.25 per game, compared to 0.57 per game in all others. (See the table following this essay for the number of games each player started in the leadoff spot.) Had they scored at that rate of 0.57 runs per first inning for the season, the Blue Jays would have produced 92 first-inning runs, 17 more than their actual total. How many more wins might those additional runs have meant? As a rule of thumb, 10 runs equals a win. Since a team scoring first is twice as likely to win as its opponent, and the Blue Jays lost the division title by just two games, it's reasonable to conclude that those 17 missing runs might have cost Toronto a trip to Oakland in October—albeit, probably, a brief one.

New Blue Jay Roberto Alomar brings to the plate exactly what the doctor ordered. His career on-base average of .339 represents an improvement over Wilson's that would move the Blue Jays slightly above the league median (.330). In addition, Alomar flourished last season when batting leadoff for San Diego, hitting .364 with a .410 OBA in 19 games—not a conclusive sample, but certainly what the Jays would love to see. That's especially good news because Alomar will be flying without a net in 1991; the departed Fernandez and Felix accounted for 97 of the 109 leadoff starts not given to Wilson.

But there's a sharp irony here. What made the leadoff problem especially critical for Toronto was the concentrated excellence of its 3–4–5 hitters; getting someone on base ahead of them seemed a top priority. The acquisition of Alomar gives them that leadoff man, but the trade of McGriff and the departure of Bell may have weakened the heart of the order to the point where a one-hitter was no longer the most pressing need. For all its fascination, this may prove to be the *Trade of the Magi*, where what's received is made superfluous by what was given away.

WON-LOST RECORD BY STARTING POSITION

Toronto Blue Jays	C	1B	2B	3B	SS	LF	CF	RF	DH	P	Leadoff	Cleanup	Starts vs. LH	Starts vs. RH	Total Starts
Jim Acker	-	-	-	-	-	-	-	-	-	-	-	-	-	-	-
George Bell	-	-	-	-	-	52-54	-	-	22-14	-	-	65-59	43	99	74-68
Bud Black	-	-	-	-	-	-	-	-	-	1-1	-	-	1	1	1-1
Willie Blair	-	-	-	-	-	-	-	-	-	3-3	-	-	4	2	3-3
Pat Borders	42-41	-	-	-	-	-	-	-	-	-	-	-	49	34	42-41
John Candelaria	-	-	-	-	-	-	-	-	-	0-2	-	-	1	1	0-2
John Cerutti	-	-	-	-	-	-	-	-	-	10-13	-	-	10	13	10-13
Steve Cummings	-	-	-	-	-	-	-	-	-	1-1	-	-	-	2	1-1
Carlos Diaz	-	-	-	-	-	-	-	-	-	-	-	-	-	-	-
Rob Ducey	-	-	-	-	-	13-5	-	-	-	-	-	-	-	18	13-5
Jim Eppard	-	-	-	-	-	-	-	-	-	-	-	-	-	-	-
Junior Felix	-	-	-	-	-	-	15-12	53-44	1-0	-	27-20	-	35	90	69-56
Tony Fernandez	-	-	-	-	86-75	-	-	-	-	-	26-24	-	49	112	86-75
Mike Flanagan	-	-	-	-	-	-	-	-	-	3-2	-	-	2	3	3-2
Thomas Gilles	-	-	-	-	-	-	-	-	-	-	-	-	-	-	-
Kelly Gruber	-	-	-	75-68	-	-	-	3-2	-	-	-	-	44	104	78-70
Tom Henke	-	-	-	-	-	-	-	-	-	-	-	-	-	-	-
Glenallen Hill	-	-	-	-	-	14-7	1-0	17-16	6-8	-	1-0	-	42	27	38-31
Jimmy Key	-	-	-	-	-	-	-	-	-	14-13	-	-	9	18	14-13
Paul Kilgus	-	-	-	-	-	-	-	-	-	-	-	-	-	-	-
Tom Lawless	-	-	-	1-0	-	1-0	-	-	0-1	-	-	-	3	-	2-1
Manny Lee	-	-	60-52	-	-	-	-	-	-	-	1-0	-	49	63	60-52
Al Leiter	-	-	-	-	-	-	-	-	-	-	-	-	-	-	-
Nelson Liriano	-	-	24-21	-	-	-	-	-	-	-	1-2	-	-	45	24-21
Rick Luecken	-	-	-	-	-	-	-	-	-	-	-	-	-	-	-
Bob MacDonald	-	-	-	-	-	-	-	-	-	-	-	-	-	-	-
Fred McGriff	-	77-70	-	-	-	-	-	-	4-2	-	-	20-16	44	109	81-72
Rance Mulliniks	-	-	-	8-6	-	-	-	-	3-3	-	-	-	-	20	11-9
Greg Myers	44-35	-	-	-	-	-	-	-	-	-	-	-	-	79	44-35
John Olerud	-	9-6	-	-	-	-	-	-	42-44	-	-	1-1	9	92	51-50
Tom Quinlan	-	-	-	0-1	-	-	-	-	-	-	-	-	1	-	0-1
Luis Sojo	-	-	2-3	2-1	0-1	1-3	-	-	1-1	-	2-3	-	7	8	6-9
Dave Stieb	-	-	-	-	-	-	-	-	-	22-11	-	-	6	27	22-11
Todd Stottlemyre	-	-	-	-	-	-	-	-	-	15-18	-	-	10	23	15-18
Ozzie Virgil	-	-	-	-	-	-	-	-	1-0	-	-	-	1	-	1-0
Duane Ward	-	-	-	-	-	-	-	-	-	-	-	-	-	-	-
Dave Wells	-	-	-	-	-	-	-	-	-	15-10	-	-	4	21	15-10
Mark Whiten	-	-	-	-	-	-	-	8-12	-	-	-	-	8	12	8-12
Ken Williams	-	-	-	-	-	2-2	2-0	5-2	0-3	-	0-2	-	13	3	9-7
Frank Wills	-	-	-	-	-	-	-	-	-	2-2	-	-	2	2	2-2
Mookie Wilson	-	-	-	-	-	3-5	68-64	-	6-0	-	28-25	-	44	102	77-69

TEAM TOTALS: BATTING

	AB	H	2B	3B	HR	RBI	BB	SO	BA	SA	OBA
Season	5589	1479	263	50	167	729	526	970	.265	.419	.328
vs. Left-Handers	1844	465	90	20	58	239	182	352	.252	.417	.318
vs. Right-Handers	3745	1014	173	30	109	490	344	618	.271	.420	.333
vs. Ground-Ballers	2535	682	111	22	64	328	226	391	.269	.406	.330
vs. Fly-Ballers	3054	797	152	28	103	401	300	579	.261	.430	.326
Home Games	2740	724	130	29	93	367	266	469	.264	.435	.330
Road Games	2849	755	133	21	74	362	260	501	.265	.404	.325
Grass Fields	2205	575	105	19	56	271	204	385	.261	.402	.323
Artificial Turf	3384	904	158	31	111	458	322	585	.267	.431	.331
April	707	201	30	5	31	105	79	110	.284	.472	.361
May	942	229	47	5	34	118	103	181	.243	.412	.317
June	1000	276	53	10	37	155	99	180	.276	.460	.340
July	896	214	32	10	21	95	69	160	.239	.367	.293
August	991	268	55	11	18	125	85	171	.270	.403	.326
Sept./Oct.	1053	291	46	9	26	131	91	168	.276	.411	.333
Leading Off Inn.	1335	361	60	12	41	41	110	226	.270	.425	.329
Bases Empty	3159	831	142	28	100	100	284	567	.263	.421	.326
Runners On	2430	648	121	22	67	629	242	403	.267	.417	.329
Runners/Scor. Pos.	1390	375	72	15	40	545	167	233	.270	.429	.339
Runners On/2 Out	1021	257	47	9	26	240	105	169	.252	.392	.327
Scor. Pos./2 Out	649	168	33	6	18	212	79	104	.259	.411	.345
Late-Inning Pressure	881	220	34	9	16	102	75	162	.250	.363	.308
Leading Off	226	50	6	3	2	2	13	45	.221	.301	.267
Runners On	351	94	15	3	10	96	38	64	.268	.413	.333
Runners/Scor. Pos.	210	51	11	2	5	84	25	37	.243	.386	.314

RUNS BATTED IN	From 1B	From 2B	From 3B	Scoring Position
Totals	101/1735	219/1082	242/603	461/1685
Percentage	5.8%	20.2%	40.1%	27.4%

TEAM TOTALS: PITCHING

	W-L	ERA	AB	H	HR	BB	SO	BA	SA	OBA
Season	86-76	3.84	5524	1434	143	445	892	.260	.398	.317
vs. Left-Handers			1979	522	43	192	273	.264	.393	.331
vs. Right-Handers			3545	912	100	253	619	.257	.401	.309
vs. Ground-Ballers			2587	691	45	197	382	.267	.384	.319
vs. Fly-Ballers			2937	743	98	248	510	.253	.410	.315
Home Games	44-37	3.86	2874	761	82	217	455	.265	.408	.319
Road Games	42-39	3.82	2650	673	61	228	437	.254	.387	.315
Grass Fields	28-35	4.23	2062	524	54	188	356	.254	.398	.319
Artificial Turf	58-41	3.60	3462	910	89	257	536	.263	.398	.316
April	12-9	4.26	702	186	21	53	115	.265	.413	.317
May	14-14	3.93	958	247	31	89	155	.258	.404	.325
June	15-13	4.27	988	272	20	83	141	.275	.408	.334
July	14-12	3.36	890	233	24	76	143	.262	.406	.320
August	13-16	3.59	987	249	19	63	156	.252	.378	.301
Sept./Oct.	18-12	3.71	999	247	28	81	182	.247	.384	.306
Leading Off Inn.			1353	353	39	96	213	.261	.402	.314
Bases Empty			3233	824	80	242	539	.255	.388	.311
Runners On			2291	610	63	203	353	.266	.412	.325
Runners/Scor. Pos.			1255	334	28	140	203	.266	.404	.336
Runners On/2 Out			978	250	24	95	157	.256	.400	.325
Scor. Pos./2 Out			598	140	9	68	102	.234	.346	.316
Late-Inning Pressure			804	199	20	66	166	.248	.378	.307
Leading Off			209	47	5	14	41	.225	.330	.277
Runners On			314	84	9	27	70	.268	.414	.326
Runners/Scor. Pos.			176	42	1	20	46	.239	.307	.317
First 9 Batters			2943	744	73	250	567	.253	.385	.312
Second 9 Batters			1468	373	36	108	195	.254	.394	.308
All Batters Thereafter			1113	317	34	87	130	.285	.436	.342

ATLANTA BRAVES

- **Been down so long—but it still looks like down.**
- **Are rookie sluggers for real?**

Five years ago, the Atlanta Braves fired manager Joe Torre. All Torre had done in Atlanta was to win a division title in 1982, his first season with the team, followed by two consecutive second-place finishes. Those near misses must have been regarded as failures by a team that had hoped for more. But five years of hindsight make Torre's teams look like scrappy overachievers. Since then, the Braves have strung together six straight seasons of misery—all below the .450 mark—and haven't landed higher than fifth in the N.L. West standings, with last-place finishes in each of the last three seasons. To paraphrase cable TV's most popular octogenarian cult hero, "They've fallen, and they can't get up."

The Braves are the first team to post six consecutive sub-.450 seasons since the New York Mets had a run of seven from 1977 through 1983. They are the first team to finish more than 20 games behind for six straight years since the San Diego Padres from 1969 through 1977 (their first nine seasons). And Atlanta has earned another distinction, one that challenges not only the worst marks of recent years but the worst of the century: The Braves have had losing records in every month since posting a 16–12 mark in May 1987. That's 22 consecutive months of losing baseball. The last time Atlanta embarked upon a winning month, Gary Hart was still a contender for the White House. At least his demise was quick (and the road leading to it rather delightful, as we recall); the fall of the Braves has been slow and constant.

Even bad teams have occasional good months. Over the past 20 years, 42 teams had sub-.400 seasons; 17 of them had at least one winning month. Four lost more than 100 games for the season, but had months with as many as 14 wins:

Year	Team	W	L	Pct.	Best Month
1971	Cleveland Indians	60	102	.370	14–12 (May)
1974	San Diego Padres	60	102	.370	17–11 (June)
1978	Toronto Blue Jays	59	102	.366	16–14 (August)
1982	Minnesota Twins	60	102	.370	14–13 (July)

But the Braves haven't reached sea level for 22 months; in fact, since May 1987 they've come within five games of the .500 mark only five times (October games are included in September totals). During that time, the team has rarely been dreadful; it's just been consistently bad. Atlanta's record of futility:

Month	1987	1988	1989	1990
April	9–12	3–16	10–15	4–13
May	16–12	13–15	12–14	13–14
June	11–16	10–18	10–17	13–15
July	9–17	9–20	11–16	10–19
August	11–17	10–19	10–18	11–19
Sept./Oct.	13–18	9–18	10–17	14–17

Atlanta's six-year slump is hardly unique in baseball history, but its streak of losing months may soon grow to record proportions. Only four N.L. teams during this century had longer streaks. Two of those began with the kickoffs of expansion franchises: the San Diego Padres and the New York Mets (the national symbol of futility in the early 1960s). All of those longer N.L. streaks are within Atlanta's reach this season. The only teams since 1900 with streaks of 20 months or longer (months with fewer than ten games not included):

Philadelphia Athletics	35	(Apr. 1915–Apr. 1922)
San Diego Padres	27	(Apr. 1969–May 1974)
St. Louis Browns	25	(July 1946–Aug. 1951)
Kansas City Athletics	25	(June 1963–May 1968)
Philadelphia Phillies	24	(Apr. 1938–Aug. 1942)
Boston Red Sox	23	(Apr. 1925–July 1929)
New York Mets	23	(Apr. 1962–June 1966)
Pittsburgh Pirates	23	(May 1951–July 1955)
Atlanta Braves	22	(June 1987–present)
St. Louis Browns	20	(Aug. 1909–Aug. 1913)

What happens from here is anyone's guess. As a general rule, negative trends spawn a corresponding positive rebound. For example, a team that falls by 200 percentage points from one season to the next almost invariably follows with at least a modest improvement. But teams that have previously fallen to Braves-like depths have proven an exception to that rule. Over the entire history of major league baseball, 25 other teams had streaks of six consecutive seasons below .450; only six of them snapped the streak at six. (More than half had at least two more seasons below .450 before reaching that level again.) Since 1900, 32 other teams finished more than 20 games behind their division or league champion in six straight years; all but four of those streaks continued beyond the sixth season, and 15 reached double figures. Apparently teams that reach such a deep and long-standing state of ineptitude aren't bound by the normal rules of resiliency—a distressing revelation for a Braves team that has grown accustomed to basement living.

As the Braves try to escape the N.L. West cellar this season, they may face an additional problem: a continuing shift of power from the National League's Eastern Division to the West, similar to the one that has already occurred in the American League. The N.L. West has lost its season series to the East in each of the past seven years, but Atlanta's own poor record is largely responsible for the division's shortfall. Eliminate all Braves games, and the West would have beaten the East three times in the past five years. Recent inter-division results:

	All Games		Without Braves	
Year	Winner	Record	Winner	Record
1984	East	235–197	East	195–165
1985	East	223–208	East	180–179
1986	East	217–214	West	182–178
1987	East	244–187	East	206–154
1988	East	214–213	West	171–186
1989	East	218–214	West	174–186
1990	East	225–207	East	186–174

Given some of the player moves of the past winter, even another 100-loss season by the Braves might not be enough to continue the East's streak for another year: Darryl Strawberry from the Mets to the Dodgers; Willie McGee from the Cardinals to the Giants (via Oakland); Bud Black and Dave Righetti from the American League to the Giants. Of course, Atlanta was involved as well, signing Terry Pendleton and Sid Bream away from N.L. East teams, further tipping the scales westward. But it may be that while the Braves have improved themselves with the addition of two useful starters, the best teams in the division have distanced themselves even further from Atlanta with superstar additions of their own.

Then again, how many consistent losers have earned a consolation prize as valuable as David Justice? Early last August, Atlanta traded its longtime franchise player, Dale Murphy, and awarded Justice his spot in right field. Three days later, Justice began a home-run tear right out of Murphy's MVP years that lasted for the remainder of the season. From August 7 on, Justice hit 20 home runs, the most in the majors during that time; only 14 other players hit even half that many. Long after New York's super rookie, Kevin Maas, had been rendered mortal, Justice kept swatting home runs like slow houseflies in the humidity of an Atlanta summer. Major league leaders from August 7 to the season's end:

National League		American League	
Justice, Atl.	20	Fielder, Det.	17
Sandberg, Chi.	15	Barfield, N.Y.	11
Bonds, Pitt.	13	McGriff, Tor.	11
Daniels, L.A.	12	McGwire, Oak.	11
Gant, Atl.	12	Maas, N.Y.	10
Williams, S.F.	12		

Should Justice continue to display that home-run swing in 1991, Atlanta could rise again, raising the following question: How reliable is a spectacular rookie season as an indicator of the year to follow? How many at-bats are needed for a great rookie season to earn our respect? Are rookies less likely to reproduce great seasons than veterans are?

Justice and Maas provide an interesting contrast. Although Justice didn't open his throttle fully until August, he played regularly throughout the season, amassing 437 at-bats; Maas didn't make his season debut until June 29, and accumulated only 254 at-bats. Does that make Justice's performance more reliable, and if so, to what extent?

Between 1900 and 1989, 83 rookies compiled slugging averages of .500 or better in at least 200 at-bats, then returned to the majors the next year. Their performances indicate that those with more than 400 at-bats are far more likely to excel as sophomores than the rookies who batted between 200 and 400 times. Not only did those with 400 or more at-bats have a higher composite slugging average as sophomores, but they were also more consistent, as the following table shows:

At-bats in Rookie Season	200–399	400–up
Number of players included	36	47
Mean sophomore slugging avg.	.441	.495
Theoretical mid-range	.329–.553	.438–.552

(The "theoretical mid-range" is a statistical concept used to estimate the distribution of an infinite population when only a limited group can be studied. The ranges listed above represent the 25th and 75th percentiles; that is, half the players should fall within its boundaries. One quarter of the population would fall below the low figure, and one quarter would exceed the high figure.)

Among rookies with slugging averages of .500 or higher, those with at least 400 rookie at-bats slugged 54 points higher as sophomores than did rookies with fewer ABs. More importantly, the theoretical mid-range indicates that half of all rookies with SAs of .500 or better and at least 400 ABs would fall within a 114-point range; in fact, among our live test group, 34 of 47 fell within that range, and only one fell below the .400 mark (Walt Dropo, .369). The corresponding range for rookies with fewer ABs was twice as wide (224 points), with one in four expected not to reach even the .330 mark as sophomores. The class of 36 players included many who didn't even earn regular starting jobs as sophomores; more than half failed once again to reach the 400 at-bat mark.

The low at-bat group produced only one Hall of Famer, Chuck Klein. The high at-bat group produced eight: Earl Averill, Joe DiMaggio, Lou Gehrig, Johnny Mize, Frank Robinson, Al Rosen, Paul Waner, and Ted Williams, along with some near misses (Shoeless Joe Jackson and Joe Gordon among them) and some strong contenders or contenders-to-be (Orlando Cepeda, Tony Oliva, Carlton Fisk, and Darryl Strawberry). At the opposite extreme, the wash-out rate was surprisingly high for those with fewer than 400 rookie at-bats. Do the names of Hal Breeden, Mandy Brooks, or Bill DeLancey ring a bell? If so, we suggest you put down your *Baseball Encyclopedia* and get out a little more often.

Do great rookie seasons warrant great expectations in proportion to the number of at-bats? Probably even more than you thought. Aside to fantasy-league owners and Yankees general manager Gene Michael: If you have a chance to trade Maas for Justice, go for it. (Aside to John Schuerholz, if you make that deal in your first months in Atlanta: Rent, don't buy.)

A related question: How should our expectations vary for rookies and veterans coming off great seasons? Our study group included all players between 1900 and 1989 with slugging averages of .500 or better in seasons of at least 200 at-bats. A comparison of rookies to veterans in that group indicates that their performances a year later follow approximately the same rules. But, as always, it's the differences that arouse our interest. Compare these patterns for veterans to those of rookies shown on page 60:

At-bats in Preceding Season	200–399	400–up
Mean slugging avg.	.458	.499
Theoretical mid-range	.369–.547	.405–.593

Among players who slugged .500 or better over 200 to 400 ABs, the range of averages a year later wasn't quite as extreme for veterans (with half falling between .369 and .547) as for rookies (.329 to .553). But for players who slugged at least .500 in fuller seasons, the range was far wider for veterans (198 points) than for rookies (114 points).

How's this for a *post facto* rationalization: Rookies capable of slugging .500 constitute a very elite subgroup of players, whose range of future performance is accordingly narrower than that of a group of veterans who include those only occasionally capable of reaching that level. But that's a surprising conclusion, one we would never have reached on our own without studying the issue statistically.

WON-LOST RECORD BY STARTING POSITION

Atlanta Braves	C	1B	2B	3B	SS	LF	CF	RF	DH	P	Leadoff	Cleanup	Starts vs. LH	Starts vs. RH	Total Starts
Steve Avery	-	-	-	-	-	-	-	-	-	6-14	-	-	8	12	6-14
Mike Bell	-	2-4	-	-	-	-	-	-	-	-	-	-	-	6	2-4
Geronimo Berroa	-	-	-	-	-	-	-	-	-	-	-	-	-	-	-
Jeff Blauser	-	-	7-5	3-1	28-61	-	-	-	-	-	-	-	34	71	38-67
Joe Boever	-	-	-	-	-	-	-	-	-	-	-	-	-	-	-
Francisco Cabrera	-	19-17	-	-	-	-	-	-	-	-	-	-	32	4	19-17
Tony Castillo	-	-	-	-	-	-	-	-	-	3-0	-	-	1	2	3-0
Marty Clary	-	-	-	-	-	-	-	-	-	3-11	-	-	6	8	3-11
Jody Davis	1-1	2-3	-	-	-	-	-	-	-	-	-	-	7	-	3-4
Nick Esasky	-	1-8	-	-	-	-	-	-	-	-	-	1-8	2	7	1-8
Marvin Freeman	-	-	-	-	-	-	-	-	-	-	-	-	-	-	-
Ron Gant	-	-	-	-	-	12-22	46-59	-	-	-	8-8	-	54	85	58-81
Tom Glavine	-	-	-	-	-	-	-	-	-	13-20	-	-	12	21	13-20
Mark Grant	-	-	-	-	-	-	-	-	-	0-1	-	-	-	1	0-1
Thomas Greene	-	-	-	-	-	-	-	-	-	1-1	-	-	-	2	1-1
Tommy Gregg	-	12-27	-	-	-	3-1	-	3-5	-	-	-	-	-	51	18-33
Dwayne Henry	-	-	-	-	-	-	-	-	-	-	-	-	-	-	-
Joe Hesketh	-	-	-	-	-	-	-	-	-	-	-	-	-	-	-
Alex Infante	-	-	3-1	-	2-1	-	-	-	-	-	-	-	4	3	5-2
David Justice	-	24-36	-	-	-	-	-	24-33	-	-	-	17-24	31	86	48-69
Charlie Kerfeld	-	-	-	-	-	-	-	-	-	-	-	-	-	-	-
Jimmy Kremers	7-14	-	-	-	-	-	-	-	-	-	-	-	-	21	7-14
Charlie Leibrandt	-	-	-	-	-	-	-	-	-	10-14	-	-	9	15	10-14
Mark Lemke	-	-	15-17	12-14	-	-	-	-	-	-	-	-	26	32	27-31
Derek Lilliquist	-	-	-	-	-	-	-	-	-	2-9	-	-	3	8	2-9
Phil Lombardi	-	-	-	-	-	-	-	-	-	-	-	-	-	-	-
Rick Luecken	-	-	-	-	-	-	-	-	-	-	-	-	-	-	-
Kelly Mann	3-4	-	-	-	-	-	-	-	-	-	-	-	4	3	3-4
Paul Marak	-	-	-	-	-	-	-	-	-	3-4	-	-	-	7	3-4
Oddibe McDowell	-	-	-	-	-	6-5	19-38	1-0	-	-	26-42	-	2	67	26-43
Kent Mercker	-	-	-	-	-	-	-	-	-	-	-	-	-	-	-
Dale Murphy	-	-	-	-	-	-	-	36-58	-	-	-	1-4	35	59	36-58
Greg Olson	37-41	-	-	-	-	-	-	-	-	-	-	-	48	30	37-41
Jeff Parrett	-	-	-	-	-	-	-	-	-	-	-	-	-	-	-
Jim Presley	-	5-2	-	48-82	-	-	-	-	-	-	-	45-61	53	84	53-84
Rusty Richards	-	-	-	-	-	-	-	-	-	-	-	-	-	-	-
Victor Rosario	-	-	-	-	0-2	-	-	-	-	-	-	-	-	2	0-2
Doug Sisk	-	-	-	-	-	-	-	-	-	-	-	-	-	-	-
Lonnie Smith	-	-	-	-	-	44-69	-	-	-	-	31-47	1-0	54	59	44-69
Pete Smith	-	-	-	-	-	-	-	-	-	6-7	-	-	6	7	6-7
John Smoltz	-	-	-	-	-	-	-	-	-	18-16	-	-	10	24	18-16
Mike Stanton	-	-	-	-	-	-	-	-	-	-	-	-	-	-	-
Andres Thomas	-	-	-	2-0	35-33	-	-	-	-	-	-	-	28	42	37-33
Jeff Treadway	-	-	40-74	-	-	-	-	-	-	-	-	-	23	91	40-74
Sergio Valdez	-	-	-	-	-	-	-	-	-	-	-	-	-	-	-
Jim Vatcher	-	-	-	-	-	-	-	1-1	-	-	-	-	2	-	1-1
Ernie Whitt	17-37	-	-	-	-	-	-	-	-	-	-	-	1	53	17-37

TEAM TOTALS: BATTING

	AB	H	2B	3B	HR	RBI	BB	SO	BA	SA	OBA
Season	5504	1376	263	26	162	636	473	1010	.250	.396	.311
vs. Left-Handers	1814	494	104	7	65	260	187	275	.272	.445	.342
vs. Right-Handers	3690	882	159	19	97	376	286	735	.239	.371	.295
vs. Ground-Ballers	2657	696	127	12	83	318	217	450	.262	.412	.320
vs. Fly-Ballers	2847	680	136	14	79	318	256	560	.239	.380	.302
Home Games	2739	717	137	9	85	329	223	476	.262	.411	.320
Road Games	2765	659	126	17	77	307	250	534	.238	.380	.302
Grass Fields	4086	1042	196	17	122	489	345	757	.255	.401	.315
Artificial Turf	1418	334	67	9	40	147	128	253	.236	.380	.299
April	545	113	22	1	7	43	49	111	.207	.290	.273
May	900	237	55	2	36	117	93	165	.263	.449	.334
June	987	261	44	5	30	123	77	177	.264	.410	.319
July	996	232	32	5	35	112	92	211	.233	.381	.299
August	1023	264	53	9	24	116	66	165	.258	.398	.304
Sept./Oct.	1053	269	57	4	30	125	96	181	.255	.403	.320
Leading Off Inn.	1355	337	77	6	47	47	87	221	.249	.418	.296
Bases Empty	3284	778	151	13	101	101	244	605	.237	.383	.293
Runners On	2220	598	112	13	61	535	229	405	.269	.414	.336
Runners/Scor. Pos.	1321	336	63	6	35	455	171	267	.254	.391	.336
Runners On/2 Out	974	245	52	5	19	203	116	188	.252	.374	.335
Scor. Pos./2 Out	640	148	34	4	12	178	96	131	.231	.353	.336
Late-Inning Pressure	791	178	34	2	25	85	61	160	.225	.368	.283
Leading Off	205	46	9	0	8	8	12	37	.224	.385	.271
Runners On	284	72	17	2	5	65	29	60	.254	.380	.323
Runners/Scor. Pos.	163	42	10	2	3	58	22	35	.258	.399	.335

RUNS BATTED IN	From 1B	From 2B	From 3B	Scoring Position
Totals	92/1536	176/1054	206/521	382/1575
Percentage	6.0%	16.7%	39.5%	24.3%

TEAM TOTALS: PITCHING

	W-L	ERA	AB	H	HR	BB	SO	BA	SA	OBA
Season	65-97	4.58	5550	1527	128	579	938	.275	.403	.343
vs. Left-Handers			2102	572	42	266	351	.272	.386	.354
vs. Right-Handers			3448	955	86	313	587	.277	.413	.337
vs. Ground-Ballers			2670	717	42	267	474	.269	.373	.335
vs. Fly-Ballers			2880	810	86	312	464	.281	.431	.351
Home Games	37-44	4.57	2874	805	70	284	498	.280	.407	.345
Road Games	28-53	4.58	2676	722	58	295	440	.270	.398	.342
Grass Fields	49-71	4.76	4193	1179	103	423	726	.281	.411	.346
Artificial Turf	16-26	4.02	1357	348	25	156	212	.256	.377	.334
April	4-13	5.63	588	172	16	61	102	.293	.435	.359
May	13-14	4.01	890	227	28	90	168	.255	.403	.323
June	13-15	5.88	1014	311	26	99	163	.307	.446	.369
July	10-19	4.64	1002	268	21	121	166	.267	.385	.343
August	11-19	4.26	1017	285	18	102	181	.280	.394	.346
Sept./Oct.	14-17	3.55	1039	264	19	106	158	.254	.369	.325
Leading Off Inn.			1317	341	28	110	197	.259	.380	.320
Bases Empty			3043	785	66	277	509	.258	.380	.323
Runners On			2507	742	62	302	429	.296	.431	.367
Runners/Scor. Pos.			1533	440	41	231	288	.287	.426	.370
Runners On/2 Out			1086	289	23	154	221	.266	.384	.360
Scor. Pos./2 Out			749	198	16	124	154	.264	.382	.370
Late-Inning Pressure			742	216	21	99	142	.291	.423	.378
Leading Off			180	45	5	20	34	.250	.389	.338
Runners On			347	107	9	57	69	.308	.435	.401
Runners/Scor. Pos.			196	62	6	51	43	.316	.464	.443
First 9 Batters			2934	815	66	340	554	.278	.399	.353
Second 9 Batters			1365	375	33	128	214	.275	.417	.337
All Batters Thereafter			1251	337	29	111	170	.269	.397	.328

CHICAGO CUBS

- **Remembering the really good, really old days.**
- **Abandoning their abandon.**

Unless you remember the Spanish-American War firsthand, you probably think the history of the Chicago Cubs has been all gloom and doom: 46 years since their last National League title, nearly that long again since their last World Series victory in 1908. But if Willard Scott ever happens to throw birthday kisses to a 103-year-old grandma in the Windy City, jot down her name and give her a call. Wish her 103 more, then ask her about the Cubs of her childhood. She'll tell you about the most dominant team in the history of the National League.

Even with that 46-year World Series vacuum, the Cubs' history has been a successful one. Take away every game that Ferguson Jenkins ever won for them, every game that Bruce Sutter ever saved for them, and every game in which Ernie Banks hit a home run, and the franchise would still have a record above the .500 mark. The more recent past may have meant a half-century of frustration, but the golden days of the Cubs franchise go all the way back to the founding of the National League in 1876, the same year that Alexander Graham Bell patented the telephone and Sitting Bull danced on General Custer.

For starters, Chicago is the only team that has represented the same city throughout the league's entire history. Even the historic Cincinnati franchise—considered the cornerstone of major league baseball—deserted the National League for the American Association for most of the 1880s. But the Chicago team remained a member club under every N.L. president from Morgan Bulkeley and William Hulbert through Bart Giamatti and Bill White. The first-year clubs were Chicago, originally called the White Stockings, the Boston Red Stockings (forerunners of the Atlanta Braves) and six other franchises no longer in operation: the Philadelphia Athletics, the New York Mutuals, the Cincinnati Red Stockings, the St. Louis Brown Stockings (creative when it came to picking names, weren't they?), the Louisville Grays, and the Hartford Dark Blues.

Chicago's first manager was Al Spalding—that's right, the guy who started the sporting goods firm that bears his name, and who made a fortune on the small, pink rubber balls that most boys and girls slapped around schoolyards until their hormones prodded them toward other diversions. Spalding's team won the first National League pennant with a record of 52–14, taking the first of Chicago's six league titles during an 11-year period from 1876 through 1886. The names of the team's stars may be familiar even to current-day baseball fans with little knowledge of the 19th-century game: Cap Anson, King Kelly, and pre-Babe home-run king Ned Williamson (see page 424), to name a few.

Chicago posted winning records in every season from 1887 through 1891 as well, finishing second or third each time, and playing 102 games above .500 for the period. That kind of record today would earn them a choker's label. But in the quaint mindset of the 1800s, such a performance was probably considered a sign of excellence. (How blissfully naive!) The team then scuffled for the rest of the 1890s, but emerged shortly thereafter to become the only team ever to rival the dominance the great Yankees teams would display nearly a half-century later.

Starting in 1904, the Cubs strung together seven consecutive seasons above the .600 mark, four of them at .675 or better. (Only the Yankees had a longer streak, 11 years from 1947 through 1957; none of those teams reached the lofty .675 level.) They won four National League titles and two World Series during that time. Their record of 116–36 in 1906 remains the best in the majors during the 1900s. And the foundation of those teams was a trio of infielders whose names have been immortalized, but whose individual talents have been ironically obscured, by a poem entitled "Baseball's Sad Lexicon," written by columnist Franklin P. Adams, which was published in the *New York Mail* in July 1910:

These are the saddest of possible words,
Tinker to Evers to Chance.
Trio of Bear Cubs and fleeter than birds,
Tinker to Evers to Chance.
Thoughtlessly pricking our gonfalon bubble,
Making a Giant hit into a double,
Words that are weighty with nothing but trouble,
Tinker to Evers to Chance.

Tinker, Evers, and Chance played together regularly from 1903 through 1910, a span that would have coincided perfectly with that run of .600 seasons had they not fallen three percentage points short in their first year together. Because of Adams's ode, baseball folklore holds that turning double plays was their hallmark. But never during their eight seasons together did the Cubs lead the National League in making double plays. On the other hand, a look at the record indicates that all three were excellent hitters and great base runners. Fielding? Well . . . at least we *know* they were excellent hitters and great base runners.

Actually, at first glance, their career batting statistics only reinforce the common notion that the three reached Cooperstown for their fielding skills. None of them was a career .300 hitter: Chance batted .297, and neither Tinker (.263) nor Evers

(.270) was even close. But the league batting average during the eight seasons they played together was just .250. It's obvious that, compared to the other players at their positions, Tinker, Evers, and Chance were all superior hitters in their day.

From 1903 to 1910, Chance was one of the toughest outs in baseball, batting .302 and ranking eighth in the majors with an eight-year total of 417 walks. (Hit-by-pitch statistics are regrettably unavailable for that period. But even discounting them, Chance—an olden-day Minnie Minoso who crowded the plate—ranked sixth with a .382 on-base average. If HBPs were included, Chance might leapfrog over Ty Cobb and Nap Lajoie, among others, into second place behind Honus Wagner.) Harry Davis had far more power, but no other first baseman compared to Chance at the plate. The eight-year batting statistics of all players with 750 or more games at first base during the period follow, along with the average performance for all first basemen telescoped down to the same number of plate appearances as Chance:

First Basemen	AB	R	H	2B	3B	HR	BB	SB	BA
Kitty Bransfield	3958	382	1041	175	49	13	173	128	.263
Frank Chance	3211	597	970	154	60	16	417	311	.302
Harry Davis	4094	598	1128	239	63	53	346	172	.276
Tom Jones	3688	320	919	115	30	3	191	134	.249
Fred Tenney	3585	527	984	115	34	10	458	112	.274
Averages	3388	395	889	131	50	16	241	129	.263

Evers was also among the best offensive second basemen of that period, second only to Nap Lajoie. Similarly, Tinker (a power-hitting infielder by deadball standards) and Bobby Wallace ran a distant and inseparable second and third to Honus Wagner among the top-hitting shortstops of the day. Those who played at least 750 games at those positions from 1903 through 1910:

Second Basemen	AB	R	H	2B	3B	HR	BB	SB	BA
Johnny Evers	3689	552	995	136	45	5	395	257	.270
Miller Huggins	3365	542	879	78	38	5	547	184	.261
Nap Lajoie	4043	577	1379	298	62	24	270	162	.341
Claude Ritchey	3074	338	811	128	40	5	341	61	.264
Jimmy Williams	3449	386	863	146	58	20	290	72	.250
Averages	3775	445	960	140	48	12	309	153	.254

Shortstops	AB	R	H	2B	3B	HR	BB	SB	BA
Bill Dahlen	3175	383	770	130	22	16	379	159	.243
Mickey Doolan	3010	253	705	133	45	8	165	82	.234
Freddy Parent	3883	453	987	125	57	13	266	152	.254
Joe Tinker	3957	474	1002	154	69	22	241	222	.253
Honus Wagner	4200	791	1454	294	107	42	440	382	.346
Bobby Wallace	4068	449	1047	171	57	8	366	107	.257
Averages	3893	441	967	139	48	12	305	165	.248

Tinker, Evers, and Chance were no worse than the second-best hitters at their three infield positions. By today's standards, they could be Eddie Murray, Steve Sax, and Barry Larkin; or Don Mattingly, Roberto Alomar, and Alan Trammell—in short, the foundation of a potentially awesome lineup, especially when you factor in their base stealing capabilities. Notice the stolen base totals above; during those eight seasons, Chance (2d), Evers (4th), and Tinker (9th) all ranked among the top 10 in the entire majors, Chance trailing only Honus Wagner.

Ironically, fielding—the skill for which Tinker, Evers, and Chance were immortalized—may have been the one at which they were merely ordinary. As we mentioned earlier, the Cubs didn't lead the National League in double plays even once during their time together; in fact, they never finished higher than third. Tinker, at least, was a good (though probably not great) fielder, having consistently ranked among the leaders in assists per game. The same standard of measure doesn't flatter Evers, however. The following table shows their major-league ranks at shortstop and second base, respectively, among players with at least 50 games played there in each season; the number of players ranked is also indicated:

	1903	1904	1905	1906	1907	1908	1909	1910
Tinker	5/17	6/18	2/17	10/16	5/18	7/17	6/19	9/18
Evers	10/17	2/17	10/17	12/18	2/18	12/19	7/17	11/17

For the period from 1903 through 1910, Tinker's average of 3.4 assists per game ranked sixth among 17 players with 500 or more games at shortstop; Evers ranked sixth among 13 second basemen with a 3.00 mark. Neither was a particularly sure-handed fielder, either. Tinker ranked eighth among those 17 shortstops in fielding percentage, with one error for every 16.1 chances. (He led the majors in fielding percentage in 1908 and 1913, and led the N.L. in 1909 and 1911.) Evers ranked only 11th among the 13 second basemen (one error per 19.3 chances). Of course, fielding is the most difficult of all baseball skills to quantify. But neither Tinker nor Evers turned an inordinate number of double plays; they didn't field an unusual number of ground balls; and they both made their share of errors—especially Evers. Have there been any great fielders in major league history who failed to distinguish themselves statistically in at least one of those categories? Among the three, it was the first baseman Chance who had the best fielding statistics. That says a lot.

Tinker, Evers, and Chance are all worthy Hall of Famers for their hitting and base stealing alone—especially in light of the N.L. championship teams they played for. That's a blessing denied many other great infields in Cubs history: not Cap Anson, Fred Pfeffer, Ned Williamson, and Tom Burns in the 1880s; but certainly Billy Jurges, Billy Herman, Stan Hack, and the first baseman of the month in the 1930s; Ernie Banks, Glenn Beckert, Don Kessinger, and Ron Santo in the 1960s; Ryne Sandberg, Shawon Dunston, and Leon Durham or Mark Grace in the 1980s. But as to whether baseball's most legendary double-play combination was anything more than adequate in the field, you'll have to take columnist Adams's word for it, if you like. That leaves only one question: What's a gonfalon?

When the Cubs won the N.L. East two years ago, they ran the bases more aggressively than any other team in the majors. They stole only a league-median 136 bases, but Chicago runners advanced from first base to third on 46 percent of all outfield singles (124 of 270); one other team in either league had a mark as high as 40 percent. Think about that: Half the teams had rates below 36 percent; 14 others were grouped between 36 and 40 percent; Pittsburgh was a clear runner-up at 42 percent; and Chicago was a runaway leader at 46 percent. An aerial view would look something like the stretch run of Secretariat's 30-length victory in the Belmont Stakes; that's Chicago way out on the right, with the Pirates in distant pursuit:

```
                  xx      xxx
xx xx   xx x xxx x xxxxxx xx      x          x
- - - - - - - - - - - - - - - - - - - - - - - - - - - - - - - - - - - -
30%          35%          40%          45%          50%
```

In addition, Cubs runners scored from second on 129 of 165 outfield singles (78%), the second-highest rate in the National League in 1989. And for all their gambling and gamboling, only 10 Cubs were thrown out on those gambits, compared to a league average of nine. (And none of them was from Gambia.)

Last season, Chicago ran the bases with renewed caution. The Cubs advanced from first to third on 110 of 294 outfield singles (37%), to rank fourth in the National League. They scored from second on only 102 of 154 outfield singles (66%), to rank tenth in the league. A summary of Cubs runners advancing on outfield singles:

Year	1st to 3d	Pct.	Rank	2d to Home	Pct.	Rank
1989	124-for-270	45.9%	1st	129-for-165	78.2%	2d
1990	110-for-294	37.4%	4th	102-for-154	66.2%	10th

When a team falls from second to tenth in any category, personnel changes would seem to be a likely cause. A comparison of individual figures from 1989 to 1990 indicates that although Chicago's decline was teamwide, it wasn't unrelated to the turnover of players. The following table shows that the five players on second base for at least 10 outfield singles in both seasons declined less than their teammates; "1B" indicates outfield singles when each player was on second, "EXB" indicates the number of times he took the extra base to score:

	1989			1990		
Player	1B	EXB	Pct.	1B	EXB	Pct.
Andre Dawson	15	7	.467	16	10	.625
Shawon Dunston	13	11	.846	11	7	.636
Mark Grace	16	12	.750	16	11	.688
Ryne Sandberg	22	20	.909	22	16	.727
Jerome Walton	12	8	.667	12	8	.667
Totals	78	58	.743	77	52	.675
Others	87	71	.816	77	50	.649

Obviously, the supporting cast was much more aggressive in 1989 than in 1990. But the decline even among the everyday starters requires a broader explanation. And the root cause of Chicago's slowdown provides an interesting illustration of how the game of baseball changes according to the situation. The 1989 Cubs were most aggressive when they had a lead, slightly less aggressive in tie games, and comparatively discreet when they trailed. Runners going from first to third on outfield singles in 1989:

Cubs winning	64-for-126	50.8%
Game tied	33-for-69	47.8%
Cubs losing	27-for-75	36.0%

Undoubtedly, much of last season's caution was attributable to the fact that Chicago was losing much more often than in 1989. But other factors were involved as well. If we assume that the Cubs were losing last season as often as they were winning in 1989—in fact, their decline wasn't that severe—that still would have accounted only for a drop from 46 percent to 43 percent (instead of the actual figure of 37 percent).

So did the Cubs run wild in 1989 because they were winning, or did they win because they ran wild? Clearly the former was true, but there may have been a reciprocal effect as well.

WON-LOST RECORD BY STARTING POSITION

Chicago Cubs	C	1B	2B	3B	SS	LF	CF	RF	DH	P	Leadoff	Cleanup	Starts vs. LH	Starts vs. RH	Total Starts
Paul Assenmacher	-	-	-	-	-	-	-	-	-	0-1	-	-	-	1	0-1
Damon Berryhill	8-7	-	-	-	-	-	-	-	-	-	-	-	3	12	8-7
Mike Bielecki	-	-	-	-	-	-	-	-	-	14-15	-	-	13	16	14-15
Kevin Blankenship	-	-	-	-	-	-	-	-	-	0-2	-	-	-	2	0-2
Shawn Boskie	-	-	-	-	-	-	-	-	-	8-7	-	-	1	14	8-7
Dave Clark	-	-	-	-	-	21-14	-	-	-	-	5-1	2-4	-	35	21-14
Kevin Coffman	-	-	-	-	-	-	-	-	-	0-2	-	-	1	1	0-2
Doug Dascenzo	-	-	-	-	-	6-10	15-16	5-2	-	-	16-16	-	36	18	26-28
Andre Dawson	-	-	-	-	-	-	-	63-76	-	-	-	61-72	52	87	63-76
Lance Dickson	-	-	-	-	-	-	-	-	-	0-3	-	-	1	2	0-3
Shawon Dunston	-	-	-	-	69-75	-	-	-	-	-	0-1	-	56	88	69-75
Joe Girardi	54-66	-	-	-	-	-	-	-	-	-	-	-	42	78	54-66
Mark Grace	-	72-74	-	-	-	-	-	-	-	-	-	6-6	43	103	72-74
Mike Harkey	-	-	-	-	-	-	-	-	-	16-11	-	-	8	19	16-11
Joe Kraemer	-	-	-	-	-	-	-	-	-	-	-	-	-	-	-
Randy Kramer	-	-	-	-	-	-	-	-	-	1-1	-	-	-	2	1-1
Les Lancaster	-	-	-	-	-	-	-	-	-	4-2	-	-	4	2	4-2
Bill Long	-	-	-	-	-	-	-	-	-	-	-	-	-	-	-
Greg Maddux	-	-	-	-	-	-	-	-	-	17-18	-	-	10	25	17-18
Derrick May	-	-	-	-	-	8-8	-	-	-	-	-	-	-	16	8-8
Lloyd McClendon	-	2-4	-	-	-	10-10	-	-	-	-	-	1-1	26	-	12-14
Jose Nunez	-	-	-	-	-	-	-	-	-	5-5	-	-	5	5	5-5
Dave Pavlas	-	-	-	-	-	-	-	-	-	-	-	-	-	-	-
Jeff Pico	-	-	-	-	-	-	-	-	-	4-4	-	-	3	5	4-4
Domingo Ramos	-	-	-	20-24	4-8	-	-	-	-	-	-	-	28	28	24-32
Luis Salazar	-	-	-	43-40	-	11-10	-	-	-	-	-	2-0	44	60	54-50
Ryne Sandberg	-	-	73-79	-	-	-	-	-	-	-	-	-	58	94	73-79
Dwight Smith	-	-	-	-	-	20-32	-	8-5	-	-	8-9	3-1	3	62	28-37
Greg Smith	-	-	2-1	-	4-2	-	-	-	-	-	-	-	-	9	6-3
Rick Sutcliffe	-	-	-	-	-	-	-	-	-	2-3	-	-	1	4	2-3
Gary Varsho	-	-	-	-	-	-	-	0-1	-	-	0-1	-	-	1	0-1
Hector Villanueva	9-8	3-7	-	-	-	-	-	-	-	-	-	-	16	11	12-15
Jerome Walton	-	-	-	-	-	-	44-53	-	-	-	44-52	-	41	56	44-53
Curt Wilkerson	-	-	2-5	14-21	-	-	-	-	-	-	0-2	-	9	33	16-26
Dean Wilkins	-	-	-	-	-	-	-	-	-	-	-	-	-	-	-
Mitch Williams	-	-	-	-	-	-	-	-	-	0-2	-	-	1	1	0-2
Steve Wilson	-	-	-	-	-	-	-	-	-	6-9	-	-	10	5	6-9
Rick Wrona	6-4	-	-	-	-	-	-	-	-	-	-	-	6	4	6-4
Marvell Wynne	-	-	-	-	-	1-1	18-16	1-1	-	-	4-3	2-1	1	37	20-18

TEAM TOTALS: BATTING

	AB	H	2B	3B	HR	RBI	BB	SO	BA	SA	OBA
Season	5600	1474	240	36	136	649	406	869	.263	.392	.314
vs. Left-Handers	1882	502	91	11	49	224	138	277	.267	.405	.316
vs. Right-Handers	3718	972	149	25	87	425	268	592	.261	.385	.312
vs. Ground-Ballers	2626	672	92	19	49	282	168	405	.256	.361	.302
vs. Fly-Ballers	2974	802	148	17	87	367	238	464	.270	.419	.324
Home Games	2796	788	125	20	75	346	202	417	.282	.421	.330
Road Games	2804	686	115	16	61	303	204	452	.245	.362	.297
Grass Fields	3971	1096	167	25	108	491	289	627	.276	.412	.325
Artificial Turf	1629	378	73	11	28	158	117	242	.232	.342	.286
April	647	162	19	2	11	56	43	104	.250	.337	.299
May	1013	281	51	5	31	131	74	155	.277	.429	.326
June	1019	272	50	8	34	128	94	157	.267	.432	.331
July	903	246	39	6	14	94	49	119	.272	.375	.311
August	953	263	40	9	23	111	61	158	.276	.409	.321
Sept./Oct.	1065	250	41	6	23	129	85	176	.235	.349	.291
Leading Off Inn.	1366	365	63	7	39	39	80	215	.267	.409	.310
Bases Empty	3245	833	140	16	81	81	202	514	.257	.385	.303
Runners On	2355	641	100	20	55	568	204	355	.272	.402	.328
Runners/Scor. Pos.	1386	357	64	11	28	492	167	241	.258	.380	.331
Runners On/2 Out	1025	251	44	7	20	217	102	160	.245	.360	.317
Scor. Pos./2 Out	665	159	31	4	11	189	90	113	.239	.347	.334
Late-Inning Pressure	841	222	31	6	18	98	71	140	.264	.379	.321
Leading Off	215	63	12	1	7	7	9	42	.293	.456	.324
Runners On	351	101	12	3	9	89	40	54	.288	.416	.356
Runners/Scor. Pos.	209	52	8	1	5	78	34	37	.249	.368	.346

RUNS BATTED IN	From 1B	From 2B	From 3B	Scoring Position
Totals	88/1626	189/1052	236/613	425/1665
Percentage	5.4%	18.0%	38.5%	25.5%

TEAM TOTALS: PITCHING

	W-L	ERA	AB	H	HR	BB	SO	BA	SA	OBA
Season	77-85	4.34	5568	1510	121	572	877	.271	.402	.340
vs. Left-Handers			2844	800	51	331	408	.281	.405	.355
vs. Right-Handers			2724	710	70	241	469	.261	.398	.323
vs. Ground-Ballers			2535	646	26	246	429	.255	.351	.322
vs. Fly-Ballers			3033	864	95	326	448	.285	.444	.354
Home Games	39-42	4.76	2907	842	73	294	441	.290	.431	.355
Road Games	38-43	3.89	2661	668	48	278	436	.251	.370	.323
Grass Fields	56-58	4.53	4011	1122	101	414	620	.280	.420	.348
Artificial Turf	21-27	3.85	1557	388	20	158	257	.249	.354	.319
April	8-11	3.63	624	142	13	77	100	.228	.335	.314
May	13-15	4.42	1000	289	26	91	142	.289	.414	.351
June	12-18	5.24	1039	299	23	123	168	.288	.432	.362
July	14-12	4.24	889	244	19	74	132	.274	.404	.331
August	15-12	3.55	925	237	16	82	146	.256	.383	.317
Sept./Oct.	15-17	4.60	1091	299	24	125	189	.274	.414	.348
Leading Off Inn.			1335	357	34	108	198	.267	.393	.325
Bases Empty			3092	797	68	276	496	.258	.377	.321
Runners On			2476	713	53	296	381	.288	.433	.362
Runners/Scor. Pos.			1473	407	29	233	250	.276	.417	.369
Runners On/2 Out			1096	302	17	148	185	.276	.401	.366
Scor. Pos./2 Out			726	189	13	125	135	.260	.390	.372
Late-Inning Pressure			833	225	15	99	158	.270	.373	.350
Leading Off			205	62	7	21	32	.302	.478	.370
Runners On			385	99	6	56	75	.257	.332	.353
Runners/Scor. Pos.			240	59	2	45	48	.246	.300	.361
First 9 Batters			2945	798	70	330	545	.271	.403	.345
Second 9 Batters			1443	381	29	138	212	.264	.393	.328
All Batters Thereafter			1180	331	22	104	120	.281	.408	.340

CINCINNATI REDS

- **On balance, a championship.**
- **Some Nasty numbers from the bullpen.**

Well, now we know: every team that leads a National League pennant race wire-to-wire in a 162-game season goes on to sweep the World Series.

After four years of second-place finishes that each led to heightened expectations for the following season, the Reds came upon this magic formula the hard way. Part One: To lower those expectations, have your manager, the ultimate homeboy-makes-good and one of baseball's all-time greats, summarily booted out of the game in the middle of the year. Part Two: Following the season, replace this legend, to whom the term "National Leaguer" was a badge of pride, with someone who in 28 years around professional baseball had never spent a minute in a National League dugout.

That's it! That's the formula! Why didn't *we* think of it? We could have bottled it, patented it, sold it. Think of the teams that would pay millions to use it: the Red Sox, the Cubs, the Angels—but why stop there? Imagine what the Cleveland Browns would pay!

Actually, since that formula can be expected to work for a particular team only once every epoch or so, Reds fans must place their hopes for the future on more tangible factors. So why in the world should the Reds become the first team since the 1977–78 Yankees to repeat as world champions, the first since the 1977–78 Dodgers to repeat as National League champions, or even the first since those same Dodgers to repeat as National League West champions?

Well, maybe because—as remarkable as it sounds for a team that spent every minute of last season in first place—there's room for improvement here. Not that they were bad last year: The Reds just missed leading the league in team ERA for the first time in 50 years, finishing at 3.39 to Montreal's 3.37; they finished fifth in the league in runs scored (693) while compiling the league's best batting average (.265); and they led the league in fielding percentage (.983), with their regular outfielders (Billy Hatcher, Paul O'Neill, and Eric Davis) becoming the first teammates in major-league history to take the Gold, Silver, and Bronze positions among all the league's outfielders.

But can you name one Reds player who had a career year, as Kevin Mitchell had the year before? We'll grant you that Chris Sabo's 25 home runs were a career high at any level of professional ball, but his 71 RBIs are only an average total for a National League third baseman. Barry Larkin had a fine all-around season with 67 RBIs and 30 steals, but do you think he isn't capable of hitting .301 again? Remember, he batted .342 in a half-season in 1989. Davis spent most of the summer hearing Riverfront catcalls and ended up with five fewer home runs and 12 fewer RBIs than he had averaged over the previous three years. Mariano Duncan surprised one and all with a .306 batting average, but with Bill Doran on hand for the full season in 1991 the Reds are well fortified if Mariano drops off. And hitting machine Hal Morris might do better than Todd Benzinger's .253 with one hand tied behind his back.

No, the Reds won their division with a group of young players who were excellent in total but did not have spectacular years as individuals. Let's take a look at just how young the Reds were, and just how unspectacular those individual performances were. Here are the Reds' 1990 regulars listed according to age:

	Age*	Avg.	HR	RBI	SB
Hatcher	29,11	.276	5	25	30
Sabo	28,8	.270	25	71	25
Davis	28,4	.260	24	86	21
Benzinger	27,7	.253	5	46	3
O'Neill	27,7	.270	16	78	13
Duncan	27,6	.306	10	55	13
Larkin	26,5	.301	7	67	30
Oliver	24,2	.231	8	52	1

* Age at end of regular season (years, months)

The average age of the Reds' lineup last season, excluding pitchers, was 27.84 years. (The average is computed by the method we've used before, with which our regular readers should be familiar: It's weighted according to the number of plate appearances that each player had during the season, so that Chris Sabo and Barry Larkin have more impact on the overall average than do Billy Bates and Terry Lee.) That gave the Reds the youngest everyday lineup in the National League, which was big news in itself. Each of the 11 other National League teams had earned that designation at least once since World War II, but the last time the Reds had fielded the league's youngest lineup was before the war—that's before World War I. It was 1909, when the name Taft identified not a broadcasting company but a broad president.

The World Series victory added another set of accomplishments: They had the youngest group of position players for a Series winner since the 1969 New York Mets, and rank among the youngest champions of the postwar era:

	Avg. Age of Position Players
1969 Mets	26.44
1946 Cardinals	27.44
1966 Orioles	27.47
1952 Yankees	27.82
1990 Reds	27.84

Hatcher, the Reds' oldest regular, did not hit the Big Three-Oh until October 4, the day the Championship Series began. (He's hitting .519 as a 30-year-old.) By that one-day margin, the Reds became only the fourth World Series champion in history on which none of the eight players with the most plate appearances during the regular season had turned 30 by season's end. The others: the 1913 Philadelphia Athletics (oldest regular: 29-year-old Rube Oldring), the 1944 Cardinals (29-year-old Walker Cooper), and the 1969 Mets (27-year-old Cleon Jones). What was the last team without a 30-year-old regular to reach the World Series? The 1970 Reds (oldest regular: 29-year-old Pete Rose), who lost that Series to the Orioles but went on to dominate the decade to come.

So even with the addition of the 32-year-old Doran, acquired from Houston late last season and re-signed as a free agent in December, it looks like the Reds will have a reasonably young team on the field again in 1991. Now take another look at the basic statistics listed above for last year's regulars. They're just like Skyline Chili: nothing fancy, just good. Lou Piniella was able to write out an everyday batting order that was dangerous from top to bottom, rather than just in the three-four-five spots. For example, the Reds' number-two hitters had a total of 205 hits and finished with a collective batting average of .307; no other team in the majors had either 200 hits or a .300 batting average from its number-two hitters. The Reds' eighth-place hitters had 16 home runs and 84 runs batted in; again, both were major-league highs. In fact, no other National League team had as many as 60 RBIs from its number-eight hitters.

But while the Reds dominated the National League West wire-to-wire, they did not have the benefit of a single dominant everyday player. No Cincinnati player finished among the National League's top 10 in batting average; none finished among the top 10 in the league in home runs; none ranked among the top 10 in runs batted in; and none made the top 10 in stolen bases. No previous team in major-league history had ever won the World Series following a season in which none of its players finished among the top 10 in the league in any of those four categories. In fact, only one other team in this century that matched this dubious achievement had won so much as a division title; the mere mention of that team's name still sends shivers down the spines of longtime Reds' fans—it's the 1973 New York Mets. (That team won its division title with a record of 82–79, the worst record in major-league history to produce a first-place finish, but then beat the favored Reds in the National League Championship Series.) While the '73 Mets were just a mediocre-to-poor offensive team (with a good pitching staff) that happened to win a division no one else seemed to want, the same cannot be said of a Reds team that led its division every day of the season. It's a tribute to Cincinnati's balance, its defense, its pitching staff, and yes, its manager, that the Reds could achieve what they did without a monster year by any of their position players.

Cincinnati's march through Pittsburgh and Oakland to the baseball championship of the planet featured some fascinating baseball. In particular, the Championship Series will surely rank with the Houston–Philadelphia series of 1980 and the Houston–New York series of 1986 as among the prime exhibits of "National League baseball" at its best. Neither team ever held a lead of more than three runs at any time during the series, and there were managerial decisions and strategy moves at every turn. Was it just coincidence that following this series (and the comparatively dull American League Championship Series, enlivened only by Roger Clemens's vocabulary) Fay Vincent declared himself a full-fledged abolitionist with regard to the designated-hitter rule?

Throughout the season, Reds pitchers demonstrated their ability to get the tough outs that kill potential rallies: Opponents batted only .230 with runners in scoring position, the lowest such average in the major leagues. Then the Reds refined that art in their 10 postseason games. During the regular season the Pirates batted a league-high .275 with runners in scoring position, and finished second in the league in runs scored, but in the playoffs the Reds held Pittsburgh's bashers to a .116 batting average—that's five hits in 43 at-bats—with runners in scoring position.

In the Big One, the Reds gave the Athletics a dose of the same medicine. Oakland produced only three hits in 27 scoring-position at-bats, a .111 batting average. How does that performance rank in the record books? Not surprisingly, it's among the best of all time. Here are the 10 best (or worst, depending on your perspective) performances with runners in scoring position in World Series history; note that seven of the 10 spots are held by teams that won in a sweep:

Year	Pitchers	Batters	Games	Avg.	AB	H
1966	Orioles	Dodgers	4	.000	22	0
1950	Yankees	Phillies	4	.067	30	2
1905	Giants	Athletics	5	.095	21	2
1911	Athletics	Giants	6	.100	40	4
1954	Giants	Indians	4	.100	40	4
1914	Braves	Athletics	4	.103	29	3
1963	Dodgers	Yankees	4	.105	19	2
1928	Yankees	Cardinals	4	.107	28	3
1984	Tigers	Padres	5	.111	36	4
1990	**Reds**	**Athletics**	4	.111	27	3

Broadening the category to include all postseason games, the Reds held their opponents to eight hits in 70 at-bats—a .114 batting average—with runners in scoring position. Since 1969, when the Championship Series was invented (we forget, was that Elias Howe or Eli Whitney?), only one World Series team has held its opponents to a lower batting average in those situations:

	Games	Avg.	AB	H
1984 Tigers	8	.104	48	5
1990 **Reds**	10	.114	70	8
1983 Orioles	9	.132	53	7
1974 Athletics	9	.133	45	6
1971 Orioles	10	.147	95	14

There were certainly some fairy-dust elements to the Reds' postseason success—or have you forgotten about Billy Bates, 0-for-27 against right-handed pitchers in his major-league career, getting a hit off Dennis Eckersley to start the winning rally in Game Two of the World Series? But when it came to pitching in the clutch, the Reds did it the old-fashioned way: They earrrrned it.

No discussion of the Reds would be complete without a nod to their bullpen. The original Nasty Boys—Randy Myers, Rob Dibble, and Norm Charlton—and the other guys as well (although Rick Mahler may have the least nasty visage in baseball) contributed some record-setting numbers on the road to the title. During the regular season, Cincinnati's relievers struck out 450 batters in 472⅔ innings, giving them the top spot on a couple of all-time single-season lists:

Most Strikeouts, Relief Pitchers		Most SO's Per Nine Innings, Relief Pitchers	
1990 **Reds**	450	1990 **Reds**	8.57
1987 Giants	442	1964 Red Sox	8.25
1987 Blue Jays	428	1986 Blue Jays	8.08
1989 Reds	427	1989 Reds	8.03
1986 Blue Jays	426	1987 Blue Jays	7.95
1964 Red Sox	425	1964 Indians	7.93
1989 Blue Jays	425	1989 Blue Jays	7.91
1967 Orioles	416	1964 Reds	7.90
1986 Padres	411	*1905 Athletics	7.83
1970 Phillies	410	1976 Phillies	7.75

* Yes, 1905. The bullpen, with 24 of its 37 appearances by Rube Waddell and Chief Bender, went 17–2 with a 1.66 ERA in 146 innings. Did Connie Mack, starched collar and all, go out to make the changes?

Last season, no team came close to the Nasty Boys. The second-highest strikeout total and strikeout rate by any bullpen both belonged to Kansas City, with 384 strikeouts and a rate of 7.26 per nine innings. In their own league, the Reds easily outdistanced the Cubs (360 strikeouts) and the Dodgers (7.03 per nine innings). In addition, the Reds tied the Expos for the league lead in saves (50), and Cincinnati's relievers led the National League in ERA (2.93), lowest opponents' batting (.233) and slugging (.343) averages, and lowest opponents' stolen-base percentage (.645). Against every other National League bullpen, more than two-thirds of stolen-base attempts were successful.

Then, in postseason play, the Reds' relievers continued to set new standards. In 10 games they yielded only one earned run in 31⅓ innings. The one earned run they allowed came in Game One of the Championship Series (Charlton has spent the winter doing appropriate penance), as they closed out the postseason with a streak of 29⅔ consecutive innings without allowing an earned run. That's an all-time record for postseason play, breaking the Yankees' record of 22⅔ innings set in 1977. And just to nip any negative thoughts in the bud, know ye that in their 10 postseason games the Reds' relievers didn't allow any inherited runners to score, either. In World Series play alone, they have thrown 27 consecutive scoreless innings; the last run allowed by the Cincinnati bullpen in a World Series game was Carlton Fisk's 12th-inning home run off Pat Darcy in Game Six of the 1975 Series. We'll all watch postseason baseball for a long time before we see again the likes of what the Nasty Boys and their extended family did in 1990.

WON-LOST RECORD BY STARTING POSITION

Cincinnati Reds	C	1B	2B	3B	SS	LF	CF	RF	DH	P	Leadoff	Cleanup	Starts vs. LH	Starts vs. RH	Total Starts
Jack Armstrong	-	-	-	-	-	-	-	-	-	16-11	-	-	7	20	16-11
Bill Bates	-	-	0-1	-	-	-	-	-	-	-	-	-	1	-	0-1
Todd Benzinger	-	52-30	-	-	-	4-4	-	-	-	-	-	19-8	44	46	56-34
Tim Birtsas	-	-	-	-	-	-	-	-	-	-	-	-	-	-	-
Glenn Braggs	-	-	-	-	-	10-14	-	16-12	-	-	-	3-3	36	16	26-26
Keith Brown	-	-	-	-	-	-	-	-	-	-	-	-	-	-	-
Tom Browning	-	-	-	-	-	-	-	-	-	20-15	-	-	19	16	20-15
Norm Charlton	-	-	-	-	-	-	-	-	-	8-8	-	-	3	13	8-8
Eric Davis	-	-	-	-	-	33-22	38-28	-	-	-	3-0	60-46	45	76	71-50
Rob Dibble	-	-	-	-	-	-	-	-	-	-	-	-	-	-	-
Bill Doran	-	-	6-5	1-2	-	-	-	-	-	-	1-3	-	-	14	7-7
Mariano Duncan	-	-	62-46	-	3-2	1-0	-	-	-	-	-	-	51	63	66-48
Ken Griffey Sr.	-	1-4	-	-	-	3-1	-	-	-	-	-	-	-	9	4-5
Kip Gross	-	-	-	-	-	-	-	-	-	-	-	-	-	-	-
Chris Hammond	-	-	-	-	-	-	-	-	-	1-2	-	-	3	-	1-2
Billy Hatcher	-	-	-	-	-	31-23	35-30	-	-	-	28-22	-	56	63	66-53
Danny Jackson	-	-	-	-	-	-	-	-	-	10-12	-	-	8	14	10-12
Barry Larkin	-	-	-	-	88-66	-	-	-	-	-	11-13	2-0	57	97	88-66
Tim Layana	-	-	-	-	-	-	-	-	-	-	-	-	-	-	-
Terry Lee	-	2-2	-	-	-	-	-	-	-	-	-	0-2	4	-	2-2
Rick Mahler	-	-	-	-	-	-	-	-	-	9-7	-	-	9	7	9-7
Terry McGriff	1-0	-	-	-	-	-	-	-	-	-	-	-	1	-	1-0
Gino Minutelli	-	-	-	-	-	-	-	-	-	-	-	-	-	-	-
Hal Morris	-	36-35	-	-	-	2-3	-	-	-	-	2-0	0-1	14	62	38-38
Randy Myers	-	-	-	-	-	-	-	-	-	-	-	-	-	-	-
Paul Noce	-	-	-	-	-	-	-	-	-	-	-	-	-	-	-
Ron Oester	-	-	17-16	0-1	-	-	-	-	-	-	-	-	5	29	17-17
Joe Oliver	62-45	-	-	-	-	-	-	-	-	-	-	-	59	48	62-45
Paul O'Neill	-	-	-	-	-	-	-	70-58	-	-	-	4-8	27	101	70-58
Luis Quinones	-	-	6-3	8-6	0-3	-	-	-	-	-	-	1-0	11	15	14-12
Jeff Reed	28-25	-	-	-	-	-	-	-	-	-	-	-	-	53	28-25
Jose Rijo	-	-	-	-	-	-	-	-	-	18-11	-	-	8	21	18-11
Ron Robinson	-	-	-	-	-	-	-	-	-	4-1	-	-	2	3	4-1
Rosario Rodriguez	-	-	-	-	-	-	-	-	-	-	-	-	-	-	-
Rolando Roomes	-	-	-	-	-	7-4	-	5-1	-	-	-	-	17	-	12-5
Chris Sabo	-	-	-	82-62	-	-	-	-	-	-	41-29	2-3	59	85	82-62
Scott Scudder	-	-	-	-	-	-	-	-	-	5-4	-	-	2	7	5-4
Glenn Sutko	-	-	-	-	-	-	-	-	-	-	-	-	-	-	-
Alex Trevino	0-1	-	-	-	-	-	-	-	-	-	-	-	1	-	0-1
Herm Winningham	-	-	-	-	-	-	18-13	-	-	-	5-4	-	-	31	18-13

TEAM TOTALS: BATTING

	AB	H	2B	3B	HR	RBI	BB	SO	BA	SA	OBA
Season	5525	1466	284	40	125	644	466	913	.265	.399	.325
vs. Left-Handers	2030	569	109	10	53	253	175	324	.280	.422	.338
vs. Right-Handers	3495	897	175	30	72	391	291	589	.257	.386	.317
vs. Ground-Ballers	2723	708	143	12	51	286	211	452	.260	.378	.317
vs. Fly-Ballers	2802	758	141	28	74	358	255	461	.271	.420	.332
Home Games	2650	691	130	14	70	313	250	420	.261	.400	.328
Road Games	2875	775	154	26	55	331	216	493	.270	.399	.322
Grass Fields	1694	445	94	12	33	188	131	303	.263	.391	.318
Artificial Turf	3831	1021	190	28	92	456	335	610	.267	.403	.328
April	565	173	25	5	16	87	66	95	.306	.453	.376
May	909	242	40	6	14	100	60	147	.266	.370	.316
June	1051	281	45	6	32	124	85	182	.267	.413	.327
July	962	231	56	6	19	100	76	168	.240	.370	.298
August	977	258	57	13	23	106	69	144	.264	.420	.315
Sept./Oct.	1061	281	61	4	21	127	110	177	.265	.389	.335
Leading Off Inn.	1341	363	68	10	36	36	104	203	.271	.417	.325
Bases Empty	3127	839	166	24	80	80	234	505	.268	.413	.324
Runners On	2398	627	118	16	45	564	232	408	.261	.380	.327
Runners/Scor. Pos.	1447	365	76	10	25	501	180	267	.252	.370	.332
Runners On/2 Out	1005	227	37	6	17	207	114	203	.226	.325	.308
Scor. Pos./2 Out	691	156	31	4	12	193	94	142	.226	.334	.322
Late-Inning Pressure	760	192	30	7	13	66	68	114	.253	.362	.317
Leading Off	189	39	3	1	3	3	18	26	.206	.280	.282
Runners On	316	74	10	3	4	57	32	53	.234	.323	.304
Runners/Scor. Pos.	181	40	3	2	3	49	26	33	.221	.309	.315

RUNS BATTED IN	From 1B	From 2B	From 3B	Scoring Position
Totals	82/1617	177/1072	260/656	437/1728
Percentage	5.1%	16.5%	39.6%	25.3%

TEAM TOTALS: PITCHING

	W-L	ERA	AB	H	HR	BB	SO	BA	SA	OBA
Season	91-71	3.39	5449	1338	124	543	1029	.246	.369	.316
vs. Left-Handers			2209	545	52	262	418	.247	.376	.328
vs. Right-Handers			3240	793	72	281	611	.245	.365	.307
vs. Ground-Ballers			2473	602	33	199	462	.243	.335	.303
vs. Fly-Ballers			2976	736	91	344	567	.247	.398	.326
Home Games	46-35	3.54	2768	679	73	278	516	.245	.377	.316
Road Games	45-36	3.24	2681	659	51	265	513	.246	.361	.316
Grass Fields	23-25	3.58	1612	413	35	145	295	.256	.384	.317
Artificial Turf	68-46	3.32	3837	925	89	398	734	.241	.363	.315
April	13-3	3.23	547	137	8	61	122	.250	.342	.331
May	17-9	2.59	889	213	16	90	158	.240	.350	.311
June	16-14	3.60	1012	249	23	93	197	.246	.378	.310
July	14-15	3.35	962	240	25	84	173	.249	.375	.313
August	15-14	3.73	976	245	22	110	155	.251	.375	.326
Sept./Oct.	16-16	3.68	1063	254	30	105	224	.239	.380	.311
Leading Off Inn.			1345	328	32	113	232	.244	.370	.305
Bases Empty			3190	768	83	289	608	.241	.374	.306
Runners On			2259	570	41	254	421	.252	.363	.329
Runners/Scor. Pos.			1367	315	19	195	305	.230	.328	.326
Runners On/2 Out			1005	247	23	131	200	.246	.370	.340
Scor. Pos./2 Out			683	163	13	111	155	.239	.354	.353
Late-Inning Pressure			871	194	14	90	225	.223	.320	.298
Leading Off			224	55	6	17	54	.246	.375	.302
Runners On			361	77	3	41	89	.213	.294	.295
Runners/Scor. Pos.			216	44	3	33	60	.204	.301	.308
First 9 Batters			2856	687	62	309	622	.241	.356	.317
Second 9 Batters			1372	337	30	130	244	.246	.378	.312
All Batters Thereafter			1221	314	32	104	163	.257	.391	.316

HOUSTON ASTROS

- **At first glance, who has the edge?**
- **Will the real Craig Biggio please crouch down?**

In last year's *Analyst*, we wrote about the strength of Houston's unheralded bullpen, especially stopper Dave Smith's extraordinarily successful set-up men: left-handers Juan Agosto and Dan Schatzeder, and righties Danny Darwin and Larry Andersen. Those four compiled a 2.63 ERA in 1989, with a record of 23–14, despite a combined career record that was six games below .500 (196–202) prior to 1989. Last season, Houston's unsung stars continued to prove that in the Astrodome bullpen, life begins at 35: their record was 26–17, with a 2.68 ERA.

Others began to notice, too. As the 1990 pennant races heated up, all four were hotly pursued by contending teams looking to strengthen their own bullpens. Eventually, Andersen became a key player for Boston down the stretch, and Schatzeder earned a bit role in the Mets' failed attempt to catch Pittsburgh. For its part, Houston rewarded Darwin with a spot in the starting rotation, and he responded by winning the league's ERA title. But the real rewards came after the season, as all four became free agents and signed lucrative contracts with new teams: Darwin with the Red Sox, Schatzeder with the Royals, Andersen with the Padres, and Agosto with the Cardinals. Even the closer, Smith, left Houston for the Cubs.

So there's little doubt that the Astros will be showcasing some new talent on the Astrodome pitchers' mound this season. As a result, the two most frequent comments on Astros broadcasts will be: (1) "Pitchers enjoy a tremendous advantage against batters who've never seen them before"; and (2) "Batters enjoy a tremendous advantage against pitchers who've never seen them before." Well, one of those comments has to be right—unless, of course, neither has an advantage on baseball's version of a blind date. Could it be that not knowing what to expect benefits neither side?

In a word, no. There is a significant advantage in these first-ever meetings, and it belongs to . . . drum roll, please . . . the pitcher. When facing a pitcher for the first time, a typical batter loses between 15 and 20 points on his batting average, and his hits are roughly 20 percent less likely to leave the ballpark. A slight (and possibly insignificant) increase in walks is the only noticeable edge for the batter.

The study group included all first-ever matchups since 1980 in which the participants faced each other at least 15 times by the end of the following season. The following table contrasts the 6942 first meetings with a proportional slice of the combined results of the subsequent 14 times the players faced each other:

	PA	AB	H	2B	3B	HR	RBI	BA	SA	OBA
First Time	6942	6248	1562	291	35	114	603	.250	.362	.316
Next 14 PAs	6942	6260	1673	294	47	154	568	.267	.403	.327

(This factor sheds new light on one of our favorite moments from baseball history. We've all heard the story about Ted Williams refusing to sit out the last-day doubleheader in 1941 when his batting average was .39955, not wanting to back into a ".400" average. Connie Mack started two young pitchers, Fred Caligiuri and Dick Fowler, against Boston that day; Williams had never batted against either before. He also had not faced Porter Vaughn, a reliever brought in by Mack in the first game. Williams went six-for-eight in the doubleheader—quite an accomplishment given what we now know about such matchups!)

The pitcher's edge apparently evaporates after the first meeting. Let's supplement that table with another line that represents the combined results of meetings 2 through 5. Notice that it mirrors the later plate appearances almost exactly:

	PA	AB	H	2B	3B	HR	RBI	BA	SA	OBA
Meetings 2–5	6942	6260	1673	294	47	154	568	.267	.403	.327
Meetings 6–15	6942	6270	1685	298	53	150	562	.269	.405	.326

But perhaps the most interesting trend that we discovered was that the pitchers' initial short-lived advantage was not only exaggerated for a certain group of pitchers, but it lasted longer for them as well. Pitchers with low strikeout rates—finesse pitchers if you will—had an enormous first-time edge, far greater than that of other pitchers.

The pitchers were classified into three groups: those with fewer than 10 strikeouts per 100 batters faced during the years under study; those with more than 18 per 100 opponents; and all those in between. The following table shows the enormous disparity in the advantages for finesse pitchers and those in either of the other groups:

	First Time	Subsequent	Diff.
Low-strikeout pitchers	.237	.285	.048
Middle group	.256	.271	.016
High-strikeout pitchers	.228	.242	.014

Home run rates against the low-strikeout groups were particularly sensitive, increasing by 57 percent from one per 67 at-bats at first (literally) to one per 42 ABs after that. And as we mentioned, low-strikeout pitchers maintained their edge beyond that first plate appearance: Opponents batted .278 on their second through their fifth meetings—far better than that .237 mark in initial encounters, but still significantly below the .288 level to which they rose from the sixth meeting on.

Incidentally, there were no discernible skews based on the strikeout tendencies of batters. (Inquiring minds want to know.)

As hard as it will be for Houston to replace its bullpen, you might think that those five former Astros relievers will have even more trouble coping with life away from the Astrodome. The Astrodome's tendency to suppress scoring has been well documented in past editions of the *Analyst,* but last season Houston's pitchers benefited from their home park to an extreme degree. The Astros had the best home-game ERA in the National League (2.73) but ranked next to last in road games (4.55). Houston allowed the fewest home runs at home (47, the same as St. Louis) and by far the most on the road (83, 11 more than runner-up Pittsburgh).

But a look at pitchers who've left the Astros over the past 25 years indicates that most, surprisingly, have thrived. The following table lists all pitchers who left Houston after pitching at least 100 innings, and then pitched at least 100 innings the next year for their new teams. The startling truth: Nine of 10 had better ERAs for their new teams:

	Last Year with Astros				----Next Season----				
Pitcher	**Year**	**W**	**L**	**ERA**	**Year**	**W**	**L**	**ERA**	**Team**
Nolan Ryan	1988	12	11	3.52	1989	16	10	3.20	Tex.
Vern Ruhle	1984	1	9	4.58	1985	2	10	4.32	Clev.
Ken Forsch	1980	12	13	3.20	1981	11	7	2.88	Cal.
Floyd Bannister	1978	3	9	4.81	1979	10	15	4.05	Sea.
Jim Crawford	1975	3	5	3.63	1976	1	8	4.53	Det.
Dave Roberts	1975	8	14	4.27	1976	16	17	4.00	Det.
Jerry Reuss	1973	16	13	3.74	1974	16	11	3.50	Pitt.
Jack Billingham	1971	10	16	3.39	1972	12	12	3.18	Cin.
Mike Cuellar	1968	8	11	2.74	1969	23	11	2.38	Balt.
Don Nottebart	1965	4	15	4.67	1966	5	4	3.07	Cin.

Particularly skeptical readers might wonder (as we ourselves did) whether pitchers joining new teams off 100-inning seasons tend to improve—the rationalization being that teams generally trade pitchers coming off poor seasons, not good ones, and that pitchers coming off poor seasons tend to improve, not decline. But it proves not to be the case: Among 83 pitchers who joined new teams between 1985 and 1990 and had 100-inning seasons before and after the move, 42 had ERAs that increased, 41 had ERAs that declined.

Is it time to conclude that leaving the Astrodome has a beneficial effect on pitchers? Could it be that they're just happy to be back pitching in the great outdoors? (And then how do we account for Floyd Bannister?)

Early last summer, the Astros approached an impending problem with a novel solution. Concerned that their young catcher, Craig Biggio, would sacrifice his speed to a career of squatting behind home plate, Houston began to prepare him for a nearly unprecedented transition: Biggio began taking pregame ground balls at second base. Without question, the anticipated loss of second baseman Bill Doran (who was eventually traded to Cincinnati) served to accelerate the timetable for Biggio's move. But Houston's primary incentive was to preserve Biggio's uncatcherlike offensive skills.

By the end of the season, the proposed transition had been tabled for several reasons. Despite the addition of Rich Gedman and Alex Trevino, Houston was unable to replace Biggio adequately behind the plate. And Biggio himself, despite the supposed long-term career advantages of shedding his mask, chest protector, and shin guards, was reported to have opposed the move. But the experiment was so unconventional and it raised so many interesting issues that it's worth a closer look.

As we note in the Player Section, Biggio is one of only 12 catchers in major league history to steal 20 bases in a season; he is only the third player since 1900 to steal at least 20 bases and catch at least 100 games in two consecutive seasons. But his peculiarities as a catcher are much more broadly based than those examples of a single attribute—namely, his speed. Players throughout major league history with similar statistical profiles have played the entire range of infield and outfield positions, but few were catchers.

To identify the players most similar to Biggio, we used our own souped-up version of a method first published in *The 1986 Bill James Baseball Abstract.* James developed a series of equations to match current rookies to the past players with the most similar first-year statistics. We've tinkered with those equations and made two significant enhancements: First, we expanded the scope beyond a player's rookie season, so that stat-clones could be found at any point during a player's career. Second, we added a step to select players based not only on similar seasons, but also on comparable career profiles at the time of those seasons. (Incidentally, a player's age is one of the elements considered as a basis for likeness.) The tables below show the five players most similar to Biggio, first based only on his 1990 season, then on his career totals:

Year	Player	AB	R	H	2B	3B	HR	RBI	BB	SO	SB	BA
1990	**Craig Biggio**	555	53	153	24	2	4	42	53	79	25	.276
1976	Al Cowens	581	71	154	23	6	3	59	26	50	23	.265
1975	Dave Chalk	513	59	140	24	2	3	56	66	49	6	.273
1982	Rafael Ramirez	609	74	169	24	4	10	52	36	49	27	.278
1968	Mike Andrews	536	77	145	22	1	7	45	81	57	3	.271
1910	Rube Ellis	550	87	142	18	8	4	54	62	70	25	.258

Year	Player	AB	R	H	2B	3B	HR	RBI	BB	SO	SB	BA
1990	**Craig Biggio**	1121	131	293	51	5	20	107	109	172	52	.261
1976	Al Cowens	1178	143	310	43	15	8	126	77	124	40	.263
1975	Dave Chalk	1047	117	273	35	5	8	93	105	119	16	.261
1982	Rafael Ramirez	1081	121	280	46	7	14	83	62	129	36	.259
1968	Mike Andrews	1048	157	278	42	1	15	85	143	131	10	.265
1910	Rube Ellis	1125	163	296	28	17	7	100	116	70	41	.263

Such short lists don't prove anything, but they certainly suggest that Biggio's skills aren't position-specific: Cowens and Ellis were outfielders, Ramirez was a shortsop, Andrews was a second baseman, and Chalk was a utility infielder who played more than 100 games apiece at second, third, and short during his career. On the other hand, the most similar catcher, Johnny Edwards, ranked only 72d among all players in his similarity to Biggio. We won't waste an entire page by printing a list of the 100 players most similar to Biggio, but the next table indicates that the short lists above are typical. The primary positions of the 100 players with statistical profiles most similar to Biggio's:

C	1B	2B	3B	SS	OF
3	7	26	11	17	36

But no matter how sensible a Biggio-to-second switch seemed on that basis alone, an even more compelling reason was the consideration that as a catcher, Biggio supposedly faced a shorter and less productive career than he would have playing a physically less demanding position. Does history support this view? Are catchers' careers compromised and curtailed more often than those of players at other positions? We selected the 20 players at each position currently most similar to Biggio. The following table shows their average performances over the remainder of their careers:

Position	G	AB	R	H	2B	3B	HR	RBI	BB	SO	SB
Catchers	768	2397	255	630	103	19	28	286	227	182	23
First Basemen	637	2249	283	617	100	27	26	277	190	153	41
Second Basemen	821	2886	373	764	127	23	30	293	287	274	76
Third Basemen	971	3363	440	915	158	32	56	421	352	342	68
Shortstops	979	3206	371	810	120	24	28	287	262	310	66
Outfielders	822	2679	359	730	124	31	53	333	238	309	67

Comparable catchers had shorter careers than any other position except for first base. First basemen, of course, are expected to provide greater production than Biggio and his clones have shown; the shortfall in games played there probably reflects their teams' dissatisfaction with their performance. But the difference in future games between the highest average (979 for shortstops) and that of the catchers (768) is considerable—nearly two seasons' worth of games—suggesting that catchers' careers are at greater risk than those of other players.

But even having established that Biggio's skills are typical of infielders and outfielders, and that a switch from behind the plate would probably extend his career, there's an historical hurdle: Only one catcher in the entire history of major league baseball has made a successful transition to second base, and that was 100 years ago. Like Biggio, Tom Daly was a good-hitting, weak-armed catcher. He played for the Chicago White Stockings and the Washington Statesmen in the late 1880s, joined the Brooklyn Bridegrooms in 1890, and two years later was moved to second base. Daly was eventually considered a good fielder at that position, but as a means of compensating for his weak arm, he became known for making long throws to first base *underhanded*.

No major leaguer other than Daly has played as many as 100 games at both catcher and second base. Still, in an era when six-foot-eight point guards and 14-year-old tennis prodigies have defied the previously established rules of order, even a vacuum of 100 years means little given Biggio's talents and Houston's incentive to find him a new home (incentive that may have been lessened by his improved throwing in 1990). It's too bad the plan is on hold, at least for now.

WON-LOST RECORD BY STARTING POSITION

Houston Astros	C	1B	2B	3B	SS	LF	CF	RF	DH	P	Leadoff	Cleanup	Starts vs. LH	Starts vs. RH	Total Starts
Juan Agosto	-	-	-	-	-	-	-	-	-	-	-	-	-	-	-
Larry Andersen	-	-	-	-	-	-	-	-	-	-	-	-	-	-	-
Eric Anthony	-	-	-	-	-	4-8	-	24-32	-	-	-	-	19	49	28-40
Jeff Baldwin	-	-	-	-	-	-	-	-	-	-	-	-	-	-	-
Craig Biggio	46-55	-	-	-	-	4-6	17-17	-	-	-	1-4	-	66	79	67-78
Ken Caminiti	-	-	-	68-72	-	-	-	-	-	-	-	3-1	70	70	68-72
Casey Candaele	-	-	14-21	-	0-2	7-3	1-4	1-0	-	-	1-1	-	29	24	23-30
Jose Cano	-	-	-	-	-	-	-	-	-	-	-	-	-	-	-
Andujar Cedeno	-	-	-	-	1-1	-	-	-	-	-	-	-	1	1	1-1
Jim Clancy	-	-	-	-	-	-	-	-	-	3-7	-	-	5	5	3-7
Terry Clark	-	-	-	-	-	-	-	-	-	0-1	-	-	1	-	0-1
Danny Darwin	-	-	-	-	-	-	-	-	-	11-6	-	-	8	9	11-6
Mark Davidson	-	-	-	-	-	9-8	0-1	8-8	-	-	-	-	31	3	17-17
Glenn Davis	-	41-47	-	-	-	-	-	-	-	-	-	41-47	40	48	41-47
Jim Deshaies	-	-	-	-	-	-	-	-	-	15-19	-	-	15	19	15-19
Bill Doran	-	-	44-52	-	-	-	-	-	-	-	6-6	-	42	54	44-52
Brian Fisher	-	-	-	-	-	-	-	-	-	-	-	-	-	-	-
Rich Gedman	16-17	-	-	-	-	-	-	-	-	-	-	-	-	33	16-17
Luis Gonzalez	-	0-1	-	1-2	-	-	-	-	-	-	-	-	-	4	1-3
Bill Gullickson	-	-	-	-	-	-	-	-	-	14-18	-	-	13	19	14-18
Randy Hennis	-	-	-	-	-	-	-	-	-	1-0	-	-	1	-	1-0
Xavier Hernandez	-	-	-	-	-	-	-	-	-	0-1	-	-	-	1	0-1
Charlie Kerfeld	-	-	-	-	-	-	-	-	-	-	-	-	-	-	-
Steve Lombardozzi	-	-	-	-	-	-	-	-	-	-	-	-	-	-	-
Terry McGriff	0-1	-	-	-	-	-	-	-	-	-	-	-	-	1	0-1
Louie Meadows	-	-	-	-	-	2-1	-	-	-	-	-	-	-	3	2-1
Brian Meyer	-	-	-	-	-	-	-	-	-	-	-	-	-	-	-
Carl Nichols	6-4	1-2	-	-	-	-	-	-	-	-	-	-	13	-	7-6
Ken Oberkfell	-	3-4	2-5	6-12	-	-	-	-	-	-	-	-	1	31	11-21
Joseph Ortiz	-	-	-	-	-	6-11	-	3-1	-	-	-	-	11	10	9-12
Al Osuna	-	-	-	-	-	-	-	-	-	-	-	-	-	-	-
Mark Portugal	-	-	-	-	-	-	-	-	-	16-16	-	-	13	19	16-16
Terry Puhl	-	-	-	-	-	1-3	0-1	-	-	-	0-1	-	-	5	1-4
Rafael Ramirez	-	-	-	-	55-65	-	-	-	-	-	-	-	57	63	55-65
Karl Rhodes	-	-	-	-	-	7-6	4-5	2-0	-	-	0-4	-	2	22	13-11
David Rohde	-	-	10-7	0-1	-	-	-	-	-	-	-	-	10	8	10-8
Dan Schatzeder	-	-	-	-	-	-	-	-	-	0-2	-	-	2	-	0-2
Mike Scott	-	-	-	-	-	-	-	-	-	15-17	-	-	13	19	15-17
Mike Simms	-	1-0	-	-	-	-	-	-	-	-	-	1-0	1	-	1-0
Dave Smith	-	-	-	-	-	-	-	-	-	-	-	-	-	-	-
Franklin Stubbs	-	29-32	-	-	-	27-30	-	1-2	-	-	-	19-22	41	80	57-64
Alex Trevino	7-10	0-1	-	-	-	-	-	-	-	-	-	-	13	5	7-11
Glenn Wilson	-	-	-	-	-	6-10	-	36-43	-	-	-	11-17	49	46	42-53
Eric Yelding	-	-	5-2	-	19-19	2-1	38-38	0-1	-	-	57-56	-	63	62	64-61
Gerald Young	-	-	-	-	-	-	15-21	-	-	-	10-15	-	9	27	15-21

TEAM TOTALS: BATTING

	AB	H	2B	3B	HR	RBI	BB	SO	BA	SA	OBA
Season	5379	1301	209	32	94	536	548	997	.242	.345	.313
vs. Left-Handers	2173	549	94	14	37	225	210	349	.253	.360	.318
vs. Right-Handers	3206	752	115	18	57	311	338	648	.235	.335	.310
vs. Ground-Ballers	2911	693	113	18	46	264	276	490	.238	.337	.305
vs. Fly-Ballers	2468	608	96	14	48	272	272	507	.246	.355	.322
Home Games	2637	654	109	23	35	276	286	471	.248	.347	.323
Road Games	2742	647	100	9	59	260	262	526	.236	.344	.303
Grass Fields	1644	408	56	7	38	172	161	298	.248	.360	.316
Artificial Turf	3735	893	153	25	56	364	387	699	.239	.338	.312
April	636	156	24	3	14	65	53	128	.245	.358	.307
May	969	242	29	2	18	105	91	160	.250	.340	.315
June	905	208	35	5	25	93	103	188	.230	.362	.307
July	944	240	41	7	10	96	97	194	.254	.344	.322
August	871	207	40	6	12	81	87	140	.238	.339	.306
Sept./Oct.	1054	248	40	9	15	96	117	187	.235	.333	.317
Leading Off Inn.	1340	327	46	6	20	20	117	236	.244	.332	.308
Bases Empty	3130	742	120	18	54	54	287	606	.237	.339	.303
Runners On	2249	559	89	14	40	482	261	391	.249	.354	.326
Runners/Scor. Pos.	1339	324	43	9	27	425	194	278	.242	.348	.333
Runners On/2 Out	945	215	29	3	19	187	134	176	.228	.325	.328
Scor. Pos./2 Out	641	139	20	2	13	167	106	135	.217	.315	.332
Late-Inning Pressure	905	218	30	7	15	92	117	183	.241	.339	.329
Leading Off	236	62	11	3	4	4	24	48	.263	.386	.333
Runners On	399	91	15	3	4	81	54	78	.228	.311	.321
Runners/Scor. Pos.	234	58	4	2	3	70	43	56	.248	.321	.360

RUNS BATTED IN	From 1B	From 2B	From 3B	Scoring Position
Totals	71/1582	171/1079	200/532	371/1611
Percentage	4.5%	15.8%	37.6%	23.0%

TEAM TOTALS: PITCHING

	W-L	ERA	AB	H	HR	BB	SO	BA	SA	OBA
Season	75-87	3.61	5481	1396	130	496	854	.255	.382	.318
vs. Left-Handers			2630	709	51	270	369	.270	.384	.339
vs. Right-Handers			2851	687	79	226	485	.241	.381	.297
vs. Ground-Ballers			2644	672	45	225	434	.254	.364	.316
vs. Fly-Ballers			2837	724	85	271	420	.255	.399	.319
Home Games	49-32	2.73	2777	660	47	229	482	.238	.342	.296
Road Games	26-55	4.55	2704	736	83	267	372	.272	.424	.340
Grass Fields	17-31	4.59	1638	451	54	136	224	.275	.428	.332
Artificial Turf	58-56	3.21	3843	945	76	360	630	.246	.363	.311
April	9-10	2.91	639	151	9	62	112	.236	.341	.306
May	11-17	4.17	977	268	22	87	124	.274	.415	.332
June	12-16	3.80	950	253	26	88	155	.266	.396	.332
July	11-18	4.70	969	260	32	89	168	.268	.421	.330
August	16-11	2.88	926	232	17	63	142	.251	.364	.298
Sept./Oct.	16-15	3.01	1020	232	24	107	153	.227	.344	.304
Leading Off Inn.			1347	336	34	102	221	.249	.380	.306
Bases Empty			3172	808	80	253	495	.255	.385	.313
Runners On			2309	588	50	243	359	.255	.378	.323
Runners/Scor. Pos.			1365	344	33	186	232	.252	.385	.334
Runners On/2 Out			996	222	19	121	172	.223	.331	.314
Scor. Pos./2 Out			668	147	13	94	124	.220	.329	.324
Late-Inning Pressure			877	215	20	95	158	.245	.358	.322
Leading Off			228	56	4	20	45	.246	.320	.312
Runners On			352	81	8	46	68	.230	.349	.320
Runners/Scor. Pos.			201	38	5	37	41	.189	.313	.312
First 9 Batters			2925	728	54	262	516	.249	.360	.311
Second 9 Batters			1371	339	36	122	196	.247	.381	.312
All Batters Thereafter			1185	329	40	112	142	.278	.438	.340

LOS ANGELES DODGERS

- **Rebuilding a Straw Man.**
- **Did the short spring cause injuries?**

Give the Dodgers credit. For years, Brooklyn's baseball refugees drooled Dodger blue at the thought of poaching another of New York's plums—an underappreciated outfielder named Strawberry. Finally given that opportunity last November, the Dodgers wasted no time in signing the best ballplayer to reach the free-agent market in his prime in the 10 years since George Steinbrenner (to his everlasting credit and chagrin) swathed Dave Winfield in pinstripes.

And give New York credit. The Big Apple didn't break down or back down. True to eight years of insult and abuse, the entire community, it seemed, rose up to salute Strawberry with one final raspberry upon hearing that he was leaving on the first plane west. Local talk shows were deluged by an endless flow of unsubstantiated slurs about the Straw Man's playing ability, work ethic, lack of motivation, and character. The litany included: He wouldn't play hurt; he wouldn't take treatment for his injuries; he's drinking again; he never fulfilled his potential. The unanimity left one wondering how such an unqualified twit ever stayed on a major-league roster in the first place.

But fortunately for Strawberry, he hasn't been playing on Pluto for the past eight years (one of the few transgressions he *wasn't* accused of). As a result, he's left behind a few statistical clues that illustrate his true abilities more objectively and accurately than the blatherings of a bunch of call-in show blowhards. The time has come to set the record straight on the five most common myths about Strawberry.

He hasn't fulfilled his potential.

A look at the record shows that during his first eight seasons in the majors, Strawberry hit 252 home runs, the highest total in the majors during that time. He hit two more than Dale Murphy, and 38 more (in other words, a full season's worth) than any other player. Eddie Murray (214), Andre Dawson (213), Jesse Barfield (202), and Tom Brunansky (201) are the only others with even 200 during that period.

Strawberry drove in 733 runs to rank eighth since 1983, a somewhat deceiving rank in that he trails fifth-place Dave Parker by only 12. (And, for what it's worth, this is an appropriate opportunity to point out that Strawberry spotted the rest of the group about a month, since he spent the first five weeks of the 1983 season at Tidewater.)

Strawberry's slugging average of .520 ranks second among players with at least 2500 at-bats during his tenure with the Mets; only Eric Davis compiled a higher mark (.522). Straw outslugged Mike Schmidt by eight points, Jose Canseco by 10, and crosstown icon Don Mattingly by 15 points. No wonder Mattingly himself urged the Yankees to make a strong bid to put Strawberry alongside him in the Yankees clubhouse.

Now, in an era where everyone is club crazy (20/20, 30/30, 30/50, .300/300, whatever), try this one on for size: Strawberry has hit 252 home runs and stolen 191 bases. During those same eight seasons, only four other players attained even the 150 level in both categories: Ryne Sandberg, Eric Davis, Kirk Gibson, and Howard Johnson. Only Straw reached 175 in both, and he exceeded that figure substantially.

It's important to bear in mind that these weren't eight great seasons hand-picked from Strawberry's prime. They were his *first* eight seasons, a period of development for any young player, be it Strawberry, Throneberry, or Ruthberry, incorporating all the errors along the learning curve. (And for those who think that Strawberry is simply a natural talent but is beyond learning his trade, consider this evidence to the contrary: He struck out once every 4.2 plate appearances over his first four seasons, but once per 5.3 PAs over the last four years—a noteworthy decrease of 19 percent.)

Strawberry's first eight seasons look good on any basis. Compared to the same period in other careers, his accomplishments really sparkle. Strawberry has hit more than 25 home runs in every season of his major-league career, the longest start-of-career streak in major-league history. That's right, even longer than the all-time home-run king, Hank Aaron. Frank Robinson came closest; his streak was snapped at seven years. And only one player besides Robinson in the entire history of major-league baseball had a streak more than half as long as Strawberry's: Joe DiMaggio (six). For the benefit of the loophole-minded among us, we must point out that crumbs of seasons prior to each player's true rookie year haven't even been considered. (For example, Mark McGwire's current four-year streak discounts his three home runs in 18 games in 1986, prior to his record-breaking 1987 rookie season.)

By the way, should Strawberry exceed 25 home runs in each season for the life of his new contract, he would equal the longest streak ever *at any point in a player's career*, established by Mays from 1954 through 1966.

(The recently passed Truth in Statistics Act requires us to divulge the following information: Eddie Mathews hit exactly 25 home runs as a rookie in 1952, his first of 11 consecutive seasons of 25 or more. If it makes you feel better to include Mathews, go right ahead. Then Strawberry isn't the first player to manifest his power to such a consistent degree right out of the gate. He's the second.)

Which players had the most similar statistical profiles to Strawberry's at similar stages of their careers? Try these:

Player	After	AB	R	H	2B	3B	HR	RBI	BB	BA
Darryl Strawberry	1990	3903	662	1025	187	30	252	733	580	.263
Reggie Jackson	1974	3757	623	1004	181	23	218	629	533	.267
Willie McCovey	1968	3958	659	1100	151	36	268	733	551	.278
Harmon Killebrew	1965	3828	651	998	131	13	297	745	634	.261
Mike Schmidt	1979	3713	674	947	183	31	235	666	689	.255

Strawberry hasn't fulfilled his potential? He's clearly on the fast track to Cooperstown. Makes you wonder what anyone was expecting of him in the first place.

Strawberry can't hit left-handers.

It's true that Strawberry often looks overmatched against left-handers. He sometimes looks overmatched against right-handers too. That's irrelevant, unless baseball suddenly forsakes the scoreboard and adopts scoring procedures similar to those of international figure skating. Strawberry hits far better against right-handers than against southpaws, without a doubt. But the man can flat-out hit left-handers.

Would it surprise you to discover that Strawberry has hit more home runs against left-handers since 1983 than Andre Dawson, who ranked 11th in the majors with 63? Actually, he even hit more than Dave Winfield, who ranked eighth. Surely you'd expect that George Bell hit more than Strawberry, especially considering that Bell ranked fourth since 1983 with 74 HRs vs. lefties. But no, Strawberry hit more than Bell as well—more, in fact, than any other player, right-handed or otherwise, with the exception of Dale Murphy. Murphy led the majors with 81 home runs against southpaws; Strawberry hit 80—over 50 percent more than any other left-handed hitter during that period. (Runner-up lefty George Brett hit 53.)

Back in 1988, Strawberry actually hit 20 home runs off southpaws (one more than he hit against righties). Such records unfortunately don't exist prior to 1975, but in the 16 years since then, only Cecil Fielder has hit more than 20 homers off left-handers in a single season. Was 1988 a fluke? Nope. He hit 16 against southpaws in 1987.

To the extent that Strawberry's alleged inability to hit left-handers is fact-based (and, frankly, that's a very limited extent), detractors cite his low career batting average vs. southpaws (.236). Fine, we'll take it, along with the strikeouts; the whole package still adds up to a pretty dangerous hitter, especially considering his truly awesome performance against right-handers (35 HRs, 98 RBIs, 88 BBs and a .278 batting average per 500 at-bats).

The batting average issue is one often used to discredit Strawberry, not only against left-handers but overall as well. Granted, Strawberry has a mediocre career mark (.263). But he has also averaged 73 walks per season, a significant ballast to any criticism of his batting average. The bottom line: 179 players had at least 2500 plate appearances from 1983 through 1990. Strawberry's on-base average, which factors in his walks, ranks 30th among that group. If that's the weakest link, Strawberry's chain is pretty strong.

Strawberry is inconsistent.

This one's a beauty. There's an entire radio station in New York City devoted to this particular subject. Inconsistency means different things to different people, but the "I" word has been draped around Straw's neck like an albatross throughout his career.

Guys and gals, wake up. Strawberry's average annual production (31.5 home runs, 91.6 runs batted in per season) does not demand that he produce 1.21 home runs and 3.52 RBIs in each of the 26 weeks that make up a baseball season. Every player goes into streaks and slumps, Strawberry included, but it's bottom-line, year-end totals that determine whether a player is consistent or not, not those little 3-for-22 or 9-for-19 snippets of a season. And when it comes to bottom-line numbers, few can stand toe-to-toe with the man who never met a barber he didn't like.

We did a little test to determine the consistency of Darryl's year-to-year production compared to that of other veteran players. There are 30 other players who, like Strawberry, had at least 400 at-bats in every season from 1983 through 1990. We looked at how much year-to-year variance there was in their batting and slugging averages and compared that variance with Strawberry's.

Some of you may be familiar with the statistical tool that measures such things: standard deviation. To those who are unfamiliar, don't let it throw you. It simply measures how far each of a group of numbers strays from the average of those numbers. In Strawberry's case, his collective batting average over the eight-year period was .263, and his yearly marks in that category averaged a deviation of 18 batting-average points (.018) from that .263 average.

How does that deviation compare with the 30 other guys? Would it surprise you to know that only seven players had less annual variance in their batting averages than Strawberry? They were Tom Brunansky, Harold Baines, Johnny Ray, Brett Butler, Julio Franco, Kent Hrbek, and Ozzie Smith. The other 23 players had more year-to-year inconsistency in their batting averages than Strawberry did; among those with far greater standard deviations than Darryl were Dwight Evans, Wade Boggs, Eddie Murray, Cal Ripken, Steve Sax, Tim Wallach, and Alan Trammell.

Taking note that Darryl is a power hitter, we repeated the test for slugging percentage. The results were much the same: Nine players showed more consistency, 21 showed less.

Does this means that Darryl hits a home run a week, or that he comes through every time in the clutch? Of course not. Darryl has failed plenty, sometimes in important situations, and sometimes those failures have resulted in a loss for his team. But too often, the tendency is to judge modern players by a different, more critical standard than we applied to their predecessors. You can spend hours marveling at Lou Gehrig's numbers in *The Baseball Encyclopedia* and walk away (or turn to Dick Gernert's page, depending on the depth of your devotion) with the feeling that Gehrig came through in the clutch every time—a flame that is fanned by various myths about the Iron Horse. But let's be logical: *No one comes through every time.* It's just that we see Gehrig's accomplishments only after they've been reduced to a single line of type in a book; Darryl's failures are there in color every night, live and on replay. And if you miss them, they're repeated on the "Late Sports Wrap."

Want to judge consistency? Just look at the numbers, baby.

Strawberry doesn't produce in the heat of a pennant race.

Once again, look at the record. The following table shows Strawberry's performance in regular-season September and October games for those seasons in which the Mets were involved in a pennant race. (We've excluded 1983, when the Mets weren't contenders, and 1986 and 1988, when the Mets had already built insurmountable leads by the end of August). As it worked out, the Mets played a total of 164 games in September and October of those seasons, so you might want to think of Strawberry's totals as those for a single full season. And what a season that would have been! Did someone mention MVP?

Year	G	AB	R	H	2B	3B	HR	RBI	BB	SB	BA
1984	27	92	19	25	4	2	9	30	12	3	.272
1985	31	131	21	31	6	1	8	22	21	5	.237
1987	28	106	25	34	10	0	8	28	16	13	.321
1989	19	79	8	15	2	0	2	8	9	0	.190
1990	26	100	17	27	5	0	8	23	6	0	.270
Totals	131	474	91	132	27	3	35	111	64	21	.278

Strawberry is a lousy fielder.

Actually, this one is true. So?

Well, that's it. Was Strawberry worth the money? You make the call. Frank Cashen and the Mets decided he was not—above all, a business decision based not only on his playing ability but on many other factors as well. For all we know, Cashen might have kept Strawberry on his fantasy-league team, where he can overlook the unattractive baggage that comes along with the package: scrapes with the law, a bout of substance abuse, and a penchant for rubbing some teammates the wrong way. Still, as closely as baseball and its players are reported, how many players have a clean slate? You just won't see many Christy Mathewsons anymore. And frankly, it's interesting to speculate how even Matty himself might have reacted to life in a fishbowl, with more money to his name at age 26—even in 1906 dollars—than he'd ever dreamed of. Strawberry's no angel, but he plays baseball like he's out of this world.

The injury that wiped out Orel Hershiser's 1990 season prompted widespread criticism of a schedule that provided little preparation time for opening day in the wake of last spring's lockout. Critics suggested that the owners, in their haste to construct a schedule of 162 games despite losing a week, had failed to anticipate the number of injuries that could occur, particularly to pitchers, on account of this expedited training period. Some criticism came immediately, but the chant grew in intensity when starting pitchers like Scott Bankhead, John Dopson, Danny Jackson, and Pascual Perez were placed on the disabled list before the season was even a month old. The loss of Hershiser for the entire season raised the chorus to its highest level. But did anyone bother to check whether the incidence of injuries had actually increased?

CBS broadcaster Jim Kaat, whose 25-year pitching career and successful stint as Reds pitching coach qualify him as something of an expert on how to keep a pitcher's arm sound, asked us early in the season to check those numbers. They told an interesting story that, in the wake of Hershiser's injury, has remained largely untold. The figures showed 14 fewer players on the disabled list on opening day of 1990 than a year earlier. By the end of the month, the total remained lower than at the corresponding point in 1989, and that trend continued throughout the season. The number of players on the disabled list at various times in each of the past three seasons:

	1990 Season			1989 Season			1988 Season		
	All	Bat.	Pit.	All	Bat.	Pit.	All	Bat.	Pit.
Any time	229	117	112	263	145	118	234	118	116
Opening day	45	16	29	59	29	30	43	21	22
End of April	65	26	39	72	35	37	55	24	31

We don't pretend to understand the level of preparation needed to tune an athlete's body for the rigors of six months of baseball. (We needed the family-sized tube of Ben-Gay simply to deal with the soreness from all the channel switching last summer—CBS, ESPN, TBS, WGN, WWOR, and so on.) Nor can we, or even Orel himself for that matter, say for sure that given a full seven-week training regimen Hershiser might not have won 20 games last season. But the longer you study the numbers above, the harder it is to accept the claim that the shortened spring training was responsible for more injuries than would have occurred under normal conditions.

WON-LOST RECORD BY STARTING POSITION

Los Angeles Dodgers	C	1B	2B	3B	SS	LF	CF	RF	DH	P	Leadoff	Cleanup	Starts vs. LH	Starts vs. RH	Total Starts
Don Aase	-	-	-	-	-	-	-	-	-	-	-	-	-	-	-
Tim Belcher	-	-	-	-	-	-	-	-	-	12-12	-	-	7	17	12-12
Hubie Brooks	-	-	-	-	-	-	-	79-71	-	-	-	4-5	55	95	79-71
Dennis Cook	-	-	-	-	-	-	-	-	-	1-2	-	-	-	3	1-2
Tim Crews	-	-	-	-	-	-	-	-	-	1-1	-	-	2	-	1-1
Kal Daniels	-	-	-	-	-	68-58	-	-	-	-	-	2-0	37	89	68-58
Rick Dempsey	13-20	-	-	-	-	-	-	-	-	-	-	-	30	3	13-20
Darrin Fletcher	-	-	-	-	-	-	-	-	-	-	-	-	-	-	-
Kirk Gibson	-	-	-	-	-	4-7	37-32	-	-	-	-	-	18	62	41-39
Jose Gonzalez	-	-	-	-	-	4-2	5-3	0-1	-	-	4-2	-	14	1	9-6
Jim Gott	-	-	-	-	-	-	-	-	-	-	-	-	-	-	-
Alfredo Griffin	-	-	-	-	70-66	-	-	-	-	-	-	-	49	87	70-66
Chris Gwynn	-	-	-	-	-	7-4	2-2	3-0	-	-	-	-	-	18	12-6
Jeff Hamilton	-	-	-	3-3	-	-	-	-	-	-	-	-	2	4	3-3
Dave Hansen	-	-	-	0-1	-	-	-	-	-	-	-	-	-	1	0-1
Lenny Harris	-	-	16-13	38-36	-	-	-	-	-	-	44-36	-	2	101	54-49
Mike Hartley	-	-	-	-	-	-	-	-	-	3-3	-	-	2	4	3-3
Mickey Hatcher	-	2-4	-	4-2	-	2-5	-	-	-	-	-	0-1	17	2	8-11
Carlos Hernandez	3-2	-	-	-	-	-	-	-	-	-	-	-	3	2	3-2
Orel Hershiser	-	-	-	-	-	-	-	-	-	2-2	-	-	1	3	2-2
Darren Holmes	-	-	-	-	-	-	-	-	-	-	-	-	-	-	-
Jay Howell	-	-	-	-	-	-	-	-	-	-	-	-	-	-	-
Stan Javier	-	-	-	-	-	1-0	28-22	4-3	-	-	15-11	-	27	31	33-25
Luis Lopez	-	-	-	-	-	-	-	-	-	-	-	-	-	-	-
Barry Lyons	-	-	-	-	-	-	-	-	-	-	-	-	-	-	-
Mike Maddux	-	-	-	-	-	-	-	-	-	1-1	-	-	-	2	1-1
Ramon Martinez	-	-	-	-	-	-	-	-	-	22-11	-	-	12	21	22-11
Mike Morgan	-	-	-	-	-	-	-	-	-	16-17	-	-	16	17	16-17
Mike Munoz	-	-	-	-	-	-	-	-	-	-	-	-	-	-	-
Eddie Murray	-	80-70	-	-	-	-	-	-	-	-	-	80-70	50	100	80-70
Jim Neidlinger	-	-	-	-	-	-	-	-	-	8-4	-	-	2	10	8-4
Jose Offerman	-	-	-	-	7-6	-	-	-	-	-	2-1	-	4	9	7-6
Pat Perry	-	-	-	-	-	-	-	-	-	-	-	-	-	-	-
Jim Poole	-	-	-	-	-	-	-	-	-	-	-	-	-	-	-
Willie Randolph	-	-	11-15	-	-	-	-	-	-	-	-	-	10	16	11-15
Juan Samuel	-	-	55-46	-	-	-	14-17	-	-	-	17-21	-	49	83	69-63
Mike Scioscia	70-54	-	-	-	-	-	-	-	-	-	-	-	23	101	70-54
Ray Searage	-	-	-	-	-	-	-	-	-	-	-	-	-	-	-
Mike Sharperson	-	4-1	4-1	41-34	4-2	-	-	-	-	-	4-5	-	54	37	53-38
John Shelby	-	-	-	-	-	-	-	0-1	-	-	-	-	1	-	0-1
Brian Traxler	-	0-1	-	-	-	-	-	-	-	-	-	-	-	1	0-1
Fernando Valenzuela	-	-	-	-	-	-	-	-	-	16-17	-	-	10	23	16-17
Jose Vizcaino	-	-	0-1	-	5-2	-	-	-	-	-	-	-	3	5	5-3
Dave Walsh	-	-	-	-	-	-	-	-	-	-	-	-	-	-	-
Terry Wells	-	-	-	-	-	-	-	-	-	3-2	-	-	1	4	3-2
John Wetteland	-	-	-	-	-	-	-	-	-	1-4	-	-	3	2	1-4

TEAM TOTALS: BATTING

	AB	H	2B	3B	HR	RBI	BB	SO	BA	SA	OBA
Season	5491	1436	222	27	129	669	538	952	.262	.382	.328
vs. Left-Handers	2048	528	73	9	45	251	207	359	.258	.368	.329
vs. Right-Handers	3443	908	149	18	84	418	331	593	.264	.391	.328
vs. Ground-Ballers	2804	755	108	10	65	352	276	467	.269	.384	.335
vs. Fly-Ballers	2687	681	114	17	64	317	262	485	.253	.380	.321
Home Games	2695	707	96	14	54	321	276	452	.262	.368	.331
Road Games	2796	729	126	13	75	348	262	500	.261	.396	.326
Grass Fields	4039	1057	149	16	92	489	407	705	.262	.375	.329
Artificial Turf	1452	379	73	11	37	180	131	247	.261	.403	.325
April	687	173	26	3	13	72	67	106	.252	.355	.317
May	923	252	37	9	23	118	74	170	.273	.407	.331
June	877	214	31	4	21	98	79	167	.244	.360	.305
July	921	253	47	3	18	117	96	143	.275	.391	.343
August	1017	256	32	4	26	120	113	198	.252	.368	.328
Sept./Oct.	1066	288	49	4	28	144	109	168	.270	.402	.339
Leading Off Inn.	1338	351	65	11	31	31	101	207	.262	.397	.318
Bases Empty	3154	800	146	14	73	73	252	550	.254	.378	.312
Runners On	2337	636	76	13	56	596	286	402	.272	.388	.349
Runners/Scor. Pos.	1365	363	48	9	32	536	211	258	.266	.385	.358
Runners On/2 Out	988	246	30	6	18	229	147	206	.249	.346	.351
Scor. Pos./2 Out	659	161	23	6	13	215	113	150	.244	.357	.361
Late-Inning Pressure	690	178	28	3	16	79	80	135	.258	.377	.339
Leading Off	178	40	6	1	5	5	11	39	.225	.354	.281
Runners On	291	78	11	1	5	68	42	51	.268	.364	.357
Runners/Scor. Pos.	175	39	8	0	3	62	34	36	.223	.320	.341

RUNS BATTED IN	From 1B	From 2B	From 3B	Scoring Position
Totals	75/1713	194/1058	271/625	465/1683
Percentage	4.4%	18.3%	43.4%	27.6%

TEAM TOTALS: PITCHING

	W-L	ERA	AB	H	HR	BB	SO	BA	SA	OBA
Season	86-76	3.72	5477	1364	137	478	1021	.249	.378	.310
vs. Left-Handers			2632	681	55	247	475	.259	.378	.324
vs. Right-Handers			2845	683	82	231	546	.240	.377	.298
vs. Ground-Ballers			2460	596	37	181	466	.242	.339	.295
vs. Fly-Ballers			3017	768	100	297	555	.255	.409	.322
Home Games	47-34	3.27	2804	675	73	232	541	.241	.361	.299
Road Games	39-42	4.20	2673	689	64	246	480	.258	.395	.322
Grass Fields	66-54	3.45	4097	1008	103	344	758	.246	.370	.305
Artificial Turf	20-22	4.53	1380	356	34	134	263	.258	.401	.325
April	11-10	3.42	702	172	17	41	135	.245	.356	.288
May	14-13	4.45	919	249	21	89	177	.271	.407	.337
June	11-15	3.66	896	223	28	85	192	.249	.396	.318
July	16-11	3.24	889	201	20	87	161	.226	.351	.293
August	18-12	2.89	996	236	20	79	176	.237	.340	.295
Sept./Oct.	16-15	4.58	1075	283	31	97	180	.263	.407	.324
Leading Off Inn.			1344	322	36	91	252	.240	.372	.292
Bases Empty			3246	760	79	237	644	.234	.355	.290
Runners On			2231	604	58	241	377	.271	.411	.339
Runners/Scor. Pos.			1287	323	31	183	253	.251	.386	.338
Runners On/2 Out			964	235	19	114	192	.244	.363	.326
Scor. Pos./2 Out			622	135	13	98	140	.217	.338	.325
Late-Inning Pressure			796	197	18	80	143	.247	.353	.321
Leading Off			199	43	6	15	30	.216	.322	.278
Runners On			334	86	6	43	58	.257	.356	.346
Runners/Scor. Pos.			196	49	5	31	40	.250	.357	.353
First 9 Batters			2870	651	68	268	599	.227	.345	.295
Second 9 Batters			1350	369	33	105	232	.273	.408	.326
All Batters Thereafter			1257	344	36	105	190	.274	.420	.330

MONTREAL EXPOS

- **Opposite-field hitting—a closer look.**
- **Delineating Delino.**

One of the most misunderstood aspects of baseball is hitting to the opposite field, an insider's topic that even a casual fan can appreciate. What baseball fan hasn't admired the ability of great left-handed hitters like Wade Boggs, Don Mattingly, Keith Hernandez, and Tony Gwynn to protect the outside of the plate with two strikes and stroke clean singles to left field? And who hasn't heard of a manager or a hitting instructor encouraging his students to "go with the pitch"? But the appeal of opposite-field hitting has created a nearly universal but nevertheless mistaken impression that most players hit better to the opposite field than to the pull field. In fact, the opposite is true.

Here are some general rules based on a study of the 1990 season: Most players hit far better when they pull the ball than when they go the other way. Ground-ball hitters and left-handed hitters are more likely than their counterparts to hit well to the opposite field.

Last season, 84 different players accumulated at least 400 at-bats on balls put in play—a total that excludes strikeouts. Switch hitters were excluded unless they had 400 ABs from one side of the plate or the other; in that case, only those at-bats were included. Another ground rule: Outs hit to the catcher, pitcher, or center fielder and hits to straightaway center were assigned to neither the player's pull- nor opposite-field statistics. Only 13 of those 84 players had higher batting averages to the opposite field than to the pull field; for all but four of those, the margin was less than 30 points (G/A below is ground outs-to-air outs ratio):

Bats	G/A	Player	Opp. Field	Pull Field	Diff.
R	1.95	Tony Pena	.324	.232	.092
L	1.16	Wade Boggs	.326	.283	.043
L	1.42	Jim Eisenreich	.298	.256	.042
L	1.81	Lenny Harris	.314	.284	.030
L	1.27	Robin Ventura	.268	.240	.028
R	0.99	Todd Zeile	.306	.288	.018
L	1.55	Brett Butler	.322	.305	.017
L	1.78	Delino DeShields	.329	.314	.015
R	1.23	Hubie Brooks	.323	.313	.010
L	1.72	Steve Finley	.287	.278	.009
L	1.14	B.J. Surhoff	.293	.284	.009
R	2.03	Kirby Puckett	.315	.308	.007
R	1.11	Chris James	.306	.304	.002

Although only four players hit at least 30 points higher to the opposite field, 23 hit more than 100 points higher to the pull field—including four (all right-handed fly-ball hitters) with margins greater than 200 points:

Bats	G/A	Player	Opp. Field	Pull Field	Diff.
R	0.59	Mark McGwire	.122	.411	.289
R	0.60	Kevin McReynolds	.157	.397	.240
R	0.61	George Bell	.164	.402	.238
R	0.69	Tom Brunansky	.159	.384	.225

As we mentioned, two classifications of hitters produced noteworthy skews. Right-handed hitters tended to be dominant pull hitters, while left-handers were more likely to hit well to the opposite field. And ground-ball hitters were far more likely to excel at opposite-field hitting than were fly-ball hitters. The following table shows the evidence for left- and right-handed batters; while 8 of the 13 players who hit better to the opposite field were left-handed hitters, 49 of 71 who were better as pull hitters were righties:

	LHB	RHB
100+ points better to pull field	5	18
50–100 pts. better to pull field	8	16
0–50 points better to pull field	9	15
Better to the opposite field	8	5

On average, the left-handers hit 44 points better to the pull field (.329) than to the opposite field (.285). The marginwas more than twice as large for right-handed hitters; right-handers hit .338 pulling the ball, 90 points higher than their .258 going the other way.

The corresponding figures for ground-ball and fly-ball hitters were even more divergent. Groundballers hit 37 points better to the pull field (.316) than to the opposite field (.279), while the margin for fly-ballers was 98 points (.353 pulling the ball, .255 going the other way). For simplicity's sake, players with ground outs-to-air outs ratios above 1.00 were considered ground-ball hitters (GBH); players below that mark were fly-ballers (FBH):

	GBH	FBH
100+ points better to pull field	6	17
50–100 pts. better to pull field	11	13
0–50 points better to pull field	14	10
Better to the opposite field	12	1

The only fly-ball hitter with a higher batting average to the opposite field was Todd Zeile. The opposite-field hitters' composite G/A ratio was 1.47, compared to 1.08 for the entire sample of 84 players, a disparity that would occur by chance only once in a quarter of a million chances. We're convinced: Ground-ball hitters comprise the group most likely to excel at opposite-field hitting.

Furthermore, if we divide the 84 qualifiers into four equal groups based on their ground-ball/fly-ball tendencies, we can see that the higher a player's ground-ball rate, the more likely he is to be an opposite-field hitter:

	Better to Opp. Field	Better to Pull Field
Extreme FBH (0.59–0.86)	0	21
Moderate FBH (0.87–1.00)	1	20
Moderate GBH (1.02–1.21)	3	18
Extreme GBH (1.21–2.03)	9	12

This study represents ground-breaking research; no one has previously published statistical evidence of the considerable overlap between successful opposite-field hitters and ground-ball hitters. We have also established that the relationship forms a continuum: The more extreme a player's tendency to hit ground balls, the greater should be his success hitting to the opposite field. And surely few would have expected such a distinct league-wide tendency to hit better to the pull field than going the other way. On the other hand, this is a relationship that most baseball fans can instinctively understand. Doesn't a ball hit to the opposite field often represent a "victory" for the pitcher, when the batter is fooled and hits the ball weakly to the opposite field? And isn't that particularly true for power-hitting, right-handed fly-ball hitters, like Gary Carter, Mark McGwire, or Joe Carter, who look to drive the ball to the pull field even when behind in the count? Contact hitters are more likely to submit to the realities of a two-strike pitch and be ready to stroke the ball the other way, so fewer of their opposite-field at-bats represent pitches on which they were fooled.

Setting aside the question of improvement, who were the best opposite-field hitters in baseball last year? The following were the top 10 batting averages among the group of 84:

George Brett	.348
Alan Trammell	.331
Rafael Palmeiro	.329
Delino DeShields	.329
Roberto Kelly	.327
Gary Sheffield	.327
Wade Boggs	.326
Paul O'Neill	.325
Tony Pena	.324
Hubie Brooks	.323

So the next time you watch Wade Boggs or George Brett spank a single to left field, feel free to admire his talent and recognize what an important talent it is. And the next time you see a Mark McGwire or Kevin McReynolds hit a weak fly to right, ask yourself just how much he's giving up with his single-minded determination to pull.

For years, it seemed that Montreal was fighting a losing battle in the war to keep its players happy in Quebec. Over a five-year period from 1984 through 1989, the Expos watched Gary Carter, Andre Dawson, Hubie Brooks, Pascual Perez, Bryn Smith, and Mark Langston leave for the land of the free and the home of the Braves. But the events of the past off-season proved that Montreal has plenty of company when it comes to losing key players. As we detailed in the San Francisco Giants essay, more major contributors changed uniforms over the past off-season than during the previous four winters combined.

Surprisingly, the Expos were among the few teams left intact after the smoke cleared. Except for a swap of Tim Raines to the White Sox for Ivan Calderon (in which the Expos also added middle reliever Barry Jones), Montreal should field the same team in 1991 that closed the 1990 season. We won't know for several years whether that pause signals the end of the mass exodus from Montreal, or if it represents simply a futile finger in the dike. Regardless, it provides us with an opportunity to note that the Expos organization has continued to provide enough talent to keep a winning team on the field despite that one-way flow of talent through baseball's underground railroad.

Only four other teams have played .500 or better in each of the last four seasons: New York and San Francisco in the National League, and Oakland and Toronto in the American League. Last season was typical: The Expos were expected to crumble after losing Brooks and the three starting pitchers mentioned above to free agency, but they remained in the hunt for a division title until the final two weeks, posting a final mark of 85–77. And they emerged from the season with several of baseball's most productive rookies: Delino DeShields, Larry Walker, and Marquis Grissom.

None of those players seriously challenged Atlanta's David Justice for the league's rookie-of-the-year award. But our system of rookie projections indicates that two of the three have some star potential. We won't keep you guessing: Ironically, it appears that Grissom, whose quick rise from college baseball to the National League had fantasy-league owners drooling last spring, will soon take a backseat to his teammates.

We've written often in the past about the difficulty of selecting from among a group of solid rookies the few who are to become stars. Even superstars like Joe Morgan and Dale Murphy were overshadowed as rookies by freshman teammates Sonny Jackson and Bob Horner. Just for fun, we'd like to present what might be a better method for divining the future career tracks of each season's rookies. The method involves finding 40 players throughout major league history with the most similar statistical profiles during their rookie seasons, and using their careers as a guide to the current rookie's future potential. Stat-clones contribute to a rookie's projected profile in proportion to the similarity between their own rookie seasons and that of the current player in question. The degree of similarity is based on a complex series of equations, but can be demonstrated better through an example.

The table below includes the three players with rookie seasons judged to be most similar to DeShields's, along with the three least similar players among the top 40. The shades of difference between Burns, Lansford, and Carew are insignificant, as are those among Guillen, Meusel, and Rowell. And while the rookie seasons of the latter group bears considerable similarity to that of DeShields, the former group is clearly *more* similar; for that reason, they will contribute more heavily to the end product—a projection of DeShields's career:

Year	Player	G	AB	R	H	2B	3B	HR	RBI	BB	SO	SB	BA
1990	**Delino DeShields**	129	499	69	144	28	6	4	45	66	96	42	.289
1914	George Burns	137	478	55	139	22	5	5	57	32	56	23	.291
1978	Carney Lansford	121	453	63	133	23	2	8	52	31	67	20	.294
1967	Rod Carew	137	514	66	150	22	7	8	51	37	91	5	.292
1985	Ozzie Guillen	150	491	71	134	21	9	1	33	12	36	7	.273
1918	Irish Meusel	124	473	48	132	25	6	4	62	30	21	18	.279
1940	Bama Rowell	130	486	46	148	19	8	3	58	18	22	12	.305

Generally, no single player accounts for more than 5 percent of any rookie's projection. In the case above, Burns contributes 4.9 percent of the DeShields projection pie, Lansford 3.6 percent, and Carew 3.5 percent. By comparison, Guillen, Meusel, and Rowell will combine for less than 3 percent.

Based on that method, the following career totals are projected for Montreal's three rookies and some of last season's other leading first-year players:

Player	G	AB	R	H	2B	3B	HR	RBI	BB	SO	SB	BA
Alomar	960	3281	443	929	160	30	66	439	289	329	45	.283
DeShields	1230	4506	656	1315	220	50	56	522	440	408	169	.292
Grissom	718	2278	290	596	99	22	28	248	207	238	66	.262
Justice	1060	3559	538	985	170	26	161	582	439	548	43	.277
Maas	587	1918	268	507	83	15	79	296	225	333	22	.264
Morris	787	2691	440	801	147	41	50	317	277	234	81	.298
Olerud	1191	3984	563	1097	180	31	143	602	457	559	47	.275
Ventura	988	3193	372	821	129	26	35	319	292	346	55	.257
Walker	929	2981	415	774	129	22	112	404	340	587	67	.260
Zeile	876	2877	370	741	131	16	96	392	342	449	24	.258

You may have seen projections like these based on similarly complex formulas in other publications. In one case, the authors are, ahem, bold enough to forecast the statistics for the upcoming season for every player in the majors. We find such an endeavor utterly inane, because projections like those in the table above are *averages,* which melt the peaks and valleys off any graph. (Ever wonder why those lists only project seven or eight 30-home-run hitters, although there have been nearly twice that many per year, on average, over the last decade?) Such lists, including the one above, are useful only for purposes of comparing one player's potential to that of another—as long as one understands that they obscure the wide range of career tracks that any rookie might subsequently take. After all, we are making judgments based on a single season at an early stage in a player's development. (Ask Joe Charboneau about the downside potential for even an apparent superstar-to-be.)

But as we said, for comparison of one player to another, these averages can be useful. And those above show DeShields to have potential at least equal to that of any other rookie in the class of 1990. The similarity of his rookie season to that of accomplished hitters like Carew and Lansford implies a genuine shot at 2000 or more career hits. And here's where our method allows us to express more directly a player's chance for stardom: Five others among DeShields's clones reached the 2000-hit level as well: George Brett, George Burns, Charlie Gehringer, Ed McKean, and Jack Tobin. Because they, along with Carew and Lansford, account for 19 percent of DeShields's projection, we would estimate that he has a 19 percent chance to reach the 2000-hit mark. Among the other rookies listed above, only Olerud has a higher probability (21 percent), based on corresponding calculations.

Walker's composite figures also disguise his potential to become an outstanding home-run hitter. Among the 40 rookies with the most similar profiles, seven hit at least 200 career home runs: Harold Baines, Jesse Barfield, George Foster, Ralph Kiner, Rick Monday, Ken Singleton, and Bill White; they represent 16 percent of Walker's projection. It ain't likely, but it's possible. The table below shows the estimated probabilities of the leading members of the Class of 1990 reaching these more modest career totals: 1500 games, 750 runs, 1500 hits, 150 home runs, and 750 RBIs:

Player	Games	Runs	Hits	HR	RBI
Alomar	19%	18%	5%	12%	20%
DeShields	35%	41%	36%	7%	27%
Grissom	11%	7%	6%	3%	4%
Justice	27%	25%	27%	31%	26%
Maas	3%	6%	2%	15%	10%
Morris	16%	18%	15%	2%	8%
Olerud	35%	33%	30%	33%	32%
Ventura	18%	10%	14%	2%	4%
Walker	17%	15%	11%	26%	17%
Zeile	14%	12%	12%	18%	14%

These figures suggest that DeShields and Olerud have a greater chance for ultimate stardom than either of last season's rookie award winners, Justice or Alomar. And our method appears to label Maas a potential washout, despite his unprecendented home-run streak last summer. How this table will look five years from now, no one knows. But given everybody's collective poor record in identifying the true potential stars from rookie pretenders, we think it merits your attention.

WON-LOST RECORD BY STARTING POSITION

Montreal Expos	C	1B	2B	3B	SS	LF	CF	RF	DH	P	Leadoff	Cleanup	Starts vs. LH	Starts vs. RH	Total Starts
Mike Aldrete	-	4-7	-	-	-	11-9	-	4-3	-	-	-	3-2	-	38	19-19
Moises Alou	-	-	-	-	-	-	-	1-1	-	-	-	-	2	-	1-1
Scott Anderson	-	-	-	-	-	-	-	-	-	2-1	-	-	1	2	2-1
Brian Barnes	-	-	-	-	-	-	-	-	-	3-1	-	-	3	1	3-1
Oil Can Boyd	-	-	-	-	-	-	-	-	-	19-12	-	-	14	17	19-12
Eric Bullock	-	-	-	-	-	-	-	-	-	-	-	-	-	-	-
Tim Burke	-	-	-	-	-	-	-	-	-	-	-	-	-	-	-
John Costello	-	-	-	-	-	-	-	-	-	-	-	-	-	-	-
Delino DeShields	-	-	63-57	-	-	-	-	-	-	-	52-46	-	35	85	63-57
Howard Farmer	-	-	-	-	-	-	-	-	-	2-2	-	-	-	4	2-2
Mike Fitzgerald	49-35	-	-	-	-	1-0	-	1-3	-	-	-	-	46	43	51-38
Tom Foley	-	-	8-8	-	10-16	-	-	-	-	-	-	-	-	42	18-24
Steve Frey	-	-	-	-	-	-	-	-	-	-	-	-	-	-	-
Andres Galarraga	-	80-65	-	-	-	-	-	-	-	-	-	27-18	60	85	80-65
Mark Gardner	-	-	-	-	-	-	-	-	-	13-13	-	-	5	21	13-13
Brett Gideon	-	-	-	-	-	-	-	-	-	-	-	-	-	-	-
Jerry Goff	12-20	0-3	-	0-1	-	-	-	-	-	-	-	-	-	36	12-24
Marquis Grissom	-	-	-	-	-	4-6	16-13	20-9	-	-	1-1	-	49	19	40-28
Kevin Gross	-	-	-	-	-	-	-	-	-	12-14	-	-	9	17	12-14
Drew Hall	-	-	-	-	-	-	-	-	-	-	-	-	-	-	-
Joe Hesketh	-	-	-	-	-	-	-	-	-	-	-	-	-	-	-
Rex Hudler	-	-	-	-	-	-	-	-	-	-	-	-	-	-	-
Wallace Johnson	-	1-2	-	-	-	-	-	-	-	-	-	-	-	3	1-2
Bob Malloy	-	-	-	-	-	-	-	-	-	-	-	-	-	-	-
Dave Martinez	-	-	-	-	-	-	46-48	1-1	-	-	9-8	-	10	86	47-49
Dennis Martinez	-	-	-	-	-	-	-	-	-	15-17	-	-	10	22	15-17
Orlando Mercado	0-3	-	-	-	-	-	-	-	-	-	-	-	2	1	0-3
Dale Mohorcic	-	-	-	-	-	-	-	-	-	-	-	-	-	-	-
Chris Nabholz	-	-	-	-	-	-	-	-	-	8-3	-	-	8	3	8-3
Otis Nixon	-	-	-	-	-	3-5	21-16	-	-	-	13-13	-	37	8	24-21
Junior Noboa	-	-	13-11	-	-	-	-	3-2	-	-	-	-	28	1	16-13
Spike Owen	-	-	-	-	75-61	-	-	-	-	-	0-1	-	60	76	75-61
Johnny Paredes	-	-	1-1	-	-	-	-	-	-	-	-	-	2	-	1-1
Tim Raines	-	-	-	-	-	66-55	-	-	-	-	10-8	-	44	77	66-55
Mel Rojas	-	-	-	-	-	-	-	-	-	-	-	-	-	-	-
Rolando Roomes	-	-	-	-	-	0-2	2-0	-	-	-	-	-	4	-	2-2
Scott Ruskin	-	-	-	-	-	-	-	-	-	-	-	-	-	-	-
Bill Sampen	-	-	-	-	-	-	-	-	-	3-1	-	-	2	2	3-1
Nelson Santovenia	24-19	-	-	-	-	-	-	-	-	-	-	-	17	26	24-19
Dave Schmidt	-	-	-	-	-	-	-	-	-	-	-	-	-	-	-
Zane Smith	-	-	-	-	-	-	-	-	-	8-13	-	-	8	13	8-13
Rich Thompson	-	-	-	-	-	-	-	-	-	-	-	-	-	-	-
Larry Walker	-	-	-	-	-	-	-	55-58	-	-	-	-	24	89	55-58
Tim Wallach	-	-	-	85-76	-	-	-	-	-	-	-	55-57	60	101	85-76

TEAM TOTALS: BATTING

	AB	H	2B	3B	HR	RBI	BB	SO	BA	SA	OBA
Season	5453	1363	227	43	114	607	576	1024	.250	.370	.322
vs. Left-Handers	2066	494	79	19	41	227	206	358	.239	.355	.307
vs. Right-Handers	3387	869	148	24	73	380	370	666	.257	.379	.331
vs. Ground-Ballers	3019	793	135	24	64	346	314	516	.263	.387	.332
vs. Fly-Ballers	2434	570	92	19	50	261	262	508	.234	.349	.309
Home Games	2624	662	120	24	48	302	289	480	.252	.371	.327
Road Games	2829	701	107	19	66	305	287	544	.248	.369	.317
Grass Fields	1467	365	49	10	41	173	141	302	.249	.380	.314
Artificial Turf	3986	998	178	33	73	434	435	722	.250	.367	.325
April	628	158	40	4	7	58	67	126	.252	.361	.322
May	907	240	42	7	24	106	97	170	.265	.406	.336
June	1001	252	46	11	20	118	129	194	.252	.380	.337
July	894	210	33	7	24	110	86	164	.235	.368	.305
August	950	239	24	3	22	97	85	163	.252	.353	.314
Sept./Oct.	1073	264	42	11	17	118	112	207	.246	.353	.317
Leading Off Inn.	1351	354	56	11	27	27	115	221	.262	.380	.322
Bases Empty	3169	785	129	23	69	69	304	584	.248	.368	.316
Runners On	2284	578	98	20	45	538	272	440	.253	.373	.330
Runners/Scor. Pos.	1402	334	63	11	30	478	223	299	.238	.363	.337
Runners On/2 Out	983	219	36	5	16	186	129	204	.223	.318	.317
Scor. Pos./2 Out	682	138	25	2	12	166	111	157	.202	.298	.318
Late-Inning Pressure	1000	260	36	6	18	112	110	176	.260	.362	.335
Leading Off	255	70	6	0	7	7	24	34	.275	.380	.342
Runners On	428	110	19	3	7	101	64	78	.257	.364	.353
Runners/Scor. Pos.	260	68	9	2	6	92	56	46	.262	.381	.390

RUNS BATTED IN	From 1B	From 2B	From 3B	Scoring Position
Totals	79/1505	181/1085	233/607	414/1692
Percentage	5.2%	16.7%	38.4%	24.5%

TEAM TOTALS: PITCHING

	W-L	ERA	AB	H	HR	BB	SO	BA	SA	OBA
Season	85-77	3.37	5506	1349	127	510	991	.245	.366	.311
vs. Left-Handers			2645	657	62	273	465	.248	.370	.318
vs. Right-Handers			2861	692	65	237	526	.242	.362	.304
vs. Ground-Ballers			2410	567	38	204	465	.235	.336	.296
vs. Fly-Ballers			3096	782	89	306	526	.253	.389	.322
Home Games	47-34	2.93	2776	661	62	225	516	.238	.355	.299
Road Games	38-43	3.81	2730	688	65	285	475	.252	.377	.323
Grass Fields	20-22	3.95	1430	371	36	142	253	.259	.385	.327
Artificial Turf	65-55	3.17	4076	978	91	368	738	.240	.359	.305
April	10-9	3.14	628	153	13	68	104	.244	.361	.319
May	15-12	3.22	917	236	18	81	177	.257	.375	.318
June	17-13	3.20	983	232	24	87	167	.236	.357	.299
July	13-14	3.77	924	235	22	80	168	.254	.376	.317
August	13-14	3.49	968	243	21	88	176	.251	.370	.316
Sept./Oct.	17-15	3.33	1086	250	29	106	199	.230	.356	.300
Leading Off Inn.			1361	356	32	113	244	.262	.392	.321
Bases Empty			3222	786	76	257	597	.244	.368	.303
Runners On			2284	563	51	253	394	.246	.363	.321
Runners/Scor. Pos.			1375	328	29	194	256	.239	.348	.331
Runners On/2 Out			974	216	16	132	195	.222	.314	.318
Scor. Pos./2 Out			650	129	7	105	126	.198	.266	.314
Late-Inning Pressure			1014	254	28	104	158	.250	.370	.321
Leading Off			257	62	6	23	45	.241	.354	.306
Runners On			412	113	12	52	62	.274	.391	.352
Runners/Scor. Pos.			251	67	9	44	38	.267	.410	.370
First 9 Batters			2911	694	56	298	568	.238	.342	.311
Second 9 Batters			1403	352	36	114	246	.251	.390	.308
All Batters Thereafter			1192	303	35	98	177	.254	.394	.314

NEW YORK METS

• **Why can't they win the close ones?**
• **Why can't they beat lefties?**

In 162 games last season, the Mets outscored their opponents by exactly 162 runs—just enough to win every game if they could have distributed that margin to their best advantage. Of course, not even the once-mighty Mets could be expected to win every game, even with a season's surplus of runs theoretically large enough to do so, but a less-than-perfect rearrangement of that surplus should still have left the Mets enough breathing room to win their division. After all, over the course of the season, division-champion Pittsburgh scored 42 fewer runs and allowed six more runs than the Mets did. Instead, the Mets' shortcomings in close games haunted them throughout the season, and they finished four games back. The Mets became the first National League team since the 1951 Brooklyn Dodgers—yes, *those* Brooklyn Dodgers, who lost the pennant playoff on Bobby Thomson's home run—to outscore its opponents by a margin of at least a run per game and not finish in first place.

Oh, the Mets made it close. For the seventh consecutive year, the Mets provided their fans with either a division title or the next best thing, pennant-race excitement. They took their pursuit of the Pirates down to the last four days of the season, but in the final analysis, they weren't meant to win. No National League team in this century has ever finished in first place (in the league or a division) with as poor a record in one- and two-run games as the 1990 Mets. And it's happened only once in the American League: the 1988 Red Sox won the American League East despite a 32–42 record in one- and two-run games.

The records of each National League team broken down by margin of victory leave little to the imagination:

	Decided By 1–2 Runs W-L	Pct.	Decided By 3+ Runs W-L	Pct.	Diff.
Houston	41–37	.526	34–50	.405	121
San Francisco	45–33	.577	40–44	.476	101
Chicago	41–37	.526	36–48	.429	97
St.Louis	38–43	.469	32–49	.395	74
Philadelphia	38–36	.514	39–49	.443	71
Pittsburgh	46–29	.613	49–38	.563	50
Los Angeles	39–31	.557	47–45	.511	46
Atlanta	31–42	.425	34–55	.382	43
San Diego	33–48	.407	42–39	.519	−112
Cincinnati	37–37	.500	54–34	.614	−114
Montreal	45–51	.469	40–26	.606	−137
New York	32–42	.432	59–29	.670	−238

Since the first edition of the *Analyst* six years ago, we've repeatedly stressed that poor records in close games are mostly the result of bad luck. (See the Texas Rangers essay in this edition for our latest installment.) But when a team plays poorly in one- *and* two-run games, and does so in consecutive seasons, even cynics like us are inclined to examine the idiosyncracies of the team itself for a possible explanation. The Mets, who played below .500 in one-run games in 1989 as well (22–30), are such a team.

The Mets were criticized regularly last season for their reliance on the home run and their inability to manufacture runs. However, the game-by-game distribution of their scoring, which seemed at the root of the team's close-game problems, was fairly typical of teams that scored at approximately the same rate for the season. The Mets scored an average of 4.78 runs per game; over the past three years, five other teams came within one-tenth of a run of that average. Compare their scoring patterns with that of the 1990 Mets:

Year	Team	0-1	2-7	7-up	0	1	2	3	4-up
1990	**Mets**	25	98	39	8	17	18	18	101
1990	Blue Jays	25	93	44	10	15	20	19	98
1989	Red Sox	24	97	41	9	15	20	16	102
1988	Twins	23	98	41	9	14	18	27	94
1988	Yankees	19	107	35	6	13	18	22	102
1988	Blue Jays	25	99	38	3	22	18	27	92
	Averages	23	99	40	7	16	19	22	98

The averages listed above don't include the Mets' totals, but they correspond to them quite closely. Notice in the first set of figures that the Mets had a typical number of games in which they scored between two and seven runs, without a skew to very high- or low-scoring games. But since it seemed possible that low-scoring games produced the imbalance that led to such a poor record in close games, we examined them in detail—the set of figures on the right. Even that breakdown indicated that New York's distribution was absolutely normal.

So why did the Mets lose so many close games? If they distribute their runs in a typical pattern, why do they lose an atypical number of one- and two-run games? One factor appears to have been the team's abject inability to hit left-handed pitching, which left them easy prey for manipulation by opposing managers. Rarely in recent baseball history has one team demonstrated so much hitting ability against pitchers who throw the ball from one side, and so little against pitchers of the opposite persuasion. Here are the batting averages for National League teams last season:

vs. Right-Handers		vs. Left-Handers	
New York	.271	Cincinnati	.280
Los Angeles	.264	San Francisco	.276
Chicago	.261	Atlanta	.272
Pittsburgh	.260	Chicago	.267
St. Louis	.260	San Diego	.261
Cincinnati	.257	Los Angeles	.258
Montreal	.257	Pittsburgh	.257

(continued)

Philadelphia	.256	Houston	.253
San Diego	.255	Philadelphia	.253
San Francisco	.254	St. Louis	.250
Atlanta	.239	Montreal	.239
Houston	.235	**New York**	.233

We've been keeping breakdowns against left- and right-handed pitchers for 16 years now, and the 1990 Mets were the first team during that time to finish with the highest batting average in their league against one type, and with the lowest in the league the other way. In fact, we're even understating the case, since the Mets' .2711 average vs. right-handers actually was the highest *in the major leagues* (Toronto finished second at .2708), while their .233 mark against lefties was the lowest *in the majors*. (Baltimore's .242 mark was lowest in the American League.)

New York's problems against southpaws were hardly a secret. Pittsburgh's acquisition of Zane Smith in late July was made with the Mets in mind. Jim Leyland set his pitching rotation weeks ahead of time for the two key series against the Mets in September (and for the October series that was rendered moot by the early clinching). The formula: Doug Drabek and any southpaw within a thousand-mile radius. The Pirates even resurrected Jerry Reuss, last seen during the Paleozoic Era, to serve as a potential intimidator. Other teams noticed what was going on and juggled their rotations accordingly, and the more lefties the Mets saw, the more helpless against them they became. Over the six-week period from late August until September 30 (the day the Pirates clinched the title), the Mets won only four of 16 games in which they faced left-handed starters, and their portside conquerors included a veritable who's who of minor-league baseball: Steve Wilson, Chris Nabholz, Randy Tomlin, and Brian Barnes. All throw left-handed, all started against the Mets down the stretch, and all helped the Mets return home in plenty of time to plan family observances of Columbus Day. Could Pete Falcone, Doug Rau, and Billy Pierce be far behind? Why not Boomer Esiason, Kenny Stabler, or Lefty Driesell?

Recent history indicates that a poor record in one-run games is often symptomatic of such an imbalance (in either direction). Over the past 16 years (actually 15 of the last 16, since 1981 wasn't included), 27 teams batted at least 25 points better one way than the other. They played below .500 in one-run games and above .500 in games decided by more than one run:

Margin of Game	W	L	Pct.
One run	643	651	.491
Two runs or more	1576	1497	.513

Those figures aren't conclusive, but they suggest that teams that hit far better against one type of pitching than the other may be at a slight disadvantage in close games. Was that why New York played so poorly in close games last season? Let's bite the bullet and concede that it was part of the problem.

Actually, the Mets have chosen the worst possible time to display such an extreme preference for right-handed opposition. Even with Driesell safely tucked away at James Madison, the use of left-handed pitchers in the National League last season was at a level that should alarm left-handed batters from Montreal to San Diego. Of the 17,381⅓ innings pitched in the league's 972 games last season, 6,428 were pitched by left-handers. That's a rate of 37 percent, a significant increase over the corresponding National League rates of recent years: 32.4 percent in 1987, 31.7 in 1988, and 33.1 in 1989. In fact, it tops the list as the highest rate of innings pitched by left-handers in one league in any season in this century:

	RHP Innings	LHP Innings	LHP Pct.
1990 N.L.	10,953.1	6,428.0	37.0
1949 N.L.	7,039.0	4,059.0	36.6
1950 A.L.	7,007.2	3,955.1	36.1
1974 A.L.	11,225.1	6,223.0	35.7
1949 A.L.	7,081.2	3,859.1	35.3

Historically, it's interesting that left-handed pitching was not nearly as prevalent throughout the first part of this century as it is today. Using the same barometer (the percentage of innings thrown by left-handers), only once in the years before World War II did the rate for either league reach 30 percent in two consecutive years (the American League in 1925–26). Not until after the war did either league reach the 30-percent mark with regularity. Even so, there were still large swings back the other way; in 1959, the A.L. rate fell to 20.6, the lowest in either league over the past 40 years.

Last year's 37-percent figure is the culmination—at least to this point—of a decade-long buildup of left-handed pitchers in the National League. And the man most responsible for the rise—and thus indirectly for the Mets' second-place finish in 1990—is their old nemesis, Dorrel Norman Elvert Herzog. Whitey spent most of the eighties collecting the switch-hitting speed demons with whom he won three National League pennants. Other teams countered by importing pitchers of various levels of ability, all of whom shared the ability to throw a baseball sixty feet, six inches, with their left hands—both to increase the switchers' distance to first base and to hold them closer to it once they got there. Then Herzog himself started to gather up left-handers, partly to deal with the arch-rival Mets, partly to give the rest of the league a graduate course in how to lefty/righty opponents to death in the late innings. (Bullpen By Something-or-other; the exact phrase escapes us.)

The result: By 1990, left-handed pitchers were everywhere. Some of the National League buildup has been the result of a migration of left-handers (John Tudor, Bob Ojeda, Danny Jackson, etc.—see the San Francisco Giants essay). The percentage of innings accounted for by lefties in each league on a year-by-year basis:

Year	A.L.	N.L.	Year	A.L.	N.L.
1980	34.9	26.8	1986	29.5	33.4
1981	32.5	25.3	1987	32.2	32.4
1982	33.5	26.2	1988	29.9	31.7
1983	34.6	27.1	1989	30.7	33.1
1984	31.7	29.9	1990	31.2	37.0
1985	31.3	31.2			

In each of the first six years of the 1980s, the American League figure was higher; in each of the past five seasons, the National League has been higher.

But while the quantity of left-handers is at an all-time high, the quality of the group leaves something to be desired. When the Royals signed Dan Schatzeder for a $700,000 salary during the offseason, the signal sent out to the children of the Western world was clear: If you can throw with your left hand, there's room for you in major-league baseball. For a second straight season in each league, the cumulative batting average against left-handed pitchers was higher than against right-handers. And the won-lost record of left-handers fell shy of the .500 mark in consecutive seasons for the first time since 1950 and 1951. Apparently, not all the left-handers out there are Sandy Koufaxes:

	Batting Avg.		By LHP	
	vs. RHP	vs. LHP	W-L	Pct.
1989 A.L.	.258	.266	318–362	.468
1989 N.L.	.244	.251	316–323	.495
1990 A.L.	.256	.266	332–364	.477
1990 N.L.	.256	.258	356–374	.488

All of this makes the Mets' failures against southpaws even more galling. Of course, there were some extenuating circumstances that contributed to their poor record, especially down the stretch. In August, they lost the services of their two best role players against left-handers. On August 15, platoon center fielder Keith Miller hurt his back while making a rare start at second base, leading to three weeks on the sidelines; at the time, his .321 batting average vs. lefties was tops on the team. Five days later, Mark Carreon tore up his knee while running the bases at San Diego and missed the remainder of the season; at the time he went down, Carreon led the Mets with seven home runs off left-handers.

But the season-long problems ran all through the Mets' batting order. Of the eight players with the most at-bats during the season, seven hit for higher batting averages against right-handers than against lefties:

	vs. RHP		vs. LHP		
	AB	BA	AB	BA	Diff.
Sasser	217	.332	53	.208	−124
Magadan	283	.371	168	.256	−115
McReynolds	327	.291	194	.232	− 59
Johnson	369	.266	221	.208	− 58
Strawberry	325	.298	217	.244	− 54
Boston	306	.278	60	.250	− 28
Jefferies	382	.293	222	.266	− 27
Elster	195	.195	119	.227	+ 32

Four of the seven regulars who hit right-handers harder than left-handers—Sasser, Magadan, Strawberry, and Boston—are left-handed batters. The two switch-hitters, Howard Johnson and Gregg Jefferies, were both disappointments when batting right-handed, although with Johnson, that's part of the package; he has generally been a better hitter from the left side. But the man who must accept a large part of the blame for the Mets' problems against southpaws was the only pure right-handed hitter in the team's everyday lineup, Kevin McReynolds.

Not only did Not-So-Big Mac bat only .232 against lefties, but he did not compensate by delivering his share of extra-base hits. His slugging average vs. left-handers was .351, inadequate for a player of McReynolds's past ability and current salary. In 194 at-bats vs. lefties, he drove in only 15 runs and hit only four home runs—none in 127 at-bats after June 19.

Because the batters hitting behind him were similarly poor against left-handers, McReynolds was often pitched around in key situations early in the season. He seemed to accept that treatment all too docilely. Left-handed pitchers walked him 38 times last season (only Jack Clark had more), including 21 times with runners in scoring position. But even when given his opportunities to produce, Mac didn't. He batted only .225 (9-for-40) against lefties with runners in scoring position.

With Darryl Strawberry summering in Chavez Ravine in 1991, you'd think that opposing managers wouldn't have quite the incentive to start southpaws against the Mets as they did last year. But Vince Coleman, who spent much of the winter singing the "I ain't Darryl" blues, nevertheless brings with him enough speed to keep a steady diet of those lefties coming. The pickup of Hubie Brooks should provide some help for Jefferies, Johnson, and McReynolds against this portside onslaught, since his career average of .296 against lefties is 30 points higher than his average against normal people. (However, that average has declined for four consecutive seasons, dropping to .240 in 1990.) With a strong pitching staff at his disposal, Bud Harrelson has a team that again seems a good bet to score more runs than it allows; maybe this year Harrelson can get out his ouija board to figure out how to get the most mileage out of that surplus.

WON-LOST RECORD BY STARTING POSITION

New York Mets	C	1B	2B	3B	SS	LF	CF	RF	DH	P	Leadoff	Cleanup	Starts vs. LH	Starts vs. RH	Total Starts
Kevin Baez	-	-	-	-	2-1	-	-	-	-	-	-	-	3	-	2-1
Blaine Beatty	-	-	-	-	-	-	-	-	-	-	-	-	-	-	-
Daryl Boston	-	-	-	-	-	1-0	55-34	-	-	-	14-8	-	4	86	56-34
Kevin D. Brown	-	-	-	-	-	-	-	-	-	-	-	-	-	-	-
Chuck Carr	-	-	-	-	-	-	-	-	-	-	-	-	-	-	-
Mark Carreon	-	-	-	-	-	6-4	16-10	1-4	-	-	10-5	-	27	14	23-18
Dave Cone	-	-	-	-	-	-	-	-	-	19-11	-	-	15	15	19-11
Ron Darling	-	-	-	-	-	-	-	-	-	10-8	-	-	7	11	10-8
Mario Diaz	-	-	-	-	2-2	-	-	-	-	-	-	-	2	2	2-2
Kevin Elster	-	-	-	-	54-37	-	-	-	-	-	-	-	34	57	54-37
Sid Fernandez	-	-	-	-	-	-	-	-	-	11-19	-	-	14	16	11-19
John Franco	-	-	-	-	-	-	-	-	-	-	-	-	-	-	-
Dwight Gooden	-	-	-	-	-	-	-	-	-	22-12	-	-	7	27	22-12
Tommy Herr	-	-	13-13	-	-	-	-	-	-	-	3-2	-	12	14	13-13
Keith Hughes	-	-	-	-	-	-	-	-	-	-	-	-	-	-	-
Todd Hundley	9-10	-	-	-	-	-	-	-	-	-	-	-	8	11	9-10
Jeff Innis	-	-	-	-	-	-	-	-	-	-	-	-	-	-	-
Gregg Jefferies	-	-	62-51	20-14	-	-	-	-	-	-	23-26	-	51	96	82-65
Chris Jelic	-	-	-	-	-	2-1	-	-	-	-	-	-	3	-	2-1
Howard Johnson	-	-	-	52-37	33-30	-	-	-	-	-	25-14	3-1	53	99	85-67
Dave Liddell	-	-	-	-	-	-	-	-	-	-	-	-	-	-	-
Barry Lyons	11-11	-	-	-	-	-	-	-	-	-	-	-	9	13	11-11
Julio Machado	-	-	-	-	-	-	-	-	-	-	-	-	-	-	-
Dave Magadan	-	64-36	-	7-8	-	-	-	-	-	-	-	-	35	80	71-44
Mike Marshall	-	19-23	-	-	-	-	-	1-0	-	-	-	-	19	24	20-23
Kevin McReynolds	-	-	-	-	-	79-63	-	-	-	-	-	10-15	55	87	79-63
Orlando Mercado	16-11	-	-	-	-	-	-	-	-	-	-	-	23	4	16-11
Keith Miller	-	-	5-1	-	0-1	1-2	18-24	1-0	-	-	14-15	-	33	20	25-28
Jeff Musselman	-	-	-	-	-	-	-	-	-	-	-	-	-	-	-
Charlie O'Brien	11-14	-	-	-	-	-	-	-	-	-	-	-	15	10	11-14
Bob Ojeda	-	-	-	-	-	-	-	-	-	7-5	-	-	4	8	7-5
Tom O'Malley	-	1-0	-	8-8	-	-	-	-	-	-	-	-	2	15	9-8
Alejandro Pena	-	-	-	-	-	-	-	-	-	-	-	-	-	-	-
Darren Reed	-	-	-	-	-	0-1	2-3	2-0	-	-	2-1	-	7	1	4-4
Mackey Sasser	44-23	-	-	-	-	-	-	-	-	-	-	-	3	64	44-23
Dan Schatzeder	-	-	-	-	-	-	-	-	-	-	-	-	-	-	-
Darryl Strawberry	-	-	-	-	-	-	-	82-64	-	-	-	76-53	48	98	82-64
Pat Tabler	-	-	-	-	-	2-0	-	4-3	-	-	-	-	5	4	6-3
Tim Teufel	-	3-9	11-6	4-4	-	-	-	-	-	-	-	2-2	27	10	18-19
Lou Thornton	-	-	-	-	-	-	-	-	-	-	-	-	-	-	-
Kelvin Torve	-	4-3	-	-	-	-	-	-	-	-	-	-	-	7	4-3
Alex Trevino	0-2	-	-	-	-	-	-	-	-	-	-	-	2	-	0-2
Julio Valera	-	-	-	-	-	-	-	-	-	2-1	-	-	1	2	2-1
Frank Viola	-	-	-	-	-	-	-	-	-	20-15	-	-	12	23	20-15
Wally Whitehurst	-	-	-	-	-	-	-	-	-	-	-	-	-	-	-

TEAM TOTALS: BATTING

	AB	H	2B	3B	HR	RBI	BB	SO	BA	SA	OBA
Season	5504	1410	278	21	172	734	536	851	.256	.408	.323
vs. Left-Handers	2144	499	108	6	48	214	205	363	.233	.356	.300
vs. Right-Handers	3360	911	170	15	124	520	331	488	.271	.441	.337
vs. Ground-Ballers	2686	730	130	9	90	400	255	413	.272	.427	.335
vs. Fly-Ballers	2818	680	148	12	82	334	281	438	.241	.390	.311
Home Games	2645	662	124	9	86	376	267	391	.250	.402	.320
Road Games	2859	748	154	12	86	358	269	460	.262	.414	.326
Grass Fields	3840	998	187	12	126	556	384	572	.260	.413	.328
Artificial Turf	1664	412	91	9	46	178	152	279	.248	.396	.311
April	640	139	24	3	17	69	61	113	.217	.344	.288
May	829	212	36	2	34	112	71	127	.256	.427	.314
June	984	292	65	5	39	161	104	130	.297	.492	.364
July	942	248	52	5	29	136	90	146	.263	.421	.328
August	1019	261	43	1	22	115	96	156	.256	.365	.323
Sept./Oct.	1090	258	58	5	31	141	114	179	.237	.384	.307
Leading Off Inn.	1310	335	60	3	54	54	118	203	.256	.430	.321
Bases Empty	3151	763	150	9	97	97	275	476	.242	.388	.306
Runners On	2353	647	128	12	75	637	261	375	.275	.435	.344
Runners/Scor. Pos.	1367	374	69	9	45	550	187	237	.274	.436	.352
Runners On/2 Out	1040	273	50	10	25	264	134	186	.262	.402	.349
Scor. Pos./2 Out	668	173	29	8	16	234	106	124	.259	.398	.363
Late-Inning Pressure	844	212	31	2	22	92	75	145	.251	.371	.315
Leading Off	210	50	6	0	7	7	17	35	.238	.367	.298
Runners On	350	87	12	0	8	78	41	63	.249	.351	.327
Runners/Scor. Pos.	195	50	7	0	4	67	28	40	.256	.354	.343

RUNS BATTED IN	From 1B	From 2B	From 3B	Scoring Position
Totals	102/1671	218/1092	242/569	460/1661
Percentage	6.1%	20.0%	42.5%	27.7%

TEAM TOTALS: PITCHING

	W-L	ERA	AB	H	HR	BB	SO	BA	SA	OBA
Season	91-71	3.42	5443	1339	119	444	1217	.246	.365	.304
vs. Left-Handers			2204	530	41	199	534	.240	.356	.306
vs. Right-Handers			3239	809	78	245	683	.250	.370	.303
vs. Ground-Ballers			2695	634	32	212	638	.235	.322	.293
vs. Fly-Ballers			2748	705	87	232	579	.257	.406	.315
Home Games	52-29	3.07	2754	644	52	217	633	.234	.344	.291
Road Games	39-42	3.79	2689	695	67	227	584	.258	.386	.317
Grass Fields	68-46	3.39	3862	933	93	301	883	.242	.364	.297
Artificial Turf	23-25	3.51	1581	406	26	143	334	.257	.367	.320
April	9-10	3.39	643	147	13	56	164	.229	.355	.293
May	11-13	3.51	806	186	26	59	175	.231	.364	.285
June	21-7	3.96	982	271	21	76	189	.276	.400	.326
July	17-11	2.98	897	204	19	79	223	.227	.353	.291
August	16-14	3.64	1023	257	21	78	216	.251	.366	.308
Sept./Oct.	17-16	3.09	1092	274	19	96	250	.251	.347	.312
Leading Off Inn.			1326	348	42	111	246	.262	.415	.322
Bases Empty			3167	776	75	254	712	.245	.368	.305
Runners On			2276	563	44	190	505	.247	.360	.303
Runners/Scor. Pos.			1363	315	25	137	332	.231	.338	.297
Runners On/2 Out			951	197	14	93	211	.207	.299	.279
Scor. Pos./2 Out			640	121	8	73	153	.189	.273	.273
Late-Inning Pressure			738	174	14	66	145	.236	.343	.298
Leading Off			179	49	8	18	25	.274	.469	.340
Runners On			320	77	1	30	62	.241	.303	.304
Runners/Scor. Pos.			207	46	1	23	44	.222	.290	.294
First 9 Batters			2694	658	52	210	617	.244	.355	.301
Second 9 Batters			1380	352	29	121	311	.255	.376	.316
All Batters Thereafter			1369	329	38	113	289	.240	.372	.298

PHILADELPHIA PHILLIES

- **Leapin' Lenny!**
- **One Hall of Fame vote for a Phillie fixture.**

Among the biggest surprises of the 1990 season was the emergence of Phillies center fielder Len Dykstra as an All-Star starter. Only a year earlier, Mets fans were crowing over how their team "stole" Juan Samuel from Philadelphia for Dykstra and Roger McDowell. By last June 18, the first anniversary of the trade, Samuel had already been foisted upon the Dodgers (for another pair of underachievers, Mike Marshall and Alejandro Pena), while McDowell shared the National League lead in saves and Dykstra was batting .387, 41 points higher than his nearest rival.

Although Dykstra sputtered as the season wound down (he hit just .255 during September and October), his season's average of .325 represented an 88-point increase from the .237 mark he compiled in 1989—one of the biggest jumps in recent history. Only one player in the previous 30 years improved that much in one season: Keith Hernandez, who batted .344 in his 1979 co-MVP season, 89 points higher than his 1978 mark of .255. (Only players with enough plate appearances to qualify for the batting title in both seasons have been considered.)

But Dykstra wasn't alone; two other National League players boosted their 1989 batting averages by more than 80 points last season: major-league leader Eddie Murray and Bill Doran. Not since 1921 had three players increased their batting averages by at least 80 points in the same season. The largest gains of the last 50 years:

Years	Player	Year 1	Year 2	Increase
1952–53	Carl Furillo	.247	.344	.097
1957–58	Pete Runnels	.230	.322	.092
1978–79	Keith Hernandez	.255	.344	.089
1989–90	**Len Dykstra**	.237	.325	.088
1952–53	Mickey Vernon	.251	.337	.086
1945–46	Mickey Vernon	.268	.353	.085
1989–90	**Eddie Murray**	.247	.330	.083
1947–48	Gerry Priddy	.214	.296	.082
1983–84	Chili Davis	.233	.315	.082
1989–90	**Bill Doran**	.219	.300	.081

Sometimes the simultaneous occurrence of several rare events is simply a logical extension of another trend that may have been overlooked. Last season's triple Salchow was a tip-off that the National League's 10-point increase from .246 to .256, modest as it sounds, was more drastic than you might think. In fact, it was the National League's first double-digit increase in nearly 40 years—since 1953, when the league standard jumped from .253 to .266, and Carl Furillo netted the largest individual gain of this century.

Conditions were similar in 1921, the last time three different regular starters made 80-point jumps. The major league average increased from .276 in 1920 to .291, the third-highest mark of this century. The most conspicuous beneficiaries of that escalation were Nemo Leibold (.220 to .306), Harry Heilmann (.309 to .394), and Ray Powell (.225 to .306).

There's a simple message here: For an individual player like Todd Benzinger (.245 in 1989, .253 in 1990), an increase of roughly 10 points is insignificant. But one small step for a man is a giant leap for an entire league, where a 10-point surge can produce uncommon results.

Now if you're like us, you've already heard more than you cared to about last season's rash of no-hitters, so we won't be insulted if you skip past this next tangent. As we just mentioned, subtle shifts occasionally spawn delightfully daffy individual performances (though one would hardly expect nine no-hitters to accompany an increase in batting averages). On the other hand, there are times when shockingly extraordinary events have no explanation at all and should be appreciated on that account alone.

There's an old cliché that goes something like this: Sit a million monkeys in front of a million typewriters for a million years, and one of them is bound to produce *King Lear*. (In fact, there is a monkey named Ralph who came remarkably close—some missing punctuation marks here and there, stuff like that. Elias recently hired Ralph to produce the 1992 *Analyst* even before the start of the 1991 season. No luck yet, but we're pleased to report that Ralph has reproduced the screenplay for *Rocky* and completed several episodes of "Love American Style." The only problem is, now he wants to direct!) But the proliferation of baseball statistics over the past decade has produced an unfortunate side effect: a growing tendency on the part of writers, broadcasters, and fans (in roughly that order) to try to explain the inexplicable. We guarantee that if some prodigious primate had produced Shakespeare's entire corpus last summer, an overly analytical baseball writer would have tied it to the shortened spring training.

But if any explanation is needed for the nine no-hitters pitched in 1990, it is this: Baseball is played 10 times a day, seven days a week, six months a year. After more than 100 years of such constant activity, it would be peculiar for random events—like the simian *King Lear* or nine no-hitters in a season—*not* to have occurred at some point. The gods of baseball, for whatever whimsical reason, decided that 1990 was the right time for this little celestial prank. God knows, after Bart Giamatti's death, Pete Rose's expulsion, and a World Series earthquake, we needed the diversion.

For those poor souls unwilling to accept that little gift without an interpretation of some sort, we offer the following. Despite nine no-hitters in 1990 (or nine more than in 1989), even the seeming black-and-white difference between 1989 and 1990 had more than a touch of gray that was overlooked last summer. The following table shows that there were only a few more games in 1990 than there were a year earlier in which pitchers had no-hitters through six innings:

	1989	1990
No-hitters through six	28	35
Broken up in 7th inning	12	15
Broken up in 8th inning	9	6
Broken up in 9th inning	7	5
No-hitters	0	9

Sure, there wasn't a single no-hitter in 1989. But the difference between 28 six-inning no-hitters in 1989 and 35 last season fails to pass the raised eyebrow test; it's not a significant margin. So the anomaly of 1990 simply represents greater success in putting the final touches on a similar number of masterpieces—an obviously random result, we trust, for even the most zealous analysts. Now, back to our show.

So where were we? Dykstra, right? Quite a season, as we said. He ranked fourth in the N.L. with a .325 batting average and drew 89 walks, for a league-high .418 on-base average. He scored 106 runs (fifth most in the league), and stole 33 bases in 38 attempts. He also led all center fielders with an average of 3.07 putouts per nine innings. An all-around superstar season.

For sake of argument, let's say that over the next 10 years, Dykstra has three more seasons just like 1990. And in his "off seasons" he bats in the .280 to .300 range, and continues to draw close to 100 walks a year from the leadoff spot, score 100 runs, steal 25 or so bases, and play the hell out of center field. And just to complete the picture, let's say he doubles his yearly assists from six to twelve. Boys and girls, can you say "Cooperstown"? Obviously this kind of record should. But for at least one other great Phillies center fielder, it did not.

During the 1950s, Richie Ashburn was the quintessential leadoff hitter: a .300-plus hitter who averaged more than 80 walks per season, a great base stealer, and perhaps the best center fielder of his day, Mays notwithstanding—maybe the best of all time. His exclusion from Cooperstown remains one of the Hall's greatest oversights.

Ashburn actually had four seasons over an eight-year period from 1951 through 1958 any one of which could be mistaken for Dykstra's 1990 season:

Year	Player	BA	G	AB	R	H	2B	3B	HR	RBI	BB	SB
1990	Dykstra	.325	149	590	106	192	35	3	9	60	89	33
1951	Ashburn	.344	154	643	92	221	31	5	4	63	50	29
1953	Ashburn	.330	156	622	110	205	25	9	2	57	61	14
1955	Ashburn	.338	140	533	91	180	32	9	3	42	105	12
1958	Ashburn	.350	152	615	97	215	24	13	2	33	97	30

His "bad" seasons during that period yielded a composite .298 batting average. But we're getting ahead of ourselves.

Ashburn joined the Phillies in 1948 and made an immediate impact: He was the first rookie since Kiki Cuyler 24 years earlier to steal 30 bases and compile a .300 batting average. (Ashburn's actual figures were 32 and .333.) He spent 12 seasons with Philadelphia, was traded to the Cubs in 1960, and finished his career in 1962 with the Mets. But it was the 10 seasons from 1950 through 1959 that marked Ashburn's greatness. During the 1950s, Ashburn accumulated 1875 hits, 300 more than any other National League player. His .313 batting average was seventh best in the majors. He drew 828 walks, second in the majors to Eddie Yost and 150 more than N.L. runner-up Gil Hodges. Throughout the decade, only one N.L. player was a tougher out: Stan Musial.

Once on the bases, Ashburn was a terror. He led the majors with 158 stolen bases from 1950 through 1959, and scored more runs than anyone else (952, 108 more than N.L. runner-up Duke Snider).

All that should probably have been enough to merit serious consideration for the Hall of Fame even if Ashburn had been a poor fielder at an inconsequential position. In fact, Ashburn had a reputation as Willie Mays's equal in center field, and the statistics suggest he was better than Mays. During the '50s, Ashburn made an average of 3.03 putouts per game, the highest average in the majors by a comfortable margin over three tightly bunched rivals: Mays (2.79), Bill Virdon (2.74), and Jim Busby (2.72). (That list, incidentally, ought to dispel any notion that putouts are not an accurate measure of an outfielder's range.) All were outstanding fly-catchers, but Ashburn was in a class by himself: He compiled six of the 10 highest single-season putout totals ever recorded by outfielders. The list of all-time leaders in putouts per game is a combination of contemporary players we know to have been great fielders and others from earlier generations who probably deserve that recognition as well (minimum: 1000 games):

Taylor Douthit	3.00	Kirby Puckett	2.77	Billy North	2.65
Richie Ashburn	2.89	Sammy West	2.73	Garry Maddox	2.64
Mike Kreevich	2.81	Sam Chapman	2.73	Vince DiMaggio	2.63
Dwayne Murphy	2.81	Fred Schulte	2.69	Max Carey	2.63
Dom DiMaggio	2.81	Lloyd Waner	2.67	Joe DiMaggio	2.62

As a center fielder, Ashburn could do more than just run down a baseball three times a game (as though that weren't an enormous contribution on its own); he also threw out more base runners during the 1950s than any other outfielder, and by a wide margin. Ashburn had 127 assists; only two others had more than 100: Gus Bell (109) and Carl Furillo (107). Ashburn led the majors in assists three times, one short of the all-time record shared by three recent players renowned for their arms (Roberto Clemente, Johnny Callison, and Jesse Barfield) and a 19th-century star whose throwing apparently rivaled his speaking ability (Orator Shaffer).

Despite his status as the premier leadoff hitter and center fielder of his era, Ashburn wasn't even a borderline contender for the Hall until 16 years after his retirement. Over his first five seasons of eligibility (1968 through 1972), he never received more than 11 votes (or less than 3 percent of the electorate, a sort of Mendoza line of voting). No matter how you feel about whether or not Ashburn belongs, 11 votes is a monumental blunder. Like Nellie Fox, Bill Mazeroski, and for a time Luis Aparicio, Ashburn had skills apparent to the connoisseur, but overlooked by the vast majority of fans, including those entrusted with the keys to Cooperstown. Hall of Fame voters look for meat and potatoes; Ashburn gave them *haute cuisine* and they spit it out.

Even the baseball writers became aware of their mistake midway through the 1970s, when the Ashburn bandwagon began to roll. (The resurgence of the running game may have increased the voters' awareness of the value of a great leadoff hitter.) He more than doubled his previous high with 25 votes in 1973, and again with 56 in 1974. By 1978, Ashburn had become a long-shot contender when he peaked at 158 votes, still 126 short of the total needed for election. But it was too little, too late. Four years later, Ashburn's only hope of induction was placed in perpetuity in the hands of the controversial veterans' committee.

Some borderline contenders for Cooperstown now seem to have unofficial lobbyists among the writers promoting their Hall of Fame candidacies (a practice we don't find nearly as distasteful as having our legislators swayed by the, ahem, charms of special-interest representatives). Even though baseball, to its credit, has always maintained a rigorously high standard for its Hall, we'd have no problem with the induction of many of those legitimate candidates: Bill Mazeroski, Tony Oliva, and Phil Rizzuto, to name a few. But no matter where you draw the line, some players will always be near misses, so the question of where to draw it will never end the debate over who belongs and who doesn't. For those particular judgments, we are at the mercy of the voters. And their collective judgment on Richie Ashburn, for one, indicates that momentous mistakes have been and will continue to be made.

WON-LOST RECORD BY STARTING POSITION

Philadelphia Phillies	C	1B	2B	3B	SS	LF	CF	RF	DH	P	Leadoff	Cleanup	Starts vs. LH	Starts vs. RH	Total Starts
Darrell Akerfelds	-	-	-	-	-	-	-	-	-	-	-	-	-	-	-
Tommy Barrett	-	-	-	-	-	-	-	-	-	-	-	-	-	-	-
Joe Boever	-	-	-	-	-	-	-	-	-	-	-	-	-	-	-
Rod Booker	-	-	2-3	1-2	9-12	-	-	-	-	-	-	-	-	29	12-17
Sil Campusano	-	-	-	-	-	0-2	6-4	-	-	-	6-4	-	10	2	6-6
Don Carman	-	-	-	-	-	-	-	-	-	0-1	-	-	-	1	0-1
Wes Chamberlain	-	-	-	-	-	6-4	-	-	-	-	-	-	6	4	6-4
Pat Combs	-	-	-	-	-	-	-	-	-	14-17	-	-	13	18	14-17
Dennis Cook	-	-	-	-	-	-	-	-	-	8-5	-	-	4	9	8-5
Darren Daulton	55-68	-	-	-	-	-	-	-	-	-	-	-	24	99	55-68
Jose DeJesus	-	-	-	-	-	-	-	-	-	12-10	-	-	3	19	12-10
Len Dykstra	-	-	-	-	-	-	70-78	-	-	-	70-78	-	42	106	70-78
Darrin Fletcher	3-3	-	-	-	-	-	-	-	-	-	-	-	2	4	3-3
Curt Ford	-	-	-	-	-	-	-	-	-	-	-	-	-	-	-
Marvin Freeman	-	-	-	-	-	-	-	-	-	0-3	-	-	1	2	0-3
Todd Frohwirth	-	-	-	-	-	-	-	-	-	-	-	-	-	-	-
Thomas Greene	-	-	-	-	-	-	-	-	-	3-4	-	-	2	5	3-4
Jason Grimsley	-	-	-	-	-	-	-	-	-	7-4	-	-	2	9	7-4
Charlie Hayes	-	3-0	0-1	69-72	-	-	-	-	-	-	-	6-3	50	95	72-73
Von Hayes	-	-	-	-	-	19-26	1-2	40-38	-	-	-	9-7	37	89	60-66
Tommy Herr	-	-	53-56	-	-	-	-	-	-	-	-	-	32	77	53-56
David Hollins	-	1-0	-	7-11	-	-	-	-	-	-	-	-	6	13	8-11
Ken Howell	-	-	-	-	-	-	-	-	-	9-9	-	-	5	13	9-9
Ron Jones	-	-	-	-	-	2-5	-	4-4	-	-	-	1-2	1	14	6-9
Ricky Jordan	-	38-43	-	-	-	-	-	-	-	-	-	24-25	32	49	38-43
John Kruk	-	16-26	-	-	-	29-28	-	9-10	-	-	-	4-4	18	100	54-64
Steve Lake	14-10	-	-	-	-	-	-	-	-	-	-	-	18	6	14-10
Chuck Malone	-	-	-	-	-	-	-	-	-	-	-	-	-	-	-
Carmelo Martinez	-	19-16	-	-	-	6-9	-	1-0	-	-	-	11-12	24	27	26-25
Roger McDowell	-	-	-	-	-	-	-	-	-	-	-	-	-	-	-
Chuck McElroy	-	-	-	-	-	-	-	-	-	-	-	-	-	-	-
Louie Meadows	-	-	-	-	-	-	-	-	-	-	-	-	-	-	-
Brad Moore	-	-	-	-	-	-	-	-	-	-	-	-	-	-	-
Mickey Morandini	-	-	12-11	-	-	-	-	-	-	-	-	-	2	21	12-11
Terry Mulholland	-	-	-	-	-	-	-	-	-	12-14	-	-	11	15	12-14
Dale Murphy	-	-	-	-	-	-	0-1	22-30	-	-	-	22-31	19	34	22-31
Tom Nieto	5-4	-	-	-	-	-	-	-	-	-	-	-	9	-	5-4
Dickie Noles	-	-	-	-	-	-	-	-	-	-	-	-	-	-	-
Steve Ontiveros	-	-	-	-	-	-	-	-	-	-	-	-	-	-	-
Jeff Parrett	-	-	-	-	-	-	-	-	-	2-3	-	-	3	2	2-3
Randy Ready	-	-	10-14	-	-	14-9	-	-	-	-	1-3	0-1	33	14	24-23
Bruce Ruffin	-	-	-	-	-	-	-	-	-	10-15	-	-	9	16	10-15
Dickie Thon	-	-	-	-	68-73	-	-	-	-	-	-	-	53	88	68-73
Jim Vatcher	-	-	-	-	-	1-2	-	1-3	-	-	-	-	6	1	2-5
Floyd Youmans	-	-	-	-	-	-	-	-	-	-	-	-	-	-	-

TEAM TOTALS: BATTING

	AB	H	2B	3B	HR	RBI	BB	SO	BA	SA	OBA
Season	5535	1410	237	27	103	619	582	915	.255	.363	.327
vs. Left-Handers	1940	490	78	10	38	207	191	314	.253	.362	.322
vs. Right-Handers	3595	920	159	17	65	412	391	601	.256	.364	.330
vs. Ground-Ballers	2938	751	120	11	47	322	277	471	.256	.352	.321
vs. Fly-Ballers	2597	659	117	16	56	297	305	444	.254	.376	.333
Home Games	2691	685	110	12	47	298	288	451	.255	.357	.326
Road Games	2844	725	127	15	56	321	294	464	.255	.369	.327
Grass Fields	1475	383	67	7	26	162	160	246	.260	.367	.334
Artificial Turf	4060	1027	170	20	77	457	422	669	.253	.362	.324
April	630	157	29	2	9	68	72	89	.249	.344	.330
May	877	255	43	8	19	122	94	142	.291	.423	.359
June	953	234	36	1	17	93	107	143	.246	.339	.323
July	908	226	37	6	21	118	106	161	.249	.372	.327
August	1050	264	49	3	17	108	111	163	.251	.352	.326
Sept./Oct.	1117	274	43	7	20	110	92	217	.245	.350	.302
Leading Off Inn.	1326	331	57	6	26	26	116	220	.250	.360	.317
Bases Empty	3078	723	123	11	57	57	295	540	.235	.338	.306
Runners On	2457	687	114	16	46	562	287	375	.280	.395	.352
Runners/Scor. Pos.	1446	380	60	9	24	485	214	247	.263	.367	.352
Runners On/2 Out	1068	286	51	6	17	233	156	180	.268	.375	.364
Scor. Pos./2 Out	711	173	30	4	11	207	126	127	.243	.343	.359
Late-Inning Pressure	864	235	26	4	17	98	110	154	.272	.370	.357
Leading Off	207	54	5	1	3	3	17	38	.261	.338	.329
Runners On	404	117	11	2	9	90	69	71	.290	.394	.391
Runners/Scor. Pos.	257	61	7	2	5	81	53	49	.237	.339	.363

RUNS BATTED IN	From 1B	From 2B	From 3B	Scoring Position
Totals	88/1817	176/1116	252/641	428/1757
Percentage	4.8%	15.8%	39.3%	24.4%

TEAM TOTALS: PITCHING

	W-L	ERA	AB	H	HR	BB	SO	BA	SA	OBA
Season	77-85	4.07	5451	1381	124	651	840	.253	.384	.334
vs. Left-Handers			2035	520	49	308	311	.256	.386	.354
vs. Right-Handers			3416	861	75	343	529	.252	.383	.321
vs. Ground-Ballers			2554	654	35	302	428	.256	.354	.336
vs. Fly-Ballers			2897	727	89	349	412	.251	.411	.331
Home Games	41-40	4.00	2795	692	67	333	440	.248	.392	.329
Road Games	36-45	4.14	2656	689	57	318	400	.259	.376	.339
Grass Fields	18-24	4.35	1375	361	36	159	194	.263	.383	.341
Artificial Turf	59-61	3.97	4076	1020	88	492	646	.250	.385	.331
April	10-9	3.58	615	162	10	71	85	.263	.372	.338
May	14-11	4.53	860	235	25	96	113	.273	.415	.348
June	11-17	4.17	924	228	24	111	150	.247	.387	.329
July	14-13	4.03	912	233	24	102	149	.255	.405	.330
August	11-19	4.47	1037	281	21	124	161	.271	.391	.349
Sept./Oct.	17-16	3.58	1103	242	20	147	182	.219	.342	.312
Leading Off Inn.			1298	336	22	153	189	.259	.370	.338
Bases Empty			3023	746	61	330	453	.247	.370	.323
Runners On			2428	635	63	321	387	.262	.402	.346
Runners/Scor. Pos.			1449	365	35	227	238	.252	.388	.349
Runners On/2 Out			1015	255	19	153	184	.251	.370	.355
Scor. Pos./2 Out			684	169	14	131	131	.247	.386	.376
Late-Inning Pressure			790	200	9	91	116	.253	.339	.331
Leading Off			197	44	1	24	29	.223	.264	.308
Runners On			338	90	4	44	46	.266	.358	.351
Runners/Scor. Pos.			195	55	1	32	19	.282	.369	.383
First 9 Batters			2988	742	66	375	514	.248	.374	.333
Second 9 Batters			1361	355	32	170	189	.261	.393	.343
All Batters Thereafter			1102	284	26	106	137	.258	.401	.324

PITTSBURGH PIRATES

- **Pittsburgh's sacrificial lamb.**
- **How long do great outfields last?**

From *The New York Times,* April 16, 1990: "The Pirates are hardly shoo-ins to win the National League pennant, but don't rule them out, [according to] *The 1990 Elias Baseball Analyst.*

"For one thing, the Pirates had an especially poor record in one-run games [in 1989], one of the strongest signs, according to Elias records, that a team will win more games the following season.

"For another, the Pirates had a much better record during the 1990 exhibition season than they had over the course of the 1989 season, another strong indicator that their record will improve.

"Either indicator gives a team about a 70 percent chance of improving. Together they amount to a statistical lock.

"According to Elias records dating back to 1981, of the 21 teams that had both especially poor records in one-run games the previous season and especially large improvements in their won-lost records in spring training over the previous season, all 21 had season-to-season improvements. The average gain was 15 victories, enough to put the 1990 Pirates on the threshold of contention.

"The cutoffs were five games below .500 in one-run games, and spring training records at least 100 points above the previous season's winning percentage.

"Technically, the Atlanta Braves . . . also met both tests. But [Elias], which prepared the basic research before the lockout-shortened 1990 exhibition season, notes that to match the statistical significance of a 100-point improvement in a 30-game exhibition season takes a 130-point improvement in a 15-game season.

"Under the lockout-adjusted 130-point test, only the Pirates qualify as certain to improve."

We'd also like to remind you that among the other longshot division winners identified by this system were the 1987 Minnesota Twins (coming off a 71–91 mark the year before), the 1988 Los Angeles Dodgers (73–89 a year earlier), and the granddaddy of all longshots, the 1989 Baltimore Orioles (67–95 in 1988).

That having been said, here's a list of teams who played at least five games below the .500 mark in one-run games last season. That's step one. The rest is up to you. Keep your eye on these teams during spring training, while everyone else is telling you that spring results are as meaningless as earthquake predictions. Should they compile winning percentages at least 100 points higher than their regular-season marks for 1990 (see table), you've found yourself an upset contender for postseason play in 1991. Note that the records needed in spring training are approximate, based on 30-game schedules:

Team	1-Run	Overall Record	Needed in Spring
Baltimore Orioles	22–28	.472 (76–85)	18–12
Cleveland Indians	16–24	.475 (77–85)	18–12
Kansas City Royals	21–26	.466 (75–86)	17–13
Milwaukee Brewers	18–23	.457 (74–88)	17–13
New York Yankees	23–29	.414 (67–95)	16–14
Seattle Mariners	20–28	.475 (77–85)	18–12
Chicago Cubs	24–29	.475 (77–85)	18–12
New York Mets	23–28	.562 (91–71)	20–10
San Diego Padres	19–27	.463 (75–87)	17–13

One final caution: Don't be afraid to blaze a trail for one of those teams on account of a poor record in 1990, should they qualify this spring. Remember the examples mentioned earlier, along with the words of *Sports Illustrated*'s Ralph Wiley, who, following Cincinnati's World Series sweep over Oakland, advised, "Whenever you see a bandwagon loading, especially one of sportswriters—jump off."

In addition to the one-run factor, the Pirates were a much healthier bunch in 1990 than they had been the year before when, by April 16, Andy Van Slyke, Sid Bream, Mike LaValliere and Jim Gott had already suffered injuries that put them on the disabled list. There were some nicks in 1990, but most of them affected secondary pitchers and role-playing extra men. John Smiley, who suffered a fractured hand, and Bob Walk, with a troublesome groin, were the only core players (starting lineup, starting rotation, closer) who were disabled during the season.

But the most significant on-field development for the Pirates last season, one that could have implications beyond the winning of a single division title, may have been their filling two revolving-door positions. Consider that, excluding the pitching position, there are 96 "team/positions" in the National League. From 1985 through 1989, there had been only three team/positions without a 100-game starter in any of the five seasons: Pirates/shortstop, Pirates/right field and Expos/catcher. But with Jay Bell at shortstop and Bobby Bonilla in right field, Jim Leyland had no worries at the very positions that had troubled him and his predecessors for most of the '80s. (The Expos/catcher streak still lives, by the way: Mike Fitzgerald led the team with 84 starts. The last Montreal catcher to start 100 games was Gary Carter in 1984.)

In Bonilla's case, of course, Leyland shifted a player to the outfield who had played third base for most of his time in Pittsburgh. But Bell was a *deus ex machina* who followed the Pirates' League of Nations series of shortstops that included Dale Berra, Sammy Khalifa, Rey Quinones, and Rafael

Belliard. Bell had a strong second half after being recalled from Buffalo in 1989, and followed with a steady 1990 at-bat and in the field. Among his offensive achievements were the highest batting average on the team (.328) in Late-Inning Pressure Situations and the best on-base average on the team (.389) when leading off an inning. But if there was one facet of the game that Bell brought to baseball fans better than anyone since Gene Mauch's last days as a general, it was the manly art of sacrifice bunting.

Watching Bell bunt the ball must have warmed the heart of Mauch, baseball's most firmly devoted disciple of Little Ball. Bell's team-record 39 sacrifice bunts were the most by any National League player since 1922, when ol' Zebulon Terry, the second baseman for the Cubs, had the same total. Under Leyland's direction, the second spot in the Pirates' order had more sacrifice bunts than the ninth spot (40 to 35). But what really branded the technique unusual was the number of times that the Pirates bunted in the first inning—three times as often as the next-nearest team, in fact. The following table lists the total of sacrifice bunts for each major-league team in 1990, followed by the number of sacrifices in the first inning:

	Total	1st Inn.		Total	1st Inn.
Chicago	75	0	**Pittsburgh**	96	18
Baltimore	72	1	Cincinnati	88	4
Oakland	60	2	Montreal	87	2
Milwaukee	59	2	Houston	79	3
California	58	2	San Diego	79	6
Cleveland	54	4	St. Louis	77	2
Texas	54	2	San Francisco	76	3
Boston	48	2	Philadelphia	73	2
Seattle	41	0	Los Angeles	71	5
Minnesota	40	3	Chicago	61	1
New York	37	1	Atlanta	58	3
Detroit	36	1	New York	54	1
Kansas City	31	1			
Toronto	18	2			

By season's end, Bell's early bunting had become the trademark of the Pirates' offense, one that would inspire among Pirates fans the kind of knowledgeable applause with which Miami Beach audiences would greet Jackie Gleason's "How Swwwwweet It Is" pronouncements. The first-inning sacrifice is a tactic available to, and eschewed by, all other major-league managers. Leyland's adoption of it as his own brings to mind other managerial or coaching idiosyncrasies. When he managed the Pirates in the 1950s, Bobby Bragan at one point gave a trial run to a batting order that featured his power hitters at the top and his pitcher hitting seventh. In the seventies, Tom Landry once shuffled quarterbacks, alternating Craig Morton and Roger Staubach on every down. And this past season, Paul Westhead adapted Mouse Davis's run-and-shoot offense to the NBA.

Bell accounted for 17 of the Pirates' 18 first-inning sacrifices (the other was a squeeze play in a five-run first inning by that noted bat manipulator, Dann Bilardello). The decision to sacrifice so often in the first inning was obviously aimed at gaining an early lead. Two-thirds of all major-league games are won by the team scoring the first run, and the Pirates last season were not, after all, a great comeback team: They had a 5–53 record in games in which they trailed after six innings. The Cubs (6–65) and the Cardinals (5–69) were the only National League teams with poorer records in that category. The Leyland solution: bunt early and often.

But the scoring-the-first-run factor applies to all teams, not just the Pirates, and there are other teams that are nearly as bad at late-game comebacks. The question is, was there a unique combination of circumstances present in Pittsburgh that would force this one manager to adopt a strategem that his colleagues uniformly avoid?

A part of the answer is the speed, or lack of it, of the Pirates' leadoff hitters. Wally Backman (81 starts leading off) and Gary Redus (41) were the players used most often at the top of the order; those two would not win any races against the other leadoff hitters in the National League. Rather than let them steal their way into scoring position (Pittsburgh's leadoff hitters stole only 13 bases, the fewest in the National League), Leyland chose to bunt them over.

In addition, look beyond Bell in the Pirates' lineup to the 3-4-5 spots, usually manned by the regular outfielders, Andy Van Slyke, Bobby Bonilla, and Barry Bonds. Here are the statistics generated in those spots:

	AB	H	2B	3B	HR	RBI	BB	BA
#3 Hitters	627	173	36	9	20	91	75	.276
#4 Hitters	638	178	39	8	32	122	46	.279
#5 Hitters	583	173	32	2	34	120	90	.297
Totals	1848	524	107	19	86	333	211	.284

Most impressive are the RBI totals for the fourth and fifth spots, each of which was the highest in the National League. Collectively, the Pirates' total of 333 runs batted in was the highest in the majors by any team's 3-4-5 hitters; here are the numbers for the top five teams:

	AB	H	2B	3B	HR	RBI	BB	BA
Pittsburgh	1848	524	107	19	86	333	211	.284
San Francisco	1920	539	88	10	88	332	169	.281
Los Angeles	1889	544	81	5	80	321	197	.288
Oakland	1835	466	73	5	97	310	258	.254
Toronto	1894	523	91	6	95	310	203	.276

Leyland possessed the most productive 3-4-5 hitters in the major leagues. To get those guys into position to drive in a run, and to minimize the possibility of his number-two hitter grounding into a double play or striking out (Bell fanned 109 times), Leyland was more than willing to sacrifice Bell's position in the batting order.

So much for the rationale; what were the results? The Pirates' leadoff hitter in the first inning reached first base and stayed there in 47 innings last season. (By "and stayed there" we're excluding his advancing during the number-two hitter's at-bat on a stolen base, wild pitch, passed ball, wild pickoff throw, etc.) On 14 occasions, Jay Bell sacrificed the runner to second; 33 other times (including twice when Bell bunted for a hit), the inning proceeded without a sacrifice bunt. Even with all of the reasons outlined above that led Jim Leyland to use Bell to sacrifice, the Pirates still scored runs more frequently when not bunting than they did when they bunted:

	Sac.	No Sac.
Innings	14	33
Scored 1+ Runs	7	19
Pct. Scored	50%	58%
Total Runs	13	43
Runs per Inning	0.93	1.30

Somewhere in Florida, Earl Weaver has a smile on his face!

As an adjunct to the tables on the Pirates' 3-4-5 hitters, the following chart shows the collective offensive numbers generated by a team's outfielders in 1990. For years, a popular discussion point has been which team in baseball at any given moment has the best outfield. In any such discussion related to last season, all logical signs point to Three Rivers Stadium. Since Van Slyke, Bonilla, and Bonds batted 3-4-5 most of the season, the Pittsburgh numbers in this chart are similar to those listed above. But they do include cameo appearances in the outfield by R.J. Reynolds, Gary Redus, and others. Remember, these totals include only times at bat by players while playing the outfield. (Note to wise guys: We know, we know, nobody bats *while playing the outfield*. The technical definition: plate appearances and base running after playing an outfield position at the end of the previous half-inning, or, in the case of a visting-team player, first-inning plate appearances and base running of players whose first defensive position in the bottom of the first is in the outfield. To our regular readers: Sorry, but wise guys are everywhere.) We've listed them by league and ranked them by total runs batted in:

	AB	H	2B	3B	HR	RBI	BB	SB	BA
Pittsburgh	1837	532	106	17	80	318	228	83	.290
N.Y. Mets	1841	498	86	6	86	277	209	58	.271
Los Angeles	1908	524	88	10	65	267	194	66	.275
Atlanta	1895	537	97	15	86	256	199	73	.283
Cincinnati	1879	506	99	13	56	243	184	72	.269
San Diego	1924	512	90	15	39	242	152	64	.266
Philadelphia	1857	524	85	12	45	232	279	64	.282
San Francisco	1906	549	81	12	51	227	197	66	.288
Chi. Cubs	1914	509	83	14	50	221	166	67	.266
Montreal	1837	487	65	18	43	207	221	142	.265
Houston	1825	456	68	12	39	177	178	78	.250
St. Louis	1929	538	94	27	26	175	169	157	.279

	AB	H	2B	3B	HR	RBI	BB	SB	BA
Oakland	1855	516	89	7	86	259	232	88	.278
Kansas City	1805	500	96	17	48	251	167	53	.277
Milwaukee	1806	436	69	10	65	249	198	51	.241
Boston	1842	526	96	21	52	243	182	24	.286
California	1897	496	69	17	56	241	178	49	.261
Seattle	1856	514	92	13	42	238	175	55	.277
Texas	1823	470	97	11	50	238	173	56	.258
Toronto	1880	499	95	14	50	234	129	54	.265
Cleveland	1883	489	101	16	47	232	129	71	.260
Minnesota	1869	514	94	16	36	210	145	50	.275
N.Y. Yankees	1843	461	85	9	57	208	149	62	.250
Chi. White Sox	1856	496	103	23	27	206	145	97	.267
Detroit	1708	428	67	17	40	197	163	28	.251
Baltimore	1868	469	68	10	36	187	165	65	.251

Besides leading the majors in runs batted in, Pittsburgh's outfielders also led in batting average, slugging average (.496), doubles, and total extra-base hits (203). The Bucs drove in 59 more runs than Oakland's heralded outfielders; to give the A's their due, their outfielders did lead the majors in runs scored (319).

Defensively, it's true that the Reds' outfielders ranked 1-2-3 in the league in fielding percentage, and Cincinnati led the majors in most outfield assists (47) and fewest outfield errors (10). But Cincinnati's outfielders didn't come close to the offensive production of the Pirates' gardeners (ah, the old *Sporting News* lingo). And the Pirates weren't exactly chopped liver out there; they were the only major-league team that had two Gold Glovers (Bonds and Van Slyke) among their suburbanites (ah, the *really* old *Sporting News* lingo).

We're satisfied that the Pirates were the best. The key question then becomes, how long will they stay around? Even the best outfields in baseball history have characteristically had life spans shorter than you might expect.

Only eight outfields in major-league history have remained intact for as long as five consecutive years, with the same three players ranking 1-2-3 on the team in outfield games played in each of those years:

Period	Team	Years	Outfielders
1910–15	Red Sox	6	Hooper-Lewis-Speaker
1957–62	Pirates	6	Clemente-Skinner-Virdon
1891–95	Phillies	5	Delahanty-Hamilton-Thompson
1912–16	Senators	5	Milan-Moeller-Shanks
1920–24	Browns	5	Jacobson-Tobin-Williams
1925–29	Yankees	5	Combs-Meusel-Ruth
1954–58	Red Sox	5	Jensen-Piersall-Williams
1975–79	Reds	5	Foster-Geronimo-Griffey

Only one other team in the past 50 years has kept a regular outfield intact for even four years. That was Toronto from 1985 to 1988, with Barfield, Bell, and Moseby. Given the direction of salaries and the born-again mobility of free agents, the Pirates have our best (though probably vain) wishes for retaining what it took them so long to assemble.

WON-LOST RECORD BY STARTING POSITION

Pittsburgh Pirates	C	1B	2B	3B	SS	LF	CF	RF	DH	P	Leadoff	Cleanup	Starts vs. LH	Starts vs. RH	Total Starts
Moises Alou	-	-	-	-	-	0-1	-	-	-	-	0-1	-	1	-	0-1
Wally Backman	-	-	7-7	38-30	-	-	-	-	-	-	44-37	-	1	81	45-37
Doug Bair	-	-	-	-	-	-	-	-	-	-	-	-	-	-	-
Stan Belinda	-	-	-	-	-	-	-	-	-	-	-	-	-	-	-
Jay Bell	-	-	-	-	89-64	-	-	-	-	-	-	-	68	85	89-64
Rafael Belliard	-	-	4-0	-	6-3	-	-	-	-	-	-	-	4	9	10-3
Dann Bilardello	8-3	-	-	-	-	-	-	-	-	-	-	-	6	5	8-3
Barry Bonds	-	-	-	-	-	85-59	0-1	-	-	-	9-4	-	57	88	85-60
Bobby Bonilla	-	1-1	-	4-4	-	-	-	88-61	-	-	-	93-66	67	92	93-66
Sid Bream	-	57-43	-	-	-	-	-	-	-	-	-	-	10	90	57-43
John Cangelosi	-	-	-	-	-	0-2	4-5	-	-	-	4-4	-	9	2	4-7
Steve Carter	-	-	-	-	-	-	-	-	-	-	-	-	-	-	-
Doug Drabek	-	-	-	-	-	-	-	-	-	25-8	-	-	18	15	25-8
Carlos Garcia	-	-	-	-	-	-	-	-	-	-	-	-	-	-	-
Neal Heaton	-	-	-	-	-	-	-	-	-	15-9	-	-	11	13	15-9
Mark Huismann	-	-	-	-	-	-	-	-	-	-	-	-	-	-	-
Jeff King	-	-	-	53-33	-	-	-	-	-	-	7-1	1-0	68	18	53-33
Bob Kipper	-	-	-	-	-	-	-	-	-	0-1	-	-	-	1	0-1
Randy Kramer	-	-	-	-	-	-	-	-	-	0-2	-	-	1	1	0-2
Bill Landrum	-	-	-	-	-	-	-	-	-	-	-	-	-	-	-
Mike LaValliere	47-40	-	-	-	-	-	-	-	-	-	-	-	8	79	47-40
Jose Lind	-	-	84-60	-	-	-	-	-	-	-	-	-	66	78	84-60
Carmelo Martinez	-	2-0	-	-	-	0-1	-	-	-	-	-	-	2	1	2-1
Lloyd McClendon	-	-	-	-	-	-	-	-	-	-	-	-	-	-	-
Orlando Merced	-	-	-	-	-	-	-	-	-	-	-	-	-	-	-
Vicente Palacios	-	-	-	-	-	-	-	-	-	-	-	-	-	-	-
Bob Patterson	-	-	-	-	-	-	-	-	-	3-2	-	-	3	2	3-2
Ted Power	-	-	-	-	-	-	-	-	-	-	-	-	-	-	-
Tom Prince	1-2	-	-	-	-	-	-	-	-	-	-	-	2	1	1-2
Gary Redus	-	35-23	-	-	-	4-0	0-1	1-0	-	-	26-15	-	63	1	40-24
Rick Reed	-	-	-	-	-	-	-	-	-	5-3	-	-	2	6	5-3
Jerry Reuss	-	-	-	-	-	-	-	-	-	0-1	-	-	1	-	0-1
R.J. Reynolds	-	-	-	-	-	6-3	15-8	6-6	-	-	4-5	1-1	28	16	27-17
Mike Roesler	-	-	-	-	-	-	-	-	-	-	-	-	-	-	-
Mark Ross	-	-	-	-	-	-	-	-	-	-	-	-	-	-	-
Scott Ruskin	-	-	-	-	-	-	-	-	-	-	-	-	-	-	-
Mark Ryal	-	-	-	-	-	0-1	-	-	-	-	-	-	-	1	0-1
Don Slaught	39-22	-	-	-	-	-	-	-	-	-	1-0	-	53	8	39-22
John Smiley	-	-	-	-	-	-	-	-	-	13-12	-	-	8	17	13-12
Zane Smith	-	-	-	-	-	-	-	-	-	7-3	-	-	6	4	7-3
Walt Terrell	-	-	-	-	-	-	-	-	-	8-8	-	-	5	11	8-8
Jay Tibbs	-	-	-	-	-	-	-	-	-	-	-	-	-	-	-
Randy Tomlin	-	-	-	-	-	-	-	-	-	6-6	-	-	4	8	6-6
Andy Van Slyke	-	-	-	-	-	-	76-52	-	-	-	-	-	39	89	76-52
Bob Walk	-	-	-	-	-	-	-	-	-	12-12	-	-	10	14	12-12
Mike York	-	-	-	-	-	-	-	-	-	1-0	-	-	-	1	1-0

TEAM TOTALS: BATTING

	AB	H	2B	3B	HR	RBI	BB	SO	BA	SA	OBA
Season	5388	1395	288	42	138	693	582	914	.259	.405	.330
vs. Left-Handers	2338	602	126	21	63	296	243	371	.257	.410	.326
vs. Right-Handers	3050	793	162	21	75	397	339	543	.260	.401	.333
vs. Ground-Ballers	2716	728	147	25	62	351	271	448	.268	.409	.335
vs. Fly-Ballers	2672	667	141	17	76	342	311	466	.250	.400	.325
Home Games	2585	655	145	19	59	330	284	426	.253	.393	.327
Road Games	2803	740	143	23	79	363	298	488	.264	.416	.333
Grass Fields	1463	402	67	9	47	205	143	283	.275	.429	.337
Artificial Turf	3925	993	221	33	91	488	439	631	.253	.396	.328
April	685	181	29	5	22	89	61	121	.264	.418	.329
May	875	256	56	11	20	127	98	142	.293	.450	.361
June	877	226	49	9	13	99	78	156	.258	.379	.316
July	885	217	42	2	23	120	105	142	.245	.375	.322
August	1032	263	53	7	32	127	111	157	.255	.413	.326
Sept./Oct.	1034	252	59	8	28	131	129	196	.244	.397	.327
Leading Off Inn.	1306	348	75	7	31	31	127	210	.266	.406	.335
Bases Empty	3096	782	173	20	75	75	284	520	.253	.394	.318
Runners On	2292	613	115	22	63	618	298	394	.267	.419	.346
Runners/Scor. Pos.	1370	377	67	15	35	531	211	250	.275	.423	.361
Runners On/2 Out	997	240	49	6	28	243	151	195	.241	.386	.344
Scor. Pos./2 Out	649	151	30	3	17	207	125	133	.233	.367	.360
Late-Inning Pressure	721	183	38	1	11	76	93	130	.254	.355	.337
Leading Off	186	59	14	0	2	2	25	32	.317	.425	.401
Runners On	319	79	14	1	3	68	41	62	.248	.326	.325
Runners/Scor. Pos.	182	48	6	1	1	59	33	36	.264	.324	.361

RUNS BATTED IN	From 1B	From 2B	From 3B	Scoring Position
Totals	94/1596	192/1056	269/617	461/1673
Percentage	5.9%	18.2%	43.6%	27.6%

TEAM TOTALS: PITCHING

	W-L	ERA	AB	H	HR	BB	SO	BA	SA	OBA
Season	95-67	3.40	5448	1367	135	413	848	.251	.381	.305
vs. Left-Handers			2190	559	53	198	326	.255	.385	.318
vs. Right-Handers			3258	808	82	215	522	.248	.378	.297
vs. Ground-Ballers			2549	640	36	177	437	.251	.348	.301
vs. Fly-Ballers			2899	727	99	236	411	.251	.409	.309
Home Games	49-32	3.24	2737	674	63	213	450	.246	.373	.302
Road Games	46-35	3.56	2711	693	72	200	398	.256	.388	.309
Grass Fields	25-17	3.89	1419	372	47	88	211	.262	.412	.308
Artificial Turf	70-50	3.23	4029	995	88	325	637	.247	.369	.304
April	14-6	2.61	660	155	14	49	108	.235	.333	.287
May	15-11	3.92	868	223	26	63	147	.257	.403	.310
June	14-13	3.87	906	241	30	93	122	.266	.430	.336
July	15-11	3.79	909	223	21	79	143	.245	.367	.307
August	17-14	3.33	1071	290	23	70	157	.271	.394	.317
Sept./Oct.	20-12	2.80	1034	235	21	59	171	.227	.345	.270
Leading Off Inn.			1362	363	45	78	189	.267	.421	.311
Bases Empty			3245	804	87	219	506	.248	.383	.300
Runners On			2203	563	48	194	342	.256	.377	.313
Runners/Scor. Pos.			1263	313	31	149	205	.248	.371	.322
Runners On/2 Out			941	223	15	113	154	.237	.335	.321
Scor. Pos./2 Out			623	142	10	92	101	.228	.324	.330
Late-Inning Pressure			809	196	15	87	157	.242	.350	.316
Leading Off			203	57	4	17	34	.281	.399	.339
Runners On			350	84	5	42	69	.240	.329	.316
Runners/Scor. Pos.			211	51	4	36	44	.242	.332	.342
First 9 Batters			3000	736	74	250	524	.245	.368	.305
Second 9 Batters			1368	336	27	84	200	.246	.369	.292
All Batters Thereafter			1080	295	34	79	124	.273	.431	.324

ST. LOUIS CARDINALS

- **Farewell to fielding percentage.**
- **What's black and white and scanned all over?**

Two years ago, Jose Oquendo broke Ryne Sandberg's single-season National League record for fielding percentage by a second baseman. Last season he eclipsed his own year-old mark. Now, most right-thinking baseball fans agree that fielding is an underappreciated talent. And the significance of Oquendo's achievement is undeniable: He became only the second player in the last 50 years to break his league's fielding percentage record at any position in two consecutive seasons. (The other was Larry Bowa, 1971–72.) Nevertheless, Oquendo's two-season, record-breaking performance received almost no attention for an obvious reason: Fielding percentage, one of our most venerable measures, has become obsolete. At a time when baseball fans have access to more statistics than ever before, and a greater capacity to interpret them, fielding percentage is a vestige of a simpler, less accomplished age.

Fielding percentage has been a part of every player's statistical profile throughout the entire history of major league baseball. The 1877 *Constitution and Playing Rules of the National League of Professional Base Ball Clubs* didn't take note of doubles, triples, home runs, walks, or strikeouts (or batting average in Late-Inning Pressure Situations) for batters. But its fielding section was remarkably similar to those found in modern publications: games, putouts, assists, errors, total chances, and fielding percentage. The players were ranked within their positions according to fielding percentage. But more than 100 years later, fielding percentages have been rendered useless by two shortcomings, one of credibility, the other of comprehension.

First, the name implies too much. A fielding percentage is nothing more than the inverse of the rate at which a player commits errors. It tells us nothing about his range, his ability to position himself properly, his arm, or his speed in the field—only how likely he is not to commit an error. It is a critical evaluation of a player's minimum level of competence: when a ball is hit to him, how likely is he to field it cleanly? But because the name is so vague, failing to describe precisely what it measures, a fielding percentage seems to promise more than it delivers, and so its credibility has been greatly diminished.

But more importantly, fielding percentages are unintelligible: a decimal point, a nine, another high number or two, and a tie-breaking digit. Fielding proficiency has improved to such a degree that it has eclipsed our ability to measure it reasonably with the outdated standards of 100 years ago. Does anyone remember the slide rule? It was an elegant instrument for basic computations before electronic calculators put eight-place decimal accuracy in the palms of our hands. Divide 893 by 26 with a slide rule? No problem: thirtysomething. Today, any 10-year-old can whip out his Casio and tell you the answer: 34.346153something. Fielding percentages are the slide rules of baseball. The combined effect of more skillful players, larger gloves, better lighting, and artificial turf has created ever-increasing levels of excellence, while fielding percentages put the focus on the opposite: ever-diminishing levels of incompetence.

The following table illustrates this trend by showing the major league averages, along with the best and worst marks among players with at least 100 games, at the four infield positions at 25-year intervals throughout history:

		1890	1915	1940	1965	1990
1B	Best	.985	.996	.995	.997	.998
	Average	.974	.988	.990	.991	.992
	Worst	.963	.983	.985	.984	.987
2B	Best	.952	.974	.980	.988	.996
	Average	.921	.954	.967	.976	.984
	Worst	.893	.936	.941	.963	.972
3B	Best	.933	.969	.962	.976	.970
	Average	.867	.938	.942	.955	.945
	Worst	.811	.917	.926	.919	.928
SS	Best	.936	.968	.970	.981	.996
	Average	.886	.932	.949	.963	.970
	Worst	.856	.898	.936	.938	.953

As a result, the differences between the best and second-best players at some positions have grown too narrow to be expressed in the conventional three-digit form. The all-time career leaders and runners-up at three infield positions (minimum: 1000 games):

First Base		Second Base		Shortstop	
Steve Garvey	.996	Ryne Sandberg	.989	Tony Fernandez	.980
Wes Parker	.996	Tommy Herr	.989	Larry Bowa	.980

The Oquendo problem is similar. Sandberg set his single-season record of .994 in 1986. Three years later, Oquendo broke that mark, but his percentage appeared as .994 as well. To measure such minute differences, we need a tool that respects such narrow margins to replace the one that hides them.

That tool is chances per error, which eliminates both the ambiguity of the term "fielding percentage," and the imprecise way in which it is expressed. Oquendo's record would be expressed as one error for every 227 chances, clearly in excess of both his previous mark (one per 170) and Sandberg's earlier record (one per 161). Chances per error magnifies the distinctions between superlatives, where fielding percentage blurs them. And the name describes exactly what is being measured. Even the otherwise imperceptible differences between the best career averages shown above would become immediately evident. Garvey would lead Parker as the all-time leader at first base by 15 chances per error (one per 246 chances to one per 231), Sandberg would lead Herr by four (92 to 88), and Fernandez would lead Bowa by two (51 to 49).

Use the following table to orient yourself to our new standard. It lists the major league averages for last season (and, for purposes of comparison, for 1900), along with the all-time career and single-season leaders. The record holders are listed following the table:

	P	C	1B	2B	3B	SS	OF
1900 Average	13	20	47	16	10	13	17
1990 Average	22	90	128	61	18	33	53
Career Record	104	149	246	92	35	51	147
Season Record	∞	∞	∞	303	94	227	∞

Career record holders are (in the order of the positions listed above; minimums are 1000 games or 1500 innings pitched): Don Mossi, Bill Freehan, Steve Garvey, Ryne Sandberg, Brooks Robinson, Tony Fernandez, and Terry Puhl. Many qualifying pitchers and outfielders have played error-free seasons, as did Buddy Rosar at catcher (1946) and Garvey at first base (1984). Single-season record holders at the other infield positions: Bobby Grich (1985), Don Money (1974), and Cal Ripken (1990).

Comparisons between players now make more sense. Let's assume two shortstops each had 500 chances in a season. If one made 10 errors and the other made 20, which would more clearly express this relationship: their fielding percentages of .990 and .980, or their chances per error of 50 and 25? Now think about the player with the .990 fielding percentage (or one error per 50 chances): When we say he's twice as reliable as the other player, do we mean that other player has a .445 fielding percentage, or that he makes one error for every 25 chances?

This change in terminology still doesn't resolve the other problems inherent in measuring a player's overall fielding ability. Maybe in time we'll develop reliable measures for a player's range, speed, arm, and so on. And maybe official scoring will become more standardized, so that an error in one city means the same thing as an error anywhere else. Maybe not. But a change from fielding percentage to chances per error does take a very important concept and express it in a straightforward, intuitively satisfying way.

Of course, it's never easy to institute new standards; look around the outfield walls at some major league stadiums and you'll see the remnants of a similar but failed attempt. But we vow that after this hybrid edition, fielding percentages will be totally eradicated from the *Analyst*. We can only hope that chances per error receives greater popular acceptance than 125-meter center field fences and beautiful 25-degree summer days at the ballpark.

Since we're already up on our soapbox, there's something else we'd like to get off our chests. The time has come for a general back-to-basics movement in baseball reporting. Even the problems inherent in fielding percentages don't adequately explain how Jose Oquendo's record can be given less attention than any of the following quasi-news items (and hundreds of others like them): Cal Ripken is within 50 months of Lou Gehrig's consecutive-game mark . . . Carlton Fisk and Jerry Reuss form the oldest opening-day battery since who-knows-when . . . George Brett becomes the first player to win batting titles in three different "decades" . . . Barry Bonds joins the .300/50/30/whatever club . . . Pat Tabler maintains his .500 career batting average with the bases loaded . . . Reuss spends an entire season in the minors to earn a September call-up, allowing him to become, what, the 117th player to hang on long enough to call himself a four-decade player?

Don't get us wrong; following baseball should be fun. And God knows we've played a considerable role in the explosion of sports data. But last season provided a striking, high-profile example of how an emphasis on statistical trivia can crowd out items of greater importance. We are referring to the "Box-Score Wars" between *USA Today* and *The National*.

Remember when a newspaper was something you read? One day, our grandchildren will sit wide-eyed as we tell them about the good old days, before computers produced the glandular box scores that threaten to do to game stories what Bill Cody did to the great American buffalo. We'll describe how we would trudge miles and miles through rain and snow—What's that? It doesn't snow during baseball season? Well, um . . . in *our* day it did! That's right, snowed like the dickens! Miles and miles we'd struggle through blizzards and hailstorms simply to buy a local paper for the baseball coverage—not sidebar events, who-cares lists of this and that, and (in our national sports dailies, at least) box scores that tell us everything from the number of fans wearing red shirts to whether the infield grass was rye or Bermuda, but *stories* about baseball *games*.

Looks of astonishment will turn to awe as our grandchildren hear of the extensive coverage given to even a late-season laugher between the Kansas City A's and the Washington Senators; or the details of two futile innings erased by rain in some obscure town halfway across the continent (to be made up, of course, as part of another dinosaur, a Sunday doubleheader); or even of a simple waiver transaction involving Hank Foiles or Lou Klimchock. Finally, when they can stand it no longer, those awestruck kids will ask the question that gnaws at them: "Radical, Dad. But with all that reading, like, how'd you dudes find time for rotisserie?"

Well, kids, in that more casual age, we just weren't sophisticated enough to take an individual's performance, strip it from the context of the game he played in, and use it as the basis for a six-month-long bet. We didn't have all those clubs (30/30, 20/50, .300/300, and so on), we didn't hold our breath for years while someone pursued a statistical milestone, and we didn't try to come up with reasons and probabilities for every single thing, as if baseball were some kind of natural science instead of a game played by people. If you can believe this, we rooted like hell for certain players not because we "owned" them, but because we liked them. Quaint, huh?

Baseball's a game of stories, not stat lines. When Eddie Gaedel, all 43 inches of him, stepped to the plate for the St. Louis Browns, a lot of people laughed, some gasped, a few harrumphed (you can always pick the harrumphers out in a crowd), and some even called upon baseball to wipe this tiny blight out of its historical record to preserve the sanctity of baseball statistics. Now there's a phrase—how much sanctity do you suppose those people would find if they could see how such an event would be covered today . . .

To begin with, every paper in the country would have scrambled to compose the following list:

Shortest Players Since 1900

Eddie Gaedel	3′7″
Harry Chappas	5′3″
Yo-Yo Davalillo	5′3″
Bob Emmerich	5′3″
Stubby Magner	5′3″

That would have been only the start. *The New York Times* would have run an illustration of Gaedel's strike zone compared to that of a crouching Rickey Henderson. Tony Kubek would have explained how a major league pitcher, under the guidance of a proper instructor like Johnny Podres or Dick Such, should have no trouble striking out an amateur (sound of disgust) like Gaedel. Yes, the next edition of *The Elias Baseball Analyst* would have included a table of walk frequencies classified according to batters' heights. And in all the blather, the fun, spontaneity, and incongruity would have been lost.

Of course, this book is full of numbers, and every one of them represents a fact about baseball. Used as a companion to the games themselves, it can broaden your understanding and deepen your appreciation of baseball. But if you tried to figure out what happened in baseball last year by studying nothing but our numbers, you'd come no closer than the blind men who tried to understand an elephant by feel. You'd miss how Cincinnati's wire-to-wire victory lifted the cloud that had hung over a franchise for a year and a half. You'd miss the tragicomedy of George Steinbrenner's plea-bargaining a two-year suspension down to a lifetime ban. You'd miss the haughty disdain with which the Oakland A's dismissed their nearest challengers, the upstart Chicago White Sox. You'd miss the will-he-won't-he-will-he of Roger Clemens's rumored return to the mound in September. You'd have all the facts, but you'd be missing the things that make us care about them.

A box score is neither steak nor sizzle; it's just the nutritional information. "HR: Sanders (2)" does nothing to convey the excitement of Deion's dash around the bases or his mad sprawl across the plate while Bo lay injured in center field. It takes a game story to tell you about that, or about the timing of a double-switch or an overshift, successful or not; about Fisk's double-tag; about Steve Lyons's mistaking a regular-season game for an exhibition contest. (Incidentally, we know someone who honestly believes that Lyons's stunt was not, repeat *not,* premeditated.) Our national sports dailies seem bent on weaning us away from those stories, so that when we're no longer reading them, they won't have to write them.

Fans around the country asked us last April what we thought of the expanded box scores, and most were surprised to learn that we were horrified by them. How, they wondered, could "stats guys" not like more stats? Well, we happen to be baseball fans, not number freaks. Bigger box scores aren't necessarily better box scores, especially when that extra space is being used to provide daily doses of runners left in scoring position, inherited base runners, relief pitcher "holds" (whatever they are), batting over the last 10 games (whether they took place over the last two weeks or the last four months), umpires, weather conditions, and so on (along with a daily box score–sized explanation of how to decipher the new box scores). Couldn't those facts have been reported within the game story in the rare cases in which they'd mattered? Sure, it's important to know which pitcher stranded the highest percentage of runners over the course of a season. On a game-by-game basis, who needs it? If it was important that day, tell us about it in the story. Otherwise, forget it.

But what surprised us most, considering the initial furor, was how quickly the debate died. Did the fans who disliked the new box scores suddenly grow to enjoy them? Or did they simply realize how easy they were to ignore? If the latter was true—and we think it was—then a lot of time and space was wasted on the efforts of a few rotisserie-crazed editors to outdo each other for an audience consisting mostly of themselves.

WON-LOST RECORD BY STARTING POSITION

St. Louis Cardinals	C	1B	2B	3B	SS	LF	CF	RF	DH	P	Leadoff	Cleanup	Starts vs. LH	Starts vs. RH	Total Starts
Rod Brewer	-	0-4	-	-	-	-	-	-	-	-	-	-	-	4	0-4
Tom Brunansky	-	-	-	-	-	-	-	8-9	-	-	-	-	10	7	8-9
Ernie Camacho	-	-	-	-	-	-	-	-	-	-	-	-	-	-	-
Cris Carpenter	-	-	-	-	-	-	-	-	-	-	-	-	-	-	-
Stan Clarke	-	-	-	-	-	-	-	-	-	-	-	-	-	-	-
Vince Coleman	-	-	-	-	-	46-67	-	1-1	-	-	45-67	-	44	71	47-68
Dave Collins	-	0-1	-	-	-	1-2	-	-	-	-	1-1	-	4	-	1-3
John Costello	-	-	-	-	-	-	-	-	-	-	-	-	-	-	-
Danny Cox	-	-	-	-	-	-	-	-	-	-	-	-	-	-	-
Ken Dayley	-	-	-	-	-	-	-	-	-	-	-	-	-	-	-
Jose DeLeon	-	-	-	-	-	-	-	-	-	8-24	-	-	15	17	8-24
Frank DiPino	-	-	-	-	-	-	-	-	-	-	-	-	-	-	-
Bernard Gilkey	-	-	-	-	-	6-11	-	-	-	-	6-11	-	9	8	6-11
Pedro Guerrero	-	57-75	-	-	-	-	-	-	-	-	-	51-69	51	81	57-75
Ken Hill	-	-	-	-	-	-	-	-	-	6-8	-	-	7	7	6-8
Howard Hilton	-	-	-	-	-	-	-	-	-	-	-	-	-	-	-
Ricky Horton	-	-	-	-	-	-	-	-	-	-	-	-	-	-	-
Rex Hudler	-	3-2	1-4	1-3	-	9-4	2-0	13-9	-	-	4-1	2-2	35	16	29-22
Tim Jones	-	-	3-3	-	10-11	-	-	-	-	-	0-1	-	5	22	13-14
Felix Jose	-	-	-	-	-	0-1	1-1	7-13	-	-	-	0-3	11	12	8-15
Ray Lankford	-	-	-	-	-	-	9-21	-	-	-	-	-	9	21	9-21
Joe Magrane	-	-	-	-	-	-	-	-	-	13-18	-	-	14	17	13-18
Greg Mathews	-	-	-	-	-	-	-	-	-	1-9	-	-	5	5	1-9
Willie McGee	-	-	-	-	-	-	54-63	2-4	-	-	3-2	1-1	47	76	56-67
John Morris	-	-	-	-	-	-	-	1-0	-	-	-	-	-	1	1-0
Tom Niedenfuer	-	-	-	-	-	-	-	-	-	-	-	-	-	-	-
Omar Olivares	-	-	-	-	-	-	-	-	-	3-3	-	-	1	5	3-3
Jose Oquendo	-	-	59-78	-	1-3	-	-	-	-	-	-	-	55	86	60-81
Tom Pagnozzi	28-31	1-0	-	-	-	-	-	-	-	-	-	-	27	33	29-31
Geronimo Pena	-	-	5-6	-	-	-	-	-	-	-	1-0	-	4	7	5-6
Terry Pendleton	-	-	-	51-62	-	-	-	-	-	-	-	-	42	71	51-62
Mike Perez	-	-	-	-	-	-	-	-	-	-	-	-	-	-	-
Tim Sherrill	-	-	-	-	-	-	-	-	-	-	-	-	-	-	-
Bryn Smith	-	-	-	-	-	-	-	-	-	13-12	-	-	10	15	13-12
Lee Smith	-	-	-	-	-	-	-	-	-	-	-	-	-	-	-
Ozzie Smith	-	-	-	-	59-78	-	-	-	-	-	3-3	-	56	81	59-78
Ray Stephens	2-3	-	-	-	-	-	-	-	-	-	-	-	2	3	2-3
Scott Terry	-	-	-	-	-	-	-	-	-	1-1	-	-	-	2	1-1
Bob Tewksbury	-	-	-	-	-	-	-	-	-	10-10	-	-	6	14	10-10
Milt Thompson	-	-	-	-	-	4-4	4-7	36-50	-	-	6-6	-	26	79	44-61
John Tudor	-	-	-	-	-	-	-	-	-	15-7	-	-	5	17	15-7
Denny Walling	-	5-3	-	4-7	-	1-1	-	0-2	-	-	-	-	-	23	10-13
Craig Wilson	-	-	2-1	6-4	-	3-2	-	2-4	-	-	1-0	5-2	17	7	13-11
Todd Worrell	-	-	-	-	-	-	-	-	-	-	-	-	-	-	-
Todd Zeile	40-58	4-7	-	8-16	-	-	-	-	-	-	-	11-15	50	83	52-81

TEAM TOTALS: BATTING

	AB	H	2B	3B	HR	RBI	BB	SO	BA	SA	OBA
Season	5462	1398	255	41	73	554	517	844	.256	.358	.320
vs. Left-Handers	2012	502	111	18	31	196	159	307	.250	.369	.305
vs. Right-Handers	3450	896	144	23	42	358	358	537	.260	.351	.329
vs. Ground-Ballers	2675	705	128	26	29	283	259	411	.264	.363	.327
vs. Fly-Ballers	2787	693	127	15	44	271	258	433	.249	.352	.314
Home Games	2694	690	125	22	43	293	277	395	.256	.367	.325
Road Games	2768	708	130	19	30	261	240	449	.256	.349	.315
Grass Fields	1456	372	60	11	15	131	118	244	.255	.343	.311
Artificial Turf	4006	1026	195	30	58	423	399	600	.256	.363	.323
April	674	169	28	3	9	76	79	97	.251	.341	.326
May	882	197	31	7	10	77	87	141	.223	.308	.293
June	962	255	43	12	14	119	103	157	.265	.378	.333
July	897	219	39	4	10	79	78	140	.244	.330	.304
August	1021	300	59	8	12	106	88	159	.294	.403	.350
Sept./Oct.	1026	258	55	7	18	97	82	150	.251	.371	.310
Leading Off Inn.	1352	332	54	9	22	22	102	183	.246	.348	.300
Bases Empty	3090	792	127	27	49	49	276	473	.256	.362	.320
Runners On	2372	606	128	14	24	505	241	371	.255	.352	.321
Runners/Scor. Pos.	1474	357	84	8	14	459	189	249	.242	.339	.322
Runners On/2 Out	1046	246	61	9	10	199	111	169	.235	.339	.309
Scor. Pos./2 Out	727	165	42	7	6	179	96	122	.227	.329	.318
Late-Inning Pressure	840	208	41	4	9	78	101	142	.248	.338	.327
Leading Off	216	57	10	1	4	4	15	32	.264	.375	.312
Runners On	368	88	14	1	2	71	53	65	.239	.299	.329
Runners/Scor. Pos.	235	58	10	1	1	67	47	45	.247	.311	.363

RUNS BATTED IN	From 1B	From 2B	From 3B	Scoring Position
Totals	56/1530	199/1152	226/611	425/1763
Percentage	3.7%	17.3%	37.0%	24.1%

TEAM TOTALS: PITCHING

	W-L	ERA	AB	H	HR	BB	SO	BA	SA	OBA
Season	70-92	3.87	5488	1432	98	475	833	.261	.380	.320
vs. Left-Handers			2449	675	39	245	365	.276	.390	.340
vs. Right-Handers			3039	757	59	230	468	.249	.373	.304
vs. Ground-Ballers			2452	616	23	219	408	.251	.343	.315
vs. Fly-Ballers			3036	816	75	256	425	.269	.410	.324
Home Games	34-47	4.01	2859	756	47	243	404	.264	.390	.323
Road Games	36-45	3.72	2629	676	51	232	429	.257	.370	.317
Grass Fields	18-24	3.91	1407	379	32	110	234	.269	.390	.321
Artificial Turf	52-68	3.86	4081	1053	66	365	599	.258	.377	.320
April	9-11	3.92	686	188	9	60	72	.274	.376	.335
May	11-16	3.68	929	246	17	63	158	.265	.391	.315
June	11-17	4.83	981	278	20	106	158	.283	.420	.352
July	15-13	3.07	921	226	10	74	149	.245	.330	.302
August	14-14	3.03	957	227	18	72	146	.237	.357	.292
Sept./Oct.	10-21	4.68	1014	267	24	100	150	.263	.403	.327
Leading Off Inn.			1340	337	23	101	189	.251	.369	.306
Bases Empty			3141	775	57	244	467	.247	.365	.305
Runners On			2347	657	41	231	366	.280	.401	.340
Runners/Scor. Pos.			1427	394	18	186	241	.276	.383	.349
Runners On/2 Out			1000	228	13	111	188	.228	.326	.309
Scor. Pos./2 Out			667	153	6	96	130	.229	.319	.330
Late-Inning Pressure			792	219	12	75	134	.277	.390	.337
Leading Off			198	47	4	18	39	.237	.359	.304
Runners On			341	95	5	38	58	.279	.390	.341
Runners/Scor. Pos.			192	52	0	28	37	.271	.339	.346
First 9 Batters			2982	770	45	288	472	.258	.368	.324
Second 9 Batters			1358	350	25	104	209	.258	.374	.310
All Batters Thereafter			1148	312	28	83	152	.272	.422	.323

SAN DIEGO PADRES

- **What is so rare as a trade of a shortstop?**
- **Another reason to admire Tony Gwynn.**

Roberto Alomar and Joe Carter for Tony Fernandez and Fred McGriff! It certainly didn't take long for Joe McIlvaine not only to perpetuate Jack McKeon's fine tradition of big deals by San Diego general managers, but to exceed it. Trader Mac outdid Trader Jack with this one; it was only the second trade in the history of major league baseball to involve four players who had appeared in 140 or more games the previous season. The other? The big Reds-Astros trade following the 1971 season in which Cincinnati received Joe Morgan and Denis Menke (among others) for Lee May and Tommy Helms (among others).

That trade, which also brought Cesar Geronimo and Jack Billingham to Cincinnati, provided the final cogs for the Big Red Machine. In the five years following that trade, the Reds finished with baseball's best record three times and its second-best record twice. It's conceivable that years from now we'll look back on this one to find the foundation of a Big Blue Machine. The question is, will it be the Canadian dark blue of Toronto, or the new navy blue of the Padres?

Because of the quality of the players involved, it's hard to pinpoint any one individual as the key to the deal. After all, this is one of the few trades ever made in which any or all of the players could wind up at the next All-Star Game—or, for that matter, win next year's MVP Award. But it strikes us that a pivotal factor in eventually determining who got the best of whom will be how well Fernandez fills the San Diego shortstop position, which has been manned on a regular basis by only two players, Ozzie Smith and Garry Templeton, over the past 13 years.

Alomar is only 23 years old as the 1991 season begins, while Fernandez will celebrate his 29th birthday on June 30. On the surface, that might seem like a major advantage for the Blue Jays, especially since quickness is such an important commodity for middle infielders and very few shortstops last into baseball middle-age. Ozzie Smith and Garry Templeton were the only shortstops to start more than one game in the majors last season who were at least 33 years old when the season ended.

But while age is a factor to consider in any exchange of players, perhaps it's not quite as important as it once was. After all, even if a team found nine 18-year olds who could hit like Babe Ruth and pitch like him too, it would no longer have any assurance of keeping them beyond the first six years of their careers, after which they could become free agents.

Regular shortstops are traded only about as often as Chris Berman comes up for air, and they seem to change leagues less frequently than players at other positions. Consider that among the ten players in major league history with the most games at the position, not one has played in both the American and National Leagues. Shortstop is the only position for which that is true:

	Majors	A.L.	N.L.
Luis Aparicio	2,581	2,581	0
Larry Bowa	2,222	0	2,222
Luke Appling	2,218	2,218	0
Dave Concepcion	2,178	0	2,178
Rabbit Maranville	2,154	0	2,154
Bill Dahlen	2,132	0	2,132
Bert Campaneris	2,097	2,097	0
*Tommy Corcoran	2,073	0	1,817
Roy McMillan	2,028	0	2,028
Pee Wee Reese	2,014	0	2,014

*Played first two seasons in Players League and American Association.

Ozzie Smith stands 108 games behind Reese and should crack the top ten sometime this season, but since he has played only in the National League, he'll preserve the rule.

Accordingly, we expected that the number of off-season deals that have sent a shortstop between leagues has been relatively low, but little did we realize how low. In the 90-year history of the American and National leagues as organized baseball's two major leagues, here are the only players who appeared in 100 or more games at shortstop in different leagues in successive seasons:

Monte Cross	1901 Phillies	1902 Athletics
George Davis	1901 Giants	1902 White Sox
Bobby Wallace	1901 Cardinals	1902 Browns
Dick Bartell	1939 Cubs	1940 Tigers
Zoilo Versalles	1967 Twins	1968 Dodgers
Leo Cardenas	1968 Reds	1969 Twins
Craig Reynolds	1978 Mariners	1979 Astros
Pepe Frias	1979 Braves	1980 Rangers
Rafael Santana	1987 Mets	1988 Yankees

Among these nine shortstops, only the last six changed leagues as the result of actual trades. Cross, Davis and Wallace—three of the preeminent shortstops of the turn-of-the-century era—all jumped leagues following the expiration of their National League contracts during the period of war between the National and American Leagues after the latter reached major league status in 1901.

Of the six who were traded, none was a player of the quality of Fernandez. All right, Versalles was the American League's Most Valuable Player when the Twins won the pennant in 1965. But Zoilo declined quickly after that season, and by the time he was traded to the Dodgers he was coming off a season in which he batted .200 with eroding defensive skills.

Late last season, Fernandez reached the 1000-game minimum necessary to qualify as the top-fielding shortstop in major league history with a career rate of 51.2 chances per error. (That's a .980 fielding percentage for those of you who have not yet read our Cardinals essay. Yes, we're really serious about this.) He supplanted as champion mild-mannered former Padres manager Larry Bowa, who averaged one error every 49.2 chances in his 16-year career. Now, however, Fernandez will not only be changing leagues, he'll be changing playing surfaces as well, moving from the artificial turf of the Skydome (and previously of Exhibition Stadium) to the California grass of Jack Murphy Stadium. The Blue Jays play 99 games per season on artificial turf; the Padres play only 42 on the rug. And that could allow Bowa to exact sweet revenge against the team that fired him by reclaiming his all-time fielding record from its incumbent shortstop.

For each of the infield positions, the rate of errors committed on grass fields is higher than it is on artificial turf. But while natural surfaces increase errors across the board, there are significant differences in the size of the increases at the four positions. And the position at which grass fields increase errors the most is shortstop.

In 1990, the rate of shortstops' errors on grass fields was 29 percent higher than it was on artificial turf. Here are the figures for the four infield positions (expressed, naturally, in chances per error—no kidding around; we're *serious*):

	Grass Fields	Artificial Turf	Error Increase on Grass
Shortstop	30.2	39.0	29%
Third Base	17.1	20.5	20%
First Base	124.0	135.9	10%
Second Base	59.7	62.3	4%

The positions on the left side of the infield are unforgiving of momentary bobbles, and the slight variations in the bounce of the ball caused by a grass field contribute to the relatively high error rate. (A second baseman or first baseman generally has more time to recover from a momentary bad hop than do his brothers on the other side of the diamond.)

Bowa underwent a turf-to-grass conversion, albeit somewhat later in his career, when he was traded by the Phillies to the Cubs. But since he played only four of his 16 seasons on a grass home field, his fielding statistics did not suffer terribly. Fernandez, with a longer baseball life ahead of him, will have to adapt to his new environment successfully if he is to hold onto the record. And in so doing, he would push the Padres closer toward becoming that Big Blue Machine.

* * *

In sports as well as life, we're always fascinated by those who can overcome some sort of handicap to achieve greatness. In the most obvious cases, the handicap is a physical one. Tom Dempsey's 63-yard field goal has stood as the longest in NFL history for 20 years now, and we frankly hope that it stands forever as a monument to what someone can do after he has been told that he can't do it.

In other instances, an athlete's environment serves as an effective handicap in his pursuit of excellence. The extent to which Glenn Davis was hurt by playing in the Astrodome is well known; we've pointed out in these pages and elsewhere that similar factors work against Jose Canseco and Mark McGwire in the Oakland Coliseum. And we can't help but feel that Ferguson Jenkins might have had an earlier induction into the Hall of Fame if he had not spent so many years pitching in Wrigley Field and Fenway Park, two places that tend to fluff up the old ERA.

A more subtle and less recognized environmental handicap surrounds Tony Gwynn, who has the distinction of being one of baseball's most difficult batters to strike out while playing his home games in a stadium that is the most conducive in baseball to strikeouts.

To paraphrase the ever-nimble Richard Nixon (hey, we know that San Diego is Republican country), let us explain the second part of that statement first. As reported in the Ballparks Section, we have studied the effect that each stadium has on the games that are played there. Some familiar examples: Wrigley Field promotes home runs, Royals Stadium retards them; artificial turf increases extra-base hits and stolen-base percentages. But perhaps the most consistently mystifying effect that we have seen since we introduced the section in the 1987 *Analyst* is the tendency of Jack Murphy Stadium to increase strikeouts.

Remember the methodology we use: we compare the frequency of an event in all of a team's home games with the frequency in all of that team's road games. To broaden the base of the data, we look at the statistics over a five-year span. And the San Diego story has been the same every time we have measured it: there are far more strikeouts in Padres home games than in their road games, and the difference in the rates is greater than it is for any other team. Here are the most recent figures (expressed as plate appearances per strikeout), showing the five parks that have done their best to increase strikeouts over the last five years:

	Home Games PA/SO	Road Games PA/SO	Pct. Diff.
Jack Murphy Stadium	6.25	6.99	11.7
Tiger Stadium	6.76	7.19	6.8
Oakland Coliseum	6.29	6.67	5.9
Shea Stadium	5.92	6.21	5.3
Memorial Stadium	7.04	7.35	4.8

Look at the mammoth difference—over hundreds of games and thousands of plate appearances over the past five years—between the "Pct. Diff." column at Jack Murphy Stadium and at the next-highest park, Tiger Stadium. For whatever reason—hitting background, lights, seven o'clock start for night games—Padres batters and their opponents strike out at a much higher rate at Jack Murphy than they do in road games. But far from sinking under the weight of that kind of albatross, Gwynn has overcome it to an extraordinary degree.

Last season, Gwynn struck out once every 27.3 times at the plate, the lowest rate in the major leagues by far. (Brian Harper, the Twins catcher, finished a distant second with a strikeout every 18.9 plate appearances; Ozzie Smith was next with one whiff every 17.9 ups.) But that's nothing new for Gwynn; since he became an everyday player in 1984, the Padres' National League championship season, he has never ranked lower than fifth in the National League's toughest-to-fan statistics:

	PA/SO	NL Rank
1984	29.3	*1st
1985	20.3	4th
1986	20.0	2nd
1987	19.4	4th
1988	14.5	5th
1989	22.6	1st
1990	27.3	*1st

*Led major leagues.

Gwynn's ranking as the toughest batter to strike out in the majors is the statistical equivalent of Canseco leading the majors in home runs or Clemens leading in earned run average: it's an example of a player succeeding in spite of his surroundings. It may not be as obvious as the other examples, but that's just typical of Gwynn, baseball's most overlooked superstar of the eighties.

WON-LOST RECORD BY STARTING POSITION

San Diego Padres	C	1B	2B	3B	SS	LF	CF	RF	DH	P	Leadoff	Cleanup	Starts vs. LH	Starts vs. RH	Total Starts
Shawn Abner	-	-	-	-	-	4-3	13-17	3-0	-	-	-	-	24	16	20-20
Roberto Alomar	-	-	63-73	-	1-4	-	-	-	-	-	9-10	1-3	51	90	64-77
Andy Benes	-	-	-	-	-	-	-	-	-	15-16	-	-	11	20	15-16
Joe Carter	-	6-7	-	-	-	16-27	52-53	-	-	-	-	39-45	58	103	74-87
Jack Clark	-	47-59	-	-	-	-	-	-	-	-	-	33-37	42	64	47-59
Jerald Clark	-	4-4	-	-	-	0-2	-	2-5	-	-	-	1-0	13	4	6-11
Pat Clements	-	-	-	-	-	-	-	-	-	-	-	-	-	-	-
Joey Cora	-	-	7-5	-	2-7	-	-	-	-	-	5-3	-	6	15	9-12
John Davis	-	-	-	-	-	-	-	-	-	-	-	-	-	-	-
Mike Dunne	-	-	-	-	-	-	-	-	-	2-4	-	-	2	4	2-4
Paul Faries	-	-	4-2	0-1	2-1	-	-	-	-	-	-	-	6	4	6-4
Mark Grant	-	-	-	-	-	-	-	-	-	-	-	-	-	-	-
Tony Gwynn	-	-	-	-	-	-	-	65-76	-	-	1-4	-	51	90	65-76
Atlee Hammaker	-	-	-	-	-	-	-	-	-	0-1	-	-	1	-	0-1
Greg W. Harris	-	-	-	-	-	-	-	-	-	-	-	-	-	-	-
Thomas Howard	-	-	-	-	-	2-3	0-2	0-1	-	-	1-3	-	2	6	2-6
Bruce Hurst	-	-	-	-	-	-	-	-	-	16-17	-	-	13	20	16-17
Darrin Jackson	-	-	-	-	-	-	9-10	2-1	-	-	-	-	16	6	11-11
Tom Lampkin	8-7	-	-	-	-	-	-	-	-	-	-	-	-	15	8-7
Craig Lefferts	-	-	-	-	-	-	-	-	-	-	-	-	-	-	-
Derek Lilliquist	-	-	-	-	-	-	-	-	-	3-4	-	-	2	5	3-4
Fred Lynn	-	-	-	-	-	18-18	1-5	3-4	-	-	-	0-1	1	48	22-27
Rob Nelson	-	-	-	-	-	-	-	-	-	-	-	-	-	-	-
Mike Pagliarulo	-	-	-	49-54	-	-	-	-	-	-	-	-	23	80	49-54
Mark Parent	22-33	-	-	-	-	-	-	-	-	-	-	-	24	31	22-33
Dennis Rasmussen	-	-	-	-	-	-	-	-	-	13-19	-	-	12	20	13-19
Ronn Reynolds	1-2	-	-	-	-	-	-	-	-	-	-	-	1	2	1-2
Bip Roberts	-	-	1-7	21-25	7-6	35-34	-	-	-	-	59-66	-	56	80	64-72
Rich Rodriguez	-	-	-	-	-	-	-	-	-	-	-	-	-	-	-
Benito Santiago	44-45	-	-	-	-	-	-	-	-	-	-	-	34	55	44-45
Calvin Schiraldi	-	-	-	-	-	-	-	-	-	2-6	-	-	2	6	2-6
Eric Show	-	-	-	-	-	-	-	-	-	5-7	-	-	3	9	5-7
Phil Stephenson	-	18-17	-	-	-	-	-	-	-	-	0-1	-	2	33	18-17
Garry Templeton	-	-	-	-	63-69	-	-	-	-	-	-	-	52	80	63-69
Rafael Valdez	-	-	-	-	-	-	-	-	-	-	-	-	-	-	-
Ed Whitson	-	-	-	-	-	-	-	-	-	19-13	-	-	13	19	19-13
Eddie Williams	-	-	-	5-7	-	-	-	-	-	-	-	1-1	10	2	5-7

TEAM TOTALS: BATTING

	AB	H	2B	3B	HR	RBI	BB	SO	BA	SA	OBA
Season	5554	1429	243	35	123	628	509	902	.257	.380	.320
vs. Left-Handers	1953	509	86	8	44	212	176	327	.261	.380	.323
vs. Right-Handers	3601	920	157	27	79	416	333	575	.255	.380	.319
vs. Ground-Ballers	2886	739	133	16	48	327	264	464	.256	.363	.319
vs. Fly-Ballers	2668	690	110	19	75	301	245	438	.259	.398	.322
Home Games	2727	697	106	21	63	323	237	444	.256	.379	.316
Road Games	2827	732	137	14	60	305	272	458	.259	.381	.324
Grass Fields	4110	1065	172	29	96	481	373	663	.259	.385	.321
Artificial Turf	1444	364	71	6	27	147	136	239	.252	.366	.317
April	636	165	24	4	20	78	60	99	.259	.404	.321
May	896	251	50	5	16	109	71	137	.280	.401	.333
June	930	242	48	8	25	115	92	156	.260	.410	.334
July	994	253	40	7	24	107	84	161	.255	.381	.311
August	969	233	41	4	10	94	94	159	.240	.322	.307
Sept./Oct.	1129	285	40	7	28	125	108	190	.252	.375	.317
Leading Off Inn.	1364	339	51	8	36	36	106	215	.249	.377	.304
Bases Empty	3216	797	131	17	69	69	245	538	.248	.363	.304
Runners On	2338	632	112	18	54	559	264	364	.270	.403	.342
Runners/Scor. Pos.	1355	345	56	11	32	488	200	227	.255	.383	.345
Runners On/2 Out	1010	256	44	7	24	243	138	175	.253	.382	.348
Scor. Pos./2 Out	683	168	27	5	19	220	114	123	.246	.384	.359
Late-Inning Pressure	919	224	31	3	18	88	111	167	.244	.343	.327
Leading Off	228	52	5	1	6	6	33	31	.228	.338	.326
Runners On	399	93	13	1	8	78	51	76	.233	.331	.320
Runners/Scor. Pos.	225	46	5	1	6	71	40	41	.204	.316	.325

RUNS BATTED IN	From 1B	From 2B	From 3B	Scoring Position
Totals	77/1659	193/1068	235/587	428/1655
Percentage	4.6%	18.1%	40.0%	25.9%

TEAM TOTALS: PITCHING

	W-L	ERA	AB	H	HR	BB	SO	BA	SA	OBA
Season	75-87	3.68	5566	1437	147	507	928	.258	.390	.320
vs. Left-Handers			2313	622	56	246	373	.269	.396	.339
vs. Right-Handers			3253	815	91	261	555	.251	.386	.307
vs. Ground-Ballers			2602	679	43	214	463	.261	.359	.317
vs. Fly-Ballers			2964	758	104	293	465	.256	.418	.323
Home Games	37-44	3.68	2843	728	78	256	517	.256	.394	.317
Road Games	38-43	3.67	2723	709	69	251	411	.260	.386	.323
Grass Fields	56-64	3.75	4196	1077	120	365	710	.257	.397	.316
Artificial Turf	19-23	3.44	1370	360	27	142	218	.263	.371	.332
April	9-10	4.10	651	173	23	50	103	.266	.422	.318
May	15-12	3.88	912	229	31	86	166	.251	.396	.316
June	11-15	3.88	915	216	27	104	167	.236	.379	.313
July	10-19	3.75	998	269	18	87	152	.270	.387	.327
August	15-13	2.86	962	242	21	93	153	.252	.367	.318
Sept./Oct.	15-18	3.75	1128	308	27	87	187	.273	.399	.327
Leading Off Inn.			1357	356	47	104	217	.262	.422	.318
Bases Empty			3227	831	96	249	542	.258	.399	.313
Runners On			2339	606	51	258	386	.259	.379	.330
Runners/Scor. Pos.			1354	346	30	195	250	.256	.383	.342
Runners On/2 Out			1031	257	27	125	176	.249	.386	.332
Scor. Pos./2 Out			673	167	19	95	122	.248	.403	.343
Late-Inning Pressure			837	224	22	88	137	.268	.398	.338
Leading Off			218	68	9	16	31	.312	.505	.364
Runners On			357	97	6	50	61	.272	.378	.357
Runners/Scor. Pos.			218	59	6	43	45	.271	.404	.379
First 9 Batters			2869	707	68	288	567	.246	.368	.316
Second 9 Batters			1448	369	38	118	223	.255	.394	.311
All Batters Thereafter			1249	361	41	101	138	.289	.437	.341

SAN FRANCISCO GIANTS

- **A baseball winter to remember.**
- **New N. L. lefties finish in the Black.**

Go ahead, call him irresponsible. You won't be the first. Even Al Rosen himself admits that he may overspend a wee bit from time to time when it comes to bulking up his roster with prime-time talent. And while his comments occasionally have a "Stop me before I kill again" quality, colleagues have been much harsher in their characterization of Rosen's acquisitive nature, blaming his generosity for everything from the price of coffee to the national debt. It's tough to say who's right: Baseball salaries have risen so sharply that it's become impossible to say whether free spenders move the market or simply anticipate the shift. But one thing's for certain: Rosen, who became the Giants general manager in September 1985, has overseen a miraculous turnaround.

The Giants lost 100 games in 1985, but have since posted winning records in each of Rosen's five full seasons as general manager. Five consecutive winning seasons may not seem like much, but not even the Giants' baymates have a streak that long; the only other teams with winning records in each of the last five seasons are the Toronto Blue Jays and the New York Mets. San Francisco's streak is all the more impressive considering its disastrous 1985 season—the first time in franchise history that the Giants lost 100 games. From 1900 through 1989, 114 teams lost in triple figures; only 11 had winning seasons a year later.

Rosen hardly needs our accolades; two titles in five years probably mean a little more to him than a tip of the proverbial Elias Sports Bureau cap. (See the back of this book for information on the complete line of officially licensed proverbial ESB products.) But along with millions of other baseball fans, we were delighted by his leadership role in making the 1990–91 offseason the most memorable in decades for those of us who still get a shiver when name players change teams.

Major trades were among the most memorable events of our baseball childhoods. More than 30 years later, we can still hear the echo of Yankees broadcaster Phil Rizzuto repeating again and again, "Kuenn for Colavito!" when news of that blockbuster broke during a late preseason telecast in 1960. But trades didn't have to be so grand to send us back to our rooms for another hour or two of cavorting with baseball cards. Frank Sullivan for Gene Conley was a fine way to warm up during a cold January day in 1962. And we'd be willing to bet that a new generation of young fans was smitten by Cory Snyder for Eric King and Shawn Hillegas this past winter. (Too bad they don't play with their cards any more; they're too busy "protecting their investments.")

Of course, kids don't have a monopoly on this passion for player moves; it is, after all, fantasy leagues' *raison d'être*. But even in the real world, trades and free-agent signings keep baseball in the newspapers throughout the winter, even as Joe Montana, Michael Jordan, and Wayne Gretzky fight each other for space on the sports pages. But over the past few years, the number of trades and free-agent signings sadly dwindled—until this winter, that is, when Rosen lit a spark with his signing of Bud Black and the whole damned thing exploded.

More impact players changed teams during the past offseason than at any other time in this century—nearly twice as many, in fact, as during any other offseason. Between the end of the 1990 season and New Year's Day, 26 players who met one of the various statistical thresholds described in the next paragraph joined new teams—more than over the previous five offseasons combined. The turnaround was remarkable: There were only three such changes between the 1989 and 1990 seasons (Joe Carter, Gary Pettis, and Mark Langston). Only once in the past 75 years had there been more than 10 team changes among players who met the criteria: 16 in 1963, when some of the traded stars included Joe Adcock (Braves to Indians), Luis Aparicio (White Sox to Orioles), Dick Groat (Pirates to Cardinals), Pete Runnels (Red Sox to Colt .45s), Bill Skowron (Yankees to Dodgers), Dick Stuart (Pirates to Red Sox), Larry Jackson (Cardinals to Cubs), Lindy McDaniel (Cardinals to Cubs), Stu Miller (Giants to Orioles), and Hoyt Wilhelm (Orioles to White Sox).

To be included, batters had to rank among the major-league leaders in runs or RBIs, pitchers had to rank among the leaders in wins or saves. The number of players included in a season depended upon the number of teams in operation at the time: four batters and two starting pitchers per team, and one reliever for every two teams. For instance, with 26 teams in operation last season, players were included if they ranked in the top 104 in runs or RBIs, the top 52 in wins, or the top 13 in saves. Arbitrary, inexact, but utterly useful as a measure for tracing the movement of impact players. The following table shows what a drastic change occurred in the marketplace last winter. The number of qualifying players who changed teams after each of the past 10 seasons:

1981	1982	1983	1984	1985	1986	1987	1988	1989	1990*
6	5	6	7	3	4	6	5	3	26

*Through 12/31/90

Among the reasons for this about-face were a large and talented group of free agents, an additional group of 15 "new-look" free agents, revenue from lucrative network television contracts that began in 1990, and the anticipated revenue from upcoming National League expansion. (Incidentally, that last reason has received a disproportionate amount of attention. Among the 13 free agents who changed leagues before we went to press, only five went from the American League to the National League: Black, Willie McGee, and Dave Righetti to the Giants; George Bell to the Cubs; and Gerald Perry to the Cardinals. Eight players headed in the opposite direction: Jack Clark, Ken Dayley, Kirk Gibson, Bill Gullickson, Dan Schatzeder, Eric Show, Franklin Stubbs, and Pat Tabler.)

Of course, Giants fans are probably less concerned with the reasons for such a shift than its results. Their scoreboard goes something like this: The addition of McGee offsets the loss of Butler; the loss of Bedrosian cancels the addition of Righetti; the addition of Bud Black is a net profit. The question becomes: How have teams fared after adding a player of that stature during the offseason?

Commensurate with our past surveys that indicated the value of even a superstar to be only about five wins per season, these players had little overall impact on the records of the teams they joined. The following table shows the combined Before and After records of teams adding players between 1983 and 1990 who met the criteria outlined earlier. Teams that added and lost players in the same season weren't included; teams that added more than one such player were double-counted:

	W	L	Pct.
Previous seasons	2740	2764	.498
With new players	2733	2725	.501

Of course, those numbers don't take into account the Rosen Guarantee. After being criticized for signing a pitcher of Bud Black's modest credentials to such an enormous contract last winter, Rosen stated that Black would win more games in 1991 than any other free-agent pitcher. Considering Black's competition will include Bob Welch (who re-signed with Oakland) and Mike Boddicker (who joined the Royals), that's a bold statement—and one that demands another look at the first-season results of southpaw pitchers moving to the National League.

The recent past has provided a pair of outstanding examples of American League southpaws who enjoyed fabulous first seasons in the National League: Bob Ojeda in 1986 and Danny Jackson in 1988. Only seven other left-handed pitchers joined National League teams over the past 10 years after making 20 or more starts for an American League team the year before. (Pitchers who made fewer than 10 starts in their first N.L. seasons, like Jerry Reuss in 1990, were excluded.) The pitchers, with their records in their last A.L. season and their first N.L. season:

Year	Player	A.L.	N.L.
1984	John Tudor	13–12	12–11
1984	Jerry Koosman	11–7	14–15
1985	Ray Fontenot	8–9	6–10
1986	Bob Ojeda	9–11	18–5
1987	Neal Heaton	7–15	13–10
1988	Danny Jackson	9–18	23–8
1989	Paul Kilgus	12–15	6–10
1989	Bruce Hurst	18–6	15–11
1990	Charlie Leibrandt	5–11	9–11

Those pitchers had a combined record of 92–104 (.469) in their last American League seasons, and improved to 116–91 (.560) a year later in the National League. During that same period, 13 right-handed starters traveled the same road; they fell from a combined record of 135–148 (.477) in the A.L. to 100–122 (.450) in the N.L. Let's restate that for emphasis: Over the past 10 years, 22 regular American League starters joined the National League. The nine left-handers and 13 right-handers had nearly identical winning percentages in their final A.L. seasons (.469 and .477, respectively), but in their first seasons in the N.L. the southpaws thrived (.560) and the right-handers floundered (.450).

We detailed in the New York Mets essay the recent proliferation of left-handed pitchers in the National League. That change took place over the past five years, prompting us to consider whether this trend might also be a recent development. But among pitchers who switched to the National League from 1971 through 1980, left-handers improved more than right-handers in their first National League seasons. The breakdowns:

Years	Left-Handed Pitchers Last in A.L.	First in N.L.	Right-Handed Pitchers Last in A.L.	First in N.L.
1971–80	161–175 .479	158–131 .547	174–179 .493	152–148 .507
1981–90	92–104 .469	116–91 .560	135–148 .477	100–122 .450
Totals	253–279 .476	274–222 .552	309–327 .486	252–270 .483

Over a 20-year period, right-handed A.L. starters who switched leagues had a slightly better winning percentage than southpaws in their final A.L. seasons. Nevertheless, the left-handed pitchers were far more successful upon arrival in the N.L. Ojeda and Jackson weren't isolated cases; Vida Blue and Ross Grimsley in 1978 and Bill Lee in 1979 combined to go 54–31 in their first N.L. seasons after going 38–38 in their last seasons in the A.L. During the first half of the decade, Al Downing (1971), San McDowell (1972), and Tommy John (1972) all pitched at least three games below .500 in their final A.L. seasons; their combined record as first-year National Leaguers was 41–22. As with most general rules, there were exceptions: Left-handers Dave McNally (1975) and Rudy May (1978) both pitched poorly after leaving the American League, and right-handers Jim McGlothlin (1970) and Gaylord Perry (1978) excelled in their new N.L. homes. But this is a noteworthy trend, and one that has existed for at least 20 years.

Maybe that's what Al Rosen had in mind when he vowed that Bud Black would outwin Welch, Boddicker, and the rest of his free-agent class in 1991. It appears that Black could well be the next Bob Ojeda. (Just in case, Bud, we've got the name of some reliable gardeners that are probably in your price range.)

One of the most frustrating aspects of Giants history has been the team's inclination to dispose of players with a flair for hitting baseballs over outfield fences. Twelve different players have hit at least 100 home runs for other teams after leaving the Giants. Four of them also hit 100 for the Giants, but most of these, great as they were, won't have prominent roles in any "History of the Giants" videos:

Player	Giants	After	Player	Giants	After
Dave Kingman	77	365	Darrell Evans	142	152
George Foster	4	344	Bobby Bonds	186	146
Hack Wilson	16	228	Jack Clark	163	144
Bill White	23	179	Jose Cardenal	0	138
Gary Matthews	64	170	Rob Deer	11	137
Orlando Cepeda	226	153	Felipe Alou	85	121

Given the criticism aimed at the Giants over the years for such notorious deals, we wondered whether other teams might not have similar skeletons in their closets. Do 12 such players over an entire century of baseball really constitute a poor record, or are they simply the inevitable scars of doing battle in the traditional baseball marketplace? The totals for all other long-standing National League franchises follow. They show that one team traded away even more home-run hitters than the Giants did, and that most other teams traded away nearly as many: Reds, 13; Giants, 12; Pirates, 11; Dodgers, 10; Cardinals, 9; Cubs, 9; Phillies, 8; Braves, 6.

Cincinnati's "mistakes" included Joe Adcock (305 for other teams), Frank Robinson (262), Hank Sauer (242), Lee May (207), Ken Williams (196), Hal McRae (169), Deron Johnson (147), George McQuinn (135), Eddie Joost (123), Frank Thomas the Elder (111), Tommy Harper (102), George Foster (100), and Tony Gonzalez (100). Of course, no team was without a major error. The highest totals on each of the other teams: Frank Howard, Dodgers (259); Tony Armas, Pirates (251); Dolf Camilli, Cubs (233); Johnny Mize, Cardinals (201); Oscar Gamble, Phillies (191); and Bill Robinson, Braves (166).

Rather than crucifying the Giants all these years for the ones that got away, maybe we should have been praising the record of the Braves. They traded away the fewest sluggers-to-be, and were the only team not to deal one who would hit more than 175 more home runs. So that's it—the Giants are off the hook (unless Brett Butler goes bonkers in Chavez Ravine).

WON-LOST RECORD BY STARTING POSITION

San Francisco Giants	C	1B	2B	3B	SS	LF	CF	RF	DH	P	Leadoff	Cleanup	Starts vs. LH	Starts vs. RH	Total Starts
Jose Alvarez	-	-	-	-	-	-	-	-	-	-	-	-	-	-	-
Dave Anderson	-	1-0	0-4	-	6-5	-	-	-	-	-	-	-	9	7	7-9
Mark Bailey	-	-	-	-	-	-	-	-	-	-	-	-	-	-	-
Kevin Bass	-	-	-	-	-	-	-	26-28	-	-	-	-	25	29	26-28
Bill Bathe	1-1	-	-	-	-	-	-	-	-	-	-	-	2	-	1-1
Steve Bedrosian	-	-	-	-	-	-	-	-	-	-	-	-	-	-	-
Mike Benjamin	-	-	-	-	12-4	-	-	-	-	-	-	-	9	7	12-4
Greg Booker	-	-	-	-	-	-	-	-	-	-	-	-	-	-	-
Jeff Brantley	-	-	-	-	-	-	-	-	-	-	-	-	-	-	-
John Burkett	-	-	-	-	-	-	-	-	-	18-14	-	-	7	25	18-14
Brett Butler	-	-	-	-	-	-	84-74	-	-	-	84-74	-	56	102	84-74
Ernie Camacho	-	-	-	-	-	-	-	-	-	-	-	-	-	-	-
Gary Carter	32-26	2-1	-	-	-	-	-	-	-	-	-	-	46	15	34-27
Will Clark	-	81-71	-	-	-	-	-	-	-	-	-	-	55	97	81-71
Steve Decker	9-5	-	-	-	-	-	-	-	-	-	-	1-0	8	6	9-5
Mark Dewey	-	-	-	-	-	-	-	-	-	-	-	-	-	-	-
Kelly Downs	-	-	-	-	-	-	-	-	-	7-2	-	-	3	6	7-2
Scott Garrelts	-	-	-	-	-	-	-	-	-	14-17	-	-	10	21	14-17
Eric Gunderson	-	-	-	-	-	-	-	-	-	1-3	-	-	1	3	1-3
Atlee Hammaker	-	-	-	-	-	-	-	-	-	3-3	-	-	2	4	3-3
Chuck Jackson	-	-	-	-	-	-	-	-	-	-	-	-	-	-	-
Terry Kennedy	41-43	-	-	-	-	-	-	-	-	-	-	-	2	82	41-43
Mike Kingery	-	-	-	-	-	4-2	-	17-18	-	-	-	-	-	41	21-20
Bob Knepper	-	-	-	-	-	-	-	-	-	5-2	-	-	4	3	5-2
Brad Komminsk	-	-	-	-	-	-	-	-	-	-	-	-	-	-	-
Mike LaCoss	-	-	-	-	-	-	-	-	-	6-6	-	-	7	5	6-6
Mike Laga	-	1-2	-	-	-	-	-	-	-	-	-	-	1	2	1-2
Rick Leach	-	0-3	-	-	-	6-3	-	22-11	-	-	-	-	2	43	28-17
Mark Leonard	-	-	-	-	-	1-0	-	0-3	-	-	-	-	2	2	1-3
Greg Litton	-	-	4-3	1-0	-	4-1	-	12-14	-	-	-	-	33	6	21-18
Kirt Manwaring	2-2	-	-	-	-	-	-	-	-	-	-	-	3	1	2-2
Randy McCament	-	-	-	-	-	-	-	-	-	-	-	-	-	-	-
Paul McClellan	-	-	-	-	-	-	-	-	-	0-1	-	-	-	1	0-1
Andy McGaffigan	-	-	-	-	-	-	-	-	-	-	-	-	-	-	-
Kevin Mitchell	-	-	-	-	-	68-70	-	-	-	-	-	68-70	51	87	68-70
Rafael Novoa	-	-	-	-	-	-	-	-	-	1-1	-	-	-	2	1-1
Francisco Oliveras	-	-	-	-	-	-	-	-	-	1-1	-	-	2	-	1-1
Randy O'Neal	-	-	-	-	-	-	-	-	-	-	-	-	-	-	-
Rick Parker	-	-	-	-	-	2-1	1-3	8-3	-	-	1-3	-	18	-	11-7
Tony Perezchica	-	-	-	-	-	-	-	-	-	-	-	-	-	-	-
Dan Quisenberry	-	-	-	-	-	-	-	-	-	-	-	-	-	-	-
Rick Reuschel	-	-	-	-	-	-	-	-	-	5-8	-	-	6	7	5-8
Ernest Riles	-	-	11-6	2-2	3-9	-	-	-	-	-	-	1-0	-	33	16-17
Don Robinson	-	-	-	-	-	-	-	-	-	15-10	-	-	14	11	15-10
Rick Rodriguez	-	-	-	-	-	-	-	-	-	-	-	-	-	-	-
Andres Santana	-	-	-	-	1-0	-	-	-	-	-	-	-	1	-	1-0
Russ Swan	-	-	-	-	-	-	-	-	-	0-1	-	-	-	1	0-1
Robby Thompson	-	-	70-64	-	-	-	-	-	-	-	-	-	53	81	70-64
Mark Thurmond	-	-	-	-	-	-	-	-	-	-	-	-	-	-	-
Jose Uribe	-	-	-	-	63-59	-	-	-	-	-	-	-	44	78	63-59
Ed Vosberg	-	-	-	-	-	-	-	-	-	-	-	-	-	-	-
Matt Williams	-	-	-	82-75	-	-	-	-	-	-	-	15-7	60	97	82-75
Trevor Wilson	-	-	-	-	-	-	-	-	-	9-8	-	-	4	13	9-8

TEAM TOTALS: BATTING

	AB	H	2B	3B	HR	RBI	BB	SO	BA	SA	OBA
Season	5573	1459	221	35	152	681	488	973	.262	.396	.323
vs. Left-Handers	2000	552	82	12	60	270	172	321	.276	.419	.336
vs. Right-Handers	3573	907	139	23	92	411	316	652	.254	.383	.315
vs. Ground-Ballers	2520	665	94	12	72	309	231	431	.264	.396	.328
vs. Fly-Ballers	3053	794	127	23	80	372	257	542	.260	.395	.318
Home Games	2743	742	116	14	81	355	269	471	.271	.412	.336
Road Games	2830	717	105	21	71	326	219	502	.253	.381	.309
Grass Fields	4130	1125	175	25	116	539	374	713	.272	.411	.333
Artificial Turf	1443	334	46	10	36	142	114	260	.231	.352	.291
April	708	196	32	6	16	86	56	122	.277	.407	.332
May	970	232	34	2	33	108	88	166	.239	.380	.304
June	976	278	35	5	29	153	86	162	.285	.420	.344
July	915	245	37	10	22	109	77	161	.268	.402	.326
August	969	239	38	4	24	104	89	191	.247	.368	.312
Sept./Oct.	1035	269	45	8	28	121	92	171	.260	.400	.321
Leading Off Inn.	1329	345	42	9	40	40	115	208	.260	.395	.321
Bases Empty	3170	802	111	21	93	93	265	563	.253	.389	.313
Runners On	2403	657	110	14	59	588	223	410	.273	.404	.335
Runners/Scor. Pos.	1383	362	58	7	31	507	174	251	.262	.381	.339
Runners On/2 Out	1042	260	36	10	20	224	113	191	.250	.361	.329
Scor. Pos./2 Out	669	169	23	5	10	192	93	124	.253	.347	.350
Late-Inning Pressure	791	214	31	4	23	94	75	147	.271	.407	.335
Leading Off	186	52	11	2	7	7	24	30	.280	.473	.362
Runners On	358	101	17	1	7	78	30	62	.282	.394	.340
Runners/Scor. Pos.	209	57	10	0	4	67	25	42	.273	.378	.346

RUNS BATTED IN	From 1B	From 2B	From 3B	Scoring Position
Totals	91/1773	179/1060	259/604	438/1664
Percentage	5.1%	16.9%	42.9%	26.3%

TEAM TOTALS: PITCHING

	W-L	ERA	AB	H	HR	BB	SO	BA	SA	OBA
Season	85-77	4.08	5541	1477	131	553	788	.267	.394	.333
vs. Left-Handers			2703	737	59	282	325	.273	.401	.341
vs. Right-Handers			2838	740	72	271	463	.261	.387	.325
vs. Ground-Ballers			2477	624	34	211	373	.252	.349	.310
vs. Fly-Ballers			3064	853	97	342	415	.278	.430	.350
Home Games	49-32	3.78	2848	751	70	269	432	.264	.390	.327
Road Games	36-45	4.39	2693	726	61	284	356	.270	.398	.339
Grass Fields	70-50	3.97	4135	1092	100	399	605	.264	.390	.329
Artificial Turf	15-27	4.39	1406	385	31	154	183	.274	.405	.343
April	8-12	4.57	698	190	16	78	104	.272	.390	.341
May	11-17	4.49	983	296	22	103	117	.301	.444	.364
June	19-8	3.05	920	214	27	72	141	.233	.360	.293
July	17-10	3.58	889	217	18	80	126	.244	.354	.307
August	12-17	4.65	993	272	29	109	144	.274	.411	.346
Sept./Oct.	18-13	4.11	1058	288	19	111	156	.272	.397	.341
Leading Off Inn.			1346	347	34	104	168	.258	.383	.312
Bases Empty			3142	800	70	278	445	.255	.378	.317
Runners On			2399	677	61	275	343	.282	.414	.352
Runners/Scor. Pos.			1399	384	37	205	221	.274	.397	.359
Runners On/2 Out			1064	293	28	150	155	.275	.403	.367
Scor. Pos./2 Out			700	187	20	126	110	.267	.386	.381
Late-Inning Pressure			867	210	17	98	120	.242	.351	.321
Leading Off			223	56	3	20	26	.251	.336	.316
Runners On			370	85	6	47	56	.230	.330	.316
Runners/Scor. Pos.			202	37	2	38	37	.183	.233	.312
First 9 Batters			3013	782	72	293	452	.260	.385	.324
Second 9 Batters			1354	359	29	153	187	.265	.374	.340
All Batters Thereafter			1174	336	30	107	149	.286	.439	.345

BATTER SECTION

The Batter Section is an alphabetical listing of every player who had at least 200 plate appearances last season. Players are listed alphabetically within each league; if he played for both leagues, he is listed in the league where he finished the season.

Column Headings Information

For each player, information is provided in 11 offensive categories.

Sandy Alomar, Jr.

Cleveland Indians	AB	H	2B	3B	HR	RBI	BB	SO	BA	SA	OBA

AB	At-Bats
H	Hits
2B	Doubles
3B	Triples
HR	Home Runs
RBI	Runs Batted In
BB	Bases on Balls
SO	Strikeouts
BA	Batting Average
SA	Slugging Average
OBA	On-Base Average

Season Summary Information

Season	445	129	26	2	9	66	25	46	.290	.418	.326
vs. Left-Handers	117	44	5	0	2	18	8	13	.376	.470	.403
vs. Right-Handers	328	85	21	2	7	48	17	33	.259	.399	.298
vs. Ground-Ballers	214	59	11	1	4	33	14	16	.276	.393	.323
vs. Fly-Ballers	231	70	15	1	5	33	11	30	.303	.442	.329
Home Games	227	68	12	0	5	30	13	22	.300	.419	.335
Road Games	218	61	14	2	4	36	12	24	.280	.417	.318
Grass Fields	370	112	21	2	7	50	21	34	.303	.427	.337
Artificial Turf	75	17	5	0	2	16	4	12	.227	.373	.275
April	57	16	3	0	1	9	3	6	.281	.386	.323
May	69	21	3	1	2	13	4	13	.304	.464	.338
June	87	25	2	1	0	8	6	11	.287	.333	.330
July	68	18	5	0	2	11	4	3	.265	.426	.306
August	81	21	4	0	2	10	5	6	.259	.383	.299
Sept./Oct.	83	28	9	0	2	15	3	7	.337	.518	.360

Each player's performance for the season is broken down into a variety of special categories. The first line for each player gives his totals for the whole season. This is followed by breakdowns of his performance against left- and right-handed pitchers, against ground-ball and fly-ball pitchers (defined by whether their ground outs-to-air outs ratio is above or below the league average; our research indicates that this is nearly as effective a basis for platooning as "handedness"), in home and road games, on grass fields and artificial turf, and in each month (regular-season October games are grouped with September). For players who played for more than one team, all totals are combined; the "home" totals for Mike Marshall, for example, include games played at Shea Stadium while with the New York Mets, and at Fenway Park while with the Red Sox.

Leading Off Inn.	101	31	2	1	3	3	4	12	.307	.436	.346
Bases Empty	250	70	9	2	8	8	10	31	.280	.428	.313
Runners On	195	59	17	0	1	58	15	15	.303	.405	.343
Runners/Scor. Pos.	127	39	12	0	0	54	11	9	.307	.402	.347
Runners On/2 Out	98	29	8	0	0	27	12	9	.296	.378	.373
Scor. Pos./2 Out	68	23	6	0	0	26	8	6	.338	.426	.408

Following these breakdowns, each batter's performance is divided into specific game situations. Totals are given for each batter when he led off an inning, when he batted with bases empty or runners on, with runners in scoring position (on second or third base, or both), with runners on and two out, and with runners in scoring position and two out.

Late-Inning Pressure	84	25	5	1	3	14	6	10	.298	.488	.344
Leading Off	22	8	1	0	2	2	1	2	.364	.682	.391
Runners On	33	11	4	0	0	11	4	4	.333	.455	.405
Runners/Scor. Pos.	26	8	2	0	0	11	4	3	.308	.385	.400

The next group shows the batter's performance in Late-Inning Pressure Situations (LIPS): any plate appearance occurring in the seventh inning or later with the score tied or with the batter's team trailing by one, two, or three runs (or four runs if there are two or more runners on base).

Each player's totals are listed for all late-inning pressure situations, then broken out for his performance leading off the inning, with runners on base, and runners in scoring position.

RUNS BATTED IN	From 1B	From 2B	From 3B	Scoring Position
Totals	7/144	23/104	27/55	50/159
Percentage	4.9%	22.1%	49.1%	31.4%

The next section, labeled "Runs Batted In," is a measure of the player's ability to drive in runners from each base. For every base, two numbers are listed in the "Totals" line: The first is the number of RBIs credited to the batter for bringing home runners from that base; the second is the total number of opportunities he faced for that situation. Plate appearances that result in a base on balls, hit batsman, sacrifice bunt, or an award of first base for catcher's interference are not treated as "opportunities" if they do not result in a run.

If there is more than one runner on base, there is an "opportunity" to drive in each runner. A single with the bases loaded that scores only the runner from third is an opportunity and an RBI in the "From 3B" line, but an unsuccessful opportunity for both "From 2B" and "From 1B." (The exceptions to this are listed above; a bases-loaded walk is an RBI and opportunity under "From 3B," but goes unrecorded for the other two.)

Also given is the percentage of successful opportunities for each base and a combined total of "From

2B" and "From 3B" to represent runners driven in from scoring position.

The tables are followed by comments for each player. The first of these is a listing of pitchers each batter "loves to face" and "hates to face." The statistics listed for each individual match-up are from all regular season games since 1975 inclusive. Next are miscellaneous statistics given in text form; these include: the batter's ground outs-to-air outs ratio; his total of double-play ground outs and opportunities (plate appearances with a runner on first and less than two outs); the number and percentage of runners driven in from third base with less than two outs; the direction of balls that reach the outfield, either in the air or on the ground (these may total more than 100 percent because they've been rounded to the nearest whole percentage); the number and percentage of times he advanced from first to third or scored from second on outfield singles; and fielding statistics (assists per nine innings for infielders, putouts per nine innings for outfielders, and the success rate of opposing base stealers for catchers).

For purposes of comparison, the league totals in all of these categories are listed in the introduction to the Team Section (see page 2).

Sandy Alomar, Jr.

Bats Right

Cleveland Indians	AB	H	2B	3B	HR	RBI	BB	SO	BA	SA	OBA
Season	445	129	26	2	9	66	25	46	.290	.418	.326
vs. Left-Handers	117	44	5	0	2	18	8	13	.376	.470	.403
vs. Right-Handers	328	85	21	2	7	48	17	33	.259	.399	.298
vs. Ground-Ballers	214	59	11	1	4	33	14	16	.276	.393	.323
vs. Fly-Ballers	231	70	15	1	5	33	11	30	.303	.442	.329
Home Games	227	68	12	0	5	30	13	22	.300	.419	.335
Road Games	218	61	14	2	4	36	12	24	.280	.417	.318
Grass Fields	370	112	21	2	7	50	21	34	.303	.427	.337
Artificial Turf	75	17	5	0	2	16	4	12	.227	.373	.275
April	57	16	3	0	1	9	3	6	.281	.386	.323
May	69	21	3	1	2	13	4	13	.304	.464	.338
June	87	25	2	1	0	8	6	11	.287	.333	.330
July	68	18	5	0	2	11	4	3	.265	.426	.306
August	81	21	4	0	2	10	5	6	.259	.383	.299
Sept./Oct.	83	28	9	0	2	15	3	7	.337	.518	.360
Leading Off Inn.	101	31	2	1	3	3	4	12	.307	.436	.346
Bases Empty	250	70	9	2	8	8	10	31	.280	.428	.313
Runners On	195	59	17	0	1	58	15	15	.303	.405	.343
Runners/Scor. Pos.	127	39	12	0	0	54	11	9	.307	.402	.347
Runners On/2 Out	98	29	8	0	0	27	12	9	.296	.378	.373
Scor. Pos./2 Out	68	23	6	0	0	26	8	6	.338	.426	.408
Late-Inning Pressure	84	25	5	1	3	14	6	10	.298	.488	.344
Leading Off	22	8	1	0	2	2	1	2	.364	.682	.391
Runners On	33	11	4	0	0	11	4	4	.333	.455	.405
Runners/Scor. Pos.	26	8	2	0	0	11	4	3	.308	.385	.400

RUNS BATTED IN	From 1B	From 2B	From 3B	Scoring Position
Totals	7/144	23/104	27/55	50/159
Percentage	4.9%	22.1%	49.1%	31.4%

Loves to face: Greg A. Harris (.600, 3-for-5, 1 HR)
Brian Holman (.667, 2-for-3, 1 2B, 1 HR)
Matt Young (.455, 5-for-11)

Hates to face: Jim Acker (0-for-6)
Andy Hawkins (0-for-7)
Mike Jackson (0-for-3, 3 SO)

Miscellaneous statistics: Ground outs-to-air outs ratio: 0.93 last season, 0.95 for career.... Grounded into 10 double plays in 80 opportunities (one per 8.0).... Drove in 20 of 27 runners from third base with less than two outs (74%), shared 4th-highest rate in A.L.... Direction of balls hit to the outfield: 32% to left field, 33% to center, 34% to right.... Base running: Advanced from first base to third on 6 of 22 outfield singles (27%); scored from second on 12 of 17 (71%).... Opposing base stealers: 77-for-118 (65%).

Comments: Led American League rookies with 66 RBIs.... The first rookie catcher ever to start an All-Star Game.... Opposed his brother Roberto in the 1990 All-Star game. Other brothers named to All-Star teams in the same season: Felipe and Matty Alou (once), Mort and Walker Cooper (3), Dom and Joe DiMaggio (6), Rick and Wes Ferrell (2), Carlos and Lee May (2), and Gaylord and Jim Perry (once).... Sixth catcher to win the Rookie of the Year Award since its inception in 1947. The others: Johnny Bench, Cin. (1968); Thurman Munson, N.Y. (1970); Earl Williams, Atl. (1971); Carlton Fisk, Bos. (1972); Benito Santiago, S.D. (1987), Alomar (1990).... Made his debut with the Padres in 1988. Only two other winners of the A.L. rookie award had previous major-league experience for a different club: Lou Piniella (debuted with the Orioles in 1964, won the award with the 1969 Royals) and Alfredo Griffin (parts of three seasons with Cleveland before winning the award with Toronto in 1979).... Batted only .190 in 21 first-inning at-bats, .281 from the second through the sixth innings, .325 from the seventh through the ninth, and .400 (2-for-5) in extra innings.... Alomar and Joel Skinner were the only catchers to play for the Indians last season. No other A.L. club had as few as two players combine for all of their innings at *any* position.... Committed 14 errors, tying Mackey Sasser for the most among major league backstops.

Brady Anderson

Bats Left

Baltimore Orioles	AB	H	2B	3B	HR	RBI	BB	SO	BA	SA	OBA
Season	234	54	5	2	3	24	31	46	.231	.308	.327
vs. Left-Handers	46	7	1	0	0	4	5	11	.152	.174	.250
vs. Right-Handers	188	47	4	2	3	20	26	35	.250	.340	.347
vs. Ground-Ballers	111	25	1	1	2	11	9	23	.225	.306	.302
vs. Fly-Ballers	123	29	4	1	1	13	22	23	.236	.309	.349
Home Games	126	22	1	2	1	10	15	33	.175	.238	.272
Road Games	108	32	4	0	2	14	16	13	.296	.389	.391
Grass Fields	204	43	2	2	2	18	23	42	.211	.270	.298
Artificial Turf	30	11	3	0	1	6	8	4	.367	.567	.500
April	13	4	0	0	0	4	6	4	.308	.308	.524
May	32	7	0	0	0	1	0	5	.219	.219	.265
June	4	1	0	0	0	1	0	1	.250	.250	.250
July	30	15	3	2	2	9	6	5	.500	.933	.583
August	71	13	1	0	1	6	10	13	.183	.239	.286
Sept./Oct.	84	14	1	0	0	3	9	18	.167	.179	.250
Leading Off Inn.	71	10	1	0	0	0	6	12	.141	.155	.228
Bases Empty	133	23	2	0	2	2	19	25	.173	.233	.286
Runners On	101	31	3	2	1	22	12	21	.307	.406	.380
Runners/Scor. Pos.	61	17	1	1	1	20	9	15	.279	.377	.364
Runners On/2 Out	39	13	1	2	1	8	6	5	.333	.538	.458
Scor. Pos./2 Out	30	8	1	1	1	7	4	5	.267	.467	.389
Late-Inning Pressure	32	8	0	1	0	6	3	5	.250	.313	.297
Leading Off	11	2	0	0	0	0	0	2	.182	.182	.182
Runners On	10	4	0	1	0	6	3	1	.400	.600	.467
Runners/Scor. Pos.	7	3	0	1	0	6	3	1	.429	.714	.500

RUNS BATTED IN	From 1B	From 2B	From 3B	Scoring Position
Totals	3/73	6/46	12/30	18/76
Percentage	4.1%	13.0%	40.0%	23.7%

Loves to face: Mark Davis (2-for-2, 1 BB)
Jack Morris (.438, 7-for-16)
Scott Sanderson (.500, 2-for-4)

Hates to face: Mike Moore (.063, 1-for-16, 2 BB)
Dave Stieb (0-for-14, 1 BB)
Bob Welch (0-for-13, 1 BB)

Miscellaneous statistics: Ground outs-to-air outs ratio: 1.04 last season, 0.87 for career.... Grounded into 4 double plays in 53 opportunities (one per 13.3).... Drove in 10 of 19 runners from third base with less than two outs (53%).... Direction of balls hit to the outfield: 43% to left field, 26% to center, 31% to right.... Base running: Advanced from first base to third on 1 of 9 outfield singles (11%); scored from second on 0 of 2.... Made 2.81 putouts per nine innings in left field.

Comments: Earned a "can't-miss" label several years ago after out-hitting Ellis Burks at every level of Boston's organizational ladder, as he followed one rung behind Burks. Career minor league batting averages: Anderson .294, Burks .256. Burks has out-hit Anderson by 75 points in the big show (.291 to .216).... Last season's .231 mark was his *highest* batting average in three seasons in the majors. Only two other outfielders in major league history batted .231 or lower in each of their first three seasons (minimum: 60 OF games): Ed Kennedy (1883–85) and Bob Coluccio (1973–75). Their careers lasted a combined total of 31 more games. Brady, we hardly knew ye!. . .For what it's worth, he's still improving as a base stealer: 10-for-16 in 1988 (63%), 16-for-20 in 1989 (80%), 15-for-17 last season (88%) for the best mark in the American League.... Batted 134 points higher with runners on base (.307) than with the bases empty (.173) last season, the 3d-largest margin in the majors.... Batted .167 in the first inning, 3d-lowest mark in the A.L. Who was the worst? Turn the page.... His career average of .211 on grass fields is right on the Mendoza line—the *real* one, that is; Mario also hit .211 on natural turf.... Has a career batting average of .185 at Memorial Stadium, .239 elsewhere.

Oscar Azocar

Bats Left

New York Yankees	AB	H	2B	3B	HR	RBI	BB	SO	BA	SA	OBA
Season	214	53	8	0	5	19	2	15	.248	.355	.257
vs. Left-Handers	60	12	2	0	1	7	1	2	.200	.283	.210
vs. Right-Handers	154	41	6	0	4	12	1	13	.266	.383	.276
vs. Ground-Ballers	95	29	4	0	4	12	2	4	.305	.474	.320
vs. Fly-Ballers	119	24	4	0	1	7	0	11	.202	.261	.207
Home Games	109	31	5	0	3	11	2	6	.284	.413	.301
Road Games	105	22	3	0	2	8	0	9	.210	.295	.210
Grass Fields	191	47	7	0	4	16	2	13	.246	.346	.256
Artificial Turf	23	6	1	0	1	3	0	2	.261	.435	.261
April	0	0	0	0	0	0	0	0	—	—	—
May	0	0	0	0	0	0	0	0	—	—	—
June	0	0	0	0	0	0	0	0	—	—	—
July	57	22	4	0	4	9	0	3	.386	.667	.386
August	124	24	4	0	0	9	2	10	.194	.226	.205
Sept./Oct.	33	7	0	0	1	1	0	2	.212	.303	.235
Leading Off Inn.	48	12	2	0	1	1	0	2	.250	.354	.250
Bases Empty	129	34	5	0	3	3	1	5	.264	.372	.275
Runners On	85	19	3	0	2	16	1	10	.224	.329	.230
Runners/Scor. Pos.	52	10	1	0	1	13	1	5	.192	.269	.204
Runners On/2 Out	35	8	2	0	1	6	1	4	.229	.371	.250
Scor. Pos./2 Out	23	4	0	0	0	3	1	4	.174	.174	.208
Late-Inning Pressure	33	8	3	0	0	2	0	4	.242	.333	.242
Leading Off	12	3	1	0	0	0	0	0	.250	.333	.250
Runners On	12	4	2	0	0	2	0	2	.333	.500	.333
Runners/Scor. Pos.	5	1	0	0	0	1	0	0	.200	.200	.200

RUNS BATTED IN	From 1B	From 2B	From 3B	Scoring Position
Totals	2/51	4/40	8/21	12/61
Percentage	3.9%	10.0%	38.1%	19.7%

Loves to chase: Bad pitches.
Hates to face: Dave Stewart (.125, 1-for-8)
Matt Young (0-for-8)

Miscellaneous statistics: Ground outs-to-air outs ratio: 1.31 last season, his first in the majors. . . . Grounded into 1 double play in 29 opportunities (one per 29.0). . . . Drove in 7 of 10 runners from third base with less than two outs (70%). . . . Direction of balls hit to the outfield: 31% to left field, 36% to center, 33% to right. . . . Base running: Advanced from first base to third on 4 of 10 outfield singles (40%); scored from second on 2 of 3 (67%). . . . Made 2.24 putouts per nine innings in left field.

Comments: Began his major league career with 129 plate appearances before drawing his first walk, the longest streak in the majors last season. . . . Batted .305 over his first 32 games before things turned sour. A turning point came when Mariners pitcher Vance Lovelace did what no other player in major league history had ever accomplished—he walked Azocar. From that point on, Azocar batted only .163 with no home runs. . . . A total of two walks in 218 PAs gave him the lowest rate in club history. The previous record, one walk per 49 plate appearances by Hal Chase in 1906, would have been broken by Mel Hall last season (one BB for 62 PAs) were it not for Oscar. . . . Recent Yankees who averaged 40 or more plate appearances between walks: Mickey Rivers in 1976, Andre Robertson in 1983. . . . Great opportunity for an automobile endorsement deal: "Buy an Azo-Car, and you'll never walk again.". . .The Azo-Car runs pretty well, too: He stole seven bases without getting caught. . . . Was hitless in 12 at-bats at the Oakland Coliseum. . . . Batted .143 during the first inning, the lowest mark in the American League.

Carlos Baerga

Bats Left and Right

Cleveland Indians	AB	H	2B	3B	HR	RBI	BB	SO	BA	SA	OBA
Season	312	81	17	2	7	47	16	57	.260	.394	.300
vs. Left-Handers	103	25	4	0	2	16	1	22	.243	.340	.250
vs. Right-Handers	209	56	13	2	5	31	15	35	.268	.421	.323
vs. Ground-Ballers	157	39	10	1	1	24	8	27	.248	.344	.285
vs. Fly-Ballers	155	42	7	1	6	23	8	30	.271	.445	.315
Home Games	150	45	10	1	3	28	9	22	.300	.440	.348
Road Games	162	36	7	1	4	19	7	35	.222	.352	.254
Grass Fields	258	70	16	2	7	42	12	45	.271	.430	.308
Artificial Turf	54	11	1	0	0	5	4	12	.204	.222	.262
April	36	7	0	1	1	5	2	4	.194	.333	.231
May	56	13	1	0	0	4	3	7	.232	.250	.267
June	48	10	5	0	2	10	4	12	.208	.438	.269
July	28	5	1	0	0	0	2	4	.179	.214	.233
August	55	20	4	0	2	11	1	8	.364	.545	.397
Sept./Oct.	89	26	6	1	2	17	4	22	.292	.449	.327
Leading Off Inn.	67	19	3	0	1	1	3	8	.284	.373	.314
Bases Empty	182	47	8	0	4	4	10	29	.258	.368	.308
Runners On	130	34	9	2	3	43	6	28	.262	.431	.289
Runners/Scor. Pos.	87	23	4	0	3	37	5	18	.264	.414	.296
Runners On/2 Out	53	13	5	0	0	15	3	8	.245	.340	.286
Scor. Pos./2 Out	43	10	2	0	0	12	2	6	.233	.279	.267
Late-Inning Pressure	62	15	4	0	1	12	7	15	.242	.355	.324
Leading Off	16	5	1	0	1	1	1	4	.313	.563	.353
Runners On	27	5	3	0	0	11	3	7	.185	.296	.281
Runners/Scor. Pos.	16	4	2	0	0	10	3	4	.250	.375	.381

RUNS BATTED IN	From 1B	From 2B	From 3B	Scoring Position
Totals	8/85	10/71	22/40	32/111
Percentage	9.4%	14.1%	55.0%	28.8%

Loves to face: Joe Price (2-for-2)
Walt Terrell (.500, 2-for-4, 1 2B)
Hates to face: Bobby Witt (0-for-4, 1 BB)
Matt Young (0-for-6, 1 BB)

Miscellaneous statistics: Ground outs-to-air outs ratio: 1.33 last season, his first in the majors. . . . Grounded into 4 double plays in 55 opportunities (one per 13.8). . . . Drove in 16 of 19 runners from third base with less than two outs (84%), highest rate in majors. . . . Direction of balls hit to the outfield: 31% to left field, 41% to center, 29% to right batting left-handed; 40% to left, 29% to center, 31% to right batting right-handed. . . . Base running: Advanced from first base to third on 6 of 21 outfield singles (29%); scored from second on 10 of 14 (71%). . . . Made 2.29 assists per nine innings at third base.

Comments: The "unknown" in the deal that sent Joe Carter to San Diego, Baerga combined with Sandy Alomar and Chris James, the Tribe's other acquisitions in that deal, for 28 home runs and 183 RBIs. . . . Had 15 go-ahead RBIs, the most of any American League rookie last season; 10 of those stood up as game-winners, the most of any rookie in the majors. . . . Batted .355 (11-for-31) as a pinch-hitter. . . . Drew only one walk in 109 plate appearances against left-handed pitchers, but averaged one walk per 15.3 PA vs. right-handers. . . . One of five American League players to start at least one game in each of eight different batting order slots. Baerga missed only the cleanup spot. . . . Batted .178 during the first inning, 7th-lowest average in the American League (minimum: 40 AB). . . . Hit three home runs in 150 at-bats in home games, and three more in 17 ABs at Memorial Stadium. . . . Participated in 27 double plays: 10 at shortstop, nine at third base, eight at second base. The last rookie to take part in at least eight DPs at each of those three positions: Billy Grabarkewitz (1970). . . . Comparable rookie seasons at the plate: Charlie Hayes (1989), Jim Gosger (1965), and Dick McAuliffe (1961).

Harold Baines

Bats Left

Rangers/A's	AB	H	2B	3B	HR	RBI	BB	SO	BA	SA	OBA
Season	415	118	15	1	16	65	67	80	.284	.441	.378
vs. Left-Handers	91	23	3	0	3	15	12	22	.253	.385	.330
vs. Right-Handers	324	95	12	1	13	50	55	58	.293	.457	.392
vs. Ground-Ballers	222	70	10	0	7	34	28	39	.315	.455	.387
vs. Fly-Ballers	193	48	5	1	9	31	39	41	.249	.425	.369
Home Games	200	56	4	0	9	40	28	40	.280	.435	.359
Road Games	215	62	11	1	7	25	39	40	.288	.447	.396
Grass Fields	341	97	9	0	14	56	58	67	.284	.434	.383
Artificial Turf	74	21	6	1	2	9	9	13	.284	.473	.357
April	64	15	2	0	4	10	8	17	.234	.453	.319
May	67	17	4	0	1	9	12	13	.254	.358	.358
June	81	29	3	1	4	13	15	18	.358	.568	.454
July	43	15	1	0	2	7	3	6	.349	.512	.391
August	71	18	0	0	2	5	11	9	.254	.338	.354
Sept./Oct.	89	24	5	0	3	21	18	17	.270	.427	.378
Leading Off Inn.	89	23	3	0	5	5	13	19	.258	.461	.353
Bases Empty	217	66	10	1	14	14	31	45	.304	.553	.391
Runners On	198	52	5	0	2	51	36	35	.263	.318	.365
Runners/Scor. Pos.	122	31	3	0	1	47	30	25	.254	.303	.384
Runners On/2 Out	83	20	1	0	1	17	20	17	.241	.289	.388
Scor. Pos./2 Out	57	13	0	0	1	16	18	11	.228	.281	.413
Late-Inning Pressure	52	18	5	0	3	8	14	6	.346	.615	.485
Leading Off	15	6	2	0	1	1	5	2	.400	.733	.550
Runners On	17	3	1	0	0	5	6	1	.176	.235	.391
Runners/Scor. Pos.	10	1	1	0	0	5	5	1	.100	.200	.400

RUNS BATTED IN	From 1B	From 2B	From 3B	Scoring Position
Totals	5/147	22/97	22/56	44/153
Percentage	3.4%	22.7%	39.3%	28.8%

Loves to face: Terry Leach (.500, 5-for-10, 1 HR)
Mike Schooler (.667, 4-for-6, 1 HR)
Jay Tibbs (.538, 7-for-13, 2 HR)

Hates to face: John Candelaria (.217, 5-for-23, 10 SO)
Mark Langston (.139, 5-for-36, 1 HR, 0 BB)
Dave Stieb (.228, 18-for-79, 1 HR)

Miscellaneous statistics: Ground outs-to-air outs ratio: 1.41 last season, 1.29 for career. . . . Grounded into 17 double plays in 92 opportunities (one per 5.4). . . . Drove in 18 of 28 runners from third base with less than two outs (64%). . . . Direction of balls hit to the outfield: 44% to left field, 32% to center, 24% to right. . . . Base running: Advanced from first base to third on 7 of 27 outfield singles (26%); scored from second on 6 of 12 (50%).

Comments: Didn't start against a left-hander for the Athletics until the third game of the World Series. Then, against southpaw Tom Browning, he hit a home run in his first at-bat. . . . Sacrifice bunt in the first game of the A.L.C.S. was his first since 1984, while playing for the White Sox and manager Tony LaRussa. . . . Fans taking their gloves to the ballpark better play this guy straightaway. He hit five home runs to left field, six to center, and five to right. . . . Ranked third in the league with a .340 batting average in the first inning, behind Wade Boggs (.352) and Jody Reed (.343). . . . Baines has hit opening-day home runs in each of the past two seasons, and for two different teams (the White Sox and Rangers). Only two players in American League history hit opening-day homers for three different clubs: Frank Robinson (Baltimore, California, and Cleveland) and Don Baylor (Baltimore, Oakland, and Boston). (Robinson, who hit three with the Reds, is the only player in major league history to do so for four different clubs.) Only three players in A.L. history hit O-D HRs in three consecutive years: Yogi Berra (4 years, 1955–58), Gus Triandos (1957–59), and Dave Winfield (1982–84). . . . Has hit at least one home run in every American League ballpark in which he has played, including Metropolitan Stadium and Exhibition Stadium. . . . Has played only three regular-season games in the field since being traded from Chicago to Texas in July 1989.

Steve Balboni

Bats Right

New York Yankees	AB	H	2B	3B	HR	RBI	BB	SO	BA	SA	OBA
Season	266	51	6	0	17	34	35	91	.192	.406	.291
vs. Left-Handers	161	34	4	0	14	27	30	53	.211	.497	.340
vs. Right-Handers	105	17	2	0	3	7	5	38	.162	.267	.205
vs. Ground-Ballers	125	27	1	0	8	18	19	35	.216	.416	.319
vs. Fly-Ballers	141	24	5	0	9	16	16	56	.170	.397	.265
Home Games	123	26	5	0	8	17	18	40	.211	.447	.315
Road Games	143	25	1	0	9	17	17	51	.175	.371	.270
Grass Fields	210	39	6	0	11	27	28	75	.186	.371	.285
Artificial Turf	56	12	0	0	6	7	7	16	.214	.536	.313
April	26	5	1	0	0	2	2	10	.192	.231	.250
May	33	7	0	0	4	7	6	9	.212	.576	.381
June	56	13	1	0	3	9	7	16	.232	.411	.308
July	52	9	2	0	4	4	10	14	.173	.442	.306
August	37	6	0	0	2	4	7	17	.162	.324	.295
Sept./Oct.	62	11	2	0	4	8	3	25	.177	.403	.215
Leading Off Inn.	70	7	1	0	4	4	10	27	.100	.286	.213
Bases Empty	160	27	2	0	14	14	22	60	.169	.444	.273
Runners On	106	24	4	0	3	20	13	31	.226	.349	.317
Runners/Scor. Pos.	67	12	1	0	0	13	7	19	.179	.194	.260
Runners On/2 Out	47	9	1	0	1	7	8	16	.191	.277	.309
Scor. Pos./2 Out	32	6	0	0	0	4	5	10	.188	.188	.297
Late-Inning Pressure	61	12	0	0	4	8	7	21	.197	.393	.286
Leading Off	14	1	0	0	0	0	1	6	.071	.071	.133
Runners On	27	6	0	0	0	4	3	8	.222	.222	.313
Runners/Scor. Pos.	21	4	0	0	0	4	2	6	.190	.190	.280

RUNS BATTED IN	From 1B	From 2B	From 3B	Scoring Position
Totals	4/73	4/55	9/24	13/79
Percentage	5.5%	7.3%	37.5%	16.5%

Loves to face: Jim Clancy (.375, 6-for-16, 1 2B, 3 HR)
Rick Honeycutt (.500, 3-for-6, 1 2B, 1 HR)
Walt Terrell (.424, 14-for-33, 4 HR)

Hates to face: Charlie Hough (.121, 4-for-33, 2 HR)
Paul Kilgus (.118, 2-for-17, 1 HR)
Dave Stewart (.107, 3-for-28)

Miscellaneous statistics: Ground outs-to-air outs ratio: 0.77 last season, 0.69 for career. . . . Grounded into 4 double plays in 52 opportunities (one per 13.0). . . . Drove in 8 of 14 runners from third base with less than two outs (57%). . . . Direction of balls hit to the outfield: 52% to left field, 33% to center, 15% to right. . . . Base running: Advanced from first base to third on 2 of 12 outfield singles (17%); scored from second on 2 of 2. . . . Made 0.34 assists per nine innings at first base.

Comments: Started 54 of 55 games in which the Yankees faced a left-handed pitcher, but only one of 107 games vs. right-handers. . . . Ranked fourth in the majors with 14 home runs vs. left-handed pitchers, behind Cecil Fielder (25), Barry Bonds (17), and Rob Deer (16). . . . Began the season with a 21-game homerless streak, then hit five HRs in his next five games. . . . Hit one home run per 15.6 at-bats, 6th-highest rate in the A.L. . . . Batted .164 from the fourth spot in the batting order, the lowest of any major leaguer with at least 100 cleanup at-bats. . . . Had a streak of 24 consecutive leadoff plate appearances without reaching base, the longest in the majors last season. . . . Came to the plate as a pinch hitter 49 times, 2d most of any A.L. player. The top five: Jack Daugherty (52), Balboni (49), Kevin Reimer (45), Dave Bergman (43), Scott Bradley (40). He batted .200 as a pinch hitter, with two homers in 40 ABs. . . . He did it! Was credited with the first (and, to date, the only) sacrifice bunt of his career in game 908 on July 7 vs. Minnesota. . . . Has compiled higher batting averages against ground-ball pitchers than against fly-ball pitchers in each of the last five seasons. Career averages: .243 vs. GBP, .218 vs. FBP. . . . Has the 2d-lowest career batting average among players with 150 home runs (.228). Gorman Thomas trails the pack (.225). . . . Our favorite chrome-domed New York athletes: Balboni, Barry Lyons, Y.A. Tittle.

Jesse Barfield

Bats Right

New York Yankees	AB	H	2B	3B	HR	RBI	BB	SO	BA	SA	OBA
Season	476	117	21	2	25	78	82	150	.246	.456	.359
vs. Left-Handers	162	42	7	0	13	25	33	51	.259	.543	.394
vs. Right-Handers	314	75	14	2	12	53	49	99	.239	.411	.341
vs. Ground-Ballers	208	47	8	0	6	25	29	64	.226	.351	.318
vs. Fly-Ballers	268	70	13	2	19	53	53	86	.261	.537	.390
Home Games	239	52	10	0	12	35	33	79	.218	.410	.314
Road Games	237	65	11	2	13	43	49	71	.274	.502	.403
Grass Fields	401	94	17	2	21	66	67	129	.234	.444	.345
Artificial Turf	75	23	4	0	4	12	15	21	.307	.520	.435
April	49	11	3	1	3	8	8	17	.224	.510	.333
May	85	22	3	0	5	17	11	28	.259	.471	.340
June	96	26	7	0	4	13	13	32	.271	.469	.357
July	70	17	5	0	2	7	9	21	.243	.400	.338
August	83	16	2	1	6	16	20	22	.193	.458	.352
Sept./Oct.	93	25	1	0	5	17	21	30	.269	.441	.410
Leading Off Inn.	114	24	4	1	5	5	13	38	.211	.395	.291
Bases Empty	287	66	11	1	14	14	39	90	.230	.422	.326
Runners On	189	51	10	1	11	64	43	60	.270	.508	.404
Runners/Scor. Pos.	110	29	8	1	4	49	25	35	.264	.464	.394
Runners On/2 Out	80	24	5	1	3	26	24	25	.300	.500	.467
Scor. Pos./2 Out	55	17	4	1	1	21	12	17	.309	.473	.441
Late-Inning Pressure	85	18	2	0	4	11	17	35	.212	.376	.352
Leading Off	23	4	1	0	0	0	4	11	.174	.217	.296
Runners On	31	8	0	0	3	10	3	13	.258	.548	.333
Runners/Scor. Pos.	19	5	0	0	1	6	2	11	.263	.421	.348

RUNS BATTED IN	From 1B	From 2B	From 3B	Scoring Position
Totals	13/147	16/85	24/53	40/138
Percentage	8.8%	18.8%	45.3%	29.0%

Loves to face: Andy Hawkins (3-for-3, 1 HR)
Rick Honeycutt (.400, 4-for-10, 1 2B, 3 HR)
Randy Johnson (.444, 4-for-9, 2 HR)

Hates to face: Mike Jackson (0-for-9, 1 BB)
Dennis Lamp (.125, 2-for-16)
Nolan Ryan (0-for-9, 8 SO)

Miscellaneous statistics: Ground outs-to-air outs ratio: 0.76 last season, 1.07 for career.... Grounded into 6 double plays in 108 opportunities (one per 18.0).... Drove in 14 of 25 runners from third base with less than two outs (56%).... Direction of balls hit to the outfield: 48% to left field, 29% to center, 23% to right.... Base running: Advanced from first base to third on 14 of 26 outfield singles (54%); scored from second on 8 of 11 (73%).... Made 2.24 putouts per nine innings in right field.

Comments: His total of 220 home runs starting with his rookie season of 1982 ranks fourth in a photo finish for the A.L. lead over that period, behind Dwight Evans (229), Cal Ripken (225), and Kent Hrbek (222).... The first outfielder with as many as 12 assists in six consecutive seasons since Johnny Callison (1962–67). The last streak of seven years or more: Bob Johnson from 1933 through 1942, his first 10 seasons in the majors.... Both Barfield and Roberto Kelly had strikeout totals higher than the previous Yankees single-season record (141), set by Jack Clark in 1988, his only season with the team. Mickey Mantle, once the K-K-K-King of strikeouts, now hardly gets a call on the team's all-time single season list. His highest total (126 in 1956) trails not only Barfield, Kelly, and Clark, but also Bobby Bonds (137 in 1975) and Reggie Jackson (133 in 1978; 129 in 1977).... Barfield and Kelly shared another trait: They hit five and eight opposite-field home runs, respectively. The only other teammates to hit five apiece were Will Clark and Kevin Mitchell.... Was thrown out trying to advance a base on a batted ball six times last season, the most of any player on the Yankees.... Was removed for a pinch hitter only once; Mel Hall batted for him against Gene Nelson in August.... His career average of .184 at the Oakland Coliseum is his lowest at any ballpark.... Has played 150 or more games in five of the last six seasons.

George Bell

Bats Right

Toronto Blue Jays	AB	H	2B	3B	HR	RBI	BB	SO	BA	SA	OBA
Season	562	149	25	0	21	86	32	80	.265	.422	.303
vs. Left-Handers	149	37	6	0	5	22	15	17	.248	.389	.315
vs. Right-Handers	413	112	19	0	16	64	17	63	.271	.433	.298
vs. Ground-Ballers	247	67	11	0	7	40	17	35	.271	.401	.315
vs. Fly-Ballers	315	82	14	0	14	46	15	45	.260	.438	.293
Home Games	274	70	12	0	11	41	16	41	.255	.420	.299
Road Games	288	79	13	0	10	45	16	39	.274	.424	.306
Grass Fields	222	59	12	0	8	35	16	31	.266	.428	.309
Artificial Turf	340	90	13	0	13	51	16	49	.265	.418	.298
April	83	22	2	0	6	16	2	6	.265	.506	.282
May	109	29	5	0	2	14	8	18	.266	.367	.317
June	114	36	7	0	9	26	9	16	.316	.614	.360
July	63	16	4	0	2	7	5	12	.254	.413	.304
August	91	21	3	0	1	14	4	10	.231	.297	.257
Sept./Oct.	102	25	4	0	1	9	4	18	.245	.314	.278
Leading Off Inn.	150	40	4	0	9	9	3	20	.267	.473	.281
Bases Empty	307	84	12	0	13	13	12	46	.274	.440	.303
Runners On	255	65	13	0	8	73	20	34	.255	.400	.302
Runners/Scor. Pos.	149	41	8	0	6	67	17	21	.275	.450	.328
Runners On/2 Out	126	33	7	0	4	29	8	21	.262	.413	.306
Scor. Pos./2 Out	77	20	5	0	2	24	6	12	.260	.403	.313
Late-Inning Pressure	81	14	1	0	3	10	6	18	.173	.296	.227
Leading Off	24	3	0	0	1	1	1	7	.125	.250	.160
Runners On	36	6	0	0	2	9	5	7	.167	.333	.262
Runners/Scor. Pos.	22	3	0	0	1	7	4	6	.136	.273	.259

RUNS BATTED IN	From 1B	From 2B	From 3B	Scoring Position
Totals	10/172	22/111	33/72	55/183
Percentage	5.8%	19.8%	45.8%	30.1%

Loves to face: Neal Heaton (.409, 9-for-22, 3 2B, 3 HR)
Jay Howell (.833, 5-for-6, 1 HR, 1 SO)
Jose Rijo (.636, 7-for-11, 1 HR)

Hates to face: Doug Drabek (0-for-8)
Mike Jackson (0-for-7, 5 SO)
Nolan Ryan (.143, 2-for-14)

Miscellaneous statistics: Ground outs-to-air outs ratio: 0.61 last season, 4th-lowest rate in A.L.; 0.75 for career.... Grounded into 14 double plays in 100 opportunities (one per 7.1).... Drove in 26 of 43 runners from third base with less than two outs (60%).... Direction of balls hit to the outfield: 40% to left field, 32% to center, 28% to right.... Base running: Advanced from first base to third on 6 of 26 outfield singles (23%); scored from second on 11 of 14 (79%).... Made 2.21 putouts per nine innings in left field.

Comments: The Orioles essay details the problems of home-run hitters who switch leagues or teams. But the Cubs are a special case. The last four players to join the Cubs off 20-HR seasons all matched or surpassed their totals for Chicago: Bobby Murcer (23 for S.F. in 1976, 27 for the Cubs), Dave Kingman (26 for four teams in 1977, 28 for the Cubs), Ron Cey (24 for L.A. in 1982, 24 for the Cubs), and Andre Dawson (20 for Mtl. in 1986, 49 for the Cubs). They don't call them the "friendly confines" for nothing.... Batted .324 in his first-inning at bats, .256 thereafter.... Averaged only one walk per 51 plate appearances leading off innings.... Batted .311 in day games, .247 at night.... Made 222 outs in the air, the most in the A.L.... Had eight at-bats with the bases loaded last season; his only hit was a grand slam. Has a career total of 79 plate appearances with the bases loaded, the most among active players who haven't drawn an RBI walk.... Had homerless streaks of 121 at-bats last season, 155 ABs the year before.... Has played 1181 career games, the most among any active player without a sacrifice bunt.... Has hit for a higher average against ground-ball pitchers than he has against fly-ball pitchers in each of the last five seasons. He also has a five-year streak of higher averages with runners in scoring position than in other at-bats.

Dave Bergman

Bats Left

Detroit Tigers	AB	H	2B	3B	HR	RBI	BB	SO	BA	SA	OBA
Season	205	57	10	1	2	26	33	17	.278	.366	.375
vs. Left-Handers	13	3	2	0	0	2	1	3	.231	.385	.286
vs. Right-Handers	192	54	8	1	2	24	32	14	.281	.365	.381
vs. Ground-Ballers	107	31	5	0	1	13	15	7	.290	.364	.371
vs. Fly-Ballers	98	26	5	1	1	13	18	10	.265	.367	.379
Home Games	109	27	8	1	1	13	18	9	.248	.367	.354
Road Games	96	30	2	0	1	13	15	8	.313	.365	.398
Grass Fields	181	47	10	1	2	25	26	15	.260	.359	.349
Artificial Turf	24	10	0	0	0	1	7	2	.417	.417	.548
April	18	4	0	0	0	3	2	1	.222	.222	.300
May	24	5	1	0	0	1	2	1	.208	.250	.259
June	37	9	2	0	1	5	7	3	.243	.378	.356
July	60	18	2	1	1	11	7	6	.300	.417	.373
August	35	15	4	0	0	5	6	3	.429	.543	.512
Sept./Oct.	31	6	1	0	0	1	9	3	.194	.226	.375
Leading Off Inn.	36	7	2	0	0	0	6	1	.194	.250	.310
Bases Empty	106	30	8	0	1	1	21	10	.283	.387	.402
Runners On	99	27	2	1	1	25	12	7	.273	.343	.345
Runners/Scor. Pos.	59	14	1	1	0	23	9	6	.237	.288	.329
Runners On/2 Out	29	6	0	1	1	6	9	1	.207	.379	.395
Scor. Pos./2 Out	21	3	0	1	0	4	7	1	.143	.238	.357
Late-Inning Pressure	31	6	1	0	0	3	8	4	.194	.226	.350
Leading Off	8	0	0	0	0	0	1	1	.000	.000	.111
Runners On	18	4	0	0	0	3	4	2	.222	.222	.348
Runners/Scor. Pos.	11	2	0	0	0	3	2	2	.182	.182	.286

RUNS BATTED IN	From 1B	From 2B	From 3B	Scoring Position
Totals	1/79	8/49	15/28	23/77
Percentage	1.3%	16.3%	53.6%	29.9%

Loves to face: Storm Davis (.444, 8-for-18, 1 HR)
Dennis Lamp (.467, 7-for-15)
Pascual Perez (.556, 5-for-9)

Hates to face: Mike Moore (.129, 4-for-31, 4 BB)
Jeff Reardon (.091, 1-for-11)
Dave Stewart (.130, 3-for-23, 4 BB)

Miscellaneous statistics: Ground outs-to-air outs ratio: 1.24 last season, 1.02 for career. . . . Grounded into 7 double plays in 61 opportunities (one per 8.7). . . . Drove in 12 of 21 runners from third base with less than two outs (57%). . . . Direction of balls hit to the outfield: 29% to left field, 42% to center, 29% to right. . . . Base running: Advanced from first base to third on 2 of 13 outfield singles (15%); scored from second on 6 of 7 (86%). . . . Made 0.59 assists per nine innings at first base.

Comments: Only three players in major league history have reached the 1000-game mark with fewer than 500 career hits. Bergman is one of them. The other two are Hoyt Wilhelm and Kent Tekulve. . . . Has started only 10 games vs. left-handed pitchers since 1978, all during the 1989 season. Last season, he started 53 games, all against right-handers. . . . Struck out only once in 42 leadoff plate appearances. . . . One of two players in the majors to start at least two games in both the cleanup spot and the ninth spot in the batting order. . . . Bergman batted .182 in 41 pinch-hit at-bats, .297 in his other at-bats. . . . Career averages are .213 as a pinch hitter, .316 as a designated hitter. . . . Could become the first Detroit player to start two consecutive opening days as designated hitter since John Wockenfuss did it in 1982 and 1983. . . . Batting average in Late-Inning Pressure Situations has been lower than his overall average in each of the last five seasons. . . . Has hit for a higher average in day games than he has in night games in each of the last five years. . . . Made his major league debut on August 26, 1975, for the Yankees. Only one other player from that game was active last season (Claudell Washington), but two have sons in the majors: Bobby Bonds and Sandy Alomar.

Dante Bichette

Bats Right

California Angels	AB	H	2B	3B	HR	RBI	BB	SO	BA	SA	OBA
Season	349	89	15	1	15	53	16	79	.255	.433	.292
vs. Left-Handers	146	40	8	1	5	21	7	30	.274	.445	.312
vs. Right-Handers	203	49	7	0	10	32	9	49	.241	.424	.278
vs. Ground-Ballers	155	42	7	0	7	27	10	33	.271	.452	.315
vs. Fly-Ballers	194	47	8	1	8	26	6	46	.242	.418	.272
Home Games	159	41	6	0	8	26	6	33	.258	.447	.296
Road Games	190	48	9	1	7	27	10	46	.253	.421	.289
Grass Fields	298	78	14	1	13	44	12	66	.262	.446	.296
Artificial Turf	51	11	1	0	2	9	4	13	.216	.353	.268
April	75	21	4	0	3	10	3	12	.280	.453	.308
May	92	26	7	0	3	15	4	17	.283	.457	.316
June	54	7	1	0	2	6	2	18	.130	.259	.161
July	66	14	1	0	5	14	5	18	.212	.455	.264
August	35	13	0	1	1	6	2	7	.371	.514	.436
Sept./Oct.	27	8	2	0	1	2	0	7	.296	.481	.296
Leading Off Inn.	83	18	5	0	4	4	4	20	.217	.422	.261
Bases Empty	178	51	11	0	9	9	10	38	.287	.500	.332
Runners On	171	38	4	1	6	44	6	41	.222	.363	.250
Runners/Scor. Pos.	95	24	3	0	5	40	5	26	.253	.442	.284
Runners On/2 Out	68	16	2	0	3	17	3	15	.235	.397	.278
Scor. Pos./2 Out	42	10	2	0	3	17	3	11	.238	.500	.289
Late-Inning Pressure	55	18	3	1	3	12	5	11	.327	.582	.387
Leading Off	9	4	1	0	1	1	1	1	.444	.889	.545
Runners On	30	8	1	1	1	10	2	7	.267	.467	.303
Runners/Scor. Pos.	18	6	1	0	1	9	2	5	.333	.556	.381

RUNS BATTED IN	From 1B	From 2B	From 3B	Scoring Position
Totals	8/139	12/65	18/44	30/109
Percentage	5.8%	18.5%	40.9%	27.5%

Loves to face: Mark Langston (.429, 3-for-7, 2 2B)
Curt Young (.600, 3-for-5, 2 HR, 4 BB)

Hates to face: Mike Jeffcoat (.077, 1-for-13)
Lance McCullers (0-for-5, 3 SO)
Mike Moore (0-for-8)

Miscellaneous statistics: Ground outs-to-air outs ratio: 1.10 last season, 1.03 for career. . . . Grounded into 9 double plays in 87 opportunities (one per 9.7). . . . Drove in 14 of 26 runners from third base with less than two outs (54%). . . . Direction of balls hit to the outfield: 41% to left field, 32% to center, 27% to right. . . . Base running: Advanced from first base to third on 3 of 16 outfield singles (19%); scored from second on 9 of 11 (82%). . . . Made 1.99 putouts per nine innings in right field.

Comments: After Bichette threw out five runners from the outfield in his first six games last season, Angels manager Doug Rader cracked that he might become a 30/30 player—30 home runs and 30 assists! Well, it might surprise Rader to find out that baseball has already had a 40/40 player—and we don't mean Jose Canseco. Hall of Famer Chuck Klein hit 40 home runs while collecting 44 outfield assists in 1930. Over the last 50 years, the only player to reach 25 in both categories was Johnny Callison (26 apiece in 1963). . . . Incidentally, Bichette finished the season with 12 outfield assists. . . . Was one of three players to start at least 15 games at each of the three outfield positions. Career outfield starts: 46 in left, 34 in center, 57 in right. . . . Bichette started 43 of the 48 games in which the Angels faced left-handed starters, only 43 of 114 (and only three of the last 42) vs. right-handers. . . . Career batting averages: .194 in day games, .261 at night. . . . Over his career has driven in 41 percent of runners from scoring position in Late-Inning Pressure Situations, 27 percent at other times.

Wade Boggs

Bats Left

Boston Red Sox	AB	H	2B	3B	HR	RBI	BB	SO	BA	SA	OBA
Season	619	187	44	5	6	63	87	68	.302	.418	.386
vs. Left-Handers	230	63	14	2	1	30	21	39	.274	.365	.332
vs. Right-Handers	389	124	30	3	5	33	66	29	.319	.450	.415
vs. Ground-Ballers	247	95	20	1	4	32	38	17	.385	.522	.462
vs. Fly-Ballers	372	92	24	4	2	31	49	51	.247	.349	.334
Home Games	309	111	30	1	3	32	52	42	.359	.492	.449
Road Games	310	76	14	4	3	31	35	26	.245	.345	.320
Grass Fields	530	164	42	5	6	62	75	63	.309	.442	.392
Artificial Turf	89	23	2	0	0	1	12	5	.258	.281	.347
April	72	24	6	0	1	12	18	7	.333	.458	.467
May	96	23	6	1	1	5	16	13	.240	.354	.345
June	103	33	8	1	3	12	18	9	.320	.505	.423
July	122	38	9	2	0	12	9	12	.311	.418	.353
August	117	39	6	0	0	11	12	14	.333	.385	.395
Sept./Oct.	109	30	9	1	1	11	14	13	.275	.404	.352
Leading Off Inn.	195	63	16	1	3	3	21	22	.323	.462	.389
Bases Empty	366	106	29	3	4	4	41	42	.290	.418	.363
Runners On	253	81	15	2	2	59	46	26	.320	.419	.416
Runners/Scor. Pos.	139	47	9	2	1	55	37	15	.338	.453	.462
Runners On/2 Out	108	36	7	1	0	25	17	8	.333	.417	.424
Scor. Pos./2 Out	68	22	4	1	0	24	16	7	.324	.412	.452
Late-Inning Pressure	86	26	3	2	0	6	17	11	.302	.384	.417
Leading Off	23	9	2	0	0	0	2	4	.391	.478	.440
Runners On	39	9	0	1	0	6	11	5	.231	.282	.400
Runners/Scor. Pos.	24	6	0	1	0	6	10	5	.250	.333	.471

RUNS BATTED IN	From 1B	From 2B	From 3B	Scoring Position
Totals	5/194	20/108	32/62	52/170
Percentage	2.6%	18.5%	51.6%	30.6%

Loves to face: Juan Berenguer (.405, 15-for-37, 1 HR, 7 BB)
Mike Moore (.371, 13-for-35, 14 BB)
Jeff Russell (.455, 5-for-11, 1 HR)

Hates to face: Randy D. Johnson (0-for-7, 5 SO)
Dave LaPoint (.211, 4-for-19)
Bob Welch (0-for-18, 3 BB)

Miscellaneous statistics: Ground outs-to-air outs ratio: 1.16 last season, 1.35 for career.... Grounded into 14 double plays in 125 opportunities (one per 8.9).... Drove in 20 of 31 runners from third base with less than two outs (65%).... Direction of balls hit to the outfield: 55% to left field, 34% to center, 11% to right.... Base running: Advanced from first base to third on 13 of 41 outfield singles (32%); scored from second on 19 of 29 (66%).... Made 1.62 assists per nine innings at third base, 2d lowest in A.L.

Comments: His career average dropped six points to .346 last season, but Boggs still ranks fifth in major league history among players with 2500 career at-bats, behind Ty Cobb (.367), Rogers Hornsby (.358), Shoeless Joe Jackson (.356), and Lefty O'Doul (.347).... Trivia question: Among players with at least 500 games, who has the highest career batting average? Answer below.... Reached base on 275 times on hits, walks, and hit batters, and didn't steal a base. Ted Williams had consecutive seasons of 334 and 345 (without stealing) in 1946 and 1947.... Led the majors with 81 hits to the opposite field; only one other player was close—Willie McGee (75). Bip Roberts ranked third with 62.... Boggs hit 41 of his 55 extra-base hits to the opposite field; 27 of his 44 doubles were hit to left field at Fenway Park.... Had the highest first-inning batting average in the majors last season: .352, compared to .287 thereafter.... Strikeout rate vs. left-handers (one per 6.5 PA) was more than double his rate vs. right-handers (one per 15.9 PA).... Batted 137 points higher vs. ground-ballers (.385) than vs. fly-ballers (.247) last season, the largest margin in the majors.... Started his fifth straight All-Star game last season, tying the record for third basemen shared by Brooks Robinson and George Brett.... Needs 73 games to become the team's all-time leader at third base. Frank Malzone currently holds the mark (1335).... Answer to trivia question: Terry Forster, .397 in 619 games (31-for-78).

Pat Borders

Bats Right

Toronto Blue Jays	AB	H	2B	3B	HR	RBI	BB	SO	BA	SA	OBA
Season	346	99	24	2	15	49	18	57	.286	.497	.319
vs. Left-Handers	186	53	16	2	10	27	15	29	.285	.554	.337
vs. Right-Handers	160	46	8	0	5	22	3	28	.287	.431	.297
vs. Ground-Ballers	144	44	4	1	6	18	5	21	.306	.472	.329
vs. Fly-Ballers	202	55	20	1	9	31	13	36	.272	.515	.312
Home Games	164	45	13	1	10	28	12	23	.274	.549	.318
Road Games	182	54	11	1	5	21	6	34	.297	.451	.319
Grass Fields	138	41	7	1	2	14	6	24	.297	.406	.326
Artificial Turf	208	58	17	1	13	35	12	33	.279	.558	.314
April	31	11	2	0	3	4	1	5	.355	.710	.375
May	84	23	7	0	4	10	3	17	.274	.500	.295
June	54	16	4	1	3	13	2	4	.296	.574	.321
July	56	17	5	0	2	9	3	9	.304	.500	.339
August	65	18	3	0	2	8	6	9	.277	.415	.333
Sept./Oct.	56	14	3	1	1	5	3	13	.250	.393	.283
Leading Off Inn.	72	27	7	1	5	5	3	10	.375	.708	.400
Bases Empty	188	59	15	2	8	8	9	29	.314	.543	.345
Runners On	158	40	9	0	7	41	9	28	.253	.443	.288
Runners/Scor. Pos.	89	20	5	0	2	28	7	15	.225	.348	.273
Runners On/2 Out	67	18	1	0	4	20	5	11	.269	.463	.319
Scor. Pos./2 Out	45	12	1	0	2	16	4	8	.267	.422	.327
Late-Inning Pressure	61	13	3	0	1	6	4	14	.213	.311	.262
Leading Off	14	2	1	0	0	0	0	3	.143	.214	.143
Runners On	22	7	1	0	1	6	1	5	.318	.500	.348
Runners/Scor. Pos.	13	4	1	0	0	4	0	3	.308	.385	.308

RUNS BATTED IN	From 1B	From 2B	From 3B	Scoring Position
Totals	10/123	13/68	11/38	24/106
Percentage	8.1%	19.1%	28.9%	22.6%

Loves to face: Allan Anderson (.412, 7-for-17, 2 HR)
Mark Davis (2-for-2, 1 BB)
Jamie Moyer (.500, 5-for-10, 1 HR)

Hates to face: Mark Langston (.111, 1-for-9)
Dave LaPoint (.136, 3-for-22, 1 HR)
Dave West (.100, 1-for-10, 1 2B)

Miscellaneous statistics: Ground outs-to-air outs ratio: 1.27 last season, 1.16 for career.... Grounded into 17 double plays in 81 opportunities (one per 4.8), 3d-worst rate in A.L.... Drove in 7 of 18 runners from third base with less than two outs (39%).... Direction of balls hit to the outfield: 43% to left field, 26% to center, 32% to right.... Base running: Advanced from first base to third on 4 of 12 outfield singles (33%); scored from second on 1 of 5 (20%).... Opposing base stealers: 54-for-94 (57%), 3d-lowest rate in A.L.

Comments: Started all 49 games in which the Blue Jays faced a left-handed starter, but only 34 of 113 vs. right-handers.... His batting average was higher against right-handers than against southpaws, but he averaged one extra-base hit per 6.6 at-bats vs. left-handers, compared to one per 12.3 ABs vs. righties. Now look at the walks: only three vs. right-handers. That's why Greg Myers starts against righties.... Batted .207 (19-for-92) against right-handers in two previous seasons.... Played 115 games behind the plate, including 32 in which he was the relief catcher.... Averaged one home run per 16.4 at-bats at the Skydome, one per 36.4 ABs on the road.... Ranked third in the majors with 15 home runs as a catcher.... Had never before hit as many as 15 home runs in any season at any level of professional ball.... Career batting-average breakdowns: .292 with the bases empty, .252 with runners on base, .249 with runners in scoring position, .226 with two outs and RISP.... Spent his first two pro seasons (1982–83) playing only third base, but led both the Pioneer and South Atlantic Leagues in errors, prompting his conversion to first base. He caught his first pro game in 1986, and has done nothing but catch since 1988, except for one game each at second and third base for the Jays.

Phil Bradley

Bats Right

Orioles/White Sox	AB	H	2B	3B	HR	RBI	BB	SO	BA	SA	OBA
Season	422	108	14	2	4	31	50	61	.256	.327	.349
vs. Left-Handers	161	38	7	2	2	9	22	24	.236	.342	.339
vs. Right-Handers	261	70	7	0	2	22	28	37	.268	.318	.356
vs. Ground-Ballers	198	55	7	0	1	11	28	27	.278	.328	.381
vs. Fly-Ballers	224	53	7	2	3	20	22	34	.237	.326	.320
Home Games	190	45	8	0	4	16	25	28	.237	.342	.336
Road Games	232	63	6	2	0	15	25	33	.272	.315	.360
Grass Fields	323	81	10	1	4	24	40	47	.251	.325	.347
Artificial Turf	99	27	4	1	0	7	10	14	.273	.333	.357
April	79	19	3	0	0	3	4	9	.241	.278	.274
May	83	20	2	0	0	4	12	13	.241	.265	.364
June	61	22	3	1	1	4	9	5	.361	.492	.451
July	69	17	1	0	3	15	6	9	.246	.391	.325
August	85	23	4	1	0	4	9	15	.271	.341	.354
Sept./Oct.	45	7	1	0	0	1	10	10	.156	.178	.333
Leading Off Inn.	149	47	7	0	1	1	11	13	.315	.383	.378
Bases Empty	284	74	12	0	2	2	25	39	.261	.324	.335
Runners On	138	34	2	2	2	29	25	22	.246	.333	.375
Runners/Scor. Pos.	76	20	1	0	2	27	21	14	.263	.355	.430
Runners On/2 Out	55	14	1	2	0	11	10	12	.255	.345	.397
Scor. Pos./2 Out	36	8	1	0	0	9	8	9	.222	.250	.378
Late-Inning Pressure	63	14	3	1	1	12	3	9	.222	.349	.254
Leading Off	14	4	0	0	0	0	1	2	.286	.286	.333
Runners On	22	6	1	1	1	12	1	3	.273	.545	.292
Runners/Scor. Pos.	14	5	1	0	1	11	1	3	.357	.643	.375

RUNS BATTED IN	From 1B	From 2B	From 3B	Scoring Position
Totals	5/98	10/65	12/32	22/97
Percentage	5.1%	15.4%	37.5%	22.7%

Loves to face: Greg A. Harris (.529, 9-for-17)
Greg Maddux (.500, 6-for-12, 1 HR)
Don Robinson (.556, 5-for-9, 2 2B, 1 3B, 1 HR)

Hates to face: David Cone (.077, 1-for-13, 7 SO)
Mike Henneman (0-for-11)
Jack Morris (.080, 2-for-25, 1 3B, 1 HR)

Miscellaneous statistics: Ground outs-to-air outs ratio: 1.94 last season, 5th-highest rate in A.L.; 1.76 for career.... Grounded into 11 double plays in 81 opportunities (one per 7.4).... Drove in 9 of 15 runners from third base with less than two outs (60%).... Direction of balls hit to the outfield: 19% to left field, 29% to center, 52% to right.... Base running: Advanced from first base to third on 11 of 24 outfield singles (46%); scored from second on 12 of 12.... Made 2.27 putouts per nine innings in left field.

Comments: Had one hit in six pinch-hit at bats, but it was a grand slam home run, which broke a career-long 0-for-15 as a pinch hitter.... Was hit by 11 pitches, the lowest total to lead the majors in more than 40 years. In 1949, Andy Pafko led the majors with nine; a year earlier, Joe DiMaggio led the majors with eight.... His strikeout rate (one every 8.1 plate appearances) was the best of his career (excluding 23 games in 1983), but he also had his lowest-ever rate of walks. More importantly, his batting average was 8 points lower than his previous nadir (.264 in 1988, his only season in the National League).... Batted .270 in 72 games for the Orioles, .226 in 45 games for the White Sox.... Had hit for a higher average in home games than in road games in each of the previous six seasons, despite spending that time playing for three different teams (Seattle, Philadelphia, and Baltimore).... Had at least 10 outfield assists in each of four straight seasons (1985–88), but has only eight in two years since then.

Scott Bradley

Bats Left

Seattle Mariners	AB	H	2B	3B	HR	RBI	BB	SO	BA	SA	OBA
Season	233	52	9	0	1	28	15	20	.223	.275	.264
vs. Left-Handers	25	4	0	0	0	4	3	2	.160	.160	.233
vs. Right-Handers	208	48	9	0	1	24	12	18	.231	.288	.268
vs. Ground-Ballers	100	23	4	0	0	11	7	9	.230	.270	.275
vs. Fly-Ballers	133	29	5	0	1	17	8	11	.218	.278	.255
Home Games	112	28	5	0	1	19	9	12	.250	.321	.296
Road Games	121	24	4	0	0	9	6	8	.198	.231	.233
Grass Fields	93	19	4	0	0	8	2	6	.204	.247	.219
Artificial Turf	140	33	5	0	1	20	13	14	.236	.293	.291
April	20	6	3	0	0	4	0	1	.300	.450	.300
May	63	14	2	0	0	5	3	9	.222	.254	.250
June	50	10	1	0	1	8	4	3	.200	.280	.250
July	31	9	0	0	0	6	2	1	.290	.290	.324
August	38	8	3	0	0	4	3	2	.211	.289	.268
Sept./Oct.	31	5	0	0	0	1	3	4	.161	.161	.229
Leading Off Inn.	59	10	2	0	0	0	3	7	.169	.203	.210
Bases Empty	133	23	5	0	0	0	6	13	.173	.211	.209
Runners On	100	29	4	0	1	28	9	7	.290	.360	.330
Runners/Scor. Pos.	60	18	4	0	1	28	6	3	.300	.417	.333
Runners On/2 Out	53	19	2	0	1	18	4	1	.358	.453	.404
Scor. Pos./2 Out	38	13	2	0	1	18	3	1	.342	.474	.390
Late-Inning Pressure	53	15	2	0	1	8	3	6	.283	.377	.316
Leading Off	13	3	0	0	0	0	2	3	.231	.231	.333
Runners On	21	9	2	0	1	8	1	2	.429	.667	.435
Runners/Scor. Pos.	13	5	2	0	1	8	0	1	.385	.769	.357

RUNS BATTED IN	From 1B	From 2B	From 3B	Scoring Position
Totals	2/76	14/54	11/26	25/80
Percentage	2.6%	25.9%	42.3%	31.3%

Loves to face: Andy Hawkins (.385, 5-for-13, 3 2B, 1 HR)
Tim Leary (.462, 6-for-13)
Jeff Montgomery (.500, 4-for-8, 1 HR)

Hates to face: Jeff Russell (.111, 1-for-9, 1 2B)
Nolan Ryan (.100, 1-for-10)
Bobby Witt (.091, 1-for-11, 1 2B)

Miscellaneous statistics: Ground outs-to-air outs ratio: 1.63 last season, 1.51 for career.... Grounded into 6 double plays in 46 opportunities (one per 7.7).... Drove in 8 of 10 runners from third base with less than two outs (80%).... Direction of balls hit to the outfield: 28% to left field, 40% to center, 32% to right.... Base running: Advanced from first base to third on 2 of 9 outfield singles (22%); scored from second on 2 of 5 (40%).... Opposing base stealers: 43-for-60 (72%).

Comments: Started 54 games vs. right-handers, but only three vs. southpaws.... Struck out only once in 57 plate appearances with two outs and runners on base.... Career average of one strikeout per 18.6 plate appearances against right-handed pitchers is better than Wade Boggs's (one per 18.5).... Games played year-by-year since 1987: 102, 103, 103, 101.... Bradley ranks second in Mariners history in games caught, behind only his current platoonmate, Dave Valle. Prior to last season, Bob Stinson topped the list.... In this era of specialization, here's what Bradley does best: He has a career batting average of .409 with two outs and runners on base in Late-Inning Pressure Situations—the highest of any active player. Really.... Has led off 356 innings in his career, but drawn only eight walks, an average of one per 45 leadoff PAs. That's the lowest rate of any active major leaguer with 150 leadoff PAs, except Fernando Valenzuela (who has two BBs in 201 PAs).... Has hit 14 home runs in 668 career at-bats at the Kingdome (one every 48 AB), and four home runs in 802 at-bats (one every 200 AB) in all other parks combined.... Had the last hit in old Comiskey Park.

George Brett

Bats Left

Kansas City Royals	AB	H	2B	3B	HR	RBI	BB	SO	BA	SA	OBA
Season	544	179	45	7	14	87	56	63	.329	.515	.387
vs. Left-Handers	187	59	11	3	5	28	16	26	.316	.487	.366
vs. Right-Handers	357	120	34	4	9	59	40	37	.336	.529	.398
vs. Ground-Ballers	249	92	24	2	8	42	23	30	.369	.578	.420
vs. Fly-Ballers	295	87	21	5	6	45	33	33	.295	.461	.360
Home Games	288	92	18	5	3	46	27	27	.319	.448	.373
Road Games	256	87	27	2	11	41	29	36	.340	.590	.403
Grass Fields	209	68	21	1	9	34	27	31	.325	.565	.399
Artificial Turf	335	111	24	6	5	53	29	32	.331	.484	.379
April	69	15	2	0	0	5	8	12	.217	.246	.295
May	105	30	5	2	1	10	12	14	.286	.400	.356
June	60	15	2	0	0	7	8	6	.250	.283	.329
July	116	45	18	1	6	24	12	13	.388	.716	.442
August	103	38	11	2	3	24	9	11	.369	.602	.416
Sept./Oct.	91	36	7	2	4	17	7	7	.396	.648	.434
Leading Off Inn.	103	30	7	0	3	3	6	8	.291	.447	.330
Bases Empty	299	89	17	5	10	10	17	40	.298	.488	.335
Runners On	245	90	28	2	4	77	39	23	.367	.547	.443
Runners/Scor. Pos.	136	49	15	0	2	68	34	15	.360	.515	.469
Runners On/2 Out	87	27	7	1	1	23	15	11	.310	.448	.412
Scor. Pos./2 Out	58	17	6	0	1	22	12	10	.293	.448	.414
Late-Inning Pressure	75	20	4	0	3	8	10	8	.267	.440	.353
Leading Off	19	3	0	0	1	1	1	0	.158	.316	.200
Runners On	32	10	2	0	1	6	6	5	.313	.469	.421
Runners/Scor. Pos.	17	3	1	0	0	4	5	3	.176	.235	.364

RUNS BATTED IN	From 1B	From 2B	From 3B	Scoring Position
Totals	14/175	29/99	30/59	59/158
Percentage	8.0%	29.3%	50.8%	37.3%

Loves to face: Gene Nelson (.400, 10-for-25, 5 HR, 0 SO)
Jeff Russell (.400, 6-for-15, 3 HR)
Matt Young (.421, 8-for-19)

Hates to face: Allan Anderson (.130, 3-for-23)
Bert Blyleven (.240, 23-for-96, 2 HR)
John Candelaria (.105, 2-for-19, 2 HR)

Miscellaneous statistics: Ground outs-to-air outs ratio: 1.44 last season, 1.05 for career.... Grounded into 18 double plays in 126 opportunities (one per 7.0).... Drove in 24 of 33 runners from third base with less than two outs (73%).... Direction of balls hit to the outfield: 29% to left field, 31% to center, 39% to right.... Base running: Advanced from first base to third on 10 of 33 outfield singles (30%); scored from second on 13 of 18 (72%).... Made 0.68 assists per nine innings at first base.

Comments: Brett won the 1990 A.L. crown 14 years after winning his first batting title in 1976. The longest such span in major league history belongs to Ted Williams: 17 years, from 1941 to 1958. (But, of course, that spanned only two decades. Big deal.)... Brett's most recent title had been in 1980, so he became the first player in major league history to win batting titles 10 years apart *without winning one in between*.... Overcame a 71-point deficit as of July 4 to win the title, the largest such comeback in the A.L. over the past 45 years. Ken Griffey, Jr. was the July 4 leader at .337.... At 37, Brett became the oldest player to hit as many as 45 doubles since Pete Rose hit 51 at age 37 in 1977.... Career total of 559 doubles is the fifth-highest in American League history. Brett trails Charlie Gehringer by only 15.... Brett is the only player to drive in at least 35 percent of runners in scoring position in each of the last three seasons. He's hit the 30-percent mark in every season for which we have those figures (1975–90)—a 16-year streak that's more than three times as long as the second-longest current streak (Paul Molitor, 5 years).... Leads all active players with 967 extra-base hits, which ranks him 21st all-time. Only eighteen players have reached four figures in XBH.... The only player in the majors to hit for the cycle last season.... Batted .341 as a first baseman, .298 in other at-bats.... Has played only one game at third base over the last three years.

Greg Briley

Bats Left

Seattle Mariners	AB	H	2B	3B	HR	RBI	BB	SO	BA	SA	OBA
Season	337	83	18	2	5	29	37	48	.246	.356	.319
vs. Left-Handers	33	7	1	0	0	3	4	7	.212	.242	.297
vs. Right-Handers	304	76	17	2	5	26	33	41	.250	.368	.322
vs. Ground-Ballers	125	30	7	0	2	13	15	14	.240	.344	.319
vs. Fly-Ballers	212	53	11	2	3	16	22	34	.250	.363	.319
Home Games	166	41	8	1	4	17	17	23	.247	.380	.312
Road Games	171	42	10	1	1	12	20	25	.246	.333	.326
Grass Fields	144	35	9	1	1	9	18	19	.243	.340	.325
Artificial Turf	193	48	9	1	4	20	19	29	.249	.368	.315
April	51	11	6	0	0	2	2	4	.216	.333	.245
May	78	21	4	0	2	11	6	11	.269	.397	.322
June	53	15	6	0	0	3	4	9	.283	.396	.333
July	48	13	1	0	1	7	6	8	.271	.354	.345
August	65	11	1	2	2	6	11	9	.169	.338	.286
Sept./Oct.	42	12	0	0	0	0	8	7	.286	.286	.400
Leading Off Inn.	68	15	1	0	0	0	8	11	.221	.235	.312
Bases Empty	202	46	7	1	2	2	19	33	.228	.302	.297
Runners On	135	37	11	1	3	27	18	15	.274	.437	.350
Runners/Scor. Pos.	71	20	4	1	2	23	9	9	.282	.451	.345
Runners On/2 Out	50	16	7	1	0	12	8	4	.320	.500	.414
Scor. Pos./2 Out	34	12	4	1	0	11	5	2	.353	.529	.436
Late-Inning Pressure	44	12	3	1	1	5	2	9	.273	.455	.304
Leading Off	7	0	0	0	0	0	0	2	.000	.000	.000
Runners On	16	6	3	1	1	5	2	2	.375	.875	.444
Runners/Scor. Pos.	10	3	1	1	1	5	1	2	.300	.900	.364

RUNS BATTED IN	From 1B	From 2B	From 3B	Scoring Position
Totals	5/95	5/59	14/31	19/90
Percentage	5.3%	8.5%	45.2%	21.1%

Loves to face: Kevin Brown (.714, 5-for-7)
Mike Henneman (.500, 3-for-6)

Hates to face: Bert Blyleven (.071, 1-for-14)
Scott Sanderson (0-for-11)
Bobby Witt (.167, 2-for-12)

Miscellaneous statistics: Ground outs-to-air outs ratio: 1.26 last season, 1.18 for career.... Grounded into 6 double plays in 70 opportunities (one per 11.7).... Drove in 7 of 13 runners from third base with less than two outs (54%).... Direction of balls hit to the outfield: 37% to left field, 32% to center, 32% to right.... Base running: Advanced from first base to third on 8 of 22 outfield singles (36%); scored from second on 10 of 16 (63%).... Made 2.18 putouts per nine innings in right field.

Comments: Started 86 games vs. right-handed pitchers, but only three vs. left-handers.... In parts of three seasons, he has accumulated 539 plate appearances vs. right-handers, but only 96 vs. lefties.... His 1989 home run off Kevin Hickey remains his only one against a southpaw. He has hit 18 against right-handers.... Comes out swinging like Mike Tyson (the boxer, not the ex-Cardinals third baseman) in the first round. Averaged one walk per 24 plate appearances during the first inning, one per 9.1 plate appearances thereafter.... Played 43 games in left field and 66 games in right, but all four of his assists came from left field.... He'd better take advantage of Memorial Stadium while he can. He has a career batting average of .407 there, with three home runs in 27 at-bats.... Career average of .219 as a pinch hitter (7-for-32).... Played second base exclusively in his first two seasons of pro ball (1986 and 1987). Was converted to an outfielder after leading Southern League second basemen with 29 errors in 1987. (Think that was easy? Ron Gant played second base in that league!) But he committed only one error in 52 chances in 10 games at second base in 1989.

Greg Brock

Bats Left

Milwaukee Brewers	AB	H	2B	3B	HR	RBI	BB	SO	BA	SA	OBA
Season	367	91	23	0	7	50	43	45	.248	.368	.324
vs. Left-Handers	86	18	5	0	2	17	10	12	.209	.337	.283
vs. Right-Handers	281	73	18	0	5	33	33	33	.260	.377	.336
vs. Ground-Ballers	162	38	10	0	1	19	19	15	.235	.315	.310
vs. Fly-Ballers	205	53	13	0	6	31	24	30	.259	.410	.335
Home Games	176	42	9	0	3	28	23	22	.239	.341	.319
Road Games	191	49	14	0	4	22	20	23	.257	.393	.329
Grass Fields	317	80	19	0	7	46	41	39	.252	.379	.335
Artificial Turf	50	11	4	0	0	4	2	6	.220	.300	.245
April	49	16	4	0	1	10	7	4	.327	.469	.407
May	76	13	4	0	0	8	6	8	.171	.224	.224
June	87	24	9	0	1	12	11	10	.276	.414	.354
July	72	19	2	0	2	10	8	11	.264	.375	.346
August	37	9	0	0	2	6	2	5	.243	.405	.275
Sept./Oct.	46	10	4	0	1	4	9	7	.217	.370	.339
Leading Off Inn.	69	18	5	0	3	3	2	5	.261	.464	.282
Bases Empty	202	47	11	0	4	4	21	23	.233	.347	.311
Runners On	165	44	12	0	3	46	22	22	.267	.394	.338
Runners/Scor. Pos.	97	24	8	0	1	41	20	14	.247	.361	.352
Runners On/2 Out	71	17	2	0	2	18	10	8	.239	.352	.333
Scor. Pos./2 Out	52	11	2	0	1	16	10	7	.212	.308	.339
Late-Inning Pressure	50	6	2	0	1	4	2	6	.120	.220	.154
Leading Off	12	1	0	0	0	0	0	2	.083	.083	.083
Runners On	23	3	0	0	1	4	2	2	.130	.261	.200
Runners/Scor. Pos.	16	2	0	0	1	4	2	1	.125	.313	.222

RUNS BATTED IN	From 1B	From 2B	From 3B	Scoring Position
Totals	4/132	16/83	23/45	39/128
Percentage	3.0%	19.3%	51.1%	30.5%

Loves to face: Andy Hawkins (.394, 13-for-33, 2 HR)
Rob Murphy (.556, 5-for-9)
Bob Welch (.500, 6-for-12, 1 HR)

Hates to face: Jeff Reardon (.167, 3-for-18)
Dave Stewart (.129, 4-for-31, 4 BB)
Bobby Witt (.111, 2-for-18, 1 3B)

Miscellaneous statistics: Ground outs-to-air outs ratio: 1.06 last season, 1.08 for career. . . . Grounded into 6 double plays in 81 opportunities (one per 13.5). . . . Drove in 18 of 22 runners from third base with less than two outs (82%), 2d-highest rate in A.L. . . . Direction of balls hit to the outfield: 25% to left field, 27% to center, 47% to right. . . . Base running: Advanced from first base to third on 3 of 10 outfield singles (30%); scored from second on 4 of 9 (44%). . . . Made 0.63 assists per nine innings at first base.

Comments: Has driven in between 50 and 52 runs and struck out between 45 and 49 times in each of the past three seasons. . . . Played 899⅔ innings at first base, and started only four double plays, the fewest among those who played at least 700 innings there. The league average: one per 129 innings. . . . Less selective as a leadoff batter: He averaged one walk per 35.5 plate appearances leading off innings, one per 8.6 plate appearances at other times. . . . Batting average vs. left-handers dropped from a career-high .333 mark in 1989. His average vs. right-handers was his highest since batting .304 against them in 1987. . . . Batted 148 points lower in Late-Inning Pressure Situations (.120) than in other at-bats (.268) last season, the 3d-largest margin in the majors, dropping his career average to .189 in LIPS. . . . Has batted below .200 in LIPS six times in nine seasons in the majors. . . . Has had higher batting averages with runners on base than with the bases empty in each of the last six seasons, batting 59 points higher with runners on base (.286) than with the bases empty (.227)—the largest margin in the majors during that period (minimum: 1000 ABs with ROB). . . . Has homered at least once in every current major league ballpark except Fenway Park (78 AB), Royals Stadium (50 AB), the Kingdome (62 AB), and Busch Stadium (33 AB). . . . Has a career batting average of .159 as a pinch hitter, with no home runs in 69 at-bats.

Jerry Browne

Bats Left and Right

Cleveland Indians	AB	H	2B	3B	HR	RBI	BB	SO	BA	SA	OBA
Season	513	137	26	5	6	50	72	46	.267	.372	.353
vs. Left-Handers	139	39	9	3	0	14	26	8	.281	.388	.392
vs. Right-Handers	374	98	17	2	6	36	46	38	.262	.366	.337
vs. Ground-Ballers	254	67	15	2	1	23	31	23	.264	.350	.341
vs. Fly-Ballers	259	70	11	3	5	27	41	23	.270	.394	.364
Home Games	250	68	12	4	2	22	40	20	.272	.376	.369
Road Games	263	69	14	1	4	28	32	26	.262	.369	.337
Grass Fields	425	120	23	4	6	48	62	40	.282	.398	.369
Artificial Turf	88	17	3	1	0	2	10	6	.193	.250	.273
April	52	8	1	0	0	0	1	7	.154	.173	.170
May	104	26	1	1	1	8	6	8	.250	.308	.288
June	103	30	5	0	2	8	17	6	.291	.398	.388
July	102	29	6	3	1	8	17	9	.284	.431	.382
August	64	22	5	1	2	13	9	9	.344	.547	.421
Sept./Oct.	88	22	8	0	0	13	22	7	.250	.341	.386
Leading Off Inn.	189	43	7	3	2	2	18	25	.228	.328	.295
Bases Empty	352	92	19	5	4	4	42	36	.261	.378	.343
Runners On	161	45	7	0	2	46	30	10	.280	.360	.371
Runners/Scor. Pos.	100	26	5	0	1	42	20	5	.260	.340	.351
Runners On/2 Out	66	14	2	0	0	12	14	3	.212	.242	.350
Scor. Pos./2 Out	44	8	2	0	0	12	10	3	.182	.227	.333
Late-Inning Pressure	69	18	2	0	1	6	15	9	.261	.333	.388
Leading Off	26	5	1	0	0	0	3	6	.192	.231	.276
Runners On	22	7	1	0	1	6	9	2	.318	.500	.500
Runners/Scor. Pos.	11	4	1	0	1	6	4	0	.364	.727	.500

RUNS BATTED IN	From 1B	From 2B	From 3B	Scoring Position
Totals	4/105	14/76	26/53	40/129
Percentage	3.8%	18.4%	49.1%	31.0%

Loves to face: Kevin Brown (.556, 5-for-9)
Brian Holton (.833, 5-for-6)
Mark Knudson (.545, 6-for-11)

Hates to face: Allan Anderson (.118, 2-for-17, 1 3B)
Jeff Reardon (0-for-8, 1 BB)
Dave Stieb (.167, 4-for-24)

Miscellaneous statistics: Ground outs-to-air outs ratio: 1.23 last season, 1.29 for career. . . . Grounded into 12 double plays in 86 opportunities (one per 7.2). . . . Drove in 18 of 29 runners from third base with less than two outs (62%). . . . Direction of balls hit to the outfield: 25% to left field, 35% to center, 40% to right batting left-handed; 31% to left, 42% to center, 27% to right batting right-handed. . . . Base running: Advanced from first base to third on 20 of 38 outfield singles (53%); scored from second on 17 of 21 (81%). . . . Made 2.91 assists per nine innings at second base.

Comments: Only three A.L. players as young as Browne started as many games as him last season: Robin Ventura, Sammy Sosa, and Ken Griffey. Browne was 24 years, nine months old when the season ended. . . . One of two A.L. players to draw walks in five consecutive plate appearances last season. The other: Chili Davis. . . . Struck out only once per 27.4 plate appearances with runners in scoring position, the best rate in the league. . . . Average of one strikeout per 22 plate appearances vs. left-handed pitchers was 2d best in the American League, behind Harold Reynolds. . . . Had higher batting averages hitting right-handed than from the left side in each of his five seasons in the majors. Career averages: .295 right-handed, .269 left-handed. But he has hit 10 of his 13 home runs batting left-handed. . . . Started the 1990 season with two hits in his first 32 at-bats from the left side. . . . Batting averages with two outs and runners in scoring position year by year since 1988: .083, .109, .182. . . . Has drawn 11 walks in 38 career plate appearances with the bases loaded. That's the highest rate of any player over the past 16 years. . . . Career batting average of .306 vs. ground-ball pitchers, .253 vs. fly-ballers.

Tom Brunansky

Bats Right

Cardinals/Red Sox	AB	H	2B	3B	HR	RBI	BB	SO	BA	SA	OBA
Season	518	132	27	5	16	73	66	115	.255	.419	.338
vs. Left-Handers	179	51	11	3	6	29	16	32	.285	.480	.333
vs. Right-Handers	339	81	16	2	10	44	50	83	.239	.386	.341
vs. Ground-Ballers	227	60	10	0	4	31	26	47	.264	.361	.344
vs. Fly-Ballers	291	72	17	5	12	42	40	68	.247	.464	.334
Home Games	252	84	19	5	13	52	27	47	.333	.603	.394
Road Games	266	48	8	0	3	21	39	68	.180	.244	.288
Grass Fields	403	109	21	5	15	66	51	84	.270	.459	.351
Artificial Turf	115	23	6	0	1	7	15	31	.200	.278	.295
April	50	9	3	0	1	2	11	7	.180	.300	.333
May	89	21	5	0	4	13	10	23	.236	.427	.310
June	92	30	8	2	1	13	14	16	.326	.489	.411
July	105	22	3	2	1	14	14	26	.210	.305	.298
August	89	24	4	0	2	11	7	24	.270	.382	.330
Sept./Oct.	93	26	4	1	7	20	10	19	.280	.570	.346
Leading Off Inn.	117	29	8	0	3	3	11	27	.248	.393	.318
Bases Empty	258	68	12	2	7	7	27	56	.264	.407	.340
Runners On	260	64	15	3	9	66	39	59	.246	.431	.337
Runners/Scor. Pos.	150	32	8	2	7	59	32	32	.213	.433	.335
Runners On/2 Out	114	26	7	0	5	25	17	32	.228	.421	.328
Scor. Pos./2 Out	72	14	3	0	4	21	13	18	.194	.403	.318
Late-Inning Pressure	72	15	3	0	0	3	11	18	.208	.250	.313
Leading Off	21	1	1	0	0	0	2	9	.048	.095	.130
Runners On	31	7	2	0	0	3	6	6	.226	.290	.351
Runners/Scor. Pos.	14	3	2	0	0	3	5	1	.214	.357	.421

RUNS BATTED IN	From 1B	From 2B	From 3B	Scoring Position
Totals	9/197	15/112	33/82	48/194
Percentage	4.6%	13.4%	40.2%	24.7%

Loves to face: Jim Acker (.389, 7-for-18, 2 HR)
Mark Eichhorn (.444, 8-for-18, 1 HR)
Tim Leary (.387, 12-for-31)

Hates to face: Bert Blyleven (.111, 2-for-18)
Jack Morris (.146, 6-for-41, 5 BB)
Scott Sanderson (.071, 1-for-14)

Miscellaneous statistics: Ground outs-to-air outs ratio: 0.69 last season, 0.69 for career.... Grounded into 13 double plays in 136 opportunities (one per 10.4).... Drove in 22 of 38 runners from third base with less than two outs (58%).... Direction of balls hit to the outfield: 47% to left field, 33% to center, 20% to right.... Base running: Advanced from first base to third on 12 of 21 outfield singles (57%), 12 of 20 in A.L. (60%), shared 4th-highest rate in league; scored from second on 8 of 12 (67%).... Made 2.32 putouts per nine innings in right field.

Comments: Last season marked the first time Bruno failed to hit 20 home runs since 1981, when he hit three in 11 games. Only 13 other players in major league history had streaks that long starting with their rookie seasons. (See Cal Ripken comments for more.)...Became the first Red Sox player to hit three home runs in one game since Jim Rice in 1983, and the first with HRs in three consecutive at-bats since Rice in 1977.... Slugging percentage of .626 at Fenway Park was the highest of any A.L. player on his home turf.... Had a streak of 34 consecutive hitless at-bats in July. It was the longest streak by a Red Sox player since 1978, when George Scott snapped an 0-for-36 streak with a two-strike double after the Boomer had fouled off two bunts.... Batted .224 with only one home run in 61 first-inning at-bats.... Batted .286 from the cleanup spot, .209 from the sixth spot.... His 1-for-21 performance leading off innings in Late-Inning Pressure Situations dropped his career mark to .188 in such situations.... Has a career average of .207 (23-for-111, 3 HR) with the bases loaded.... Has hit a home run in every current major league ballpark except the Skydome (11 AB) and Three Rivers Stadium (65 AB).... Has only eight hits in 63 at-bats with the bases loaded over the past five seasons (.127). His career batting average is .196 with the bases loaded.

Steve Buechele

Bats Right

Texas Rangers	AB	H	2B	3B	HR	RBI	BB	SO	BA	SA	OBA
Season	251	54	10	0	7	30	27	63	.215	.339	.294
vs. Left-Handers	80	22	5	0	4	12	12	18	.275	.488	.372
vs. Right-Handers	171	32	5	0	3	18	15	45	.187	.269	.255
vs. Ground-Ballers	128	27	2	0	6	19	11	37	.211	.367	.284
vs. Fly-Ballers	123	27	8	0	1	11	16	26	.220	.309	.305
Home Games	136	33	6	0	5	21	13	28	.243	.397	.316
Road Games	115	21	4	0	2	9	14	35	.183	.270	.269
Grass Fields	202	48	9	0	6	24	20	45	.238	.371	.311
Artificial Turf	49	6	1	0	1	6	7	18	.122	.204	.228
April	31	9	2	0	3	7	5	4	.290	.645	.405
May	15	2	1	0	0	0	2	6	.133	.200	.235
June	52	8	2	0	0	3	4	16	.154	.192	.214
July	34	9	3	0	1	6	8	7	.265	.441	.395
August	53	14	1	0	2	10	3	14	.264	.396	.316
Sept./Oct.	66	12	1	0	1	4	5	16	.182	.242	.236
Leading Off Inn.	56	14	3	0	1	1	3	10	.250	.357	.288
Bases Empty	127	25	5	0	3	3	11	24	.197	.307	.266
Runners On	124	29	5	0	4	27	16	39	.234	.371	.322
Runners/Scor. Pos.	65	16	5	0	2	23	11	17	.246	.415	.354
Runners On/2 Out	60	15	4	0	3	16	8	23	.250	.467	.338
Scor. Pos./2 Out	37	10	4	0	1	12	7	11	.270	.459	.386
Late-Inning Pressure	30	8	1	0	0	2	2	11	.267	.300	.303
Leading Off	8	3	1	0	0	0	1	3	.375	.500	.444
Runners On	13	3	0	0	0	2	0	6	.231	.231	.214
Runners/Scor. Pos.	5	1	0	0	0	2	0	2	.200	.200	.167

RUNS BATTED IN	From 1B	From 2B	From 3B	Scoring Position
Totals	4/98	9/54	10/26	19/80
Percentage	4.1%	16.7%	38.5%	23.8%

Loves to face: Wes Gardner (.462, 6-for-13, 2 HR)
Tim Leary (.571, 4-for-7, 1 3B, 1 HR, 2 BB)
Dave West (.800, 4-for-5, 2 2B, 1 HR)

Hates to face: Mike Henneman (0-for-11, 1 BB)
Dave Schmidt (0-for-15, 2 BB)
Curt Young (.056, 1-for-18, 1 2B, 2 BB)

Miscellaneous statistics: Ground outs-to-air outs ratio: 1.18 last season, 1.15 for career.... Grounded into 5 double plays in 64 opportunities (one per 12.8).... Drove in 6 of 13 runners from third base with less than two outs (46%).... Direction of balls hit to the outfield: 38% to left field, 31% to center, 31% to right.... Base running: Advanced from first base to third on 4 of 9 outfield singles (44%); scored from second on 1 of 5 (20%).... Made 2.06 assists per nine innings at third base.

Comments: The Rangers will need more from their third basemen in 1991. Their combined batting average from that position (.210) was the lowest in the majors, and their total of 52 RBIs ranked 12th in the American League, beating only New York (49) and Kansas City (44).... No third baseman in franchise history has reached the 1000-game mark. Buechele ranks third with 715 games, behind Buddy Bell (904) and Ken McMullen (742).... Played only 91 games last season, after topping the 150 mark three times in the previous four years.... Spent 33 days on the disabled list after an Eric Plunk pitch broke his wrist in April. Buechele returned too soon, batting .149 during a three-week stretch, then returned to the D.L. for another 32 days.... Both his overall batting average and his average vs. right-handed pitchers were career lows.... Career batting averages: .266 vs. left-handers, .222 vs. right-handers.... Has hit 76 career home runs, but only 21 with runners on base.... Has driven in only 12 of 75 runners from scoring position in Late-Inning Pressure Situations (16%), compared to a career mark of 26 percent in other at-bats.

Ellis Burks

Bats Right

Boston Red Sox	AB	H	2B	3B	HR	RBI	BB	SO	BA	SA	OBA
Season	588	174	33	8	21	89	48	82	.296	.486	.349
vs. Left-Handers	188	56	10	2	5	24	20	26	.298	.452	.365
vs. Right-Handers	400	118	23	6	16	65	28	56	.295	.503	.341
vs. Ground-Ballers	249	80	11	4	6	36	21	38	.321	.470	.373
vs. Fly-Ballers	339	94	22	4	15	53	27	44	.277	.499	.332
Home Games	297	91	20	4	10	48	23	39	.306	.502	.357
Road Games	291	83	13	4	11	41	25	43	.285	.471	.341
Grass Fields	505	150	28	6	20	78	38	74	.297	.495	.346
Artificial Turf	83	24	5	2	1	11	10	8	.289	.434	.366
April	80	17	5	0	0	8	6	12	.213	.275	.267
May	94	30	7	3	4	16	9	11	.319	.585	.379
June	104	35	7	2	6	16	8	11	.337	.615	.384
July	71	24	5	0	1	10	6	11	.338	.451	.397
August	116	37	6	2	5	22	12	17	.319	.534	.377
Sept./Oct.	123	31	3	1	5	17	7	20	.252	.415	.292
Leading Off Inn.	152	44	7	2	8	8	9	12	.289	.520	.333
Bases Empty	294	90	12	3	12	12	27	39	.306	.490	.366
Runners On	294	84	21	5	9	77	21	43	.286	.483	.331
Runners/Scor. Pos.	170	52	9	4	7	72	14	27	.306	.529	.355
Runners On/2 Out	143	41	10	2	4	40	7	22	.287	.469	.320
Scor. Pos./2 Out	82	28	5	2	4	40	4	10	.341	.598	.372
Late-Inning Pressure	82	24	6	1	1	9	9	11	.293	.427	.359
Leading Off	25	5	1	0	0	0	3	3	.200	.240	.286
Runners On	40	14	5	1	1	9	2	4	.350	.600	.372
Runners/Scor. Pos.	18	4	0	0	1	8	2	2	.222	.389	.286

RUNS BATTED IN	From 1B	From 2B	From 3B	Scoring Position
Totals	9/220	34/141	25/66	59/207
Percentage	4.1%	24.1%	37.9%	28.5%

Loves to face: Jesse Orosco (.667, 2-for-3, 1 HR)
Jeff Russell (.533, 8-for-15, 2 HR)
Nolan Ryan (.571, 4-for-7)

Hates to face: Bert Blyleven (.176, 3-for-17)
Dennis Eckersley (.077, 1-for-13, 1 2B)
Jack Morris (.190, 4-for-21)

Miscellaneous statistics: Ground outs-to-air outs ratio: 0.91 last season, 1.01 for career. . . . Grounded into 18 double plays in 127 opportunities (one per 7.1). . . . Drove in 11 of 30 runners from third base with less than two outs (37%), 5th-lowest rate in A.L. . . . Direction of balls hit to the outfield: 41% to left field, 30% to center, 29% to right. . . . Base running: Advanced from first base to third on 15 of 37 outfield singles (41%); scored from second on 13 of 18 (72%). . . . Made 2.30 putouts per nine innings in center field, 2d-lowest rate in A.L.

Comments: Led the Red Sox with nine stolen bases, the lowest total to lead a major league club since Gary Pettis led the 1983 California Angels with eight (in 22 games). . . . Burks was caught stealing 11 times in 20 attempts. His success rate over three previous seasons was 78 percent (73 SBs in 93 attempts). . . . Was thrown out trying to advance a base on a batted ball six times last season, the most of any player on the Red Sox. (Marty Barrett was thrown out five times in considerably less playing time.). . .Burks was one of five A.L. players to start at least 10 games in five different lineup slots—in his case, the third through seventh slots. Burks also started twice as the leadoff batter. . . . Batted over .300 with runners in scoring position for the third consecutive season. . . . Led the league with a .341 average with two outs and runners in scoring position. Before 1990, his career mark was only .211 in those situations. . . . Career batting average of .309 at Fenway, .274 on the road. . . . Damaged his growing reputation as a poor man's Pat Tabler (at least among regular readers of *USA Today*'s Insiders section) with only four hits (no HRs) in 19 at-bats last season. His previous career average: .364 (12-for-44 with five HRs). . . . His total of seven at-bats against Nolan Ryan is the most of any active batter who has never struck out against the old man, except for Fernando Valenzuela (9 AB).

Randy Bush

Bats Left

Minnesota Twins	AB	H	2B	3B	HR	RBI	BB	SO	BA	SA	OBA
Season	181	44	8	0	6	18	21	27	.243	.387	.338
vs. Left-Handers	4	1	1	0	0	1	0	1	.250	.500	.333
vs. Right-Handers	177	43	7	0	6	17	21	26	.243	.384	.338
vs. Ground-Ballers	82	23	4	0	3	11	7	6	.280	.439	.355
vs. Fly-Ballers	99	21	4	0	3	7	14	21	.212	.343	.325
Home Games	98	29	7	0	4	12	10	12	.296	.490	.375
Road Games	83	15	1	0	2	6	11	15	.181	.265	.296
Grass Fields	63	9	1	0	1	1	6	11	.143	.206	.239
Artificial Turf	118	35	7	0	5	17	15	16	.297	.483	.388
April	37	7	2	0	1	4	2	4	.189	.324	.220
May	31	7	2	0	1	2	3	1	.226	.387	.333
June	0	0	0	0	0	0	0	0	—	—	—
July	26	10	3	0	1	2	3	0	.385	.615	.484
August	36	13	0	0	3	9	6	7	.361	.611	.465
Sept./Oct.	51	7	1	0	0	1	7	15	.137	.157	.254
Leading Off Inn.	48	8	1	0	0	0	3	9	.167	.188	.216
Bases Empty	115	30	5	0	2	2	8	14	.261	.357	.341
Runners On	66	14	3	0	4	16	13	13	.212	.439	.333
Runners/Scor. Pos.	40	6	1	0	1	9	11	10	.150	.250	.321
Runners On/2 Out	33	6	1	0	1	6	4	5	.182	.303	.270
Scor. Pos./2 Out	25	5	1	0	1	6	4	5	.200	.360	.310
Late-Inning Pressure	30	8	0	0	1	3	6	7	.267	.367	.389
Leading Off	9	2	0	0	0	0	1	2	.222	.222	.300
Runners On	15	3	0	0	1	3	3	5	.200	.400	.333
Runners/Scor. Pos.	12	2	0	0	0	1	3	3	.167	.167	.333

RUNS BATTED IN	From 1B	From 2B	From 3B	Scoring Position
Totals	5/46	3/34	4/14	7/48
Percentage	10.9%	8.8%	28.6%	14.6%

Loves to face: Tim Leary (.625, 5-for-8, 1 HR)
Jack Morris (.276, 16-for-58, 4 HR, 7 BB)
Gene Nelson (.545, 6-for-11, 1 HR)

Hates to face: Bert Blyleven (.229, 8-for-35, 1 HR)
Storm Davis (.081, 3-for-37, 3 BB)
Dave Stieb (.200, 12-for-60)

Miscellaneous statistics: Ground outs-to-air outs ratio: 0.87 last season, 0.88 for career. . . . Grounded into 2 double plays in 33 opportunities (one per 16.5). . . . Drove in 3 of 5 runners from third base with less than two outs (60%). . . . Direction of balls hit to the outfield: 12% to left field, 36% to center, 52% to right. . . . Base running: Advanced from first base to third on 0 of 6 outfield singles; scored from second on 0 of 1. . . . Made 2.24 putouts per nine innings in right field.

Comments: Started 52 games, all vs. right-handed pitchers. He had only one start against a left-hander in 1989. . . . Has hit 88 career home runs, all vs. right-handed pitchers. . . . Career totals of 2930 plate appearances vs. right-handers, 108 vs. left-handers. He has never had more than 20 at-bats in a season vs. southpaws. . . . Had batted over .280 with runners in scoring position in each of the previous three seasons. . . . He ain't exactly "Mr. Twin," but his career total of 991 games is the fifth highest (and about to be fourth) among players who never played for another team, behind Tony Oliva (1626), Gary Gaetti (1361), Kent Hrbek (1299), and Kirby Puckett (1070). . . . Had only two opposite field hits last season, the fewest among players with a total of at least 30 hits. . . . Two terms on the disabled list, for knee and hamstring injuries, limited Bush to 73 games, his lowest total since 1982. He stole no bases last season after stealing 28 over the four previous years. . . . One of five different players to start as many as 19 games in right field for the Twins last season. More is less: Twins right fielders drove in the fewest runs in the American League (57), and only Milwaukee's Rob Deer kept Minnesota from compiling the lowest batting average as well (.243).

Ivan Calderon

Bats Right

Chicago White Sox	AB	H	2B	3B	HR	RBI	BB	SO	BA	SA	OBA
Season	607	166	44	2	14	74	51	79	.273	.422	.327
vs. Left-Handers	227	67	19	2	6	27	21	25	.295	.476	.353
vs. Right-Handers	380	99	25	0	8	47	30	54	.261	.389	.311
vs. Ground-Ballers	269	76	24	0	5	28	18	38	.283	.428	.324
vs. Fly-Ballers	338	90	20	2	9	46	33	41	.266	.417	.329
Home Games	284	87	24	2	6	40	30	37	.306	.468	.370
Road Games	323	79	20	0	8	34	21	42	.245	.381	.287
Grass Fields	508	150	39	2	12	66	41	61	.295	.451	.345
Artificial Turf	99	16	5	0	2	8	10	18	.162	.273	.236
April	58	17	6	0	2	13	7	12	.293	.500	.368
May	104	31	6	0	2	12	12	15	.298	.413	.368
June	96	29	8	0	3	14	11	15	.302	.479	.367
July	98	27	6	2	0	10	8	9	.276	.378	.327
August	130	37	11	0	4	16	4	10	.285	.462	.304
Sept./Oct.	121	25	7	0	3	9	9	18	.207	.339	.260
Leading Off Inn.	128	35	10	0	3	3	15	17	.273	.422	.350
Bases Empty	346	91	24	1	5	5	29	53	.263	.382	.322
Runners On	261	75	20	1	9	69	22	26	.287	.475	.333
Runners/Scor. Pos.	131	43	9	0	8	60	16	12	.328	.580	.381
Runners On/2 Out	86	24	6	1	4	23	5	8	.279	.512	.319
Scor. Pos./2 Out	48	13	4	0	4	20	4	4	.271	.604	.327
Late-Inning Pressure	68	14	5	0	0	1	8	6	.206	.279	.289
Leading Off	21	4	2	0	0	0	5	1	.190	.286	.346
Runners On	31	6	1	0	0	1	3	3	.194	.226	.265
Runners/Scor. Pos.	10	0	0	0	0	0	2	2	.000	.000	.167

RUNS BATTED IN	From 1B	From 2B	From 3B	Scoring Position
Totals	10/179	20/89	30/69	50/158
Percentage	5.6%	22.5%	43.5%	31.6%

Loves to face: Dale Mohorcic (.600, 6-for-10, 2 HR)
Mike Morgan (.600, 3-for-5, 2 2B, 1 HR)
Dennis Rasmussen (.357, 5-for-14, 3 HR)

Hates to face: Mark Eichhorn (0-for-9)
Charlie Leibrandt (.133, 2-for-15)
Dave Schmidt (.091, 1-for-11)

Miscellaneous statistics: Ground outs-to-air outs ratio: 1.25 last season, 0.98 for career. . . . Grounded into 26 double plays in 128 opportunities (one per 4.9), 5th-worst rate in A.L. . . . Drove in 21 of 37 runners from third base with less than two outs (57%). . . . Direction of balls hit to the outfield: 29% to left field, 34% to center, 37% to right. . . . Base running: Advanced from first base to third on 11 of 24 outfield singles (46%); scored from second on 14 of 16 (88%). . . . Made 2.16 putouts per nine innings in left field.

Comments: Stole 32 bases last season, three more than he had in 502 games over six previous seasons. . . . Had a higher stolen base percentage against left-handed pitchers (14-for-20, 70%) than against right-handers (18-for-28, 64%). . . . Grounded into 26 double plays, the most in the majors, including 11 in the first inning. . . . Tied Bobby Bonilla and Brian Harper for the major league lead in doubles vs. left-handed pitchers. . . . His batting average with runners in scoring position was a career high. . . . Although the distribution of his batted balls to the outfield leans toward the opposite field, 12 of his 14 home runs were hit to left, the other two to center. . . . Has hit exactly 14 home runs in each of the last three seasons, after hitting 28 in 1987, the year of the home run. . . . Has homered at least once in every current American League ballpark with the exception of Cleveland Stadium (74 career AB). . . . Batting averages in Late-Inning Pressure Situations year by year since 1986: .345, .342, .211, .208, .206. . . . Finished his White Sox career (or Phase I, at least) with 70 career home runs, 20th on their all-time list, despite playing only four full seasons with the club. . . . Market value has increased a tad since he was the player to be named later for Scott Bradley in 1986.

Jose Canseco

Bats Right

Oakland A's	AB	H	2B	3B	HR	RBI	BB	SO	BA	SA	OBA
Season	481	132	14	2	37	101	72	158	.274	.543	.371
vs. Left-Handers	123	34	3	1	12	28	15	41	.276	.610	.362
vs. Right-Handers	358	98	11	1	25	73	57	117	.274	.520	.374
vs. Ground-Ballers	250	77	6	1	21	54	36	72	.308	.592	.400
vs. Fly-Ballers	231	55	8	1	16	47	36	86	.238	.489	.341
Home Games	217	56	7	0	18	43	45	71	.258	.539	.386
Road Games	264	76	7	2	19	58	27	87	.288	.545	.358
Grass Fields	409	109	11	1	30	80	64	131	.267	.518	.369
Artificial Turf	72	23	3	1	7	21	8	27	.319	.681	.383
April	70	21	0	0	5	12	18	22	.300	.514	.444
May	102	36	3	0	13	35	14	30	.353	.765	.424
June	31	5	0	0	2	3	3	16	.161	.355	.278
July	110	33	3	1	12	27	11	30	.300	.673	.368
August	85	18	4	0	3	11	10	28	.212	.365	.295
Sept./Oct.	83	19	4	1	2	13	16	32	.229	.373	.354
Leading Off Inn.	80	17	0	1	3	3	12	25	.213	.350	.315
Bases Empty	250	66	6	1	19	19	36	82	.264	.524	.361
Runners On	231	66	8	1	18	82	36	76	.286	.563	.382
Runners/Scor. Pos.	126	33	4	1	6	57	25	46	.262	.452	.376
Runners On/2 Out	77	21	2	0	4	24	12	28	.273	.455	.371
Scor. Pos./2 Out	46	10	1	0	0	16	9	22	.217	.239	.345
Late-Inning Pressure	51	9	3	0	1	6	9	22	.176	.294	.300
Leading Off	19	2	0	0	0	0	2	7	.105	.105	.190
Runners On	19	4	2	0	1	6	3	7	.211	.474	.318
Runners/Scor. Pos.	11	3	2	0	0	4	3	4	.273	.455	.429

RUNS BATTED IN	From 1B	From 2B	From 3B	Scoring Position
Totals	18/163	22/89	24/61	46/150
Percentage	11.0%	24.7%	39.3%	30.7%

Loves to face: Allan Anderson (.409, 9-for-22, 2 2B, 5 HR)
Tim Leary (.444, 8-for-18, 3 HR)
Dave West (2-for-2, 2 HR)

Hates to face: Greg A. Harris (0-for-13, 9 SO)
Dave LaPoint (.118, 2-for-17, 8 SO)
Bobby Witt (.167, 4-for-24, 5 BB, 15 SO)

Miscellaneous statistics: Ground outs-to-air outs ratio: 0.85 last season, 0.80 for career. . . . Grounded into 9 double plays in 123 opportunities (one per 13.7). . . . Drove in 18 of 41 runners from third base with less than two outs (44%). . . . Direction of balls hit to the outfield: 42% to left field, 34% to center, 24% to right. . . . Base running: Advanced from first base to third on 5 of 23 outfield singles (22%); scored from second on 14 of 16 (88%). . . . Made 2.21 putouts per nine innings in right field.

Comments: His total of 35 RBIs in May was the highest by any player in any month last season. . . . Drove in 17 game-winning runs, to rank second in the American League to Bo Jackson (19). . . . Hit only three home runs in 45 regular-season games after August 2. Batted only .212 over his last 39 games. . . . Led the majors with 11 first-inning home runs. . . . He has a career total of 76 home runs (one per 16.5 AB) at home, 89 homers (one per 15.6 AB) on the road, a negligible difference (5 percent lower at home), especially compared to the career rate of Mark McGwire (33 percent lower at home). So why is Canseco doing all the whining about moving the fences in?. . .Has higher batting averages with runners on base than with the bases empty in each of his six major league seasons. Career averages: .298 with runners on, .246 with no one on. . . . Career batting average of .300 with runners in scoring position, .398 with RISP in Late-Inning Pressure Situations. . . . Has 40 career at-bats with the bases loaded, but only one regular-season grand slam. . . . Given all the publicity surrounding that 40/40 thing in 1988, we dutifully report that since then, Canseco was one of 83 players in the 6/6 Club in 1989, and one of 11 in the 19/19 Club last season.

Alex Cole

Bats Left

Cleveland Indians	AB	H	2B	3B	HR	RBI	BB	SO	BA	SA	OBA
Season	227	68	5	4	0	13	28	38	.300	.357	.379
vs. Left-Handers	52	13	0	1	0	4	10	11	.250	.288	.381
vs. Right-Handers	175	55	5	3	0	9	18	27	.314	.377	.378
vs. Ground-Ballers	122	37	4	1	0	8	15	18	.303	.352	.380
vs. Fly-Ballers	105	31	1	3	0	5	13	20	.295	.362	.378
Home Games	121	37	2	3	0	9	18	23	.306	.372	.400
Road Games	106	31	3	1	0	4	10	15	.292	.340	.353
Grass Fields	194	60	4	4	0	11	26	34	.309	.371	.394
Artificial Turf	33	8	1	0	0	2	2	4	.242	.273	.286
April	0	0	0	0	0	0	0	0	—	—	—
May	0	0	0	0	0	0	0	0	—	—	—
June	0	0	0	0	0	0	0	0	—	—	—
July	22	7	0	0	0	0	0	3	.318	.318	.318
August	106	34	4	2	0	9	14	22	.321	.396	.405
Sept./Oct.	99	27	1	2	0	4	14	13	.273	.323	.363
Leading Off Inn.	79	22	1	1	0	0	16	14	.278	.316	.400
Bases Empty	144	44	4	2	0	0	22	26	.306	.361	.401
Runners On	83	24	1	2	0	13	6	12	.289	.349	.337
Runners/Scor. Pos.	50	16	1	0	0	11	6	10	.320	.340	.393
Runners On/2 Out	38	11	1	1	0	6	4	6	.289	.368	.357
Scor. Pos./2 Out	29	9	1	0	0	5	4	5	.310	.345	.394
Late-Inning Pressure	24	8	0	0	0	0	3	3	.333	.333	.407
Leading Off	6	1	0	0	0	0	1	1	.167	.167	.286
Runners On	9	3	0	0	0	0	1	1	.333	.333	.400
Runners/Scor. Pos.	3	1	0	0	0	0	1	1	.333	.333	.500

RUNS BATTED IN	From 1B	From 2B	From 3B	Scoring Position
Totals	2/54	4/35	7/20	11/55
Percentage	3.7%	11.4%	35.0%	20.0%

Loves to face: Mike Macfarlane (6-for-6)
Mark Salas (5-for-5)
B.J. Surhoff (3-for-3)

Hates to face: Andy McGaffigan (0-for-5, 1 BB)
Walt Terrell (.143, 1-for-7)

Miscellaneous statistics: Ground outs-to-air outs ratio: 1.32 last season, 1.32 for career.... Grounded into 2 double plays in 34 opportunities (one per 17.0).... Drove in 4 of 10 runners from third base with less than two outs (40%).... Direction of balls hit to the outfield: 46% to left field, 34% to center, 20% to right.... Base running: Advanced from first base to third on 5 of 5 outfield singles; scored from second on 7 of 7.... Made 2.65 putouts per nine innings in center field.

Comments: Stole 40 bases, 10 shy of John Cangelosi's American League record for a rookie.... Played only 63 games, but his stolen base total was the 10th highest in club history, and Cleveland's fourth-highest in the last 70 years. The team record of 61 steals was set in 1980 by Miguel Dilone.... Stole 37 bases in 43 attempts (86%) on grass fields, but was only 3-for-6 on artificial turf.... Stole 27 bases in 32 attempts (84%) against right-handers, 13 bases in 17 attempts (76%) vs. left-handers.... It's true—no one asked. But for the record, Cole is ahead of Rickey Henderson's pace. Rickey didn't reach the 40-steal mark until his 106th game. Only two players in this century reached 40 steals faster than Cole: Vince Coleman (44 games, the all-time "record") and Tim Raines (51).... His final at-bat of the season dropped him below the .300 mark to .2995.... Batted .389 in day games, .283 at night.... Eleven of his 68 hits were infield hits.

Darnell Coles

Bats Right

Mariners/Tigers	AB	H	2B	3B	HR	RBI	BB	SO	BA	SA	OBA
Season	215	45	7	1	3	20	16	38	.209	.293	.265
vs. Left-Handers	121	26	4	1	1	11	13	18	.215	.289	.287
vs. Right-Handers	94	19	3	0	2	9	3	20	.202	.298	.235
vs. Ground-Ballers	81	17	2	1	2	7	6	9	.210	.333	.261
vs. Fly-Ballers	134	28	5	0	1	13	10	29	.209	.269	.267
Home Games	124	30	5	0	3	17	9	17	.242	.355	.296
Road Games	91	15	2	1	0	3	7	21	.165	.209	.222
Grass Fields	121	26	3	1	1	4	9	23	.215	.281	.269
Artificial Turf	94	19	4	0	2	16	7	15	.202	.309	.260
April	24	4	2	0	1	2	0	4	.167	.375	.200
May	69	14	3	1	0	10	4	9	.203	.275	.247
June	24	8	0	0	1	4	1	9	.333	.458	.346
July	27	4	2	0	0	1	8	3	.148	.222	.343
August	29	7	0	0	0	1	2	3	.241	.241	.281
Sept./Oct.	42	8	0	0	1	2	1	10	.190	.262	.209
Leading Off Inn.	42	8	0	0	1	1	5	8	.190	.262	.277
Bases Empty	113	22	2	1	1	1	10	21	.195	.257	.266
Runners On	102	23	5	0	2	19	6	17	.225	.333	.264
Runners/Scor. Pos.	58	9	1	0	0	12	4	10	.155	.172	.203
Runners On/2 Out	47	5	1	0	0	5	4	10	.106	.128	.176
Scor. Pos./2 Out	30	4	1	0	0	5	3	6	.133	.167	.212
Late-Inning Pressure	35	6	1	1	0	3	2	6	.171	.257	.211
Leading Off	7	0	0	0	0	0	1	0	.000	.000	.125
Runners On	21	5	1	0	0	3	0	3	.238	.286	.227
Runners/Scor. Pos.	12	2	0	0	0	2	0	2	.167	.167	.154

RUNS BATTED IN	From 1B	From 2B	From 3B	Scoring Position
Totals	6/82	3/46	8/32	11/78
Percentage	7.3%	6.5%	25.0%	14.1%

Loves to face: Andy Hawkins (.583, 7-for-12, 1 HR)
Mike Jeffcoat (.600, 6-for-10)
Mike Moore (.444, 4-for-9, 1 3B, 3 HR)

Hates to face: Cecilio Guante (0-for-8)
Greg A. Harris (0-for-10)
Eric Show (.100, 1-for-10)

Miscellaneous statistics: Ground outs-to-air outs ratio: 0.67 last season, 0.82 for career.... Grounded into 4 double plays in 45 opportunities (one per 11.3).... Drove in 5 of 14 runners from third base with less than two outs (36%).... Direction of balls hit to the outfield: 47% to left field, 27% to center, 25% to right.... Base running: Advanced from first base to third on 0 of 7 outfield singles; scored from second on 6 of 6.... Made 1.88 putouts per nine innings in right field.

Comments: Batted .215 with the Mariners, .204 with the Tigers.... Had only 31 plate appearances vs. right-handed pitchers after joining the Tigers in mid-June.... Hitless in 89 at-bats in which he failed to get the ball out of the infield. No other batter in the majors had that many without at least one infield hit.... Drove in only 11 of 78 runners from scoring position (14%), lowest percentage in the majors (minimum: 50 opportunities).... He also had the lowest batting average in the American League with two outs and runners on base (minimum: 40 AB).... Batted .297 in 27 at-bats as a pinch hitter.... Batted .309 in day games, .175 at night. Has hit for a higher average in day games than he has at night in each of the last three seasons.... Has batted below .215 in Late-Inning Pressure Situations in six of his eight seasons in the majors. Career average: .207.... Career average of .180 (11-for-61) as a pinch hitter.... Sparky must be waxing nostalgic in his twilight years. In addition to Coles's second tour of duty in Motown, the Tigers reacquired Walt Terrell and Dan Petry last season. There's been only one other two-term Tiger who rejoined the team during Sparky's tenure: Jim Slaton, who pitched for Detroit in 1978 and again in 1986.

Scott Coolbaugh

Bats Right

Texas Rangers	AB	H	2B	3B	HR	RBI	BB	SO	BA	SA	OBA
Season	180	36	6	0	2	13	15	47	.200	.267	.264
vs. Left-Handers	54	17	4	0	0	7	6	6	.315	.389	.377
vs. Right-Handers	126	19	2	0	2	6	9	41	.151	.214	.213
vs. Ground-Ballers	68	15	1	0	1	6	2	15	.221	.279	.239
vs. Fly-Ballers	112	21	5	0	1	7	13	32	.188	.259	.278
Home Games	86	20	4	0	1	6	5	27	.233	.314	.280
Road Games	94	16	2	0	1	7	10	20	.170	.223	.250
Grass Fields	157	31	6	0	1	10	11	43	.197	.255	.253
Artificial Turf	23	5	0	0	1	3	4	4	.217	.348	.333
April	19	2	0	0	0	0	3	8	.105	.105	.227
May	48	9	1	0	0	2	4	16	.188	.208	.250
June	42	15	1	0	2	9	3	7	.357	.524	.404
July	48	7	2	0	0	2	3	12	.146	.188	.196
August	0	0	0	0	0	0	0	0	—	—	—
Sept./Oct.	23	3	2	0	0	0	2	4	.130	.217	.200
Leading Off Inn.	44	11	2	0	2	2	2	13	.250	.432	.298
Bases Empty	97	23	4	0	2	2	8	28	.237	.340	.302
Runners On	83	13	2	0	0	11	7	19	.157	.181	.220
Runners/Scor. Pos.	41	7	0	0	0	11	5	7	.171	.171	.255
Runners On/2 Out	39	8	2	0	0	5	2	10	.205	.256	.244
Scor. Pos./2 Out	20	5	0	0	0	5	2	4	.250	.250	.318
Late-Inning Pressure	10	0	0	0	0	0	0	4	.000	.000	.000
Leading Off	4	0	0	0	0	0	0	1	.000	.000	.000
Runners On	4	0	0	0	0	0	0	1	.000	.000	.000
Runners/Scor. Pos.	2	0	0	0	0	0	0	0	.000	.000	.000

RUNS BATTED IN	From 1B	From 2B	From 3B	Scoring Position
Totals	0/61	5/37	6/15	11/52
Percentage	0.0%	13.5%	40.0%	

Loves to face: Juan Berenguer (.500, 1-for-2, 2 BB)
Randy Johnson (3-for-3)

Hates to face: Jack Morris (0-for-5, 3 SO)

Miscellaneous statistics: Ground outs-to-air outs ratio: 0.96 last season, 0.93 for career.... Grounded into 2 double plays in 40 opportunities (one per 20.0).... Drove in 5 of 9 runners from third base with less than two outs (56%).... Direction of balls hit to the outfield: 41% to left field, 25% to center, 34% to right.... Base running: Advanced from first base to third on 1 of 9 outfield singles (11%); scored from second on 5 of 7 (71%).... Made 2.21 assists per nine innings at third base.

Comments: Rangers pitching staff allowed an average of 4.98 runs per nine innings with Coolbaugh at third base, compared to 4.16 runs per nine innings with Steve Buechele there. Coolbaugh, however, started more than twice as many double plays (11) as did Buechele (5), despite playing fewer innings.... Started only seven games after his September recall.... The lowest single-season batting average in franchise history for a player with at least 200 plate appearances was .179 by Rich Billings in 1973.... His .151 batting average against right-handers was the 2d lowest in the majors last season (minimum: 100 AB). Only Claudell Washington was worse (.147).... But look before you leap—to any conclusions, that is—regarding Coolbaugh's inability to hit right-handers. He batted .324 vs. right-handers, .176 vs. lefties between sips of Colombian in 1989. And, as in 1990, both his home runs in 1989 were hit against right-handers.... Distressingly comparable rookie seasons during the 1980s: Terry Blocker (1988), Luis Rivera (1986), and Doug Strange (1990).

Henry Cotto

Bats Right

Seattle Mariners	AB	H	2B	3B	HR	RBI	BB	SO	BA	SA	OBA
Season	355	92	14	3	4	33	22	52	.259	.349	.307
vs. Left-Handers	192	50	7	2	2	19	13	25	.260	.349	.308
vs. Right-Handers	163	42	7	1	2	14	9	27	.258	.350	.307
vs. Ground-Ballers	134	38	4	3	2	10	9	22	.284	.403	.338
vs. Fly-Ballers	221	54	10	0	2	23	13	30	.244	.317	.288
Home Games	173	45	7	2	2	15	13	21	.260	.358	.321
Road Games	182	47	7	1	2	18	9	31	.258	.341	.294
Grass Fields	122	31	4	1	0	12	8	19	.254	.303	.303
Artificial Turf	233	61	10	2	4	21	14	33	.262	.373	.310
April	27	7	2	0	0	1	1	3	.259	.333	.276
May	79	26	0	0	1	5	5	14	.329	.367	.369
June	69	22	3	2	1	10	4	9	.319	.464	.360
July	83	19	6	0	1	8	4	14	.229	.337	.278
August	38	3	0	0	0	1	4	7	.079	.079	.167
Sept./Oct.	59	15	3	1	1	8	4	5	.254	.390	.313
Leading Off Inn.	61	18	6	0	1	1	8	10	.295	.443	.377
Bases Empty	191	47	9	1	2	2	11	32	.246	.335	.291
Runners On	164	45	5	2	2	31	11	20	.274	.366	.326
Runners/Scor. Pos.	93	21	1	1	0	24	9	9	.226	.258	.299
Runners On/2 Out	68	20	1	1	1	12	6	6	.294	.382	.368
Scor. Pos./2 Out	48	10	0	1	0	10	4	3	.208	.250	.283
Late-Inning Pressure	53	13	0	0	1	5	5	9	.245	.302	.328
Leading Off	13	4	0	0	0	0	1	1	.308	.308	.357
Runners On	25	6	0	0	0	4	4	5	.240	.240	.375
Runners/Scor. Pos.	13	2	0	0	0	4	4	1	.154	.154	.368

RUNS BATTED IN	From 1B	From 2B	From 3B	Scoring Position
Totals	6/120	10/73	13/35	23/108
Percentage	5.0%	13.7%	37.1%	21.3%

Loves to face: Rick Honeycutt (.444, 4-for-9, 1 HR)
Bill Long (.833, 5-for-6, 1 HR)
Jack Morris (.538, 7-for-13, 1 HR)

Hates to face: Bruce Hurst (.133, 2-for-15)
Mark Langston (.067, 1-for-15)
Frank Viola (.059, 1-for-17, 1 2B)

Miscellaneous statistics: Ground outs-to-air outs ratio: 1.45 last season, 1.28 for career.... Grounded into 13 double plays in 79 opportunities (one per 6.1).... Drove in 9 of 18 runners from third base with less than two outs (50%).... Direction of balls hit to the outfield: 40% to left field, 32% to center, 28% to right.... Base running: Advanced from first base to third on 8 of 14 outfield singles (57%); scored from second on 6 of 13 (46%).... Made 2.11 putouts per nine innings in right field.

Comments: News flash! The Mariners were 10 games above .500 last season—in games in which Cotto started and batted second.... Last year was his seventh season in the majors; he has never had as many as 400 at-bats in a season.... He started all 48 games in which the Mariners faced a left-hander, but only 32 of 114 games vs. right-handers. Started only one game against a right-hander in September.... Why platoon a player with such outstanding defensive skills? His career batting average against left-handers (.257) is only three points lower than vs. right-handers (.260).... Career average of .211 with two outs and runners in scoring position.... Batted 83 points lower in Late-Inning Pressure Situations (.182) than in other at-bats (.266) over the last five seasons, the 2d-largest margin in the majors. Batting average in LIPS was lower than his overall average in each of those five seasons.... Has hit for a higher average with runners on base than he has with the bases empty in each of the last six seasons.... Has stolen 58 bases in 68 attempts over the last three seasons.

Jack Daugherty

Bats Left and Right

Texas Rangers	AB	H	2B	3B	HR	RBI	BB	SO	BA	SA	OBA
Season	310	93	20	2	6	47	22	49	.300	.435	.347
vs. Left-Handers	77	21	3	0	0	10	7	20	.273	.312	.337
vs. Right-Handers	233	72	17	2	6	37	15	29	.309	.476	.351
vs. Ground-Ballers	123	38	7	1	3	19	13	12	.309	.455	.374
vs. Fly-Ballers	187	55	13	1	3	28	9	37	.294	.422	.328
Home Games	164	51	9	1	5	25	13	24	.311	.470	.369
Road Games	146	42	11	1	1	22	9	25	.288	.397	.323
Grass Fields	269	78	16	1	6	41	21	41	.290	.424	.344
Artificial Turf	41	15	4	1	0	6	1	8	.366	.512	.372
April	15	3	1	0	0	1	2	2	.200	.267	.294
May	57	16	3	0	0	5	3	5	.281	.333	.311
June	46	16	5	1	0	8	2	10	.348	.500	.380
July	81	27	8	0	2	12	7	18	.333	.506	.386
August	41	9	3	0	0	3	2	5	.220	.293	.273
Sept./Oct.	70	22	0	1	4	18	6	9	.314	.514	.364
Leading Off Inn.	64	18	4	0	1	1	5	17	.281	.391	.333
Bases Empty	172	51	9	1	2	2	12	29	.297	.395	.342
Runners On	138	42	11	1	4	45	10	20	.304	.486	.353
Runners/Scor. Pos.	80	22	5	0	0	32	8	12	.275	.338	.344
Runners On/2 Out	60	21	8	0	2	20	4	7	.350	.583	.409
Scor. Pos./2 Out	37	8	3	0	0	12	4	4	.216	.297	.326
Late-Inning Pressure	56	10	2	0	2	5	1	18	.179	.321	.203
Leading Off	12	3	1	0	1	1	1	5	.250	.583	.308
Runners On	27	5	1	0	1	4	0	8	.185	.333	.207
Runners/Scor. Pos.	13	1	0	0	0	2	0	4	.077	.077	.133

RUNS BATTED IN	From 1B	From 2B	From 3B	Scoring Position
Totals	11/98	14/63	16/33	30/96
Percentage	11.2%	22.2%	48.5%	31.3%

Loves to face: Terry Leach (.800, 4-for-5)
Jack Morris (.500, 4-for-8)

Hates to face: Chuck Cary (0-for-5, 1 BB)
Dennis Eckersley (.167, 1-for-6)

Miscellaneous statistics: Ground outs-to-air outs ratio: 1.06 last season, 0.98 for career. . . . Grounded into 4 double plays in 60 opportunities (one per 15.0). . . . Drove in 11 of 17 runners from third base with less than two outs (65%). . . . Direction of balls hit to the outfield: 32% to left field, 28% to center, 39% to right batting left-handed; 31% to left, 25% to center, 44% to right batting right-handed. . . . Base running: Advanced from first base to third on 6 of 15 outfield singles (40%); scored from second on 9 of 10 (90%). . . . Made 1.47 putouts per nine innings in left field.

Comments: Might be a serious hitter; he batted .302 in 52 games in 1989. . . . Collected four or more hits in four different games last season. The only players in the American League with more were Rafael Palmeiro (6), Fred McGriff (5), and George Brett (5). . . . Led the American League with 52 appearances as a pinch hitter, but batted only .222 (10-for-45) in that role. . . . Aside from Daugherty, last season's most frequently used switch-hitting pinch hitters were Carlos Baerga, John Moses, R.J. Reynolds, Dave Hollins, and Wallace Johnson. . . . All-time leaders in pinch hits by switch hitters: Dave Philley (93), Dave Collins (84) and Jerry Hairston (82). . . . Batted 148 points lower in Late-Inning Pressure Situations (.179) than in other at-bats (.327) last season, the 2d-largest margin in the majors. Has only one hit in 16 career at-bats with runners in scoring position in LIPS. . . . Has hit six home runs in 226 career at-bats at Arlington Stadium, but has only one home run in 200 at-bats elsewhere. . . . Has drawn three walks in 11 career plate appearances with the bases loaded. . . . The same guys who say the .400 hitter is dead probably think Montana is a suburb of San Francisco; Daugherty batted .402 for Helena of the Pioneer League in 1984.

Alvin Davis

Bats Left

Seattle Mariners	AB	H	2B	3B	HR	RBI	BB	SO	BA	SA	OBA
Season	494	140	21	0	17	68	85	68	.283	.429	.387
vs. Left-Handers	168	43	7	0	6	29	28	24	.256	.405	.360
vs. Right-Handers	326	97	14	0	11	39	57	44	.298	.442	.401
vs. Ground-Ballers	182	60	6	0	11	30	30	25	.330	.544	.423
vs. Fly-Ballers	312	80	15	0	6	38	55	43	.256	.362	.366
Home Games	252	70	11	0	12	40	47	38	.278	.464	.392
Road Games	242	70	10	0	5	28	38	30	.289	.393	.381
Grass Fields	182	47	7	0	3	20	32	22	.258	.346	.364
Artificial Turf	312	93	14	0	14	48	53	46	.298	.478	.400
April	68	18	4	0	1	5	16	8	.265	.368	.405
May	101	35	2	0	4	9	14	10	.347	.485	.422
June	75	17	2	0	0	8	10	9	.227	.253	.322
July	59	17	3	0	3	14	14	10	.288	.492	.413
August	98	32	6	0	4	14	20	13	.327	.510	.430
Sept./Oct.	93	21	4	0	5	18	11	18	.226	.430	.321
Leading Off Inn.	105	25	2	0	5	5	16	15	.238	.400	.350
Bases Empty	268	72	13	0	11	11	42	47	.269	.440	.372
Runners On	226	68	8	0	6	57	43	21	.301	.416	.404
Runners/Scor. Pos.	125	35	6	0	4	53	34	11	.280	.424	.411
Runners On/2 Out	90	20	3	0	3	23	17	8	.222	.356	.352
Scor. Pos./2 Out	52	13	3	0	2	21	14	5	.250	.423	.409
Late-Inning Pressure	74	21	6	0	3	6	9	9	.284	.486	.361
Leading Off	17	1	0	0	0	0	2	3	.059	.059	.158
Runners On	29	7	0	0	1	4	3	3	.241	.345	.313
Runners/Scor. Pos.	18	3	0	0	0	2	1	1	.167	.167	.211

RUNS BATTED IN	From 1B	From 2B	From 3B	Scoring Position
Totals	6/170	19/109	26/47	45/156
Percentage	3.5%	17.4%	55.3%	28.8%

Loves to face: Jim Acker (.667, 6-for-9, 1 HR)
Allan Anderson (.474, 9-for-19)
Dan Schatzeder (3-for-3, 1 HR)

Hates to face: Bert Blyleven (.148, 9-for-61, 1 HR)
Mark Knudson (.059, 1-for-17, 2 BB)
Dennis Martinez (0-for-13, 2 BB)

Miscellaneous statistics: Ground outs-to-air outs ratio: 0.75 last season, 0.89 for career. . . . Grounded into 9 double plays in 118 opportunities (one per 13.1). . . . Drove in 19 of 26 runners from third base with less than two outs (73%). . . . Direction of balls hit to the outfield: 23% to left field, 32% to center, 45% to right. . . . Base running: Advanced from first base to third on 5 of 32 outfield singles (16%); scored from second on 9 of 16 (56%). . . . Made 0.63 assists per nine innings at first base.

Comments: Hit three grand slam home runs last season, tying Kal Daniels for the major league lead. Has a career total of nine slams in seven seasons, including at least one in each of the last five. Only three players in American League history have hit grand slams in at least six straight seasons: Vern Stephens (7 seasons, 1944–50), Lou Gehrig (6 seasons, 1927–32), and Eddie Murray (6 seasons, 1981–86). The all-time record is nine seasons, by Willie McCovey (1964–71). . . . Hit only one home run in 84 first-inning at-bats. . . . Hit all 17 home runs to right field. . . . Has hit more home runs at the Kingdome than he has in road games in each of his seven years in the majors. Career totals: 95 at home, 53 on the road (including the last two hit at old Comiskey Park). . . . Has homered in every A.L. ballpark stateside, but has never homered at either Exhibition Stadium (101 career AB) or the Skydome (22 AB). . . . His career average at Fenway Park (.387) is higher than Wade Boggs's (.380). . . . Davis, Bo Jackson, Keith Hernandez, and Tracy Jones are the only four players, other than pitchers and catchers, to have been on the disabled list in each of the last three seasons.

Chili Davis

Bats Left and Right

California Angels	AB	H	2B	3B	HR	RBI	BB	SO	BA	SA	OBA
Season	412	109	17	1	12	58	61	89	.265	.398	.357
vs. Left-Handers	126	32	5	0	4	20	18	29	.254	.389	.345
vs. Right-Handers	286	77	12	1	8	38	43	60	.269	.402	.363
vs. Ground-Ballers	193	50	7	1	3	26	22	37	.259	.352	.333
vs. Fly-Ballers	219	59	10	0	9	32	39	52	.269	.438	.377
Home Games	216	66	9	1	10	39	30	46	.306	.495	.389
Road Games	196	43	8	0	2	19	31	43	.219	.291	.323
Grass Fields	355	94	14	1	11	48	50	80	.265	.403	.353
Artificial Turf	57	15	3	0	1	10	11	9	.263	.368	.382
April	74	19	5	0	2	8	10	17	.257	.405	.345
May	105	31	4	1	2	16	12	16	.295	.410	.361
June	91	25	4	0	6	16	18	23	.275	.516	.394
July	32	7	0	0	0	0	4	6	.219	.219	.306
August	66	17	2	0	2	14	8	15	.258	.379	.333
Sept./Oct.	44	10	2	0	0	4	9	12	.227	.273	.358
Leading Off Inn.	86	21	4	0	2	2	16	19	.244	.360	.363
Bases Empty	224	62	10	1	3	3	30	42	.277	.371	.362
Runners On	188	47	7	0	9	55	31	47	.250	.431	.351
Runners/Scor. Pos.	105	23	4	0	4	44	22	27	.219	.371	.346
Runners On/2 Out	75	17	2	0	5	20	13	18	.227	.453	.341
Scor. Pos./2 Out	40	10	1	0	3	16	10	10	.250	.500	.400
Late-Inning Pressure	55	17	3	1	0	5	10	10	.309	.400	.409
Leading Off	14	5	2	0	0	0	2	3	.357	.500	.438
Runners On	18	4	1	0	0	5	6	3	.222	.278	.400
Runners/Scor. Pos.	10	2	0	0	0	5	6	1	.200	.200	.471

RUNS BATTED IN	From 1B	From 2B	From 3B	Scoring Position
Totals	9/132	12/78	25/56	37/134
Percentage	6.8%	15.4%	44.6%	27.6%

Loves to face: Rick Honeycutt (.417, 10-for-24, 4 HR, 0 SO)
Mark Knudson (.563, 9-for-16, 1 HR)
Walt Terrell (.385, 10-for-26, 1 HR)

Hates to face: Bill Gullickson (.149, 7-for-47, 2 HR)
Nolan Ryan (.167, 11-for-66, 1 HR)
Bob Welch (.200, 13-for-65, 2 HR)

Miscellaneous statistics: Ground outs-to-air outs ratio: 1.38 last season, 1.22 for career.... Grounded into 14 double plays in 92 opportunities (one per 6.6).... Drove in 19 of 35 runners from third base with less than two outs (54%).... Direction of balls hit to the outfield: 32% to left field, 33% to center, 34% to right batting left-handed; 39% to left, 37% to center, 24% to right batting right-handed.... Base running: Advanced from first base to third on 7 of 28 outfield singles (25%); scored from second on 12 of 18 (67%).... Made 1.70 putouts per nine innings in left field.

Comments: Was Chili swinging from the heels with runners on base? Despite batting 27 points higher with the bases empty, he hit all but three of his 12 home runs with runners on base.... Was thrown out trying to advance a base on a batted ball seven times last season, the most of any player on the Angels.... Batted .164 during the first inning, lowest in the American League (minimum: 50 AB).... Hit only one home run in 122 at-bats from the seventh inning on.... Career total of 156 home runs is the 10th highest among switch-hitters. He starts the 1991 season three ahead of Tom Tresh, three behind Howard Johnson.... He was one of two A.L. players to draw walks in five consecutive plate appearances last season. The other: Jerry Browne.... Was removed for a pinch hitter only once last season; Luis Polonia batted for him on September 26.... Has homered in every current major league park with the exception of Memorial Stadium (52 AB) and the Skydome (19 AB).... Stole only 13 bases in three seasons with California (only one in 1990), compared to an average of 15.5 a year in six seasons with the Giants.... The end of an era: Davis had between 20 and 29 doubles in each of his previous nine seasons.

Rob Deer

Bats Right

Milwaukee Brewers	AB	H	2B	3B	HR	RBI	BB	SO	BA	SA	OBA
Season	440	92	15	1	27	69	64	147	.209	.432	.313
vs. Left-Handers	140	41	5	0	16	34	25	40	.293	.671	.399
vs. Right-Handers	300	51	10	1	11	35	39	107	.170	.320	.271
vs. Ground-Ballers	192	41	8	1	12	35	34	60	.214	.453	.330
vs. Fly-Ballers	248	51	7	0	15	34	30	87	.206	.415	.299
Home Games	214	40	7	0	11	30	35	67	.187	.374	.310
Road Games	226	52	8	1	16	39	29	80	.230	.487	.317
Grass Fields	378	81	14	1	24	59	55	120	.214	.447	.317
Artificial Turf	62	11	1	0	3	10	9	27	.177	.339	.292
April	37	8	2	0	3	9	9	12	.216	.514	.388
May	66	13	3	0	4	11	14	29	.197	.424	.338
June	76	17	2	0	6	18	10	21	.224	.487	.318
July	76	16	2	0	5	10	13	24	.211	.434	.326
August	98	24	4	1	8	17	11	37	.245	.551	.324
Sept./Oct.	87	14	2	0	1	4	7	24	.161	.218	.223
Leading Off Inn.	104	25	2	0	6	6	9	30	.240	.433	.301
Bases Empty	248	48	8	0	13	13	21	85	.194	.383	.262
Runners On	192	44	7	1	14	56	43	62	.229	.495	.371
Runners/Scor. Pos.	112	24	2	0	10	44	35	35	.214	.500	.397
Runners On/2 Out	90	23	3	0	6	28	21	26	.256	.489	.396
Scor. Pos./2 Out	59	17	1	0	5	24	19	14	.288	.559	.462
Late-Inning Pressure	60	16	3	0	2	9	12	21	.267	.417	.405
Leading Off	14	3	0	0	0	0	1	6	.214	.214	.267
Runners On	21	6	1	0	1	8	8	7	.286	.476	.500
Runners/Scor. Pos.	18	5	0	0	1	8	8	7	.278	.444	.519

RUNS BATTED IN	From 1B	From 2B	From 3B	Scoring Position
Totals	10/134	18/89	14/43	32/132
Percentage	7.5%	20.2%	32.6%	24.2%

Loves to face: Storm Davis (.412, 7-for-17, 2 HR)
Charlie Hough (.667, 6-for-9, 2 HR, 2 SO)
Mike Moore (.367, 11-for-30, 4 HR)

Hates to face: Nolan Ryan (0-for-12, 8 SO)
Dave Stewart (.083, 3-for-36, 1 HR, 4 BB, 18 SO)
Dave Stieb (.045, 1-for-22, 3 BB)

Miscellaneous statistics: Ground outs-to-air outs ratio: 0.44 last season, lowest rate in majors; 0.58 for career.... Grounded into 0 double plays in 85 opportunities, best rate in majors.... Drove in 7 of 22 runners from third base with less than two outs (32%), 2d-lowest rate in A.L.... Direction of balls hit to the outfield: 63% to left field, 22% to center, 15% to right.... Base running: Advanced from first base to third on 10 of 17 outfield singles (59%); scored from second on 4 of 7 (57%).... Made 2.40 putouts per nine innings in right field.

Comments: Thought we were seeing double when we compared the "Season" line above to his 1989 figures: 466 AB, 98 hits, 15 2B, 1 3B, 26 HR, 69 RBI, 60 BB, 158 SO, .210 BA, .425 SA, .305 OBA.... Our favorite season clones: Eddie Collins, 1913–14; Rabbit Maranville, 1929–30; and Willie Randolph, 1985–86. ...Only one other player in major league history has hit 25 or more home runs while batting under .210 in the same season: Dave Kingman, 37 homers, .204 batting average in 1982.... Career average of .225 is the 2d lowest of any active nonpitcher with at least 500 games, 15 points ahead of Steve Jeltz.... The most important characteristic of hitters who don't ground into double plays? Not speed, but hitting the ball in the air (or not at all). How else to explain the fact that Deer hasn't grounded into a DP since July 17, 1989?. . .Career ratio of ground outs-to-air outs (0.58) is the lowest of any player in the 16 years we've been tracking such things.... Batted 123 points higher vs. left-handers (.293) than vs. right-handers (.170) last season, the 5th-largest margin in the majors. Batting average vs. left-handed pitchers was a career high, while his average vs. right-handers was a career low, courtesy of an 0-for-34 streak.... Batted 82 points higher in night games (.234) than in day games (.152) last season, the 5th-largest margin in the majors.... Career batting average of .280 at Tiger Stadium, with an average of one home run every 15.5 at bats.

Mike Devereaux

Bats Right

Baltimore Orioles	AB	H	2B	3B	HR	RBI	BB	SO	BA	SA	OBA
Season	367	88	18	1	12	49	28	48	.240	.392	.291
vs. Left-Handers	160	37	7	0	7	22	10	15	.231	.406	.273
vs. Right-Handers	207	51	11	1	5	27	18	33	.246	.382	.304
vs. Ground-Ballers	162	36	8	1	4	21	16	16	.222	.358	.291
vs. Fly-Ballers	205	52	10	0	8	28	12	32	.254	.420	.291
Home Games	150	35	7	0	6	21	16	25	.233	.400	.304
Road Games	217	53	11	1	6	28	12	23	.244	.387	.281
Grass Fields	296	74	15	1	12	44	25	40	.250	.429	.305
Artificial Turf	71	14	3	0	0	5	3	8	.197	.239	.230
April	35	5	0	0	0	0	3	4	.143	.143	.211
May	31	7	3	0	0	5	0	1	.226	.323	.219
June	50	12	2	0	2	7	5	9	.240	.400	.298
July	96	32	5	1	4	17	6	15	.333	.531	.373
August	62	11	3	0	1	9	8	10	.177	.274	.271
Sept./Oct.	93	21	5	0	5	11	6	9	.226	.441	.270
Leading Off Inn.	91	23	5	0	4	4	8	10	.253	.440	.313
Bases Empty	198	46	10	0	7	7	17	22	.232	.389	.293
Runners On	169	42	8	1	5	42	11	26	.249	.396	.288
Runners/Scor. Pos.	92	22	6	1	3	37	3	14	.239	.424	.253
Runners On/2 Out	71	21	7	0	2	22	4	11	.296	.479	.333
Scor. Pos./2 Out	37	12	5	0	2	21	1	6	.324	.622	.342
Late-Inning Pressure	58	16	3	0	1	6	8	8	.276	.379	.358
Leading Off	17	4	0	0	0	0	1	2	.235	.235	.278
Runners On	26	8	1	0	0	5	3	3	.308	.346	.367
Runners/Scor. Pos.	10	4	1	0	0	5	2	0	.400	.500	.462

RUNS BATTED IN	From 1B	From 2B	From 3B	Scoring Position
Totals	8/130	12/74	17/38	29/112
Percentage	6.2%	16.2%	44.7%	25.9%

Loves to face: Allan Anderson (.385, 5-for-13, 1 HR)
Mike Henneman (.500, 2-for-4, 1 3B, 1 HR)
Nolan Ryan (.500, 4-for-8, 1 HR)

Hates to face: Chuck Cary (.071, 1-for-14)
Jeff Montgomery (0-for-6, 4 SO)
Curt Young (.091, 1-for-11)

Miscellaneous statistics: Ground outs-to-air outs ratio: 1.01 last season, 1.00 for career. . . . Grounded into 10 double plays in 83 opportunities (one per 8.3). . . . Drove in 10 of 18 runners from third base with less than two outs (56%). . . . Direction of balls hit to the outfield: 43% to left field, 30% to center, 27% to right. . . . Base running: Advanced from first base to third on 9 of 14 outfield singles (64%); scored from second on 9 of 10 (90%). . . . Made 2.99 putouts per nine innings in center field, 2d-highest rate in A.L.

Comments: On a team of excellent fielding outfielders, Devereaux played exclusively in center field last season. . . . One of five American League players to start at least one game in each of eight different batting order slots. Devereaux missed only the cleanup spot. In September alone, he started in six different batting-order positions. . . . Stole 22 bases in 1989, the most by an Orioles rookie since Al Bumbry (23 in 1973). Then, Devereaux stole 13 bases in his first 19 attempts in 1990, but was 0-for-6 after August 20. . . . Batted .297 in day games, to raise his career mark to .288; he batted .218 under the lights, to lower his career mark to .228. During Devereaux's four-year career, seven players have wider margins in favor of day games: Randy Ready (112 points), Mike Fitzgerald (77), Craig Biggio (74), Dan Pasqua (69), Leon Durham (66), Jim Eisenreich (62), and Mackey Sasser (61) (minimum: 200 AB, day and night). . . . Career batting averages: .244 vs. right-handers, .245 vs. left-handers. . . . Career average of .125 as a pinch-hitter, with no extra-base hits in 32 at-bats. . . . Has a career mark of .229 in Late-Inning Pressure Situations, divided rather well: .291 with runners on base, .184 with the bases empty. . . . Never batted below .300 in four years in the minors. . . . One of the few Wyoming natives in the majors. Both Devereaux and Tom Browning were born in Casper.

Edgar Diaz

Bats Right

Milwaukee Brewers	AB	H	2B	3B	HR	RBI	BB	SO	BA	SA	OBA
Season	218	59	2	2	0	14	21	32	.271	.298	.338
vs. Left-Handers	95	27	2	0	0	2	9	11	.284	.305	.346
vs. Right-Handers	123	32	0	2	0	12	12	21	.260	.293	.331
vs. Ground-Ballers	81	22	1	0	0	10	8	14	.272	.284	.344
vs. Fly-Ballers	137	37	1	2	0	4	13	18	.270	.307	.333
Home Games	102	28	0	1	0	4	12	16	.275	.294	.357
Road Games	116	31	2	1	0	10	9	16	.267	.302	.320
Grass Fields	180	48	0	1	0	12	18	26	.267	.278	.337
Artificial Turf	38	11	2	1	0	2	3	6	.289	.395	.341
April	63	18	0	0	0	8	4	7	.286	.286	.338
May	56	11	0	1	0	1	6	13	.196	.232	.274
June	25	10	0	1	0	1	4	3	.400	.480	.483
July	21	7	0	0	0	2	0	4	.333	.333	.333
August	32	7	2	0	0	1	6	3	.219	.281	.342
Sept./Oct.	21	6	0	0	0	1	1	2	.286	.286	.318
Leading Off Inn.	42	12	1	1	0	0	5	3	.286	.357	.362
Bases Empty	124	37	2	1	0	0	13	17	.298	.331	.370
Runners On	94	22	0	1	0	14	8	15	.234	.255	.294
Runners/Scor. Pos.	58	8	0	0	0	13	4	11	.138	.138	.194
Runners On/2 Out	45	10	0	1	0	5	6	4	.222	.267	.314
Scor. Pos./2 Out	31	3	0	0	0	4	3	4	.097	.097	.176
Late-Inning Pressure	16	3	0	0	0	0	1	4	.188	.188	.235
Leading Off	7	1	0	0	0	0	0	1	.143	.143	.143
Runners On	2	0	0	0	0	0	1	0	.000	.000	.333
Runners/Scor. Pos.	1	0	0	0	0	0	0	0	.000	.000	.000

RUNS BATTED IN	From 1B	From 2B	From 3B	Scoring Position
Totals	1/61	4/43	9/28	13/71
Percentage	1.6%	9.3%	32.1%	18.3%

Loves to face: Kevin Tapani (.667, 4-for-6)
Sergio Valdez (.667, 2-for-3)

Hates to face: Mark Langston (.143, 1-for-7)

Miscellaneous statistics: Ground outs-to-air outs ratio: 2.29 last season, highest rate in A.L.; 2.46 for career. . . . Grounded into 3 double plays in 36 opportunities (one per 12.0). . . . Drove in 7 of 10 runners from third base with less than two outs (70%). . . . Direction of balls hit to the outfield: 19% to left field, 35% to center, 45% to right. . . . Base running: Advanced from first base to third on 3 of 10 outfield singles (30%); scored from second on 5 of 5. . . . Made 2.95 assists per nine innings at shortstop.

Comments: Milwaukee opened the season with Paul Molitor, Jim Gantner, and Bill Spiers on the disabled list. Diaz started each of the Brewers' first 30 games, but only 36 thereafter. . . . Committed 14 errors in just under 500 innings at shortstop. Spiers committed only 12 errors in more than 900 innings at that position. Nevertheless, the Brewers had a 31–26 record with Diaz starting at short, 43–62 with other players there. . . . Six of his 14 RBIs were recorded on balls that did not leave the infield. To put that in perspective, Rob Deer had only two such RBIs all season . . . . His streak of 25 consecutive hitless at-bats with runners in scoring position was the 2d longest in the American League last year. . . . Average of one extra-base hit per 55 ABs was the lowest in the majors (minimum: 200 AB). The last major leaguer with a lower rate was Rafael Belliard in 1988 (4 XBH in 286 AB); the last A.L. player was Julio Cruz in 1986 (2 XBH in 209 AB). . . . Has two extra-base hits in 16 career at-bats at the Metrodome, and another two in 215 at-bats elsewhere. . . . He'll have to step it up a notch to join Cuyler, Dee, and Vandeweghe in the Kiki Hall of Fame.

Brian Downing

Bats Right

California Angels	AB	H	2B	3B	HR	RBI	BB	SO	BA	SA	OBA
Season	330	90	18	2	14	51	50	45	.273	.467	.374
vs. Left-Handers	119	41	8	1	5	16	25	14	.345	.555	.466
vs. Right-Handers	211	49	10	1	9	35	25	31	.232	.417	.318
vs. Ground-Ballers	134	40	8	0	7	22	16	12	.299	.515	.383
vs. Fly-Ballers	196	50	10	2	7	29	34	33	.255	.434	.369
Home Games	162	49	9	0	11	26	24	14	.302	.562	.403
Road Games	168	41	9	2	3	25	26	31	.244	.375	.347
Grass Fields	286	77	14	2	14	45	40	38	.269	.479	.365
Artificial Turf	44	13	4	0	0	6	10	7	.295	.386	.429
April	43	8	1	0	1	6	4	5	.186	.279	.271
May	24	5	0	0	2	4	3	1	.208	.458	.296
June	38	11	4	0	1	2	2	1	.289	.474	.372
July	83	26	5	1	4	13	13	12	.313	.542	.402
August	65	22	6	0	4	18	16	11	.338	.615	.463
Sept./Oct.	77	18	2	1	2	8	12	15	.234	.364	.344
Leading Off Inn.	92	22	3	1	2	2	11	11	.239	.359	.327
Bases Empty	191	46	9	1	7	7	29	25	.241	.408	.350
Runners On	139	44	9	1	7	44	21	20	.317	.547	.407
Runners/Scor. Pos.	79	23	5	1	3	35	15	13	.291	.494	.400
Runners On/2 Out	49	16	4	0	2	13	7	7	.327	.531	.441
Scor. Pos./2 Out	24	6	3	0	1	11	4	3	.250	.500	.400
Late-Inning Pressure	62	13	2	0	2	5	7	9	.210	.339	.290
Leading Off	16	1	1	0	0	0	0	2	.063	.125	.063
Runners On	28	7	0	0	1	4	5	4	.250	.357	.364
Runners/Scor. Pos.	13	2	0	0	0	2	3	3	.154	.154	.313

RUNS BATTED IN	From 1B	From 2B	From 3B	Scoring Position
Totals	8/101	11/61	18/39	29/100
Percentage	7.9%	18.0%	46.2%	29.0%

Loves to face: Cecilio Guante (.800, 4-for-5, 1 2B, 2 HR)
Mike Jeffcoat (.474, 9-for-19, 1 HR)
Curt Young (.393, 11-for-28, 3 HR)

Hates to face: Jim Acker (.077, 1-for-13, 2 BB)
Mark Knudson (0-for-12)
Mike Moore (.125, 6-for-48, 1 HR)

Miscellaneous statistics: Ground outs-to-air outs ratio: 0.94 last season, 1.09 for career.... Grounded into 11 double plays in 73 opportunities (one per 6.6).... Drove in 13 of 26 runners from third base with less than two outs (50%).... Direction of balls hit to the outfield: 44% to left field, 34% to center, 22% to right.... Base running: Advanced from first base to third on 7 of 27 outfield singles (26%); scored from second on 8 of 11 (73%).

Comments: Thanks to Dave Henderson, Downing is the oldest active player who has never appeared in a World Series. Since the start of World Series play, only 12 players have played in as many regular-season games as Downing (2114) without appearing in the Fall Classic. Ernie Banks heads that list with 2528 games.... Career total of 2114 games ranks 10th among players active at the end of last season.... The all-time leader in games played for the Angels (1661). No other player currently on their roster has reached 1000 games with the club.... Has played 373 games over the last three seasons, but hasn't played the field during that time.... Was removed for a pinch hitter only once last season (Chili Davis batted for him on May 15).... Batting average vs. left-handed pitchers was his highest since 1980. During 1979 and 1980, Downing batted .383 vs. southpaws.... Has hit for a higher average against ground-ball pitchers than he has against fly-ball pitchers in each of the last five seasons.... Career average of .141 as a pinch hitter; hitless in his last 10 AB (0-for-8 last season).... Surpassed 1000 runs in 1989, 1000 walks last season; begins 1991 with 999 strikeouts and 985 RBIs. Most comparable career statistics: Bobby Grich.

Jim Eisenreich

Bats Left

Kansas City Royals	AB	H	2B	3B	HR	RBI	BB	SO	BA	SA	OBA
Season	496	139	29	7	5	51	42	51	.280	.397	.335
vs. Left-Handers	156	35	9	2	1	16	10	18	.224	.327	.268
vs. Right-Handers	340	104	20	5	4	35	32	33	.306	.429	.365
vs. Ground-Ballers	216	62	14	1	2	24	20	16	.287	.389	.346
vs. Fly-Ballers	280	77	15	6	3	27	22	35	.275	.404	.327
Home Games	236	61	12	5	2	29	25	19	.258	.377	.327
Road Games	260	78	17	2	3	22	17	32	.300	.415	.343
Grass Fields	189	57	12	1	2	13	16	27	.302	.407	.357
Artificial Turf	307	82	17	6	3	38	26	24	.267	.391	.321
April	51	12	3	1	1	5	2	9	.235	.392	.264
May	100	33	7	0	0	15	7	10	.330	.400	.373
June	84	22	4	1	1	7	12	8	.262	.369	.351
July	110	32	11	4	0	8	11	8	.291	.464	.355
August	87	28	1	1	3	13	6	7	.322	.460	.362
Sept./Oct.	64	12	3	0	0	3	4	9	.188	.234	.235
Leading Off Inn.	128	38	11	1	2	2	7	13	.297	.445	.333
Bases Empty	287	83	19	6	3	3	22	32	.289	.429	.340
Runners On	209	56	10	1	2	48	20	19	.268	.354	.329
Runners/Scor. Pos.	137	33	5	1	1	46	16	14	.241	.314	.316
Runners On/2 Out	84	25	2	1	1	21	10	9	.298	.381	.379
Scor. Pos./2 Out	55	16	2	1	0	19	9	8	.291	.364	.400
Late-Inning Pressure	78	19	3	1	2	11	6	12	.244	.385	.298
Leading Off	20	3	1	0	1	1	0	4	.150	.350	.150
Runners On	30	11	1	0	1	10	3	3	.367	.500	.424
Runners/Scor. Pos.	19	7	1	0	0	8	3	1	.368	.421	.455

RUNS BATTED IN	From 1B	From 2B	From 3B	Scoring Position
Totals	1/135	25/118	20/45	45/163
Percentage	0.7%	21.2%	44.4%	27.6%

Loves to face: Dennis Eckersley (.667, 4-for-6)
Wes Gardner (.500, 5-for-10, 1 HR)
Dave Stewart (.333, 6-for-18, 2 HR)

Hates to face: Bert Blyleven (.074, 2-for-27)
Nolan Ryan (.063, 1-for-16, 2 BB)
Bob Welch (.095, 2-for-21, 1 HR)

Miscellaneous statistics: Ground outs-to-air outs ratio: 1.42 last season, 1.18 for career.... Grounded into 7 double plays in 87 opportunities (one per 12.4).... Drove in 14 of 27 runners from third base with less than two outs (52%).... Direction of balls hit to the outfield: 42% to left field, 35% to center, 23% to right.... Base running: Advanced from first base to third on 9 of 32 outfield singles (28%); scored from second on 9 of 14 (64%).... Made 2.01 putouts per nine innings in left field.

Comments: One of three major league players to start at least 15 games at each of the three outfield positions.... Ended the season with a streak of 89 errorless games in the outfield.... Number of plate appearances has increased in each of his last five seasons.... Drove in only seven runs over his last 29 games, and none of those runs gave the Royals a lead.... Stole only 12 bases in 26 attempts, including only four in 10 attempts vs. left-handed pitchers. His previous career average was 76 percent (39-for-51).... Two of his five home runs were hit in consecutive games at the Oakland Coliseum.... Had four hits and a walk in nine pinch-hit appearances.... Batted 84 points higher in day games (.345) than in night games (.261) last season, the 5th-largest margin in the majors. That marks the fifth consecutive season that he has had a higher mark in day games. Career breakdown: .322 in day games, .253 at night.... Through 1989, he had career batting averages of .335 vs. left-handers, .254 vs. right-handers. Even after last season, his career mark against southpaws (.281) is still 11 points higher than against right-handers.... Career batting average of .317 as a pinch hitter (13-for-41, 2 HR).

Alvaro Espinoza

Bats Right

New York Yankees	AB	H	2B	3B	HR	RBI	BB	SO	BA	SA	OBA
Season	438	98	12	2	2	20	16	54	.224	.274	.258
vs. Left-Handers	144	36	2	1	1	9	9	13	.250	.299	.294
vs. Right-Handers	294	62	10	1	1	11	7	41	.211	.262	.240
vs. Ground-Ballers	186	45	7	1	2	9	4	22	.242	.323	.264
vs. Fly-Ballers	252	53	5	1	0	11	12	32	.210	.238	.254
Home Games	219	47	7	2	0	9	9	21	.215	.265	.251
Road Games	219	51	5	0	2	11	7	33	.233	.283	.265
Grass Fields	370	77	9	2	1	15	15	44	.208	.251	.248
Artificial Turf	68	21	3	0	1	5	1	10	.309	.397	.314
April	55	11	3	0	0	4	2	11	.200	.255	.237
May	76	15	1	0	0	4	2	6	.197	.211	.218
June	78	19	2	1	1	1	3	9	.244	.333	.272
July	76	21	1	0	1	4	4	10	.276	.329	.313
August	82	13	2	1	0	3	1	10	.159	.207	.176
Sept./Oct.	71	19	3	0	0	4	4	8	.268	.310	.333
Leading Off Inn.	92	20	3	1	0	0	3	11	.217	.272	.250
Bases Empty	268	58	7	1	2	2	12	38	.216	.272	.258
Runners On	170	40	5	1	0	18	4	16	.235	.276	.258
Runners/Scor. Pos.	74	14	2	1	0	18	3	6	.189	.243	.225
Runners On/2 Out	65	17	1	1	0	7	1	7	.262	.308	.273
Scor. Pos./2 Out	32	7	1	1	0	7	1	5	.219	.313	.242
Late-Inning Pressure	49	12	2	0	1	3	4	4	.245	.347	.302
Leading Off	11	5	1	0	0	0	0	0	.455	.545	.455
Runners On	16	4	0	0	0	2	2	2	.250	.250	.333
Runners/Scor. Pos.	9	3	0	0	0	2	2	1	.333	.333	.455

RUNS BATTED IN	From 1B	From 2B	From 3B	Scoring Position
Totals	0/138	9/63	9/24	18/87
Percentage	0.0%	14.3%	37.5%	20.7%

Loves to face: Mike Jackson (.571, 4-for-7)
Jack Morris (.385, 5-for-13)
Scott Sanderson (.600, 3-for-5)

Hates to face: Bert Blyleven (0-for-8)
Kevin Brown (.071, 1-for-14)
Greg A. Harris (0-for-7)

Miscellaneous statistics: Ground outs-to-air outs ratio: 1.42 last season, 1.55 for career.... Grounded into 13 double plays in 102 opportunities (one per 7.8).... Drove in 8 of 16 runners from third base with less than two outs (50%).... Direction of balls hit to the outfield: 30% to left field, 33% to center, 37% to right.... Base running: Advanced from first base to third on 6 of 22 outfield singles (27%); scored from second on 9 of 10 (90%).... Made 3.33 assists per nine innings at shortstop, highest rate in majors.

Comments: Appeared to be a serious candidate to break the record of former Red Sox outfielder Tom Oliver, who had 1931 career at-bats without a home run. But Espinoza hit two last season: one over the Green Monster, the other inside the Blue Monster (the Metrodome).... The first player since John Shelby in 1986 to gather fewer than 100 hits and fewer than 20 walks in more than 400 at-bats.... Batting average decreased 58 points from 1989 to 1990. Among the players with the 10 largest drops last season, three were Yankees: Espinoza, Steve Sax (55 points), and Don Mattingly (47) (minimum: 300 AB in both seasons).... Batted .383 vs. left-handed pitchers and .318 with runners in scoring position in 1989.... Batted 108 points higher vs. left-handers (.326) than vs. right-handers (.218) over the last five seasons, the largest margin in the majors.... Career average of one walk per 59 plate appearances vs. right-handed pitchers.... Started the season batting second in the New York batting order, but he eventually accumulated 300 at-bats in the nine hole.... The latest in a long line of weak-hitting Yankees shortstops. His predecessors included Tom Tresh (who batted .195 in 1968), Gene Michael (.214 in 1970), Bobby Meacham (.218 in 1985), and Ruben Amaro (.223 in 1967).

Dwight Evans

Bats Right

Boston Red Sox	AB	H	2B	3B	HR	RBI	BB	SO	BA	SA	OBA
Season	445	111	18	3	13	63	67	73	.249	.391	.349
vs. Left-Handers	147	39	10	2	3	16	25	29	.265	.422	.375
vs. Right-Handers	298	72	8	1	10	47	42	44	.242	.376	.335
vs. Ground-Ballers	188	49	10	1	1	20	27	28	.261	.340	.350
vs. Fly-Ballers	257	62	8	2	12	43	40	45	.241	.428	.348
Home Games	218	55	10	2	7	31	30	42	.252	.413	.348
Road Games	227	56	8	1	6	32	37	31	.247	.370	.349
Grass Fields	380	94	14	3	10	52	58	62	.247	.379	.348
Artificial Turf	65	17	4	0	3	11	9	11	.262	.462	.355
April	74	18	2	0	3	12	8	18	.243	.392	.317
May	91	23	6	0	1	11	15	14	.253	.352	.370
June	93	21	3	1	5	17	20	16	.226	.441	.359
July	39	7	1	0	1	4	6	7	.179	.282	.289
August	84	26	3	1	3	11	12	9	.310	.476	.402
Sept./Oct.	64	16	3	1	0	8	6	9	.250	.328	.301
Leading Off Inn.	96	23	4	0	3	3	16	17	.240	.375	.348
Bases Empty	225	58	9	2	7	7	35	40	.258	.409	.360
Runners On	220	53	9	1	6	56	32	33	.241	.373	.337
Runners/Scor. Pos.	123	33	4	0	5	51	21	22	.268	.423	.364
Runners On/2 Out	82	21	4	0	4	19	18	15	.256	.451	.390
Scor. Pos./2 Out	54	14	1	0	4	18	13	13	.259	.500	.403
Late-Inning Pressure	79	24	2	0	7	17	9	14	.304	.595	.382
Leading Off	20	6	1	0	2	2	3	3	.300	.650	.391
Runners On	33	8	0	0	3	13	5	7	.242	.515	.359
Runners/Scor. Pos.	20	6	0	0	3	13	4	4	.300	.750	.417

RUNS BATTED IN	From 1B	From 2B	From 3B	Scoring Position
Totals	8/172	19/96	23/67	42/163
Percentage	4.7%	19.8%	34.3%	25.8%

Loves to face: Dennis Eckersley (.292, 7-for-24, 4 HR)
Dennis Lamp (.474, 9-for-19)
Curt Young (.400, 10-for-25, 3 HR)

Hates to face: Dave LaPoint (.158, 3-for-19)
Nolan Ryan (.103, 3-for-29, 1 HR, 3 BB)
Bob Welch (.071, 1-for-14)

Miscellaneous statistics: Ground outs-to-air outs ratio: 1.04 last season, 1.05 for career.... Grounded into 18 double plays in 119 opportunities (one per 6.6).... Drove in 20 of 40 runners from third base with less than two outs (50%).... Direction of balls hit to the outfield: 39% to left field, 30% to center, 32% to right.... Base running: Advanced from first base to third on 10 of 28 outfield singles (36%); scored from second on 14 of 18 (78%).

Comments: The first time Dewey steps on the field for Baltimore, he will renounce his membership in an exclusive club. Only six others in major league history played 2500 or more games and spent their entire careers with a single club: Carl Yastrzemski, Stan Musial, Brooks Robinson, Al Kaline, Mel Ott, and Ernie Banks.... Has something else in common with Brooks and Yaz. His five opening-day home runs leave him one short of the A.L. record that they share with the Bambino.... Career total of games ranks Evans ninth in American League history, 94 behind Luis Aparicio.... Starts the 1991 season with a share of the career home-run lead among active players in a race that rivals the 1967 A.L. pennant race: Evans and Eddie Murray are tied with 379, with Dale Murphy and Dave Winfield just one behind.... The retirement of Darrell Evans last season left baseball without an active 400-HR hitter for the first time since 1956, when Ted Williams reached the 400-mark (filling a void that had existed since the retirement of Mel Ott in 1947).... His seven home runs in Late-Inning Pressure Situations tied Kevin Mitchell for the major league lead.... Of his 63 RBIs, 24 gave the Red Sox a lead. Only Ellis Burks drove in more tie-breaking runs for the Sox (27). Starting with a home run in a 1–0 victory over the Blue Jays on August 25, Evans drove in the winning runs in five games during Boston's pennant drive.

Mike Felder

Bats Left and Right

Milwaukee Brewers	AB	H	2B	3B	HR	RBI	BB	SO	BA	SA	OBA
Season	237	65	7	2	3	27	22	17	.274	.359	.330
vs. Left-Handers	80	22	2	2	3	14	6	5	.275	.463	.315
vs. Right-Handers	157	43	5	0	0	13	16	12	.274	.306	.337
vs. Ground-Ballers	118	32	3	1	1	15	4	10	.271	.339	.288
vs. Fly-Ballers	119	33	4	1	2	12	18	7	.277	.378	.367
Home Games	110	29	3	1	1	10	8	11	.264	.336	.311
Road Games	127	36	4	1	2	17	14	6	.283	.378	.345
Grass Fields	198	50	5	1	3	20	15	16	.253	.333	.298
Artificial Turf	39	15	2	1	0	7	7	1	.385	.487	.478
April	12	3	0	0	0	2	2	2	.250	.250	.333
May	29	5	0	0	0	2	4	0	.172	.172	.265
June	65	19	4	0	0	6	7	3	.292	.354	.361
July	49	11	0	0	2	3	2	5	.224	.347	.255
August	37	12	1	1	1	9	2	3	.324	.486	.341
Sept./Oct.	45	15	2	1	0	5	5	4	.333	.422	.392
Leading Off Inn.	70	19	5	0	2	2	5	3	.271	.429	.320
Bases Empty	141	41	6	0	3	3	10	8	.291	.397	.338
Runners On	96	24	1	2	0	24	12	9	.250	.302	.319
Runners/Scor. Pos.	67	19	1	1	0	23	7	7	.284	.328	.329
Runners On/2 Out	47	9	1	1	0	8	6	4	.191	.255	.283
Scor. Pos./2 Out	40	8	1	1	0	8	6	4	.200	.275	.304
Late-Inning Pressure	46	12	2	1	0	7	5	6	.261	.348	.327
Leading Off	11	2	1	0	0	0	1	0	.182	.273	.250
Runners On	20	6	1	1	0	7	3	3	.300	.450	.375
Runners/Scor. Pos.	14	6	1	1	0	7	3	2	.429	.643	.500

RUNS BATTED IN	From 1B	From 2B	From 3B	Scoring Position
Totals	2/60	6/56	16/32	22/88
Percentage	3.3%	10.7%	50.0%	25.0%

Loves to face: Mark Thurmond (.667, 4-for-6)
Duane Ward (.500, 4-for-8)

Hates to face: Greg A. Harris (0-for-7, 1 BB)
Walt Terrell (.077, 1-for-13)
Bobby Witt (.176, 3-for-17, 3 BB)

Miscellaneous statistics: Ground outs-to-air outs ratio: 1.51 last season, 1.42 for career.... Grounded into 0 double plays in 45 opportunities, 2d best in A.L.... Drove in 13 of 18 runners from third base with less than two outs (72%).... Direction of balls hit to the outfield: 25% to left field, 28% to center, 47% to right batting left-handed; 34% to left, 26% to center, 40% to right batting right-handed.... Base running: Advanced from first base to third on 6 of 13 outfield singles (46%); scored from second on 9 of 10 (90%).... Made 2.57 putouts per nine innings in left field.

Comments: Made 20 appearances as a pinch-runner last season, third most in the American League. The top five: Kenny Williams (31), Rodney McCray (24), Felder (20), teammate Darryl Hamilton (20), Wayne Tolleson (20).... Tom Trebelhorn used the fewest pinch hitters in the majors last season (69), as he did in each of his three previous full seasons as Brewers manager. But Milwaukee had the most pinch runners in the majors last season (62), and only one A.L. team used more defensive substitutes (Texas, 159 to 143).... Batted .342 in 38 1st-inning at-bats.... Didn't ground into a double play last season, although he batted 45 times with a runner on first and less than two outs. That says a lot about his speed, because he does not strike out often, and he hits a lot of ground balls.... Entered the 1990 season with a career stolen base percentage of .830 (88-for-106), but stole at a 69 percent rate last season (20-for-29).... Consistency from both sides of the plate in 1990 was a surprise. His career batting average through 1989 was more than 50 points higher vs. left-handers than it was against right-handers. Current career figures: .275 vs. LHP, .234 vs. RHP.... There's an even wider gap (67 points) between his career averages against ground-ball (.283) and fly-ball (.216) pitchers.

Junior Felix

Bats Left and Right

Toronto Blue Jays	AB	H	2B	3B	HR	RBI	BB	SO	BA	SA	OBA
Season	463	122	23	7	15	65	45	99	.263	.441	.328
vs. Left-Handers	152	32	8	1	9	22	15	41	.211	.454	.282
vs. Right-Handers	311	90	15	6	6	43	30	58	.289	.434	.351
vs. Ground-Ballers	204	57	8	4	6	30	21	39	.279	.446	.345
vs. Fly-Ballers	259	65	15	3	9	35	24	60	.251	.436	.315
Home Games	236	58	13	6	7	29	24	50	.246	.441	.316
Road Games	227	64	10	1	8	36	21	49	.282	.441	.341
Grass Fields	172	45	8	1	6	23	17	37	.262	.424	.326
Artificial Turf	291	77	15	6	9	42	28	62	.265	.450	.329
April	66	23	7	2	3	17	10	13	.348	.652	.449
May	89	25	4	0	6	13	12	16	.281	.528	.356
June	117	31	7	2	1	11	13	26	.265	.385	.336
July	28	6	0	1	1	5	0	9	.214	.393	.214
August	74	17	5	1	1	5	4	19	.230	.365	.269
Sept./Oct.	89	20	0	1	3	14	6	16	.225	.348	.271
Leading Off Inn.	130	32	6	2	2	2	16	29	.246	.369	.329
Bases Empty	273	70	14	5	9	9	28	63	.256	.443	.326
Runners On	190	52	9	2	6	56	17	36	.274	.437	.332
Runners/Scor. Pos.	105	31	7	0	3	48	10	18	.295	.448	.352
Runners On/2 Out	83	22	4	1	1	20	4	12	.265	.373	.315
Scor. Pos./2 Out	52	16	4	0	1	19	3	8	.308	.442	.368
Late-Inning Pressure	72	11	2	1	1	6	4	21	.153	.250	.195
Leading Off	23	4	2	1	0	0	2	6	.174	.348	.240
Runners On	28	5	0	0	1	6	0	8	.179	.286	.172
Runners/Scor. Pos.	16	2	0	0	0	4	0	4	.125	.125	.118

RUNS BATTED IN	From 1B	From 2B	From 3B	Scoring Position
Totals	9/126	18/82	23/48	41/130
Percentage	7.1%	22.0%	47.9%	31.5%

Loves to face: Dennis Lamp (.400, 4-for-10, 1 2B, 1 3B, 1 HR)
Bob Welch (.500, 5-for-10, 1 HR)
Curt Young (.600, 3-for-5, 2 HR)

Hates to face: Allan Anderson (.167, 3-for-18)
Juan Berenguer (0-for-5)
Mike Moore (.100, 1-for-10)

Miscellaneous statistics: Ground outs-to-air outs ratio: 1.58 last season, 1.48 for career.... Grounded into 4 double plays in 85 opportunities (one per 21.3), 5th-best rate in A.L.... Drove in 16 of 27 runners from third base with less than two outs (59%).... Direction of balls hit to the outfield: 37% to left field, 30% to center, 33% to right batting left-handed; 40% to left, 34% to center, 26% to right batting right-handed.... Base running: Advanced from first base to third on 9 of 18 outfield singles (50%); scored from second on 15 of 17 (88%).... Made 1.91 putouts per nine innings in right field, 2d-lowest rate in A.L.

Comments: Joins the Angels with a rather noteworthy skew. Felix has batted .300 or better at four A.L. ballparks, including all three in the Pacific Time Zone: .385 in the Kingdome, .346 at Oakland Coliseum, .317 at Fenway Park, and .304 at Anaheim Stadium. His composite average on the west coast is .347, compared to .253 at points further east.... Tied teammate Kelly Gruber for the major league lead with 12 extra-base hits in April. Rode a similar hot streak in June 1989, when he led the major leagues with 26 RBIs for the month.... Streaky throwers *do* exist! Felix collected seven outfield assists by the end of May, then no more until September, when he added another four.... Batted .308 from the left side of the plate on artificial turf. Benchmarks: he batted .177 batting right-handed on plastic, .259 batting left-handed on grass fields.... A career .275 hitter through the end of July, but only .235 thereafter.... Career average of .286 batting left-handed, .206 batting right-handed.... His career average against ground-ball pitchers (.288) is 51 points higher than his mark vs. fly-ballers (.237).... Career average of .150 in Late-Inning Pressure Situations is the lowest of any player over the 16 years since we first compiled those figures (minimum: 100 AB). The bottom four: Felix, Rusty Torrez (.151), Stan Jefferson (.156), and Dave Hostetler (.164).

Felix Fermin

Bats Right

Cleveland Indians	AB	H	2B	3B	HR	RBI	BB	SO	BA	SA	OBA
Season	414	106	13	2	1	40	26	22	.256	.304	.297
vs. Left-Handers	130	34	3	0	0	15	9	4	.262	.285	.303
vs. Right-Handers	284	72	10	2	1	25	17	18	.254	.313	.294
vs. Ground-Ballers	205	62	5	0	1	18	14	14	.302	.341	.345
vs. Fly-Ballers	209	44	8	2	0	22	12	8	.211	.268	.249
Home Games	205	57	12	1	1	24	8	13	.278	.361	.301
Road Games	209	49	1	1	0	16	18	9	.234	.249	.293
Grass Fields	351	86	13	1	1	32	21	18	.245	.296	.285
Artificial Turf	63	20	0	1	0	8	5	4	.317	.349	.362
April	36	9	1	1	1	4	1	1	.250	.417	.270
May	59	12	1	1	0	4	4	6	.203	.254	.254
June	84	20	5	0	0	6	4	3	.238	.298	.270
July	86	19	1	0	0	5	1	3	.221	.233	.227
August	72	22	5	0	0	12	7	3	.306	.375	.358
Sept./Oct.	77	24	0	0	0	9	9	6	.312	.312	.379
Leading Off Inn.	91	18	0	1	1	1	6	6	.198	.253	.247
Bases Empty	231	56	4	2	1	1	15	13	.242	.290	.289
Runners On	183	50	9	0	0	39	11	9	.273	.322	.307
Runners/Scor. Pos.	115	29	5	0	0	37	5	7	.252	.296	.272
Runners On/2 Out	92	24	7	0	0	23	8	5	.261	.337	.320
Scor. Pos./2 Out	65	16	5	0	0	22	4	4	.246	.323	.290
Late-Inning Pressure	28	10	1	0	0	1	2	0	.357	.393	.400
Leading Off	6	2	0	0	0	0	0	0	.333	.333	.333
Runners On	9	2	0	0	0	1	0	0	.222	.222	.222
Runners/Scor. Pos.	6	2	0	0	0	1	0	0	.333	.333	.333

RUNS BATTED IN	From 1B	From 2B	From 3B	Scoring Position
Totals	5/141	16/87	18/51	34/138
Percentage	3.5%	18.4%	35.3%	24.6%

Loves to face: Storm Davis (.444, 4-for-9)
Terry Leach (.571, 4-for-7)
Bobby Witt (.500, 5-for-10)

Hates to face: Bert Blyleven (.091, 1-for-11)
Wes Gardner (.100, 1-for-10)
Nolan Ryan (.083, 1-for-12)

Miscellaneous statistics: Ground outs-to-air outs ratio: 1.76 last season, 2.46 for career.... Grounded into 13 double plays in 82 opportunities (one per 6.3).... Drove in 11 of 25 runners from third base with less than two outs (44%).... Direction of balls hit to the outfield: 24% to left field, 36% to center, 39% to right.... Base running: Advanced from first base to third on 12 of 30 outfield singles (40%); scored from second on 7 of 12 (58%).... Made 3.21 assists per nine innings at shortstop.

Comments: Career ground outs-to-air outs ratio of 2.46 is the highest of any player over the 16 years we've bothered to take notice.... Led the majors with 32 sacrifice bunts in 1989, but had only 14 in 148 games last season. Cleveland's team total dropped from 72 to 54, reflecting only Fermin's shortfall.... One of three A.L. players to start 100 games from the ninth spot in the batting order: Ozzie Guillen (152), Fermin (112), and Mike Gallego (102). So despite playing 148 games, Fermin finished the season 44 plate appearances shy of the minimum for the batting title.... He batted .317 in 101 at-bats in the 7th inning or later, but was lifted for pinch hitters 56 times—all in the 7th inning or later. Carlos Baerga alone took his place 34 times.... Broke a streak of 654 homerless at-bats with his first (and, to date, his only) career home run on April 22 against Don Pall of the White Sox.... His streak of 104 plate appearances between strikeouts was the longest in the majors. Scott Sanderson finally got him.... Averaged one strikeout per 36.5 plate appearances vs. left-handed pitchers.... Error total dropped from 26 in 1989 to 16 last season.... Has a career batting average of .245 at Cleveland Stadium, .224 on other grass fields, .287 on artificial surfaces.

Tony Fernandez

Bats Left and Right

Toronto Blue Jays	AB	H	2B	3B	HR	RBI	BB	SO	BA	SA	OBA
Season	635	175	27	17	4	66	71	70	.276	.391	.352
vs. Left-Handers	202	48	6	2	1	13	31	18	.238	.302	.340
vs. Right-Handers	433	127	21	15	3	53	40	52	.293	.432	.358
vs. Ground-Ballers	287	77	11	7	2	28	25	30	.268	.376	.330
vs. Fly-Ballers	348	98	16	10	2	38	46	40	.282	.402	.369
Home Games	321	99	17	12	2	38	31	36	.308	.455	.376
Road Games	314	76	10	5	2	28	40	34	.242	.325	.328
Grass Fields	237	57	5	5	1	20	33	26	.241	.316	.335
Artificial Turf	398	118	22	12	3	46	38	44	.296	.435	.363
April	87	27	3	2	1	15	6	11	.310	.425	.368
May	111	24	3	1	1	3	17	17	.216	.288	.326
June	106	27	5	5	0	14	15	15	.255	.396	.352
July	101	23	3	5	0	8	11	11	.228	.356	.298
August	101	30	6	3	1	15	13	5	.297	.446	.385
Sept./Oct.	129	44	7	1	1	11	9	11	.341	.434	.381
Leading Off Inn.	151	38	6	2	1	1	22	20	.252	.338	.358
Bases Empty	376	95	14	8	1	1	45	46	.253	.340	.339
Runners On	259	80	13	9	3	65	26	24	.309	.463	.371
Runners/Scor. Pos.	152	47	8	6	3	60	20	16	.309	.500	.387
Runners On/2 Out	100	34	6	3	1	28	10	6	.340	.490	.405
Scor. Pos./2 Out	70	24	4	2	1	26	8	4	.343	.500	.418
Late-Inning Pressure	84	28	0	3	0	4	11	1	.333	.405	.412
Leading Off	19	6	0	0	0	0	1	0	.316	.316	.381
Runners On	28	8	0	1	0	4	6	0	.286	.357	.400
Runners/Scor. Pos.	18	3	0	1	0	4	4	0	.167	.278	.304

RUNS BATTED IN	From 1B	From 2B	From 3B	Scoring Position
Totals	9/165	25/116	28/67	53/183
Percentage	5.5%	21.6%	41.8%	29.0%

Loves to face: Dale Mohorcic (.714, 5-for-7)
Mike Morgan (.538, 7-for-13)
Dave Schmidt (.368, 7-for-19)

Hates to face: Neal Heaton (.250, 4-for-16)
Randy O'Neal (0-for-8)
Mark Thurmond (0-for-7)

Miscellaneous statistics: Ground outs-to-air outs ratio: 1.29 last season, 1.29 for career.... Grounded into 17 double plays in 118 opportunities (one per 6.9).... Drove in 18 of 31 runners from third base with less than two outs (58%).... Direction of balls hit to the outfield: 37% to left field, 28% to center, 35% to right batting left-handed; 18% to left, 42% to center, 40% to right batting right-handed.... Base running: Advanced from first base to third on 10 of 32 outfield singles (31%); scored from second on 13 of 16 (81%).... Made 3.12 assists per nine innings at shortstop.

Comments: Over the last six seasons, the Blue Jays had a record of 19–36 (.345) without Fernandez in the starting lineup.... Led the major leagues with 17 triples, the most by any player since Willie Wilson hit 21 in 1985. Over the last 40 years, only three players have hit 20 or more three-baggers in a season: Wilson, George Brett (20 in 1979), and Willie Mays (20 in 1957).... Batted much higher from the left side of the plate (.347) than from the right side (.225) at the Skydome last season, but on the road his averages were virtually the same from both sides of the plate.... Stole 26 bases in 39 attempts. His success rate of .667 was down from .750 over the previous three seasons.... Was thrown out trying to advance a base on a batted ball six times last season, tied for the most on the Blue Jays.... Struck out only once in 97 plate appearances in Late-Inning Pressure Situations, by far the best rate in the majors last season.... Has batted over .300 in Late-Inning Pressure Situations in five of the last six seasons. His LIPS average has been higher than his overall average in each of the last seven seasons. Has a career average of .326 in LIPS.... Batting average with two outs and runners in scoring position year by year since 1985: .324, .404, .375, .386, .138, .343.... Career average of one error per 51 chances at shortstop is best in baseball history. Previous leader: Larry Bowa (one per 49).

Cecil Fielder

Bats Right

Detroit Tigers	AB	H	2B	3B	HR	RBI	BB	SO	BA	SA	OBA
Season	573	159	25	1	51	132	90	182	.277	.592	.377
vs. Left-Handers	178	66	11	0	25	54	37	47	.371	.854	.479
vs. Right-Handers	395	93	14	1	26	78	53	135	.235	.473	.330
vs. Ground-Ballers	274	69	8	0	18	50	35	85	.252	.478	.343
vs. Fly-Ballers	299	90	17	1	33	82	55	97	.301	.696	.408
Home Games	271	76	13	0	25	60	52	81	.280	.605	.396
Road Games	302	83	12	1	26	72	38	101	.275	.579	.359
Grass Fields	484	131	21	0	43	107	77	152	.271	.581	.374
Artificial Turf	89	28	4	1	8	25	13	30	.315	.652	.394
April	70	17	1	0	7	19	8	19	.243	.557	.325
May	103	38	10	0	11	23	15	31	.369	.786	.458
June	99	26	1	0	8	23	16	33	.263	.515	.359
July	98	25	5	0	7	21	19	36	.255	.520	.373
August	94	28	7	1	9	25	21	31	.298	.681	.432
Sept./Oct.	109	25	1	0	9	21	11	32	.229	.486	.300
Leading Off Inn.	137	41	7	0	13	13	9	41	.299	.635	.347
Bases Empty	295	80	13	0	26	26	34	93	.271	.580	.348
Runners On	278	79	12	1	25	106	56	89	.284	.604	.405
Runners/Scor. Pos.	151	40	5	1	11	74	42	51	.265	.530	.426
Runners On/2 Out	129	37	4	0	13	45	24	36	.287	.620	.410
Scor. Pos./2 Out	67	15	1	0	5	28	18	22	.224	.463	.409
Late-Inning Pressure	65	13	2	0	2	6	15	25	.200	.323	.358
Leading Off	9	4	0	0	0	0	2	1	.444	.444	.545
Runners On	38	5	0	0	1	5	10	18	.132	.211	.327
Runners/Scor. Pos.	25	2	0	0	1	5	8	11	.080	.200	.324

RUNS BATTED IN	From 1B	From 2B	From 3B	Scoring Position
Totals	23/218	26/117	32/80	58/197
Percentage	10.6%	22.2%	40.0%	29.4%

Loves to face: Ron Robinson (3-for-3, 1 HR)
Dave Stewart (.571, 4-for-7, 2 HR)
Bobby Witt (.600, 3-for-5, 1 2B, 2 HR)

Hates to face: John Candelaria (.182, 4-for-22, 2 HR)
Chuck Cary (0-for-6, 1 BB, 5 SO)
Bob Welch (0-for-10, 2 BB)

Miscellaneous statistics: Ground outs-to-air outs ratio: 1.03 last season, 1.04 for career. . . . Grounded into 15 double plays in 133 opportunities (one per 8.9). . . . Drove in 20 of 44 runners from third base with less than two outs (45%). . . . Direction of balls hit to the outfield: 50% to left field, 26% to center, 24% to right. . . . Base running: Advanced from first base to third on 7 of 33 outfield singles (21%); scored from second on 12 of 15 (80%). . . . Made 0.81 assists per nine innings at first base.

Comments: Of the previous 15 players who led the major leagues in both home runs and RBIs in the same season, only one failed to win his league's MVP Award: Tony Armas in 1984, when Willie Hernandez was the A.L. MVP. . . . There have been 18 seasons of 50 or more home runs in major league history, but only twice have players reached that mark while batting below .300: Fielder and Roger Maris, who hit .269 in 1961. . . . Home runs and strikeouts seem to go hand in hand, but Fielder became only the sixth player to lead the majors in both categories in the same season. The others: Babe Ruth (1918, 1923–24, 1930), Hack Wilson (1927), Jimmie Foxx (1933), Mike Schmidt (1974–76), and Reggie Jackson (1982). . . . Prior to Fielder, the most strikeouts by a player with 50 or more home runs was 112, by Mickey Mantle in 1961, when he hit 54 homers. . . . Fielder's total of 132 RBIs was the highest by a Tigers player since 1961, when Rocky Colavito had 140 and Norm Cash had 132. . . . His total of 25 home runs vs. left-handers was five more than the highest total over the previous 15 years. . . . Batted 135 points higher vs. left-handers (.371) than vs. right-handers (.235) last season, the 3d-largest margin in the majors. . . . Batted 89 points higher in night games (.301) than in day games (.213) last season, the 3d-largest margin in the majors. . . . How'd he do against southpaws at night? Oh, mama! A .368 batting average with nine doubles and 18 home runs in 133 at-bats.

Steve Finley

Bats Left

Baltimore Orioles	AB	H	2B	3B	HR	RBI	BB	SO	BA	SA	OBA
Season	464	119	16	4	3	37	32	53	.256	.328	.304
vs. Left-Handers	114	22	2	0	1	9	2	15	.193	.237	.202
vs. Right-Handers	350	97	14	4	2	28	30	38	.277	.357	.336
vs. Ground-Ballers	210	59	7	1	1	19	14	26	.281	.338	.326
vs. Fly-Ballers	254	60	9	3	2	18	18	27	.236	.319	.286
Home Games	247	57	9	3	1	14	15	31	.231	.304	.274
Road Games	217	62	7	1	2	23	17	22	.286	.355	.338
Grass Fields	405	104	15	4	1	29	29	46	.257	.321	.307
Artificial Turf	59	15	1	0	2	8	3	7	.254	.373	.286
April	58	17	2	2	0	5	7	7	.293	.397	.369
May	75	14	3	1	0	4	6	9	.187	.253	.247
June	81	20	5	0	0	4	4	7	.247	.309	.299
July	50	14	1	0	1	4	4	9	.280	.360	.327
August	78	24	3	0	0	6	5	5	.308	.346	.341
Sept./Oct.	122	30	2	1	2	14	6	16	.246	.328	.277
Leading Off Inn.	142	27	8	2	0	0	12	15	.190	.275	.253
Bases Empty	280	70	13	3	3	3	20	30	.250	.350	.302
Runners On	184	49	3	1	0	34	12	23	.266	.293	.307
Runners/Scor. Pos.	102	26	1	1	0	34	9	20	.255	.284	.308
Runners On/2 Out	62	15	1	0	0	14	4	7	.242	.258	.288
Scor. Pos./2 Out	48	13	1	0	0	14	4	6	.271	.292	.327
Late-Inning Pressure	68	15	1	0	1	3	4	11	.221	.279	.270
Leading Off	16	0	0	0	0	0	2	0	.000	.000	.111
Runners On	29	8	1	0	0	2	2	5	.276	.310	.313
Runners/Scor. Pos.	12	2	0	0	0	2	1	3	.167	.167	.214

RUNS BATTED IN	From 1B	From 2B	From 3B	Scoring Position
Totals	0/131	14/88	20/42	34/130
Percentage	0.0%	15.9%	47.6%	26.2%

Loves to face: Charlie Hough (.455, 5-for-11)
Mike Moore (.429, 6-for-14)
Jack Morris (.400, 4-for-10)

Hates to face: Bob Welch (.063, 1-for-16)
Matt Young (0-for-7, 7 ground outs)

Miscellaneous statistics: Ground outs-to-air outs ratio: 1.72 last season, 1.54 for career. . . . Grounded into 8 double plays in 112 opportunities (one per 14.0). . . . Drove in 15 of 24 runners from third base with less than two outs (63%). . . . Direction of balls hit to the outfield: 28% to left field, 31% to center, 41% to right. . . . Base running: Advanced from first base to third on 6 of 22 outfield singles (27%); scored from second on 10 of 16 (63%). . . . Made 2.54 putouts per nine innings in right field, 2d-highest rate in A.L. The leader was teammate Joe Orsulak.

Comments: Was thrown out trying to advance a base on a batted ball six times last season, the most of any player on the Orioles. . . . One of four Orioles to play all three outfield positions, along with Brady Anderson, Dave Gallagher, and Brad Komminsk. Finley played 21 games in left field, 44 in center, 73 in right. . . . Drove in 37 runs, of which only six gave the Orioles a lead, and none of which proved to be a game-winner. . . . Orioles left fielders drove in 50 runs, fewer than any other team's LFs. . . . Batted 84 points higher vs. right-handers (.277) than vs. left-handers (.193) last season, the 4th-largest margin in the majors. He averaged one walk per 61 plate appearances vs. southpaws, one per 13 vs. right-handers. . . . He batted 110 points higher vs. right-handers than lefties in 1989 (.268 to .158). . . . Hitless in 12 at-bats as a pinch-hitter last season to lower his career average in that role to .059 (1-for-17). . . . Just in case you overlooked it, he was 0-for-16 leading off innings in Late-Inning Pressure Situations. . . . Career average of .143 (3-for-21) with the bases loaded. . . . This could be the only hitter ever thrilled at the thought of leaving Memorial Stadium for the Astrodome. His two-year composite: .227, one HR at home; .284, four HR on the road.

Carlton Fisk

Bats Right

Chicago White Sox	AB	H	2B	3B	HR	RBI	BB	SO	BA	SA	OBA
Season	452	129	21	0	18	65	61	73	.285	.451	.378
vs. Left-Handers	165	52	10	0	9	30	21	23	.315	.539	.397
vs. Right-Handers	287	77	11	0	9	35	40	50	.268	.401	.367
vs. Ground-Ballers	198	56	12	0	5	29	21	28	.283	.419	.366
vs. Fly-Ballers	254	73	9	0	13	36	40	45	.287	.476	.387
Home Games	219	63	13	0	5	37	33	30	.288	.416	.387
Road Games	233	66	8	0	13	28	28	43	.283	.485	.370
Grass Fields	378	112	19	0	14	57	51	60	.296	.458	.386
Artificial Turf	74	17	2	0	4	8	10	13	.230	.419	.337
April	55	17	4	0	0	5	4	10	.309	.382	.356
May	84	21	1	0	3	13	13	15	.250	.369	.364
June	54	15	1	0	3	6	11	5	.278	.463	.400
July	70	21	5	0	3	10	11	6	.300	.500	.398
August	85	21	5	0	4	13	10	19	.247	.447	.340
Sept./Oct.	104	34	5	0	5	18	12	18	.327	.519	.407
Leading Off Inn.	97	37	7	0	7	7	11	12	.381	.670	.450
Bases Empty	262	82	12	0	14	14	30	42	.313	.519	.392
Runners On	190	47	9	0	4	51	31	31	.247	.358	.360
Runners/Scor. Pos.	131	29	6	0	3	47	26	21	.221	.336	.360
Runners On/2 Out	94	23	6	0	4	29	15	15	.245	.436	.355
Scor. Pos./2 Out	76	17	4	0	3	25	13	11	.224	.395	.344
Late-Inning Pressure	60	16	5	0	2	11	9	14	.267	.450	.362
Leading Off	11	4	1	0	0	0	2	2	.364	.455	.462
Runners On	25	7	2	0	2	11	6	4	.280	.600	.419
Runners/Scor. Pos.	20	6	2	0	2	11	6	4	.300	.700	.462

RUNS BATTED IN	From 1B	From 2B	From 3B	Scoring Position
Totals	7/116	18/101	22/52	40/153
Percentage	6.0%	17.8%	42.3%	26.1%

Loves to face: John Candelaria (.417, 5-for-12, 3 HR)
Mike Jeffcoat (.444, 4-for-9, 1 2B, 1 3B, 1 HR)
Dan Schatzeder (.667, 4-for-6, 2 2B, 1 HR)

Hates to face: Mike Moore (.161, 5-for-31)
Jack Morris (.150, 9-for-60, 2 HR)
Curt Young (.077, 2-for-26)

Miscellaneous statistics: Ground outs-to-air outs ratio: 1.10 last season, 0.80 for career. . . . Grounded into 12 double plays in 73 opportunities (one per 6.1). . . . Drove in 13 of 21 runners from third base with less than two outs (62%). . . . Direction of balls hit to the outfield: 44% to left field, 30% to center, 27% to right. . . . Base running: Advanced from first base to third on 9 of 31 outfield singles (29%); scored from second on 9 of 17 (53%). . . . Opposing base stealers: 71-for-113 (63%).

Comments: Set three major career home run records within six weeks: most at Comiskey (94), most in White Sox history (192), and most by a catcher (332). . . . Despite holding the club record for career home runs (192), Fisk ranks only fourth among White Sox in home-run rate, with an average of one HR per 21.8 at-bats (minimum: 50 HR), behind Dick Allen (one HR per 14.3 AB), Ron Kittle (one per 15.5 AB), and Roy Sievers (one per 17.0 AB). . . . Did not hit his first home run until his 25th game last season. . . . Struck out only twice in 59 1st-inning plate appearances, while batting .319 in the first frame last season. . . . Has higher batting averages in each of the last two seasons (.293 and .285, in that order) than in any of the previous five, during which he batted .242 combined. . . . Started only 12 games as a designated hitter last season, six of them in September. . . . Has now caught 206 games since his 40th birthday. Only two other players in major league history caught more than 100: Bob Boone (290) and Chief Zimmer (116). . . . Enters the 1991 season with 2041 games behind the plate, 184 fewer than Boone, baseball's all-time leader. . . . The White Sox have had only two All-Star starters over the last 12 seasons: Fisk (catcher, 1981–82 and 1985) and Harold Baines (designated hitter, 1989). The last Chisox pitcher to start an All-Star game was Early Wynn, in 1959.

Scott Fletcher

Bats Right

Chicago White Sox	AB	H	2B	3B	HR	RBI	BB	SO	BA	SA	OBA
Season	509	123	18	3	4	56	45	63	.242	.312	.304
vs. Left-Handers	173	49	4	0	1	13	21	16	.283	.324	.365
vs. Right-Handers	336	74	14	3	3	43	24	47	.220	.307	.271
vs. Ground-Ballers	230	60	7	2	2	25	14	26	.261	.335	.306
vs. Fly-Ballers	279	63	11	1	2	31	31	37	.226	.294	.303
Home Games	265	64	9	1	1	29	20	32	.242	.294	.291
Road Games	244	59	9	2	3	27	25	31	.242	.332	.319
Grass Fields	421	102	15	1	4	48	38	54	.242	.311	.304
Artificial Turf	88	21	3	2	0	8	7	9	.239	.318	.306
April	52	9	1	0	0	3	10	12	.173	.192	.302
May	87	20	4	2	1	7	10	11	.230	.356	.309
June	91	25	4	1	1	7	5	6	.275	.374	.327
July	82	26	3	0	1	13	7	9	.317	.390	.367
August	91	20	0	0	0	11	4	10	.220	.220	.250
Sept./Oct.	106	23	6	0	1	15	9	15	.217	.302	.280
Leading Off Inn.	128	19	3	0	0	0	10	18	.148	.172	.216
Bases Empty	292	53	8	1	1	1	24	39	.182	.226	.248
Runners On	217	70	10	2	3	55	21	24	.323	.429	.377
Runners/Scor. Pos.	126	34	6	1	2	50	12	16	.270	.381	.322
Runners On/2 Out	100	26	3	1	2	21	6	13	.260	.370	.308
Scor. Pos./2 Out	59	13	2	0	1	17	5	9	.220	.305	.281
Late-Inning Pressure	74	15	2	0	1	7	11	11	.203	.270	.310
Leading Off	21	3	0	0	0	0	2	3	.143	.143	.217
Runners On	27	6	0	0	1	7	5	4	.222	.333	.353
Runners/Scor. Pos.	16	4	0	0	1	7	3	4	.250	.438	.350

RUNS BATTED IN	From 1B	From 2B	From 3B	Scoring Position
Totals	8/148	21/105	23/55	44/160
Percentage	5.4%	20.0%	41.8%	27.5%

Loves to face: John Candelaria (.579, 11-for-19)
Dave LaPoint (.483, 14-for-29)
Gene Nelson (.412, 7-for-17, 1 HR)

Hates to face: Dennis Lamp (.125, 2-for-16, 1 3B)
Dave Schmidt (.125, 3-for-24)
Dave Stieb (.171, 7-for-41)

Miscellaneous statistics: Ground outs-to-air outs ratio: 0.94 last season, 1.43 for career. . . . Grounded into 10 double plays in 104 opportunities (one per 10.4). . . . Drove in 18 of 32 runners from third base with less than two outs (56%). . . . Direction of balls hit to the outfield: 39% to left field, 30% to center, 30% to right. . . . Base running: Advanced from first base to third on 10 of 26 outfield singles (38%); scored from second on 14 of 18 (78%). . . . Made 2.97 assists per nine innings at second base.

Comments: Batted 141 points higher with runners on base (.323) than with the bases empty (.182) last season, the 2d-largest margin in the majors. Career breakdown: .294 with runners on base, .245 with the bases empty. . . . His overall batting average declined for the fourth consecutive season. Year by year since 1986: .300, .287, .276, .253, .242. . . . His streak of hits in eight consecutive at-bats, the longest in the majors last season, was stopped by Roger Clemens. . . . Played 151 games at second base last season, compared to only 154 there over nine previous years (including 53 errorless games following his acquisition from Texas in 1989). . . . Career average of one error per 85 chances at second base ranks fourth among players with 300 or more games there, behind Jose Oquendo (157), Ryne Sandberg (92), and Tommy Herr (88). . . . This will surprise you (or else): Fletcher has played at least 140 games and accumulated at least 500 at-bats in each of the last five seasons. . . . Batting average in Late-Inning Pressure Situations has been lower than his overall average in each of the last five seasons. Hit a game-tying, 7th-inning, 3-run home run off Dan Petry on July 16 last season, the only HR he has hit in 485 career at-bats in Late-Inning Pressure Situations.

Julio Franco

Bats Right

Texas Rangers	AB	H	2B	3B	HR	RBI	BB	SO	BA	SA	OBA
Season	582	172	27	1	11	69	82	83	.296	.402	.383
vs. Left-Handers	179	53	9	0	3	19	31	25	.296	.397	.398
vs. Right-Handers	403	119	18	1	8	50	51	58	.295	.404	.376
vs. Ground-Ballers	273	72	12	0	4	29	38	33	.264	.352	.354
vs. Fly-Ballers	309	100	15	1	7	40	44	50	.324	.447	.409
Home Games	303	96	16	0	4	27	41	37	.317	.409	.399
Road Games	279	76	11	1	7	42	41	46	.272	.394	.366
Grass Fields	485	145	23	0	9	53	68	70	.299	.402	.385
Artificial Turf	97	27	4	1	2	16	14	13	.278	.402	.375
April	81	20	4	0	1	10	7	14	.247	.333	.315
May	97	33	7	0	3	12	13	17	.340	.505	.418
June	114	33	3	1	2	17	12	13	.289	.386	.357
July	86	27	6	0	1	9	14	12	.314	.419	.406
August	97	30	3	0	0	10	17	11	.309	.340	.409
Sept./Oct.	107	29	4	0	4	11	19	16	.271	.421	.386
Leading Off Inn.	119	30	5	0	1	1	12	22	.252	.319	.321
Bases Empty	332	88	18	1	2	2	39	55	.265	.343	.344
Runners On	250	84	9	0	9	67	43	28	.336	.480	.432
Runners/Scor. Pos.	144	43	4	0	5	58	29	16	.299	.431	.415
Runners On/2 Out	90	27	5	0	3	23	21	12	.300	.456	.438
Scor. Pos./2 Out	66	17	2	0	2	20	18	11	.258	.379	.424
Late-Inning Pressure	89	32	4	0	2	8	12	12	.360	.472	.441
Leading Off	29	10	1	0	1	1	0	4	.345	.483	.345
Runners On	38	14	1	0	1	7	9	3	.368	.474	.489
Runners/Scor. Pos.	23	7	0	0	1	7	8	3	.304	.435	.484

RUNS BATTED IN	From 1B	From 2B	From 3B	Scoring Position
Totals	9/174	23/110	26/57	49/167
Percentage	5.2%	20.9%	45.6%	29.3%

Loves to face: Allan Anderson (.583, 7-for-12)
Scott Sanderson (.375, 3-for-8, 2 HR)
Bob Welch (.519, 14-for-27, 0 BB)

Hates to face: Bert Blyleven (.188, 6-for-32)
Andy Hawkins (.063, 1-for-16, 2 BB)
Dennis Lamp (.174, 4-for-23)

Miscellaneous statistics: Ground outs-to-air outs ratio: 1.35 last season, 1.55 for career.... Grounded into 12 double plays in 130 opportunities (one per 10.8).... Drove in 17 of 27 runners from third base with less than two outs (63%).... Direction of balls hit to the outfield: 25% to left field, 31% to center, 44% to right.... Base running: Advanced from first base to third on 30 of 50 outfield singles (60%), shared 4th-highest rate in A.L.; scored from second on 16 of 20 (80%).... Made 3.05 assists per nine innings at second base.

Comments: One of three players in major league history with at least 150 hits and 10 stolen bases in his rookie season and for at least seven seasons thereafter. The others: Ben Chapman (11 years, 1930–40) and Ryne Sandberg (a current nine-year streak that started in 1982). Honus Wagner's 15-year streak (1898–1912), which started in his second season, is the longest overall.... His average of one error for every 41 chances last season was the worst among American League second basemen, and his 19 errors there tied Harold Reynolds for most in the majors. However, he led all second basemen by starting 46 double plays.... Stole 20 bases in 22 attempts with right-handers on the mound (91%), but only 11 of 19 vs. southpaws (58%).... Of his 172 hits, 61 were hit to the opposite field, tying him with Kirby Puckett for second most in the league, behind Wade Boggs (81).... Was recalled for a pinch hitter only three times last season, twice with the Rangers leading by eight runs, and once with them trailing by 12.... Grounded into only 12 double plays, roughly half his average over the previous seven years (23).... Year by year walk totals, starting with 1986: 32, 57, 56, 66, 82; next thing you know, he'll be telling us you *can* walk off the island!

Travis Fryman

Bats Right

Detroit Tigers	AB	H	2B	3B	HR	RBI	BB	SO	BA	SA	OBA
Season	232	69	11	1	9	27	17	51	.297	.470	.348
vs. Left-Handers	88	28	7	0	5	12	8	16	.318	.568	.375
vs. Right-Handers	144	41	4	1	4	15	9	35	.285	.410	.331
vs. Ground-Ballers	110	29	3	1	2	10	6	28	.264	.364	.308
vs. Fly-Ballers	122	40	8	0	7	17	11	23	.328	.566	.383
Home Games	108	28	3	0	5	8	14	26	.259	.426	.350
Road Games	124	41	8	1	4	19	3	25	.331	.508	.346
Grass Fields	205	63	9	1	9	24	16	42	.307	.493	.360
Artificial Turf	27	6	2	0	0	3	1	9	.222	.296	.250
April	0	0	0	0	0	0	0	0	—	—	—
May	0	0	0	0	0	0	0	0	—	—	—
June	0	0	0	0	0	0	0	0	—	—	—
July	53	14	1	0	4	7	4	12	.264	.509	.316
August	87	29	5	0	2	4	7	20	.333	.460	.389
Sept./Oct.	92	26	5	1	3	16	6	19	.283	.457	.327
Leading Off Inn.	47	15	3	0	1	1	3	11	.319	.447	.360
Bases Empty	132	43	6	0	6	6	8	26	.326	.508	.364
Runners On	100	26	5	1	3	21	9	25	.260	.420	.327
Runners/Scor. Pos.	55	12	2	1	2	17	6	14	.218	.400	.295
Runners On/2 Out	39	11	3	1	2	16	4	7	.282	.564	.349
Scor. Pos./2 Out	27	8	2	1	2	15	2	5	.296	.667	.345
Late-Inning Pressure	16	8	2	0	0	2	1	3	.500	.625	.529
Leading Off	7	5	1	0	0	0	0	0	.714	.857	.714
Runners On	3	2	1	0	0	2	0	1	.667	1.000	.667
Runners/Scor. Pos.	2	1	1	0	0	2	0	1	.500	1.000	.500

RUNS BATTED IN	From 1B	From 2B	From 3B	Scoring Position
Totals	7/75	8/46	3/15	11/61
Percentage	9.3%	17.4%	20.0%	18.0%

Loves to face: Allan Anderson (.600, 3-for-5, 1 HR)
Greg A. Harris (.500, 3-for-6)

Hates to face: Bobby Witt (0-for-3, 2 SO)

Miscellaneous statistics: Ground outs-to-air outs ratio: 0.93 last season, his first in the majors.... Grounded into 3 double plays in 49 opportunities (one per 16.3).... Drove in 0 of 5 runners from third base with less than two outs.... Direction of balls hit to the outfield: 43% to left field, 32% to center, 26% to right.... Base running: Advanced from first base to third on 2 of 7 outfield singles (29%); scored from second on 4 of 10 (40%), shared 2d-lowest rate in A.L.... Made 2.20 assists per nine innings at third base.

Comments: Had the 3d-highest batting average among rookies with at least 250 plate appearances last season. The top five: Hal Morris, Cin. (.340); Alex Cole, Clev. (.300); Fryman, Det. (.297); Sandy Alomar, Clev. (.290); Delino DeShields, Mtl. (.289).... The highest batting average by a Tigers rookie with 200 or more at-bats was .352 in 1922, by a man more known for leading the Braves to consecutive N.L. titles in the 1950s: Fred Haney.... Averaged one home run per 17.4 at-bats vs. left-handed pitchers, 2d-best rate among American League rookies, behind Frank Thomas (one per 14.2 AB). Hector Villanueva of the Cubs led N.L. rookies (one per 10.5 AB).... He was the 2d-youngest player to appear in at least 50 games last season. He was born in March 1969, eight months before Ken Griffey, Jr.... Batted .342 in 73 at-bats in the seventh inning or later.... Batted .379 in day games, .270 at night.... Batted 72 points higher in road games than at Tiger Stadium.... So naturally you'll wonder, "How did he do in day games on the road?" He started four such games, and collected at least two hits in each of them. His totals: .500 (9-for-18), with a double and two home runs.... Some pretty talented players compiled similar statistics as rookies: Bill Nicholson (1939), Donn Clendenon (1962), and Joe Carter (1984).

Gary Gaetti

Bats Right

Minnesota Twins	AB	H	2B	3B	HR	RBI	BB	SO	BA	SA	OBA
Season	577	132	27	5	16	85	36	101	.229	.376	.274
vs. Left-Handers	166	37	8	0	5	18	14	28	.223	.361	.283
vs. Right-Handers	411	95	19	5	11	67	22	73	.231	.382	.270
vs. Ground-Ballers	251	56	10	3	5	35	17	45	.223	.347	.277
vs. Fly-Ballers	326	76	17	2	11	50	19	56	.233	.399	.271
Home Games	286	68	15	3	7	43	16	40	.238	.385	.279
Road Games	291	64	12	2	9	42	20	61	.220	.368	.269
Grass Fields	216	50	9	1	6	33	18	42	.231	.366	.289
Artificial Turf	361	82	18	4	10	52	18	59	.227	.382	.265
April	62	16	2	1	1	5	7	13	.258	.371	.329
May	97	25	7	1	5	26	7	17	.258	.505	.299
June	97	22	5	0	3	11	4	19	.227	.371	.260
July	108	27	8	1	3	19	12	15	.250	.426	.328
August	101	16	2	1	2	8	3	20	.158	.257	.183
Sept./Oct.	112	26	3	1	2	16	3	17	.232	.330	.256
Leading Off Inn.	144	34	6	2	4	4	6	25	.236	.389	.267
Bases Empty	309	65	13	4	7	7	11	60	.210	.346	.240
Runners On	268	67	14	1	9	78	25	41	.250	.410	.310
Runners/Scor. Pos.	156	41	9	1	7	71	17	28	.263	.468	.324
Runners On/2 Out	113	34	8	1	4	33	12	22	.301	.496	.373
Scor. Pos./2 Out	72	23	4	1	4	31	8	15	.319	.569	.395
Late-Inning Pressure	83	17	1	1	1	8	5	13	.205	.277	.244
Leading Off	20	4	0	0	0	0	1	5	.200	.200	.238
Runners On	38	9	1	0	1	8	3	4	.237	.342	.279
Runners/Scor. Pos.	21	5	1	0	0	6	1	2	.238	.286	.250

RUNS BATTED IN	From 1B	From 2B	From 3B	Scoring Position
Totals	13/192	15/117	41/74	56/191
Percentage	6.8%	12.8%	55.4%	29.3%

Loves to face: Greg A. Harris (.625, 10-for-16, 1 HR, 6 SO)
Gene Nelson (.414, 12-for-29, 2 HR)
Joe Price (.500, 2-for-4, 2 HR)

Hates to face: Jeff Russell (.063, 1-for-16)
Bobby Witt (.125, 3-for-24)
Matt Young (.171, 6-for-35)

Miscellaneous statistics: Ground outs-to-air outs ratio: 1.04 last season, 0.99 for career. . . . Grounded into 22 double plays in 135 opportunities (one per 6.1). . . . Drove in 25 of 41 runners from third base with less than two outs (61%). . . . Direction of balls hit to the outfield: 50% to left field, 32% to center, 18% to right. . . . Base running: Advanced from first base to third on 3 of 23 outfield singles (13%); scored from second on 9 of 14 (64%). . . . Made 2.22 assists per nine innings at third base, 2d-highest rate in A.L.

Comments: Sixth player in A.L. history to reach 1000 games at third base with 200 home runs. The others: Sal Bando, George Brett, Doug DeCinces, Graig Nettles, and Brooks Robinson. . . . Was thrown out trying to advance a base on a batted ball nine times last season, the most on the Twins. . . . Started 33 double plays, to lead major league third basemen, and started two triple plays in the same game!. . .Some trends just don't figure. During the 10 seasons from 1956 through 1965, there were no around-the-horn triple-play ground outs. Since then, 29 of 110 TPs have been of that ilk. Of those 29, Gaetti has started four of the last six. He also started a TP on a line drive in 1984. . . . Drove in 85 runs for the season, 28 of which broke a tie to give the Twins a lead (16 stood up as game-winners). Only the leader and runner-up in *overall* RBIs had more go-aheads: Cecil Fielder (30) and Kelly Gruber (29). . . . Overall batting average was his lowest in any full season in the majors. . . . Has hit for a higher average against fly-ball pitchers than he has against ground-ballers in each of the last five seasons. . . . His home run totals have declined by at least three each year since 1987. The last five seasons: 34, 31, 28, 19, 16. Only four players declined by three or more for five straight years: Curt Blefary (1968–72), George Foster (1978–82), Babe Ruth (1931–35), and Norm Siebern (1963–67). Those streaks ended the careers of Blefary and the Babe.

Greg Gagne

Bats Right

Minnesota Twins	AB	H	2B	3B	HR	RBI	BB	SO	BA	SA	OBA
Season	388	91	22	3	7	38	24	76	.235	.361	.280
vs. Left-Handers	124	37	12	1	3	18	10	27	.298	.484	.353
vs. Right-Handers	264	54	10	2	4	20	14	49	.205	.303	.244
vs. Ground-Ballers	178	45	11	1	2	22	12	23	.253	.360	.298
vs. Fly-Ballers	210	46	11	2	5	16	12	53	.219	.362	.263
Home Games	182	45	13	2	3	20	13	37	.247	.390	.298
Road Games	206	46	9	1	4	18	11	39	.223	.335	.263
Grass Fields	163	39	9	1	2	13	8	26	.239	.344	.275
Artificial Turf	225	52	13	2	5	25	16	50	.231	.373	.283
April	56	16	4	0	3	8	11	10	.286	.518	.403
May	73	15	3	2	0	4	2	19	.205	.301	.227
June	81	18	6	1	1	9	2	19	.222	.358	.238
July	75	16	4	0	1	6	3	10	.213	.307	.253
August	62	18	4	0	1	8	4	10	.290	.403	.328
Sept./Oct.	41	8	1	0	1	3	2	8	.195	.293	.233
Leading Off Inn.	86	22	5	2	1	1	3	10	.256	.395	.281
Bases Empty	220	54	12	3	4	4	13	35	.245	.382	.291
Runners On	168	37	10	0	3	34	11	41	.220	.333	.265
Runners/Scor. Pos.	89	16	4	0	0	26	9	26	.180	.225	.250
Runners On/2 Out	72	17	6	0	1	8	6	17	.236	.361	.295
Scor. Pos./2 Out	36	4	2	0	0	5	4	13	.111	.167	.200
Late-Inning Pressure	45	17	5	1	0	1	2	6	.378	.533	.396
Leading Off	12	5	2	0	0	0	1	1	.417	.583	.462
Runners On	15	2	1	0	0	1	0	4	.133	.200	.125
Runners/Scor. Pos.	5	1	0	0	0	1	0	1	.200	.200	.167

RUNS BATTED IN	From 1B	From 2B	From 3B	Scoring Position
Totals	7/124	10/76	14/32	24/108
Percentage	5.6%	13.2%	43.8%	22.2%

Loves to face: Chuck Cary (.364, 4-for-11, 2 2B, 1 HR)
Storm Davis (.400, 8-for-20, 2 HR)
Jeff D. Robinson (.500, 2-for-4, 1 HR)

Hates to face: Wes Gardner (0-for-7, 4 SO)
Walt Terrell (.118, 4-for-34, 4 BB)
Bobby Witt (.148, 4-for-27, 1 HR)

Miscellaneous statistics: Ground outs-to-air outs ratio: 1.03 last season, 0.98 for career. . . . Grounded into 5 double plays in 76 opportunities (one per 15.2). . . . Drove in 12 of 19 runners from third base with less than two outs (63%). . . . Direction of balls hit to the outfield: 31% to left field, 30% to center, 39% to right. . . . Base running: Advanced from first base to third on 6 of 17 outfield singles (35%); scored from second on 8 of 11 (73%). . . . Made 3.16 assists per nine innings at shortstop.

Comments: Started 121 games, all but one of them from either the eighth or ninth slots in the batting order. . . . Established a personal best with one error per 41 chances at shortstop. His errors at that position year by year since 1986: 26, 18, 18, 18, 14. . . . Has batted over .290 vs. left-handed pitchers in each of the last three seasons, but compiled a .227 mark against right-handers during that time. . . . Career average of .195 with two outs and runners in scoring position. Year by year since 1987: .211, .194, .164, and .111. Has manager Tom Kelly noticed? You bet—Gagne was removed for a pinch hitter a team-high 31 times last season, and batted only once with two outs and RISP in Late-Inning Pressure Situations. . . . Had a career-high batting average in LIPS, but the breakdown wasn't flattering: .500 with the bases empty (15-for-30), .133 with men on base (2-for-15). . . . Has a career average of .140 (6-for-43, 1 HR) with the bases loaded. . . . Career average of .159 at Tiger Stadium is his lowest at any ballpark. . . . Consistency, thy name is not Gagne. His batting averages have moved by an average of 28 points per season over the last five seasons. Year by year since 1985: .225, .250, .265, .236, .272, .235.

Mike Gallego

Bats Right

Oakland A's	AB	H	2B	3B	HR	RBI	BB	SO	BA	SA	OBA
Season	389	80	13	2	3	34	35	50	.206	.272	.277
vs. Left-Handers	128	23	5	0	1	9	9	19	.180	.242	.234
vs. Right-Handers	261	57	8	2	2	25	26	31	.218	.287	.297
vs. Ground-Ballers	217	49	8	1	2	22	17	27	.226	.300	.288
vs. Fly-Ballers	172	31	5	1	1	12	18	23	.180	.238	.263
Home Games	187	40	4	1	1	14	24	20	.214	.262	.305
Road Games	202	40	9	1	2	20	11	30	.198	.282	.249
Grass Fields	324	70	9	2	2	27	31	36	.216	.275	.289
Artificial Turf	65	10	4	0	1	7	4	14	.154	.262	.214
April	44	4	1	0	1	4	5	4	.091	.182	.184
May	57	16	4	2	0	8	6	10	.281	.421	.349
June	57	14	2	0	0	5	4	9	.246	.281	.290
July	93	19	5	0	1	9	5	8	.204	.290	.253
August	66	14	0	0	1	7	9	3	.212	.258	.303
Sept./Oct.	72	13	1	0	0	1	6	16	.181	.194	.272
Leading Off Inn.	90	13	2	0	2	2	12	13	.144	.233	.245
Bases Empty	207	33	7	1	2	2	25	30	.159	.232	.250
Runners On	182	47	6	1	1	32	10	20	.258	.319	.308
Runners/Scor. Pos.	94	19	3	0	0	27	8	13	.202	.234	.287
Runners On/2 Out	83	21	3	1	0	11	5	14	.253	.313	.311
Scor. Pos./2 Out	43	9	1	0	0	8	3	9	.209	.233	.292
Late-Inning Pressure	32	8	1	0	0	4	4	4	.250	.281	.333
Leading Off	9	2	1	0	0	0	1	2	.222	.333	.300
Runners On	15	4	0	0	0	4	1	0	.267	.267	.313
Runners/Scor. Pos.	10	3	0	0	0	4	1	0	.300	.300	.364

RUNS BATTED IN	From 1B	From 2B	From 3B	Scoring Position
Totals	6/140	10/72	15/40	25/112
Percentage	4.3%	13.9%	37.5%	22.3%

Loves to face: Brian Holman (.333, 3-for-9)
Danny Jackson (.625, 5-for-8)
Lance McCullers (.500, 2-for-4, 2 2B)

Hates to face: Dennis Lamp (0-for-7)
Mark Langston (.083, 1-for-12, 2 BB, 6 SO)

Miscellaneous statistics: Ground outs-to-air outs ratio: 1.24 last season, 1.34 for career. . . . Grounded into 13 double plays in 96 opportunities (one per 7.4). . . . Drove in 12 of 21 runners from third base with less than two outs (57%). . . . Direction of balls hit to the outfield: 29% to left field, 33% to center, 38% to right. . . . Base running: Advanced from first base to third on 7 of 20 outfield singles (35%); scored from second on 6 of 9 (67%). . . . Made 3.51 assists per nine innings at second base, highest rate in majors.

Comments: Has never committed an error in 111 chances at shortstop on artificial turf—regular-season, of course. . . . Athletics pitchers allowed an average of 3.2 runs per nine innings with Gallego at second base, 3.8 with Willie Randolph there. . . . Started 102 games from the ninth slot in the batting order. Only two other A.L. players started at least 100 games there: Ozzie Guillen (152) and Felix Fermin (112). . . . His April batting average was the lowest in the major leagues. . . . Had 17 sacrifice bunts, tying him with Billy Ripken for the American League lead. . . . Was removed for a pinch hitter 32 times last season, edging out Lance Blankenship (29) for the team lead. . . . Batting average vs. left-handed pitchers was by far a career low. Career breakdown now stands at .242 vs. left-handers, .217 vs. right-handers. . . . His .250 batting average in Late-Inning Pressure Situations raised his career average to .167. . . . Despite last season's breakdown, he still has a career mark 35 points higher on artificial turf (.255) than on grass (.220). . . . Has a career average of .057 (2-for-35) at Memorial Stadium, the only ballpark in which he has never had an extra-base hit. (And time is running out.). . . Played all four games of the World Series after batting only once in Oakland's two previous Series appearances. (He had only one hit in 11 trips to the plate, and committed an error in Game 1.)

Jim Gantner

Bats Left

Milwaukee Brewers	AB	H	2B	3B	HR	RBI	BB	SO	BA	SA	OBA
Season	323	85	8	5	0	25	29	19	.263	.319	.328
vs. Left-Handers	88	27	2	0	0	9	12	6	.307	.330	.390
vs. Right-Handers	235	58	6	5	0	16	17	13	.247	.315	.303
vs. Ground-Ballers	145	43	4	1	0	14	9	5	.297	.338	.338
vs. Fly-Ballers	178	42	4	4	0	11	20	14	.236	.303	.320
Home Games	158	44	5	0	0	12	17	9	.278	.310	.356
Road Games	165	41	3	5	0	13	12	10	.248	.327	.299
Grass Fields	279	76	8	3	0	19	27	16	.272	.323	.341
Artificial Turf	44	9	0	2	0	6	2	3	.205	.295	.239
April	0	0	0	0	0	0	0	0	—	—	—
May	0	0	0	0	0	0	0	0	—	—	—
June	33	9	1	0	0	2	5	2	.273	.303	.385
July	96	22	1	0	0	10	12	7	.229	.240	.315
August	89	26	1	3	0	9	3	5	.292	.371	.315
Sept./Oct.	105	28	5	2	0	4	9	5	.267	.352	.330
Leading Off Inn.	77	24	2	1	0	0	10	4	.312	.364	.398
Bases Empty	189	56	6	3	0	0	16	8	.296	.360	.357
Runners On	134	29	2	2	0	25	13	11	.216	.261	.286
Runners/Scor. Pos.	76	18	2	2	0	25	11	8	.237	.316	.333
Runners On/2 Out	49	11	0	1	0	11	7	3	.224	.265	.321
Scor. Pos./2 Out	30	8	0	1	0	11	5	3	.267	.333	.371
Late-Inning Pressure	44	9	1	0	0	3	3	4	.205	.227	.255
Leading Off	10	3	1	0	0	0	2	1	.300	.400	.417
Runners On	19	4	0	0	0	3	0	3	.211	.211	.211
Runners/Scor. Pos.	14	3	0	0	0	3	0	2	.214	.214	.214

RUNS BATTED IN	From 1B	From 2B	From 3B	Scoring Position
Totals	1/88	9/50	15/34	24/84
Percentage	1.1%	18.0%	44.1%	28.6%

Loves to face: Jack Morris (.301, 25-for-83)
Jeff Russell (.455, 5-for-11)
Curt Young (.440, 11-for-25)

Hates to face: Danny Darwin (.200, 5-for-25, 1 HR)
Storm Davis (.200, 8-for-40)
Bobby Witt (.175, 7-for-40)

Miscellaneous statistics: Ground outs-to-air outs ratio: 1.35 last season, 1.40 for career. . . . Grounded into 10 double plays in 59 opportunities (one per 5.9). . . . Drove in 9 of 19 runners from third base with less than two outs (47%). . . . Direction of balls hit to the outfield: 34% to left field, 35% to center, 31% to right. . . . Base running: Advanced from first base to third on 10 of 22 outfield singles (45%); scored from second on 10 of 16 (63%). . . . Made 2.93 assists per nine innings at second base.

Comments: Brewers pitchers allowed 4.40 runs per nine innings with Gantner at second base, and almost a full run more per nine innings with Molitor there (5.26). . . . Batted 80 points higher with the bases empty (.296) than with runners on base (.216) last season, the 5th-largest margin in the majors. Over last five years, he's batted 45 points higher with the bases empty (.290) than with runners on base (.246). . . . Stole 18 bases, after stealing 20 in 1988 and 1989, despite being limited to 88 games after off-season knee surgery. That's a total of 58 stolen bases in the three seasons since he turned 34; he had never stolen more than 13 in a season previously. . . Enters 1991 with a streak of 1350 at bats since his last home run (June 14, 1987). He hasn't connected in front of the home fans since 1986. . . . The franchise leader with 1322 games played at second base, 889 more than runner-up Pedro Garcia, a member of the Brewers from 1973 to 1976. . . . Has hit better than .290 against ground-ball pitchers and below .270 against fly-ball pitchers in each of the last five seasons. . . . Bring back that crisp Canadian air! Had a career average of .297 at Exhibition Stadium, but has only one hit in 19 career at-bats at the Skydome.

Bob Geren

Bats Right

New York Yankees	AB	H	2B	3B	HR	RBI	BB	SO	BA	SA	OBA
Season	277	59	7	0	8	31	13	73	.213	.325	.259
vs. Left-Handers	114	29	4	0	4	10	7	25	.254	.395	.309
vs. Right-Handers	163	30	3	0	4	21	6	48	.184	.276	.224
vs. Ground-Ballers	131	31	3	0	5	15	7	26	.237	.374	.273
vs. Fly-Ballers	146	28	4	0	3	16	6	47	.192	.281	.247
Home Games	143	31	5	0	4	15	5	41	.217	.336	.250
Road Games	134	28	2	0	4	16	8	32	.209	.313	.269
Grass Fields	223	47	7	0	5	20	11	63	.211	.309	.261
Artificial Turf	54	12	0	0	3	11	2	10	.222	.389	.250
April	26	9	3	0	0	2	1	5	.346	.462	.370
May	71	12	1	0	3	6	4	21	.169	.310	.231
June	45	11	2	0	1	5	1	12	.244	.356	.277
July	62	14	0	0	3	11	2	17	.226	.371	.246
August	43	11	1	0	1	6	2	7	.256	.349	.289
Sept./Oct.	30	2	0	0	0	1	3	11	.067	.067	.200
Leading Off Inn.	66	11	1	0	1	1	1	18	.167	.227	.191
Bases Empty	159	32	3	0	4	4	8	46	.201	.296	.262
Runners On	118	27	4	0	4	27	5	27	.229	.364	.256
Runners/Scor. Pos.	70	16	0	0	3	23	3	17	.229	.357	.253
Runners On/2 Out	62	16	2	0	3	19	1	14	.258	.435	.270
Scor. Pos./2 Out	40	9	0	0	2	15	0	11	.225	.375	.225
Late-Inning Pressure	51	11	1	0	2	5	1	14	.216	.353	.231
Leading Off	13	3	0	0	0	0	0	5	.231	.231	.231
Runners On	24	6	1	0	1	4	0	5	.250	.417	.250
Runners/Scor. Pos.	15	4	0	0	1	4	0	3	.267	.467	.267

RUNS BATTED IN	From 1B	From 2B	From 3B	Scoring Position
Totals	5/86	9/58	9/32	18/90
Percentage	5.8%	15.5%	28.1%	20.0%

Loves to face: Mike Dunne (.667, 2-for-3, 1 HR)
Brian Holman (.444, 4-for-9, 1 HR)

Hates to face: Rob Murphy (0-for-4, 3 SO)
Curt Young (0-for-5)

Miscellaneous statistics: Ground outs-to-air outs ratio: 1.03 last season, 1.08 for career. . . . Grounded into 7 double plays in 49 opportunities (one per 7.0). . . . Drove in 4 of 11 runners from third base with less than two outs (36%). . . . Direction of balls hit to the outfield: 50% to left field, 34% to center, 17% to right. . . . Base running: Advanced from first base to third on 1 of 15 outfield singles (7%), 2d-lowest rate in majors; scored from second on 4 of 7 (57%). . . . Opposing base stealers: 55-for-97 (57%), 2d-lowest rate in A.L.

Comments: Played a majority of innings behind the plate for the Yankees (52%), sharing the job with Matt Nokes (21%), Rick Cerone (18%), Jim Leyritz (5%), and Brian Dorsett (3%). . . . Yankees pitchers allowed 4.21 runs per nine innings with Geren calling the signals, compared to 5.05 with Cerone, and 5.51 with Nokes. . . . New York had three of the league's top six catchers in opponents' stolen-base percentage (minimum: 25 attempts): Cerone ranked first in the majors, Geren ranked fourth, and Nokes ranked sixth. . . . Drove in only one run over his last 25 games. . . . Batting average vs. right-handed pitchers dropped over 100 points from 1989, when he batted .290 against them. . . . Career average of .287 in day games, .222 at night. . . . Has hit three home runs in 42 career at-bats with runners on base in Late-Inning Pressure Situations. . . . For those of you who think of this third-year catcher as a promising youngster, two surprising facts: (1) Geren was a first-round selection in the 1979 draft, which also produced Tim Wallach, Scott Garrelts, Steve Howe, and Atlee Hammaker; (2) Geren was included along with Rollie Fingers and Gene Tenace in the 1980 blockbuster deal that brought Terry Kennedy and a cast of thousands from the Cardinals to the Padres.

Dan Gladden

Bats Right

Minnesota Twins	AB	H	2B	3B	HR	RBI	BB	SO	BA	SA	OBA
Season	534	147	27	6	5	40	26	67	.275	.376	.314
vs. Left-Handers	163	44	8	0	2	16	5	18	.270	.356	.297
vs. Right-Handers	371	103	19	6	3	24	21	49	.278	.385	.322
vs. Ground-Ballers	238	72	13	4	2	17	9	23	.303	.416	.340
vs. Fly-Ballers	296	75	14	2	3	23	17	44	.253	.345	.293
Home Games	263	79	15	5	2	17	14	27	.300	.418	.339
Road Games	271	68	12	1	3	23	12	40	.251	.336	.290
Grass Fields	204	49	8	1	2	18	9	33	.240	.319	.282
Artificial Turf	330	98	19	5	3	22	17	34	.297	.412	.334
April	67	22	7	0	1	7	3	4	.328	.478	.370
May	115	36	5	1	3	10	6	17	.313	.452	.347
June	101	25	3	1	0	5	4	17	.248	.297	.274
July	83	21	3	1	0	5	5	9	.253	.313	.295
August	93	21	5	1	1	7	4	11	.226	.333	.277
Sept./Oct.	75	22	4	2	0	6	4	9	.293	.400	.333
Leading Off Inn.	209	61	11	3	3	3	10	28	.292	.416	.333
Bases Empty	351	97	18	5	3	3	20	47	.276	.382	.321
Runners On	183	50	9	1	2	37	6	20	.273	.366	.301
Runners/Scor. Pos.	117	33	5	1	2	35	4	15	.282	.393	.302
Runners On/2 Out	92	25	5	1	1	22	2	14	.272	.380	.287
Scor. Pos./2 Out	69	19	3	1	1	20	1	11	.275	.391	.286
Late-Inning Pressure	76	15	3	0	0	6	6	12	.197	.237	.253
Leading Off	14	5	1	0	0	0	1	3	.357	.429	.400
Runners On	40	8	2	0	0	6	3	4	.200	.250	.250
Runners/Scor. Pos.	27	7	1	0	0	5	2	3	.259	.296	.300

RUNS BATTED IN	From 1B	From 2B	From 3B	Scoring Position
Totals	4/120	12/83	19/59	31/142
Percentage	3.3%	14.5%	32.2%	21.8%

Loves to face: Andy McGaffigan (.400, 4-for-10, 1 HR)
Ted Power (.600, 6-for-10, 1 HR)

Hates to face: Andy Hawkins (.105, 2-for-19)
Jeff Russell (.148, 4-for-27, 0 BB)
Bobby Witt (.080, 2-for-25, 3 BB)

Miscellaneous statistics: Ground outs-to-air outs ratio: 0.91 last season, 1.00 for career. . . . Grounded into 17 double plays in 71 opportunities (one per 4.2), worst rate in majors. . . . Drove in 11 of 28 runners from third base with less than two outs (39%). . . . Direction of balls hit to the outfield: 30% to left field, 33% to center, 37% to right. . . . Base running: Advanced from first base to third on 11 of 20 outfield singles (55%); scored from second on 11 of 15 (73%). . . . Made 2.32 putouts per nine innings in left field, 2d-highest rate in A.L.

Comments: Has stolen 23 or more bases in every season since his rookie year of 1984. . . . Stole 20 bases in 26 attempts (.769) against right-handed pitchers, but only five bases in eight attempts (.625) against left-handers. . . . Matched his single-season career high with 12 outfield assists last season. . . . Drew only one walk in 70 plate appearances with two outs and runners in scoring position, and that one was intentional (on the pitcher's part). . . . Career batting average of .290 vs. ground-ball pitchers, .262 vs. fly-ball pitchers. Difference of 28 points is greater than the 20-point difference between his career averages vs. left-handers (.289) and right-handers (.269). . . . Batted under .200 in Late-Inning Pressure Situations for the fourth time in his eight-year career. . . . Other players involved in the trade that brought him to the Twins from San Francisco in 1987 are either long forgotten or were never known. Do the names David Blakley, Jose Diminguez, Bryan Hickerson, or Ray Valasquez ring a bell? If they do, get your hearing checked. . . . Gladden is still waiting to continue his eight-game postseason hitting streak from 1987. He may have a long wait.

Mike Greenwell

Bats Left

Boston Red Sox	AB	H	2B	3B	HR	RBI	BB	SO	BA	SA	OBA
Season	610	181	30	6	14	73	65	43	.297	.434	.367
vs. Left-Handers	202	52	8	2	3	22	17	19	.257	.361	.326
vs. Right-Handers	408	129	22	4	11	51	48	24	.316	.471	.386
vs. Ground-Ballers	261	81	13	3	7	36	32	21	.310	.464	.387
vs. Fly-Ballers	349	100	17	3	7	37	33	22	.287	.413	.351
Home Games	306	95	21	2	6	41	34	24	.310	.451	.379
Road Games	304	86	9	4	8	32	31	19	.283	.418	.354
Grass Fields	525	161	29	5	11	66	56	37	.307	.444	.375
Artificial Turf	85	20	1	1	3	7	9	6	.235	.376	.316
April	68	15	1	0	2	4	9	8	.221	.324	.325
May	96	24	2	0	0	3	13	7	.250	.271	.339
June	112	35	5	1	0	17	13	7	.313	.375	.384
July	107	32	6	1	3	10	11	7	.299	.458	.370
August	108	33	4	1	4	17	9	5	.306	.472	.361
Sept./Oct.	119	42	12	3	5	22	10	9	.353	.630	.400
Leading Off Inn.	138	31	7	0	2	2	10	5	.225	.319	.282
Bases Empty	328	97	17	3	9	9	31	20	.296	.448	.358
Runners On	282	84	13	3	5	64	34	23	.298	.418	.376
Runners/Scor. Pos.	162	37	6	2	1	52	30	15	.228	.309	.350
Runners On/2 Out	115	28	6	1	2	22	11	13	.243	.365	.315
Scor. Pos./2 Out	74	13	2	1	0	16	10	7	.176	.230	.282
Late-Inning Pressure	85	21	3	3	3	12	8	6	.247	.459	.323
Leading Off	21	2	1	0	0	0	2	1	.095	.143	.208
Runners On	35	11	1	2	2	11	5	2	.314	.629	.405
Runners/Scor. Pos.	17	4	0	1	0	6	3	0	.235	.353	.364

RUNS BATTED IN	From 1B	From 2B	From 3B	Scoring Position
Totals	10/212	17/129	32/80	49/209
Percentage	4.7%	13.2%	40.0%	23.4%

Loves to face: Mike Moore (.692, 9-for-13)
Jeff Reardon (.800, 4-for-5, 1 2B, 2 HR)
Dave Schmidt (.500, 8-for-16, 3 HR, 8 fly outs)

Hates to face: Kevin Brown (.071, 1-for-14, 2 BB)
Mark Knudson (.091, 1-for-11, 1 2B)
Curt Young (.167, 2-for-12)

Miscellaneous statistics: Ground outs-to-air outs ratio: 1.21 last season, 0.99 for career.... Grounded into 19 double plays in 139 opportunities (one per 7.3).... Drove in 22 of 43 runners from third base with less than two outs (51%).... Direction of balls hit to the outfield: 36% to left field, 30% to center, 35% to right.... Base running: Advanced from first base to third on 14 of 41 outfield singles (34%); scored from second on 14 of 20 (70%).... Made 1.87 putouts per nine innings in left field.

Comments: Hitless in 14 at-bats in the A.L.C.S. against Oakland last season. In L.C.S. history, only Gene Alley (0-for-16 in 1972 for Pittsburgh) and Aurelio Rodriguez (0-for-16 in 1972 for Detroit) had worse marks.... Finished the season at .297, two hits shy of the .300 mark. He had topped that mark in each of his previous five major league seasons.... Led the American League in hits vs. right-handed pitchers.... Average of one strikeout per 15.9 plate appearances was 2d best in the A.L., behind Brian Harper. Among N.L. players, Tony Gwynn, Ozzie Smith, and Gregg Jefferies were tougher to fan.... Batted 93 points lower with runners in scoring position (.228) than in other at-bats (.321) last season, the 5th-largest margin in the majors. That's not bad, considering he started the season going 0-for-29 with RISP.... Led American League left fielders with 13 assists.... Hit all 14 of his home runs to right field. In other words, none of the Green Monster variety.... Career batting-average breakdowns: .325 at Fenway, .302 on the road; .288 vs. left-handers, .324 vs. right-handers; .330 in day games, .305 at night.... Has batted more often with the bases loaded than any other player during his four full seasons in the majors (102 PAs); true to his Red Sox heritage, he has grounded into 13 bases-loaded double plays. (Major league average: one GIDP for every 18 bases-loaded PA-s.)...Has homered at every current American League ballpark except County Stadium (89 career AB).

Ken Griffey, Jr.

Bats Left

Seattle Mariners	AB	H	2B	3B	HR	RBI	BB	SO	BA	SA	OBA
Season	597	179	28	7	22	80	63	81	.300	.481	.366
vs. Left-Handers	219	67	14	1	5	22	17	45	.306	.447	.357
vs. Right-Handers	378	112	14	6	17	58	46	36	.296	.500	.371
vs. Ground-Ballers	218	62	6	4	7	26	29	31	.284	.445	.371
vs. Fly-Ballers	379	117	22	3	15	54	34	50	.309	.501	.364
Home Games	305	89	17	4	8	45	34	33	.292	.452	.364
Road Games	292	90	11	3	14	35	29	48	.308	.510	.369
Grass Fields	232	75	10	2	12	32	22	35	.323	.539	.380
Artificial Turf	365	104	18	5	10	48	41	46	.285	.444	.358
April	80	31	2	1	5	17	5	14	.387	.625	.419
May	111	35	5	1	5	14	13	9	.315	.514	.387
June	104	32	8	0	2	7	16	11	.308	.442	.400
July	104	29	8	0	3	11	10	16	.279	.442	.339
August	108	28	5	2	3	14	12	17	.259	.426	.333
Sept./Oct.	90	24	0	3	4	17	7	14	.267	.467	.327
Leading Off Inn.	130	35	2	2	3	3	4	8	.269	.385	.296
Bases Empty	345	104	14	3	13	13	27	43	.301	.472	.354
Runners On	252	75	14	4	9	67	36	38	.298	.492	.382
Runners/Scor. Pos.	135	42	7	2	4	53	30	22	.311	.481	.429
Runners On/2 Out	92	22	6	2	1	20	20	18	.239	.380	.375
Scor. Pos./2 Out	64	15	4	1	1	19	18	11	.234	.375	.402
Late-Inning Pressure	85	18	2	1	2	9	7	19	.212	.329	.277
Leading Off	27	5	0	0	1	1	0	4	.185	.296	.214
Runners On	29	5	0	1	1	8	4	10	.172	.345	.265
Runners/Scor. Pos.	18	3	0	0	1	7	2	7	.167	.333	.238

RUNS BATTED IN	From 1B	From 2B	From 3B	Scoring Position
Totals	14/192	17/107	27/50	44/157
Percentage	7.3%	15.9%	54.0%	28.0%

Loves to face: Shawn Hillegas (3-for-3, 1 HR, 1 BB)
Jack Morris (.400, 4-for-10, 2 2B, 1 HR)
Dave Stewart (.467, 7-for-15, 4 2B)

Hates to face: Storm Davis (.100, 1-for-10)
Kevin Tapani (0-for-8)
Bob Welch (.154, 2-for-13)

Miscellaneous statistics: Ground outs-to-air outs ratio: 1.04 last season, 1.03 for career.... Grounded into 12 double plays in 135 opportunities (one per 11.3).... Drove in 18 of 25 runners from third base with less than two outs (72%).... Direction of balls hit to the outfield: 27% to left field, 33% to center, 40% to right.... Base running: Advanced from first base to third on 19 of 42 outfield singles (45%); scored from second on 14 of 16 (88%).... Made 2.23 putouts per nine innings in center field, lowest rate in majors.

Comments: Became the first player in Mariners history to start an All-Star game. He was the 3d-youngest player in history to start an All-Star game, behind Al Kaline (1955) and Jerry Walker (1959).... Was batting over .320 as late as August 17, but a seven-game 1-for-26 slump dropped him out of the batting race.... Did little Griff follow in Dad's footsteps and sit out Seattle's last three games to protect his status as a .300 hitter? Somebody give that man a calculator; he actually batted only .2998.... Turned 21 two months after the season ended. Only two younger players in major league history played that many games: Ken Hubbs in 1962 (160 games) and Cesar Cedeno in 1971 (161).... Career average of .302 with runners in scoring position, .279 in other at-bats.... Has only one hit in 14 career at-bats in everybody's favorite category, two outs and runners in scoring position in Late-Inning Pressure Situations.... Last year we told you that his rookie season was comparable to those of Willie Mays, Gene Freese, and Harold Baines. Well, to paraphrase Lloyd Bentsen, we saw Willie Mays; and, Ken Jr., you're no Willie Mays. After a .300 sophomore season, Griffey's statistical profile now most closely resembles those of Vern Stephens (after the 1943 season), Ellis Burks (1988), and Willie Davis (1962).

Kelly Gruber

Bats Right

Toronto Blue Jays	AB	H	2B	3B	HR	RBI	BB	SO	BA	SA	OBA
Season	592	162	36	6	31	118	48	94	.274	.512	.330
vs. Left-Handers	166	49	11	4	8	34	16	27	.295	.554	.349
vs. Right-Handers	426	113	25	2	23	84	32	67	.265	.495	.322
vs. Ground-Ballers	252	68	15	2	8	46	20	36	.270	.440	.335
vs. Fly-Ballers	340	94	21	4	23	72	28	58	.276	.565	.326
Home Games	305	89	13	4	23	62	17	47	.292	.587	.331
Road Games	287	73	23	2	8	56	31	47	.254	.432	.328
Grass Fields	233	56	21	2	7	43	22	37	.240	.438	.311
Artificial Turf	359	106	15	4	24	75	26	57	.295	.560	.343
April	83	27	5	0	7	20	4	15	.325	.639	.367
May	100	30	9	0	6	20	12	20	.300	.570	.377
June	116	35	7	2	7	24	10	14	.302	.578	.349
July	89	15	2	0	2	11	5	15	.169	.258	.235
August	102	21	4	1	1	12	4	18	.206	.294	.236
Sept./Oct.	102	34	9	3	8	31	13	12	.333	.716	.400
Leading Off Inn.	103	27	7	1	3	3	4	13	.262	.437	.309
Bases Empty	326	85	24	3	14	14	26	59	.261	.482	.325
Runners On	266	77	12	3	17	104	22	35	.289	.549	.336
Runners/Scor. Pos.	149	47	7	3	13	93	15	17	.315	.664	.361
Runners On/2 Out	100	28	6	2	8	41	7	12	.280	.620	.339
Scor. Pos./2 Out	68	19	4	2	7	37	6	5	.279	.706	.355
Late-Inning Pressure	92	30	9	1	3	24	4	13	.326	.543	.357
Leading Off	19	5	0	0	0	0	0	3	.263	.263	.263
Runners On	43	17	5	1	2	23	3	3	.395	.698	.426
Runners/Scor. Pos.	26	10	3	1	2	23	2	1	.385	.808	.414

RUNS BATTED IN	From 1B	From 2B	From 3B	Scoring Position
Totals	18/183	29/116	40/75	69/191
Percentage	9.8%	25.0%	53.3%	36.1%

Loves to face: Tom Niedenfuer (4-for-4, 1 2B, 2 HR)
Jeff Reardon (.571, 4-for-7, 1 2B, 1 HR)
Bob Welch (.462, 6-for-13, 1 HR)

Hates to face: Greg A. Harris (.091, 1-for-11)
Andy Hawkins (.130, 3-for-23)
Mark Langston (.053, 1-for-19)

Miscellaneous statistics: Ground outs-to-air outs ratio: 0.95 last season, 1.01 for career.... Grounded into 14 double plays in 130 opportunities (one per 9.3).... Drove in 30 of 45 runners from third base with less than two outs (67%).... Direction of balls hit to the outfield: 43% to left field, 26% to center, 31% to right.... Base running: Advanced from first base to third on 9 of 27 outfield singles (33%); scored from second on 20 of 21 (95%), 5th-highest rate in A.L.... Made 1.99 assists per nine innings at third base.

Comments: Made errors on consecutive batters to allow an eighth-inning tie-breaking run in key loss to Boston on the final weekend of the season. It was his only two-error game of the season.... Started 148 games, all from the 3d slot in the batting order. That may change with the departure of Bell and McGriff.... Collected three or more hits in 17 games, the most in the American League last season.... Has batted over .300 in Late-Inning Pressure Situations in each of the last three seasons. He has a career mark of .301 in LIPS, 41 points higher than in other at-bats. Career LIPS average jumps to .338 with runners on base.... His first 12 home runs of the season were all hit at the Skydome. His 40 extra-base hits there were the most of any A.L. player in his home ballpark.... Hit 26 home runs to left field, two to center, and three to the opposite field.... His home-run total has increased in every year since 1985: 0, 5, 12, 16, 18, 31. Only five players in major league history have increased their totals in six straight seasons: Cy Williams (1918–23), Eddie Robinson (1946–51), Jimmy Piersall (1952–57), Tim McCarver (1961–67), and John Shelby (1982–87).... Career batting average of only .217 (10-for-46, 1 HR) with the bases loaded.... Career average of .238 in day games, .279 at night.... Has hit for a higher average with runners on base than he has with the bases empty in each of his seven major league seasons.

Ozzie Guillen

Bats Left

Chicago White Sox	AB	H	2B	3B	HR	RBI	BB	SO	BA	SA	OBA
Season	516	144	21	4	1	58	26	37	.279	.341	.312
vs. Left-Handers	206	55	8	1	0	28	6	19	.267	.316	.288
vs. Right-Handers	310	89	13	3	1	30	20	18	.287	.358	.327
vs. Ground-Ballers	230	61	10	3	0	30	14	18	.265	.335	.301
vs. Fly-Ballers	286	83	11	1	1	28	12	19	.290	.346	.321
Home Games	247	69	10	3	1	25	14	19	.279	.356	.318
Road Games	269	75	11	1	0	33	12	18	.279	.327	.306
Grass Fields	429	117	16	3	1	43	22	33	.273	.331	.307
Artificial Turf	87	27	5	1	0	15	4	4	.310	.391	.337
April	54	16	2	2	0	5	2	3	.296	.407	.316
May	94	36	3	2	0	8	5	4	.383	.457	.410
June	82	22	3	0	0	10	1	6	.268	.305	.274
July	94	26	2	0	0	10	7	7	.277	.298	.333
August	101	23	6	0	1	13	4	5	.228	.317	.252
Sept./Oct.	91	21	5	0	0	12	7	12	.231	.286	.286
Leading Off Inn.	108	30	2	1	0	0	4	7	.278	.315	.304
Bases Empty	290	75	5	2	1	1	12	27	.259	.300	.288
Runners On	226	69	16	2	0	57	14	10	.305	.394	.341
Runners/Scor. Pos.	133	44	12	2	0	56	14	6	.331	.451	.386
Runners On/2 Out	107	29	7	0	0	17	6	5	.271	.336	.310
Scor. Pos./2 Out	68	17	5	0	0	17	6	3	.250	.324	.311
Late-Inning Pressure	84	24	3	0	0	13	9	10	.286	.321	.362
Leading Off	19	6	0	0	0	0	1	1	.316	.316	.350
Runners On	36	14	2	0	0	13	7	2	.389	.444	.500
Runners/Scor. Pos.	24	9	2	0	0	13	7	2	.375	.458	.531

RUNS BATTED IN	From 1B	From 2B	From 3B	Scoring Position
Totals	4/162	24/101	29/62	53/163
Percentage	2.5%	23.8%	46.8%	32.5%

Loves to face: Dennis Lamp (.500, 7-for-14)
Mark Langston (.450, 9-for-20)
Mike Moore (.370, 17-for-46, 1 HR)

Hates to face: Kevin Brown (0-for-12)
Rick Honeycutt (.100, 2-for-20)
Matt Young (0-for-17)

Miscellaneous statistics: Ground outs-to-air outs ratio: 1.27 last season, 1.38 for career.... Grounded into 6 double plays in 97 opportunities (one per 16.2).... Drove in 22 of 32 runners from third base with less than two outs (69%).... Direction of balls hit to the outfield: 42% to left field, 35% to center, 23% to right.... Base running: Advanced from first base to third on 11 of 25 outfield singles (44%); scored from second on 10 of 12 (83%).... Made 3.14 assists per nine innings at shortstop.

Comments: May batting average was the highest in the American League. He had hits in seven consecutive at-bats with runners on base during the month.... Led the league in batting average through June 24, reminding us that no White Sox player has won the batting title since Luke Appling in 1943.... Was thrown out trying to take an extra base on a batted ball only once.... Started 152 games, all in the ninth spot in the batting order. Why would you want to bury a such a talented hitter so deep in the order, especially when Chicago's leadoff hitters batted only .237 (11th in the A.L.), with the lowest on-base percentage in the league (.288)? Over the course of the season, the Sox's leadoff spot came to the plate 138 more times than its ninth-place hitters.... Has only one hit in 18 career at-bats as a pinch hitter.... Career breakdown: .250 with the bases empty, .288 with runners on base, .301 with runners in scoring position. He has hit for a higher average with runners in scoring position than he has in other at-bats in each of his six years in the majors.... Has averaged 155 games per season over his six-year career.... First White Sox shortstop to appear in an All-Star Game since Bucky Dent in 1975.... We get the darndest requests. Someone asked whether Guillen was a "second-half fielder." His career averages: one error per 43 chances before the All-Star break, one per 37 thereafter.

Mel Hall

Bats Left

New York Yankees	AB	H	2B	3B	HR	RBI	BB	SO	BA	SA	OBA
Season	360	93	23	2	12	46	6	46	.258	.433	.272
vs. Left-Handers	58	12	3	0	1	5	0	11	.207	.310	.203
vs. Right-Handers	302	81	20	2	11	41	6	35	.268	.457	.285
vs. Ground-Ballers	152	35	11	1	5	22	4	19	.230	.414	.252
vs. Fly-Ballers	208	58	12	1	7	24	2	27	.279	.447	.288
Home Games	187	51	13	2	3	25	3	27	.273	.412	.287
Road Games	173	42	10	0	9	21	3	19	.243	.457	.256
Grass Fields	303	74	17	2	9	38	6	38	.244	.403	.261
Artificial Turf	57	19	6	0	3	8	0	8	.333	.596	.333
April	44	12	2	1	2	7	1	6	.273	.500	.289
May	81	18	8	0	2	7	0	6	.222	.395	.220
June	91	26	6	0	5	15	3	10	.286	.516	.309
July	40	13	4	0	0	6	1	6	.325	.425	.333
August	76	16	3	0	2	7	1	14	.211	.329	.241
Sept./Oct.	28	8	0	1	1	4	0	4	.286	.464	.276
Leading Off Inn.	89	21	5	0	4	4	3	12	.236	.427	.261
Bases Empty	195	46	12	0	7	7	3	32	.236	.405	.251
Runners On	165	47	11	2	5	39	3	14	.285	.467	.297
Runners/Scor. Pos.	96	24	7	2	2	32	2	11	.250	.427	.265
Runners On/2 Out	78	23	5	2	2	18	1	8	.295	.487	.304
Scor. Pos./2 Out	48	14	4	2	1	16	1	7	.292	.521	.306
Late-Inning Pressure	64	16	3	1	4	11	1	7	.250	.516	.258
Leading Off	15	3	1	0	1	1	0	2	.200	.467	.200
Runners On	27	8	1	1	2	9	1	2	.296	.630	.310
Runners/Scor. Pos.	19	4	1	1	2	9	0	2	.211	.684	.200

RUNS BATTED IN	From 1B	From 2B	From 3B	Scoring Position
Totals	7/121	12/68	15/41	27/109
Percentage	5.8%	17.6%	36.6%	24.8%

Loves to face: Bert Blyleven (.400, 12-for-30, 2 HR)
Brian Holman (.368, 7-for-19, 2 HR)
Wes Gardner (.455, 5-for-11, 2 2B)

Hates to face: Mark Knudson (.211, 4-for-19)
Gene Nelson (.182, 4-for-22)
Dave Stewart (.157, 8-for-51, 3 HR)

Miscellaneous statistics: Ground outs-to-air outs ratio: 0.86 last season, 0.91 for career. . . . Grounded into 7 double plays in 69 opportunities (one per 9.9). . . . Drove in 8 of 15 runners from third base with less than two outs (53%). . . . Direction of balls hit to the outfield: 20% to left field, 32% to center, 48% to right. . . . Base running: Advanced from first base to third on 3 of 12 outfield singles (25%); scored from second on 6 of 8 (75%). . . . Made 1.67 putouts per nine innings in left field.

Comments: Drove in only 46 runs for the season, but he led the Yankees with 21 go-ahead RBIs. By way of comparison, Steve Sax had 42 RBIs, but only 10 gave the Yankees a lead. . . . Batted .390 in 41 first-inning at-bats. . . . Percentage of runners driven in from scoring position was the lowest of his career. . . . Started 84 of 107 games in which the Yankees faced a right-handed pitcher, but only nine of 55 games vs. southpaws. . . . Was removed for a pinch hitter 25 times last season, but never against a right-handed pitcher. Against lefties was another story: even Randy Velarde batted for him!. . .Last season's .207 mark was only his second sortie across the .200 barrier into the land of respectability against southpaws. . . . Career average of .290 vs. right-handed pitchers (one home run per 29 at-bats), .163 vs. left-handers (4 HR in 355 ABs; one in each of the last four seasons). . . . During Hall's 10-year career, only one other player with as many as 300 ABs vs. southpaws has hit 100 points better against right-handers: Wally Backman (.296 vs. RHP, .170 vs. LHP). . . . His average of one walk per 62 plate appearances would have set a club record, except for Oscar Azocar, the human "Don't Walk" sign. . . . Has never walked with the bases loaded in 72 plate appearances. . . . An unusual trait: Over the past five seasons, Hall's home-run rate is considerably higher against ground-ball pitchers (one HR per 28 AB) than fly-ball pitchers (one HR per 39 AB).

Brian Harper

Bats Right

Minnesota Twins	AB	H	2B	3B	HR	RBI	BB	SO	BA	SA	OBA
Season	479	141	42	3	6	54	19	27	.294	.432	.328
vs. Left-Handers	146	46	19	1	4	20	8	10	.315	.541	.357
vs. Right-Handers	333	95	23	2	2	34	11	17	.285	.384	.315
vs. Ground-Ballers	203	60	20	0	3	23	7	9	.296	.438	.326
vs. Fly-Ballers	276	81	22	3	3	31	12	18	.293	.428	.330
Home Games	230	65	18	2	1	24	12	15	.283	.391	.325
Road Games	249	76	24	1	5	30	7	12	.305	.470	.331
Grass Fields	192	57	18	0	4	21	5	10	.297	.453	.313
Artificial Turf	287	84	24	3	2	33	14	17	.293	.418	.338
April	54	15	5	0	1	6	2	2	.278	.426	.333
May	83	28	8	0	3	15	3	7	.337	.542	.356
June	77	22	3	1	0	9	4	4	.286	.351	.329
July	98	37	11	0	1	13	5	4	.378	.520	.415
August	87	20	9	1	1	8	1	4	.230	.391	.247
Sept./Oct.	80	19	6	1	0	3	4	6	.237	.338	.271
Leading Off Inn.	112	36	13	0	2	2	2	4	.321	.491	.339
Bases Empty	260	76	22	2	4	4	8	13	.292	.438	.324
Runners On	219	65	20	1	2	50	11	14	.297	.425	.333
Runners/Scor. Pos.	122	37	9	0	2	44	7	9	.303	.426	.341
Runners On/2 Out	85	23	6	1	1	20	3	8	.271	.400	.311
Scor. Pos./2 Out	58	17	3	0	1	17	2	6	.293	.397	.328
Late-Inning Pressure	72	22	1	0	1	11	6	4	.306	.361	.367
Leading Off	19	6	0	0	0	0	1	0	.316	.316	.350
Runners On	27	10	0	0	1	11	2	2	.370	.481	.414
Runners/Scor. Pos.	17	8	0	0	1	11	0	2	.471	.647	.471

RUNS BATTED IN	From 1B	From 2B	From 3B	Scoring Position
Totals	8/166	19/95	21/52	40/147
Percentage	4.8%	20.0%	40.4%	27.2%

Loves to face: Mark Knudson (.667, 4-for-6)
Lance McCullers (.600, 3-for-5, 1 HR)

Hates to face: Charlie Hough (0-for-7)
Craig McMurtry (0-for-7)

Miscellaneous statistics: Ground outs-to-air outs ratio: 1.11 last season, 0.93 for career. . . . Grounded into 20 double plays in 116 opportunities (one per 5.8). . . . Drove in 16 of 31 runners from third base with less than two outs (52%). . . . Direction of balls hit to the outfield: 36% to left field, 29% to center, 36% to right. . . . Base running: Advanced from first base to third on 4 of 18 outfield singles (22%); scored from second on 17 of 23 (74%). . . . Opposing base stealers: 86-for-136 (63%).

Comments: Here's one that slipped through the cracks (in other words, one we discovered after the deadline for the 1990 *Analyst*). In 1989, Harper played 101 games behind the plate and batted .325—the 3d-highest batting average over the last 50 years by an A.L. player who caught at least 100 games. The A.L. record for a regular starting catcher is .362, set in 1936 by Bill Dickey. . . . Harper's 25-game hitting streak was the longest in the major leagues last season. He collected at least two hits in 13 of those 25 games. . . . One of five A.L. players to hit .300 or better with runners in scoring position in each of the last two seasons (minimum: 100 AB). The others: Wade Boggs, Ellis Burks, Kirby Puckett, and Ruben Sierra. . . . Harper led the majors with 44 extra-base hits as a catcher. . . . Average of one strikeout per 20.8 plate appearances was the best in the A.L. last season. . . . Twins pitchers allowed 4.75 runs per nine innings with Harper catching, 4.29 runs per nine with Junior Ortiz behind the plate. Ortiz played errorless ball in 68 games. . . . Has 864 at-bats over the last two seasons, compared to 556 from 1979 through 1988. . . . Caught 269 games over the last three seasons. Prior to that, he played in 265 major league games for five different clubs, but only six as a catcher. He's the Dave Stewart of backstops, having drifted through the Angels, Pirates, Cardinals, Tigers, and Athletics organizations.

Ron Hassey

Bats Left

Oakland A's	AB	H	2B	3B	HR	RBI	BB	SO	BA	SA	OBA
Season	254	54	7	0	5	22	27	29	.213	.299	.288
vs. Left-Handers	33	3	0	0	0	1	1	4	.091	.091	.143
vs. Right-Handers	221	51	7	0	5	21	26	25	.231	.330	.308
vs. Ground-Ballers	144	39	4	0	4	15	11	15	.271	.382	.321
vs. Fly-Ballers	110	15	3	0	1	7	16	14	.136	.191	.246
Home Games	125	27	4	0	2	13	12	15	.216	.296	.281
Road Games	129	27	3	0	3	9	15	14	.209	.302	.295
Grass Fields	222	49	7	0	5	21	25	28	.221	.320	.299
Artificial Turf	32	5	0	0	0	1	2	1	.156	.156	.206
April	32	9	2	0	1	3	4	4	.281	.438	.361
May	36	7	0	0	1	1	2	0	.194	.278	.237
June	54	6	2	0	0	3	7	10	.111	.148	.222
July	41	11	1	0	2	8	3	6	.268	.439	.311
August	53	14	1	0	1	5	6	4	.264	.340	.333
Sept./Oct.	38	7	1	0	0	2	5	5	.184	.211	.279
Leading Off Inn.	66	20	4	0	2	2	4	8	.303	.455	.343
Bases Empty	155	33	4	0	5	5	13	21	.213	.335	.274
Runners On	99	21	3	0	0	17	14	8	.212	.242	.308
Runners/Scor. Pos.	54	12	1	0	0	17	8	5	.222	.241	.318
Runners On/2 Out	47	8	1	0	0	5	5	5	.170	.191	.250
Scor. Pos./2 Out	29	5	0	0	0	5	3	3	.172	.172	.250
Late-Inning Pressure	27	5	0	0	0	1	4	5	.185	.185	.290
Leading Off	9	3	0	0	0	0	1	3	.333	.333	.400
Runners On	12	1	0	0	0	1	1	1	.083	.083	.154
Runners/Scor. Pos.	5	1	0	0	0	1	1	0	.200	.200	.333

RUNS BATTED IN	From 1B	From 2B	From 3B	Scoring Position
Totals	1/77	8/43	8/26	16/69
Percentage	1.3%	18.6%	30.8%	23.2%

Loves to face: Bert Blyleven (.405, 15-for-37, 1 HR)
Danny Darwin (.636, 7-for-11)
Storm Davis (.500, 8-for-16, 1 HR)

Hates to face: Bob McClure (0-for-9, 1 BB)
Jeff Russell (0-for-8)
Dave Stieb (.194, 14-for-72)

Miscellaneous statistics: Ground outs-to-air outs ratio: 0.87 last season, 1.24 for career.... Grounded into 3 double plays in 47 opportunities (one per 15.7).... Drove in 7 of 12 runners from third base with less than two outs (58%).... Direction of balls hit to the outfield: 34% to left field, 32% to center, 34% to right.... Base running: Advanced from first base to third on 1 of 10 outfield singles (10%); scored from second on 3 of 5 (60%).... Opposing base stealers: 20-for-32 (63%).

Comments: Innings and ERAs of Oakland's catchers last season: Afenir, 9.82 ERA in 33 innings; Hassey, 2.89 in 489⅔; Quirk, 3.75 in 252; Steinbach, 3.29 in 681⅓.... Overall batting average was his lowest since he broke into the majors with a .203 mark in 74 at-bats for the Indians in 1978.... June batting average was lowest in the major leagues.... Batted 134 points higher vs. ground-ballers (.271) than vs. fly-ballers (.136) last season, the 2d-largest margin in the majors. His average against fly-ballers was the lowest in the American League over the last 10 years.... Has a career average of .242 vs. left-handed pitchers, but has batted only .129 against them over the last four seasons.... He has a career average of one home run per 47 at-bats, but he has 77 AB with the bases loaded without a grand slam.... Has hit only one home run in 211 career at-bats in domed stadiums, while averaging one for every 45 AB outdoors.... Played three games at first base last season, raising his career total to 23 games there.... Career batting average of .323 in postseason games (10-for-31, 1 HR).

Mike Heath

Bats Right

Detroit Tigers	AB	H	2B	3B	HR	RBI	BB	SO	BA	SA	OBA
Season	370	100	18	2	7	38	19	71	.270	.386	.311
vs. Left-Handers	149	34	6	0	3	15	8	28	.228	.329	.264
vs. Right-Handers	221	66	12	2	4	23	11	43	.299	.425	.342
vs. Ground-Ballers	147	40	6	2	1	17	8	24	.272	.361	.314
vs. Fly-Ballers	223	60	12	0	6	21	11	47	.269	.404	.308
Home Games	169	46	9	2	3	15	10	35	.272	.402	.321
Road Games	201	54	9	0	4	23	9	36	.269	.373	.302
Grass Fields	313	84	17	2	7	36	18	60	.268	.403	.312
Artificial Turf	57	16	1	0	0	2	1	11	.281	.298	.305
April	36	16	2	2	0	2	1	3	.444	.611	.462
May	85	27	6	0	1	9	4	14	.318	.424	.341
June	56	17	2	0	1	3	4	9	.304	.393	.350
July	72	13	1	0	3	12	2	22	.181	.319	.224
August	57	12	3	0	1	5	6	11	.211	.316	.286
Sept./Oct.	64	15	4	0	1	7	2	12	.234	.344	.269
Leading Off Inn.	83	26	3	1	2	2	1	14	.313	.446	.329
Bases Empty	206	63	12	2	4	4	13	33	.306	.442	.353
Runners On	164	37	6	0	3	34	6	38	.226	.317	.257
Runners/Scor. Pos.	100	21	1	0	2	29	5	24	.210	.280	.255
Runners On/2 Out	66	11	2	0	1	10	3	21	.167	.242	.214
Scor. Pos./2 Out	42	5	0	0	0	7	2	13	.119	.119	.178
Late-Inning Pressure	49	11	0	0	2	4	3	16	.224	.347	.269
Leading Off	13	3	0	0	1	1	0	5	.231	.462	.231
Runners On	12	1	0	0	1	3	1	8	.083	.333	.154
Runners/Scor. Pos.	8	1	0	0	1	3	1	6	.125	.500	.222

RUNS BATTED IN	From 1B	From 2B	From 3B	Scoring Position
Totals	5/122	9/72	17/44	26/116
Percentage	4.1%	12.5%	38.6%	22.4%

Loves to face: Doug Bair (.625, 5-for-8, 1 HR)
Oil Can Boyd (.500, 7-for-14, 2 HR)
Neal Heaton (.400, 6-for-15)

Hates to face: Jim Clancy (.162, 6-for-37, 0 BB)
Dennis Martinez (.154, 4-for-26)
Fernando Valenzuela (.077, 1-for-13)

Miscellaneous statistics: Ground outs-to-air outs ratio: 1.60 last season, 1.35 for career.... Grounded into 12 double plays in 74 opportunities (one per 6.2).... Drove in 14 of 27 runners from third base with less than two outs (52%).... Direction of balls hit to the outfield: 38% to left field, 34% to center, 28% to right.... Base running: Advanced from first base to third on 8 of 18 outfield singles (44%); scored from second on 6 of 7 (86%).... Opposing base stealers: 84-for-117 (72%), 5th-highest rate in A.L.

Comments: Started 46 of 49 games in which the Tigers were opposed by a left-handed pitcher, but started less than half of their games vs. right-handers (55 of 113).... Played 117 games behind the plate, matching the career high he set in 1989.... His .980 fielding percentage (one error per 50 chances) was the lowest among qualifying American League catchers.... Don't put too much stock in last season's lefty/righty breakdown. He has a career average of .279 vs. left-handers, .232 vs. right-handers.... Batted 80 points higher with the bases empty (.306) than with runners on base (.226) last season, the 4th-largest margin in the majors.... Batted 80 points lower in Late-Inning Pressure Situations (.192) than in other at-bats (.272) over the last five seasons, the 3d-largest margin in the majors. Has a career mark of .218 in LIPS.... Played in the 1978 World Series in his rookie season for the Yankees, but hasn't returned to the Series since. Heath had the misfortune to leave Oakland the year Canseco arrived; spend time with the Cardinals in between their 1985 and 1987 N.L. titles; and hit Motown two years after Detroit's last league title.... Aside to Mike: Don't give up. Jim Kaat went a record 17 seasons between Series appearances (1965–82). The record for a nonpitcher is 14 years, by Rabbit Maranville (1914–27).... Had he played for winning teams, Heath's career would look at lot more like John Roseboro's than you might think.

Dave Henderson

Bats Right

Oakland A's	AB	H	2B	3B	HR	RBI	BB	SO	BA	SA	OBA
Season	450	122	28	0	20	63	40	105	.271	.467	.331
vs. Left-Handers	133	47	7	0	11	23	10	22	.353	.654	.400
vs. Right-Handers	317	75	21	0	9	40	30	83	.237	.388	.302
vs. Ground-Ballers	224	60	14	0	9	31	25	49	.268	.451	.341
vs. Fly-Ballers	226	62	14	0	11	32	15	56	.274	.482	.320
Home Games	222	67	14	0	11	36	18	46	.302	.514	.353
Road Games	228	55	14	0	9	27	22	59	.241	.421	.310
Grass Fields	384	107	23	0	18	55	33	81	.279	.479	.336
Artificial Turf	66	15	5	0	2	8	7	24	.227	.394	.301
April	65	13	2	0	3	7	10	15	.200	.369	.307
May	88	25	8	0	3	13	6	17	.284	.477	.330
June	99	26	7	0	8	21	5	28	.263	.576	.298
July	108	33	6	0	3	7	12	20	.306	.444	.377
August	67	19	5	0	2	11	4	16	.284	.448	.324
Sept./Oct.	23	6	0	0	1	4	3	9	.261	.391	.333
Leading Off Inn.	97	27	5	0	4	4	4	23	.278	.454	.307
Bases Empty	256	70	15	0	11	11	22	62	.273	.461	.333
Runners On	194	52	13	0	9	52	18	43	.268	.474	.327
Runners/Scor. Pos.	115	29	8	0	2	37	16	30	.252	.374	.338
Runners On/2 Out	89	24	5	0	5	25	8	17	.270	.494	.330
Scor. Pos./2 Out	58	14	3	0	2	18	8	13	.241	.397	.333
Late-Inning Pressure	56	15	4	0	1	7	2	15	.268	.393	.293
Leading Off	9	5	0	0	0	0	0	2	.556	.556	.556
Runners On	30	6	1	0	1	7	2	8	.200	.333	.250
Runners/Scor. Pos.	17	6	1	0	1	7	2	4	.353	.588	.421

RUNS BATTED IN	From 1B	From 2B	From 3B	Scoring Position
Totals	10/146	16/88	17/53	33/141
Percentage	6.8%	18.2%	32.1%	23.4%

Loves to face: Paul Kilgus (.833, 5-for-6, 1 HR)
Mark Knudson (.667, 6-for-9, 2 SO)
Ray Searage (5-for-5, 1 HR, 1 BB)

Hates to face: Rick Aguilera (.100, 1-for-10, 5 SO)
Bert Blyleven (.080, 2-for-25)
Andy Hawkins (0-for-9, 1 BB)

Miscellaneous statistics: Ground outs-to-air outs ratio: 0.64 last season, 0.76 for career.... Grounded into 5 double plays in 90 opportunities (one per 18.0).... Drove in 11 of 26 runners from third base with less than two outs (42%).... Direction of balls hit to the outfield: 38% to left field, 37% to center, 25% to right.... Base running: Advanced from first base to third on 11 of 25 outfield singles (44%); scored from second on 15 of 19 (79%).... Made 2.96 putouts per nine innings in center field.

Comments: Played his first five major league seasons in Seattle; his teams have reached the postseason in each of five seasons since. Add your own punch line.... Has seven career postseason home runs, tied with Jose Canseco for 2d among active players, behind George Brett (10).... Has played in four League Championship Series, and his team has advanced to the World Series on all four occasions. Only Steve Garvey has played on more Championship Series winners without ever tasting defeat (5). Five other players have done it four times each: Gary Nolan, Jerry Grote, Lee Lacy, Dave Stewart, and Henderson's insurance policy, Willie McGee. (Lacy was on the Pirates' roster in 1979, but did not play during the NLCS. We'll give him the benefit of the doubt.)...Oakland Coliseum reduces batting averages by about six percent (the 2d-largest reduction in the majors, behind Tiger Stadium), but Henderson seems not to notice. His career batting average there is .278, 21 points higher than elsewhere. His home-run rate is 15 percent higher there (one HR per 24 AB) than in other stadiums (one per 27 AB).... His career batting average is only .167 with two outs and runners on base in Late-Inning Pressure Situations (16-for-96, 1 HR)—in the regular season, that is. Postseason: 4-for-16, 1 HR. (Isn't it amazing how much emotion can be obscured by the simple accounting notation *"1 HR"*?).... Career average of .205 (18-for-88, 1 HR) with the bases loaded.

Rickey Henderson

Bats Right

Oakland A's	AB	H	2B	3B	HR	RBI	BB	SO	BA	SA	OBA
Season	489	159	33	3	28	61	97	60	.325	.577	.439
vs. Left-Handers	134	42	12	0	9	17	24	22	.313	.604	.421
vs. Right-Handers	355	117	21	3	19	44	73	38	.330	.566	.446
vs. Ground-Ballers	246	81	19	3	13	34	48	30	.329	.589	.441
vs. Fly-Ballers	243	78	14	0	15	27	49	30	.321	.564	.437
Home Games	220	67	12	2	8	22	44	26	.305	.486	.425
Road Games	269	92	21	1	20	39	53	34	.342	.651	.451
Grass Fields	408	124	23	2	22	44	84	55	.304	.532	.426
Artificial Turf	81	35	10	1	6	17	13	5	.432	.802	.505
April	65	22	7	0	3	7	11	9	.338	.585	.429
May	94	31	7	1	5	10	19	5	.330	.585	.447
June	85	29	5	1	5	11	20	10	.341	.600	.462
July	88	31	4	1	7	15	12	9	.352	.659	.430
August	66	18	4	0	3	7	16	12	.273	.470	.415
Sept./Oct.	91	28	6	0	5	11	19	15	.308	.538	.442
Leading Off Inn.	206	59	13	1	12	12	39	20	.286	.534	.400
Bases Empty	336	112	29	2	20	20	60	39	.333	.610	.434
Runners On	153	47	4	1	8	41	37	21	.307	.503	.449
Runners/Scor. Pos.	85	23	1	0	6	35	29	18	.271	.494	.458
Runners On/2 Out	64	16	2	0	1	12	22	14	.250	.328	.448
Scor. Pos./2 Out	40	6	1	0	0	9	21	12	.150	.175	.452
Late-Inning Pressure	47	21	3	1	4	7	16	5	.447	.809	.587
Leading Off	10	4	0	0	2	2	6	1	.400	1.000	.625
Runners On	20	10	1	0	1	4	3	4	.500	.700	.565
Runners/Scor. Pos.	9	4	0	0	1	4	3	2	.444	.778	.583

RUNS BATTED IN	From 1B	From 2B	From 3B	Scoring Position
Totals	7/108	10/64	16/44	26/108
Percentage	6.5%	15.6%	36.4%	24.1%

Loves to face: Juan Berenguer (.423, 11-for-26)
Jamie Moyer (.800, 4-for-5, 3 2B)
Bobby Witt (.370, 10-for-27, 1 HR)

Hates to face: John Mitchell (0-for-7)
Nolan Ryan (.143, 2-for-14)
Kevin Tapani (0-for-6)

Miscellaneous statistics: Ground outs-to-air outs ratio: 0.90 last season, 1.11 for career.... Grounded into 13 double plays in 83 opportunities (one per 6.4).... Drove in 12 of 22 runners from third base with less than two outs (55%).... Direction of balls hit to the outfield: 45% to left field, 28% to center, 27% to right.... Base running: Advanced from first base to third on 11 of 30 outfield singles (37%); scored from second on 27 of 32 (84%).... Made 2.62 putouts per nine innings in left field, highest rate in majors.

Comments: Led the major leagues in runs scored for the fifth time in his career. Only three players in major league history, all Hall of Famers, have led as often: Babe Ruth (8 times), Mickey Mantle (6), and Ted Williams (5). Four others have led three times: Ty Cobb, Eddie Collins, Lou Gehrig, and Pete Rose.... In an interview in *Playboy* (and, by the way, we only read the articles—Rosanna or not), Rickey said that he had trouble stealing against left-handed pitchers. Well, last season, he was 18-for-22 vs. lefties (82%), 47-for-53 vs. right-handers (89%). That's trouble?...Ranked fourth in the majors with 20 home runs in road games. (Oakland Coliseum has reduced home runs by 17 percent over the last five years.)...Led off with first-inning home runs in consecutive games (May 5–6). No player has ever done that in three games in a row; only Felipe Alou has hit first-inning leadoff home runs in consecutive games on two occasions.... Has hit for a lower average with runners in scoring position than he has in other at bats in each of the last seven seasons, tying the *Player Analysis* record shared by Steve Kemp and Johnny Oates.... Has 20 career stolen bases in 23 postseason games, to share the all-time record with Davey Lopes, who played in nearly twice as many games (45).... His 15-game postseason hitting streak was snapped in the fourth game of the World Series, two games shy of Hank Bauer's all-time record.

Donnie Hill

Bats Left and Right

California Angels	AB	H	2B	3B	HR	RBI	BB	SO	BA	SA	OBA
Season	352	93	18	2	3	32	29	27	.264	.352	.319
vs. Left-Handers	98	23	8	0	1	12	12	10	.235	.347	.315
vs. Right-Handers	254	70	10	2	2	20	17	17	.276	.354	.320
vs. Ground-Ballers	145	38	8	1	1	15	10	11	.262	.352	.310
vs. Fly-Ballers	207	55	10	1	2	17	19	16	.266	.353	.325
Home Games	169	42	9	0	0	9	18	11	.249	.302	.319
Road Games	183	51	9	2	3	23	11	16	.279	.399	.318
Grass Fields	296	77	14	0	1	20	22	21	.260	.318	.308
Artificial Turf	56	16	4	2	2	12	7	6	.286	.536	.369
April	18	6	2	0	0	1	1	5	.333	.444	.368
May	69	17	4	1	1	6	8	4	.246	.377	.333
June	80	18	7	0	0	7	5	7	.225	.313	.267
July	75	20	1	1	1	10	9	8	.267	.347	.337
August	73	19	3	0	0	1	3	2	.260	.301	.289
Sept./Oct.	37	13	1	0	1	7	3	1	.351	.459	.390
Leading Off Inn.	63	20	3	1	0	0	6	4	.317	.397	.377
Bases Empty	198	51	10	1	1	1	13	14	.258	.333	.307
Runners On	154	42	8	1	2	31	16	13	.273	.377	.333
Runners/Scor. Pos.	79	20	5	1	1	29	10	9	.253	.380	.323
Runners On/2 Out	65	14	1	1	1	8	8	7	.215	.308	.301
Scor. Pos./2 Out	36	6	1	1	0	6	6	6	.167	.250	.286
Late-Inning Pressure	54	15	2	1	1	6	7	4	.278	.407	.361
Leading Off	9	3	0	0	0	0	1	0	.333	.333	.400
Runners On	21	4	1	1	1	6	3	3	.190	.476	.292
Runners/Scor. Pos.	14	3	1	1	0	4	3	3	.214	.429	.353

RUNS BATTED IN	From 1B	From 2B	From 3B	Scoring Position
Totals	4/119	9/64	16/31	25/95
Percentage	3.4%	14.1%	51.6%	26.3%

Loves to face: Juan Berenguer (.417, 5-for-12)
Neal Heaton (.455, 5-for-11)

Hates to face: Mark Langston (.152, 5-for-33, 1 HR, 0 BB)
Mike Moore (.250, 10-for-40, 0 BB)
Dave Stewart (.217, 5-for-23)

Miscellaneous statistics: Ground outs-to-air outs ratio: 1.02 last season, 0.97 for career.... Grounded into 10 double plays in 83 opportunities (one per 8.3).... Drove in 14 of 20 runners from third base with less than two outs (70%).... Direction of balls hit to the outfield: 43% to left field, 34% to center, 24% to right batting left-handed; 37% to left, 33% to center, 31% to right batting right-handed.... Base running: Advanced from first base to third on 6 of 17 outfield singles (35%); scored from second on 11 of 12 (92%).... Made 3.34 assists per nine innings at second base.

Comments: Played 50 consecutive errorless games at second base from April 20 through August 21, the 3d-longest streak at the position in the A.L. last season.... Angels pitchers allowed 4.13 runs per nine innings with Hill at second, compared to 4.48 with other second basemen.... California had a 27–19 record with Hill in the starting lineup, but were 10 games below .500 without him (53–63).... One of four American League players to start at least one game at all four infield positions; he played three games at first base, 60 at second, 21 at third, and 24 games at shortstop.... Although he's played for three different clubs, he has hit only three of his 25 career home runs in home games.... Hill was released from both the Athletics and White Sox systems in 1989, without appearing in a major league game.... Became only the second position player in team history to pitch: one inning, no hits, one walk, and one strikeout (Rob Deer, of course).... The only other position player to pitch for the Angels was Willie Smith (who began his career as a pitcher) in 1964.... He's more than a switch-hitter; like Boston's Greg Harris, Hill is ambidextrous. In case you're wondering, Hill is 1-for-7 in his career against Harris.

Glenallen Hill

Bats Right

Toronto Blue Jays	AB	H	2B	3B	HR	RBI	BB	SO	BA	SA	OBA
Season	260	60	11	3	12	32	18	62	.231	.435	.281
vs. Left-Handers	143	32	5	3	5	12	10	36	.224	.406	.275
vs. Right-Handers	117	28	6	0	7	20	8	26	.239	.470	.288
vs. Ground-Ballers	124	33	7	2	4	14	7	26	.266	.452	.305
vs. Fly-Ballers	136	27	4	1	8	18	11	36	.199	.419	.259
Home Games	140	33	8	0	7	17	11	29	.236	.443	.291
Road Games	120	27	3	3	5	15	7	33	.225	.425	.268
Grass Fields	99	23	2	2	4	13	5	31	.232	.414	.269
Artificial Turf	161	37	9	1	8	19	13	31	.230	.447	.287
April	42	13	3	0	2	4	3	5	.310	.524	.356
May	56	9	2	0	3	8	4	14	.161	.357	.217
June	36	8	1	0	1	6	3	6	.222	.333	.282
July	34	9	1	0	3	5	1	7	.265	.559	.286
August	71	17	4	3	3	9	6	23	.239	.507	.299
Sept./Oct.	21	4	0	0	0	0	1	7	.190	.190	.227
Leading Off Inn.	74	19	4	2	3	3	5	17	.257	.486	.304
Bases Empty	152	33	7	2	8	8	6	37	.217	.447	.247
Runners On	108	27	4	1	4	24	12	25	.250	.417	.325
Runners/Scor. Pos.	56	14	2	1	2	20	7	12	.250	.429	.333
Runners On/2 Out	44	10	3	0	1	10	3	10	.227	.364	.277
Scor. Pos./2 Out	24	5	2	0	1	10	1	6	.208	.417	.240
Late-Inning Pressure	38	8	1	0	0	0	2	8	.211	.237	.250
Leading Off	9	1	0	0	0	0	0	3	.111	.111	.111
Runners On	11	2	0	0	0	0	1	5	.182	.182	.250
Runners/Scor. Pos.	4	0	0	0	0	0	1	4	.000	.000	.200

RUNS BATTED IN	From 1B	From 2B	From 3B	Scoring Position
Totals	5/86	8/47	7/22	15/69
Percentage	5.8%	17.0%	31.8%	21.7%

Loves to face: Jack Morris (2-for-2, 1 BB)

Hates to face: Allan Anderson (.100, 1-for-10)
Dave LaPoint (.125, 1-for-8)
Jamie Moyer (1-for-7)

Miscellaneous statistics: Ground outs-to-air outs ratio: 0.88 last season, 0.85 for career.... Grounded into 5 double plays in 55 opportunities (one per 11.0).... Drove in 5 of 12 runners from third base with less than two outs (42%).... Direction of balls hit to the outfield: 51% to left field, 28% to center, 21% to right.... Base running: Advanced from first base to third on 2 of 11 outfield singles (18%); scored from second on 7 of 8 (88%).... Made 1.98 putouts per nine innings in right field.

Comments: Started 42 of 49 games in which the Blue Jays faced left-handed pitchers, but only 27 of 113 games vs. right-handers.... Made 33 starts in right field, 21 in left. He has his pick this season, since the regulars at both those positions are now gone (Junior Felix and George Bell, respectively).... Started only one game after September 4.... Hit one home run for every 22 at-bats, cracking the American League's top 20 at number 16 (minimum: 10 HR).... Only four of his 32 RBIs gave Toronto a lead.... Has never driven in a run in 46 career at-bats in Late-Inning Pressure Situations.... Career breakdown: .221 with the bases empty, .267 with runners on base, .270 with runners in scoring position.... Has hit two grand slams in only 11 career at-bats with the bases loaded.... Career average of .212 in day games, .255 at night.... A mediocre season for a much heralded rookie who was highly prized in fantasy-league drafts last April. Comparable rookie seasons: Darrell Evans (1971), Ken Gerhart (1987), Bob Speake (1955).

Sam Horn

Bats Left

Baltimore Orioles	AB	H	2B	3B	HR	RBI	BB	SO	BA	SA	OBA
Season	246	61	13	0	14	45	32	62	.248	.472	.332
vs. Left-Handers	17	1	0	0	0	0	0	7	.059	.059	.059
vs. Right-Handers	229	60	13	0	14	45	32	55	.262	.502	.350
vs. Ground-Ballers	122	30	6	0	7	26	14	27	.246	.467	.321
vs. Fly-Ballers	124	31	7	0	7	19	18	35	.250	.476	.343
Home Games	120	30	6	0	8	21	22	38	.250	.500	.364
Road Games	126	31	7	0	6	24	10	24	.246	.444	.299
Grass Fields	207	47	11	0	9	31	29	60	.227	.411	.319
Artificial Turf	39	14	2	0	5	14	3	2	.359	.795	.405
April	56	16	2	0	2	10	8	16	.286	.429	.375
May	19	3	1	0	1	2	0	3	.158	.368	.158
June	4	1	0	0	0	0	1	1	.250	.250	.400
July	45	12	2	0	5	9	7	12	.267	.644	.352
August	56	12	2	0	2	5	11	10	.214	.357	.343
Sept./Oct.	66	17	6	0	4	19	5	20	.258	.530	.310
Leading Off Inn.	66	14	2	0	6	6	2	16	.212	.515	.235
Bases Empty	128	35	5	0	8	8	14	30	.273	.500	.345
Runners On	118	26	8	0	6	37	18	32	.220	.441	.319
Runners/Scor. Pos.	68	18	4	0	5	34	10	16	.265	.544	.350
Runners On/2 Out	57	9	4	0	1	8	12	15	.158	.281	.304
Scor. Pos./2 Out	34	5	1	0	1	8	6	9	.147	.265	.275
Late-Inning Pressure	36	11	0	0	1	6	3	8	.306	.389	.359
Leading Off	10	1	0	0	0	0	0	3	.100	.100	.100
Runners On	15	4	0	0	1	6	1	3	.267	.467	.313
Runners/Scor. Pos.	10	3	0	0	1	6	0	2	.300	.600	.300

RUNS BATTED IN	From 1B	From 2B	From 3B	Scoring Position
Totals	8/98	14/51	9/33	23/84
Percentage	8.2%	27.5%	27.3%	27.4%

Loves to face: Jose Nunez (.750, 3-for-4, 2 HR, 1 SO)
Bob Welch (.538, 7-for-13, 1 HR)

Hates to face: Bert Blyleven (.077, 1-for-13, 1 2B)
Jack Morris (.083, 1-for-12, 2 BB, 6 SO)
Bobby Witt (0-for-7, 2 BB, 4 SO)

Miscellaneous statistics: Ground outs-to-air outs ratio: 1.15 last season, 1.17 for career.... Grounded into 8 double plays in 58 opportunities (one per 7.3).... Drove in 8 of 19 runners from third base with less than two outs (42%).... Direction of balls hit to the outfield: 37% to left field, 31% to center, 31% to right.... Base running: Advanced from first base to third on 3 of 14 outfield singles (21%); scored from second on 5 of 5.... Made 0.71 assists per nine innings at first base.

Comments: Hit a pair of three-run home runs on opening day; didn't drive in another run in his next seven games, or hit his third home run until May 4 in his 18th game of the season.... Hit four of his 14 home runs to the opposite field.... Had four hits in nine at-bats as a pinch-hitter, including two home runs and seven RBIs.... Wasn't thrown out trying to advance an extra base on any batted ball last season.... Started 68 games last season, all against right-handed pitchers. He has started only five games vs. left-handers in his career, none since October 1987.... Career batting average of .182 vs. left-handers (3 HR in 55 AB), .241 vs. right-handers (27 HR, one per 17 AB—nearly the same rate).... Career batting-average breakdowns: .215 vs. ground-ball pitchers, .254 vs. fly-ballers; .225 on grass fields, .297 on artificial surfaces.... Has driven in over 38 percent of runners from scoring position in Late-Inning Pressure Situations during his career, but only 23 percent of such runners in other at-bats.... His career total of 592 plate appearances over four years approximates one full season. He has batted .235 (122-for-519), but with 68 walks, 22 doubles, 30 HR and 92 RBIs (not to mention 153 strikeouts).... Fewest at-bats to reach 30 home runs? No contest—Rudy York (285).... If this were 1976, Horn would be Tony Solaita.

Jack Howell

Bats Left

California Angels	AB	H	2B	3B	HR	RBI	BB	SO	BA	SA	OBA
Season	316	72	19	1	8	33	46	61	.228	.370	.326
vs. Left-Handers	62	11	2	0	0	5	9	16	.177	.210	.292
vs. Right-Handers	254	61	17	1	8	28	37	45	.240	.409	.334
vs. Ground-Ballers	139	28	7	1	3	15	20	30	.201	.331	.298
vs. Fly-Ballers	177	44	12	0	5	18	26	31	.249	.401	.348
Home Games	156	34	9	0	3	17	20	31	.218	.333	.305
Road Games	160	38	10	1	5	16	26	30	.237	.406	.346
Grass Fields	271	59	15	1	7	30	43	55	.218	.358	.323
Artificial Turf	45	13	4	0	1	3	3	6	.289	.444	.347
April	50	14	6	0	1	5	9	6	.280	.460	.390
May	59	13	5	1	2	7	3	11	.220	.441	.266
June	49	6	1	0	1	4	6	11	.122	.204	.218
July	56	12	2	0	2	3	14	13	.214	.357	.371
August	14	5	0	0	0	2	1	1	.357	.357	.400
Sept./Oct.	88	22	5	0	2	12	13	19	.250	.375	.343
Leading Off Inn.	71	15	4	0	1	1	6	19	.211	.310	.273
Bases Empty	181	37	10	1	5	5	24	35	.204	.354	.298
Runners On	135	35	9	0	3	28	22	26	.259	.393	.363
Runners/Scor. Pos.	66	11	4	0	1	21	16	18	.167	.273	.329
Runners On/2 Out	71	16	2	0	0	9	14	15	.225	.254	.353
Scor. Pos./2 Out	39	7	1	0	0	9	12	12	.179	.205	.373
Late-Inning Pressure	50	11	3	0	1	3	10	13	.220	.340	.350
Leading Off	14	3	1	0	0	0	1	3	.214	.286	.267
Runners On	18	5	1	0	0	2	6	6	.278	.333	.458
Runners/Scor. Pos.	6	1	0	0	0	1	3	3	.167	.167	.444

RUNS BATTED IN	From 1B	From 2B	From 3B	Scoring Position
Totals	6/110	8/56	11/34	19/90
Percentage	5.5%	14.3%	32.4%	21.1%

Loves to face: Bill Gullickson (2-for-2, 1 HR, 1 BB)
Dave Stieb (.440, 11-for-25, 3 HR)

Hates to face: Storm Davis (.071, 1-for-14, 3 BB, 8 SO)
Charlie Hough (.045, 1-for-22, 5 BB)
Mark Langston (.158, 3-for-19, 1 HR, 12 SO)

Miscellaneous statistics: Ground outs-to-air outs ratio: 0.91 last season, 1.02 for career.... Grounded into 3 double plays in 63 opportunities (one per 21.0).... Drove in 8 of 14 runners from third base with less than two outs (57%).... Direction of balls hit to the outfield: 37% to left field, 32% to center, 31% to right.... Base running: Advanced from first base to third on 3 of 17 outfield singles (18%); scored from second on 5 of 8 (63%).... Made 2.13 assists per nine innings at third base.

Comments: Of his 33 RBIs, 13 gave the Angels a lead. By comparison, teammate Lance Parrish had 70 RBIs for the season, but only 16 go-ahead RBIs.... Hit four home runs to the opposite field, one to center, and three to right field last season.... Has batted under .200 with runners in scoring position in three of the last four years. His career mark: .221.... Batted 82 points higher vs. right-handers (.262) than vs. left-handers (.180) over the last five seasons, the largest margin in the majors. His career average vs. southpaws (.179) is the 2d lowest of any player over the last 16 years (minimum: 400 AB). Only Wally Backman has a lower average (.170).... Batted 62 points higher on artificial turf (.294) than on grass fields (.232) over the last five seasons, the 3d-largest margin in the majors.... Career average of .306 (15-for-49, 3 HR) as a pinch hitter.... Had only one hit in 14 at-bats with the bases loaded last season, to lower his career average to .216 (11-for-51, 1 HR) with the bags full.

Kent Hrbek

Bats Left

Minnesota Twins	AB	H	2B	3B	HR	RBI	BB	SO	BA	SA	OBA
Season	492	141	26	0	22	79	69	45	.287	.474	.377
vs. Left-Handers	129	37	3	0	2	17	17	13	.287	.357	.377
vs. Right-Handers	363	104	23	0	20	62	52	32	.287	.515	.376
vs. Ground-Ballers	204	54	10	0	6	28	25	20	.265	.402	.347
vs. Fly-Ballers	288	87	16	0	16	51	44	25	.302	.524	.397
Home Games	247	69	15	0	8	43	32	16	.279	.437	.362
Road Games	245	72	11	0	14	36	37	29	.294	.510	.391
Grass Fields	177	52	7	0	12	28	29	17	.294	.537	.401
Artificial Turf	315	89	19	0	10	51	40	28	.283	.438	.363
April	53	15	4	0	3	13	16	6	.283	.528	.457
May	99	29	3	0	5	16	9	10	.293	.475	.354
June	85	17	9	0	2	8	13	12	.200	.376	.306
July	90	32	6	0	6	13	14	3	.356	.622	.458
August	97	29	2	0	5	18	7	10	.299	.474	.336
Sept./Oct.	68	19	2	0	1	11	10	4	.279	.353	.370
Leading Off Inn.	102	32	9	0	6	6	13	8	.314	.578	.402
Bases Empty	264	71	16	0	12	12	30	25	.269	.466	.352
Runners On	228	70	10	0	10	67	39	20	.307	.482	.403
Runners/Scor. Pos.	127	35	6	0	4	53	27	13	.276	.417	.390
Runners On/2 Out	74	16	2	0	2	13	16	8	.216	.324	.370
Scor. Pos./2 Out	40	8	1	0	1	10	12	4	.200	.300	.407
Late-Inning Pressure	69	21	5	0	0	6	14	9	.304	.377	.419
Leading Off	12	5	2	0	0	0	1	1	.417	.583	.462
Runners On	29	10	1	0	0	6	10	5	.345	.379	.488
Runners/Scor. Pos.	14	4	1	0	0	6	7	3	.286	.357	.478

RUNS BATTED IN	From 1B	From 2B	From 3B	Scoring Position
Totals	10/165	21/101	26/54	47/155
Percentage	6.1%	20.8%	48.1%	30.3%

Loves to face: Dennis Eckersley (.409, 9-for-22, 4 2B, 2 HR)
Mike Jackson (.571, 4-for-7, 1 2B, 2 HR)
Jeff Montgomery (.556, 5-for-9, 1 HR)

Hates to face: Wes Gardner (.125, 2-for-16)
Bob McClure (0-for-12, 2 BB)
Dave Stieb (.211, 16-for-76, 5 HR)

Miscellaneous statistics: Ground outs-to-air outs ratio: 1.02 last season, 1.14 for career.... Grounded into 17 double plays in 131 opportunities (one per 7.7).... Drove in 24 of 38 runners from third base with less than two outs (63%).... Direction of balls hit to the outfield: 28% to left field, 30% to center, 42% to right.... Base running: Advanced from first base to third on 7 of 33 outfield singles (21%); scored from second on 4 of 7 (57%).... Made 0.71 assists per nine innings at first base.

Comments: Needs 34 home runs to pass Bob Allison as the runner-up to Harmon Killebrew among home-run hitters in the history of the franchise, including its 60 years in Washington. The top five: Killer, 559; Allison, 256; Hrbek, 223; Tony Oliva, 220; Gary Gaetti, 201.... Hrbek and Gaetti have started every opening day for the Twins since 1982.... The toughest man in the majors to strike out during the first inning last season; he fanned only once in 72 plate appearances.... The only American League player to reach base safely in eight consecutive innings in which he led off last season.... Leads the majors with 115 home runs vs. right-handed pitchers over the past five seasons, three more than runner-up Darryl Strawberry.... Hit fewer home runs in the Metrodome than on the road for the first time since 1985. Career totals: 119 at home, 104 on the road.... He has hit 30 more doubles at the Metrodome than in road games (140 to 110), and has hit only one of his 16 triples on the road (at Royals Stadium in 1983). He has 1762 career at-bats without a triple on grass fields.... Is everyone still bemoaning his not being selected to the All-Star team? In the words of Ed Norton, "Look at the facts." Among A.L. first basemen, Hrbek ranked 7th in batting average, 5th in home runs, 7th in extra-base hits, and 7th in RBIs. And that's in a season without Don Mattingly. Sure, he led the league in fielding percentage (one error per 380 chances); ask Wes Parker how many All-Star starts that will earn.

Jeff Huson

Bats Left

Texas Rangers	AB	H	2B	3B	HR	RBI	BB	SO	BA	SA	OBA
Season	396	95	12	2	0	28	46	54	.240	.280	.320
vs. Left-Handers	46	12	1	0	0	3	4	9	.261	.283	.327
vs. Right-Handers	350	83	11	2	0	25	42	45	.237	.280	.319
vs. Ground-Ballers	179	35	3	2	0	8	21	28	.196	.235	.279
vs. Fly-Ballers	217	60	9	0	0	20	25	26	.276	.318	.354
Home Games	191	42	8	1	0	11	18	33	.220	.272	.291
Road Games	205	53	4	1	0	17	28	21	.259	.288	.346
Grass Fields	327	78	10	2	0	24	37	48	.239	.281	.318
Artificial Turf	69	17	2	0	0	4	9	6	.246	.275	.329
April	36	10	1	0	0	5	8	6	.278	.306	.400
May	78	23	7	0	0	3	6	8	.295	.385	.349
June	78	21	2	1	0	4	10	9	.269	.321	.352
July	77	18	2	1	0	7	7	9	.234	.286	.302
August	66	11	0	0	0	4	10	12	.167	.167	.276
Sept./Oct.	61	12	0	0	0	5	5	10	.197	.197	.258
Leading Off Inn.	134	30	7	0	0	0	15	20	.224	.276	.307
Bases Empty	253	57	9	0	0	0	31	32	.225	.261	.312
Runners On	143	38	3	2	0	28	15	22	.266	.315	.333
Runners/Scor. Pos.	88	22	1	1	0	26	10	13	.250	.284	.324
Runners On/2 Out	58	13	0	1	0	12	5	8	.224	.259	.286
Scor. Pos./2 Out	43	10	0	1	0	12	3	6	.233	.279	.283
Late-Inning Pressure	53	16	1	0	0	5	11	11	.302	.321	.415
Leading Off	16	6	1	0	0	0	3	3	.375	.438	.474
Runners On	15	5	0	0	0	5	3	4	.333	.333	.421
Runners/Scor. Pos.	9	5	0	0	0	5	3	2	.556	.556	.615

RUNS BATTED IN	From 1B	From 2B	From 3B	Scoring Position
Totals	3/103	9/72	16/38	25/110
Percentage	2.9%	12.5%	42.1%	22.7%

Loves to face: Juan Berenguer (.750, 3-for-4)
Storm Davis (.429, 3-for-7)

Hates to face: Dave Stieb (.182, 2-for-11)
Duane Ward (0-for-5)
Bob Welch (0-for-8)

Miscellaneous statistics: Ground outs-to-air outs ratio: 1.17 last season, 1.34 for career.... Grounded into 8 double plays in 73 opportunities (one per 9.1).... Drove in 10 of 16 runners from third base with less than two outs (63%).... Direction of balls hit to the outfield: 31% to left field, 33% to center, 36% to right.... Base running: Advanced from first base to third on 14 of 22 outfield singles (64%), 3d-highest rate in A.L.; scored from second on 10 of 11 (91%).... Made 2.93 assists per nine innings at shortstop.

Comments: Started 97 games vs. right-handed pitchers, but only seven games vs. left-handers.... Played 119 games at shortstop, 36 at third base, and 12 at second base.... The Rangers allowed an average of 3.59 runs per nine innings with Huson at third base, compared to 4.16 runs per nine with Steve Buechele there, and 4.98 with Scott Coolbaugh.... His fielding percentage at shortstop was 2d worst among A.L. players at that position (.960, one error per 25 chances).... Ranked high among American League rookies in games (2d with 145), at-bats (3d), runs (2d with 57), hits (tied for 3d), walks (3d), and stolen bases (2d with 12).... Ended the season with a streak of 128 consecutive at-bats without an extra-base hit.... His career total of 512 at-bats is the highest of any player active in 1990 who has never hit a home run. Only two other active players have more than 300 career at-bats and no homers: Joey Cora (360) and Junior Noboa (309).... Career batting average of .314 in 70 at-bats in Late-Inning Pressure Situations.... Career average of .192 vs. ground-ballers, .271 vs. fly-ballers.... Batted .199 from the first slot in the batting order, the lowest of any player in the American League (minimum: 100 AB). But he was one of two players to bat over .300 from the ninth slot.... Robert Stack will investigate on "Unsolved Mysteries."

Pete Incaviglia

Bats Right

Texas Rangers	AB	H	2B	3B	HR	RBI	BB	SO	BA	SA	OBA
Season	529	123	27	0	24	85	45	146	.233	.420	.302
vs. Left-Handers	169	42	9	0	8	30	21	36	.249	.444	.347
vs. Right-Handers	360	81	18	0	16	55	24	110	.225	.408	.279
vs. Ground-Ballers	235	54	8	0	10	42	16	57	.230	.391	.292
vs. Fly-Ballers	294	69	19	0	14	43	29	89	.235	.442	.309
Home Games	247	61	13	0	15	45	28	73	.247	.482	.333
Road Games	282	62	14	0	9	40	17	73	.220	.365	.272
Grass Fields	435	99	22	0	20	64	37	128	.228	.416	.297
Artificial Turf	94	24	5	0	4	21	8	18	.255	.436	.321
April	70	17	5	0	4	15	6	24	.243	.486	.303
May	76	15	4	0	3	10	6	25	.197	.368	.274
June	106	30	5	0	5	16	9	22	.283	.472	.347
July	95	25	7	0	5	19	10	25	.263	.495	.330
August	84	15	1	0	2	9	4	26	.179	.262	.247
Sept./Oct.	98	21	5	0	5	16	10	24	.214	.418	.291
Leading Off Inn.	104	24	2	0	7	7	7	33	.231	.452	.292
Bases Empty	272	60	12	0	13	13	21	79	.221	.408	.289
Runners On	257	63	15	0	11	72	24	67	.245	.432	.315
Runners/Scor. Pos.	152	35	10	0	4	56	17	42	.230	.375	.313
Runners On/2 Out	100	24	6	0	3	26	10	25	.240	.390	.327
Scor. Pos./2 Out	67	18	6	0	2	24	8	18	.269	.448	.372
Late-Inning Pressure	87	18	6	0	4	18	4	27	.207	.414	.239
Leading Off	13	1	0	0	0	0	1	7	.077	.077	.143
Runners On	44	11	4	0	2	16	3	11	.250	.477	.292
Runners/Scor. Pos.	24	6	4	0	0	12	3	6	.250	.417	.321

RUNS BATTED IN	From 1B	From 2B	From 3B	Scoring Position
Totals	17/196	16/109	28/72	44/181
Percentage	8.7%	14.7%	38.9%	24.3%

Loves to face: Andy Hawkins (.429, 6-for-14, 2 2B, 2 HR)
Mike Jackson (.500, 4-for-8)
Walt Terrell (.294, 5-for-17, 1 3B, 2 HR)

Hates to face: Storm Davis (.063, 1-for-16, 3 BB)
Dave Stieb (.148, 4-for-27, 4 BB)
Bob Welch (0-for-12, 5 SO)

Miscellaneous statistics: Ground outs-to-air outs ratio: 1.12 last season, 1.16 for career.... Grounded into 18 double plays in 131 opportunities (one per 7.3).... Drove in 17 of 39 runners from third base with less than two outs (44%).... Direction of balls hit to the outfield: 30% to left field, 35% to center, 35% to right.... Base running: Advanced from first base to third on 13 of 32 outfield singles (41%); scored from second on 5 of 6 (83%).... Made 2.10 putouts per nine innings in left field.

Comments: Was removed for a pinch hitter three times last season; in each case it was Thad Bosley.... Career total of 826 games with no sacrifice bunts is 2d most among active players. George Bell tops the list with 1181 games.... Half of his 24 home runs were hit to center field, seven to left, and five to the opposite field. Cecil Fielder (10) was the only other player in the majors to hit at least 10 home runs to center field.... Batting average vs. right-handed pitchers was a career low, as was his overall average.... Batted .161 in day games last season, with no home runs in 87 at-bats. Career breakdown: .225 in day games, .253 at night.... Has hit more home runs at Arlington Stadium than he has on the road in four of his five seasons. Career totals: 68 at home, 56 on the road.... Career average of .160 (4-for-25, 2 HR) as a pinch hitter.... Had only one hit in 18 at-bats with the bases loaded last season, and lowered his career average with the bases loaded and two outs (no easy task) to .061 (2-for-33, 1 HR).... Has played 1470 fewer games than Lou Gehrig, but Incaviglia's first strikeout of the 1991 season will match the career total of Ol' Biscuit Pants.

Bo Jackson

Bats Right

Kansas City Royals	AB	H	2B	3B	HR	RBI	BB	SO	BA	SA	OBA
Season	405	110	16	1	28	78	44	128	.272	.523	.342
vs. Left-Handers	143	39	4	0	10	24	16	46	.273	.510	.348
vs. Right-Handers	262	71	12	1	18	54	28	82	.271	.531	.339
vs. Ground-Ballers	176	45	8	1	10	33	16	53	.256	.483	.318
vs. Fly-Ballers	229	65	8	0	18	45	28	75	.284	.555	.360
Home Games	192	59	15	0	12	37	21	58	.307	.573	.370
Road Games	213	51	1	1	16	41	23	70	.239	.479	.317
Grass Fields	156	38	1	1	11	30	18	48	.244	.474	.322
Artificial Turf	249	72	15	0	17	48	26	80	.289	.554	.355
April	53	18	3	0	1	5	6	20	.340	.453	.407
May	106	28	4	0	5	14	12	34	.264	.443	.336
June	97	23	4	0	6	15	12	36	.237	.464	.327
July	44	12	1	1	7	23	5	10	.273	.818	.327
August	16	8	1	0	3	7	3	0	.500	1.125	.550
Sept./Oct.	89	21	3	0	6	14	6	28	.236	.472	.292
Leading Off Inn.	105	26	4	0	5	5	4	35	.248	.429	.282
Bases Empty	212	59	13	0	12	12	14	63	.278	.509	.326
Runners On	193	51	3	1	16	66	30	65	.264	.539	.358
Runners/Scor. Pos.	113	27	3	0	11	55	20	36	.239	.558	.345
Runners On/2 Out	82	22	1	1	8	27	13	25	.268	.598	.368
Scor. Pos./2 Out	48	13	1	0	5	20	10	11	.271	.604	.397
Late-Inning Pressure	62	15	0	0	6	12	5	27	.242	.532	.309
Leading Off	20	4	0	0	2	2	1	9	.200	.500	.273
Runners On	29	7	0	0	2	8	3	14	.241	.448	.313
Runners/Scor. Pos.	21	4	0	0	2	8	3	10	.190	.476	.292

RUNS BATTED IN	From 1B	From 2B	From 3B	Scoring Position
Totals	13/135	15/91	22/53	37/144
Percentage	9.6%	16.5%	41.5%	25.7%

Loves to face: Andy Hawkins (.500, 3-for-6, 3 HR, 2 SO)
Paul Kilgus (.500, 7-for-14, 2 HR, 4 SO)
Mike Morgan (.667, 6-for-9)

Hates to face: Mike Henneman (0-for-9, 1 BB)
Mark Langston (.056, 1-for-18, 1 HR, 13 SO)
Curt Young (.133, 2-for-15, 1 HR)

Miscellaneous statistics: Ground outs-to-air outs ratio: 1.76 last season, 1.45 for career.... Grounded into 10 double plays in 91 opportunities (one per 9.1).... Drove in 14 of 27 runners from third base with less than two outs (52%).... Direction of balls hit to the outfield: 26% to left field, 33% to center, 41% to right.... Base running: Advanced from first base to third on 11 of 21 outfield singles (52%); scored from second on 9 of 11 (82%).... Made 2.49 putouts per nine innings in center field.

Comments: Became only the 12th player in major league history to homer in four consecutive plate appearances. Bo was the first of those 12 to visit the disabled list in the middle of such a streak.... Led the American League with 19 game-winning RBIs despite driving in only 78 runs for the season. Since 1980, no player has had that many game-winners with so few total RBIs.... His batting average has increased in each of his seasons with the Royals.... Bo led the American League in opposite-field home runs for the second straight season, hitting 12 of his home runs to left field, five to center, and 11 to the opposite field.... Has hit 49 career doubles at Royals Stadium compared to only 17 on the road. He was double-less on the road last season until the final week.... Committed 12 errors last season, and ranked last in the majors in fielding percentage (.952, one error per 21 chances).... Bo has already made more errors in his 464 games in the outfield (40) than Jimmy Piersall made in his entire career of 1610 games there.... Hasn't produced at crunch time, driving in only 12 percent of runners from scoring position in Late-Inning Pressure Situations, compared to 29 percent at other times. Career batting average with RISP in LIPS is .139. Well, it's better than Cecil Fielder (.116) and Barry Bonds (.111).... Has hit for a higher average with the bases empty than he has with runners on base in each of his four seasons in the majors.

Brook Jacoby

Bats Right

Cleveland Indians	AB	H	2B	3B	HR	RBI	BB	SO	BA	SA	OBA
Season	553	162	24	4	14	75	63	58	.293	.427	.365
vs. Left-Handers	158	50	4	1	3	18	16	13	.316	.411	.383
vs. Right-Handers	395	112	20	3	11	57	47	45	.284	.433	.358
vs. Ground-Ballers	274	77	14	2	5	31	34	25	.281	.401	.362
vs. Fly-Ballers	279	85	10	2	9	44	29	33	.305	.452	.367
Home Games	261	75	10	3	10	41	36	21	.287	.464	.374
Road Games	292	87	14	1	4	34	27	37	.298	.394	.356
Grass Fields	468	141	20	3	14	69	52	50	.301	.447	.371
Artificial Turf	85	21	4	1	0	6	11	8	.247	.318	.333
April	54	18	2	2	1	4	6	3	.333	.500	.400
May	93	21	3	1	3	9	8	16	.226	.376	.282
June	104	41	4	1	6	21	11	8	.394	.625	.452
July	103	26	1	0	2	13	14	10	.252	.320	.342
August	94	21	4	0	1	12	14	8	.223	.298	.330
Sept./Oct.	105	35	10	0	1	16	10	13	.333	.457	.391
Leading Off Inn.	111	28	2	0	2	2	15	11	.252	.324	.341
Bases Empty	295	81	12	2	10	10	35	29	.275	.431	.352
Runners On	258	81	12	2	4	65	28	29	.314	.422	.380
Runners/Scor. Pos.	140	41	5	0	1	54	24	13	.293	.350	.387
Runners On/2 Out	102	36	3	0	2	30	15	12	.353	.441	.441
Scor. Pos./2 Out	64	23	2	0	0	25	14	4	.359	.391	.474
Late-Inning Pressure	88	23	4	0	2	9	6	11	.261	.375	.309
Leading Off	20	2	0	0	0	0	1	3	.100	.100	.143
Runners On	34	9	3	0	0	7	2	5	.265	.353	.306
Runners/Scor. Pos.	19	4	1	0	0	6	2	3	.211	.263	.286

RUNS BATTED IN	From 1B	From 2B	From 3B	Scoring Position
Totals	9/196	24/104	28/61	52/165
Percentage	4.6%	23.1%	45.9%	31.5%

Loves to face: Dennis Lamp (.435, 10-for-23, 2 HR)
Bobby Witt (.350, 7-for-20, 2 2B, 1 3B, 2 HR, 7 BB)

Hates to face: Greg A. Harris (.167, 3-for-18)
Randy Johnson (0-for-12, 1 BB)
Gene Nelson (.138, 4-for-29)

Miscellaneous statistics: Ground outs-to-air outs ratio: 0.95 last season, 1.01 for career.... Grounded into 20 double plays in 126 opportunities (one per 6.3).... Drove in 17 of 35 runners from third base with less than two outs (49%).... Direction of balls hit to the outfield: 33% to left field, 36% to center, 30% to right.... Base running: Advanced from first base to third on 6 of 36 outfield singles (17%); scored from second on 17 of 23 (74%).... Made 1.84 assists per nine innings at third base; made 0.45 assists per nine innings at first base, lowest rate in majors.

Comments: His June batting average was the highest in the American League.... Had a league-high 36-game errorless streak at third base, followed by a 30-game streak to end the season.... Jacoby led the Tribe in innings played at both first base and third base, and he led the team in fielding at both as well. In fact, he led the league in fielding with an average of one error per 52 chances at third base (minimum: 81 games).... Jacoby hit 32 home runs in 1987, but has hit only 36 homers in three seasons since then.... Strikeouts year by year since 1988: 101, 90, 58.... Indians all-time top five in games at third base: Ken Keltner (1492), Bill Bradley (1191), Jacoby (983), Max Alvis (935), Al Rosen (932).... Has been in the opening-day lineup in each of the last seven seasons, the longest streak for an Indians player since Jim Hegan started 11 in a row from 1947 through 1957.... Has hit for a higher average on the road than he has at home in each of his seven seasons with the Indians. Career breakdown: .267 at Cleveland Stadium, .283 everywhere else.... Has hit for a higher average in night games than he has in day games in each of the last six seasons.... Doesn't it seem like Jacoby and Brett Butler for Len Barker in 1983, then Joe Carter, Mel Hall, and Ron Hassey for Rick Sutcliffe nine months later should have added up to more than one winning season in the last six?

Chris James

Bats Right

Cleveland Indians	AB	H	2B	3B	HR	RBI	BB	SO	BA	SA	OBA
Season	528	158	32	4	12	70	31	71	.299	.443	.341
vs. Left-Handers	162	49	7	1	4	22	15	25	.302	.432	.361
vs. Right-Handers	366	109	25	3	8	48	16	46	.298	.448	.332
vs. Ground-Ballers	266	82	15	2	4	40	13	36	.308	.425	.340
vs. Fly-Ballers	262	76	17	2	8	30	18	35	.290	.462	.342
Home Games	234	67	13	1	6	33	15	33	.286	.427	.333
Road Games	294	91	19	3	6	37	16	38	.310	.456	.347
Grass Fields	449	138	27	3	9	58	28	59	.307	.441	.351
Artificial Turf	79	20	5	1	3	12	3	12	.253	.456	.280
April	41	5	0	0	1	3	0	7	.122	.195	.140
May	81	26	6	0	1	11	5	10	.321	.432	.375
June	104	33	5	2	2	17	6	16	.317	.462	.348
July	98	28	7	1	2	8	9	15	.286	.439	.352
August	112	40	8	1	4	17	7	12	.357	.554	.395
Sept./Oct.	92	26	6	0	2	14	4	11	.283	.413	.313
Leading Off Inn.	102	27	6	0	5	5	6	15	.265	.471	.318
Bases Empty	281	78	17	3	10	10	14	33	.278	.466	.319
Runners On	247	80	15	1	2	60	17	38	.324	.417	.366
Runners/Scor. Pos.	145	47	7	1	2	58	14	20	.324	.428	.377
Runners On/2 Out	98	30	3	0	2	28	6	15	.306	.398	.346
Scor. Pos./2 Out	66	20	2	0	2	27	6	6	.303	.424	.361
Late-Inning Pressure	72	15	2	0	0	4	6	15	.208	.236	.278
Leading Off	18	0	0	0	0	0	2	6	.000	.000	.143
Runners On	25	8	1	0	0	4	3	5	.320	.360	.393
Runners/Scor. Pos.	15	4	0	0	0	3	3	4	.267	.267	.389

RUNS BATTED IN	From 1B	From 2B	From 3B	Scoring Position
Totals	5/169	26/111	27/66	53/177
Percentage	3.0%	23.4%	40.9%	29.9%

Loves to face: Brian Fisher (.467, 7-for-15)
Randy Johnson (.400, 4-for-10, 1 3B, 2 HR)
Pascual Perez (.417, 5-for-12, 2 HR)

Hates to face: Mike Dunne (.118, 2-for-17)
Jack Morris (.130, 3-for-23, 4 BB)
Nolan Ryan (.050, 1-for-20, 2 BB)

Miscellaneous statistics: Ground outs-to-air outs ratio: 1.11 last season, 1.09 for career.... Grounded into 11 double plays in 117 opportunities (one per 10.6).... Drove in 19 of 35 runners from third base with less than two outs (54%).... Direction of balls hit to the outfield: 35% to left field, 32% to center, 33% to right.... Base running: Advanced from first base to third on 8 of 37 outfield singles (22%); scored from second on 9 of 14 (64%).... Made 1.88 putouts per nine innings in left field.

Comments: James and teammate Candy Maldonado both increased their batting averages by 56 points from 1989 to 1990, the second and third biggest gains in the A.L. last season (minimum: 300 at-bats in both seasons), behind Alan Trammell (61 points).... Over the 30 seasons from 1961 through 1990, 165 players accumulated at least 300 at-bats in consecutive seasons in different leagues; 91 of them (55%) improved their batting averages, but only three by more than James or Maldonado: Frank Howard (1965), Don Money (1973), and Greg Brock (1987).... Led designated hitters with a .296 batting average. He started 12 games in the field, but only two after the All-Star break.... Led the Indians with 40 hits to the opposite field last season.... Batting average with runners in scoring position year by year since 1987: .233, .204, .259, .324.... He has a career total of 52 plate appearances with the bases loaded. Who cares that he hasn't walked—he's hit three grand slams.... Over the last two seasons he has only two hits and two walks in 39 at-bats leading off innings in Late-Inning Pressure Situations.... Flashed his potential in 1983 when he led the South Atlantic League with 121 RBIs, 34 more than his nearest rival. Among the distant pursuers: a 19-year-old named Cecil Fielder, with 94 RBIs. Vince Coleman led the league in batting average (.350) and stolen bases (145 in 113 games).

Dion James

Bats Left

Cleveland Indians	AB	H	2B	3B	HR	RBI	BB	SO	BA	SA	OBA
Season	248	68	15	2	1	22	27	23	.274	.363	.347
vs. Left-Handers	9	1	1	0	0	1	1	0	.111	.222	.200
vs. Right-Handers	239	67	14	2	1	21	26	23	.280	.368	.352
vs. Ground-Ballers	121	39	9	2	1	15	14	9	.322	.455	.397
vs. Fly-Ballers	127	29	6	0	0	7	13	14	.228	.276	.298
Home Games	123	40	12	1	0	10	15	12	.325	.439	.400
Road Games	125	28	3	1	1	12	12	11	.224	.288	.292
Grass Fields	216	60	14	2	1	20	25	20	.278	.375	.354
Artificial Turf	32	8	1	0	0	2	2	3	.250	.281	.294
April	33	8	1	0	0	2	4	3	.242	.273	.316
May	55	14	3	0	0	3	5	7	.255	.309	.317
June	49	14	4	1	0	3	6	3	.286	.408	.364
July	34	10	3	1	0	5	5	2	.294	.441	.400
August	56	16	3	0	1	7	4	5	.286	.393	.333
Sept./Oct.	21	6	1	0	0	2	3	3	.286	.333	.375
Leading Off Inn.	56	15	2	1	0	0	5	6	.268	.339	.339
Bases Empty	147	35	9	1	0	0	16	17	.238	.313	.317
Runners On	101	33	6	1	1	22	11	6	.327	.436	.389
Runners/Scor. Pos.	47	13	2	1	0	18	9	3	.277	.362	.386
Runners On/2 Out	35	8	3	0	0	6	4	2	.229	.314	.308
Scor. Pos./2 Out	20	4	1	0	0	4	4	1	.200	.250	.333
Late-Inning Pressure	44	9	2	0	0	1	4	4	.205	.250	.271
Leading Off	8	2	1	0	0	0	1	1	.250	.375	.333
Runners On	20	4	0	0	0	1	2	3	.200	.200	.273
Runners/Scor. Pos.	10	2	0	0	0	1	2	1	.200	.200	.333

RUNS BATTED IN	From 1B	From 2B	From 3B	Scoring Position
Totals	4/72	2/28	15/25	17/53
Percentage	5.6%	7.1%	60.0%	32.1%

Loves to face: Brian Fisher (.467, 7-for-15)
Ted Power (.500, 6-for-12)
Bob Walk (.455, 10-for-22, 6 2B)

Hates to face: Jack Morris (.130, 3-for-23, 4 BB)
Nolan Ryan (.050, 1-for-20, 2 BB)
Bryn Smith (.105, 2-for-19)

Miscellaneous statistics: Ground outs-to-air outs ratio: 1.57 last season, 1.50 for career. . . . Grounded into 6 double plays in 54 opportunities (one per 9.0). . . . Drove in 11 of 13 runners from third base with less than two outs (85%). . . . Direction of balls hit to the outfield: 28% to left field, 33% to center, 39% to right. . . . Base running: Advanced from first base to third on 1 of 14 outfield singles (7%), 3d-lowest rate in A.L.; scored from second on 5 of 8 (63%). . . . Made 0.61 assists per nine innings at first base.

Comments: Started 66 games, all against right-handed pitchers. . . . Batted against left-handers only 113 times over the last three seasons, compiling a .167 batting average. But in 1987, the only year he played against southpaws on even a semiregular basis, he batted .303 vs. LHP. His only career home run off of a left-handed pitcher was against Bob Knepper in that season. . . . Was removed for a pinch hitter 20 times last season, all against left-handed pitchers. . . . One of four major league outfielders to play at least 200 innings last season without an assist. The others: Jeffrey Leonard, Kevin Romine, and Darnell Coles. . . . Threw out seven runners as a rookie in 1984. Underwent shoulder surgery in 1985, and has only 10 assists in 373 games in the outfield since then. . . . Appeared headed for stardom after hitting .295 as a rookie in 1984, then .312 in his 1987 comeback. He missed most of '85 following the shoulder separation, and spent all of 1986 at Vancouver. . . . Has batted over .300 with runners on base in three of the last four years, and has hit for a higher average with runners on base than with the bases empty in each of the last six years. Career breakdown: .307 with runners on base, .269 with the bases empty. . . . Career average of .170 (15-for-88, 1 HR) as a pinch hitter. . . . Was released by the Indians after starting only three of their last 28 games. . . . If there's no room on the roster for a 28-year-old hitter of this caliber, someone ought to have his head examined.

Lance Johnson

Bats Left

Chicago White Sox	AB	H	2B	3B	HR	RBI	BB	SO	BA	SA	OBA
Season	541	154	18	9	1	51	33	45	.285	.357	.325
vs. Left-Handers	156	50	3	3	0	19	9	18	.321	.378	.353
vs. Right-Handers	385	104	15	6	1	32	24	27	.270	.348	.313
vs. Ground-Ballers	264	80	10	2	0	25	16	21	.303	.356	.342
vs. Fly-Ballers	277	74	8	7	1	26	17	24	.267	.357	.309
Home Games	265	80	9	6	0	25	15	20	.302	.381	.336
Road Games	276	74	9	3	1	26	18	25	.268	.333	.314
Grass Fields	458	130	16	9	1	43	26	42	.284	.365	.321
Artificial Turf	83	24	2	0	0	8	7	3	.289	.313	.344
April	58	16	2	0	0	8	3	7	.276	.310	.311
May	101	29	4	0	0	8	10	6	.287	.327	.348
June	83	23	4	2	0	10	4	9	.277	.373	.307
July	97	24	2	1	1	10	6	7	.247	.320	.288
August	85	20	2	4	0	8	4	7	.235	.353	.267
Sept./Oct.	117	42	4	2	0	7	6	9	.359	.427	.395
Leading Off Inn.	158	43	6	2	0	0	9	11	.272	.335	.311
Bases Empty	330	87	11	4	0	0	25	25	.264	.321	.315
Runners On	211	67	7	5	1	51	8	20	.318	.412	.339
Runners/Scor. Pos.	116	40	3	4	1	49	7	10	.345	.466	.375
Runners On/2 Out	90	26	3	2	0	20	3	11	.289	.367	.319
Scor. Pos./2 Out	55	18	1	2	0	20	3	7	.327	.418	.373
Late-Inning Pressure	73	19	2	3	0	7	7	9	.260	.370	.321
Leading Off	19	6	0	1	0	0	1	2	.316	.421	.350
Runners On	28	9	2	2	0	7	4	5	.321	.536	.394
Runners/Scor. Pos.	16	7	1	2	0	7	4	2	.438	.750	.524

RUNS BATTED IN	From 1B	From 2B	From 3B	Scoring Position
Totals	4/138	17/75	29/64	46/139
Percentage	2.9%	22.7%	45.3%	33.1%

Loves to face: Kevin Brown (.833, 5-for-6)
Ron Robinson (.556, 5-for-9)

Hates to face: Storm Davis (.091, 1-for-11)
Nolan Ryan (.077, 1-for-13, 1 3B, 2 BB)
Scott Sanderson (.091, 1-for-11, 1 3B)

Miscellaneous statistics: Ground outs-to-air outs ratio: 1.84 last season, 2.09 for career. . . . Grounded into 12 double plays in 100 opportunities (one per 8.3). . . . Drove in 17 of 32 runners from third base with less than two outs (53%). . . . Direction of balls hit to the outfield: 37% to left field, 28% to center, 35% to right. . . . Base running: Advanced from first base to third on 21 of 26 outfield singles (81%), highest rate in majors; scored from second on 15 of 18 (83%). . . . Made 2.70 putouts per nine innings in center field.

Comments: Batting average vs. southpaws was the 2d highest in the league by a left-handed batter (minimum: 100 AB). Only Rafael Palmeiro was better (.339). . . . Batted .337 from the 2d spot in the batting order, the highest of any player in the American League (minimum: 100 AB). . . . Ended the season with a 14-game hitting streak. . . . Stole 36 bases in 58 attempts. The list of American League leaders in times caught stealing is littered with White Sox: Johnson (22), Ozzie Guillen (17), Roberto Kelly (17), Ivan Calderon (16), Harold Reynolds (16), and Sammy Sosa (16). Chicago led the league with 90 runners caught. . . . His only home run in more than 900 career at-bats was hit against Andy Hawkins in the game in which Melido Perez pitched his rain-shortened no-hitter. Johnson also saved that no-hitter with a great catch against Alvaro Espinoza. . . . Sox pitchers allowed 3.84 runs per nine innings with Johnson in center field, nearly a half-run more with others there (4.30). . . . Has batted over .300 with runners in scoring position in three of his four seasons in the majors. Career breakdown: .249 with the bases empty, .305 with runners on base, .312 with runners in scoring position. . . . Last season was no fluke—he played three seasons at the Triple-A level and batted .316.

Tracy Jones

Bats Right

Tigers/Mariners	AB	H	2B	3B	HR	RBI	BB	SO	BA	SA	OBA
Season	204	53	8	1	6	24	9	25	.260	.397	.307
vs. Left-Handers	112	29	4	0	4	13	6	11	.259	.402	.308
vs. Right-Handers	92	24	4	1	2	11	3	14	.261	.391	.306
vs. Ground-Ballers	82	20	4	0	2	11	3	13	.244	.366	.295
vs. Fly-Ballers	122	33	4	1	4	13	6	12	.270	.418	.315
Home Games	114	30	4	0	3	17	5	14	.263	.377	.317
Road Games	90	23	4	1	3	7	4	11	.256	.422	.295
Grass Fields	106	23	1	0	5	11	6	10	.217	.368	.278
Artificial Turf	98	30	7	1	1	13	3	15	.306	.429	.340
April	31	11	4	1	0	1	2	5	.355	.548	.444
May	58	12	0	0	3	7	4	4	.207	.362	.258
June	60	15	3	0	1	8	0	8	.250	.350	.262
July	36	10	0	0	2	4	3	4	.278	.444	.350
August	19	5	1	0	0	4	0	4	.263	.316	.263
Sept./Oct.	0	0	0	0	0	0	0	0	—	—	—
Leading Off Inn.	36	9	2	1	2	2	0	4	.250	.528	.250
Bases Empty	100	28	6	1	6	6	3	12	.280	.540	.314
Runners On	104	25	2	0	0	18	6	13	.240	.260	.301
Runners/Scor. Pos.	59	15	2	0	0	18	5	11	.254	.288	.333
Runners On/2 Out	46	11	1	0	0	8	1	6	.239	.261	.271
Scor. Pos./2 Out	27	8	1	0	0	8	1	6	.296	.333	.321
Late-Inning Pressure	34	4	1	0	0	2	2	4	.118	.147	.189
Leading Off	7	0	0	0	0	0	0	1	.000	.000	.000
Runners On	18	4	1	0	0	2	2	2	.222	.278	.333
Runners/Scor. Pos.	9	2	1	0	0	2	2	2	.222	.333	.417

RUNS BATTED IN	From 1B	From 2B	From 3B	Scoring Position
Totals	2/81	7/48	9/20	16/68
Percentage	2.5%	14.6%	45.0%	23.5%

Loves to face: Mark Davis (.571, 8-for-14)
Rick Honeycutt (.429, 3-for-7, 1 HR)
Jamie Moyer (.500, 4-for-8, 1 HR)

Hates to face: Allan Anderson (0-for-7)
Mark Langston (0-for-7)
Jesse Orosco (0-for-8, 1 BB)

Miscellaneous statistics: Ground outs-to-air outs ratio: 0.96 last season, 1.36 for career.... Grounded into 7 double plays in 50 opportunities (one per 7.1).... Drove in 6 of 9 runners from third base with less than two outs (67%).... Direction of balls hit to the outfield: 49% to left field, 28% to center, 24% to right.... Base running: Advanced from first base to third on 2 of 11 outfield singles (18%); scored from second on 5 of 6 (83%).... Made 1.92 putouts per nine innings in left field.

Comments: Hit for a higher average against right-handers than against left-handers for the first time in his career. Career averages: .318 vs. left-handers, .236 vs. right-handers.... The only player to play for five different teams over the past three seasons.... Played for two clubs in each of the last three seasons (Reds and Expos in 1988, Giants and Tigers in 1989, Tigers and Mariners in 1990.) The record for such nonsense—my, they keep records on the oddest things!—is four consecutive split seasons: Bob Kennedy (1954–57), Sal Maglie (1955–58), Don McMahon (1966–69), and Willie Montanez (1979–82).... Wore out his welcome in Detroit after one year. He played his last game for them exactly one year to the day after making his Tigers debut.... Career average of .519 (14-for-27) with the bases loaded is better than Pat Tabler's.... Career average of .232 on grass fields, .312 on artificial surfaces.... Batting average in Late-Inning Pressure Situations has dropped in each of his five seasons in the majors: .391, .278, .271, .220, .188.... Career average of .217 (20-for-92, 2 HR) as a pinch hitter.... Has played 298 games in the outfield, the most of any active player who has never been involved in a double play at that position.

Wally Joyner

Bats Left

California Angels	AB	H	2B	3B	HR	RBI	BB	SO	BA	SA	OBA
Season	310	83	15	0	8	41	41	34	.268	.394	.350
vs. Left-Handers	106	24	2	0	2	17	10	15	.226	.302	.291
vs. Right-Handers	204	59	13	0	6	24	31	19	.289	.441	.379
vs. Ground-Ballers	147	40	8	0	5	22	21	13	.272	.429	.363
vs. Fly-Ballers	163	43	7	0	3	19	20	21	.264	.362	.339
Home Games	135	37	5	0	5	21	21	13	.274	.422	.367
Road Games	175	46	10	0	3	20	20	21	.263	.371	.337
Grass Fields	255	64	12	0	7	36	36	26	.251	.380	.340
Artificial Turf	55	19	3	0	1	5	5	8	.345	.455	.400
April	74	18	5	0	2	7	9	8	.243	.392	.318
May	101	34	3	0	5	22	18	9	.337	.515	.438
June	94	22	3	0	1	9	12	13	.234	.298	.315
July	41	9	4	0	0	3	2	4	.220	.317	.256
August	0	0	0	0	0	0	0	0	—	—	—
Sept./Oct.	0	0	0	0	0	0	0	0	—	—	—
Leading Off Inn.	76	13	1	0	3	3	10	9	.171	.303	.267
Bases Empty	185	44	7	0	6	6	26	19	.238	.373	.335
Runners On	125	39	8	0	2	35	15	15	.312	.424	.372
Runners/Scor. Pos.	78	22	3	0	1	33	11	11	.282	.359	.351
Runners On/2 Out	43	13	2	0	1	13	9	6	.302	.419	.423
Scor. Pos./2 Out	33	8	1	0	1	13	6	4	.242	.364	.359
Late-Inning Pressure	49	8	5	0	0	4	4	6	.163	.265	.222
Leading Off	11	0	0	0	0	0	1	2	.000	.000	.083
Runners On	21	5	3	0	0	4	2	3	.238	.381	.292
Runners/Scor. Pos.	11	2	1	0	0	4	1	1	.182	.273	.231

RUNS BATTED IN	From 1B	From 2B	From 3B	Scoring Position
Totals	4/89	14/61	15/37	29/98
Percentage	4.5%	23.0%	40.5%	29.6%

Loves to face: Paul Kilgus (.455, 5-for-11, 2 HR)
Al Nipper (.583, 7-for-12, 1 2B, 4 HR)
Walt Terrell (.389, 7-for-18, 3 2B, 1 3B, 2 HR)

Hates to face: Mark Langston (.130, 3-for-23, 1 HR)
Nolan Ryan (.143, 2-for-14)
Bob Welch (.071, 1-for-14, 4 BB)

Miscellaneous statistics: Ground outs-to-air outs ratio: 1.07 last season, 0.89 for career.... Grounded into 10 double plays in 66 opportunities (one per 6.6).... Drove in 10 of 20 runners from third base with less than two outs (50%).... Direction of balls hit to the outfield: 34% to left field, 36% to center, 30% to right.... Base running: Advanced from first base to third on 9 of 17 outfield singles (53%); scored from second on 7 of 8 (88%).... Made 0.77 assists per nine innings at first base.

Comments: Missed 79 games last season, compared to a total of 28 in his first four seasons in the majors.... Has played 699 games at first base, 19 fewer than Rod Carew, the Angels' all-time leader at that position.... Career batting average of .257 vs left-handers, .301 vs. right-handers.... The following review of the 1986 American League Rookie of the Year voting is sponsored by the Ruben Sierra fan club: Jose Canseco, 110; Joyner, 98; Mark Eichhorn, 23; Cory Snyder, 16; Danny Tartabull, 4; Sierra, 1.... Although his batting average in road games has dropped steadily from a career high of .315 in 1987, his averages at Anaheim Stadium have remained consistent—never below .260 or above .280 in five seasons.... Career batting averages: .273 at Anaheim Stadium, .285 on other grass fields, .329 on artificial turf.... Has never batted below .287 against right-handed pitchers.... One of 17 players in major league history with 100 RBIs in both his rookie and sophomore seasons. The others drove in an average of 282 runs over their next three seasons; Joyner has 205 RBIs in three seasons since. The only players with fewer than Joyner: Dale Alexander (187), Babe Young (171), Ray Jablonski (151), and Luke Easter (128).

Ron Karkovice

Bats Right

Chicago White Sox	AB	H	2B	3B	HR	RBI	BB	SO	BA	SA	OBA
Season	183	45	10	0	6	20	16	52	.246	.399	.308
vs. Left-Handers	64	14	4	0	2	9	6	24	.219	.375	.282
vs. Right-Handers	119	31	6	0	4	11	10	28	.261	.412	.323
vs. Ground-Ballers	81	24	5	0	4	9	4	22	.296	.506	.333
vs. Fly-Ballers	102	21	5	0	2	11	12	30	.206	.314	.289
Home Games	83	18	5	0	0	6	9	24	.217	.277	.293
Road Games	100	27	5	0	6	14	7	28	.270	.500	.321
Grass Fields	151	39	9	0	5	15	14	43	.258	.417	.323
Artificial Turf	32	6	1	0	1	5	2	9	.188	.313	.235
April	4	0	0	0	0	0	1	2	.000	.000	.200
May	27	9	1	0	1	4	3	7	.333	.481	.400
June	41	11	2	0	2	3	3	11	.268	.463	.333
July	35	9	5	0	1	3	3	6	.257	.486	.316
August	39	10	2	0	1	7	3	14	.256	.385	.302
Sept./Oct.	37	6	0	0	1	3	3	12	.162	.243	.225
Leading Off Inn.	37	13	2	0	1	1	5	7	.351	.486	.442
Bases Empty	98	25	5	0	5	5	8	24	.255	.459	.318
Runners On	85	20	5	0	1	15	8	28	.235	.329	.298
Runners/Scor. Pos.	44	10	2	0	1	15	7	16	.227	.341	.327
Runners On/2 Out	38	5	1	0	0	3	3	14	.132	.158	.195
Scor. Pos./2 Out	18	2	0	0	0	3	2	7	.111	.111	.200
Late-Inning Pressure	26	12	1	0	1	1	1	4	.462	.615	.481
Leading Off	7	4	1	0	0	0	0	1	.571	.714	.571
Runners On	10	5	0	0	0	0	1	2	.500	.500	.545
Runners/Scor. Pos.	5	1	0	0	0	0	1	1	.200	.200	.333

RUNS BATTED IN	From 1B	From 2B	From 3B	Scoring Position
Totals	1/62	6/38	7/18	13/56
Percentage	1.6%	15.8%	38.9%	23.2%

Loves to face: Bert Blyleven (.667, 2-for-3, 1 HR)
Curt Young (.571, 4-for-7, 2 SO)

Hates to face: John Candelaria (.077, 1-for-13, 1 HR, 7 SO)
Nolan Ryan (.167, 2-for-12)
Matt Young (0-for-9, 5 SO)

Miscellaneous statistics: Ground outs-to-air outs ratio: 0.64 last season, 0.87 for career.... Grounded into 1 double play in 37 opportunities (one per 37.0).... Drove in 6 of 9 runners from third base with less than two outs (67%).... Direction of balls hit to the outfield: 54% to left field, 29% to center, 17% to right.... Base running: Advanced from first base to third on 5 of 11 outfield singles (45%); scored from second on 4 of 10 (40%), shared 2d-lowest rate in A.L.... Opposing base stealers: 18-for-36 (50%).

Comments: Karkovice is a living, breathing endorsement for White Sox hitting instructor Walt Hriniak. He has batted a modest .255 over the last two seasons, but that's a vast improvement over his .168 career mark prior to Hriniak's change of Sox from Red to White.... That's great for Hriniak, whose own career batting statistics don't look too good on a resume: 26 hits—all singles—in 99 at-bats.... Karkovice has also reduced his strikeout rate by 20 percent over the past two seasons: one SO per 3.1 plate appearances before, one per 3.8 PA after.... White Sox pitchers allowed 3.71 runs per nine innings with Karkovice catching, 4.05 with Fisk.... Has only three hits in 14 career at-bats with the bases loaded, but two of those hits are grand slams, one in each of the last two seasons.... Why was Karkovice smiling at the Comiskey Park wake? He had a .189 career average there, with only three home runs in 312 at-bats. His career numbers on the road are respectable: .240, 15 home runs (one per 23 AB).... Has stranded 21 runners in scoring position in Late-Inning Pressure Situations during his career without driving a single runner home.... Career batting average of .244 in day games (despite going 0-for-27 in 1987), .197 at night.

Roberto Kelly

Bats Right

New York Yankees	AB	H	2B	3B	HR	RBI	BB	SO	BA	SA	OBA
Season	641	183	32	4	15	61	33	148	.285	.418	.323
vs. Left-Handers	181	55	10	0	5	17	12	46	.304	.442	.352
vs. Right-Handers	460	128	22	4	10	44	21	102	.278	.409	.311
vs. Ground-Ballers	296	87	9	4	7	33	10	63	.294	.422	.321
vs. Fly-Ballers	345	96	23	0	8	28	23	85	.278	.414	.324
Home Games	315	96	22	2	5	25	14	57	.305	.435	.334
Road Games	326	87	10	2	10	36	19	91	.267	.402	.311
Grass Fields	542	154	28	3	13	48	26	120	.284	.419	.319
Artificial Turf	99	29	4	1	2	13	7	28	.293	.414	.343
April	60	19	2	0	0	4	1	10	.317	.350	.328
May	107	30	6	1	2	15	8	32	.280	.411	.328
June	110	31	4	1	2	3	7	33	.282	.391	.325
July	120	33	7	1	4	18	3	24	.275	.450	.296
August	122	39	9	0	6	11	7	27	.320	.541	.362
Sept./Oct.	122	31	4	1	1	10	7	22	.254	.328	.301
Leading Off Inn.	208	63	14	0	9	9	10	46	.303	.500	.344
Bases Empty	421	121	20	1	12	12	22	109	.287	.425	.327
Runners On	220	62	12	3	3	49	11	39	.282	.405	.314
Runners/Scor. Pos.	122	30	5	1	1	39	7	25	.246	.328	.284
Runners On/2 Out	90	26	4	0	1	20	4	13	.289	.367	.319
Scor. Pos./2 Out	54	15	3	0	1	18	3	8	.278	.389	.316
Late-Inning Pressure	106	27	4	0	3	10	7	30	.255	.377	.301
Leading Off	27	10	3	0	1	1	3	8	.370	.593	.433
Runners On	47	10	1	0	1	8	0	8	.213	.298	.213
Runners/Scor. Pos.	23	4	1	0	0	5	0	6	.174	.217	.174

RUNS BATTED IN	From 1B	From 2B	From 3B	Scoring Position
Totals	8/152	19/92	19/54	38/146
Percentage	5.3%	20.7%	35.2%	26.0%

Loves to face: John Candelaria (.750, 3-for-4, 1 HR, 1 SO)
Storm Davis (.500, 7-for-14, 1 HR)
Nolan Ryan (.556, 5-for-9, 1 HR)

Hates to face: Kevin Brown (.200, 3-for-15)
Brian Holman (.200, 3-for-15)
Jack Morris (.188, 3-for-16)

Miscellaneous statistics: Ground outs-to-air outs ratio: 0.93 last season, 1.10 for career.... Grounded into 7 double plays in 100 opportunities (one per 14.3).... Drove in 13 of 27 runners from third base with less than two outs (48%).... Direction of balls hit to the outfield: 34% to left field, 31% to center, 35% to right.... Base running: Advanced from first base to third on 7 of 21 outfield singles (33%); scored from second on 15 of 24 (63%).... Made 2.79 putouts per nine innings in center field.

Comments: The only players to equal or surpass Kelly's 1990 season totals in both stolen bases and home runs were the A.L. and N.L. MVPs, Rickey Henderson and Barry Bonds.... Ranked second in the league to Mike Greenwell in hits vs. right-handed pitchers.... Hit eight of his 15 home runs to the opposite field. Only two players in the majors hit more dingers to the opposite field last season: Kal Daniels (15) and Bo Jackson (11).... Who led the majors in complete games last season? Not Ramon Martinez, but Roberto Kelly, who played 154 games in their entirety, the most of any player in the majors.... Kelly was one of three players not to miss a game last season. The others: Cal Ripken and Joe Carter.... Kelly is only the second player in Yankees history to play 160 or more games in the outfield. He tied the team record, set by Roger Maris in 1961. (If you're going to match one of Roger's records from 1961, that's probably not the one you would choose.)... Can anyone explain why Kelly struck out only 57 times at Yankee Stadium, but 91 times on the road? It's not a random occurrence; his strikeout rate was 36 percent lower at home from 1987 through 1989 as well.... Career batting-average breakdown: .299 at Yankee Stadium, .257 on other grass fields, .317 on artificial surfaces.

Ron Kittle

Bats Right

White Sox/Orioles	AB	H	2B	3B	HR	RBI	BB	SO	BA	SA	OBA
Season	338	78	16	0	18	46	26	91	.231	.438	.293
vs. Left-Handers	151	34	6	0	13	25	13	38	.225	.523	.291
vs. Right-Handers	187	44	10	0	5	21	13	53	.235	.369	.294
vs. Ground-Ballers	132	19	3	0	5	15	15	39	.144	.280	.236
vs. Fly-Ballers	206	59	13	0	13	31	11	52	.286	.539	.330
Home Games	185	42	13	0	8	20	14	53	.227	.427	.289
Road Games	153	36	3	0	10	26	12	38	.235	.451	.298
Grass Fields	293	69	16	0	14	39	24	75	.235	.433	.302
Artificial Turf	45	9	0	0	4	7	2	16	.200	.467	.229
April	53	15	3	0	2	8	5	12	.283	.453	.367
May	70	21	4	0	6	21	8	24	.300	.614	.367
June	86	15	3	0	6	7	4	26	.174	.419	.211
July	74	18	5	0	2	7	7	16	.243	.392	.317
August	35	5	1	0	1	2	2	11	.143	.257	.211
Sept./Oct.	20	4	0	0	1	1	0	2	.200	.350	.200
Leading Off Inn.	86	14	3	0	6	6	4	24	.163	.407	.209
Bases Empty	196	45	11	0	13	13	13	50	.230	.485	.284
Runners On	142	33	5	0	5	33	13	41	.232	.373	.304
Runners/Scor. Pos.	83	17	2	0	1	23	8	31	.205	.265	.287
Runners On/2 Out	63	16	1	0	3	15	7	16	.254	.413	.338
Scor. Pos./2 Out	38	10	0	0	0	9	5	12	.263	.263	.364
Late-Inning Pressure	45	9	0	0	2	6	7	11	.200	.333	.308
Leading Off	9	1	0	0	0	0	1	1	.111	.111	.200
Runners On	18	4	0	0	1	5	5	6	.222	.389	.391
Runners/Scor. Pos.	10	2	0	0	0	3	4	3	.200	.200	.429

RUNS BATTED IN	From 1B	From 2B	From 3B	Scoring Position
Totals	8/95	11/67	9/32	20/99
Percentage	8.4%	16.4%	28.1%	20.2%

Loves to face: Bert Blyleven (.318, 14-for-44, 1 2B, 9 HR)
Jim Clancy (.500, 9-for-18, 4 HR)
Mark Knudson (4-for-4, 1 HR, 1 HP)

Hates to face: Storm Davis (.063, 1-for-16, 1 HR)
Dave Stewart (.083, 2-for-24)
Dave Stieb (.071, 2-for-28)

Miscellaneous statistics: Ground outs-to-air outs ratio: 0.61 last season, 5th-lowest rate in A.L.; 0.69 for career.... Grounded into 6 double plays in 61 opportunities (one per 10.2).... Drove in 6 of 15 runners from third base with less than two outs (40%).... Direction of balls hit to the outfield: 55% to left field, 26% to center, 20% to right.... Base running: Advanced from first base to third on 4 of 16 outfield singles (25%); scored from second on 3 of 6 (50%).... Made 0.28 assists per nine innings at first base.

Comments: Only five players in major league history hit more home runs than Kittle in their first 2500 at-bats. The leaders: Babe Ruth, 197; Ralph Kiner, 196; Harmon Killebrew, 192; Eddie Mathews, 182; Rocky Colavito, 169; and Kittle, 166.... Career average of one HR per 15.3 at-bats is the 10th highest among players with at least 150 homers. Kittle ranks just below Jimmie Foxx and Mike Schmidt, slightly above Hank Greenberg, Willie McCovey, and Hank Aaron.... Has a career rate of only one home run per 33.5 at-bats in Late-Inning Pressure Situations.... Has 174 career home runs, but no grand slams. Only one player in major league history has hit more home runs without a slam: Kirk. Gibson (192). Kittle has 59 career at-bats with the bases loaded...Kittle has a career batting average of only .205 as a pinch hitter, but has six home runs in 83 at-bats in that role.... Kittle came to the plate 369 times in 1990, his highest total since 422 in 1986.... Batted only .164 with three RBIs in 22 games after being traded to the Orioles. He didn't play during the final two weeks of the season.... Batted 142 points higher vs. fly-ballers (.286) than vs. ground-ballers (.144) last season, the largest margin in the majors.... His batting average against ground-ball pitchers was the lowest in the American League since 1975, when Jim Mason batted .142 and Harmon Killebrew batted .145.

Jeff Kunkel

Bats Right

Texas Rangers	AB	H	2B	3B	HR	RBI	BB	SO	BA	SA	OBA
Season	200	34	11	1	3	17	11	66	.170	.280	.221
vs. Left-Handers	118	27	8	1	2	14	8	39	.229	.364	.278
vs. Right-Handers	82	7	3	0	1	3	3	27	.085	.159	.138
vs. Ground-Ballers	85	14	3	1	0	5	4	29	.165	.224	.211
vs. Fly-Ballers	115	20	8	0	3	12	7	37	.174	.322	.228
Home Games	93	14	6	1	1	10	7	34	.151	.269	.218
Road Games	107	20	5	0	2	7	4	32	.187	.290	.223
Grass Fields	169	31	9	1	3	17	11	57	.183	.302	.242
Artificial Turf	31	3	2	0	0	0	0	9	.097	.161	.097
April	40	4	1	1	0	2	2	16	.100	.175	.163
May	34	5	2	0	0	1	1	11	.147	.206	.171
June	24	5	2	0	0	3	3	11	.208	.292	.296
July	7	2	1	0	1	1	0	3	.286	.857	.286
August	62	14	4	0	2	9	2	17	.226	.387	.262
Sept./Oct.	33	4	1	0	0	1	3	8	.121	.152	.194
Leading Off Inn.	36	4	0	0	1	1	4	13	.111	.194	.200
Bases Empty	101	18	5	0	2	2	8	33	.178	.287	.245
Runners On	99	16	6	1	1	15	3	33	.162	.273	.194
Runners/Scor. Pos.	48	8	4	0	0	12	2	17	.167	.250	.200
Runners On/2 Out	45	7	3	0	0	7	2	14	.156	.222	.191
Scor. Pos./2 Out	31	5	3	0	0	7	1	9	.161	.258	.188
Late-Inning Pressure	30	4	2	0	0	2	3	10	.133	.200	.212
Leading Off	5	1	0	0	0	0	2	3	.200	.200	.429
Runners On	11	1	1	0	0	2	0	3	.091	.182	.091
Runners/Scor. Pos.	2	1	1	0	0	2	0	0	.500	1.000	.500

RUNS BATTED IN	From 1B	From 2B	From 3B	Scoring Position
Totals	3/75	4/35	7/24	11/59
Percentage	4.0%	11.4%	29.2%	18.6%

Loves to face: Allan Anderson (.833, 5-for-6)
Dave West (.444, 4-for-9, 1 HR)

Hates to face: Storm Davis (.118, 2-for-17, 1 HR)
Mark Langston (.143, 2-for-14, 1 HR)
Gene Nelson (0-for-5)

Miscellaneous statistics: Ground outs-to-air outs ratio: 1.29 last season, 1.28 for career.... Grounded into 7 double plays in 52 opportunities (one per 7.4).... Drove in 3 of 8 runners from third base with less than two outs (38%).... Direction of balls hit to the outfield: 37% to left field, 32% to center, 32% to right.... Base running: Advanced from first base to third on 4 of 10 outfield singles (40%); scored from second on 3 of 5 (60%).... Made 3.10 assists per nine innings at shortstop.

Comments: The third pick in the 1983 June free-agent draft, behind Tim Belcher and Kurt Stillwell. Roger Clemens was the 19th selection.... Only two players since 1980 had lower batting averages in seasons of at least 200 at-bats: Kenny Williams (.159 in 1988) and Jody Davis (.169 in 1989). The all-time record for lowest single-season batting average (minimum: 200 AB): .132, by Dodgers catcher Bill Bergen in 1911. The A.L. record: .135, by Tigers shortstop Ray Oyler in 1968.... Batted 102 points higher vs. left-handers (.277) than vs. right-handers (.175) over the last five seasons, the 4th-largest margin in the majors.... Kunkel's high-water mark was a dreadful .187 on August 10.... Was removed in favor of a pinch hitter 29 times last season, all against right-handed pitchers.... Had batted above .300 vs. left-handed pitchers in each of the two previous seasons. Career batting averages: .261 vs. left-handers, .188 vs. right-handers.... Has hit 18 career home runs, only two with runners on base.... Among 44 players active in 1990 with 200 or more games at shortstop, Kunkel has the lowest career fielding percentage (one error per 16 chances).

Carney Lansford

Bats Right

Oakland A's	AB	H	2B	3B	HR	RBI	BB	SO	BA	SA	OBA
Season	507	136	15	1	3	50	45	50	.268	.320	.333
vs. Left-Handers	119	41	5	1	1	11	19	13	.345	.429	.439
vs. Right-Handers	388	95	10	0	2	39	26	37	.245	.286	.298
vs. Ground-Ballers	252	55	8	0	1	27	18	22	.218	.262	.280
vs. Fly-Ballers	255	81	7	1	2	23	27	28	.318	.376	.383
Home Games	215	64	5	0	1	19	23	22	.298	.335	.376
Road Games	292	72	10	1	2	31	22	28	.247	.308	.300
Grass Fields	437	115	12	0	3	44	40	44	.263	.311	.331
Artificial Turf	70	21	3	1	0	6	5	6	.300	.371	.347
April	81	24	5	0	1	9	3	4	.296	.395	.329
May	99	31	3	0	0	14	10	7	.313	.343	.375
June	93	21	2	0	1	7	7	12	.226	.280	.282
July	56	14	0	0	1	4	5	5	.250	.304	.311
August	108	32	4	0	0	13	7	10	.296	.333	.345
Sept./Oct.	70	14	1	1	0	3	13	12	.200	.243	.341
Leading Off Inn.	91	26	2	1	0	0	6	6	.286	.330	.330
Bases Empty	268	71	9	1	3	3	17	21	.265	.340	.314
Runners On	239	65	6	0	0	47	28	29	.272	.297	.353
Runners/Scor. Pos.	138	37	3	0	0	47	19	16	.268	.290	.356
Runners On/2 Out	84	20	0	0	0	16	15	9	.238	.238	.366
Scor. Pos./2 Out	61	15	0	0	0	16	14	5	.246	.246	.395
Late-Inning Pressure	54	9	1	0	0	6	5	8	.167	.185	.233
Leading Off	11	2	1	0	0	0	1	0	.182	.273	.250
Runners On	29	5	0	0	0	6	2	7	.172	.172	.219
Runners/Scor. Pos.	17	3	0	0	0	6	2	4	.176	.176	.250

RUNS BATTED IN	From 1B	From 2B	From 3B	Scoring Position
Totals	0/162	22/114	25/50	47/164
Percentage	0.0%	19.3%	50.0%	28.7%

Loves to face: Randy Johnson (.417, 5-for-12)
Mark Langston (.349, 15-for-43, 1 HR)
Sergio Valdez (.667, 4-for-6, 1 HR)

Hates to face: Danny Darwin (.220, 11-for-50, 1 HR)
Mike Henneman (0-for-10)
Charlie Hough (.211, 15-for-71, 2 HR)

Miscellaneous statistics: Ground outs-to-air outs ratio: 1.26 last season, 1.05 for career.... Grounded into 10 double plays in 121 opportunities (one per 12.1).... Drove in 20 of 27 runners from third base with less than two outs (74%), shared 4th-highest rate in A.L.... Direction of balls hit to the outfield: 34% to left field, 29% to center, 38% to right.... Base running: Advanced from first base to third on 7 of 24 outfield singles (29%); scored from second on 9 of 11 (82%).... Made 1.69 assists per nine innings at third base.

Comments: Led American League third basemen in fielding percentage for the fourth time in his career, and the third time in the last four years. Brooks Robinson led the league 11 times, the most of any third baseman in history.... Lansford's career fielding percentage of .966 (one error per 29 chances) ranks fifth in American League history (minimum: 1000 games), behind Robinson (.971), George Kell (.969), Don Wert (.968), and Willie Kamm (.967).... Batting average dropped 68 points from 1989 to 1990, the 2d-largest decrease in the American League last season (minimum: 300 AB in both seasons).... Batted 75 points lower in Late-Inning Pressure Situations (.226) than in other at-bats (.301) over the last five seasons, the 5th-largest margin in the majors. Batting average in LIPS has been lower than his overall average in each of the last seven seasons.... Has hit only 12 home runs over the last three seasons, after hitting 19 home runs in each of the two previous years.... Lansford will miss his first opening-day start since his rookie season of 1978, when he watched Dave Chalk open the season as the Angels' starting third baseman.... What can Oakland expect from its platoon of Vance Law and Ernest Riles? Law is a career .268 hitter vs. left-handers, with six HR per 200 AB; Riles has a career .276 mark vs. right-handers, with eight HR per 400 AB. Should they combine for a .270 mark with 14 homers, the difference will be more in the field and on the bases than at the plate.

Gene Larkin

Bats Left and Right

Minnesota Twins	AB	H	2B	3B	HR	RBI	BB	SO	BA	SA	OBA
Season	401	108	26	4	5	42	42	55	.269	.392	.343
vs. Left-Handers	121	30	6	2	0	12	10	14	.248	.331	.303
vs. Right-Handers	280	78	20	2	5	30	32	41	.279	.418	.359
vs. Ground-Ballers	180	48	9	1	1	18	17	25	.267	.344	.332
vs. Fly-Ballers	221	60	17	3	4	24	25	30	.271	.430	.352
Home Games	199	57	16	2	5	26	20	25	.286	.462	.348
Road Games	202	51	10	2	0	16	22	30	.252	.322	.338
Grass Fields	145	36	7	2	0	13	17	18	.248	.324	.339
Artificial Turf	256	72	19	2	5	29	25	37	.281	.430	.345
April	64	22	6	1	0	9	5	8	.344	.469	.403
May	84	26	8	0	3	16	12	13	.310	.512	.388
June	84	16	4	1	1	4	9	16	.190	.298	.274
July	42	12	2	1	0	3	4	4	.286	.381	.362
August	82	23	4	1	1	10	8	10	.280	.390	.344
Sept./Oct.	45	9	2	0	0	0	4	4	.200	.244	.280
Leading Off Inn.	80	19	2	1	0	0	13	9	.237	.287	.344
Bases Empty	205	61	14	2	3	3	27	22	.298	.429	.385
Runners On	196	47	12	2	2	39	15	33	.240	.352	.298
Runners/Scor. Pos.	105	26	7	2	2	37	9	18	.248	.410	.314
Runners On/2 Out	87	23	6	1	1	21	7	11	.264	.391	.333
Scor. Pos./2 Out	59	16	6	1	1	21	2	7	.271	.458	.317
Late-Inning Pressure	55	10	0	1	0	3	6	12	.182	.218	.274
Leading Off	17	3	0	0	0	0	2	3	.176	.176	.263
Runners On	28	4	0	1	0	3	1	6	.143	.214	.172
Runners/Scor. Pos.	15	3	0	1	0	3	1	2	.200	.333	.250

RUNS BATTED IN	From 1B	From 2B	From 3B	Scoring Position
Totals	4/141	13/79	20/48	33/127
Percentage	2.8%	16.5%	41.7%	26.0%

Loves to face: Jim Acker (.600, 3-for-5)
Andy Hawkins (.667, 4-for-6)

Hates to face: Jeff Montgomery (0-for-7, 1 BB)
Bob Welch (.071, 1-for-14, 5 BB)
Bobby Witt (.077, 1-for-13, 3 BB)

Miscellaneous statistics: Ground outs-to-air outs ratio: 0.90 last season, 0.98 for career.... Grounded into 6 double plays in 92 opportunities (one per 15.3).... Drove in 10 of 19 runners from third base with less than two outs (53%).... Direction of balls hit to the outfield: 29% to left field, 30% to center, 40% to right batting left-handed; 39% to left, 31% to center, 30% to right batting right-handed.... Base running: Advanced from first base to third on 8 of 20 outfield singles (40%); scored from second on 6 of 9 (67%).... Made 1.89 putouts per nine innings in right field.

Comments: Larkin's year by year batting averages, starting with his rookie season of 1987: .266, 267, .267, .269.... It's hard to believe, but the margin between Larkin's highest and lowest averages (.0032, or 3.2 batting-average points) was *not* the smallest ever over four consecutive seasons of 200 or more at-bats. That distinction belongs to Hod Ford, from 1922 through 1925, whose range was only 2.1 points. One other player had a range narrower than Larkin's: Mookie Wilson (2.7 points, 1982–85).... Despite that consistency, Larkin's yearly averages in Late-Inning Pressure Situations have dropped steadily: .359, .323, .258, .182. His career average with runners in scoring position in those situations (RISP/LIPS in Elias-speak) remains a robust .344.... Hit all five of his home runs batting left-handed at the Metrodome.... Batted .336 in 140 at-bats as a designated hitter, .234 in other at bats. But he started only six games as a DH after the All-Star break.... Twins right fielders had only 57 RBIs last season, the fewest in the A.L. Larkin led the team with 367 innings there, but seven others shared the time, including Shane Mack (324 innings), John Moses (216), Randy Bush (202⅔), Pedro Munoz (161), Carmelo Castillo (89), Kirby Puckett (76), and Jim Dwyer (2).... Career batting average of .216 as a pinch hitter (8-for-37, 0 HR).

Manny Lee

Bats Left and Right

Toronto Blue Jays	AB	H	2B	3B	HR	RBI	BB	SO	BA	SA	OBA
Season	391	95	12	4	6	41	26	90	.243	.340	.288
vs. Left-Handers	178	43	8	2	6	20	6	41	.242	.410	.265
vs. Right-Handers	213	52	4	2	0	21	20	49	.244	.282	.306
vs. Ground-Ballers	184	41	4	1	0	20	12	41	.223	.255	.268
vs. Fly-Ballers	207	54	8	3	6	21	14	49	.261	.415	.306
Home Games	190	50	4	2	2	19	11	45	.263	.337	.302
Road Games	201	45	8	2	4	22	15	45	.224	.343	.275
Grass Fields	161	34	4	2	3	19	11	32	.211	.317	.259
Artificial Turf	230	61	8	2	3	22	15	58	.265	.357	.309
April	36	11	0	0	0	3	2	8	.306	.306	.342
May	48	13	0	2	5	8	3	13	.271	.667	.314
June	62	17	4	0	1	6	4	17	.274	.387	.318
July	69	11	1	1	0	6	1	13	.159	.203	.171
August	95	21	3	0	0	11	8	21	.221	.253	.276
Sept./Oct.	81	22	4	1	0	7	8	18	.272	.346	.333
Leading Off Inn.	95	23	3	0	2	2	8	24	.242	.337	.301
Bases Empty	220	54	4	1	5	5	22	51	.245	.341	.314
Runners On	171	41	8	3	1	36	4	39	.240	.339	.253
Runners/Scor. Pos.	101	25	5	2	1	35	3	21	.248	.366	.262
Runners On/2 Out	63	15	1	2	1	14	2	17	.238	.365	.262
Scor. Pos./2 Out	41	11	1	1	1	13	1	9	.268	.415	.286
Late-Inning Pressure	65	13	1	1	0	2	4	17	.200	.246	.246
Leading Off	19	4	0	0	0	0	0	3	.211	.211	.211
Runners On	26	5	0	1	0	2	1	9	.192	.269	.222
Runners/Scor. Pos.	12	1	0	0	0	1	0	3	.083	.083	.083

RUNS BATTED IN	From 1B	From 2B	From 3B	Scoring Position
Totals	2/124	16/82	17/40	33/122
Percentage	1.6%	19.5%	42.5%	27.0%

Loves to face: Dave LaPoint (.429, 6-for-14, 1 HR)
Frank Viola (.455, 5-for-11)

Hates to face: Allan Anderson (.143, 2-for-14, 2 2B)
Rick Honeycutt (0-for-9, 1 BB)
Walt Terrell (.133, 2-for-15, 3 BB)

Miscellaneous statistics: Ground outs-to-air outs ratio: 1.64 last season, 1.77 for career. . . . Grounded into 9 double plays in 78 opportunities (one per 8.7). . . . Drove in 14 of 25 runners from third base with less than two outs (56%). . . . Direction of balls hit to the outfield: 46% to left field, 40% to center, 14% to right batting left-handed; 35% to left, 28% to center, 37% to right batting right-handed. . . . Base running: Advanced from first base to third on 9 of 22 outfield singles (41%); scored from second on 6 of 11 (55%). . . . Made 2.69 assists per nine innings at second base, lowest rate in A.L.

Comments: Although he had playoff experience in 1985 at the age of 20, Lee was still the 2d-youngest regular second baseman in the league last season. Only the Tribe's Jerry Browne is younger. . . . Ended the season with 36 consecutive errorless games at second base, his longest streak of the year. . . . Nevertheless, the departure of Tony Fernandez may send Lee back to shortstop, where he played only 43 innings last season—albeit error-free. . . . Drove in only one of 13 base runners from scoring position in Late-Inning Pressure Situations last season. In unpressured at-bats he drove in 29 percent. . . . Hit only seven home runs in 920 career at-bats prior to last season. . . . A better hitter from the right side of the plate for both average and power. Career breakdown: .282 (one HR per 59 AB) batting right-handed; .243 (one HR per 196 AB) batting left-handed. . . . Has had higher batting averages against fly-ball pitchers than against ground-ballers in each of his six seasons in the majors. He has a career mark of only .226 vs. ground-ballers, compared to .282 against fly-ballers. . . . Our favorite baseball places: Volcano—Manuel Lona Lee; Retirement Community—Glenallen Hill; Irish Racetrack—Kelly Downs.

Chet Lemon

Bats Right

Detroit Tigers	AB	H	2B	3B	HR	RBI	BB	SO	BA	SA	OBA
Season	322	83	16	4	5	32	48	61	.258	.379	.359
vs. Left-Handers	138	39	4	3	3	12	21	22	.283	.420	.375
vs. Right-Handers	184	44	12	1	2	20	27	39	.239	.348	.347
vs. Ground-Ballers	149	41	6	2	2	15	24	28	.275	.383	.383
vs. Fly-Ballers	173	42	10	2	3	17	24	33	.243	.376	.338
Home Games	133	34	6	1	2	17	25	27	.256	.361	.380
Road Games	189	49	10	3	3	15	23	34	.259	.392	.343
Grass Fields	261	63	13	3	3	26	42	51	.241	.349	.353
Artificial Turf	61	20	3	1	2	6	6	10	.328	.508	.388
April	44	9	2	0	1	6	4	7	.205	.318	.280
May	42	14	3	1	3	7	4	5	.333	.667	.391
June	28	7	1	0	0	3	6	3	.250	.286	.382
July	62	19	4	1	0	3	13	10	.306	.403	.434
August	75	15	4	2	0	8	12	22	.200	.307	.322
Sept./Oct.	71	19	2	0	1	5	9	14	.268	.338	.350
Leading Off Inn.	79	21	7	1	2	2	7	11	.266	.456	.341
Bases Empty	184	44	9	1	5	5	26	32	.239	.380	.340
Runners On	138	39	7	3	0	27	22	29	.283	.377	.384
Runners/Scor. Pos.	71	16	3	1	0	24	13	19	.225	.296	.337
Runners On/2 Out	53	13	0	2	0	8	11	17	.245	.321	.385
Scor. Pos./2 Out	29	6	0	0	0	6	6	13	.207	.207	.343
Late-Inning Pressure	41	6	1	1	0	5	8	2	.146	.220	.286
Leading Off	9	1	0	0	0	0	0	0	.111	.111	.111
Runners On	21	4	1	1	0	5	6	0	.190	.333	.370
Runners/Scor. Pos.	13	4	1	1	0	5	4	0	.308	.538	.471

RUNS BATTED IN	From 1B	From 2B	From 3B	Scoring Position
Totals	4/111	4/55	19/34	23/89
Percentage	3.6%	7.3%	55.9%	25.8%

Loves to face: Allan Anderson (.452, 14-for-31, 2 HR)
Jeff Reardon (.750, 3-for-4, 1 HR, 1 SO)
Matt Young (.571, 12-for-21, 4 HR)

Hates to face: Dennis Lamp (.189, 7-for-37)
Nolan Ryan (.122, 5-for-41, 5 BB)
Bob Welch (0-for-13)

Miscellaneous statistics: Ground outs-to-air outs ratio: 1.24 last season, 1.16 for career. . . . Grounded into 8 double plays in 78 opportunities (one per 9.8). . . . Drove in 15 of 19 runners from third base with less than two outs (79%), 3d-highest rate in A.L. . . . Direction of balls hit to the outfield: 36% to left field, 32% to center, 32% to right. . . . Base running: Advanced from first base to third on 11 of 19 outfield singles (58%); scored from second on 5 of 6 (83%). . . . Made 2.41 putouts per nine innings in right field.

Comments: Only two older players appeared in more games in the outfield than Lemon did last season: Andre Dawson and Dave Winfield. . . . Has a career total of 1925 games in the outfield, the 15th-highest total in American League history. Mickey Mantle stands 14th on that list, 94 games ahead of Lemon. . . . His career average of 2.59 putouts per game in the outfield ranks eighth in major league history (minimum: 1500 games). Only two of the players above him reached the 2000-game mark: Richie Ashburn (2.89) and Max Carey (2.63). . . . Once baseball's best center fielder, he played only three games there last season; he played more than half of the Tigers' innings in right field. . . . Came to bat 378 times last season, his lowest total since playing nine games for the White Sox in 1975. . . . Percentage of runners driven in from third base with less than two outs (78.9) was 3d highest in the A.L. last season. . . . Has hit for a higher average on artificial turf than on grass fields in each of the last six seasons, the longest streak by any active player. . . . Also has a five-year streak of hitting for a higher average with runners on base than with the bases empty. . . . Lemon has been hit by 151 pitches in his career, the most among active players. He ranks fifth on the all-time list, behind Ron Hunt (243), Don Baylor (267), Frank Robinson (198), and Minnie Minoso (192).

Jeffrey Leonard

Bats Right

Seattle Mariners	AB	H	2B	3B	HR	RBI	BB	SO	BA	SA	OBA
Season	478	120	20	0	10	75	37	97	.251	.356	.305
vs. Left-Handers	175	54	9	0	6	40	15	28	.309	.463	.361
vs. Right-Handers	303	66	11	0	4	35	22	69	.218	.294	.272
vs. Ground-Ballers	187	49	10	0	3	27	14	37	.262	.364	.315
vs. Fly-Ballers	291	71	10	0	7	48	23	60	.244	.351	.298
Home Games	234	52	12	0	7	37	21	50	.222	.363	.285
Road Games	244	68	8	0	3	38	16	47	.279	.348	.325
Grass Fields	193	55	7	0	1	26	15	32	.285	.337	.335
Artificial Turf	285	65	13	0	9	49	22	65	.228	.368	.284
April	80	22	3	0	3	13	3	8	.275	.425	.298
May	116	27	4	0	4	21	3	19	.233	.371	.252
June	106	24	4	0	2	15	8	29	.226	.321	.280
July	88	20	3	0	1	14	5	21	.227	.295	.269
August	61	12	4	0	0	2	11	15	.197	.262	.319
Sept./Oct.	27	15	2	0	0	10	7	5	.556	.630	.657
Leading Off Inn.	111	22	4	0	2	2	8	21	.198	.288	.252
Bases Empty	226	52	8	0	3	3	15	45	.230	.305	.278
Runners On	252	68	12	0	7	72	22	52	.270	.401	.327
Runners/Scor. Pos.	147	45	7	0	4	63	15	31	.306	.435	.359
Runners On/2 Out	111	28	3	0	3	26	11	30	.252	.360	.331
Scor. Pos./2 Out	69	18	2	0	1	21	7	19	.261	.333	.338
Late-Inning Pressure	68	5	0	0	0	5	13	17	.074	.074	.226
Leading Off	18	1	0	0	0	0	3	3	.056	.056	.190
Runners On	30	2	0	0	0	5	7	9	.067	.067	.250
Runners/Scor. Pos.	17	2	0	0	0	5	5	6	.118	.118	.320

RUNS BATTED IN	From 1B	From 2B	From 3B	Scoring Position
Totals	9/192	25/106	31/72	56/178
Percentage	4.7%	23.6%	43.1%	31.5%

Loves to face: Craig Lefferts (.500, 6-for-12, 1 HR)
Dennis Powell (.714, 5-for-7, 2 HR)
Jeff D. Robinson (3-for-3, 2 HR)

Hates to face: Jose DeLeon (.150, 3-for-20, 9 SO)
Dwight Gooden (.067, 1-for-15)
Jeff Reardon (.111, 2-for-18)

Miscellaneous statistics: Ground outs-to-air outs ratio: 0.87 last season, 1.02 for career. . . . Grounded into 20 double plays in 126 opportunities (one per 6.3). . . . Drove in 22 of 39 runners from third base with less than two outs (56%). . . . Direction of balls hit to the outfield: 31% to left field, 37% to center, 32% to right. . . . Base running: Advanced from first base to third on 8 of 25 outfield singles (32%); scored from second on 5 of 9 (56%). . . . Made 1.64 putouts per nine innings in left field, lowest rate in majors.

Comments: Drove in 40 runs against left-handed pitchers, 2d most of any A.L. player. Cecil Fielder led the league (54). . . . Leonard was the sixth different opening day designated hitter for the Mariners in the last six years. . . . Played the most innings of any major league outfielder without an assist last season (651). Leonard threw out 41 runners over a three-year period from 1983 through 1985, but only 17 since 1986, when an injury to his right wrist required surgery. . . . Batting average in Late-Inning Pressure Situations was the fourth lowest we've ever seen, beating only Greg Brock (.058 in 1986), Walt Weiss (.071 in 1988), and Garry Maddox (.073 in 1984). Leonard had a streak of 30 consecutive hitless LIPS at-bats, the 2d-longest streak over the last 10 years. Stan Jefferson had a drought of 33 LIPS at bats in 1987. . . . The 207-point gap between his batting averages in LIPS and in unpressured at-bats (.280) was the largest in the majors. . . . His first three walks of the season were intentional. He didn't earn a base on balls until his 28th game of the season. . . . His career batting average is 43 points higher against left-handed pitchers (.295) than vs. right-handers (.252). . . . Has homered in every current major league ballpark with the exception of Memorial Stadium (53 AB) and the Metrodome (52 AB).

Jim Leyritz

Bats Right

New York Yankees	AB	H	2B	3B	HR	RBI	BB	SO	BA	SA	OBA
Season	303	78	13	1	5	25	27	51	.257	.356	.331
vs. Left-Handers	103	30	7	1	2	7	15	15	.291	.437	.392
vs. Right-Handers	200	48	6	0	3	18	12	36	.240	.315	.298
vs. Ground-Ballers	141	39	5	1	3	10	13	21	.277	.390	.358
vs. Fly-Ballers	162	39	8	0	2	15	14	30	.241	.327	.307
Home Games	166	44	11	1	1	13	15	25	.265	.361	.335
Road Games	137	34	2	0	4	12	12	26	.248	.350	.327
Grass Fields	257	65	12	1	4	21	23	46	.253	.354	.325
Artificial Turf	46	13	1	0	1	4	4	5	.283	.370	.365
April	0	0	0	0	0	0	0	0	—	—	—
May	0	0	0	0	0	0	0	0	—	—	—
June	67	23	3	0	2	7	2	8	.343	.478	.362
July	88	20	1	0	1	4	15	16	.227	.273	.358
August	84	22	4	1	1	4	6	16	.262	.369	.326
Sept./Oct.	64	13	5	0	1	10	4	11	.203	.328	.268
Leading Off Inn.	62	17	2	0	2	2	3	10	.274	.403	.328
Bases Empty	176	48	8	1	3	3	14	29	.273	.381	.347
Runners On	127	30	5	0	2	22	13	22	.236	.323	.310
Runners/Scor. Pos.	66	13	2	0	1	18	8	10	.197	.273	.280
Runners On/2 Out	57	16	3	0	1	12	4	11	.281	.386	.339
Scor. Pos./2 Out	31	8	1	0	1	11	1	5	.258	.387	.281
Late-Inning Pressure	58	16	2	0	0	5	3	9	.276	.310	.323
Leading Off	13	5	0	0	0	0	1	1	.385	.385	.429
Runners On	26	6	1	0	0	5	2	5	.231	.269	.310
Runners/Scor. Pos.	14	3	1	0	0	5	2	2	.214	.286	.313

RUNS BATTED IN	From 1B	From 2B	From 3B	Scoring Position
Totals	3/96	7/57	10/26	17/83
Percentage	3.1%	12.3%	38.5%	20.5%

Loves to face: Matt Young (.600, 3-for-5)

Hates to face: Jack Morris (0-for-6, 1 BB)
Dave Stewart (.143, 1-for-7)

Miscellaneous statistics: Ground outs-to-air outs ratio: 1.40 last season, his first in the majors. . . . Grounded into 11 double plays in 59 opportunities (one per 5.4). . . . Drove in 5 of 10 runners from third base with less than two outs (50%). . . . Direction of balls hit to the outfield: 43% to left field, 30% to center, 27% to right. . . . Base running: Advanced from first base to third on 3 of 20 outfield singles (15%); scored from second on 7 of 12 (58%). . . . Made 1.57 assists per nine innings at third base, lowest rate in majors.

Comments: His value to the 1991 Yankees is yet to be determined, but one factor in his favor is his versatility. Leyritz started 67 games at third base, 10 behind the plate, eight in left field, and one in right field. . . . Allowed only two stolen bases in five attempts in 74 innings behind the plate. The A.L. average: one steal every 13 innings. . . . Seven Yankees rookies accumulated more than 1000 at-bats among them—more than the rookie at-bat total for the previous five years combined. . . . The Yankees had three rookies with 200 or more at-bats (Leyritz, Maas, and Azocar) for the first time since consecutive years during World War II: 1943—Billy Johnson (SS), Bud Metheny (OF), and Snuffy Stirnweiss (SS); 1944—Mike Garbark (C), Mike Milosevich (SS), and Don Savage (3B). . . . Leyritz's first major league at-bat was a 9th-inning game-tying single off of Baltimore's Gregg Olson on June 8. At the time, Olson had 14 saves in as many opportunities, and a 0.26 ERA. . . . Batted .325 from the 7th-spot in the batting order, the highest average of any American League player with at least 100 such at bats. . . . Comparable rookie seasons: Milt Bolling (brother of Frank), 1953; Faye Throneberry (brother of Marv), 1952; Ricky Nelson (brother of Dave?), 1983.

Nelson Liriano

Bats Left and Right

Blue Jays/Twins	AB	H	2B	3B	HR	RBI	BB	SO	BA	SA	OBA
Season	355	83	12	9	1	28	38	44	.234	.327	.308
vs. Left-Handers	67	13	1	3	0	6	11	12	.194	.299	.308
vs. Right-Handers	288	70	11	6	1	22	27	32	.243	.333	.308
vs. Ground-Ballers	160	41	8	4	1	12	18	12	.256	.375	.335
vs. Fly-Ballers	195	42	4	5	0	16	20	32	.215	.287	.286
Home Games	178	45	6	6	1	22	21	23	.253	.371	.328
Road Games	177	38	6	3	0	6	17	21	.215	.282	.287
Grass Fields	110	25	3	3	0	2	9	10	.227	.309	.292
Artificial Turf	245	58	9	6	1	26	29	34	.237	.335	.315
April	38	7	1	1	1	3	8	5	.184	.342	.326
May	54	11	3	1	0	8	2	6	.204	.296	.228
June	49	12	2	0	0	2	3	5	.245	.286	.302
July	38	7	1	0	0	2	5	4	.184	.211	.279
August	101	29	4	3	0	8	8	13	.287	.386	.339
Sept./Oct.	75	17	1	4	0	5	12	11	.227	.347	.330
Leading Off Inn.	101	20	3	0	1	1	12	8	.198	.257	.283
Bases Empty	208	46	8	3	1	1	23	23	.221	.303	.299
Runners On	147	37	4	6	0	27	15	21	.252	.361	.321
Runners/Scor. Pos.	82	21	3	3	0	24	11	13	.256	.366	.337
Runners On/2 Out	54	10	1	1	0	4	11	9	.185	.241	.333
Scor. Pos./2 Out	35	4	0	0	0	3	7	7	.114	.114	.262
Late-Inning Pressure	56	7	1	0	0	2	4	9	.125	.143	.180
Leading Off	17	1	0	0	0	0	1	1	.059	.059	.111
Runners On	21	3	0	0	0	2	1	5	.143	.143	.174
Runners/Scor. Pos.	12	1	0	0	0	2	1	3	.083	.083	.143

RUNS BATTED IN	From 1B	From 2B	From 3B	Scoring Position
Totals	6/101	11/66	10/31	21/97
Percentage	5.9%	16.7%	32.3%	21.6%

Loves to face: Rob Murphy (.667, 4-for-6)
Walt Terrell (.750, 6-for-8)

Hates to face: Bert Blyleven (.083, 1-for-12)
Mike Schooler (0-for-6)
Bob Welch (.091, 1-for-11)

Miscellaneous statistics: Ground outs-to-air outs ratio: 1.66 last season, 1.42 for career.... Grounded into 8 double plays in 72 opportunities (one per 9.0).... Drove in 10 of 14 runners from third base with less than two outs (71%).... Direction of balls hit to the outfield: 27% to left field, 29% to center, 43% to right batting left-handed, 21% to left, 42% to center, 38% to right batting right-handed.... Base running: Advanced from first base to third on 9 of 16 outfield singles (56%); scored from second on 1 of 5 (20%).... Made 2.82 assists per nine innings at second base, 2d-lowest rate in A.L.

Comments: All 45 of his starts with the Blue Jays were against right-handed pitchers, but he made 10 starts against southpaws after being traded to the Twins.... Batted .254 in 53 games for Minnesota, mostly from the first and second spots in the batting order. In 50 games with the Blue Jays, mostly from the eighth and ninth spots in the order, he batted .212.... Has a career average 19 points higher batting left-handed (.257) than batting right-handed (.238).... Had the lowest fielding percentage of any American League second baseman who played at least 81 games last season (.975, one error per 41 chances).... Career breakdown: .243 with the bases empty, .264 with runners on base, .284 with runners in scoring position.... Has a career average of .379 (11-for-29, 1 HR) as a pinch hitter.... What does Liriano have in common with Luis Gomez, Dave McKay, and Hosken Powell? They are the only four players in history to play at least 50 games for both the Blue Jays and the Twins.... Should Cito Gaston have batted Liriano for Tony Fernandez, who made the last out in Dave Stewart's no-hitter against the Blue Jays last June? In 1989, Liriano broke up two ninth-inning no-hit bids within a week's time, by Nolan Ryan on April 23 and Kirk McCaskill on April 28.

Kevin Maas

Bats Left

New York Yankees	AB	H	2B	3B	HR	RBI	BB	SO	BA	SA	OBA
Season	254	64	9	0	21	41	43	76	.252	.535	.367
vs. Left-Handers	67	11	1	0	3	8	10	28	.164	.313	.273
vs. Right-Handers	187	53	8	0	18	33	33	48	.283	.615	.399
vs. Ground-Ballers	111	21	4	0	8	15	18	28	.189	.441	.313
vs. Fly-Ballers	143	43	5	0	13	26	25	48	.301	.608	.408
Home Games	135	38	6	0	12	27	23	38	.281	.593	.390
Road Games	119	26	3	0	9	14	20	38	.218	.471	.340
Grass Fields	217	57	9	0	18	38	36	63	.263	.553	.375
Artificial Turf	37	7	0	0	3	3	7	13	.189	.432	.318
April	0	0	0	0	0	0	0	0	—	—	—
May	0	0	0	0	0	0	0	0	—	—	—
June	6	2	0	0	0	1	1	1	.333	.333	.429
July	63	17	1	0	8	14	13	21	.270	.667	.395
August	104	27	6	0	8	15	12	31	.260	.548	.342
Sept./Oct.	81	18	2	0	5	11	17	23	.222	.432	.370
Leading Off Inn.	58	13	3	0	5	5	9	16	.224	.534	.328
Bases Empty	143	41	6	0	15	15	19	41	.287	.643	.374
Runners On	111	23	3	0	6	26	24	35	.207	.396	.358
Runners/Scor. Pos.	58	12	2	0	2	18	21	18	.207	.345	.432
Runners On/2 Out	54	10	1	0	2	11	13	19	.185	.315	.353
Scor. Pos./2 Out	33	6	1	0	1	9	10	11	.182	.303	.386
Late-Inning Pressure	40	7	0	0	3	5	13	18	.175	.400	.377
Leading Off	8	2	0	0	1	1	4	4	.250	.625	.500
Runners On	13	1	0	0	0	2	7	5	.077	.077	.400
Runners/Scor. Pos.	10	1	0	0	0	2	5	4	.100	.100	.400

RUNS BATTED IN	From 1B	From 2B	From 3B	Scoring Position
Totals	4/87	6/46	10/21	16/67
Percentage	4.6%	13.0%	47.6%	23.9%

Loves to face: Jack Morris (.429, 3-for-7, 1 HR)
Walt Terrell (.500, 2-for-4, 2 HR)

Hates to face: Mark Langston (0-for-3, 2 SO)
Matt Young (0-for-4, 2 SO)

Miscellaneous statistics: Ground outs-to-air outs ratio: 0.57 last season, his first in majors, 2d-lowest rate in A.L.... Grounded into 2 double plays in 52 opportunities (one per 26.0), 3d-best rate in A.L.... Drove in 5 of 9 runners from third base with less than two outs (56%).... Direction of balls hit to the outfield: 16% to left field, 27% to center, 57% to right.... Base running: Advanced from first base to third on 5 of 13 outfield singles (38%); scored from second on 3 of 3.... Made 0.66 assists per nine innings at first base.

Comments: Rookie home-run leaders: Dave Justice (28), Maas (21), Larry Walker (19), Greg Vaughn (17).... Average of one home run per 12.1 at-bats was 2d best in the majors, behind Cecil Fielder.... His total of 21 home runs was the 3d highest ever by a Yankees rookie. The top five: Joe DiMaggio, 29 (1936); Joe Gordon, 25 (1938); Maas, 21 (1990); Lou Gehrig, 20 (1926); Tom Tresh, 20 (1962).... Among players with at least 50 hits, no one had fewer hits to the opposite field (3).... Maas set a record for the fewest RBIs by a player with at least 20 home runs. The previous record was 43 by Carlton Fisk (1984) and Fred McGriff (1987).... Drew 43 walks in 300 plate appearances, the highest rate of any major league rookie last season.... Fielding percentages of Yankees first basemen: Mattingly, .997; Steve Balboni, .984; Maas, .983.... Batted 112 points higher vs. fly-ballers (.301) than vs. ground-ballers (.189) last season, the 2d-largest margin in the majors.... Hit six home runs in his last 121 at-bats after reaching 15 home runs in the fewest at-bats in major league history (133). Fewest ABs to reach other HR totals: 10 HR—133 AB, Kevin Maas; 20 HR—178 AB, Mark McGwire; 50 HR—530 AB, Rudy York; 100 HR—1330 AB, Ken Phelps; 200 HR—2537 AB, Ralph Kiner; 250 HR—3097 AB, Harmon Killebrew.

Mike Macfarlane

Bats Right

Kansas City Royals	AB	H	2B	3B	HR	RBI	BB	SO	BA	SA	OBA
Season	400	102	24	4	6	58	25	69	.255	.380	.306
vs. Left-Handers	147	36	8	3	2	12	9	26	.245	.381	.300
vs. Right-Handers	253	66	16	1	4	46	16	43	.261	.379	.309
vs. Ground-Ballers	178	52	10	2	3	26	7	23	.292	.421	.328
vs. Fly-Ballers	222	50	14	2	3	32	18	46	.225	.347	.289
Home Games	191	49	13	3	1	30	13	32	.257	.372	.307
Road Games	209	53	11	1	5	28	12	37	.254	.388	.305
Grass Fields	156	40	8	1	3	22	10	27	.256	.378	.312
Artificial Turf	244	62	16	3	3	36	15	42	.254	.381	.302
April	26	9	4	0	0	3	0	4	.346	.500	.346
May	70	19	5	2	1	11	4	15	.271	.443	.320
June	82	18	2	1	0	9	3	8	.220	.268	.261
July	81	27	8	0	2	16	7	14	.333	.506	.389
August	75	15	2	0	3	16	6	16	.200	.347	.250
Sept./Oct.	66	14	3	1	0	3	5	12	.212	.288	.293
Leading Off Inn.	92	20	3	1	3	3	4	18	.217	.370	.258
Bases Empty	215	51	12	3	4	4	11	40	.237	.377	.284
Runners On	185	51	12	1	2	54	14	29	.276	.384	.330
Runners/Scor. Pos.	118	30	4	1	1	47	11	19	.254	.331	.319
Runners On/2 Out	89	25	6	1	1	29	10	12	.281	.404	.379
Scor. Pos./2 Out	63	16	3	1	0	24	8	9	.254	.333	.365
Late-Inning Pressure	64	20	7	0	2	10	4	15	.313	.516	.362
Leading Off	16	2	0	0	1	1	0	4	.125	.313	.125
Runners On	27	11	4	0	1	9	4	7	.407	.667	.500
Runners/Scor. Pos.	15	5	2	0	0	6	3	5	.333	.467	.474

RUNS BATTED IN	From 1B	From 2B	From 3B	Scoring Position
Totals	9/124	17/96	26/58	43/154
Percentage	7.3%	17.7%	44.8%	27.9%

Loves to face: Wes Gardner (.333, 1-for-3, 1 HR, 2 BB)
Tim Leary (.500, 3-for-6, 2 2B, 1 HR)

Hates to face: Randy Johnson (0-for-6)
Mike Moore (.100, 1-for-10, 1 3B)
Dave Stewart (0-for-8, 1 BB)

Miscellaneous statistics: Ground outs-to-air outs ratio: 0.78 last season, 0.90 for career.... Grounded into 9 double plays in 71 opportunities (one per 7.9).... Drove in 13 of 26 runners from third base with less than two outs (50%).... Direction of balls hit to the outfield: 44% to left field, 34% to center, 22% to right.... Base running: Advanced from first base to third on 6 of 17 outfield singles (35%); scored from second on 7 of 9 (78%).... Opposing base stealers: 68-for-82 (83%), highest rate in majors.

Comments: Batting average at season's end was at its lowest point since the first week of the season.... Was removed for a pinch hitter only once last season, replaced by Gerald Perry to face Bobby Thigpen—despite the fact that Macfarlane has three hits in six career at-bats vs. Thigpen.... Career batting average of .224 with the bases empty, .283 with runners on base.... Led American League catchers with four triples last season, the first four of his career.... Time out for trivia: Who holds the modern record for triples in a season by a catcher? The record for this century is 13, set by Johnny Kling in 1903, and tied by Tim McCarver in 1966.... McCarver suggested to us a while back that catchers who played regularly during the first half of the season might become automatic outs in the late innings of late-season games, due to the physical strain of the position. But Macfarlane had a season-long batting average of .214 during the first six innings, compared to .324 thereafter. So we looked a little deeper, and were surprised to find that Macfarlane was actually *typical.* There were 13 catchers (Mac included) who started at least 60 games by the end of July. From that point on, they compiled these batting averages in games they started: .255 on their first time up, .235 on their second, then .305 and .298 on their third and fourth times, respectively. Home run rates remained fairly constant through the game, and strikeout rates declined as batting averages rose.

Shane Mack

Bats Right

Minnesota Twins	AB	H	2B	3B	HR	RBI	BB	SO	BA	SA	OBA
Season	313	102	10	4	8	44	29	69	.326	.460	.392
vs. Left-Handers	146	54	9	1	5	27	15	26	.370	.548	.439
vs. Right-Handers	167	48	1	3	3	17	14	43	.287	.383	.350
vs. Ground-Ballers	126	36	3	3	3	16	14	29	.286	.429	.362
vs. Fly-Ballers	187	66	7	1	5	28	15	40	.353	.481	.413
Home Games	141	52	6	3	5	21	14	33	.369	.560	.433
Road Games	172	50	4	1	3	23	15	36	.291	.378	.358
Grass Fields	137	42	3	1	1	13	13	23	.307	.365	.379
Artificial Turf	176	60	7	3	7	31	16	46	.341	.534	.402
April	18	6	2	0	1	2	3	1	.333	.611	.478
May	33	14	1	2	0	5	3	6	.424	.576	.486
June	39	9	0	0	2	5	3	12	.231	.385	.286
July	72	22	1	1	2	6	8	18	.306	.431	.375
August	63	13	2	0	1	9	5	15	.206	.286	.275
Sept./Oct.	88	38	4	1	2	17	7	17	.432	.568	.479
Leading Off Inn.	76	27	2	2	3	3	6	15	.355	.553	.402
Bases Empty	182	57	6	2	6	6	13	40	.313	.467	.365
Runners On	131	45	4	2	2	38	16	29	.344	.450	.427
Runners/Scor. Pos.	72	26	4	1	0	33	14	16	.361	.444	.477
Runners On/2 Out	55	21	1	1	1	17	5	10	.382	.491	.433
Scor. Pos./2 Out	31	11	1	0	0	14	5	5	.355	.387	.444
Late-Inning Pressure	38	12	1	1	1	7	3	7	.316	.474	.366
Leading Off	9	3	0	0	0	0	2	2	.333	.333	.455
Runners On	19	6	1	1	1	7	1	4	.316	.632	.350
Runners/Scor. Pos.	8	4	1	0	0	4	0	1	.500	.625	.500

RUNS BATTED IN	From 1B	From 2B	From 3B	Scoring Position
Totals	4/94	17/57	15/32	32/89
Percentage	4.3%	29.8%	46.9%	36.0%

Loves to face: Bob Kipper (.400, 2-for-5, 2 HR, 2 SO)

Hates to face: Tom Browning (0-for-5)
Joe Magrane (.182, 2-for-11)
Bobby Witt (0-for-6)

Miscellaneous statistics: Ground outs-to-air outs ratio: 1.82 last season, 1.86 for career.... Grounded into 7 double plays in 65 opportunities (one per 9.3).... Drove in 8 of 16 runners from third base with less than two outs (50%).... Direction of balls hit to the outfield: 17% to left field, 38% to center, 46% to right.... Base running: Advanced from first base to third on 10 of 24 outfield singles (42%); scored from second on 5 of 5.... Made 2.44 putouts per nine innings in right field.

Comments: Batted .241 in 161 games for San Diego in 1987 and 1988, then spent first two months of 1989 season at Las Vegas and the rest on the D.L. following surgery on his right elbow.... He threw out eight runners last season, in case you were wondering about that elbow.... Hit five of his eight home runs to the opposite field. Among major league players with with at least five home runs last season, only Mack, Roberto Kelly (8 of 15) and Jay Buhner (4 of 7) hit a majority of their homers to the opposite field.... His .438 batting average as a pinch hitter (7-for-16) was the highest in the majors (minimum: 15 AB).... Batted .371 in day games, .306 in night games. That brings his career averages to .321 during the day, .262 at night.... Has driven in 37 percent of runners from scoring position over the last two seasons. The major league average is slightly more than 26 percent. Don Mattingly has a career rate of 36 percent, the highest among players with at least 100 RBIs over the past 16 years.... Career average of .306 (one HR per 37 AB) vs. left-handers, .255 (one HR per 112 AB) vs. right-handers.... Career breakdown: .262 with the bases empty, .304 with runners on base, .338 with two outs and runners on base.

Candy Maldonado

Bats Right

Cleveland Indians	AB	H	2B	3B	HR	RBI	BB	SO	BA	SA	OBA
Season	590	161	32	2	22	95	49	134	.273	.446	.330
vs. Left-Handers	175	58	7	0	10	34	16	32	.331	.543	.387
vs. Right-Handers	415	103	25	2	12	61	33	102	.248	.405	.306
vs. Ground-Ballers	296	87	17	1	12	56	23	62	.294	.480	.350
vs. Fly-Ballers	294	74	15	1	10	39	26	72	.252	.412	.311
Home Games	298	80	11	0	12	48	19	73	.268	.426	.307
Road Games	292	81	21	2	10	47	30	61	.277	.466	.353
Grass Fields	500	136	25	1	18	81	40	112	.272	.434	.325
Artificial Turf	90	25	7	1	4	14	9	22	.278	.511	.356
April	69	22	4	0	4	12	3	16	.319	.551	.365
May	90	27	6	0	6	20	10	24	.300	.567	.363
June	98	20	7	0	3	12	12	20	.204	.367	.292
July	112	30	5	0	2	13	12	30	.268	.366	.336
August	109	31	5	0	3	19	7	21	.284	.413	.325
Sept./Oct.	112	31	5	2	4	19	5	23	.277	.464	.317
Leading Off Inn.	161	44	9	0	4	4	8	37	.273	.404	.320
Bases Empty	318	84	19	1	13	13	17	69	.264	.453	.308
Runners On	272	77	13	1	9	82	32	65	.283	.438	.355
Runners/Scor. Pos.	164	44	8	1	5	73	22	41	.268	.421	.342
Runners On/2 Out	117	31	5	1	3	29	13	27	.265	.402	.344
Scor. Pos./2 Out	74	20	2	1	2	26	8	17	.270	.405	.341
Late-Inning Pressure	82	22	6	0	2	12	7	22	.268	.415	.322
Leading Off	25	7	3	0	0	0	1	8	.280	.400	.308
Runners On	27	9	2	0	0	10	6	7	.333	.407	.441
Runners/Scor. Pos.	19	7	2	0	0	10	6	5	.368	.474	.500

RUNS BATTED IN	From 1B	From 2B	From 3B	Scoring Position
Totals	10/164	30/133	33/74	63/207
Percentage	6.1%	22.6%	44.6%	30.4%

Loves to face: Dan Boone (2-for-2, 1 HR, 1 BB)
Frank DiPino (.615, 8-for-13, 1 HR)
Bob McClure (.800, 4-for-5, 1 HR)

Hates to face: Sid Fernandez (.120, 3-for-25)
Andy Hawkins (.189, 7-for-37, 1 HR, 0 BB)
Tim Leary (.045, 1-for-22, 3 BB)

Miscellaneous statistics: Ground outs-to-air outs ratio: 0.97 last season, 1.03 for career.... Grounded into 13 double plays in 114 opportunities (one per 8.8).... Drove in 28 of 48 runners from third base with less than two outs (58%).... Direction of balls hit to the outfield: 39% to left field, 33% to center, 28% to right.... Base running: Advanced from first base to third on 6 of 33 outfield singles (18%); scored from second on 13 of 18 (72%).... Made 2.16 putouts per nine innings in left field.

Comments: Batted 98 points higher in day games (.343) than in night games (.245) last season, the 2d-largest margin in the majors.... Batting average vs. left-handed pitchers was a career high.... Established career highs in games (155), at-bats, runs (76), hits, doubles, home runs, RBIs, walks, and strikeouts.... Batted in the cleanup spot in 129 of his last 130 starts.... Has hit nine career home runs in 157 at-bats as a pinch hitter. That rate of one HR per 17 AB is nearly double his rate at other times (one per 32 AB). It's conceivable that he could challenge the all-time record for pinch-hit home runs—20, by Goose Gossage's shower-room buddy, Cliff Johnson.... Has hit for a higher average in road games than he has in home games in each of the last seven seasons, during which time he has called three different stadiums home: Dodger Stadium, Candlestick Park, and Cleveland Stadium.... Maldonado became only the tenth player in major league history to play at least one game for the Dodgers, Giants, and Indians. The most recent, aside from Maldonado, was Mike Vail. The most famous, including Maldonado, are Hoyt Wilhelm and Sal Maglie.

Fred Manrique

Bats Right

Minnesota Twins	AB	H	2B	3B	HR	RBI	BB	SO	BA	SA	OBA
Season	228	54	10	0	5	29	4	35	.237	.346	.254
vs. Left-Handers	61	15	2	0	1	8	1	13	.246	.328	.254
vs. Right-Handers	167	39	8	0	4	21	3	22	.234	.353	.254
vs. Ground-Ballers	91	25	5	0	2	11	1	11	.275	.396	.280
vs. Fly-Ballers	137	29	5	0	3	18	3	24	.212	.314	.238
Home Games	100	24	4	0	3	19	3	15	.240	.370	.274
Road Games	128	30	6	0	2	10	1	20	.234	.328	.238
Grass Fields	100	18	3	0	2	6	1	14	.180	.270	.186
Artificial Turf	128	36	7	0	3	23	3	21	.281	.406	.306
April	40	11	1	0	2	9	1	6	.275	.450	.286
May	79	20	4	0	2	10	1	10	.253	.380	.262
June	70	18	4	0	0	6	0	11	.257	.314	.264
July	39	5	1	0	1	4	2	8	.128	.231	.190
August	0	0	0	0	0	0	0	0	—	—	—
Sept./Oct.	0	0	0	0	0	0	0	0	—	—	—
Leading Off Inn.	40	10	3	0	1	1	2	6	.250	.400	.286
Bases Empty	127	29	6	0	1	1	3	23	.228	.299	.258
Runners On	101	25	4	0	4	28	1	12	.248	.406	.250
Runners/Scor. Pos.	58	14	2	0	2	23	1	6	.241	.379	.246
Runners On/2 Out	34	7	0	0	0	9	0	5	.206	.206	.206
Scor. Pos./2 Out	25	6	0	0	0	9	0	3	.240	.240	.240
Late-Inning Pressure	25	6	1	0	0	2	1	3	.240	.280	.269
Leading Off	2	0	0	0	0	0	1	0	.000	.000	.333
Runners On	12	4	1	0	0	2	0	2	.333	.417	.333
Runners/Scor. Pos.	5	2	1	0	0	2	0	1	.400	.600	.400

RUNS BATTED IN	From 1B	From 2B	From 3B	Scoring Position
Totals	5/69	7/45	12/21	19/66
Percentage	7.2%	15.6%	57.1%	28.8%

Loves to face: Brian Holton (.600, 3-for-5, 2 HR)
Bruce Hurst (.500, 7-for-14, 1 HR)
Terry Leach (.667, 6-for-9)

Hates to face: Kevin Brown (0-for-8)
Charlie Hough (0-for-7, 1 BB)
Curt Young (.125, 2-for-16)

Miscellaneous statistics: Ground outs-to-air outs ratio: 1.78 last season, 1.29 for career.... Grounded into 8 double plays in 52 opportunities (one per 6.5).... Drove in 7 of 10 runners from third base with less than two outs (70%).... Direction of balls hit to the outfield: 39% to left field, 33% to center, 29% to right.... Base running: Advanced from first base to third on 3 of 9 outfield singles (33%); scored from second on 2 of 3 (67%).... Made 2.87 assists per nine innings at second base.

Comments: Posted similar numbers in 1988, but batted .294 in 119 games in 1989.... Batting average peaked at .285 in mid-June, but six weeks later it had dropped to .237. He was released on July 27 when Nelson Liriano (acquired in a trade for John Candelaria) was added to Minnesota's roster. The Twins also added Pedro Munoz on that day.... Batted 101 points higher on artificial turf (.281) than on grass fields (.180) last season, the 3d-largest margin in the majors.... Played only one position in the field for the first time since 1984.... Stole six bases in seven attempts over the last two seasons, compared to a 12-for-25 mark prior to that.... Career batting averages: .241 with the bases empty, .278 with runners on base, .306 with runners in scoring position.... Despite those numbers, he has never driven in more than 52 runs in a season.... Career batting averages of .273 vs. left-handed pitchers, .244 vs. right-handers.... Has played with six different clubs over a career of fewer than 500 games (489 to be exact). And before you get any funny ideas about that being some sort of record, check the Greg A. Harris comments.

Mike Marshall

Bats Right

Mets/Red Sox	AB	H	2B	3B	HR	RBI	BB	SO	BA	SA	OBA
Season	275	71	14	2	10	39	11	66	.258	.433	.294
vs. Left-Handers	96	21	6	0	4	9	5	27	.219	.406	.257
vs. Right-Handers	179	50	8	2	6	30	6	39	.279	.447	.313
vs. Ground-Ballers	130	38	5	2	3	19	3	29	.292	.431	.319
vs. Fly-Ballers	145	33	9	0	7	20	8	37	.228	.434	.271
Home Games	146	37	8	0	7	22	6	32	.253	.452	.293
Road Games	129	34	6	2	3	17	5	34	.264	.411	.294
Grass Fields	227	58	11	2	9	35	9	53	.256	.441	.292
Artificial Turf	48	13	3	0	1	4	2	13	.271	.396	.300
April	57	13	2	1	2	9	1	13	.228	.404	.254
May	62	14	3	0	2	11	3	15	.226	.371	.265
June	38	12	3	0	2	6	3	8	.316	.553	.381
July	6	0	0	0	0	1	0	4	.000	.000	.000
August	39	13	1	0	2	7	1	6	.333	.513	.350
Sept./Oct.	73	19	5	1	2	5	3	20	.260	.438	.299
Leading Off Inn.	63	20	2	0	5	5	3	16	.317	.587	.348
Bases Empty	144	39	7	1	6	6	8	40	.271	.458	.318
Runners On	131	32	7	1	4	33	3	26	.244	.405	.266
Runners/Scor. Pos.	78	16	3	1	1	25	1	19	.205	.308	.207
Runners On/2 Out	54	12	2	1	2	15	0	7	.222	.407	.236
Scor. Pos./2 Out	37	8	0	1	1	12	0	7	.216	.351	.216
Late-Inning Pressure	45	11	1	0	1	10	1	9	.244	.333	.271
Leading Off	4	2	0	0	1	1	0	1	.500	1.250	.500
Runners On	26	7	1	0	0	9	1	3	.269	.308	.310
Runners/Scor. Pos.	16	6	1	0	0	9	0	2	.375	.438	.353

RUNS BATTED IN	From 1B	From 2B	From 3B	Scoring Position
Totals	7/96	13/62	9/33	22/95
Percentage	7.3%	21.0%	27.3%	23.2%

Loves to face: Mark Davis (.355, 11-for-31, 2 HR)
Joe Price (.350, 7-for-20, 3 HR)
Walt Terrell (.353, 6-for-17)

Hates to face: John Candelaria (.053, 1-for-19, 2 BB)
Bill Gullickson (.167, 5-for-30, 0 BB)
Pascual Perez (.125, 3-for-24)

Miscellaneous statistics: Ground outs-to-air outs ratio: 1.34 last season, 1.08 for career.... Grounded into 4 double plays in 62 opportunities (one per 15.5).... Drove in 8 of 20 runners from third base with less than two outs (40%).... Direction of balls hit to the outfield: 42% to left field, 33% to center, 25% to right.... Base running: Advanced from first base to third on 5 of 14 outfield singles (36%); scored from second on 2 of 7 (29%).... Made 0.72 assists per nine innings at first base.

Comments: Batted .238 in 53 games with the Mets, .286 in 30 games with Boston.... Batting average has dropped in each of the last three seasons: .294 in 1987, then .277, .260, .258.... Batting average leading off innings was a career high, but his averages vs. left-handed pitchers and with runners in scoring position were career lows.... Drove in 45 percent of runners from scoring position in Late-Inning Pressure Situations. The league average is 26 percent.... Didn't pinch-hit for the Red Sox during the regular season, but made two appearances in that role during the A.L.C.S. Has a career batting average of .203 as a pinch-hitter (13-for-64, 1 HR).... Batted .230 in innings one through six, but raised his average to .321 from the seventh inning on.... This right-handed hitter has things backwards: He has batted at least 20 points higher vs. right-handers than vs. left-handers in each of the past four seasons. His career averages: .278 vs. RHP, .254 vs. LHP.... First, the Mets traded Len Dykstra and Roger McDowell for Juan Samuel. Then they unloaded Samuel to the Dodgers for Marshall. When Dave Magadan got hot, Marshall became unhappy and was dealt to the Red Sox for three minor leaguers. Here's the punch line: In August, not only are the Mets searching for a veteran right-handed bat to come off the bench, but they have nothing to show for Dykstra and McDowell.

Carlos Martinez

Bats Right

Chicago White Sox	AB	H	2B	3B	HR	RBI	BB	SO	BA	SA	OBA
Season	272	61	6	5	4	24	10	40	.224	.327	.252
vs. Left-Handers	140	31	2	2	2	7	5	20	.221	.307	.248
vs. Right-Handers	132	30	4	3	2	17	5	20	.227	.348	.255
vs. Ground-Ballers	104	31	5	1	2	14	2	15	.298	.423	.311
vs. Fly-Ballers	168	30	1	4	2	10	8	25	.179	.268	.216
Home Games	147	33	5	3	2	16	6	24	.224	.340	.255
Road Games	125	28	1	2	2	8	4	16	.224	.312	.248
Grass Fields	230	53	6	5	3	23	9	36	.230	.339	.259
Artificial Turf	42	8	0	0	1	1	1	4	.190	.262	.209
April	54	13	2	1	2	10	2	7	.241	.426	.268
May	76	11	2	1	1	8	4	13	.145	.237	.188
June	51	15	1	0	0	2	2	9	.294	.314	.321
July	37	10	1	2	0	1	1	3	.270	.405	.289
August	42	8	0	1	1	1	1	3	.190	.310	.209
Sept./Oct.	12	4	0	0	0	2	0	5	.333	.333	.333
Leading Off Inn.	60	12	1	1	1	1	0	8	.200	.300	.200
Bases Empty	147	36	3	3	3	3	4	20	.245	.367	.265
Runners On	125	25	3	2	1	21	6	20	.200	.280	.237
Runners/Scor. Pos.	65	19	3	2	1	21	5	11	.292	.446	.343
Runners On/2 Out	53	13	3	0	1	16	1	5	.245	.358	.259
Scor. Pos./2 Out	37	13	3	0	1	16	1	3	.351	.514	.368
Late-Inning Pressure	24	6	2	0	0	1	1	4	.250	.333	.280
Leading Off	7	1	0	0	0	0	0	2	.143	.143	.143
Runners On	9	1	0	0	0	1	1	1	.111	.111	.200
Runners/Scor. Pos.	7	1	0	0	0	1	1	1	.143	.143	.250

RUNS BATTED IN	From 1B	From 2B	From 3B	Scoring Position
Totals	1/96	12/55	7/18	19/73
Percentage	1.0%	21.8%	38.9%	26.0%

Loves to face: Brian Holman (.667, 4-for-6, 1 HR)
Jamie Moyer (.571, 4-for-7)

Hates to face: Mark Langston (.100, 1-for-10)
Charlie Leibrandt (.125, 1-for-8, 4 SO)
Dave Stieb (.182, 2-for-11)

Miscellaneous statistics: Ground outs-to-air outs ratio: 1.22 last season, 1.40 for career.... Grounded into 8 double plays in 65 opportunities (one per 8.1).... Drove in 2 of 7 runners from third base with less than two outs (29%).... Direction of balls hit to the outfield: 29% to left field, 40% to center, 31% to right.... Base running: Advanced from first base to third on 3 of 9 outfield singles (33%); scored from second on 5 of 5.... Made 0.55 assists per nine innings at first base, 2d-lowest rate in A.L.

Comments: Started 68 of 73 games for the White Sox after the All-Star break in 1989. Last season, he started 72 games at first base, but only 12 after the arrival of Frank Thomas on August 2. Just short of his 25th birthday, he lost his job to a younger man. Now he knows how former members of Menudo feel.... Batting average dropped 76 points from his 1989 level, when he was the only rookie in the American League to bat .300.... Batted 119 points higher vs. ground-ballers (.298) than vs. fly-ballers (.179) last season, the 4th-largest margin in the majors.... May batting average was the lowest in the major leagues.... Started only one double play in 626 innings at first base. The A.L. average: one per 129 innings.... Didn't play an inning of first base in his first five seasons of pro ball (1984–88). Signed as a six-foot-five shortstop, and was converted to a third baseman and an outfielder before someone just threw up his arms in frustration and gave him a first baseman's mitt in 1989.... His career average is 40 points higher with the bases empty (.277) than with runners on base (.237), the 5th-largest margin in the majors over the last five seasons.... Career average of .184 in day games, .285 in night games.

Edgar Martinez

Bats Right

Seattle Mariners	AB	H	2B	3B	HR	RBI	BB	SO	BA	SA	OBA
Season	487	147	27	2	11	49	74	62	.302	.433	.397
vs. Left-Handers	156	48	8	1	6	24	27	21	.308	.487	.412
vs. Right-Handers	331	99	19	1	5	25	47	41	.299	.408	.390
vs. Ground-Ballers	185	53	10	0	4	21	31	30	.286	.405	.395
vs. Fly-Ballers	302	94	17	2	7	28	43	32	.311	.450	.398
Home Games	244	73	17	1	3	20	42	31	.299	.414	.401
Road Games	243	74	10	1	8	29	32	31	.305	.453	.393
Grass Fields	190	57	7	1	7	22	23	24	.300	.458	.382
Artificial Turf	297	90	20	1	4	27	51	38	.303	.418	.406
April	53	17	3	0	2	4	3	5	.321	.491	.368
May	103	36	2	2	5	16	16	10	.350	.553	.442
June	90	24	7	0	0	4	20	20	.267	.344	.405
July	90	27	5	0	2	10	11	13	.300	.422	.375
August	88	23	7	0	2	8	12	8	.261	.409	.356
Sept./Oct.	63	20	3	0	0	7	12	6	.317	.365	.421
Leading Off Inn.	119	36	11	0	2	2	10	12	.303	.445	.357
Bases Empty	274	90	23	2	5	5	31	35	.328	.482	.401
Runners On	213	57	4	0	6	44	43	27	.268	.371	.393
Runners/Scor. Pos.	118	29	2	0	3	37	28	16	.246	.339	.395
Runners On/2 Out	94	21	1	0	3	21	21	15	.223	.330	.381
Scor. Pos./2 Out	64	16	0	0	2	18	14	9	.250	.344	.407
Late-Inning Pressure	82	29	6	0	4	14	17	12	.354	.573	.465
Leading Off	30	11	3	0	1	1	2	2	.367	.567	.406
Runners On	30	12	2	0	3	13	11	5	.400	.767	.561
Runners/Scor. Pos.	18	6	1	0	1	8	7	4	.333	.556	.520

RUNS BATTED IN	From 1B	From 2B	From 3B	Scoring Position
Totals	6/158	14/101	18/47	32/148
Percentage	3.8%	13.9%	38.3%	21.6%

Loves to face: Andy Hawkins (.429, 3-for-7, 1 HR)
Bill Long (.667, 4-for-6)

Hates to face: Tim Leary (0-for-9)
Nolan Ryan (.100, 1-for-10)

Miscellaneous statistics: Ground outs-to-air outs ratio: 0.89 last season, 0.82 for career.... Grounded into 13 double plays in 112 opportunities (one per 8.6).... Drove in 13 of 25 runners from third base with less than two outs (52%).... Direction of balls hit to the outfield: 30% to left field, 27% to center, 43% to right.... Base running: Advanced from first base to third on 2 of 38 outfield singles (5%), lowest rate in majors; scored from second on 15 of 21 (71%).... Made 1.95 assists per nine innings at third base.

Comments: The fourth-highest batting average in 14 years of Mariners baseball, behind Bruce Bochte, .316 (1979); Phil Bradley, .310 (1986); and Alvin Davis, .305 (1989).... His on-base percentage was the 3d highest in the American League.... With competition from Wade Boggs, Kelly Gruber, Carney Lansford, Gary Gaetti, Gary Sheffield, Brook Jacoby, and Kevin Seitzer, it might be difficult for a third baseman from Seattle to get a little recognition. But Martinez ranked second among that group in batting average, third in slugging percentage, first in on-base percentage, and third in home runs.... His average of one error per 13.8 chances was the worst among regular major league third basemen. Martinez's predecessor, Jim Presley, ranked last in the National League (one per 14.3).... His career average of .120 (3-for-25) with the bases loaded is the lowest of any player over the last 10 years (minimum: 25 AB).... Take a look at these career batting-average breakdowns: .290 vs. right-handers, .291 vs. left-handers; .292 vs. ground-ballers, .290 vs. fly-ballers; .285 at the Kingdome, .296 on the road; .284 with runners on base, .296 with the bases empty.

Don Mattingly

Bats Left

New York Yankees	AB	H	2B	3B	HR	RBI	BB	SO	BA	SA	OBA
Season	394	101	16	0	5	42	28	20	.256	.335	.308
vs. Left-Handers	126	33	6	0	0	17	7	8	.262	.310	.301
vs. Right-Handers	268	68	10	0	5	25	21	12	.254	.347	.312
vs. Ground-Ballers	164	35	5	0	1	15	13	8	.213	.262	.274
vs. Fly-Ballers	230	66	11	0	4	27	15	12	.287	.387	.333
Home Games	183	45	4	0	4	20	16	11	.246	.333	.308
Road Games	211	56	12	0	1	22	12	9	.265	.336	.308
Grass Fields	315	81	12	0	5	34	24	15	.257	.343	.311
Artificial Turf	79	20	4	0	0	8	4	5	.253	.304	.298
April	64	20	4	0	2	6	5	3	.313	.469	.366
May	108	29	5	0	3	18	6	11	.269	.398	.319
June	116	25	3	0	0	9	6	4	.216	.241	.252
July	55	10	1	0	0	2	5	2	.182	.200	.250
August	0	0	0	0	0	0	0	0	—	—	—
Sept./Oct.	51	17	3	0	0	7	6	0	.333	.392	.397
Leading Off Inn.	81	17	4	0	2	2	1	6	.210	.333	.220
Bases Empty	227	51	9	0	2	2	8	13	.225	.291	.257
Runners On	167	50	7	0	3	40	20	7	.299	.395	.372
Runners/Scor. Pos.	96	28	3	0	1	35	16	6	.292	.354	.383
Runners On/2 Out	48	13	2	0	0	10	12	2	.271	.313	.417
Scor. Pos./2 Out	33	8	2	0	0	10	10	2	.242	.303	.419
Late-Inning Pressure	70	15	5	0	2	9	8	4	.214	.371	.304
Leading Off	21	1	1	0	0	0	0	2	.048	.095	.048
Runners On	30	10	3	0	2	9	7	1	.333	.633	.459
Runners/Scor. Pos.	16	2	0	0	0	4	7	1	.125	.125	.391

RUNS BATTED IN	From 1B	From 2B	From 3B	Scoring Position
Totals	5/112	12/66	20/45	32/111
Percentage	4.5%	18.2%	44.4%	28.8%

Loves to face: Bert Blyleven (.410, 16-for-39, 3 HR)
Dickie Noles (.556, 5-for-9, 1 HR)
Jeff Russell (.500, 8-for-16, 1 HR)

Hates to face: Kevin Brown (.190, 4-for-21)
Storm Davis (.190, 8-for-42, 1 HR)
Bobby Witt (.174, 4-for-23, 3 2B, 4 BB)

Miscellaneous statistics: Ground outs-to-air outs ratio: 0.89 last season, 0.88 for career.... Grounded into 13 double plays in 87 opportunities (one per 6.7).... Drove in 15 of 27 runners from third base with less than two outs (56%).... Direction of balls hit to the outfield: 25% to left field, 35% to center, 39% to right.... Base running: Advanced from first base to third on 6 of 22 outfield singles (27%); scored from second on 5 of 10 (50%).... Made 0.90 assists per nine innings at first base.

Comments: Batted .362 in 16 games after returning from 47 days on the disabled list. Of those 16 games, he started seven at first base, five as designated hitter, and pinch-hit four times.... Didn't strike out in 74 plate appearances after his return.... Started 13 double plays, to rank 2d among American League first basemen despite playing only 89 games there. George Brett led the league with 14.... Committed only three errors while playing 54 percent of the Yankees' innings at first base. Steve Balboni and Kevin Maas combined for the other 46 percent, and committed 12 errors between them.... Hasn't homered in 261 at-bats since May 20, the longest home-run drought of his career. He had a streak of 171 homerless at-bats from September 1988 to May 1989.... That drought will probably end at Yankee Stadium. Over the last two seasons, all of his 28 home runs have been hit to right field, and 23 were hit at home.... On May 14, Mattingly homered off Minnesota's Roy Smith to become the 11th player ever to hit 100 home runs at Yankee Stadium. His career breakdown: 102 at Yankee Stadium, 67 on the road.... Has driven in 36 percent of runners from scoring position in his career, the best rate of any player over the 16 years we've kept track (minimum: 100 RBI).... Has homered in every current American League ballpark except County Stadium (191 career AB).... Has batted over .300 in day games in each of the last seven seasons.

Willie McGee

Bats Left and Right

Cardinals/A's	AB	H	2B	3B	HR	RBI	BB	SO	BA	SA	OBA
Season	614	199	35	7	3	77	48	104	.324	.419	.373
vs. Left-Handers	225	73	11	3	2	27	10	43	.324	.427	.352
vs. Right-Handers	389	126	24	4	1	50	38	61	.324	.414	.385
vs. Ground-Ballers	312	112	22	6	0	50	20	49	.359	.468	.398
vs. Fly-Ballers	302	87	13	1	3	27	28	55	.288	.368	.348
Home Games	328	110	18	4	1	47	24	45	.335	.424	.379
Road Games	286	89	17	3	2	30	24	59	.311	.413	.367
Grass Fields	218	67	7	3	1	26	21	43	.307	.381	.371
Artificial Turf	396	132	28	4	2	51	27	61	.333	.439	.374
April	83	30	8	1	0	12	7	18	.361	.482	.411
May	107	29	3	1	1	7	6	11	.271	.346	.310
June	112	36	6	2	0	15	14	22	.321	.411	.394
July	97	38	7	0	1	15	5	19	.392	.495	.427
August	106	35	8	1	1	14	6	16	.330	.453	.363
Sept./Oct.	109	31	3	2	0	14	10	18	.284	.349	.345
Leading Off Inn.	123	40	5	0	1	1	7	22	.325	.390	.362
Bases Empty	319	107	15	2	3	3	24	51	.335	.423	.382
Runners On	295	92	20	5	0	74	24	53	.312	.414	.363
Runners/Scor. Pos.	187	58	15	3	0	69	22	38	.310	.422	.382
Runners On/2 Out	99	25	8	2	0	26	9	22	.253	.374	.315
Scor. Pos./2 Out	77	22	7	2	0	25	9	19	.286	.429	.360
Late-Inning Pressure	82	30	7	1	1	17	7	15	.366	.512	.416
Leading Off	21	5	0	0	1	1	0	7	.238	.381	.238
Runners On	39	15	4	1	0	16	4	6	.385	.538	.442
Runners/Scor. Pos.	30	14	4	1	0	16	4	4	.467	.667	.529

RUNS BATTED IN	From 1B	From 2B	From 3B	Scoring Position
Totals	9/163	36/151	29/64	65/215
Percentage	5.5%	23.8%	45.3%	30.2%

Loves to face: Derek Lilliquist (.500, 6-for-12, 1 HR)
Craig McMurtry (.474, 9-for-19)
Mike Scott (.548, 23-for-42)

Hates to face: Tom Browning (.097, 3-for-31, 1 HR)
Bob Knepper (.191, 13-for-68, 0 BB)
Walt Terrell (.105, 2-for-19)

Miscellaneous statistics: Ground outs-to-air outs ratio: 2.66 last season, 2d-highest rate in majors; 2.26 for career. . . . Grounded into 13 double plays in 126 opportunities (one per 9.7). . . . Drove in 19 of 33 runners from third base with less than two outs (58%). . . . Direction of balls hit to the outfield: 54% to left field, 32% to center, 14% to right batting left-handed; 19% to left, 39% to center, 42% to right batting right-handed. . . . Base running: Advanced from first base to third on 24 of 42 outfield singles (57%); scored from second on 21 of 24 (88%). . . . Made 2.85 putouts per nine innings in center field.

Comments: McGee's only previous .300 season was in 1985, when he led the National League with a .353 mark. . . . Had 168 hits when traded from St. Louis to the Athletics. The last in-season trade involving a player with as many hits was in 1892, when George van Haltren was traded to the Pittsburgh Pirates after collecting 168 hits for the Baltimore Orioles. Other high contemporary totals: 147, Matty Alou (1973); 137, Bob Oliver (1972); 132, Alex Johnson (1974); 132, Willie Montanez (1980); 129, Johnny Ray (Pirates). . . . Led major league outfielders with 17 errors last season. . . . Averaged one walk per 24 plate appearances batting left-handed, one per 11 plate appearances batting right-handed. . . . The next time you hear someone describe McGee as an "artificial-turf hitter," mention that he's also a pretty fair "grass-field hitter." Career batting averages: .297 on synthetics, .295 on grass. . . . His career average of .265 at Candlestick is his 2d lowest at any National League ballpark. (He has a .250 mark at the Astrodome.). . .McGee has started 41 postseason games in the outfield. That's 5th most in major league history, behind Mickey Mantle (63), Reggie Jackson (58), Joe DiMaggio (51), and Hank Bauer (45). . . . Has played in four League Championship Series, and his club has advanced to the World Series all four times.

Fred McGriff

Bats Left

Toronto Blue Jays	AB	H	2B	3B	HR	RBI	BB	SO	BA	SA	OBA
Season	557	167	21	1	35	88	94	108	.300	.530	.400
vs. Left-Handers	202	52	5	1	8	30	21	48	.257	.411	.324
vs. Right-Handers	355	115	16	0	27	58	73	60	.324	.597	.440
vs. Ground-Ballers	251	80	9	0	17	37	45	44	.319	.558	.425
vs. Fly-Ballers	306	87	12	1	18	51	49	64	.284	.507	.380
Home Games	264	73	10	0	14	38	55	37	.277	.473	.399
Road Games	293	94	11	1	21	50	39	71	.321	.580	.401
Grass Fields	233	77	10	1	14	34	28	56	.330	.562	.402
Artificial Turf	324	90	11	0	21	54	66	52	.278	.506	.399
April	60	17	0	0	4	7	22	17	.283	.483	.482
May	81	16	3	0	3	12	11	18	.198	.346	.301
June	94	30	3	0	9	23	17	15	.319	.638	.420
July	97	29	4	0	7	16	14	21	.299	.557	.381
August	105	39	8	1	5	15	18	22	.371	.610	.460
Sept./Oct.	120	36	3	0	7	15	12	15	.300	.500	.364
Leading Off Inn.	155	49	6	1	8	8	15	27	.316	.523	.376
Bases Empty	331	106	14	1	24	24	51	59	.320	.586	.413
Runners On	226	61	7	0	11	64	43	49	.270	.447	.383
Runners/Scor. Pos.	129	34	2	0	5	48	33	31	.264	.395	.404
Runners On/2 Out	101	25	3	0	3	22	22	19	.248	.366	.387
Scor. Pos./2 Out	60	15	1	0	2	18	19	14	.250	.367	.430
Late-Inning Pressure	85	22	6	1	4	11	11	17	.259	.494	.337
Leading Off	31	8	2	1	1	1	2	7	.258	.484	.303
Runners On	26	6	2	0	1	8	4	4	.231	.423	.313
Runners/Scor. Pos.	16	2	0	0	0	5	3	4	.125	.125	.238

RUNS BATTED IN	From 1B	From 2B	From 3B	Scoring Position
Totals	13/166	21/102	19/51	40/153
Percentage	7.8%	20.6%	37.3%	26.1%

Loves to face: Oil Can Boyd (.444, 4-for-9)
Cecilio Guante (.571, 4-for-7, 2 HR, 2 SO)
Gene Harris (3-for-3, 2 HR, 1 BB)

Hates to face: Jose DeLeon (.125, 1-for-8, 4 SO)
Dave Schmidt (.091, 1-for-11)
Frank Viola (.214, 3-for-14, 1 HR)

Miscellaneous statistics: Ground outs-to-air outs ratio: 1.00 last season, 1.07 for career. . . . Grounded into 7 double plays in 108 opportunities (one per 15.4). . . . Drove in 14 of 28 runners from third base with less than two outs (50%). . . . Direction of balls hit to the outfield: 28% to left field, 33% to center, 38% to right. . . . Base running: Advanced from first base to third on 12 of 41 outfield singles (29%); scored from second on 9 of 13 (69%). . . . Made 0.87 assists per nine innings at first base.

Comments: Platooned with Cecil Fielder as Toronto's DH in 1987. Combine McGriff's 1990 performance vs. right-handers with Fielder's vs. left-handers, and you'd have 52 home runs with a .340 batting average. Only four players in history reached those figures in the same season: Babe Ruth (1920–21, 1927), Hack Wilson (1930), Jimmie Foxx (1932), and Mickey Mantle (1956). . . . August batting average was the highest in the American League. . . . Has a career average of one home run per 12.8 at bats vs. right-handers, but only one per 30.1 at bats vs. left-handers. . . . Has had no fewer than 34 home runs and no more than 92 RBIs for three consecutive seasons. Only one other player in major league history had two such seasons in his entire *career*: Dave Kingman. . . . Why, you ask? He's hit for a higher average with the bases empty than with runners on base in each of his five seasons in the majors. Career mark of .294 with the bases empty, .256 with runners on base. His average continues to decline as the importance of the situation grows: .239 with runners in scoring position, .208 with two outs and RISP. . . . Career slugging percentage of .593 vs. right-handed pitchers is the highest of any player over the 16 years we've kept track. . . . As most of us were sitting at home waiting (and waiting, and waiting. . .) for a replay of Tom Brunansky's pennant-clinching catch, McGriff was in Baltimore, where he had just dropped his average for the season below the .300 mark. He finished at .2998.

Mark McGwire

Bats Right

Oakland A's	AB	H	2B	3B	HR	RBI	BB	SO	BA	SA	OBA
Season	523	123	16	0	39	108	110	116	.235	.489	.370
vs. Left-Handers	132	34	3	0	11	38	29	19	.258	.530	.387
vs. Right-Handers	391	89	13	0	28	70	81	97	.228	.476	.364
vs. Ground-Ballers	276	63	8	0	20	55	54	42	.228	.475	.361
vs. Fly-Ballers	247	60	8	0	19	53	56	74	.243	.506	.379
Home Games	245	55	8	0	14	37	54	61	.224	.429	.369
Road Games	278	68	8	0	25	71	56	55	.245	.543	.370
Grass Fields	436	101	13	0	34	91	96	96	.232	.495	.369
Artificial Turf	87	22	3	0	5	17	14	20	.253	.460	.371
April	61	15	0	0	7	18	15	10	.246	.590	.390
May	83	16	3	0	5	14	23	15	.193	.410	.374
June	88	22	2	0	8	18	12	21	.250	.545	.340
July	109	22	2	0	7	16	15	24	.202	.413	.302
August	89	20	3	0	6	21	20	21	.225	.461	.366
Sept./Oct.	93	28	6	0	6	21	25	25	.301	.559	.455
Leading Off Inn.	124	31	4	0	11	11	28	19	.250	.548	.396
Bases Empty	278	68	10	0	20	20	56	55	.245	.496	.381
Runners On	245	55	6	0	19	88	54	61	.224	.482	.358
Runners/Scor. Pos.	129	32	2	0	6	60	32	36	.248	.403	.380
Runners On/2 Out	124	29	1	0	10	43	29	35	.234	.484	.383
Scor. Pos./2 Out	71	18	0	0	2	26	18	21	.254	.338	.411
Late-Inning Pressure	50	12	1	0	4	10	18	13	.240	.500	.457
Leading Off	9	0	0	0	0	0	2	2	.000	.000	.250
Runners On	23	5	0	0	3	9	12	8	.217	.609	.500
Runners/Scor. Pos.	11	2	0	0	1	5	11	6	.182	.455	.609

RUNS BATTED IN	From 1B	From 2B	From 3B	Scoring Position
Totals	18/193	21/102	30/77	51/179
Percentage	9.3%	20.6%	39.0%	28.5%

Loves to face: Greg A. Harris (.385, 5-for-13, 3 HR)
Paul Kilgus (.625, 5-for-8, 2 2B, 2 HR)
Rob Murphy (.750, 3-for-4, 1 2B, 2 HR, 1 SO)

Hates to face: Allan Anderson (.083, 2-for-24)
Dennis Lamp (0-for-11, 1 BB)
Dave Stieb (.143, 3-for-21, 3 BB)

Miscellaneous statistics: Ground outs-to-air outs ratio: 0.59 last season, 3d-lowest rate in A.L.; 0.61 for career. . . . Grounded into 13 double plays in 126 opportunities (one per 9.7). . . . Drove in 20 of 37 runners from third base with less than two outs (54%). . . . Direction of balls hit to the outfield: 43% to left field, 36% to center, 22% to right. . . . Base running: Advanced from first base to third on 5 of 35 outfield singles (14%); scored from second on 15 of 16 (94%). . . . Made 0.64 assists per nine innings at first base.

Comments: The first player in major league history to hit 30 or more home runs as a rookie, and in his next three seasons as well. The only other player with a comparable streak of even three years: Jose Canseco. . . . Career average of one home run per 11.7 at-bats on the road is the highest of any player over the 16 years we've kept track. His overall rate of one home run per 13.9 at-bats is 2d best in major league history behind the Babe's 11.8 (minimum: 100 HR). . . . Career home run totals: 96 on the road, 60 at home. . . . Mark McGwire and Joe Carter became the fifth and sixth players in major league history to drive in at least 100 runs while batting below .240. The others: Roy Sievers, 1954 (.232 BA, 102 RBI); Gorman Thomas, 1980 (.239, 105); Tony Armas, 1983 (.218, 107); and Carlton Fisk, 1985 (.238, 107). . . . McGwire batted .413 on balls hit to the left side of the field, .304 on balls up the middle, and .121 on balls hit to the right side. Among A.L. players with at least 100 hits, McGwire and Gary Gaetti had the fewest to the opposite field (11). . . . Started the season with a streak of 91 consecutive errorless games at first base, the longest streak by any major league first baseman last season. . . . His 154 games at first base matched his 1988 total, the 3d highest in Athletics history, behind Norm Siebern (162 games for Kansas City in 1962) and Eddie Robinson (155 games for Philadelphia in 1953). . . . Career batting average of .292 with runners in scoring position, .240 in other at-bats.

Bob Melvin

Bats Right

Baltimore Orioles	AB	H	2B	3B	HR	RBI	BB	SO	BA	SA	OBA
Season	301	73	14	1	5	37	11	53	.243	.346	.267
vs. Left-Handers	152	42	11	0	3	16	6	18	.276	.408	.298
vs. Right-Handers	149	31	3	1	2	21	5	35	.208	.282	.234
vs. Ground-Ballers	121	26	2	0	1	14	5	19	.215	.256	.242
vs. Fly-Ballers	180	47	12	1	4	23	6	34	.261	.406	.283
Home Games	121	21	3	1	3	13	3	28	.174	.289	.190
Road Games	180	52	11	0	2	24	8	25	.289	.383	.317
Grass Fields	243	57	11	1	5	32	8	43	.235	.350	.256
Artificial Turf	58	16	3	0	0	5	3	10	.276	.328	.311
April	37	6	2	0	1	5	2	7	.162	.297	.200
May	56	18	5	0	1	10	2	8	.321	.464	.345
June	47	9	3	0	0	4	2	13	.191	.255	.224
July	54	9	0	1	0	5	1	13	.167	.204	.179
August	53	14	1	0	2	7	1	3	.264	.396	.278
Sept./Oct.	54	17	3	0	1	6	3	9	.315	.426	.345
Leading Off Inn.	77	14	4	0	0	0	4	17	.182	.234	.222
Bases Empty	160	32	10	0	2	2	7	30	.200	.300	.234
Runners On	141	41	4	1	3	35	4	23	.291	.397	.304
Runners/Scor. Pos.	98	27	2	1	2	32	3	18	.276	.378	.288
Runners On/2 Out	75	22	2	1	2	19	3	10	.293	.427	.321
Scor. Pos./2 Out	57	17	1	1	2	18	2	8	.298	.456	.322
Late-Inning Pressure	47	8	2	0	0	4	3	7	.170	.213	.212
Leading Off	15	1	0	0	0	0	1	2	.067	.067	.125
Runners On	17	3	0	0	0	4	1	4	.176	.176	.200
Runners/Scor. Pos.	13	3	0	0	0	4	1	4	.231	.231	.250

RUNS BATTED IN	From 1B	From 2B	From 3B	Scoring Position
Totals	4/108	14/68	14/47	28/115
Percentage	3.7%	20.6%	29.8%	24.3%

Loves to face: Randy Johnson (.533, 8-for-15)
John Tudor (.500, 5-for-10)
Curt Young (.429, 3-for-7, 2 2B, 1 HR)

Hates to face: Andy Hawkins (.125, 2-for-16, 1 HR)
Tim Leary (.133, 2-for-15)
Nolan Ryan (.222, 4-for-18, 8 SO)

Miscellaneous statistics: Ground outs-to-air outs ratio: 1.20 last season, 1.31 for career. . . . Grounded into 8 double plays in 58 opportunities (one per 7.3). . . . Drove in 9 of 23 runners from third base with less than two outs (39%). . . . Direction of balls hit to the outfield: 34% to left field, 33% to center, 33% to right. . . . Base running: Advanced from first base to third on 2 of 9 outfield singles (22%); scored from second on 3 of 3. . . . Opposing base stealers: 44-for-63 (70%).

Comments: Compiled a career-high batting average last season. His career average is .229 over six seasons. . . . Orioles pitchers allowed a half-run less per nine innings with Melvin catching (4.16) than with Mickey Tettleton (4.65) behind the plate. . . . Melvin committed only one error and one passed ball in 633⅔ innings; Tettleton had four of each in only 120 more innings. . . . Melvin's 70-game errorless streak to start the season was the 2d longest by any major league catcher last year. . . . Melvin started 51 of 56 games in which Baltimore faced a left-handed starter, but only 23 of 105 vs. right-handers. . . . Was hitless in his first 28 at-bats at Memorial Stadium last season; during that time, he hit .325 on the road (27-for-83). . . . Batted 75 points higher with runners on base (.271) than with the bases empty (.196) over the last five seasons, the 4th-largest margin in the majors. . . . Batted 94 points higher vs. left-handers (.283) than vs. right-handers (.188) over the last five seasons, the 5th-largest margin in the majors. His career average of .189 vs. right-handers is the lowest among active players (minimum: 600 AB). . . . Has driven in an average of only 39 percent of runners from third base with less than two outs during his career. Over the last 16 years, only three batters had lower marks: Bill Schroeder (33%), Steve Lombardozzi (37%), and Bob Knepper (38%) (minimum: 50 opportunities).

Randy Milligan

Bats Right

Baltimore Orioles	AB	H	2B	3B	HR	RBI	BB	SO	BA	SA	OBA
Season	362	96	20	1	20	60	88	68	.265	.492	.408
vs. Left-Handers	100	33	9	1	8	22	28	14	.330	.680	.473
vs. Right-Handers	262	63	11	0	12	38	60	54	.240	.420	.382
vs. Ground-Ballers	172	45	12	0	4	25	29	30	.262	.401	.369
vs. Fly-Ballers	190	51	8	1	16	35	59	38	.268	.574	.440
Home Games	166	44	10	1	11	31	45	33	.265	.536	.419
Road Games	196	52	10	0	9	29	43	35	.265	.454	.398
Grass Fields	300	80	18	1	16	50	75	58	.267	.493	.411
Artificial Turf	62	16	2	0	4	10	13	10	.258	.484	.395
April	58	15	1	0	2	9	17	14	.259	.379	.416
May	78	16	6	0	3	10	27	17	.205	.397	.415
June	101	33	8	0	8	24	21	17	.327	.644	.439
July	101	25	5	0	7	15	20	14	.248	.505	.369
August	14	3	0	1	0	0	3	4	.214	.357	.389
Sept./Oct.	10	4	0	0	0	2	0	2	.400	.400	.400
Leading Off Inn.	71	15	2	0	6	6	21	11	.211	.493	.391
Bases Empty	191	47	8	1	17	17	48	37	.246	.565	.402
Runners On	171	49	12	0	3	43	40	31	.287	.409	.414
Runners/Scor. Pos.	95	24	6	0	3	39	26	21	.253	.411	.400
Runners On/2 Out	72	17	6	0	1	18	20	16	.236	.361	.402
Scor. Pos./2 Out	53	11	2	0	1	16	10	14	.208	.302	.333
Late-Inning Pressure	59	14	2	0	4	10	17	9	.237	.475	.408
Leading Off	20	2	0	0	1	1	5	3	.100	.250	.280
Runners On	21	8	2	0	0	6	10	2	.381	.476	.581
Runners/Scor. Pos.	10	4	2	0	0	6	5	1	.400	.600	.600

RUNS BATTED IN	From 1B	From 2B	From 3B	Scoring Position
Totals	8/121	17/75	15/43	32/118
Percentage	6.6%	22.7%	34.9%	27.1%

Loves to face: Tom Filer (3-for-3, 2 2B)
Andy Hawkins (.667, 2-for-3, 2 HR, 1 SO)
Bobby Witt (.583, 7-for-12, 1 HR, 6 BB)

Hates to face: Kevin Brown (.091, 1-for-11, 3 BB)
Mike Moore (0-for-6, 5 SO)
Jack Morris (.100, 1-for-10, 1 2B)

Miscellaneous statistics: Ground outs-to-air outs ratio: 0.84 last season, 0.95 for career. . . . Grounded into 11 double plays in 85 opportunities (one per 7.7). . . . Drove in 9 of 18 runners from third base with less than two outs (50%). . . . Direction of balls hit to the outfield: 24% to left field, 40% to center, 37% to right. . . . Base running: Advanced from first base to third on 8 of 25 outfield singles (32%); scored from second on 17 of 19 (89%). . . . Made 0.92 assists per nine innings at first base, 2d-highest rate in A.L.

Comments: Reached base in 10 consecutive plate appearances last May, tying Kirby Puckett for the longest streak in the majors last season. . . . Average of one walk per 5.2 plate appearances was the best in the American League. . . . Batted 37 points higher in day games (.293) than night games (.256), a smaller margin than in 1989. Career averages: .287 in day games, .254 at night. . . . Prior to 1990, Milligan had hit 85 points higher against right-handed pitchers (.302) than vs. left-handers (.217). . . . Orioles were in striking distance of first place, trailing by six games, when Milligan went down with a separated shoulder on August 7. . . . His injury allowed the O's to take a long look at David Segui at first base. . . . Segui, by the way, grounded into 12 double plays in 26 opportunities, by far the highest rate of any major leaguer (minimum: 5 GIDPs). . . . Career average of .280 in Late-Inning Pressure Situations, .258 in other at-bats. His LIPS average breaks down as follows: .431 with runners on base, .176 with the bases empty. . . . He has driven in 11 of 22 runners from scoring position in LIPS, compared to only 22 percent in other situations (50-for-223). . . . No sacrifice bunts in 1005 career plate appearances.

Paul Molitor

Bats Right

Milwaukee Brewers	AB	H	2B	3B	HR	RBI	BB	SO	BA	SA	OBA
Season	418	119	27	6	12	45	37	51	.285	.464	.343
vs. Left-Handers	112	35	9	2	5	14	9	16	.313	.563	.364
vs. Right-Handers	306	84	18	4	7	31	28	35	.275	.428	.335
vs. Ground-Ballers	170	48	6	2	6	16	19	19	.282	.447	.354
vs. Fly-Ballers	248	71	21	4	6	29	18	32	.286	.476	.335
Home Games	185	53	14	1	6	19	17	20	.286	.470	.343
Road Games	233	66	13	5	6	26	20	31	.283	.459	.343
Grass Fields	325	87	21	5	7	28	33	43	.268	.428	.335
Artificial Turf	93	32	6	1	5	17	4	8	.344	.591	.371
April	17	4	1	0	1	3	1	3	.235	.471	.278
May	105	30	6	0	4	11	10	12	.286	.457	.348
June	67	21	7	0	2	11	6	6	.313	.507	.360
July	8	4	1	0	0	0	1	2	.500	.625	.556
August	120	39	9	3	2	11	11	16	.325	.500	.382
Sept./Oct.	101	21	3	3	3	9	8	12	.208	.386	.273
Leading Off Inn.	162	48	7	5	4	4	10	17	.296	.475	.337
Bases Empty	274	78	18	6	7	7	16	28	.285	.471	.324
Runners On	144	41	9	0	5	38	21	23	.285	.451	.375
Runners/Scor. Pos.	80	25	6	0	1	30	17	10	.313	.425	.430
Runners On/2 Out	67	22	4	0	2	21	10	8	.328	.478	.423
Scor. Pos./2 Out	44	15	3	0	1	19	9	6	.341	.477	.463
Late-Inning Pressure	48	11	2	0	2	5	4	7	.229	.396	.283
Leading Off	8	4	0	0	1	1	1	0	.500	.875	.556
Runners On	25	3	0	0	1	4	1	6	.120	.240	.148
Runners/Scor. Pos.	10	2	0	0	0	2	1	1	.200	.200	.250

RUNS BATTED IN	From 1B	From 2B	From 3B	Scoring Position
Totals	5/90	16/61	12/31	28/92
Percentage	5.6%	26.2%	38.7%	30.4%

Loves to face: Tom Niedenfuer (.600, 3-for-5, 1 HR)
Walt Terrell (.485, 16-for-33, 2 HR)
John Tudor (.500, 6-for-12, 1 HR)

Hates to face: Juan Berenguer (.212, 7-for-33)
Mike Moore (.146, 6-for-41)
Jeff Russell (.158, 3-for-19)

Miscellaneous statistics: Ground outs-to-air outs ratio: 0.93 last season, 1.22 for career. . . . Grounded into 7 double plays in 54 opportunities (one per 7.7). . . . Drove in 5 of 11 runners from third base with less than two outs (45%). . . . Direction of balls hit to the outfield: 47% to left field, 23% to center, 30% to right. . . . Base running: Advanced from first base to third on 9 of 21 outfield singles (43%); scored from second on 5 of 10 (50%). . . . Made 3.40 assists per nine innings at second base.

Comments: Stole only 18 bases last season, snapping a streak of five consecutive years of 20 or more. But his percentage was a career high (86%). . . . Career batting average of .299 ranks eighth among active players with at least 1000 hits. . . . Batting average was above .300 as late as September 9, but he batted only .197 (13-for-66) thereafter to end his streak of consecutive .300 seasons at three. . . . Has batted over .300 with runners in scoring position in each of the last five years. . . . Has hit for a higher average at County Stadium than he has in road games in each of the last seven seasons. . . . Has also had higher averages with runners on base than with the bases empty in each of those seven seasons. . . . Has driven in only four of 29 runners from scoring position in Late-Inning Pressure Situations over the last two seasons (14 percent), compared to 33 percent in other at-bats during that time. . . . Had to make room for a new glove in his locker last season when he appeared in 37 games at first base. If he plays 13 more games there, he will become only the eighth player in history to play at least 50 games in the outfield, and 50 at all four infield positions as well. The others: Joe Quinn, Honus Wagner, Germany Schaefer, Red Kress, Chico Salmon, Don Money, and Bill Almon. . . . Molitor hasn't played the outfield since 1986, and hasn't done that shortstop thing since 1982.

Lloyd Moseby

Bats Left

Detroit Tigers	AB	H	2B	3B	HR	RBI	BB	SO	BA	SA	OBA
Season	431	107	16	5	14	51	48	77	.248	.406	.329
vs. Left-Handers	132	24	2	0	2	9	10	26	.182	.242	.264
vs. Right-Handers	299	83	14	5	12	42	38	51	.278	.478	.358
vs. Ground-Ballers	206	56	9	3	7	29	19	32	.272	.447	.332
vs. Fly-Ballers	225	51	7	2	7	22	29	45	.227	.369	.327
Home Games	221	53	4	3	8	25	31	39	.240	.394	.341
Road Games	210	54	12	2	6	26	17	38	.257	.419	.316
Grass Fields	381	92	11	4	12	42	44	69	.241	.386	.328
Artificial Turf	50	15	5	1	2	9	4	8	.300	.560	.339
April	66	22	4	1	0	4	7	12	.333	.424	.397
May	95	19	1	1	6	11	9	21	.200	.421	.290
June	68	17	2	0	1	6	7	10	.250	.324	.320
July	46	14	1	1	3	10	11	8	.304	.565	.439
August	79	18	4	1	3	17	8	16	.228	.418	.308
Sept./Oct.	77	17	4	1	1	3	6	10	.221	.338	.277
Leading Off Inn.	108	29	5	1	1	1	12	17	.269	.361	.347
Bases Empty	240	64	10	3	10	10	25	46	.267	.458	.346
Runners On	191	43	6	2	4	41	23	31	.225	.340	.309
Runners/Scor. Pos.	114	23	3	2	2	37	18	17	.202	.316	.306
Runners On/2 Out	87	13	1	0	2	15	12	16	.149	.230	.253
Scor. Pos./2 Out	55	10	1	0	1	13	11	9	.182	.255	.318
Late-Inning Pressure	65	16	1	1	1	8	5	13	.246	.338	.306
Leading Off	18	6	0	0	0	0	1	3	.333	.333	.400
Runners On	34	9	1	1	0	7	3	5	.265	.353	.316
Runners/Scor. Pos.	23	5	1	1	0	7	3	2	.217	.348	.296

RUNS BATTED IN	From 1B	From 2B	From 3B	Scoring Position
Totals	8/158	16/91	13/50	29/141
Percentage	5.1%	17.6%	26.0%	20.6%

Loves to face: Andy Hawkins (.417, 5-for-12, 2 HR)
Mike Jeffcoat (.417, 5-for-12, 1 HR)
Rick Sutcliffe (.467, 7-for-15, 1 2B, 3 3B, 2 HR, 6 BB)

Hates to face: Juan Berenguer (.105, 2-for-19, 1 3B, 10 SO)
John Candelaria (.056, 1-for-18, 1 2B)
Dave Stewart (.128, 6-for-47, 7 BB)

Miscellaneous statistics: Ground outs-to-air outs ratio: 0.91 last season, 1.09 for career. . . . Grounded into 14 double plays in 102 opportunities (one per 7.3). . . . Drove in 11 of 28 runners from third base with less than two outs (39%). . . . Direction of balls hit to the outfield: 31% to left field, 35% to center, 34% to right. . . . Base running: Advanced from first base to third on 13 of 22 outfield singles (59%); scored from second on 11 of 11. . . . Made 2.74 putouts per nine innings in center field.

Comments: Batted 96 points higher vs. right-handers (.278) than vs. left-handers (.182) last season, the 2d-largest margin in the majors. His yearly averages vs. lefties have been on the decline since 1987: .278, .253, .196, .182. . . . Batting average with runners in scoring position was the lowest of his career. . . . He was hitless in seven at-bats as a pinch-hitter last season, dropping his career PH average to .182 (6-for-33, no HR). . . . Participated in five double plays from the outfield last season, equalling his total of the previous five seasons. . . . Moseby played 60 percent of the Tigers' innings in center field, but moved to left field in September so the Tigers could take a look at Milt Cuyler in center. . . . Superstars have their 30/30 and 40/40 clubs. For the *hoi polloi* there's the 10/10 club. Moseby's been a member for eight straight seasons, tying Darryl Strawberry for the longest current streak. The all-time record: 12, Andre Dawson (1977–88). . . . Another streak: Only two others played 100 or more games in the outfield while batting below .250 in each of the last three seasons: his old outfieldmate, Jesse Barfield, and Dale Murphy. The only four-year streaks in major league history: Jim Busby (1955–58) and Jim Landis (1962–65), both known as great fly-hawks.

Greg Myers

Bats Left

Toronto Blue Jays	AB	H	2B	3B	HR	RBI	BB	SO	BA	SA	OBA
Season	250	59	7	1	5	22	22	33	.236	.332	.293
vs. Left-Handers	23	4	0	0	0	2	3	4	.174	.174	.259
vs. Right-Handers	227	55	7	1	5	20	19	29	.242	.348	.297
vs. Ground-Ballers	136	33	5	1	2	15	13	16	.243	.338	.303
vs. Fly-Ballers	114	26	2	0	3	7	9	17	.228	.325	.282
Home Games	122	29	2	0	3	13	13	19	.238	.328	.307
Road Games	128	30	5	1	2	9	9	14	.234	.336	.281
Grass Fields	96	24	4	1	2	7	9	9	.250	.375	.308
Artificial Turf	154	35	3	0	3	15	13	24	.227	.305	.284
April	43	13	1	0	2	8	6	2	.302	.465	.380
May	14	0	0	0	0	0	2	3	.000	.000	.125
June	59	15	2	0	2	3	3	11	.254	.390	.290
July	41	9	0	1	0	8	2	6	.220	.268	.239
August	43	14	3	0	0	1	2	7	.326	.395	.356
Sept./Oct.	50	8	1	0	1	2	7	4	.160	.240	.263
Leading Off Inn.	51	17	2	0	2	2	5	6	.333	.490	.393
Bases Empty	126	33	4	0	3	3	11	18	.262	.365	.321
Runners On	124	26	3	1	2	19	11	15	.210	.298	.266
Runners/Scor. Pos.	71	12	1	1	2	19	6	12	.169	.296	.222
Runners On/2 Out	64	7	0	1	0	5	2	10	.109	.141	.136
Scor. Pos./2 Out	37	4	0	1	0	5	1	7	.108	.162	.132
Late-Inning Pressure	26	10	1	0	1	3	1	3	.385	.538	.407
Leading Off	9	3	1	0	0	0	1	1	.333	.444	.400
Runners On	10	3	0	0	1	3	0	1	.300	.600	.300
Runners/Scor. Pos.	6	1	0	0	1	3	0	1	.167	.667	.167

RUNS BATTED IN	From 1B	From 2B	From 3B	Scoring Position
Totals	3/102	6/54	8/29	14/83
Percentage	2.9%	11.1%	27.6%	16.9%

Loves to face: Andy Hawkins (.364, 4-for-11, 1 HR)

Hates to face: Brian Holman (0-for-8, 1 BB)
Nolan Ryan (0-for-6)
Dave Stewart (.125, 1-for-8)

Miscellaneous statistics: Ground outs-to-air outs ratio: 1.43 last season, 1.40 for career. . . . Grounded into 12 double plays in 57 opportunities (one per 4.8), 2d-worst rate in A.L. . . . Drove in 6 of 11 runners from third base with less than two outs (55%). . . . Direction of balls hit to the outfield: 30% to left field, 31% to center, 39% to right. . . . Base running: Advanced from first base to third on 2 of 18 outfield singles (11%); scored from second on 7 of 13 (54%). . . . Opposing base stealers: 40-for-66 (61%), 5th-lowest rate in A.L.

Comments: Blue Jays pitchers allowed about as many runs per nine innings with Myers behind the plate (4.05) as with Pat Borders (4.15). . . . Has started 95 games in his career (including 79 last season), all vs. right-handed pitchers. He has only 30 career plate appearances vs. left-handers, over 300 against right-handers. . . . Career batting averages: .192 vs. left-handers, .217 vs. right-handers. . . . Other batting-average breakdowns: .232 with the bases empty, .196 with runners on base, .151 with runners in scoring position, .095 with two outs and RISP, .000 (0-for-7) with the bases loaded. . . . Has a career BA of .323 in Late-Inning Pressure Situations (10-for-31). . . . Was removed in favor of a pinch hitter 34 times last season, the most of any player on the Blue Jays. In 33 of those 34 cases, he was due to face a left-handed pitcher; in 32 of those 33 cases, the pinch hitter was Pat Borders. Myers batted for Borders seven times (his only seven pinch-hit appearances of the season). . . . Has one hit in 20 career at-bats at the Kingdome. . . . Was the only Blue Jays selection from the June 1984 draft to hit the big time—in baseball, that is. Toronto also chose Detroit Lions quarterback Rodney Peete (a shortstop at Shawnee Mission HS in Kansas) and Rams safety Anthony Newman (an outfielder at Beaverton HS in Portland, Oregon).

Al Newman

Bats Left and Right

Minnesota Twins	AB	H	2B	3B	HR	RBI	BB	SO	BA	SA	OBA
Season	388	94	14	0	0	30	33	34	.242	.278	.304
vs. Left-Handers	123	31	6	0	0	6	15	14	.252	.301	.333
vs. Right-Handers	265	63	8	0	0	24	18	20	.238	.268	.289
vs. Ground-Ballers	165	40	4	0	0	16	14	13	.242	.267	.306
vs. Fly-Ballers	223	54	10	0	0	14	19	21	.242	.287	.302
Home Games	199	52	8	0	0	19	23	13	.261	.302	.338
Road Games	189	42	6	0	0	11	10	21	.222	.254	.265
Grass Fields	152	37	5	0	0	8	8	18	.243	.276	.286
Artificial Turf	236	57	9	0	0	22	25	16	.242	.280	.314
April	43	9	3	0	0	3	4	5	.209	.279	.277
May	68	18	2	0	0	7	2	4	.265	.294	.288
June	54	12	2	0	0	5	4	4	.222	.259	.276
July	94	26	6	0	0	7	10	7	.277	.340	.346
August	58	14	0	0	0	2	3	3	.241	.241	.279
Sept./Oct.	71	15	1	0	0	6	10	11	.211	.225	.317
Leading Off Inn.	96	25	2	0	0	0	9	7	.260	.281	.324
Bases Empty	223	56	6	0	0	0	16	21	.251	.278	.304
Runners On	165	38	8	0	0	30	17	13	.230	.279	.303
Runners/Scor. Pos.	110	24	5	0	0	29	9	7	.218	.264	.273
Runners On/2 Out	80	15	2	0	0	9	9	6	.188	.213	.270
Scor. Pos./2 Out	60	11	2	0	0	9	3	4	.183	.217	.222
Late-Inning Pressure	59	11	4	0	0	3	3	7	.186	.254	.238
Leading Off	19	5	2	0	0	0	1	2	.263	.368	.300
Runners On	23	3	1	0	0	3	2	1	.130	.174	.200
Runners/Scor. Pos.	15	2	1	0	0	3	0	1	.133	.200	.133

RUNS BATTED IN	From 1B	From 2B	From 3B	Scoring Position
Totals	1/108	9/85	20/48	29/133
Percentage	0.9%	10.6%	41.7%	21.8%

Loves to face: Brian Holman (.500, 3-for-6)
Bobby Witt (.391, 9-for-23)
Curt Young (.533, 8-for-15)

Hates to face: Dennis Eckersley (0-for-8)
Mike Moore (.158, 3-for-19)
Bob Welch (.105, 2-for-19)

Miscellaneous statistics: Ground outs-to-air outs ratio: 1.59 last season, 1.68 for career. . . . Grounded into 7 double plays in 71 opportunities (one per 10.1). . . . Drove in 18 of 25 runners from third base with less than two outs (72%). . . . Direction of balls hit to the outfield: 34% to left field, 40% to center, 27% to right batting left-handed; 46% to left, 38% to center, 16% to right batting right-handed. . . . Base running: Advanced from first base to third on 9 of 18 outfield singles (50%); scored from second on 8 of 9 (89%). . . . Made 2.95 assists per nine innings at second base.

Comments: Enters 1991 with a streak of 1479 at-bats since the only home run of his career, the longest current streak by any active player. . . . His only career home run was hit off of Zane Smith in 1986, while Newman played for the Montreal Expos. He has 1401 American League at-bats, the 5th most in league history among players without a home run. The top four: Tom Oliver, 1931 AB; Irv Hall, 1904 AB; Hal Rhyne, 1497 AB; Roxy Walters, 1426 AB. . . . His 388 at-bats without either a triple or a home run were the most by an American League player since 1945, when Mike Tresh had 458 at-bats with nothing longer than a double. In A.L. history, only nine players, including Newman, have accumulated at least 388 AB without a three- or four-bagger. The last National Leaguers to do it were Frank Taveras in 1980 and Ron Hunt in 1972–74, the last three years of his career. . . . Has hit for a higher average in day games than he has in night games in each of his six seasons in the majors. Career averages: .270 in day games, .213 at night. . . . Batted .390 in 41 first-inning at-bats, .225 in subsequent at bats. . . . Committed only two errors in 293 chances at second base. Fielding titles are based on 108 games (two-thirds of the schedule), and Newman played in only 89 at second. . . . Has played at least 25 games apiece at second base, third base, and shortstop in each of the last three seasons. The only other player in baseball history with a three-year streak: Jim Davenport (1964–66).

Matt Nokes

Bats Left

Tigers/Yankees	AB	H	2B	3B	HR	RBI	BB	SO	BA	SA	OBA
Season	351	87	9	1	11	40	24	47	.248	.373	.306
vs. Left-Handers	14	2	0	0	0	2	0	5	.143	.143	.200
vs. Right-Handers	337	35	9	1	11	38	24	42	.252	.383	.311
vs. Ground-Ballers	162	40	3	1	6	19	9	20	.247	.389	.289
vs. Fly-Ballers	189	47	6	0	5	21	15	27	.249	.360	.321
Home Games	157	40	3	0	4	20	12	13	.255	.350	.306
Road Games	194	47	6	1	7	20	12	34	.242	.392	.307
Grass Fields	283	66	6	0	7	28	21	32	.233	.329	.292
Artificial Turf	68	21	3	1	4	12	3	15	.309	.559	.365
April	51	15	3	0	0	2	3	4	.294	.353	.333
May	55	15	2	1	3	6	1	8	.273	.509	.305
June	65	16	1	0	4	16	2	8	.246	.446	.269
July	68	17	1	0	2	5	7	12	.250	.353	.354
August	60	15	1	0	2	6	9	7	.250	.367	.348
Sept./Oct.	52	9	1	0	0	5	2	8	.173	.192	.204
Leading Off Inn.	86	21	5	0	5	5	5	12	.244	.477	.301
Bases Empty	201	47	6	1	8	8	12	28	.234	.393	.290
Runners On	150	40	3	0	3	32	12	19	.267	.347	.327
Runners/Scor. Pos.	80	24	2	0	3	32	10	8	.300	.438	.380
Runners On/2 Out	71	15	2	0	0	12	6	9	.211	.239	.273
Scor. Pos./2 Out	48	12	1	0	0	12	5	5	.250	.271	.321
Late-Inning Pressure	51	12	1	0	1	4	2	6	.235	.314	.264
Leading Off	13	4	0	0	1	1	1	2	.308	.538	.357
Runners On	22	5	1	0	0	3	0	2	.227	.273	.227
Runners/Scor. Pos.	12	2	0	0	0	3	0	2	.167	.167	.167

RUNS BATTED IN	From 1B	From 2B	From 3B	Scoring Position
Totals	2/115	14/62	13/36	27/98
Percentage	1.7%	22.6%	36.1%	27.6%

Loves to face: Mike Moore (.381, 8-for-21, 2 HR)
Jeff Russell (.455, 5-for-11, 1 HR)
Dave Schmidt (.500, 4-for-8, 1 HR)

Hates to face: Charlie Hough (.118, 2-for-17, 4 BB)
Nolan Ryan (.083, 1-for-12, 1 2B)
Bob Welch (.067, 1-for-15, 2 BB)

Miscellaneous statistics: Ground outs-to-air outs ratio: 0.85 last season, 0.97 for career. . . . Grounded into 11 double plays in 68 opportunities (one per 6.2). . . . Drove in 7 of 14 runners from third base with less than two outs (50%). . . . Direction of balls hit to the outfield: 28% to left field, 27% to center, 45% to right. . . . Base running: Advanced from first base to third on 6 of 17 outfield singles (35%); scored from second on 4 of 6 (67%). . . . Opposing base stealers: 41-for-71 (58%), 4th-lowest rate in A.L.

Comments: Batting averages year by year since 1986: .333 (in seven games), .289, .251, .250, .248. Nine other players had batting averages in 1990 that declined for at least a fourth consecutive season, including two of Nokes's Yankees teammates: Don Mattingly and Mel Hall (the only player with a five-year streak). . . . Started 99 games, including three for three different managers over a four-day period. He played his last game for Sparky Anderson on June 3, his only for Bucky Dent on June 5, and his first for Stump Merrill on June 6. By way of comparison, Dock Ellis played for three teams and six managers in 1977, including the one-day wonder, Eddie Stanky. . . . Sparky, Bucky, Stump. Is there a manager named "Fluffy" out there just waiting for a chance to manage Nokes?. . .Batted only 15 times against left-handers, his lowest total since 1986. . . . Career batting average of .220 (one HR per 23.3 AB) vs. left-handers, .267 (one HR per 21.5 AB) vs. right-handers. . . . Nokes batted .222 (6-for-27) with two home runs and seven RBIs as a pinch hitter for the Yankees last season. Prior to joining New York, he had a .172 average in 58 career at-bats as a pinch hitter, with no home runs and only eight RBIs. . . . There were 27 pinch-hit home runs in the American League last season; six were hit by the Yankees: Nokes 2, Balboni 2, Barfield 1, Hall 1.

Pete O'Brien

Bats Left

Seattle Mariners	AB	H	2B	3B	HR	RBI	BB	SO	BA	SA	OBA
Season	366	82	18	0	5	27	44	33	.224	.314	.308
vs. Left-Handers	130	26	2	0	1	12	16	13	.200	.238	.291
vs. Right-Handers	236	56	16	0	4	15	28	20	.237	.356	.317
vs. Ground-Ballers	131	29	9	0	1	6	20	13	.221	.313	.325
vs. Fly-Ballers	235	53	9	0	4	21	24	20	.226	.315	.298
Home Games	172	45	10	0	3	14	26	13	.262	.372	.361
Road Games	194	37	8	0	2	13	18	20	.191	.263	.257
Grass Fields	151	28	5	0	1	10	15	15	.185	.238	.256
Artificial Turf	215	54	13	0	4	17	29	18	.251	.367	.343
April	73	11	1	0	1	7	6	6	.151	.205	.213
May	13	4	1	0	1	2	1	3	.308	.615	.357
June	37	8	2	0	0	1	5	5	.216	.270	.341
July	92	19	4	0	1	8	14	5	.207	.283	.308
August	77	21	4	0	2	5	7	8	.273	.403	.333
Sept./Oct.	74	19	6	0	0	4	11	6	.257	.338	.345
Leading Off Inn.	82	29	6	0	3	3	11	7	.354	.537	.436
Bases Empty	200	56	15	0	5	5	25	21	.280	.430	.366
Runners On	166	26	3	0	0	22	19	12	.157	.175	.238
Runners/Scor. Pos.	96	15	2	0	0	21	9	9	.156	.177	.220
Runners On/2 Out	71	8	1	0	0	4	11	5	.113	.127	.232
Scor. Pos./2 Out	43	4	0	0	0	3	5	3	.093	.093	.188
Late-Inning Pressure	59	11	2	0	0	1	5	7	.186	.220	.262
Leading Off	10	6	1	0	0	0	2	0	.600	.700	.667
Runners On	29	2	0	0	0	1	2	2	.069	.069	.129
Runners/Scor. Pos.	17	2	0	0	0	1	0	1	.118	.118	.118

RUNS BATTED IN	From 1B	From 2B	From 3B	Scoring Position
Totals	2/134	7/79	13/49	20/128
Percentage	1.5%	8.9%	26.5%	15.6%

Loves to face: Jim Acker (.545, 6-for-11)
Randy O'Neal (.500, 3-for-6, 1 HR)
Rick Sutcliffe (.455, 5-for-11, 1 HR)

Hates to face: Mike Moore (.167, 10-for-60, 9 BB)
Dennis Rasmussen (.118, 2-for-17)
Dave Stieb (.173, 9-for-52, 2 HR)

Miscellaneous statistics: Ground outs-to-air outs ratio: 0.99 last season, 0.98 for career.... Grounded into 12 double plays in 84 opportunities (one per 7.0).... Drove in 12 of 29 runners from third base with less than two outs (41%).... Direction of balls hit to the outfield: 21% to left field, 31% to center, 48% to right.... Base running: Advanced from first base to third on 2 of 18 outfield singles (11%); scored from second on 3 of 12 (25%), lowest rate in A.L.... Made 0.86 assists per nine innings at first base.

Comments: Fractured his right thumb and missed 54 games last season, more than he had missed in the seven previous seasons combined (51). That ended his streak of five consecutive seasons with at least 154 games at first base, the longest in American League history, the "Iron Horse" notwithstanding.... Mariners first basemen combined to drive in only 48 runs, the fewest at that position in the majors.... His batting average has dropped in every year since 1986: .290, .286, .272, .260, .224. RBI total has dropped in every season since 1985.... Batted 123 points higher with the bases empty (.280) than with runners on base (.157) last season, the largest margin in the majors. Batting average with runners on was the lowest of any major leaguer with at least 100 at-bats in those situations.... Drove in only 20 of 128 runners from scoring position, the lowest percentage of any player in the majors (15.6%) (minimum: 100 opportunities). He was even worse in Late-Inning Pressure Situations, driving in only one of 21 runners from scoring position.... Had only one hit in 18 at-bats with the bases loaded, lowering his career average to .197 in those situations.... Played six games in the outfield last season, doubling his total of the previous six seasons. He played 27 games there for the Rangers in 1983.

John Olerud

Bats Left

Toronto Blue Jays	AB	H	2B	3B	HR	RBI	BB	SO	BA	SA	OBA
Season	358	95	15	1	14	48	57	75	.265	.430	.364
vs. Left-Handers	73	25	5	0	3	15	15	18	.342	.534	.444
vs. Right-Handers	285	70	10	1	11	33	42	57	.246	.404	.342
vs. Ground-Ballers	169	50	10	0	7	25	26	29	.296	.479	.391
vs. Fly-Ballers	189	45	5	1	7	23	31	46	.238	.386	.341
Home Games	187	51	7	1	11	26	29	43	.273	.497	.372
Road Games	171	44	8	0	3	22	28	32	.257	.357	.356
Grass Fields	135	38	8	0	3	19	24	26	.281	.407	.385
Artificial Turf	223	57	7	1	11	29	33	49	.256	.444	.351
April	48	12	2	0	2	5	8	7	.250	.417	.357
May	71	17	1	1	2	10	16	19	.239	.366	.375
June	75	25	5	0	4	15	8	16	.333	.560	.393
July	67	19	3	0	3	7	8	11	.284	.463	.364
August	66	14	4	0	2	7	8	14	.212	.364	.293
Sept./Oct.	31	8	0	0	1	4	9	8	.258	.355	.425
Leading Off Inn.	54	16	1	1	3	3	12	13	.296	.519	.424
Bases Empty	185	44	5	1	8	8	31	42	.238	.405	.347
Runners On	173	51	10	0	6	40	26	33	.295	.457	.382
Runners/Scor. Pos.	85	25	5	0	2	27	17	20	.294	.424	.402
Runners On/2 Out	63	20	6	0	2	17	13	12	.317	.508	.442
Scor. Pos./2 Out	30	12	3	0	1	12	11	4	.400	.600	.571
Late-Inning Pressure	66	20	4	0	2	14	6	17	.303	.455	.356
Leading Off	9	1	0	0	0	0	3	4	.111	.111	.333
Runners On	32	14	2	0	2	14	3	8	.438	.688	.472
Runners/Scor. Pos.	20	9	2	0	1	12	2	4	.450	.700	.478

RUNS BATTED IN	From 1B	From 2B	From 3B	Scoring Position
Totals	9/142	15/75	10/22	25/97
Percentage	6.3%	20.0%	45.5%	25.8%

Loves to face: Andy Hawkins (.500, 3-for-6, 1 HR, 3 BB)
Dennis Lamp (2-for-2, 1 HR, 1 BB)

Hates to face: Dave Stewart (0-for-7, 4 SO)
Bob Welch (0-for-5, 1 BB, 4 SO)

Miscellaneous statistics: Ground outs-to-air outs ratio: 1.25 last season, 1.22 for career.... Grounded into 5 double plays in 97 opportunities (one per 19.4).... Drove in 9 of 14 runners from third base with less than two outs (64%).... Direction of balls hit to the outfield: 35% to left field, 29% to center, 37% to right.... Base running: Advanced from first base to third on 3 of 17 outfield singles (18%); scored from second on 4 of 9 (44%).... Made 0.63 assists per nine innings at first base.

Comments: Olerud was Toronto's opening-day designated hitter last season, a role no player has reprised since Cliff Johnson (1983–84).... Led American League rookies with 57 walks.... He started 101 games last season. Only four players younger than Olerud started as many as 100 games last year: Ken Griffey, Delino DeShields, Gary Sheffield, and Sammy Sosa.... Started 92 games vs. right-handed pitchers, but only nine games vs. left-handers.... Batted .198 with one home run in 96 at-bats in day games, .294 with an average of one HR per 20.2 AB at night.... Drove in 46 percent of runners from scoring position in Late-Inning Pressure Situations (11-of-25), but drove in only 19 percent at other times.... Batting average vs. left-handed pitchers was the highest of any left-handed batter in the American League (minimum: 50 AB).... An auspicious list of comparable rookie seasons: Enos Slaughter (1938), Ray Lamanno (1942), Mickey Mantle (1951), Tommy Davis (1960), Willie Stargell (1963). That list reminds us of Robert Klein's parody of IQ tests—"Pick out the one that doesn't fit: (a) gorilla, (b) elephant, (c) rhinocerous, (d) mouse."...But seriously, folks, Lamanno was a catcher for the Reds whose career was derailed by three years of military service immediately following his promising rookie season (1943–45).

Joe Orsulak

Bats Left

Baltimore Orioles	AB	H	2B	3B	HR	RBI	BB	SO	BA	SA	OBA
Season	413	111	14	3	11	57	46	48	.269	.397	.343
vs. Left-Handers	72	18	0	1	0	7	8	8	.250	.278	.325
vs. Right-Handers	341	93	14	2	11	50	38	40	.273	.422	.346
vs. Ground-Ballers	192	50	5	1	4	30	20	21	.260	.359	.330
vs. Fly-Ballers	221	61	9	2	7	27	26	27	.276	.430	.353
Home Games	202	55	5	1	9	34	23	28	.272	.441	.348
Road Games	211	56	9	2	2	23	23	20	.265	.355	.338
Grass Fields	356	96	10	1	11	53	38	42	.270	.396	.341
Artificial Turf	57	15	4	2	0	4	8	6	.263	.404	.354
April	58	17	2	1	1	6	6	8	.293	.414	.369
May	78	26	5	2	5	23	11	7	.333	.641	.416
June	89	22	2	0	0	6	8	4	.247	.270	.309
July	91	28	4	0	3	12	7	8	.308	.451	.354
August	76	14	1	0	2	10	8	16	.184	.276	.262
Sept./Oct.	21	4	0	0	0	0	6	5	.190	.190	.370
Leading Off Inn.	85	29	3	0	2	2	6	7	.341	.447	.385
Bases Empty	223	63	8	2	5	5	17	25	.283	.404	.333
Runners On	190	48	6	1	6	52	29	23	.253	.389	.353
Runners/Scor. Pos.	110	33	5	0	4	47	24	13	.300	.455	.426
Runners On/2 Out	83	21	2	1	4	30	13	10	.253	.446	.354
Scor. Pos./2 Out	60	16	2	0	3	27	11	8	.267	.450	.380
Late-Inning Pressure	62	13	2	0	1	3	11	8	.210	.290	.329
Leading Off	13	4	1	0	1	1	2	1	.308	.615	.400
Runners On	28	4	0	0	0	2	8	3	.143	.143	.333
Runners/Scor. Pos.	15	3	0	0	0	2	7	1	.200	.200	.455

RUNS BATTED IN	From 1B	From 2B	From 3B	Scoring Position
Totals	6/151	19/85	21/52	40/137
Percentage	4.0%	22.4%	40.4%	29.2%

Loves to face: Kevin Brown (.455, 5-for-11, 1 HR)
Scott Sanderson (.375, 6-for-16, 2 2B, 2 HR)
Bobby Witt (.545, 6-for-11, 1 HR)

Hates to face: Rick Aguilera (.208, 5-for-24)
Ron Robinson (0-for-13, 1 BB)
Nolan Ryan (.056, 1-for-18)

Miscellaneous statistics: Ground outs-to-air outs ratio: 0.93 last season, 1.13 for career. . . . Grounded into 7 double plays in 98 opportunities (one per 14.0). . . . Drove in 11 of 21 runners from third base with less than two outs (52%). . . . Direction of balls hit to the outfield: 26% to left field, 29% to center, 46% to right. . . . Base running: Advanced from first base to third on 15 of 28 outfield singles (54%); scored from second on 7 of 9 (78%). . . . Made 2.91 putouts per nine innings in right field, highest rate in majors.

Comments: Started at least one game in every batting order position except the leadoff and ninth spots. . . . Not only did he make 16 starts as Baltimore cleanup hitter, he batted .371 from the number-four slot (23-for-62). Other Orioles cleanup hitters batted just .205. (See the Orioles essay for more.). . .Had hits in seven consecutive at bats, 2d-longest streak in the American League last season. . . . Batting average in Late-Inning Pressure Situations has been lower than his overall average in each of the last five seasons. Owns a career average of .240 in LIPS, .283 in other at-bats. . . . Career average of .237 vs. left-handers, .285 vs. right-handers. All 28 of his career home runs have been hit against right-handed pitchers. . . . Career average of .359 (14-for-39, no HR, six BB) with the bases loaded. . . . Had no home runs in his first 497 career at-bats, 28 in 1561 at-bats since then (one per 56 AB). . . . Stole 24 bases in both 1985 and 1986 for the Pirates but has stolen only 20 in three years in Baltimore. . . . Career stolen-base totals of 31-for-53 on grass fields (58%), 40-for-61 on artificial turf (66%). . . . Has played 372 games with the Orioles after playing 298 games with the Pirates. Only one other player in history has played at least that many games for both franchises: Lee Lacy.

Rafael Palmeiro

Bats Left

Texas Rangers	AB	H	2B	3B	HR	RBI	BB	SO	BA	SA	OBA
Season	598	191	35	6	14	89	40	59	.319	.468	.361
vs. Left-Handers	189	64	9	1	5	32	8	17	.339	.476	.361
vs. Right-Handers	409	127	26	5	9	57	32	42	.311	.465	.360
vs. Ground-Ballers	282	92	19	3	5	32	14	22	.326	.468	.360
vs. Fly-Ballers	316	99	16	3	9	57	26	37	.313	.468	.361
Home Games	295	85	19	5	9	46	30	31	.288	.478	.354
Road Games	303	106	16	1	5	43	10	28	.350	.459	.367
Grass Fields	510	162	29	6	14	84	37	50	.318	.480	.363
Artificial Turf	88	29	6	0	0	5	3	9	.330	.398	.348
April	69	23	4	2	3	12	7	9	.333	.580	.390
May	100	29	6	0	2	13	7	15	.290	.410	.333
June	102	35	6	0	2	13	2	11	.343	.461	.367
July	96	32	4	1	4	22	8	10	.333	.521	.377
August	111	33	9	1	1	13	7	6	.297	.423	.333
Sept./Oct.	120	39	6	2	2	16	9	8	.325	.458	.372
Leading Off Inn.	101	31	4	2	4	4	2	10	.307	.505	.320
Bases Empty	327	93	15	2	8	8	17	37	.284	.416	.324
Runners On	271	98	20	4	6	81	23	22	.362	.531	.403
Runners/Scor. Pos.	148	48	9	2	1	65	19	16	.324	.432	.383
Runners On/2 Out	96	34	8	2	3	37	6	12	.354	.573	.398
Scor. Pos./2 Out	69	22	5	1	1	30	5	9	.319	.464	.365
Late-Inning Pressure	97	31	5	0	4	12	5	9	.320	.495	.353
Leading Off	18	5	2	0	2	2	0	4	.278	.722	.278
Runners On	58	18	1	0	1	9	4	4	.310	.379	.355
Runners/Scor. Pos.	34	7	0	0	0	6	3	3	.206	.206	.270

RUNS BATTED IN	From 1B	From 2B	From 3B	Scoring Position
Totals	16/196	29/119	30/60	59/179
Percentage	8.2%	24.4%	50.0%	33.0%

Loves to face: Mike Dunne (.667, 4-for-6, 2 HR)
Brian Holman (.636, 7-for-11)
Mike Jackson (.714, 5-for-7, 1 HR)

Hates to face: Steve Bedrosian (0-for-9)
Randy Johnson (.071, 1-for-14)
Bob Welch (.133, 2-for-15)

Miscellaneous statistics: Ground outs-to-air outs ratio: 0.97 last season, 1.04 for career. . . . Grounded into 24 double plays in 150 opportunities (one per 6.3). . . . Drove in 20 of 31 runners from third base with less than two outs (65%). . . . Direction of balls hit to the outfield: 31% to left field, 26% to center, 43% to right. . . . Base running: Advanced from first base to third on 14 of 33 outfield singles (42%); scored from second on 15 of 21 (71%). . . . Made 0.65 assists per nine innings at first base.

Comments: Became the third player in franchise history to finish as high as third in an American League batting race. Chuck Hinton batted .310 for the Washington Senators in 1962, to rank third among A.L. batters. Al Oliver batted .324 for Texas in 1978, runner-up to Rod Carew. . . . No Texas player, either for the Rangers or the Astros, has ever led his league in batting. . . . Only American League player to collect 100 or more hits in road games last season. . . . Collected four or more hits in six different games to lead the majors; that included two five-hit games. . . . Led the American League with 136 singles. . . . Has hit for a higher average on artificial turf than he has on grass fields in each of his five seasons in the majors. Career averages: .325 on the artificial stuff, .288 on real turf. . . Set career-high marks in at-bats, hits, triples, home runs, RBIs, and batting average. . . . Was removed in favor of a pinch hitter 11 times last season (nine times with southpaws on the mound) but only twice after the end of June. . . . Had the highest batting average by a left-handed hitter vs. left-handed pitchers since 1986, when Wade Boggs batted .352 and Don Mattingly batted .358 vs. LHP (minimum: 150 AB). . . . A statistical double for Al Oliver after "Scoops's" first four seasons in the majors.

Dave Parker

Bats Left

Milwaukee Brewers	AB	H	2B	3B	HR	RBI	BB	SO	BA	SA	OBA
Season	610	176	30	3	21	92	41	102	.289	.451	.330
vs. Left-Handers	185	48	6	0	6	24	5	35	.259	.389	.282
vs. Right-Handers	425	128	24	3	15	68	36	67	.301	.478	.350
vs. Ground-Ballers	280	85	16	2	11	47	18	45	.304	.493	.345
vs. Fly-Ballers	330	91	14	1	10	45	23	57	.276	.415	.318
Home Games	293	80	16	1	9	46	20	58	.273	.427	.316
Road Games	317	96	14	2	12	46	21	44	.303	.473	.344
Grass Fields	514	143	28	2	16	83	33	88	.278	.434	.319
Artificial Turf	96	33	2	1	5	9	8	14	.344	.542	.394
April	65	20	7	1	1	11	5	12	.308	.492	.347
May	90	32	4	2	1	17	5	19	.356	.478	.378
June	116	35	6	0	7	22	9	18	.302	.534	.349
July	104	27	5	0	5	16	12	13	.260	.452	.336
August	119	38	5	0	6	19	5	15	.319	.513	.341
Sept./Oct.	116	24	3	0	1	7	5	25	.207	.259	.248
Leading Off Inn.	155	48	5	2	9	9	6	21	.310	.542	.335
Bases Empty	316	91	15	3	13	13	16	59	.288	.478	.324
Runners On	294	85	15	0	8	79	25	43	.289	.422	.336
Runners/Scor. Pos.	156	41	9	0	4	67	22	26	.263	.397	.338
Runners On/2 Out	132	33	8	0	1	19	15	18	.250	.333	.331
Scor. Pos./2 Out	66	15	7	0	1	19	13	10	.227	.379	.363
Late-Inning Pressure	67	13	1	0	0	1	10	12	.194	.209	.295
Leading Off	14	3	0	0	0	0	2	4	.214	.214	.313
Runners On	32	6	0	0	0	1	6	3	.188	.188	.308
Runners/Scor. Pos.	14	0	0	0	0	1	5	2	.000	.000	.250

RUNS BATTED IN	From 1B	From 2B	From 3B	Scoring Position
Totals	12/224	26/125	33/69	59/194
Percentage	5.4%	20.8%	47.8%	30.4%

Loves to face: Jimmy Jones (.714, 10-for-14)
Greg Minton (.500, 12-for-24)
Eric Show (.362, 17-for-47, 5 HR)

Hates to face: Mark Davis (.138, 4-for-29)
Barry Jones (0-for-8, 3 SO)
Jesse Orosco (.105, 2-for-19)

Miscellaneous statistics: Ground outs-to-air outs ratio: 1.08 last season, 1.20 for career.... Grounded into 18 double plays in 139 opportunities (one per 7.7).... Drove in 29 of 45 runners from third base with less than two outs (64%).... Direction of balls hit to the outfield: 33% to left field, 33% to center, 35% to right.... Base running: Advanced from first base to third on 5 of 29 outfield singles (17%); scored from second on 11 of 15 (73%).

Comments: Turned 39 years old in June, during a season in which he played 157 games. Only one player as old as Parker has ever played that many games in a season: Pete Rose, who did it twice (162 games in both 1980 and 1982).... He is one of 18 players in major league history to accumulate 2000 hits and 300 home runs. Of the other 17, 15 have already been inducted into the Hall of Fame, and the other two are strong contenders who haven't yet become eligible: Reggie Jackson and Tony Perez.... Led the American League with 14 sacrifice flies. His previous single-season high was nine.... Ranked second in the league to Mike Greenwell in hits vs. right-handed pitchers.... Brewers have not had the same designated hitter in their opening day lineup in consecutive seasons since Ted Simmons (1984–85).... Has hit for a higher average with runners on base than he has with the bases empty in each of the last eight seasons, the 2d-longest streak among active players. Keith Hernandez has done it for 13 straight years.... Has hit for a higher average in night games than he has in day games in each of the last five seasons.... Has averaged over 96 RBIs per season in seven years since leaving the Pirates.... So far, he's the only player to play in All-Star Games in the 1970s, 1980s, and 1990s. Nine years from now, he can become the first four-decade and two-millennium All-Star in the same game.

Lance Parrish

Bats Right

California Angels	AB	H	2B	3B	HR	RBI	BB	SO	BA	SA	OBA
Season	470	126	14	0	24	70	46	107	.268	.451	.338
vs. Left-Handers	125	38	2	0	7	17	13	27	.304	.488	.370
vs. Right-Handers	345	88	12	0	17	53	33	80	.255	.438	.327
vs. Ground-Ballers	196	51	7	0	10	28	20	48	.260	.449	.336
vs. Fly-Ballers	274	75	7	0	14	42	26	59	.274	.453	.340
Home Games	235	65	7	0	14	39	23	55	.277	.485	.346
Road Games	235	61	7	0	10	31	23	52	.260	.417	.331
Grass Fields	401	111	13	0	22	65	40	88	.277	.474	.349
Artificial Turf	69	15	1	0	2	5	6	19	.217	.319	.276
April	48	9	1	0	2	4	4	12	.188	.333	.250
May	75	24	4	0	5	17	7	12	.320	.573	.381
June	92	30	3	0	7	17	13	18	.326	.587	.421
July	79	23	2	0	3	12	8	20	.291	.430	.364
August	82	16	0	0	4	11	9	29	.195	.341	.283
Sept./Oct.	94	24	4	0	3	9	5	16	.255	.394	.290
Leading Off Inn.	97	24	3	0	6	6	10	23	.247	.464	.318
Bases Empty	244	60	6	0	11	11	21	57	.246	.406	.311
Runners On	226	66	8	0	13	59	25	50	.292	.500	.367
Runners/Scor. Pos.	115	29	2	0	5	41	13	28	.252	.400	.328
Runners On/2 Out	108	30	3	0	7	30	12	19	.278	.500	.355
Scor. Pos./2 Out	62	15	1	0	3	21	7	11	.242	.403	.329
Late-Inning Pressure	80	20	0	0	5	10	6	22	.250	.438	.310
Leading Off	24	5	0	0	2	2	3	8	.208	.458	.296
Runners On	36	10	0	0	2	7	2	6	.278	.444	.316
Runners/Scor. Pos.	22	5	0	0	1	5	0	4	.227	.364	.227

RUNS BATTED IN	From 1B	From 2B	From 3B	Scoring Position
Totals	13/178	21/96	12/44	33/140
Percentage	7.3%	21.9%	27.3%	23.6%

Loves to face: Bruce Hurst (.478, 11-for-23, 6 HR)
Jamie Moyer (.360, 9-for-25, 4 HR)
Jay Tibbs (.455, 5-for-11, 4 HR)

Hates to face: Dennis Lamp (.143, 6-for-42, 2 HR)
Dave LaPoint (0-for-14, 2 BB)
Pascual Perez (0-for-11)

Miscellaneous statistics: Ground outs-to-air outs ratio: 1.04 last season, 1.03 for career.... Grounded into 12 double plays in 109 opportunities (one per 9.1).... Drove in 7 of 19 runners from third base with less than two outs (37%).... Direction of balls hit to the outfield: 47% to left field, 31% to center, 22% to right.... Base running: Advanced from first base to third on 3 of 24 outfield singles (13%); scored from second on 4 of 8 (50%).... Opposing base stealers: 62-for-117 (53%), lowest rate in majors.

Comments: Parrish and Brook Jacoby are the only players to improve their batting averages by at least 20 points in each of the last two seasons (minimum: 400 AB in each). The last player to make three consecutive 20-point jumps: Lee Mazzilli (1977–79).... Caught 76 percent of California's innings, followed by Orton (15%), Schroeder (8%), and Tingley (1%).... He was one of seven catchers in the majors to log more than 1000 innings behing the plate last season. Carlton Fisk missed by 30 innings.... Angels' opponents scored 4.00 runs per nine innings with Parrish behind the plate, and over one-and-one-half more with Orton, Schroeder, and Tingley calling the signals (5.51).... Opponents were successful in only 53 percent of attempted steals with Parrish catching, 67 percent with others behind the plate.... Led major league catchers with 88 assists.... Parrish led major league catchers with 22 home runs.... Batting average in Late-Inning Pressure Situations has been worse than his overall average in each of the last seven seasons.... Parrish hits on his birthday like Pat Tabler hits with the bases loaded. He was 1-for-4 with a home run on June 15 last season, dropping his average on that date to .393, with four home runs in 28 at-bats. Happy birthday, indeed!

Dan Pasqua

Bats Left

Chicago White Sox	AB	H	2B	3B	HR	RBI	BB	SO	BA	SA	OBA
Season	325	89	27	3	13	58	37	66	.274	.495	.347
vs. Left-Handers	31	6	3	0	0	4	2	8	.194	.290	.265
vs. Right-Handers	294	83	24	3	13	54	35	58	.282	.517	.355
vs. Ground-Ballers	150	49	17	0	5	25	18	20	.327	.540	.398
vs. Fly-Ballers	175	40	10	3	8	33	19	46	.229	.457	.303
Home Games	157	50	15	3	4	29	19	28	.318	.529	.392
Road Games	168	39	12	0	9	29	18	38	.232	.464	.303
Grass Fields	273	76	22	3	10	48	33	57	.278	.491	.356
Artificial Turf	52	13	5	0	3	10	4	9	.250	.519	.298
April	7	1	1	0	0	0	2	4	.143	.286	.333
May	58	21	4	1	4	13	13	12	.362	.672	.479
June	56	15	3	0	4	12	3	9	.268	.536	.305
July	77	21	8	1	3	16	4	17	.273	.519	.306
August	59	15	7	0	2	9	6	14	.254	.475	.328
Sept./Oct.	68	16	4	1	0	8	9	10	.235	.324	.321
Leading Off Inn.	99	26	10	0	2	2	3	20	.263	.424	.291
Bases Empty	185	46	16	1	6	6	11	40	.249	.443	.298
Runners On	140	43	11	2	7	52	26	26	.307	.564	.404
Runners/Scor. Pos.	93	26	10	1	3	42	18	18	.280	.505	.379
Runners On/2 Out	62	16	5	1	1	17	15	7	.258	.419	.403
Scor. Pos./2 Out	44	10	4	1	0	14	9	4	.227	.364	.358
Late-Inning Pressure	48	10	2	1	2	7	6	11	.208	.417	.296
Leading Off	12	3	2	0	1	1	0	3	.250	.667	.250
Runners On	20	5	0	0	1	6	5	5	.250	.400	.400
Runners/Scor. Pos.	14	3	0	0	0	4	4	3	.214	.214	.389

RUNS BATTED IN	From 1B	From 2B	From 3B	Scoring Position
Totals	9/89	18/74	18/45	36/119
Percentage	10.1%	24.3%	40.0%	30.3%

Loves to face: Andy McGaffigan (2-for-2, 1 BB)
Dale Mohorcic (.571, 4-for-7, 1 HR, 2 SO)

Hates to face: Gene Nelson (.200, 3-for-15, 7 SO)
Nolan Ryan (.143, 2-for-14)
Walt Terrell (.077, 2-for-26, 1 HR, 4 BB)

Miscellaneous statistics: Ground outs-to-air outs ratio: 0.72 last season, 0.78 for career.... Grounded into 4 double plays in 59 opportunities (one per 14.8).... Drove in 13 of 25 runners from third base with less than two outs (52%).... Direction of balls hit to the outfield: 32% to left field, 30% to center, 38% to right.... Base running: Advanced from first base to third on 5 of 10 outfield singles (50%); scored from second on 8 of 10 (80%).... Made 2.15 putouts per nine innings in right field.

Comments: Established a career high for extra-base hits.... Started 86 of 97 games in which the White Sox were opposed by a right-handed starter, but only four of 65 games vs. left-handers.... Has hit 86 career home runs, all but six against right-handed pitchers.... Career batting averages: .178 vs. left-handers, .264 vs. right-handers. His career-high average vs. lefties was .224 in 1989.... A similar difference between his career averages against fly-ballers and ground-ballers: .223 and .280, respectively.... Has batted over .300 in day games in each of the last three seasons. His career average during the day (.289) is 58 points higher than his nighttime average (.231).... Has driven in over 30 percent of runners from scoring position in each of the last two seasons.... Career average of .210 in Late-Inning Pressure Situations, .256 in other at-bats.... What's the antidote for a Yankee Stadium swing? Walt Hriniak. Pasqua hit four home runs to the opposite field, three to center, and six to right field last season. Among A.L. left-handers, only Fred McGriff (7) hit more opposite-field dingers than Pasqua. Sam Horn and Jack Howell also hit four each.

Bill Pecota

Bats Right

Kansas City Royals	AB	H	2B	3B	HR	RBI	BB	SO	BA	SA	OBA
Season	240	58	15	2	5	20	33	39	.242	.383	.336
vs. Left-Handers	100	29	11	1	2	6	13	12	.290	.480	.372
vs. Right-Handers	140	29	4	1	3	14	20	27	.207	.314	.311
vs. Ground-Ballers	102	23	5	1	2	12	19	21	.225	.353	.347
vs. Fly-Ballers	138	35	10	1	3	8	14	18	.254	.406	.327
Home Games	102	21	5	1	3	7	14	15	.206	.363	.308
Road Games	138	37	10	1	2	13	19	24	.268	.399	.357
Grass Fields	94	24	5	0	1	11	12	19	.255	.340	.340
Artificial Turf	146	34	10	2	4	9	21	20	.233	.411	.333
April	0	0	0	0	0	0	0	0	—	—	—
May	0	0	0	0	0	0	0	0	—	—	—
June	36	14	3	0	0	1	4	7	.389	.472	.450
July	83	19	5	1	1	9	10	19	.229	.349	.312
August	66	13	4	1	3	6	7	7	.197	.424	.284
Sept./Oct.	55	12	3	0	1	4	12	6	.218	.327	.358
Leading Off Inn.	54	14	3	0	1	1	7	13	.259	.370	.344
Bases Empty	143	39	12	1	4	4	14	26	.273	.455	.338
Runners On	97	19	3	1	1	16	19	13	.196	.278	.333
Runners/Scor. Pos.	58	12	3	0	1	15	14	8	.207	.310	.361
Runners On/2 Out	37	5	0	0	0	5	8	6	.135	.135	.304
Scor. Pos./2 Out	23	4	0	0	0	5	7	4	.174	.174	.367
Late-Inning Pressure	29	5	1	0	0	1	5	6	.172	.207	.294
Leading Off	11	1	0	0	0	0	1	4	.091	.091	.167
Runners On	7	1	0	0	0	1	3	1	.143	.143	.400
Runners/Scor. Pos.	4	1	0	0	0	1	3	1	.250	.250	.571

RUNS BATTED IN	From 1B	From 2B	From 3B	Scoring Position
Totals	1/65	7/42	7/26	14/68
Percentage	1.5%	16.7%	26.9%	20.6%

Loves to face: Randy Johnson (.500, 3-for-6, 1 2B, 2 HR)
Dennis Powell (.750, 3-for-4)

Hates to face: Jose DeLeon (0-for-7)
Jerry Reuss (0-for-5)
Bob Welch (0-for-8, 2 BB)

Miscellaneous statistics: Ground outs-to-air outs ratio: 0.90 last season, 1.12 for career.... Grounded into 5 double plays in 51 opportunities (one per 10.2).... Drove in 5 of 14 runners from third base with less than two outs (36%).... Direction of balls hit to the outfield: 53% to left field, 24% to center, 24% to right.... Base running: Advanced from first base to third on 7 of 14 outfield singles (50%); scored from second on 8 of 8.... Made 3.16 assists per nine innings at second base.

Comments: One of six players in the majors to start at least one game at five different fielding positions. Pecota started at all four infield positions and left field.... Has played second base, third base, and shortstop in each of the last four seasons.... Batting average in Late-Inning Pressure Situations has been under .200 in each of his five seasons in the majors. Career averages: .147 in LIPS, .245 in other at-bats.... Even putting LIPS aside, take a look at how his career batting average suffers in the most important areas of situational hitting: .248 with the bases empty, .215 with runners on base, .211 with runners in scoring position, .174 with two outs and RISP.... Drove in only 21 percent of runners from scoring position, but that's still light-years ahead of his performance in that area in 1989, when he drove in only one of 25.... Career average of .263 vs. left-handers, .218 vs. right-handers.... Was removed for a pinch hitter 16 times last season, all against right-handed pitchers. Steve Jeltz was also removed for a pinch hitter 16 times, tying Pecota for the club lead.... Was on the Royals' roster from opening day until his demotion to Omaha on April 30 without stepping into the batter's box.

Tony Pena

Bats Right

Boston Red Sox	AB	H	2B	3B	HR	RBI	BB	SO	BA	SA	OBA
Season	491	129	19	1	7	56	43	71	.263	.348	.322
vs. Left-Handers	155	45	4	0	5	22	12	14	.290	.413	.341
vs. Right-Handers	336	84	15	1	2	34	31	57	.250	.318	.313
vs. Ground-Ballers	211	56	8	0	0	23	10	25	.265	.303	.300
vs. Fly-Ballers	280	73	11	1	7	33	33	46	.261	.382	.337
Home Games	247	68	9	0	3	30	27	41	.275	.348	.344
Road Games	244	61	10	1	4	26	16	30	.250	.348	.298
Grass Fields	418	114	18	1	6	51	39	60	.273	.364	.334
Artificial Turf	73	15	1	0	1	5	4	11	.205	.260	.247
April	72	29	5	0	2	13	0	9	.403	.556	.403
May	91	19	2	0	2	8	5	16	.209	.297	.250
June	70	17	2	1	0	8	10	8	.243	.300	.333
July	86	15	1	0	0	5	3	15	.174	.186	.202
August	79	21	2	0	2	9	14	14	.266	.367	.383
Sept./Oct.	93	28	7	0	1	13	11	9	.301	.409	.368
Leading Off Inn.	103	25	5	0	2	2	17	20	.243	.350	.350
Bases Empty	252	61	12	0	5	5	31	42	.242	.349	.325
Runners On	239	68	7	1	2	51	12	29	.285	.347	.318
Runners/Scor. Pos.	127	38	5	0	2	50	7	17	.299	.386	.333
Runners On/2 Out	93	29	2	1	2	24	4	17	.312	.419	.340
Scor. Pos./2 Out	57	17	1	0	2	23	3	12	.298	.421	.333
Late-Inning Pressure	89	31	5	1	0	9	3	20	.348	.427	.370
Leading Off	20	5	1	0	0	0	1	7	.250	.300	.286
Runners On	46	18	3	1	0	9	0	9	.391	.500	.391
Runners/Scor. Pos.	18	8	2	0	0	8	0	3	.444	.556	.444

RUNS BATTED IN	From 1B	From 2B	From 3B	Scoring Position
Totals	3/182	19/93	27/63	46/156
Percentage	1.6%	20.4%	42.9%	29.5%

Loves to face: Rick Aguilera (.316, 6-for-19)
Dave LaPoint (.382, 13-for-34)
Dave West (3-for-3, 2 2B, 1 BB)

Hates to face: Juan Berenguer (0-for-7)
Nolan Ryan (.172, 5-for-29, 0 BB)
Walt Terrell (.118, 2-for-17)

Miscellaneous statistics: Ground outs-to-air outs ratio: 1.95 last season, 4th-highest rate in A.L.; 1.63 for career. . . . Grounded into 23 double plays in 122 opportunities (one per 5.3). . . . Drove in 18 of 32 runners from third base with less than two outs (56%). . . . Direction of balls hit to the outfield: 24% to left field, 31% to center, 45% to right. . . . Base running: Advanced from first base to third on 2 of 18 outfield singles (11%); scored from second on 18 of 21 (86%). . . . Opposing base stealers: 99-for-145 (68%).

Comments: April batting average was the highest in the American League. Lost the league batting lead to Kurt Stillwell on May 1. . . . Was caught stealing in each of his first six American League attempts, but was a perfect 8-for-8 after that. . . . Red Sox pitchers allowed an average of 4.05 runs per nine innings with Pena behind the plate, 4.57 with other catchers: Gedman (4.47) and Marzano (4.59). . . . Led the American League with 142 games played behind the plate. It was the 4th-highest single-season total in Red Sox history, behind Carlton Fisk (154 in 1978, 151 in 1977) and Sammy White (143 in 1955). . . . Was removed for a pinch hitter only once. (Danny Heep on Sept. 9). . . . Grounded into 23 double plays, 3d most in the American League, but teammate Kevin Romine actually had a higher *rate*, averaging one GIDP for every 4.6 opportunities, compared to Pena's rate of one per 5.3 opportunities. . . . Batted above .300 in Late-Inning Pressure Situations for the first time since 1983, which was the last of three consecutive seasons of .340 or better in LIPS. . . . Went 3-for-14 in the A.L.C.S., dropping his career postseason batting average to .351 (20-for-57), the 13th highest in major league history (minimum: 50 AB). The all-time leader: Will Clark (.426, 26-for-61).

Gerald Perry

Bats Left

Kansas City Royals	AB	H	2B	3B	HR	RBI	BB	SO	BA	SA	OBA
Season	465	118	22	2	8	57	39	56	.254	.361	.313
vs. Left-Handers	134	28	5	0	1	14	7	19	.209	.269	.252
vs. Right-Handers	331	90	17	2	7	43	32	37	.272	.399	.336
vs. Ground-Ballers	212	53	8	0	2	19	21	19	.250	.316	.324
vs. Fly-Ballers	253	65	14	2	6	38	18	37	.257	.399	.303
Home Games	238	68	15	1	3	30	17	28	.286	.395	.333
Road Games	227	50	7	1	5	27	22	28	.220	.326	.291
Grass Fields	185	42	5	1	5	24	17	21	.227	.346	.296
Artificial Turf	280	76	17	1	3	33	22	35	.271	.371	.324
April	63	17	1	0	1	4	8	8	.270	.333	.352
May	109	30	7	1	3	20	5	13	.275	.440	.302
June	79	16	4	0	0	8	7	10	.203	.253	.264
July	96	27	6	0	3	13	12	11	.281	.438	.358
August	67	21	3	1	0	10	3	8	.313	.388	.347
Sept./Oct.	51	7	1	0	1	2	4	6	.137	.216	.228
Leading Off Inn.	108	30	4	0	4	4	6	12	.278	.426	.328
Bases Empty	245	56	10	2	7	7	18	33	.229	.371	.287
Runners On	220	62	12	0	1	50	21	23	.282	.350	.340
Runners/Scor. Pos.	133	34	10	0	1	49	18	13	.256	.353	.338
Runners On/2 Out	89	25	3	0	0	19	16	14	.281	.315	.396
Scor. Pos./2 Out	63	17	3	0	0	19	14	9	.270	.317	.410
Late-Inning Pressure	66	17	2	1	1	7	5	7	.258	.364	.306
Leading Off	19	4	0	0	0	0	1	3	.211	.211	.250
Runners On	25	6	1	0	0	6	4	1	.240	.280	.333
Runners/Scor. Pos.	15	3	1	0	0	6	4	1	.200	.267	.350

RUNS BATTED IN	From 1B	From 2B	From 3B	Scoring Position
Totals	4/148	19/97	26/58	45/155
Percentage	2.7%	19.6%	44.8%	29.0%

Loves to face: Tom Browning (.429, 9-for-21, 1 HR)
Scott Garrelts (.385, 5-for-13, 3 HR)
Dennis Rasmussen (.467, 7-for-15, 2 HR)

Hates to face: Don Carman (.167, 3-for-18)
Bob Ojeda (.091, 1-for-11)
Mike Scott (.128, 5-for-39, 1 HR)

Miscellaneous statistics: Ground outs-to-air outs ratio: 1.23 last season, 1.49 for career. . . . Grounded into 14 double plays in 94 opportunities (one per 6.7). . . . Drove in 16 of 27 runners from third base with less than two outs (59%). . . . Direction of balls hit to the outfield: 32% to left field, 36% to center, 32% to right. . . . Base running: Advanced from first base to third on 8 of 20 outfield singles (40%); scored from second on 10 of 13 (77%). . . . Made 0.86 assists per nine innings at first base.

Comments: Started 98 of 109 games in which the Royals faced a right-handed pitcher, 19 of 52 games vs. left-handers. . . . Had hits in seven consecutive at-bats with runners in scoring position, the longest streak of its kind in the majors last season. Alas, the end of that streak was the start of 25 consecutive hitless at-bats with RISP. . . . Hitless in 12 at-bats as a pinch hitter last season, dropping his career batting average as a pinch hitter to .240 (25-for-104, 1 HR). . . . Stole 17 bases in 21 attempts last season (81%), well above his percentage during seven years with the Braves (66%). . . . His middle name, and his favorite month, is June. Career monthly batting averages build to a summer peak and decline thereafter: April, .249; May, .258; June, .283; July, .281; August, .259; September, .236; and October, .159. . . . Career batting average of .333 at Busch Stadium (30-for-90, 2 HR). He has higher marks at only two other parks: venerable old Fenway Park (.435, 10-for-23, 0 HR) and venerable old Wrigley Field (.353, 30-for-85, 2 HR). . . . Hasn't played the outfield since 1987, and has played only 29 games there over the last six seasons. That will change, unless St. Louis is prepared to move Pedro Guerrero off first base.

Geno Petralli

Bats Left

Texas Rangers	AB	H	2B	3B	HR	RBI	BB	SO	BA	SA	OBA
Season	325	83	13	1	0	21	50	49	.255	.302	.357
vs. Left-Handers	20	6	0	0	0	3	8	1	.300	.300	.483
vs. Right-Handers	305	77	13	1	0	18	42	48	.252	.302	.347
vs. Ground-Ballers	146	36	3	1	0	10	26	16	.247	.281	.365
vs. Fly-Ballers	179	47	10	0	0	11	24	33	.263	.318	.350
Home Games	170	45	7	0	0	11	28	31	.265	.306	.373
Road Games	155	38	6	1	0	10	22	18	.245	.297	.339
Grass Fields	282	71	11	1	0	20	39	44	.252	.298	.344
Artificial Turf	43	12	2	0	0	1	11	5	.279	.326	.436
April	45	13	3	0	0	3	10	7	.289	.356	.418
May	61	13	2	1	0	5	7	9	.213	.279	.304
June	37	8	1	0	0	4	2	4	.216	.243	.286
July	51	10	1	0	0	3	10	7	.196	.216	.317
August	64	22	2	0	0	5	8	11	.344	.375	.417
Sept./Oct.	67	17	4	0	0	1	13	11	.254	.313	.375
Leading Off Inn.	82	24	5	0	0	0	15	11	.293	.354	.414
Bases Empty	198	51	9	0	0	0	29	36	.258	.303	.358
Runners On	127	32	4	1	0	21	21	13	.252	.299	.355
Runners/Scor. Pos.	61	14	2	1	0	20	13	8	.230	.295	.351
Runners On/2 Out	60	19	1	1	0	10	11	9	.317	.367	.423
Scor. Pos./2 Out	33	7	1	1	0	10	6	7	.212	.303	.333
Late-Inning Pressure	55	12	2	0	0	1	7	8	.218	.255	.302
Leading Off	16	3	1	0	0	0	3	3	.188	.250	.316
Runners On	16	3	0	0	0	1	3	1	.188	.188	.300
Runners/Scor. Pos.	6	1	0	0	0	1	2	0	.167	.167	.333

RUNS BATTED IN	From 1B	From 2B	From 3B	Scoring Position
Totals	3/97	7/49	11/26	18/75
Percentage	3.1%	14.3%	42.3%	24.0%

Loves to face: Dennis Lamp (.500, 6-for-12, 1 HR)
Mike Moore (.370, 10-for-27)
Dave Stieb (.444, 8-for-18)

Hates to face: Bert Blyleven (.125, 2-for-16, 3 BB)
Mike Henneman (0-for-7)
Dave Stewart (0-for-15, 1 BB)

Miscellaneous statistics: Ground outs-to-air outs ratio: 1.01 last season, 0.98 for career. . . . Grounded into 12 double plays in 59 opportunities (one per 4.9), 4th-worst rate in A.L. . . . Drove in 7 of 12 runners from third base with less than two outs (58%). . . . Direction of balls hit to the outfield: 29% to left field, 36% to center, 35% to right. . . . Base running: Advanced from first base to third on 7 of 16 outfield singles (44%); scored from second on 4 of 8 (50%). . . . Opposing base stealers: 58-for-93 (62%).

Comments: Each of his last 191 starts, including all 99 in 1990, have been against right-handed pitchers. . . . Career batting averages: .203 vs. left-handers (two extra-base hits in 118 at-bats), .287 vs. right-handers (one XBH per 15 AB). . . . Petralli had a .200 average vs. left-handers as a switch-hitter, from 1982 through 1987. Since swinging exclusively from the left side of the plate, Petralli has improved his average vs. southpaws by a full five points. . . . Texas needs to improve its production from behind the plate. Rangers catchers drove in only 35 runs last season, while hitting only three home runs. Both figures are major league lows for backstops. . . . Played in 133 games last year, a career high in his ninth major league season. . . . Rangers pitchers allowed runs at roughly the same rate regardless of who was catching: Petralli, 4.38 per nine innings; Stanley, 4.27; Russell, 4.31. . . . Career total of 87 passed balls is 2d highest among active catchers, behind Lance Parrish (106). (Good riddance, Charlie Hough!). . .A career .300 hitter in day games, 27 points higher than at night. . . . Batted higher than .340 vs. ground-ball pitchers in each of the two previous seasons.

Gary Pettis

Bats Left and Right

Texas Rangers	AB	H	2B	3B	HR	RBI	BB	SO	BA	SA	OBA
Season	423	101	16	8	3	31	57	118	.239	.336	.333
vs. Left-Handers	152	33	6	3	0	7	23	38	.217	.296	.320
vs. Right-Handers	271	68	10	5	3	24	34	80	.251	.358	.340
vs. Ground-Ballers	210	47	6	2	1	9	24	59	.224	.286	.310
vs. Fly-Ballers	213	54	10	6	2	22	33	59	.254	.385	.355
Home Games	221	56	7	4	3	21	30	59	.253	.362	.348
Road Games	202	45	9	4	0	10	27	59	.223	.307	.316
Grass Fields	352	83	13	5	3	27	49	98	.236	.327	.333
Artificial Turf	71	18	3	3	0	4	8	20	.254	.380	.329
April	64	14	3	1	0	3	9	19	.219	.297	.333
May	76	17	2	0	2	8	10	18	.224	.329	.314
June	73	20	4	2	1	10	8	17	.274	.425	.349
July	54	12	3	1	0	2	5	17	.222	.315	.288
August	95	23	2	3	0	4	17	26	.242	.326	.357
Sept./Oct.	61	15	2	1	0	4	8	21	.246	.311	.333
Leading Off Inn.	171	31	4	2	1	1	24	60	.181	.246	.286
Bases Empty	280	63	8	4	3	3	39	86	.225	.314	.324
Runners On	143	38	8	4	0	28	18	32	.266	.378	.349
Runners/Scor. Pos.	77	17	4	2	0	24	11	24	.221	.325	.323
Runners On/2 Out	71	19	2	3	0	10	6	12	.268	.380	.342
Scor. Pos./2 Out	39	8	1	2	0	8	5	9	.205	.333	.326
Late-Inning Pressure	56	14	2	1	1	3	6	16	.250	.375	.323
Leading Off	18	6	1	1	1	1	3	6	.333	.667	.429
Runners On	21	6	1	0	0	2	3	2	.286	.333	.375
Runners/Scor. Pos.	8	1	0	0	0	1	1	2	.125	.125	.222

RUNS BATTED IN	From 1B	From 2B	From 3B	Scoring Position
Totals	4/102	12/61	12/27	24/88
Percentage	3.9%	19.7%	44.4%	27.3%

Loves to face: Jim Acker (.571, 4-for-7, 2 SO)
John Davis (.500, 4-for-8)
Rich Thompson (3-for-3, 1 BB)

Hates to face: Juan Berenguer (0-for-11, 1 BB, 9 SO)
Bert Blyleven (.128, 5-for-39)
Mike Moore (.148, 9-for-61)

Miscellaneous statistics: Ground outs-to-air outs ratio: 2.15 last season, 2d-highest rate in A.L.; 2.07 for career. . . . Grounded into 6 double plays in 76 opportunities (one per 12.7). . . . Drove in 11 of 19 runners from third base with less than two outs (58%). . . . Direction of balls hit to the outfield: 47% to left field, 20% to center, 33% to right batting left-handed; 22% to left, 24% to center, 53% to right batting right-handed. . . . Base running: Advanced from first base to third on 9 of 27 outfield singles (33%); scored from second on 16 of 20 (80%). . . . Made 2.49 putouts per nine innings in center field.

Comments: Career average of 2.69 putouts per game. He needs 58 more games in the outfield to reach the 1000-mark and crack the all-time top 10 in that category (see page 88). . . . Pettis has had six seasons of 100 or more strikeouts and fewer than 10 home runs. The only other player in major league history to do that six times is Omar Moreno. Two other players, Lou Brock and Bobby Knoop, did it four times. . . . Was thrown out trying to advance a base on a batted ball nine times last season, the most of any player on the Rangers. . . . Texas center fielders combined to drive in only 48 runs last season, the fewest of any outfield position on any team in the American League. . . . And while we're at it, let's give Pettis the blame for the Rangers' leadoff spot batting only .217, the lowest of any club in the majors. . . . Batted .177 in 79 first-inning at-bats, .253 in subsequent at-bats. . . . From our "Why Bother" Dept.: Pettis's career batting average of .239 ranks 22nd among the 23 active switch-hitters with at least 3000 career at-bats. Among that group, only Spike Owen has a lower average (.239). . . . Hasn't hit a home run with a runner on base since July 16, 1988. . . . Within two weeks last summer, Pettis notched the 300th stolen base of his career and then-teammate Harold Baines hit his 200th home run. Which do you think was more unusual? Baines was the 158th player to reach the 200-HR mark; Pettis was only the 118th to steal 300 bases.

Tony Phillips

Bats Left and Right

Detroit Tigers	AB	H	2B	3B	HR	RBI	BB	SO	BA	SA	OBA
Season	573	144	23	5	8	55	99	85	.251	.351	.364
vs. Left-Handers	202	50	11	2	2	19	27	22	.248	.351	.341
vs. Right-Handers	371	94	12	3	6	36	72	63	.253	.350	.377
vs. Ground-Ballers	255	61	6	0	4	20	39	36	.239	.310	.347
vs. Fly-Ballers	318	83	17	5	4	35	60	49	.261	.384	.378
Home Games	286	69	7	2	4	23	50	53	.241	.322	.360
Road Games	287	75	16	3	4	32	49	32	.261	.380	.369
Grass Fields	478	118	17	4	5	43	83	73	.247	.331	.362
Artificial Turf	95	26	6	1	3	12	16	12	.274	.453	.378
April	89	18	1	2	0	8	5	11	.202	.258	.245
May	113	29	6	2	2	14	19	15	.257	.398	.378
June	82	17	3	0	3	9	17	13	.207	.354	.350
July	97	21	3	1	0	5	23	14	.216	.268	.367
August	93	31	5	0	1	9	16	14	.333	.419	.427
Sept./Oct.	99	28	5	0	2	10	19	18	.283	.394	.395
Leading Off Inn.	191	45	8	1	1	1	30	25	.236	.304	.345
Bases Empty	357	83	16	2	3	3	61	51	.232	.314	.348
Runners On	216	61	7	3	5	52	38	34	.282	.412	.391
Runners/Scor. Pos.	114	32	4	2	3	46	23	17	.281	.430	.404
Runners On/2 Out	96	28	5	1	4	27	15	17	.292	.490	.393
Scor. Pos./2 Out	55	17	3	0	2	21	11	8	.309	.473	.433
Late-Inning Pressure	59	17	4	0	1	4	15	6	.288	.407	.447
Leading Off	15	4	0	0	0	0	3	2	.267	.267	.421
Runners On	28	7	1	0	1	4	7	1	.250	.393	.417
Runners/Scor. Pos.	13	2	0	0	0	2	4	0	.154	.154	.389

RUNS BATTED IN	From 1B	From 2B	From 3B	Scoring Position
Totals	5/148	15/86	27/50	42/136
Percentage	3.4%	17.4%	54.0%	30.9%

Loves to face: Andy Hawkins (.714, 5-for-7)
Bob Welch (.556, 5-for-9, 1 HR)
Matt Young (.273, 3-for-11, 1 HR, 4 BB)

Hates to face: Chuck Cary (.143, 2-for-14)
Danny Darwin (.063, 1-for-16)
Brian Holman (0-for-11, 2 BB)

Miscellaneous statistics: Ground outs-to-air outs ratio: 1.12 last season, 1.16 for career.... Grounded into 10 double plays in 108 opportunities (one per 10.8).... Drove in 17 of 27 runners from third base with less than two outs (63%).... Direction of balls hit to the outfield: 39% to left field, 36% to center, 25% to right batting left-handed; 33% to left, 30% to center, 37% to right batting right-handed.... Base running: Advanced from first base to third on 15 of 36 outfield singles (42%); scored from second on 14 of 17 (82%).... Made 2.27 assists per nine innings at third base, highest rate in A.L.

Comments: The only player in either league to play every inning of every game through the end of May.... Was thrown out trying to advance a base on a batted ball 13 times last season, the most in the majors.... One of six players to start at least one game at five different fielding positions. Phillips started at second base, third base, shortstop, left and right fields.... Tigers pitchers allowed only 3.34 runs per nine innings with Phillips at second base, compared to 5.27 with Lou Whitaker there.... Walked 99 times, to rank third in the American League. His previous career high in that category was 76.... Established a career high in RBIs as well. His previous best: 47 in 1989.... Stole 19 bases last season after stealing only three over the two previous seasons (all in 1989).... Has hit for a higher average with runners on base than he has with the bases empty in each of the last five years.... Career average of .274 batting right-handed (one HR per 88 AB), .239 batting left-handed (one HR per 73 AB).... Phillips and Fielder, two players not with the Tigers in 1989, combined to score 201 runs for them last season, about equally divided (Fielder, 104; Phillips, 97). They also combined for 59 home runs.

Luis Polonia

Bats Left

Yankees/Angels	AB	H	2B	3B	HR	RBI	BB	SO	BA	SA	OBA
Season	403	135	7	9	2	35	25	43	.335	.412	.372
vs. Left-Handers	51	15	0	2	0	3	4	11	.294	.373	.345
vs. Right-Handers	352	120	7	7	2	32	21	32	.341	.418	.376
vs. Ground-Ballers	172	50	3	3	1	19	13	21	.291	.360	.339
vs. Fly-Ballers	231	85	4	6	1	16	12	22	.368	.450	.398
Home Games	207	73	2	4	2	23	8	23	.353	.430	.378
Road Games	196	62	5	5	0	12	17	20	.316	.393	.366
Grass Fields	336	114	5	8	2	29	21	34	.339	.420	.377
Artificial Turf	67	21	2	1	0	6	4	9	.313	.373	.347
April	22	7	0	0	0	3	0	1	.318	.318	.304
May	67	19	0	1	1	3	2	9	.284	.358	.300
June	59	19	2	1	0	5	8	5	.322	.390	.397
July	89	26	1	3	0	3	2	10	.292	.371	.315
August	69	24	2	1	1	14	1	8	.348	.449	.357
Sept./Oct.	97	40	2	3	0	7	12	10	.412	.495	.473
Leading Off Inn.	157	57	2	6	1	1	9	18	.363	.471	.398
Bases Empty	266	94	2	7	1	1	16	31	.353	.425	.392
Runners On	137	41	5	2	1	34	9	12	.299	.387	.333
Runners/Scor. Pos.	83	27	4	2	1	34	7	5	.325	.458	.362
Runners On/2 Out	54	17	1	1	1	16	3	3	.315	.426	.351
Scor. Pos./2 Out	37	14	1	1	1	16	2	3	.378	.541	.410
Late-Inning Pressure	58	18	1	0	0	5	5	6	.310	.328	.359
Leading Off	16	7	1	0	0	0	2	3	.438	.500	.500
Runners On	26	7	0	0	0	5	2	2	.269	.269	.310
Runners/Scor. Pos.	15	5	0	0	0	5	2	1	.333	.333	.389

RUNS BATTED IN	From 1B	From 2B	From 3B	Scoring Position
Totals	2/99	12/69	19/36	31/105
Percentage	2.0%	17.4%	52.8%	29.5%

Loves to face: Jim Acker (3-for-3)
Jose DeLeon (.538, 7-for-13)
Mike Jackson (.750, 3-for-4, 2 BB)

Hates to face: Charlie Hough (.091, 1-for-11)
Nolan Ryan (.267, 4-for-15)
Dave Stieb (.242, 8-for-33)

Miscellaneous statistics: Ground outs-to-air outs ratio: 1.74 last season, 1.67 for career.... Grounded into 9 double plays in 62 opportunities (one per 6.9).... Drove in 13 of 20 runners from third base with less than two outs (65%).... Direction of balls hit to the outfield: 41% to left field, 37% to center, 23% to right.... Base running: Advanced from first base to third on 16 of 28 outfield singles (57%); scored from second on 5 of 9 (56%).... Made 1.81 putouts per nine innings in left field, 2d-lowest rate in A.L.

Comments: Only the second player in this century to steal at least 20 bases and bat at least .280 in each of his first four seasons (rookie or otherwise). The other: Willie McGee (1982–85).... Batted .336 after joining the Angels, the 2d-highest single-season average in franchise history, behind Rod Carew's .339 in 1983 (minimum: 400 PA).... Overall batting average year by year since 1987: .287, .292, .300, .335 ... Batted .334 as an outfielder last season, the highest such average in the majors.... Started 94 games, only seven against left-handers. Has a career BA of .311 vs. right-handers, .266 vs. lefties. Has hit 11 career home runs, all against right-handers.... Led the major leagues with a .363 batting average leading off innings.... Had 30 infield hits, tying Kirby Puckett for the American League lead.... First player since Craig Robinson in 1974 to hit more triples than doubles in a season of at least 400 at-bats. Last American Leaguer to do it was Jorge Orta in 1973.... Career average of .327 with two outs and runners in scoring position is the 3d highest in *Player Analysis* history, behind Larry Hisle (.332) and Wade Boggs (.328).... Career batting average of .340 (17-for-50) as a pinch hitter.... In what may go down as the last worst deal of the Steinbrenner era, New York gave the 25-year-old Polonia to the Angels for Claudell Washington, who batted 36 times for the Yankees and was released after the end of the season.

Kirby Puckett

Bats Right

Minnesota Twins	AB	H	2B	3B	HR	RBI	BB	SO	BA	SA	OBA
Season	551	164	40	3	12	80	57	73	.298	.446	.365
vs. Left-Handers	164	49	11	1	4	22	22	21	.299	.451	.382
vs. Right-Handers	387	115	29	2	8	58	35	52	.297	.444	.357
vs. Ground-Ballers	226	57	13	0	1	27	29	35	.252	.323	.336
vs. Fly-Ballers	325	107	27	3	11	53	28	38	.329	.532	.386
Home Games	273	94	24	1	6	47	27	40	.344	.505	.403
Road Games	278	70	16	2	6	33	30	33	.252	.388	.328
Grass Fields	212	52	10	2	6	27	25	24	.245	.396	.331
Artificial Turf	339	112	30	1	6	53	32	49	.330	.478	.387
April	74	20	4	1	2	11	10	9	.270	.432	.357
May	102	39	13	1	6	21	13	9	.382	.706	.457
June	99	24	5	1	2	11	8	16	.242	.374	.303
July	106	33	8	0	2	19	13	17	.311	.443	.388
August	74	21	5	0	0	7	6	17	.284	.351	.333
Sept./Oct.	96	27	5	0	0	11	7	5	.281	.333	.330
Leading Off Inn.	115	38	12	0	1	1	9	15	.330	.461	.379
Bases Empty	309	81	22	0	5	5	27	43	.262	.382	.323
Runners On	242	83	18	3	7	75	30	30	.343	.529	.415
Runners/Scor. Pos.	137	46	10	1	5	62	24	20	.336	.533	.430
Runners On/2 Out	80	21	2	0	5	22	11	8	.262	.475	.352
Scor. Pos./2 Out	51	15	1	0	3	17	9	5	.294	.490	.400
Late-Inning Pressure	78	17	3	1	2	7	9	18	.218	.359	.299
Leading Off	22	4	2	0	1	1	4	5	.182	.409	.308
Runners On	29	8	0	1	1	6	2	8	.276	.448	.323
Runners/Scor. Pos.	16	3	0	0	1	5	2	5	.188	.375	.278

RUNS BATTED IN	From 1B	From 2B	From 3B	Scoring Position
Totals	16/165	21/101	31/51	52/152
Percentage	9.7%	20.8%	60.8%	34.2%

Loves to face: Jose DeLeon (.538, 7-for-13, 2 HR)
Mark Knudson (.727, 8-for-11, 1 HR)
Curt Young (.441, 15-for-34, 2 HR)

Hates to face: Danny Darwin (.125, 3-for-24)
Gene Nelson (.200, 6-for-30)
Bobby Witt (.214, 9-for-42)

Miscellaneous statistics: Ground outs-to-air outs ratio: 2.03 last season, 3d-highest rate in A.L.; 1.69 for career. . . . Grounded into 15 double plays in 121 opportunities (one per 8.1). . . . Drove in 25 of 36 runners from third base with less than two outs (69%). . . . Direction of balls hit to the outfield: 17% to left field, 32% to center, 51% to right. . . . Base running: Advanced from first base to third on 8 of 25 outfield singles (32%); scored from second on 15 of 19 (79%). . . . Made 2.75 putouts per nine innings in center field.

Comments: Has hit only 21 home runs over the past two seasons, fewer than in any of the three seasons immediately preceding them: 31 in 1986, 28 in 1987, and 24 in 1988. Stranger still, he hit just four in 1984–85, in 1248 at-bats. . . . Had hits in seven consecutive at bats, 2d-longest streak in the American League last season, and longest by a Minnesota player since Mickey Hatcher in 1985 (9). . . . Advanced from first to second base on four outfield fly outs to lead the American League last season. . . . Career batting average of .334 vs. left-handed pitchers is the highest of any player in 16 years of *The Player Analysis*. . . . Has batted over .300 at the Metrodome in each of his seven seasons in the majors. His road game average has been below .300 in five of those seven years. Career breakdown: .352 at the Metrodome, .288 on the road. . . . Has a .293 batting average on grass fields, and a mark of .272 on artificial surfaces other than the Metrodome. . . . One of two players to drive in over 30 percent of runners from scoring position in each of the last six years. The other: George Brett. . . . Played his 1000th game in July. Only one active player accumulated more hits over his first 1000 games: Wade Boggs. The top five: Boggs, 1351; Puckett, 1329; Don Mattingly, 1284; Tony Gwynn, 1280; and George Brett, 1254. Puckett's total is nowhere near the all-time record; two players topped the 1500 mark: Nap Lajoie (1505) and Willie Keeler, by far the all-time champ (1635).

Carlos Quintana

Bats Right

Boston Red Sox	AB	H	2B	3B	HR	RBI	BB	SO	BA	SA	OBA
Season	512	147	28	0	7	67	52	74	.287	.383	.354
vs. Left-Handers	182	64	12	0	3	27	16	24	.352	.467	.407
vs. Right-Handers	330	83	16	0	4	40	36	50	.252	.336	.325
vs. Ground-Ballers	201	64	9	0	3	35	23	34	.318	.408	.391
vs. Fly-Ballers	311	83	19	0	4	32	29	40	.267	.367	.329
Home Games	251	75	11	0	3	31	26	36	.299	.378	.368
Road Games	261	72	17	0	4	36	26	38	.276	.387	.340
Grass Fields	432	135	25	0	6	59	49	56	.313	.412	.384
Artificial Turf	80	12	3	0	1	8	3	18	.150	.225	.181
April	22	8	2	0	0	0	5	4	.364	.455	.481
May	75	23	6	0	1	14	4	5	.307	.427	.350
June	101	30	3	0	2	12	4	18	.297	.386	.324
July	106	35	9	0	4	20	17	15	.330	.528	.419
August	100	24	4	0	0	11	17	17	.240	.280	.356
Sept./Oct.	108	27	4	0	0	10	5	15	.250	.287	.281
Leading Off Inn.	95	23	3	0	1	1	6	9	.242	.305	.301
Bases Empty	264	73	13	0	3	3	28	39	.277	.360	.350
Runners On	248	74	15	0	4	64	24	35	.298	.407	.358
Runners/Scor. Pos.	129	40	7	0	1	52	15	24	.310	.388	.377
Runners On/2 Out	111	36	9	0	1	35	10	17	.324	.432	.380
Scor. Pos./2 Out	69	22	5	0	0	29	9	15	.319	.391	.397
Late-Inning Pressure	69	21	5	0	0	8	4	13	.304	.377	.338
Leading Off	20	6	1	0	0	0	1	0	.300	.350	.333
Runners On	32	8	3	0	0	8	2	9	.250	.344	.286
Runners/Scor. Pos.	14	2	0	0	0	5	2	5	.143	.143	.235

RUNS BATTED IN	From 1B	From 2B	From 3B	Scoring Position
Totals	11/188	20/95	29/64	49/159
Percentage	5.9%	21.1%	45.3%	30.8%

Loves to face: Mike Jeffcoat (.625, 5-for-8)
Jamie Moyer (3-for-3, 1 HR)
Sergio Valdez (.556, 5-for-9)

Hates to face: Chuck Cary (.182, 2-for-11)
Storm Davis (0-for-5)
Duane Ward (0-for-7, 5 SO)

Miscellaneous statistics: Ground outs-to-air outs ratio: 1.68 last season, 1.77 for career. . . . Grounded into 19 double plays in 124 opportunities (one per 6.5). . . . Drove in 11 of 27 runners from third base with less than two outs (41%). . . . Direction of balls hit to the outfield: 24% to left field, 35% to center, 40% to right. . . . Base running: Advanced from first base to third on 8 of 42 outfield singles (19%); scored from second on 8 of 12 (67%). . . . Made 1.03 assists per nine innings at first base, highest rate in A.L.

Comments: Hit 55 balls to left or left-center field (in the air or otherwise) last season, and all but four were hits. Yes, that's 51 of 55, a .927 average. But as you can see above, he is, alas, not a pull hitter. . . . Fewest home runs by a regular Red Sox first baseman since 1969, when Dalton Jones hit three. . . . Had a streak of hits in seven consecutive at bats snapped by Toronto's John Barfield. . . . Had the most errors (17) and lowest fielding percentage (.987) of any first baseman in the majors, but led A.L. first basemen with 137 assists. . . . At 25 years of age, he was the youngest American Leaguer to appear in at least 100 games at first base last season. The league's youngest to play that many games at other positions, along with their ages at the end of the 1990 season: 2B, Jerry Browne (24); 3B, Gary Sheffield (21); SS, Bill Spiers (23); LF, Greg Vaughn (25); CF, Ken Griffey (20); RF, Sammy Sosa (21); C, Sandy Alomar (23). . . . Batted 85 points higher vs. left-handed pitchers (.263) than vs. right-handers (.178) in two previous season fragments. Current career totals: .336 vs. LHP, .243 vs. RHP. . . . Career batting average of .299 on grass fields, .188 on artificial surfaces. . . . Hitless in 26 career at-bats at Royals Stadium. . . . No triples in 595 career at-bats.

Willie Randolph

Bats Right

Dodgers/A's	AB	H	2B	3B	HR	RBI	BB	SO	BA	SA	OBA
Season	388	101	13	3	2	30	45	34	.260	.325	.339
vs. Left-Handers	116	41	8	1	0	12	10	5	.353	.440	.405
vs. Right-Handers	272	60	5	2	2	18	35	29	.221	.276	.313
vs. Ground-Ballers	185	47	4	0	1	10	16	17	.254	.292	.320
vs. Fly-Ballers	203	54	9	3	1	20	29	17	.266	.355	.356
Home Games	164	41	5	1	1	11	18	12	.250	.311	.326
Road Games	224	60	8	2	1	19	27	22	.268	.335	.349
Grass Fields	305	79	9	3	1	19	36	31	.259	.318	.340
Artificial Turf	83	22	4	0	1	11	9	3	.265	.349	.337
April	66	18	0	0	1	7	7	7	.273	.318	.342
May	76	18	4	0	1	3	10	4	.237	.329	.333
June	69	15	4	0	0	7	7	8	.217	.275	.286
July	38	11	3	1	0	3	3	2	.289	.421	.357
August	63	16	0	1	0	2	3	5	.254	.286	.288
Sept./Oct.	76	23	2	1	0	8	15	8	.303	.355	.418
Leading Off Inn.	93	20	2	0	0	0	12	7	.215	.237	.305
Bases Empty	211	51	5	1	2	2	29	20	.242	.303	.336
Runners On	177	50	8	2	0	28	16	14	.282	.350	.344
Runners/Scor. Pos.	104	26	3	2	0	26	13	8	.250	.317	.336
Runners On/2 Out	75	21	4	2	0	13	5	4	.280	.387	.325
Scor. Pos./2 Out	52	14	3	2	0	13	3	3	.269	.404	.309
Late-Inning Pressure	35	10	2	0	1	3	5	7	.286	.429	.366
Leading Off	6	1	0	0	0	0	2	1	.167	.167	.375
Runners On	18	5	1	0	0	2	1	2	.278	.333	.300
Runners/Scor. Pos.	10	2	0	0	0	2	1	1	.200	.200	.250

RUNS BATTED IN	From 1B	From 2B	From 3B	Scoring Position
Totals	2/122	12/83	14/37	26/120
Percentage	1.6%	14.5%	37.8%	21.7%

Loves to face: Tom Browning (.533, 8-for-15, 1 HR)
Bruce Hurst (.393, 33-for-84, 1 HR)
Charlie Leibrandt (.357, 10-for-28, 1 HR)

Hates to face: Mike Moore (.091, 2-for-22)
Nolan Ryan (.115, 3-for-26, 5 BB)
Mike Scott (.053, 1-for-19, 2 BB)

Miscellaneous statistics: Ground outs-to-air outs ratio: 1.57 last season, 1.44 for career.... Grounded into 14 double plays in 82 opportunities (one per 5.9).... Drove in 9 of 18 runners from third base with less than two outs (50%).... Direction of balls hit to the outfield: 34% to left field, 35% to center, 31% to right.... Base running: Advanced from first base to third on 10 of 32 outfield singles (31%); scored from second on 14 of 16 (88%).... Made 3.06 assists per nine innings at second base.

Comments: Batted 133 points higher vs. left-handers (.353) than vs. right-handers (.221) last season, the 4th-largest margin in the majors. That's his career high vs. southpaws, and his career low vs. right-handers.... Has played more postseason games than any active player (47). Theoretically, he could increase that total to 61 this season, which would rank him fifth on the all-time list, behind Reggie Jackson (77), Yogi Berra (75), Pete Rose (67), and Mickey Mantle (65).... Career total of 46 postseason games at second base is 2d highest in major league history, behind Joe Morgan (50). Willie passed Frank White, Frankie Frisch, and Davey Lopes on that list last October. Randolph has handled 209 postseason chances in the field, all at second base, without ever committing an error. The only players to handle more postseason chances without an error: catcher Gary Carter (220) and first baseman Wally Pipp (213).... Played one regular-season game at third base for the Pirates in 1975, his only appearance at any position other than second base. His 1952 games at second rank ninth in major league history.... A's second basemen combined for a .218 batting average last season, driving in 38 runs, and scoring 53 runs. All three figures were lowest in the league for that position.... Has hit only four home runs over the last two seasons, but two of them have been in Late-Inning Pressure Situations.... Acquired by the defending World Champions in two straight seasons: the Dodgers in 1989, the Athletics in 1990.

Johnny Ray

Bats Left and Right

California Angels	AB	H	2B	3B	HR	RBI	BB	SO	BA	SA	OBA
Season	404	112	23	0	5	43	19	44	.277	.371	.308
vs. Left-Handers	120	36	5	0	0	15	3	14	.300	.342	.317
vs. Right-Handers	284	76	18	0	5	28	16	30	.268	.384	.304
vs. Ground-Ballers	173	52	12	0	2	23	6	24	.301	.405	.320
vs. Fly-Ballers	231	60	11	0	3	20	13	20	.260	.346	.298
Home Games	210	57	9	0	5	21	10	19	.271	.386	.302
Road Games	194	55	14	0	0	22	9	25	.284	.356	.314
Grass Fields	356	100	18	0	5	41	17	37	.281	.374	.311
Artificial Turf	48	12	5	0	0	2	2	7	.250	.354	.280
April	55	12	1	0	1	6	6	6	.218	.291	.290
May	76	22	6	0	1	10	6	7	.289	.408	.337
June	27	3	1	0	0	0	0	6	.111	.148	.111
July	87	29	4	0	1	5	2	9	.333	.414	.344
August	61	18	4	0	0	6	2	6	.295	.361	.317
Sept./Oct.	98	28	7	0	2	16	3	10	.286	.418	.307
Leading Off Inn.	72	21	5	0	1	1	3	5	.292	.403	.320
Bases Empty	222	64	13	0	4	4	12	26	.288	.401	.325
Runners On	182	48	10	0	1	39	7	18	.264	.335	.286
Runners/Scor. Pos.	100	29	6	0	1	39	5	12	.290	.380	.315
Runners On/2 Out	75	15	3	0	1	16	4	10	.200	.280	.241
Scor. Pos./2 Out	49	12	3	0	1	16	3	8	.245	.367	.288
Late-Inning Pressure	78	20	4	0	1	11	4	8	.256	.346	.293
Leading Off	17	4	1	0	0	0	0	2	.235	.294	.235
Runners On	38	10	3	0	1	11	2	5	.263	.421	.300
Runners/Scor. Pos.	27	9	3	0	1	11	2	4	.333	.556	.379

RUNS BATTED IN	From 1B	From 2B	From 3B	Scoring Position
Totals	2/140	18/74	18/44	36/118
Percentage	1.4%	24.3%	40.9%	30.5%

Loves to face: Rick Aguilera (.429, 6-for-14, 2 HR, 6 BB)
Juan Berenguer (.583, 7-for-12)
Dave Stewart (.438, 14-for-32)

Hates to face: Charlie Hough (.172, 5-for-29)
Mike Jeffcoat (.091, 1-for-11)
Dave LaPoint (.200, 11-for-55)

Miscellaneous statistics: Ground outs-to-air outs ratio: 1.30 last season, 1.08 for career.... Grounded into 10 double plays in 88 opportunities (one per 8.8).... Drove in 14 of 24 runners from third base with less than two outs (58%).... Direction of balls hit to the outfield: 47% to left field, 26% to center, 27% to right batting left-handed; 26% to left, 31% to center, 43% to right batting right-handed.... Base running: Advanced from first base to third on 4 of 16 outfield singles (25%); scored from second on 7 of 13 (54%).... Made 3.11 assists per nine innings at second base.

Comments: Ended the season with 38 consecutive errorless games at second base, his longest streak of the season.... Led the Angels with 41 hits to the opposite field last season.... Homered against Brian Holman in the first inning on opening day, the third opening-day home run of his career.... All five of his home runs were hit to right field batting left-handed at Anaheim Stadium.... Has always been one of the toughest batters in the majors to strike out, with a career average of one SO per 18.3 plate appearances through the 1989 season. But last season, he averaged one per 9.8 times up, the highest of his career.... Career batting average of .290 ranks fifth among the 55 active switch-hitters with at least 1000 at-bats.... Career batting breakdown is the opposite of 1990's. Career: .264 batting right-handed, .301 batting left-handed.... Has batted above .300 in day games in each of the last five years.... At 33 years of age, he was the oldest player to appear in 100 American League games at second base last season. The league's oldest to play that many games at other positions, and their ages at the end of the 1990 season: 1B, George Brett (36); 3B, Carney Lansford (33); SS, Alan Trammell (32); LF, Dan Gladden (33); CF, Robin Yount (35); RF, Dave Winfield (39); C, Carlton Fisk (41).

Jody Reed

Bats Right

Boston Red Sox	AB	H	2B	3B	HR	RBI	BB	SO	BA	SA	OBA
Season	598	173	45	0	5	51	75	65	.289	.390	.371
vs. Left-Handers	184	55	16	0	0	14	23	17	.299	.386	.376
vs. Right-Handers	414	118	29	0	5	37	52	48	.285	.391	.368
vs. Ground-Ballers	255	68	13	0	2	27	29	26	.267	.341	.348
vs. Fly-Ballers	343	105	32	0	3	24	46	39	.306	.426	.387
Home Games	311	91	26	0	3	31	34	39	.293	.405	.365
Road Games	287	82	19	0	2	20	41	26	.286	.373	.377
Grass Fields	512	148	37	0	5	47	71	53	.289	.391	.379
Artificial Turf	86	25	8	0	0	4	4	12	.291	.384	.319
April	63	21	4	0	2	12	8	5	.333	.492	.408
May	100	25	7	0	0	4	11	15	.250	.320	.330
June	104	32	12	0	1	11	9	9	.308	.452	.360
July	106	39	14	0	1	6	14	13	.368	.528	.438
August	109	30	4	0	1	13	10	10	.275	.339	.336
Sept./Oct.	116	26	4	0	0	5	23	13	.224	.259	.364
Leading Off Inn.	161	43	9	0	1	1	19	19	.267	.342	.348
Bases Empty	351	98	26	0	4	4	38	41	.279	.387	.356
Runners On	247	75	19	0	1	47	37	24	.304	.393	.390
Runners/Scor. Pos.	119	33	6	0	0	44	28	13	.277	.328	.407
Runners On/2 Out	93	27	4	0	0	21	16	9	.290	.333	.394
Scor. Pos./2 Out	58	17	2	0	0	21	16	7	.293	.328	.446
Late-Inning Pressure	84	24	3	0	1	8	18	9	.286	.357	.412
Leading Off	15	6	1	0	0	0	7	2	.400	.467	.591
Runners On	47	11	1	0	0	7	6	4	.234	.255	.321
Runners/Scor. Pos.	19	5	0	0	0	7	5	0	.263	.263	.417

RUNS BATTED IN	From 1B	From 2B	From 3B	Scoring Position
Totals	4/187	19/104	23/51	42/155
Percentage	2.1%	18.3%	45.1%	27.1%

Loves to face: Mike Dunne (.600, 3-for-5, 2 2B)
Rick Honeycutt (2-for-2, 1 HR, 1 BB)
Curt Young (.556, 5-for-9)

Hates to face: Mike Moore (.100, 1-for-10)
Duane Ward (0-for-9)
Bob Welch (.077, 1-for-13)

Miscellaneous statistics: Ground outs-to-air outs ratio: 0.95 last season, 0.99 for career. . . . Grounded into 19 double plays in 142 opportunities (one per 7.5). . . . Drove in 16 of 25 runners from third base with less than two outs (64%). . . . Direction of balls hit to the outfield: 49% to left field, 30% to center, 21% to right. . . . Base running: Advanced from first base to third on 14 of 42 outfield singles (33%); scored from second on 14 of 18 (78%). . . . Made 3.42 assists per nine innings at second base, 2d-highest rate in A.L.

Comments: The Sox have had a winning record with Reed in the starting lineup and a losing record without him in each of the last three seasons. Three-year records: 214–173 with him (.553); 46–53 without him (.465). . . . Red Sox opponents scored an average of 3.55 runs per nine innings with Reed at second base, 4.70 runs per nine innings with Marty Barrett there. . . . Played at least 50 games at both second base and shortstop for the second consecutive season. Only four other players in major league history did that: Jimmy Johnston (1922–23), Ted Kubiak (1970–71), Bob Bailor (1982–83), and Tony Phillips (1983–84). . . . Shared the major league lead in doubles with George Brett. It was the most doubles ever by a player without a triple. . . . No kidding. . . . Reed was one of four Red Sox players to hit at least 20 doubles at Fenway Park and fewer than 20 on the road. The others: Wade Boggs, Mike Greenwell, and Ellis Burks. Over the last five seasons, Fenway Park has increased doubles by 29 percent over "your average American League ballpark.". . .Of Reed's 26 Fenway doubles, 23 were hit to left field. . . . Batted .343 in the first inning, 2d-highest average in the American League. The league leader was Wade Boggs (.352). . . . Career batting average is higher vs. left-handers (.297) than against right-handers (.287), but only one of his nine home runs has been hit against a southpaw (a pinch-hit homer off Rick Honeycutt in 1989).

Harold Reynolds

Bats Left and Right

Seattle Mariners	AB	H	2B	3B	HR	RBI	BB	SO	BA	SA	OBA
Season	642	162	36	5	5	55	81	52	.252	.347	.336
vs. Left-Handers	207	59	15	2	1	22	17	7	.285	.391	.335
vs. Right-Handers	435	103	21	3	4	33	64	45	.237	.326	.337
vs. Ground-Ballers	242	65	15	3	1	27	31	23	.269	.368	.353
vs. Fly-Ballers	400	97	21	2	4	28	50	29	.243	.335	.326
Home Games	297	75	15	1	0	21	46	18	.253	.310	.350
Road Games	345	87	21	4	5	34	35	34	.252	.380	.324
Grass Fields	268	69	17	3	4	30	23	25	.257	.388	.317
Artificial Turf	374	93	19	2	1	25	58	27	.249	.318	.349
April	83	16	2	1	1	6	7	5	.193	.277	.256
May	118	30	10	1	0	13	15	13	.254	.356	.336
June	97	25	4	2	0	9	20	7	.258	.340	.378
July	105	31	5	1	1	10	16	4	.295	.390	.385
August	114	24	8	0	0	2	12	10	.211	.281	.297
Sept./Oct.	125	36	7	0	3	15	11	13	.288	.416	.345
Leading Off Inn.	260	63	16	2	1	1	39	21	.242	.331	.348
Bases Empty	412	99	22	3	2	2	58	33	.240	.323	.338
Runners On	230	63	14	2	3	53	23	19	.274	.391	.332
Runners/Scor. Pos.	123	37	6	2	2	47	15	13	.301	.431	.361
Runners On/2 Out	103	32	7	2	2	25	14	8	.311	.476	.393
Scor. Pos./2 Out	66	20	4	2	1	21	10	7	.303	.470	.395
Late-Inning Pressure	90	29	8	1	1	23	11	10	.322	.467	.394
Leading Off	17	5	2	0	0	0	4	3	.294	.412	.455
Runners On	47	17	5	1	1	23	3	6	.362	.574	.385
Runners/Scor. Pos.	26	8	2	1	1	20	2	3	.308	.577	.333

RUNS BATTED IN	From 1B	From 2B	From 3B	Scoring Position
Totals	9/166	17/95	24/56	41/151
Percentage	5.4%	17.9%	42.9%	27.2%

Loves to face: Allan Anderson (.458, 11-for-24)
Jeff Reardon (.833, 5-for-6)
Dave Stieb (.448, 13-for-29, 0 BB)

Hates to face: Greg A. Harris (.150, 3-for-20)
Charlie Hough (.200, 10-for-50)
Dave Stewart (.087, 4-for-46, 5 BB)

Miscellaneous statistics: Ground outs-to-air outs ratio: 1.05 last season, 1.24 for career. . . . Grounded into 9 double plays in 107 opportunities (one per 11.9). . . . Drove in 15 of 26 runners from third base with less than two outs (58%). . . . Direction of balls hit to the outfield: 27% to left field, 30% to center, 43% to right batting left-handed; 47% to left, 36% to center, 16% to right batting right-handed. . . . Base running: Advanced from first base to third on 11 of 29 outfield singles (38%); scored from second on 17 of 21 (81%). . . . Made 3.19 assists per nine innings at second base.

Comments: Has played eight major league seasons, all with the Mariners. Translation: He has never played for a team with a winning record. . . . Related trivia: The longest streak of seasons with losing teams—16, Cy Williams (1915–30). The longest from the start of a career—14, Ken Raffensberger (1940–54). The longest career spent entirely with losing teams—11 seasons, Roy Sievers (1949–59). For those figures, we considered the team of record to be the one with which a player finished the season (or the last team he played for in that year). . . . Had a streak of 27 consecutive hitless at-bats with runners on base in June, the longest streak of its kind in the majors last season. . . . Total of walks has increased in every season since 1984: 0, 17, 29, 39, 51, 55, 81. . . . Average of one strikeout per 32.9 plate appearances vs. left-handed pitchers was the best in the majors last season (minimum: 150 PA). . . . Played 160 games at second base, becoming only the eighth second baseman in history to reach that mark in two different seasons. Only Bill Mazeroski has had three such seasons. . . . Led major league second basemen in putouts (331) and assists (500). . . . Made the final out in Comiskey Park. . . . Batting average dropped 48 points from his .300 mark in 1989, 6th-largest drop of any major leaguer with at least 300 at bats in both seasons.

Billy Ripken

Bats Right

Baltimore Orioles	AB	H	2B	3B	HR	RBI	BB	SO	BA	SA	OBA
Season	406	118	28	1	3	38	28	43	.291	.387	.342
vs. Left-Handers	140	44	9	0	2	11	12	16	.314	.421	.370
vs. Right-Handers	266	74	19	1	1	27	16	27	.278	.368	.326
vs. Ground-Ballers	173	58	12	1	2	21	8	18	.335	.451	.373
vs. Fly-Ballers	233	60	16	0	1	17	20	25	.258	.339	.319
Home Games	198	55	17	0	2	20	13	16	.278	.394	.329
Road Games	208	63	11	1	1	18	15	27	.303	.380	.354
Grass Fields	352	97	24	0	2	33	24	38	.276	.361	.325
Artificial Turf	54	21	4	1	1	5	4	5	.389	.556	.450
April	43	9	3	0	0	1	5	2	.209	.279	.292
May	67	18	3	1	0	7	2	10	.269	.343	.296
June	90	25	4	0	1	8	1	6	.278	.356	.293
July	76	25	5	0	0	4	7	4	.329	.395	.386
August	37	13	4	0	0	3	6	5	.351	.459	.442
Sept./Oct.	93	28	9	0	2	15	7	16	.301	.462	.363
Leading Off Inn.	80	23	7	1	1	1	10	6	.287	.438	.374
Bases Empty	236	61	18	1	2	2	21	24	.258	.369	.327
Runners On	170	57	10	0	1	36	7	19	.335	.412	.363
Runners/Scor. Pos.	100	31	2	0	0	32	5	14	.310	.330	.346
Runners On/2 Out	76	21	4	0	0	14	4	10	.276	.329	.313
Scor. Pos./2 Out	52	12	1	0	0	14	2	7	.231	.250	.259
Late-Inning Pressure	55	18	1	0	0	2	5	2	.327	.345	.393
Leading Off	17	3	1	0	0	0	3	0	.176	.235	.300
Runners On	21	8	0	0	0	2	1	1	.381	.381	.435
Runners/Scor. Pos.	10	4	0	0	0	2	1	0	.400	.400	.500

RUNS BATTED IN	From 1B	From 2B	From 3B	Scoring Position
Totals	3/118	16/76	16/40	32/116
Percentage	2.5%	21.1%	40.0%	27.6%

Loves to face: Storm Davis (.500, 6-for-12)
Mark Langston (.381, 8-for-21)
Sergio Valdez (.571, 4-for-7)

Hates to face: Mike Moore (.158, 3-for-19)
Dave Stewart (.083, 1-for-12, 1 2B)
Walt Terrell (0-for-11, 2 BB)

Miscellaneous statistics: Ground outs-to-air outs ratio: 1.27 last season, 1.54 for career. . . . Grounded into 7 double plays in 87 opportunities (one per 12.4). . . . Drove in 10 of 19 runners from third base with less than two outs (53%). . . . Direction of balls hit to the outfield: 35% to left field, 32% to center, 33% to right. . . . Base running: Advanced from first base to third on 10 of 28 outfield singles (36%); scored from second on 10 of 15 (67%). . . . Made 3.15 assists per nine innings at second base.

Comments: Orioles played .500 ball (61–61) with Billy starting at second base, but were nine games under the break-even point without him there (15–24). . . . Batted .304 from the ninth slot in the lineup, the highest average of any player with at least 100 at-bats batting ninth last season. . . . Had an errorless streak of 53 games at second base, while his bro' was setting the record for consecutive errorless games at shortstop. . . . The last player to hit as well coming off consecutive seasons below .240 (with 300 or more AB in all three years) was Jose Uribe in 1987. . . . Was outhit by only one A.L. second baseman last season: Julio Franco, who batted .296 while playing there. . . . File this one away for future reference: No brothers have ever shared the same infield, either as opponents or teammates, in an All-Star Game. . . . The Rips are entering their fifth consecutive season as teammates. The last pair of brothers with as long a tenure together was Walker and Mort Cooper, who shared a locker room with the St. Louis Cardinals from 1940 to 1945. The Aaron brothers were teammates with the Braves for seven seasons, but never for more than four years in a row. The brothers who were teammates for the longest time were the Waners, who played together for 15 straight years with the Pirates (1927–40) and the Braves (1941) before parting company, only to be reunited with the Dodgers in 1944.

Cal Ripken

Bats Right

Baltimore Orioles	AB	H	2B	3B	HR	RBI	BB	SO	BA	SA	OBA
Season	600	150	28	4	21	84	82	66	.250	.415	.341
vs. Left-Handers	182	48	9	1	9	24	30	17	.264	.473	.363
vs. Right-Handers	418	102	19	3	12	60	52	49	.244	.390	.332
vs. Ground-Ballers	263	62	15	1	8	32	37	27	.236	.392	.329
vs. Fly-Ballers	337	88	13	3	13	52	45	39	.261	.433	.351
Home Games	300	64	13	2	8	42	35	33	.213	.350	.295
Road Games	300	86	15	2	13	42	47	33	.287	.480	.386
Grass Fields	511	123	23	4	17	68	66	59	.241	.401	.330
Artificial Turf	89	27	5	0	4	16	16	7	.303	.494	.404
April	76	17	1	1	2	11	15	10	.224	.342	.359
May	97	20	4	1	5	15	18	8	.206	.423	.333
June	110	34	8	0	1	11	11	8	.309	.409	.369
July	94	26	6	0	3	16	18	11	.277	.436	.397
August	102	27	5	2	6	21	11	15	.265	.529	.333
Sept./Oct.	121	26	4	0	4	10	9	14	.215	.347	.271
Leading Off Inn.	103	26	5	0	9	9	11	6	.252	.563	.336
Bases Empty	310	81	16	0	17	17	32	27	.261	.477	.336
Runners On	290	69	12	4	4	67	50	39	.238	.348	.347
Runners/Scor. Pos.	167	34	8	1	2	59	40	19	.204	.299	.349
Runners On/2 Out	123	27	3	1	3	24	25	18	.220	.333	.356
Scor. Pos./2 Out	81	16	2	0	2	20	21	10	.198	.296	.363
Late-Inning Pressure	91	24	5	0	4	13	11	11	.264	.451	.343
Leading Off	22	8	1	0	4	4	1	0	.364	.955	.417
Runners On	42	9	0	0	0	9	7	8	.214	.214	.314
Runners/Scor. Pos.	23	5	0	0	0	9	7	4	.217	.217	.375

RUNS BATTED IN	From 1B	From 2B	From 3B	Scoring Position
Totals	11/220	20/133	32/86	52/219
Percentage	5.0%	15.0%	37.2%	23.7%

Loves to face: Rick Honeycutt (.571, 4-for-7, 2 2B, 1 HR)
Mark Langston (.346, 18-for-52, 1 HR, 8 BB)
Gene Nelson (.357, 10-for-28, 2 2B, 2 3B, 3 HR)

Hates to face: Tom Filer (0-for-12, 2 BB)
Mike Moore (.203, 16-for-79, 3 HR)
Dave Stieb (.203, 13-for-64, 1 HR)

Miscellaneous statistics: Ground outs-to-air outs ratio: 0.91 last season, 0.99 for career. . . . Grounded into 12 double plays in 148 opportunities (one per 12.3). . . . Drove in 27 of 44 runners from third base with less than two outs (61%). . . . Direction of balls hit to the outfield: 49% to left field, 27% to center, 23% to right. . . . Base running: Advanced from first base to third on 15 of 31 outfield singles (48%); scored from second on 15 of 15. . . . Made 2.79 assists per nine innings at shortstop, 2d-lowest rate in A.L.

Comments: Has hit at least 20 home runs in nine consecutive seasons starting with his rookie year, the longest such streak since Eddie Murray's (1977–85). The all-time record: 14, Eddie Mathews (1952–65). . . . Had 219 opportunities to drive in runners from scoring position, an A.L. high last season. Among 49 A.L. players with at least 150 chances, only Steve Sax and Mike Greenwell drove in a lower percentage than Ripken did. . . . Played all of Baltimore's 161 games, starting every one, and missing only 31 innings at shortstop. He's played at least 161 games at shortstop in each of the last eight seasons. Only one other player in major league history has ever done that in even two consecutive seasons (Alfredo Griffin, 1985–86). . . . Did anyone really expect Ripken to sacrifice his pursuit of Gehrig's consecutive-game record for the good of the team during a 25-game 15-of-93 slump last spring? Remember, this is the same man whose determination/bullheadedness (take your pick) dictated that he play through an 0-for-29 slump in April 1988. . . . Why are we such grumps on this subject? Look, Cal and the O's can do whatever they like; it's really none of our business. But is it a coincidence that for three consecutive seasons, Ripken has hit below .220 during September and October (for a composite .213 mark)? And in the event of a pennant race, might not some of Ripken's own teammates ask whether another September swoon was the result of his single-minded quest for individual glory?

Luis Rivera

Bats Right

Boston Red Sox	AB	H	2B	3B	HR	RBI	BB	SO	BA	SA	OBA
Season	346	78	20	0	7	45	25	58	.225	.344	.279
vs. Left-Handers	116	20	5	0	2	15	8	24	.172	.267	.226
vs. Right-Handers	230	58	15	0	5	30	17	34	.252	.383	.305
vs. Ground-Ballers	142	38	10	0	4	31	6	13	.268	.423	.300
vs. Fly-Ballers	204	40	10	0	3	14	19	45	.196	.289	.265
Home Games	177	41	12	0	4	32	14	24	.232	.367	.286
Road Games	169	37	8	0	3	13	11	34	.219	.320	.271
Grass Fields	284	65	17	0	6	43	22	46	.229	.352	.286
Artificial Turf	62	13	3	0	1	2	3	12	.210	.306	.246
April	8	0	0	0	0	1	2	1	.000	.000	.200
May	72	24	3	0	1	9	4	11	.333	.417	.364
June	84	14	3	0	1	6	6	15	.167	.238	.231
July	45	7	4	0	2	6	1	9	.156	.378	.174
August	64	15	3	0	3	14	5	8	.234	.422	.290
Sept./Oct.	73	18	7	0	0	9	7	14	.247	.342	.313
Leading Off Inn.	81	12	4	0	0	0	3	22	.148	.198	.179
Bases Empty	185	38	9	0	4	4	12	38	.205	.319	.254
Runners On	161	40	11	0	3	41	13	20	.248	.373	.307
Runners/Scor. Pos.	105	26	6	0	3	40	7	13	.248	.390	.298
Runners On/2 Out	76	20	8	0	0	15	5	9	.263	.368	.309
Scor. Pos./2 Out	53	13	4	0	0	14	4	7	.245	.321	.298
Late-Inning Pressure	45	11	4	0	0	2	2	8	.244	.333	.277
Leading Off	14	2	1	0	0	0	0	5	.143	.214	.143
Runners On	18	4	2	0	0	2	2	2	.222	.333	.300
Runners/Scor. Pos.	9	2	1	0	0	2	2	2	.222	.333	.364

RUNS BATTED IN	From 1B	From 2B	From 3B	Scoring Position
Totals	4/105	15/89	19/36	34/125
Percentage	3.8%	16.9%	52.8%	27.2%

Loves to face: Kevin Brown (.500, 4-for-8)
Mike Henneman (.750, 3-for-4, 1 HR)
Jimmy Jones (.625, 5-for-8)

Hates to face: Chuck Cary (0-for-12)
Jamie Moyer (.048, 1-for-21)
Bobby Witt (0-for-11, 1 BB)

Miscellaneous statistics: Ground outs-to-air outs ratio: 1.01 last season, 0.85 for career. . . . Grounded into 10 double plays in 77 opportunities (one per 7.7). . . . Drove in 13 of 21 runners from third base with less than two outs (62%). . . . Direction of balls hit to the outfield: 49% to left field, 30% to center, 22% to right. . . . Base running: Advanced from first base to third on 11 of 17 outfield singles (65%) 2d-highest rate in A.L.; scored from second on 7 of 9 (78%). . . . Made 3.00 assists per nine innings at shortstop.

Comments: Anyone who saw Rivera worry every throw to first base last September won't be surprised that his rate of one error per 11 chances at shortstop in Late-Inning Pressure Situations was the highest in the majors (minimum: 25 chances). Worst rates at other positions: 1B, Dave Bergman (one error in 25 chances); 2B, Mariano Duncan (one per 16); 3B, Robin Ventura (one per 8); LF, Lonnie Smith (one per 11); CF, Devon White (one per 12); RF, Hubie Brooks (one per 12). . . . Among players with at least 75 hits last season, none had fewer to the opposite field than Rivera (5). . . . His .179 on-base percentage leading off innings was the lowest by an American League player since Bill Melton (.167) in 1976 (minimum: 75 PA). . . . Batting average vs. left-handed pitchers was the lowest of any right-handed batter in the American League last season (minimum: 100 AB). . . . Thank God for Fenway, where he has a career .261 batting average. He has a career mark of .216 outside of Beantown, and has batted under .220 on the road in each of his five seasons in the majors. . . . Was removed in favor of a pinch hitter 16 times last season, the most of any player on the club. . . . Has hit for a higher average against ground-ball pitchers than he has against fly-ball pitchers in each of his five seasons in the majors. Career average vs. ground-ballers (.267) is 76 points higher than vs. fly-ballers (.191), the 3d-largest margin in the majors over the last five years. . . . Year-by-year batting averages vs. fly-ballers: .198, .111, .189, .188, .196.

Steve Sax

Bats Right

New York Yankees	AB	H	2B	3B	HR	RBI	BB	SO	BA	SA	OBA
Season	615	160	24	2	4	42	49	46	.260	.325	.316
vs. Left-Handers	177	44	7	1	0	11	20	10	.249	.299	.325
vs. Right-Handers	438	116	17	1	4	31	29	36	.265	.336	.312
vs. Ground-Ballers	268	70	10	1	2	21	18	25	.261	.328	.307
vs. Fly-Ballers	347	90	14	1	2	21	31	21	.259	.323	.323
Home Games	294	76	13	2	3	27	30	22	.259	.347	.327
Road Games	321	84	11	0	1	15	19	24	.262	.305	.305
Grass Fields	505	129	20	2	4	36	44	37	.255	.327	.315
Artificial Turf	110	31	4	0	0	6	5	9	.282	.318	.319
April	68	20	1	0	1	5	7	3	.294	.353	.360
May	101	26	4	0	0	5	9	5	.257	.297	.324
June	109	32	5	1	0	8	6	12	.294	.358	.331
July	114	28	6	0	2	13	9	11	.246	.351	.296
August	112	22	3	0	0	4	7	11	.196	.223	.248
Sept./Oct.	111	32	5	1	1	7	11	4	.288	.378	.355
Leading Off Inn.	154	35	7	0	2	2	13	10	.227	.312	.292
Bases Empty	388	105	19	0	3	3	30	25	.271	.343	.325
Runners On	227	55	5	2	1	39	19	21	.242	.295	.302
Runners/Scor. Pos.	134	32	3	2	1	37	12	17	.239	.313	.299
Runners On/2 Out	90	21	2	0	0	11	10	6	.233	.256	.310
Scor. Pos./2 Out	58	14	2	0	0	11	9	5	.241	.276	.343
Late-Inning Pressure	89	27	4	1	0	8	10	6	.303	.371	.366
Leading Off	22	5	2	0	0	0	2	1	.227	.318	.292
Runners On	43	10	0	1	0	8	4	4	.233	.279	.286
Runners/Scor. Pos.	26	6	0	1	0	8	3	2	.231	.308	.290

RUNS BATTED IN	From 1B	From 2B	From 3B	Scoring Position
Totals	6/149	12/114	20/48	32/162
Percentage	4.0%	10.5%	41.7%	19.8%

Loves to face: Jeff D. Robinson (.471, 8-for-17)
Ron Robinson (.436, 17-for-39)
Dave Stewart (.526, 10-for-19)

Hates to face: Terry Leach (.143, 3-for-21)
Eric Show (.208, 10-for-48)
Bob Welch (0-for-11)

Miscellaneous statistics: Ground outs-to-air outs ratio: 1.87 last season, 1.98 for career. . . . Grounded into 13 double plays in 105 opportunities (one per 8.1). . . . Drove in 16 of 28 runners from third base with less than two outs (57%). . . . Direction of balls hit to the outfield: 30% to left field, 34% to center, 36% to right. . . . Base running: Advanced from first base to third on 11 of 30 outfield singles (37%); scored from second on 13 of 20 (65%). . . . Made 3.03 assists per nine innings at second base.

Comments: He was the fifth different A.L. second baseman to start the All-Star Game in the last five years. Other than pitcher, no other position for either league has had a different starter in each of those games. . . . Became the fourth second baseman in Yankees history to start an All-Star game. The others: Joe Gordon (1939–40, 1942); Bobby Richardson (1964); Willie Randolph (1977, 1980–81, 1987). . . . In 1989, he became the fifth player in major league history to have had seasons of 200 or more hits in both the American and the National Leagues. The others: Nap Lajoie, George Sisler, Al Oliver, and Bill Buckner. . . . Batted 87 points higher in day games (.322) than in night games (.235) last season, the 3d-largest margin in the majors. . . . Had a streak of 35 consecutive plate appearances in which he didn't bat with a runner in scoring position, the longest streak in the A.L. last season. . . . Had a higher stolen-base percentage against left-handed pitchers (17-of-20, .850) than he had against right-handers (26-of-32, .813). . . . Sax, Rickey Henderson, and Vince Coleman are the only players to steal at least 40 bases in each of the last three seasons. . . . Extended his streak of hitting for a higher average in Late-Inning Pressure Situations than in other at-bats to eight consecutive seasons—the longest current streak, one year short of Garth Iorg's *Player Analysis* record. Sax has a career average of .319 in LIPS, .278 at other times.

Dick Schofield

Bats Right

California Angels	AB	H	2B	3B	HR	RBI	BB	SO	BA	SA	OBA
Season	310	79	8	1	1	18	52	61	.255	.297	.363
vs. Left-Handers	89	25	2	0	1	6	18	14	.281	.337	.404
vs. Right-Handers	221	54	6	1	0	12	34	47	.244	.281	.346
vs. Ground-Ballers	141	41	4	0	1	10	23	21	.291	.340	.392
vs. Fly-Ballers	169	38	4	1	0	8	29	40	.225	.260	.340
Home Games	158	43	4	1	1	12	30	26	.272	.329	.384
Road Games	152	36	4	0	0	6	22	35	.237	.263	.341
Grass Fields	265	69	6	1	1	15	47	51	.260	.302	.373
Artificial Turf	45	10	2	0	0	3	5	10	.222	.267	.300
April	0	0	0	0	0	0	0	0	—	—	—
May	0	0	0	0	0	0	0	0	—	—	—
June	66	13	0	0	1	1	13	13	.197	.242	.338
July	74	13	0	0	0	2	8	20	.176	.176	.256
August	80	25	3	0	0	7	19	15	.313	.350	.446
Sept./Oct.	90	28	5	1	0	8	12	13	.311	.389	.388
Leading Off Inn.	91	21	3	0	1	1	12	20	.231	.297	.327
Bases Empty	188	45	7	0	1	1	23	38	.239	.293	.329
Runners On	122	34	1	1	0	17	29	23	.279	.303	.412
Runners/Scor. Pos.	54	16	0	1	0	17	14	10	.296	.333	.429
Runners On/2 Out	65	11	0	1	0	6	14	13	.169	.200	.316
Scor. Pos./2 Out	30	5	0	1	0	6	7	6	.167	.233	.324
Late-Inning Pressure	42	11	0	0	0	2	9	15	.262	.262	.392
Leading Off	14	3	0	0	0	0	2	7	.214	.214	.313
Runners On	15	4	0	0	0	2	6	4	.267	.267	.476
Runners/Scor. Pos.	6	3	0	0	0	2	4	2	.500	.500	.700

RUNS BATTED IN	From 1B	From 2B	From 3B	Scoring Position
Totals	0/98	6/45	11/27	17/72
Percentage	0.0%	13.3%	40.7%	23.6%

Loves to face: Allan Anderson (.444, 8-for-18)
Mike Henneman (.500, 5-for-10)
Matt Young (.333, 4-for-12, 1 HR)

Hates to face: Juan Berenguer (.059, 1-for-17, 2 BB, 9 SO)
Danny Darwin (0-for-15, 2 BB)
Nolan Ryan (0-for-13, 3 BB, 9 SO)

Miscellaneous statistics: Ground outs-to-air outs ratio: 0.94 last season, 0.92 for career.... Grounded into 3 double plays in 66 opportunities (one per 22.0), 4th-best rate in A.L.... Drove in 7 of 13 runners from third base with less than two outs (54%).... Direction of balls hit to the outfield: 26% to left field, 36% to center, 38% to right.... Base running: Advanced from first base to third on 7 of 24 outfield singles (29%); scored from second on 9 of 11 (82%).... Made 3.31 assists per nine innings at shortstop, 2d-highest rate in A.L.

Comments: Needs 74 games to become the fourth player in Angels history to reach the 1000-game mark. Three of the club's top five players in that category were catchers (part-time, at least): Brian Downing (1661), Jim Fregosi (1429), Bobby Grich (1222), Bob Boone (968), and Buck Rodgers (932).... His 1990 batting average was a career high; he topped .250 only once before (.251 in 1987).... Had a streak of 134 consecutive at-bats without an extra-base hit, the longest such streak of any American League player last season.... Averaged one walk per 7.3 plate appearances, the best rate of his career. His previous career rate was one walk every 13.2 times up.... Had a career stolen-base percentage of .798 entering last season, but stole only three bases in seven attempts (.428) in 1990.... Participated in 77 double plays in only 99 games at shortstop. The last shortstop with as many DPs in so few games: Robin Yount (83 DPs in 93 games in 1981). The most DPs by a shortstop in less than 100 games: Eddie Pellagrini, 85 in 98 games in 1948.... Has had higher batting averages against ground-ball pitchers than against fly-ballers in each of his eight seasons in the majors. Career averages: .258 vs. ground-ballers, .216 vs. fly-ballers.... Has batted below .200 with two outs and runners on base five times in his seven full seasons. His career average (.184) is the 2d lowest over the 16 years those figures have been compiled (minimum: 500 AB).... Only two of his 2968 career at-bats have come as a pinch hitter.

Kevin Seitzer

Bats Right

Kansas City Royals	AB	H	2B	3B	HR	RBI	BB	SO	BA	SA	OBA
Season	622	171	31	5	6	38	67	66	.275	.370	.346
vs. Left-Handers	209	58	17	4	4	23	22	22	.278	.455	.345
vs. Right-Handers	413	113	14	1	2	15	45	44	.274	.327	.347
vs. Ground-Ballers	291	92	13	3	4	21	29	30	.316	.423	.377
vs. Fly-Ballers	331	79	18	2	2	17	38	36	.239	.323	.320
Home Games	308	96	22	3	5	26	35	32	.312	.451	.384
Road Games	314	75	9	2	1	12	32	34	.239	.290	.308
Grass Fields	233	54	5	2	0	8	26	24	.232	.270	.308
Artificial Turf	389	117	26	3	6	30	41	42	.301	.429	.370
April	78	18	2	0	0	2	2	7	.231	.256	.250
May	108	35	6	1	1	6	14	12	.324	.426	.403
June	109	36	9	1	2	9	9	7	.330	.486	.381
July	116	29	3	2	1	8	13	13	.250	.336	.328
August	109	28	6	1	0	7	14	12	.257	.330	.341
Sept./Oct.	102	25	5	0	2	6	15	15	.245	.353	.342
Leading Off Inn.	218	60	13	1	1	1	18	26	.275	.358	.336
Bases Empty	414	110	20	2	4	4	45	46	.266	.353	.341
Runners On	208	61	11	3	2	34	22	20	.293	.404	.358
Runners/Scor. Pos.	127	34	8	2	0	27	18	13	.268	.362	.354
Runners On/2 Out	84	27	5	0	1	14	9	6	.321	.417	.387
Scor. Pos./2 Out	64	16	4	0	0	11	9	5	.250	.313	.342
Late-Inning Pressure	81	16	1	0	0	3	8	11	.198	.210	.267
Leading Off	17	2	0	0	0	0	0	2	.118	.118	.118
Runners On	29	7	0	0	0	3	3	4	.241	.241	.303
Runners/Scor. Pos.	19	4	0	0	0	3	2	4	.211	.211	.273

RUNS BATTED IN	From 1B	From 2B	From 3B	Scoring Position
Totals	8/137	13/94	11/46	24/140
Percentage	5.8%	13.8%	23.9%	17.1%

Loves to face: Allan Anderson (.478, 11-for-23, 1 HR)
Mark Langston (.400, 10-for-25, 5 BB)
Dave LaPoint (.571, 4-for-7)

Hates to face: Wes Gardner (.133, 2-for-15, 2 2B)
Kevin Tapani (0-for-7)
Bobby Witt (.200, 4-for-20, 7 BB)

Miscellaneous statistics: Ground outs-to-air outs ratio: 1.14 last season, 1.45 for career.... Grounded into 11 double plays in 93 opportunities (one per 8.5).... Drove in 6 of 18 runners from third base with less than two outs (33%), 4th-lowest rate in A.L.... Direction of balls hit to the outfield: 27% to left field, 30% to center, 43% to right.... Base running: Advanced from first base to third on 15 of 43 outfield singles (35%); scored from second on 16 of 21 (76%).... Made 1.87 assists per nine innings at third base.

Comments: Batted above .300 in each of his first three seasons, below .300 in each of the last two.... Had extra-base hits in five consecutive at-bats in May, equalling the longest streaks of the past 12 seasons. The others (and *pay attention*—this is the most improbable list in the book): Dave Skaggs (1979), Tim Teufel (1987), and Mike Fitzgerald (1989).... Had a streak of 20 consecutive plate appearances in which he batted with the bases empty, the longest streak of any A.L. player last season.... Drew 35 fewer walks than in 1989, in only 15 fewer plate appearances.... Of his 171 hits, 57 were hit to the opposite field, the 4th-highest total in the A.L.... Was thrown out trying to advance a base on a batted ball nine times last season, the most of any player on the Royals.... Has hit for a higher average on artificial turf than he has on grass fields, and for a higher average at Royals Stadium than in road games in each of his five seasons in the majors. Career averages: .325 at Royals Stadium (higher than at *any* other ballpark), .283 on other artificially surfaced fields, .265 on grass fields.... Has hit 73 of 117 doubles and 14 of 21 triples at Royals Stadium.... Has no home runs in 319 career at-bats in Late-Inning Pressure Situations. He has averaged one HR per 69 at-bats at other times.... Has nine hits in 25 career at-bats, along with seven walks, with the bases loaded.

Larry Sheets

Bats Left

Detroit Tigers	AB	H	2B	3B	HR	RBI	BB	SO	BA	SA	OBA
Season	360	94	17	2	10	52	24	42	.261	.403	.308
vs. Left-Handers	17	4	0	0	0	1	1	3	.235	.235	.278
vs. Right-Handers	343	90	17	2	10	51	23	39	.262	.411	.309
vs. Ground-Ballers	180	50	10	1	4	20	14	22	.278	.411	.330
vs. Fly-Ballers	180	44	7	1	6	32	10	20	.244	.394	.286
Home Games	179	44	8	1	7	30	11	27	.246	.419	.288
Road Games	181	50	9	1	3	22	13	15	.276	.387	.327
Grass Fields	308	80	16	2	9	39	20	38	.260	.412	.306
Artificial Turf	52	14	1	0	1	13	4	4	.269	.346	.317
April	44	13	4	0	0	5	5	5	.295	.386	.353
May	61	20	2	0	3	7	2	2	.328	.508	.359
June	56	12	3	1	1	6	5	7	.214	.357	.274
July	72	19	3	1	3	17	5	11	.264	.458	.308
August	72	22	3	0	2	12	4	7	.306	.431	.342
Sept./Oct.	55	8	2	0	1	5	3	10	.145	.236	.203
Leading Off Inn.	74	22	3	0	1	1	6	4	.297	.378	.366
Bases Empty	177	48	7	0	5	5	14	19	.271	.395	.332
Runners On	183	46	10	2	5	47	10	23	.251	.410	.284
Runners/Scor. Pos.	101	28	5	1	5	45	8	14	.277	.495	.319
Runners On/2 Out	82	19	5	0	3	23	5	11	.232	.402	.276
Scor. Pos./2 Out	49	15	3	0	3	23	4	6	.306	.551	.358
Late-Inning Pressure	38	13	4	0	2	9	5	6	.342	.605	.419
Leading Off	9	3	0	0	0	0	1	1	.333	.333	.400
Runners On	19	7	2	0	2	9	2	2	.368	.789	.429
Runners/Scor. Pos.	12	6	1	0	2	9	2	1	.500	1.083	.571

RUNS BATTED IN	From 1B	From 2B	From 3B	Scoring Position
Totals	7/134	16/83	19/43	35/126
Percentage	5.2%	19.3%	44.2%	27.8%

Loves to face: Paul Kilgus (.600, 6-for-10, 2 HR)
Nolan Ryan (.467, 7-for-15, 2 HR)
Bobby Witt (.357, 5-for-14, 2 HR)

Hates to face: Storm Davis (.083, 1-for-12)
Charlie Hough (.167, 5-for-30, 1 HR)
Curt Young (.083, 1-for-12)

Miscellaneous statistics: Ground outs-to-air outs ratio: 1.08 last season, 1.22 for career. . . . Grounded into 13 double plays in 77 opportunities (one per 5.9). . . . Drove in 14 of 23 runners from third base with less than two outs (61%). . . . Direction of balls hit to the outfield: 29% to left field, 40% to center, 31% to right. . . . Base running: Advanced from first base to third on 2 of 12 outfield singles (17%); scored from second on 7 of 13 (54%). . . . Made 1.69 putouts per nine innings in left field.

Comments: Remember the lively-ball controversy of 1987? Well, Sheets is one of five players to have hit more home runs in '87 (31) than in the three years since (27), despite playing at least 100 games in each of those seasons. The others: Wade Boggs (24 and 14), Carney Lansford (19 and 12), Mike Pagliarulo (32 and 29), and John Shelby (22 and 15). . . . Started 104 games last season, all against right-handed pitchers. Number of opportunities to bat against left-handers has decreased in each of the last three seasons. Year-by-year since 1987: 155, 131, 43, 18. . . . Career batting averages: .231 vs. left-handers (one HR per 30 AB), .274 vs. right-handers (one HR per 23 AB). . . . Has driven in 35 percent of runners from scoring position in Late-Inning Pressure Situations during his career. That ranks sixth among active players with at least 20 RBIs in those situations, behind some names from the high-rent district: Eddie Murray (39%), Pedro Guerrero (39%), Jose Canseco (39%), Kelly Gruber (38%), and Don Mattingly (37%). . . . Career average as a pinch hitter (.279) is higher than his average in other at-bats (.266). . . . One of 15 players to have played under both Earl Weaver and Sparky Anderson. The others: Doyle Alexander, Enos Cabell, Terry Crowley, Roger Freed, Ross Grimsley, Brad Havens, Wayne Krenchicki, Fred Lynn, Lee May, Bob Molinaro, Roger Nelson, Merv Rettenmund, John Shelby, and Nate Snell. . . . Check the John Shelby comments on the next page for those who played for both Sparky and Lasorda.

Gary Sheffield

Bats Right

Milwaukee Brewers	AB	H	2B	3B	HR	RBI	BB	SO	BA	SA	OBA
Season	487	143	30	1	10	67	44	41	.294	.421	.350
vs. Left-Handers	135	37	12	1	3	18	14	15	.274	.444	.338
vs. Right-Handers	352	106	18	0	7	49	30	26	.301	.412	.355
vs. Ground-Ballers	219	64	15	0	3	23	21	17	.292	.402	.354
vs. Fly-Ballers	268	79	15	1	7	44	23	24	.295	.437	.347
Home Games	239	65	15	1	3	28	24	22	.272	.381	.338
Road Games	248	78	15	0	7	39	20	19	.315	.460	.361
Grass Fields	418	126	28	1	9	55	40	37	.301	.438	.361
Artificial Turf	69	17	2	0	1	12	4	4	.246	.319	.286
April	60	16	5	0	0	10	5	4	.267	.350	.328
May	69	25	7	0	1	3	6	6	.362	.507	.413
June	98	27	8	0	3	18	9	15	.276	.449	.321
July	117	43	7	1	3	21	6	4	.368	.521	.403
August	104	23	2	0	2	12	12	10	.221	.298	.300
Sept./Oct.	39	9	1	0	1	3	6	2	.231	.333	.333
Leading Off Inn.	95	26	5	0	2	2	8	7	.274	.389	.330
Bases Empty	270	65	16	0	6	6	22	25	.241	.367	.305
Runners On	217	78	14	1	4	61	22	16	.359	.488	.403
Runners/Scor. Pos.	124	42	10	1	0	50	18	13	.339	.435	.397
Runners On/2 Out	76	27	4	1	3	23	9	8	.355	.553	.424
Scor. Pos./2 Out	59	18	4	1	0	16	7	5	.305	.407	.379
Late-Inning Pressure	55	20	4	0	2	7	8	2	.364	.545	.453
Leading Off	20	9	1	0	2	2	4	0	.450	.800	.542
Runners On	21	9	3	0	0	5	3	1	.429	.571	.500
Runners/Scor. Pos.	16	5	2	0	0	5	2	1	.313	.438	.389

RUNS BATTED IN	From 1B	From 2B	From 3B	Scoring Position
Totals	7/143	25/95	25/55	50/150
Percentage	4.9%	26.3%	45.5%	33.3%

Loves to face: Greg A. Harris (.500, 3-for-6, 1 HR)
Jamie Moyer (.750, 3-for-4, 1 HR, 3 BB)
Bob Welch (.357, 5-for-14, 2 2B, 1 HR)

Hates to face: Mike Moore (.200, 4-for-20)
Jerry Reuss (0-for-17)
Dave Stieb (.100, 1-for-10)

Miscellaneous statistics: Ground outs-to-air outs ratio: 0.78 last season, 0.80 for career. . . . Grounded into 11 double plays in 115 opportunities (one per 10.5). . . . Drove in 22 of 32 runners from third base with less than two outs (69%). . . . Direction of balls hit to the outfield: 46% to left field, 31% to center, 23% to right. . . . Base running: Advanced from first base to third on 9 of 28 outfield singles (32%); scored from second on 14 of 14. . . . Made 2.14 assists per nine innings at third base.

Comments: Had the American League's 3d-highest batting average with runners in scoring position despite only five hits in 32 at-bats after August 8. . . . Career average of .314 in Late-Inning Pressure Situations, .264 in other at-bats. . . . Batted .202 in 109 at-bats during the first inning, but raised his average to .320 after that. . . . Played 125 games last season, all at third base, after playing mostly shortstop in his first two seasons. . . . Only two third basemen had higher batting averages: Wade Boggs (.307 while playing third base) and Edgar Martinez (.299). . . . His career average of one error per 15.2 chances at third base ranks 48th among the 60 active players with at least 100 games there. Among those below Sheffield: Nick Esasky (53d, one error per 13.7 chances), Pedro Guerrero (54th, one per 13.4 chances), Mickey Hatcher (55th, one per 13.1 chances), and Jamie Quirk (57th, one per 12.7 chances). . . . A career .314 hitter in Late-Inning Pressure Situations, with only nine strikeouts in 139 plate appearances. . . . He's eight days younger than Sammy Sosa, two months older than Delino DeShields. Needs to play until he's 41 years old in order to become a four-decade player in 2010. . . . Sheffield's career to date is a duplicate of Don Money's first three seasons, 20 years ago. Money, who eventually played 687 games at third base for the Brewers, also began his career as a can't-miss shortstop, making his debut for the Phillies in 1968.

John Shelby

Bats Left and Right

Dodgers/Tigers	AB	H	2B	3B	HR	RBI	BB	SO	BA	SA	OBA
Season	246	61	10	3	4	22	10	58	.248	.362	.277
vs. Left-Handers	78	14	2	1	2	6	3	21	.179	.308	.210
vs. Right-Handers	168	47	8	2	2	16	7	37	.280	.387	.309
vs. Ground-Ballers	112	23	2	1	1	8	6	23	.205	.268	.246
vs. Fly-Ballers	134	38	8	2	3	14	4	35	.284	.440	.304
Home Games	114	29	6	1	3	11	6	27	.254	.404	.292
Road Games	132	32	4	2	1	11	4	31	.242	.326	.265
Grass Fields	199	48	8	2	4	19	9	44	.241	.362	.274
Artificial Turf	47	13	2	1	0	3	1	14	.277	.362	.292
April	6	1	0	0	0	0	0	2	.167	.167	.167
May	14	5	1	0	0	2	0	4	.357	.429	.357
June	51	13	2	0	1	5	0	9	.255	.353	.255
July	60	13	2	1	1	5	5	17	.217	.333	.277
August	57	17	4	2	2	8	2	13	.298	.544	.322
Sept./Oct.	58	12	1	0	0	2	3	13	.207	.224	.246
Leading Off Inn.	63	18	3	2	1	1	1	11	.286	.444	.297
Bases Empty	143	38	4	3	1	1	2	33	.266	.357	.276
Runners On	103	23	6	0	3	21	8	25	.223	.369	.279
Runners/Scor. Pos.	61	13	4	0	2	19	6	18	.213	.377	.284
Runners On/2 Out	45	10	2	0	0	8	6	9	.222	.267	.314
Scor. Pos./2 Out	28	7	2	0	0	8	4	6	.250	.321	.344
Late-Inning Pressure	33	8	2	0	0	3	0	11	.242	.303	.242
Leading Off	13	4	1	0	0	0	0	2	.308	.385	.308
Runners On	12	2	1	0	0	3	0	7	.167	.250	.167
Runners/Scor. Pos.	10	2	1	0	0	3	0	6	.200	.300	.200

RUNS BATTED IN	From 1B	From 2B	From 3B	Scoring Position
Totals	4/81	8/46	6/23	14/69
Percentage	4.9%	17.4%	26.1%	20.3%

Loves to face: Mark Langston (.333, 7-for-21, 2 HR)
Jeff Montgomery (.750, 3-for-4)
Ron Robinson (.440, 11-for-25)

Hates to face: Bert Blyleven (0-for-11)
Danny Darwin (.182, 6-for-33, 1 HR, 0 BB)
Jamie Moyer (.091, 1-for-11)

Miscellaneous statistics: Ground outs-to-air outs ratio: 1.15 last season, 0.95 for career.... Grounded into 7 double plays in 54 opportunities (one per 7.7).... Drove in 1 of 8 runners from third base with less than two outs (13%).... Direction of balls hit to the outfield: 32% to left field, 36% to center, 33% to right batting left-handed; 31% to left, 38% to center, 31% to right batting right-handed.... Base running: Advanced from first base to third on 5 of 13 outfield singles (38%); scored from second on 6 of 6.... Made 2.50 putouts per nine innings in center field.

Comments: Drove in 21 runs last season, but only one of those runs gave his team a lead. An average of one out of every five RBIs by Tigers players were go-ahead RBIs.... Has scored and driven in fewer than 30 runs in each of the last two seasons, despite playing at least 100 games in each. The last player with a similar two-year streak: Angel Salazar (1986–87).... Has driven in only two of 23 runners from scoring position in Late-Inning Pressure Situations over the last two seasons.... Batted .320 from the right side of the plate in 1987, compared to a .204 average over the last three seasons.... Stole only four bases last season, compared to 60 over the four previous seasons.... One of three players to have played under Earl Weaver, Tommy Lasorda, and Sparky Anderson. The others: Enos Cabell and Brad Havens. Others to play under Lasorda and Anderson only: Rick Auerbach, Billy Bean, Ivan DeJesus, Kirk Gibson, Bill Madlock, Orlando Mercado, Ted Power, Elias ("Baseball Analyst") Sosa, and Pat Zachry.... For those who played under Weaver and Anderson, see the Larry Sheets comments on the previous page.

Ruben Sierra

Bats Left and Right

Texas Rangers	AB	H	2B	3B	HR	RBI	BB	SO	BA	SA	OBA
Season	608	170	37	2	16	96	49	86	.280	.426	.330
vs. Left-Handers	216	70	16	0	3	31	14	25	.324	.440	.361
vs. Right-Handers	392	100	21	2	13	65	35	61	.255	.418	.314
vs. Ground-Ballers	289	78	18	0	5	41	23	42	.270	.384	.322
vs. Fly-Ballers	319	92	19	2	11	55	26	44	.288	.464	.338
Home Games	301	80	17	1	10	46	23	51	.266	.429	.317
Road Games	307	90	20	1	6	50	26	35	.293	.423	.343
Grass Fields	502	130	30	1	15	80	42	73	.259	.412	.313
Artificial Turf	106	40	7	1	1	16	7	13	.377	.491	.416
April	80	25	5	0	4	16	7	15	.313	.525	.368
May	87	16	4	0	2	7	10	15	.184	.299	.265
June	115	36	6	1	2	16	9	14	.313	.435	.360
July	95	26	7	0	4	23	7	9	.274	.474	.314
August	114	36	12	1	3	17	7	16	.316	.518	.350
Sept./Oct.	117	31	3	0	1	17	9	17	.265	.316	.320
Leading Off Inn.	174	54	11	1	7	7	7	21	.310	.506	.341
Bases Empty	329	89	20	1	8	8	13	44	.271	.410	.300
Runners On	279	81	17	1	8	88	36	42	.290	.444	.362
Runners/Scor. Pos.	168	54	13	1	6	82	23	24	.321	.518	.387
Runners On/2 Out	133	37	9	1	2	30	22	18	.278	.406	.381
Scor. Pos./2 Out	74	20	6	1	1	26	14	7	.270	.419	.386
Late-Inning Pressure	86	24	5	0	4	18	8	12	.279	.477	.340
Leading Off	22	7	0	0	2	2	0	3	.318	.591	.318
Runners On	39	14	4	0	2	16	7	5	.359	.615	.457
Runners/Scor. Pos.	22	10	4	0	1	14	7	3	.455	.773	.586

RUNS BATTED IN	From 1B	From 2B	From 3B	Scoring Position
Totals	11/207	33/127	36/71	69/198
Percentage	5.3%	26.0%	50.7%	34.8%

Loves to face: Storm Davis (.324, 11-for-34, 2 2B, 5 HR)
Mark Knudson (.500, 2-for-4, 2 HR)
Terry Leach (.500, 3-for-6, 1 HR)

Hates to face: Allan Anderson (.067, 1-for-15)
Juan Berenguer (.130, 3-for-23)
Dave Stieb (.214, 6-for-28)

Miscellaneous statistics: Ground outs-to-air outs ratio: 1.19 last season, 0.88 for career.... Grounded into 15 double plays in 135 opportunities (one per 9.0).... Drove in 26 of 44 runners from third base with less than two outs (59%).... Direction of balls hit to the outfield: 24% to left field, 29% to center, 47% to right batting left-handed; 40% to left, 40% to center, 19% to right batting right-handed.... Base running: Advanced from first base to third on 11 of 39 outfield singles (28%); scored from second on 14 of 20 (70%).... Made 1.95 putouts per nine innings in right field.

Comments: Ranks third in the American League with 415 RBIs over the past four seasons, behind George Bell (421) and Mark McGwire (420).... Sierra is one of five players to exceed 154 games—a full season in the old days—in each of the last four seasons. The others: Eddie Murray, Cal Ripken, Steve Sax, and Robin Yount.... Led the American League with 70 hits vs. left-handed pitchers last season.... Batted 118 points higher on artificial turf (.377) than on grass fields (.259) last season, the 2d-largest margin in the majors.... Had a streak of hits in seven consecutive at-bats in Late-Inning Pressure Situations last April. Minus those hits, he batted only .215 in LIPS. Still, his .279 LIPS mark was a *good* .279: .359 with runners on base, .213 with the bases empty.... Stole nine bases in nine attempts last season.... Career average of .294 from the right side, .264 from the left side.... Career total of 114 home runs ranks fourth among active switch-hitters, behind Eddie Murray (379), Howard Johnson (159), and Chili Davis (156).... Has homered in every major league ballpark in which he has played, with the exception of Yankee Stadium (97 career AB).... Has not had a sacrifice bunt since 1986, his rookie season.... Even after five strong seasons with Texas, Sierra is younger than Todd Stottlemyre, Kevin Maas, Greg Vaughn, Todd Zeile, and Jerome Walton. And he probably always will be.

Cory Snyder

Bats Right

Cleveland Indians	AB	H	2B	3B	HR	RBI	BB	SO	BA	SA	OBA
Season	438	102	27	3	14	55	21	118	.233	.404	.268
vs. Left-Handers	135	30	6	1	4	14	12	36	.222	.370	.291
vs. Right-Handers	303	72	21	2	10	41	9	82	.238	.419	.256
vs. Ground-Ballers	212	53	12	2	8	33	10	44	.250	.439	.284
vs. Fly-Ballers	226	49	15	1	6	22	11	74	.217	.372	.252
Home Games	196	46	13	1	3	17	14	55	.235	.357	.287
Road Games	242	56	14	2	11	38	7	63	.231	.442	.251
Grass Fields	377	86	20	3	11	45	17	101	.228	.385	.262
Artificial Turf	61	16	7	0	3	10	4	17	.262	.525	.303
April	70	23	6	0	3	13	2	16	.329	.543	.338
May	88	16	6	0	2	8	3	32	.182	.318	.215
June	100	29	8	2	6	19	6	17	.290	.590	.327
July	89	17	5	1	1	7	6	27	.191	.303	.240
August	74	15	2	0	1	6	2	19	.203	.270	.231
Sept./Oct.	17	2	0	0	1	2	2	7	.118	.294	.211
Leading Off Inn.	95	22	7	0	3	3	2	31	.232	.400	.247
Bases Empty	219	47	13	2	7	7	7	66	.215	.388	.239
Runners On	219	55	14	1	7	48	14	52	.251	.420	.295
Runners/Scor. Pos.	110	25	6	1	2	36	8	33	.227	.355	.272
Runners On/2 Out	98	22	6	1	3	21	6	23	.224	.398	.269
Scor. Pos./2 Out	50	12	4	1	1	16	3	14	.240	.420	.283
Late-Inning Pressure	72	14	6	2	1	3	3	23	.194	.375	.227
Leading Off	15	2	2	0	0	0	0	7	.133	.267	.133
Runners On	33	7	3	0	0	2	3	7	.212	.303	.278
Runners/Scor. Pos.	18	3	1	0	0	2	2	6	.167	.222	.250

RUNS BATTED IN	From 1B	From 2B	From 3B	Scoring Position
Totals	12/175	11/79	18/51	29/130
Percentage	6.9%	13.9%	35.3%	22.3%

Loves to face: Wes Gardner (.400, 4-for-10, 1 2B, 2 HR)
Dennis Lamp (.429, 6-for-14, 1 HR)
Tim Leary (.667, 6-for-9, 2 HR)

Hates to face: Mark Langston (.143, 5-for-35, 19 SO)
Scott Sanderson (0-for-10)
Walt Terrell (.059, 1-for-17)

Miscellaneous statistics: Ground outs-to-air outs ratio: 0.75 last season, 0.81 for career.... Grounded into 11 double plays in 108 opportunities (one per 9.8).... Drove in 14 of 35 runners from third base with less than two outs (40%).... Direction of balls hit to the outfield: 43% to left field, 26% to center, 30% to right.... Base running: Advanced from first base to third on 8 of 16 outfield singles (50%); scored from second on 7 of 9 (78%).... Made 2.05 putouts per nine innings in right field.

Comments: One of three players in major league history to strike out 100 times in each of his first five seasons. The others: Pete Incaviglia (like Snyder's, a current streak, 1986–90) and Bobby Knoop (1964–68).... Snyder's career average of 4.8 strikeouts per walk is the highest in major league history among players with as many strikeouts as he has (642).... His career average of one assist per 9.2 games in the outfield ranks second among active players to Jesse Barfield (one per 8.6 games; minimum: 500 games).... Batted .375 with eight extra-base hits over his first 12 games last season, after working with White Sox hitting instructor Walt Hriniak during the offseason.... Has hit an opening-day home run in three of the last four seasons, missing only 1989.... Needed only seven more home runs to break into Cleveland's all-time top 10. His total of 115 home runs in five seasons with the Indians was slightly more than halfway to the all-time team record of 226, held by Earl Averill.... His home run output has dropped in every season since 1987: 33, 26, 18, 14.... Has a career average of .370 at Memorial Stadium, with 10 home runs in 92 at-bats.... Hopefully, the new Comiskey will be a kinder, gentler ballpark to Snyder, who had a career average of .206 at the old one.... Snyder's dad Jim played second base at Vancouver in 1962. His DP partners were former and future major leaguers—Jose Valdivielso and Al Moran, respectively.

Sammy Sosa

Bats Right

Chicago White Sox	AB	H	2B	3B	HR	RBI	BB	SO	BA	SA	OBA
Season	532	124	26	10	15	70	33	150	.233	.404	.282
vs. Left-Handers	233	61	14	3	12	37	20	59	.262	.502	.316
vs. Right-Handers	299	63	12	7	3	33	13	91	.211	.328	.255
vs. Ground-Ballers	221	50	14	4	3	32	12	57	.226	.367	.271
vs. Fly-Ballers	311	74	12	6	12	38	21	93	.238	.431	.290
Home Games	266	68	15	7	10	36	19	72	.256	.477	.314
Road Games	266	56	11	3	5	34	14	78	.211	.331	.251
Grass Fields	454	104	23	10	14	58	30	125	.229	.416	.280
Artificial Turf	78	20	3	0	1	12	3	25	.256	.333	.294
April	57	17	2	2	2	9	4	16	.298	.509	.333
May	94	20	4	0	2	6	4	28	.213	.319	.250
June	96	30	6	5	3	13	4	25	.313	.573	.350
July	100	19	7	2	2	16	6	29	.190	.360	.236
August	98	18	3	0	3	13	9	24	.184	.306	.259
Sept./Oct.	87	20	4	1	3	13	6	28	.230	.402	.289
Leading Off Inn.	162	34	4	3	5	5	11	47	.210	.364	.269
Bases Empty	311	71	13	5	9	9	21	88	.228	.389	.284
Runners On	221	53	13	5	6	61	12	62	.240	.425	.281
Runners/Scor. Pos.	141	34	9	3	4	53	11	39	.241	.433	.294
Runners On/2 Out	90	25	5	2	3	25	6	21	.278	.478	.337
Scor. Pos./2 Out	63	17	4	1	2	22	5	12	.270	.460	.333
Late-Inning Pressure	69	12	2	0	0	3	3	26	.174	.203	.208
Leading Off	12	2	0	0	0	0	0	4	.167	.167	.167
Runners On	30	4	2	0	0	3	3	14	.133	.200	.212
Runners/Scor. Pos.	22	3	2	0	0	3	3	10	.136	.227	.240

RUNS BATTED IN	From 1B	From 2B	From 3B	Scoring Position
Totals	11/146	23/113	21/59	44/172
Percentage	7.5%	20.4%	35.6%	25.6%

Loves to face: Dave LaPoint (.333, 4-for-12, 2 HR)
Mike Moore (.400, 4-for-10, 1 2B, 1 3B, 1 HR)
Dave West (.556, 5-for-9, 2 2B, 1 3B, 1 HR)

Hates to face: Rick Aguilera (0-for-6, 4 SO)
Charlie Hough (.111, 1-for-9)
Nolan Ryan (0-for-10, 2 BB)

Miscellaneous statistics: Ground outs-to-air outs ratio: 1.17 last season, 1.25 for career.... Grounded into 10 double plays in 91 opportunities (one per 9.1).... Drove in 14 of 29 runners from third base with less than two outs (48%).... Direction of balls hit to the outfield: 35% to left field, 34% to center, 31% to right.... Base running: Advanced from first base to third on 8 of 19 outfield singles (42%); scored from second on 12 of 16 (75%).... Made 2.26 putouts per nine innings in right field.

Comments: There have been 596 "player-seasons" in major league history of double figures in doubles, triples, and home runs. Only nine were by players younger than Sosa; six of those players are in the Hall of Fame. The list: Mike Tiernan, the only 20-year-old (1887), Sam Crawford (1901), Jimmie Foxx (1928), Ben Chapman (1930), Joe Medwick (1933), Joe DiMaggio (1936), Ted Williams (1939), Al Kaline (1956), and Ruben Sierra (1986).... Struck out 150 times, tied for the 4th-highest total in the American League last season, equaling the 2d-highest total in White Sox history. Dave "Swish" Nicholson holds the team record (175 in 1963); Ron Kittle (1983) shares the runner-up spot with Sosa.... Had the lowest fielding percentage (.962) of any American League outfielder last season, committing 13 errors in 152 games (one per 22 chances).... Led the majors in grass-field triples.... Stole 15 bases in 20 attempts with right-handers on the mound (75%), 17 of 28 against left-handers (61%).... Was thrown out trying to advance a base on a batted ball seven times last season, the most of any player on the White Sox.... Has driven in only two of 29 runners from scoring position in Late-Inning Pressure Situations during his career. He has driven in 27 percent at other times.... Career batting-average breakdowns: .283 vs. left-handers, .205 vs. right-handers; .198 in day games, .251 at night.

Bill Spiers

Bats Left

Milwaukee Brewers	AB	H	2B	3B	HR	RBI	BB	SO	BA	SA	OBA
Season	363	88	15	3	2	36	16	45	.242	.317	.274
vs. Left-Handers	81	19	3	1	0	7	5	13	.235	.296	.279
vs. Right-Handers	282	69	12	2	2	29	11	32	.245	.323	.273
vs. Ground-Ballers	176	45	6	2	0	22	8	21	.256	.313	.290
vs. Fly-Ballers	187	43	9	1	2	14	8	24	.230	.321	.259
Home Games	176	47	7	3	2	22	9	19	.267	.375	.305
Road Games	187	41	8	0	0	14	7	26	.219	.262	.245
Grass Fields	312	77	13	3	2	32	12	41	.247	.327	.275
Artificial Turf	51	11	2	0	0	4	4	4	.216	.255	.268
April	0	0	0	0	0	0	0	0	—	—	—
May	39	5	1	0	0	4	2	6	.128	.154	.171
June	89	28	8	1	1	9	5	10	.315	.461	.351
July	80	20	3	0	1	10	4	14	.250	.325	.282
August	67	12	1	1	0	3	3	4	.179	.224	.222
Sept./Oct.	88	23	2	1	0	10	2	11	.261	.307	.275
Leading Off Inn.	105	27	5	1	0	0	0	10	.257	.324	.257
Bases Empty	220	55	9	1	1	1	7	25	.250	.314	.273
Runners On	143	33	6	2	1	35	9	20	.231	.322	.276
Runners/Scor. Pos.	90	23	5	2	0	33	7	14	.256	.356	.300
Runners On/2 Out	62	13	3	1	0	9	4	9	.210	.290	.258
Scor. Pos./2 Out	47	10	3	1	0	9	3	9	.213	.319	.260
Late-Inning Pressure	60	15	0	0	0	6	1	11	.250	.250	.254
Leading Off	18	6	0	0	0	0	0	2	.333	.333	.333
Runners On	23	5	0	0	0	6	1	5	.217	.217	.231
Runners/Scor. Pos.	15	4	0	0	0	6	1	4	.267	.267	.278

RUNS BATTED IN	From 1B	From 2B	From 3B	Scoring Position
Totals	3/98	13/74	18/42	31/116
Percentage	3.1%	17.6%	42.9%	26.7%

Loves to face: Walt Terrell (.600, 3-for-5)
Bob Welch (.417, 5-for-12)

Hates to face: Bert Blyleven (.083, 1-for-12)
Nolan Ryan (.143, 2-for-14)
Dave Stieb (.125, 2-for-16, 3 BB)

Miscellaneous statistics: Ground outs-to-air outs ratio: 1.41 last season, 1.34 for career. . . . Grounded into 12 double plays in 74 opportunities (one per 6.2). . . . Drove in 15 of 25 runners from third base with less than two outs (60%). . . . Direction of balls hit to the outfield: 35% to left field, 35% to center, 29% to right. . . . Base running: Advanced from first base to third on 5 of 8 outfield singles (63%); scored from second on 12 of 13 (92%). . . . Made 3.15 assists per nine innings at shortstop.

Comments: Led off 105 innings without drawing a walk last season, the 5th-highest total in the 16 years that such figures have been compiled. Steve Garvey holds the *Player Analysis* record with 161 leadoff PAs without a walk in 1982. Rounding out the top five: Jody Davis (123 in 1983), Al Oliver (110 in 1975), Tim Foli (109 in 1977), and Spiers. In 1989, Spiers drew eight leadoff walks in 101 plate appearances. . . . Has a career average of .270 at County Stadium, .228 on the road. . . . Had the exact same number of runs (44), hits (88), and total bases (115) in each of his first two seasons in the majors. . . . Spiers committed 12 errors in 111 games at short; teammate Edgar Diaz made 14 errors in only 65 games there. . . . Played 111 games in the field last season, all at shortstop. In 1989, Spiers was moved around the field, starting at least once at all four infield positions, before displacing Gary Sheffield as Milwaukee's regular shortstop. . . . Spiers was the first rookie to start at all four infield positions since Ozzie Chavarria in 1966. Ozzie also started in both right and left field (different games). . . . Played football at Clemson, appearing in the 1986 Gator Bowl with several current NFL players, including Terrence Flagler, Delton Hall, and the Refrigerator's brother, Michael Dean Perry.

Mike Stanley

Bats Right

Texas Rangers	AB	H	2B	3B	HR	RBI	BB	SO	BA	SA	OBA
Season	189	47	8	1	2	19	30	25	.249	.333	.350
vs. Left-Handers	137	38	6	1	2	17	24	18	.277	.380	.385
vs. Right-Handers	52	9	2	0	0	2	6	7	.173	.212	.254
vs. Ground-Ballers	73	18	3	1	0	9	8	12	.247	.315	.317
vs. Fly-Ballers	116	29	5	0	2	10	22	13	.250	.345	.370
Home Games	85	24	4	1	1	10	14	9	.282	.388	.384
Road Games	104	23	4	0	1	9	16	16	.221	.288	.322
Grass Fields	158	42	7	1	2	16	26	21	.266	.361	.368
Artificial Turf	31	5	1	0	0	3	4	4	.161	.194	.257
April	21	5	0	0	1	4	2	3	.238	.381	.304
May	37	5	0	0	1	4	4	1	.135	.216	.214
June	38	9	2	0	0	3	5	7	.237	.289	.326
July	32	11	1	1	0	2	2	2	.344	.438	.382
August	31	12	4	0	0	3	8	5	.387	.516	.513
Sept./Oct.	30	5	1	0	0	3	9	7	.167	.200	.359
Leading Off Inn.	50	12	2	0	0	0	4	8	.240	.280	.296
Bases Empty	106	24	5	0	0	0	15	17	.226	.274	.322
Runners On	83	23	3	1	2	19	15	8	.277	.410	.384
Runners/Scor. Pos.	49	14	2	0	1	15	10	2	.286	.388	.400
Runners On/2 Out	35	5	2	1	0	3	4	4	.143	.257	.231
Scor. Pos./2 Out	23	2	1	0	0	1	3	2	.087	.130	.192
Late-Inning Pressure	22	4	1	0	0	1	9	6	.182	.227	.419
Leading Off	3	1	0	0	0	0	2	1	.333	.333	.600
Runners On	8	2	0	0	0	1	7	2	.250	.250	.600
Runners/Scor. Pos.	6	1	0	0	0	1	5	1	.167	.167	.545

RUNS BATTED IN	From 1B	From 2B	From 3B	Scoring Position
Totals	4/65	7/42	6/17	13/59
Percentage	6.2%	16.7%	35.3%	22.0%

Loves to face: Cecilio Guante (.500, 2-for-4, 2 HR)
Dave West (.750, 6-for-8)

Hates to face: Juan Berenguer (0-for-6, 4 SO)
Randy Johnson (0-for-10, 2 BB)
Jeff Montgomery (0-for-6, 4 SO)

Miscellaneous statistics: Ground outs-to-air outs ratio: 1.25 last season, 1.11 for career. . . . Grounded into 4 double plays in 52 opportunities (one per 13.0). . . . Drove in 6 of 8 runners from third base with less than two outs (75%). . . . Direction of balls hit to the outfield: 17% to left field, 40% to center, 43% to right. . . . Base running: Advanced from first base to third on 4 of 15 outfield singles (27%); scored from second on 6 of 6. . . . Opposing base stealers: 41-for-53 (77%), 2d-highest rate in A.L.

Comments: Started 47 of 53 games in which the Rangers faced a left-handed starter, but only nine of 109 vs. right-handers. The numbers support Bobby Valentine on this one. Stanley has career batting averages of .272 vs. lefties, .227 vs. righties. . . . That makes him a suitable, though marginal, complement for his platoon partner, Gino Petralli. Stanley vs. LHP last season plus Petralli vs. RHP equaled: .260 (115-for-442), 19 2B, 2 3B, 2 HR, 35 RBI, 66 BB, 66 SO. . . . Stanley was removed for a pinch hitter 24 times, all against right-handed pitchers. . . . Of his first 13 starts last season, only four were behind the plate. Three were at third base, and the other six were as the designated hitter. . . . Batted .284 after the All-Star break. . . . Career average in home games (.284) is 65 points higher than in road games (.219). . . . Has a career average of .289 (22-for-76, 2 HR) as a pinch hitter. . . . Has only one hit in 16 career at-bats with two outs and the bases loaded. . . . Career average of .233 with the bases empty, .276 with runners on base. . . . Has stolen six bases over five seasons, which ain't much, but he hasn't been caught at all. . . . Has made only one error in 32 career games at first base.

Terry Steinbach

Bats Right

Oakland A's	AB	H	2B	3B	HR	RBI	BB	SO	BA	SA	OBA
Season	379	95	15	2	9	57	19	66	.251	.372	.291
vs. Left-Handers	109	31	6	1	3	16	8	15	.284	.440	.336
vs. Right-Handers	270	64	9	1	6	41	11	51	.237	.344	.273
vs. Ground-Ballers	196	48	6	2	2	26	12	28	.245	.327	.292
vs. Fly-Ballers	183	47	9	0	7	31	7	38	.257	.421	.290
Home Games	185	46	5	0	3	28	12	33	.249	.324	.302
Road Games	194	49	10	2	6	29	7	33	.253	.418	.281
Grass Fields	315	80	11	0	9	50	17	49	.254	.375	.299
Artificial Turf	64	15	4	2	0	7	2	17	.234	.359	.254
April	53	12	4	0	1	5	4	7	.226	.358	.281
May	83	14	2	0	2	7	4	15	.169	.265	.205
June	83	27	3	2	2	14	3	18	.325	.482	.349
July	22	5	0	0	0	3	2	5	.227	.227	.320
August	75	19	3	0	2	7	2	13	.253	.373	.291
Sept./Oct.	63	18	3	0	2	21	4	8	.286	.429	.329
Leading Off Inn.	71	13	4	1	0	0	9	11	.183	.268	.275
Bases Empty	201	47	9	2	4	4	13	37	.234	.358	.284
Runners On	178	48	6	0	5	53	6	29	.270	.388	.300
Runners/Scor. Pos.	101	30	4	0	2	46	3	17	.297	.396	.321
Runners On/2 Out	84	21	2	0	3	24	4	11	.250	.381	.292
Scor. Pos./2 Out	57	15	1	0	1	20	3	8	.263	.333	.311
Late-Inning Pressure	59	14	1	0	0	6	3	10	.237	.254	.274
Leading Off	12	2	0	0	0	0	1	1	.167	.167	.231
Runners On	26	9	1	0	0	6	1	2	.346	.385	.370
Runners/Scor. Pos.	15	5	1	0	0	6	1	1	.333	.400	.375

RUNS BATTED IN	From 1B	From 2B	From 3B	Scoring Position
Totals	6/146	20/81	22/50	42/131
Percentage	4.1%	24.7%	44.0%	32.1%

Loves to face: Paul Kilgus (.800, 4-for-5, 1 HR)
Cecilio Guante (.500, 2-for-4, 1 HR)
Mark Knudson (.667, 4-for-6, 1 HR)

Hates to face: Mike Henneman (.100, 1-for-10, 5 SO)
Dave Stieb (.083, 1-for-12)
Bobby Witt (0-for-9)

Miscellaneous statistics: Ground outs-to-air outs ratio: 1.03 last season, 1.03 for career. . . . Grounded into 11 double plays in 92 opportunities (one per 8.4). . . . Drove in 14 of 24 runners from third base with less than two outs (58%). . . . Direction of balls hit to the outfield: 36% to left field, 33% to center, 31% to right. . . . Base running: Advanced from first base to third on 8 of 16 outfield singles (50%); scored from second on 6 of 14 (43%), 5th-lowest rate in A.L. . . . Opposing base stealers: 43-for-63 (68%).

Comments: Career-low batting average, but a career high in RBIs despite a 25-day stint on the disabled list in July. . . . Was thrown out trying to advance a base on a batted ball seven times last season, matching the departed Felix Jose for the most on the Athletics. . . . A mediocre career batting average in Late-Inning Pressure Situations masks a favorable breakdown: .294 with runners on base, .205 with the bases empty. . . . Batted .579 (11-for-18) with the bases loaded last season, the highest average and the most hits of any player in the majors. He drove in 57 runs for the season, and 25 of them came with the bags full. He has a .462 career average with the bases loaded (24-for-52), second to Pat Tabler (.500, 40-for-80) among active players. Steinbach has hit a grand slam in each of the last three seasons. . . . Has a career average of .266 at the Oakland Coliseum, .288 on other grass fields, and .233 on artificial surfaces. . . . Career average of .371 (13-for-35, 4 HR) as a pinch hitter. That's four home runs in 35 PH at-bats. . . . Has handled 92 postseason chances without an error. No fewer than five catchers have perfect records on 100 or more chances: Gary Carter (220), Tim McCarver (200), Johnny Roseboro (174), Ray Fosse (119), and Gus Mancuso (106). . . . What must Steinbach have thought about sitting the final game of the 1990 World Series in favor of Jamie Quirk?

Lee Stevens

Bats Left

California Angels	AB	H	2B	3B	HR	RBI	BB	SO	BA	SA	OBA
Season	248	53	10	0	7	32	22	75	.214	.339	.275
vs. Left-Handers	54	11	1	0	1	9	5	19	.204	.278	.267
vs. Right-Handers	194	42	9	0	6	23	17	56	.216	.356	.277
vs. Ground-Ballers	92	16	2	0	1	10	8	31	.174	.228	.235
vs. Fly-Ballers	156	37	8	0	6	22	14	44	.237	.404	.298
Home Games	133	34	6	0	4	20	12	38	.256	.391	.313
Road Games	115	19	4	0	3	12	10	37	.165	.278	.230
Grass Fields	216	46	8	0	6	28	20	67	.213	.333	.276
Artificial Turf	32	7	2	0	1	4	2	8	.219	.375	.265
April	0	0	0	0	0	0	0	0	—	—	—
May	0	0	0	0	0	0	0	0	—	—	—
June	0	0	0	0	0	0	0	0	—	—	—
July	56	13	4	0	2	8	4	16	.232	.411	.283
August	103	24	1	0	3	13	11	29	.233	.330	.304
Sept./Oct.	89	16	5	0	2	11	7	30	.180	.303	.235
Leading Off Inn.	63	17	4	0	2	2	3	19	.270	.429	.303
Bases Empty	134	28	7	0	3	3	10	44	.209	.328	.264
Runners On	114	25	3	0	4	29	12	31	.219	.351	.287
Runners/Scor. Pos.	68	16	2	0	4	28	6	22	.235	.441	.286
Runners On/2 Out	49	10	1	0	4	15	3	17	.204	.469	.250
Scor. Pos./2 Out	36	8	1	0	4	15	1	14	.222	.583	.243
Late-Inning Pressure	37	8	2	0	1	3	6	13	.216	.351	.326
Leading Off	7	2	0	0	0	0	0	3	.286	.286	.286
Runners On	17	2	0	0	1	3	3	6	.118	.294	.250
Runners/Scor. Pos.	11	1	0	0	1	3	1	5	.091	.364	.167

RUNS BATTED IN	From 1B	From 2B	From 3B	Scoring Position
Totals	3/91	11/54	11/30	22/84
Percentage	3.3%	20.4%	36.7%	26.2%

Loves to face: Ron Robinson (3-for-3)
Scott Sanderson (.600, 3-for-5)

Hates to face: Tim Leary (0-for-5, 5 SO)
Dave Stewart (0-for-10)

Miscellaneous statistics: Ground outs-to-air outs ratio: 0.73 last season, his first in the majors. . . . Grounded into 8 double plays in 65 opportunities (one per 8.1). . . . Drove in 10 of 18 runners from third base with less than two outs (56%). . . . Direction of balls hit to the outfield: 36% to left field, 35% to center, 29% to right. . . . Base running: Advanced from first base to third on 3 of 11 outfield singles (27%); scored from second on 4 of 10 (40%), shared 2d-lowest rate in A.L. . . . Made 0.57 assists per nine innings at first base.

Comments: Only 12 players in Angels history had lower batting averages than Stevens's mark last season (minimum: 275 PA). Paul Schaal's .188 average in 1967 is the lowest, but other names among the dirty dozen include Reggie Jackson (.194 in 1983), Roger Repoz (.199 in 1971), and Dick Schofield (.193 in 1984). . . . Was batting .310 after 22 games, but hit only .161 after August 8. . . . Batted .202 from the fifth spot in the order, the 2d lowest of any major leaguer with at least 100 such at-bats. . . . Went hitless in nine at-bats with the bases loaded, including six strikeouts. . . . Batted .130 in day games, .246 at night. . . . Drove in only one of 12 runners from scoring position in Late-Inning Pressure Situations. . . . Among major leaguers with at least 100 at-bats in road games, only the Cubs' Curtis Wilkerson had a lower road game batting average than Stevens. . . . The major league player closest in age to Stevens is Robin Ventura, who is four days younger. . . . From the "Feel Old Dept.": Stevens was born the day before the 15-inning All-Star game in Anaheim, won by the National League when Tony Perez homered off Catfish Hunter. . . . Not a very impressive season, but his numbers are very similar to the numbers posted by Hawk Harrelson in his rookie season. You can look it up.

Kurt Stillwell

Bats Left and Right

Kansas City Royals	AB	H	2B	3B	HR	RBI	BB	SO	BA	SA	OBA
Season	506	126	35	4	3	51	39	60	.249	.352	.304
vs. Left-Handers	128	27	9	2	0	20	17	15	.211	.313	.302
vs. Right-Handers	378	99	26	2	3	31	22	45	.262	.365	.305
vs. Ground-Ballers	227	60	15	1	1	20	16	21	.264	.352	.317
vs. Fly-Ballers	279	66	20	3	2	31	23	39	.237	.351	.293
Home Games	254	68	20	4	3	34	20	32	.268	.413	.319
Road Games	252	58	15	0	0	17	19	28	.230	.290	.289
Grass Fields	211	47	12	0	0	13	15	21	.223	.280	.277
Artificial Turf	295	79	23	4	3	38	24	39	.268	.403	.323
April	57	22	7	1	1	9	5	11	.386	.596	.444
May	99	27	4	1	0	7	15	11	.273	.333	.368
June	87	23	8	2	0	12	5	9	.264	.402	.312
July	99	18	4	0	1	10	4	13	.182	.253	.210
August	87	20	4	0	0	6	3	10	.230	.276	.253
Sept./Oct.	77	16	8	0	1	7	7	6	.208	.351	.276
Leading Off Inn.	91	18	7	0	0	0	7	12	.198	.275	.255
Bases Empty	277	61	20	0	1	1	24	34	.220	.303	.289
Runners On	229	65	15	4	2	50	15	26	.284	.410	.321
Runners/Scor. Pos.	123	30	6	4	1	45	15	16	.244	.382	.310
Runners On/2 Out	91	24	5	3	1	19	6	12	.264	.418	.309
Scor. Pos./2 Out	63	15	2	3	0	16	6	10	.238	.365	.304
Late-Inning Pressure	73	22	4	0	1	4	5	10	.301	.397	.342
Leading Off	13	5	1	0	0	0	2	1	.385	.462	.467
Runners On	27	9	0	0	1	4	0	5	.333	.444	.321
Runners/Scor. Pos.	17	4	0	0	0	2	0	2	.235	.235	.222

RUNS BATTED IN	From 1B	From 2B	From 3B	Scoring Position
Totals	7/164	15/96	26/57	41/153
Percentage	4.3%	15.6%	45.6%	26.8%

Loves to face: Storm Davis (.625, 5-for-8)
Brian Holman (.400, 10-for-25)
Matt Young (.571, 4-for-7)

Hates to face: Jeff D. Robinson (0-for-10)
Bobby Witt (.133, 2-for-15)
Curt Young (.118, 2-for-17)

Miscellaneous statistics: Ground outs-to-air outs ratio: 1.04 last season, 0.91 for career.... Grounded into 11 double plays in 108 opportunities (one per 9.8).... Drove in 18 of 25 runners from third base with less than two outs (72%).... Direction of balls hit to the outfield: 41% to left field, 29% to center, 30% to right batting left-handed; 43% to left, 22% to center, 35% to right batting right-handed.... Base running: Advanced from first base to third on 10 of 25 outfield singles (40%); scored from second on 13 of 14 (93%).... Made 2.76 assists per nine innings at shortstop, lowest rate in A.L.

Comments: Has batted at least 60 points higher with runners on base than with the bases empty in each of the last four seasons. As a rookie in 1986, he batted a career-low 39 points higher with runners on. Career averages: .293 with runners on base, .222 with the bases empty.... Committed 24 errors last season, six more than any other A.L. shortstop. His average of one error per 23 chances was the worst in the league, and considerably worse than his average for the two previous seasons (one per 36 chances).... His career average of one error per 25 chances ranks 18th among 20 active players with at least 500 games at shortstop. The only two players below him are Andres Thomas (one per 24) and Rafael Ramirez (one per 21).... Stole no bases last season, after stealing 25 in his first four seasons.... Batting average from the right side of the plate was the lowest of his career. From the left side, his yearly averages have remained consistent since 1987: .268, .260, .260, .262.... Drove in only two of 23 runners from scoring position in Late-Inning Pressure Situations.... If you want a switch-hitting infielder with a career average of .251, you can take your pick. Three active players meet those specs: Stillwell, Curtis Wilkerson, and Tony Phillips. Or how about Alfredo Griffin, whose career average is one point lower?

B.J. Surhoff

Bats Left

Milwaukee Brewers	AB	H	2B	3B	HR	RBI	BB	SO	BA	SA	OBA
Season	474	131	21	4	6	59	41	37	.276	.376	.331
vs. Left-Handers	104	33	4	1	2	17	8	9	.317	.433	.353
vs. Right-Handers	370	98	17	3	4	42	33	28	.265	.359	.324
vs. Ground-Ballers	200	52	12	1	2	27	21	12	.260	.360	.327
vs. Fly-Ballers	274	79	9	3	4	32	20	25	.288	.387	.333
Home Games	235	72	10	2	4	35	22	18	.306	.417	.364
Road Games	239	59	11	2	2	24	19	19	.247	.335	.298
Grass Fields	406	110	18	3	6	52	35	31	.271	.374	.326
Artificial Turf	68	21	3	1	0	7	6	6	.309	.382	.360
April	47	12	4	1	1	9	5	6	.255	.447	.315
May	75	19	2	0	2	9	7	6	.253	.360	.313
June	100	32	7	1	2	6	2	8	.320	.470	.340
July	70	18	2	0	0	8	9	7	.257	.286	.338
August	74	22	2	1	0	10	6	4	.297	.351	.346
Sept./Oct.	108	28	4	1	1	17	12	6	.259	.343	.328
Leading Off Inn.	115	31	2	0	2	2	5	6	.270	.339	.300
Bases Empty	276	74	10	1	4	4	23	22	.268	.355	.327
Runners On	198	57	11	3	2	55	18	15	.288	.404	.336
Runners/Scor. Pos.	120	33	6	3	2	52	12	13	.275	.425	.324
Runners On/2 Out	81	20	5	1	1	19	10	7	.247	.370	.330
Scor. Pos./2 Out	58	13	4	1	1	18	7	6	.224	.379	.308
Late-Inning Pressure	62	13	3	0	0	7	5	4	.210	.258	.265
Leading Off	12	1	0	0	0	0	1	0	.083	.083	.154
Runners On	30	9	2	0	0	7	2	1	.300	.367	.333
Runners/Scor. Pos.	17	5	1	0	0	6	2	0	.294	.353	.350

RUNS BATTED IN	From 1B	From 2B	From 3B	Scoring Position
Totals	8/139	17/99	28/55	45/154
Percentage	5.8%	17.2%	50.9%	29.2%

Loves to face: Walt Terrell (.333, 9-for-27, 2 HR)
Duane Ward (.500, 4-for-8)
Bobby Witt (.382, 13-for-34, 2 HR)

Hates to face: Mark Langston (.143, 2-for-14)
Jeff Montgomery (0-for-7)
Nolan Ryan (.091, 1-for-11)

Miscellaneous statistics: Ground outs-to-air outs ratio: 1.14 last season, 1.23 for career.... Grounded into 8 double plays in 91 opportunities (one per 11.4).... Drove in 21 of 30 runners from third base with less than two outs (70%).... Direction of balls hit to the outfield: 33% to left field, 36% to center, 31% to right.... Base running: Advanced from first base to third on 12 of 37 outfield singles (32%); scored from second on 9 of 13 (69%).... Opposing base stealers: 89-for-120 (74%), 3d-highest rate in A.L.

Comments: He was the first selection in the June 1985 free-agent draft. The next five selections were Will Clark, Bobby Witt, Barry Larkin, Kurt Brown (White Sox), and Barry Bonds.... Surhoff was one of five A.L. players to start at least 10 games in five different lineup spots.... Has batted with the bases loaded 47 times without drawing a walk.... This lefty swinger has a higher career average vs. southpaws (.278) than he does against right-handers (.262). He has batted over .300 vs. left-handers in three of his four seasons in the majors. His .317 average vs. southpaws last season was the 3d highest in the American League by a left-handed batter (minimum: 100 AB), behind Rafael Palmeiro (.339) and Lance Johnson (.321).... Has stolen 64 bases over the last four seasons, considerably more than some noteworthy base stealers: Ruben Sierra (51), Alan Trammell (50), Alfredo Griffin (49), Andre Dawson (47).... That, along with his occasional appearances at third base, add to his value as a catcher for your fantasy-league team.... Four consecutive seasons of 10 or more steals tied a record for catchers, set by John Wathan from 1980 to 1983.... Brewers pitchers allowed 4.80 runs per nine innings with Surhoff catching, a quarter-run more than with Charlie O'Brien behind the plate.

Danny Tartabull

Bats Right

Kansas City Royals	AB	H	2B	3B	HR	RBI	BB	SO	BA	SA	OBA
Season	313	84	19	0	15	60	36	93	.268	.473	.341
vs. Left-Handers	106	34	5	0	5	17	21	28	.321	.509	.426
vs. Right-Handers	207	50	14	0	10	43	15	65	.242	.454	.291
vs. Ground-Ballers	134	37	10	0	5	26	16	35	.276	.463	.351
vs. Fly-Ballers	179	47	9	0	10	34	20	58	.263	.480	.333
Home Games	142	33	4	0	5	25	13	40	.232	.366	.291
Road Games	171	51	15	0	10	35	23	53	.298	.561	.381
Grass Fields	134	40	12	0	7	23	15	42	.299	.545	.369
Artificial Turf	179	44	7	0	8	37	21	51	.246	.419	.320
April	5	2	0	0	1	2	0	1	.400	1.000	.400
May	42	5	0	0	1	4	3	13	.119	.190	.174
June	89	27	6	0	6	19	9	28	.303	.573	.367
July	27	6	3	0	0	6	4	7	.222	.333	.313
August	100	29	3	0	6	16	14	31	.290	.500	.374
Sept./Oct.	50	15	7	0	1	13	6	13	.300	.500	.375
Leading Off Inn.	69	21	6	0	5	5	6	21	.304	.609	.360
Bases Empty	150	39	9	0	7	7	19	47	.260	.460	.343
Runners On	163	45	10	0	8	53	17	46	.276	.485	.339
Runners/Scor. Pos.	100	26	8	0	3	42	13	30	.260	.430	.336
Runners On/2 Out	72	18	3	0	3	14	10	19	.250	.417	.341
Scor. Pos./2 Out	39	6	1	0	1	9	8	12	.154	.256	.298
Late-Inning Pressure	44	14	5	0	3	7	3	14	.318	.636	.362
Leading Off	10	6	3	0	2	2	0	3	.600	1.500	.600
Runners On	19	6	1	0	1	5	3	5	.316	.526	.409
Runners/Scor. Pos.	9	3	1	0	1	5	3	2	.333	.778	.500

RUNS BATTED IN	From 1B	From 2B	From 3B	Scoring Position
Totals	10/114	14/73	21/49	35/122
Percentage	8.8%	19.2%	42.9%	28.7%

Loves to face: Greg Minton (.800, 4-for-5, 1 HR)
Mike Moore (.462, 6-for-13, 3 2B, 1 HR)
Mike Morgan (.727, 8-for-11, 1 HR)

Hates to face: Juan Berenguer (0-for-12, 4 BB, 8 SO)
Charlie Hough (.152, 5-for-33, 1 HR, 8 BB)
Nolan Ryan (0-for-11)

Miscellaneous statistics: Ground outs-to-air outs ratio: 1.18 last season, 1.07 for career.... Grounded into 9 double plays in 69 opportunities (one per 7.7).... Drove in 16 of 25 runners from third base with less than two outs (64%).... Direction of balls hit to the outfield: 30% to left field, 40% to center, 30% to right.... Base running: Advanced from first base to third on 5 of 19 outfield singles (26%); scored from second on 5 of 9 (56%).... Made 1.75 putouts per nine innings in right field.

Comments: Posted respectable numbers in a injury-filled season of only 88 games. Over the past 50 years, only three players drove in as many as 60 runs in so few games: Hank Greenberg (60 RBIs in 78 games in 1945), Joe DiMaggio (67 RBIs in 76 games in 1949), and Ellis Valentine (67 RBIs in 86 games in 1980).... Drove in only two fewer runs than in 1989, when he played 45 more games.... Visited the disabled list twice, for muscle tears in both legs. His right leg cost him 37 days (April 11–May 18), his left one only 17 days (July 14–31).... Was understandably limited to only one stolen base; he stole 25 over the four previous seasons.... Batted .176 during the first inning, 2d lowest of any player in the American League (minimum: 50 at-bats). He batted nearly twice as high in his second plate appearance of each start (.352) as in his first time up (.181).... Career batting average of .216 with two outs and runners in scoring position. He has batted under .200 in those situations in four of the last six seasons.... Has batted .268 in each of the last two seasons, but in both years he has batted above .300 in Late-Inning Pressure Situations. Owns a .310 career average with runners in scoring position in LIPS.... Has batted .289 or better vs. left-handers in each of the last five seasons.

Mickey Tettleton

Bats Left and Right

Baltimore Orioles	AB	H	2B	3B	HR	RBI	BB	SO	BA	SA	OBA
Season	444	99	21	2	15	51	106	160	.223	.381	.376
vs. Left-Handers	128	30	8	0	5	18	24	50	.234	.414	.351
vs. Right-Handers	316	69	13	2	10	33	82	110	.218	.367	.385
vs. Ground-Ballers	208	49	11	0	7	26	53	73	.236	.389	.396
vs. Fly-Ballers	236	50	10	2	8	25	53	87	.212	.373	.357
Home Games	215	51	11	2	8	27	56	79	.237	.419	.394
Road Games	229	48	10	0	7	24	50	81	.210	.345	.358
Grass Fields	365	84	18	2	15	48	86	131	.230	.414	.379
Artificial Turf	79	15	3	0	0	3	20	29	.190	.228	.360
April	57	12	4	0	0	6	14	26	.211	.281	.366
May	79	20	5	0	5	15	15	28	.253	.506	.379
June	86	24	1	2	6	16	30	29	.279	.547	.463
July	83	12	3	0	1	5	19	31	.145	.217	.304
August	78	16	3	0	0	2	15	23	.205	.244	.337
Sept./Oct.	61	15	5	0	3	7	13	23	.246	.475	.387
Leading Off Inn.	117	21	6	1	3	3	23	44	.179	.325	.314
Bases Empty	247	55	13	2	9	9	45	87	.223	.401	.347
Runners On	197	44	8	0	6	42	61	73	.223	.355	.408
Runners/Scor. Pos.	110	17	3	0	3	34	45	41	.155	.264	.401
Runners On/2 Out	94	19	3	0	2	12	30	31	.202	.298	.400
Scor. Pos./2 Out	57	7	0	0	2	10	23	20	.123	.228	.383
Late-Inning Pressure	72	16	2	0	6	11	17	25	.222	.500	.374
Leading Off	17	2	0	0	1	1	7	5	.118	.294	.375
Runners On	30	5	0	0	2	7	7	16	.167	.367	.333
Runners/Scor. Pos.	16	2	0	0	0	3	4	8	.125	.125	.318

RUNS BATTED IN	From 1B	From 2B	From 3B	Scoring Position
Totals	8/150	11/93	17/48	28/141
Percentage	5.3%	11.8%	35.4%	19.9%

Loves to face: Jerry Reuss (.364, 4-for-11, 1 2B, 2 HR)
Mike Moore (.313, 10-for-32)
Bobby Witt (.350, 7-for-20)

Hates to face: Bert Blyleven (.056, 1-for-18, 1 3B, 3 BB)
Mark Langston (.194, 6-for-31)
Jeff Russell (0-for-7)

Miscellaneous statistics: Ground outs-to-air outs ratio: 0.96 last season, 1.18 for career.... Grounded into 7 double plays in 108 opportunities (one per 15.4).... Drove in 15 of 28 runners from third base with less than two outs (54%).... Direction of balls hit to the outfield: 21% to left field, 25% to center, 54% to right batting left-handed; 45% to left, 28% to center, 28% to right batting right-handed.... Base running: Advanced from first base to third on 8 of 34 outfield singles (24%); scored from second on 15 of 21 (71%).... Opposing base stealers: 55-for-76 (72%), 4th-highest rate in A.L.

Comments: Major league home run leaders in Late-Inning Pressure Situations: Dwight Evans (7), Kevin Mitchell (7), Tettleton (6), Bo Jackson (6), Franklin Stubbs (6).... July batting average was the lowest in the American League.... Ranked second in the league with 106 walks. The only catcher ever to lead the league in walks was Darrell Porter (1979).... Had 271 plate appearances in which he didn't put the ball in play (106 walks, 160 strikeouts, five hit by pitch). See page 24 for the PAWOP-BIP honor roll.... Drew five walks with the bases loaded last season, the most in the majors. He has batted 69 times with the bases loaded in seven seasons, and put only 33 balls in play. He's drawn 15 walks and struck out 21 times. His batting average with the bags full: .154 (8-for-52, 0 HR).... Career batting average with runners in scoring position (.185) is 17 points lower than Fernando Valenzuela's (.202). His 1990 average with RISP was the lowest of any American Leaguer since Paul Blair's mark of .154 in 1975 (minimum: 100 at-bats). In seven seasons in the majors, he has never hit above .218 with RISP.... His .123 average with two outs and RISP was one point better than in 1989.... Only three switch hitters active in 1990 have career batting averages worse than Tettleton's .236 mark (minimum: 1000 AB): Al Newman (.232), Otis Nixon (.228), and Steve Jeltz (.210).

Frank Thomas

Bats Right

Chicago White Sox	AB	H	2B	3B	HR	RBI	BB	SO	BA	SA	OBA
Season	191	63	11	3	7	31	44	54	.330	.529	.454
vs. Left-Handers	71	29	6	1	5	12	21	17	.408	.732	.538
vs. Right-Handers	120	34	5	2	2	19	23	37	.283	.408	.401
vs. Ground-Ballers	86	24	4	0	2	11	23	19	.279	.395	.423
vs. Fly-Ballers	105	39	7	3	5	20	21	35	.371	.638	.481
Home Games	73	25	4	2	2	13	26	24	.342	.534	.510
Road Games	118	38	7	1	5	18	18	30	.322	.525	.413
Grass Fields	141	46	9	3	5	27	36	43	.326	.539	.462
Artificial Turf	50	17	2	0	2	4	8	11	.340	.500	.431
April	0	0	0	0	0	0	0	0	—	—	—
May	0	0	0	0	0	0	0	0	—	—	—
June	0	0	0	0	0	0	0	0	—	—	—
July	0	0	0	0	0	0	0	0	—	—	—
August	89	27	7	3	2	13	21	22	.303	.517	.436
Sept./Oct.	102	36	4	0	5	18	23	32	.353	.539	.469
Leading Off Inn.	47	14	5	1	3	3	9	19	.298	.638	.411
Bases Empty	104	32	7	1	5	5	23	32	.308	.538	.433
Runners On	87	31	4	2	2	26	21	22	.356	.517	.478
Runners/Scor. Pos.	53	18	1	2	1	24	11	15	.340	.491	.441
Runners On/2 Out	40	15	1	2	1	14	8	8	.375	.575	.490
Scor. Pos./2 Out	26	10	1	2	1	14	5	6	.385	.692	.484
Late-Inning Pressure	21	8	2	1	1	7	5	9	.381	.714	.500
Leading Off	6	2	1	0	0	0	3	2	.333	.500	.556
Runners On	10	4	1	1	0	6	2	4	.400	.700	.500
Runners/Scor. Pos.	8	3	0	1	0	6	2	4	.375	.625	.500

RUNS BATTED IN	From 1B	From 2B	From 3B	Scoring Position
Totals	4/57	8/38	12/26	20/64
Percentage	7.0%	21.1%	46.2%	31.3%

Loves to face: Randy Johnson (.400, 2-for-5, 1 HR)
Matt Young (.400, 2-for-5, 3 BB)

Hates to face: Jeff Montgomery (0-for-3, 2 SO)
Nolan Ryan (0-for-4, 4 SO)

Miscellaneous statistics: Ground outs-to-air outs ratio: 0.95 last season, his first in the majors. . . . Grounded into 5 double plays in 43 opportunities (one per 8.6). . . . Drove in 6 of 12 runners from third base with less than two outs (50%). . . . Direction of balls hit to the outfield: 33% to left field, 34% to center, 34% to right. . . . Base running: Advanced from first base to third on 2 of 12 outfield singles (17%); scored from second on 9 of 9. . . . Made 0.56 assists per nine innings at first base.

Comments: His 13-game hitting-streak was the longest by an American League rookie last season. . . . Drove in 31 runs (in only 60 games), nine of which broke a tie to give the White Sox a lead. Compare that to Carlos Martinez, who drove in 24 runs, but had only one go-ahead RBI all season. . . . The only other active players who, as rookies, drove in at least 30 runs in as few as 60 games: Eric Davis (30 RBIs in 57 games in 1984) and Sam Horn (34 RBIs in 46 games in 1987); 19 other rookies to do so in this century run the gamut from Dick Gray to Willie McCovey. . . . Drove in five of nine runners from scoring position in Late-Inning Pressure Situations. . . . Averaged one walk per 5.5 plate appearances, 3d-best rate among A.L. players. . . . Sixth youngest American Leaguer to play at least 50 games last season, but only the 2d youngest on his own team to do so, thanks to Sammy Sosa. . . . Only two White Sox rookies in the last 50 years have batted .330 or better in a season of at least 175 at-bats: Thomas and Taffy Wright (.333 in 1942). . . . By the method described in the Expos essay, Thomas rates a 13 percent chance of reaching 2000 hits for his career, and a 29 percent chance of batting .300 or better. . . . Comparable rookie seasons: Nap Lajoie (1896), Tommy Henrich (1937), Ron Blomberg (1971), and Kal Daniels (1986).

Alan Trammell

Bats Right

Detroit Tigers	AB	H	2B	3B	HR	RBI	BB	SO	BA	SA	OBA
Season	559	170	37	1	14	89	68	55	.304	.449	.377
vs. Left-Handers	173	50	11	1	7	27	23	14	.289	.486	.367
vs. Right-Handers	386	120	26	0	7	62	45	41	.311	.433	.382
vs. Ground-Ballers	247	80	17	1	8	44	22	22	.324	.498	.377
vs. Fly-Ballers	312	90	20	0	6	45	46	33	.288	.410	.377
Home Games	271	92	18	1	9	59	36	24	.339	.513	.413
Road Games	288	78	19	0	5	30	32	31	.271	.389	.342
Grass Fields	470	145	32	1	11	83	61	44	.309	.451	.385
Artificial Turf	89	25	5	0	3	6	7	11	.281	.438	.333
April	80	26	7	1	1	11	11	9	.325	.475	.407
May	100	29	4	0	2	17	14	12	.290	.390	.371
June	108	32	2	0	3	18	12	12	.296	.398	.364
July	93	30	8	0	1	10	19	7	.323	.441	.442
August	103	36	13	0	6	21	7	7	.350	.650	.384
Sept./Oct.	75	17	3	0	1	12	5	8	.227	.307	.272
Leading Off Inn.	100	25	5	0	4	4	4	11	.250	.420	.279
Bases Empty	296	82	18	1	7	7	31	34	.277	.416	.346
Runners On	263	88	19	0	7	82	37	21	.335	.487	.410
Runners/Scor. Pos.	145	55	12	0	4	75	26	12	.379	.545	.461
Runners On/2 Out	79	25	3	0	2	25	13	5	.316	.430	.419
Scor. Pos./2 Out	57	18	3	0	2	25	11	5	.316	.474	.435
Late-Inning Pressure	63	21	7	0	1	12	8	9	.333	.492	.417
Leading Off	14	5	0	0	0	0	1	3	.357	.357	.400
Runners On	37	12	6	0	0	11	5	4	.324	.486	.419
Runners/Scor. Pos.	22	8	4	0	0	11	5	3	.364	.545	.500

RUNS BATTED IN	From 1B	From 2B	From 3B	Scoring Position
Totals	10/189	30/113	35/65	65/178
Percentage	5.3%	26.5%	53.8%	36.5%

Loves to face: Greg A. Harris (.455, 10-for-22)
Duane Ward (.714, 5-for-7)
Matt Young (.393, 11-for-28, 1 HR)

Hates to face: Bert Blyleven (.234, 15-for-64, 1 HR)
Dennis Lamp (.237, 9-for-38)
Bobby Witt (.148, 4-for-27, 5 BB)

Miscellaneous statistics: Ground outs-to-air outs ratio: 0.77 last season, 0.81 for career. . . . Grounded into 11 double plays in 161 opportunities (one per 14.6). . . . Drove in 26 of 40 runners from third base with less than two outs (65%). . . . Direction of balls hit to the outfield: 40% to left field, 28% to center, 32% to right. . . . Base running: Advanced from first base to third on 16 of 32 outfield singles (50%); scored from second on 14 of 16 (88%). . . . Made 3.03 assists per nine innings at shortstop.

Comments: Needs 71 hits to become the sixth player in Tigers club history to reach 2000. The top five: Ty Cobb (3902), Al Kaline (3007), Charlie Gehringer (2839), Harry Heilmann (2499), and Sam Crawford (2466). Lou Whitaker is 169 hits shy of 2000. Of the 26 franchises in baseball, only the Pirates have more than six players with 2000 hits. They have eight: Roberto Clemente, Honus Wagner, Paul Waner, Max Carey, Pie Traynor, Lloyd Waner, Willie Stargell, and Bill Mazeroski. . . . Increased his overall average 61 points from the previous season, the largest gain by any A.L. player with at least 300 at-bats in both 1989 and 1990. . . . Batted 102 points higher with runners in scoring position (.379) than in other at-bats (.278) last season, the 3d-largest margin in the majors. . . . Drove in 36.5 percent of runners from scoring position, the 2d-highest rate in the A.L. last season, and the highest rate of his career. . . . Batted 68 points higher in Late-Inning Pressure Situations (.357) than in other at-bats (.289) over the last five seasons, the 4th-largest margin in the majors. His LIPS average was higher than his overall average in each of those five seasons. . . . Oldest regular shortstop in the American League, but not in the majors. Older N.L. shortstops: Ozzie Smith, Garry Templeton, Alfredo Griffin, and Rafael Ramirez. . . . Participated in 102 double plays last season, the first time in his 14-year career that Trammell reached the 100 mark.

Dave Valle

Bats Right

Seattle Mariners	AB	H	2B	3B	HR	RBI	BB	SO	BA	SA	OBA
Season	308	66	15	0	7	33	45	48	.214	.331	.328
vs. Left-Handers	104	21	4	0	2	10	14	17	.202	.298	.308
vs. Right-Handers	204	45	11	0	5	23	31	31	.221	.348	.338
vs. Ground-Ballers	122	29	4	0	2	13	14	26	.238	.320	.340
vs. Fly-Ballers	186	37	11	0	5	20	31	22	.199	.339	.320
Home Games	131	26	9	0	1	13	23	21	.198	.290	.340
Road Games	177	40	6	0	6	20	22	27	.226	.362	.318
Grass Fields	139	32	3	0	6	18	15	26	.230	.381	.310
Artificial Turf	169	34	12	0	1	15	30	22	.201	.290	.341
April	56	14	2	0	3	7	4	8	.250	.446	.311
May	39	11	4	0	0	6	7	6	.282	.385	.391
June	31	6	1	0	1	4	1	6	.194	.323	.219
July	58	9	2	0	0	6	6	8	.155	.190	.258
August	57	9	0	0	2	4	8	10	.158	.263	.284
Sept./Oct.	67	17	6	0	1	6	19	10	.254	.388	.432
Leading Off Inn.	74	12	4	0	2	2	9	10	.162	.297	.253
Bases Empty	165	35	10	0	5	5	25	22	.212	.364	.323
Runners On	143	31	5	0	2	28	20	26	.217	.294	.333
Runners/Scor. Pos.	90	21	4	0	1	25	10	16	.233	.311	.337
Runners On/2 Out	52	10	2	0	0	11	9	12	.192	.231	.323
Scor. Pos./2 Out	38	9	2	0	0	11	5	9	.237	.289	.341
Late-Inning Pressure	41	7	3	0	0	0	6	8	.171	.244	.320
Leading Off	15	3	2	0	0	0	1	1	.200	.333	.250
Runners On	12	2	0	0	0	0	3	1	.167	.167	.412
Runners/Scor. Pos.	6	1	0	0	0	0	2	1	.167	.167	.444

RUNS BATTED IN	From 1B	From 2B	From 3B	Scoring Position
Totals	3/109	14/76	9/34	23/110
Percentage	2.8%	18.4%	26.5%	20.9%

Loves to face: John Candelaria (.400, 4-for-10, 2 2B, 1 HR)
Nolan Ryan (.375, 3-for-8, 1 HR)
Scott Sanderson (.500, 3-for-6, 1 2B, 1 BB)

Hates to face: Allan Anderson (.077, 1-for-13)
Dennis Eckersley (0-for-6)
Dave Stewart (.100, 1-for-10)

Miscellaneous statistics: Ground outs-to-air outs ratio: 1.13 last season, 1.33 for career. . . . Grounded into 11 double plays in 85 opportunities (one per 7.7). . . . Drove in 6 of 19 runners from third base with less than two outs (32%), lowest rate in majors. . . . Direction of balls hit to the outfield: 53% to left field, 24% to center, 24% to right. . . . Base running: Advanced from first base to third on 2 of 15 outfield singles (13%); scored from second on 9 of 14 (64%). . . . Opposing base stealers: 65-for-93 (70%).

Comments: August batting average was lowest in the American League. . . . Had 11 at-bats with the bases loaded, the most among players without a hit in that situation last season. . . . Was thrown out trying to advance a base on a batted ball five times last season, tied with Harold Reynolds for the most of any player on the Mariners. . . . Ended the season with 93 consecutive errorless games behind the plate, the longest streak by any catcher in the majors last season. The all-time record for catchers is 159 games by Rick Cerone. . . . Led major league catchers with a .997 fielding percentage, commiting only two errors in 677 chances. . . . Combined with the rest of the Mariners' backstops for a .225 batting average, the lowest of any catching corps in the league. . . . He's the Mariners all-time leader with 412 games played behind the plate. And they've had some great ones. . . . Has hit for a higher average against ground-ball pitchers than he has against fly-ball pitchers in each of the last six seasons. Career averages: .248 vs. ground-ballers, .226 vs. fly-ballers. . . . Has hit for a higher average with runners on base than with the bases empty in each of his seven seasons in the majors. Career breakdown: .207 with the bases empty, .273 with runners on base, .284 with runners in scoring position. . . . Has more career home runs on the road (22) than he has in the Kingdome (20).

Greg Vaughn

Bats Right

Milwaukee Brewers	AB	H	2B	3B	HR	RBI	BB	SO	BA	SA	OBA
Season	382	84	26	2	17	61	33	91	.220	.432	.280
vs. Left-Handers	127	25	10	1	4	12	10	29	.197	.386	.254
vs. Right-Handers	255	59	16	1	13	49	23	62	.231	.455	.292
vs. Ground-Ballers	160	42	14	2	10	39	10	29	.262	.563	.301
vs. Fly-Ballers	222	42	12	0	7	22	23	62	.189	.338	.265
Home Games	193	42	13	1	9	32	17	42	.218	.435	.277
Road Games	189	42	13	1	8	29	16	49	.222	.429	.282
Grass Fields	343	76	23	2	16	56	32	79	.222	.440	.286
Artificial Turf	39	8	3	0	1	5	1	12	.205	.359	.220
April	51	14	6	0	1	9	5	13	.275	.451	.333
May	42	8	2	0	3	11	9	9	.190	.452	.327
June	66	17	6	1	1	6	3	15	.258	.424	.296
July	92	19	4	1	5	18	8	27	.207	.435	.267
August	36	4	1	0	1	2	0	10	.111	.222	.108
Sept./Oct.	95	22	7	0	6	15	8	17	.232	.495	.288
Leading Off Inn.	92	15	3	0	5	5	7	21	.163	.359	.222
Bases Empty	210	40	8	2	10	10	12	51	.190	.390	.234
Runners On	172	44	18	0	7	51	21	40	.256	.483	.330
Runners/Scor. Pos.	92	26	12	0	4	43	13	25	.283	.543	.351
Runners On/2 Out	70	13	5	0	3	15	9	21	.186	.386	.278
Scor. Pos./2 Out	38	7	3	0	2	12	6	12	.184	.421	.295
Late-Inning Pressure	35	5	2	0	2	6	3	9	.143	.371	.205
Leading Off	8	1	0	0	1	1	0	1	.125	.500	.125
Runners On	16	3	1	0	1	5	3	4	.188	.438	.300
Runners/Scor. Pos.	10	1	0	0	0	2	3	3	.100	.100	.286

RUNS BATTED IN	From 1B	From 2B	From 3B	Scoring Position
Totals	8/134	18/70	18/47	36/117
Percentage	6.0%	25.7%	38.3%	30.8%

Loves to face: Dennis Lamp (.400, 4-for-10, 2 2B)
Mike Moore (.500, 2-for-4, 1 3B)

Hates to face: Brian Holman (0-for-5)
Nolan Ryan (0-for-7)

Miscellaneous statistics: Ground outs-to-air outs ratio: 0.93 last season, 0.94 for career. . . . Grounded into 11 double plays in 94 opportunities (one per 8.5). . . . Drove in 16 of 31 runners from third base with less than two outs (52%). . . . Direction of balls hit to the outfield: 59% to left field, 24% to center, 17% to right. . . . Base running: Advanced from first base to third on 5 of 14 outfield singles (36%); scored from second on 8 of 10 (80%). . . . Made 2.11 putouts per nine innings in left field.

Comments: Led American League rookies with 45 extra-base hits, a far cry from Hal Trosky's rookie record of 89 XBH in 1934. . . . Had a streak of 38 consecutive hitless at-bats from late July to mid-August. Only Robin Ventura (0-for-41) had a longer hitless streak last season. . . . Batted 83 points higher with runners in scoring position (.283) than in other at-bats (.200) last season, the 4th-largest margin in the majors. . . . His one opposite field home run was the only one by a Brewers player other than Robin Yount. . . . Vaughn and Todd Zeile were the only two players in the majors to start at least 20 games from each of four different batting order positions. Vaughn regularly found himself batting anywhere from fifth through eighth, but exactly where, only Tom Trebelhorn knew. . . . Career batting averages of .192 in day games, .243 at night. . . . Platoon him at your own risk: His career average is only .201 against left-handed pitchers. He was one of four right-handed batters in the American League to hit below .200 against southpaws last season (minimum: 100 AB). The others: Luis Rivera, Mike Gallego, and Ken Williams. . . . Comparable rookie seasons: Daryl Spencer (1953), Ron Swoboda (1965), and John Milner (1972).

Randy Velarde

Bats Right

New York Yankees	AB	H	2B	3B	HR	RBI	BB	SO	BA	SA	OBA
Season	229	48	6	2	5	19	20	53	.210	.319	.275
vs. Left-Handers	65	18	2	1	1	2	4	15	.277	.385	.314
vs. Right-Handers	164	30	4	1	4	17	16	38	.183	.293	.260
vs. Ground-Ballers	94	21	4	1	1	5	5	16	.223	.319	.263
vs. Fly-Ballers	135	27	2	1	4	14	15	37	.200	.319	.283
Home Games	105	22	4	0	1	9	14	23	.210	.276	.306
Road Games	124	26	2	2	4	10	6	30	.210	.355	.246
Grass Fields	188	43	6	1	5	19	17	42	.229	.351	.295
Artificial Turf	41	5	0	1	0	0	3	11	.122	.171	.182
April	16	2	1	0	0	0	3	4	.125	.188	.300
May	47	9	0	1	0	1	5	10	.191	.234	.269
June	49	11	1	1	1	4	1	8	.224	.347	.240
July	21	3	1	0	0	0	3	8	.143	.190	.250
August	28	7	1	0	2	6	2	7	.250	.500	.300
Sept./Oct.	68	16	2	0	2	8	6	16	.235	.353	.293
Leading Off Inn.	56	8	2	0	0	0	4	19	.143	.179	.200
Bases Empty	138	26	3	1	1	1	13	35	.188	.246	.258
Runners On	91	22	3	1	4	18	7	18	.242	.429	.300
Runners/Scor. Pos.	54	11	2	0	3	15	4	13	.204	.407	.267
Runners On/2 Out	44	7	1	1	1	6	2	13	.159	.295	.213
Scor. Pos./2 Out	31	3	1	0	1	5	1	10	.097	.226	.152
Late-Inning Pressure	33	7	3	0	1	2	5	8	.212	.394	.316
Leading Off	9	2	1	0	0	0	0	3	.222	.333	.222
Runners On	12	4	1	0	1	2	2	2	.333	.667	.429
Runners/Scor. Pos.	8	1	0	0	1	2	1	2	.125	.500	.222

RUNS BATTED IN	From 1B	From 2B	From 3B	Scoring Position
Totals	4/65	4/41	6/21	10/62
Percentage	6.2%	9.8%	28.6%	16.1%

Loves to face: Terry Clark (.500, 2-for-4, 2 2B)
Duane Ward (.667, 2-for-3, 1 3B)

Hates to face: Jeff Montgomery (0-for-5, 3 SO)
Dave Stewart (.091, 1-for-11, 1 2B)
Bob Welch (0-for-7)

Miscellaneous statistics: Ground outs-to-air outs ratio: 1.40 last season, 1.58 for career.... Grounded into 6 double plays in 42 opportunities (one per 7.0).... Drove in 5 of 7 runners from third base with less than two outs (71%).... Direction of balls hit to the outfield: 27% to left field, 37% to center, 36% to right.... Base running: Advanced from first base to third on 4 of 8 outfield singles (50%); scored from second on 3 of 4 (75%).... Made 2.34 assists per nine innings at third base.

Comments: His career batting average settles in at .227 after compiling marks as high as .340 (1989) and as low as .174 (1988) in parts of four seasons.... Yankees third base corps consisted of three players, each of whose fielding percentage was below the major league average for third basemen (.946, one error per 18.2 chances): Velarde (.945, one error per 18.1 chances), Jim Leyritz (.929, one per 14.1 chances), and Mike Blowers (.899, one per 9.9 chances).... Velarde started 10 double plays at third base while playing fewer innings than Leyritz, who started only four.... Yankees need more offense from third base in 1991. Their .226 batting average from that position ranked 13th in the league, ahead of only the Rangers (.210), and their 49 RBIs also ranked next to last, ahead of the Royals (44).... Drove in only 10 of 62 runners from scoring position last season, the 4th-lowest percentage among A.L. players with at least 50 opportunities.... Career average of .247 on grass fields, .098 on artificial surfaces (6-for-61).... Hitless in 19 career at-bats at Royals Stadium.... Has stolen only one base in 184 career games; has been caught seven times.

Max Venable

Bats Left

California Angels	AB	H	2B	3B	HR	RBI	BB	SO	BA	SA	OBA
Season	189	49	9	3	4	21	24	31	.259	.402	.340
vs. Left-Handers	25	6	2	0	0	4	3	6	.240	.320	.321
vs. Right-Handers	164	43	7	3	4	17	21	25	.262	.415	.342
vs. Ground-Ballers	75	19	3	1	2	8	10	13	.253	.400	.337
vs. Fly-Ballers	114	30	6	2	2	13	14	18	.263	.404	.341
Home Games	84	21	5	1	3	8	13	12	.250	.440	.347
Road Games	105	28	4	2	1	13	11	19	.267	.371	.333
Grass Fields	167	43	8	2	4	18	19	27	.257	.401	.330
Artificial Turf	22	6	1	1	0	3	5	4	.273	.409	.407
April	20	3	2	0	0	0	2	5	.150	.250	.227
May	26	12	1	0	2	3	2	5	.462	.731	.500
June	36	10	2	0	0	4	4	3	.278	.333	.350
July	43	11	1	1	1	6	3	9	.256	.395	.298
August	33	6	1	1	1	5	5	4	.182	.364	.282
Sept./Oct.	31	7	2	1	0	3	8	5	.226	.355	.385
Leading Off Inn.	49	9	1	1	1	1	5	9	.184	.306	.259
Bases Empty	114	30	6	1	4	4	11	17	.263	.439	.328
Runners On	75	19	3	2	0	17	13	14	.253	.347	.356
Runners/Scor. Pos.	40	11	2	2	0	17	11	6	.275	.425	.415
Runners On/2 Out	26	10	2	0	0	9	6	8	.385	.462	.500
Scor. Pos./2 Out	19	8	2	0	0	9	6	5	.421	.526	.560
Late-Inning Pressure	37	6	1	0	0	3	5	7	.162	.189	.262
Leading Off	13	0	0	0	0	0	1	2	.000	.000	.071
Runners On	15	3	1	0	0	3	4	3	.200	.267	.368
Runners/Scor. Pos.	8	2	1	0	0	3	4	1	.250	.375	.500

RUNS BATTED IN	From 1B	From 2B	From 3B	Scoring Position
Totals	2/57	6/29	9/18	15/47
Percentage	3.5%	20.7%	50.0%	31.9%

Loves to face: Mark Knudson (.500, 7-for-14, 1 HR)
Greg Minton (.600, 3-for-5, 1 HR)

Hates to face: Steve Bedrosian (.100, 1-for-10)
Bill Gullickson (.125, 2-for-16)
Bob Welch (.238, 5-for-21)

Miscellaneous statistics: Ground outs-to-air outs ratio: 1.20 last season, 0.96 for career.... Grounded into 3 double plays in 47 opportunities (one per 15.7).... Drove in 5 of 9 runners from third base with less than two outs (56%).... Direction of balls hit to the outfield: 30% to left field, 28% to center, 43% to right.... Base running: Advanced from first base to third on 7 of 15 outfield singles (47%); scored from second on 2 of 5 (40%).... Made 2.42 putouts per nine innings in center field.

Comments: Played 93 games last season, his 3d-highest total in 11 major league seasons. It was only the third time in his 14 seasons in professional ball that he was spared the honor of touring the minors.... Started 40 games last season, but only one against a left-handed pitcher.... Has hit 15 career home runs, all against right-handed pitchers. He has only three extra-base hits, all doubles, in 128 career at-bats vs. left-handers.... Rate of walks (one per 9.3 plate appearances) was much higher than in 1989, when he walked only once in 57 plate appearances.... Has hit for a higher average in night games than he has in day games in each of the last six seasons, matching Brook Jacoby for the longest current streak. That's one year shy of the *Player Analysis* record, held by Mitchell Page.... We'll probably be accused of jumping the gun on this one, but there are certain facts that are essential to a proper understanding of baseball. So here goes: Having made his debut in 1979, Venable is three-quarters of the way to becoming a four-decade player.... How many pairs of ballplayers have been named after consecutive 19th-century presidents? How about Grover Cleveland Alexander and William McKinley Venable?

Robin Ventura

Bats Left

Chicago White Sox	AB	H	2B	3B	HR	RBI	BB	SO	BA	SA	OBA
Season	493	123	17	1	5	54	55	53	.249	.318	.324
vs. Left-Handers	154	34	2	1	0	12	22	26	.221	.247	.315
vs. Right-Handers	339	89	15	0	5	42	33	27	.263	.351	.329
vs. Ground-Ballers	217	56	7	0	2	31	24	17	.258	.318	.329
vs. Fly-Ballers	276	67	10	1	3	23	31	36	.243	.319	.320
Home Games	238	65	4	1	2	25	27	24	.273	.324	.348
Road Games	255	58	13	0	3	29	28	29	.227	.314	.302
Grass Fields	427	108	14	1	4	46	45	46	.253	.319	.324
Artificial Turf	66	15	3	0	1	8	10	7	.227	.318	.325
April	42	7	1	1	1	3	8	10	.167	.310	.314
May	72	13	1	0	2	7	11	8	.181	.278	.289
June	94	28	5	0	0	11	10	15	.298	.351	.365
July	107	28	3	0	1	11	6	7	.262	.318	.301
August	75	13	2	0	0	7	10	8	.173	.200	.267
Sept./Oct.	103	34	5	0	1	15	10	5	.330	.408	.383
Leading Off Inn.	100	24	3	0	1	1	9	10	.240	.300	.303
Bases Empty	305	66	9	1	2	2	36	37	.216	.272	.299
Runners On	188	57	8	0	3	52	19	16	.303	.394	.365
Runners/Scor. Pos.	120	36	3	0	0	43	16	15	.300	.325	.379
Runners On/2 Out	85	24	2	0	0	20	7	8	.282	.306	.337
Scor. Pos./2 Out	61	19	1	0	0	20	6	8	.311	.328	.373
Late-Inning Pressure	62	15	0	0	1	7	6	10	.242	.290	.309
Leading Off	21	7	0	0	0	0	2	3	.333	.333	.391
Runners On	20	5	0	0	0	6	0	3	.250	.250	.250
Runners/Scor. Pos.	16	4	0	0	0	6	0	3	.250	.250	.250

RUNS BATTED IN	From 1B	From 2B	From 3B	Scoring Position
Totals	6/114	18/93	25/56	43/149
Percentage	5.3%	19.4%	44.6%	28.9%

Loves to face: Tim Leary (.600, 3-for-5)
Scott Sanderson (.500, 4-for-8)

Hates to face: Mark Knudson (0-for-5)
Nolan Ryan (0-for-7, 3 BB, 4 SO)

Miscellaneous statistics: Ground outs-to-air outs ratio: 1.27 last season, 1.28 for career. . . . Grounded into 5 double plays in 82 opportunities (one per 16.4). . . . Drove in 17 of 28 runners from third base with less than two outs (61%). . . . Direction of balls hit to the outfield: 38% to left field, 37% to center, 25% to right. . . . Base running: Advanced from first base to third on 8 of 22 outfield singles (36%); scored from second on 7 of 9 (78%). . . . Made 1.99 assists per nine innings at third base.

Comments: Led major league rookies in games (150) and games started (135). . . . One of five A.L. rookies in opening-day lineups last season. The others: Sandy Alomar (Clev.), Mike Blowers (N.Y.), John Olerud (Tor.), and Billy Bates (Mil.). . . Ventura had a 58-game hitting streak as a sophomore at Oklahoma State, but so far is no threat to Joltin' Joe as a major leaguer. His longest hitting streak last season was seven games. . . . Snapped an 0-for-41 streak with a hit against Bret Saberhagen in May. That was the longest streak of hitless at-bats in the American League since Tony Bernazard went 0-for-44 in 1984. . . . Was promoted from the eighth spot in the batting order to the second slot in late May, a time at which his batting average stood at .135. But Ventura went on to bat .274 in 74 games from that spot in the order. . . . Stole only one base in five attempts. . . . Committed 25 errors last season, the most by a rookie third baseman since Dale Sveum committed 26 in 1986. Ventura can take comfort in the fact that Dick Allen committed 41 errors at that position as a rookie with the Phillies in 1964. . . . Has only one hit in 25 career at-bats at Royals Stadium. . . . Comparable season to those of many rookies in the mid-1970s: Mike Tyson (1973), Dave Chalk (1974), Manny Trillo (1975), Jerry Royster (1976), and Craig Reynolds (1977).

Omar Vizquel

Bats Left and Right

Seattle Mariners	AB	H	2B	3B	HR	RBI	BB	SO	BA	SA	OBA
Season	255	63	3	2	2	18	18	22	.247	.298	.295
vs. Left-Handers	81	19	2	0	1	8	5	8	.235	.296	.279
vs. Right-Handers	174	44	1	2	1	10	13	14	.253	.299	.302
vs. Ground-Ballers	102	30	1	1	1	5	10	12	.294	.353	.357
vs. Fly-Ballers	153	33	2	1	1	13	8	10	.216	.261	.252
Home Games	114	27	2	0	0	6	11	14	.237	.254	.299
Road Games	141	36	1	2	2	12	7	8	.255	.333	.291
Grass Fields	100	26	1	1	1	7	6	7	.260	.320	.302
Artificial Turf	155	37	2	1	1	11	12	15	.239	.284	.290
April	0	0	0	0	0	0	0	0	—	—	—
May	0	0	0	0	0	0	0	0	—	—	—
June	0	0	0	0	0	0	0	0	—	—	—
July	71	20	1	0	2	8	1	6	.282	.380	.292
August	93	19	1	1	0	6	5	10	.204	.237	.242
Sept./Oct.	91	24	1	1	0	4	12	6	.264	.297	.346
Leading Off Inn.	51	16	1	1	0	0	5	5	.314	.373	.375
Bases Empty	135	39	1	1	1	1	11	12	.289	.333	.342
Runners On	120	24	2	1	1	17	7	10	.200	.258	.240
Runners/Scor. Pos.	70	12	1	0	1	15	5	6	.171	.229	.221
Runners On/2 Out	56	10	2	1	1	9	3	5	.179	.304	.220
Scor. Pos./2 Out	33	5	1	0	1	7	2	3	.152	.273	.200
Late-Inning Pressure	36	9	0	0	0	1	3	3	.250	.250	.308
Leading Off	9	1	0	0	0	0	1	1	.111	.111	.200
Runners On	16	2	0	0	0	1	1	2	.125	.125	.176
Runners/Scor. Pos.	9	1	0	0	0	1	1	1	.111	.111	.200

RUNS BATTED IN	From 1B	From 2B	From 3B	Scoring Position
Totals	3/89	5/59	8/29	13/88
Percentage	3.4%	8.5%	27.6%	14.8%

Loves to face: Terry Leach (.500, 2-for-4, 1 3B)
David West (.677, 2-for-3, 1 HR)

Hates to face: Allan Anderson (.100, 1-for-10)
Dave Stewart (0-for-10)
Walt Terrell (0-for-10, 1 BB)

Miscellaneous statistics: Ground outs-to-air outs ratio: 1.28 last season, 1.37 for career. . . . Grounded into 7 double plays in 63 opportunities (one per 9.0). . . . Drove in 6 of 15 runners from third base with less than two outs (40%). . . . Direction of balls hit to the outfield: 36% to left field, 39% to center, 25% to right batting left-handed; 48% to left, 24% to center, 27% to right batting right-handed. . . . Base running: Advanced from first base to third on 2 of 17 outfield singles (12%); scored from second on 5 of 7 (71%). . . . Made 3.16 assists per nine innings at shortstop.

Comments: Silly quiz: What does Vizquel have in common with Mike Devereaux, Bob Tewksbury, and 28 other players in major league history? Answer below. . . . Vizquel played 47 percent of Seattle's innings at shortstop, sharing time with Mike Brumley (24%), Brian Giles (18%), and Jeff Schaefer (11%). . . . His average of one error per 50 chances was the fifth best among shortstops who played at least half their teams' games. Only Cal Ripken, Spike Owen, Tony Fernandez, and Ozzie Smith had better marks. . . . Batted 89 points higher with the bases empty (.289) than with runners on base (.200) last season, the 3d-largest margin in the majors. . . . Drove in only 13 of 88 runners from scoring position, the 2d-lowest percentage (.148) of any player in the majors (minimum: 50 opportunities). . . . Career average with runners in scoring position (.175) is 74 points lower than in other at-bats (.249), the 5th-largest margin in the majors over the last five seasons. . . . Career batting average of .258 vs. ground-ball pitchers, .206 vs. fly-ball pitchers. . . . Has only two hits in 24 career at-bats with runners on base in Late-Inning Pressure Situations. . . . Has a career average of .175 with runners in scoring position. . . . Quiz answer: They have three of the last six letters of the alphabet in their last names, as did Klu, Fernando, and many others. But no player has had more than three of the last six. You heard it here first.

Gary Ward

Bats Right

Detroit Tigers	AB	H	2B	3B	HR	RBI	BB	SO	BA	SA	OBA
Season	309	79	11	2	9	46	30	50	.256	.392	.322
vs. Left-Handers	152	39	6	2	5	20	14	22	.257	.421	.315
vs. Right-Handers	157	40	5	0	4	26	16	28	.255	.363	.328
vs. Ground-Ballers	145	35	6	0	4	19	5	22	.241	.366	.272
vs. Fly-Ballers	164	44	5	2	5	27	25	28	.268	.415	.361
Home Games	131	34	7	2	2	17	14	24	.260	.389	.331
Road Games	178	45	4	0	7	29	16	26	.253	.393	.314
Grass Fields	254	63	9	2	6	38	24	44	.248	.370	.313
Artificial Turf	55	16	2	0	3	8	6	6	.291	.491	.361
April	57	17	1	0	2	9	7	6	.298	.421	.369
May	81	19	4	0	1	7	5	7	.235	.321	.279
June	35	5	0	0	1	3	3	8	.143	.229	.231
July	27	9	2	0	1	8	4	5	.333	.519	.419
August	64	16	2	1	2	10	3	13	.250	.406	.279
Sept./Oct.	45	13	2	1	2	9	8	11	.289	.511	.396
Leading Off Inn.	71	21	3	1	0	0	2	11	.296	.366	.315
Bases Empty	178	47	8	2	5	5	10	32	.264	.416	.303
Runners On	131	32	3	0	4	41	20	18	.244	.359	.344
Runners/Scor. Pos.	71	20	3	0	3	39	13	12	.282	.451	.391
Runners On/2 Out	58	14	1	0	1	18	6	8	.241	.310	.323
Scor. Pos./2 Out	37	9	1	0	0	16	5	6	.243	.270	.349
Late-Inning Pressure	41	12	2	0	0	8	3	6	.293	.341	.356
Leading Off	11	6	1	0	0	0	0	0	.545	.636	.545
Runners On	19	4	0	0	0	8	2	4	.211	.211	.318
Runners/Scor. Pos.	13	3	0	0	0	8	1	4	.231	.231	.333

RUNS BATTED IN	From 1B	From 2B	From 3B	Scoring Position
Totals	3/103	15/58	19/36	34/94
Percentage	2.9%	25.9%	52.8%	36.2%

Loves to face: Larry Andersen (.800, 4-for-5, 1 HR)
Allan Anderson (.429, 9-for-21, 2 HR)
Mark Portugal (.750, 6-for-8, 2 HR)

Hates to face: Dennis Eckersley (.100, 2-for-20)
Rick Honeycutt (.100, 2-for-20)
Jack Morris (.130, 7-for-54)

Miscellaneous statistics: Ground outs-to-air outs ratio: 1.11 last season, 1.20 for career.... Grounded into 12 double plays in 70 opportunities (one per 5.8).... Drove in 10 of 15 runners from third base with less than two outs (67%).... Direction of balls hit to the outfield: 30% to left field, 37% to center, 33% to right.... Base running: Advanced from first base to third on 6 of 16 outfield singles (38%); scored from second on 3 of 4 (75%).... Made 2.24 putouts per nine innings in left field.

Comments: Had exactly the same number of doubles, triples, and home runs as in 1989.... Percentage of runners driven in from scoring position (36.2%) was the 3d highest in the American League last season, behind George Brett (37.3%) and Alan Trammell (36.2%). Ward drove in 42 percent of runners from scoring position in Late-Inning Pressure Situations.... Was removed for a pinch hitter 24 times, all against right-handed pitchers, despite almost identical statistics vs. left- and right-handers.... Hit four home runs against right-handed pitchers after hitting none in 208 at-bats over the two previous seasons.... The margin between his career averages against ground-ballers (.293) and fly-ballers (.264) is greater than his margin between left-handers (.288) and right-handers (.268).... Had seven hits, including a home run, in 13 at-bats with the bases loaded. His slam in the Tigers' season finale was overshadowed by Cecil Fielder's 50th and 51st home runs. Ward also drove in four runs with bases-loaded walks (different games).... Has hit for a higher average in home games than on the road in each of the last seven seasons. During that time he has spent at least one full season with the Rangers, the Yankees, and the Tigers.... Had five hits in 14 at-bats as a pinch hitter, raising his career average to .288 in that role.

Mitch Webster

Bats Left and Right

Cleveland Indians	AB	H	2B	3B	HR	RBI	BB	SO	BA	SA	OBA
Season	437	110	20	6	12	55	20	61	.252	.407	.285
vs. Left-Handers	192	56	11	2	8	33	7	14	.292	.495	.320
vs. Right-Handers	245	54	9	4	4	22	13	47	.220	.339	.259
vs. Ground-Ballers	214	56	13	3	5	28	12	29	.262	.421	.296
vs. Fly-Ballers	223	54	7	3	7	27	8	32	.242	.395	.275
Home Games	231	57	7	2	6	35	12	32	.247	.372	.284
Road Games	206	53	13	4	6	20	8	29	.257	.447	.287
Grass Fields	369	91	13	6	9	45	17	53	.247	.388	.279
Artificial Turf	68	19	7	0	3	10	3	8	.279	.515	.319
April	48	18	4	1	2	8	1	5	.375	.625	.392
May	99	19	2	2	3	12	6	19	.192	.343	.243
June	84	21	2	2	0	6	2	18	.250	.321	.261
July	100	30	7	1	2	10	4	7	.300	.450	.333
August	58	13	3	0	4	14	2	8	.224	.483	.242
Sept./Oct.	48	9	2	0	1	5	5	4	.188	.292	.264
Leading Off Inn.	87	25	7	1	1	1	6	15	.287	.425	.347
Bases Empty	256	59	12	3	5	5	9	39	.230	.359	.265
Runners On	181	51	8	3	7	50	11	22	.282	.475	.313
Runners/Scor. Pos.	94	25	7	1	4	42	6	14	.266	.489	.292
Runners On/2 Out	66	17	3	1	5	23	1	11	.258	.561	.269
Scor. Pos./2 Out	43	10	3	0	3	18	1	8	.233	.512	.250
Late-Inning Pressure	65	14	2	1	2	11	2	16	.215	.369	.239
Leading Off	12	3	0	0	0	0	0	1	.250	.250	.250
Runners On	31	7	2	1	2	11	2	6	.226	.548	.273
Runners/Scor. Pos.	17	5	2	0	1	8	0	3	.294	.588	.294

RUNS BATTED IN	From 1B	From 2B	From 3B	Scoring Position
Totals	8/129	17/74	18/41	35/115
Percentage	6.2%	23.0%	43.9%	30.4%

Loves to face: Jim Acker (.833, 5-for-6, 1 HR)
Mike Dunne (.444, 12-for-27, 3 HR)
John Mitchell (.556, 5-for-9, 3 2B, 4 BB)

Hates to face: Randy Johnson (.077, 1-for-13)
Nolan Ryan (.105, 2-for-19, 2 3B, 12 SO)
Bobby Witt (0-for-7)

Miscellaneous statistics: Ground outs-to-air outs ratio: 0.73 last season, 0.76 for career.... Grounded into 5 double plays in 101 opportunities (one per 20.2).... Drove in 14 of 21 runners from third base with less than two outs (67%).... Direction of balls hit to the outfield: 29% to left field, 31% to center, 40% to right batting left-handed; 38% to left, 34% to center, 28% to right batting right-handed.... Base running: Advanced from first base to third on 10 of 20 outfield singles (50%); scored from second on 6 of 8 (75%).... Made 3.35 putouts per nine innings in center field, highest rate in majors.

Comments: The Indians had a 55–49 record with Webster in the starting lineup, but were 22–36 without him. However, before we award him a spot on the All-Star team by acclamation, consider the following: Because Cleveland's lineup was predominantly right-handed (Maldonado, Snyder, Alomar, Jacoby, the James gang), the Indians had a much better record in games against left-handed starters (34–20) than vs. right-handers (43–65). Because Webster was one of two part-time starters on the team to start as many games vs. southpaws as he did vs. right-handers (the other was Tom Brookens), his won-lost record as a starter is weighted heavily with games in which the Tribe had its strongest lineup on the field.... Career average of .293 batting right-handed (one HR per 34 AB), .257 batting left-handed (one HR per 61 AB).... Last season's average batting left-handed was a career low.... Consistently hit for a higher average on grass fields than on artificial turf in his years in Canada; but over the last three seasons, first with the Cubs and then the Indians, he has reversed that trend. His career BAs in those categories are now separated by only four points (advantage: artificial turf).... Career average of .207 (18-for-87, 1 HR) as a pinch hitter.... Has hit between .250 and .260 in each of the last three seasons, compared to a range of .270 to .290 over the three previous years.

Walt Weiss

Bats Left and Right

Oakland A's	AB	H	2B	3B	HR	RBI	BB	SO	BA	SA	OBA
Season	445	118	17	1	2	35	46	53	.265	.321	.337
vs. Left-Handers	115	30	5	0	0	12	8	10	.261	.304	.306
vs. Right-Handers	330	88	12	1	2	23	38	43	.267	.327	.347
vs. Ground-Ballers	234	61	9	0	1	17	16	31	.261	.312	.315
vs. Fly-Ballers	211	57	8	1	1	18	30	22	.270	.332	.359
Home Games	235	58	5	0	1	16	22	33	.247	.281	.316
Road Games	210	60	12	1	1	19	24	20	.286	.367	.360
Grass Fields	367	97	13	1	2	26	36	47	.264	.322	.333
Artificial Turf	78	21	4	0	0	9	10	6	.269	.321	.352
April	70	21	4	0	2	6	2	7	.300	.443	.319
May	84	23	3	0	0	3	9	7	.274	.310	.351
June	83	23	5	1	0	5	8	14	.277	.361	.355
July	95	22	3	0	0	9	9	9	.232	.263	.299
August	55	16	2	0	0	8	6	9	.291	.327	.349
Sept./Oct.	58	13	0	0	0	4	12	7	.224	.224	.357
Leading Off Inn.	116	29	8	0	0	0	7	17	.250	.319	.298
Bases Empty	267	67	14	0	2	2	22	31	.251	.326	.313
Runners On	178	51	3	1	0	33	24	22	.287	.315	.370
Runners/Scor. Pos.	98	22	2	0	0	32	18	15	.224	.245	.339
Runners On/2 Out	75	20	2	0	0	14	13	7	.267	.293	.382
Scor. Pos./2 Out	47	10	1	0	0	14	9	5	.213	.234	.351
Late-Inning Pressure	59	26	3	1	0	8	5	5	.441	.525	.492
Leading Off	17	6	2	0	0	0	0	4	.353	.471	.389
Runners On	28	14	0	1	0	8	3	0	.500	.571	.548
Runners/Scor. Pos.	14	6	0	0	0	7	1	0	.429	.429	.467

RUNS BATTED IN	From 1B	From 2B	From 3B	Scoring Position
Totals	2/138	15/78	16/38	31/116
Percentage	1.4%	19.2%	42.1%	26.7%

Loves to face: Bert Blyleven (.368, 7-for-19, 4 2B)
Andy Hawkins (.667, 4-for-6, 1 HR)
Bill Long (.625, 5-for-8, 2 SO)

Hates to face: Allan Anderson (.133, 2-for-15)
Mark Langston (.100, 1-for-10)
Jack Morris (0-for-8, 1 BB)

Miscellaneous statistics: Ground outs-to-air outs ratio: 1.40 last season, 1.31 for career.... Grounded into 7 double plays in 92 opportunities (one per 13.1).... Drove in 10 of 19 runners from third base with less than two outs (53%).... Direction of balls hit to the outfield: 43% to left field, 29% to center, 29% to right batting left-handed; 45% to left, 25% to center, 30% to right batting right-handed.... Base running: Advanced from first base to third on 12 of 24 outfield singles (50%); scored from second on 10 of 11 (91%).... Made 2.91 assists per nine innings at shortstop.

Comments: Batted 202 points higher in Late-Inning Pressure Situations (.441) than in other at-bats (.238) last season, the largest margin in the majors. His LIPS batting average was the highest in the American League in the 16 years we've kept track. The previous high during that time was .439 by Mickey Rivers in 1977.... Drove in seven of 15 runners from scoring position in LIPS (47%), 3d-highest rate in the majors (minimum: 15 opportunities).... Led the Athletics with 38 hits to the opposite field.... A's pitchers allowed 3.41 runs per nine innings with Weiss at shortstop, compared to 3.96 runs with other shortstops.... Career average vs. fly-ballers (.293) is 70 points higher than his average vs. ground-ballers (.222), the largest margin in the majors over the last five seasons.... Has hit eight career home runs, all against right-handed pitchers.... Had batted only .203 in two previous Aprils in the majors.... Hit both of his home runs in April, ending the season with a streak of 388 homerless at-bats.... The 10 lowest career batting averages in postseason play (minimum: 50 AB): Billy North, .051; Gorman Thomas, .102; Dal Maxvill, .114; Taylor Douthit, .140; Al Bumbry, .141; Weiss, .145; Travis Jackson, .149; Andy Etchebarren and Johnny Logan, .154; and Dick Green, .155.

Lou Whitaker

Bats Left

Detroit Tigers	AB	H	2B	3B	HR	RBI	BB	SO	BA	SA	OBA
Season	472	112	22	2	18	60	74	71	.237	.407	.338
vs. Left-Handers	99	16	1	1	2	7	16	19	.162	.253	.278
vs. Right-Handers	373	96	21	1	16	53	58	52	.257	.448	.353
vs. Ground-Ballers	214	58	13	1	10	33	37	27	.271	.481	.373
vs. Fly-Ballers	258	54	9	1	8	27	37	44	.209	.345	.307
Home Games	219	47	10	0	8	27	34	36	.215	.370	.316
Road Games	253	65	12	2	10	33	40	35	.257	.439	.356
Grass Fields	395	92	19	2	14	49	61	63	.233	.397	.332
Artificial Turf	77	20	3	0	4	11	13	8	.260	.455	.367
April	64	12	1	0	2	8	11	9	.188	.297	.299
May	87	17	1	0	4	11	13	20	.195	.345	.297
June	92	21	6	0	4	10	12	13	.228	.424	.311
July	97	29	8	2	3	14	12	14	.299	.515	.376
August	73	24	5	0	3	11	19	7	.329	.521	.467
Sept./Oct.	59	9	1	0	2	6	7	8	.153	.271	.242
Leading Off Inn.	132	33	8	0	1	1	12	18	.250	.333	.313
Bases Empty	264	64	16	1	5	5	43	34	.242	.367	.349
Runners On	208	48	6	1	13	55	31	37	.231	.457	.324
Runners/Scor. Pos.	114	25	3	1	7	42	17	24	.219	.447	.309
Runners On/2 Out	70	16	2	1	4	19	9	10	.229	.457	.316
Scor. Pos./2 Out	46	12	1	1	3	17	4	6	.261	.522	.320
Late-Inning Pressure	60	8	3	0	0	0	11	14	.133	.183	.268
Leading Off	9	1	1	0	0	0	2	3	.111	.222	.273
Runners On	28	4	0	0	0	0	5	8	.143	.143	.273
Runners/Scor. Pos.	14	0	0	0	0	0	4	5	.000	.000	.222

RUNS BATTED IN	From 1B	From 2B	From 3B	Scoring Position
Totals	12/153	15/88	15/52	30/140
Percentage	7.8%	17.0%	28.8%	21.4%

Loves to face: Brian Holman (.444, 4-for-9, 1 2B, 2 HR)
Charlie Hough (.350, 21-for-60, 3 HR)
Bob Welch (.346, 9-for-26, 3 2B, 3 HR)

Hates to face: Dave Stieb (.184, 14-for-76)
Curt Young (.172, 5-for-29, 0 BB)
Matt Young (.217, 5-for-23)

Miscellaneous statistics: Ground outs-to-air outs ratio: 0.79 last season, 1.11 for career.... Grounded into 10 double plays in 120 opportunities (one per 12.0).... Drove in 10 of 31 runners from third base with less than two outs (32%), 3d-lowest rate in A.L.... Direction of balls hit to the outfield: 29% to left field, 31% to center, 41% to right.... Base running: Advanced from first base to third on 15 of 30 outfield singles (50%); scored from second on 14 of 16 (88%).... Made 3.23 assists per nine innings at second base.

Comments: The fourth player in major league history to hit at least 10 home runs and play 100 games at second base in as many as nine consecutive seasons. The others: Bobby Doerr, 12 (1939–51), Joe Gordon, 11 (1938–50, his entire career), and Charlie Gehringer, 9 (1932–40). Ryne Sandberg has a current seven-year streak.... Tigers pitchers allowed 5.27 runs per nine innings with Whitaker at second base, but only 3.34 runs per nine with Tony Phillips at that position.... An error in his last game of the season snapped a 67-game streak without one, the longest among A.L. second baseman last season.... Percentage of runners driven in from scoring position was the lowest of his career.... Started only 13 of 49 games in which the Tigers faced a left-handed starter.... Batted 75 points higher vs. right-handers (.281) than vs. left-handers (.206) over the last five seasons, the 3d-largest margin in the majors. His streak of 28 consecutive hitless at-bats vs. left-handers was the longest in the American League last season.... Has batted below .230 vs. LHP in each of the last seven seasons, but his 1990 average vs. RHP was one point short of a career low.... Batting average in Late-Inning Pressure Situations was 4th lowest among A.L. players with at least 50 at-bats.... Has hit for a higher average against ground-ball pitchers than he has against fly-ball pitchers in each of the last five seasons.

Devon White

Bats Left and Right

California Angels	AB	H	2B	3B	HR	RBI	BB	SO	BA	SA	OBA
Season	443	96	17	3	11	44	44	116	.217	.343	.290
vs. Left-Handers	130	32	5	0	3	10	12	22	.246	.354	.315
vs. Right-Handers	313	64	12	3	8	34	32	94	.204	.339	.280
vs. Ground-Ballers	192	44	9	1	4	19	17	42	.229	.349	.294
vs. Fly-Ballers	251	52	8	2	7	25	27	74	.207	.339	.287
Home Games	219	47	9	3	5	20	19	55	.215	.352	.278
Road Games	224	49	8	0	6	24	25	61	.219	.335	.302
Grass Fields	372	83	16	3	10	38	34	94	.223	.363	.289
Artificial Turf	71	13	1	0	1	6	10	22	.183	.239	.298
April	66	12	3	0	1	2	4	19	.182	.273	.239
May	108	25	8	1	3	10	11	21	.231	.407	.306
June	69	15	2	0	3	9	9	23	.217	.377	.304
July	37	9	2	0	0	2	4	12	.243	.297	.317
August	91	18	2	2	3	12	9	19	.198	.363	.267
Sept./Oct.	72	17	0	0	1	9	7	22	.236	.278	.313
Leading Off Inn.	112	21	5	1	2	2	8	24	.188	.304	.242
Bases Empty	252	55	12	2	6	6	18	67	.218	.353	.273
Runners On	191	41	5	1	5	38	26	49	.215	.330	.311
Runners/Scor. Pos.	111	22	2	1	3	34	17	36	.198	.315	.303
Runners On/2 Out	81	16	2	1	3	20	6	24	.198	.358	.261
Scor. Pos./2 Out	52	10	1	1	2	18	4	19	.192	.365	.263
Late-Inning Pressure	81	15	1	0	2	5	9	23	.185	.272	.267
Leading Off	22	2	0	0	0	0	0	4	.091	.091	.091
Runners On	31	5	0	0	1	4	8	12	.161	.258	.333
Runners/Scor. Pos.	20	3	0	0	1	4	6	10	.150	.300	.346

RUNS BATTED IN	From 1B	From 2B	From 3B	Scoring Position
Totals	5/136	8/85	20/52	28/137
Percentage	3.7%	9.4%	38.5%	20.4%

Loves to face: Andy Hawkins (.556, 5-for-9, 3 2B)
Mike Henneman (.500, 4-for-8)
Dave LaPoint (.308, 8-for-26, 2 HR)

Hates to face: Kevin Brown (0-for-9)
Mark Langston (.080, 2-for-25)
Nolan Ryan (.045, 1-for-22)

Miscellaneous statistics: Ground outs-to-air outs ratio: 1.37 last season, 1.44 for career. . . . Grounded into 6 double plays in 102 opportunities (one per 17.0). . . . Drove in 12 of 27 runners from third base with less than two outs (44%). . . . Direction of balls hit to the outfield: 38% to left field, 23% to center, 39% to right batting left-handed; 44% to left, 25% to center, 31% to right batting right-handed. . . . Base running: Advanced from first base to third on 9 of 22 outfield singles (41%); scored from second on 6 of 8 (75%). . . . Made 2.68 putouts per nine innings in center field.

Comments: Batting averages year-by-year since 1987: .263, .259, .245, .217. . . . His streak of 22 consecutive plate appearances leading off innings without reaching base was the 3d longest in the majors last season. . . . A sign of hope: His total of 44 walks was a career high. . . . Has hit for a higher average in road games than he has in Anaheim in each of his six seasons in the majors. Career averages: .236 at Anaheim Stadium, .257 on the road. . . . He has only five hits in 29 career at-bats at the Skydome (.172). His career batting average on artificial turf is 16 points lower than on grass fields (.234 to .250). . . . There's something else he's done in each of his six seasons. He's hit for a lower average with runners in scoring position than he has in other at-bats. . . . He's batted below .200 with two outs and runners in scoring position in five of his six seasons. . . . His career average of 2.65 putouts per game in the outfield is excellent, but not world class. He ranks 17th in major league history among players with at least 500 games, which is to say slightly ahead of Vince (20th, with 2.63) and Joe (22d, with 2.62) but way behind Dom (6th, with 2.81). . . . Batted below .220 in each of his first two minor league seasons.

Frank White

Bats Right

Kansas City Royals	AB	H	2B	3B	HR	RBI	BB	SO	BA	SA	OBA
Season	241	52	14	1	2	21	10	32	.216	.307	.253
vs. Left-Handers	93	18	5	0	1	6	6	15	.194	.280	.240
vs. Right-Handers	148	34	9	1	1	15	4	17	.230	.324	.261
vs. Ground-Ballers	110	28	5	1	1	12	5	12	.255	.345	.300
vs. Fly-Ballers	131	24	9	0	1	9	5	20	.183	.275	.212
Home Games	145	36	9	1	2	15	6	20	.248	.366	.281
Road Games	96	16	5	0	0	6	4	12	.167	.219	.212
Grass Fields	68	14	5	0	0	5	0	10	.206	.279	.225
Artificial Turf	173	38	9	1	2	16	10	22	.220	.318	.263
April	42	6	2	0	1	7	1	5	.143	.262	.178
May	16	5	1	0	0	1	0	3	.313	.375	.313
June	55	12	4	0	0	2	3	10	.218	.291	.254
July	37	12	1	1	1	5	3	4	.324	.486	.381
August	53	9	2	0	0	4	2	8	.170	.208	.200
Sept./Oct.	38	8	4	0	0	2	1	2	.211	.316	.250
Leading Off Inn.	56	11	7	0	0	0	3	8	.196	.321	.262
Bases Empty	132	27	8	1	0	0	7	16	.205	.280	.261
Runners On	109	25	6	0	2	21	3	16	.229	.339	.243
Runners/Scor. Pos.	60	13	3	0	1	18	1	8	.217	.317	.219
Runners On/2 Out	48	13	2	0	2	12	0	7	.271	.438	.271
Scor. Pos./2 Out	26	8	2	0	1	10	0	3	.308	.500	.308
Late-Inning Pressure	31	2	1	0	0	1	1	4	.065	.097	.091
Leading Off	7	0	0	0	0	0	1	1	.000	.000	.125
Runners On	12	0	0	0	0	1	0	1	.000	.000	.000
Runners/Scor. Pos.	9	0	0	0	0	1	0	0	.000	.000	.000

RUNS BATTED IN	From 1B	From 2B	From 3B	Scoring Position
Totals	4/79	6/52	9/25	15/77
Percentage	5.1%	11.5%	36.0%	19.5%

Loves to face: Oil Can Boyd (.406, 13-for-32, 6 2B, 1 3B, 2 HR, 0 BB)
Bruce Hurst (.400, 18-for-45, 8 2B, 4 HR)
Jerry Reuss (.467, 7-for-15, 2 HR)

Hates to face: Dennis Eckersley (.082, 4-for-49)
Nolan Ryan (.180, 9-for-50, 1 HR)
Dave Stieb (.161, 10-for-62)

Miscellaneous statistics: Ground outs-to-air outs ratio: 0.94 last season, 0.97 for career. . . . Grounded into 7 double plays in 48 opportunities (one per 6.9). . . . Drove in 5 of 13 runners from third base with less than two outs (38%). . . . Direction of balls hit to the outfield: 45% to left field, 31% to center, 24% to right. . . . Base running: Advanced from first base to third on 3 of 7 outfield singles (43%); scored from second on 1 of 5 (20%). . . . Made 3.13 assists per nine innings at second base.

Comments: Career total of 2150 games played at second base is highest among players active in 1990, 4th highest in A.L. history, and higher than the total of all other second basemen in Royals history put together (1939). Kansas City's all-time top five: White, Cookie Rojas (792), Jerry Adair (116), Brad Wellman (110), Bobby Knoop (85). Among those with only one game: George Brett, Ed Kirkpatrick, and Joe Zdeb. . . . White accounted for less than half of Kansas City's innings at second base last season (44%), but the staff allowed an average of 4.12 runs per nine innings with him there, compared to 4.79 runs with other second basemen (Jeltz, Pecota, Seitzer, and Shumpert). . . . His batting average was as low as .205 as late as September 10. The only player to hit below .200 for the Royals in a season of at least 200 at-bats was Harmon Killebrew, who batted .199 in 1975. . . . Only one of his 21 RBIs gave the Royals a lead. . . . White has the longest current streak of consecutive opening-day starts (1976–90), which will probably end in 1991. . . . Ranks fourth in major league history with an average of one error per 63 chances at second base (minimum: 1000 games), behind Ryne Sandberg (one per 92), Tommy Herr (one per 88), and Jim Gantner (one per 66). . . . Coming off a 418-AB season in 1989, we were skeptical of our projections (method described on page 427) that showed 84 games for 1990 (he played in 82), a .264 batting average (a little high) in 241 at-bats, with 11 doubles, one triple, two homers, and 25 RBIs. Bull's-eye!

Mookie Wilson

Bats Left and Right

Toronto Blue Jays	AB	H	2B	3B	HR	RBI	BB	SO	BA	SA	OBA
Season	588	156	36	4	3	51	31	102	.265	.355	.300
vs. Left-Handers	188	46	10	2	2	21	14	36	.245	.351	.294
vs. Right-Handers	400	110	26	2	1	30	17	66	.275	.357	.303
vs. Ground-Ballers	256	67	13	2	0	26	7	35	.262	.328	.278
vs. Fly-Ballers	332	89	23	2	3	25	24	67	.268	.377	.317
Home Games	271	67	16	2	0	20	12	50	.247	.321	.279
Road Games	317	89	20	2	3	31	19	52	.281	.385	.318
Grass Fields	245	67	16	1	3	22	14	37	.273	.384	.309
Artificial Turf	343	89	20	3	0	29	17	65	.259	.335	.294
April	78	16	3	0	0	2	6	13	.205	.244	.262
May	91	23	7	0	1	8	9	12	.253	.363	.317
June	96	24	6	0	0	11	7	26	.250	.313	.298
July	93	25	6	1	0	3	3	20	.269	.355	.289
August	99	33	8	2	1	16	3	13	.333	.485	.353
Sept./Oct.	131	35	6	1	1	11	3	18	.267	.351	.281
Leading Off Inn.	156	40	8	1	0	0	6	28	.256	.321	.284
Bases Empty	353	93	17	3	3	3	16	66	.263	.354	.295
Runners On	235	63	19	1	0	48	15	36	.268	.357	.307
Runners/Scor. Pos.	136	35	11	1	0	46	6	20	.257	.353	.281
Runners On/2 Out	97	24	6	0	0	16	10	14	.247	.309	.318
Scor. Pos./2 Out	68	16	5	0	0	16	6	9	.235	.309	.297
Late-Inning Pressure	94	27	4	1	1	10	6	13	.287	.383	.327
Leading Off	22	8	0	0	0	0	1	3	.364	.364	.391
Runners On	42	9	3	0	0	9	4	8	.214	.286	.277
Runners/Scor. Pos.	25	6	3	0	0	9	1	3	.240	.360	.259

RUNS BATTED IN	From 1B	From 2B	From 3B	Scoring Position
Totals	5/163	17/97	26/67	43/164
Percentage	3.1%	17.5%	38.8%	26.2%

Loves to face: Joe Hesketh (.563, 9-for-16)
Brian Holman (.500, 8-for-16, 1 HR)
Rick Honeycutt (.444, 8-for-18, 1 HR)

Hates to face: Greg A. Harris (.063, 1-for-16)
Andy Hawkins (.071, 2-for-28, 3 BB)
Bob Welch (.074, 2-for-27, 1 3B)

Miscellaneous statistics: Ground outs-to-air outs ratio: 1.57 last season, 1.65 for career. . . . Grounded into 10 double plays in 117 opportunities (one per 11.7). . . . Drove in 19 of 32 runners from third base with less than two outs (59%). . . . Direction of balls hit to the outfield: 43% to left field, 30% to center, 28% to right batting left-handed; 35% to left, 34% to center, 31% to right batting right-handed. . . . Base running: Advanced from first base to third on 14 of 26 outfield singles (54%); scored from second on 21 of 24 (88%). . . . Made 2.71 putouts per nine innings in center field.

Comments: Played in 146 games last season, his highest total since the pre-Dykstra days in New York. . . . Was the Blue Jays' leadoff batter in each of his last 37 games, after spending most of the season batting either second or ninth. . . . Batting average leading off innings was the lowest of his career. . . . Stolen base percentage was the highest of his career (23-for-27, 85%). Mookie stole 20 bases in 21 attempts against right-handers, but was cautious with lefties on the mound, stealing only three bases in six attempts. . . . Was thrown out trying to advance a base on a batted ball six times last season, tied with Tony Fernandez for the team lead. . . . One of four active players with at least 50 career home runs, and more triples than homers. The others: Garry Templeton, Willie McGee, and Willie Randolph. . . . Has hit eight home runs over the last two seasons, all solo shots. . . . Mookie has a career batting average of .276 despite never hitting .300 or better in his 11 seasons in the majors. The only player with a higher average in a career that included at least 10 seasons of 100 at-bats or more but no .300 seasons: Sam Mertes (.279). Others above .270: Billy Nash, Jim Gantner, Frank Howard, Billy Bruton, Rick Burleson, Ossie Bluege, Don Kolloway, and Burt Shotton.

Willie Wilson

Bats Left and Right

Kansas City Royals	AB	H	2B	3B	HR	RBI	BB	SO	BA	SA	OBA
Season	307	89	13	3	2	42	30	57	.290	.371	.354
vs. Left-Handers	103	28	6	1	0	17	5	19	.272	.350	.306
vs. Right-Handers	204	61	7	2	2	25	25	38	.299	.382	.377
vs. Ground-Ballers	138	37	4	0	2	21	8	30	.268	.341	.309
vs. Fly-Ballers	169	52	9	3	0	21	22	27	.308	.396	.389
Home Games	166	55	8	2	1	22	13	27	.331	.422	.381
Road Games	141	34	5	1	1	20	17	30	.241	.312	.323
Grass Fields	103	25	4	0	1	16	14	21	.243	.311	.333
Artificial Turf	204	64	9	3	1	26	16	36	.314	.402	.365
April	55	19	4	1	1	10	6	5	.345	.509	.419
May	43	7	1	0	0	4	5	11	.163	.186	.245
June	67	21	1	1	0	9	4	13	.313	.358	.347
July	50	15	3	1	0	11	5	11	.300	.400	.357
August	62	17	3	0	1	7	5	13	.274	.371	.328
Sept./Oct.	30	10	1	0	0	1	5	4	.333	.367	.444
Leading Off Inn.	66	11	0	1	1	1	8	16	.167	.242	.257
Bases Empty	153	38	4	1	1	1	17	32	.248	.307	.324
Runners On	154	51	9	2	1	41	13	25	.331	.435	.384
Runners/Scor. Pos.	101	30	5	1	1	40	11	20	.297	.396	.368
Runners On/2 Out	68	25	4	1	1	20	8	11	.368	.500	.442
Scor. Pos./2 Out	51	17	3	0	1	19	8	9	.333	.451	.433
Late-Inning Pressure	51	9	0	1	1	4	6	9	.176	.275	.276
Leading Off	15	2	0	1	1	1	1	2	.133	.467	.188
Runners On	27	4	0	0	0	3	3	5	.148	.148	.258
Runners/Scor. Pos.	19	3	0	0	0	3	3	3	.158	.158	.304

RUNS BATTED IN	From 1B	From 2B	From 3B	Scoring Position
Totals	2/104	17/81	21/47	38/128
Percentage	1.9%	21.0%	44.7%	29.7%

Loves to face: Storm Davis (.429, 15-for-35)
Paul Kilgus (.429, 6-for-14)
Rob Murphy (.667, 4-for-6)

Hates to face: Nolan Ryan (.189, 7-for-37)
Dave Stieb (.224, 19-for-85, 1 HR)
Bobby Witt (.188, 3-for-16)

Miscellaneous statistics: Ground outs-to-air outs ratio: 1.06 last season, 1.48 for career. . . . Grounded into 4 double plays in 67 opportunities (one per 16.8). . . . Drove in 12 of 24 runners from third base with less than two outs (50%). . . . Direction of balls hit to the outfield: 32% to left field, 39% to center, 29% to right batting left-handed; 26% to left, 28% to center, 47% to right batting right-handed. . . . Base running: Advanced from first base to third on 9 of 14 outfield singles (64%); scored from second on 15 of 15. . . . Made 2.28 putouts per nine innings in left field.

Comments: Batted 136 points lower in Late-Inning Pressure Situations (.176) than in other at-bats (.313) last season, the 5th-largest margin in the majors. . . . Batting average with two outs and runners in scoring position was a career high. His overall average was his highest since 1984. . . . Has ended his Kansas City career with 1732 games in the outfield, 2d most in franchise history, 113 games behind Amos Otis. No other outfielder in Royals history has played as many as 1000 games. . . . Leads active players with 133 triples, six more than George Brett. . . . The last Royals player to start an opening-day game in center field before Wilson was Pat Sheridan in 1984, while Willie served a suspension imposed by Bowie Kuhn. . . . Career average of .257 at the Oakland Coliseum is his 2d lowest at any current A.L. ballpark. (He has a career mark of .226 at the Kingdome.). . .He has hit for a higher average on rugs than he has on grass in each of the last three seasons, but there is only a five-point difference between his career averages on grass fields (.286) and artificial surfaces (.291). . . . Has played at least 100 games in each of the last 13 seasons, but has never driven in as many as 50 runs. . . . He has stolen at least 20 bases for 13 years running. The only longer streaks: 18, Honus Wagner (1898–1915); 15, Lou Brock (1963–77); 14, Bert Campaneris (1965–78), Ty Cobb (1906–19), Herman Long (1889–1902), and George Van Haltren (1888–1901).

Dave Winfield

Bats Right

Yankees/Angels	AB	H	2B	3B	HR	RBI	BB	SO	BA	SA	OBA
Season	475	127	21	2	21	78	52	81	.267	.453	.338
vs. Left-Handers	156	45	9	2	5	32	20	22	.288	.468	.365
vs. Right-Handers	319	82	12	0	16	46	32	59	.257	.445	.324
vs. Ground-Ballers	205	57	11	0	10	33	26	35	.278	.478	.356
vs. Fly-Ballers	270	70	10	2	11	45	26	46	.259	.433	.323
Home Games	238	62	12	1	13	41	27	44	.261	.483	.333
Road Games	237	65	9	1	8	37	25	37	.274	.422	.342
Grass Fields	407	105	19	2	18	65	49	67	.258	.447	.335
Artificial Turf	68	22	2	0	3	13	3	14	.324	.485	.352
April	47	9	2	0	2	5	3	11	.191	.362	.250
May	62	14	1	0	2	4	3	11	.226	.339	.262
June	81	21	5	1	5	15	11	11	.259	.531	.344
July	100	26	3	0	4	16	8	15	.260	.410	.309
August	84	28	7	0	2	13	17	19	.333	.488	.447
Sept./Oct.	101	29	3	1	6	25	10	14	.287	.515	.345
Leading Off Inn.	110	31	6	0	7	7	14	16	.282	.527	.373
Bases Empty	247	67	12	0	12	12	28	40	.271	.466	.350
Runners On	228	60	9	2	9	66	24	41	.263	.439	.324
Runners/Scor. Pos.	125	31	3	1	5	55	19	20	.248	.408	.331
Runners On/2 Out	97	21	5	0	4	22	12	20	.216	.392	.303
Scor. Pos./2 Out	60	10	2	0	2	16	9	14	.167	.300	.275
Late-Inning Pressure	78	22	2	1	4	12	6	11	.282	.487	.333
Leading Off	19	5	1	0	0	0	1	3	.263	.316	.300
Runners On	34	11	1	1	3	11	1	3	.324	.676	.343
Runners/Scor. Pos.	18	4	0	0	2	8	1	2	.222	.556	.263

RUNS BATTED IN	From 1B	From 2B	From 3B	Scoring Position
Totals	11/174	15/91	31/73	46/164
Percentage	6.3%	16.5%	42.5%	28.0%

Loves to face: Mike Moore (.500, 13-for-26, 2 HR)
Jeff Russell (.700, 7-for-10, 2 SO)
Scott Sanderson (.571, 8-for-14, 1 HR)

Hates to face: Dennis Lamp (.205, 9-for-44, 1 HR)
Nolan Ryan (.050, 1-for-20, 3 BB)
Duane Ward (0-for-7)

Miscellaneous statistics: Ground outs-to-air outs ratio: 1.37 last season, 1.34 for career. . . . Grounded into 17 double plays in 120 opportunities (one per 7.1). . . . Drove in 25 of 42 runners from third base with less than two outs (60%). . . . Direction of balls hit to the outfield: 42% to left field, 29% to center, 29% to right. . . . Base running: Advanced from first base to third on 16 of 30 outfield singles (53%); scored from second on 5 of 7 (71%). . . . Made 1.61 putouts per nine innings in right field, lowest rate in majors.

Comments: Played 132 games in 1990 after missing the entire 1989 season. It had been 74 years since a player as old as Winfield missed a full major league season and returned to play as many as 100 games the next season. Dave Shean, who spent 1916 in the minors but played 131 games for the Reds in 1917, was the most recent of five players ever to have done it. The others: Charlie Reilly (1897), Dummy Hoy (1901), Jimmy Ryan (1902), and Fred Tenney, the most recent among them who, like Winfield, missed the season due to injury (1911). . . . The Angels have had a different right fielder in their opening-day lineup every year since 1984: Fred Lynn, Reggie Jackson, Ruppert Jones, George Hendrick, Chili Davis, Tony Armas, and Claudell Washington. . . . Leads active players with 1516 career RBIs. . . . Had driven in at least 97 runs, and at least 30 percent of runners from scoring position in seven seasons from 1982 to '88. . . . Hit three grand slams with the Yankees, five with the Padres. In major league history, only four players hit at least four grand slams in each league: Darrell Evans, Dave Kingman, Lee May, and Dick Stuart. . . . Averaged 1.7 chances per nine innings, the lowest of any regular outfielder in the majors last season. . . . Career average of .313 (25-for-80, 1 HR) as a pinch hitter. . . . They said it couldn't be done, and it wasn't. But Winfield came within three months of outlasting Steinbrenner in New York.

Craig Worthington

Bats Right

Baltimore Orioles	AB	H	2B	3B	HR	RBI	BB	SO	BA	SA	OBA
Season	425	96	17	0	8	44	63	96	.226	.322	.328
vs. Left-Handers	126	32	7	0	2	12	27	21	.254	.357	.387
vs. Right-Handers	299	64	10	0	6	32	36	75	.214	.308	.301
vs. Ground-Ballers	206	54	15	0	3	25	30	51	.262	.379	.361
vs. Fly-Ballers	219	42	2	0	5	19	33	45	.192	.269	.297
Home Games	209	49	10	0	3	20	29	49	.234	.325	.331
Road Games	216	47	7	0	5	24	34	47	.218	.319	.325
Grass Fields	347	81	15	0	5	34	54	77	.233	.320	.339
Artificial Turf	78	15	2	0	3	10	9	19	.192	.333	.276
April	73	19	5	0	2	10	10	20	.260	.411	.345
May	86	16	3	0	1	6	8	22	.186	.256	.263
June	79	19	1	0	4	12	11	15	.241	.405	.333
July	71	12	1	0	1	9	14	14	.169	.225	.315
August	54	13	2	0	0	3	9	9	.241	.278	.349
Sept./Oct.	62	17	5	0	0	4	11	16	.274	.355	.384
Leading Off Inn.	79	23	6	0	2	2	13	12	.291	.443	.398
Bases Empty	224	55	13	0	7	7	32	43	.246	.397	.342
Runners On	201	41	4	0	1	37	31	53	.204	.239	.312
Runners/Scor. Pos.	111	22	3	0	0	35	20	28	.198	.225	.319
Runners On/2 Out	94	21	3	0	1	19	19	26	.223	.287	.360
Scor. Pos./2 Out	62	13	2	0	0	17	14	17	.210	.242	.364
Late-Inning Pressure	77	21	4	0	3	6	11	12	.273	.442	.378
Leading Off	13	5	1	0	0	0	2	0	.385	.462	.500
Runners On	35	7	1	0	0	3	5	8	.200	.229	.317
Runners/Scor. Pos.	16	3	0	0	0	3	3	4	.188	.188	.316

RUNS BATTED IN	From 1B	From 2B	From 3B	Scoring Position
Totals	1/161	14/91	21/50	35/141
Percentage	0.6%	15.4%	42.0%	24.8%

Loves to face: Mike Moore (.313, 5-for-16, 1 HR)
Mike Schooler (.600, 3-for-5)
Curt Young (.429, 3-for-7)

Hates to face: Storm Davis (0-for-7)
Mark Knudson (.091, 1-for-11)
Bob Welch (.154, 2-for-13)

Miscellaneous statistics: Ground outs-to-air outs ratio: 1.35 last season, 1.26 for career. . . . Grounded into 13 double plays in 106 opportunities (one per 8.2). . . . Drove in 12 of 22 runners from third base with less than two outs (55%). . . . Direction of balls hit to the outfield: 46% to left field, 28% to center, 26% to right. . . . Base running: Advanced from first base to third on 6 of 29 outfield singles (21%); scored from second on 8 of 16 (50%). . . . Made 1.82 assists per nine innings at third base.

Comments: Orioles had a 53–71 record with Worthington in the starting lineup, 23–14 with him on the bench. Baltimore also had a better record without Worthington in the starting lineup (14–4) than with him (73–71) in 1989. . . . Orioles pitchers allowed 4.63 runs per nine innings with Worthington at third base, compared to 3.63 with others there (Brown, Gomez, Gonzales, and Hulett). . . . He had only one infield hit last season, the fewest of any regular player in the majors. . . . Drove in seven runners from first base in 1989, in the same number of opportunities. . . . One of four players in major league history with at least 1000 career at-bats but no triples: Gaylord Perry (1076 AB); Earl Averill—the son, not the Hall of Fame father (1031); Whitey Ford (1023); and Worthington (1003). The 2d most among active players is Dann Bilardello, with 890 AB. Among players who eventually tripled, none took longer than Willie Aikens (1717 AB). . . . Career batting averages of .262 vs. ground-ball pitchers, .208 vs. fly-ball pitchers. . . . Had a fielding percentage of .981 on artificial surfaces (one error in 51 chances), the best of any third baseman in the majors, but had only a .938 mark on grass fields (one error per 16 chances).

Robin Yount

Bats Right

Milwaukee Brewers	AB	H	2B	3B	HR	RBI	BB	SO	BA	SA	OBA
Season	587	145	17	5	17	77	78	89	.247	.380	.337
vs. Left-Handers	156	42	5	1	5	20	22	27	.269	.410	.356
vs. Right-Handers	431	103	12	4	12	57	56	62	.239	.369	.331
vs. Ground-Ballers	256	69	6	2	6	36	39	34	.270	.379	.367
vs. Fly-Ballers	331	76	11	3	11	41	39	55	.230	.381	.313
Home Games	293	65	10	4	8	35	36	42	.222	.365	.310
Road Games	294	80	7	1	9	42	42	47	.272	.395	.364
Grass Fields	495	123	15	5	15	67	65	73	.248	.390	.339
Artificial Turf	92	22	2	0	2	10	13	16	.239	.326	.327
April	70	19	2	1	2	11	8	8	.271	.414	.363
May	97	23	2	1	1	11	10	16	.237	.309	.312
June	106	26	2	0	4	13	17	14	.245	.377	.344
July	103	25	3	3	3	13	18	17	.243	.417	.355
August	110	19	2	0	3	10	13	20	.173	.273	.262
Sept./Oct.	101	33	6	0	4	19	12	14	.327	.505	.400
Leading Off Inn.	122	32	7	1	2	2	10	15	.262	.385	.318
Bases Empty	336	79	11	4	7	7	50	54	.235	.354	.339
Runners On	251	66	6	1	10	70	28	35	.263	.414	.334
Runners/Scor. Pos.	167	38	3	0	7	62	18	24	.228	.371	.297
Runners On/2 Out	92	18	1	1	2	21	12	16	.196	.293	.288
Scor. Pos./2 Out	74	14	0	0	2	19	10	11	.189	.270	.286
Late-Inning Pressure	69	16	2	0	1	14	8	14	.232	.304	.313
Leading Off	14	2	1	0	0	0	1	3	.143	.214	.200
Runners On	32	9	1	0	1	14	5	8	.281	.406	.359
Runners/Scor. Pos.	21	6	0	0	0	11	4	4	.286	.286	.370

RUNS BATTED IN	From 1B	From 2B	From 3B	Scoring Position
Totals	10/158	21/130	29/67	50/197
Percentage	6.3%	16.2%	43.3%	25.4%

Loves to face: Jim Acker (.500, 7-for-14, 3 BB)
Brian Holman (.400, 4-for-10, 1 HR, 4 BB)
Dave Stieb (.326, 28-for-86, 3 2B, 2 3B, 3 HR, 13 BB)

Hates to face: Bert Blyleven (.190, 19-for-100, 1 HR)
Mark Langston (.204, 11-for-54)
Walt Terrell (.162, 6-for-37)

Miscellaneous statistics: Ground outs-to-air outs ratio: 0.74 last season, 0.98 for career.... Grounded into 7 double plays in 122 opportunities (one per 17.4).... Drove in 23 of 36 runners from third base with less than two outs (64%).... Direction of balls hit to the outfield: 28% to left field, 28% to center, 43% to right.... Base running: Advanced from first base to third on 15 of 39 outfield singles (38%); scored from second on 13 of 14 (93%).... Made 2.79 putouts per nine innings in center field.

Comments: Has played 1479 games at shortstop, 848 in the outfield. Here's a surprise—only two other players reached even the 400 mark at both positions: Yount's former manager Harvey Kuenn (748 at short, 826 in the pasture) and Woodie Held (526 and 448, respectively).... The Brewers' all-time leader in singles, doubles, triples, and homers. Stan Musial is the only other man to be a franchise leader in all four of those categories. The distinctive element is leading in both triples and home runs, something that only Earl Averill (the Hall of Fame father, not the son), Musial, and Yount have done.... Enters 1991 as baseball's active leader in hits (2747), 40 ahead of George Brett, who narrowed Yount's lead by 34 last season.... Hit eight of his 17 home runs to the opposite field last season. Only two players in the majors hit more opposite-field homers: Kal Daniels (15) and Bo Jackson (11).... Had batted over .300 at County Stadium in seven of the previous eight seasons. He batted .297 in the one year he missed.... Batting average dropped 71 points from 1989 to 1990, the largest decrease of any player in the American League last season (minimum: 300 AB in both seasons).... In a lost season, Yount managed a career-high total of 78 walks.... Has missed only 10 games over the last four seasons.... Made his major league debut on April 5, 1974, one day after the first appearance of pinch-runner Herb Washington. Somehow, we just knew Yount would last longer.

Mike Aldrete

Bats Left

Montreal Expos	AB	H	2B	3B	HR	RBI	BB	SO	BA	SA	OBA
Season	161	39	7	1	1	18	37	31	.242	.317	.385
vs. Left-Handers	9	0	0	0	0	0	3	2	.000	.000	.250
vs. Right-Handers	152	39	7	1	1	18	34	29	.257	.336	.394
vs. Ground-Ballers	96	26	5	0	0	9	23	18	.271	.323	.413
vs. Fly-Ballers	65	13	2	1	1	9	14	13	.200	.308	.342
Home Games	81	20	3	1	0	9	27	16	.247	.309	.436
Road Games	80	19	4	0	1	9	10	15	.237	.325	.322
Grass Fields	44	11	3	0	1	5	6	6	.250	.386	.340
Artificial Turf	117	28	4	1	0	13	31	25	.239	.291	.400
April	6	3	0	0	0	1	2	1	.500	.500	.625
May	23	5	0	0	0	1	5	4	.217	.217	.357
June	52	10	4	0	0	4	13	11	.192	.269	.364
July	24	6	3	1	0	6	7	5	.250	.458	.419
August	31	8	0	0	1	3	2	3	.258	.355	.303
Sept./Oct.	25	7	0	0	0	3	8	7	.280	.280	.441
Leading Off Inn.	40	17	0	1	1	1	5	5	.425	.550	.489
Bases Empty	88	25	1	1	1	1	16	11	.284	.352	.394
Runners On	73	14	6	0	0	17	21	20	.192	.274	.375
Runners/Scor. Pos.	45	5	2	0	0	14	14	15	.111	.156	.328
Runners On/2 Out	28	5	2	0	0	3	8	11	.179	.250	.361
Scor. Pos./2 Out	19	1	0	0	0	1	4	9	.053	.053	.217
Late-Inning Pressure	46	13	1	0	1	4	4	10	.283	.370	.340
Leading Off	12	8	0	0	1	1	2	1	.667	.917	.714
Runners On	21	3	1	0	0	3	2	6	.143	.190	.217
Runners/Scor. Pos.	10	1	0	0	0	2	2	4	.100	.100	.250

RUNS BATTED IN	From 1B	From 2B	From 3B	Scoring Position
Totals	4/54	5/33	8/25	13/58
Percentage	7.4%	15.2%	32.0%	22.4%

Loves to face: Brian Holton (.800, 4-for-5, 1 HR)
Calvin Schiraldi (.800, 4-for-5, 1 SO)
John Smoltz (.500, 4-for-8)

Hates to face: David Cone (.154, 2-for-13)
Rob Dibble (0-for-5, 4 SO)
Rick Sutcliffe (.190, 4-for-21)

Miscellaneous statistics: Ground outs-to-air outs ratio: 1.41 last season, 1.69 for career. . . . Grounded into 2 double plays in 44 opportunities (one per 22.0). . . . Drove in 8 of 15 runners from third base with less than two outs (53%). . . . Direction of balls hit to the outfield: 39% to left field, 45% to center, 16% to right. . . . Base running: Advanced from first base to third on 5 of 10 outfield singles (50%); scored from second on 2 of 4 (50%). . . . Made 1.88 putouts per nine innings in left field.

Comments: Started 38 games last season, all against right-handed pitchers. Two-year totals with Expos: 66 starts vs. right-handers, none vs. left-handers. Buck Rodgers allowed him to come to bat only 12 times against lefties last season, despite a career average of .267 vs. southpaws. . . . His only career home run against a left-handed pitcher was hit off Dennis Rasmussen in 1988. . . . His only home run in 186 career at-bats at Olympic Stadium came while wearing a Giants uniform in 1987. . . . His only home run last season came as a pinch hitter, August 17, off Jay Howell. . . . Batted .250 (9-for-36) as a pinch hitter last season; including nine walks, his pinch-hit on-base average was a neat .391. His career batting average as a pinch hitter is .288 to rank sixth among active players with at least 100 pinch at-bats. . . . Annual batting averages with runners in scoring position since 1987: .419, .298, .171, .111. Has only three hits in 33 at-bats with two outs and RISP over the past two seasons. . . . His true niche: leading off innings. His .489 on-base percentage in those situations was the highest in the majors among players with at least 40 such plate appearances. . . . His .999 fielding percentage (one error in 762 chances) is the best of any active player with at least 100 career games at first base, but don't hold your breath on his beating out *Le Gros Chat.*

Roberto Alomar

Bats Left and Right

San Diego Padres	AB	H	2B	3B	HR	RBI	BB	SO	BA	SA	OBA
Season	586	168	27	5	6	60	48	72	.287	.381	.340
vs. Left-Handers	204	53	13	1	3	17	21	38	.260	.377	.330
vs. Right-Handers	382	115	14	4	3	43	27	34	.301	.382	.345
vs. Ground-Ballers	290	80	15	2	1	32	29	32	.276	.352	.343
vs. Fly-Ballers	296	88	12	3	5	28	19	40	.297	.409	.338
Home Games	298	85	9	4	4	36	23	37	.285	.383	.334
Road Games	288	83	18	1	2	24	25	35	.288	.378	.346
Grass Fields	425	123	19	4	4	45	33	52	.289	.381	.340
Artificial Turf	161	45	8	1	2	15	15	20	.280	.379	.341
April	73	22	0	1	1	8	6	10	.301	.370	.346
May	108	37	9	0	0	13	9	10	.343	.426	.390
June	111	35	9	2	1	13	10	10	.315	.459	.379
July	108	26	1	1	1	10	9	17	.241	.296	.297
August	120	30	6	0	1	8	9	18	.250	.325	.302
Sept./Oct.	66	18	2	1	2	8	5	7	.273	.424	.324
Leading Off Inn.	113	32	6	0	3	3	12	13	.283	.416	.352
Bases Empty	322	86	16	0	3	3	26	39	.267	.345	.322
Runners On	264	82	11	5	3	57	22	33	.311	.424	.362
Runners/Scor. Pos.	139	47	4	3	2	50	13	22	.338	.453	.390
Runners On/2 Out	88	28	4	1	0	22	9	13	.318	.386	.388
Scor. Pos./2 Out	57	18	1	1	0	19	7	9	.316	.368	.400
Late-Inning Pressure	94	20	3	0	0	8	11	16	.213	.245	.292
Leading Off	20	4	0	0	0	0	5	4	.200	.200	.360
Runners On	48	9	1	0	0	8	3	8	.188	.208	.231
Runners/Scor. Pos.	25	6	1	0	0	8	2	4	.240	.280	.286

RUNS BATTED IN	From 1B	From 2B	From 3B	Scoring Position
Totals	6/176	29/119	19/43	48/162
Percentage	3.4%	24.4%	44.2%	29.6%

Loves to face: Neal Heaton (.400, 8-for-20, 3 2B, 2 HR)
Mike Scott (.444, 12-for-27, 1 HR)
Zane Smith (.571, 4-for-7)

Hates to face: Scott Garrelts (.167, 3-for-18)
Bryn Smith (.182, 6-for-33, 0 BB)
Fernando Valenzuela (.148, 4-for-27)

Miscellaneous statistics: Ground outs-to-air outs ratio: 1.46 last season, 1.41 for career. . . . Grounded into 16 double plays in 137 opportunities (one per 8.6). . . . Drove in 12 of 23 runners from third base with less than two outs (52%). . . . Direction of balls hit to the outfield: 42% to left field, 31% to center, 27% to right batting left-handed; 41% to left, 27% to center, 32% to right batting right-handed. . . . Base running: Advanced from first base to third on 19 of 34 outfield singles (56%); scored from second on 15 of 18 (83%). . . . Made 2.88 assists per nine innings at second base.

Comments: Batted .364 from the leadoff spot in the lineup, the 3d-highest average of any player in the majors last season (minimum: 50 AB). That would be a useful skill in Toronto, where leadoff batters batted only .252 (11th in A.L.) with a .306 on-base average (12th in A.L.) last season. Two of the guys chiefly responsible for those figures (Mookie Wilson, Tony Fernandez, and Junior Felix combined for 150 starts) have all left the country. . . . For breakdown freaks only: in road games, he hit .325 batting left-handed, but only .216 from the right side. In Jack Murphy Stadium, he hit .277 left-handed, .299 right-handed. . . . Batted .344 in 128 first-inning at-bats, .271 thereafter. . . . Hit 22 home runs in his three seasons with San Diego. In his 15-year career, Senor Sandy Senior hit 13 homers, including one off a young Dennis Eckersley in 1975. . . . With Roberto's acquisition by Toronto, he and Sandy Jr. have a shot at joining Lee and Carlos May as the only brothers who have been both teammates and opponents on All-Star squads. . . . Career and most-recent season batting statistics closely resemble those of Tony Taylor (through 1960), Rennie Stennett (1974), and Julio Franco (1985).

Eric Anthony

Bats Left

Houston Astros	AB	H	2B	3B	HR	RBI	BB	SO	BA	SA	OBA
Season	239	46	8	0	10	29	29	78	.192	.351	.279
vs. Left-Handers	84	18	3	0	3	10	8	23	.214	.357	.284
vs. Right-Handers	155	28	5	0	7	19	21	55	.181	.348	.276
vs. Ground-Ballers	125	25	7	0	4	15	17	43	.200	.352	.292
vs. Fly-Ballers	114	21	1	0	6	14	12	35	.184	.351	.265
Home Games	110	24	4	0	5	14	13	34	.218	.391	.305
Road Games	129	22	4	0	5	15	16	44	.171	.318	.257
Grass Fields	69	10	1	0	4	12	10	23	.145	.333	.247
Artificial Turf	170	36	7	0	6	17	19	55	.212	.359	.292
April	5	1	0	0	0	0	1	1	.200	.200	.333
May	74	18	3	0	4	8	11	24	.243	.446	.345
June	65	14	4	0	3	9	6	20	.215	.415	.278
July	36	2	0	0	0	3	4	18	.056	.056	.140
August	0	0	0	0	0	0	0	0	—	—	—
Sept./Oct.	59	11	1	0	3	9	7	15	.186	.356	.279
Leading Off Inn.	59	8	0	0	2	2	6	14	.136	.237	.227
Bases Empty	137	21	1	0	7	7	17	48	.153	.314	.252
Runners On	102	25	7	0	3	22	12	30	.245	.402	.314
Runners/Scor. Pos.	49	8	4	0	2	19	6	16	.163	.367	.242
Runners On/2 Out	44	12	3	0	1	8	3	14	.273	.409	.319
Scor. Pos./2 Out	25	5	2	0	1	8	2	8	.200	.400	.259
Late-Inning Pressure	43	12	2	0	3	4	9	15	.279	.535	.415
Leading Off	12	2	0	0	1	1	1	3	.167	.417	.231
Runners On	18	6	2	0	0	1	3	6	.333	.444	.455
Runners/Scor. Pos.	5	0	0	0	0	0	1	4	.000	.000	.286

RUNS BATTED IN	From 1B	From 2B	From 3B	Scoring Position
Totals	5/79	6/41	8/20	14/61
Percentage	6.3%	14.6%	40.0%	23.0%

Loves to face: Scott Garrelts (.400, 2-for-5, 1 HR)
Hates to face: Jack Armstrong (0-for-5, 1 BB, 5 SO)
Dwight Gooden (0-for-8, 1 BB, 8 SO)

Miscellaneous statistics: Ground outs-to-air outs ratio: 1.07 last season, 1.09 for career.... Grounded into 4 double plays in 52 opportunities (one per 13.0).... Drove in 6 of 9 runners from third base with less than two outs (67%).... Direction of balls hit to the outfield: 23% to left field, 30% to center, 47% to right.... Base running: Advanced from first base to third on 0 of 8 outfield singles; scored from second on 4 of 6 (67%).... Made 2.00 putouts per nine innings in right field.

Comments: Led his minor league in home runs in each of three consecutive seasons (1987–88–89). Career totals: 77 home runs in 1289 at-bats in the minor leagues, an average of one homer every 16.7 at-bats. How good is that figure? It approximates the career rate of Hall-of-Famer Eddie Mathews, who spent some of his baseball dotage in an Astros uniform.... In the majors, Anthony has seven home runs in 135 at-bats at the Astrodome, and another seven in 165 at-bats in road games.... Road-game batting average was 2d lowest among National League players with at least 100 at-bats last season. Only Chicago's Curtis Wilkerson (.162) had a lower average.... Only three players in Houston's major league history have had a lower single-season batting average than Anthony's .192 with as many at-bats as Eric had last season: Jerry Grote (.181 in 1964), Roger Metzger (.186 in 1977), and John Bateman (.190 in 1967).... He has struck out 94 times in 347 career plate appearances in the majors, or once every 3.69 times up. Quick now, we're looking for an instinctive answer: Is that a higher or a lower rate of strikeouts than Nolan Ryan has achieved from the mound? The answer: Ryan has struck out 5308 of the 20,927 batters he has faced in his career, a rate of one strikeout every 3.94 batters faced. To this point, if you want to see a strikeout, you're better off watching Anthony batting than Ryan pitching.

Wally Backman

Bats Left and Right

Pittsburgh Pirates	AB	H	2B	3B	HR	RBI	BB	SO	BA	SA	OBA
Season	315	92	21	3	2	28	42	53	.292	.397	.374
vs. Left-Handers	31	6	1	0	0	3	7	9	.194	.226	.359
vs. Right-Handers	284	86	20	3	2	25	35	44	.303	.415	.376
vs. Ground-Ballers	156	44	6	3	1	17	16	24	.282	.378	.353
vs. Fly-Ballers	159	48	15	0	1	11	26	29	.302	.415	.394
Home Games	154	43	12	1	0	12	21	28	.279	.370	.364
Road Games	161	49	9	2	2	16	21	25	.304	.422	.384
Grass Fields	87	32	6	1	2	11	9	14	.368	.529	.418
Artificial Turf	228	60	15	2	0	17	33	39	.263	.346	.357
April	43	16	2	1	0	2	4	10	.372	.465	.438
May	61	20	4	0	1	10	8	8	.328	.443	.400
June	64	12	4	1	1	5	5	12	.188	.328	.243
July	46	13	4	0	0	3	11	11	.283	.370	.414
August	43	9	3	0	0	4	8	5	.209	.279	.333
Sept./Oct.	58	22	4	1	0	4	6	7	.379	.483	.438
Leading Off Inn.	148	41	9	0	2	2	17	26	.277	.378	.352
Bases Empty	235	64	14	2	2	2	24	43	.272	.374	.340
Runners On	80	28	7	1	0	26	18	10	.350	.463	.461
Runners/Scor. Pos.	53	19	4	1	0	24	9	8	.358	.472	.431
Runners On/2 Out	39	12	4	0	0	9	10	5	.308	.410	.460
Scor. Pos./2 Out	28	8	2	0	0	8	6	5	.286	.357	.412
Late-Inning Pressure	32	7	4	0	0	2	7	8	.219	.344	.359
Leading Off	12	3	2	0	0	0	3	3	.250	.417	.400
Runners On	6	3	2	0	0	2	2	0	.500	.833	.625
Runners/Scor. Pos.	3	1	1	0	0	1	2	0	.333	.667	.600

RUNS BATTED IN	From 1B	From 2B	From 3B	Scoring Position
Totals	4/53	9/38	13/25	22/63
Percentage	7.5%	23.7%	52.0%	34.9%

Loves to face: Larry Andersen (.500, 7-for-14)
Shawn Boskie (.667, 4-for-6, 2 2B)
Rick Mahler (.500, 24-for-48)
Hates to face: Tim Belcher (.083, 1-for-12)
Bob Sebra (0-for-15, 2 BB)
Fernando Valenzuela (.059, 1-for-17)

Miscellaneous statistics: Ground outs-to-air outs ratio: 1.97 last season, 4th-highest rate in N.L.; 2.41 for career.... Grounded into 5 double plays in 34 opportunities (one per 6.8).... Drove in 9 of 15 runners from third base with less than two outs (60%).... Direction of balls hit to the outfield: 51% to left field, 33% to center, 16% to right batting left-handed; 57% to left, 14% to center, 29% to right batting right-handed.... Base running: Advanced from first base to third on 2 of 14 outfield singles (14%); scored from second on 13 of 20 (65%).... Made 1.81 assists per nine innings at third base.

Comments: Rejoins former Metsmate Lenny Dykstra in Philadelphia; they started 270 games as one-two hitters for Mets between 1985 and 1988; Mets had 173–97 (.641) record in those games.... Backman has alternated good and poor seasons throughout his entire career. He has a career average of .296 in even-numbered years, .253 in odd-numbered years.... Started 81 games vs. right-handed pitchers last season, but only one against a left-hander. Career batting average (.170) vs. lefties is the lowest by any player over the last 16 years (minimum: 400 AB). Ditto his .206 slugging percentage vs. lefties.... Owns .298 career batting average vs. right-handers.... His percentage of runners driven in from scoring position and his batting average with RISP were career highs.... Did not have a sacrifice bunt last season, and Jim Leyland bypassed him as potential pinch-hitter for Carmelo Martinez in key bunt situation vs. Norm Charlton in final game of National League playoffs. Martinez popped up the bunt, and Pirates went on to lose by a run.... Has hit three home runs over the last three seasons, all while leading off innings.... In eight seasons with Mets, Backman hit only two home runs at Shea Stadium; as a visitor there last season, he took David Cone deep.... His average of one error per 12.5 chances at third base was worse than Bobby Bonilla's (one per 13.0) or Jeff King's (one per 16.2).... Became the first major league player to go 6-for-6 in a game since Kirby Puckett in 1987.

Kevin Bass

Bats Left and Right

San Francisco Giants	AB	H	2B	3B	HR	RBI	BB	SO	BA	SA	OBA
Season	214	54	9	1	7	32	14	26	.252	.402	.303
vs. Left-Handers	90	23	4	0	5	16	4	10	.256	.467	.302
vs. Right-Handers	124	31	5	1	2	16	10	16	.250	.355	.304
vs. Ground-Ballers	107	34	5	1	6	21	5	10	.318	.551	.354
vs. Fly-Ballers	107	20	4	0	1	11	9	16	.187	.252	.254
Home Games	115	26	4	0	3	16	9	15	.226	.339	.282
Road Games	99	28	5	1	4	16	5	11	.283	.475	.327
Grass Fields	169	39	5	1	6	28	11	23	.231	.379	.276
Artificial Turf	45	15	4	0	1	4	3	3	.333	.489	.400
April	80	20	2	1	3	12	3	9	.250	.412	.277
May	69	20	5	0	3	13	4	8	.290	.493	.329
June	0	0	0	0	0	0	0	0	—	—	—
July	0	0	0	0	0	0	0	0	—	—	—
August	0	0	0	0	0	0	0	0	—	—	—
Sept./Oct.	65	14	2	0	1	7	7	9	.215	.292	.307
Leading Off Inn.	40	4	1	0	0	0	2	3	.100	.125	.143
Bases Empty	118	23	3	1	3	3	6	13	.195	.314	.240
Runners On	96	31	6	0	4	29	8	13	.323	.510	.377
Runners/Scor. Pos.	49	20	3	0	2	25	5	4	.408	.592	.455
Runners On/2 Out	33	9	1	0	1	8	4	3	.273	.394	.351
Scor. Pos./2 Out	21	7	0	0	1	8	1	1	.333	.476	.364
Late-Inning Pressure	35	9	1	0	1	4	3	5	.257	.371	.316
Leading Off	6	0	0	0	0	0	1	1	.000	.000	.143
Runners On	17	3	1	0	0	3	2	3	.176	.235	.263
Runners/Scor. Pos.	11	3	1	0	0	3	2	1	.273	.364	.385

RUNS BATTED IN	From 1B	From 2B	From 3B	Scoring Position
Totals	3/74	11/37	11/20	22/57
Percentage	4.1%	29.7%	55.0%	38.6%

Loves to face: Neal Heaton (.471, 8-for-17, 3 2B, 3 HR)
Rick Mahler (.435, 20-for-46, 1 HR)
John Smiley (.458, 11-for-24)

Hates to face: Norm Charlton (0-for-12)
Alejandro Pena (.111, 2-for-18)
Fernando Valenzuela (.194, 12-for-62, 1 HR)

Miscellaneous statistics: Ground outs-to-air outs ratio: 1.18 last season, 1.08 for career.... Grounded into 5 double plays in 52 opportunities (one per 10.4).... Drove in 9 of 13 runners from third base with less than two outs (69%).... Direction of balls hit to the outfield: 28% to left field, 46% to center, 26% to right batting left-handed; 43% to left, 27% to center, 30% to right batting right-handed.... Base running: Advanced from first base to third on 2 of 11 outfield singles (18%); scored from second on 3 of 5 (60%).... Made 1.73 putouts per nine innings in right field.

Comments: Knee surgery limited him to only 61 games last season. He has played in only 148 games over the last two years, after playing 150 or more in each of the previous four seasons.... Giants right fielders batted only .224 in 1989, so they signed Bass at (then) big bucks. He hit .254 as the right fielder last season; the players who combined to replace him during his time on the disabled list batted .282.... Bass hit 131 points higher vs. ground-ball pitchers (.318) than vs. fly-ballers (.187), the 3d-largest margin in the majors last season.... Has never drawn a walk in 71 career plate appearances with the bases loaded. Only two active players have more bases-loaded plate appearances without a walk.... A good clutch hitter: he has driven in over 30 percent of runners from scoring position in each of the last four seasons. Career breakdown: .263 with the bases empty, .287 with runners on base, .300 with runners in scoring position.... Even so, only one of his 32 RBIs gave the Giants a lead. Among all the players in the majors with at least 30 RBIs last season, no other player had fewer than three go-ahead RBIs. Don Robinson, who drove in all of seven runs for the season, had four go-ahead RBIs for the Giants.... Career average of .310 (39-for-126, 2 HR) as a pinch hitter, the highest by any active National League player with at least 100 pinch at-bats.

Jay Bell

Bats Right

Pittsburgh Pirates	AB	H	2B	3B	HR	RBI	BB	SO	BA	SA	OBA
Season	583	148	28	7	7	52	65	109	.254	.362	.329
vs. Left-Handers	251	69	13	4	2	17	34	42	.275	.382	.359
vs. Right-Handers	332	79	15	3	5	35	31	67	.238	.346	.305
vs. Ground-Ballers	297	86	16	3	3	31	29	53	.290	.394	.352
vs. Fly-Ballers	286	62	12	4	4	21	36	56	.217	.329	.305
Home Games	287	75	14	4	1	17	31	56	.261	.348	.336
Road Games	296	73	14	3	6	35	34	53	.247	.375	.321
Grass Fields	149	36	6	0	3	14	16	31	.242	.342	.311
Artificial Turf	434	112	22	7	4	38	49	78	.258	.369	.335
April	69	18	3	0	1	7	8	18	.261	.348	.338
May	99	28	9	2	0	7	8	15	.283	.414	.333
June	92	24	4	3	1	8	10	22	.261	.402	.330
July	103	28	2	0	2	12	6	10	.272	.350	.306
August	121	32	3	1	2	8	6	18	.264	.355	.297
Sept./Oct.	99	18	7	1	1	10	27	26	.182	.303	.369
Leading Off Inn.	94	28	5	1	1	1	14	20	.298	.404	.389
Bases Empty	350	80	18	1	4	4	43	75	.229	.320	.315
Runners On	233	68	10	6	3	48	22	34	.292	.425	.350
Runners/Scor. Pos.	121	34	3	4	3	44	15	22	.281	.446	.354
Runners On/2 Out	84	25	3	1	1	19	12	10	.298	.393	.385
Scor. Pos./2 Out	60	16	1	1	1	18	10	10	.267	.367	.371
Late-Inning Pressure	67	22	1	0	0	7	9	17	.328	.343	.397
Leading Off	20	9	1	0	0	0	1	5	.450	.500	.476
Runners On	27	10	0	0	0	7	2	5	.370	.370	.387
Runners/Scor. Pos.	17	8	0	0	0	7	2	5	.471	.471	.476

RUNS BATTED IN	From 1B	From 2B	From 3B	Scoring Position
Totals	7/170	16/92	22/51	38/143
Percentage	4.1%	17.4%	43.1%	26.6%

Loves to face: Mike Bielecki (.667, 8-for-12)
Tom Browning (.400, 4-for-10, 1 HR)

Hates to face: David Cone (.067, 1-for-15, 3 BB)
Mike Morgan (.071, 1-for-14, 1 2B)
Rick Reuschel (0-for-8)
Frank Viola (.158, 3-for-19)

Miscellaneous statistics: Ground outs-to-air outs ratio: 1.19 last season, 1.15 for career.... Grounded into 14 double plays in 160 opportunities (one per 11.4).... Drove in 14 of 25 runners from third base with less than two outs (56%).... Direction of balls hit to the outfield: 28% to left field, 32% to center, 40% to right.... Base running: Advanced from first base to third on 18 of 29 outfield singles (62%); scored from second on 10 of 17 (59%).... Made 3.00 assists per nine innings at shortstop.

Comments: Led National League shortstops in games played (159), complete games (149), putouts (260), and double plays started (51); became first Pittsburgh shortstop to start at least 100 games since Dale Berra in 1984.... Finished with 696 plate appearances, 3d-highest total in the league behind Brett Butler (732) and Joe Carter (697).... Led the majors with 39 sacrifice bunts, the most by any National League player since Zebulon Terry had that number in 1922; 17 of Bell's 39 sacrifices came in the first inning. When he wasn't sacrificing, he had the lowest first-inning batting average (.200) of any major leaguer who had at least 100 first-inning at-bats.... Jim Leyland sacrificed more with the 2d spot in his batting order (40) than he did with the 9th spot (35).... His .328 average in Late-Inning Pressure Situations was the best on the team. In LIPS with runners in scoring position, he batted .471 (8-for-17).... Has hit for a higher average with runners on base than he has with the bases empty in each of his five seasons in the majors. Career figures: .280 with runners on base, .221 with the bases empty.... Even though he batted only .182 from September 1 to the end of the season, he helped out by drawing 27 walks.... Bell struck out 108 times as a shortstop last season, 21 more than any other major league shortstop.

Todd Benzinger

Bats Left and Right

Cincinnati Reds	AB	H	2B	3B	HR	RBI	BB	SO	BA	SA	OBA
Season	376	95	14	2	5	46	19	69	.253	.340	.291
vs. Left-Handers	172	49	7	0	2	17	6	15	.285	.360	.306
vs. Right-Handers	204	46	7	2	3	29	13	54	.225	.324	.279
vs. Ground-Ballers	197	49	8	0	4	24	2	36	.249	.350	.256
vs. Fly-Ballers	179	46	6	2	1	22	17	33	.257	.330	.325
Home Games	190	49	8	1	4	23	10	30	.258	.374	.296
Road Games	186	46	6	1	1	23	9	39	.247	.306	.285
Grass Fields	87	19	2	0	0	6	5	16	.218	.241	.277
Artificial Turf	289	76	12	2	5	40	14	53	.263	.370	.295
April	59	20	3	0	1	9	9	6	.339	.441	.408
May	106	29	6	1	0	14	1	16	.274	.349	.273
June	91	24	2	0	3	16	6	20	.264	.385	.320
July	42	5	1	0	0	0	1	13	.119	.143	.140
August	51	12	2	1	1	5	0	7	.235	.373	.250
Sept./Oct.	27	5	0	0	0	2	2	7	.185	.185	.267
Leading Off Inn.	82	20	0	0	0	0	6	17	.244	.244	.303
Bases Empty	203	49	3	1	4	4	8	37	.241	.325	.277
Runners On	173	46	11	1	1	42	11	32	.266	.358	.306
Runners/Scor. Pos.	116	29	6	1	1	40	10	24	.250	.345	.304
Runners On/2 Out	74	14	3	0	1	10	5	15	.189	.270	.241
Scor. Pos./2 Out	57	8	3	0	1	10	5	13	.140	.246	.210
Late-Inning Pressure	54	14	1	1	2	8	1	10	.259	.426	.281
Leading Off	14	2	0	0	0	0	1	4	.143	.143	.250
Runners On	22	6	1	1	0	6	0	3	.273	.409	.261
Runners/Scor. Pos.	15	5	1	1	0	6	0	1	.333	.533	.313

RUNS BATTED IN	From 1B	From 2B	From 3B	Scoring Position
Totals	4/122	7/80	30/63	37/143
Percentage	3.3%	8.8%	47.6%	25.9%

Loves to face: Tom Glavine (.400, 10-for-25, 2 HR)
Derek Lilliquist (.688, 11-for-16)
Jay Howell (.500, 3-for-6, 1 2B, 1 HR)

Hates to face: Greg W. Harris (.063, 1-for-16)
Bruce Hurst (.059, 1-for-17)
Frank Viola (.059, 1-for-17)

Miscellaneous statistics: Ground outs-to-air outs ratio: 1.26 last season, 1.04 for career.... Grounded into 3 double plays in 79 opportunities (one per 26.3), 5th-best rate in N.L. ... Drove in 25 of 31 runners from third base with less than two outs (81%), shared 2d-highest rate in N.L.... Direction of balls hit to the outfield: 32% to left field, 22% to center, 46% to right batting left-handed; 25% to left, 30% to center, 45% to right batting right-handed.... Base running: Advanced from first base to third on 9 of 27 outfield singles (33%); scored from second on 6 of 11 (55%).... Made 0.63 assists per nine innings at first base.

Comments: Total of plate appearances fell from 686 in 1989 to 408 last season. Most of the 278 missing plate appearances were found by Hal Morris.... Started 64 of the Reds' first 70 games last season, but made only 26 starts in their last 92 games. He then made four postseason starts (including Games Three and Four of the World Series, played under DH rules).... Started at least one game in each lineup slot except the leadoff and ninth spots.... Has come up with the bases loaded 69 times in his four years in the majors; over that span, only five players in majors have been up more often with the bags full. Career numbers with three on: batting .333 with three home runs, one walk, 13 strikeouts.... Has played four years in the majors, split between Fenway and Riverfront, two of the top five parks for batting average in our five-year survey. That's apparent in Todd's career batting-average breakdown: .275 in home games, .232 in road games.... Hit for a higher average with runners on base than he did with the bases empty for the first time in his career.... Has been caught stealing 18 times in his career, with only 13 stolen bases to show for it.... Career average of .182 as a pinch hitter.... Caught Carney Lansford's foul pop for final out of the Reds' World Series sweep; that more than made up for Oakland's sweep of his Red Sox in 1988 American League Championship Series.

Craig Biggio

Bats Right

Houston Astros	AB	H	2B	3B	HR	RBI	BB	SO	BA	SA	OBA
Season	555	153	24	2	4	42	53	79	.276	.348	.342
vs. Left-Handers	218	50	6	1	2	13	27	27	.229	.294	.316
vs. Right-Handers	337	103	18	1	2	29	26	52	.306	.383	.359
vs. Ground-Ballers	294	88	18	2	2	23	29	33	.299	.395	.362
vs. Fly-Ballers	261	65	6	0	2	19	24	46	.249	.295	.318
Home Games	277	76	11	1	2	21	25	39	.274	.343	.338
Road Games	278	77	13	1	2	21	28	40	.277	.353	.345
Grass Fields	166	50	8	1	2	12	12	21	.301	.398	.352
Artificial Turf	389	103	16	1	2	30	41	58	.265	.326	.337
April	72	20	2	0	1	5	10	14	.278	.347	.366
May	102	30	2	0	1	10	9	19	.294	.343	.351
June	98	26	5	0	1	7	13	13	.265	.347	.351
July	108	32	7	1	1	9	7	10	.296	.407	.350
August	93	24	2	1	0	6	5	11	.258	.301	.296
Sept./Oct.	82	21	6	0	0	5	9	12	.256	.329	.333
Leading Off Inn.	99	21	6	1	1	1	11	10	.212	.323	.291
Bases Empty	311	82	16	1	3	3	27	43	.264	.350	.324
Runners On	244	71	8	1	1	39	26	36	.291	.344	.363
Runners/Scor. Pos.	138	41	3	0	1	35	18	25	.297	.341	.384
Runners On/2 Out	89	24	4	0	1	18	14	14	.270	.348	.375
Scor. Pos./2 Out	59	18	3	0	1	17	12	10	.305	.407	.431
Late-Inning Pressure	100	21	2	1	0	5	7	16	.210	.250	.262
Leading Off	21	5	1	1	0	0	2	3	.238	.381	.304
Runners On	42	7	1	0	0	5	3	5	.167	.190	.222
Runners/Scor. Pos.	22	6	0	0	0	5	2	2	.273	.273	.333

RUNS BATTED IN	From 1B	From 2B	From 3B	Scoring Position
Totals	4/175	14/107	20/52	34/159
Percentage	2.3%	13.1%	38.5%	21.4%

Loves to face: Orel Hershiser (.526, 10-for-19)
Danny Jackson (.667, 6-for-9)
John Wetteland (.625, 5-for-8, 2 HR, 3 SO)

Hates to face: Tom Browning (.056, 1-for-18, 3 BB)
Kevin Gross (0-for-14)
Ed Whitson (.100, 2-for-20)

Miscellaneous statistics: Ground outs-to-air outs ratio: 1.08 last season, 1.14 for career.... Grounded into 11 double plays in 131 opportunities (one per 11.9).... Drove in 13 of 29 runners from third base with less than two outs (45%).... Direction of balls hit to the outfield: 41% to left field, 31% to center, 28% to right.... Base running: Advanced from first base to third on 6 of 21 outfield singles (29%); scored from second on 9 of 13 (69%).... Opposing base stealers: 117-for-155 (75%).

Comments: The youngest regular catcher in the National League last season; he didn't turn 25 until December. He's three months younger than Todd Zeile, five months younger than Joe Oliver.... Had the 2d-highest day-game batting average (.374) in the National League last season, and his 131-point difference between day-game and night-game (.243) averages was the largest margin in the majors. Career numbers: .315 in day games, .241 at night, the 2d-largest margin in the majors over the last five years.... Despite hitting .297 with runners in scoring position, he drove in only 21 percent of runners from second or third base last season, the 4th-lowest rate in the league among players who batted with 150 or more runners in scoring position. Zeile, Juan Samuel, and Dickie Thon were the only players with lower rates.... Became the third player since 1900 with at least 20 steals in two consecutive seasons in which he caught 100 or more games. The others: Johnny Kling (1902–03) and John Wathan (1982–83). In major league history, only 12 catchers (minimum: 100 games caught) have had 20 or more steals in a season, including active players Biggio, B.J. Surhoff, and Benito Santiago.... Caught 113 games, played 50 in the outfield. The last player with 50 games at those positions in the same season: Joe Ferguson (1979).... Only one player in baseball history played 100 games at both catcher and second base in his *career*: Tom Daly (1887–1903). For more on the possibility of Biggio moving to second base, see the Astros essay.

Jeff Blauser

Bats Right

Atlanta Braves	AB	H	2B	3B	HR	RBI	BB	SO	BA	SA	OBA
Season	386	104	24	3	8	39	35	70	.269	.409	.338
vs. Left-Handers	136	40	12	1	3	17	16	20	.294	.463	.373
vs. Right-Handers	250	64	12	2	5	22	19	50	.256	.380	.319
vs. Ground-Ballers	184	55	15	0	3	16	20	30	.299	.429	.380
vs. Fly-Ballers	202	49	9	3	5	23	15	40	.243	.391	.298
Home Games	172	51	12	2	3	21	19	25	.297	.442	.373
Road Games	214	53	12	1	5	18	16	45	.248	.383	.309
Grass Fields	288	76	19	3	7	36	32	51	.264	.424	.346
Artificial Turf	98	28	5	0	1	3	3	19	.286	.367	.314
April	38	8	0	0	0	0	4	8	.211	.211	.286
May	30	9	3	0	3	6	5	12	.300	.700	.417
June	97	31	8	1	1	11	6	14	.320	.454	.365
July	62	13	2	1	0	5	8	11	.210	.274	.300
August	58	13	3	0	1	5	5	8	.224	.328	.308
Sept./Oct.	101	30	8	1	3	12	7	17	.297	.485	.349
Leading Off Inn.	90	29	10	0	2	2	5	11	.322	.500	.358
Bases Empty	228	61	15	0	5	5	16	38	.268	.399	.324
Runners On	158	43	9	3	3	34	19	32	.272	.424	.358
Runners/Scor. Pos.	79	19	3	2	1	25	14	14	.241	.367	.362
Runners On/2 Out	71	15	4	2	0	17	10	18	.211	.324	.317
Scor. Pos./2 Out	45	10	2	2	0	15	9	10	.222	.356	.364
Late-Inning Pressure	62	12	3	1	4	10	3	14	.194	.468	.242
Leading Off	17	1	1	0	0	0	1	5	.059	.118	.111
Runners On	24	7	1	1	2	8	2	5	.292	.667	.370
Runners/Scor. Pos.	13	4	1	1	1	6	1	2	.308	.769	.357

RUNS BATTED IN	From 1B	From 2B	From 3B	Scoring Position
Totals	9/122	12/61	10/30	22/91
Percentage	7.4%	19.7%	33.3%	24.2%

Loves to face: Jim Deshaies (.355, 11-for-31, 2 HR)
Fernando Valenzuela (.364, 8-for-22, 1 HR)
Jose Rijo (.600, 6-for-10)

Hates to face: Jose DeLeon (0-for-8, 450)
Scott Garrelts (.100, 2-for-20)
Ramon Martinez (.143, 2-for-14, 1 HR, 10 SO)

Miscellaneous statistics: Ground outs-to-air outs ratio: 0.86 last season, 0.96 for career. . . . Grounded into 4 double plays in 84 opportunities (one per 21.0). . . . Drove in 3 of 8 runners from third base with less than two outs (38%). . . . Direction of balls hit to the outfield: 49% to left field, 29% to center, 23% to right. . . . Base running: Advanced from first base to third on 13 of 23 outfield singles (57%); scored from second on 4 of 7 (57%). . . . Made 2.97 assists per nine innings at shortstop.

Comments: Like most fly-ball hitters, he has a better career batting average vs. ground-ball pitchers (.301) than vs. fly-ball pitchers (.229). . . . Has hit more career home runs on the road (13) than he has at Atlanta-Fulton County Stadium (11). He has hit five in 29 at-bats at Wrigley Field, where he has a .345 career average. . . . Hit four home runs in 62 at-bats in Late-Inning Pressure Situations, and four home runs in 324 at bats at other times. Eight of his 12 hits in Late-Inning Pressure Situations were extra-base hits. Through the 1989 season, Blauser had only one career home run in 125 LIPS at-bats. . . . Remember the hot trade rumor from the spring of 1988? Blauser to the Yankees for Roberto Kelly. . . . Batted .272 as a shortstop last season, 2d highest in the league at that position, behind Barry Larkin. . . . Played 54 percent of Braves' innings at shortstop last season; Andres Thomas played 42 percent. But there was a large difference in runs allowed: Atlanta allowed 5.73 runs per nine innings with Blauser at shortstop, but only 4.49 runs per nine innings with Thomas there. . . . Who was the last (and only) Braves shortstop to start for the National League in the All-Star Game? Eddie Miller for the Boston Braves in 1942. They traded him that winter, and they have been damned with mediocre shortstops ever since.

Barry Bonds

Bats Left

Pittsburgh Pirates	AB	H	2B	3B	HR	RBI	BB	SO	BA	SA	OBA
Season	519	156	32	3	33	114	93	83	.301	.565	.406
vs. Left-Handers	240	73	14	2	17	58	31	41	.304	.592	.386
vs. Right-Handers	279	83	18	1	16	56	62	42	.297	.541	.422
vs. Ground-Ballers	275	91	20	2	19	63	42	37	.331	.625	.419
vs. Fly-Ballers	244	65	12	1	14	51	51	46	.266	.496	.391
Home Games	239	66	9	3	14	46	50	43	.276	.515	.401
Road Games	280	90	23	0	19	68	43	40	.321	.607	.410
Grass Fields	146	51	13	0	10	40	21	22	.349	.644	.429
Artificial Turf	373	105	19	3	23	74	72	61	.282	.534	.397
April	60	19	4	1	4	13	8	10	.317	.617	.400
May	88	27	7	1	6	24	14	18	.307	.614	.402
June	84	31	9	1	3	16	11	10	.369	.607	.442
July	86	28	4	0	5	22	22	13	.326	.547	.450
August	101	25	5	0	7	22	20	17	.248	.505	.374
Sept./Oct.	100	26	3	0	8	17	18	15	.260	.530	.375
Leading Off Inn.	131	39	8	1	10	10	27	17	.298	.603	.421
Bases Empty	298	80	16	2	19	19	49	59	.268	.527	.375
Runners On	221	76	16	1	14	95	44	24	.344	.615	.445
Runners/Scor. Pos.	138	52	12	1	7	79	30	15	.377	.630	.471
Runners On/2 Out	105	35	7	1	6	48	20	13	.333	.590	.444
Scor. Pos./2 Out	80	28	6	1	4	43	17	8	.350	.600	.464
Late-Inning Pressure	71	19	3	0	4	8	15	13	.268	.479	.395
Leading Off	18	7	2	0	1	1	6	4	.389	.667	.542
Runners On	35	6	1	0	1	5	4	6	.171	.286	.256
Runners/Scor. Pos.	21	3	1	0	0	3	3	4	.143	.190	.250

RUNS BATTED IN	From 1B	From 2B	From 3B	Scoring Position
Totals	15/150	28/104	38/74	66/178
Percentage	10.0%	26.9%	51.4%	37.1%

Loves to face: Dwight Gooden (.372, 16-for-43, 2 HR, 8 BB)
Tom Browning (.400, 10-for-25, 4 HR, 10 BB)
Bruce Hurst (.476, 10-for-21, 2 HR)

Hates to face: Paul Assenmacher (.063, 1-for-16, 2 BB)
Mike Bielecki (.040, 1-for-25, 1 2B, 5 BB)
Randy Myers (.158, 3-for-19, 3 BB)

Miscellaneous statistics: Ground outs-to-air outs ratio: 0.74 last season, 0.86 for career. . . . Grounded into 8 double plays in 95 opportunities (one per 11.9). . . . Drove in 22 of 33 runners from third base with less than two outs (67%). . . . Direction of balls hit to the outfield: 31% to left field, 33% to center, 36% to right. . . . Base running: Advanced from first base to third on 14 of 25 outfield singles (56%); scored from second on 15 of 21 (71%). . . . Made 2.36 putouts per nine innings in left field, highest rate in N.L.

Comments: First major league player in the 30/50/.300 Club for homers, steals, and batting average. . . . Led the majors with 58 RBIs vs. left-handed pitchers (Cecil Fielder had 54), and led National League with 17 home runs off lefties, after hitting only 4 in 1989. . . . Batted 104 points higher with runners in scoring position (.377) than in other at-bats (.273) last season, the 2d-largest margin in the majors. Coming into 1990, he had been a .213 career hitter in those situations. . . . Even with his MVP year, however, he went only 3-for-21 with RISP in Late-Inning Pressure Situations. His career average of .111 (11-for-99) in those situations is the lowest by any player over the last 16 years (minimum: 40 AB). He has driven in only 13 percent of runners from scoring poasition in LIPS, compared to a rate of 30 percent in other at-bats. . . . Led the majors with a .349 batting average on grass fields last season. His favorite grass field: Jack Murphy Stadium, with a .447 career batting average and six home runs in 85 at-bats. . . . Led major league left fielders with 335 putouts, and had 14 assists to tie Kevin McReynolds for National League lead among outfielders. . . . Bonds has played 717 games in his major league career. Father/son comparison at 717-game mark of their respective careers: Daddy Bobby leads in batting average (.275–.265), home runs (128–117), RBIs (393–337), and steals (181–169); Barry has more walks (377–321) and a lot fewer strikeouts (448–743).

Bobby Bonilla

Bats Left and Right

Pittsburgh Pirates	AB	H	2B	3B	HR	RBI	BB	SO	BA	SA	OBA
Season	625	175	39	7	32	120	45	103	.280	.518	.322
vs. Left-Handers	280	73	19	2	14	48	20	32	.261	.493	.303
vs. Right-Handers	345	102	20	5	18	72	25	71	.296	.539	.338
vs. Ground-Ballers	314	98	22	3	16	66	21	50	.312	.554	.349
vs. Fly-Ballers	311	77	17	4	16	54	24	53	.248	.482	.295
Home Games	310	81	19	2	13	52	17	44	.261	.461	.295
Road Games	315	94	20	5	19	68	28	59	.298	.575	.347
Grass Fields	171	57	13	3	14	44	11	32	.333	.690	.368
Artificial Turf	454	118	26	4	18	76	34	71	.260	.454	.305
April	86	24	4	0	7	21	2	16	.279	.570	.295
May	103	33	8	4	5	19	7	16	.320	.621	.360
June	95	20	5	0	5	14	6	17	.211	.421	.248
July	104	25	8	0	4	14	11	19	.240	.433	.305
August	112	40	6	2	9	23	15	15	.357	.688	.426
Sept./Oct.	125	33	8	1	2	29	4	20	.264	.392	.281
Leading Off Inn.	161	45	9	3	7	7	6	29	.280	.503	.305
Bases Empty	323	97	22	5	20	20	14	51	.300	.585	.329
Runners On	302	78	17	2	12	100	31	52	.258	.447	.315
Runners/Scor. Pos.	188	53	13	1	7	86	25	29	.282	.473	.345
Runners On/2 Out	139	27	4	1	6	34	22	22	.194	.367	.309
Scor. Pos./2 Out	81	17	4	1	3	28	18	12	.210	.395	.360
Late-Inning Pressure	70	17	3	0	2	11	9	14	.243	.371	.321
Leading Off	14	2	0	0	0	0	0	5	.143	.143	.143
Runners On	30	5	1	0	1	10	8	7	.167	.300	.326
Runners/Scor. Pos.	14	2	0	0	0	7	5	3	.143	.143	.333

RUNS BATTED IN	From 1B	From 2B	From 3B	Scoring Position
Totals	16/212	27/139	45/103	72/242
Percentage	7.5%	19.4%	43.7%	29.8%

Loves to face: Mike Bielecki (.407, 11-for-27, 3 2B, 4 HR)
Tom Browning (.387, 12-for-31, 4 2B, 5 HR, 0 BB)
Pete Smith (.467, 7-for-15, 3 HR)

Hates to face: Dennis Cook (0-for-10)
Craig Lefferts (.071, 1-for-14)
Mike Scott (.130, 3-for-23)

Miscellaneous statistics: Ground outs-to-air outs ratio: 0.70 last season, 0.91 for career.... Grounded into 11 double plays in 128 opportunities (one per 11.6).... Drove in 36 of 57 runners from third base with less than two outs (63%).... Direction of balls hit to the outfield: 32% to left field, 32% to center, 36% to right batting left-handed; 41% to left, 31% to center; 28% to right batting right-handed.... Base running: Advanced from first base to third on 12 of 22 outfield singles (55%); scored from second on 12 of 16 (75%).... Made 2.00 putouts per nine innings in right field.

Comments: First Pirates hitter since Willie Stargell in 1973 to lead majors in extra-base hits. Bo also led majors with 15 sacrifice flies, helping Pirates to drive in league-leading 58.5 percent of runners from third base with less than two outs.... Enters 1991 with a career total of 98 home runs. Only 17 switch-hitters in baseball history have hit 100 or more home runs; only five have hit 200, a likely Bonilla target.... One of 11 major leaguers to have hit for a higher batting average in day games than in night games in each of the last five seasons.... Led National League right fielders with 12 errors.... Pirates have had a different opening-day right fielder in each of the last eight seasons: Dave Parker, Doug Frobel, George Hendrick, Joe Orsulak, Andy Van Slyke, Darnell Coles, Glenn Wilson, and Bonilla. Last year, he became the first Pittsburgh player since Parker in 1983 to make 100 or more starts in right field.... His grand-slam homer on May 18 was first by a Pirates player in nearly three years; Barry Bonds, Jeff King, Gary Redus, and Bonilla himself hit grannies later in the season.... Batted .425 (17-for-40, 4 HR) in the Pirates' five doubleheaders last season. Pittsburgh swept all 10 games, becoming the first team in this century to play as many as five doubleheaders in a season and sweep them all.

Daryl Boston

Bats Left

White Sox/Mets	AB	H	2B	3B	HR	RBI	BB	SO	BA	SA	OBA
Season	367	100	21	2	12	45	28	50	.272	.439	.327
vs. Left-Handers	60	15	2	0	0	8	7	11	.250	.283	.328
vs. Right-Handers	307	85	19	2	12	37	21	39	.277	.469	.327
vs. Ground-Ballers	186	56	11	1	8	29	15	24	.301	.500	.360
vs. Fly-Ballers	181	44	10	1	4	16	13	26	.243	.376	.294
Home Games	186	50	12	1	4	17	16	27	.269	.409	.327
Road Games	181	50	9	1	8	28	12	23	.276	.470	.328
Grass Fields	275	76	18	2	7	32	25	36	.276	.433	.339
Artificial Turf	92	24	3	0	5	13	3	14	.261	.457	.292
April	1	0	0	0	0	0	0	0	.000	.000	.000
May	59	17	6	1	3	9	5	4	.288	.576	.344
June	73	20	5	0	2	10	8	13	.274	.425	.361
July	72	23	4	1	2	8	2	13	.319	.486	.338
August	96	25	5	0	1	6	4	11	.260	.344	.290
Sept./Oct.	66	15	1	0	4	12	9	9	.227	.424	.320
Leading Off Inn.	94	28	4	0	3	3	8	18	.298	.436	.359
Bases Empty	209	57	12	1	6	6	17	33	.273	.426	.330
Runners On	158	43	9	1	6	39	11	17	.272	.456	.324
Runners/Scor. Pos.	98	27	4	1	4	33	8	10	.276	.459	.336
Runners On/2 Out	69	21	5	1	3	22	4	9	.304	.536	.351
Scor. Pos./2 Out	46	15	3	1	2	19	4	5	.326	.565	.392
Late-Inning Pressure	54	12	5	0	1	5	3	9	.222	.370	.263
Leading Off	14	2	1	0	0	0	0	4	.143	.214	.143
Runners On	21	6	1	0	0	4	2	0	.286	.333	.348
Runners/Scor. Pos.	15	4	0	0	0	4	0	0	.267	.267	.267

RUNS BATTED IN	From 1B	From 2B	From 3B	Scoring Position
Totals	6/110	16/85	11/33	27/118
Percentage	5.5%	18.8%	33.3%	22.9%

Loves to face: Xavier Hernandez (2-for-2, 2 HR)
Mike Morgan (.375, 6-for-16, 3 2B, 2 HR)
Jeff Russell (.667, 6-for-9, 3 2B, 1 HR)

Hates to face: Oil Can Boyd (.176, 3-for-17)
Mike Moore (.087, 2-for-23, 2 2B)
Jack Morris (.120, 3-for-25, 1 HR, 3 BB)

Miscellaneous statistics: Ground outs-to-air outs ratio: 0.68 last season, 0.92 for career.... Grounded into 7 double plays in 68 opportunities (one per 9.7).... Drove in 4 of 12 runners from third base with less than two outs (33%).... Direction of balls hit to the outfield: 34% to left field, 31% to center, 35% to right.... Base running: Advanced from first base to third on 13 of 19 outfield singles (68%), shared highest rate in N.L.; scored from second on 12 of 15 (80%).... Made 2.25 putouts per nine innings in center field, lowest rate in N.L.

Comments: Released by White Sox in April, he went on to establish career highs in starts (90), batting average (.272), and RBIs (45).... Batting average stood above .300 as late as August 17, but batted only .207 over remainder of season.... Started 86 games in which the Mets faced a right-handed starter, but only four games in which they faced a lefty.... After never being hit by a pitch through the first 1594 plate appearances of his career, Boston was plunked in consecutive games in June.... Has had serious career-long problems in Late-Inning Pressure Situations. He has hit for a lower average in LIPS than in other at-bats in each of seven seasons in the majors. Career averages: .195 in LIPS, .256 at other times. He has driven in only 14 percent of runners from scoring position in LIPS over his career, the 6th-lowest rate by any player since 1975 (minimum: 50 opportunities). Eclectic group: the five players with worse rates are Roger Metzger, Rick Schu, Buck Martinez, Bo Jackson, and Barry Bonds.... Has hit 50 career home runs: 49 against right-handed pitchers, one against Mark Thurmond. He's also hitless in 20 career at-bats with two outs and the bases loaded. Those trends were known, thanks to last year's *Analyst*, when Boston was due to bat against Thurmond with two outs and the bags full in the seventh inning of a one-run game in May. In one of those great *Elias Analyst* moments, Davey Johnson sent Mark Carreon to bat for Boston. Carreon struck out.

Glenn Braggs

Bats Right

Brewers/Reds	AB	H	2B	3B	HR	RBI	BB	SO	BA	SA	OBA
Season	314	88	14	1	9	41	38	64	.280	.417	.365
vs. Left-Handers	149	43	5	1	6	19	26	26	.289	.456	.399
vs. Right-Handers	165	45	9	0	3	22	12	38	.273	.382	.332
vs. Ground-Ballers	161	52	5	1	6	25	18	32	.323	.478	.398
vs. Fly-Ballers	153	36	9	0	3	16	20	32	.235	.353	.330
Home Games	161	45	8	1	5	25	20	37	.280	.435	.368
Road Games	153	43	6	0	4	16	18	27	.281	.399	.360
Grass Fields	144	33	8	0	3	18	17	32	.229	.347	.317
Artificial Turf	170	55	6	1	6	23	21	32	.324	.476	.405
April	34	9	3	0	1	5	4	5	.265	.441	.350
May	68	18	1	0	2	8	7	13	.265	.368	.342
June	61	18	1	1	2	7	4	16	.295	.443	.348
July	66	20	6	0	1	10	10	17	.303	.439	.397
August	36	7	0	0	0	4	6	4	.194	.194	.310
Sept./Oct.	49	16	3	0	3	7	7	9	.327	.571	.421
Leading Off Inn.	89	24	2	1	2	2	10	17	.270	.382	.343
Bases Empty	194	50	5	1	7	7	21	42	.258	.402	.342
Runners On	120	38	9	0	2	34	17	22	.317	.442	.399
Runners/Scor. Pos.	69	21	4	0	0	26	13	13	.304	.362	.409
Runners On/2 Out	52	13	2	0	0	9	7	8	.250	.288	.350
Scor. Pos./2 Out	35	7	1	0	0	8	7	6	.200	.229	.349
Late-Inning Pressure	54	16	1	0	0	4	4	10	.296	.315	.367
Leading Off	12	3	0	0	0	0	3	2	.250	.250	.400
Runners On	23	9	1	0	0	4	1	4	.391	.435	.440
Runners/Scor. Pos.	15	5	0	0	0	3	1	3	.333	.333	.412

RUNS BATTED IN	From 1B	From 2B	From 3B	Scoring Position
Totals	7/90	7/48	18/38	25/86
Percentage	7.8%	14.6%	47.4%	29.1%

Loves to face: Steve Avery (.500, 4-for-8, 1 3B, 2 HR)
Charlie Hough (.667, 4-for-6, 1 HR)

Hates to face: Jim Clancy (.133, 2-for-15)
Scott Garrelts (.111, 1-for-9)
Bruce Hurst (.174, 4-for-23)
Charlie Leibrandt (.226, 7-for-31, 1 HR, 0 BB)

Miscellaneous statistics: Ground outs-to-air outs ratio: 0.83 last season, 1.23 for career.... Grounded into 4 double plays in 62 opportunities (one per 15.5).... Drove in 13 of 18 runners from third base with less than two outs (72%).... Direction of balls hit to the outfield: 42% to left field, 33% to center, 25% to right.... Base running: Advanced from first base to third on 7 of 20 outfield singles (35%); scored from second on 6 of 8 (75%).... Made 2.69 putouts per nine innings in right field.

Comments: The only player in history who has not had a hit but has driven in two runs in World Series play. Both RBIs were pivotal; each came in the 8th inning of games in last year's Series and tied up the game. In Game Two, he produced a fielder's choice grounder off Rick Honeycutt to tie the score at 4–4; in Game Four, he did the same against Dave Stewart, tying the game 1–1. The next batter, Hal Morris, hit a sacrifice fly to score what proved to be winning run.... Batted .248 in 37 games for the Brewers, .299 in 72 games for the Reds.... Hit .339 vs. left-handed pitchers, and .395 with runners on base, after coming to Cincinnati on June 9.... Batted 94 points higher on artificial turf (.324) than on grass fields (.229) last season, the 4th-largest margin in the majors. He had a very similar breakdown in 1989 (.321 on artificial, .233 on grass), making his move from Milwaukee's County Stadium to Cincinnati's Riverfront Stadium a fortuitous move for all involved.... Had 10 outfield assists in 60 games in the field with the Reds, after averaging one every 21 games in the outfield over parts of five seasons with Milwaukee.... Owns a career fielding percentage of .964 (one error per 28 chances), which ranks 77th among the 80 active outfielders with as many career games as Braggs. The only outfielders with worse percentages: Lonnie Smith, Pete Incaviglia, and Bo Jackson.

Sid Bream

Bats Left

Pittsburgh Pirates	AB	H	2B	3B	HR	RBI	BB	SO	BA	SA	OBA
Season	389	105	23	2	15	67	48	65	.270	.455	.349
vs. Left-Handers	96	25	8	1	2	12	6	16	.260	.427	.308
vs. Right-Handers	293	80	15	1	13	55	42	49	.273	.464	.362
vs. Ground-Ballers	186	49	11	1	3	23	22	26	.263	.382	.341
vs. Fly-Ballers	203	56	12	1	12	44	26	39	.276	.522	.356
Home Games	181	50	11	1	8	36	21	26	.276	.481	.356
Road Games	208	55	12	1	7	31	27	39	.264	.433	.343
Grass Fields	106	24	4	0	4	16	14	23	.226	.377	.309
Artificial Turf	283	81	19	2	11	51	34	42	.286	.484	.364
April	43	10	1	0	1	4	3	10	.233	.326	.283
May	62	17	6	0	2	12	10	14	.274	.468	.378
June	64	20	2	1	2	11	4	9	.313	.469	.348
July	69	16	1	0	5	18	11	9	.232	.464	.337
August	75	25	9	0	2	12	11	11	.333	.533	.419
Sept./Oct.	76	17	4	1	3	10	9	12	.224	.421	.302
Leading Off Inn.	71	21	4	1	2	2	8	12	.296	.465	.367
Bases Empty	205	54	10	1	6	6	21	36	.263	.410	.335
Runners On	184	51	13	1	9	61	27	29	.277	.505	.364
Runners/Scor. Pos.	117	34	6	0	6	49	20	19	.291	.496	.385
Runners On/2 Out	85	19	6	1	2	21	10	15	.224	.388	.313
Scor. Pos./2 Out	59	11	3	0	1	16	9	12	.186	.288	.304
Late-Inning Pressure	53	16	5	0	1	8	8	4	.302	.453	.387
Leading Off	9	3	1	0	0	0	3	1	.333	.444	.500
Runners On	27	9	3	0	0	7	5	1	.333	.444	.424
Runners/Scor. Pos.	13	4	1	0	0	5	5	0	.308	.385	.474

RUNS BATTED IN	From 1B	From 2B	From 3B	Scoring Position
Totals	11/117	23/97	18/41	41/138
Percentage	9.4%	23.7%	43.9%	29.7%

Loves to face: Kevin Gross (.364, 16-for-44, 4 HR)
Rick Mahler (.421, 8-for-19)
Ramon Martinez (.750, 3-for-4, 1 2B, 2 HR)

Hates to face: Tim Belcher (.125, 2-for-16)
Sid Fernandez (.063, 1-for-16)
Ed Whitson (.077, 1-for-13, 1 2B)

Miscellaneous statistics: Ground outs-to-air outs ratio: 0.71 last season, 1.00 for career.... Grounded into 6 double plays in 75 opportunities (one per 12.5).... Drove in 13 of 20 runners from third base with less than two outs (65%).... Direction of balls hit to the outfield: 32% to left field, 31% to center, 38% to right.... Base running: Advanced from first base to third on 6 of 28 outfield singles (21%); scored from second on 3 of 10 (30%), shared 2d-lowest rate in N.L.... Made 0.96 assists per nine innings at first base, 2d-highest rate in N.L.

Comments: Missed almost all of the 1989 season with repeat visits to a knee surgeon, but proved that he was 100 percent recovered by putting up numbers in 1990 that were carbon copies of his lines for both 1987 and 1988: games (149 in 1987, 148 in 1988, 147 in 1990); home runs (13, 10, 15); RBIs (65, 65, 67); walks (49, 47, 48); strikeouts (69, 64, 65); stolen bases (9, 9, 8); batting average (.275, .264, .270).... Started 90 of the 93 games in which the Pirates faced a right-handed pitcher, 10 of 69 games vs. left-handers.... Batted only .190 vs. lefties in his last full season (1988), but has a career average of .236 vs. southpaws, compared to .275 vs. right-handers.... Owns .304 career batting average with the bases loaded, including four hits in eight at-bats in 1990, but he has never hit a home run in 46 career at-bats with the bags full.... Neither had he ever hit a home run in 78 regular-season at-bats at Riverfront Stadium; then he connected off Jose Rijo in Game One of last year's playoffs.... The Pirates won all 15 games in which he homered last season; they also won Game One of the Championship Series.... Someone in Atlanta is on the ball: both Bream (.323) and Terry Pendleton (.313) have higher career batting averages in the Braves' home ballpark than they do at any other park in the majors. But take that with a grain of salt, remembering that both players compiled those averages against Braves pitching.

Hubie Brooks

Bats Right

Los Angeles Dodgers	AB	H	2B	3B	HR	RBI	BB	SO	BA	SA	OBA
Season	568	151	28	1	20	91	33	108	.266	.424	.307
vs. Left-Handers	217	52	12	0	9	34	17	41	.240	.419	.294
vs. Right-Handers	351	99	16	1	11	57	16	67	.282	.427	.316
vs. Ground-Ballers	283	82	8	1	11	52	20	46	.290	.442	.334
vs. Fly-Ballers	285	69	20	0	9	39	13	62	.242	.407	.280
Home Games	275	69	8	1	9	44	21	49	.251	.385	.303
Road Games	293	82	20	0	11	47	12	59	.280	.461	.312
Grass Fields	414	104	16	1	16	70	24	85	.251	.411	.292
Artificial Turf	154	47	12	0	4	21	9	23	.305	.461	.349
April	82	19	4	0	4	12	3	14	.232	.427	.253
May	96	23	3	1	3	10	4	19	.240	.385	.284
June	79	21	3	0	3	12	4	14	.266	.418	.299
July	101	28	5	0	2	19	4	20	.277	.386	.306
August	106	37	7	0	5	19	8	20	.349	.557	.400
Sept./Oct.	104	23	6	0	3	19	10	21	.221	.365	.286
Leading Off Inn.	132	35	8	0	4	4	4	26	.265	.417	.297
Bases Empty	307	78	16	0	12	12	8	60	.254	.423	.280
Runners On	261	73	12	1	8	79	25	48	.280	.425	.337
Runners/Scor. Pos.	150	40	7	0	6	72	21	29	.267	.433	.346
Runners On/2 Out	112	30	7	0	3	30	15	28	.268	.411	.369
Scor. Pos./2 Out	72	18	5	0	3	29	13	19	.250	.444	.386
Late-Inning Pressure	69	20	4	0	3	13	7	14	.290	.478	.372
Leading Off	13	2	0	0	0	0	2	5	.154	.154	.313
Runners On	36	13	3	0	2	12	4	4	.361	.611	.425
Runners/Scor. Pos.	17	6	1	0	1	9	4	1	.353	.588	.476

RUNS BATTED IN	From 1B	From 2B	From 3B	Scoring Position
Totals	10/214	20/114	41/75	61/189
Percentage	4.7%	17.5%	54.7%	32.3%

Loves to face: Pat Combs (.500, 6-for-12, 2 2B, 2 HR, 4 SO)
Tom Glavine (.440, 11-for-25, 1 HR)
Bob Walk (.378, 17-for-45, 2 HR)

Hates to face: Jose DeLeon (.149, 7-for-47, 2 HR)
Kevin Gross (.205, 9-for-44)
Joe Magrane (.135, 5-for-37)

Miscellaneous statistics: Ground outs-to-air outs ratio: 1.23 last season, 1.37 for career.... Grounded into 13 double plays in 132 opportunities (one per 10.2).... Drove in 27 of 40 runners from third base with less than two outs (68%).... Direction of balls hit to the outfield: 34% to left field, 32% to center, 33% to right.... Base running: Advanced from first base to third on 9 of 27 outfield singles (33%); scored from second on 12 of 20 (60%).... Made 1.83 putouts per nine innings in right field, lowest rate in N.L.

Comments: Here's news: Hubie *did not* hit a grand-slam home run last season after hitting one in each of the previous five seasons. In 1990, all he did with the bases loaded was hit .471 (8-for-17) with 24 RBIs in 22 plate appearances.... A real Mr. Consistency, he has hit at least .260 with at least 10 home runs for seven consecutive years. Ryne Sandberg is the only other National League player who can make that claim.... Has struck out exactly 108 times in each of the last three seasons.... Has not had a sacrifice bunt in more than seven years, since September of 1983. How long ago is that? His manager was Frank Howard.... Batting average vs. left-handed pitchers (.240) was his lowest since he broke into the majors with 24 games in 1980.... Has batted .290 or better in Late-Inning Pressure Situations in six of the last seven years.... Owns .272 batting average in a Mets uniform, 10th best in team history. Immediate goal: pass Joel Youngblood (9th place, .274).... Played 516 games at third base in his first tour with the Mets to rank third in team history behind Wayne Garrett (709) and Howard Johnson (664). But he hasn't played in the infield since he was the Expos' regular shortstop in 1987.... Hubie becomes the 14th player in Mets history to be brought back for an encore. The most famous: Tom Seaver, Lee Mazzilli, Rusty Staub, and Dave Kingman. The least famous: Jim Gosger, Bob Miller, and Alex Trevino.

Brett Butler

Bats Left

San Francisco Giants	AB	H	2B	3B	HR	RBI	BB	SO	BA	SA	OBA
Season	622	192	20	9	3	44	90	62	.309	.384	.397
vs. Left-Handers	245	74	6	2	1	20	33	28	.302	.355	.389
vs. Right-Handers	377	118	14	7	2	24	57	34	.313	.403	.403
vs. Ground-Ballers	293	92	8	1	1	15	42	26	.314	.358	.407
vs. Fly-Ballers	329	100	12	8	2	29	48	36	.304	.407	.389
Home Games	312	105	12	1	3	25	50	28	.337	.410	.427
Road Games	310	87	8	8	0	19	40	34	.281	.358	.367
Grass Fields	464	150	19	6	3	35	69	42	.323	.409	.409
Artificial Turf	158	42	1	3	0	9	21	20	.266	.310	.362
April	82	30	5	1	1	7	13	4	.366	.488	.453
May	110	20	0	0	0	3	16	15	.182	.182	.291
June	99	29	4	0	0	8	20	9	.293	.333	.412
July	107	37	3	3	1	10	12	11	.346	.458	.413
August	103	32	4	1	0	9	14	10	.311	.369	.390
Sept./Oct.	121	44	4	4	1	7	15	13	.364	.488	.436
Leading Off Inn.	270	82	8	3	2	2	41	26	.304	.378	.399
Bases Empty	453	138	13	6	2	2	69	45	.305	.373	.400
Runners On	169	54	7	3	1	42	21	17	.320	.414	.390
Runners/Scor. Pos.	103	29	3	2	0	37	14	9	.282	.350	.357
Runners On/2 Out	74	27	4	1	0	14	11	4	.365	.446	.460
Scor. Pos./2 Out	47	16	2	1	0	12	9	3	.340	.426	.466
Late-Inning Pressure	85	25	3	0	1	9	10	14	.294	.365	.371
Leading Off	22	7	0	0	0	0	5	3	.318	.318	.444
Runners On	36	12	3	0	1	9	1	6	.333	.500	.359
Runners/Scor. Pos.	21	7	2	0	0	6	0	3	.333	.429	.318

RUNS BATTED IN	From 1B	From 2B	From 3B	Scoring Position
Totals	5/112	11/83	25/50	36/133
Percentage	4.5%	13.3%	50.0%	27.1%

Loves to face: Jose DeLeon (.440, 11-for-25, 3 2B, 3 3B, 1 HR)
Neal Heaton (.500, 6-for-12)
Mike Morgan (.459, 17-for-37, 0 SO)

Hates to face: Frank DiPino (.190, 4-for-21)
Danny Jackson (.205, 8-for-39)
Steve Wilson (0-for-8, 2 BB)

Miscellaneous statistics: Ground outs-to-air outs ratio: 1.55 last season, 1.25 for career.... Grounded into 3 double plays in 80 opportunities (one per 26.7), 4th-best rate in N.L.... Drove in 20 of 30 runners from third base with less than two outs (67%).... Direction of balls hit to the outfield: 37% to left field, 33% to center, 30% to right.... Base running: Advanced from first base to third on 25 of 46 outfield singles (54%); scored from second on 17 of 21 (81%).... Made 2.72 putouts per nine innings in center field.

Comments: An underrated player whose specialty, scoring runs, is often overlooked in statistical discussions. Butler has scored 100 or more runs in five different seasons, yet he has never been selected to an All-Star team. There have been 97 other players in baseball history with five or more seasons of at least 100 runs; but Butler is the only one of them who has played his entire career in the "All-Star era" and yet has never been selected for one.... Tied Len Dykstra for major league lead in hits, becoming first Giants league-leader in that category since Willie Mays in 1960.... Led the National League with 44 RBIs from the first spot in the lineup.... His 159 games in the outfield led the National League and ranked second in club history (Mays played 161 games there in 1962).... One of those left-handed batters with a higher career batting average vs. left-handed pitchers (.290) than he has vs. right-handed pitchers (.283).... His .365 average with two outs and runners on base was 4th-best in the league behind Dykstra (.446), Dave Magadan (.406), and teammate Will Clark (.371).... Had streak of 148 consecutive at-bats without an extra-base hit (in April and May), the longest by any player in the majors last season.... Stole 51 bases last season, one short of his career high set with Cleveland in 1984. He was caught 19 times, giving him the best success rate (.729) in any full season of his career.

Ken Caminiti

Bats Left and Right

Houston Astros	AB	H	2B	3B	HR	RBI	BB	SO	BA	SA	OBA
Season	541	131	20	2	4	51	48	97	.242	.309	.302
vs. Left-Handers	240	59	9	1	2	23	13	35	.246	.317	.280
vs. Right-Handers	301	72	11	1	2	28	35	62	.239	.302	.318
vs. Ground-Ballers	293	78	9	2	2	25	26	51	.266	.331	.324
vs. Fly-Ballers	248	53	11	0	2	26	22	46	.214	.282	.276
Home Games	285	82	15	0	2	31	27	47	.288	.361	.348
Road Games	256	49	5	2	2	20	21	50	.191	.250	.250
Grass Fields	159	31	4	1	1	10	15	33	.195	.252	.261
Artificial Turf	382	100	16	1	3	41	33	64	.262	.332	.319
April	64	17	2	0	0	4	6	17	.266	.297	.329
May	96	29	3	0	2	13	8	13	.302	.396	.356
June	97	20	3	0	0	9	6	15	.206	.237	.248
July	87	24	4	0	0	8	10	15	.276	.322	.347
August	93	21	5	1	0	6	8	19	.226	.301	.284
Sept./Oct.	104	20	3	1	2	11	10	18	.192	.298	.263
Leading Off Inn.	124	38	5	1	1	1	8	20	.306	.387	.348
Bases Empty	298	72	12	1	2	2	23	59	.242	.309	.296
Runners On	243	59	8	1	2	49	25	38	.243	.309	.309
Runners/Scor. Pos.	142	37	5	0	2	45	22	27	.261	.338	.351
Runners On/2 Out	106	22	2	0	1	21	12	20	.208	.255	.288
Scor. Pos./2 Out	76	17	2	0	1	20	10	15	.224	.289	.314
Late-Inning Pressure	90	25	2	2	0	8	9	26	.278	.344	.343
Leading Off	21	7	1	1	0	0	2	8	.333	.476	.391
Runners On	42	11	0	1	0	8	5	10	.262	.310	.340
Runners/Scor. Pos.	23	6	0	0	0	7	5	7	.261	.261	.393

RUNS BATTED IN	From 1B	From 2B	From 3B	Scoring Position
Totals	6/176	16/116	25/53	41/169
Percentage	3.4%	13.8%	47.2%	24.3%

Loves to face: Mike Bielecki (.600, 6-for-10)
Mark Grant (.400, 4-for-10, 2 HR)
Kevin Gross (.455, 5-for-11, 1 HR, 4 SO)

Hates to face: Tim Belcher (.087, 2-for-23)
Norm Charlton (0-for-15)
Jay Howell (0-for-8, 5 SO)

Miscellaneous statistics: Ground outs-to-air outs ratio: 0.95 last season, 0.97 for career.... Grounded into 15 double plays in 111 opportunities (one per 7.4).... Drove in 15 of 25 runners from third base with less than two outs (60%).... Direction of balls hit to the outfield: 26% to left field, 35% to center, 38% to right batting left-handed; 41% to left, 25% to center, 34% to right batting right-handed.... Base running: Advanced from first base to third on 10 of 28 outfield singles (36%); scored from second on 14 of 16 (88%).... Made 1.75 assists per nine innings at third base, 2d-lowest rate in N.L.

Comments: Here's a guy who actually *looks forward* to hitting in the Astrodome. He's the only National League player with 200 or more at bats who hit below .200 on the road last season. He has hit for a higher average at the Astrodome than in road games in each of his four years in the majors. Career averages: .267 at home, .222 on the road.... Batted .217 from the 3d spot in the batting order, the lowest of any National League player with at least 100 at-bats from that spot. The Astros' 3d-place hitters batted .232, the lowest in the league. They stood 50 points below the National League average for the 3d spot last season.... Margin of difference between his average against left- and right-handed pitchers was much smaller than usual. He has a career average of .274 vs. lefties, .227 vs. right-handers.... He has hit for a higher average against ground-ball pitchers than he has against fly-ball pitchers in each of his four seasons in the majors.... His best work last season came with the bases loaded: eight hits in 15 at-bats. (Aside: Keep in mind that the league averages for bases-loaded batting average are comparatively high: .273 in the American League, .271 in the National.)...Started the only triple play in the National League last season, a 5–4–3 job, grounded into by the Braves' Francisco Cabrera.

Casey Candaele

Bats Left and Right

Houston Astros	AB	H	2B	3B	HR	RBI	BB	SO	BA	SA	OBA
Season	262	75	8	6	3	22	31	42	.286	.397	.364
vs. Left-Handers	126	43	3	2	2	10	14	12	.341	.444	.407
vs. Right-Handers	136	32	5	4	1	12	17	30	.235	.353	.325
vs. Ground-Ballers	144	43	2	3	1	14	16	25	.299	.375	.373
vs. Fly-Ballers	118	32	6	3	2	8	15	17	.271	.424	.353
Home Games	126	36	3	5	1	12	17	18	.286	.413	.375
Road Games	136	39	5	1	2	10	14	24	.287	.382	.353
Grass Fields	75	26	2	1	2	10	10	10	.347	.480	.424
Artificial Turf	187	49	6	5	1	12	21	32	.262	.364	.340
April	11	3	0	0	1	1	1	3	.273	.545	.333
May	42	10	0	0	0	1	7	8	.238	.238	.347
June	25	6	0	2	2	4	4	5	.240	.640	.345
July	46	17	1	2	0	1	7	10	.370	.478	.453
August	37	9	4	1	0	6	3	5	.243	.405	.300
Sept./Oct.	101	30	3	1	0	9	9	11	.297	.347	.360
Leading Off Inn.	67	12	2	0	0	0	11	17	.179	.209	.295
Bases Empty	155	43	6	3	2	2	19	24	.277	.394	.356
Runners On	107	32	2	3	1	20	12	18	.299	.402	.375
Runners/Scor. Pos.	66	20	1	3	1	19	9	13	.303	.455	.395
Runners On/2 Out	44	11	1	0	0	7	4	6	.250	.273	.327
Scor. Pos./2 Out	29	6	0	0	0	6	3	5	.207	.207	.303
Late-Inning Pressure	61	13	1	2	1	7	10	8	.213	.344	.324
Leading Off	13	2	0	0	0	0	5	3	.154	.154	.389
Runners On	28	6	1	2	1	7	3	5	.214	.500	.290
Runners/Scor. Pos.	19	4	0	2	1	6	2	3	.211	.579	.286

RUNS BATTED IN	From 1B	From 2B	From 3B	Scoring Position
Totals	2/79	13/59	4/22	17/81
Percentage	2.5%	22.0%	18.2%	21.0%

Loves to face: Rick Mahler (.545, 6-for-11, 1 HR)
Jamie Moyer (.462, 6-for-13, 4 2B)
Fernando Valenzuela (.476, 10-for-21, 2 HR)

Hates to face: Ron Darling (.167, 4-for-24)
Sid Fernandez (0-for-8)
Rick Sutcliffe (.158, 3-for-19, 2 2B)

Miscellaneous statistics: Ground outs-to-air outs ratio: 1.25 last season, 1.26 for career.... Grounded into 4 double plays in 52 opportunities (one per 13.0).... Drove in 2 of 10 runners from third base with less than two outs (20%).... Direction of balls hit to the outfield: 43% to left field, 34% to center, 23% to right batting left-handed; 33% to left, 35% to center, 32% to right batting right-handed.... Base running: Advanced from first base to third on 4 of 13 outfield singles (31%); scored from second on 5 of 7 (71%).... Made 3.05 assists per nine innings at second base.

Comments: Those two home runs off Fernando in his *Loves to face* list are his only homers in 343 major league at-bats vs. left-handed pitchers.... Hit his three home runs last season over a span of 68 at bats, but he has only one home run in his other 894 career at-bats.... Started games at five different fielding positions (2B-SS-LF-CF-RF) last season. Rex Hudler led National League players with starts at six positions; Keith Miller and Eric Yelding also started at five positions.... Of Candy's 53 starts, 35 came at second base. He played second base regularly after Bill Doran was traded to Cincinnati in late August.... Started 29 of 71 games vs. left-handers, 24 of 91 vs. right-handers. The Astros faced more left-handed starters than any team in the majors in the past three seasons.... His .341 batting average against left-handers lifted his career mark against lefties to .300. He's a .231 career hitter against right-handed pitchers.... He was hitting .302 as late as September 24, but went 4-for-27 over the last nine days of the season to fall short of the .300 mark.... Has batted with the bases loaded 24 times in his career, with only six RBIs to show for it.... Has driven in only 19 percent of runners from scoring position during his career. That's only slightly better than teammate Mike Scott (18 percent).

Mark Carreon

Bats Right

New York Mets	AB	H	2B	3B	HR	RBI	BB	SO	BA	SA	OBA
Season	188	47	12	0	10	26	15	29	.250	.473	.312
vs. Left-Handers	116	30	9	0	7	17	9	20	.259	.517	.312
vs. Right-Handers	72	17	3	0	3	9	6	9	.236	.403	.313
vs. Ground-Ballers	93	29	6	0	8	17	5	11	.312	.634	.360
vs. Fly-Ballers	95	18	6	0	2	9	10	18	.189	.316	.267
Home Games	87	20	7	0	1	7	6	16	.230	.345	.295
Road Games	101	27	5	0	9	19	9	13	.267	.584	.327
Grass Fields	131	34	11	0	5	17	10	23	.260	.458	.322
Artificial Turf	57	13	1	0	5	9	5	6	.228	.509	.290
April	44	11	3	0	3	6	3	8	.250	.523	.313
May	29	6	3	0	1	3	2	6	.207	.414	.258
June	41	14	2	0	4	7	4	3	.341	.683	.400
July	45	8	3	0	2	7	5	8	.178	.378	.260
August	29	8	1	0	0	3	1	4	.276	.310	.323
Sept./Oct.	0	0	0	0	0	0	0	0	—	—	—
Leading Off Inn.	49	13	6	0	4	4	4	8	.265	.633	.321
Bases Empty	106	26	7	0	6	6	10	15	.245	.481	.310
Runners On	82	21	5	0	4	20	5	14	.256	.463	.315
Runners/Scor. Pos.	49	14	3	0	2	16	2	10	.286	.469	.340
Runners On/2 Out	42	13	3	0	3	16	1	8	.310	.595	.341
Scor. Pos./2 Out	29	10	2	0	1	12	1	6	.345	.517	.387
Late-Inning Pressure	38	7	1	0	1	3	3	12	.184	.289	.244
Leading Off	8	2	1	0	0	0	1	4	.250	.375	.333
Runners On	19	1	0	0	0	2	0	6	.053	.053	.053
Runners/Scor. Pos.	13	1	0	0	0	2	0	6	.077	.077	.077

RUNS BATTED IN	From 1B	From 2B	From 3B	Scoring Position
Totals	2/57	9/38	5/19	14/57
Percentage	3.5%	23.7%	26.3%	24.6%

Loves to face: Neal Heaton (.714, 5-for-7, 2 HR)
Jeff Pico (.714, 5-for-7, 1 HR)

Hates to face: Craig Lefferts (0-for-9, 5 SO)
Bruce Ruffin (0-for-6)

Miscellaneous statistics: Ground outs-to-air outs ratio: 0.74 last season, 0.82 for career.... Grounded into 1 double play in 36 opportunities (one per 36.0).... Drove in 1 of 8 runners from third base with less than two outs (13%).... Direction of balls hit to the outfield: 47% to left field, 30% to center, 23% to right.... Base running: Advanced from first base to third on 2 of 9 outfield singles (22%); scored from second on 3 of 8 (38%).... Made 2.38 putouts per nine innings in center field.

Comments: Tore up his knee in game at San Diego on August 20 and missed the rest of the season. That injury might have had a more profound effect on the division race than you might expect. At the time he was injured, Carreon was the team leader with seven home runs off left-handed pitchers. Mets went 4–12 vs. left-handed starters from mid-August through September 30, the date that Pittsburgh clinched the division.... Has a career rate of one home run every 15.5 at-bats vs. left-handers. Hank Aaron's career rate against all types of pitching: one homer every 16.4 at-bats.... Carreon and Rickey Henderson were the only two nonpitchers in the majors last season to throw left-handed but bat exclusively from the right side.... Played 60 games in the field last season without committing an error.... In addition, as Darryl Strawberry's backup, he made five starts in right field, and might have gotten additional calls while Strawberry nursed a bad back in late September.... He's played 166 games in his career, slightly more than a full season for a regular player, but he has never had any kind of sacrifice, bunt or fly.... Mark's father Camillo was a major league catcher with an eight-year career with the White Sox, Indians, and Orioles. They are perhaps the most second-most obscure father-son combination among today's active players. First place: the Stillwells.

Gary Carter

Bats Right

San Francisco Giants	AB	H	2B	3B	HR	RBI	BB	SO	BA	SA	OBA
Season	244	62	10	0	9	27	25	31	.254	.406	.324
vs. Left-Handers	127	30	7	0	3	11	16	13	.236	.362	.322
vs. Right-Handers	117	32	3	0	6	16	9	18	.274	.453	.325
vs. Ground-Ballers	124	34	4	0	8	20	16	17	.274	.500	.355
vs. Fly-Ballers	120	28	6	0	1	7	9	14	.233	.308	.290
Home Games	127	39	7	0	6	19	9	13	.307	.504	.350
Road Games	117	23	3	0	3	8	16	18	.197	.299	.296
Grass Fields	181	54	9	0	9	24	18	20	.298	.497	.360
Artificial Turf	63	8	1	0	0	3	7	11	.127	.143	.222
April	36	7	3	0	0	1	6	6	.194	.278	.310
May	42	11	2	0	1	4	5	2	.262	.381	.354
June	46	15	4	0	3	6	8	5	.326	.609	.418
July	32	14	0	0	3	10	0	3	.438	.719	.438
August	67	9	0	0	1	3	5	13	.134	.179	.192
Sept./Oct.	21	6	1	0	1	3	1	2	.286	.476	.318
Leading Off Inn.	52	19	1	0	6	6	5	4	.365	.731	.421
Bases Empty	137	35	3	0	7	7	16	17	.255	.431	.333
Runners On	107	27	7	0	2	20	9	14	.252	.374	.311
Runners/Scor. Pos.	65	15	2	0	1	18	7	11	.231	.308	.307
Runners On/2 Out	44	8	2	0	0	8	6	8	.182	.227	.280
Scor. Pos./2 Out	32	7	1	0	0	8	5	7	.219	.250	.324
Late-Inning Pressure	48	13	3	0	1	4	5	5	.271	.396	.340
Leading Off	10	2	1	0	1	1	2	0	.200	.600	.333
Runners On	21	5	2	0	0	3	1	3	.238	.333	.273
Runners/Scor. Pos.	15	3	1	0	0	3	1	3	.200	.267	.250

RUNS BATTED IN	From 1B	From 2B	From 3B	Scoring Position
Totals	2/75	8/54	8/29	16/83
Percentage	2.7%	14.8%	27.6%	19.3%

Loves to face: Greg Booker (.833, 5-for-6, 2 HR)
Ron Darling (.444, 4-for-9, 2 HR)
Mark Thurmond (.429, 9-for-21, 1 HR)

Hates to face: Tim Burke (.091, 2-for-22)
Dennis Martinez (.080, 2-for-25)
Don Robinson (.143, 8-for-56)

Miscellaneous statistics: Ground outs-to-air outs ratio: 0.58 last season, 2d-lowest rate in N.L.; 0.78 for career.... Grounded into 2 double plays in 51 opportunities (one per 25.5).... Drove in 5 of 14 runners from third base with less than two outs (36%).... Direction of balls hit to the outfield: 46% to left field, 30% to center, 24% to right.... Base running: Advanced from first base to third on 5 of 15 outfield singles (33%); scored from second on 4 of 4.... Opposing base stealers: 66-for-87 (76%), 5th-highest rate in N.L.

Comments: Broke Al Lopez's National League record for games as a catcher; new mark should stand for a while, since his closest N.L. pursuer, Mike Scioscia, is 731 behind him. Carter stands 97 shy of the 2000 mark attained only by Bob Boone (2225) and Carlton Fisk (2041).... No player active in 1990 has played more National League games than Carter's 2100 without playing at least one game in the American League.... For a player nicknamed "Camera," best day of the season had to be 5-for-5 game vs. Cubs on July 7 that was nationally televised by CBS.... Batted .301 through July, but only .170 thereafter. August batting average was the lowest in the majors.... Started 46 of 60 games in which Giants faced a left-handed starter, 15 of 102 vs. right-handers.... Batted 111 points higher in home games (.307) than in road games (.197), the 3d-largest margin in the majors.... Has hit for a higher average with the bases empty than with runners on base in each of the last two seasons, after doing it the other way in each of the previous 11 years.... Owns .197 career batting average (14-for-71, 1 HR) as a pinch hitter.... Has 287 career home runs as a catcher, 4th most in history. The last time that he approached 300 homers (for his overall career), he went into a two-month stall at 299.

Joe Carter

Bats Right

San Diego Padres	AB	H	2B	3B	HR	RBI	BB	SO	BA	SA	OBA
Season	634	147	27	1	24	115	48	93	.232	.391	.290
vs. Left-Handers	203	40	7	0	7	32	17	27	.197	.335	.258
vs. Right-Handers	431	107	20	1	17	83	31	66	.248	.418	.305
vs. Ground-Ballers	322	73	15	0	9	60	27	39	.227	.357	.287
vs. Fly-Ballers	312	74	12	1	15	55	21	54	.237	.426	.293
Home Games	322	71	11	0	12	53	18	49	.220	.366	.263
Road Games	312	76	16	1	12	62	30	44	.244	.417	.316
Grass Fields	468	105	17	0	17	80	39	67	.224	.370	.286
Artificial Turf	166	42	10	1	7	35	9	26	.253	.452	.302
April	75	17	3	0	3	17	3	6	.227	.387	.256
May	107	28	5	0	5	23	5	22	.262	.449	.304
June	105	19	6	0	5	18	7	19	.181	.381	.254
July	108	22	4	0	3	14	9	12	.204	.324	.261
August	107	27	5	1	5	26	14	13	.252	.458	.336
Sept./Oct.	132	34	4	0	3	17	10	21	.258	.356	.310
Leading Off Inn.	142	34	7	0	5	5	5	18	.239	.394	.265
Bases Empty	321	68	12	0	10	10	13	47	.212	.343	.247
Runners On	313	79	15	1	14	105	35	46	.252	.441	.330
Runners/Scor. Pos.	191	51	8	1	7	87	30	27	.267	.429	.362
Runners On/2 Out	144	30	5	0	7	39	17	18	.208	.389	.309
Scor. Pos./2 Out	94	20	2	0	5	32	15	13	.213	.394	.339
Late-Inning Pressure	111	27	3	1	4	21	7	15	.243	.396	.288
Leading Off	29	6	1	0	1	1	1	1	.207	.345	.233
Runners On	47	12	0	1	3	20	6	9	.255	.489	.340
Runners/Scor. Pos.	26	8	0	1	1	16	6	4	.308	.500	.438

RUNS BATTED IN	From 1B	From 2B	From 3B	Scoring Position
Totals	16/235	35/150	40/94	75/244
Percentage	6.8%	23.3%	42.6%	30.7%

Loves to face: Charlie Hough (.361, 13-for-36, 6 HR)
Jay Howell (.500, 5-for-10, 1 HR)
Mark Knudson (.571, 8-for-14, 4 HR)

Hates to face: Dave LaPoint (.133, 2-for-15)
Greg Minton (0-for-14, 1 BB)
Gene Nelson (.176, 3-for-17)

Miscellaneous statistics: Ground outs-to-air outs ratio: 0.74 last season, 0.66 for career.... Grounded into 12 double plays in 143 opportunities (one per 11.9).... Drove in 28 of 46 runners from third base with less than two outs (61%).... Direction of balls hit to the outfield: 42% to left field, 30% to center, 28% to right.... Base running: Advanced from first base to third on 16 of 27 outfield singles (59%); scored from second on 11 of 12 (92%), 4th-highest rate in N.L.... Made 2.78 putouts per nine innings in center field.

Comments: His batting average against left-handers was the lowest of any right-handed hitter in the National League last season (minimum: 100 AB). He had a streak of 37 consecutive hitless at-bats vs. lefties starting in late May, the 2d-longest streak by any player over the last 16 years. (Graig Nettles had an 0-for-39 stretch vs. lefties in 1981.) ... The only N.L. player to appear in all of his team's games last season, and the only player in the majors this side of Cal Ripken who has played every game in each of the last two years. He enters 1991 with 343 consecutive games played.... Batted .220 from the 4th slot in the order, the lowest of any of the 24 National League players with at least 50 cleanup at-bats.... Became only the second player in this century with 100 or more RBIs in consecutive seasons in different leagues; Frank Robinson did it in 1965–66. Back in the A.L. this season, Carter can try to go Robinson one better.... Had 115 RBIs despite a .232 batting average; that's the most RBIs in major league history by any player with less than a .240 batting average.... How can a player do that, especially when his scoring-position batting average (.267) isn't much better? Answer: Carter batted with 244 runners in scoring position last season, the highest total for any player in the majors. Over the last 16 years, only seven players have had seasons in which they had more opportunities to drive runners in from scoring position. Remember, *RBIs are not an equal opportunity statistic.*

Jack Clark

Bats Right

San Diego Padres	AB	H	2B	3B	HR	RBI	BB	SO	BA	SA	OBA
Season	334	89	12	1	25	62	104	91	.266	.533	.441
vs. Left-Handers	114	43	4	1	9	21	41	29	.377	.667	.541
vs. Right-Handers	220	46	8	0	16	41	63	62	.209	.464	.386
vs. Ground-Ballers	169	48	7	0	11	27	62	51	.284	.521	.474
vs. Fly-Ballers	165	41	5	1	14	35	42	40	.248	.545	.405
Home Games	176	45	5	1	16	39	50	53	.256	.568	.419
Road Games	158	44	7	0	9	23	54	38	.278	.494	.465
Grass Fields	265	69	10	1	20	50	76	72	.260	.532	.426
Artificial Turf	69	20	2	0	5	12	28	19	.290	.536	.495
April	54	11	1	0	4	9	20	21	.204	.444	.413
May	13	6	2	0	1	1	4	3	.462	.846	.588
June	63	12	2	0	4	11	13	16	.190	.413	.338
July	87	27	0	0	9	20	17	20	.310	.621	.419
August	40	14	5	1	2	9	18	10	.350	.675	.559
Sept./Oct.	77	19	2	0	5	12	32	21	.247	.468	.468
Leading Off Inn.	83	19	0	1	8	8	21	22	.229	.542	.385
Bases Empty	180	45	1	1	16	16	44	54	.250	.533	.400
Runners On	154	44	11	0	9	46	60	37	.286	.532	.484
Runners/Scor. Pos.	90	25	5	0	6	39	47	22	.278	.533	.521
Runners On/2 Out	61	16	3	0	4	21	33	18	.262	.508	.521
Scor. Pos./2 Out	39	10	1	0	3	19	27	11	.256	.513	.561
Late-Inning Pressure	55	13	2	0	5	7	23	11	.236	.545	.462
Leading Off	11	3	0	0	2	2	4	1	.273	.818	.467
Runners On	27	4	1	0	1	3	12	5	.148	.296	.410
Runners/Scor. Pos.	13	1	0	0	1	2	11	3	.077	.308	.500

RUNS BATTED IN	From 1B	From 2B	From 3B	Scoring Position
Totals	8/105	14/71	15/39	29/110
Percentage	7.6%	19.7%	38.5%	26.4%

Loves to face: Bert Blyleven (.417, 10-for-24, 3 2B, 2 HR)
Rick Honeycutt (.533, 8-for-15, 2 HR, 7 BB)
Ken Dayley (.333, 4-for-12, 3 HR, 4 BB)

Hates to face: Dennis Eckersley (.083, 1-for-12, 5 SO)
Ron Robinson (.182, 2-for-11)
Dan Schatzeder (.192, 5-for-26, 1 HR, 5 BB)

Miscellaneous statistics: Ground outs-to-air outs ratio: 0.85 last season, 0.91 for career.... Grounded into 12 double plays in 78 opportunities (one per 6.5).... Drove in 8 of 24 runners from third base with less than two outs (33%), lowest rate in N.L.... Direction of balls hit to the outfield: 50% to left field, 31% to center, 19% to right.... Base running: Advanced from first base to third on 3 of 30 outfield singles (10%), shared 4th-lowest rate in N.L.; scored from second on 6 of 10 (60%).... Made 0.70 assists per nine innings at first base.

Comments: Has had seasons of 25 or more home runs for four different teams (Giants, Cardinals, Yankees, Padres), and has a chance to add the Red Sox this season. Only one player has had 25-HR seasons for five teams: Bobby Bonds. Like Clark, Don Baylor, Reggie Jackson, and Dave Kingman hit 25 homers for four different teams.... Batted 168 points higher vs. left-handers (.377) than vs. right-handers (.209) last season, the 2d-largest margin in the majors.... Has hit for a higher average on artificial turf than on grass fields in each of the last five seasons.... Let's talk walks. Clark has walked 485 times in the last four years, the highest four-year total since Mickey Mantle drew 500 walks, 1955–58. (All-time record: 606 by Ted Williams, 1946–49.) Clark has drawn at least 100 in each of the last four seasons; the last player with a five-year streak: Joe Morgan (six years, 1972–77). Major league record streak: Mel Ott (seven years, 1936–42).... Clark wasn't always a big walker. Career breakdown: 1975–84 (his years with Giants), one walk every 8.7 plate appearances; 1985–90 (starting with his Cardinals tenure), one every 4.9 times up. In his first full season (exactly what constitutes a "full" season for this guy?), he walked only 50 times in 156 games.... A Clark has led the National League in walks in each of the last four seasons—Jack in 1987, 1989, and 1990, and Will in 1988. It's up to Will to keep the streak going in 1991.

Will Clark

Bats Left

San Francisco Giants	AB	H	2B	3B	HR	RBI	BB	SO	BA	SA	OBA
Season	600	177	25	5	19	95	62	97	.295	.448	.357
vs. Left-Handers	249	79	7	4	9	47	22	35	.317	.486	.372
vs. Right-Handers	351	98	18	1	10	48	40	62	.279	.422	.347
vs. Ground-Ballers	283	81	11	2	10	46	28	50	.286	.445	.347
vs. Fly-Ballers	317	96	14	3	9	49	34	47	.303	.451	.366
Home Games	296	94	14	2	8	44	37	49	.318	.459	.384
Road Games	304	83	11	3	11	51	25	48	.273	.438	.329
Grass Fields	439	135	21	3	13	73	48	71	.308	.458	.370
Artificial Turf	161	42	4	2	6	22	14	26	.261	.422	.320
April	84	26	4	1	3	17	3	13	.310	.488	.337
May	110	23	3	0	6	17	10	15	.209	.400	.281
June	110	38	5	1	5	24	13	17	.345	.545	.408
July	95	29	3	2	0	10	13	18	.305	.379	.378
August	94	26	3	1	2	10	10	20	.277	.394	.340
Sept./Oct.	107	35	7	0	3	17	13	14	.327	.477	.389
Leading Off Inn.	118	37	8	1	5	5	11	16	.314	.525	.372
Bases Empty	314	89	15	4	10	10	28	49	.283	.452	.344
Runners On	286	88	10	1	9	85	34	48	.308	.444	.370
Runners/Scor. Pos.	172	50	7	1	4	73	27	34	.291	.413	.366
Runners On/2 Out	89	33	3	1	2	31	15	11	.371	.494	.467
Scor. Pos./2 Out	58	21	2	1	1	28	13	7	.362	.483	.486
Late-Inning Pressure	85	22	5	0	2	9	11	21	.259	.388	.347
Leading Off	17	7	3	0	1	1	4	3	.412	.765	.524
Runners On	46	12	1	0	1	8	5	15	.261	.348	.340
Runners/Scor. Pos.	31	8	1	0	1	8	4	11	.258	.387	.351

RUNS BATTED IN	From 1B	From 2B	From 3B	Scoring Position
Totals	11/205	27/123	38/77	65/200
Percentage	5.4%	22.0%	49.4%	32.5%

Loves to face: Derek Lilliquist (.526, 10-for-19, 2 HR)
Jim Clancy (.556, 5-for-9, 2 2B, 2 HR)
Pete Smith (.476, 10-for-21, 3 HR)

Hates to face: Dennis Cook (.067, 1-for-15)
Tom Glavine (.130, 3-for-23, 3 BB)
Terry Mulholland (.063, 1-for-16, 1 2B)

Miscellaneous statistics: Ground outs-to-air outs ratio: 0.94 last season, 0.85 for career.... Grounded into 7 double plays in 152 opportunities (one per 21.7).... Drove in 22 of 43 runners from third base with less than two outs (51%).... Direction of balls hit to the outfield: 36% to left field, 34% to center, 31% to right.... Base running: Advanced from first base to third on 13 of 34 outfield singles (38%); scored from second on 12 of 16 (75%).... Made 0.80 assists per nine innings at first base.

Comments: Baseball's all-time top five postseason slugging percentages (minimum: 50 AB): Babe Ruth .744, Lou Gehrig .731, Hank Aaron .710, Will Clark .705, Gary Matthews .677.... High anxiety with the bases loaded? His figures in 56 plate appearances with the bags full: batting .185 (10-for-54) with one home run, no walks and 17 strikeouts.... The only National League player with fewer than 20 home runs who hit at least five to the opposite field last season.... Has cut his strikeouts from 125 in 1988 to 103 and 97 in the last two seasons, but his power has dwindled along with it. His yearly home run totals since 1987: 35, 29, 23, 19.... With an overall career average of .302, he has career averages of over .300 against both left-handed (.305) and right-handed (.3002) pitchers. He has hit over .300 against lefties in four of his five years in the majors, the only exception being a .262 mark in 1988.... Career breakdown: .316 at Candlestick Park, .299 on other grass fields, .277 on artificial surfaces.... Became the first Giants first baseman to start three consecutive All-Star Games since Johnny Mize (1946–49). Giants have had the league's starting first baseman in 20 of the 61 All-Star Games. Besides Clark (three times) and Mize (5) there were Orlando Cepeda (4), Willie McCovey (4), Bill Terry (3) and Whitey Lockman (1).

Vince Coleman

Bats Left and Right

St. Louis Cardinals	AB	H	2B	3B	HR	RBI	BB	SO	BA	SA	OBA
Season	497	145	18	9	6	39	35	88	.292	.400	.340
vs. Left-Handers	191	50	13	4	5	18	9	37	.262	.450	.297
vs. Right-Handers	306	95	5	5	1	21	26	51	.310	.369	.366
vs. Ground-Ballers	249	76	14	6	2	13	17	37	.305	.434	.348
vs. Fly-Ballers	248	69	4	3	4	26	18	51	.278	.367	.332
Home Games	259	77	10	6	5	21	22	48	.297	.440	.352
Road Games	238	68	8	3	1	18	13	40	.286	.357	.327
Grass Fields	139	38	5	1	0	6	7	27	.273	.324	.306
Artificial Turf	358	107	13	8	6	33	28	61	.299	.430	.353
April	80	24	2	0	0	3	5	9	.300	.325	.341
May	101	31	1	4	2	10	8	23	.307	.455	.358
June	118	35	8	1	1	8	6	29	.297	.407	.331
July	77	20	3	1	2	4	5	10	.260	.403	.301
August	95	32	4	3	1	12	10	12	.337	.474	.411
Sept./Oct.	26	3	0	0	0	2	1	5	.115	.115	.148
Leading Off Inn.	214	58	7	5	3	3	18	43	.271	.393	.330
Bases Empty	330	100	10	9	5	5	27	60	.303	.433	.358
Runners On	167	45	8	0	1	34	8	28	.269	.335	.305
Runners/Scor. Pos.	112	29	6	0	1	34	8	20	.259	.339	.311
Runners On/2 Out	80	20	5	0	0	19	3	15	.250	.313	.277
Scor. Pos./2 Out	61	14	4	0	0	19	3	13	.230	.295	.266
Late-Inning Pressure	74	24	3	2	1	3	5	9	.324	.459	.367
Leading Off	25	10	1	0	0	0	2	5	.400	.440	.444
Runners On	31	9	1	0	0	2	1	4	.290	.323	.313
Runners/Scor. Pos.	17	2	0	0	0	2	1	3	.118	.118	.167

RUNS BATTED IN	From 1B	From 2B	From 3B	Scoring Position
Totals	1/99	14/92	18/45	32/137
Percentage	1.0%	15.2%	40.0%	23.4%

Loves to face: Mike Bielecki (.455, 10-for-22)
John Smiley (.391, 9-for-23)
Zane Smith (.425, 17-for-40)

Hates to face: Tom Browning (.040, 1-for-25, 1 2B, 5 BB)
Dennis Rasmussen (.083, 1-for-12)
Fernando Valenzuela (.133, 8-for-60)

Miscellaneous statistics: Ground outs-to-air outs ratio: 1.27 last season, 1.48 for career.... Grounded into 6 double plays in 58 opportunities (one per 9.7).... Drove in 10 of 18 runners from third base with less than two outs (56%).... Direction of balls hit to the outfield: 37% to left field, 36% to center, 27% to right batting left-handed; 45% to left, 24% to right, 32% to right batting right-handed.... Base running: Advanced from first base to third on 6 of 17 outfield singles (35%); scored from second on 16 of 22 (73%).... Made 2.14 putouts per nine innings in left field.

Comments: Has averaged 91.5 stolen bases per season in his six years in the majors; Mets have had only eight players in their history who have had that many steals in their careers with the team. Club record: 281 by Mookie Wilson. The over/under on Coleman breaking that record: three full seasons.... Stole 29 bases in 32 attempts (.906) vs. left-handed pitchers, but "only" 48 bases in 62 attempts (.774) vs. right-handers.... Ended the 1990 season with 549 steals in 878 games, eight steals ahead of Rickey Henderson's pace.... Has 12 career home runs at Busch Stadium, three elsewhere. That replicates his breakdown from either side of the plate: 12 right-handed, three left-handed.... It seems like wearing a Cardinals' uniform during the 1980s was akin to wearing an "artificial-turf hitter" label. But look at Coleman's career breakdown: .280 at Busch Stadium, only .245 on other carpets, .253 on grass fields.... Sure, he's a leadoff hitter who's not paid to drive in runs, but when opportunities arise, he should be doing a better job. He has driven in only 22 percent of runners from scoring position in his career, the fifth-lowest rate among players in the majors since 1975 (minimum: 500 opportunities). Players with lower rates: Barry Foote, Wayne Tolleson, Frank Taveras, and Jeff Newman.... Very quietly had a career-high batting average in his option year.... Owns a career batting average of .233 at Shea Stadium, but remember, that's against Mets' pitching.

Kal Daniels

Bats Left

Los Angeles Dodgers	AB	H	2B	3B	HR	RBI	BB	SO	BA	SA	OBA
Season	450	133	23	1	27	94	68	104	.296	.531	.389
vs. Left-Handers	151	43	6	0	6	30	25	33	.285	.444	.393
vs. Right-Handers	299	90	17	1	21	64	43	71	.301	.575	.387
vs. Ground-Ballers	247	72	12	0	18	57	42	57	.291	.559	.399
vs. Fly-Ballers	203	61	11	1	9	37	26	47	.300	.498	.378
Home Games	231	67	10	1	12	43	35	48	.290	.498	.379
Road Games	219	66	13	0	15	51	33	56	.301	.566	.400
Grass Fields	334	100	18	1	19	72	51	79	.299	.530	.389
Artificial Turf	116	33	5	0	8	22	17	25	.284	.534	.390
April	52	18	4	0	1	6	13	8	.346	.481	.470
May	90	28	3	0	8	23	6	21	.311	.611	.357
June	56	14	4	0	2	7	10	13	.250	.429	.364
July	92	27	6	0	4	16	15	12	.293	.489	.393
August	81	18	1	1	4	11	13	29	.222	.407	.330
Sept./Oct.	79	28	5	0	8	31	11	21	.354	.722	.441
Leading Off Inn.	78	20	4	0	3	3	11	17	.256	.423	.356
Bases Empty	232	65	10	0	11	11	32	55	.280	.466	.372
Runners On	218	68	13	1	16	83	36	49	.312	.601	.407
Runners/Scor. Pos.	130	38	10	1	10	69	24	31	.292	.615	.399
Runners On/2 Out	67	20	4	1	6	31	14	20	.299	.657	.420
Scor. Pos./2 Out	44	13	3	1	4	25	9	15	.295	.682	.415
Late-Inning Pressure	45	15	2	0	4	11	9	12	.333	.644	.444
Leading Off	8	4	1	0	1	1	2	2	.500	1.000	.600
Runners On	22	6	1	0	2	9	5	7	.273	.591	.407
Runners/Scor. Pos.	16	3	1	0	2	9	4	6	.188	.625	.350

RUNS BATTED IN	From 1B	From 2B	From 3B	Scoring Position
Totals	20/152	22/97	25/54	47/151
Percentage	13.2%	22.7%	46.3%	31.1%

Loves to face: Cris Carpenter (4-for-4)
Orel Hershiser (.429, 12-for-28, 4 HR)
Greg Maddux (.471, 8-for-17, 2 HR)

Hates to face: Bob Kipper (.067, 1-for-15)
Dennis Martinez (.125, 3-for-24, 1 HR)
Ed Whitson (.125, 4-for-32, 2 2B, 1 HR)

Miscellaneous statistics: Ground outs-to-air outs ratio: 1.36 last season, 1.54 for career.... Grounded into 9 double plays in 115 opportunities (one per 12.8).... Drove in 18 of 32 runners from third base with less than two outs (56%).... Direction of balls hit to the outfield: 43% to left field, 32% to center, 26% to right.... Base running: Advanced from first base to third on 8 of 43 outfield singles (19%); scored from second on 9 of 15 (60%).... Made 1.90 putouts per nine innings in left field, 2d-lowest rate in N.L.

Comments: Hit 15 opposite-field home runs last season, by far the most in the majors. Bo Jackson, with 11, was the only other player in the majors to hit more than eight. Daniels's teammates *combined* for only 10 opposite-field shots last season, led by Eddie Murray with four.... Owns .572 career slugging average vs. right-handed pitchers, second to Fred McGriff (.593) among active players. He ranked fourth in the majors in that category.... Career average vs. right-handers (.320) is 74 points higher than vs. left-handers (.246), the 4th-largest margin in the majors over the last five seasons. The good news is that 1990 was, by far, his best season against southpaws. Career home-run rates: one every 17 at-bats vs. right-handers, one run every 41 vs. lefties.... Owns .341 career batting average (15-for-44) as a pinch hitter.... Became first player in Dodgers' 101-year history to hit three grand-slam homers in a season. They helped lift his career bases-loaded batting average to .423 (11-for-26).... Contrast in career batting averages in Late-Inning Pressure Situations: .414 leading off innings, but only .189 with runners in scoring position.... Scratch Daniels off the long list of players who achieved their career high in home runs in 1987, when the balls and/or the bats were jacked up. He hit 26 in 108 games that year, his high mark until last season.

Doug Dascenzo

Bats Left and Right

Chicago Cubs	AB	H	2B	3B	HR	RBI	BB	SO	BA	SA	OBA
Season	241	61	9	5	1	26	21	18	.253	.344	.312
vs. Left-Handers	136	38	9	0	1	19	9	11	.279	.368	.322
vs. Right-Handers	105	23	0	5	0	7	12	7	.219	.314	.300
vs. Ground-Ballers	119	33	5	5	0	17	8	11	.277	.403	.323
vs. Fly-Ballers	122	28	4	0	1	9	13	7	.230	.287	.301
Home Games	119	33	4	3	1	13	11	6	.277	.387	.336
Road Games	122	28	5	2	0	13	10	12	.230	.303	.288
Grass Fields	173	48	6	4	1	21	13	13	.277	.376	.326
Artificial Turf	68	13	3	1	0	5	8	5	.191	.265	.276
April	11	2	0	0	1	2	1	0	.182	.455	.250
May	33	7	1	1	0	7	1	3	.212	.303	.229
June	22	6	2	1	0	2	2	3	.273	.455	.360
July	67	18	3	0	0	4	1	1	.269	.313	.279
August	54	19	3	2	0	6	8	4	.352	.481	.429
Sept./Oct.	54	9	0	1	0	5	8	7	.167	.204	.270
Leading Off Inn.	82	25	6	2	0	0	7	6	.305	.427	.360
Bases Empty	157	37	7	3	0	0	16	12	.236	.318	.306
Runners On	84	24	2	2	1	26	5	6	.286	.393	.323
Runners/Scor. Pos.	47	15	2	0	0	22	4	1	.319	.362	.352
Runners On/2 Out	35	10	1	1	0	11	2	3	.286	.371	.342
Scor. Pos./2 Out	22	9	1	0	0	10	2	0	.409	.455	.458
Late-Inning Pressure	26	5	1	2	0	5	5	3	.192	.385	.313
Leading Off	8	0	0	0	0	0	0	2	.000	.000	.000
Runners On	8	2	1	1	0	5	2	1	.250	.625	.364
Runners/Scor. Pos.	4	1	1	0	0	4	1	0	.250	.500	.333

RUNS BATTED IN	From 1B	From 2B	From 3B	Scoring Position
Totals	4/60	7/36	14/26	21/62
Percentage	6.7%	19.4%	53.8%	33.9%

Loves to face: Jose DeJesus (2-for-2, 1 3B, 1 BB)
Mark Portugal (.750, 3-for-4)
Dennis Rasmussen (.455, 5-for-11)

Hates to face: Jose DeLeon (0-for-14)
Jim Deshaies (.083, 1-for-12)
Jose Rijo (0-for-10)

Miscellaneous statistics: Ground outs-to-air outs ratio: 0.78 last season, 1.07 for career.... Grounded into 3 double plays in 44 opportunities (one per 14.7).... Drove in 9 of 14 runners from third base with less than two outs (64%).... Direction of balls hit to the outfield: 22% to left field, 36% to center, 42% to right batting left-handed; 44% to left, 32% to center, 24% to right batting right-handed.... Base running: Advanced from first base to third on 3 of 10 outfield singles (30%); scored from second on 6 of 7 (86%).... Made 2.58 putouts per nine innings in center field.

Comments: Has a career average of .269 batting right-handed, but only .176 batting left-handed. That's a switch-hitter? They should revoke switch-hitting privileges from players who can't top the .200 mark from both sides. How much worse could he hit batting right-handed against right-handed pitchers?...A .230 career hitter in the United States, .040 (1-for-25) in Canada.... Hitless in 11 career at-bats as a pinch hitter.... Played 107 games in the outfield without committing an error last season. The minimum qualification for the fielding percentage leadership is two-thirds of a club's scheduled games (108), which left Dascenzo one game shy of the title, which went to Billy Hatcher (.997). We have no grudge against Dascenzo, but what goes 'round, comes 'round. You'll recall that in 1989 Don Zimmer manipulated the record books, playing Ryne Sandberg for only one or two innings of games in the final week of the season to facilitate his record for consecutive errorless games at second base. Had Zim known about Dascenzo's situation, similar shenanigans would no doubt have occurred.... Doug's career total of 172 games in the outfield is the most by any player in major league history who has never committed an outfield error. He's just 54 games shy of Curt Flood's National League record of 226 consecutive errorless games in the outfield. The major league record of 266 games by Don Demeter is also within reach. (P.S. Don't tell Zimmer.)

Darren Daulton

Bats Left

Philadelphia Phillies	AB	H	2B	3B	HR	RBI	BB	SO	BA	SA	OBA
Season	459	123	30	1	12	57	72	72	.268	.416	.367
vs. Left-Handers	113	29	8	0	1	9	22	23	.257	.354	.378
vs. Right-Handers	346	94	22	1	11	48	50	49	.272	.436	.363
vs. Ground-Ballers	249	79	21	0	6	34	30	32	.317	.474	.389
vs. Fly-Ballers	210	44	9	1	6	23	42	40	.210	.348	.343
Home Games	224	56	15	0	5	24	34	31	.250	.384	.345
Road Games	235	67	15	1	7	33	38	41	.285	.447	.388
Grass Fields	129	37	7	0	2	14	20	25	.287	.388	.384
Artificial Turf	330	86	23	1	10	43	52	47	.261	.427	.360
April	47	11	4	0	0	4	9	11	.234	.319	.357
May	64	12	2	0	0	4	16	11	.188	.219	.346
June	79	20	5	0	2	5	9	10	.253	.392	.326
July	79	21	7	1	4	16	9	12	.266	.532	.337
August	102	32	7	0	4	11	19	13	.314	.500	.426
Sept./Oct.	88	27	5	0	2	17	10	15	.307	.432	.380
Leading Off Inn.	101	20	6	0	1	1	10	14	.198	.287	.277
Bases Empty	259	61	9	0	7	7	39	45	.236	.351	.340
Runners On	200	62	21	1	5	50	33	27	.310	.500	.401
Runners/Scor. Pos.	117	33	11	0	3	42	23	20	.282	.453	.389
Runners On/2 Out	86	25	9	0	3	25	17	13	.291	.500	.408
Scor. Pos./2 Out	59	15	4	0	2	20	16	11	.254	.424	.413
Late-Inning Pressure	78	18	1	0	2	8	5	18	.231	.321	.282
Leading Off	18	4	0	0	0	0	1	1	.222	.222	.300
Runners On	35	6	1	0	1	7	2	8	.171	.286	.211
Runners/Scor. Pos.	25	3	1	0	0	5	1	7	.120	.160	.148

RUNS BATTED IN	From 1B	From 2B	From 3B	Scoring Position
Totals	9/141	17/92	19/50	36/142
Percentage	6.4%	18.5%	38.0%	25.4%

Loves to face: David Cone (.278, 5-for-18, 1 2B, 3 HR, 6 BB)
Mike LaCoss (.417, 5-for-12, 1 HR)
Scott Terry (.444, 4-for-9, 1 2B, 2 HR)

Hates to face: Jose Rijo (.143, 2-for-14)
John Smoltz (0-for-18, 1 BB)
Ed Whitson (0-for-13)

Miscellaneous statistics: Ground outs-to-air outs ratio: 0.78 last season, 0.83 for career.... Grounded into 6 double plays in 98 opportunities (one per 16.3).... Drove in 13 of 27 runners from third base with less than two outs (48%).... Direction of balls hit to the outfield: 21% to left field, 28% to center, 51% to right.... Base running: Advanced from first base to third on 10 of 31 outfield singles (32%); scored from second on 4 of 13 (31%), 4th-lowest rate in N.L.... Opposing base stealers: 78-for-120 (65%), 4th-lowest rate in N.L.

Comments: In view of the contract he signed in October, his season must rank as the best-timed .268, 57-RBI season in baseball history.... Batting average increased 67 points from 1989 to 1990, the 5th-largest gain among players with at least 300 at-bats in both seasons.... Moved to second spot in lineup in early July, he responded with .349 batting average and .453 on-base average in first innings, with four home runs in 43 at-bats.... Caught 139 games last season, becoming first Phillies catcher to lead league in that category since Spud Davis in 1931. That total was the 6th-highest one-year total in Phillies' history. The highest: Bob Boone (146 in 1974, 145 in 1973), Bo Diaz (144 in 1982), Clay Dalrymple (142 in 1963), and Red Dooin (140 in 1909). Catchers whose surnames start from *E* through *Z* need not apply.... Stole seven bases in eight attempts last season, with all of his attempts coming after the All-Star break.... Has hit only two of his 36 career home runs off of left-handed pitchers: Bob Knepper (1989) and Jeff Musselman (1990).... Batted 108 points higher vs. ground-ball pitchers (.317) than vs. fly-ballers (.210), the 5th-largest margin in the majors last season, and *de rigeur* for a fly-ball hitter. His career average of .185 vs. fly-ball pitchers is the 3d-worst of any player over the last 16 years (minimum: 400 AB). Who's worse? Jim Mason (.175) and Dann Bilardello (.176), of course.

Eric Davis

Bats Right

Cincinnati Reds	AB	H	2B	3B	HR	RBI	BB	SO	BA	SA	OBA
Season	453	118	26	2	24	86	60	100	.260	.486	.347
vs. Left-Handers	150	43	11	0	8	36	19	32	.287	.520	.365
vs. Right-Handers	303	75	15	2	16	50	41	68	.248	.469	.339
vs. Ground-Ballers	218	56	10	1	10	39	32	58	.257	.450	.356
vs. Fly-Ballers	235	62	16	1	14	47	28	42	.264	.519	.340
Home Games	193	45	8	1	13	34	32	42	.233	.487	.344
Road Games	260	73	18	1	11	52	28	58	.281	.485	.351
Grass Fields	171	50	11	0	9	40	18	42	.292	.515	.359
Artificial Turf	282	68	15	2	15	46	42	58	.241	.468	.340
April	43	8	2	1	1	8	6	11	.186	.349	.280
May	28	5	1	0	1	4	6	8	.179	.321	.324
June	96	28	4	1	9	22	18	19	.292	.635	.404
July	93	18	5	0	3	16	14	21	.194	.344	.306
August	95	25	7	0	3	12	6	22	.263	.432	.304
Sept./Oct.	98	34	7	0	7	24	10	19	.347	.633	.409
Leading Off Inn.	111	32	4	1	9	9	12	29	.288	.586	.358
Bases Empty	232	64	9	1	14	14	25	53	.276	.504	.346
Runners On	221	54	17	1	10	72	35	47	.244	.466	.349
Runners/Scor. Pos.	131	33	12	1	6	61	26	31	.252	.496	.377
Runners On/2 Out	97	20	4	0	5	23	16	22	.206	.402	.325
Scor. Pos./2 Out	57	13	3	0	3	19	12	14	.228	.439	.371
Late-Inning Pressure	67	14	3	0	2	11	4	14	.209	.343	.254
Leading Off	19	1	0	0	0	0	0	7	.053	.053	.053
Runners On	26	6	1	0	2	11	2	5	.231	.500	.286
Runners/Scor. Pos.	20	4	0	0	2	10	1	5	.200	.500	.238

RUNS BATTED IN	From 1B	From 2B	From 3B	Scoring Position
Totals	16/140	20/92	26/64	46/156
Percentage	11.4%	21.7%	40.6%	29.5%

Loves to face: Don Carman (.571, 8-for-14, 1 2B, 5 HR)
Bruce Ruffin (.500, 9-for-18, 1 HR)
John Smoltz (.643, 9-for-14, 2 2B, 4 HR)

Hates to face: Rick Reuschel (.048, 1-for-21, 2 BB)
Brian Holton (0-for-8, 4 SO)
John Tudor (.059, 1-for-17)

Miscellaneous statistics: Ground outs-to-air outs ratio: 1.13 last season, 1.05 for career.... Grounded into 7 double plays in 96 opportunities (one per 13.7).... Drove in 19 of 37 runners from third base with less than two outs (51%).... Direction of balls hit to the outfield: 35% to left field, 34% to center, 31% to right.... Base running: Advanced from first base to third on 10 of 24 outfield singles (42%); scored from second on 11 of 13 (85%).... Made 2.54 putouts per nine innings in center field.

Comments: Owns the best career home run rate in the history of a franchise that has seen some pretty good power hitters: The top five (minimum: 50 HR): Davis (15.5), Frank Robinson (17.1), Wally Post (17.6), George Foster (18.3), and Lee May (19.3). In fact, among players with at least 100 N.L. home runs, Davis's rate is fifth best in the history of the National League. Ahead of him: Ralph Kiner (13.9), Dave Kingman (14.6), Mike Schmidt (15.2), and Darryl Strawberry (15.488 to Davis's 15.494). His career rate of one homer every 13.5 at-bats vs. left-handed pitchers is tops among active N.L. players.... Hit seven opposite-field homers last season, 2d most in N.L. behind Kal Daniels (15).... Has missed 155 games in his five "full" seasons with Cincinnati, and hasn't played more than 135 games in any of those seasons. Nevertheless, he has a streak of five straight years with at least 100 strikeouts.... Had his best statistical year in the outfield, with career highs in assists (11) and fielding percentage (.993, two errors in 270 chances).... Batting average stood at .224 as late as August 19; he hit .351 from then until the end of the regular season.... Started 55 games in left field last season to cut the wear and tear on those knees, after only four starts there in 1989.... Owns .869 career stolen-base percentage, higher than baseball's all-time record holder, Tim Raines (.857). Qualification for the record is based on 300 attempts. Davis starts 1991 with 233 steals in 268 attempts.

Glenn Davis

Bats Right

Houston Astros	AB	H	2B	3B	HR	RBI	BB	SO	BA	SA	OBA
Season	327	82	15	4	22	64	46	54	.251	.523	.357
vs. Left-Handers	123	31	6	0	11	27	21	11	.252	.569	.378
vs. Right-Handers	204	51	9	4	11	37	25	43	.250	.495	.343
vs. Ground-Ballers	189	49	8	2	12	31	26	22	.259	.513	.361
vs. Fly-Ballers	138	33	7	2	10	33	20	32	.239	.536	.352
Home Games	175	38	7	2	4	22	21	35	.217	.349	.315
Road Games	152	44	8	2	18	42	25	19	.289	.724	.403
Grass Fields	92	29	4	2	13	30	14	13	.315	.826	.427
Artificial Turf	235	53	11	2	9	34	32	41	.226	.404	.328
April	70	24	5	0	6	14	9	21	.343	.671	.439
May	107	23	6	0	4	18	6	13	.215	.383	.263
June	57	12	1	1	9	16	10	14	.211	.737	.328
July	0	0	0	0	0	0	0	0	—	—	—
August	4	0	0	0	0	0	1	0	.000	.000	.200
Sept./Oct.	89	23	3	3	3	16	20	6	.258	.461	.416
Leading Off Inn.	99	20	4	1	4	4	7	16	.202	.384	.269
Bases Empty	174	44	7	3	12	12	16	28	.253	.534	.333
Runners On	153	38	8	1	10	52	30	26	.248	.510	.382
Runners/Scor. Pos.	99	26	5	1	6	43	27	20	.263	.515	.421
Runners On/2 Out	85	18	4	0	6	24	22	13	.212	.471	.380
Scor. Pos./2 Out	53	11	3	0	3	18	19	11	.208	.434	.417
Late-Inning Pressure	59	14	3	1	2	9	12	8	.237	.424	.375
Leading Off	17	4	2	0	0	0	2	3	.235	.353	.350
Runners On	21	6	1	0	0	7	8	3	.286	.333	.483
Runners/Scor. Pos.	13	5	1	0	0	7	8	2	.385	.462	.619

RUNS BATTED IN	From 1B	From 2B	From 3B	Scoring Position
Totals	12/102	17/76	13/38	30/114
Percentage	11.8%	22.4%	34.2%	26.3%

Loves to face: Tim Burke (.500, 8-for-16, 2 HR)
Ricky Horton (.500, 6-for-12, 3 2B, 2 HR)
Dennis Martinez (.481, 13-for-27, 6 HR)

Hates to face: Mike Bielecki (0-for-16, 2 BB)
Orel Hershiser (.207, 12-for-58)
Jose Rijo (.083, 2-for-24)

Miscellaneous statistics: Ground outs-to-air outs ratio: 0.87 last season, 0.91 for career.... Grounded into 5 double plays in 55 opportunities (one per 11.0).... Drove in 7 of 17 runners from third base with less than two outs (41%), 5th-lowest rate in N.L.... Direction of balls hit to the outfield: 50% to left field, 28% to center, 23% to right.... Base running: Advanced from first base to third on 7 of 17 outfield singles (41%); scored from second on 2 of 4 (50%).... Made 0.64 assists per nine innings at first base.

Comments: With 18 home runs in 152 at-bats in road games, Davis was on his way to challenging Babe Ruth's major league record of 32 road homers in a season. But 65 days on the disabled list due to a rib injury ended that pursuit.... In September, he passed Bob Watson (790) to become the Astros' all-time leader in games at first base (810); four months later, he was traded to Baltimore.... His career total of 166 home runs is 2d highest in Astros history, three ahead of Cesar Cedeno, 57 behind Jim Wynn.... Career average: one home run every 18.3 at-bats. But he has never homered in 52 career at-bats with the bases loaded.... Hit only 72 home runs at the Astrodome compared to 94 on the road, but his career batting average was over 40 points higher at home (.283) than on the road (.241).... Owns a .229 career batting average in Late-Inning Pressure Situations, .269 in other at-bats. He hasn't been so hot in early-inning pressure situations either: he has a .217 career average with two outs and runners in scoring position.... Hit four triples in his last 145 at-bats last season, compared to six triples in 2941 career at-bats until then. Now let's see him do it in Baltimore. We've said it before, we'll say it again: It's easier to hit a triple at Pimlico than at Memorial Stadium.

Andre Dawson

Bats Right

Chicago Cubs	AB	H	2B	3B	HR	RBI	BB	SO	BA	SA	OBA
Season	529	164	28	5	27	100	42	65	.310	.535	.358
vs. Left-Handers	181	54	10	2	8	25	14	19	.298	.508	.343
vs. Right-Handers	348	110	18	3	19	75	28	46	.316	.549	.366
vs. Ground-Ballers	257	68	7	1	9	32	19	31	.265	.405	.313
vs. Fly-Ballers	272	96	21	4	18	68	23	34	.353	.658	.400
Home Games	266	84	10	3	14	51	27	26	.316	.534	.374
Road Games	263	80	18	2	13	49	15	39	.304	.536	.342
Grass Fields	376	114	16	3	22	77	37	45	.303	.537	.360
Artificial Turf	153	50	12	2	5	23	5	20	.327	.529	.352
April	59	20	2	1	4	15	2	9	.339	.610	.349
May	100	35	7	1	9	28	10	7	.350	.710	.395
June	99	28	8	0	5	9	14	10	.283	.515	.377
July	76	27	3	0	1	10	7	8	.355	.434	.412
August	89	21	3	2	2	12	1	15	.236	.382	.242
Sept./Oct.	106	33	5	1	6	26	8	16	.311	.547	.360
Leading Off Inn.	125	35	4	0	6	6	4	15	.280	.456	.302
Bases Empty	264	79	9	3	16	16	11	34	.299	.538	.330
Runners On	265	85	19	2	11	84	31	31	.321	.532	.384
Runners/Scor. Pos.	145	43	13	1	4	69	27	21	.297	.483	.392
Runners On/2 Out	121	36	6	0	5	28	17	16	.298	.471	.388
Scor. Pos./2 Out	68	20	4	0	2	22	16	12	.294	.441	.435
Late-Inning Pressure	80	22	2	0	3	12	13	7	.275	.412	.376
Leading Off	17	5	1	0	1	1	0	1	.294	.529	.294
Runners On	45	13	1	0	2	11	10	2	.289	.444	.418
Runners/Scor. Pos.	18	4	0	0	0	7	9	2	.222	.222	.481

RUNS BATTED IN	From 1B	From 2B	From 3B	Scoring Position
Totals	14/188	29/110	30/66	59/176
Percentage	7.4%	26.4%	45.5%	33.5%

Loves to face: Mark Grant (.571, 12-for-21, 3 HR)
John Smiley (.533, 16-for-30, 4 HR, 0 BB)
Pete Smith (.368, 7-for-19, 2 2B, 4 HR)

Hates to face: Bob Kipper (0-for-12, 1 BB)
Don Robinson (.226, 14-for-62, 3 HR)
John Smoltz (.059, 1-for-17)

Miscellaneous statistics: Ground outs-to-air outs ratio: 0.95 last season, 1.00 for career.... Grounded into 12 double plays in 121 opportunities (one per 10.1).... Drove in 26 of 36 runners from third base with less than two outs (72%).... Direction of balls hit to the outfield: 49% to left field, 30% to center, 22% to right.... Base running: Advanced from first base to third on 11 of 33 outfield singles (33%); scored from second on 10 of 16 (63%).... Made 1.93 putouts per nine innings in right field.

Comments: Set a career high for batting average at the age of 36. Finished the season four steals shy of becoming the oldest player in major league history to hit 20 home runs and steal 20 bases in the same season. Had a perfect 11-for-11 record stealing on natural surfaces.... Drove in 33.5 percent of runners from scoring position, also a career high, and the 5th-highest rate in the National League last season.... Annual batting averages vs. left-handed pitchers since 1986: .331, .298, .296, .298, .298.... Once again, last season he hit for a higher average in day games (.326) than he did at night (.294). He's done that in 14 of his 15 seasons in the majors. His career breakdown: .305 in day games, .266 at night.... Walked 42 times last season, with half of them being of the intentional persuasion.... Alternated between the 4th- and 5th-spots in the Cubs' batting order through the first two weeks of the season, but his last 127 starts were all in the cleanup spot.... Career totals: 2201 hits, 346 home runs, 300 stolen bases. The only two players in history to surpass him in both steals and homers are Willie Mays and Bobby Bonds. Add hits to the equation and Bonds (1886) drops out.... His career total of 1962 games in the outfield is the 3d highest among players active in 1990, behind Dave Winfield (2296) and Dwight Evans (2079).

Delino DeShields

Bats Left

Montreal Expos	AB	H	2B	3B	HR	RBI	BB	SO	BA	SA	OBA
Season	499	144	28	6	4	45	66	96	.289	.393	.375
vs. Left-Handers	193	51	9	3	2	17	26	48	.264	.373	.356
vs. Right-Handers	306	93	19	3	2	28	40	48	.304	.405	.387
vs. Ground-Ballers	272	73	16	4	2	25	33	54	.268	.379	.354
vs. Fly-Ballers	227	71	12	2	2	20	33	42	.313	.410	.400
Home Games	226	71	15	2	3	27	32	41	.314	.438	.402
Road Games	273	73	13	4	1	18	34	55	.267	.355	.352
Grass Fields	140	34	5	2	1	6	12	32	.243	.329	.305
Artificial Turf	359	110	23	4	3	39	54	64	.306	.418	.400
April	70	23	7	0	0	4	10	13	.329	.429	.412
May	96	28	5	2	2	8	16	19	.292	.448	.393
June	58	17	1	2	0	2	8	13	.293	.379	.388
July	61	17	5	0	0	8	8	6	.279	.361	.362
August	104	28	4	2	1	8	11	17	.269	.375	.342
Sept./Oct.	110	31	6	0	1	15	13	28	.282	.364	.365
Leading Off Inn.	192	62	6	3	1	1	15	27	.323	.401	.378
Bases Empty	338	101	15	4	4	4	36	62	.299	.402	.373
Runners On	161	43	13	2	0	41	30	34	.267	.373	.378
Runners/Scor. Pos.	106	30	12	2	0	40	24	22	.283	.434	.409
Runners On/2 Out	76	17	3	1	0	13	13	16	.224	.289	.337
Scor. Pos./2 Out	56	12	3	1	0	13	12	12	.214	.304	.353
Late-Inning Pressure	84	16	2	0	0	4	12	19	.190	.214	.299
Leading Off	23	5	1	0	0	0	2	5	.217	.261	.280
Runners On	32	5	0	0	0	4	8	7	.156	.156	.325
Runners/Scor. Pos.	17	5	0	0	0	4	7	2	.294	.294	.500

RUNS BATTED IN	From 1B	From 2B	From 3B	Scoring Position
Totals	4/94	17/84	20/42	37/126
Percentage	4.3%	20.2%	47.6%	29.4%

Loves to face: Ken Howell (.600, 3-for-5, 3 BB)
Joe Magrane (.500, 4-for-8)
Ramon Martinez (.500, 3-for-6, 4 BB)

Hates to face: John Franco (0-for-5, 3 SO)
Fernando Valenzuela (.111, 1-for-9, 2 BB)
Frank Viola (.214, 3-for-14)

Miscellaneous statistics: Ground outs-to-air outs ratio: 1.78 last season, his first in the majors. . . . Grounded into 10 double plays in 62 opportunities (one per 6.2). . . . Drove in 15 of 24 runners from third base with less than two outs (63%). . . . Direction of balls hit to the outfield: 40% to left field, 36% to center, 25% to right. . . . Base running: Advanced from first base to third on 8 of 27 outfield singles (30%); scored from second on 9 of 19 (47%), 5th-lowest rate in N.L. . . . Made 2.99 assists per nine innings at second base.

Comments: Expos may have *finally* secured someone to solve their long-standing second base problem. After 21 years, the Expos record for games by a second baseman is only 388 by Ron Hunt. How low is that total? It's lower than the club record for games by a *pitcher*: 399 by Steve Rogers. No other National League team has a similar situation, in which the team record for games by a pitcher exceeds the corresponding mark for any other position. . . . There were 10 rookies in the opening-day lineups of major league teams last season. DeShields was the only one who had never before played a major league game. His four hits on Opening Day tied a 20th-century N.L. record for most hits in a major league debut. . . . His 15-game hitting streak was the longest by any rookie in the majors last season. He also led all rookies in doubles and stolen bases (42). That's a pretty high total of steals, but 21 rookies have had higher totals since 1900, including seven in the 1980s and five in the 1970s. Yes, Expos fans, Larry Lintz was one of them. . . . Removed in favor of a pinch hitter only once last season. . . . He played 129 games last season at age 21; no other National League player that young appeared in even 50 games. . . . Batted .255 in 110 first-inning at-bats, .298 in subsequent at bats. . . . Highest batting averages by Expos rookies (minimum: 200 AB): Tim Raines, .304 (1981); DeShields, .289 (1990); Boots Day, .283 (1971).

Bill Doran

Bats Left and Right

Astros/Reds	AB	H	2B	3B	HR	RBI	BB	SO	BA	SA	OBA
Season	403	121	29	2	7	37	79	58	.300	.434	.411
vs. Left-Handers	142	38	12	1	2	12	35	19	.268	.408	.408
vs. Right-Handers	261	83	17	1	5	25	44	39	.318	.448	.412
vs. Ground-Ballers	222	61	16	1	3	20	37	28	.275	.396	.375
vs. Fly-Ballers	181	60	13	1	4	17	42	30	.331	.481	.451
Home Games	199	66	14	2	4	18	38	26	.332	.482	.432
Road Games	204	55	15	0	3	19	41	32	.270	.387	.390
Grass Fields	141	44	15	0	2	15	29	20	.312	.461	.427
Artificial Turf	262	77	14	2	5	22	50	38	.294	.420	.402
April	63	14	4	0	1	7	8	10	.222	.333	.306
May	77	22	4	0	0	11	13	9	.286	.338	.380
June	69	20	3	0	0	2	18	13	.290	.333	.432
July	52	14	3	1	3	7	13	8	.269	.538	.409
August	83	29	7	1	2	5	19	13	.349	.530	.471
Sept./Oct.	59	22	8	0	1	5	8	5	.373	.559	.448
Leading Off Inn.	91	34	9	1	1	1	18	11	.374	.527	.477
Bases Empty	255	78	19	2	4	4	47	41	.306	.443	.414
Runners On	148	43	10	0	3	33	32	17	.291	.419	.405
Runners/Scor. Pos.	93	21	3	0	2	28	21	15	.226	.323	.353
Runners On/2 Out	59	12	0	0	1	8	15	8	.203	.254	.365
Scor. Pos./2 Out	45	7	0	0	0	6	10	8	.156	.156	.309
Late-Inning Pressure	50	11	2	0	0	1	18	9	.220	.260	.426
Leading Off	13	6	0	0	0	0	4	0	.462	.462	.588
Runners On	24	2	1	0	0	1	7	5	.083	.125	.290
Runners/Scor. Pos.	16	1	0	0	0	1	7	4	.063	.063	.348

RUNS BATTED IN	From 1B	From 2B	From 3B	Scoring Position
Totals	7/89	11/69	12/39	23/108
Percentage	7.9%	15.9%	30.8%	21.3%

Loves to face: Tom Glavine (.563, 9-for-16)
Craig Lefferts (.483, 14-for-29)
Mike Maddux (.833, 5-for-6, 1 HR, 1 SO)

Hates to face: David Cone (.174, 4-for-23)
Rick Reuschel (.130, 6-for-46, 0 SO)
Jose Rijo (.056, 1-for-18, 3 BB)

Miscellaneous statistics: Ground outs-to-air outs ratio: 1.01 last season, 1.08 for career. . . . Grounded into 3 double plays in 66 opportunities (one per 22.0). . . . Drove in 9 of 17 runners from third base with less than two outs (53%). . . . Direction of balls hit to the outfield: 19% to left field, 30% to center, 51% to right batting left-handed; 43% to left, 35% to center, 22% to right batting right-handed. . . . Base running: Advanced from first base to third on 11 of 27 outfield singles (41%); scored from second on 11 of 19 (58%). . . . Made 2.92 assists per nine innings at second base.

Comments: Batting average increased 81 points from 1989 to 1990, the 10th-largest one-year gain by an everyday player in major league history. Yet both Len Dykstra and Eddie Murray had larger increases last season. . . . If you were to combine Mariano Duncan's 1990 statistics vs. left-handed pitchers with Doran's vs. right-handers, you'd have a second base platoon that batted .356 with nine home runs and 52 RBIs. Good numbers, but we'd still rather have Ryne Sandberg. . . . Batted 97 points lower with runners in scoring position (.226) than in other at-bats (.323) last season, the 3d-largest drop in the majors. . . . Also hit 87 points higher in day games (.361) than at night (.274) last season, the 4th-largest disparity in the majors. . . . Batted .397 from leadoff spot in lineup, highest by any player in the majors (minimum: 50 AB). . . . His .477 on-base average leading off innings was best in majors last year and 6th highest in the majors since 1975 (minimum: 100 leadoff PA). Rod Carew set the record with .523 in 1982 (Full list appears on page 400). With Reds in September, Doran reached base safely in eight consecutive leadoff appearances. . . . Has career total of 26 home runs at the Astrodome, 42 elsewhere. Has homered at every current National League stadium except Busch, where he has 158 at-bats. . . . His streak of eight straight years in Houston's opening-day starting lineup ends one shy of Jose Cruz's club record (1977–85).

Mariano Duncan

Bats Right

Cincinnati Reds	AB	H	2B	3B	HR	RBI	BB	SO	BA	SA	OBA
Season	435	133	22	11	10	55	24	67	.306	.476	.345
vs. Left-Handers	188	77	17	4	4	27	10	22	.410	.606	.437
vs. Right-Handers	247	56	5	7	6	28	14	45	.227	.377	.276
vs. Ground-Ballers	219	66	14	2	1	19	10	33	.301	.397	.332
vs. Fly-Ballers	216	67	8	9	9	36	14	34	.310	.556	.357
Home Games	230	71	12	5	5	30	13	30	.309	.470	.346
Road Games	205	62	10	6	5	25	11	37	.302	.483	.344
Grass Fields	117	34	7	4	1	14	9	26	.291	.444	.351
Artificial Turf	318	99	15	7	9	41	15	41	.311	.487	.342
April	49	20	4	1	4	14	8	5	.408	.776	.483
May	43	15	2	1	0	1	3	5	.349	.442	.391
June	98	23	5	1	2	6	1	13	.235	.367	.265
July	60	19	4	2	1	7	2	8	.317	.500	.339
August	109	35	4	4	1	13	5	15	.321	.459	.351
Sept./Oct.	76	21	3	2	2	14	5	21	.276	.447	.318
Leading Off Inn.	97	29	3	4	3	3	8	12	.299	.505	.352
Bases Empty	244	80	14	7	6	6	15	37	.328	.516	.369
Runners On	191	53	8	4	4	49	9	30	.277	.424	.314
Runners/Scor. Pos.	105	27	5	1	1	40	7	19	.257	.352	.299
Runners On/2 Out	77	20	1	2	2	20	7	14	.260	.403	.321
Scor. Pos./2 Out	48	13	1	1	1	17	7	10	.271	.396	.364
Late-Inning Pressure	60	17	1	0	0	4	5	13	.283	.300	.343
Leading Off	15	3	0	0	0	0	4	3	.200	.200	.368
Runners On	23	4	0	0	0	4	0	6	.174	.174	.200
Runners/Scor. Pos.	14	3	0	0	0	4	0	4	.214	.214	.200

RUNS BATTED IN	From 1B	From 2B	From 3B	Scoring Position
Totals	8/144	16/83	21/46	37/129
Percentage	5.6%	19.3%	45.7%	28.7%

Loves to face: Sid Fernandez (.440, 11-for-25)
John Franco (.538, 7-for-13)
Craig Lefferts (.417, 5-for-12, 1 HR)

Hates to face: Dwight Gooden (.063, 1-for-16, 1 HR, 8 SO)
Mike Scott (.167, 5-for-30, 1 HR)
Rick Sutcliffe (0-for-11)

Miscellaneous statistics: Ground outs-to-air outs ratio: 1.41 last season, 1.26 for career.... Grounded into 10 double plays in 99 opportunities (one per 9.9).... Drove in 17 of 26 runners from third base with less than two outs (65%).... Direction of balls hit to the outfield: 28% to left field, 35% to center, 37% to right.... Base running: Advanced from first base to third on 11 of 24 outfield singles (46%); scored from second on 7 of 11 (64%).... Made 2.79 assists per nine innings at second base.

Comments: Batting average vs. left-handed pitchers (.410) was the best by any player in majors since 1980 (minimum: 40 hits). The last players with higher marks: Sixto Lezcano (.411 in 1979) and Rennie Stennett (.435 in 1977). Duncan hit 183 points higher vs. left-handers than vs. right-handers (.227), the largest difference in the majors; the difference over his last five seasons: .318 vs. lefties, .211 vs. righties.... Owns a .310 career batting average in Late-Inning Pressure Situations.... First Cincinnati player to lead the National League in triples since Vada Pinson in 1967.... April batting average was the highest in the league.... Batted .368 from the 2d spot in the batting order, highest in majors among players with at least 100 such at-bats last season.... Hitless in eight at-bats with the bases loaded last season, lowering his career average in those situations to .195 (8-for-41, 1 HR).... Stole 86 bases over the first 250 games of his career, but has stolen only 33 bases in 296 games since then.... Downside: fielding statistics. Duncan's rate of errors (one every 36.5 chances) was second worst in majors last season among regular second basemen; only Juan Samuel (35.8) made errors more rapidly.... As a shortstop, Duncan's career rate of 19.2 chances per error ranks as the worst among the 39 players active in 1990 with 300+ career games at short. Yes, even worse than Rafael Ramirez (21.3).

Shawon Dunston

Bats Right

Chicago Cubs	AB	H	2B	3B	HR	RBI	BB	SO	BA	SA	OBA
Season	545	143	22	8	17	66	15	87	.262	.426	.283
vs. Left-Handers	188	54	6	4	9	23	3	24	.287	.505	.295
vs. Right-Handers	357	89	16	4	8	43	12	63	.249	.384	.277
vs. Ground-Ballers	253	67	9	7	6	28	3	40	.265	.427	.273
vs. Fly-Ballers	292	76	13	1	11	38	12	47	.260	.425	.291
Home Games	268	67	12	4	7	25	7	46	.250	.403	.275
Road Games	277	76	10	4	10	41	8	41	.274	.448	.291
Grass Fields	400	104	17	4	15	50	10	73	.260	.435	.281
Artificial Turf	145	39	5	4	2	16	5	14	.269	.400	.289
April	73	21	4	0	3	7	1	12	.288	.466	.293
May	99	34	3	1	5	16	1	10	.343	.545	.347
June	97	21	5	0	2	14	4	23	.216	.330	.252
July	88	28	3	4	3	16	5	13	.318	.545	.354
August	96	26	5	2	3	11	2	12	.271	.458	.286
Sept./Oct.	92	13	2	1	1	2	2	17	.141	.217	.167
Leading Off Inn.	124	36	7	1	2	2	3	20	.290	.411	.313
Bases Empty	328	91	14	4	8	8	10	56	.277	.418	.301
Runners On	217	52	8	4	9	58	5	31	.240	.438	.257
Runners/Scor. Pos.	122	28	6	2	5	48	5	22	.230	.434	.259
Runners On/2 Out	105	30	6	2	5	32	2	12	.286	.524	.306
Scor. Pos./2 Out	68	20	5	1	4	29	2	9	.294	.574	.324
Late-Inning Pressure	86	24	5	0	2	10	3	14	.279	.407	.311
Leading Off	17	6	2	0	0	0	0	4	.353	.471	.389
Runners On	34	11	2	0	2	10	1	5	.324	.559	.343
Runners/Scor. Pos.	19	7	2	0	2	10	1	4	.368	.789	.400

RUNS BATTED IN	From 1B	From 2B	From 3B	Scoring Position
Totals	12/150	19/87	18/58	37/145
Percentage	8.0%	21.8%	31.0%	25.5%

Loves to face: Mark Langston (.800, 4-for-5)
John Smiley (.400, 8-for-20, 2 HR)
Scott Terry (.375, 6-for-16, 2 HR)

Hates to face: Jose DeLeon (.135, 5-for-37, 0 BB)
Dwight Gooden (.143, 6-for-42, 3 2B, 1 HR)
Rick Reuschel (.190, 8-for-42, 1 HR)

Miscellaneous statistics: Ground outs-to-air outs ratio: 0.84 last season, 1.04 for career.... Grounded into 9 double plays in 95 opportunities (one per 10.6).... Drove in 13 of 25 runners from third base with less than two outs (52%).... Direction of balls hit to the outfield: 40% to left field, 33% to center, 26% to right.... Base running: Advanced from first base to third on 15 of 24 outfield singles (63%); scored from second on 7 of 11 (64%).... Made 2.83 assists per nine innings at shortstop.

Comments: Dunston has played 749 games at shortstop; with his third game this season, he'll move past Charlie Hollocher into fifth place in team history for games at short. The top four: Don Kessinger (1618), Joe Tinker (1500), Ernie Banks (1125), and Billy Jurges (960).... Became the first Cubs shortstop to appear in an All-Star game since Don Kessinger in 1974.... Became the first National League player since Craig Reynolds in 1981 to hit three triples in a nine-inning game.... Led the majors with 46 runs and 45 RBIs from the seventh slot in the batting order.... The only player with more home runs than walks last season (minimum: 400 AB). That distinction was earned previously by Andres Thomas (1989) and Kirby Puckett (1988).... Has walked 111 times, including 33 intentional walks, in six years in majors, or once every 26.4 plate appearances. (To put that in perspective: Nolan Ryan has averaged one walk every 25.2 plate appearances.) But last year, Dunston proved incapable of maintaining that furious rate; it slowed to, well, a non-walk: once every 38.2 times up.... Career breakdown reveals a pretty consistent performer at the plate: .257 overall; .256 with the bases empty, .259 with runners on base; .257 with runners in scoring position, .258 with two outs and RISP; .259 leading off innings; .264 vs. left-handers, .255 vs. right-handers.

Lenny Dykstra

Bats Left

Philadelphia Phillies	AB	H	2B	3B	HR	RBI	BB	SO	BA	SA	OBA
Season	590	192	35	3	9	60	89	48	.325	.441	.418
vs. Left-Handers	200	58	6	1	1	17	29	20	.290	.345	.385
vs. Right-Handers	390	134	29	2	8	43	60	28	.344	.490	.434
vs. Ground-Ballers	301	84	16	0	1	23	39	32	.279	.342	.368
vs. Fly-Ballers	289	108	19	3	8	37	50	16	.374	.543	.468
Home Games	280	95	15	1	6	27	52	23	.339	.464	.445
Road Games	310	97	20	2	3	33	37	25	.313	.419	.392
Grass Fields	153	46	14	1	1	19	27	11	.301	.425	.410
Artificial Turf	437	146	21	2	8	41	62	37	.334	.446	.421
April	58	19	5	0	1	7	3	7	.328	.466	.381
May	102	44	9	1	1	12	16	5	.431	.569	.512
June	109	37	4	0	2	11	21	10	.339	.431	.446
July	94	27	6	1	1	6	24	11	.287	.404	.437
August	117	37	10	0	2	11	11	6	.316	.453	.382
Sept./Oct.	110	28	1	1	2	13	14	9	.255	.336	.336
Leading Off Inn.	240	70	11	2	7	7	37	25	.292	.442	.393
Bases Empty	413	118	22	3	8	8	51	34	.286	.412	.371
Runners On	177	74	13	0	1	52	38	14	.418	.508	.518
Runners/Scor. Pos.	111	47	8	0	0	47	33	7	.423	.495	.547
Runners On/2 Out	74	33	8	0	0	25	20	7	.446	.554	.568
Scor. Pos./2 Out	53	22	4	0	0	22	18	5	.415	.491	.563
Late-Inning Pressure	83	28	4	0	0	14	18	8	.337	.386	.461
Leading Off	16	1	0	0	0	0	3	4	.063	.063	.211
Runners On	42	19	1	0	0	14	11	4	.452	.476	.566
Runners/Scor. Pos.	27	14	1	0	0	13	9	1	.519	.556	.639

RUNS BATTED IN	From 1B	From 2B	From 3B	Scoring Position
Totals	6/119	20/87	25/49	45/136
Percentage	5.0%	23.0%	51.0%	33.1%

Loves to face: Mike Bielecki (.371, 13-for-35, 2 HR)
Oil Can Boyd (.500, 5-for-10, 2 HR)
Bob Walk (.424, 14-for-33)

Hates to face: Doug Drabek (.167, 7-for-42)
Joe Magrane (.087, 2-for-23)
Rick Sutcliffe (.191, 9-for-47, 1 HR)

Miscellaneous statistics: Ground outs-to-air outs ratio: 0.99 last season, 1.00 for career.... Grounded into 5 double plays in 82 opportunities (one per 16.4).... Drove in 16 of 22 runners from third base with less than two outs (73%), 5th-highest rate in N.L.... Direction of balls hit to the outfield: 34% to left field, 28% to center, 38% to right.... Base running: Advanced from first base to third on 19 of 42 outfield singles (45%); scored from second on 15 of 21 (71%).... Made 3.07 putouts per nine innings in center field, highest rate in N.L.

Comments: Became the third Phillies center fielder to start an All-Star game. The others: Harry Walker (1947) and Richie Ashburn (1948 and 1951).... Batting average increased 88 points from 1989 to 1990, the largest gain of any player with at least 300 at-bats in both years.... Batted 121 points higher with runners in scoring position (.423) than in other at-bats (.303) last season, the largest margin in the majors.... Batted 132 points higher with runners on base (.418) than with the bases empty (.286) last season, the 4th-largest margin in the majors.... Batting average with two outs and runners on base was the highest single-season average in the 16-year history of *The Player Analysis*.... Batted 95 points higher vs. fly-ballers (.374) than vs. ground-ballers (.279) last season, the 4th-largest margin in the majors.... Dykstra and Brett Butler were the only full-time leadoff hitters in the National League last season, each making every one of their starts from the leadoff spot in the batting order.... Was thrown out trying to advance an extra base on a batted ball ten times last season, the most of any player in the National League.... Batted only .252 in 123 first-inning at-bats, but hit at a .345 clip in his subsequent at-bats.... The Dykstra trade may have been the Phillies' best deal since they acquired Lefty. Which Lefty? Take your pick—O'Doul (for Freddy Leach in 1928) or Carlton (for Rick Wise in 1972).

Kevin Elster

Bats Right

New York Mets	AB	H	2B	3B	HR	RBI	BB	SO	BA	SA	OBA
Season	314	65	20	1	9	45	30	54	.207	.363	.274
vs. Left-Handers	119	27	7	0	2	8	10	16	.227	.336	.282
vs. Right-Handers	195	38	13	1	7	37	20	38	.195	.379	.268
vs. Ground-Ballers	152	35	8	0	4	25	16	27	.230	.362	.299
vs. Fly-Ballers	162	30	12	1	5	20	14	27	.185	.364	.249
Home Games	163	32	11	1	2	24	15	30	.196	.313	.262
Road Games	151	33	9	0	7	21	15	24	.219	.417	.286
Grass Fields	223	46	15	1	6	38	23	39	.206	.363	.278
Artificial Turf	91	19	5	0	3	7	7	15	.209	.363	.263
April	62	6	1	1	1	5	6	15	.097	.194	.174
May	80	19	4	0	4	13	12	11	.237	.438	.337
June	89	24	11	0	1	16	6	16	.270	.427	.306
July	79	15	4	0	3	11	5	11	.190	.354	.238
August	4	1	0	0	0	0	1	1	.250	.250	.400
Sept./Oct.	0	0	0	0	0	0	0	0	—	—	—
Leading Off Inn.	78	16	2	0	4	4	4	9	.205	.385	.253
Bases Empty	189	32	8	0	6	6	16	33	.169	.307	.238
Runners On	125	33	12	1	3	39	14	21	.264	.448	.324
Runners/Scor. Pos.	78	20	8	1	2	36	11	15	.256	.462	.326
Runners On/2 Out	51	13	5	1	1	15	6	11	.255	.451	.333
Scor. Pos./2 Out	34	9	4	1	1	14	4	7	.265	.529	.342
Late-Inning Pressure	44	6	3	0	0	3	4	4	.136	.205	.208
Leading Off	18	2	1	0	0	0	1	2	.111	.167	.158
Runners On	9	3	1	0	0	3	3	0	.333	.444	.500
Runners/Scor. Pos.	4	2	1	0	0	3	3	0	.500	.750	.714

RUNS BATTED IN	From 1B	From 2B	From 3B	Scoring Position
Totals	6/91	11/69	19/35	30/104
Percentage	6.6%	15.9%	54.3%	28.8%

Loves to face: Oil Can Boyd (.571, 4-for-7, 2 2B, 1 HR)
Doug Drabek (.391, 9-for-23, 1 HR)
Bruce Hurst (.455, 5-for-11)

Hates to face: Jim Deshaies (0-for-11, 1 BB)
Rob Dibble (0-for-7, 1 BB, 5 SO)
Pete Smith (0-for-9, 7 SO)

Miscellaneous statistics: Ground outs-to-air outs ratio: 0.75 last season, 0.78 for career.... Grounded into 4 double plays in 64 opportunities (one per 16.0).... Drove in 14 of 20 runners from third base with less than two outs (70%).... Direction of balls hit to the outfield: 36% to left field, 37% to center, 27% to right.... Base running: Advanced from first base to third on 4 of 10 outfield singles (40%); scored from second on 7 of 10 (70%).... Made 2.84 assists per nine innings at shortstop.

Comments: Mets opponents scored an average of 3.63 runs per nine innings with Elster at shortstop, compared to 4.08 runs with other shortstops. But with New York's inclination to cede Elster's spot to Howard Johnson, it's important to note that HoJo wasn't the problem (3.82 runs); the Mets allowed 5.89 runs with Baez, Diaz, or Miller at short.... Set a major league record with 88 consecutive errorless games from 1988 to 1989, but couldn't put together a streak longer than 17 games in 1990. Johnson, by the way, committed two errors in the season finale to snap a 39-game errorless streak of his own at shortstop.... Batted 113 points higher in night games (.245) than in day games (.132) last season, the largest margin in the majors. He batted .098 in day games at Shea Stadium last season. Career average of .191 in day games is the lowest of any nonpitcher over the last 16 years (minimum: 400 AB).... April batting average was the lowest in the National League. His 11 doubles in June tied Howard Johnson for the most in the league in that month.... There were *two* automatic outs at the bottom of the Mets' batting order last season. Elster (.145 batting eighth) and Charlie O'Brien (.171) contributed to New York's major-league-low .207 mark from the eight hole.

Mike Fitzgerald

Bats Right

Montreal Expos	AB	H	2B	3B	HR	RBI	BB	SO	BA	SA	OBA
Season	313	76	18	1	9	41	60	60	.243	.393	.365
vs. Left-Handers	138	31	4	0	5	20	30	21	.225	.362	.359
vs. Right-Handers	175	45	14	1	4	21	30	39	.257	.417	.370
vs. Ground-Ballers	189	44	9	1	4	21	29	38	.233	.354	.336
vs. Fly-Ballers	124	32	9	0	5	20	31	22	.258	.452	.405
Home Games	134	33	10	0	2	14	27	23	.246	.366	.374
Road Games	179	43	8	1	7	27	33	37	.240	.413	.358
Grass Fields	91	23	5	0	4	17	17	18	.253	.440	.364
Artificial Turf	222	53	13	1	5	24	43	42	.239	.374	.366
April	20	4	1	0	1	2	10	1	.200	.400	.467
May	60	16	8	0	1	6	4	15	.267	.450	.313
June	66	16	3	1	2	9	14	14	.242	.409	.378
July	62	13	1	0	3	9	11	14	.210	.371	.333
August	45	7	0	0	1	5	12	4	.156	.222	.328
Sept./Oct.	60	20	5	0	1	10	9	12	.333	.467	.420
Leading Off Inn.	68	19	5	0	2	2	18	11	.279	.441	.430
Bases Empty	179	37	10	1	5	5	38	38	.207	.358	.349
Runners On	134	39	8	0	4	36	22	22	.291	.440	.387
Runners/Scor. Pos.	82	23	7	0	1	29	20	11	.280	.402	.415
Runners On/2 Out	60	18	3	0	0	14	11	6	.300	.350	.408
Scor. Pos./2 Out	39	10	2	0	0	13	11	4	.256	.308	.420
Late-Inning Pressure	74	13	4	0	0	7	12	9	.176	.230	.291
Leading Off	14	2	0	0	0	0	3	1	.143	.143	.294
Runners On	35	8	4	0	0	7	6	3	.229	.343	.341
Runners/Scor. Pos.	22	7	4	0	0	7	6	0	.318	.500	.464

RUNS BATTED IN	From 1B	From 2B	From 3B	Scoring Position
Totals	6/89	14/58	12/36	26/94
Percentage	6.7%	24.1%	33.3%	27.7%

Loves to face: Sid Fernandez (.400, 6-for-15, 2 2B, 2 HR)
Pete Smith (3-for-3, 2 2B, 1 BB)
Bob Walk (.412, 7-for-17, 1 HR)

Hates to face: Jose DeLeon (.067, 1-for-15)
Doug Drabek (.130, 3-for-23)
Bob Ojeda (.059, 1-for-17, 3 BB)

Miscellaneous statistics: Ground outs-to-air outs ratio: 1.24 last season, 1.22 for career. . . . Grounded into 5 double plays in 60 opportunities (one per 12.0). . . . Drove in 7 of 19 runners from third base with less than two outs (37%), 2d-lowest rate in N.L. . . . Direction of balls hit to the outfield: 46% to left field, 26% to center, 28% to right. . . . Base running: Advanced from first base to third on 3 of 14 outfield singles (21%); scored from second on 6 of 8 (75%). . . . Opposing base stealers: 103-for-129 (80%), 3d-highest rate in N.L.

Comments: Six years after joining the Expos in the Gary Carter deal, Fitzgerald still hasn't played even half as many games behind the plate for Montreal as Carter, the team's all-time leader. The current score: Kid, 1257; Fitz, 505; John Bateman, 347. . . . Expos pitchers allowed 3.65 runs per nine innings with Fitzgerald catching, compared to 3.40 with Nelson Santovenia behind the plate and 4.12 with Jerry Goff there. . . . Fitzgerald and Santovenia combined for nine passed balls in over 1100 innings of work behind the plate. But their rookie teammate, Goff, was charged with 12 passed balls in less than 300 innings. . . . Stole eight bases in nine attempts last season. He had previous career totals of 14 steals, 11 times caught. . . . Career-high total of walks was nearly 50 percent more than his previous high (42 in 1987). . . . Average of one walk per 4.8 plate appearances leading off innings was the best in the National League last season. . . . Had the best walk-to-strikeout ratio of his career. . . . Batted 62 points higher in day games (.292) than in night games (.230) over the last five seasons, the 5th-largest margin in the majors. . . . Career average of .225 with the bases empty, .261 with runners on base. . . . Pencil him in for 11 home runs in 1991; his year-by-year totals starting with 1987: 3, 5, 7, 9.

Andres Galarraga

Bats Right

Montreal Expos	AB	H	2B	3B	HR	RBI	BB	SO	BA	SA	OBA
Season	579	148	29	0	20	87	40	169	.256	.409	.306
vs. Left-Handers	217	49	9	0	9	35	11	62	.226	.392	.260
vs. Right-Handers	362	99	20	0	11	52	29	107	.273	.420	.332
vs. Ground-Ballers	308	78	15	0	10	44	24	85	.253	.399	.308
vs. Fly-Ballers	271	70	14	0	10	43	16	84	.258	.421	.303
Home Games	286	76	20	0	6	42	21	82	.266	.399	.317
Road Games	293	72	9	0	14	45	19	87	.246	.420	.294
Grass Fields	147	32	2	0	7	25	9	44	.218	.374	.269
Artificial Turf	432	116	27	0	13	62	31	125	.269	.421	.318
April	66	15	3	0	1	6	11	20	.227	.318	.329
May	98	28	5	0	4	19	6	27	.286	.459	.330
June	104	26	6	0	1	10	5	28	.250	.337	.291
July	98	26	7	0	6	21	5	28	.265	.520	.308
August	93	19	1	0	4	10	5	32	.204	.344	.253
Sept./Oct.	120	34	7	0	4	21	8	34	.283	.442	.323
Leading Off Inn.	128	37	11	0	2	2	8	37	.289	.422	.336
Bases Empty	301	74	19	0	10	10	21	82	.246	.409	.299
Runners On	278	74	10	0	10	77	19	87	.266	.410	.313
Runners/Scor. Pos.	169	45	7	0	7	69	18	58	.266	.432	.328
Runners On/2 Out	142	33	5	0	4	31	11	56	.232	.352	.292
Scor. Pos./2 Out	97	21	4	0	3	28	10	42	.216	.351	.290
Late-Inning Pressure	104	29	5	0	2	15	7	29	.279	.385	.333
Leading Off	25	8	3	0	1	1	3	6	.320	.560	.414
Runners On	49	16	1	0	1	14	3	15	.327	.408	.358
Runners/Scor. Pos.	32	11	1	0	1	14	3	11	.344	.469	.389

RUNS BATTED IN	From 1B	From 2B	From 3B	Scoring Position
Totals	11/181	24/131	32/78	56/209
Percentage	6.1%	18.3%	41.0%	26.8%

Loves to face: Joe Boever (.500, 8-for-16, 2 HR, 5 SO)
Bruce Ruffin (.478, 11-for-23, 1 HR)
Zane Smith (.450, 9-for-20, 1 HR)

Hates to face: Jose DeLeon (.040, 1-for-25, 3 BB)
Roger McDowell (.111, 2-for-18)
Ron Robinson (0-for-15, 1 BB)

Miscellaneous statistics: Ground outs-to-air outs ratio: 1.21 last season, 1.50 for career. . . . Grounded into 14 double plays in 104 opportunities (one per 7.4). . . . Drove in 22 of 36 runners from third base with less than two outs (61%). . . . Direction of balls hit to the outfield: 31% to left field, 35% to center, 34% to right. . . . Base running: Advanced from first base to third on 11 of 30 outfield singles (37%); scored from second on 8 of 10 (80%). . . . Made 0.64 assists per nine innings at first base.

Comments: First player to lead the National League in strikeouts for three straight seasons since Mike Schmidt (1974–76). This season, he could become the first player since Vince DiMaggio (1942–45) to do it four straight years. . . . Career rate of one strikeout for every four plate appearances vs. right-handed pitchers is the worst of any player (excluding pitchers) active in the National League last season (minimum: 150 strikeouts). . . . His strikeout total has increased in each of his six seasons in the majors. His totals of doubles, triples, and home runs have all fallen in each of the last two. . . . The only National League player to start at least 40 games in each of three different batting order positions. He started 45 games as a cleanup hitter, 41 games in the fifth slot, and 48 games batting sixth. Mookie Wilson did it in the American League, starting at least 40 games each in the first, second, and ninth spots. . . . Had the 2d-lowest first-inning batting average (.156) of any player in the majors last season (minimum: 50 AB). . . . His overall batting average has declined (if slightly) in every year since 1987: .305, .302, .257, .256. . . . Although his overall batting average dropped only one point from 1989 to 1990, his average vs. left-handed pitchers plummeted 159 points from his career-high mark of .385 in 1989. . . . Despite last season's breakdown, he still has a career mark of .299 vs. left-handers, compared to .265 vs. right-handers.

Ron Gant

Bats Right

Atlanta Braves	AB	H	2B	3B	HR	RBI	BB	SO	BA	SA	OBA
Season	575	174	34	3	32	84	50	86	.303	.539	.357
vs. Left-Handers	204	61	15	0	10	32	21	20	.299	.520	.361
vs. Right-Handers	371	113	19	3	22	52	29	66	.305	.550	.355
vs. Ground-Ballers	272	96	16	2	20	51	24	41	.353	.647	.405
vs. Fly-Ballers	303	78	18	1	12	33	26	45	.257	.442	.314
Home Games	288	90	15	1	18	47	22	37	.313	.559	.362
Road Games	287	84	19	2	14	37	28	49	.293	.519	.352
Grass Fields	429	131	20	1	26	68	40	65	.305	.538	.364
Artificial Turf	146	43	14	2	6	16	10	21	.295	.541	.338
April	25	5	2	0	0	1	2	3	.200	.280	.259
May	93	33	6	0	7	14	6	14	.355	.645	.386
June	108	33	7	1	8	18	11	13	.306	.611	.370
July	116	29	6	0	5	17	8	20	.250	.431	.296
August	114	36	8	2	5	13	11	14	.316	.553	.373
Sept./Oct.	119	38	5	0	7	21	12	22	.319	.538	.386
Leading Off Inn.	127	46	9	0	15	15	8	10	.362	.787	.400
Bases Empty	330	108	21	2	22	22	28	43	.327	.603	.382
Runners On	245	66	13	1	10	62	22	43	.269	.453	.325
Runners/Scor. Pos.	144	37	9	0	3	47	16	28	.257	.382	.323
Runners On/2 Out	96	19	4	0	2	15	8	20	.198	.302	.260
Scor. Pos./2 Out	64	13	4	0	2	15	6	13	.203	.359	.271
Late-Inning Pressure	76	19	4	0	4	7	7	13	.250	.461	.313
Leading Off	17	7	1	0	2	2	1	0	.412	.824	.444
Runners On	29	3	1	0	1	4	3	8	.103	.241	.188
Runners/Scor. Pos.	21	2	1	0	0	2	3	6	.095	.143	.208

RUNS BATTED IN	From 1B	From 2B	From 3B	Scoring Position
Totals	12/168	17/103	23/63	40/166
Percentage	7.1%	16.5%	36.5%	24.1%

Loves to face: Jeff Brantley (.571, 4-for-7, 1 2B, 2 HR)
Ron Darling (.500, 7-for-14, 1 HR)
Mark Portugal (.750, 6-for-8, 1 HR)

Hates to face: Alejandro Pena (0-for-10)
Calvin Schiraldi (.077, 1-for-13, 1 HR, 2 BB)
Bryn Smith (0-for-18, 1 BB)

Miscellaneous statistics: Ground outs-to-air outs ratio: 0.74 last season, 0.72 for career.... Grounded into 8 double plays in 111 opportunities (one per 13.9).... Drove in 17 of 33 runners from third base with less than two outs (52%).... Direction of balls hit to the outfield: 48% to left field, 33% to center, 19% to right.... Base running: Advanced from first base to third on 20 of 31 outfield singles (65%); scored from second on 15 of 17 (88%), shared 5th-highest rate in N.L.... Made 2.64 putouts per nine innings in center field.

Comments: Raised his batting average from .177 in 1989, the largest single-season increase since George Burns raised his average by 126 points, from .226 in 1917 to .352 in 1918 (minimum: 250 AB in each season).... Batted .387 from the first-spot in the batting order, the 2d-highest average in the majors (minimum: 50 AB).... Batting average leading off innings was the highest in the National League. Additionally, he led the league in leadoff home runs and extra-base hits.... Ended the season with a 13-game hitting streak, the longest by any Braves player last season.... Drove in only two of 24 runners from scoring position in Late-Inning Pressure Situations last season, compared to 27 percent at other times.... Was not thrown out trying to advance an extra base on any batted ball last season.... Batted 49 points higher in night games (.273) than in day games (.224) over the last five seasons, the 4th-largest margin in the majors.... Batted .114 vs. left-handed pitchers, and .119 in Late-Inning Pressure Situations in 1989.... Was successful on 74 percent of stolen base attempts against right-handed pitchers (23 of 31) but on only 56 percent of his attempts against southpaws (10 of 18).... Last season, Gant and Barry Bonds joined an exclusive branch of the 30/30 club by hitting over .300 while stealing 30 bases and hitting 30 home runs. Only five other players in history have done that, and none has done it twice. The members: Ken Williams (1922), Willie Mays (1957), Hank Aaron (1963), Dale Murphy (1988), and Jose Canseco (1988).

Kirk Gibson

Bats Left

Los Angeles Dodgers	AB	H	2B	3B	HR	RBI	BB	SO	BA	SA	OBA
Season	315	82	20	0	8	38	39	65	.260	.400	.345
vs. Left-Handers	102	26	7	0	3	15	12	30	.255	.412	.347
vs. Right-Handers	213	56	13	0	5	23	27	35	.263	.394	.344
vs. Ground-Ballers	156	37	6	0	3	16	19	32	.237	.333	.328
vs. Fly-Ballers	159	45	14	0	5	22	20	33	.283	.465	.363
Home Games	157	39	8	0	2	19	20	29	.248	.338	.339
Road Games	158	43	12	0	6	19	19	36	.272	.462	.352
Grass Fields	239	58	12	0	6	31	30	51	.243	.368	.331
Artificial Turf	76	24	8	0	2	7	9	14	.316	.500	.391
April	0	0	0	0	0	0	0	0	—	—	—
May	0	0	0	0	0	0	0	0	—	—	—
June	60	12	2	0	3	10	7	14	.200	.383	.279
July	92	31	10	0	1	11	8	9	.337	.478	.390
August	94	28	4	0	4	13	13	25	.298	.468	.385
Sept./Oct.	69	11	4	0	0	4	11	17	.159	.217	.293
Leading Off Inn.	58	15	6	0	1	1	3	15	.259	.414	.317
Bases Empty	169	45	16	0	3	3	20	33	.266	.414	.351
Runners On	146	37	4	0	5	35	19	32	.253	.384	.339
Runners/Scor. Pos.	62	18	3	0	2	28	9	18	.290	.435	.378
Runners On/2 Out	55	14	1	0	0	11	6	12	.255	.273	.339
Scor. Pos./2 Out	29	8	1	0	0	11	1	8	.276	.310	.323
Late-Inning Pressure	50	14	3	0	0	5	7	14	.280	.340	.373
Leading Off	16	1	1	0	0	0	1	5	.063	.125	.167
Runners On	24	9	0	0	0	5	4	6	.375	.375	.448
Runners/Scor. Pos.	12	3	0	0	0	5	2	5	.250	.250	.333

RUNS BATTED IN	From 1B	From 2B	From 3B	Scoring Position
Totals	8/114	11/47	11/26	22/73
Percentage	7.0%	23.4%	42.3%	30.1%

Loves to face: Steve Bedrosian (3-for-3, 1 HR, 1 BB)
Greg A. Harris (.444, 4-for-9, 1 HR, 6 BB)
Steve Ontiveros (.750, 6-for-8, 2 HR)

Hates to face: Tim Leary (.125, 1-for-8)
Eric Show (.154, 2-for-13)
Curt Young (.214, 3-for-14)

Miscellaneous statistics: Ground outs-to-air outs ratio: 0.64 last season, 0.98 for career.... Grounded into 4 double plays in 79 opportunities (one per 19.8).... Drove in 6 of 14 runners from third base with less than two outs (43%).... Direction of balls hit to the outfield: 38% to left field, 25% to center, 37% to right.... Base running: Advanced from first base to third on 4 of 13 outfield singles (31%); scored from second on 10 of 16 (63%).... Made 2.51 putouts per nine innings in center field, 2d-lowest rate in N.L.

Comments: Since the first All-Star game in 1933, Gibson is the only player who has won an MVP Award but has never been selected to an All-Star team.... Has played only 160 games over the last two seasons, and has played as many as 130 games only once in the last five years. Which MVP Award winners played the fewest games after winning the award (excluding pitchers)? Willie Stargell had only 179 games left after his 1979 season, and Mickey Cochrane played only 186 games after winning the award in 1934.... His major league career has spanned two leagues and 12 years, but Gibson has played for only two managers. Matt Nokes played for more than that over a span of four days last summer.... Needs eight more home runs to reach the 200 mark, to go with his 200-plus stolen bases. Only 12 players have reached 200 in both categories; three are still active: Dave Winfield, Andre Dawson, and Robin Yount.... Has the most career home runs of any player who has never hit a grand slam (192).... Has no home runs in 80 career at-bats in the state of Pennsylvania.... Career average of .218 (12-for-55) with no home runs as a pinch hitter. Of course, that doesn't include postseason.... Hasn't hit a home run in 94 at-bats in Late-Inning Pressure Situations since, well, you know when.... His career average of .190 at Royals Stadium is his lowest at any A.L. ballpark.... Stole 26 bases in 28 attempts, giving him the highest percentage of any player in the majors last season (93%).

Joe Girardi

Bats Right

Chicago Cubs	AB	H	2B	3B	HR	RBI	BB	SO	BA	SA	OBA
Season	419	113	24	2	1	38	17	50	.270	.344	.300
vs. Left-Handers	141	46	15	1	1	16	3	11	.326	.468	.336
vs. Right-Handers	278	67	9	1	0	22	14	39	.241	.281	.283
vs. Ground-Ballers	196	50	8	1	0	16	5	23	.255	.306	.282
vs. Fly-Ballers	223	63	16	1	1	22	12	27	.283	.377	.316
Home Games	202	55	11	1	1	25	7	26	.272	.351	.296
Road Games	217	58	13	1	0	13	10	24	.267	.336	.304
Grass Fields	284	81	15	1	1	30	12	30	.285	.356	.318
Artificial Turf	135	32	9	1	0	8	5	20	.237	.319	.262
April	45	15	1	0	0	1	0	5	.333	.356	.354
May	79	18	6	1	0	11	5	10	.228	.329	.279
June	76	22	6	1	1	7	2	11	.289	.434	.308
July	73	25	4	0	0	9	3	3	.342	.397	.359
August	85	22	5	0	0	5	5	11	.259	.318	.300
Sept./Oct.	61	11	2	0	0	5	2	10	.180	.213	.206
Leading Off Inn.	106	28	6	0	0	0	1	16	.264	.321	.284
Bases Empty	232	59	13	1	0	0	4	27	.254	.319	.273
Runners On	187	54	11	1	1	38	13	23	.289	.374	.332
Runners/Scor. Pos.	105	29	6	0	1	34	12	18	.276	.362	.344
Runners On/2 Out	73	19	4	0	0	14	12	9	.260	.315	.365
Scor. Pos./2 Out	44	12	2	0	0	12	11	8	.273	.318	.418
Late-Inning Pressure	60	20	2	1	0	6	0	7	.333	.400	.333
Leading Off	12	6	0	0	0	0	0	1	.500	.500	.500
Runners On	24	10	2	0	0	6	0	3	.417	.500	.417
Runners/Scor. Pos.	16	5	1	0	0	5	0	3	.313	.375	.313

RUNS BATTED IN	From 1B	From 2B	From 3B	Scoring Position
Totals	5/125	11/74	21/48	32/122
Percentage	4.0%	14.9%	43.8%	26.2%

Loves to face: Mark Portugal (.471, 8-for-17)
Bruce Ruffin (.545, 6-for-11, 1 HR)
Fernando Valenzuela (.667, 6-for-9)

Hates to face: Jose DeLeon (.063, 1-for-16, 1 2B, 3 BB, 9 SO)
Alejandro Pena (0-for-7)
Bob Tewksbury (.100, 1-for-10)

Miscellaneous statistics: Ground outs-to-air outs ratio: 1.59 last season, 1.44 for career.... Grounded into 13 double plays in 79 opportunities (one per 6.1).... Drove in 12 of 24 runners from third base with less than two outs (50%).... Direction of balls hit to the outfield: 24% to left field, 38% to center, 38% to right.... Base running: Advanced from first base to third on 3 of 16 outfield singles (19%); scored from second on 9 of 14 (64%).... Opposing base stealers: 80-for-127 (63%), 3d-lowest rate in N.L.

Comments: Walked only 17 times last season, and 11 of them were intentional. He drew only one nonintentional walk in his first 359 plate appearances. Discounting free passes, he has drawn only eight walks in 611 career plate appearances.... The all-time record for at-bats in a season without a walk: 274, by Tom Carey in 1877. The next season, Carey had 253 ABs without a walk, the 2d-highest total ever. (In both seasons, a walk required nine balls.) The 20th-century record is 154, by Big Ed Walsh—too large a strike zone?—in 1907. The most since 1900 by a nonpitcher: 146, by Giants infielder Craig Robinson in 1973.... Caught 133 games last season; only two other players in Cubs history caught that many in a season: Gabby Hartnett (twice) and Randy Hundley (four times).... Was charged with 16 passed balls last season, tying him with Joe Oliver for the National League lead.... Cubs pitchers allowed 4.71 runs per nine innings with Girardi catching, compared to 5.16 with other catchers.... Cubs catchers hit only four home runs last season. Among major league teams, only the two Lone Star State franchises had lower totals: the Rangers and the Astros had three each.... Of his 38 RBIs, 14 gave the Cubs a lead. By comparison, only 11 of Shawon Dunston's 66 RBIs were go-ahead RBIs.... Was removed for pinch-hitters 27 times last season, the most of any player on the Cubs.... Career batting average of .347 in 75 at-bats in Late-Inning Pressure Situations.

Mark Grace

Bats Left

Chicago Cubs	AB	H	2B	3B	HR	RBI	BB	SO	BA	SA	OBA
Season	589	182	32	1	9	82	59	54	.309	.413	.372
vs. Left-Handers	185	57	12	0	3	33	20	21	.308	.422	.378
vs. Right-Handers	404	125	20	1	6	49	39	33	.309	.408	.369
vs. Ground-Ballers	288	89	14	1	3	37	23	23	.309	.396	.360
vs. Fly-Ballers	301	93	18	0	6	45	36	31	.309	.429	.384
Home Games	308	102	18	0	4	46	29	24	.331	.429	.391
Road Games	281	80	14	1	5	36	30	30	.285	.395	.352
Grass Fields	428	133	23	0	6	60	42	41	.311	.407	.372
Artificial Turf	161	49	9	1	3	22	17	13	.304	.429	.374
April	65	17	2	0	0	4	12	8	.262	.292	.375
May	113	29	5	0	1	9	3	11	.257	.327	.281
June	103	33	7	1	1	17	14	7	.320	.437	.398
July	87	25	4	0	1	6	5	9	.287	.368	.326
August	108	43	8	0	4	26	10	11	.398	.583	.451
Sept./Oct.	113	35	6	0	2	20	15	8	.310	.416	.391
Leading Off Inn.	103	37	2	1	3	3	4	8	.359	.485	.383
Bases Empty	333	107	18	1	9	9	30	33	.321	.462	.381
Runners On	256	75	14	0	0	73	29	21	.293	.348	.361
Runners/Scor. Pos.	170	56	12	0	0	72	26	17	.329	.400	.411
Runners On/2 Out	93	23	4	0	0	19	10	8	.247	.290	.333
Scor. Pos./2 Out	64	18	3	0	0	19	9	6	.281	.328	.387
Late-Inning Pressure	88	27	2	0	1	9	13	6	.307	.364	.402
Leading Off	23	8	0	0	0	0	1	2	.348	.348	.375
Runners On	37	9	2	0	0	8	4	3	.243	.297	.333
Runners/Scor. Pos.	23	5	2	0	0	8	4	2	.217	.304	.357

RUNS BATTED IN	From 1B	From 2B	From 3B	Scoring Position
Totals	4/167	32/130	37/76	69/206
Percentage	2.4%	24.6%	48.7%	33.5%

Loves to face: Doug Drabek (.471, 16-for-34, 1 HR)
Scott Garrelts (.579, 11-for-19, 1 HR)
Mike Maddux (.583, 7-for-12, 1 HR)

Hates to face: Ron Darling (.056, 1-for-18, 1 2B, 4 BB)
Jose DeLeon (.161, 5-for-31, 1 HR, 5 BB)
Mike Scott (.103, 3-for-29, 1 HR)

Miscellaneous statistics: Ground outs-to-air outs ratio: 1.21 last season, 1.28 for career.... Grounded into 10 double plays in 110 opportunities (one per 11.0).... Drove in 31 of 45 runners from third base with less than two outs (69%).... Direction of balls hit to the outfield: 31% to left field, 34% to center, 34% to right.... Base running: Advanced from first base to third on 10 of 35 outfield singles (29%); scored from second on 11 of 16 (69%).... Made 1.23 assists per nine innings at first base, highest rate in majors.

Comments: As a three-year player, Grace is the least senior of five active players to reach base at least 200 times on walks or hits in every season starting with their rookie years. The others: Alvin Davis (7 years), Cal Ripken (9), Ryne Sandberg (9), and Kevin Seitzer (4).... Set a National League record for first basemen with 180 assists.... Had seven consecutive hits vs. left-handed pitchers in August, tying him for the longest string in the majors last season. In the 11 years we've tracked such streaks, no left-handed batter has had a longer one against left-handed pitchers. The other lefty swingers with seven in a row: Jorge Orta (1980), Rod Carew (1980), Don Mattingly (1984), and Brett Butler (1986).... Led the Cubs with 46 opposite-field hits last season.... Played 15 more games in 1990 than he did the previous season, but drew 21 fewer walks.... Stole 15 bases last season, a career high, which makes you wonder how Jim Belushi could run him down.... Has a career average of .440 with the bases loaded (11-for-25, 4 BB).... Career batting average of .357, with a .401 on-base percentage, leading off innings.... Has driven in over 30 percent of runners from scoring position in each of his three seasons in the majors, but his career rate is only 22 percent in Late-Inning Pressure Situations.... Comparable statistical profiles: Zack Wheat (through 1912), Tony Cuccinello (1932), Mike Hargrove (1976), and Tony Gwynn (1985).

Tommy Gregg

Bats Left

Atlanta Braves	AB	H	2B	3B	HR	RBI	BB	SO	BA	SA	OBA
Season	239	63	13	1	5	32	20	39	.264	.389	.322
vs. Left-Handers	19	2	0	0	0	0	3	6	.105	.105	.227
vs. Right-Handers	220	61	13	1	5	32	17	33	.277	.414	.331
vs. Ground-Ballers	112	31	5	0	3	20	7	18	.277	.402	.322
vs. Fly-Ballers	127	32	8	1	2	12	13	21	.252	.378	.321
Home Games	122	30	5	0	2	19	8	17	.246	.336	.290
Road Games	117	33	8	1	3	13	12	22	.282	.444	.354
Grass Fields	192	53	8	1	5	30	13	30	.276	.406	.320
Artificial Turf	47	10	5	0	0	2	7	9	.213	.319	.327
April	22	1	0	0	0	0	2	8	.045	.045	.125
May	24	2	1	0	1	1	5	3	.083	.250	.267
June	25	6	2	0	0	4	1	5	.240	.320	.269
July	37	14	1	0	3	9	1	7	.378	.649	.395
August	65	22	6	1	0	9	5	7	.338	.462	.386
Sept./Oct.	66	18	3	0	1	9	6	9	.273	.364	.329
Leading Off Inn.	48	9	3	0	0	0	0	7	.188	.250	.188
Bases Empty	144	36	10	0	2	2	6	23	.250	.361	.285
Runners On	95	27	3	1	3	30	14	16	.284	.432	.373
Runners/Scor. Pos.	70	20	2	1	3	30	10	14	.286	.471	.370
Runners On/2 Out	43	12	2	0	0	10	8	7	.279	.326	.392
Scor. Pos./2 Out	36	10	2	0	0	10	8	7	.278	.333	.409
Late-Inning Pressure	46	13	5	0	2	8	4	7	.283	.522	.340
Leading Off	8	1	0	0	0	0	0	1	.125	.125	.125
Runners On	11	5	2	0	1	7	2	1	.455	.909	.538
Runners/Scor. Pos.	8	4	1	0	1	7	0	1	.500	1.000	.500

RUNS BATTED IN	From 1B	From 2B	From 3B	Scoring Position
Totals	5/63	11/51	11/25	22/76
Percentage	7.9%	21.6%	44.0%	28.9%

Loves to face: Andy Benes (.545, 6-for-11)
Jim Deshaies (3-for-3, 1 BB)
Mike Morgan (.500, 8-for-16)

Hates to face: Ron Darling (.091, 1-for-11, 1 HR)
Scott Scudder (.077, 1-for-13)
Ed Whitson (.077, 1-for-13)

Miscellaneous statistics: Ground outs-to-air outs ratio: 1.11 last season, 1.05 for career. . . . Grounded into 1 double play in 41 opportunities (one per 41.0), best rate in N.L. . . . Drove in 7 of 12 runners from third base with less than two outs (58%). . . . Direction of balls hit to the outfield: 37% to left field, 32% to center, 31% to right. . . . Base running: Advanced from first base to third on 3 of 9 outfield singles (33%); scored from second on 3 of 5 (60%). . . . Made 0.88 assists per nine innings at first base.

Comments: Started 51 games last season, all against right-handed pitchers. . . . Started only 19 of 103 games for the Braves before Dale Murphy was traded, but started 32 of 59 thereafter. . . . Hitless in 32 at-bats from April 22 through May 6, but batted .301 thereafter. . . . Career batting averages of .193 vs. left-handers (no HR), .267 vs. right-handers (12 HR). He has only one extra-base hit (a double) in 83 career at-bats against southpaws. . . . Other career batting averages: .330 in day games, but only .237 at night. . . . Has only one hit in 25 career at-bats at Shea Stadium. . . . Made 63 appearances as a pinch hitter, 2d most in the majors to Chris Gwynn (66), and batted .353 with four home runs (18-for-51). . . . His total of 18 pinch-hits ranks second in franchise history to Chris Chambliss, who had 20 in 1986. Mike Lum, the Braves' career leader with 70, had more than 13 only once; his single-season high was 17 (in 1979). . . . Since the Big Bang, only five players have compiled higher batting averages in as many as 50 at-bats as pinch hitters: Peanuts Lowrey (.373 in 1953), Ken Oberkfell (.360 in 1989), Bob Fothergill (.358 in 1929), Greg Gross (.358 in 1982), and Doc Miller (.357 in 1913).

Alfredo Griffin

Bats Left and Right

Los Angeles Dodgers	AB	H	2B	3B	HR	RBI	BB	SO	BA	SA	OBA
Season	461	97	11	3	1	35	29	65	.210	.254	.258
vs. Left-Handers	169	35	2	0	1	12	11	30	.207	.237	.257
vs. Right-Handers	292	62	9	3	0	23	18	35	.212	.264	.259
vs. Ground-Ballers	235	45	7	1	0	12	14	32	.191	.230	.239
vs. Fly-Ballers	226	52	4	2	1	23	15	33	.230	.279	.278
Home Games	218	48	4	1	0	22	14	36	.220	.248	.268
Road Games	243	49	7	2	1	13	15	29	.202	.259	.249
Grass Fields	330	67	8	1	0	24	22	54	.203	.233	.253
Artificial Turf	131	30	3	2	1	11	7	11	.229	.305	.271
April	70	23	5	1	0	5	8	5	.329	.429	.392
May	93	24	3	0	0	8	6	14	.258	.290	.310
June	92	16	0	1	1	10	4	18	.174	.228	.210
July	66	12	1	0	0	3	3	9	.182	.197	.217
August	81	13	1	0	0	3	5	12	.160	.173	.209
Sept./Oct.	59	9	1	1	0	6	3	7	.153	.203	.194
Leading Off Inn.	113	28	3	1	1	1	5	13	.248	.319	.280
Bases Empty	256	50	8	1	1	1	12	40	.195	.246	.234
Runners On	205	47	3	2	0	34	17	25	.229	.263	.286
Runners/Scor. Pos.	122	26	2	2	0	34	15	18	.213	.262	.296
Runners On/2 Out	90	20	0	2	0	16	10	9	.222	.267	.307
Scor. Pos./2 Out	58	15	0	2	0	16	9	8	.259	.328	.368
Late-Inning Pressure	59	13	1	0	0	2	5	9	.220	.237	.292
Leading Off	29	7	1	0	0	0	1	5	.241	.276	.267
Runners On	15	3	0	0	0	2	2	0	.200	.200	.294
Runners/Scor. Pos.	8	2	0	0	0	2	2	0	.250	.250	.400

RUNS BATTED IN	From 1B	From 2B	From 3B	Scoring Position
Totals	2/153	12/98	20/48	32/146
Percentage	1.3%	12.2%	41.7%	21.9%

Loves to face: Tom Browning (.367, 11-for-30, 1 HR)
Rick Mahler (.387, 12-for-31, 0 BB)
John Tudor (.357, 10-for-28)

Hates to face: Oil Can Boyd (.136, 3-for-22)
Don Robinson (.050, 1-for-20)
Calvin Schiraldi (.067, 1-for-15, 2 BB)

Miscellaneous statistics: Ground outs-to-air outs ratio: 0.90 last season, 1.14 for career. . . . Grounded into 5 double plays in 93 opportunities (one per 18.6). . . . Drove in 15 of 30 runners from third base with less than two outs (50%). . . . Direction of balls hit to the outfield: 31% to left field, 30% to center, 40% to right batting left-handed; 36% to left, 28% to center, 36% to right batting right-handed. . . . Base running: Advanced from first base to third on 8 of 22 outfield singles (36%); scored from second on 12 of 14 (86%). . . . Made 2.98 assists per nine innings at shortstop.

Comments: Finished the season with 502 plate appearances, giving him the distinction of having the lowest batting average of any National League player to qualify for the batting title since Dave Kingman batted .204 in 1982. . . . Started 136 games last season, all from the eighth spot in the batting order. . . . Eleven of his 29 walks were intentional. . . . This switch-hitter has a career average of .250 from both sides of the plate. His career slugging percentage is slighty better batting left-handed (.330) than from the right side (.311). . . . Has hit for a higher average with runners on base than with the bases empty in each of the last six seasons. . . . In three seasons in the National League, he has hit only two home runs, neither at Dodger Stadium, where he has 626 at-bats. . . . Has stolen only 23 bases in his three seasons with Los Angeles; he stole more than that in each of his three years with Oakland. . . . Career total of 1684 games at shortstop ranks fourth among players active in 1990, behind Garry Templeton (1923), Ozzie Smith (1906), and Alan Trammell (1791). In September, Griffin passed Phil Rizzuto (1647) on the all-time list. . . . The Blue Jays (1985) and the Athletics (1988) both won division titles the season after trading Griffin, whose only postseason appearance was with the 1988 world champion Dodgers.

Marquis Grissom

Bats Right

Montreal Expos	AB	H	2B	3B	HR	RBI	BB	SO	BA	SA	OBA
Season	288	74	14	2	3	29	27	40	.257	.351	.320
vs. Left-Handers	181	44	11	2	2	16	20	20	.243	.359	.317
vs. Right-Handers	107	30	3	0	1	13	7	20	.280	.336	.325
vs. Ground-Ballers	144	38	6	0	1	15	16	18	.264	.326	.338
vs. Fly-Ballers	144	36	8	2	2	14	11	22	.250	.375	.301
Home Games	146	36	5	2	2	17	16	22	.247	.349	.321
Road Games	142	38	9	0	1	12	11	18	.268	.352	.318
Grass Fields	71	16	1	0	0	1	7	10	.225	.239	.291
Artificial Turf	217	58	13	2	3	28	20	30	.267	.387	.329
April	74	17	8	0	0	5	7	12	.230	.338	.296
May	76	20	2	0	0	4	5	8	.263	.289	.309
June	4	2	1	0	0	1	1	1	.500	.750	.600
July	57	16	1	2	1	6	6	9	.281	.421	.349
August	37	8	1	0	1	6	2	3	.216	.324	.256
Sept./Oct.	40	11	1	0	1	7	6	7	.275	.375	.362
Leading Off Inn.	62	18	3	1	1	1	6	11	.290	.419	.353
Bases Empty	169	40	8	1	2	2	15	26	.237	.331	.299
Runners On	119	34	6	1	1	27	12	14	.286	.378	.348
Runners/Scor. Pos.	75	19	4	0	1	24	9	13	.253	.347	.329
Runners On/2 Out	45	12	4	0	0	10	8	6	.267	.356	.377
Scor. Pos./2 Out	35	9	3	0	0	9	7	6	.257	.343	.381
Late-Inning Pressure	57	17	2	0	2	10	6	11	.298	.439	.365
Leading Off	11	3	0	0	0	0	2	2	.273	.273	.385
Runners On	24	9	1	0	1	9	4	5	.375	.542	.464
Runners/Scor. Pos.	18	7	0	0	1	8	4	4	.389	.556	.500

RUNS BATTED IN	From 1B	From 2B	From 3B	Scoring Position
Totals	5/73	8/60	13/31	21/91
Percentage	6.8%	13.3%	41.9%	23.1%

Loves to face: Bruce Hurst (.500, 6-for-12)
Greg Maddux (.455, 5-for-11, 1 HR)
John Smiley (.455, 5-for-11, 1 HR)

Hates to face: Pat Combs (.133, 2-for-15)
Randy Myers (0-for-5)
Frank Viola (.077, 1-for-13)

Miscellaneous statistics: Ground outs-to-air outs ratio: 1.12 last season, 1.12 for career.... Grounded into 3 double plays in 54 opportunities (one per 18.0).... Drove in 10 of 19 runners from third base with less than two outs (53%).... Direction of balls hit to the outfield: 38% to left field, 44% to center, 18% to right.... Base running: Advanced from first base to third on 7 of 16 outfield singles (44%); scored from second on 8 of 10 (80%).... Made 1.99 putouts per nine innings in right field.

Comments: One of three rookies in Montreal's opening-day lineup last season, along with Larry Walker and Delino Deshields. The other 11 National League teams produced only two rookie starters in their opening-day lineups: Eric Anthony (Astros) and Todd Zeile (Cardinals).... Started 49 of 60 games in which the Expos faced a left-handed starter, but only 19 of 102 against right-handers. That's an example of blindly following a general rule that may not apply to the individual players involved: Grissom hit 37 points higher vs. RHP than vs. LHP, and he even outhit his platoonmate, Larry Walker, against right-handers (.280 to .254).... Grissom was the youngest National Leaguer to play at least 100 games last season, almost a full year younger than runner-up Roberto Alomar. In fact, Grissom was the third-youngest position player to appear in the N.L. last season. Only Todd Hundley (35 games for New York), and Andujar Cedeno (seven games for Houston) are younger.... The third Expos rookie in the last 10 years to steal at least 20 bases in fewer than 100 games: Tim Raines (71 SB in 88 games in 1981), Rex Hudler (29 in 77 in 1988), and Grissom (22 in 98 last season).... Stole his 22 bases in only 24 attempts, the 2d-highest average in the majors (92%). Only Kirk Gibson had a higher mark (93%). Anybody have that exacta?

Pedro Guerrero

Bats Right

St. Louis Cardinals	AB	H	2B	3B	HR	RBI	BB	SO	BA	SA	OBA
Season	498	140	31	1	13	80	44	70	.281	.426	.334
vs. Left-Handers	168	46	17	0	4	30	13	28	.274	.446	.319
vs. Right-Handers	330	94	14	1	9	50	31	42	.285	.415	.341
vs. Ground-Ballers	262	72	16	1	6	37	19	43	.275	.412	.321
vs. Fly-Ballers	236	68	15	0	7	43	25	27	.288	.441	.348
Home Games	261	72	18	0	8	50	26	42	.276	.437	.333
Road Games	237	68	13	1	5	30	18	28	.287	.414	.335
Grass Fields	139	40	6	1	5	19	13	15	.288	.453	.344
Artificial Turf	359	100	25	0	8	61	31	55	.279	.415	.330
April	78	23	2	0	5	20	7	10	.295	.513	.349
May	87	24	9	0	1	13	11	14	.276	.414	.350
June	109	33	8	1	2	15	9	18	.303	.450	.344
July	93	25	7	0	3	17	5	12	.269	.441	.297
August	51	12	1	0	1	4	7	8	.235	.314	.328
Sept./Oct.	80	23	4	0	1	11	5	8	.287	.375	.333
Leading Off Inn.	115	33	7	0	3	3	5	16	.287	.426	.317
Bases Empty	242	72	15	1	7	7	17	36	.298	.455	.344
Runners On	256	68	16	0	6	73	27	34	.266	.398	.325
Runners/Scor. Pos.	159	40	11	0	3	64	25	19	.252	.377	.337
Runners On/2 Out	117	30	8	0	2	20	17	16	.256	.376	.356
Scor. Pos./2 Out	72	15	4	0	0	13	16	9	.208	.264	.360
Late-Inning Pressure	70	17	6	0	2	8	9	13	.243	.414	.321
Leading Off	14	6	1	0	1	1	0	1	.429	.714	.429
Runners On	34	5	0	0	0	6	7	7	.147	.147	.279
Runners/Scor. Pos.	19	3	0	0	0	6	7	6	.158	.158	.357

RUNS BATTED IN	From 1B	From 2B	From 3B	Scoring Position
Totals	10/167	29/120	28/75	57/195
Percentage	6.0%	24.2%	37.3%	29.2%

Loves to face: Tom Glavine (.474, 9-for-19, 2 HR)
Ricky Horton (.778, 7-for-9, 2 HR)
Dennis Rasmussen (.733, 11-for-15)

Hates to face: David Cone (.179, 7-for-39, 2 2B, 3 HR, 0 BB)
Sid Fernandez (.176, 6-for-34, 1 HR)
Scott Garrelts (.091, 2-for-22, 5 BB)

Miscellaneous statistics: Ground outs-to-air outs ratio: 0.85 last season, 0.85 for career.... Grounded into 14 double plays in 105 opportunities (one per 7.5).... Drove in 23 of 44 runners from third base with less than two outs (52%).... Direction of balls hit to the outfield: 29% to left field, 36% to center, 35% to right.... Base running: Advanced from first base to third on 3 of 17 outfield singles (18%); scored from second on 5 of 9 (56%).... Made 0.61 assists per nine innings at first base, 2d-lowest rate in N.L.

Comments: Current career totals: 206 HR, 812 RBI, .305 batting average at age 35. Could reach 250 HR and 1000 RBIs while maintaining a .300 BA, something only 15 other players have done—14 Hall of Famers and one active player (George Brett).... His rate of one error per 90 chances was the highest among regular National League first baseman last season. But it was *low* enough to improve his career average to one flub per 89 chances, the 2d worst among active players to his new teammate Gerald Perry, who's averaged one error per 82 (minimum: 400 games).... Challenge to ESPN camera crews: First shot of Guerrero giving fielding tips to Perry earns a mention in next year's *Analyst*.... Hit eight of his 13 home runs at Busch Stadium after hitting only three of 17 there in 1989.... Hit the third grand slam of his career last season. His career average with the bases full now stands at .345 (29-for-84).... Batting average with runners in scoring position, year by year since 1987: .344, .371, .405, .252.... Has not been credited with a sacrifice bunt since 1984.... His career average of .309 in road games is the fourth highest among active players. For a list of the top three, see the Tony Gwynn comments on the next page.... Can anyone think of a worse deal for the Dodgers, either Brooklyn of Los Angeles, than Pedro Guerrero for John Tudor? Or a better one for them than the 1974 deal in which Los Angeles acquired Guerrero from Cleveland for a reputed pitcher named Bruce Ellingsen—even up? Easy come, easy go.

Tony Gwynn

Bats Left

San Diego Padres	AB	H	2B	3B	HR	RBI	BB	SO	BA	SA	OBA
Season	573	177	29	10	4	72	44	23	.309	.415	.357
vs. Left-Handers	228	64	8	2	3	28	8	10	.281	.373	.307
vs. Right-Handers	345	113	21	8	1	44	36	13	.328	.443	.388
vs. Ground-Ballers	308	99	21	4	1	37	21	17	.321	.425	.363
vs. Fly-Ballers	265	78	8	6	3	35	23	6	.294	.404	.351
Home Games	306	95	16	6	2	42	22	10	.310	.422	.356
Road Games	267	82	13	4	2	30	22	13	.307	.408	.358
Grass Fields	422	129	23	9	2	54	34	17	.306	.417	.357
Artificial Turf	151	48	6	1	2	18	10	6	.318	.411	.356
April	76	23	6	1	1	5	5	2	.303	.447	.346
May	104	34	7	1	1	11	8	4	.327	.442	.381
June	108	34	4	3	0	15	12	8	.315	.407	.380
July	117	35	7	2	2	15	5	4	.299	.444	.328
August	109	35	3	0	0	14	9	4	.321	.349	.367
Sept./Oct.	59	16	2	3	0	12	5	1	.271	.407	.323
Leading Off Inn.	100	20	3	1	2	2	6	6	.200	.310	.245
Bases Empty	314	87	10	4	3	3	13	15	.277	.363	.308
Runners On	259	90	19	6	1	69	31	8	.347	.479	.412
Runners/Scor. Pos.	151	46	9	2	0	59	25	5	.305	.391	.394
Runners On/2 Out	78	26	7	4	0	23	14	2	.333	.526	.435
Scor. Pos./2 Out	56	17	5	2	0	20	13	2	.304	.464	.435
Late-Inning Pressure	95	27	3	0	0	6	10	6	.284	.316	.352
Leading Off	22	3	0	0	0	0	2	1	.136	.136	.208
Runners On	46	12	3	0	0	6	8	4	.261	.326	.370
Runners/Scor. Pos.	20	5	1	0	0	5	7	2	.250	.300	.444

RUNS BATTED IN	From 1B	From 2B	From 3B	Scoring Position
Totals	12/176	25/118	31/55	56/173
Percentage	6.8%	21.2%	56.4%	32.4%

Loves to face: Jeff Brantley (.727, 8-for-11)
Don Carman (.469, 15-for-32, 1 HR)
Greg Maddux (.542, 13-for-24, 0 SO)

Hates to face: Jose DeLeon (.206, 7-for-34)
Frank DiPino (.053, 1-for-19)
Dan Schatzeder (.111, 2-for-18)

Miscellaneous statistics: Ground outs-to-air outs ratio: 1.27 last season, 1.71 for career. . . . Grounded into 13 double plays in 145 opportunities (one per 11.2). . . . Drove in 21 of 34 runners from third base with less than two outs (62%). . . . Direction of balls hit to the outfield: 43% to left field, 29% to center, 28% to right. . . . Base running: Advanced from first base to third on 7 of 23 outfield singles (30%); scored from second on 11 of 14 (79%). . . . Made 2.33 putouts per nine innings in right field.

Comments: His career batting average of .329 ranks 12th in National League history, .0002 ahead of Honus Wagner, and two points behind Stan Musial (minimum: 1000 games). . . . The top three active players in career batting average are Wade Boggs (.346), Gwynn (.329), and Kirby Puckett (.320), but both Boggs and Puckett benefit greatly from their home ballparks. On the road, Gwynn is number one. The top three: Gwynn, .324; Mattingly, .317; Boggs, .313. Where's Puckett? He doesn't even make the top 10. . . . Has never struck out more than 40 times in a season. His streak of seven consecutive seasons of 500 or more ABs and 40 or fewer strikeouts is the longest since Nellie Fox's 13-year streak ended in 1963. . . . Enters the 1991 season 53 games behind Garry Templeton as San Diego's all-time leader. Only three players have appeared in 1000 or more games for the Padres: Templeton (1254), Gwynn (1201), and Dave Winfield (1117). . . . Has a career average of at least .290 in every National League ballpark except Shea Stadium, where he isn't even close (.254). He has homered in every one except Veterans Stadium (164 career AB). . . . Had five hits in nine at-bats with the bases loaded last season, raising his career average to .422 (27-for-64). . . . Had batted over .300 in Late-Inning Pressure Situations in each of his previous eight seasons in the majors, but hasn't hit a home run in 335 LIPS at-bats since 1987.

Lenny Harris

Bats Left

Los Angeles Dodgers	AB	H	2B	3B	HR	RBI	BB	SO	BA	SA	OBA
Season	431	131	16	4	2	29	29	31	.304	.374	.348
vs. Left-Handers	42	10	0	1	0	6	3	5	.238	.286	.304
vs. Right-Handers	389	121	16	3	2	23	26	26	.311	.383	.353
vs. Ground-Ballers	241	72	6	1	0	17	12	15	.299	.332	.331
vs. Fly-Ballers	190	59	10	3	2	12	17	16	.311	.426	.370
Home Games	217	60	8	2	0	9	15	15	.276	.332	.322
Road Games	214	71	8	2	2	20	14	16	.332	.416	.376
Grass Fields	318	99	11	3	1	22	22	23	.311	.374	.355
Artificial Turf	113	32	5	1	1	7	7	8	.283	.372	.331
April	40	9	0	1	0	5	3	1	.225	.275	.273
May	76	28	4	2	0	9	3	6	.368	.474	.392
June	75	21	3	0	1	1	4	6	.280	.360	.316
July	78	23	3	1	0	3	7	4	.295	.359	.360
August	81	21	1	0	0	7	4	6	.259	.272	.294
Sept./Oct.	81	29	5	0	1	4	8	8	.358	.457	.416
Leading Off Inn.	166	49	6	2	1	1	10	5	.295	.373	.335
Bases Empty	303	92	15	2	2	2	22	18	.304	.386	.353
Runners On	128	39	1	2	0	27	7	13	.305	.344	.338
Runners/Scor. Pos.	73	22	1	2	0	27	4	10	.301	.370	.333
Runners On/2 Out	45	11	0	1	0	9	2	7	.244	.289	.277
Scor. Pos./2 Out	37	7	0	1	0	9	1	7	.189	.243	.211
Late-Inning Pressure	47	12	0	0	0	1	4	4	.255	.255	.314
Leading Off	7	2	0	0	0	0	0	0	.286	.286	.286
Runners On	20	6	0	0	0	1	0	2	.300	.300	.300
Runners/Scor. Pos.	13	2	0	0	0	1	0	2	.154	.154	.154

RUNS BATTED IN	From 1B	From 2B	From 3B	Scoring Position
Totals	2/82	10/60	15/33	25/93
Percentage	2.4%	16.7%	45.5%	26.9%

Loves to face: Mark Gardner (.500, 3-for-6, 1 HR)
Scott Garrelts (.556, 5-for-9)
Paul Marak (.800, 4-for-5)

Hates to face: Jose DeJesus (0-for-7)
Ken Hill (0-for-5, 1 BB)
Rick Mahler (.214, 3-for-14)

Miscellaneous statistics: Ground outs-to-air outs ratio: 1.81 last season, 1.75 for career. . . . Grounded into 8 double plays in 64 opportunities (one per 8.0). . . . Drove in 11 of 19 runners from third base with less than two outs (58%). . . . Direction of balls hit to the outfield: 31% to left field, 30% to center, 40% to right. . . . Base running: Advanced from first base to third on 19 of 30 outfield singles (63%), 5th-highest rate in N.L.; scored from second on 9 of 12 (75%). . . . Made 1.87 assists per nine innings at third base.

Comments: Harris batted .331 in his at-bats as a third baseman. Only three third basemen in the majors batted over .300 last season (minimum: 100 AB at 3B): Harris, Wade Boggs (.307), and Mike Sharperson (.301). Combined primarily with Mike Sharperson's .301 mark, Harris made the Dodgers the only team in the majors—regardless of sock color—whose third basemen batted .300 or better. . . . Prior to 1990, Harris and Sharperson had a .247 composite batting average. . . . Batting average increased 68 points from 1989 to 1990, the 4th-largest gain of any player with at least 300 at-bats in both seasons. . . . Was thrown out trying to advance an extra base on a batted ball a team-high nine times last season. . . . Started 101 of 106 games in which the Dodgers faced a right-handed starter but only two of 56 games in which they were opposed by a left-hander. . . . Harris was removed for a pinch-hitter 30 times last season (all against left-handed pitchers), the most of any player on the Dodgers and the most of any nonpitcher in the National League. . . . Career averages of .221 vs. left-handers, .289 vs. right-handers. . . . Has driven in only one of 29 runners from scoring position in Late-Inning Pressure Situations over the last two seasons. One of 29! Harris has only two RBIs in 108 career at-bats in LIPS.

Billy Hatcher

Bats Right

Cincinnati Reds	AB	H	2B	3B	HR	RBI	BB	SO	BA	SA	OBA
Season	504	139	28	5	5	25	33	42	.276	.381	.327
vs. Left-Handers	207	51	10	1	1	8	16	16	.246	.319	.299
vs. Right-Handers	297	88	18	4	4	17	17	26	.296	.424	.347
vs. Ground-Ballers	253	72	14	3	3	13	13	18	.285	.399	.328
vs. Fly-Ballers	251	67	14	2	2	12	20	24	.267	.363	.326
Home Games	246	65	16	3	2	11	16	18	.264	.378	.314
Road Games	258	74	12	2	3	14	17	24	.287	.384	.339
Grass Fields	150	40	4	2	2	8	15	11	.267	.360	.337
Artificial Turf	354	99	24	3	3	17	18	31	.280	.390	.323
April	63	21	2	2	1	4	4	6	.333	.476	.373
May	99	31	5	1	0	3	3	11	.313	.384	.355
June	103	30	5	2	0	5	10	10	.291	.379	.354
July	78	18	4	0	1	2	3	7	.231	.321	.259
August	85	21	11	0	3	6	3	5	.247	.482	.289
Sept./Oct.	76	18	1	0	0	5	10	3	.237	.250	.326
Leading Off Inn.	168	49	16	1	3	3	8	17	.292	.452	.328
Bases Empty	322	92	23	3	5	5	17	28	.286	.422	.329
Runners On	182	47	5	2	0	20	16	14	.258	.308	.323
Runners/Scor. Pos.	106	21	3	1	0	18	11	10	.198	.245	.283
Runners On/2 Out	85	20	2	1	0	8	5	6	.235	.282	.278
Scor. Pos./2 Out	57	10	1	1	0	8	4	3	.175	.228	.230
Late-Inning Pressure	68	16	1	2	0	1	9	7	.235	.309	.333
Leading Off	20	5	0	1	0	0	2	3	.250	.350	.348
Runners On	29	5	0	0	0	1	5	3	.172	.172	.294
Runners/Scor. Pos.	11	2	0	0	0	1	5	1	.182	.182	.438

RUNS BATTED IN	From 1B	From 2B	From 3B	Scoring Position
Totals	2/112	7/83	11/35	18/118
Percentage	1.8%	8.4%	31.4%	15.3%

Loves to face: Mike Harkey (.571, 4-for-7, 3 2B, 1 HR)
Bill Landrum (.643, 9-for-14)
Randy O'Neal (.500, 5-for-10, 1 HR)

Hates to face: Orel Hershiser (.176, 6-for-34)
Joe Magrane (.100, 3-for-30)
Ed Whitson (.107, 3-for-28, 1 HR, 0 BB)

Miscellaneous statistics: Ground outs-to-air outs ratio: 0.98 last season, 1.21 for career.... Grounded into 4 double plays in 71 opportunities (one per 17.8).... Drove in 9 of 18 runners from third base with less than two outs (50%).... Direction of balls hit to the outfield: 37% to left field, 34% to center, 30% to right.... Base running: Advanced from first base to third on 8 of 29 outfield singles (28%); scored from second on 11 of 15 (73%).... Made 2.80 putouts per nine innings in center field.

Comments: Baseball's all-time top five postseason batting averages (minimum: 50 AB): Will Clark, .426; Pepper Martin, .418; Fred Lynn, .407; Hatcher, .404; and Lou Brock, .391.... Broke a record with hits in seven consecutive at-bats in one World Series. The previous record was six, by Goose Goslin (1924) and Thurman Munson (1976). (With a hit in his first at-bat in the '77 Series, Munson set the overall series record of seven, which Hatcher tied.)... Hatcher was also the first player to reach base in nine consecutive plate appearances in the same Series. Joe Gordon set the previous record of eight in 1941.... Batted 98 points lower with runners in scoring position (.198) than in other at-bats (.296) last season, the 2d-largest margin in the majors.... Drove in only 15 percent of runners from scoring position last season, the lowest rate of any player in the National League (minimum: 75 opportunities).... Led National League outfielders with a .997 fielding percentage (one error in 319 chances).... Stole 12 bases in 13 attempts against left-handed pitchers (92%), but only 18 in 27 attempts vs. right-handers (67%).... Has homered in every current National League ballpark except Three Rivers Stadium, his home field briefly in 1989 (148 career AB).... Has a career average of one home run per 45 at-bats in day games, one home run every 114 at-bats at night.... Has played on four different teams in his seven years in the majors, and has already played on three division winners: the 1984 Cubs, the 1986 Astros, and the 1990 Reds.

Charlie Hayes

Bats Right

Philadelphia Phillies	AB	H	2B	3B	HR	RBI	BB	SO	BA	SA	OBA
Season	561	145	20	0	10	57	28	91	.258	.348	.293
vs. Left-Handers	193	57	10	0	5	22	8	26	.295	.425	.324
vs. Right-Handers	368	88	10	0	5	35	20	65	.239	.307	.277
vs. Ground-Ballers	292	85	12	0	6	33	17	44	.291	.394	.328
vs. Fly-Ballers	269	60	8	0	4	24	11	47	.223	.297	.254
Home Games	282	69	9	0	3	26	12	47	.245	.309	.272
Road Games	279	76	11	0	7	31	16	44	.272	.387	.314
Grass Fields	146	43	9	0	3	13	8	22	.295	.418	.329
Artificial Turf	415	102	11	0	7	44	20	69	.246	.323	.281
April	65	15	2	0	0	5	4	10	.231	.262	.275
May	86	27	3	0	3	9	7	16	.314	.453	.366
June	109	33	5	0	2	13	2	13	.303	.404	.319
July	95	24	2	0	4	16	5	14	.253	.400	.284
August	108	23	6	0	0	4	4	17	.213	.269	.246
Sept./Oct.	98	23	2	0	1	10	6	21	.235	.286	.274
Leading Off Inn.	127	33	7	0	2	2	5	16	.260	.362	.288
Bases Empty	314	84	15	0	5	5	17	57	.268	.363	.305
Runners On	247	61	5	0	5	52	11	34	.247	.328	.278
Runners/Scor. Pos.	141	33	2	0	2	46	6	19	.234	.291	.260
Runners On/2 Out	105	26	1	0	2	21	6	13	.248	.314	.301
Scor. Pos./2 Out	66	14	1	0	0	17	4	5	.212	.227	.268
Late-Inning Pressure	91	25	2	0	2	7	4	15	.275	.363	.305
Leading Off	22	8	0	0	0	0	2	2	.364	.364	.417
Runners On	41	9	1	0	2	7	1	8	.220	.390	.238
Runners/Scor. Pos.	23	5	0	0	2	7	1	4	.217	.478	.250

RUNS BATTED IN	From 1B	From 2B	From 3B	Scoring Position
Totals	5/190	13/105	29/73	42/178
Percentage	2.6%	12.4%	39.7%	23.6%

Loves to face: Tom Glavine (.500, 6-for-12, 1 HR)
Kevin Gross (.462, 6-for-13, 1 HR)
Rick Reed (.500, 7-for-14, 2 HR)

Hates to face: David Cone (0-for-9)
Sid Fernandez (.077, 1-for-13, 2 BB, 7 SO)
Greg Maddux (.063, 1-for-16)

Miscellaneous statistics: Ground outs-to-air outs ratio: 1.04 last season, 0.96 for career.... Grounded into 12 double plays in 114 opportunities (one per 9.5).... Drove in 19 of 40 runners from third base with less than two outs (48%).... Direction of balls hit to the outfield: 26% to left field, 37% to center, 37% to right.... Base running: Advanced from first base to third on 15 of 28 outfield singles (54%); scored from second on 10 of 14 (71%).... Made 2.36 assists per nine innings at third base, highest rate in majors.

Comments: The only player in the N.L. to start more than five games in both the cleanup spot and the eighth slot in the batting order.... His average of 3.4 chances per nine innings at third base was the highest in the majors last season. Hayes committed 22 errors in 82 games at third base in 1989, only 20 in 146 games last season.... Wondering how Hayes's fielding statistics match up against Mike Schmidt's? Hayes made one error per 23 chances last season; Schmidt topped that in only six of his 17 years at Philadelphia's hot corner. But Hayes's average of 2.22 assists per game at third base last season, 19th best in team history, ranks behind 10 of Schmidt's single-season averages.... His snatch of Gary Carter's liner to secure Terry Mulholland's no-hitter on August 15 may have been the best fielding play we've ever seen end a no-no.... Batted 25 times with the bases loaded, tying Joe Carter for the National League high last season. Hayes batted .238 with the bases full (5-for-21).... Career batting average of .297 vs. ground-ballers is 83 points higher than vs. fly-ballers (.214), the largest margin in the majors over the last five seasons.... Hitless in 12 career at-bats with—look out, here it comes!—two outs and runners in scoring position in Late-Inning Pressure Situations.... Has hit three home runs in 36 career at-bats at Three Rivers Stadium. He has an average of one per 56 at-bats elsewhere.

Von Hayes

Bats Left

Philadelphia Phillies	AB	H	2B	3B	HR	RBI	BB	SO	BA	SA	OBA
Season	467	122	14	3	17	73	87	81	.261	.413	.375
vs. Left-Handers	179	49	6	1	6	28	24	36	.274	.419	.365
vs. Right-Handers	288	73	8	2	11	45	63	45	.253	.410	.381
vs. Ground-Ballers	244	67	5	2	7	38	41	46	.275	.398	.379
vs. Fly-Ballers	223	55	9	1	10	35	46	35	.247	.430	.371
Home Games	203	56	5	3	10	36	40	33	.276	.478	.392
Road Games	264	66	9	0	7	37	47	48	.250	.364	.362
Grass Fields	141	34	4	0	3	22	27	25	.241	.333	.359
Artificial Turf	326	88	10	3	14	51	60	56	.270	.448	.382
April	64	19	1	0	2	7	17	9	.297	.406	.446
May	93	27	5	2	6	23	15	12	.290	.581	.381
June	52	10	1	0	1	7	14	12	.192	.269	.373
July	61	16	0	0	1	7	9	13	.262	.311	.352
August	117	29	4	1	6	18	19	17	.248	.453	.348
Sept./Oct.	80	21	3	0	1	11	13	18	.262	.338	.365
Leading Off Inn.	91	20	1	1	5	5	17	19	.220	.418	.360
Bases Empty	241	52	4	1	10	10	41	43	.216	.365	.339
Runners On	226	70	10	2	7	63	46	38	.310	.465	.411
Runners/Scor. Pos.	134	34	3	1	2	49	32	19	.254	.336	.375
Runners On/2 Out	79	18	2	1	2	15	22	18	.228	.354	.396
Scor. Pos./2 Out	50	8	0	0	1	11	17	8	.160	.220	.373
Late-Inning Pressure	72	21	1	1	3	9	16	15	.292	.458	.424
Leading Off	24	7	0	1	1	1	4	6	.292	.500	.414
Runners On	25	9	1	0	1	7	11	4	.360	.520	.526
Runners/Scor. Pos.	15	3	0	0	0	5	10	3	.200	.200	.481

RUNS BATTED IN	From 1B	From 2B	From 3B	Scoring Position
Totals	13/165	16/103	27/58	43/161
Percentage	7.9%	15.5%	46.6%	26.7%

Loves to face: Jim Deshaies (.583, 7-for-12, 6 BB)
Rick Sutcliffe (.441, 26-for-59, 5 HR)
Bob Walk (.417, 15-for-36, 3 HR)

Hates to face: Atlee Hammaker (.091, 2-for-22, 3 BB)
Bob Ojeda (.125, 4-for-32)
Frank Viola (.150, 3-for-20)

Miscellaneous statistics: Ground outs-to-air outs ratio: 0.80 last season, 1.21 for career. . . . Grounded into 10 double plays in 118 opportunities (one per 11.8). . . . Drove in 23 of 35 runners from third base with less than two outs (66%). . . . Direction of balls hit to the outfield: 22% to left field, 28% to center, 50% to right. . . . Base running: Advanced from first base to third on 14 of 34 outfield singles (41%); scored from second on 14 of 17 (82%). . . . Made 2.33 putouts per nine innings in right field, 2d-highest rate in N.L.

Comments: Has played fewer than 130 games in two of the last three seasons, after four straight years of 150 or more (1984–87). . . . All 17 of his home runs were hit to right field. . . . Stole 12 bases in 15 attempts on artificial surfaces (80%), but only four bases in eight attempts on grass fields (50%). . . . Has hit for a higher average with runners on base than with the bases empty in each of the last six seasons. Career averages: .291 with runners on base, .257 with the bases empty. . . . Has homered in every current National League ballpark except Dodger Stadium (157 career AB). . . . Don't be fooled by last season's lefty/righty breakdown. He had hit for a higher average against right-handers than against left-handers in each of the previous six seasons. His batting average vs. right-handed pitchers was a career low. Career breakdown: .236 vs. LHP, .287 vs. RHP. Other career totals: 160 walks and 256 strikeouts vs. LHP, but more BB (484) than SO (452) vs. RHP. . . . Led the National League with 46 doubles in 1986. Year-by-year totals since then: 36, 28, 27, 14. . . . Batted .232 in his first three plate appearances of each start, but .320 thereafter—not what you'd expect from the only man ever to hit two home runs in the first inning of a ballgame. . . . Career total of 233 stolen bases is already higher than that of some fine contemporary base stealers: Reggie Jackson (228), Rudy Law (228), and Cesar Tovar (226). . . . It's official—the experiment is over: Hayes played 127 games in the field last season, all in the outfield. In other words: No first base.

Tommy Herr

Bats Left and Right

Phillies/Mets	AB	H	2B	3B	HR	RBI	BB	SO	BA	SA	OBA
Season	547	143	26	3	5	60	50	58	.261	.347	.324
vs. Left-Handers	208	55	8	1	1	20	20	19	.264	.327	.329
vs. Right-Handers	339	88	18	2	4	40	30	39	.260	.360	.322
vs. Ground-Ballers	274	72	12	1	2	21	23	22	.263	.336	.322
vs. Fly-Ballers	273	71	14	2	3	39	27	36	.260	.359	.327
Home Games	265	72	15	2	4	38	27	31	.272	.389	.338
Road Games	282	71	11	1	1	22	23	27	.252	.309	.312
Grass Fields	185	50	6	0	2	14	17	19	.270	.335	.335
Artificial Turf	362	93	20	3	3	46	33	39	.257	.354	.319
April	69	21	5	0	2	5	6	4	.304	.464	.360
May	84	23	5	0	0	14	9	12	.274	.333	.340
June	102	22	3	1	1	10	6	10	.216	.294	.259
July	100	29	5	2	1	14	8	14	.290	.410	.343
August	92	23	3	0	0	7	7	7	.250	.283	.314
Sept./Oct.	100	25	5	0	1	10	14	11	.250	.330	.342
Leading Off Inn.	86	22	5	0	1	1	6	9	.256	.349	.304
Bases Empty	284	66	12	0	3	3	26	34	.232	.306	.301
Runners On	263	77	14	3	2	57	24	24	.293	.392	.349
Runners/Scor. Pos.	153	36	6	3	1	48	14	17	.235	.333	.296
Runners On/2 Out	102	26	3	1	1	16	8	10	.255	.333	.309
Scor. Pos./2 Out	68	15	2	1	1	15	5	9	.221	.324	.274
Late-Inning Pressure	81	14	2	0	0	4	8	12	.173	.198	.247
Leading Off	16	3	1	0	0	0	2	2	.188	.250	.278
Runners On	43	9	1	0	0	4	4	6	.209	.233	.277
Runners/Scor. Pos.	30	2	0	0	0	3	4	5	.067	.067	.176

RUNS BATTED IN	From 1B	From 2B	From 3B	Scoring Position
Totals	12/185	21/120	22/53	43/173
Percentage	6.5%	17.5%	41.5%	24.9%

Loves to face: Jim Clancy (.714, 5-for-7)
Frank DiPino (.480, 12-for-25)
Rick Mahler (.377, 20-for-53)

Hates to face: Andy Benes (0-for-12, 2 BB)
Scott Garrelts (.087, 2-for-23)
Rick Sutcliffe (.152, 7-for-46)

Miscellaneous statistics: Ground outs-to-air outs ratio: 1.37 last season, 1.27 for career. . . . Grounded into 11 double plays in 132 opportunities (one per 12.0). . . . Drove in 16 of 33 runners from third base with less than two outs (48%). . . . Direction of balls hit to the outfield: 34% to left field, 41% to center, 25% to right batting left-handed; 18% to left, 45% to center, 37% to right batting right-handed. . . . Base running: Advanced from first base to third on 9 of 32 outfield singles (28%); scored from second on 6 of 12 (50%). . . . Made 2.68 assists per nine innings at second base.

Comments: Enters the season with a career average of one error for every 88 chances at second base, to rank second in major league history behind Ryne Sandberg's average of one error per 92 chances (minimum: 1000 games). That margin represents approximately four errors; that is, if Sandberg were charged with errors on his first four chances of the season, Herr would assume the lead. . . . His major league experience at positions other than second base has been limited to 16 games at shortstop (14 in 1980, the other two in 1988). . . . Took 1161 at-bats to hit his first career home run (on May 10, 1983); has hit one home run per 147 at-bats since then. . . . Has batted in the .260s five times in the past 10 seasons. . . . Has career batting averages of .275 batting right-handed, .273 batting left-handed. . . . Career batting average of .347 as a pinch hitter (17-for-49). . . . If you noticed his performance with runners in scoring position in Late-Inning Pressure Situations above, it won't surprise you to discover that he drove in only three of 35 runners from scoring position in LIPS. . . . Mets pitchers allowed 3.59 runs per nine innings with Herr at second base, compared to 3.78 with Gregg Jefferies there, and 4.22 with Tim Teufel. . . . One of five ex–Minnesota Twins to play for the Mets last season, all acquired in different deals. The others: Dan Schatzeder, Tim Teufel, Kelvin Torve, and Frank Viola.

Rex Hudler

Bats Right

Expos/Cardinals	AB	H	2B	3B	HR	RBI	BB	SO	BA	SA	OBA
Season	220	62	11	2	7	22	12	32	.282	.445	.323
vs. Left-Handers	137	32	5	1	5	11	9	22	.234	.394	.281
vs. Right-Handers	83	30	6	1	2	11	3	10	.361	.530	.393
vs. Ground-Ballers	115	34	6	1	2	11	10	15	.296	.417	.349
vs. Fly-Ballers	105	28	5	1	5	11	2	17	.267	.476	.294
Home Games	89	22	3	1	2	7	6	15	.247	.371	.302
Road Games	131	40	8	1	5	15	6	17	.305	.496	.338
Grass Fields	72	26	5	0	3	9	6	7	.361	.556	.405
Artificial Turf	148	36	6	2	4	13	6	25	.243	.392	.282
April	7	1	0	0	0	0	0	1	.143	.143	.143
May	29	6	0	0	1	1	2	4	.207	.310	.258
June	26	4	2	0	0	1	2	7	.154	.231	.214
July	32	9	1	0	0	2	5	2	.281	.313	.378
August	74	28	7	2	4	15	1	9	.378	.689	.395
Sept./Oct.	52	14	1	0	2	3	2	9	.269	.404	.304
Leading Off Inn.	53	14	0	0	1	1	2	4	.264	.321	.291
Bases Empty	121	34	3	1	5	5	5	16	.281	.446	.315
Runners On	99	28	8	1	2	17	7	16	.283	.444	.333
Runners/Scor. Pos.	55	14	5	1	1	14	5	11	.255	.436	.323
Runners On/2 Out	49	12	6	1	1	10	2	9	.245	.469	.275
Scor. Pos./2 Out	32	9	5	1	1	9	1	8	.281	.594	.303
Late-Inning Pressure	36	9	0	0	3	4	2	7	.250	.500	.289
Leading Off	5	1	0	0	1	1	1	0	.200	.800	.333
Runners On	23	5	0	0	1	2	0	6	.217	.348	.217
Runners/Scor. Pos.	14	3	0	0	0	0	0	5	.214	.214	.214

RUNS BATTED IN	From 1B	From 2B	From 3B	Scoring Position
Totals	2/67	8/41	5/23	13/64
Percentage	3.0%	19.5%	21.7%	20.3%

Loves to face: Ron Darling (.667, 4-for-6)
Bruce Ruffin (.400, 4-for-10, 2 2B)
John Tudor (.556, 5-for-9)

Hates to face: Danny Jackson (.182, 2-for-11)
Terry Mulholland (.071, 1-for-14)
Bob Ojeda (.150, 3-for-20)

Miscellaneous statistics: Ground outs-to-air outs ratio: 1.30 last season, 0.99 for career. . . . Grounded into 3 double plays in 40 opportunities (one per 13.3). . . . Drove in 3 of 11 runners from third base with less than two outs (27%). . . . Direction of balls hit to the outfield: 49% to left field, 26% to center, 25% to right. . . . Base running: Advanced from first base to third on 3 of 5 outfield singles (60%); scored from second on 5 of 7 (71%). . . . Made 2.29 putouts per nine innings in right field.

Comments: Hudler is well on his way to becoming the Oquendo of the 1990s, now that Jose has settled in at second base. Hudler was the only player in the majors to start at least one game at six different positions last season (everywhere except shortstop and the battery positions). At one point in September, Joe Torre had Hudler at a different position in four straight starts. . . . Hudler has carved a nice little niche for himself, symbolized not only by his versatility, but also by his streak of three consecutive seasons with at least 15 stolen bases in fewer than 100 games. It takes an excellent base stealer to do that; only eight others have had streaks as long, including Davey Lopes (1984–86) and Alan Wiggins (1985–87). Among the others: Connie Mack (1887–89)—sans suit jacket, we presume. . .Was removed in favor of a pinch hitter 11 times, all against right-handed pitchers. . . . Has a career average of only .157 as a pinch hitter, but has four home runs in 51 pinch-hit at-bats. . . . Career batting-average breakdown: .274 with the bases empty, .234 with runners on base, .199 with runners in scoring position, .182 with two outs and RISP (are you getting the picture? The more crucial the situation, the lower his BA), .111 with the bases loaded, .000 (0-for-6) with two outs and the bases loaded.

Stan Javier

Bats Left and Right

A's/Dodgers	AB	H	2B	3B	HR	RBI	BB	SO	BA	SA	OBA
Season	309	92	9	6	3	27	40	50	.298	.395	.376
vs. Left-Handers	124	39	2	3	1	10	18	14	.315	.403	.401
vs. Right-Handers	185	53	7	3	2	17	22	36	.286	.389	.359
vs. Ground-Ballers	167	57	6	3	1	12	17	22	.341	.431	.398
vs. Fly-Ballers	142	35	3	3	2	15	23	28	.246	.352	.352
Home Games	161	46	3	2	1	16	21	24	.286	.348	.366
Road Games	148	46	6	4	2	11	19	26	.311	.446	.387
Grass Fields	245	61	4	2	1	20	36	40	.249	.294	.343
Artificial Turf	64	31	5	4	2	7	4	10	.484	.781	.515
April	26	6	0	2	0	3	0	6	.231	.385	.231
May	51	13	1	2	0	7	11	7	.255	.353	.387
June	65	26	4	1	1	6	5	10	.400	.538	.437
July	37	10	0	0	0	4	5	7	.270	.270	.357
August	52	9	2	1	0	3	10	13	.173	.250	.302
Sept./Oct.	78	28	2	0	2	4	9	7	.359	.462	.425
Leading Off Inn.	76	24	4	1	2	2	10	15	.316	.474	.395
Bases Empty	191	57	8	3	3	3	28	35	.298	.419	.388
Runners On	118	35	1	3	0	24	12	15	.297	.356	.356
Runners/Scor. Pos.	68	20	1	1	0	22	10	10	.294	.338	.375
Runners On/2 Out	46	12	1	0	0	9	5	9	.261	.283	.333
Scor. Pos./2 Out	34	8	1	0	0	9	4	7	.235	.265	.316
Late-Inning Pressure	61	15	2	1	0	6	4	13	.246	.311	.284
Leading Off	15	1	0	0	0	0	1	5	.067	.067	.125
Runners On	27	8	0	1	0	6	2	4	.296	.370	.323
Runners/Scor. Pos.	14	5	0	0	0	5	2	2	.357	.357	.389

RUNS BATTED IN	From 1B	From 2B	From 3B	Scoring Position
Totals	3/81	10/55	11/31	21/86
Percentage	3.7%	18.2%	35.5%	24.4%

Loves to face: Joe Price (2-for-2, 1 3B, 1 BB)
Scott Terry (3-for-3)

Hates to face: Dave LaPoint (.133, 2-for-15)
Dave Schmidt (0-for-9)
Frank Viola (.150, 3-for-20)

Miscellaneous statistics: Ground outs-to-air outs ratio: 1.23 last season, 1.62 for career. . . . Grounded into 6 double plays in 60 opportunities (one per 10.0). . . . Drove in 6 of 13 runners from third base with less than two outs (46%). . . . Direction of balls hit to the outfield: 48% to left field, 25% to center, 28% to right batting left-handed; 19% to left, 32% to center, 49% to right batting right-handed. . . . Base running: Advanced from first base to third on 11 of 24 outfield singles (46%); scored from second on 10 of 13 (77%). . . . Made 3.26 putouts per nine innings in center field.

Comments: Batted .351 from the leadoff spot in the batting order last season, the highest mark in the majors (minimum: 100 AB). Juan Samuel, whom Javier replaced as L.A.'s leadoff hitter, batted only .184 from that spot, the *lowest* average among the 47 major leaguers with at least 100 AB. See the Samuel comment for more (p. 243). . . . Tom Lasorda pinch-hit for his leadoff hitter 30 times last season; only Texas's Bobby Valentine (otherwise known as "Tommy, Jr.") did that more often (38 times). . . . Made his major league debut with the Yankees in 1984. He's played under Yogi Berra, Tony LaRussa, and Lasorda. Now that's Italian!. . .Had the highest batting average on artificial turf in the majors last season. Career marks: .336 on artificial turf, .233 on grass fields. . . . Last season was the first in a six-year career in which Javier had a higher batting average batting right-handed than left-handed. Career breakdown: .235 right-handed, .258 left-handed. . . . Julian and Stan are one of three father-son pairs to have played on World Series winners. The others: Jim and Mike Hegan and Ray and Bob Boone. (Jim Hegan and Ray Boone played on the same championship team, the 1948 Indians.) Four other pairs played in the Series: Jim Bagby, Jr. and Sr.; Don and Ernie Johnson; Billy Sullivan, Jr. and Sr.; and Bob and Terry Kennedy.

Gregg Jefferies

Bats Left and Right

New York Mets	AB	H	2B	3B	HR	RBI	BB	SO	BA	SA	OBA
Season	604	171	40	3	15	68	46	40	.283	.434	.337
vs. Left-Handers	222	59	15	2	5	23	13	17	.266	.419	.308
vs. Right-Handers	382	112	25	1	10	45	33	23	.293	.442	.353
vs. Ground-Ballers	290	96	21	1	7	35	21	18	.331	.483	.379
vs. Fly-Ballers	314	75	19	2	8	33	25	22	.239	.389	.298
Home Games	311	99	26	1	9	41	28	17	.318	.495	.380
Road Games	293	72	14	2	6	27	18	23	.246	.369	.290
Grass Fields	442	135	35	1	10	49	39	26	.305	.457	.366
Artificial Turf	162	36	5	2	5	19	7	14	.222	.370	.256
April	75	19	5	0	1	3	7	8	.253	.360	.325
May	93	30	9	0	6	14	4	5	.323	.613	.354
June	107	37	6	0	3	16	8	4	.346	.486	.391
July	95	27	7	1	3	13	9	7	.284	.474	.358
August	124	35	8	1	1	17	7	7	.282	.387	.323
Sept./Oct.	110	23	5	1	1	5	11	9	.209	.300	.276
Leading Off Inn.	141	28	8	0	3	3	18	9	.199	.319	.289
Bases Empty	352	100	23	0	11	11	30	20	.284	.443	.344
Runners On	252	71	17	3	4	57	16	20	.282	.421	.327
Runners/Scor. Pos.	144	39	11	2	0	45	10	13	.271	.375	.314
Runners On/2 Out	103	27	7	3	2	28	7	11	.262	.447	.309
Scor. Pos./2 Out	74	19	5	2	0	22	5	8	.257	.378	.304
Late-Inning Pressure	91	25	3	0	0	9	8	4	.275	.308	.330
Leading Off	30	7	0	0	0	0	4	0	.233	.233	.324
Runners On	33	11	2	0	0	9	2	2	.333	.394	.361
Runners/Scor. Pos.	17	7	1	0	0	8	2	0	.412	.471	.450

RUNS BATTED IN	From 1B	From 2B	From 3B	Scoring Position
Totals	10/174	19/111	24/52	43/163
Percentage	5.7%	17.1%	46.2%	26.4%

Loves to face: Joe Magrane (.417, 5-for-12, 3 2B)
Mark Portugal (.385, 5-for-13, 2 HR)
John Smiley (.300, 6-for-20, 1 2B, 3 HR)

Hates to face: Pat Combs (.100, 2-for-20)
Neal Heaton (.143, 2-for-14)
Zane Smith (.167, 3-for-18)

Miscellaneous statistics: Ground outs-to-air outs ratio: 0.72 last season, 0.86 for career. . . . Grounded into 12 double plays in 117 opportunities (one per 9.8). . . . Drove in 15 of 26 runners from third base with less than two outs (58%). . . . Direction of balls hit to the outfield: 33% to left field, 24% to center, 44% to right batting left-handed; 62% to left, 24% to center, 14% to right batting right-handed. . . . Base running: Advanced from first base to third on 9 of 31 outfield singles (29%); scored from second on 15 of 18 (83%). . . . Made 2.51 assists per nine innings at second base, lowest rate in majors.

Comments: Ended the season with 37 consecutive hitless at-bats with runners in scoring position, the longest streak by any major leaguer over the 16 years we've kept track. When Mike Greenwell started the season 0-for-29 in that situation it was literally front-page news (at least in the *USA Today* sports section), but Jefferies's streak, which started on August 14, went unnoticed. . . . Became only the second New York player in the last 49 years to lead the National League in doubles. The other was Al Dark, who did it for the Giants in 1951. . . . The toughest player in the National League to strike out in Late-Inning Pressure Situations last season, averaging one SO per 25 plate appearances. He has hit only one home run in 177 career at-bats in LIPS. . . . Batted 83 points higher on grass fields (.305) than on artificial turf (.222) last season, the largest margin in the majors. . . . The 67-point gap between his career averages at home (.310) and on the road (.243) is the 5th-largest margin over the last five years. . . . Batted 67 points higher in 1989 against ground-ball pitchers (.291) than vs. fly-ballers (.224). . . . Has a career batting average of .156 at Riverfront Stadium (5-for-32), the only ballpark in which he has never had an extra-base hit. . . . Among the 84 players active in 1990 with at least 50 games at third base, Jefferies has the 11th-best error rate (one per 26 chances). At second base, it's a different story: he ranks 49th among 69 players (one error per 41 chances).

Howard Johnson

Bats Left and Right

New York Mets	AB	H	2B	3B	HR	RBI	BB	SO	BA	SA	OBA
Season	590	144	37	3	23	90	69	100	.244	.434	.319
vs. Left-Handers	221	46	12	0	6	23	29	50	.208	.344	.296
vs. Right-Handers	369	98	25	3	17	67	40	50	.266	.488	.333
vs. Ground-Ballers	293	74	23	1	9	50	27	53	.253	.430	.310
vs. Fly-Ballers	297	70	14	2	14	40	42	47	.236	.438	.327
Home Games	291	68	12	1	13	45	27	49	.234	.416	.297
Road Games	299	76	25	2	10	45	42	51	.254	.452	.339
Grass Fields	425	106	23	1	19	69	44	71	.249	.442	.317
Artificial Turf	165	38	14	2	4	21	25	29	.230	.412	.323
April	72	18	4	0	4	12	6	11	.250	.472	.308
May	91	23	2	0	4	11	11	19	.253	.407	.324
June	108	23	11	2	4	18	7	15	.213	.463	.254
July	101	27	6	1	3	16	15	21	.267	.436	.362
August	114	29	8	0	5	19	15	16	.254	.456	.341
Sept./Oct.	104	24	6	0	3	14	15	18	.231	.375	.320
Leading Off Inn.	163	41	8	1	10	10	11	31	.252	.497	.299
Bases Empty	340	76	14	3	14	14	30	57	.224	.406	.286
Runners On	250	68	23	0	9	76	39	43	.272	.472	.359
Runners/Scor. Pos.	139	42	14	0	6	68	27	29	.302	.532	.394
Runners On/2 Out	107	26	8	0	3	28	19	21	.243	.402	.357
Scor. Pos./2 Out	71	18	4	0	3	27	14	16	.254	.437	.376
Late-Inning Pressure	94	27	5	1	4	10	9	25	.287	.489	.346
Leading Off	28	9	1	0	2	2	1	7	.321	.571	.345
Runners On	43	8	2	0	0	6	7	17	.186	.233	.294
Runners/Scor. Pos.	25	4	2	0	0	6	5	14	.160	.240	.290

RUNS BATTED IN	From 1B	From 2B	From 3B	Scoring Position
Totals	14/190	24/110	29/61	53/171
Percentage	7.4%	21.8%	47.5%	31.0%

Loves to face: Frank DiPino (.350, 7-for-20, 4 HR)
Mike LaCoss (.350, 7-for-20, 2 2B, 3 HR)
Pat Perry (.462, 6-for-13, 1 2B, 4 HR)

Hates to face: Tom Browning (.067, 2-for-30, 1 HR)
Jim Deshaies (.056, 1-for-18)
John Smiley (.069, 2-for-29, 0 BB)

Miscellaneous statistics: Ground outs-to-air outs ratio: 0.49 last season, lowest rate in N.L.; 0.59 for career. . . . Grounded into 7 double plays in 124 opportunities (one per 17.7). . . . Drove in 20 of 32 runners from third base with less than two outs (63%). . . . Direction of balls hit to the outfield: 28% to left field, 26% to center, 46% to right batting left-handed; 54% to left, 23% to center, 22% to right batting right-handed. . . . Base running: Advanced from first base to third on 18 of 30 outfield singles (60%); scored from second on 17 of 20 (85%). . . . Made 1.85 assists per nine innings at third base.

Comments: Has played for teams with winning records in every season of his major league career. Frank Crosetti's 17-year career (1932–48, all with the Yankees) was the longest by a played who played only for winning teams—on a technicality. Yogi Berra spoiled his 18-year mark by playing four games with the 1965 Mets. One active player has a longer career-long streak than HoJo's: Rick Leach (10 years with four different teams). . . . Career total of 159 home runs ranks ninth among switch-hitters. He could eventually become the all-time N.L. leader; his league total of 140 trails only Ted Simmons (182) Reggie Smith (165), and Pete Rose (160). . . . Has hit below .250 in four of his six seasons with the Mets. . . . Batted .165 in the first plate appearance of each start last season, but improved that with each time up: .232, .258, .291, .320, and .429 (3-for-7) on his second through sixth PAs, respectively. . . . His average of one error per 11.6 chances at third base was the worst in the majors (minimum: 81 games). Mets pitchers allowed 3.88 runs per nine innings with Johnson at third base, compared to 3.39 runs with Gregg Jefferies there. . . . Johnson had a streak of 39 consecutive errorless games at shortstop, which ended with two errors in the season finale. . . . Enters this season 45 games behind Wayne Garrett as the Mets' franchise leader in games played at third base. Garrett, who holds about as many records as his brother Adrian, is hoping that HoJo's move to shortstop is permanent.

Ricky Jordan

Bats Right

Philadelphia Phillies	AB	H	2B	3B	HR	RBI	BB	SO	BA	SA	OBA
Season	324	78	21	0	5	44	13	39	.241	.352	.277
vs. Left-Handers	118	29	9	0	2	12	10	9	.246	.373	.313
vs. Right-Handers	206	49	12	0	3	32	3	30	.238	.340	.256
vs. Ground-Ballers	180	44	11	0	2	24	7	20	.244	.339	.274
vs. Fly-Ballers	144	34	10	0	3	20	6	19	.236	.368	.282
Home Games	145	34	6	0	2	18	2	26	.234	.317	.250
Road Games	179	44	15	0	3	26	11	13	.246	.380	.299
Grass Fields	90	24	8	0	3	17	1	6	.267	.456	.280
Artificial Turf	234	54	13	0	2	27	12	33	.231	.312	.277
April	60	16	4	0	0	9	5	6	.267	.333	.324
May	87	23	4	0	3	13	0	11	.264	.414	.270
June	39	8	4	0	1	5	5	6	.205	.385	.304
July	59	11	4	0	0	8	2	10	.186	.254	.226
August	17	3	2	0	0	2	0	1	.176	.294	.176
Sept./Oct.	62	17	3	0	1	7	1	5	.274	.371	.297
Leading Off Inn.	72	22	2	0	2	2	0	7	.306	.417	.315
Bases Empty	167	40	9	0	2	2	1	15	.240	.329	.253
Runners On	157	38	12	0	3	42	12	24	.242	.376	.301
Runners/Scor. Pos.	95	21	7	0	1	34	11	20	.221	.326	.304
Runners On/2 Out	73	18	7	0	0	17	8	10	.247	.342	.337
Scor. Pos./2 Out	49	9	4	0	0	14	7	9	.184	.265	.298
Late-Inning Pressure	44	14	2	0	1	8	1	6	.318	.432	.362
Leading Off	8	3	0	0	0	0	0	1	.375	.375	.444
Runners On	23	8	1	0	1	8	1	3	.348	.522	.400
Runners/Scor. Pos.	16	5	1	0	1	8	0	3	.313	.563	.313

RUNS BATTED IN	From 1B	From 2B	From 3B	Scoring Position
Totals	9/123	11/68	19/49	30/117
Percentage	7.3%	16.2%	38.8%	25.6%

Loves to face: Jose DeLeon (.438, 7-for-16, 2 HR)
Ramon Martinez (.462, 6-for-13, 1 HR)
Frank Viola (.385, 5-for-13, 4 2B)

Hates to face: Doug Drabek (0-for-13)
Rick Reuschel (.111, 2-for-18)
Calvin Schiraldi (0-for-10)

Miscellaneous statistics: Ground outs-to-air outs ratio: 1.12 last season, 1.13 for career.... Grounded into 9 double plays in 73 opportunities (one per 8.1).... Drove in 13 of 25 runners from third base with less than two outs (52%).... Direction of balls hit to the outfield: 29% to left field, 39% to center, 32% to right.... Base running: Advanced from first base to third on 9 of 18 outfield singles (50%); scored from second on 5 of 7 (71%).... Made 0.48 assists per nine innings at first base, lowest rate in N.L.

Comments: Eight years after being selected in the first round of the 1983 free-agent draft (22d overall, three picks after Roger Clemens), Jordan remains a question mark. In six minor league seasons, Jordan never hit below .274 or above .318; he batted .293 in 213 major league games prior to 1990. But he has played as many as 100 games for the Phillies only once (1989).... Became Philadelphia's cleanup hitter in late 1989, and remained there until a 21-day stay on the disabled list last June. When Jordan returned, he was placed mostly in the fifth or sixth slot for the remainder of the season.... His first-inning batting average (.132) was the lowest in the majors last season.... Career batting-average breakdowns: .281 with the bases empty, .274 with runners on base, .269 with runners in scoring position, .205 with two outs and RISP; .303 vs. left-handed pitchers, .264 vs. right-handers.... Has hit home runs with much greater frequency with runners on base (one HR per 30 at-bats) than with the bases empty (one per 57 AB).... Impressive *Loves to Face* group, isn't it?...One of six active nonpitchers with at least 300 career games and no sacrifice bunts. The other five players, are guys you want swinging away with the game on the line: George Bell, Ron Kittle, Pete Incaviglia, Mike Greenwell, and Cecil Fielder. But Ricky Jordan?

Felix Jose

Bats Left and Right

A's/Cardinals	AB	H	2B	3B	HR	RBI	BB	SO	BA	SA	OBA
Season	426	113	16	1	11	52	24	81	.265	.385	.311
vs. Left-Handers	103	31	5	1	2	16	7	21	.301	.427	.348
vs. Right-Handers	323	82	11	0	9	36	17	60	.254	.372	.299
vs. Ground-Ballers	228	62	9	0	5	29	6	41	.272	.377	.303
vs. Fly-Ballers	198	51	7	1	6	23	18	40	.258	.394	.321
Home Games	210	49	7	1	5	27	16	44	.233	.348	.296
Road Games	216	64	9	0	6	25	8	37	.296	.421	.327
Grass Fields	319	86	11	0	6	33	17	59	.270	.361	.314
Artificial Turf	107	27	5	1	5	19	7	22	.252	.458	.304
April	32	12	2	0	2	6	2	5	.375	.625	.412
May	68	14	0	0	2	9	3	12	.206	.294	.239
June	70	15	5	0	0	4	2	13	.214	.286	.236
July	86	26	3	0	4	14	6	20	.302	.477	.365
August	89	25	2	0	0	6	3	16	.281	.303	.319
Sept./Oct.	81	21	4	1	3	13	8	15	.259	.444	.326
Leading Off Inn.	94	23	2	0	2	2	7	21	.245	.330	.297
Bases Empty	223	52	7	1	4	4	19	49	.233	.327	.299
Runners On	203	61	9	0	7	48	5	32	.300	.448	.325
Runners/Scor. Pos.	117	38	8	0	4	42	1	20	.325	.496	.339
Runners On/2 Out	86	24	3	0	4	21	3	17	.279	.453	.319
Scor. Pos./2 Out	54	14	3	0	2	17	1	13	.259	.426	.286
Late-Inning Pressure	49	12	1	0	1	7	6	17	.245	.327	.339
Leading Off	14	1	0	0	0	0	3	6	.071	.071	.235
Runners On	25	9	1	0	1	7	1	7	.360	.520	.385
Runners/Scor. Pos.	14	7	1	0	1	7	1	3	.500	.786	.533

RUNS BATTED IN	From 1B	From 2B	From 3B	Scoring Position
Totals	5/137	19/90	17/39	36/129
Percentage	3.6%	21.1%	43.6%	27.9%

Loves to face: Pat Combs (.667, 2-for-3, 1 3B, 1 HR)
Jay Tibbs (.429, 3-for-7, 1 HR)

Hates to face: Mike Jackson (0-for-5)
Terry Mulholland (0-for-6)

Miscellaneous statistics: Ground outs-to-air outs ratio: 1.37 last season, 1.43 for career.... Grounded into 9 double plays in 83 opportunities (one per 9.2).... Drove in 10 of 16 runners from third base with less than two outs (63%).... Direction of balls hit to the outfield: 32% to left field, 38% to center, 30% to right batting left-handed; 29% to left, 27% to center, 44% to right batting right-handed.... Base running: Advanced from first base to third on 7 of 21 outfield singles (33%); scored from second on 10 of 12 (83%).... Made 2.04 putouts per nine innings in right field.

Comments: Made the opening-day roster of the defending American League champions in each of the last two seasons (although his 1989 spot was due to Jose Canseco's wrist injury).... One of three rookies with at least 10 home runs and 10 steals last season. The others: Dave Justice and Larry Walker.... Batted 82 points higher with runners in scoring position (.325) than in other at-bats (.243) last season, the 5th-largest margin in the majors.... Career batting-average breakdown: .227 with the bases empty, .293 with runners on base, .312 with RISP.... Career average is much higher from the right side of the plate (.302) than the left side (.242).... Career average of .226 in day games, .279 at night.... From Frankie Frisch to Red Schoendienst to Julian Javier to Ted Simmons to the crop of Ozzie, Coleman, McGee, Herr, Pendleton, and Oquendo in the 1980s, St. Louis has been the switch-hit capital of the National League. Jose, Luis Alicea, and Geronimo Pena will continue that legacy in the 1990s.... Comparable rookie seasons: Tito Francona (1956), Leon ("Not Bip") Roberts (1975), Brook Jacoby (1986), and Mike Devereaux (1989).

Dave Justice

Bats Left

Atlanta Braves	AB	H	2B	3B	HR	RBI	BB	SO	BA	SA	OBA
Season	439	124	23	2	28	78	64	92	.282	.535	.373
vs. Left-Handers	131	48	8	0	10	32	18	22	.366	.656	.443
vs. Right-Handers	308	76	15	2	18	46	46	70	.247	.484	.344
vs. Ground-Ballers	213	70	12	1	17	44	27	41	.329	.634	.404
vs. Fly-Ballers	226	54	11	1	11	34	37	51	.239	.442	.345
Home Games	225	72	18	1	19	48	32	49	.320	.662	.405
Road Games	214	52	5	1	9	30	32	43	.243	.402	.340
Grass Fields	336	98	21	2	22	60	46	74	.292	.563	.376
Artificial Turf	103	26	2	0	6	18	18	18	.252	.447	.364
April	0	0	0	0	0	0	0	0	—	—	—
May	54	19	6	0	2	10	5	10	.352	.574	.407
June	91	20	3	1	2	9	14	19	.220	.341	.324
July	75	16	2	0	4	9	10	21	.213	.400	.306
August	113	34	7	0	11	29	9	24	.301	.655	.352
Sept./Oct.	106	35	5	1	9	21	26	18	.330	.651	.459
Leading Off Inn.	105	25	4	0	6	6	13	26	.238	.448	.322
Bases Empty	251	58	9	2	17	17	39	52	.231	.486	.334
Runners On	188	66	14	0	11	61	25	40	.351	.601	.425
Runners/Scor. Pos.	113	36	8	0	7	50	18	28	.319	.575	.409
Runners On/2 Out	86	25	6	0	4	23	10	21	.291	.500	.365
Scor. Pos./2 Out	59	14	3	0	2	17	7	17	.237	.390	.318
Late-Inning Pressure	62	18	1	0	4	8	9	10	.290	.500	.380
Leading Off	17	6	0	0	2	2	3	3	.353	.706	.450
Runners On	21	7	1	0	0	4	1	5	.333	.381	.364
Runners/Scor. Pos.	11	3	1	0	0	4	1	4	.273	.364	.333

RUNS BATTED IN	From 1B	From 2B	From 3B	Scoring Position
Totals	11/123	19/91	20/42	39/133
Percentage	8.9%	20.9%	47.6%	29.3%

Loves to face: Derek Lilliquist (5-for-5)
Eric Show (.571, 4-for-7, 2 HR)

Hates to face: Ramon Martinez (.200, 2-for-10, 5 SO)
Jim Neidlinger (0-for-6)
Ed Whitson (0-for-10)

Miscellaneous statistics: Ground outs-to-air outs ratio: 0.61 last season, 4th-lowest rate in N.L.; 0.60 for career. . . . Grounded into 2 double plays in 75 opportunities (one per 37.5), 2d-best rate in N.L. . . . Drove in 14 of 20 runners from third base with less than two outs (70%). . . . Direction of balls hit to the outfield: 23% to left field, 22% to center, 55% to right. . . . Base running: Advanced from first base to third on 5 of 30 outfield singles (17%); scored from second on 15 of 21 (71%). . . . Made 0.64 assists per nine innings at first base.

Comments: From August 7 to the end of the season, Justice led the majors with 20 home runs, three more than runner-up Cecil Fielder, and five more than N.L. runner-up Ryne Sandberg. . . . Led the major leagues with 11 home runs and 18 extra-base hits in August. . . . His total of 28 home runs was the 3d highest ever by a Braves rookie, behind Wally Berger (38 in 1930) and Earl Williams (33 in 1971). Berger shares the National League record for rookies with Frank Robinson. . . . Became the first Braves player with back-to-back 2-homer games since Gene Oliver did it for Milwaukee in 1965 at Wrigley Field. . . . Had never hit more than 22 home runs in any season of pro ball before last season. . . . Was Justice's August explosion related to his simultaneous move from first base to right field? Could be: His average of one error per 54 chances at first base was the worst in the majors (minimum: 50 games). As a first baseman, Justice batted .235 with 8 HR and 30 RBI in 69 games; in 60 games as a right fielder, he hit .332 with 19 HR and 47 RBI. . . . Batting average vs. left-handed pitchers was the highest of any left-handed batter in the majors (minimum: 100 AB). . . . Led the major leagues with a .413 batting average in the first inning. . . . Hitless in eight extra-inning at-bats, tying Dale Murphy for the largest 0-fer in the National League last season. . . . Justice was born on April 14, 1966, two days after major league baseball debuted in Dixie.

Terry Kennedy

Bats Left

San Francisco Giants	AB	H	2B	3B	HR	RBI	BB	SO	BA	SA	OBA
Season	303	84	22	0	2	26	31	38	.277	.370	.342
vs. Left-Handers	32	6	1	0	0	1	3	4	.188	.219	.257
vs. Right-Handers	271	78	21	0	2	25	28	34	.288	.387	.352
vs. Ground-Ballers	129	32	5	0	1	12	11	18	.248	.310	.307
vs. Fly-Ballers	174	52	17	0	1	14	20	20	.299	.414	.367
Home Games	148	43	10	0	2	18	19	14	.291	.399	.369
Road Games	155	41	12	0	0	8	12	24	.265	.342	.315
Grass Fields	220	67	18	0	2	24	25	25	.305	.414	.372
Artificial Turf	83	17	4	0	0	2	6	13	.205	.253	.258
April	39	16	6	0	0	3	3	2	.410	.564	.452
May	55	16	2	0	1	6	10	8	.291	.382	.394
June	56	10	3	0	0	5	5	8	.179	.232	.246
July	60	15	5	0	1	4	5	8	.250	.383	.308
August	51	16	3	0	0	3	3	5	.314	.373	.352
Sept./Oct.	42	11	3	0	0	5	5	7	.262	.333	.333
Leading Off Inn.	70	17	3	0	0	0	4	8	.243	.286	.284
Bases Empty	184	50	12	0	0	0	16	19	.272	.337	.330
Runners On	119	34	10	0	2	26	15	19	.286	.420	.360
Runners/Scor. Pos.	63	15	7	0	1	23	14	11	.238	.397	.367
Runners On/2 Out	52	12	3	0	0	9	8	10	.231	.288	.333
Scor. Pos./2 Out	33	7	2	0	0	8	7	6	.212	.273	.350
Late-Inning Pressure	38	15	3	0	0	2	3	7	.395	.474	.439
Leading Off	11	4	1	0	0	0	1	2	.364	.455	.417
Runners On	14	5	1	0	0	2	0	4	.357	.429	.357
Runners/Scor. Pos.	10	3	1	0	0	2	0	4	.300	.400	.300

RUNS BATTED IN	From 1B	From 2B	From 3B	Scoring Position
Totals	5/94	8/51	11/31	19/82
Percentage	5.3%	15.7%	35.5%	23.2%

Loves to face: Rick Mahler (.393, 22-for-56, 2 HR)
Calvin Schiraldi (.600, 6-for-10, 1 HR)
Pete Smith (.571, 4-for-7, 2 2B)

Hates to face: Alejandro Pena (.043, 1-for-23)
Mark Portugal (.167, 4-for-24)
Fernando Valenzuela (.200, 11-for-55)

Miscellaneous statistics: Ground outs-to-air outs ratio: 1.10 last season, 1.09 for career. . . . Grounded into 7 double plays in 64 opportunities (one per 9.1). . . . Drove in 8 of 15 runners from third base with less than two outs (53%). . . . Direction of balls hit to the outfield: 32% to left field, 36% to center, 33% to right. . . . Base running: Advanced from first base to third on 3 of 11 outfield singles (27%); scored from second on 3 of 9 (33%). . . . Opposing base stealers: 63-for-87 (72%).

Comments: Started 82 games vs. right-handed pitchers, two vs. left-handers. He's batted under .200 with no home runs against left-handed pitchers in each of the last two seasons. . . . Kennedy and Carter formed an effective platoon for the Giants, whose catchers combined for a .269 average, the highest of any National League club. (That's more than you can say about the unity of their namesakes, Ted and Jimmy, who split the Democratic Party in the summer of 1980.). . .Giants pitchers allowed 4.51 runs per nine innings with Kennedy catching, compared to 3.96 runs with Carter behind the plate. . . . Has hit only 10 home runs over the past three seasons, equaling the lowest of his totals for the six previous years. . . . His grand slam on May 15 was his first in nearly 11 years. Max Carey went more than 15 years between grand slams, the longest of any player in major league history. Others with gaps of longer than 10 years: Alan Ashby, Kurt Bevacqua, Bob Boone, Tommy Corcoran, Eddie Joost, Al Kaline, Deacon McGuire, Chris Speier, and Cy Williams. Incidentally, Dwight Evans, who hit his last slam in 1975, could break Carey's record in 1991. . . . Kennedy was the oldest National Leaguer to play at least 100 games behind the plate last season. The league's oldest to play that many games at other positions, along with their ages at the end of the 1990 season: 1B, Jack Clark (34); 2B, Tommy Herr (34); 3B, Tim Wallach (33); SS, Ozzie Smith (35); LF, Lonnie Smith (34); CF, Brett Butler (35); and RF, Andre Dawson (36).

Jeff King

Bats Right

Pittsburgh Pirates	AB	H	2B	3B	HR	RBI	BB	SO	BA	SA	OBA
Season	371	91	17	1	14	53	21	50	.245	.410	.283
vs. Left-Handers	231	61	13	1	9	36	14	24	.264	.446	.303
vs. Right-Handers	140	30	4	0	5	17	7	26	.214	.350	.248
vs. Ground-Ballers	192	44	7	0	6	25	6	30	.229	.359	.251
vs. Fly-Ballers	179	47	10	1	8	28	15	20	.263	.464	.315
Home Games	179	49	9	0	9	30	9	23	.274	.475	.304
Road Games	192	42	8	1	5	23	12	27	.219	.349	.263
Grass Fields	91	19	3	0	2	10	4	17	.209	.308	.232
Artificial Turf	280	72	14	1	12	43	17	33	.257	.443	.299
April	39	4	1	0	1	4	3	8	.103	.205	.163
May	50	13	4	0	1	4	4	4	.260	.400	.315
June	51	13	1	0	0	4	2	7	.255	.275	.296
July	52	16	3	0	2	11	3	4	.308	.481	.339
August	86	22	4	1	5	16	2	15	.256	.500	.261
Sept./Oct.	93	23	4	0	5	14	7	12	.247	.452	.297
Leading Off Inn.	79	21	4	0	4	4	2	8	.266	.468	.284
Bases Empty	213	56	12	0	8	8	8	20	.263	.432	.290
Runners On	158	35	5	1	6	45	13	30	.222	.380	.274
Runners/Scor. Pos.	112	26	3	1	3	38	10	23	.232	.357	.285
Runners On/2 Out	71	18	3	0	5	25	4	13	.254	.507	.303
Scor. Pos./2 Out	53	14	3	0	3	21	4	9	.264	.491	.328
Late-Inning Pressure	57	7	2	0	0	4	4	10	.123	.158	.180
Leading Off	9	1	0	0	0	0	0	1	.111	.111	.111
Runners On	28	5	1	0	0	4	3	6	.179	.214	.258
Runners/Scor. Pos.	19	5	1	0	0	4	3	4	.263	.316	.364

RUNS BATTED IN	From 1B	From 2B	From 3B	Scoring Position
Totals	8/105	13/92	18/47	31/139
Percentage	7.6%	14.1%	38.3%	22.3%

Loves to face: Joe Magrane (.316, 6-for-19, 3 2B, 1 3B)
Fernando Valenzuela (.500, 4-for-8, 3 2B)
Steve Wilson (.300, 3-for-10, 2 HR)

Hates to face: Tim Burke (0-for-8)
John Franco (0-for-6)
Bruce Hurst (0-for-9, 1 BB)

Miscellaneous statistics: Ground outs-to-air outs ratio: 0.83 last season, 0.79 for career. . . . Grounded into 12 double plays in 69 opportunities (one per 5.8). . . . Drove in 13 of 30 runners from third base with less than two outs (43%). . . . Direction of balls hit to the outfield: 45% to left field, 34% to center, 21% to right. . . . Base running: Advanced from first base to third on 6 of 18 outfield singles (33%); scored from second on 7 of 11 (64%). . . . Made 2.30 assists per nine innings at third base, 2d-highest rate in N.L.

Comments: First picks in the June free-agent draft during the 1980s: 1980, Darryl Strawberry; 1981, Mike Moore; 1982, Shawon Dunston; 1983, Tim Belcher; 1984, Shawn Abner; 1985, B.J. Surhoff; 1986, Jeff King; 1987, Ken Griffey, Jr.; 1988, Andy Benes; 1989, Ben McDonald. . . . King has been labeled "slow to devleop." But of the six nonpitchers listed above, only Griffey and Surhoff reached the majors within two years, and it was Abner who took more than three years to make his big league debut. . . . The first player to reach the bigs from the 1986 draft was 7th-round Rangers pick Mike Loynd, who won his debut on July 26 that season. . . . Other big names from the 1986 draft include Bo Jackson (4th round), Matt Williams (1st), Gary Sheffield (1st), Greg Swindell (1st), Todd Zeile (2d), and Phoenix Suns guard Kevin Johnson (23d round). . . . Pirates third basemen combined for a National League–high 33 errors. King had 18, Wally Backman 12, and Bobby Bonilla three. That's not surprising, since Bonilla was converted to the outfield this season, and King and Backman played other positions in 1989 (first and second base, respectively). . . . Started 68 of 69 games in which the Pirates faced left-handed starters, but only 18 of 93 vs. right-handers. . . . Batted 145 points lower in Late-Inning Pressure Situations (.123) than in other at-bats (.268) last season, the 4th-largest margin in the majors. Career batting average of .147 in LIPS, .242 in other at-bats.

Mike Kingery

Bats Left

San Francisco Giants	AB	H	2B	3B	HR	RBI	BB	SO	BA	SA	OBA
Season	207	61	7	1	0	24	12	19	.295	.338	.335
vs. Left-Handers	25	10	1	0	0	4	1	1	.400	.440	.444
vs. Right-Handers	182	51	6	1	0	20	11	18	.280	.324	.320
vs. Ground-Ballers	89	26	1	1	0	8	3	8	.292	.326	.319
vs. Fly-Ballers	118	35	6	0	0	16	9	11	.297	.347	.346
Home Games	107	29	3	1	0	13	9	10	.271	.318	.333
Road Games	100	32	4	0	0	11	3	9	.320	.360	.337
Grass Fields	154	49	6	1	0	20	11	13	.318	.370	.365
Artificial Turf	53	12	1	0	0	4	1	6	.226	.245	.241
April	0	0	0	0	0	0	0	0	—	—	—
May	3	0	0	0	0	0	0	1	.000	.000	.000
June	43	12	0	0	0	9	4	2	.279	.279	.333
July	26	7	1	1	0	3	4	4	.269	.385	.387
August	58	15	3	0	0	7	1	8	.259	.310	.271
Sept./Oct.	77	27	3	0	0	5	3	4	.351	.390	.375
Leading Off Inn.	30	9	0	0	0	0	1	1	.300	.300	.323
Bases Empty	119	26	1	1	0	0	5	12	.218	.244	.250
Runners On	88	35	6	0	0	24	7	7	.398	.466	.443
Runners/Scor. Pos.	51	18	3	0	0	23	5	6	.353	.412	.404
Runners On/2 Out	36	12	2	0	0	10	4	3	.333	.389	.400
Scor. Pos./2 Out	25	9	1	0	0	10	3	3	.360	.400	.429
Late-Inning Pressure	21	8	0	1	0	7	0	3	.381	.476	.391
Leading Off	4	1	0	0	0	0	0	0	.250	.250	.250
Runners On	7	5	0	0	0	7	0	0	.714	.714	.667
Runners/Scor. Pos.	6	5	0	0	0	7	0	0	.833	.833	.714

RUNS BATTED IN	From 1B	From 2B	From 3B	Scoring Position
Totals	1/55	8/33	15/25	23/58
Percentage	1.8%	24.2%	60.0%	39.7%

Loves to face: Mike Moore (.429, 3-for-7, 1 3B, 2 HR)
Steve Ontiveros (.600, 3-for-5)

Hates to face: Jack Armstrong (0-for-8, 1 BB)
Bert Blyleven (.161, 5-for-31)
Doug Drabek (0-for-7)

Miscellaneous statistics: Ground outs-to-air outs ratio: 1.35 last season, 0.88 for career. . . . Grounded into 1 double play in 39 opportunities (one per 39.0). . . . Drove in 8 of 11 runners from third base with less than two outs (73%). . . . Direction of balls hit to the outfield: 35% to left field, 36% to center, 28% to right. . . . Base running: Advanced from first base to third on 7 of 18 outfield singles (39%); scored from second on 4 of 6 (67%). . . . Made 2.52 putouts per nine innings in right field.

Comments: Picked more splinters out of his butt than any other player in the majors last year, entering 64 games in which he wasn't in the starting lineup. He was used as a pinch hitter 20 times, a pinch runner eight times, and a defensive replacement 36 times. . . . One of three N.L. players with at least 200 at-bats but no home runs. The others: Mark Lemke (239 AB) and R.J. Reynolds (215 AB). . . . Percentage of runners driven in from scoring position (.397) was 2d highest in the majors, behind Dave Magadan (minimum: 50 opportunities). Kingery drove in seven of nine such runners (78%) in Late-Inning Pressure Situations. . . . Was not thrown out trying to advance an extra base on any batted ball last season. . . . Batted .412 (7-for-17) as a pinch hitter, raising his career mark to .283 (12-for-42, 1 HR). . . . Has a career batting average of .312 leading off innings, .251 in other at-bats. . . . Other career averages: .202 vs. left-handed pitchers, .271 against right-handers. He has hit 15 career home runs: 14 off right-handers, the other off former Twins southpaw Jack O'Connor. . . . Catchers, beware! Kingery has reached base on catcher's interference seven times, tying him with Johnny Ray for 2d most among players active in 1990, behind Andy Van Slyke (13). . . . Career total of 22 plate appearances with the bases loaded is the most of any active player who has never struck out. . . . Kingery's full name is Michael Scott Kingery; he has two hits in seven at-bats against his two-thirds namesake.

John Kruk

Bats Left

Philadelphia Phillies	AB	H	2B	3B	HR	RBI	BB	SO	BA	SA	OBA
Season	443	129	25	8	7	67	69	70	.291	.431	.386
vs. Left-Handers	117	26	2	2	2	15	14	20	.222	.325	.303
vs. Right-Handers	326	103	23	6	5	52	55	50	.316	.469	.415
vs. Ground-Ballers	237	70	11	2	5	42	32	33	.295	.422	.379
vs. Fly-Ballers	206	59	14	6	2	25	37	37	.286	.442	.393
Home Games	220	70	15	4	2	37	31	29	.318	.450	.401
Road Games	223	59	10	4	5	30	38	41	.265	.413	.372
Grass Fields	118	33	6	3	2	17	19	22	.280	.432	.380
Artificial Turf	325	96	19	5	5	50	50	48	.295	.431	.388
April	58	14	2	1	1	13	5	9	.241	.362	.302
May	79	23	5	3	1	9	10	11	.291	.468	.371
June	75	20	4	0	0	7	16	12	.267	.320	.396
July	54	16	3	0	0	5	16	9	.296	.352	.457
August	91	28	4	1	2	18	13	12	.308	.440	.390
Sept./Oct.	86	28	7	3	3	15	9	17	.326	.581	.389
Leading Off Inn.	100	23	7	0	1	1	9	17	.230	.330	.294
Bases Empty	228	60	10	2	3	3	34	37	.263	.364	.359
Runners On	215	69	15	6	4	64	35	33	.321	.502	.414
Runners/Scor. Pos.	131	39	9	3	3	56	29	23	.298	.481	.422
Runners On/2 Out	106	31	9	2	1	31	17	16	.292	.443	.390
Scor. Pos./2 Out	78	24	7	1	1	30	14	11	.308	.462	.413
Late-Inning Pressure	62	17	2	1	1	12	18	6	.274	.387	.438
Leading Off	10	2	1	0	0	0	0	1	.200	.300	.200
Runners On	35	11	1	1	1	12	13	3	.314	.486	.500
Runners/Scor. Pos.	24	6	1	1	1	12	10	2	.250	.500	.471

RUNS BATTED IN	From 1B	From 2B	From 3B	Scoring Position
Totals	12/156	23/98	25/59	48/157
Percentage	7.7%	23.5%	42.4%	30.6%

Loves to face: Jeff Pico (.714, 5-for-7, 1 HR)
Ted Power (.588, 10-for-17)
Bob Walk (.500, 12-for-24, 1 HR)

Hates to face: Frank DiPino (.111, 2-for-18, 9 SO)
Kelly Downs (.111, 3-for-27)
Bob Ojeda (.150, 3-for-20, 9 SO)

Miscellaneous statistics: Ground outs-to-air outs ratio: 1.61 last season, 1.65 for career. . . . Grounded into 11 double plays in 90 opportunities (one per 8.2). . . . Drove in 12 of 20 runners from third base with less than two outs (60%). . . . Direction of balls hit to the outfield: 51% to left field, 30% to center, 19% to right. . . . Base running: Advanced from first base to third on 10 of 33 outfield singles (30%); scored from second on 12 of 16 (75%). . . . Made 1.77 putouts per nine innings in left field.

Comments: Check Philadelphia's opening-day lineup. Kruk could become the first left fielder to start consecutive openers since Gary Matthews (1981–83). . . . Had 53 hits to the opposite field last season, 3d most in the National League, behind Willie McGee and Bip Roberts. . . . Started 100 of 109 games in which the Phillies faced a right-handed starter, 18 of 53 vs. left-handers. . . . Was removed in favor of a pinch hitter nine times, all against left-handed pitchers. . . . Batted 94 points higher vs. right-handers (.316) than vs. left-handers (.222) last season, the 3d-largest margin in the majors. He has batted over .300 against right-handers in four of his five seasons in the majors. . . . Has hit for a higher average on artificial turf than he has on grass fields in each of his five seasons in the majors. Career averages: .308 on synthetics, .277 on real turf. . . . Has played in 634 major league games, but has never been hit by a pitch. Among active batters, only Herm Winningham has played more games without getting stung (665). . . . Has homered in every current National League ballpark except the Astrodome (82 career AB). . . . Hit 20 home runs in 1987, his only season in double figures. See the Lonnie Smith comments for more (p. 247). . . . Has batted .290 or better in four of his five seasons in the majors. He hit .312 over his first two years, then slumped to .231 over the next year-and-a-half, but since joining the Phillies in mid-1989 he's hit .308.

Barry Larkin

Bats Right

Cincinnati Reds	AB	H	2B	3B	HR	RBI	BB	SO	BA	SA	OBA
Season	614	185	25	6	7	67	49	49	.301	.396	.358
vs. Left-Handers	203	54	10	3	4	21	23	10	.266	.404	.344
vs. Right-Handers	411	131	15	3	3	46	26	39	.319	.392	.365
vs. Ground-Ballers	294	85	14	2	5	33	24	26	.289	.401	.351
vs. Fly-Ballers	320	100	11	4	2	34	25	23	.313	.391	.364
Home Games	286	78	8	2	4	26	29	21	.273	.357	.349
Road Games	328	107	17	4	3	41	20	28	.326	.430	.365
Grass Fields	191	63	13	2	1	22	8	16	.330	.435	.358
Artificial Turf	423	122	12	4	6	45	41	33	.288	.378	.357
April	65	25	2	1	0	12	8	5	.385	.446	.461
May	96	31	2	1	0	14	10	7	.323	.365	.394
June	120	33	4	0	2	10	3	13	.275	.358	.294
July	109	35	12	1	3	10	7	6	.321	.532	.368
August	114	28	3	2	0	10	10	12	.246	.307	.306
Sept./Oct.	110	33	2	1	2	11	11	6	.300	.391	.369
Leading Off Inn.	133	38	6	0	0	0	9	8	.286	.331	.336
Bases Empty	358	104	17	1	5	5	23	28	.291	.385	.342
Runners On	256	81	8	5	2	62	26	21	.316	.410	.378
Runners/Scor. Pos.	159	50	4	4	1	59	22	14	.314	.409	.392
Runners On/2 Out	93	29	1	1	1	30	8	9	.312	.376	.366
Scor. Pos./2 Out	74	23	1	1	1	30	8	8	.311	.392	.378
Late-Inning Pressure	80	24	3	2	1	13	9	4	.300	.425	.374
Leading Off	17	5	2	0	0	0	2	1	.294	.412	.368
Runners On	37	12	0	1	1	13	5	2	.324	.459	.395
Runners/Scor. Pos.	24	8	0	1	0	11	3	1	.333	.417	.393

RUNS BATTED IN	From 1B	From 2B	From 3B	Scoring Position
Totals	4/161	28/126	28/64	56/190
Percentage	2.5%	22.2%	43.8%	29.5%

Loves to face: Tim Belcher (.393, 11-for-28, 1 HR)
Zane Smith (.433, 13-for-30, 3 HR)
Ed Whitson (.469, 15-for-32, 1 HR)

Hates to face: Atlee Hammaker (.172, 5-for-29, 0 SO)
Jeff Pico (.071, 1-for-14)
Bruce Ruffin (.071, 1-for-14, 2 BB)

Miscellaneous statistics: Ground outs-to-air outs ratio: 1.13 last season, 1.11 for career. . . . Grounded into 14 double plays in 116 opportunities (one per 8.3). . . . Drove in 15 of 30 runners from third base with less than two outs (50%). . . . Direction of balls hit to the outfield: 30% to left field, 34% to center, 36% to right. . . . Base running: Advanced from first base to third on 14 of 25 outfield singles (56%); scored from second on 10 of 13 (77%). . . . Made 3.14 assists per nine innings at shortstop, 2d-highest rate in N.L.

Comments: Only the fourth National League shortstop in the last 50 years to hit .300 or better in consecutive seasons (minimum: 80 games at SS). The others: Alvin Dark (1951–52), Ernie Banks (1958–59), and Garry Templeton (1979–80). The last shortstop to hit .300 in three consecutive seasons: Harvey Kuenn (four years, 1953–56). The all-time record? Larkin would have to hit .300 through the 1999 season to equal Honus Wagner's streak (1903–13). . . . Has hit .315 over the past two seasons, 2d highest in the National League to Tony Gwynn's .323 average (minimum: 800 AB). . . . Had 18 game-winning RBIs, even though he drove in a total of only 68 runs. Over the past 10 years, no other player had as many game-winners with so few total RBIs. . . . Led the Reds with 45 hits to the opposite field last season. . . . Batted .333 from the third slot in the batting order, but only .251 from the second slot. . . . Has hit for a higher average with runners on base than with the bases empty in each of his five seasons in the majors. Career breakdown: .320 with runners on base, .276 with the bases empty. . . . His 1990 batting breakdown vs. left- and right-handed pitchers is a reversal from his previous form. He has career batting averages of .312 vs. left-handers, .284 vs. right-handers. . . . Committed 29 errors at shortstop in his last full season (1988), but trimmed that total to 17 in 156 games there last season.

Mike LaValliere

Bats Left

Pittsburgh Pirates	AB	H	2B	3B	HR	RBI	BB	SO	BA	SA	OBA
Season	279	72	15	0	3	31	44	20	.258	.344	.362
vs. Left-Handers	56	21	3	0	2	11	9	6	.375	.536	.470
vs. Right-Handers	223	51	12	0	1	20	35	14	.229	.296	.335
vs. Ground-Ballers	146	42	8	0	2	20	24	13	.288	.384	.392
vs. Fly-Ballers	133	30	7	0	1	11	20	7	.226	.301	.329
Home Games	127	35	7	0	2	15	18	6	.276	.378	.374
Road Games	152	37	8	0	1	16	26	14	.243	.316	.352
Grass Fields	87	20	3	0	0	4	16	11	.230	.264	.350
Artificial Turf	192	52	12	0	3	27	28	9	.271	.380	.368
April	35	7	1	0	0	2	7	0	.200	.229	.333
May	42	17	2	0	1	7	8	4	.405	.524	.500
June	34	7	1	0	0	3	5	1	.206	.235	.308
July	49	8	2	0	0	3	9	5	.163	.204	.305
August	53	14	5	0	2	12	8	6	.264	.472	.361
Sept./Oct.	66	19	4	0	0	4	7	4	.288	.348	.360
Leading Off Inn.	73	17	7	0	0	0	8	5	.233	.329	.317
Bases Empty	166	38	9	0	1	1	19	14	.229	.301	.312
Runners On	113	34	6	0	2	30	25	6	.301	.407	.429
Runners/Scor. Pos.	66	20	4	0	2	30	19	2	.303	.455	.460
Runners On/2 Out	42	13	3	0	0	10	13	2	.310	.381	.473
Scor. Pos./2 Out	24	6	2	0	0	10	10	1	.250	.333	.471
Late-Inning Pressure	33	5	2	0	0	0	6	5	.152	.212	.300
Leading Off	8	2	1	0	0	0	0	1	.250	.375	.333
Runners On	16	2	1	0	0	0	4	2	.125	.188	.300
Runners/Scor. Pos.	9	0	0	0	0	0	4	2	.000	.000	.308

RUNS BATTED IN	From 1B	From 2B	From 3B	Scoring Position
Totals	3/79	8/46	17/31	25/77
Percentage	3.8%	17.4%	54.8%	32.5%

Loves to face: Kelly Downs (.500, 10-for-20)
John Smoltz (.500, 4-for-8)
Rick Sutcliffe (.429, 15-for-35)

Hates to face: David Cone (.158, 3-for-19, 3 BB)
Frank DiPino (.111, 2-for-18)
Rick Mahler (.217, 5-for-23, 1 HR)

Miscellaneous statistics: Ground outs-to-air outs ratio: 0.87 last season, 1.02 for career. . . . Grounded into 6 double plays in 57 opportunities (one per 9.5). . . . Drove in 10 of 16 runners from third base with less than two outs (63%). . . . Direction of balls hit to the outfield: 32% to left field, 29% to center, 39% to right. . . . Base running: Advanced from first base to third on 1 of 13 outfield singles (8%), lowest rate in N.L.; scored from second on 3 of 8 (38%). . . . Opposing base stealers: 68-for-104 (65%), 5th-lowest rate in N.L.

Comments: Started 79 games vs. right-handed pitchers, but only eight against lefties. . . . His two home runs against left-handers last season was one more than his previous career total. He nailed Bruce Ruffin in 1986, and added Pat Clements and Dennis Cook to this select list in 1990. . . . Batting average vs. left-handed pitchers was the highest of any left-handed batter in the majors last season (minimum: 50 AB)—proving how deceiving batting averages can be when based on so few at-bats; many platoon players have similar blips on their records. But LaV's career averages remain indicative of his strengths and weaknesses: .273 vs. right-handers, .239 vs. left-handers. . . . Had four hits in six at-bats with the bases loaded last season, raising his career mark to .433 (13-for-30). . . . Other career batting averages: .289 with runners in scoring position, .259 in other at-bats. . . . Has driven in over 30 percent of runners from scoring position in each of the last three seasons, but was 0-for-9 in Late-Inning Pressure Situations last season. . . . LaValliere could be gearing up for some big-time base running this summer. Back in 1986, he hit the only two triples of his career. After catching his breath in '87, he stole three bases in 1988—also his career total. Well, with two years to recuperate, there's no telling what he's planning for '91. Going first-to-third, perhaps?

Mark Lemke

Bats Left and Right

Atlanta Braves	AB	H	2B	3B	HR	RBI	BB	SO	BA	SA	OBA
Season	239	54	13	0	0	21	21	22	.226	.280	.286
vs. Left-Handers	97	26	8	0	0	11	9	6	.268	.351	.330
vs. Right-Handers	142	28	5	0	0	10	12	16	.197	.232	.256
vs. Ground-Ballers	115	25	8	0	0	7	10	13	.217	.287	.276
vs. Fly-Ballers	124	29	5	0	0	14	11	9	.234	.274	.296
Home Games	109	23	7	0	0	10	8	9	.211	.275	.265
Road Games	130	31	6	0	0	11	13	13	.238	.285	.303
Grass Fields	171	42	10	0	0	17	14	13	.246	.304	.303
Artificial Turf	68	12	3	0	0	4	7	9	.176	.221	.247
April	30	5	2	0	0	4	2	5	.167	.233	.219
May	46	8	2	0	0	2	11	5	.174	.217	.322
June	0	0	0	0	0	0	0	0	—	—	—
July	31	9	2	0	0	6	4	0	.290	.355	.371
August	60	13	1	0	0	5	2	8	.217	.233	.242
Sept./Oct.	72	19	6	0	0	4	2	4	.264	.347	.284
Leading Off Inn.	62	12	2	0	0	0	6	6	.194	.226	.265
Bases Empty	145	25	7	0	0	0	12	14	.172	.221	.236
Runners On	94	29	6	0	0	21	9	8	.309	.372	.362
Runners/Scor. Pos.	57	17	5	0	0	21	6	5	.298	.386	.354
Runners On/2 Out	32	8	2	0	0	9	6	5	.250	.313	.368
Scor. Pos./2 Out	22	6	2	0	0	9	5	2	.273	.364	.407
Late-Inning Pressure	44	9	1	0	0	3	1	5	.205	.227	.222
Leading Off	12	4	0	0	0	0	1	2	.333	.333	.385
Runners On	15	4	1	0	0	3	0	2	.267	.333	.267
Runners/Scor. Pos.	10	2	1	0	0	3	0	2	.200	.300	.200

RUNS BATTED IN	From 1B	From 2B	From 3B	Scoring Position
Totals	1/70	12/54	8/18	20/72
Percentage	1.4%	22.2%	44.4%	27.8%

Loves to face: Tom Browning (.300, 3-for-10, 1 HR)
Fernando Valenzuela (.400, 2-for-5)

Hates to face: Ramon Martinez (0-for-6, 2 BB)
Dennis Rasmussen (0-for-8, 1 BB)

Miscellaneous statistics: Ground outs-to-air outs ratio: 1.30 last season, 1.12 for career. . . . Grounded into 6 double plays in 53 opportunities (one per 8.8). . . . Drove in 6 of 11 runners from third base with less than two outs (55%). . . . Direction of balls hit to the outfield: 31% to left field, 34% to center, 34% to right batting left-handed; 45% to left, 30% to center, 26% to right batting right-handed. . . . Base running: Advanced from first base to third on 3 of 7 outfield singles (43%); scored from second on 4 of 9 (44%). . . . Made 3.71 assists per nine innings at second base.

Comments: Could be the league's best-fielding second baseman. He led his leagues in double plays at second base in each of his last three seasons in the minors (1987–89). Last season, his average of 3.71 assists per nine innings was the highest among the 38 second basemen who played at least 250 innings (500 was needed for our rankings in the miscellaneous section). . . . Braves pitchers allowed 4.69 runs per nine innings with Lemke at second base, compared to 5.29 with other second basemen. . . . The only rookie in the majors to collect five hits in a game last season, the second consecutive year that the Braves have had a rookie do that. Tommy Gregg had a five-hit game in 1989. . . . Batted .192 in 104 at-bats as a third baseman, the lowest average of any third baseman in the National League (minimum: 100 AB). . . . Had the most at-bats of any National League player who didn't hit a home run. He did, however, hit two home runs in only 55 at-bats in 1989. . . . Has hit both career home runs off left-handed pitchers: Career batting averages: .257 vs. left-handers, .190 vs. right-handers. . . . How do you make the most of a .219 career batting average? By batting only .167 with the bases empty, but .299 with runners on base, and .298 with runners in scoring position. (Lemke batted .300 with runners on base compared to only .114 with the bases empty in 55 total at-bats in 1989 to complement last season's breakdown.)

Jose Lind

Bats Right

Pittsburgh Pirates	AB	H	2B	3B	HR	RBI	BB	SO	BA	SA	OBA
Season	514	134	28	5	1	48	35	52	.261	.340	.305
vs. Left-Handers	216	50	12	3	1	19	18	21	.231	.329	.285
vs. Right-Handers	298	84	16	2	0	29	17	31	.282	.349	.321
vs. Ground-Ballers	258	64	14	4	1	22	15	32	.248	.345	.289
vs. Fly-Ballers	256	70	14	1	0	26	20	20	.273	.336	.321
Home Games	245	64	14	2	1	30	13	26	.261	.347	.293
Road Games	269	70	14	3	0	18	22	26	.260	.335	.316
Grass Fields	143	32	4	1	0	13	10	15	.224	.266	.275
Artificial Turf	371	102	24	4	1	35	25	37	.275	.369	.317
April	70	20	3	0	0	6	7	7	.286	.329	.351
May	90	30	8	1	0	13	4	6	.333	.444	.354
June	88	26	7	1	0	9	5	9	.295	.398	.330
July	80	22	3	1	1	9	5	7	.275	.375	.314
August	102	18	4	0	0	6	5	12	.176	.216	.213
Sept./Oct.	84	18	3	2	0	5	9	11	.214	.298	.290
Leading Off Inn.	112	29	11	1	0	0	2	7	.259	.375	.272
Bases Empty	274	68	21	2	0	0	10	18	.248	.339	.275
Runners On	240	66	7	3	1	48	25	34	.275	.342	.337
Runners/Scor. Pos.	130	37	5	3	0	45	22	20	.285	.369	.371
Runners On/2 Out	103	25	6	0	0	17	19	22	.243	.301	.361
Scor. Pos./2 Out	61	15	5	0	0	16	19	12	.246	.328	.425
Late-Inning Pressure	84	27	6	0	0	7	4	7	.321	.393	.348
Leading Off	26	7	4	0	0	0	0	1	.269	.423	.269
Runners On	36	13	0	0	0	7	3	5	.361	.361	.400
Runners/Scor. Pos.	21	7	0	0	0	7	3	3	.333	.333	.400

RUNS BATTED IN	From 1B	From 2B	From 3B	Scoring Position
Totals	4/185	18/103	25/57	43/160
Percentage	2.2%	17.5%	43.9%	26.9%

Loves to face: Don Carman (.500, 9-for-18, 1 HR)
Rob Dibble (.833, 5-for-6)
Bob Sebra (.455, 5-for-11, 1 HR)

Hates to face: Randy Myers (.067, 1-for-15, 3 BB)
Jose Rijo (.125, 2-for-16)
Ed Whitson (.056, 1-for-18)

Miscellaneous statistics: Ground outs-to-air outs ratio: 1.20 last season, 1.39 for career.... Grounded into 20 double plays in 116 opportunities (one per 5.8).... Drove in 17 of 26 runners from third base with less than two outs (65%).... Direction of balls hit to the outfield: 20% to left field, 32% to center, 48% to right.... Base running: Advanced from first base to third on 6 of 15 outfield singles (40%); scored from second on 10 of 15 (67%).... Made 3.17 assists per nine innings at second base.

Comments: Made only seven errors last season (one per 112 chances), but none in 129 chances in Late-Inning Pressure Situations. Only one other second baseman made at least 100 plays without an error in LIPS: Ryne Sandberg (113). Most chances handled in LIPS without an error at other positions: 1B, Mark McGwire (205); 3B, Ken Caminiti (63); SS, Tony Fernandez (110); LF, Ivan Calderon (48); CF, Brett Butler (75); RF, Tom Brunansky (64); C, Carlton Fisk (134); P, Juan Agosto (21).... During the 1980s, there were 15 second basemen with lower error rates than Lind's 1990 average. Compare that with the number of players who reached that mark in previous decades: 1970s—5; 1960s—3; 1950s—2; 1940s—2; pre-1940—1.... Led the Pirates with 44 hits to the opposite field last season.... Career batting averages: .266 at Three Rivers Stadium, .271 on other artificial surfaces, .226 on grass fields.... Has stolen 23 bases in 24 attempts over the last two seasons, raising his career average to .870 (40-for-46). He's been successful on 17 consecutive attempts on artificial surfaces.... At age 26, Lind already ranks eighth in team history with 491 games at second base (the only position he has played for Pittsburgh). He will probably rank sixth by the time he turns 27 on May 1. The top five: Bill Mazeroski (2094), Claude Ritchey (973), Rennie Stennett (919), Johnny Ray (914), and Lou Bierbauer (707).

Greg Litton

Bats Right

San Francisco Giants	AB	H	2B	3B	HR	RBI	BB	SO	BA	SA	OBA
Season	204	50	9	1	1	24	11	45	.245	.314	.284
vs. Left-Handers	139	39	9	1	1	15	5	25	.281	.381	.306
vs. Right-Handers	65	11	0	0	0	9	6	20	.169	.169	.243
vs. Ground-Ballers	82	16	5	0	0	9	6	19	.195	.256	.256
vs. Fly-Ballers	122	34	4	1	1	15	5	26	.279	.352	.305
Home Games	102	29	6	1	0	15	6	27	.284	.363	.327
Road Games	102	21	3	0	1	9	5	18	.206	.265	.241
Grass Fields	144	35	6	1	0	19	10	37	.243	.299	.293
Artificial Turf	60	15	3	0	1	5	1	8	.250	.350	.262
April	6	0	0	0	0	0	0	4	.000	.000	.000
May	30	8	0	0	1	2	1	10	.267	.367	.290
June	27	7	1	0	0	3	1	3	.259	.296	.286
July	42	11	1	0	0	6	0	7	.262	.286	.279
August	53	12	3	0	0	6	5	16	.226	.283	.293
Sept./Oct.	46	12	4	1	0	7	4	5	.261	.391	.308
Leading Off Inn.	40	15	3	1	1	1	1	6	.375	.575	.390
Bases Empty	102	25	5	1	1	1	7	23	.245	.343	.294
Runners On	102	25	4	0	0	23	4	22	.245	.284	.275
Runners/Scor. Pos.	62	15	3	0	0	23	1	15	.242	.290	.258
Runners On/2 Out	44	8	0	0	0	6	1	12	.182	.182	.217
Scor. Pos./2 Out	31	5	0	0	0	6	1	9	.161	.161	.212
Late-Inning Pressure	49	13	4	1	0	7	2	9	.265	.388	.288
Leading Off	14	7	2	1	0	0	0	3	.500	.786	.500
Runners On	21	5	2	0	0	7	1	3	.238	.333	.261
Runners/Scor. Pos.	10	2	1	0	0	7	0	1	.200	.300	.182

RUNS BATTED IN	From 1B	From 2B	From 3B	Scoring Position
Totals	1/75	10/52	12/25	22/77
Percentage	1.3%	19.2%	48.0%	28.6%

Loves to face: Dennis Cook (.615, 8-for-13, 1 HR)
Dennis Rasmussen (.500, 3-for-6, 1 HR)
Dennis Anyone?

Hates to face: Jim Deshaies (0-for-5)
Sid Fernandez (0-for-6, 1 BB, 5 SO)
Fernando Valenzuela (.143, 2-for-14)

Miscellaneous statistics: Ground outs-to-air outs ratio: 1.27 last season, 1.28 for career.... Grounded into 5 double plays in 50 opportunities (one per 10.0).... Drove in 9 of 12 runners from third base with less than two outs (75%).... Direction of balls hit to the outfield: 21% to left field, 40% to center, 39% to right.... Base running: Advanced from first base to third on 2 of 11 outfield singles (18%); scored from second on 5 of 7 (71%).... Made 2.15 putouts per nine innings in right field.

Comments: Played 56 games in the outfield, 18 games at second base, seven games at shortstop, and five games at third base.... Drove in six of 13 runners from scoring position in Late-Inning Pressure Situations (46%), the highest percentage in the National League. Career averages: 9-for-21 in LIPS (43%), 22-for-106 at other times (21%).... Has a career average of .302 with one home run every 43 at-bats in day games, but is batting only .216 and averaging one home run per 109 at-bats in night games.... Hit only one home run in 204 at-bats in 1990, after hitting four in 143 at-bats in 1989.... All five of his career home runs have been hit against left-handed pitchers. Career batting averages: .279 vs. left-handers, .178 vs. right-handers.... No new ballpark in the Bay area? That's fine with Litton, who has a career average of .301 at Candlestick Park, but only .193 on the road. His career average on artificial turf is .232, but he's batting only .145 on grass fields other than Candlestick.... Want to know the difference between the January and June free-agent drafts? Litton was San Francisco's first-round selection, chosen 10th overall, in the January 1984 draft. The 10th pick in June that year was Mark McGwire.

Fred Lynn

Bats Left

San Diego Padres	AB	H	2B	3B	HR	RBI	BB	SO	BA	SA	OBA
Season	196	47	3	1	6	23	22	44	.240	.357	.315
vs. Left-Handers	20	5	0	0	0	1	3	6	.250	.250	.348
vs. Right-Handers	176	42	3	1	6	22	19	38	.239	.369	.312
vs. Ground-Ballers	96	24	0	1	2	12	9	21	.250	.333	.308
vs. Fly-Ballers	100	23	3	0	4	11	13	23	.230	.380	.322
Home Games	112	27	3	0	2	15	12	22	.241	.321	.315
Road Games	84	20	0	1	4	8	10	22	.238	.405	.316
Grass Fields	150	40	3	0	5	20	16	30	.267	.387	.335
Artificial Turf	46	7	0	1	1	3	6	14	.152	.261	.250
April	48	11	1	0	2	3	6	9	.229	.375	.309
May	37	12	1	1	0	5	2	9	.324	.405	.350
June	30	9	1	0	3	6	6	7	.300	.633	.432
July	17	3	0	0	0	2	2	3	.176	.176	.250
August	22	2	0	0	0	1	0	8	.091	.091	.091
Sept./Oct.	42	10	0	0	1	6	6	8	.238	.310	.333
Leading Off Inn.	51	11	1	0	1	1	1	14	.216	.294	.231
Bases Empty	119	29	2	0	5	5	12	23	.244	.387	.313
Runners On	77	18	1	1	1	18	10	21	.234	.312	.319
Runners/Scor. Pos.	44	10	1	1	0	16	9	8	.227	.295	.351
Runners On/2 Out	29	8	1	1	1	8	7	4	.276	.483	.432
Scor. Pos./2 Out	21	5	1	1	0	6	6	2	.238	.381	.429
Late-Inning Pressure	44	16	0	0	2	5	6	16	.364	.500	.451
Leading Off	11	5	0	0	1	1	1	4	.455	.727	.500
Runners On	18	3	0	0	0	3	1	10	.167	.167	.250
Runners/Scor. Pos.	10	3	0	0	0	3	1	4	.300	.300	.417

RUNS BATTED IN	From 1B	From 2B	From 3B	Scoring Position
Totals	2/56	6/37	9/18	15/55
Percentage	3.6%	16.2%	50.0%	27.3%

Loves to face: Allan Anderson (.500, 4-for-8, 2 2B, 1 HR)
John Candelaria (.500, 2-for-4, 2 HR, 2 SO)
Walt Terrell (.455, 10-for-22)

Hates to face: Al Nipper (.125, 2-for-16)
Bob Ojeda (.200, 4-for-20, 1 HR, 10 SO)
Jose Rijo (0-for-14)

Miscellaneous statistics: Ground outs-to-air outs ratio: 0.72 last season, 1.02 for career.... Grounded into 1 double play in 38 opportunities (one per 38.0).... Drove in 8 of 11 runners from third base with less than two outs (73%).... Direction of balls hit to the outfield: 21% to left field, 30% to center, 49% to right.... Base running: Advanced from first base to third on 5 of 20 outfield singles (25%); scored from second on 2 of 3 (67%).... Made 1.86 putouts per nine innings in left field.

Comments: Has not made an All-Star squad since 1983, the last of his nine consecutive seasons in the midsummer classic, when he hit the only grand-slam home run in All-Star competition.... Only four of his 47 hits were to the opposite field.... Batting average has slowly but steadily eroded since 1986, when he hit .287 for the Orioles; year-by-year since then: .253, .246, .241, .240.... Had higher batting averages vs. right-handers than vs. left-handers in each of the previous 15 seasons. Of course, his 20 at-bats vs. southpaws last season was his lowest total since his "pre-rookie" season of 1974. Career batting averages: .243 vs. left-handers, .298 vs. right-handers.... His 1990 batting average in Late-Inning Pressure Situations was a career high. He had lower averages in LIPS than in other at-bats in 13 of the previous 14 seasons.... A career average of .467 at Shea Stadium is based on more than last season (his first in the N.L.); Lynn is one of several active players who played there in 1974–75, while Yankee Stadium was being renovated.... Doesn't it seem like more than 10 years ago that the Red Sox traded Lynn and Steve Renko to California for Joe Rudi and Frank Tanana?... Appeared bound for Cooperstown in the late 1970s, but his final career figures (1969 games, .283 BA, 306 HR, 1111 RBI)—if this is the end—closely approximate those of Reggie Smith (1987 games, .287 BA, 314 HR, 1092 RBI), who was knocked off the Hall of Fame ballot after receiving only three votes in his first year of eligibility.

Dave Magadan

Bats Left

New York Mets	AB	H	2B	3B	HR	RBI	BB	SO	BA	SA	OBA
Season	451	148	28	6	6	72	74	55	.328	.457	.417
vs. Left-Handers	168	43	6	2	2	27	20	22	.256	.351	.335
vs. Right-Handers	283	105	22	4	4	45	54	33	.371	.519	.462
vs. Ground-Ballers	225	73	11	4	2	37	37	31	.324	.436	.407
vs. Fly-Ballers	226	75	17	2	4	35	37	24	.332	.478	.427
Home Games	212	59	10	2	2	34	42	26	.278	.373	.391
Road Games	239	89	18	4	4	38	32	29	.372	.531	.442
Grass Fields	305	94	13	3	4	54	59	41	.308	.410	.413
Artificial Turf	146	54	15	3	2	18	15	14	.370	.555	.426
April	26	6	1	0	0	1	4	5	.231	.269	.323
May	34	12	0	0	0	2	5	6	.353	.353	.425
June	87	35	5	3	2	17	14	9	.402	.598	.485
July	102	34	8	1	2	17	13	8	.333	.490	.398
August	102	29	4	0	0	13	23	12	.284	.324	.417
Sept./Oct.	100	32	10	2	2	22	15	15	.320	.520	.398
Leading Off Inn.	94	32	4	1	2	2	18	10	.340	.468	.446
Bases Empty	271	75	17	3	3	3	47	32	.277	.395	.387
Runners On	180	73	11	3	3	69	27	23	.406	.550	.461
Runners/Scor. Pos.	110	42	7	1	2	63	15	16	.382	.518	.422
Runners On/2 Out	69	28	5	2	0	25	13	10	.406	.536	.500
Scor. Pos./2 Out	46	17	3	1	0	24	11	8	.370	.478	.491
Late-Inning Pressure	65	27	2	1	1	7	5	9	.415	.523	.472
Leading Off	15	5	0	0	0	0	1	2	.333	.333	.375
Runners On	32	15	2	0	1	7	2	4	.469	.625	.500
Runners/Scor. Pos.	16	5	1	0	0	5	1	2	.313	.375	.353

RUNS BATTED IN	From 1B	From 2B	From 3B	Scoring Position
Totals	7/116	27/92	32/48	59/140
Percentage	6.0%	29.3%	66.7%	42.1%

Loves to face: Neal Heaton (.600, 6-for-10)
Randy Kramer (.429, 3-for-7, 1 HR)
Mike Morgan (.545, 6-for-11)

Hates to face: Pat Combs (.077, 1-for-13, 1 HR, 2 BB)
Orel Hershiser (0-for-11, 1 BB)
Jose Rijo (.100, 1-for-10)

Miscellaneous statistics: Ground outs-to-air outs ratio: 1.05 last season, 1.17 for career.... Grounded into 11 double plays in 86 opportunities (one per 7.8).... Drove in 20 of 30 runners from third base with less than two outs (67%).... Direction of balls hit to the outfield: 36% to left field, 31% to center, 33% to right.... Base running: Advanced from first base to third on 8 of 29 outfield singles (28%); scored from second on 13 of 18 (72%).... Made 0.71 assists per nine innings at first base.

Comments: Had only one extra-base hit in 60 at-bats under Davey Johnson, compared to 39 XBH in 391 AB after Bud Harrelson urged him to increase his run productivity.... Batted 115 points higher vs. right-handers (.371) than vs. left-handers (.256) last season, the largest margin in the majors. Over the last 16 years, only two National League players had higher averages vs. right-handed pitchers (minimum: 75 hits): Hal Morris (.378 last season) and Tony Gwynn (.376 in 1987, and .371 in 1984).... Batted 94 points higher in road games (.372) than in home games (.278) last season, the 4th-largest margin in the majors. Only three players in the last 16 years had higher averages in road games: George Brett (.388 in 1980), Cecil Cooper (.386 in 1980), and Rod Carew (.374 in 1977).... Batted 129 points higher with runners on base (.406) than with the bases empty (.277) last season, the 5th-largest margin in the majors.... Now strap on your helmets—Magadan vs. right-handed pitchers with runners on base in road games last season: .500 (28-for-56).... Drove in 42.1 percent of runners from scoring position last season, the highest rate in the majors.... Led the Mets with 37 hits to the opposite field.... Led major league first basemen with a .998 fielding percentage (two errors in 903 chances).... Enters the 1990 season with a .305 career mark in 478 games. No player in franchise history has batted .300 in 500 or more games. Among players with 500 games for New York, only Keith Hernandez (.297) came within 15 points of the .300 mark.

Carmelo Martinez

Bats Right

Phillies/Pirates	AB	H	2B	3B	HR	RBI	BB	SO	BA	SA	OBA
Season	217	52	9	0	10	35	30	42	.240	.419	.332
vs. Left-Handers	90	21	5	0	5	16	15	15	.233	.456	.343
vs. Right-Handers	127	31	4	0	5	19	15	27	.244	.394	.324
vs. Ground-Ballers	117	30	5	0	4	23	16	23	.256	.402	.346
vs. Fly-Ballers	100	22	4	0	6	12	14	19	.220	.440	.316
Home Games	122	28	5	0	6	17	12	25	.230	.418	.299
Road Games	95	24	4	0	4	18	18	17	.253	.421	.372
Grass Fields	50	14	3	0	4	12	9	11	.280	.580	.390
Artificial Turf	167	38	6	0	6	23	21	31	.228	.371	.314
April	27	6	0	0	2	6	6	4	.222	.444	.364
May	30	9	3	0	2	7	3	6	.300	.600	.364
June	30	8	1	0	1	7	1	6	.267	.400	.290
July	69	16	2	0	3	8	14	13	.232	.391	.361
August	43	9	2	0	0	3	5	8	.209	.256	.292
Sept./Oct.	18	4	1	0	2	4	1	5	.222	.611	.263
Leading Off Inn.	45	9	2	0	1	1	2	8	.200	.311	.234
Bases Empty	112	24	4	0	5	5	14	21	.214	.384	.302
Runners On	105	28	5	0	5	30	16	21	.267	.457	.364
Runners/Scor. Pos.	72	19	5	0	4	28	14	14	.264	.500	.384
Runners On/2 Out	58	16	2	0	4	20	9	15	.276	.517	.373
Scor. Pos./2 Out	45	12	2	0	3	18	7	11	.267	.511	.365
Late-Inning Pressure	36	8	1	0	4	8	6	5	.222	.583	.333
Leading Off	5	0	0	0	0	0	0	1	.000	.000	.000
Runners On	13	4	1	0	1	5	4	1	.308	.615	.471
Runners/Scor. Pos.	10	2	1	0	1	5	2	1	.200	.600	.333

RUNS BATTED IN	From 1B	From 2B	From 3B	Scoring Position
Totals	5/73	10/51	10/30	20/81
Percentage	6.8%	19.6%	33.3%	24.7%

Loves to face: John Burkett (.667, 4-for-6, 1 HR)
Atlee Hammaker (.421, 8-for-19, 1 2B, 4 HR, 9 BB)
Bob Ojeda (.500, 8-for-16, 1 HR)

Hates to face: Norm Charlton (0-for-11)
Rob Dibble (0-for-9)
Lee Smith (.143, 2-for-14)

Miscellaneous statistics: Ground outs-to-air outs ratio: 0.64 last season, 0.85 for career.... Grounded into 3 double plays in 42 opportunities (one per 14.0).... Drove in 4 of 10 runners from third base with less than two outs (40%).... Direction of balls hit to the outfield: 52% to left field, 29% to center, 19% to right.... Base running: Advanced from first base to third on 5 of 17 outfield singles (29%); scored from second on 3 of 4 (75%).... Made 0.75 assists per nine innings at first base.

Comments: His 87 walks with the Padres in 1985 are the most ever by a Latin-American player. That record survived a challange by Julio Franco last season; he finished the season with 82 bases on balls.... Since 1987, Martinez has walked more than 35 times only once in five seasons.... Started only three games for the Pirates after his acquisition in late August. He batted .211 in 12 regular-season games for Pittsburgh.... Martinez is taking that long, slow walk down Platoon Road. His total of plate appearances vs. right-handed pitchers has decreased in every season since 1987: 302, 228, 169, 142.... Owns a career average of .194 with only one home run in 151 at-bats at the Astrodome. His career average at Candlestick Park (.320) is his highest at any ballpark.... Career stolen-base percentage is only 40 percent (10-for-25).... Career batting average of .190 in postseason (8-for-42).... Quick: For which team did Martinez make his big-league debut? See answer below.... Forget Wes Chamberlain (assuming you know who he is in the first place). If Martinez (who hit four home runs in 36 at-bats in Late-Inning Pressure Situations, the best rate in the majors) had cleared the right-field fence in Riverfront in the ninth inning of the sixth game of the N.L.C.S., the Chamberlain deal might have gone down as the greatest in Pirates history.... Martinez played 29 games for the Cubs in 1983, his first season in the majors, then was traded to the Padres in December and came back to face Chicago in the 1984 N.L.C.S.

Dave Martinez

Bats Left

Montreal Expos	AB	H	2B	3B	HR	RBI	BB	SO	BA	SA	OBA
Season	391	109	13	5	11	39	24	48	.279	.422	.321
vs. Left-Handers	78	19	0	1	1	11	11	15	.244	.308	.333
vs. Right-Handers	313	90	13	4	10	28	13	33	.288	.450	.317
vs. Ground-Ballers	231	74	11	3	8	23	10	28	.320	.498	.349
vs. Fly-Ballers	160	35	2	2	3	16	14	20	.219	.313	.282
Home Games	204	56	7	0	5	18	11	27	.275	.382	.309
Road Games	187	53	6	5	6	21	13	21	.283	.465	.333
Grass Fields	97	22	5	2	1	9	3	15	.227	.351	.250
Artificial Turf	294	87	8	3	10	30	21	33	.296	.446	.343
April	7	1	0	0	0	0	0	3	.143	.143	.143
May	47	13	2	0	1	5	2	7	.277	.383	.306
June	112	34	4	3	4	14	10	17	.304	.500	.355
July	66	22	1	0	4	5	4	6	.333	.530	.380
August	83	23	3	1	2	12	3	7	.277	.410	.302
Sept./Oct.	76	16	3	1	0	3	5	8	.211	.276	.259
Leading Off Inn.	87	26	3	1	2	2	6	7	.299	.425	.344
Bases Empty	237	67	5	2	7	7	14	28	.283	.409	.323
Runners On	154	42	8	3	4	32	10	20	.273	.442	.317
Runners/Scor. Pos.	92	22	5	1	3	28	9	14	.239	.413	.308
Runners On/2 Out	66	13	3	0	1	11	5	12	.197	.288	.254
Scor. Pos./2 Out	48	9	2	0	1	11	5	10	.188	.292	.264
Late-Inning Pressure	55	12	1	2	0	8	3	8	.218	.309	.254
Leading Off	10	1	0	0	0	0	2	1	.100	.100	.250
Runners On	21	4	1	2	0	8	1	6	.190	.429	.217
Runners/Scor. Pos.	12	2	0	1	0	7	1	4	.167	.333	.214

RUNS BATTED IN	From 1B	From 2B	From 3B	Scoring Position
Totals	5/94	15/82	8/24	23/106
Percentage	5.3%	18.3%	33.3%	21.7%

Loves to face: Jose DeJesus (.625, 5-for-8, 2 HR)
Mike Morgan (.833, 5-for-6)
Scott Terry (.556, 5-for-9, 3 2B)

Hates to face: Jose DeLeon (.143, 3-for-21, 3 BB)
Kevin Gross (.136, 3-for-22, 3 BB)
Alejandro Pena (.091, 1-for-11)

Miscellaneous statistics: Ground outs-to-air outs ratio: 0.99 last season, 1.00 for career.... Grounded into 8 double plays in 60 opportunities (one per 7.5).... Drove in 7 of 11 runners from third base with less than two outs (64%).... Direction of balls hit to the outfield: 23% to left field, 36% to center, 41% to right.... Base running: Advanced from first base to third on 10 of 22 outfield singles (45%); scored from second on 12 of 14 (86%).... Made 2.81 putouts per nine innings in center field.

Comments: His average of 2.38 putouts per game last season was the highest by an Expos outfielder since 1984, when Tim Raines had 2.63 per game (minimum: 100 games). The team record: 3.17, by Andre Dawson in 1981.... Started 86 games vs. right-handed pitchers, but only 10 games against left-handers.... Was removed in favor of a pinch-hitter 22 times last season, all against left-handed pitchers.... Career batting averages: .214 vs. lefties, .273 vs. right-handers.... Was thrown out trying to advance an extra base on a batted ball seven times last season, tying Delino DeShields and Andres Galarraga for the team lead.... Stole only 13 bases in 24 attempts last season, compared to a rate of 74 percent in four previous seasons (66-for-89).... Has no home runs in 256 career at-bats in Late-Inning Pressure Situations. He has an average of one home run per 52 at-bats at other times.... Has homered in every current National League ballpark except Jack Murphy Stadium (79 career AB).... Buck Rodgers sent Martinez and Junior Noboa to the mound in the Astros' 12–6 romp over the Expos on July 20. It was more of a romp until the Expos' six-run ninth-inning rally had Noboa dreaming of a victory. (Would *USA Today* have given Martinez a "hold"?) ... Martinez has now played 543 games in the outfield, one as a pitcher, and none in the infield.

Oddibe McDowell

Bats Left

Atlanta Braves	AB	H	2B	3B	HR	RBI	BB	SO	BA	SA	OBA
Season	305	74	14	0	7	25	21	53	.243	.357	.295
vs. Left-Handers	39	4	0	0	0	1	5	8	.103	.103	.222
vs. Right-Handers	266	70	14	0	7	24	16	45	.263	.395	.306
vs. Ground-Ballers	150	30	6	0	3	13	13	27	.200	.300	.273
vs. Fly-Ballers	155	44	8	0	4	12	8	26	.284	.413	.317
Home Games	150	41	7	0	4	14	10	21	.273	.400	.321
Road Games	155	33	7	0	3	11	11	32	.213	.316	.269
Grass Fields	230	57	9	0	7	23	16	38	.248	.378	.298
Artificial Turf	75	17	5	0	0	2	5	15	.227	.293	.284
April	50	10	2	0	2	8	4	10	.200	.360	.259
May	65	16	4	0	1	5	5	10	.246	.354	.296
June	74	24	3	0	2	10	2	11	.324	.446	.351
July	42	8	2	0	1	1	4	8	.190	.310	.261
August	45	10	3	0	0	0	5	3	.222	.289	.300
Sept./Oct.	29	6	0	0	1	1	1	11	.207	.310	.258
Leading Off Inn.	128	35	11	0	4	4	7	18	.273	.453	.311
Bases Empty	218	50	11	0	4	4	13	37	.229	.335	.276
Runners On	87	24	3	0	3	21	8	16	.276	.414	.340
Runners/Scor. Pos.	50	17	2	0	3	21	5	10	.340	.560	.404
Runners On/2 Out	44	14	1	0	2	11	3	8	.318	.477	.375
Scor. Pos./2 Out	26	8	1	0	2	11	2	5	.308	.577	.379
Late-Inning Pressure	45	8	3	0	1	2	2	7	.178	.311	.208
Leading Off	19	5	3	0	1	1	0	2	.263	.579	.263
Runners On	12	2	0	0	0	1	2	1	.167	.167	.267
Runners/Scor. Pos.	4	0	0	0	0	1	1	0	.000	.000	.167

RUNS BATTED IN	From 1B	From 2B	From 3B	Scoring Position
Totals	3/59	7/43	8/19	15/62
Percentage	5.1%	16.3%	42.1%	24.2%

Loves to face: Mike Morgan (.444, 12-for-27, 2 HR)
Calvin Schiraldi (.667, 2-for-3, 2 HR)
Frank Viola (.318, 7-for-22, 1 2B, 1 3B, 1 HR)

Hates to face: Oil Can Boyd (.179, 7-for-39)
Mark Portugal (.125, 2-for-16, 1 HR)
Bob Ojeda (.083, 1-for-12)

Miscellaneous statistics: Ground outs-to-air outs ratio: 1.12 last season, 1.08 for career.... Grounded into 3 double plays in 31 opportunities (one per 10.3).... Drove in 5 of 9 runners from third base with less than two outs (56%).... Direction of balls hit to the outfield: 22% to left field, 28% to center, 51% to right.... Base running: Advanced from first base to third on 5 of 20 outfield singles (25%); scored from second on 6 of 9 (67%).... Made 2.25 putouts per nine innings in center field.

Comments: Started 67 games against right-handed pitchers, but only two games against left-handers. Oddibe batted .244 vs. southpaws as a rookie with Texas in 1985, but hasn't reached the .230 mark since then. He hasn't homered off a left-hander since 1988.... Only eight of his 74 hits were to the opposite field.... Started from the second slot in the batting order on September 29, snapping a streak of 136 starts in the leadoff position since joining the Braves in 1989.... The Braves led the National League with 20 home runs from the leadoff spot in their batting order. McDowell and Lonnie Smith contributed seven apiece; Ron Gant added the other six homers in only 75 leadoff at-bats. With all that power, it's no surprise that Braves leadoff hitters had both the fewest stolen bases (21) and the lowest stolen-base percentage (.636) in the league.... Stole only 13 bases last season; he had stolen at least 24 in each of five previous seasons.... His batting average with runners in scoring position was 7th-highest in the National League among players with at least 50 at-bats (a level at which he just qualifies).... Hit 50 home runs over the first three years of his career, but has hit only 23 homers in three years since then.

Kevin McReynolds

Bats Right

New York Mets	AB	H	2B	3B	HR	RBI	BB	SO	BA	SA	OBA
Season	521	140	23	1	24	82	71	61	.269	.455	.353
vs. Left-Handers	194	45	11	0	4	15	38	20	.232	.351	.358
vs. Right-Handers	327	95	12	1	20	67	33	41	.291	.517	.350
vs. Ground-Ballers	242	68	9	0	14	43	35	31	.281	.492	.367
vs. Fly-Ballers	279	72	14	1	10	39	36	30	.258	.423	.340
Home Games	244	63	8	0	11	39	31	25	.258	.426	.336
Road Games	277	77	15	1	13	43	40	36	.278	.480	.368
Grass Fields	359	99	16	0	21	64	46	38	.276	.496	.354
Artificial Turf	162	41	7	1	3	18	25	23	.253	.364	.351
April	52	15	1	0	1	8	7	3	.288	.365	.367
May	83	21	3	0	5	15	12	9	.253	.470	.351
June	91	21	7	0	6	16	20	9	.231	.505	.366
July	97	27	6	1	1	12	20	10	.278	.392	.392
August	104	26	1	0	5	15	6	17	.250	.404	.286
Sept./Oct.	94	30	5	0	6	16	6	13	.319	.564	.360
Leading Off Inn.	113	26	3	0	5	5	14	15	.230	.389	.320
Bases Empty	287	73	10	0	14	14	30	27	.254	.436	.327
Runners On	234	67	13	1	10	68	41	34	.286	.479	.382
Runners/Scor. Pos.	132	39	7	1	6	58	34	19	.295	.500	.420
Runners On/2 Out	107	28	5	1	1	21	29	14	.262	.355	.419
Scor. Pos./2 Out	64	16	2	1	0	18	22	8	.250	.313	.442
Late-Inning Pressure	87	25	1	0	4	16	11	7	.287	.437	.364
Leading Off	18	5	0	0	1	1	2	1	.278	.444	.350
Runners On	37	10	0	0	2	14	7	4	.270	.432	.378
Runners/Scor. Pos.	20	6	0	0	1	12	5	3	.300	.450	.423

RUNS BATTED IN	From 1B	From 2B	From 3B	Scoring Position
Totals	12/176	17/101	29/55	46/156
Percentage	6.8%	16.8%	52.7%	29.5%

Loves to face: Bill Landrum (.636, 7-for-11)
Jeff Parrett (.429, 9-for-21, 3 HR)
Dave Smith (.389, 7-for-18, 3 HR)

Hates to face: Tim Burke (.148, 4-for-27)
Pat Combs (.105, 2-for-19)
Danny Jackson (.095, 2-for-21)

Miscellaneous statistics: Ground outs-to-air outs ratio: 0.60 last season, 3d-lowest rate in N.L.; 0.75 for career.... Grounded into 8 double plays in 106 opportunities (one per 13.3).... Drove in 16 of 25 runners from third base with less than two outs (64%).... Direction of balls hit to the outfield: 40% to left field, 32% to center, 27% to right.... Base running: Advanced from first base to third on 13 of 31 outfield singles (42%); scored from second on 13 of 13.... Made 1.72 putouts per nine innings in left field, lowest rate in N.L.

Comments: New York's inability to beat left-handers last season made McReynolds's struggle against lefties impossible to overlook. His batting average vs. LHP, year-by-year since 1986 (his last season with San Diego): .339, .290, .270, .296, .232.... In four seasons with the Mets, McReynolds has played 586 games in left field and one in center, and has only heard rumors of the existence of right field. But in four seasons with the Padres, he played 434 in center, 110 games in left, and 13 in right.... Year-to-year consistency is his forte. Over the past five seasons, his batting average has fallen within a 19-point range (.269 to .288). He has hit between 22 and 29 home runs with between 82 and 99 RBIs in each of those seasons.... Hit all 24 of his home runs to left field. Switch-hitting teammate Howard Johnson also pulled all 23 of his home runs, hitting none to either center or the opposite field. Among players with at least 20 home runs last season, only McReynolds, Johnson, Cal Ripken and Chris Sabo did that.... Drew a career-high 71 walks last season.... Batting average has been higher in road games than at Shea Stadium in each of his four seasons with the Mets.... He's been on a three-year tear with the bases loaded. Since 1988, he has batted .548 (17-for-31) with four home runs, three walks, and no strikeouts.... Has played at least 147 games in each of the last seven seasons. Among National League players, only Dale Murphy has a longer streak (9).

Keith Miller

Bats Right

New York Mets	AB	H	2B	3B	HR	RBI	BB	SO	BA	SA	OBA
Season	233	60	8	0	1	12	23	46	.258	.305	.327
vs. Left-Handers	149	43	7	0	0	8	12	27	.289	.336	.340
vs. Right-Handers	84	17	1	0	1	4	11	19	.202	.250	.306
vs. Ground-Ballers	111	32	3	0	0	6	15	26	.288	.315	.367
vs. Fly-Ballers	122	28	5	0	1	6	8	20	.230	.295	.288
Home Games	107	25	3	0	1	9	19	19	.234	.290	.349
Road Games	126	35	5	0	0	3	4	27	.278	.317	.306
Grass Fields	145	35	4	0	1	10	20	28	.241	.290	.331
Artificial Turf	88	25	4	0	0	2	3	18	.284	.330	.319
April	52	13	5	0	1	3	8	9	.250	.404	.350
May	25	7	0	0	0	0	0	4	.280	.280	.280
June	44	13	1	0	0	4	3	7	.295	.318	.327
July	28	10	0	0	0	1	0	6	.357	.357	.379
August	33	8	0	0	0	3	3	9	.242	.242	.324
Sept./Oct.	51	9	2	0	0	1	9	11	.176	.216	.300
Leading Off Inn.	90	26	4	0	0	0	13	14	.289	.333	.385
Bases Empty	166	44	8	0	0	0	17	32	.265	.313	.337
Runners On	67	16	0	0	1	12	6	14	.239	.284	.303
Runners/Scor. Pos.	35	7	0	0	0	10	5	10	.200	.200	.302
Runners On/2 Out	34	10	0	0	0	3	1	6	.294	.294	.314
Scor. Pos./2 Out	19	5	0	0	0	3	1	4	.263	.263	.300
Late-Inning Pressure	41	11	0	0	0	1	2	9	.268	.268	.318
Leading Off	16	4	0	0	0	0	2	3	.250	.250	.368
Runners On	8	1	0	0	0	1	0	3	.125	.125	.125
Runners/Scor. Pos.	3	1	0	0	0	1	0	1	.333	.333	.333

RUNS BATTED IN	From 1B	From 2B	From 3B	Scoring Position
Totals	1/45	3/30	7/14	10/44
Percentage	2.2%	10.0%	50.0%	22.7%

Loves to face: Brian Barnes (2-for-2, 2 BB)
Neal Heaton (.667, 6-for-9)

Hates to face: Paul Assenmacher (.111, 1-for-9, 7 SO)
Chris Nabholz (0-for-7)

Miscellaneous statistics: Ground outs-to-air outs ratio: 1.42 last season, 1.55 for career. . . . Grounded into 2 double plays in 29 opportunities (one per 14.5). . . . Drove in 6 of 8 runners from third base with less than two outs (75%). . . . Direction of balls hit to the outfield: 49% to left field, 28% to center, 22% to right. . . . Base running: Advanced from first base to third on 13 of 19 outfield singles (68%), shared highest rate in N.L.; scored from second on 10 of 10. . . . Made 3.23 putouts per nine innings in center field.

Comments: One of four National League players to start at least one game at five different fielding positions (2B, SS, LF, CF, and RF). . . . He was the Mets' opening-day center fielder in 1990, despite only 16 games of previous major league experience (and 25 games in the minors) in the outfield. . . . His technique often belied his lack of experience. But in fairness to Miller, his average of 3.23 putouts per nine innings in center field was third-highest among the 46 major leaguers with 250 or more innings there. . . . Excluding pitchers, Miller and Terry Puhl were the only National League players to be placed on the disabled list twice last season. . . . Career batting-average breakdowns: .263 with the bases empty, .239 with runners on base, .187 with runners in scoring position; .281 vs. left-handed pitchers, .228 vs. right-handers; .232 at Shea Stadium, .234 on other grass fields, .290 on artificial surfaces. . . . Has played for the Mets in each of the last four seasons, increasing his playing time each year. Games played year-by-year since 1987: 25, 40, 57, 88. . . . Has driven in one of 41 runners with none out in four seasons (2.4%). The major league average: 27 percent. . . . Has stolen 22 bases in 25 attempts over the past two seasons, after going 0-for-5 in 1988. . . . Where have you gone, Joe DiMaggio? Forget Mr. Coffee—the Mets would take back Lenny and Mookie in a New York minute.

Kevin Mitchell

Bats Right

San Francisco Giants	AB	H	2B	3B	HR	RBI	BB	SO	BA	SA	OBA
Season	524	152	24	2	35	93	58	87	.290	.544	.360
vs. Left-Handers	170	52	11	0	10	29	27	24	.306	.547	.395
vs. Right-Handers	354	100	13	2	25	64	31	63	.282	.542	.342
vs. Ground-Ballers	234	72	10	1	17	42	28	39	.308	.577	.383
vs. Fly-Ballers	290	80	14	1	18	51	30	48	.276	.517	.342
Home Games	241	67	10	1	15	39	31	36	.278	.515	.360
Road Games	283	85	14	1	20	54	27	51	.300	.569	.360
Grass Fields	383	111	19	1	22	63	43	64	.290	.517	.361
Artificial Turf	141	41	5	1	13	30	15	23	.291	.617	.356
April	71	22	4	0	4	9	8	15	.310	.535	.380
May	96	30	3	1	8	15	11	15	.313	.615	.380
June	91	28	6	0	7	21	10	11	.308	.604	.376
July	77	25	3	0	6	17	9	16	.325	.597	.391
August	104	28	4	0	6	18	11	15	.269	.481	.342
Sept./Oct.	85	19	4	1	4	13	9	15	.224	.435	.299
Leading Off Inn.	121	41	5	1	11	11	14	16	.339	.669	.407
Bases Empty	258	88	11	1	24	24	25	42	.341	.671	.399
Runners On	266	64	13	1	11	69	33	45	.241	.421	.324
Runners/Scor. Pos.	153	34	7	0	2	49	25	25	.222	.307	.330
Runners On/2 Out	135	30	4	1	7	28	21	23	.222	.422	.331
Scor. Pos./2 Out	75	13	2	0	0	13	17	13	.173	.200	.333
Late-Inning Pressure	77	27	3	0	7	13	10	8	.351	.662	.420
Leading Off	20	7	1	0	3	3	5	4	.350	.850	.480
Runners On	40	11	1	0	1	7	3	3	.275	.375	.318
Runners/Scor. Pos.	25	5	1	0	0	5	3	2	.200	.240	.276

RUNS BATTED IN	From 1B	From 2B	From 3B	Scoring Position
Totals	15/199	17/111	26/66	43/177
Percentage	7.5%	15.3%	39.4%	24.3%

Loves to face: Tim Crews (.467, 7-for-15, 2 HR)
Mark Grant (.421, 8-for-19, 2 2B, 3 HR)
Rick Mahler (.419, 13-for-31, 3 HR)

Hates to face: Jim Gott (0-for-9, 1 BB)
Mike Morgan (.077, 1-for-13, 2 BB)
Terry Mulholland (.125, 2-for-16)

Miscellaneous statistics: Ground outs-to-air outs ratio: 0.71 last season, 0.77 for career. . . . Grounded into 8 double plays in 111 opportunities (one per 13.9). . . . Drove in 20 of 36 runners from third base with less than two outs (56%). . . . Direction of balls hit to the outfield: 41% to left field, 34% to center, 25% to right. . . . Base running: Advanced from first base to third on 13 of 33 outfield singles (39%); scored from second on 7 of 10 (70%). . . . Made 2.25 putouts per nine innings in left field.

Comments: Mitchell's rate of one home run per 15.9 at-bats with the Giants is third highest in franchise history. The top 10 is worth at least an hour of party chatter; fewest AB per HR (minimum: 50 HR): Willie McCovey, 15.4; Johnny Mize, 15.6; Mitchell, 15.9; Dave Kingman, 16.1; Willie Mays, 16.2; Ed Bailey (!) 18.2; Orlando Cepeda, 18.5; Mel Ott, 18.5; Matt Williams, 19.6; Walker Cooper, 19.6. . . . In the Giants essay (on p. 105), we point out that 12 players have hit at least 100 home runs after being traded from the Giants. Here's the flip side: Mitchell has become the fifth player to hit 100 homers after joining the Giants from another team. The others: George Kelly, Johnny Mize, Hank Thompson, and Darrell Evans. . . . A related note: Mitchell became the 20th player to hit 100 home runs with the Giants. No other teams has had as many 100-HR players. . . . Became only the third Giants outfielder to start the All-Star game since the club moved to San Francisco. The others: Willie Mays (16 times) and Orlando Cepeda (twice, both in 1961). . . . Batted 96 points lower with runners in scoring position (.222) than in other at-bats (.318) last season, the 4th-largest margin in the majors. . . . Has a career average of one home run per 17.6 at-bats, but has 47 career at-bats with the bases loaded without ever hitting a grand slam. . . . His last 331 starts, since July 31, 1988, have all been from the cleanup spot. He has also been the N.L.'s starting cleanup hitter in both All-Star games during that time.

Hal Morris

Bats Left

Cincinnati Reds	AB	H	2B	3B	HR	RBI	BB	SO	BA	SA	OBA
Season	309	105	22	3	7	36	21	32	.340	.498	.381
vs. Left-Handers	76	17	0	0	0	5	6	13	.224	.224	.280
vs. Right-Handers	233	88	22	3	7	31	15	19	.378	.588	.414
vs. Ground-Ballers	141	42	12	0	3	16	11	20	.298	.447	.351
vs. Fly-Ballers	168	63	10	3	4	20	10	12	.375	.542	.408
Home Games	148	50	12	1	3	20	12	13	.338	.493	.383
Road Games	161	55	10	2	4	16	9	19	.342	.503	.380
Grass Fields	109	33	7	2	1	8	7	14	.303	.431	.350
Artificial Turf	200	72	15	1	6	28	14	18	.360	.535	.398
April	12	2	0	0	0	0	1	4	.167	.167	.231
May	15	4	1	0	0	1	1	1	.267	.333	.313
June	18	8	2	0	0	3	1	2	.444	.556	.500
July	75	32	3	2	3	13	3	6	.427	.640	.438
August	93	28	8	0	3	8	4	9	.301	.484	.330
Sept./Oct.	96	31	8	1	1	11	11	10	.323	.458	.393
Leading Off Inn.	70	29	6	1	2	2	3	4	.414	.614	.438
Bases Empty	160	60	14	3	5	5	9	12	.375	.594	.412
Runners On	149	45	8	0	2	31	12	20	.302	.396	.350
Runners/Scor. Pos.	84	28	4	0	1	27	9	12	.333	.417	.389
Runners On/2 Out	45	11	4	0	0	12	5	5	.244	.333	.320
Scor. Pos./2 Out	28	9	3	0	0	11	4	2	.321	.429	.406
Late-Inning Pressure	49	11	4	0	0	2	0	5	.224	.306	.240
Leading Off	8	1	0	0	0	0	0	0	.125	.125	.125
Runners On	23	6	2	0	0	2	0	5	.261	.348	.261
Runners/Scor. Pos.	12	2	0	0	0	1	0	5	.167	.167	.167

RUNS BATTED IN	From 1B	From 2B	From 3B	Scoring Position
Totals	5/99	8/58	16/38	24/96
Percentage	5.1%	13.8%	42.1%	25.0%

Loves to face: Scott Garrelts (.545, 6-for-11, 1 HR)
Calvin Schiraldi (.500, 4-for-8, 1 HR)
John Smoltz (4-for-5)

Hates to face: Mike Bielecki (.200, 2-for-10)
Doug Drabek (0-for-6)
Ramon Martinez (.182, 2-for-11)

Miscellaneous statistics: Ground outs-to-air outs ratio: 1.42 last season, 1.40 for career. . . . Grounded into 12 double plays in 78 opportunities (one per 6.5). . . . Drove in 11 of 25 runners from third base with less than two outs (44%). . . . Direction of balls hit to the outfield: 36% to left field, 35% to center, 29% to right. . . . Base running: Advanced from first base to third on 5 of 13 outfield singles (38%); scored from second on 5 of 9 (56%). . . . Made 0.75 assists per nine innings at first base.

Comments: Since 1940, only two rookies compiled higher batting averages than Morris (minimum: 300 at-bats): Wade Boggs, .349 (1982) and Dan Gladden, .351 (1984). . . . Over the last 16 years, only three players had higher batting averages against right-handed pitchers than Morris did last year (minimum: 75 hits). See page 395 for a 25-deep list. . . . . Had 10 games in which he collected at least three hits, to lead all rookies despite spending part of the season in the minors; he didn't become a regular until July. . . . Career average of .364 on artificial turf is the highest of any active player with at least 200 at-bats. . . . Had 10 hits, including three home runs, in 19 at-bats at Veterans Stadium last season. . . . Has a career average of .188 in Late-Inning Pressure Situations, .353 in other at-bats. He has driven in only one of 18 runners from scoring position in LIPS. . . . Has 84 career at-bats vs. left-handed pitchers, with no extra-base hits. Over the last four seasons, only two other players had as many at-bats against southpaws with nothing longer than a single: Franklin Stubbs (86 AB in 1987) and Mike Scioscia (78 AB in 1988). . . . Statistical profile closely resembles that of Dwight Smith in 1989. The Reds hope for more, but Morris has yet to prove he's anything other than a platoon player.

Dale Murphy

Bats Right

Braves/Phillies	AB	H	2B	3B	HR	RBI	BB	SO	BA	SA	OBA
Season	563	138	23	1	24	83	61	130	.245	.417	.318
vs. Left-Handers	180	56	11	1	14	38	31	22	.311	.617	.410
vs. Right-Handers	383	82	12	0	10	45	30	108	.214	.324	.271
vs. Ground-Ballers	280	65	11	1	8	34	30	68	.232	.364	.305
vs. Fly-Ballers	283	73	12	0	16	49	31	62	.258	.470	.331
Home Games	279	64	9	1	9	27	31	66	.229	.366	.307
Road Games	284	74	14	0	15	56	30	64	.261	.468	.329
Grass Fields	325	81	12	0	16	51	32	80	.249	.434	.317
Artificial Turf	238	57	11	1	8	32	29	50	.239	.395	.320
April	58	15	2	0	2	8	7	12	.259	.397	.338
May	95	26	7	0	5	14	15	18	.274	.505	.375
June	104	18	2	0	4	17	7	30	.173	.308	.223
July	88	22	3	0	6	16	12	23	.250	.489	.337
August	112	28	5	0	2	15	6	24	.250	.348	.286
Sept./Oct.	106	29	4	1	5	13	14	23	.274	.472	.358
Leading Off Inn.	139	25	4	1	3	3	3	32	.180	.288	.197
Bases Empty	333	67	12	1	9	9	24	78	.201	.324	.255
Runners On	230	71	11	0	15	74	37	52	.309	.552	.401
Runners/Scor. Pos.	137	40	4	0	8	56	25	37	.292	.496	.395
Runners On/2 Out	119	41	6	0	6	38	19	26	.345	.546	.439
Scor. Pos./2 Out	77	24	3	0	3	30	14	20	.312	.468	.424
Late-Inning Pressure	86	15	2	0	3	7	16	24	.174	.302	.301
Leading Off	24	5	1	0	1	1	2	7	.208	.375	.269
Runners On	33	4	0	0	0	4	9	10	.121	.121	.302
Runners/Scor. Pos.	20	3	0	0	0	4	6	8	.150	.150	.333

RUNS BATTED IN	From 1B	From 2B	From 3B	Scoring Position
Totals	18/167	25/107	16/56	41/163
Percentage	10.8%	23.4%	28.6%	25.2%

Loves to face: Atlee Hammaker (.442, 19-for-43, 5 HR)
Bob Ojeda (.632, 12-for-19, 1 HR)
Fernando Valenzuela (.318, 35-for-110, 8 HR)

Hates to face: Rob Dibble (.133, 2-for-15, 7 SO)
Scott Garrelts (.133, 6-for-45, 2 HR, 5 BB)
Greg Maddux (.111, 2-for-18)

Miscellaneous statistics: Ground outs-to-air outs ratio: 1.06 last season, 1.26 for career. . . . Grounded into 22 double plays in 102 opportunities (one per 4.6), 3d-worst rate in N.L. . . . Drove in 12 of 27 runners from third base with less than two outs (44%). . . . Direction of balls hit to the outfield: 37% to left field, 37% to center, 26% to right. . . . Base running: Advanced from first base to third on 5 of 24 outfield singles (21%); scored from second on 7 of 12 (58%). . . . Made 2.22 putouts per nine innings in right field.

Comments: Career total of 378 home runs is 13th highest in National League history, with a chance to move into the top 10 this season. He needs 11 more to move past Johnny Bench, 15 to pass Billy Williams, and 30 to pass Duke Snider. Eighth place is shared by Willie Stargell and Stan Musial with 475 apiece, out of Murphy's reach. . . . The only other active players in the N.L.'s 30 all-time leading home run hitters are Andre Dawson (18th with 346) and Gary Carter (24th with 313). . . . Has hit for a higher average on grass fields than he has on artificial surfaces in each of the last five years. Career breakdown: .279 on grass, .238 on artificial turf. . . . Grounded into 22 double plays, the most in the National League last season. Who was the toughest player to double-up? Murphy's replacement in Atlanta, Dave Justice. . . . Batting average leading off innings was the lowest in the National League. . . . Has not had a sacrifice bunt since 1981. . . . Has struck out at least 100 times in each of the last nine seasons, matching Richie Allen for the 3d-longest streak in major league history. The two players with longer streaks of 100-strikeout seasons: Reggie Jackson (13 years), and Willie Stargell (12 years). . . . Has played at least 154 games (a full slate prior to expansion) in each of the nine seasons since the strike of '81. Cal Ripken also has a nine-year streak; only three players in major league history had longer ones: Pete Rose (12, 1969–80), Ron Santo (11, 1961–71), and Billy Williams (10, 1962–71).

Eddie Murray

Bats Left and Right

Los Angeles Dodgers	AB	H	2B	3B	HR	RBI	BB	SO	BA	SA	OBA
Season	558	184	22	3	26	95	82	64	.330	.520	.414
vs. Left-Handers	206	65	7	0	8	36	25	22	.316	.466	.387
vs. Right-Handers	352	119	15	3	18	59	57	42	.338	.551	.429
vs. Ground-Ballers	275	90	9	0	13	48	41	37	.327	.502	.412
vs. Fly-Ballers	283	94	13	3	13	47	41	27	.332	.537	.415
Home Games	271	93	11	1	12	43	49	28	.343	.524	.444
Road Games	287	91	11	2	14	52	33	36	.317	.516	.384
Grass Fields	410	139	16	1	21	73	64	44	.339	.537	.429
Artificial Turf	148	45	6	2	5	22	18	20	.304	.473	.373
April	78	22	3	0	3	11	11	11	.282	.436	.371
May	71	22	4	1	2	11	11	7	.310	.479	.398
June	82	23	2	1	4	14	12	9	.280	.476	.368
July	98	35	5	0	7	18	17	16	.357	.622	.453
August	117	36	2	1	4	24	12	11	.308	.444	.372
Sept./Oct.	112	46	6	0	6	17	19	10	.411	.625	.492
Leading Off Inn.	135	45	7	2	7	7	11	17	.333	.570	.384
Bases Empty	274	89	14	2	12	12	26	36	.325	.522	.385
Runners On	284	95	8	1	14	83	56	28	.335	.518	.439
Runners/Scor. Pos.	150	49	5	1	9	73	44	15	.327	.553	.470
Runners On/2 Out	124	33	2	0	5	25	32	17	.266	.403	.417
Scor. Pos./2 Out	64	16	2	0	4	23	25	8	.250	.469	.461
Late-Inning Pressure	71	24	2	0	2	10	11	11	.338	.451	.422
Leading Off	20	5	0	0	2	2	0	3	.250	.550	.250
Runners On	31	11	2	0	0	8	7	3	.355	.419	.462
Runners/Scor. Pos.	16	4	2	0	0	8	5	2	.250	.375	.409

RUNS BATTED IN	From 1B	From 2B	From 3B	Scoring Position
Totals	10/210	28/98	31/72	59/170
Percentage	4.8%	28.6%	43.1%	34.7%

Loves to face: Jose DeLeon (.524, 11-for-21, 4 HR)
Mark Grant (.500, 4-for-8, 2 HR)
Ed Whitson (.417, 10-for-24, 3 HR)

Hates to face: Ron Darling (0-for-7)
Bruce Hurst (.145, 9-for-62, 4 HR)
Rick Mahler (.118, 2-for-17)

Miscellaneous statistics: Ground outs-to-air outs ratio: 0.97 last season, 1.04 for career. . . . Grounded into 19 double plays in 134 opportunities (one per 7.1). . . . Drove in 23 of 36 runners from third base with less than two outs (64%). . . . Direction of balls hit to the outfield: 32% to left field, 28% to center, 41% to right batting left-handed; 46% to left, 25% to center, 28% to right batting right-handed. . . . Base running: Advanced from first base to third on 13 of 46 outfield singles (28%); scored from second on 17 of 25 (68%). . . . Made 0.79 assists per nine innings at first base.

Comments: Career total of 379 home runs ties him with Dwight Evans for the most among players active in 1990. See the Evans comment on page 127 for more on the HR race. . . . Had the highest batting average in the major leagues last season, even though he did not win the National League batting title. . . . Murray increased his batting average by 83 points from 1989 to 1990, the 2d-largest gain of any player with at least 300 at-bats in both seasons. (See the Phillies essay on page 87 for the largest increases of the past 50 years.) . . . Homered from both sides of the plate in the same game for the 10th time in his career, tying Mickey Mantle's all-time record. . . . Has a career average of .407 (66-for-162) with the bases loaded. His total of 15 career grand slams ranks eighth in major league history. . . . Has homered in every major league ballpark in which he has played, except Atlanta Stadium (66 career AB). . . . Has never hit fewer than 17 home runs in his 14-year career. Only five players in major league history had longer streaks of seasons with at least 17 home runs: Hank Aaron (20 years), Mel Ott (18), Babe Ruth (16), Willie Mays (15), and Mike Schmidt (15). . . . Has missed a total of 68 games during his 14 seasons in the majors, 25 of them in 1986 when a pulled hamstring put him on the disabled list for the only time.

Otis Nixon

Bats Left and Right

Montreal Expos	AB	H	2B	3B	HR	RBI	BB	SO	BA	SA	OBA
Season	231	58	6	2	1	20	28	33	.251	.307	.331
vs. Left-Handers	151	36	3	2	1	11	15	14	.238	.305	.307
vs. Right-Handers	80	22	3	0	0	9	13	19	.275	.313	.372
vs. Ground-Ballers	133	39	4	2	0	11	17	18	.293	.353	.373
vs. Fly-Ballers	98	19	2	0	1	9	11	15	.194	.245	.273
Home Games	108	26	3	2	0	8	13	18	.241	.306	.322
Road Games	123	32	3	0	1	12	15	15	.260	.309	.338
Grass Fields	62	17	3	0	1	8	5	10	.274	.371	.324
Artificial Turf	169	41	3	2	0	12	23	23	.243	.284	.333
April	9	1	0	0	0	0	0	1	.111	.111	.111
May	19	5	0	1	0	2	4	4	.263	.368	.375
June	35	9	2	0	0	4	7	5	.257	.314	.381
July	49	11	2	0	0	3	6	4	.224	.265	.309
August	53	17	0	0	1	6	4	10	.321	.377	.368
Sept./Oct.	66	15	2	1	0	5	7	9	.227	.288	.301
Leading Off Inn.	72	19	3	0	0	0	11	8	.264	.306	.361
Bases Empty	142	34	4	0	1	1	24	21	.239	.289	.349
Runners On	89	24	2	2	0	19	4	12	.270	.337	.298
Runners/Scor. Pos.	56	15	1	0	0	16	4	8	.268	.286	.311
Runners On/2 Out	37	9	0	1	0	6	3	4	.243	.297	.300
Scor. Pos./2 Out	27	6	0	0	0	5	3	3	.222	.222	.300
Late-Inning Pressure	60	20	2	0	0	4	6	11	.333	.367	.394
Leading Off	20	8	0	0	0	0	1	1	.400	.400	.429
Runners On	19	6	1	0	0	4	1	5	.316	.368	.350
Runners/Scor. Pos.	11	3	0	0	0	3	1	3	.273	.273	.333

RUNS BATTED IN	From 1B	From 2B	From 3B	Scoring Position
Totals	3/56	6/42	10/23	16/65
Percentage	5.4%	14.3%	43.5%	24.6%

Loves to face: Juan Agosto (.500, 5-for-10)
Les Lancaster (1-for-1, 1 2B, 2 BB)
Dennis Rasmussen (.500, 3-for-6, 1 HR)

Hates to face: Tom Browning (.059, 1-for-17, 2 BB)
Don Carman (0-for-13, 1 BB)
Sid Fernandez (0-for-10, 3 BB, 9 SO)

Miscellaneous statistics: Ground outs-to-air outs ratio: 1.10 last season, 1.41 for career. . . . Grounded into 2 double plays in 41 opportunities (one per 20.5). . . . Drove in 7 of 13 runners from third base with less than two outs (54%). . . . Direction of balls hit to the outfield: 40% to left field, 43% to center, 17% to right batting left-handed; 35% to left, 26% to center, 39% to right batting right-handed. . . . Base running: Advanced from first base to third on 5 of 10 outfield singles (50%); scored from second on 7 of 11 (64%). . . . Made 2.61 putouts per nine innings in center field.

Comments: Stole 50 bases last season. No player in major league history reached the 50-steal mark in so few at-bats. Others with 50 or more SB and less than 400 AB since 1900: Miguel Dilone (50 SB, 258 AB in 1978), Tim Raines (71 SB, 313 AB in 1981), Larry Lintz (50 SB, 319 AB in 1979). . . . Enters the 1991 season with 191 career steals in 625 games. To put that in perspective, Nixon should hit the 200 mark sometime bewteen the number of games it took Ty Cobb (616) and Lou Brock (703) to get there. It surprised us to find that 42 players stole 200 bases in their first 500 games (two-thirds of them in the 1800s). Vince Coleman stole 200 bases in his first 280 games, the fastest in this century. . . . Had a higher stolen base percentage with left-handed pitchers on the mound (29-for-34, 85%) than against right-handers (21-for-29, 72%). . . . Made 26 appearances as a pinch runner last season, 2d most in the National League to Dave Collins (33). . . . Among the 55 switch-hitters active in 1989 with at least 1000 career at-bats, only Steve Jeltz (.210) had a lower career batting average than Nixon (.228). . . . Has hit for a higher average in road games than in home games in each of the last five seasons. . . . Most career games among active batters who have never been hit by a pitch: Herm Winningham (665), John Kruk (634), and Nixon (625).

Charlie O'Brien

Bats Right

Brewers/Mets	AB	H	2B	3B	HR	RBI	BB	SO	BA	SA	OBA
Season	213	38	10	2	0	20	21	34	.178	.244	.259
vs. Left-Handers	112	16	7	1	0	7	9	18	.143	.223	.211
vs. Right-Handers	101	22	3	1	0	13	12	16	.218	.267	.310
vs. Ground-Ballers	101	17	3	0	0	5	9	17	.168	.198	.257
vs. Fly-Ballers	112	21	7	2	0	15	12	17	.188	.286	.262
Home Games	88	15	2	2	0	11	10	14	.170	.239	.260
Road Games	125	23	8	0	0	9	11	20	.184	.248	.259
Grass Fields	151	26	5	2	0	16	16	23	.172	.232	.257
Artificial Turf	62	12	5	0	0	4	5	11	.194	.274	.265
April	24	4	1	0	0	2	2	5	.167	.208	.259
May	30	6	2	1	0	4	2	6	.200	.333	.273
June	23	5	2	1	0	4	2	4	.217	.391	.280
July	32	4	1	0	0	1	1	5	.125	.156	.152
August	36	8	1	0	0	0	4	6	.222	.250	.300
Sept./Oct.	68	11	3	0	0	9	10	8	.162	.206	.272
Leading Off Inn.	48	6	2	0	0	0	4	10	.125	.167	.192
Bases Empty	123	15	5	0	0	0	13	23	.122	.163	.212
Runners On	90	23	5	2	0	20	8	11	.256	.356	.324
Runners/Scor. Pos.	50	12	3	2	0	20	7	6	.240	.380	.333
Runners On/2 Out	41	13	4	1	0	11	4	3	.317	.463	.378
Scor. Pos./2 Out	26	7	3	1	0	11	4	2	.269	.462	.367
Late-Inning Pressure	27	6	1	0	0	0	2	5	.222	.259	.276
Leading Off	7	1	0	0	0	0	1	2	.143	.143	.250
Runners On	9	3	0	0	0	0	0	0	.333	.333	.333
Runners/Scor. Pos.	4	0	0	0	0	0	0	0	.000	.000	.000

RUNS BATTED IN	From 1B	From 2B	From 3B	Scoring Position
Totals	4/67	8/42	8/22	16/64
Percentage	6.0%	19.0%	36.4%	25.0%

Loves to face: Chuck Cary (.500, 2-for-4, 2 2B)
Greg Maddux (.500, 2-for-4)
Jamie Moyer (.400, 2-for-5, 1 HR)

Hates to face: Pat Combs (0-for-5)
Mark Langston (.111, 1-for-9)

Miscellaneous statistics: Ground outs-to-air outs ratio: 0.78 last season, 0.92 for career.... Grounded into 4 double plays in 46 opportunities (one per 11.5).... Drove in 5 of 7 runners from third base with less than two outs (71%).... Direction of balls hit to the outfield: 50% to left field, 33% to center, 17% to right.... Base running: Advanced from first base to third on 3 of 10 outfield singles (30%); scored from second on 5 of 6 (83%).... Opposing base stealers: 40-for-70 (57%), 4th-lowest rate in majors.

Comments: Here's some tough trivia. O'Brien is one of only two nonpitchers to have played at least one game with the Athletics, the Brewers, and the Mets. Who is the other? Answer below.... Batted .162 in 28 games for the Mets. The lowest single-season batting average in club history, excluding pitchers, was .133 by Bobby Valentine in 1977 (11-for-83).... His batting average vs. left-handers was the lowest of any right-handed batter in the majors last season (minimum: 75 AB).... Batting average vs. ground-ball pitchers was the 2d lowest in the majors, behind Ron Kittle's .145 average (minimum: 100 AB).... Has made the most of his .209 career batting average; the breakdown: .159 with the bases empty, .277 with runners on base, .284 with runners in scoring position, .292 with two outs and RISP, .333 with the bases loaded.... Brewers pitchers allowed 4.55 runs per nine innings with O'Brien behind the plate, 4.80 runs per nine innings with B.J. Surhoff calling the signals. According to those figures, O'Brien saved the Brewers about one run every four games; but his effect on Mets pitchers was negligible (3.80 runs per nine innings with O'Brien, 3.84 with other catchers).... If you knew that Tommie Reynolds also played for the A's, the Brewers, and the Mets, apply immediately for a job at the all-sports radio station nearest you.

Joe Oliver

Bats Right

Cincinnati Reds	AB	H	2B	3B	HR	RBI	BB	SO	BA	SA	OBA
Season	364	84	23	0	8	52	37	75	.231	.360	.304
vs. Left-Handers	180	51	13	0	5	28	18	34	.283	.439	.350
vs. Right-Handers	184	33	10	0	3	24	19	41	.179	.283	.260
vs. Ground-Ballers	180	42	12	0	3	23	15	36	.233	.350	.294
vs. Fly-Ballers	184	42	11	0	5	29	22	39	.228	.370	.314
Home Games	172	38	13	0	3	25	20	38	.221	.349	.306
Road Games	192	46	10	0	5	27	17	37	.240	.370	.303
Grass Fields	105	22	8	0	2	14	6	26	.210	.343	.250
Artificial Turf	259	62	15	0	6	38	31	49	.239	.367	.325
April	52	13	3	0	0	2	7	10	.250	.308	.339
May	76	20	3	0	5	16	11	10	.263	.500	.364
June	73	15	3	0	0	9	9	18	.205	.247	.293
July	70	15	5	0	1	12	6	19	.214	.329	.273
August	49	12	4	0	2	8	1	8	.245	.449	.260
Sept./Oct.	44	9	5	0	0	5	3	10	.205	.318	.271
Leading Off Inn.	84	16	4	0	3	3	5	18	.190	.345	.244
Bases Empty	191	37	9	0	4	4	16	41	.194	.304	.263
Runners On	173	47	14	0	4	48	21	34	.272	.422	.349
Runners/Scor. Pos.	106	29	11	0	3	45	17	20	.274	.462	.371
Runners On/2 Out	68	17	7	0	1	22	14	16	.250	.397	.378
Scor. Pos./2 Out	51	14	7	0	1	22	12	11	.275	.471	.413
Late-Inning Pressure	38	7	3	0	1	4	4	6	.184	.342	.262
Leading Off	15	2	0	0	0	0	1	2	.133	.133	.188
Runners On	14	2	2	0	0	3	2	2	.143	.286	.250
Runners/Scor. Pos.	11	1	1	0	0	2	1	2	.091	.182	.167

RUNS BATTED IN	From 1B	From 2B	From 3B	Scoring Position
Totals	11/126	16/77	17/42	33/119
Percentage	8.7%	20.8%	40.5%	27.7%

Loves to face: Steve Avery (.667, 4-for-6)
Zane Smith (.429, 9-for-21, 3 HR)

Hates to face: John Burkett (0-for-9)
Randy Kramer (0-for-6)
Joe Magrane (.083, 1-for-12)

Miscellaneous statistics: Ground outs-to-air outs ratio: 0.83 last season, 0.79 for career.... Grounded into 6 double plays in 85 opportunities (one per 14.2).... Drove in 9 of 18 runners from third base with less than two outs (50%).... Direction of balls hit to the outfield: 46% to left field, 26% to center, 28% to right.... Base running: Advanced from first base to third on 3 of 14 outfield singles (21%); scored from second on 9 of 11 (82%).... Opposing base stealers: 64-for-107 (60%), 2d-lowest rate in N.L.

Comments: Was charged with 16 passed balls last season, tying him with Joe Girardi for most among National League catchers.... Became only the fifth Reds catcher in more than 60 years to lead the league in fielding percentage (one error per 125 chances).... With time on his side, Oliver could become the first Cincinnati backstop to win two fielding titles since Bubbles Hargrave (1926–27). Since Bubbles's days, four other Reds catchers won one title each: Ray Mueller (1946), Johnny Edwards (1963), Johnny Bench (1976), and Joe Nolan (1981).... In 20 seasons since 1971, 18 different catchers have led the National League in fielding percentage. The only players to do it twice: Gary Carter (1980 and 1983) and Tony Pena (1988–89).... Oliver's average was the worst to lead the league since 1978, when Bob Boone led with an average of one error per 113 chances.... Started 88 of 115 games through August 15, but only 19 of 47 games thereafter.... Led the National League with 44 RBIs from the eighth slot in the batting order.... Was removed for a pinch hitter 18 times last season, all against right-handed pitchers.... Among players who batted at least 200 times against right-handed pitchers last season, only Rob Deer (.170) had a lower average.... He's a career .302 hitter vs. left-handed pitchers, but has a mark of only .183 against right-handers.... Had the lowest night-game batting average (.201) of any regular player in the National League. Has a career average of .328 in day games, .214 at night.

Greg Olson

Bats Right

Atlanta Braves	AB	H	2B	3B	HR	RBI	BB	SO	BA	SA	OBA
Season	298	78	12	1	7	36	30	51	.262	.379	.332
vs. Left-Handers	154	48	9	1	5	25	15	26	.312	.481	.374
vs. Right-Handers	144	30	3	0	2	11	15	25	.208	.271	.287
vs. Ground-Ballers	144	36	4	0	3	18	15	19	.250	.340	.323
vs. Fly-Ballers	154	42	8	1	4	18	15	32	.273	.416	.341
Home Games	151	43	6	1	4	21	12	20	.285	.417	.335
Road Games	147	35	6	0	3	15	18	31	.238	.340	.329
Grass Fields	218	56	8	1	5	25	21	32	.257	.372	.324
Artificial Turf	80	22	4	0	2	11	9	19	.275	.400	.356
April	11	3	1	0	0	1	2	3	.273	.364	.385
May	58	17	2	0	4	11	6	12	.293	.534	.379
June	78	24	2	0	2	12	10	8	.308	.410	.382
July	66	11	1	0	0	2	6	12	.167	.182	.236
August	53	20	6	1	1	9	3	10	.377	.585	.411
Sept./Oct.	32	3	0	0	0	1	3	6	.094	.094	.171
Leading Off Inn.	73	17	4	0	1	1	9	7	.233	.329	.325
Bases Empty	169	40	6	0	3	3	16	29	.237	.325	.306
Runners On	129	38	6	1	4	33	14	22	.295	.450	.366
Runners/Scor. Pos.	74	16	2	0	3	27	13	17	.216	.365	.330
Runners On/2 Out	52	13	2	1	0	7	12	11	.250	.327	.391
Scor. Pos./2 Out	28	5	1	0	0	5	11	9	.179	.214	.410
Late-Inning Pressure	44	11	2	0	0	6	3	9	.250	.295	.306
Leading Off	9	1	0	0	0	0	2	1	.111	.111	.273
Runners On	19	8	2	0	0	6	1	3	.421	.526	.455
Runners/Scor. Pos.	8	3	1	0	0	5	0	2	.375	.500	.333

RUNS BATTED IN	From 1B	From 2B	From 3B	Scoring Position
Totals	8/99	7/60	14/32	21/92
Percentage	8.1%	11.7%	43.8%	22.8%

Loves to face: Tom Niedenfuer (2-for-2, 1 BB)
Steve Wilson (3-for-3, 1 HR, 1 BB)

Hates to face: Mike Morgan (0-for-5)
Dave Schmidt (0-for-5)

Miscellaneous statistics: Ground outs-to-air outs ratio: 1.24 last season, 1.25 for career. . . . Grounded into 8 double plays in 60 opportunities (one per 7.5). . . . Drove in 11 of 14 runners from third base with less than two outs (79%). . . . Direction of balls hit to the outfield: 33% to left field, 36% to center, 31% to right. . . . Base running: Advanced from first base to third on 4 of 18 outfield singles (22%); scored from second on 8 of 12 (67%). . . . Opposing base stealers: 75-for-98 (77%), 4th-highest rate in N.L.

Comments: We don't usually think of Atlanta as a hot bed of catching talent, but since 1978 they have had four different catchers in the All-Star game: Biff Pocoroba, Bruce Benedict, Ozzie Virgil, and Olson. No other club in the majors can make that claim. . . . Olson was the oldest rookie (29) on the active roster of any major league team at the time of the All-Star break. In case you need a point of reference, he is one day younger than Candy Maldonado. He should not be confused with Gregg ("Double G") Olson of the Orioles, the youngest member of the American League All-Star squad last season. . . . Olson and starting A.L. catcher, Sandy Alomar, both participated in the 1990 All-Star Game, despite only 11 games of major league experience between them prior to the start of the season. . . . Braves pitchers allowed 5.04 runs per nine innings with Olson calling the signals, 5.50 with Jimmy Kremers, and 5.53 with Ernie Whitt. . . . Olson finished the season with an errorless streak of 36 games, his longest of the season. . . . His home run total was the highest of his nine-year professional baseball career. Olson hit only 17 home runs in 606 minor league games. . . . Hitless in 18 career at-bats at Jack Murphy Stadium. . . . His only hit in 11 career at-bats with the bases loaded was a grand slam off Danny Jackson in June.

Paul O'Neill

Bats Left

Cincinnati Reds	AB	H	2B	3B	HR	RBI	BB	SO	BA	SA	OBA
Season	503	136	28	0	16	78	53	103	.270	.421	.339
vs. Left-Handers	143	37	12	0	3	25	11	45	.259	.406	.310
vs. Right-Handers	360	99	16	0	13	53	42	58	.275	.428	.351
vs. Ground-Ballers	241	62	17	0	4	24	25	48	.257	.378	.332
vs. Fly-Ballers	262	74	11	0	12	54	28	55	.282	.462	.346
Home Games	241	70	10	0	10	36	25	48	.290	.456	.357
Road Games	262	66	18	0	6	42	28	55	.252	.389	.323
Grass Fields	152	39	7	0	5	21	14	29	.257	.401	.317
Artificial Turf	351	97	21	0	11	57	39	74	.276	.430	.348
April	60	17	3	0	2	15	8	13	.283	.433	.368
May	96	27	6	0	2	12	6	26	.281	.406	.327
June	87	25	4	0	6	15	13	13	.287	.540	.380
July	81	18	3	0	2	9	7	18	.222	.333	.292
August	92	31	9	0	3	14	10	17	.337	.533	.398
Sept./Oct.	87	18	3	0	1	13	9	16	.207	.276	.273
Leading Off Inn.	109	30	9	0	5	5	9	21	.275	.495	.331
Bases Empty	266	71	18	0	7	7	21	59	.267	.414	.323
Runners On	237	65	10	0	9	71	32	44	.274	.430	.356
Runners/Scor. Pos.	144	42	8	0	6	64	25	28	.292	.472	.385
Runners On/2 Out	89	26	3	0	4	26	15	18	.292	.461	.394
Scor. Pos./2 Out	62	18	2	0	3	24	12	13	.290	.468	.405
Late-Inning Pressure	71	19	4	0	1	5	9	13	.268	.366	.350
Leading Off	12	4	1	0	0	0	2	1	.333	.417	.429
Runners On	31	7	2	0	0	4	5	5	.226	.290	.333
Runners/Scor. Pos.	11	3	0	0	0	3	5	0	.273	.273	.500

RUNS BATTED IN	From 1B	From 2B	From 3B	Scoring Position
Totals	8/156	27/108	27/66	54/174
Percentage	5.1%	25.0%	40.9%	31.0%

Loves to face: Jay Howell (.714, 5-for-7, 1 HR)
Dennis Martinez (.385, 10-for-26, 3 HR)
Don Robinson (.313, 10-for-32, 5 HR)

Hates to face: Tom Glavine (.059, 1-for-17)
Jeff Parrett (0-for-15, 1 BB)
Mike Scott (.125, 3-for-24)

Miscellaneous statistics: Ground outs-to-air outs ratio: 0.87 last season, 0.95 for career. . . . Grounded into 12 double plays in 108 opportunities (one per 9.0). . . . Drove in 18 of 40 runners from third base with less than two outs (45%). . . . Direction of balls hit to the outfield: 30% to left field, 41% to center, 29% to right. . . . Base running: Advanced from first base to third on 2 of 18 outfield singles (11%); scored from second on 8 of 15 (53%). . . . Made 2.09 putouts per nine innings in right field.

Comments: Cincinnati's starting outfield of Billy Hatcher (.997, one error in 319 chances), Eric Davis (.993, one error in 270 chances), and O'Neill (.993, two errors in 285 chances) finished 1–2–3 in the National League in fielding percentage among outfielders. That's the first time in the 115-year history of baseball that any major league's top three outfielders came from the same team. . . . O'Neill led Reds outfielders with 12 assists, but three teammates reached double figure as well: Eric Davis (11), Glenn Braggs (10), and Billy Hatcher (10). Over the past 60 years, only one other National League team had four outfielders with 10 or more asssists: the 1977 Padres (George Hendrick, Gene Richards, Jerry Turner, and Dave Winfield). . . . Batted 47 points higher in night games (.279) than in day games (.232) over the last five seasons, the 5th-largest margin in the majors. . . . His career average vs. left-handed pitchers is only .217, but O'Neill improved dramatically last season after batting .178 against southpaws in 1989. . . . Career batting average of .186 at the Astrodome (16-for-86, 0 HR). . . . Batted .471 (8-for-17) in the N.L. Championship Series, but disappeared in the World Series, batting .083 (1-for-12). . . . O'Neill is reputedly a superstar waiting to explode. But his statistical profile tells us otherwise; cf. Pete O'Brien (through 1985) and Sid Bream (through 1988).

Jose Oquendo

Bats Left and Right

St. Louis Cardinals	AB	H	2B	3B	HR	RBI	BB	SO	BA	SA	OBA
Season	469	118	17	5	1	37	74	46	.252	.316	.350
vs. Left-Handers	164	36	4	2	1	7	24	13	.220	.287	.319
vs. Right-Handers	305	82	13	3	0	30	50	33	.269	.331	.367
vs. Ground-Ballers	235	71	5	4	1	26	40	17	.302	.370	.399
vs. Fly-Ballers	234	47	12	1	0	11	34	29	.201	.261	.300
Home Games	238	57	8	1	1	17	33	21	.239	.294	.330
Road Games	231	61	9	4	0	20	41	25	.264	.338	.371
Grass Fields	137	42	6	3	0	12	18	16	.307	.394	.385
Artificial Turf	332	76	11	2	1	25	56	30	.229	.283	.337
April	64	18	2	1	0	6	12	7	.281	.344	.395
May	82	13	2	0	0	2	15	13	.159	.183	.283
June	89	27	4	1	1	15	13	4	.303	.404	.381
July	89	20	4	1	0	2	13	12	.225	.292	.324
August	84	25	5	0	0	7	15	5	.298	.357	.404
Sept./Oct.	61	15	0	2	0	5	6	5	.246	.311	.313
Leading Off Inn.	116	26	5	1	0	0	13	12	.224	.284	.302
Bases Empty	288	67	11	2	1	1	42	32	.233	.295	.330
Runners On	181	51	6	3	0	36	32	14	.282	.348	.381
Runners/Scor. Pos.	118	31	3	3	0	35	26	12	.263	.339	.383
Runners On/2 Out	83	19	2	2	0	14	16	7	.229	.301	.354
Scor. Pos./2 Out	60	13	0	2	0	14	15	6	.217	.283	.373
Late-Inning Pressure	78	21	3	0	0	5	15	8	.269	.308	.387
Leading Off	26	4	1	0	0	0	2	3	.154	.192	.214
Runners On	25	10	0	0	0	5	7	2	.400	.400	.531
Runners/Scor. Pos.	15	7	0	0	0	5	5	1	.467	.467	.600

RUNS BATTED IN	From 1B	From 2B	From 3B	Scoring Position
Totals	3/123	15/97	18/43	33/140
Percentage	2.4%	15.5%	41.9%	23.6%

Loves to face: Mike LaCoss (.450, 9-for-20)
Pete Smith (5-for-5, 4 BB)
Ed Whitson (.409, 9-for-22)

Hates to face: Don Carman (.148, 4-for-27)
Dwight Gooden (.100, 2-for-20)
Rick Mahler (.120, 3-for-25, 0 BB)

Miscellaneous statistics: Ground outs-to-air outs ratio: 0.71 last season, 1.01 for career.... Grounded into 7 double plays in 81 opportunities (one per 11.6).... Drove in 14 of 24 runners from third base with less than two outs (58%).... Direction of balls hit to the outfield: 39% to left field, 28% to center, 34% to right batting left-handed; 38% to left, 36% to center, 26% to right batting right-handed.... Base running: Advanced from first base to third on 7 of 29 outfield singles (24%); scored from second on 7 of 11 (64%).... Made 2.94 assists per nine innings at second base.

Comments: His average of one error per 227 chances at second base was an all-time National League record.... Having broken Ryne Sandberg's record in 1989 as well, Oquendo became only the second player in the last 50 years to break his league's fielding percentage record at any position in consecutive seasons. The other was Larry Bowa, 1971–72.... Oquendo now tries to become the first second baseman to lead the N.L. in fielding for three straight seasons since Claude Ritchey (1905–07).... Enters 1991 with a streak of 188 consecutive errorless games at second base on artificial turf. Think about that: Ryne Sandberg set the all-time major league record for consecutive errorless games (regardless of ground cover) at that position last season—and it was only 123 games. Oquendo's streak on artificial turf is already 50 percent longer!... Despite all that, Sandberg won his eighth consecutive Gold Glove Award.... Oquendo batted 78 points higher on grass fields (.307) than on artificial turf (.229) last season, the 4th-largest margin in the majors. He has hit over .300 on grass fields in three of the last four seasons.... His 1990 batting average vs. left-handed pitchers was the lowest of his career.... Of his 11 career home runs, 10 have been hit against left-handed pitchers; his only home run in 1525 at-bats vs. right-handers was off Doug Bair in 1989.

Spike Owen

Bats Left and Right

Montreal Expos	AB	H	2B	3B	HR	RBI	BB	SO	BA	SA	OBA
Season	453	106	24	5	5	35	70	60	.234	.342	.333
vs. Left-Handers	201	52	16	2	3	17	23	25	.259	.403	.330
vs. Right-Handers	252	54	8	3	2	18	47	35	.214	.294	.336
vs. Ground-Ballers	246	59	14	2	2	20	39	29	.240	.337	.341
vs. Fly-Ballers	207	47	10	3	3	15	31	31	.227	.348	.324
Home Games	215	49	11	3	2	16	34	25	.228	.335	.332
Road Games	238	57	13	2	3	19	36	35	.239	.349	.335
Grass Fields	123	28	5	1	2	12	22	25	.228	.333	.342
Artificial Turf	330	78	19	4	3	23	48	35	.236	.345	.330
April	64	23	7	2	1	7	5	5	.359	.578	.400
May	74	17	1	0	1	6	15	13	.230	.284	.356
June	95	17	4	0	2	10	18	14	.179	.284	.304
July	69	14	3	1	1	3	15	11	.203	.319	.341
August	75	18	4	0	0	5	7	10	.240	.293	.305
Sept./Oct.	76	17	5	2	0	4	10	7	.224	.342	.314
Leading Off Inn.	116	25	6	2	1	1	14	12	.216	.328	.300
Bases Empty	278	70	17	3	5	5	34	36	.252	.388	.333
Runners On	175	36	7	2	0	30	36	24	.206	.269	.333
Runners/Scor. Pos.	101	17	2	2	0	27	27	17	.168	.228	.331
Runners On/2 Out	66	9	2	0	0	8	22	9	.136	.167	.352
Scor. Pos./2 Out	45	4	1	0	0	7	18	7	.089	.111	.349
Late-Inning Pressure	77	18	3	2	3	10	10	13	.234	.442	.315
Leading Off	16	2	0	0	1	1	3	1	.125	.313	.263
Runners On	27	5	1	1	0	7	6	4	.185	.296	.314
Runners/Scor. Pos.	19	4	1	1	0	7	4	4	.211	.368	.320

RUNS BATTED IN	From 1B	From 2B	From 3B	Scoring Position
Totals	3/124	6/71	21/51	27/122
Percentage	2.4%	8.5%	41.2%	22.1%

Loves to face: Juan Agosto (.500, 5-for-10, 1 HR)
Tom Browning (.533, 8-for-15)
Ed Whitson (.429, 6-for-14, 1 HR)

Hates to face: Mike Bielecki (0-for-15, 1 BB)
Tom Glavine (.063, 1-for-16, 2 BB)
Dennis Rasmussen (.069, 2-for-29, 3 BB)

Miscellaneous statistics: Ground outs-to-air outs ratio: 1.08 last season, 1.16 for career.... Grounded into 6 double plays in 96 opportunities (one per 16.0).... Drove in 17 of 30 runners from third base with less than two outs (57%).... Direction of balls hit to the outfield: 34% to left field, 33% to center, 33% to right batting left-handed; 36% to left, 40% to center, 24% to right batting right-handed.... Base running: Advanced from first base to third on 5 of 17 outfield singles (29%); scored from second on 9 of 10 (90%).... Made 2.56 assists per nine innings at shortstop, lowest rate in majors.

Comments: Led National League shortstops with a .989 fielding percentage (one error per 94 chances), the highest by an N.L. shortstop since Larry Bowa's record of .991 in 1979 (one error per 114 chances). The error Owen committed on his final play of the season did *not* cost him the record.... Spike did set another National League record for shortstops, however: 63 consecutive errorless games in one season (his first 63 of the season, as it happened).... Owen's career batting average of .239 ranks last among the 23 active switch-hitters with at least 3000 career at-bats.... Batting average with runners in scoring position was the 2d lowest of any National League player last season (minimum: 100 AB).... Has hit for a higher average batting right-handed than he has batting left-handed in each of the last five seasons.... Has hit for a higher average on artificial surfaces than he has on grass fields in each of the last six seasons, tying him with Chet Lemon for the longest current streak. He'll have to keep it up through 1994 season to match the *Player Analysis* record of 10 straight years, held by Dane Iorg.... Led the major leagues with 43 runs scored from the eighth slot in the batting order last season.... His .083 average with two outs and runners in scoring position is pretty poor, but Spike has seen worse—he was hitless in 27 at-bats in those situations in 1988. His career average is .198 (69-for-349).

Mike Pagliarulo

Bats Left

San Diego Padres	AB	H	2B	3B	HR	RBI	BB	SO	BA	SA	OBA
Season	398	101	23	2	7	38	39	66	.254	.374	.322
vs. Left-Handers	101	25	3	0	4	13	15	21	.248	.396	.353
vs. Right-Handers	297	76	20	2	3	25	24	45	.256	.367	.311
vs. Ground-Ballers	210	44	11	1	2	20	20	38	.210	.300	.283
vs. Fly-Ballers	188	57	12	1	5	18	19	28	.303	.457	.365
Home Games	169	46	10	1	1	14	19	31	.272	.361	.354
Road Games	229	55	13	1	6	24	20	35	.240	.384	.298
Grass Fields	285	77	18	2	5	29	29	46	.270	.400	.341
Artificial Turf	113	24	5	0	2	9	10	20	.212	.310	.274
April	11	1	0	0	0	1	3	6	.091	.091	.267
May	76	24	8	0	1	8	12	6	.316	.461	.418
June	80	19	3	1	2	6	5	16	.237	.375	.287
July	65	18	5	1	0	8	9	16	.277	.385	.365
August	84	15	1	0	0	5	6	15	.179	.190	.231
Sept./Oct.	82	24	6	0	4	10	4	7	.293	.512	.326
Leading Off Inn.	91	22	2	1	4	4	9	16	.242	.418	.310
Bases Empty	240	58	16	1	6	6	22	44	.242	.392	.311
Runners On	158	43	7	1	1	32	17	22	.272	.348	.339
Runners/Scor. Pos.	94	21	4	1	0	29	11	17	.223	.287	.300
Runners On/2 Out	83	21	5	0	0	16	9	13	.253	.313	.326
Scor. Pos./2 Out	61	14	4	0	0	15	6	12	.230	.295	.299
Late-Inning Pressure	63	13	5	1	0	3	10	12	.206	.317	.311
Leading Off	16	3	1	1	0	0	5	2	.188	.375	.381
Runners On	23	8	2	0	0	3	3	4	.348	.435	.407
Runners/Scor. Pos.	10	1	0	0	0	2	2	2	.100	.100	.231

RUNS BATTED IN	From 1B	From 2B	From 3B	Scoring Position
Totals	4/114	10/75	17/38	27/113
Percentage	3.5%	13.3%	44.7%	23.9%

Loves to face: Jeff Russell (.444, 4-for-9, 2 HR)
Bobby Witt (.333, 3-for-9, 2 HR, 5 BB)

Hates to face: Bert Blyleven (.065, 2-for-31)
Jim Clancy (.100, 2-for-20)
Curt Young (.063, 1-for-16)

Miscellaneous statistics: Ground outs-to-air outs ratio: 0.96 last season, 0.90 for career. . . . Grounded into 12 double plays in 64 opportunities (one per 5.3), 5th-worst rate in N.L. . . . Drove in 11 of 16 runners from third base with less than two outs (69%). . . . Direction of balls hit to the outfield: 29% to left field, 35% to center, 36% to right. . . . Base running: Advanced from first base to third on 7 of 22 outfield singles (32%); scored from second on 3 of 5 (60%). . . . Made 1.89 assists per nine innings at third base.

Comments: Padres pitchers allowed 3.99 runs per nine innings with Pags at third base, 4.43 runs per game with other third basemen. Pagliarulo finished the season with a 20-game errorless streak, his longest of the season. . . . Batted 94 points higher vs. fly-ballers (.303) than vs. ground-ballers (.210) last season, the 5th-largest margin in the majors. . . . His low batting average in Late-Inning Pressure Situations can be attributed to a hitless streak of 25 at-bats in LIPS (July 2–August 17). . . . Has hit for a higher average with runners on base than he has with the bases empty in each of the last five seasons. . . . His career-high batting average went hand in hand with the lowest strikeout rate and lowest home-run rate of his career. . . . Home runs vs. right-handed pitchers year by year since 1985: 17, 26, 28, 20, 7, 3. . . . Has no home runs in 183 at-bats in Late-Inning Pressure Situations over the last three seasons. . . . Career average of .207 vs. left-handed pitchers is the 3d lowest among players active during the 1990 season (minimum: 400 AB). He struck out in six consecutive plate appearances vs. southpaws last summer. . . . Has a career average of .153 (11-for-72, 2 HR) as a pinch hitter. . . . Over the last two seasons, 11 of his 14 home runs have been hit with the bases empty. . . . Career batting at the Metrodome: .245 (25-for-102), with six home runs.

Tom Pagnozzi

Bats Right

St. Louis Cardinals	AB	H	2B	3B	HR	RBI	BB	SO	BA	SA	OBA
Season	220	61	15	0	2	23	14	37	.277	.373	.321
vs. Left-Handers	82	24	6	0	1	9	7	17	.293	.402	.356
vs. Right-Handers	138	37	9	0	1	14	7	20	.268	.355	.299
vs. Ground-Ballers	110	29	9	0	0	15	6	21	.264	.345	.299
vs. Fly-Ballers	110	32	6	0	2	8	8	16	.291	.400	.342
Home Games	101	30	5	0	2	12	9	14	.297	.406	.357
Road Games	119	31	10	0	0	11	5	23	.261	.345	.288
Grass Fields	55	12	3	0	0	6	2	10	.218	.273	.241
Artificial Turf	165	49	12	0	2	17	12	27	.297	.406	.346
April	8	2	0	0	0	0	0	1	.250	.250	.250
May	24	6	0	0	0	1	0	5	.250	.250	.250
June	15	2	0	0	1	2	1	3	.133	.333	.188
July	27	8	2	0	0	8	6	5	.296	.370	.424
August	52	15	6	0	0	4	4	10	.288	.404	.333
Sept./Oct.	94	28	7	0	1	8	3	13	.298	.404	.323
Leading Off Inn.	46	12	2	0	1	1	1	5	.261	.370	.277
Bases Empty	124	36	8	0	2	2	9	17	.290	.403	.343
Runners On	96	25	7	0	0	21	5	20	.260	.333	.291
Runners/Scor. Pos.	54	15	4	0	0	18	2	10	.278	.352	.293
Runners On/2 Out	44	13	3	0	0	9	3	7	.295	.364	.340
Scor. Pos./2 Out	24	6	2	0	0	7	2	4	.250	.333	.308
Late-Inning Pressure	27	8	3	0	0	5	0	6	.296	.407	.296
Leading Off	7	2	0	0	0	0	0	2	.286	.286	.286
Runners On	10	4	3	0	0	5	0	3	.400	.700	.400
Runners/Scor. Pos.	6	2	1	0	0	3	0	1	.333	.500	.333

RUNS BATTED IN	From 1B	From 2B	From 3B	Scoring Position
Totals	4/64	8/45	9/20	17/65
Percentage	6.3%	17.8%	45.0%	26.2%

Loves to face: Greg W. Harris (3-for-3, 2 2B)
Jose Rijo (.600, 3-for-5, 2 2B)

Hates to face: Norm Charlton (0-for-5)
David Cone (0-for-6)
Randy Myers (.167, 2-for-12)

Miscellaneous statistics: Ground outs-to-air outs ratio: 0.81 last season, 0.97 for career. . . . Grounded into 0 double plays in 36 opportunities. . . . Drove in 7 of 10 runners from third base with less than two outs (70%). . . . Direction of balls hit to the outfield: 21% to left field, 35% to center, 45% to right. . . . Base running: Advanced from first base to third on 2 of 6 outfield singles (33%); scored from second on 5 of 6 (83%). . . . Opposing base stealers: 40-for-73 (55%), lowest rate in N.L.

Comments: Started only 45 games behind the plate in three season as Tony Pena's backup. He started 59 games there last season, and won the position from Todd Zeile by the end of the season. Pagnozzi was the starting catcher in 37 of 52 games after Joe Torre's arrival on August 2; Zeile started 24 of the Cardinals' last 27 games at third base. . . . Cardinals pitchers seemed not to notice the change, allowing 4.45 runs per nine innings with Pagnozzi catching, 4.26 runs with Zeile behind the plate. . . . Was not thrown out trying to advance an extra base on any batted ball last season. . . . His career batting average of .252 is deceptively encouraging. Pagnozzi rarely walks (one per 17 plate appearances) and has little extra-base power. His average of 1.28 bases per hit ranks 321st among 359 active nonpitchers with at least 100 career hits. . . . Has hit four career home runs, all at Busch Stadium; he's 0-for-293 at-bats elsewhere. Of course, Duane Kuiper can scoff at that figure; he had a career total of 1736 at-bats in road games without ever hitting a home run. . . . Career batting-average breakdown: .264 at Busch, .244 on other artificial surfaces, .241 on grass fields.

Mark Parent

Bats Right

San Diego Padres	AB	H	2B	3B	HR	RBI	BB	SO	BA	SA	OBA
Season	189	42	11	0	3	16	16	29	.222	.328	.283
vs. Left-Handers	85	26	7	0	2	7	10	12	.306	.459	.379
vs. Right-Handers	104	16	4	0	1	9	6	17	.154	.221	.200
vs. Ground-Ballers	104	18	4	0	0	7	6	19	.173	.212	.218
vs. Fly-Ballers	85	24	7	0	3	9	10	10	.282	.471	.358
Home Games	68	16	4	0	1	3	8	8	.235	.338	.316
Road Games	121	26	7	0	2	13	8	21	.215	.322	.264
Grass Fields	135	29	7	0	2	12	12	20	.215	.311	.279
Artificial Turf	54	13	4	0	1	4	4	9	.241	.370	.293
April	10	3	0	0	0	1	1	2	.300	.300	.364
May	18	4	1	0	0	4	0	3	.222	.278	.222
June	49	8	2	0	1	2	6	8	.163	.265	.255
July	62	16	5	0	1	3	6	7	.258	.387	.324
August	26	7	2	0	0	4	1	6	.269	.346	.296
Sept./Oct.	24	4	1	0	1	2	2	3	.167	.333	.231
Leading Off Inn.	42	9	4	0	2	2	0	7	.214	.452	.214
Bases Empty	108	27	8	0	3	3	6	15	.250	.407	.289
Runners On	81	15	3	0	0	13	10	14	.185	.222	.275
Runners/Scor. Pos.	48	10	3	0	0	13	8	10	.208	.271	.321
Runners On/2 Out	35	8	1	0	0	7	5	4	.229	.257	.325
Scor. Pos./2 Out	22	6	1	0	0	7	4	3	.273	.318	.385
Late-Inning Pressure	27	7	2	0	0	0	4	4	.259	.333	.355
Leading Off	5	1	0	0	0	0	0	1	.200	.200	.200
Runners On	11	2	0	0	0	0	2	1	.182	.182	.308
Runners/Scor. Pos.	6	0	0	0	0	0	1	1	.000	.000	.143

RUNS BATTED IN	From 1B	From 2B	From 3B	Scoring Position
Totals	1/59	6/37	6/23	12/60
Percentage	1.7%	16.2%	26.1%	20.0%

Loves to face: Tim Leary (.250, 2-for-8, 1 HR)
Scott Sanderson (.333, 1-for-3, 1 HR)
John Tudor (.571, 4-for-7, 1 HR)

Hates to face: Tom Glavine (.050, 1-for-20)
Rick Honeycutt (.167, 1-for-6)
Pascual Perez (0-for-5)

Miscellaneous statistics: Ground outs-to-air outs ratio: 0.86 last season, 1.14 for career.... Grounded into 2 double plays in 39 opportunities (one per 19.5).... Drove in 3 of 14 runners from third base with less than two outs (21%).... Direction of balls hit to the outfield: 36% to left field, 33% to center, 31% to right.... Base running: Advanced from first base to third on 2 of 9 outfield singles (22%); scored from second on 3 of 4 (75%).... Opposing base stealers: 52-for-70 (74%).

Comments: Padres pitchers allowed fewer runs per nine innings with Parent calling the signals (3.99) than with Benito Santiago behind the plate (4.06). They allowed one home run per 12.5 innings pitching to Parent, one per 9.1 innings to Santiago.... His June batting average was the lowest in the National League.... Batting average vs. ground-ball pitchers was the lowest of any player in the National League last season (minimum: 100 AB).... Last season was the fifth in which he spent time in the majors, but the first in which he batted above the .200 mark.... Has batted with 16 runners in scoring position during Late-Inning Pressure Situations in his career, and failed to drive any of those runners across the plate.... Has a career average of .240 vs. left-handed pitchers, .167 vs. right-handed pitchers. That career average vs. right-handers is the lowest of any nonpitcher over the last 16 years (minimum: 300 PA vs. RHP).... The race is on! Parent needs four hits in his first 13 at-bats this season to avoid reaching the 500-AB mark with fewer than 100 hits. The most at-bats that any nonpitcher ever needed to reach the 100-hit mark was approximately 587, by Bill Traffley. We say approximately because we couldn't track down a day-by-day record of Traff's 1886 season. Since 1900, that distinction belongs to Dave Duncan, who reached the 100-hit mark on at-bat number 559.

Terry Pendleton

Bats Left and Right

St. Louis Cardinals	AB	H	2B	3B	HR	RBI	BB	SO	BA	SA	OBA
Season	447	103	20	2	6	58	30	58	.230	.324	.277
vs. Left-Handers	158	33	12	0	4	23	6	15	.209	.361	.235
vs. Right-Handers	289	70	8	2	2	35	24	43	.242	.304	.299
vs. Ground-Ballers	210	55	11	1	4	37	15	26	.262	.381	.307
vs. Fly-Ballers	237	48	9	1	2	21	15	32	.203	.274	.249
Home Games	251	61	13	1	6	32	17	31	.243	.375	.289
Road Games	196	42	7	1	0	26	13	27	.214	.260	.262
Grass Fields	105	23	3	1	0	16	7	10	.219	.267	.263
Artificial Turf	342	80	17	1	6	42	23	48	.234	.342	.281
April	52	12	4	0	0	8	4	4	.231	.308	.276
May	78	18	2	0	2	13	6	8	.231	.333	.282
June	107	32	7	2	3	23	10	19	.299	.486	.356
July	102	13	1	0	1	6	3	15	.127	.167	.151
August	87	21	4	0	0	7	7	11	.241	.287	.302
Sept./Oct.	21	7	2	0	0	1	0	1	.333	.429	.333
Leading Off Inn.	95	20	4	1	1	1	6	9	.211	.305	.257
Bases Empty	237	55	9	1	3	3	13	32	.232	.316	.275
Runners On	210	48	11	1	3	55	17	26	.229	.333	.279
Runners/Scor. Pos.	133	31	8	1	3	53	12	15	.233	.376	.285
Runners On/2 Out	82	20	4	1	3	23	7	6	.244	.427	.303
Scor. Pos./2 Out	66	17	3	1	3	23	7	6	.258	.470	.329
Late-Inning Pressure	81	17	2	1	0	7	7	14	.210	.259	.278
Leading Off	23	5	1	1	0	0	2	0	.217	.348	.280
Runners On	36	7	1	0	0	7	2	8	.194	.222	.231
Runners/Scor. Pos.	21	6	1	0	0	7	2	4	.286	.333	.333

RUNS BATTED IN	From 1B	From 2B	From 3B	Scoring Position
Totals	7/146	19/102	26/55	45/157
Percentage	4.8%	18.6%	47.3%	28.7%

Loves to face: Jose DeLeon (.563, 9-for-16)
Kelly Downs (.500, 7-for-14, 1 HR)
Zane Smith (.442, 19-for-43, 1 HR)

Hates to face: Greg W. Harris (0-for-9)
Bill Landrum (0-for-8)
Bryn Smith (.132, 5-for-38)

Miscellaneous statistics: Ground outs-to-air outs ratio: 1.14 last season, 1.26 for career.... Grounded into 12 double plays in 102 opportunities (one per 8.5).... Drove in 19 of 29 runners from third base with less than two outs (66%).... Direction of balls hit to the outfield: 36% to left field, 36% to center, 28% to right batting left-handed; 37% to left, 35% to center, 28% to right batting right-handed.... Base running: Advanced from first base to third on 5 of 17 outfield singles (29%); scored from second on 8 of 8.... Made 2.21 assists per nine innings at third base.

Comments: Pendleton's career average of .313 at Atlanta Stadium is his highest at any National League ballpark. In fact, it's the only place that he has hit better than .280. Oddly, Atlanta is one of three N.L. cities in which he has never homered: Atlanta (134 career at-bats), Montreal (177 AB), and San Diego (136 AB).... Just asking: Wasn't Pendleton's 1990 season a lot like the one that Davey Johnson had in his last season with Baltimore, just prior to hitting 43 home runs in his debut season with the Braves? ... Had the lowest batting average of any regular third baseman in the National League last season.... July batting average was the lowest in the major leagues.... Committed one error per 19 chances at third base, his worst rate since his rookie season of 1984.... Has hit for a higher average in day games than he has at night in each of his last seven seasons in the majors, the longest such streak of any active major leaguer, and one year short of the *Player Analysis* record held by Scot Thompson. Career averages: .285 in day games (one home run every 49 at-bats), .246 at night (one HR per 110 AB).... When told by the staff of CBS sitcom "Good Sports" that the subject of his guest appearance would be the enormity of his new contract vis-a-vis his .230 batting average, Pendleton replied, "Hey, you want me to go on TV with Farrah. I can deal with that." Good attitude.

Jim Presley

Bats Right

Atlanta Braves	AB	H	2B	3B	HR	RBI	BB	SO	BA	SA	OBA
Season	541	131	34	1	19	72	29	130	.242	.414	.282
vs. Left-Handers	180	48	15	0	6	28	17	38	.267	.450	.333
vs. Right-Handers	361	83	19	1	13	44	12	92	.230	.396	.255
vs. Ground-Ballers	247	65	14	1	10	33	15	44	.263	.449	.306
vs. Fly-Ballers	294	66	20	0	9	39	14	86	.224	.384	.263
Home Games	288	75	18	0	10	38	16	64	.260	.427	.304
Road Games	253	56	16	1	9	34	13	66	.221	.399	.257
Grass Fields	415	102	27	1	14	54	21	98	.246	.417	.285
Artificial Turf	126	29	7	0	5	18	8	32	.230	.405	.274
April	66	20	6	0	1	7	1	11	.303	.439	.313
May	91	27	11	0	3	16	8	24	.297	.516	.353
June	106	25	4	0	4	14	5	25	.236	.387	.270
July	110	26	5	0	9	18	9	31	.236	.527	.300
August	96	17	2	1	1	8	4	24	.177	.250	.208
Sept./Oct.	72	16	6	0	1	9	2	15	.222	.347	.250
Leading Off Inn.	143	32	7	0	7	7	7	35	.224	.420	.260
Bases Empty	304	71	14	0	16	16	11	73	.234	.438	.263
Runners On	237	60	20	1	3	56	18	57	.253	.384	.307
Runners/Scor. Pos.	150	32	14	1	1	47	15	40	.213	.340	.287
Runners On/2 Out	107	32	14	1	0	25	8	22	.299	.449	.353
Scor. Pos./2 Out	76	18	9	1	0	21	7	17	.237	.382	.310
Late-Inning Pressure	83	15	2	0	3	10	2	30	.181	.313	.195
Leading Off	26	5	0	0	1	1	1	7	.192	.308	.222
Runners On	33	5	2	0	0	7	1	15	.152	.212	.167
Runners/Scor. Pos.	17	3	1	0	0	6	1	6	.176	.235	.200

RUNS BATTED IN	From 1B	From 2B	From 3B	Scoring Position
Totals	8/148	23/121	22/62	45/183
Percentage	5.4%	19.0%	35.5%	24.6%

Loves to face: Tom Browning (.471, 8-for-17)
Dave Schmidt (.480, 12-for-25)
Mitch Williams (.455, 5-for-11, 1 HR, 5 BB)

Hates to face: John Candelaria (.105, 2-for-19)
Greg A. Harris (.083, 1-for-12, 6 SO)
Nolan Ryan (0-for-6, 5 SO)

Miscellaneous statistics: Ground outs-to-air outs ratio: 1.03 last season, 1.07 for career. . . . Grounded into 10 double plays in 95 opportunities (one per 9.5). . . . Drove in 14 of 28 runners from third base with less than two outs (50%). . . . Direction of balls hit to the outfield: 39% to left field, 36% to center, 25% to right. . . . Base running: Advanced from first base to third on 2 of 24 outfield singles (8%), 2d-lowest rate in N.L.; scored from second on 6 of 11 (55%). . . . Made 1.90 assists per nine innings at third base.

Comments: Had the lowest fielding percentage (.930, one error per 14 chances) of any regular third baseman in the National League last season. . . . His total of 54 extra-base hits was the highest since 1986, when he had 64 XBH and drove in 107 runs for Seattle. . . . Had a streak of 29 consecutive hitless at-bats in Late-Inning Pressure Situations that started on July 29 and ran through the end of the season, the 4th-longest streak in *Player Analysis* history. . . . Has hit for a higher average in home games than he has on the road in each of the last five seasons. Of course, he has had the luxury of playing his home games in two of the best home run ballparks in baseball, the Kingdome and Atlanta Stadium. Still, that's not evident in his career home run totals: Over his seven years in the majors, he has hit 68 homers in home games, 66 on the road. . . . Batting average with runners in scoring position year by year since 1986: .294, .269, .235, .227, .213. . . . Has driven in 96 of 192 runners from third base with less than two outs over his seven-year career—exactly 50 percent. . . . Has struck out at least 100 times in each of his six full seasons in the majors. . . . You don't think Jerry Glanville moved to Atlanta because he heard someone named Presley was playing third base for the Braves, do you?

Tim Raines

Bats Left and Right

Montreal Expos	AB	H	2B	3B	HR	RBI	BB	SO	BA	SA	OBA
Season	457	131	11	5	9	62	70	43	.287	.392	.379
vs. Left-Handers	180	52	0	2	3	27	21	13	.289	.361	.357
vs. Right-Handers	277	79	11	3	6	35	49	30	.285	.412	.393
vs. Ground-Ballers	259	79	9	4	5	35	35	15	.305	.429	.385
vs. Fly-Ballers	198	52	2	1	4	27	35	28	.263	.343	.372
Home Games	202	62	6	2	6	28	28	18	.307	.446	.391
Road Games	255	69	5	3	3	34	42	25	.271	.349	.370
Grass Fields	142	41	1	1	3	19	23	15	.289	.373	.385
Artificial Turf	315	90	10	4	6	43	47	28	.286	.400	.377
April	72	17	0	1	0	10	8	8	.236	.264	.305
May	90	27	0	2	2	12	19	10	.300	.411	.420
June	49	16	3	0	0	3	8	3	.327	.388	.421
July	64	19	2	1	1	12	6	6	.297	.406	.365
August	94	26	4	0	4	14	15	10	.277	.447	.373
Sept./Oct.	88	26	2	1	2	11	14	6	.295	.409	.388
Leading Off Inn.	89	18	0	1	2	2	9	10	.202	.292	.283
Bases Empty	259	67	8	2	5	5	33	29	.259	.363	.347
Runners On	198	64	3	3	4	57	37	14	.323	.429	.418
Runners/Scor. Pos.	125	39	3	2	3	54	31	12	.312	.440	.430
Runners On/2 Out	76	23	2	1	2	21	13	7	.303	.434	.411
Scor. Pos./2 Out	56	19	2	1	2	21	11	7	.339	.518	.456
Late-Inning Pressure	79	24	1	0	1	10	12	7	.304	.354	.398
Leading Off	22	5	0	0	1	1	2	1	.227	.364	.320
Runners On	36	13	1	0	0	9	9	2	.361	.389	.478
Runners/Scor. Pos.	20	7	1	0	0	9	8	1	.350	.400	.517

RUNS BATTED IN	From 1B	From 2B	From 3B	Scoring Position
Totals	5/118	17/107	31/52	48/159
Percentage	4.2%	15.9%	59.6%	30.2%

Loves to face: Eric Show (.364, 16-for-44, 3 2B, 1 3B, 2 HR)
Dave Stewart (.500, 3-for-6, 1 2B, 1 3B, 1 HR)
Bob Welch (.361, 13-for-36)

Hates to face: Rick Aguilera (.148, 4-for-27)
Jesse Orosco (.208, 5-for-24, 1 HR, 11 SO)
Nolan Ryan (.196, 11-for-56)

Miscellaneous statistics: Ground outs-to-air outs ratio: 1.26 last season, 1.21 for career. . . . Grounded into 9 double plays in 84 opportunities (one per 9.3). . . . Drove in 25 of 31 runners from third base with less than two outs (81%), shared 2d-highest rate in N.L. . . . Direction of balls hit to the outfield: 39% to left field, 27% to center, 34% to right batting left-handed; 33% to left, 33% to center, 33% to right batting right-handed. . . . Base running: Advanced from first base to third on 12 of 31 outfield singles (39%); scored from second on 9 of 9. . . . Made 2.03 putouts per nine innings in left field.

Comments: How many players in major league history have hit .300 from both sides of the plate? Unfortunately, no one can answer that question, but certainly no more than three; at least for the moment, Raines is one. He has career averages of .301 as both a left- and right-handed hitter. Only three other switch-hitters in major league history had combined career averages of .300 or better (minimum: 1000 hits): Tuck Turner (.320), Frankie Frisch (.316), and Pete Rose (.303), who hit only .293 batting right-handed. . . . Raines has a career average of .339 in Late-Inning Pressure Situations, including a .407 mark with two outs and runners on base in LIPS. In the 16 years of data that we have compiled, Raines is the only player with a career average of .400 or better in the aforementioned category (minimum: 100 AB). . . . Raines completed the initial phase of his National League career with 634 stolen bases, 6th most in league history. He currently stands 11th in major league history, needing 15 more to crack the all-time top 10 by equaling the career total of Bert Campaneris. . . . He needs four more home runs to reach the century mark. Only 11 players in major league history with 100 home runs and 300 stolen bases have career batting averages of .300 or better. Of those 11, eight are Hall of Famers. . . . Notice anything about the pitchers listed above whom Raines loves to face? You can bet Tony LaRussa will.

Rafael Ramirez

Bats Right

Houston Astros	AB	H	2B	3B	HR	RBI	BB	SO	BA	SA	OBA
Season	445	116	19	3	2	37	24	46	.261	.330	.299
vs. Left-Handers	192	50	9	1	1	15	13	17	.260	.333	.306
vs. Right-Handers	253	66	10	2	1	22	11	29	.261	.328	.294
vs. Ground-Ballers	233	61	9	1	2	24	13	20	.262	.335	.302
vs. Fly-Ballers	212	55	10	2	0	13	11	26	.259	.325	.296
Home Games	206	55	8	3	1	20	16	21	.267	.350	.320
Road Games	239	61	11	0	1	17	8	25	.255	.314	.281
Grass Fields	140	39	6	0	0	10	4	14	.279	.321	.297
Artificial Turf	305	77	13	3	2	27	20	32	.252	.334	.301
April	63	17	1	1	0	6	1	9	.270	.317	.281
May	86	19	2	0	1	7	4	7	.221	.279	.264
June	85	26	5	1	0	5	6	7	.306	.388	.352
July	39	11	2	0	0	2	2	6	.282	.333	.310
August	86	20	6	0	1	10	6	9	.233	.337	.283
Sept./Oct.	86	23	3	1	0	7	5	8	.267	.326	.308
Leading Off Inn.	99	30	3	0	1	1	3	9	.303	.364	.324
Bases Empty	263	58	8	1	1	1	10	32	.221	.270	.252
Runners On	182	58	11	2	1	36	14	14	.319	.418	.365
Runners/Scor. Pos.	102	32	6	2	1	33	12	8	.314	.441	.383
Runners On/2 Out	70	19	2	1	1	11	7	8	.271	.371	.338
Scor. Pos./2 Out	45	10	1	1	1	10	7	6	.222	.356	.327
Late-Inning Pressure	78	20	4	0	0	6	4	11	.256	.308	.289
Leading Off	26	8	2	0	0	0	0	6	.308	.385	.308
Runners On	29	10	2	0	0	6	3	2	.345	.414	.394
Runners/Scor. Pos.	16	7	1	0	0	5	3	2	.438	.500	.500

RUNS BATTED IN	From 1B	From 2B	From 3B	Scoring Position
Totals	5/131	16/80	14/32	30/112
Percentage	3.8%	20.0%	43.8%	26.8%

Loves to face: Jim Gott (.462, 6-for-13)
Terry Mulholland (.417, 5-for-12)
John Smiley (.423, 11-for-26, 0 BB, 0 SO)

Hates to face: David Cone (.067, 1-for-15)
Sid Fernandez (.161, 5-for-31)
Ken Howell (0-for-12)

Miscellaneous statistics: Ground outs-to-air outs ratio: 1.16 last season, 1.19 for career.... Grounded into 9 double plays in 92 opportunities (one per 10.2).... Drove in 10 of 13 runners from third base with less than two outs (77%).... Direction of balls hit to the outfield: 39% to left field, 32% to center, 29% to right.... Base running: Advanced from first base to third on 7 of 21 outfield singles (33%); scored from second on 6 of 11 (55%).... Made 2.73 assists per nine innings at shortstop, 2d-lowest rate in N.L.

Comments: Career fielding percentage of .953 (one error per 21 chances) is the lowest of any active shortstop with at least 500 games.... Committed 25 errors, one fewer than Garry Templeton and Alfredo Griffin, who shared the league lead for shortstops. Ramirez has led the N.L. in errors six times, one shy of Dick Groat's league record at that position.... Astros pitchers allowed 4.27 runs per nine innings with Ramirez at shortstop, compared to 3.54 runs with other shortstops.... Had seven consecutive hits vs. left-handed pitchers in August, tying him with Mark Grace for the longest streak in the majors last season.... Has batted over .300 with runners in scoring position in three of the last four seasons. Over those four years, he has batted .286 with RISP compared to .252 in other at-bats.... Has homered in every N.L. ballpark except those located in Pennsylvania. He has a total of 389 career at-bats without a home run at Veterans Stadium and Three Rivers Stadium.... With those 25 errors, he kept alive an amazing streak. (Warning: If you don't like freak-show stats, proceed immediately to the nearest exit. This one's as freaky as they get.) Ramirez has had more errors than bases on balls in each of his 11 seasons in the majors, the longest since Art Fletcher retired with a 13-year streak after the 1922 season. Ramirez may have to become a designated hitter to end his streak. His career totals: 244 walks, 297 errors.

Domingo Ramos

Bats Right

Chicago Cubs	AB	H	2B	3B	HR	RBI	BB	SO	BA	SA	OBA
Season	226	60	5	0	2	17	27	29	.265	.314	.342
vs. Left-Handers	102	26	2	0	0	6	12	10	.255	.275	.331
vs. Right-Handers	124	34	3	0	2	11	15	19	.274	.347	.353
vs. Ground-Ballers	118	32	3	0	1	6	10	16	.271	.322	.326
vs. Fly-Ballers	108	28	2	0	1	11	17	13	.259	.306	.359
Home Games	117	32	1	0	2	10	13	12	.274	.333	.341
Road Games	109	28	4	0	0	7	14	17	.257	.294	.344
Grass Fields	167	45	1	0	2	14	17	23	.269	.311	.333
Artificial Turf	59	15	4	0	0	3	10	6	.254	.322	.366
April	21	4	0	0	0	0	1	4	.190	.190	.227
May	48	13	0	0	2	8	3	7	.271	.396	.314
June	48	11	2	0	0	3	8	7	.229	.271	.333
July	37	6	1	0	0	1	4	4	.162	.189	.244
August	33	14	2	0	0	2	6	3	.424	.485	.513
Sept./Oct.	39	12	0	0	0	3	5	4	.308	.308	.386
Leading Off Inn.	49	16	3	0	1	1	8	8	.327	.449	.421
Bases Empty	125	32	4	0	1	1	20	16	.256	.312	.363
Runners On	101	28	1	0	1	16	7	13	.277	.317	.315
Runners/Scor. Pos.	46	8	0	0	0	14	6	6	.174	.174	.255
Runners On/2 Out	45	13	0	0	1	7	4	4	.289	.356	.347
Scor. Pos./2 Out	20	3	0	0	0	5	4	2	.150	.150	.292
Late-Inning Pressure	35	4	0	0	0	2	2	8	.114	.114	.158
Leading Off	8	0	0	0	0	0	2	4	.000	.000	.200
Runners On	14	3	0	0	0	2	0	3	.214	.214	.200
Runners/Scor. Pos.	6	1	0	0	0	2	0	1	.167	.167	.143

RUNS BATTED IN	From 1B	From 2B	From 3B	Scoring Position
Totals	1/85	6/37	8/23	14/60
Percentage	1.2%	16.2%	34.8%	23.3%

Loves to face: Don Carman (.556, 5-for-9)
Mark Portugal (.556, 5-for-9)
Frank Viola (.389, 7-for-18)

Hates to face: Charlie Leibrandt (.133, 2-for-15)
Dennis Martinez (0-for-6)
Mike Scott (0-for-9)

Miscellaneous statistics: Ground outs-to-air outs ratio: 2.10 last season, 3d-highest rate in N.L.; 1.93 for career.... Grounded into 7 double plays in 51 opportunities (one per 7.3).... Drove in 6 of 11 runners from third base with less than two outs (55%).... Direction of balls hit to the outfield: 16% to left field, 34% to center, 50% to right.... Base running: Advanced from first base to third on 7 of 17 outfield singles (41%); scored from second on 5 of 8 (63%).... Made 1.03 assists per nine innings at third base.

Comments: Three Cubs third basemen split the playing time there pretty evenly last season: Luis Salazar played 727 innings, Ramos played 402⅔, and Curtis Wilkerson played 313. Although Wilkerson had by far the highest rate of errors (one per 8.9 chances), Ramos clearly had the most limited range of the three: he made 1.65 plays per nine innings, compared to 2.49 for Salazar and 2.82 for Wilkerson.... His career average of one error per 12.9 chances at third base ranks 56th among the 60 active players with at least 100 games there. So why does Zimmer play him there? Perhaps because Wilkerson ranks 60th.... Of his eight career home runs, his only one against a left-handed pitcher was off Neal Heaton in 1989.... Career batting average of .177 in Late-Inning Pressure Situations is the lowest of any active player (minimum: 150 AB). He has batted below .115 in LIPS in five of the last seven seasons.... Ramos is hitless in 13 career at-bats at Candlestick Park, and his career average at the Oakland Coliseum is only .034 (1-for-29), giving him a career batting average of .024 (1-for-42) in the Bay Area. (Thank goodness the Cubs don't have an affiliate in the California League.)... Ramos has been around longer than you might think. He made his major league debut for the Yankees on Sept. 8, 1978—the same day as Danny Darwin and two days before Ron Oester. Ramos was traded to Texas with Mike Heath and Sparky Lyle in the deal that brought Dave Righetti to New York.

Randy Ready

Bats Right

Philadelphia Phillies	AB	H	2B	3B	HR	RBI	BB	SO	BA	SA	OBA
Season	217	53	9	1	1	26	29	35	.244	.309	.332
vs. Left-Handers	128	32	8	1	1	15	17	18	.250	.352	.336
vs. Right-Handers	89	21	1	0	0	11	12	17	.236	.247	.327
vs. Ground-Ballers	132	37	4	1	1	16	19	23	.280	.348	.366
vs. Fly-Ballers	85	16	5	0	0	10	10	12	.188	.247	.278
Home Games	117	31	4	0	0	13	14	17	.265	.299	.338
Road Games	100	22	5	1	1	13	15	18	.220	.320	.325
Grass Fields	49	10	1	1	0	3	8	8	.204	.265	.316
Artificial Turf	168	43	8	0	1	23	21	27	.256	.321	.337
April	18	5	1	0	1	5	4	3	.278	.500	.417
May	33	11	0	0	0	7	2	5	.333	.333	.371
June	38	9	3	0	0	3	1	7	.237	.316	.256
July	50	12	4	1	0	7	11	11	.240	.360	.371
August	33	7	0	0	0	2	4	5	.212	.212	.297
Sept./Oct.	45	9	1	0	0	2	7	4	.200	.222	.302
Leading Off Inn.	44	7	3	0	0	0	6	8	.159	.227	.275
Bases Empty	115	20	7	0	0	0	15	22	.174	.235	.275
Runners On	102	33	2	1	1	26	14	13	.324	.392	.395
Runners/Scor. Pos.	62	21	2	0	0	23	10	9	.339	.371	.413
Runners On/2 Out	38	14	0	0	0	9	7	4	.368	.368	.467
Scor. Pos./2 Out	29	9	0	0	0	9	6	3	.310	.310	.429
Late-Inning Pressure	58	21	4	0	1	7	7	14	.362	.483	.439
Leading Off	18	4	1	0	0	0	0	7	.222	.278	.263
Runners On	28	11	1	0	1	7	5	5	.393	.536	.485
Runners/Scor. Pos.	20	6	1	0	0	5	3	5	.300	.350	.391

RUNS BATTED IN	From 1B	From 2B	From 3B	Scoring Position
Totals	2/82	12/50	11/30	23/80
Percentage	2.4%	24.0%	36.7%	28.8%

Loves to face: Jim Deshaies (.429, 6-for-14, 1 HR, 6 BB)
Bryn Smith (.471, 8-for-17, 1 HR)
Fernando Valenzuela (.370, 10-for-27, 2 HR, 8 BB)

Hates to face: Orel Hershiser (0-for-11, 1 BB)
Dennis Martinez (.154, 2-for-13)
Mike Scott (.077, 1-for-13)

Miscellaneous statistics: Ground outs-to-air outs ratio: 0.62 last season, 5th-lowest rate in N.L.; 0.84 for career. . . . Grounded into 3 double plays in 61 opportunities (one per 20.3). . . . Drove in 9 of 18 runners from third base with less than two outs (50%). . . . Direction of balls hit to the outfield: 42% to left field, 27% to center, 30% to right. . . . Base running: Advanced from first base to third on 5 of 15 outfield singles (33%); scored from second on 6 of 8 (75%). . . . Made 3.65 assists per nine innings at second base.

Comments: Started 24 games at second base and 23 in left field, but he didn't start in the outfield after the end of July. Played no third base for the first time in his career. . . . Batted 150 points higher with runners on base (.324) than with the bases empty (.174) last season, the largest margin in the majors. . . . Batted 161 points higher in Late-Inning Pressure Situations (.362) than in other at-bats (.201) last season, the 3d-largest margin in the majors. . . . Total of plate appearances has decreased in each of the last three seasons: 423 in 1987, then 380, 303, 253. . . . Batted 99 points higher in day games (.338) than in night games (.238) over the last five seasons, the largest margin in the majors. . . . He has batted .280 or better against ground-ball pitchers in each of the last four seasons, but look at the drop in his yearly averages vs. fly-ball pitchers during that time: .281, .247, .242, .188. . . . Has hit at least one home run in every National League ballpark except the Astrodome (45 AB) and Olympic Stadium (65 AB). He was also homerless in the American League's domed ballparks while playing for the Brewers. . . . He's claims he's Ready, but apparently that's not always true. His career batting average as a pinch hitter is only .227 (29-for-128, 1 HR).

Gary Redus

Bats Right

Pittsburgh Pirates	AB	H	2B	3B	HR	RBI	BB	SO	BA	SA	OBA
Season	227	56	15	3	6	23	33	38	.247	.419	.341
vs. Left-Handers	202	53	15	3	6	23	27	29	.262	.455	.345
vs. Right-Handers	25	3	0	0	0	0	6	9	.120	.120	.313
vs. Ground-Ballers	125	30	9	1	2	8	21	23	.240	.376	.353
vs. Fly-Ballers	102	26	6	2	4	15	12	15	.255	.471	.325
Home Games	108	22	7	1	2	12	21	15	.204	.343	.333
Road Games	119	34	8	2	4	11	12	23	.286	.487	.348
Grass Fields	54	15	3	1	1	4	7	13	.278	.426	.355
Artificial Turf	173	41	12	2	5	19	26	25	.237	.416	.337
April	35	7	0	2	1	5	3	3	.200	.400	.300
May	30	6	2	0	0	3	3	5	.200	.267	.250
June	42	15	4	0	0	2	6	8	.357	.452	.429
July	30	3	2	0	1	5	5	8	.100	.267	.229
August	56	17	4	1	2	4	10	9	.304	.518	.409
Sept./Oct.	34	8	3	0	2	4	6	5	.235	.500	.341
Leading Off Inn.	81	22	4	0	3	3	11	9	.272	.432	.366
Bases Empty	151	41	11	1	4	4	23	19	.272	.437	.371
Runners On	76	15	4	2	2	19	10	19	.197	.382	.283
Runners/Scor. Pos.	34	8	0	2	2	17	5	8	.235	.529	.311
Runners On/2 Out	28	3	2	0	1	5	4	10	.107	.286	.242
Scor. Pos./2 Out	13	1	0	0	1	4	2	5	.077	.308	.250
Late-Inning Pressure	36	10	2	1	0	3	7	4	.278	.389	.378
Leading Off	13	5	1	0	0	0	2	1	.385	.462	.467
Runners On	11	4	1	1	0	3	2	2	.364	.636	.400
Runners/Scor. Pos.	4	2	0	1	0	3	0	1	.500	1.000	.333

RUNS BATTED IN	From 1B	From 2B	From 3B	Scoring Position
Totals	3/53	5/30	9/18	14/48
Percentage	5.7%	16.7%	50.0%	29.2%

Loves to face: Charlie Leibrandt (.444, 8-for-18)
Rick Mahler (.417, 10-for-24, 3 HR)
Terry Mulholland (.429, 6-for-14, 4 2B, 2 HR)

Hates to face: Dwight Gooden (.067, 1-for-15, 1 2B)
Danny Jackson (0-for-17, 4 BB)
Alejandro Pena (.063, 1-for-16)

Miscellaneous statistics: Ground outs-to-air outs ratio: 0.71 last season, 0.67 for career. . . . Grounded into 1 double play in 38 opportunities (one per 38.0). . . . Drove in 8 of 10 runners from third base with less than two outs (80%). . . . Direction of balls hit to the outfield: 42% to left field, 26% to center, 32% to right. . . . Base running: Advanced from first base to third on 9 of 13 outfield singles (69%); scored from second on 6 of 8 (75%). . . . Made 0.74 assists per nine innings at first base.

Comments: Has never driven in more than 51 runs in a season, but his low RBI total in 1990 was not his fault. At one point last season, Redus had a streak of 38 consecutive plate appearances in which he did not bat with a runner in scoring position. . . . Started 63 of 69 games in which the Pirates faced a left-handed starter, but only one of 93 vs. right-handers. He has officially reached the dreaded status of "platoon player," with close to 90 percent of his plate appearances coming against left-handed pitchers; PAs vs. right-handers year-by-year since 1987: 315, 217, 190, 32. . . . Batted 82 points higher in road games (.286) than in home games (.204) last season, the 5th-largest margin in the majors. . . . Has hit for a higher average with the bases empty than with runners on base in each of the last six seasons, tying Jose ("Not Uribe") Gonzalez for the longest streak in the majors over the last 16 years. . . . Stole only 11 bases last season, breaking a streak of seven consecutive years with at least 25 steals. He barely kept his career stolen-base average above the 80 percent mark, going 11-for-16 in 1990. Current career totals: 290-for-362 (80.1%). . . . Made his postseason debut in 1990. He previously missed the boat by three years at both Cincinnati and Philadelphia, and four years with the White Sox (for whom the boat doesn't sail too often to begin with).

Jeff Reed

Bats Left

Cincinnati Reds	AB	H	2B	3B	HR	RBI	BB	SO	BA	SA	OBA
Season	175	44	8	1	3	16	24	26	.251	.360	.340
vs. Left-Handers	25	9	2	0	2	4	5	6	.360	.680	.467
vs. Right-Handers	150	35	6	1	1	12	19	20	.233	.307	.318
vs. Ground-Ballers	79	19	2	0	0	7	12	10	.241	.266	.337
vs. Fly-Ballers	96	25	6	1	3	9	12	16	.260	.438	.343
Home Games	84	20	5	0	2	8	12	12	.238	.369	.330
Road Games	91	24	3	1	1	8	12	14	.264	.352	.350
Grass Fields	65	17	3	0	1	5	7	12	.262	.354	.333
Artificial Turf	110	27	5	1	2	11	17	14	.245	.364	.344
April	7	1	0	0	1	1	0	2	.143	.571	.143
May	13	1	0	0	0	1	2	1	.077	.077	.200
June	26	6	1	0	0	1	4	2	.231	.269	.333
July	26	8	1	1	1	4	4	6	.308	.538	.400
August	43	13	1	0	1	5	7	4	.302	.395	.392
Sept./Oct.	60	15	5	0	0	4	7	11	.250	.333	.328
Leading Off Inn.	45	11	3	1	0	0	5	4	.244	.356	.320
Bases Empty	100	26	8	1	2	2	11	10	.260	.420	.333
Runners On	75	18	0	0	1	14	13	16	.240	.280	.348
Runners/Scor. Pos.	44	11	0	0	0	12	11	10	.250	.250	.393
Runners On/2 Out	29	5	0	0	0	4	8	7	.172	.172	.351
Scor. Pos./2 Out	21	5	0	0	0	4	7	5	.238	.238	.429
Late-Inning Pressure	17	0	0	0	0	0	2	3	.000	.000	.105
Leading Off	3	0	0	0	0	0	0	0	.000	.000	.000
Runners On	10	0	0	0	0	0	2	3	.000	.000	.167
Runners/Scor. Pos.	7	0	0	0	0	0	2	3	.000	.000	.222

RUNS BATTED IN	From 1B	From 2B	From 3B	Scoring Position
Totals	1/49	5/34	7/18	12/52
Percentage	2.0%	14.7%	38.9%	23.1%

Loves to face: Danny Darwin (.333, 5-for-15, 3 2B, 1 3B)
Derek Lilliquist (2-for-2, 1 HR, 1 BB)
Jeff Parrett (.750, 3-for-4)

Hates to face: Mike Bielecki (.133, 2-for-15)
Doug Drabek (.167, 3-for-18)
Ken Howell (0-for-10, 1 BB)

Miscellaneous statistics: Ground outs-to-air outs ratio: 1.56 last season, 1.22 for career.... Grounded into 4 double plays in 41 opportunities (one per 10.3).... Drove in 6 of 11 runners from third base with less than two outs (55%).... Direction of balls hit to the outfield: 38% to left field, 30% to center, 32% to right.... Base running: Advanced from first base to third on 0 of 5 outfield singles.... Opposing base stealers: 67-for-82 (82%), 2d-highest rate in N.L. (Highest rate in N.L.: Nelson Santovenia, 51-for-62 [82%].)

Comments: He can't hit lefties (.229 career batting average vs. LHP), and he hasn't had much success with the game on the line (.196 in Late-Inning Pressure Situations, including 0-for-17 in 1990 and 6-for-49 in 1989). But there he is, batting against southpaw Bob Patterson *with the Reds trailing by a run and the bases loaded in the ninth inning of the fifth game of the playoffs!* Piniella had left himself vulnerable after pinch hitting for the only other catcher on his postseason roster in the previous inning. That meant that Reed, regardless of the game situation, had to bat when his turn in the order came around. (A double-switch with the pitcher's spot would have guaranteed that Reed would not bat in the ninth inning, but obviously Piniella didn't realize his tactical error.) After the game, Piniella defended his strategy by citing Reed's .360 average vs. left-handers in 1990. Three questions: (1) Why did Reed accumulate only 25 at-bats against southpaws during the regular season? (2) Why didn't Reed start a single game against a left-hander? (3) Why was Reed removed for pinch-hitter 15 times against left-handed pitchers?... We rest our case: That manager will *never* win a division title, let alone a league championship series, or a World Series.... Reed's 17 hitless at-bats in Late-Inning Pressure Situations last season puts him in good company. Over the past 16 years, the only other player with as many LIPS at-bats and no hits was Cecil Fielder, who went 0-for-19 in 1986 with Toronto.

R.J. Reynolds

Bats Left and Right

Pittsburgh Pirates	AB	H	2B	3B	HR	RBI	BB	SO	BA	SA	OBA
Season	215	62	10	1	0	19	23	35	.288	.344	.354
vs. Left-Handers	112	33	4	0	0	8	14	13	.295	.330	.373
vs. Right-Handers	103	29	6	1	0	11	9	22	.282	.359	.333
vs. Ground-Ballers	104	29	6	0	0	10	16	21	.279	.337	.375
vs. Fly-Ballers	111	33	4	1	0	9	7	14	.297	.351	.333
Home Games	96	28	7	1	0	14	13	14	.292	.385	.369
Road Games	119	34	3	0	0	5	10	21	.286	.311	.341
Grass Fields	68	17	2	0	0	4	3	13	.250	.279	.282
Artificial Turf	147	45	8	1	0	15	20	22	.306	.374	.385
April	32	9	2	0	0	3	3	5	.281	.344	.343
May	38	11	1	1	0	4	6	5	.289	.368	.386
June	38	10	2	0	0	5	3	5	.263	.316	.310
July	54	19	4	0	0	6	4	6	.352	.426	.390
August	28	7	1	0	0	1	1	5	.250	.286	.276
Sept./Oct.	25	6	0	0	0	0	6	9	.240	.240	.387
Leading Off Inn.	52	18	1	0	0	0	4	7	.346	.365	.393
Bases Empty	116	35	5	1	0	0	10	20	.302	.362	.357
Runners On	99	27	5	0	0	19	13	15	.273	.323	.351
Runners/Scor. Pos.	54	14	3	0	0	18	7	10	.259	.315	.333
Runners On/2 Out	41	9	3	0	0	7	5	8	.220	.293	.304
Scor. Pos./2 Out	25	5	1	0	0	6	4	5	.200	.240	.310
Late-Inning Pressure	49	16	2	0	0	8	4	6	.327	.367	.364
Leading Off	12	4	0	0	0	0	1	1	.333	.333	.385
Runners On	24	9	1	0	0	8	3	1	.375	.417	.414
Runners/Scor. Pos.	15	5	0	0	0	7	2	0	.333	.333	.368

RUNS BATTED IN	From 1B	From 2B	From 3B	Scoring Position
Totals	2/77	6/40	11/24	17/64
Percentage	2.6%	15.0%	45.8%	26.6%

Loves to face: Joe Price (.533, 8-for-15, 1 HR)
Orel Hershiser (.410, 16-for-39)
Craig Lefferts (.769, 10-for-13)

Hates to face: John Franco (.158, 3-for-19)
Nolan Ryan (.125, 3-for-24, 3 BB, 11 SO)
Rick Sutcliffe (.185, 5-for-27, 14 SO)

Miscellaneous statistics: Ground outs-to-air outs ratio: 2.67 last season, highest rate in majors; 1.67 for career.... Grounded into 12 double plays in 52 opportunities (one per 4.3), worst rate in N.L.... Drove in 8 of 15 runners from third base with less than two outs (53%).... Direction of balls hit to the outfield: 45% to left field, 36% to center, 19% to right batting left-handed; 36% to left, 36% to center, 28% to right batting right-handed.... Base running: Advanced from first base to third on 2 of 10 outfield singles (20%); scored from second on 4 of 5 (80%).... Made 2.11 putouts per nine innings in center field.

Comments: Overall batting average was the highest of his career.... Batted .311 (51-for-164) in 44 games in the starting lineup. But when you've never played an inning of your major league career anywhere but the outfield, and your teammates include Andy Van Slyke, Bobby Bonilla, and Barry Bonds, here's what a .311 mark as a starter gets you: 42 appearances as a pinch hitter.... Among National League players without a home run, only Mark Lemke had more at-bats.... Among N.L. players, only Rick Dempsey grounded into double plays at a higher rate than Reynolds last season (minimum: 5 GIDP).... Stole 91 bases in 112 attempts (81%) over his six seasons with Pittsburgh.... Reynolds will be spending the summmer of 1991 in Japan, which, thanks to Cecil Fielder's Godzilla-like return from the Orient, no longer sounds like a career-ending move. But in Reynolds's case, that may still be true. By the time the 1992 season rolls around, R.J. will be pushing 31; don't forget that Fielder made his return at the age of 26.... Batted .267 in nearly 800 big-league games, but had as many as 400 at-bats only once: 402 for Pittsburgh in 1986.

Bip Roberts

Bats Left and Right

San Diego Padres	AB	H	2B	3B	HR	RBI	BB	SO	BA	SA	OBA
Season	556	172	36	3	9	44	55	65	.309	.433	.375
vs. Left-Handers	221	65	17	0	4	16	16	26	.294	.425	.350
vs. Right-Handers	335	107	19	3	5	28	39	39	.319	.439	.391
vs. Ground-Ballers	282	94	15	1	6	26	30	33	.333	.457	.402
vs. Fly-Ballers	274	78	21	2	3	18	25	32	.285	.409	.348
Home Games	287	81	14	2	4	17	19	31	.282	.387	.334
Road Games	269	91	22	1	5	27	36	34	.338	.483	.416
Grass Fields	414	115	20	3	6	27	38	46	.278	.384	.342
Artificial Turf	142	57	16	0	3	17	17	19	.401	.577	.469
April	66	17	3	1	2	5	3	5	.258	.424	.286
May	95	31	8	1	2	10	12	13	.326	.495	.402
June	102	30	7	1	1	8	11	15	.294	.412	.385
July	87	25	4	0	0	6	10	7	.287	.333	.360
August	100	34	9	0	1	6	9	12	.340	.460	.391
Sept./Oct.	106	35	5	0	3	9	10	13	.330	.462	.393
Leading Off Inn.	238	68	10	3	3	3	26	29	.286	.391	.361
Bases Empty	379	113	22	3	3	3	44	48	.298	.396	.377
Runners On	177	59	14	0	6	41	11	17	.333	.514	.371
Runners/Scor. Pos.	100	28	8	0	3	34	6	10	.280	.450	.321
Runners On/2 Out	74	22	5	0	4	24	5	10	.297	.527	.350
Scor. Pos./2 Out	56	16	4	0	3	21	2	6	.286	.518	.322
Late-Inning Pressure	83	23	2	0	1	9	9	13	.277	.337	.354
Leading Off	20	4	0	0	0	0	7	2	.200	.200	.407
Runners On	33	8	0	0	1	9	1	8	.242	.333	.270
Runners/Scor. Pos.	19	4	0	0	1	9	0	3	.211	.368	.227

RUNS BATTED IN	From 1B	From 2B	From 3B	Scoring Position
Totals	6/119	13/80	16/41	29/121
Percentage	5.0%	16.3%	39.0%	24.0%

Loves to face: Don Carman (.500, 4-for-8, 1 HR)
Greg Maddux (.462, 6-for-13, 5 BB)
Dennis Martinez (.529, 9-for-17)

Hates to face: Tim Belcher (0-for-12, 2 BB)
Rick Mahler (.190, 4-for-21)
Rick Reuschel (.133, 2-for-15)

Miscellaneous statistics: Ground outs-to-air outs ratio: 1.40 last season, 1.50 for career.... Grounded into 8 double plays in 92 opportunities (one per 11.5).... Drove in 12 of 16 runners from third base with less than two outs (75%), 4th-highest rate in N.L.... Direction of balls hit to the outfield: 47% to left field, 23% to center, 29% to right batting left-handed; 40% to left, 26% to center; 34% to right batting right-handed.... Base running: Advanced from first base to third on 12 of 39 outfield singles (31%); scored from second on 33 of 38 (87%).... Made 2.36 putouts per nine innings in left field, 2d-highest rate in N.L.

Comments: Last season, three players batted .300 or better with at least 40 extra-base hits and 40 stolen bases. Two won MVP Awards; the other was Bip. No one did it in 1989; in 1988, there was only MVP Jose ("40/40") Canseco and Paul Molitor.... The leadoff spot in San Diego's batting order led the league in runs scored (119) and ranked second to the Phillies with a .311 batting average. Roberts started 125 games in the number-one slot.... Split his time almost evenly between the infield and the outfield, batting .329 while playing third base, second base, and shortstop, and batting .296 in his at-bats as an outfielder.... Led the National League with 62 hits to the opposite field last season. Only one A.L. player had more: Wade Boggs (81).... Batted 124 points higher on artificial turf (.401) than on grass fields (.278) last season, the largest margin in the majors. In our 16 years of data, Roberts became the first player to hit .400 or better on artificial surfaces (minimum: 150 PA).... Career batting averages: .280 at Jack Murphy Stadium, .283 on other grass fields, .338 on artificial surfaces.... Career batting averages: .321 with runners on base, .283 with the bases empty.... This hardly seems like the same player who batted .253 in 101 games for San Diego, then disappeared for two years.

Wasn't there another Leon Roberts a while back?

Chris Sabo

Bats Right

Cincinnati Reds	AB	H	2B	3B	HR	RBI	BB	SO	BA	SA	OBA
Season	567	153	38	2	25	71	61	58	.270	.476	.343
vs. Left-Handers	214	70	12	1	14	33	27	12	.327	.589	.408
vs. Right-Handers	353	83	26	1	11	38	34	46	.235	.408	.303
vs. Ground-Ballers	289	83	20	1	11	30	30	21	.287	.478	.357
vs. Fly-Ballers	278	70	18	1	14	41	31	37	.252	.475	.329
Home Games	275	77	18	0	15	45	33	28	.280	.509	.361
Road Games	292	76	20	2	10	26	28	30	.260	.445	.326
Grass Fields	177	46	14	0	7	18	14	16	.260	.458	.318
Artificial Turf	390	107	24	2	18	53	47	42	.274	.485	.354
April	64	25	6	0	5	12	12	7	.391	.719	.487
May	101	28	6	0	5	15	9	7	.277	.485	.342
June	113	34	8	1	6	15	12	15	.301	.549	.373
July	98	17	6	0	2	7	11	9	.173	.296	.261
August	102	26	5	1	5	12	8	8	.255	.471	.313
Sept./Oct.	89	23	7	0	2	10	9	12	.258	.404	.323
Leading Off Inn.	170	43	6	1	7	7	20	13	.253	.424	.332
Bases Empty	353	98	24	2	17	17	40	30	.278	.501	.354
Runners On	214	55	14	0	8	54	21	28	.257	.435	.325
Runners/Scor. Pos.	136	33	10	0	5	47	16	18	.243	.426	.325
Runners On/2 Out	101	25	6	0	3	25	12	17	.248	.396	.333
Scor. Pos./2 Out	75	19	6	0	2	23	8	12	.253	.413	.333
Late-Inning Pressure	76	20	4	0	4	9	10	7	.263	.474	.349
Leading Off	19	3	0	0	2	2	1	1	.158	.474	.200
Runners On	30	8	1	0	1	6	5	5	.267	.400	.371
Runners/Scor. Pos.	17	6	1	0	1	6	4	2	.353	.588	.476

RUNS BATTED IN	From 1B	From 2B	From 3B	Scoring Position
Totals	7/128	15/99	24/60	39/159
Percentage	5.5%	15.2%	40.0%	24.5%

Loves to face: Dennis Cook (.556, 5-for-9, 1 HR)
Jim Deshaies (.417, 10-for-24, 2 HR)
Kelly Downs (.714, 5-for-7, 3 2B, 1 HR)

Hates to face: Sid Fernandez (.067, 1-for-15, 1 2B, 2 BB)
Greg Maddux (.158, 3-for-19)
John Smoltz (.083, 1-for-12)

Miscellaneous statistics: Ground outs-to-air outs ratio: 0.72 last season, 0.74 for career.... Grounded into 8 double plays in 77 opportunities (one per 9.6).... Drove in 15 of 28 runners from third base with less than two outs (54%).... Direction of balls hit to the outfield: 58% to left field, 30% to center, 11% to right.... Base running: Advanced from first base to third on 18 of 30 outfield singles (60%); scored from second on 15 of 18 (83%).... Made 1.94 assists per nine innings at third base.

Comments: Hit all 25 regular-season home runs to left field, and added three more in post-season play. Every other player with 25 or more home runs last season hit at least one to either center field or to the opposite field.... Only 13 of Sabo's 153 hits were to the opposite field.... Averaged one home run every 23 at-bats, compared to one per 50 at-bats over the first two years of his career. The increase in his home run rate vs. left-handed pitchers was even more outstanding: one per 60 AB through 1989, one per 15 last season.... Became the fourth third baseman in Reds history to start an All-Star game, joining Don Hoak (1957, the year Reds fans stuffed the ballot box), Tony Perez (1970), and Rose (1976 and 1978).... Led N.L. third basemen with a .966 fielding percentage (one error per 29 chances). Over the last 40 years, only two other Reds third basemen have led the league in that category: Hoak (1957) and Rose (1976).... Has batted between .260 and .271 in each of his three seasons in the majors. But his batting average vs. right-handed pitchers has declined year by year: .266, .245, .235.... Career average in night games (.285) is 59 points higher than in day games (.226), the 2d-largest margin in the majors over the last five seasons. Sabo has batted at least 50 points higher in night games in each of his three seasons.... Think Michigan Wolverines, and most people think football or hoops. But Sabo and two of his Reds teammates, Barry Larkin and Hal Morris, all played baseball there in the early-to-mid-1980s.

Luis Salazar

Bats Right

Chicago Cubs	AB	H	2B	3B	HR	RBI	BB	SO	BA	SA	OBA
Season	410	104	13	3	12	47	19	59	.254	.388	.293
vs. Left-Handers	157	46	7	1	6	22	6	18	.293	.465	.319
vs. Right-Handers	253	58	6	2	6	25	13	41	.229	.340	.277
vs. Ground-Ballers	182	46	5	0	4	22	10	22	.253	.346	.290
vs. Fly-Ballers	228	58	8	3	8	25	9	37	.254	.421	.295
Home Games	218	64	7	2	7	20	11	29	.294	.440	.333
Road Games	192	40	6	1	5	27	8	30	.208	.328	.246
Grass Fields	318	85	9	3	12	39	16	44	.267	.428	.306
Artificial Turf	92	19	4	0	0	8	3	15	.207	.250	.247
April	53	13	2	0	0	3	2	5	.245	.283	.273
May	45	7	0	0	2	7	7	8	.156	.289	.264
June	48	21	4	1	2	10	3	6	.438	.688	.471
July	93	22	2	1	3	12	3	12	.237	.376	.276
August	89	21	3	0	4	8	3	15	.236	.404	.277
Sept./Oct.	82	20	2	1	1	7	1	13	.244	.329	.253
Leading Off Inn.	93	32	5	0	4	4	3	10	.344	.527	.365
Bases Empty	229	62	10	1	7	7	6	27	.271	.415	.295
Runners On	181	42	3	2	5	40	13	32	.232	.354	.289
Runners/Scor. Pos.	115	28	2	1	4	37	9	17	.243	.383	.307
Runners On/2 Out	85	12	2	0	2	13	10	17	.141	.235	.232
Scor. Pos./2 Out	63	9	1	0	2	13	8	11	.143	.254	.239
Late-Inning Pressure	58	17	0	0	2	8	5	9	.293	.397	.359
Leading Off	14	5	0	0	1	1	2	2	.357	.571	.438
Runners On	23	9	0	0	1	7	2	4	.391	.522	.462
Runners/Scor. Pos.	15	7	0	0	1	7	1	1	.467	.667	.529

RUNS BATTED IN	From 1B	From 2B	From 3B	Scoring Position
Totals	6/119	12/83	17/50	29/133
Percentage	5.0%	14.5%	34.0%	21.8%

Loves to face: Bruce Hurst (.313, 5-for-16)
Randy Myers (.667, 2-for-3, 1 HR, 1 BB)
Bruce Ruffin (.353, 6-for-17)

Hates to face: Neal Heaton (.158, 3-for-19)
Mike Scott (.103, 3-for-29, 1 HR, 0 BB)
Fernando Valenzuela (.114, 8-for-70, 1 HR)

Miscellaneous statistics: Ground outs-to-air outs ratio: 0.89 last season, 1.09 for career. . . . Grounded into 4 double plays in 73 opportunities (one per 18.3). . . . Drove in 12 of 23 runners from third base with less than two outs (52%). . . . Direction of balls hit to the outfield: 33% to left field, 33% to center, 34% to right. . . . Base running: Advanced from first base to third on 9 of 22 outfield singles (41%); scored from second on 4 of 5 (80%). . . . Made 1.68 assists per nine innings at third base, lowest rate in N.L.

Comments: One of 134 players to have played for both the Chicago Cubs and the Chicago White Sox, 19 of whom (Salazar included) played at least 100 games for each. The only player to reach 300 games for both teams is Danny Green, who split an eight-year career between the Cubs (400 games from 1898 to 1901) and White Sox (523 games from 1902 to 1905). . . . Incidentally, Salazar is one of 40 players in major league history to serve three tours with the same team (San Diego, in his case). He started his career in San Diego, and returned there after stints with the White Sox (1985–86) and the Tigers (1988). If he rejoins the Padres once again, Salazar would become only the second player to play four different terms for the same team. The other: Bobo Newsom, who was a *five*-term Washington Senator. (Didn't they outlaw that after FDR?) Joe McIlvaine, are you interested in a small piece of baseball history? . . . Has had higher batting averages against left-handers than against right-handers in each of the last nine seasons. . . . Has a career home-run rate of one every 47 at-bats, but has 82 career at-bats with the bases loaded and no grand slams. His career average of .098 (4-for-41, no XBH) with two outs and the bases loaded is the 2d-lowest of any player with at least 35 at bats in those situations over the last 16 years. Only Rick Dempsey's average is worse (.048, 3-for-62, 1 HR). . . . Career average of .291 in Late-Inning Pressure Situations, .260 in other at-bats.

Juan Samuel

Bats Right

Los Angeles Dodgers	AB	H	2B	3B	HR	RBI	BB	SO	BA	SA	OBA
Season	492	119	24	3	13	52	51	126	.242	.382	.316
vs. Left-Handers	187	54	10	2	10	25	17	43	.289	.524	.350
vs. Right-Handers	305	65	14	1	3	27	34	83	.213	.295	.297
vs. Ground-Ballers	249	67	13	1	8	30	23	58	.269	.426	.332
vs. Fly-Ballers	243	52	11	2	5	22	28	68	.214	.337	.301
Home Games	224	55	8	3	6	26	25	60	.246	.388	.329
Road Games	268	64	16	0	7	26	26	66	.239	.377	.305
Grass Fields	349	88	17	3	10	35	39	86	.252	.404	.332
Artificial Turf	143	31	7	0	3	17	12	40	.217	.329	.277
April	82	17	4	1	1	4	11	29	.207	.317	.298
May	102	24	4	0	2	7	4	27	.235	.333	.278
June	76	14	5	0	2	7	8	23	.184	.329	.271
July	92	23	3	0	3	13	12	18	.250	.380	.340
August	55	9	0	1	0	3	9	17	.164	.200	.284
Sept./Oct.	85	32	8	1	5	18	7	12	.376	.671	.419
Leading Off Inn.	146	39	8	1	3	3	16	28	.267	.397	.348
Bases Empty	291	75	17	2	7	7	26	67	.258	.402	.323
Runners On	201	44	7	1	6	45	25	59	.219	.353	.308
Runners/Scor. Pos.	126	26	3	1	2	36	20	41	.206	.294	.305
Runners On/2 Out	92	18	3	1	1	18	17	31	.196	.283	.333
Scor. Pos./2 Out	66	13	1	1	1	17	15	24	.197	.288	.346
Late-Inning Pressure	64	18	4	1	2	9	5	15	.281	.469	.352
Leading Off	16	7	1	0	1	1	0	3	.438	.688	.471
Runners On	27	6	1	0	1	8	3	7	.222	.370	.323
Runners/Scor. Pos.	20	5	1	0	0	6	3	5	.250	.300	.348

RUNS BATTED IN	From 1B	From 2B	From 3B	Scoring Position
Totals	6/143	10/105	23/57	33/162
Percentage	4.2%	9.5%	40.4%	20.4%

Loves to face: Mike Bielecki (.438, 7-for-16, 1 HR)
Joe Magrane (.471, 8-for-17, 1 HR)
Trevor Wilson (2-for-2, 1 HR, 1 BB)

Hates to face: Sid Fernandez (.120, 6-for-50, 3 2B, 1 HR)
Dwight Gooden (.179, 12-for-67)
Roger McDowell (.091, 2-for-22)

Miscellaneous statistics: Ground outs-to-air outs ratio: 1.15 last season, 1.11 for career. . . . Grounded into 8 double plays in 94 opportunities (one per 11.8). . . . Drove in 16 of 32 runners from third base with less than two outs (50%). . . . Direction of balls hit to the outfield: 33% to left field, 27% to center, 40% to right. . . . Base running: Advanced from first base to third on 10 of 16 outfield singles (63%); scored from second on 9 of 11 (82%). . . . Made 2.63 assists per nine innings at second base, 2d-lowest rate in N.L.

Comments: Started the season as the Dodgers' center fielder and leadoff hitter, but lost both of those jobs by the end of May. He was permanently moved to the infield on May 15, and was dropped from the leadoff spot a week later, after batting .188 in 36 games in that role—a great move by Lasorda. Los Angeles led the league by a wide margin with 119 first-inning runs (14 more than runner-up Chicago), despite scoring only seven in the 38 games that Samuel batted leadoff. With other leadoff batters (most Lenny Harris and Stan Javier), the Dodgers scored 112 first-inning runs in 124 games. . . . His batting average was .213 on September 9, but he batted .400 over the final three weeks to raise his average almost 30 points. . . . His batting average vs. left-handers was a career-high, but his average against right-handed pitchers has declined in each season since 1987: .281, .243, .222, .213. . . . Had a streak of 23 consecutive plate appearances in which he batted with the bases empty, equalling the longest streak in the N.L. over the last 11 years. . . . Stole 38 bases, but was caught stealing a career-high 20 times. His success rate was the lowest of his career (66%). . . . Had the lowest fielding percentage of any regular second baseman in the majors last season (.972, one error per 36 chances). . . . Owns a career batting average of .347 (26-for-75, 2 HR) with the bases loaded, but has drawn only one walk in 82 bases-loaded plate appearances.

Ryne Sandberg

Bats Right

Chicago Cubs	AB	H	2B	3B	HR	RBI	BB	SO	BA	SA	OBA
Season	615	188	30	3	40	100	50	84	.306	.559	.354
vs. Left-Handers	214	54	13	0	10	23	21	34	.252	.453	.319
vs. Right-Handers	401	134	17	3	30	77	29	50	.334	.616	.373
vs. Ground-Ballers	287	90	10	1	23	54	24	41	.314	.596	.361
vs. Fly-Ballers	328	98	20	2	17	46	26	43	.299	.527	.348
Home Games	305	109	21	1	25	62	27	44	.357	.679	.405
Road Games	310	79	9	2	15	38	23	40	.255	.442	.303
Grass Fields	435	143	25	3	29	76	36	64	.329	.600	.375
Artificial Turf	180	45	5	0	11	24	14	20	.250	.461	.303
April	76	19	3	0	1	7	2	11	.250	.329	.266
May	118	44	10	0	9	21	12	13	.373	.686	.427
June	114	43	3	1	14	25	13	16	.377	.789	.438
July	98	20	4	1	1	10	6	15	.204	.296	.250
August	107	30	5	1	6	16	8	16	.280	.514	.325
Sept./Oct.	102	32	5	0	9	21	9	13	.314	.627	.366
Leading Off Inn.	116	31	3	0	14	14	9	20	.267	.655	.320
Bases Empty	378	101	20	0	24	24	23	55	.267	.511	.311
Runners On	237	87	10	3	16	76	27	29	.367	.637	.418
Runners/Scor. Pos.	124	37	3	2	9	56	20	19	.298	.573	.373
Runners On/2 Out	74	23	3	0	3	17	18	11	.311	.473	.446
Scor. Pos./2 Out	45	13	2	0	2	13	14	7	.289	.467	.458
Late-Inning Pressure	90	25	3	1	5	16	7	13	.278	.500	.324
Leading Off	21	7	1	0	2	2	1	3	.333	.667	.364
Runners On	35	9	0	1	2	13	4	5	.257	.486	.302
Runners/Scor. Pos.	24	3	0	0	1	10	3	3	.125	.250	.194

RUNS BATTED IN	From 1B	From 2B	From 3B	Scoring Position
Totals	19/181	18/101	23/50	41/151
Percentage	10.5%	17.8%	46.0%	27.2%

Loves to face: Bob Ojeda (.458, 11-for-24, 3 HR)
Randy O'Neal (.714, 5-for-7, 3 HR)
Wally Whitehurst (.571, 4-for-7, 2 HR)

Hates to face: Larry Andersen (.086, 3-for-35, 0 BB)
Jose Rijo (.077, 1-for-13)
Bryn Smith (.145, 10-for-69, 2 HR, 11 BB)

Miscellaneous statistics: Ground outs-to-air outs ratio: 0.86 last season, 1.13 for career. . . . Grounded into 8 double plays in 132 opportunities (one per 16.5). . . . Drove in 19 of 30 runners from third base with less than two outs (63%). . . . Direction of balls hit to the outfield: 45% to left field, 31% to center, 24% to right. . . . Base running: Advanced from first base to third on 18 of 33 outfield singles (55%); scored from second on 16 of 22 (73%). . . . Made 3.21 assists per nine innings at second base.

Comments: Only three players in baseball history have met the following criteria in a single season: .300 batting average, 40 home runs, 100 RBIs, 25 stolen bases. They are Hank Aaron (1963), Jose Canseco (1988), and Ryne Sandberg (1990). . . . Sandberg became the first second baseman ever to hit 30 or more home runs in consecutive seasons. He also became the only second baseman other than Rogers Hornsby to hit 30 HR and bat .300 or better in the same season. . . . Has started five consecutive All-Star Games, and six in the last seven years. Rod Carew and Nellie Fox share the record for second basemen with eight starts; Joe Morgan holds the record for *consecutive* starts there (7). . . . Not only is Sandberg the all-time leader at second with a career average of one error per 92 chances, but if you lower the qualifier to 100 games he leads active players at third base as well (one error per 33 chances). . . . Of course, if you lower the qualifier far enough, Sandberg isn't even the leader at second base on his own team (George Bell—one game, one putout, no errors). . . . Needs 133 games to pass Johnny Evers as the Cubs' all-time leader in games at second base. The top three: Evers (1368), Billy Herman (1340), Sandberg (1236). . . . Batted 82 points higher vs. right-handers (.334) than vs. left-handers (.252) last season, the 5th-largest margin in the majors. . . . Batted 103 points higher in home games (.357) than in road games (.255) last season, the 4th-largest margin in the majors. . . . Sandberg vs. southpaws at Wrigley, you ask? No problem: .320 (33-for-103), 8 2B, 9 HR.

Benito Santiago

Bats Right

San Diego Padres	AB	H	2B	3B	HR	RBI	BB	SO	BA	SA	OBA
Season	344	93	8	5	11	53	27	55	.270	.419	.323
vs. Left-Handers	116	32	3	0	1	12	9	21	.276	.328	.323
vs. Right-Handers	228	61	5	5	10	41	18	34	.268	.465	.323
vs. Ground-Ballers	161	40	5	3	3	22	15	18	.248	.373	.317
vs. Fly-Ballers	183	53	3	2	8	31	12	37	.290	.459	.328
Home Games	189	54	4	4	5	26	19	31	.286	.429	.350
Road Games	155	39	4	1	6	27	8	24	.252	.406	.287
Grass Fields	262	73	4	4	10	42	19	41	.279	.439	.330
Artificial Turf	82	20	4	1	1	11	8	14	.244	.354	.301
April	63	25	3	1	4	13	3	6	.397	.667	.433
May	88	21	1	1	2	9	3	10	.239	.341	.255
June	35	13	1	0	3	11	9	9	.371	.657	.511
July	0	0	0	0	0	0	0	0	—	—	—
August	63	16	1	2	0	7	5	10	.254	.333	.306
Sept./Oct.	95	18	2	1	2	13	7	20	.189	.295	.243
Leading Off Inn.	88	22	0	0	2	2	4	17	.250	.318	.283
Bases Empty	204	55	3	4	3	3	13	31	.270	.368	.320
Runners On	140	38	5	1	8	50	14	24	.271	.493	.327
Runners/Scor. Pos.	91	22	3	1	6	46	11	17	.242	.495	.309
Runners On/2 Out	69	21	1	0	4	23	8	11	.304	.493	.385
Scor. Pos./2 Out	49	15	1	0	4	23	8	7	.306	.571	.414
Late-Inning Pressure	62	25	2	1	3	7	5	9	.403	.613	.464
Leading Off	18	9	0	0	1	1	1	3	.500	.667	.526
Runners On	25	9	1	0	2	6	3	3	.360	.640	.448
Runners/Scor. Pos.	15	3	1	0	2	6	2	1	.200	.667	.333

RUNS BATTED IN	From 1B	From 2B	From 3B	Scoring Position
Totals	7/103	11/69	24/50	35/119
Percentage	6.8%	15.9%	48.0%	29.4%

Loves to face: Don Carman (.360, 9-for-25, 2 HR)
Mike LaCoss (.318, 7-for-22, 2 HR)
Zane Smith (.375, 6-for-16, 2 2B, 3 HR)

Hates to face: Jim Clancy (.063, 1-for-16)
Sid Fernandez (.080, 2-for-25, 0 BB, 12 SO)
Ted Power (.067, 1-for-15)

Miscellaneous statistics: Ground outs-to-air outs ratio: 0.66 last season, 0.88 for career. . . . Grounded into 4 double plays in 63 opportunities (one per 15.8). . . . Drove in 13 of 26 runners from third base with less than two outs (50%). . . . Direction of balls hit to the outfield: 42% to left field, 33% to center, 25% to right. . . . Base running: Advanced from first base to third on 6 of 19 outfield singles (32%); scored from second on 6 of 9 (67%). . . . Opposing base stealers: 60-for-91 (66%).

Comments: Santiago's reputation as a thrower won't benefit from the figures above; he ranked only 16th among 42 catchers in opponents' stolen-base percentage. But that reputation did limit the number of runners who dared challenge Santiago's arm. Only two N.L. catchers faced fewer attempts per nine innings than Santiago (1.02): Darren Daulton (0.97) and Joe Oliver (1.02). . . . Batted .342 in 120 at-bats in the seventh inning or later. He batted 162 points higher in Late-Inning Pressure Situations (.403) than in other at-bats (.241), the 2d-largest margin in the majors. Career batting averages: .325 in LIPS, .253 in other at-bats. . . . Had started 48 of San Diego's first 58 games before he was sidelined for two months with a fractured wrist, suffered when he was hit by a pitch from Jeff Brantley. . . . Has played fewer games with each season in the majors. Year by year since 1987: 146, 139, 129, 100. . . . After four full seasons in the majors, he still hasn't reattained his rookie-season figures in games (146), batting average (.300), extra-base hits (53), home runs (18), RBIs (79), or stolen bases (21). . . . Has homered at every current National League ballpark except Olympic Stadium (79 career AB). . . . Career batting-average breakdown: .278 with the bases empty, .251 with runners on base, .229 with runners in scoring position. . . . Last season, he became the first player in Padres history to hit grand slam home runs in three consecutive seasons.

Mackey Sasser

Bats Left

New York Mets	AB	H	2B	3B	HR	RBI	BB	SO	BA	SA	OBA
Season	270	83	14	0	6	41	15	19	.307	.426	.344
vs. Left-Handers	53	11	3	0	1	7	3	10	.208	.321	.250
vs. Right-Handers	217	72	11	0	5	34	12	9	.332	.452	.366
vs. Ground-Ballers	121	42	5	0	3	22	6	10	.347	.463	.372
vs. Fly-Ballers	149	41	9	0	3	19	9	9	.275	.396	.321
Home Games	143	35	9	0	3	21	10	10	.245	.371	.295
Road Games	127	48	5	0	3	20	5	9	.378	.488	.402
Grass Fields	204	56	10	0	4	32	11	16	.275	.382	.312
Artificial Turf	66	27	4	0	2	9	4	3	.409	.561	.443
April	19	1	0	0	0	0	1	2	.053	.053	.100
May	34	13	1	0	1	6	5	2	.382	.500	.462
June	71	25	5	0	1	8	5	3	.352	.465	.390
July	54	22	4	0	4	20	0	3	.407	.704	.407
August	65	16	4	0	0	3	3	7	.246	.308	.290
Sept./Oct.	27	6	0	0	0	4	1	2	.222	.222	.241
Leading Off Inn.	64	20	5	0	0	0	1	3	.313	.391	.333
Bases Empty	141	40	8	0	0	0	3	9	.284	.340	.303
Runners On	129	43	6	0	6	41	12	10	.333	.519	.385
Runners/Scor. Pos.	71	21	2	0	5	36	10	8	.296	.535	.373
Runners On/2 Out	53	16	4	0	2	23	5	8	.302	.491	.362
Scor. Pos./2 Out	33	10	1	0	2	20	5	6	.303	.515	.395
Late-Inning Pressure	49	10	2	0	1	6	2	6	.204	.306	.235
Leading Off	7	2	2	0	0	0	0	1	.286	.571	.286
Runners On	27	7	0	0	1	6	1	4	.259	.370	.286
Runners/Scor. Pos.	18	5	0	0	1	6	0	3	.278	.444	.278

RUNS BATTED IN	From 1B	From 2B	From 3B	Scoring Position
Totals	7/95	16/58	12/34	28/92
Percentage	7.4%	27.6%	35.3%	30.4%

Loves to face: Ken Howell (.600, 6-for-10)
Mark Portugal (.600, 3-for-5, 1 HR)
Ed Whitson (.579, 11-for-19, 1 HR, 8 fly outs)

Hates to face: Tim Burke (0-for-8)
Bob Kipper (0-for-6)

Miscellaneous statistics: Ground outs-to-air outs ratio: 0.88 last season, 0.90 for career.... Grounded into 7 double plays in 58 opportunities (one per 8.3).... Drove in 6 of 14 runners from third base with less than two outs (43%).... Direction of balls hit to the outfield: 26% to left field, 28% to center, 46% to right.... Base running: Advanced from first base to third on 3 of 13 outfield singles (23%); scored from second on 2 of 10 (20%), lowest rate in majors.... Opposing base stealers: 91-for-129 (71%).

Comments: Led National League catchers in errors (14) despite playing only 87 games. The last catcher to lead the N.L. in errors in fewer games: Bob Uecker in 1967 (11 errors in 76 games). John Bateman led the league in 1972 with totals identical to Sasser's.... Batted .316 in his at-bats as a catcher last season. He was the only backstop in the majors to top the .300 mark. (Uecker's career batting average was .200.) ... Only four N.L. players in the last 50 years hit .280 or better in three consecutive seasons in which they caught at least 40 games, starting with their rookie years: Ernie Lombardi (10 years, 1931–40), Manny Sanguillen (8, 1969–76), and Tony Pena (4, 1981–84).... Batted 133 points higher in road games (.378) than in home games (.245) last season, the largest margin in the majors. Career batting-average breakdown: .264 at Shea Stadium, .328 on other grass fields, .313 on artificial surfaces.... Was removed for a pinch hitter 13 times last season, all against left-handed pitchers.... Has a career batting average of .198 vs. left-handers (one home run in 91 at-bats), .309 vs. right-handers (7 HR in 511 AB). As bad as that mark against southpaws is, it's still better than Charlie O'Brien's career mark against lefties (.196).... Has a career average of .500 (18-for-36, 2 HR) at Veterans Stadium.... Has driven in at least 30 percent of runners from scoring position in each of the last three seasons.

Mike Scioscia

Bats Left

Los Angeles Dodgers	AB	H	2B	3B	HR	RBI	BB	SO	BA	SA	OBA
Season	435	115	25	0	12	66	55	31	.264	.405	.348
vs. Left-Handers	119	28	5	0	2	18	10	11	.235	.328	.295
vs. Right-Handers	316	87	20	0	10	48	45	20	.275	.434	.367
vs. Ground-Ballers	226	64	18	0	3	35	34	14	.283	.403	.375
vs. Fly-Ballers	209	51	7	0	9	31	21	17	.244	.407	.318
Home Games	208	58	12	0	5	32	29	12	.279	.409	.363
Road Games	227	57	13	0	7	34	26	19	.251	.401	.335
Grass Fields	313	86	17	0	7	46	40	18	.275	.396	.353
Artificial Turf	122	29	8	0	5	20	15	13	.238	.426	.336
April	68	20	2	0	3	8	3	3	.294	.456	.324
May	76	21	4	0	3	14	8	5	.276	.447	.345
June	77	16	2	0	2	9	7	8	.208	.312	.274
July	67	18	7	0	1	14	11	2	.269	.418	.367
August	71	22	5	0	2	13	15	8	.310	.465	.437
Sept./Oct.	76	18	5	0	1	8	11	5	.237	.342	.337
Leading Off Inn.	88	21	6	0	4	4	11	5	.239	.443	.323
Bases Empty	246	65	13	0	10	10	23	19	.264	.439	.327
Runners On	189	50	12	0	2	56	32	12	.265	.360	.373
Runners/Scor. Pos.	119	37	8	0	1	54	21	7	.311	.403	.415
Runners On/2 Out	70	16	5	0	0	22	18	7	.229	.300	.393
Scor. Pos./2 Out	49	15	5	0	0	22	13	4	.306	.408	.460
Late-Inning Pressure	54	10	5	0	1	1	8	4	.185	.333	.290
Leading Off	14	4	2	0	1	1	1	2	.286	.643	.333
Runners On	26	4	1	0	0	0	5	2	.154	.192	.290
Runners/Scor. Pos.	12	1	0	0	0	0	4	1	.083	.083	.313

RUNS BATTED IN	From 1B	From 2B	From 3B	Scoring Position
Totals	4/148	23/95	27/59	50/154
Percentage	2.7%	24.2%	45.8%	32.5%

Loves to face: Kelly Downs (.432, 16-for-37)
Todd Frohwirth (.750, 3-for-4, 1 HR)
Ken Howell (.500, 5-for-10, 1 HR)

Hates to face: Juan Agosto (.067, 1-for-15)
Larry Andersen (0-for-13, 1 BB, all ground outs)
Andy Benes (0-for-14, 2 BB)

Miscellaneous statistics: Ground outs-to-air outs ratio: 1.06 last season, 1.06 for career.... Grounded into 11 double plays in 103 opportunities (one per 9.4).... Drove in 19 of 32 runners from third base with less than two outs (59%).... Direction of balls hit to the outfield: 27% to left field, 35% to center, 38% to right.... Base running: Advanced from first base to third on 10 of 30 outfield singles (33%); scored from second on 4 of 9 (44%).... Opposing base stealers: 99-for-137 (72%).

Comments: Currently ranks fourth in games caught for the Dodgers, but should move into first place on that list in 1991. The top four: Johnny Roseboro (1218), Roy Campanella (1183), Steve Yeager (1181), Scioscia (1172).... Has been in the starting lineup on opening day in each of the last seven years; the longest streak by a Dodgers backstop: John Roseboro (1959–67).... In 1990, Scioscia became the first Dodgers catcher to start an All-Star game since Campanella in 1954.... Dodgers pitchers allowed 4.18 runs per nine innings with Scioscia catching, compared to 4.75 with Rick Dempsey behind the plate.... His total of 31 strikeouts last season matched his career high. Established more noteworthy career highs in home runs and runs batted in.... Of his 57 career home runs, only nine have been hit off left-handed pitchers. He has hit 41 home runs with the bases empty (one per 52 at-bats), but only 16 with runners on base (one every 97 at-bats).... Has hit for a higher average against ground-ball pitchers than against fly-ball pitchers in each of the last five seasons.... Career breakdown: .266 at Dodger Stadium, .286 on other grass fields, .231 on artificial surfaces.... Career batting average of .362 at Candlestick Park is his highest at any stadium.

Mike Sharperson

Bats Right

Los Angeles Dodgers	AB	H	2B	3B	HR	RBI	BB	SO	BA	SA	OBA
Season	357	106	14	2	3	36	46	39	.297	.373	.376
vs. Left-Handers	208	67	8	1	1	17	25	23	.322	.385	.396
vs. Right-Handers	149	39	6	1	2	19	21	16	.262	.356	.349
vs. Ground-Ballers	164	57	6	0	2	17	26	12	.348	.421	.435
vs. Fly-Ballers	193	49	8	2	1	19	20	27	.254	.332	.324
Home Games	195	60	7	1	1	19	21	18	.308	.369	.373
Road Games	162	46	7	1	2	17	25	21	.284	.377	.379
Grass Fields	280	89	9	1	2	27	35	29	.318	.379	.393
Artificial Turf	77	17	5	1	1	9	11	10	.221	.351	.315
April	29	8	2	0	0	3	2	1	.276	.345	.323
May	62	19	3	0	0	5	7	10	.306	.355	.371
June	56	19	1	1	0	9	9	6	.339	.393	.431
July	46	16	3	0	0	4	7	5	.348	.413	.434
August	85	24	1	0	2	6	12	10	.282	.365	.367
Sept./Oct.	79	20	4	1	1	9	9	7	.253	.367	.333
Leading Off Inn.	93	28	5	1	0	0	6	7	.301	.376	.343
Bases Empty	208	56	11	1	2	2	20	23	.269	.361	.333
Runners On	149	50	3	1	1	34	26	16	.336	.389	.430
Runners/Scor. Pos.	88	24	1	0	0	30	17	14	.273	.284	.385
Runners On/2 Out	68	19	0	0	1	14	13	9	.279	.324	.402
Scor. Pos./2 Out	51	12	0	0	0	12	11	9	.235	.235	.381
Late-Inning Pressure	48	12	2	1	1	8	8	6	.250	.396	.357
Leading Off	12	2	0	0	0	0	0	1	.167	.167	.167
Runners On	19	6	0	1	0	7	3	2	.316	.421	.409
Runners/Scor. Pos.	14	3	0	0	0	6	2	2	.214	.214	.313

RUNS BATTED IN	From 1B	From 2B	From 3B	Scoring Position
Totals	3/105	12/73	18/40	30/113
Percentage	2.9%	16.4%	45.0%	26.5%

Loves to face: Ron Darling (.800, 4-for-5, 1 HR)
Dwight Gooden (.750, 3-for-4)

Hates to face: Tom Browning (.222, 4-for-18)
Jim Deshaies (.091, 1-for-11)
Don Robinson (0-for-4)

Miscellaneous statistics: Ground outs-to-air outs ratio: 1.13 last season, 1.29 for career. . . . Grounded into 5 double plays in 77 opportunities (one per 15.4). . . . Drove in 14 of 21 runners from third base with less than two outs (67%). . . . Direction of balls hit to the outfield: 32% to left field, 29% to center, 39% to right. . . . Base running: Advanced from first base to third on 16 of 25 outfield singles (64%), 4th-highest rate in N.L.; scored from second on 8 of 9 (89%). . . . Made 2.00 assists per nine innings at third base.

Comments: Started 54 of 56 games in which the Dodgers faced a left-handed pitcher, but only 37 of 106 vs. right-handers. . . . Started 75 games at third base, six at shortstop, and five apiece at first base and second base. . . . Has played at least one game at each of the four infield positions in each of the last two seasons. . . . Dodgers opponents scored 4.02 runs per nine innings with Sharperson at third base, 4.69 runs per nine innings with Lenny Harris there. . . . Sharperson pinch-hit for Harris 16 times last season. Harris returned the favor to Sharperson 15 times. . . . See the Harris comments for more on the Harris/Sharperson platoon (p. 216). . . . His career batting average is only .189 in Late-Inning Pressure Situations, compared to .292 in other at-bats. . . . Other career breakdowns: .302 with runners on base, .257 with the bases empty; .300 vs. left-handed pitchers, .253 vs. right-handers; .325 vs. ground-ball pitchers; .234 vs. fly-ballers; .295 on grass fields, .225 on artificial surfaces; .326 in day games, .252 at night. . . . His career statistics vs. left-handed ground-ball pitchers on grass fields in day games with runners on base? Forget it—even *we* have limits! . . . But we will tell you that Sharperson has a career batting average of .619 at Shea Stadium (13-for-21, 1 HR).

Don Slaught

Bats Right

Pittsburgh Pirates	AB	H	2B	3B	HR	RBI	BB	SO	BA	SA	OBA
Season	230	69	18	3	4	29	27	27	.300	.457	.375
vs. Left-Handers	164	52	13	2	2	17	22	20	.317	.457	.393
vs. Right-Handers	66	17	5	1	2	12	5	7	.258	.455	.329
vs. Ground-Ballers	126	37	9	2	2	18	10	14	.294	.444	.350
vs. Fly-Ballers	104	32	9	1	2	11	17	13	.308	.471	.403
Home Games	113	31	10	2	1	12	19	14	.274	.425	.381
Road Games	117	38	8	1	3	17	8	13	.325	.487	.369
Grass Fields	47	18	2	0	2	9	1	5	.383	.553	.400
Artificial Turf	183	51	16	3	2	20	26	22	.279	.432	.369
April	31	15	3	0	2	5	1	0	.484	.774	.500
May	51	17	3	2	2	7	7	6	.333	.588	.424
June	41	15	4	0	0	8	3	5	.366	.463	.404
July	21	3	1	0	0	1	3	2	.143	.190	.250
August	57	13	4	1	0	5	5	6	.228	.333	.302
Sept./Oct.	29	6	3	0	0	3	8	8	.207	.310	.359
Leading Off Inn.	55	15	5	0	0	0	6	4	.273	.364	.365
Bases Empty	132	39	12	2	3	3	14	14	.295	.485	.372
Runners On	98	30	6	1	1	26	13	13	.306	.418	.379
Runners/Scor. Pos.	49	17	4	0	0	22	10	9	.347	.429	.438
Runners On/2 Out	41	12	1	1	0	6	11	5	.293	.366	.442
Scor. Pos./2 Out	23	6	1	0	0	5	8	3	.261	.304	.452
Late-Inning Pressure	40	9	4	0	1	6	4	3	.225	.400	.311
Leading Off	10	4	1	0	0	0	0	1	.400	.500	.400
Runners On	20	3	2	0	0	5	1	2	.150	.250	.227
Runners/Scor. Pos.	13	2	1	0	0	5	1	2	.154	.231	.267

RUNS BATTED IN	From 1B	From 2B	From 3B	Scoring Position
Totals	4/68	8/40	13/24	21/64
Percentage	5.9%	20.0%	54.2%	32.8%

Loves to face: Dennis Martinez (.500, 7-for-14)
Jeff Musselman (.778, 7-for-9)
Bob Ojeda (.364, 4-for-11)

Hates to face: Juan Agosto (0-for-6)
Oil Can Boyd (.100, 1-for-10, 1 HBP)
Frank Viola (.147, 5-for-34)

Miscellaneous statistics: Ground outs-to-air outs ratio: 0.68 last season, 0.92 for career. . . . Grounded into 2 double plays in 45 opportunities (one per 22.5). . . . Drove in 10 of 11 runners from third base with less than two outs (91%). . . . Direction of balls hit to the outfield: 46% to left field, 35% to center, 19% to right. . . . Base running: Advanced from first base to third on 6 of 14 outfield singles (43%); scored from second on 6 of 6. . . . Opposing base stealers: 58-for-84 (69%).

Comments: Reached the .300 mark for the first time since batting .312 for the Royals in his second season in the majors (1983), in part because he was asked to face right-handed pitchers only 74 times, his lowest total since 1982. . . . Started 53 games vs. right-handers, eight vs. left-handers. . . . Last season was the fifth in the last eight in which Slaught hit .300 or better vs. left-handed pitchers, making him an ideal complement for his platoonmate, Mike LaValliere. Reduce Slaught's career vs. LHP to a 200-plate appearance slice, add a 400-PA slice from LaValliere's career totals vs. right-handers, and here's what you get: a .279-hitting catcher (146-for-523), with 29 2B, 3 3B, 7 HR, 63 RBI, and 63 BB. There aren't many of those around. . . . Slaught pinch-hit for Mike LaValliere 16 times, tying the Sharperson-for-Harris entry for the most in the National League. . . . Last season was the first time in his career that he walked as often as he struck out. . . . Only six of his 69 hits were to the opposite field. . . . Percentage of runners driven in from scoring position was a career high, as was his batting average with RISP. . . . Batting average in Late-Inning Pressure Situations was his lowest since his rookie season. . . . He has hit 26 home runs over the last four seasons, but only three with runners on base.

Dwight Smith

Bats Left

Chicago Cubs	AB	H	2B	3B	HR	RBI	BB	SO	BA	SA	OBA
Season	290	76	15	0	6	27	28	46	.262	.376	.329
vs. Left-Handers	36	8	2	0	1	3	1	11	.222	.361	.263
vs. Right-Handers	254	68	13	0	5	24	27	35	.268	.378	.338
vs. Ground-Ballers	140	35	7	0	1	11	9	23	.250	.321	.305
vs. Fly-Ballers	150	41	8	0	5	16	19	23	.273	.427	.351
Home Games	131	33	8	0	3	12	13	25	.252	.382	.317
Road Games	159	43	7	0	3	15	15	21	.270	.371	.339
Grass Fields	197	56	12	0	5	18	20	31	.284	.421	.349
Artificial Turf	93	20	3	0	1	9	8	15	.215	.280	.288
April	41	10	2	0	1	4	6	4	.244	.366	.340
May	74	24	5	0	2	6	7	12	.324	.473	.390
June	71	17	4	0	2	5	6	12	.239	.380	.291
July	37	7	0	0	0	0	3	6	.189	.189	.250
August	27	8	1	0	0	3	1	5	.296	.333	.321
Sept./Oct.	40	10	3	0	1	9	5	7	.250	.400	.348
Leading Off Inn.	85	17	6	0	4	4	7	16	.200	.412	.269
Bases Empty	168	42	9	0	6	6	14	24	.250	.411	.311
Runners On	122	34	6	0	0	21	14	22	.279	.328	.353
Runners/Scor. Pos.	76	20	5	0	0	20	11	16	.263	.329	.348
Runners On/2 Out	48	15	5	0	0	9	7	7	.313	.417	.400
Scor. Pos./2 Out	31	9	4	0	0	8	6	4	.290	.419	.405
Late-Inning Pressure	57	16	4	0	2	8	5	9	.281	.456	.333
Leading Off	19	7	3	0	2	2	1	5	.368	.842	.400
Runners On	23	8	1	0	0	6	3	3	.348	.391	.407
Runners/Scor. Pos.	15	4	1	0	0	6	2	3	.267	.333	.333

RUNS BATTED IN	From 1B	From 2B	From 3B	Scoring Position
Totals	2/80	6/61	13/29	19/90
Percentage	2.5%	9.8%	44.8%	21.1%

Loves to face: Bob Kipper (.750, 3-for-4, 1 3B)
Don Robinson (.571, 4-for-7, 1 2B)
Ed Whitson (.429, 6-for-14, 3 2B, 1 HR)

Hates to face: Scott Garrelts (.158, 3-for-19)
Mike Morgan (.154, 2-for-13)
John Smoltz (0-for-8)

Miscellaneous statistics: Ground outs-to-air outs ratio: 1.42 last season, 1.48 for career. . . . Grounded into 7 double plays in 54 opportunities (one per 7.7). . . . Drove in 11 of 17 runners from third base with less than two outs (65%). . . . Direction of balls hit to the outfield: 34% to left field, 31% to center, 35% to right. . . . Base running: Advanced from first base to third on 7 of 16 outfield singles (44%); scored from second on 5 of 8 (63%). . . . Made 2.21 putouts per nine innings in left field.

Comments: Had the distinction of being the only player to pinch-hit for Andre Dawson last season. That may not earn him a place in baseball folklore alongside Carroll Hardy (the only man ever to pinch-hit for Ted Williams), but it's still a feather in his batting helmet. . . . Was thrown out trying to advance an extra base on a batted ball seven times last season, tying Mark Grace for the team lead. . . . Started 62 games against right-handed pitchers, only three against left-handers. . . . Averaged one walk every 11 plate appearances vs. right-handed pitchers, but drew only one walk in 38 PAs vs. left-handers. . . . Career batting-average breakdown: .231 vs. left-handers (2 HR in 65 AB), .303 vs. right-handers (13 HR, or one per 44 AB). . . . Career batting average of .313 at Wrigley Field, .341 on other grass fields, .243 on artificial surfaces. . . . Was hitless in seven at-bats with the bases loaded last season after going 4-for-7 as a rookie in 1989. . . . After Jerome Walton won the 1989 National League Rookie of the Year Award, it was widely reported that he and Smith were the only position players from the same team other than Fred Lynn and Jim Rice in 1975 to finish first and second in the voting. In fairness to Rice and Lynn, a statistical comparison of their sophomore-season totals: Lynn and Rice (1976)—.297 BA, 35 HR, 150 RBI; Walton and Smith (1990)—.262 BA, 8 HR, 48 RBI.

Lonnie Smith

Bats Right

Atlanta Braves	AB	H	2B	3B	HR	RBI	BB	SO	BA	SA	OBA
Season	466	142	27	9	9	42	58	69	.305	.459	.384
vs. Left-Handers	197	58	14	3	6	18	21	22	.294	.487	.365
vs. Right-Handers	269	84	13	6	3	24	37	47	.312	.439	.397
vs. Ground-Ballers	227	78	15	5	5	21	25	37	.344	.520	.412
vs. Fly-Ballers	239	64	12	4	4	21	33	32	.268	.402	.359
Home Games	231	72	16	4	2	16	27	34	.312	.442	.390
Road Games	235	70	11	5	7	26	31	35	.298	.477	.379
Grass Fields	336	106	22	6	6	30	44	51	.315	.470	.398
Artificial Turf	130	36	5	3	3	12	14	18	.277	.431	.347
April	55	12	2	1	1	6	8	13	.218	.345	.323
May	67	15	4	1	0	6	6	15	.224	.313	.284
June	66	24	4	2	4	7	8	9	.364	.667	.432
July	86	29	4	3	0	4	14	11	.337	.453	.437
August	88	28	7	1	0	9	7	6	.318	.420	.374
Sept./Oct.	104	34	6	1	4	10	15	15	.327	.519	.413
Leading Off Inn.	164	51	10	3	2	2	14	16	.311	.445	.369
Bases Empty	313	99	19	5	8	8	29	44	.316	.486	.382
Runners On	153	43	8	4	1	34	29	25	.281	.405	.389
Runners/Scor. Pos.	90	21	2	1	0	28	21	21	.233	.278	.364
Runners On/2 Out	57	13	3	1	1	6	14	8	.228	.368	.389
Scor. Pos./2 Out	35	5	0	1	0	4	12	6	.143	.200	.362
Late-Inning Pressure	62	18	4	0	2	4	9	12	.290	.452	.392
Leading Off	14	2	0	0	0	0	1	4	.143	.143	.250
Runners On	20	7	2	0	0	2	6	3	.350	.450	.500
Runners/Scor. Pos.	12	3	0	0	0	2	5	3	.250	.250	.444

RUNS BATTED IN	From 1B	From 2B	From 3B	Scoring Position
Totals	5/96	9/79	19/31	28/110
Percentage	5.2%	11.4%	61.3%	25.5%

Loves to face: John Burkett (.545, 6-for-11, 2 2B, 1 3B, 1 HR)
Kevin Gross (.500, 8-for-16, 2 HR)
Bob Walk (.625, 10-for-16, 2 HR)

Hates to face: Neal Heaton (.118, 2-for-17)
Ramon Martinez (0-for-8)
Dave Schmidt (0-for-8)

Miscellaneous statistics: Ground outs-to-air outs ratio: 0.74 last season, 1.02 for career. . . . Grounded into 2 double plays in 74 opportunities (one per 37.0), 3d-best rate in N.L. . . . Drove in 17 of 21 runners from third base with less than two outs (81%), highest rate in N.L. . . . Direction of balls hit to the outfield: 42% to left field, 27% to center, 32% to right. . . . Base running: Advanced from first base to third on 10 of 23 outfield singles (43%); scored from second on 10 of 14 (71%). . . . Made 2.30 putouts per nine innings in left field.

Comments: His total of nine home runs was the 2d highest of his career, after belting 21 in 1989. Even including Dave Justice and Kevin Maas, only 15 players in major league history hit 20 HR in their only season in double figures. The others: Ned Williamson (27 in 1884; see pp. 423–424), Ken Hunt (25 in 1961), Wally Moses (25 in 1937), Dale Sveum (25 in 1987), Wade Boggs (24 in 1987), Joe Charboneau (23 in 1980), Sam Bowens (22 in 1964), Bert Campaneris (22 in 1970), Roy Smalley (21 in 1950), Walt Bond (20 in 1964), Chico Fernandez (20 in 1962), and John Kruk (20 in 1987). . . . Think it's a coincidence that (putting aside Justice and Maas) 1987 is the only repeat year in the list? . . . Batted .340 from the leadoff slot in the batting order last season, the 2d-highest average in the majors (minimum: 100 AB). Batted only .238 from the third slot. . . . Led the Braves with 38 hits to the opposite field. . . . Had the lowest fielding percentage (.956, one error per 23 chances) among National League outfielders (minimum: 81 games). . . . Has hit for a higher average in home games than on the road in each of his last five seasons. . . . Has a career average of .326 at Atlanta-Fulton County Stadium. . . . Has hit for a lower average in Late-Inning Pressure Situations than in other at-bats in each of the last nine years, the longest current streak in the majors (two years shy of Jim Rice's *Player Analysis* record). Career batting averages: .253 in LIPS, .298 in other at-bats.

Ozzie Smith

Bats Left and Right

St. Louis Cardinals	AB	H	2B	3B	HR	RBI	BB	SO	BA	SA	OBA
Season	512	130	21	1	1	50	61	33	.254	.305	.330
vs. Left-Handers	201	58	12	1	1	23	21	11	.289	.373	.350
vs. Right-Handers	311	72	9	0	0	27	40	22	.232	.260	.318
vs. Ground-Ballers	263	62	8	1	0	29	27	19	.236	.274	.302
vs. Fly-Ballers	249	68	13	0	1	21	34	14	.273	.337	.359
Home Games	256	68	15	1	0	25	35	17	.266	.332	.347
Road Games	256	62	6	0	1	25	26	16	.242	.277	.313
Grass Fields	147	37	6	0	0	13	14	12	.252	.293	.317
Artificial Turf	365	93	15	1	1	37	47	21	.255	.310	.335
April	55	12	1	0	0	5	7	3	.218	.236	.292
May	96	23	6	0	0	7	9	7	.240	.302	.311
June	91	18	2	0	0	11	19	8	.198	.220	.336
July	80	27	6	0	0	10	9	3	.338	.412	.396
August	96	25	2	1	1	13	12	7	.260	.333	.333
Sept./Oct.	94	25	4	0	0	4	5	5	.266	.309	.303
Leading Off Inn.	104	24	4	1	1	1	10	4	.231	.317	.304
Bases Empty	295	74	14	1	1	1	37	22	.251	.315	.336
Runners On	217	56	7	0	0	49	24	11	.258	.290	.321
Runners/Scor. Pos.	146	35	5	0	0	49	19	8	.240	.274	.313
Runners On/2 Out	89	21	5	0	0	15	8	6	.236	.292	.299
Scor. Pos./2 Out	63	14	3	0	0	15	6	4	.222	.270	.290
Late-Inning Pressure	73	13	4	0	0	6	8	5	.178	.233	.250
Leading Off	14	4	2	0	0	0	0	0	.286	.429	.286
Runners On	37	6	1	0	0	6	6	2	.162	.189	.261
Runners/Scor. Pos.	25	4	0	0	0	6	6	1	.160	.160	.294

RUNS BATTED IN	From 1B	From 2B	From 3B	Scoring Position
Totals	1/131	13/108	35/66	48/174
Percentage	0.8%	12.0%	53.0%	27.6%

Loves to face: Larry Andersen (.500, 7-for-14, 8 BB)
Tim Crews (.625, 5-for-8, 1 HR)
Calvin Schiraldi (.636, 7-for-11)

Hates to face: Tom Browning (.143, 5-for-35)
Bruce Hurst (.105, 2-for-19)
Mike Scott (.116, 5-for-43, 5 BB)

Miscellaneous statistics: Ground outs-to-air outs ratio: 1.56 last season, 1.55 for career. . . . Grounded into 8 double plays in 87 opportunities (one per 10.9). . . . Drove in 29 of 41 runners from third base with less than two outs (71%). . . . Direction of balls hit to the outfield: 34% to left field, 38% to center, 28% to right batting left-handed; 40% to left, 34% to center, 26% to right batting right-handed. . . . Base running: Advanced from first base to third on 14 of 34 outfield singles (41%); scored from second on 19 of 26 (73%). . . . Made 2.83 assists per nine innings at shortstop.

Comments: Has appeared in 10 All-Star games and started eight, tying Luis Aparicio's records for shortstops. The record for consecutive starts at any position is 14 by Willie Mays (1957–66), who had the advantage of starting two All-Star games in four of those years. . . . Has played 1906 games at shortstop. Among players active in 1990, only Garry Templeton has more (1923). Only 10 players in major league history, and six in National League history, have reached the 2000-game mark at that position. . . . Career fielding percentage of .978 at shortstop (one error per 45 chances) ranks third, behind Tony Fernandez (.980, one error per 51 chances) and Larry Bowa (.980, one error per 49 chances). . . . The highest average of assists per game in major league history belongs to Smith—Germany Smith, that is (3.70; minimum: 1000 games). Ozzie ranks 10th, but he is the only player among the top 20 to have played in the last 40 years. . . . Ranks ninth with 1200 double plays at shortstop; all but the top three are within reach this season. The N.L. record is 1304, by Roy McMillan; the major-league mark is 1553, by Luis Aparicio. . . . Has hit for a higher average with runners on base than with the bases empty in each of the last eight seasons, the longest current streak by a National League player. . . . In the 1976 draft, the Tigers signed their 2d-round pick, Alan Trammell, but failed to come to terms with their 7th-round selection, Ozzie Smith. Detroit's shortstop at the time was Tom Veryzer.

Phil Stephenson

Bats Left

San Diego Padres	AB	H	2B	3B	HR	RBI	BB	SO	BA	SA	OBA
Season	182	38	9	1	4	19	30	43	.209	.335	.319
vs. Left-Handers	32	8	3	1	0	5	4	9	.250	.406	.333
vs. Right-Handers	150	30	6	0	4	14	26	34	.200	.320	.316
vs. Ground-Ballers	97	21	5	1	3	14	12	24	.216	.381	.300
vs. Fly-Ballers	85	17	4	0	1	5	18	19	.200	.282	.340
Home Games	75	16	4	0	2	9	12	14	.213	.347	.322
Road Games	107	22	5	1	2	10	18	29	.206	.327	.317
Grass Fields	128	30	6	1	4	17	19	32	.234	.391	.333
Artificial Turf	54	8	3	0	0	2	11	11	.148	.204	.288
April	9	4	0	0	1	2	2	1	.444	.778	.545
May	32	6	1	1	1	6	8	12	.188	.375	.350
June	31	8	4	0	1	3	5	4	.258	.484	.361
July	26	5	1	0	1	2	6	6	.192	.346	.344
August	49	7	1	0	0	3	7	10	.143	.163	.246
Sept./Oct.	35	8	2	0	0	3	2	10	.229	.286	.270
Leading Off Inn.	41	13	2	0	2	2	7	9	.317	.512	.417
Bases Empty	110	22	5	0	3	3	16	26	.200	.327	.302
Runners On	72	16	4	1	1	16	14	17	.222	.347	.345
Runners/Scor. Pos.	48	7	1	1	1	15	9	13	.146	.271	.276
Runners On/2 Out	36	6	1	0	1	6	8	13	.167	.278	.318
Scor. Pos./2 Out	28	4	1	0	1	6	5	11	.143	.286	.273
Late-Inning Pressure	45	11	1	0	1	4	11	12	.244	.333	.393
Leading Off	7	4	0	0	1	1	3	0	.571	1.000	.700
Runners On	24	5	1	0	0	3	5	7	.208	.250	.345
Runners/Scor. Pos.	15	1	0	0	0	3	4	5	.067	.067	.263

RUNS BATTED IN	From 1B	From 2B	From 3B	Scoring Position
Totals	2/45	5/35	8/22	13/57
Percentage	4.4%	14.3%	36.4%	22.8%

Loves to face: Rick Reuschel (2-for-2, 1 HR, 1 BB)

Hates to face: Oil Can Boyd (0-for-8, 2 BB)
Dwight Gooden (0-for-6, 1 BB, 4 SO)
Dennis Martinez (.182, 2-for-11)

Miscellaneous statistics: Ground outs-to-air outs ratio: 1.39 last season, 1.34 for career. . . . Grounded into 3 double plays in 29 opportunities (one per 9.7). . . . Drove in 6 of 12 runners from third base with less than two outs (50%). . . . Direction of balls hit to the outfield: 38% to left field, 25% to center, 38% to right. . . . Base running: Advanced from first base to third on 3 of 7 outfield singles (43%); scored from second on 5 of 8 (63%). . . . Made 0.84 assists per nine innings at first base.

Comments: Had only 27 games of major league experience prior to 1990, so the numbers you see above are close to career totals. Nevertheless, it's noteworthy that he was hitless in eight at-bats with runners in scoring position before last season, which gives him a career average of .125 with RISP. He has only one hit in 17 career at-bats with RISP in Late-Inning Pressure Situations. . . . His only RBIs prior to last season were produced by two solo home runs. Five of his six career homers have come with the bases empty. . . . Had only one infield hit in 213 plate appearances. The major league average was one every 45 plate appearances. . . . Played 874 games over an eight-year minor league career, but his record indicates considerable talent. His batting averages ranged from .254 (his only season below .270) to .305 (at Iowa of the American Association in 1987) with an average of 40 extra-base hits. He batted over .300 twice (1987 and 1989), walked over 100 times twice (1983 and 1986), and stole 25 or more bases twice (1986 and 1989). . . . Nevertheless, given Stephenson's age (30 when the season ended) and position (1B), the most comparable statistical profiles we found were those of Duke Carmel (through 1963) and Bob Beall (1978), whose careers lasted a combined total of 26 more games.

Darryl Strawberry

Bats Left

New York Mets	AB	H	2B	3B	HR	RBI	BB	SO	BA	SA	OBA
Season	542	150	18	1	37	108	70	110	.277	.518	.361
vs. Left-Handers	217	53	8	0	9	29	17	51	.244	.406	.300
vs. Right-Handers	325	97	10	1	28	79	53	59	.298	.594	.398
vs. Ground-Ballers	268	77	7	0	23	66	31	44	.287	.571	.362
vs. Fly-Ballers	274	73	11	1	14	42	39	66	.266	.467	.360
Home Games	268	68	5	1	24	67	31	52	.254	.549	.332
Road Games	274	82	13	0	13	41	39	58	.299	.489	.388
Grass Fields	396	106	11	1	29	82	45	76	.268	.520	.345
Artificial Turf	146	44	7	0	8	26	25	34	.301	.514	.402
April	66	19	1	1	2	9	13	17	.288	.424	.407
May	84	18	1	0	5	10	9	19	.214	.405	.295
June	93	35	3	0	10	27	17	12	.376	.731	.477
July	97	24	4	0	8	21	12	21	.247	.536	.336
August	102	27	4	0	4	18	13	20	.265	.422	.342
Sept./Oct.	100	27	5	0	8	23	6	21	.270	.560	.308
Leading Off Inn.	123	35	1	0	11	11	13	23	.285	.561	.358
Bases Empty	280	79	11	1	19	19	23	54	.282	.532	.343
Runners On	262	71	7	0	18	89	47	56	.271	.504	.378
Runners/Scor. Pos.	148	45	3	0	12	74	32	27	.304	.568	.419
Runners On/2 Out	113	31	2	0	5	30	26	29	.274	.425	.414
Scor. Pos./2 Out	62	18	1	0	3	25	19	16	.290	.452	.463
Late-Inning Pressure	83	19	2	0	5	10	12	21	.229	.434	.326
Leading Off	20	6	0	0	2	2	3	2	.300	.600	.391
Runners On	39	7	0	0	3	8	8	8	.179	.410	.319
Runners/Scor. Pos.	18	5	0	0	2	6	5	2	.278	.611	.435

RUNS BATTED IN	From 1B	From 2B	From 3B	Scoring Position
Totals	16/183	27/111	28/61	55/172
Percentage	8.7%	24.3%	45.9%	32.0%

Loves to face: Cris Carpenter (2-for-2, 2 HR)
Rick Mahler (.457, 21-for-46, 5 HR)
Don Robinson (.481, 13-for-27, 2 HR)

Hates to face: Andy Benes (0-for-9)
Bob Sebra (.105, 2-for-19, 1 HR, 10 SO)
Zane Smith (.175, 7-for-40, 1 HR)

Miscellaneous statistics: Ground outs-to-air outs ratio: 0.81 last season, 0.93 for career. . . . Grounded into 5 double plays in 118 opportunities (one per 23.6). . . . Drove in 17 of 31 runners from third base with less than two outs (55%). . . . Direction of balls hit to the outfield: 26% to left field, 35% to center, 39% to right. . . . Base running: Advanced from first base to third on 6 of 23 outfield singles (26%); scored from second on 12 of 14 (86%). . . . Made 1.91 putouts per nine innings in right field, 2d-lowest rate in N.L.

Comments: Dodger Stadium hasn't exactly been Strawberry's field of dreams. He has batted .225 there; the only stadium at which he has a lower batting average is the Astrodome (.215). Strawberry has hit only five home runs in 178 at-bats at Dodger Stadium, his lowest rate at any N.L. ballpark. . . . Has hit more than 25 home runs in every season of his career; no other player in major league history had as long a streak starting from his rookie season. (See pp. 75–77 for more on Strawberry's first eight seasons.) . . . Only six times in 28 years of Mets baseball has a player driven in more than 100 runs. Strawberry did it three times, Gary Carter, Rusty Staub, and Howard Johnson once apiece. . . . The last right fielder to start for the Mets on opening day besides Strawberry was Mike Howard in 1983. It was Howard's last major-league game. . . . Has driven in over 29 percent of runners from scoring position during his career; but over the last four seasons, he has driven in only 11 percent in Late-Inning Pressure Situations (9 of 79). During that time, he has only three hits in 27 at-bats with RISP in LIPS. . . . Let's get this straight: Strawberry can't wear uniform number 18 because *Bill Russell* won't give it up? The only numbers anyone ever associated with Bill Russell are the number *6* hanging in Boston Garden, and the number *8* in the Dodgers' batting order.

Franklin Stubbs

Bats Left

Houston Astros	AB	H	2B	3B	HR	RBI	BB	SO	BA	SA	OBA
Season	448	117	23	2	23	71	48	114	.261	.475	.334
vs. Left-Handers	159	41	10	1	7	23	10	41	.258	.465	.300
vs. Right-Handers	289	76	13	1	16	48	38	73	.263	.481	.352
vs. Ground-Ballers	232	55	9	2	9	27	23	55	.237	.409	.307
vs. Fly-Ballers	216	62	14	0	14	44	25	59	.287	.546	.362
Home Games	229	58	15	1	9	39	25	57	.253	.445	.327
Road Games	219	59	8	1	14	32	23	57	.269	.507	.342
Grass Fields	131	30	3	0	7	18	14	35	.229	.412	.308
Artificial Turf	317	87	20	2	16	53	34	79	.274	.502	.345
April	36	9	3	0	2	5	2	10	.250	.500	.289
May	49	12	2	1	3	6	8	11	.245	.510	.362
June	78	21	4	0	5	14	6	23	.269	.513	.321
July	108	22	4	0	4	13	7	33	.204	.352	.250
August	79	24	4	0	5	16	14	18	.304	.544	.404
Sept./Oct.	98	29	6	1	4	17	11	19	.296	.500	.373
Leading Off Inn.	104	33	6	0	6	6	6	25	.317	.548	.360
Bases Empty	244	68	15	2	11	11	22	65	.279	.492	.341
Runners On	204	49	8	0	12	60	26	49	.240	.456	.326
Runners/Scor. Pos.	118	26	3	0	7	45	17	36	.220	.424	.319
Runners On/2 Out	91	21	3	0	5	25	12	21	.231	.429	.320
Scor. Pos./2 Out	61	13	1	0	3	19	9	16	.213	.377	.314
Late-Inning Pressure	86	33	7	0	6	15	6	20	.384	.674	.424
Leading Off	25	13	2	0	3	3	1	3	.520	.960	.538
Runners On	35	10	3	0	1	10	4	8	.286	.457	.359
Runners/Scor. Pos.	18	6	0	0	1	7	3	6	.333	.500	.429

RUNS BATTED IN	From 1B	From 2B	From 3B	Scoring Position
Totals	14/148	19/98	15/43	34/141
Percentage	9.5%	19.4%	34.9%	24.1%

Loves to face: Steve Bedrosian (.417, 5-for-12, 2 2B, 2 HR)
Bill Gullickson (.368, 7-for-19, 1 HR)
Craig McMurtry (.364, 4-for-11, 3 HR)

Hates to face: Rick Aguilera (0-for-12)
Andy Hawkins (.174, 4-for-23, 4 BB)
Jeff D. Robinson (.083, 1-for-12, 6 SO)

Miscellaneous statistics: Ground outs-to-air outs ratio: 0.76 last season, 0.68 for career. . . . Grounded into 4 double plays in 100 opportunities (one per 25.0). . . . Drove in 12 of 25 runners from third base with less than two outs (48%). . . . Direction of balls hit to the outfield: 17% to left field, 24% to center, 59% to right. . . . Base running: Advanced from first base to third on 8 of 25 outfield singles (32%); scored from second on 12 of 17 (71%). . . . Made 0.70 assists per nine innings at first base.

Comments: Last season was the first time in seven seasons in the majors that Stubbs hit for a higher average against fly-ball pitchers than he did against ground-ball pitchers. Career averages: .255 vs. ground-ballers, .214 vs. fly-ballers. . . . Only 10 of his 117 hits were to the opposite field. . . . Played 71 games at first base, and 71 games in the outfield. . . . Was removed in favor of a pinch hitter 19 times last season, all against left-handed pitchers. . . . Batted 152 points higher in Late-Inning Pressure Situations (.384) than in other at-bats (.232) last season, the 4th-largest margin in the majors. Went 6-for-10 in extra innings. . . . Some bad news for the faithful at County Stadium: Stubbs has a career batting average of .216 on natural grass, .270 on artificial turf. He has had higher averages on artificial turf than on grass fields in each of the last five seasons, and also prefers the synthetic turf in his running game. Stubbs stole 18 bases in 21 attempts on the rug last season (86%), but was only 1-for-4 on dirt infields. Career stolen-base totals: 21-for-32 on dirt (66%), 29-for-33 on artificial surfaces (88%). . . . It's amazing how some guys are labeled "For Platoon Only" without ever having a chance to prove themselves as everyday players. In six seasons with the Dodgers, Stubbs had never had as many as 100 at-bats vs. southpaws.

Pat Tabler

Bats Right

Royals/Mets	AB	H	2B	3B	HR	RBI	BB	SO	BA	SA	OBA
Season	238	65	15	1	2	29	23	29	.273	.370	.338
vs. Left-Handers	105	35	7	1	1	14	11	13	.333	.448	.393
vs. Right-Handers	133	30	8	0	1	15	12	16	.226	.308	.295
vs. Ground-Ballers	123	35	6	0	1	19	9	19	.285	.358	.333
vs. Fly-Ballers	115	30	9	1	1	10	14	10	.261	.383	.344
Home Games	114	28	8	0	1	13	14	14	.246	.342	.328
Road Games	124	37	7	1	1	16	9	15	.298	.395	.348
Grass Fields	87	27	3	0	2	18	10	9	.310	.414	.378
Artificial Turf	151	38	12	1	0	11	13	20	.252	.344	.315
April	30	7	1	0	0	1	3	2	.233	.267	.303
May	26	6	1	0	0	3	2	5	.231	.269	.310
June	35	8	4	0	0	1	5	8	.229	.343	.325
July	67	21	6	0	1	13	8	3	.313	.448	.377
August	37	11	2	0	0	1	2	3	.297	.351	.325
Sept./Oct.	43	12	1	1	1	10	3	8	.279	.419	.340
Leading Off Inn.	49	14	6	1	0	0	4	4	.286	.449	.340
Bases Empty	107	28	9	1	1	1	12	11	.262	.393	.336
Runners On	131	37	6	0	1	28	11	18	.282	.351	.340
Runners/Scor. Pos.	84	25	5	0	1	28	10	12	.298	.393	.374
Runners On/2 Out	64	16	2	0	1	11	7	11	.250	.328	.324
Scor. Pos./2 Out	43	11	2	0	1	11	6	7	.256	.372	.347
Late-Inning Pressure	35	7	2	0	0	6	3	6	.200	.257	.275
Leading Off	6	1	1	0	0	0	1	2	.167	.333	.286
Runners On	23	6	1	0	0	6	1	4	.261	.304	.308
Runners/Scor. Pos.	16	4	1	0	0	6	1	3	.250	.313	.316

RUNS BATTED IN	From 1B	From 2B	From 3B	Scoring Position
Totals	1/87	13/67	13/31	26/98
Percentage	1.1%	19.4%	41.9%	26.5%

Loves to face: Don Aase (.667, 4-for-6, 1 HR)
John Candelaria (.583, 7-for-12, 1 HR)
Greg A. Harris (.500, 9-for-18, 1 HR)

Hates to face: Dennis Eckersley (.091, 1-for-11)
Charlie Hough (.197, 12-for-61, 1 HR)
Dave Schmidt (.217, 5-for-23)

Miscellaneous statistics: Ground outs-to-air outs ratio: 1.42 last season, 1.29 for career.... Grounded into 8 double plays in 45 opportunities (one per 5.6).... Drove in 10 of 17 runners from third base with less than two outs (59%).... Direction of balls hit to the outfield: 38% to left field, 32% to center, 29% to right.... Base running: Advanced from first base to third on 1 of 16 outfield singles (6%); scored from second on 4 of 6 (67%).... Made 2.36 putouts per nine innings in right field.

Comments: His career average with the bases loaded remains at the .500 mark (40-for-80) despite only three hits in 16 at-bats over the last two seasons.... Of his 475 career RBIs, 98 have resulted from bases-loaded situations (21 percent). For purposes of comparison, 15 percent of all RBIs in the majors in 1990 came with the bases loaded.... His reputation as a great hitter with the bases loaded has obscured the fact that he has always been an excellent situational hitter, even with only one or two runners on base. Career batting-average breakdown: .264 with the bases empty, .310 with runners on base, .322 with runners in scoring position.... He has batted over .300 against left-handed pitchers in each of the last six seasons, but his averages vs. right-handed pitchers have deteriorated. Year by year vs. RHP since 1986: .322, .281, .272, .196, .226. Career breakdown: .317 vs. left-handers, .270 vs. right-handers.... Has homered in every current American League ballpark except Yankee Stadium (137 career at-bats) and the Skydome (20 AB). But his .328 batting average at Yankee Stadium is his highest at any ballpark in the majors.... Career mark of .300 on grass fields, .249 on artificial surfaces. Difference of 51 points in those averages is the largest margin among players with at least 1000 plate appearances on both kinds of fields over the last 16 years.

Garry Templeton

Bats Left and Right

San Diego Padres	AB	H	2B	3B	HR	RBI	BB	SO	BA	SA	OBA
Season	505	125	25	3	9	59	24	59	.248	.362	.280
vs. Left-Handers	189	48	8	1	4	29	9	21	.254	.370	.286
vs. Right-Handers	316	77	17	2	5	30	15	38	.244	.358	.275
vs. Ground-Ballers	266	68	13	1	3	27	12	29	.256	.346	.287
vs. Fly-Ballers	239	57	12	2	6	32	12	30	.238	.381	.272
Home Games	255	63	12	2	6	36	12	36	.247	.380	.278
Road Games	250	62	13	1	3	23	12	23	.248	.344	.281
Grass Fields	375	97	20	2	7	51	19	44	.259	.379	.291
Artificial Turf	130	28	5	1	2	8	5	15	.215	.315	.244
April	62	14	5	0	0	7	2	5	.226	.306	.250
May	81	21	3	0	3	14	3	7	.259	.407	.279
June	83	24	3	0	2	7	5	12	.289	.398	.330
July	95	21	6	2	2	10	5	14	.221	.389	.260
August	87	23	3	0	1	7	4	10	.264	.333	.297
Sept./Oct.	97	22	5	1	1	14	5	11	.227	.330	.260
Leading Off Inn.	109	28	9	0	1	1	4	11	.257	.367	.283
Bases Empty	273	59	17	1	3	3	11	40	.216	.319	.246
Runners On	232	66	8	2	6	56	13	19	.284	.414	.317
Runners/Scor. Pos.	122	35	2	1	5	50	12	12	.287	.443	.341
Runners On/2 Out	102	33	5	1	3	30	9	7	.324	.480	.378
Scor. Pos./2 Out	66	20	2	1	3	28	9	6	.303	.500	.387
Late-Inning Pressure	95	21	4	0	1	11	6	14	.221	.295	.265
Leading Off	27	4	3	0	0	0	1	3	.148	.259	.179
Runners On	42	14	1	0	1	11	3	4	.333	.429	.370
Runners/Scor. Pos.	27	9	0	0	1	11	2	3	.333	.444	.367

RUNS BATTED IN	From 1B	From 2B	From 3B	Scoring Position
Totals	8/170	18/92	24/63	42/155
Percentage	4.7%	19.6%	38.1%	27.1%

Loves to face: Danny Darwin (.524, 11-for-21, 3 HR)
Dickie Noles (.429, 12-for-28, 0 SO)
Frank Viola (.500, 4-for-8, 1 HR)

Hates to face: Scott Garrelts (.132, 5-for-38)
Dennis Martinez (.095, 2-for-21)
Mike Scott (.171, 13-for-76)

Miscellaneous statistics: Ground outs-to-air outs ratio: 1.05 last season, 1.63 for career.... Grounded into 17 double plays in 103 opportunities (one per 6.1).... Drove in 13 of 21 runners from third base with less than two outs (62%).... Direction of balls hit to the outfield: 33% to left field, 34% to center, 32% to right batting left-handed; 36% to left, 32% to center, 32% to right batting right-handed.... Base running: Advanced from first base to third on 1 of 8 outfield singles (13%); scored from second on 8 of 11 (73%).... Made 2.83 assists per nine innings at shortstop.

Comments: Equalled his career high with nine home runs last season, raising his career total to 67 homers. Only four other players in major league history have hit that many without a season in double figures: Tony Taylor (75), George van Haltren (69), Edd Roush (68), and Fred Clarke (67).... Among N.L. shortstops, only Shawon Dunston hit more home runs than Templeton last season.... Has drawn only 224 walks over the last seven seasons, nearly half of which have been intentional (108).... Batting average on artificial turf was the lowest of his career. Career batting-average breakdown: .290 on artificial turf, .259 on grass fields.... Had the lowest fielding percentage (.957, one error per 23 chances) of any National League shortstop last season (minimum: 81 games), and his lowest since 1978. He had the 2d-highest mark on artificial surfaces (.989, two errors in 175 chances), but was dismal on grass fields (.944, one per 18).... Templeton has played 1923 games at shortstop, the most among active players, but only two games at any other position (third base).... His career total of 378 errors is the most of any shortstop who played in the post-war era.... Has any team ever had a succession of shortstops like the Padres? You can't do much better than Ozzie Smith, Garry Templeton, and Tony Fernandez. And all this from a team that traded Ozzie Guillen!

Andres Thomas

Bats Right

Atlanta Braves	AB	H	2B	3B	HR	RBI	BB	SO	BA	SA	OBA
Season	278	61	8	0	5	30	11	43	.219	.302	.248
vs. Left-Handers	102	23	2	0	4	15	5	15	.225	.363	.259
vs. Right-Handers	176	38	6	0	1	15	6	28	.216	.267	.242
vs. Ground-Ballers	143	30	4	0	2	16	2	16	.210	.280	.221
vs. Fly-Ballers	135	31	4	0	3	14	9	27	.230	.326	.276
Home Games	157	36	4	0	1	12	7	24	.229	.274	.262
Road Games	121	25	4	0	4	18	4	19	.207	.339	.230
Grass Fields	212	46	6	0	2	20	8	32	.217	.274	.245
Artificial Turf	66	15	2	0	3	10	3	11	.227	.394	.257
April	22	2	0	0	0	1	1	5	.091	.091	.130
May	59	16	2	0	1	6	5	13	.271	.356	.323
June	21	5	0	0	1	1	0	4	.238	.381	.238
July	81	15	1	0	2	5	2	11	.185	.272	.205
August	57	14	2	0	1	10	1	8	.246	.333	.259
Sept./Oct.	38	9	3	0	0	7	2	2	.237	.316	.275
Leading Off Inn.	52	16	1	0	4	4	3	6	.308	.558	.345
Bases Empty	160	34	4	0	4	4	5	26	.213	.313	.236
Runners On	118	27	4	0	1	26	6	17	.229	.288	.264
Runners/Scor. Pos.	73	19	4	0	1	26	5	9	.260	.356	.304
Runners On/2 Out	53	12	3	0	1	13	1	7	.226	.340	.241
Scor. Pos./2 Out	35	9	3	0	1	13	1	3	.257	.429	.278
Late-Inning Pressure	43	10	1	0	2	3	0	6	.233	.395	.233
Leading Off	12	8	0	0	2	2	0	0	.667	1.167	.667
Runners On	11	1	1	0	0	1	0	2	.091	.182	.091
Runners/Scor. Pos.	5	1	1	0	0	1	0	1	.200	.400	.200

RUNS BATTED IN	From 1B	From 2B	From 3B	Scoring Position
Totals	3/88	10/59	12/31	22/90
Percentage	3.4%	16.9%	38.7%	24.4%

Loves to face: Tom Browning (.370, 10-for-27, 1 HR, 0 BB)
Craig Lefferts (.353, 6-for-17, 3 HR)
Rick Reuschel (.370, 10-for-27, 3 HR)

Hates to face: Jose DeLeon (.154, 4-for-26, 1 HR, 0 BB, 12 SO)
Jim Deshaies (.121, 4-for-33, 0 BB)
Ted Power (.067, 1-for-15)

Miscellaneous statistics: Ground outs-to-air outs ratio: 0.78 last season, 0.98 for career. . . . Grounded into 10 double plays in 53 opportunities (one per 5.3), 4th-worst rate in N.L. . . . Drove in 7 of 15 runners from third base with less than two outs (47%). . . . Direction of balls hit to the outfield: 36% to left field, 36% to center, 28% to right. . . . Base running: Advanced from first base to third on 2 of 8 outfield singles (25%); scored from second on 3 of 5 (60%). . . . Made 2.87 assists per nine innings at shortstop.

Comments: With the departure of Dale Murphy, Thomas was the senior member of the Braves at the end of the 1990 season. No other player who finished the 1986 season with Atlanta remained there throughout the past four seasons. . . . The Braves were two games over the .500 mark with Thomas starting at shortstop (35–33), compared to 28–61 with Jeff Blauser at short. . . . Thomas turned 41 double plays at shortstop last season, only six fewer than Blauser, despite playing almost 200 fewer innings in the field. . . . Braves pitchers allowed more than one run per nine innings less with Thomas at shortstop (4.49) than with Blauser there (5.73). . . . Appeared in five games at third base last season, his first major league experience at any position other than shortstop. . . . Had eight hits in 12 at-bats leading off innings in Late-Inning Pressure Situations, but batted only .065 (3-for-31) in his other LIPS at-bats. . . . Career batting-average breakdown: .230 with the bases empty, .241 with runners on base, .257 with runners in scoring position, .285 with two outs and RISP. . . . Thomas and Rob Deer are the only two players to bat below .220 with at least 250 at-bats in each of the last two seasons. Over the last 75 years, only two players have had streaks of three consecutive seasons: Tom Tresh (1967–69) and Dave Duncan (1974–76).

Milt Thompson

Bats Left

St. Louis Cardinals	AB	H	2B	3B	HR	RBI	BB	SO	BA	SA	OBA
Season	418	91	14	7	6	30	39	60	.218	.328	.292
vs. Left-Handers	120	21	3	2	0	4	5	26	.175	.233	.227
vs. Right-Handers	298	70	11	5	6	26	34	34	.235	.366	.317
vs. Ground-Ballers	194	40	7	2	1	11	25	24	.206	.278	.300
vs. Fly-Ballers	224	51	7	5	5	19	14	36	.228	.371	.285
Home Games	221	47	5	4	3	20	21	27	.213	.312	.290
Road Games	197	44	9	3	3	10	18	33	.223	.345	.295
Grass Fields	111	22	6	3	1	2	11	18	.198	.333	.282
Artificial Turf	307	69	8	4	5	28	28	42	.225	.326	.296
April	35	5	1	0	1	4	5	3	.143	.257	.250
May	80	16	2	1	1	4	8	11	.200	.287	.289
June	91	23	2	4	2	11	8	11	.253	.429	.313
July	79	13	1	2	0	2	8	14	.165	.228	.258
August	67	19	5	0	0	5	5	16	.284	.358	.342
Sept./Oct.	66	15	3	0	2	4	5	5	.227	.364	.282
Leading Off Inn.	95	18	4	0	1	1	8	7	.189	.263	.267
Bases Empty	250	50	10	4	3	3	22	33	.200	.308	.275
Runners On	168	41	4	3	3	27	17	27	.244	.357	.317
Runners/Scor. Pos.	91	19	2	1	1	20	14	19	.209	.286	.314
Runners On/2 Out	53	14	0	3	1	12	9	8	.264	.434	.371
Scor. Pos./2 Out	37	7	0	1	0	8	9	7	.189	.243	.348
Late-Inning Pressure	70	16	4	1	1	10	9	12	.229	.357	.316
Leading Off	13	4	1	0	0	0	4	1	.308	.385	.471
Runners On	27	7	1	1	1	10	3	4	.259	.481	.333
Runners/Scor. Pos.	18	7	1	1	1	10	3	3	.389	.722	.476

RUNS BATTED IN	From 1B	From 2B	From 3B	Scoring Position
Totals	6/120	11/76	7/29	18/105
Percentage	5.0%	14.5%	24.1%	17.1%

Loves to face: Stan Belinda (3-for-3)
David Cone (.424, 14-for-33, 1 HR)
Rick Mahler (.500, 15-for-30)

Hates to face: Tom Browning (.071, 1-for-14)
Dwight Gooden (.167, 7-for-42, 6 BB)
Orel Hershiser (.161, 5-for-31)

Miscellaneous statistics: Ground outs-to-air outs ratio: 1.86 last season, 5th-highest rate in N.L.; 2.34 for career. . . . Grounded into 4 double plays in 94 opportunities (one per 23.5). . . . Drove in 4 of 11 runners from third base with less than two outs (36%). . . . Direction of balls hit to the outfield: 46% to left field, 27% to center, 27% to right. . . . Base running: Advanced from first base to third on 5 of 19 outfield singles (26%); scored from second on 9 of 14 (64%). . . . Made 2.18 putouts per nine innings in right field.

Comments: In 115 years of baseball, only 139 players suffered declines of 70 or more batting-average points from one season to the next (minimum: 400 AB in both seasons). Last season, Thompson (.290 to .218) and Robin Yount (.318 to .247) were the only two. . . . Only one Cardinals player in the last 80 years had a lower batting average (minimum: 400 at-bats): Leo Durocher, who batted .203 in 1934. . . . Career batting average prior to 1990 was .289 in more than 2000 at-bats. . . . Drove in only 17 percent of runners from scoring position, but turned it up a notch with the game on the line, plating 40 percent in Late-Inning Pressure Situations (8 of 20). . . . Maintains a career batting average of .307 in Late-Inning Pressure Situations, despite his disappointing 1990 season. . . . Has a career average of .225 vs. left-handers, .290 vs. right-handers. He's hit only one of his 27 career home runs off a left-handed pitcher (Fernando Valenzuela in 1989). . . . Has hit for a higher average on artificial turf than on grass fields in each of the last five seasons. . . . Has hit for a higher average with runners on base than with the bases empty in each of the last six seasons. Career batting-average breakdown: .304 with runners on base, .260 with the bases empty. . . . Has homered in every current National League ballpark except the Astrodome (93 career AB). . . . Year-by-year walk totals since 1987: 42, 39, 39, 39. . . . Has stolen 115 bases over the last four seasons.

Robby Thompson

Bats Right

San Francisco Giants	AB	H	2B	3B	HR	RBI	BB	SO	BA	SA	OBA
Season	498	122	22	3	15	56	34	96	.245	.392	.299
vs. Left-Handers	183	50	11	1	8	27	13	34	.273	.475	.325
vs. Right-Handers	315	72	11	2	7	29	21	62	.229	.343	.284
vs. Ground-Ballers	219	45	10	1	3	19	19	42	.205	.301	.280
vs. Fly-Ballers	279	77	12	2	12	37	15	54	.276	.462	.315
Home Games	248	66	14	2	8	37	24	47	.266	.435	.335
Road Games	250	56	8	1	7	19	10	49	.224	.348	.262
Grass Fields	357	94	16	2	10	43	33	67	.263	.403	.332
Artificial Turf	141	28	6	1	5	13	1	29	.199	.362	.210
April	74	17	2	1	1	7	6	18	.230	.324	.296
May	99	20	4	0	3	10	4	15	.202	.333	.240
June	91	26	1	1	4	16	6	15	.286	.451	.343
July	74	18	5	0	1	5	6	13	.243	.351	.296
August	86	24	5	1	4	11	7	22	.279	.500	.344
Sept./Oct.	74	17	5	0	2	7	5	13	.230	.378	.275
Leading Off Inn.	86	18	4	1	1	1	9	15	.209	.314	.299
Bases Empty	283	67	14	1	10	10	18	54	.237	.399	.292
Runners On	215	55	8	2	5	46	16	42	.256	.381	.309
Runners/Scor. Pos.	121	30	5	2	3	41	14	28	.248	.397	.324
Runners On/2 Out	95	26	5	1	1	20	6	19	.274	.379	.324
Scor. Pos./2 Out	59	17	4	1	1	19	5	12	.288	.441	.354
Late-Inning Pressure	77	14	2	0	3	12	3	18	.182	.325	.213
Leading Off	10	0	0	0	0	0	0	1	.000	.000	.000
Runners On	38	10	2	0	2	11	2	6	.263	.474	.300
Runners/Scor. Pos.	23	6	1	0	1	8	2	6	.261	.435	.320

RUNS BATTED IN	From 1B	From 2B	From 3B	Scoring Position
Totals	8/162	8/89	25/62	33/151
Percentage	4.9%	9.0%	40.3%	21.9%

Loves to face: Paul Assenmacher (.750, 6-for-8)
Tom Glavine (.467, 7-for-15, 3 2B, 1 3B, 1 HR)
Bob Sebra (.500, 4-for-8, 1 2B, 2 HR)

Hates to face: Tim Burke (.071, 1-for-14)
Randy Myers (0-for-8, 6 SO)
Rick Sutcliffe (.143, 4-for-28, 0 BB)

Miscellaneous statistics: Ground outs-to-air outs ratio: 1.10 last season, 1.00 for career.... Grounded into 9 double plays in 103 opportunities (one per 11.4).... Drove in 16 of 29 runners from third base with less than two outs (55%).... Direction of balls hit to the outfield: 39% to left field, 33% to center, 27% to right.... Base running: Advanced from first base to third on 13 of 26 outfield singles (50%); scored from second on 10 of 16 (63%).... Made 3.40 assists per nine innings at second base, highest rate in N.L.

Comments: Offseason word was that Thompson would inherit the leadoff slot from the departed Brett Butler, despite his career average of 109 strikeouts per season. However, Thompson's only previous stint as a leadoff hitter was successful: the Giants were 24–11 with him in the number-one slot in 1987, compared to 66–61 in other games that season. Someone mention Willie McGee? He had one season as a semiregular leadoff starter, with similar success: St. Louis was 38–25 with McGee batting leadoff in 1984, compared to 46–53 in other games. But Vince Coleman arrived the next season, and McGee has started in the leadoff slot only 47 times in six seasons since.... Only two other second basemen have struck out at least 90 times in five consecutive seasons: Bobby Knoop (1964–68) and Juan Samuel (1984–88). Samuel's streak would still be running if he hadn't moved to the outfield in 1989.... In the 108-year history of the Giants franchise, only two players have appeared in more games at second base than Thompson. The top three: Larry Doyle (1593 games, 1907–20), Tito Fuentes (842, 1965–74), and Thompson (699, 1986–90).... His 1990 average vs. left-handed pitchers was a career low; he batted over .300 against southpaws in each of the previous three seasons. Career breakdown: .298 vs. left-handers, .236 vs. right-handers.... Has a career average below .200 at three ballparks: Jack Murphy Stadium (.184), Dodger Stadium (.198), and Busch Stadium (.198).

Dickie Thon

Bats Right

Philadelphia Phillies	AB	H	2B	3B	HR	RBI	BB	SO	BA	SA	OBA
Season	552	141	20	4	8	48	37	77	.255	.350	.305
vs. Left-Handers	202	53	9	1	5	21	14	25	.262	.391	.310
vs. Right-Handers	350	88	11	3	3	27	23	52	.251	.326	.302
vs. Ground-Ballers	282	66	7	2	2	16	17	37	.234	.294	.279
vs. Fly-Ballers	270	75	13	2	6	32	20	40	.278	.407	.331
Home Games	254	63	7	0	3	28	25	37	.248	.311	.316
Road Games	298	78	13	4	5	20	12	40	.262	.383	.295
Grass Fields	153	40	7	1	1	8	8	24	.261	.340	.302
Artificial Turf	399	101	13	3	7	40	29	53	.253	.353	.306
April	62	12	1	1	0	3	5	6	.194	.242	.265
May	91	27	3	1	1	13	9	15	.297	.385	.353
June	95	24	4	0	1	5	5	13	.253	.326	.290
July	97	29	2	0	4	17	3	12	.299	.443	.327
August	107	28	5	1	1	8	11	16	.262	.355	.336
Sept./Oct.	100	21	5	1	1	2	4	15	.210	.310	.240
Leading Off Inn.	132	39	4	2	1	1	7	20	.295	.379	.340
Bases Empty	287	77	12	3	5	5	19	46	.268	.383	.318
Runners On	265	64	8	1	3	43	18	31	.242	.313	.290
Runners/Scor. Pos.	143	35	4	0	2	40	12	21	.245	.315	.299
Runners On/2 Out	118	30	6	0	2	23	14	15	.254	.356	.338
Scor. Pos./2 Out	74	19	4	0	1	21	9	12	.257	.351	.337
Late-Inning Pressure	87	28	2	1	0	4	9	9	.322	.368	.385
Leading Off	27	10	0	0	0	0	2	2	.370	.370	.414
Runners On	39	13	2	0	0	4	5	6	.333	.385	.409
Runners/Scor. Pos.	20	6	1	0	0	4	4	3	.300	.350	.417

RUNS BATTED IN	From 1B	From 2B	From 3B	Scoring Position
Totals	4/202	13/113	23/66	36/179
Percentage	2.0%	11.5%	34.8%	20.1%

Loves to face: Mike Bielecki (.417, 5-for-12)
Neal Heaton (.417, 5-for-12, 2 HR)
Mike Scott (.500, 7-for-14, 2 HR)

Hates to face: David Cone (.176, 3-for-17)
Jose DeLeon (0-for-6, 3 SO)
Bryn Smith (.121, 4-for-33, 1 HR, 0 BB)

Miscellaneous statistics: Ground outs-to-air outs ratio: 1.08 last season, 1.12 for career.... Grounded into 14 double plays in 118 opportunities (one per 8.4).... Drove in 12 of 29 runners from third base with less than two outs (41%).... Direction of balls hit to the outfield: 35% to left field, 34% to center, 31% to right.... Base running: Advanced from first base to third on 12 of 33 outfield singles (36%); scored from second on 6 of 8 (75%).... Made 3.13 assists per nine innings at shortstop.

Comments: Was hit by a pitch three times last season after being hit only once in the five seasons after the Mike Torrez incident in 1984.... Thon played 149 games last season, his highest total post-Torrez.... His span of seven years between 500–at-bat seasons is unusual, but hardly unique. Four players had 10-year gaps: Rico Carty (1966–76), Jimmy Dykes (1922–32), Al Kaline (1964–74), and Bob Kennedy (1940–50).... Batted 93 points higher in night games (.278) than in day games (.185) last season, the 2d-largest margin in the majors.... What did the beaning cost Thon? Most comparable statistical batting profiles prior to the beaning: Von Hayes, Lou Brock, Mike Davis, and Al Oliver. Current clones: Phil Garner, Dave Philley, Ron Oester, and Jim Gantner.... Grounded into a career-high 14 double plays, with seven during the month of September. His ground out-to-air out ratio was 0.89 through September 1, but 1.68 thereafter.... Had the lowest fielding percentage of any shortstop in the majors on grass fields (.936, one error per 16 chances), but had a much higher percentage on artificial surfaces (.973, one error per 37 chances).... Combined with Rod Booker to play every inning at shortstop for the Phillies last season. No other club in the National League had as few as two players combine for all of its innings at any position.... His lowest home-run rate at any National League ballpark is at Wrigley Field, where he has only one home run in 133 career at-bats.... Now that he's nearly 33 years old, can't we call him Rick?

Jeff Treadway

Bats Left

Atlanta Braves	AB	H	2B	3B	HR	RBI	BB	SO	BA	SA	OBA
Season	474	134	20	2	11	59	25	42	.283	.403	.320
vs. Left-Handers	119	36	5	0	4	20	10	10	.303	.445	.359
vs. Right-Handers	355	98	15	2	7	39	15	32	.276	.389	.307
vs. Ground-Ballers	235	68	10	0	3	22	8	19	.289	.370	.315
vs. Fly-Ballers	239	66	10	2	8	37	17	23	.276	.435	.326
Home Games	219	66	10	0	5	27	9	20	.301	.416	.336
Road Games	255	68	10	2	6	32	16	22	.267	.392	.307
Grass Fields	330	97	14	1	5	38	18	35	.294	.388	.333
Artificial Turf	144	37	6	1	6	21	7	7	.257	.438	.289
April	50	15	1	0	1	3	0	2	.300	.380	.300
May	89	28	4	1	4	17	4	4	.315	.517	.351
June	111	33	7	0	2	16	6	14	.297	.414	.336
July	67	17	0	0	3	9	4	9	.254	.388	.296
August	85	21	2	0	1	5	3	8	.247	.306	.270
Sept./Oct.	72	20	6	1	0	9	8	5	.278	.389	.349
Leading Off Inn.	89	23	5	1	3	3	2	8	.258	.438	.275
Bases Empty	262	65	12	1	6	6	16	28	.248	.370	.294
Runners On	212	69	8	1	5	53	9	14	.325	.443	.352
Runners/Scor. Pos.	123	42	3	1	3	47	6	8	.341	.455	.366
Runners On/2 Out	94	30	3	0	1	20	2	8	.319	.383	.340
Scor. Pos./2 Out	61	19	2	0	0	18	1	6	.311	.344	.333
Late-Inning Pressure	63	17	3	1	1	12	4	5	.270	.397	.313
Leading Off	18	2	1	0	0	0	0	3	.111	.167	.111
Runners On	28	13	2	1	1	12	2	0	.464	.714	.500
Runners/Scor. Pos.	19	11	1	1	1	11	2	0	.579	.895	.619

RUNS BATTED IN	From 1B	From 2B	From 3B	Scoring Position
Totals	6/148	20/94	22/50	42/144
Percentage	4.1%	21.3%	44.0%	29.2%

Loves to face: Andy Benes (.500, 7-for-14)
David Cone (.409, 9-for-22, 2 HR)
Don Robinson (.467, 7-for-15, 1 HR)

Hates to face: Tim Belcher (.150, 3-for-20, 2 2B)
Mike Scott (.115, 3-for-26, 0 BB)
Dave Smith (0-for-10)

Miscellaneous statistics: Ground outs-to-air outs ratio: 0.81 last season, 0.92 for career.... Grounded into 10 double plays in 92 opportunities (one per 9.2).... Drove in 14 of 23 runners from third base with less than two outs (61%).... Direction of balls hit to the outfield: 31% to left field, 31% to center, 38% to right.... Base running: Advanced from first base to third on 6 of 24 outfield singles (25%); scored from second on 8 of 11 (73%).... Made 3.27 assists per nine innings at second base, 2d-highest rate in N.L.

Comments: Had the highest overall batting average by a Braves second baseman since Felix Millan batted .289 in 1971.... One of six left-handed batters in the National League who hit .300 or better in at least 100 at-bats against left-handed pitchers. The others: Dave Justice (.366), Will Clark (.317), Mark Grace (.308), Barry Bonds (.304), Brett Butler (.302). Treadway had a career average of .205 with no home runs in 146 at-bats vs. left-handers prior to 1990.... Hit his 10th home run of the season on July 15, but hit only one in 177 at-bats thereafter.... His batting average in Late-Inning Pressure Situations with runners in scoring position was the highest in the National League since Bill Madlock went 13-for-17 (.765) in 1979 (minimum: 20 PA).... Committed only one error in 35 games at second base on artificial surfaces, but committed 14 errors in 87 games on grass fields. Don't blame Atlanta Stadium's sun-baked infield; Tread actually had a higher fielding percentage in home games than on grass fields on the road.... Career batting average of .385 as a pinch hitter (10-for-26).... Batted .300 or better in each of his four seasons in the minors. His composite minor league batting average was .313.

Jose Uribe

Bats Left and Right

San Francisco Giants	AB	H	2B	3B	HR	RBI	BB	SO	BA	SA	OBA
Season	415	103	8	6	1	24	29	49	.248	.304	.297
vs. Left-Handers	142	40	4	1	0	7	9	13	.282	.324	.325
vs. Right-Handers	273	63	4	5	1	17	20	36	.231	.293	.283
vs. Ground-Ballers	184	51	5	2	1	6	17	19	.277	.342	.338
vs. Fly-Ballers	231	52	3	4	0	18	12	30	.225	.273	.263
Home Games	197	44	4	2	0	8	17	27	.223	.264	.285
Road Games	218	59	4	4	1	16	12	22	.271	.339	.309
Grass Fields	297	73	5	4	0	16	22	38	.246	.290	.298
Artificial Turf	118	30	3	2	1	8	7	11	.254	.339	.296
April	52	16	1	2	0	7	2	5	.308	.404	.333
May	92	27	2	1	1	5	7	8	.293	.370	.343
June	100	27	0	1	0	6	2	8	.270	.290	.284
July	76	14	1	1	0	2	4	8	.184	.224	.225
August	56	14	3	1	0	4	9	13	.250	.339	.354
Sept./Oct.	39	5	1	0	0	0	5	7	.128	.154	.227
Leading Off Inn.	97	24	1	0	0	0	3	9	.247	.258	.270
Bases Empty	229	55	5	2	0	0	10	30	.240	.279	.272
Runners On	186	48	3	4	1	24	19	19	.258	.333	.327
Runners/Scor. Pos.	103	22	1	1	1	21	18	13	.214	.272	.331
Runners On/2 Out	91	23	0	3	1	14	13	11	.253	.352	.346
Scor. Pos./2 Out	58	13	0	1	1	12	12	8	.224	.310	.357
Late-Inning Pressure	47	14	1	0	0	2	5	3	.298	.319	.365
Leading Off	17	6	1	0	0	0	1	1	.353	.412	.389
Runners On	17	5	0	0	0	2	2	1	.294	.294	.368
Runners/Scor. Pos.	9	2	0	0	0	2	2	0	.222	.222	.364

RUNS BATTED IN	From 1B	From 2B	From 3B	Scoring Position
Totals	4/145	11/79	8/40	19/119
Percentage	2.8%	13.9%	20.0%	16.0%

Loves to face: Tim Burke (.429, 6-for-14, 1 HR)
Jose DeLeon (.474, 9-for-19)
Rick Mahler (.447, 17-for-38)

Hates to face: Tim Crews (0-for-12)
Doug Drabek (.067, 1-for-15)
Ed Whitson (.091, 3-for-33, 0 BB)

Miscellaneous statistics: Ground outs-to-air outs ratio: 1.24 last season, 1.04 for career.... Grounded into 8 double plays in 81 opportunities (one per 10.1).... Drove in 7 of 18 runners from third base with less than two outs (39%), 3d-lowest rate in N.L.... Direction of balls hit to the outfield: 29% to left field, 37% to center, 34% to right batting left-handed; 21% to left, 35% to center, 44% to right batting right-handed.... Base running: Advanced from first base to third on 5 of 18 outfield singles (28%); scored from second on 8 of 9 (89%).... Made 3.24 assists per nine innings at shortstop, highest rate in N.L.

Comments: Batted .289 before the All-Star break, but only .174 in the second half of the season. That's been a career-long problem for Uribe, who has played an average of 147 games per season, excluding 1987 when he missed most of the first half of the season, played only 95 games, and batted .291, a career high.... Started only 14 of the Giants' last 31 games last season, as the club took a look at Mike Benjamin at shortstop.... Giants pitchers didn't like what they saw, allowing 4.19 runs per nine innings with Uribe at shorstop, 4.52 with Benjamin there, and 5.25 with other shortstops.... Batted 85 points higher in night games (.282) than in day games (.196) last season, the 4th-largest margin in the majors.... Has hit for a higher average against ground-ball pitchers than against fly-ball pitchers in each of his seven seasons in the majors, the longest streak by a National League player. Career averages: .265 vs. ground-ballers, .220 vs. fly-ballers.... He has also hit for a higher average with runners on base than with the bases empty in each of his six full seasons.... Walked 29 times last season, but 13 of them were intentional. Intentional walks account for roughly one-third of his career walks (71 of 214).... Each of his last 302 starts have been from the eight slot in the batting order. Career totals: 792 starts, 755 from the eight slot.... Uribe has played 820 games at shortstop, tying him with Buddy Kerr for sixth most in franchise history.

Andy Van Slyke

Bats Left

Pittsburgh Pirates	AB	H	2B	3B	HR	RBI	BB	SO	BA	SA	OBA
Season	493	140	26	6	17	77	66	89	.284	.465	.367
vs. Left-Handers	188	49	3	2	5	28	26	35	.261	.378	.349
vs. Right-Handers	305	91	23	4	12	49	40	54	.298	.518	.378
vs. Ground-Ballers	238	64	10	5	6	30	36	44	.269	.429	.367
vs. Fly-Ballers	255	76	16	1	11	47	30	45	.298	.498	.367
Home Games	219	63	15	1	6	35	31	40	.288	.447	.373
Road Games	274	77	11	5	11	42	35	49	.281	.478	.362
Grass Fields	150	49	6	3	8	26	24	28	.327	.567	.420
Artificial Turf	343	91	20	3	9	51	42	61	.265	.420	.343
April	69	20	3	1	4	11	8	11	.290	.536	.364
May	83	30	2	0	2	15	14	12	.361	.458	.449
June	83	21	5	2	1	11	10	18	.253	.398	.330
July	84	19	5	0	3	6	9	12	.226	.393	.305
August	68	21	2	1	3	12	13	12	.309	.500	.420
Sept./Oct.	106	29	9	2	4	22	12	24	.274	.509	.345
Leading Off Inn.	80	24	6	0	2	2	11	15	.300	.450	.385
Bases Empty	254	71	13	3	8	8	25	42	.280	.449	.344
Runners On	239	69	13	3	9	69	41	47	.289	.481	.389
Runners/Scor. Pos.	140	41	7	2	2	51	26	28	.293	.414	.398
Runners On/2 Out	80	22	4	1	3	22	11	19	.275	.463	.363
Scor. Pos./2 Out	45	14	1	0	1	15	10	12	.311	.400	.436
Late-Inning Pressure	64	16	3	0	2	10	6	14	.250	.391	.310
Leading Off	17	7	1	0	1	1	2	3	.412	.647	.474
Runners On	31	6	1	0	0	8	3	9	.194	.226	.257
Runners/Scor. Pos.	16	6	1	0	0	8	2	3	.375	.438	.421

RUNS BATTED IN	From 1B	From 2B	From 3B	Scoring Position
Totals	13/159	24/112	23/52	47/164
Percentage	8.2%	21.4%	44.2%	28.7%

Loves to face: Rick Mahler (.500, 24-for-48, 3 HR)
Rick Reuschel (.450, 18-for-40, 1 HR)
Steve Wilson (.500, 6-for-12, 1 HR)

Hates to face: Dennis Cook (0-for-7)
Randy Myers (.087, 2-for-23, 1 3B)
Mike Scott (.026, 1-for-38, 3 BB)

Miscellaneous statistics: Ground outs-to-air outs ratio: 0.87 last season, 0.91 for career. . . . Grounded into 6 double plays in 124 opportunities (one per 20.7). . . . Drove in 19 of 32 runners from third base with less than two outs (59%). . . . Direction of balls hit to the outfield: 29% to left field, 28% to center, 43% to right. . . . Base running: Advanced from first base to third on 7 of 22 outfield singles (32%); scored from second on 9 of 15 (60%). . . . Made 2.58 putouts per nine innings in center field.

Comments: Won a third consecutive Gold Glove (has there ever been a *one-time* winner?) despite having more errors (8) than assists (6) for the first time in his career. Previous career totals in the outfield: 64 assists, 23 errors. . . . Of Van Slyke's 77 RBIs, 22 gave the Pirates a lead and 17 held up as game-winners. He shared the team lead in go-ahead RBIs with Bobby Bonilla, who drove in 120 runs overall, and led the team outright in GWs with one more than Bonilla. . . . Became the fourth Pirates player to hit a pair of opening-day home runs, joining Willie Stargell (1975), Richie Hebner (1974), and Dale Long (1956). . . . Averaged 28 stolen bases per season over the first six years of his career, but stole only 16 in 1989 and 14 last season. . . . Batted 74 points higher vs. right-handers (.302) than vs. left-handers (.228) over the last five seasons, the 5th-largest margin in the majors. Last season's batting average vs. left-handers was his highest since batting .262 in only 42 at-bats in 1984. . . . Batting average in Late-Inning Pressure Situations has been lower than his overall average in each of the last four seasons. . . . Career batting average of .182 at the Astrodome is his lowest at any ballpark. . . . Has only five hits in 30 at-bats with the bases loaded since joining the Pirates in 1987. . . . Has reached base on catcher's interference 13 times in his career, the most of any active player. . . . Career batting average is only .152 in 17 postseason games, and note the breakdown: 2-for-27 vs. right-handers (.074), 5-for-19 vs. left-handers (.263).

Larry Walker

Bats Left

Montreal Expos	AB	H	2B	3B	HR	RBI	BB	SO	BA	SA	OBA
Season	419	101	18	3	19	51	49	112	.241	.434	.326
vs. Left-Handers	116	24	6	0	6	18	8	30	.207	.414	.264
vs. Right-Handers	303	77	12	3	13	33	41	82	.254	.442	.349
vs. Ground-Ballers	223	49	8	0	11	30	29	55	.220	.404	.311
vs. Fly-Ballers	196	52	10	3	8	21	20	57	.265	.469	.344
Home Games	196	50	8	2	9	27	22	50	.255	.454	.338
Road Games	223	51	10	1	10	24	27	62	.229	.417	.316
Grass Fields	105	30	4	1	7	17	16	29	.286	.543	.385
Artificial Turf	314	71	14	2	12	34	33	83	.226	.398	.306
April	53	13	6	0	1	5	7	20	.245	.415	.339
May	65	18	3	1	2	6	6	13	.277	.446	.338
June	73	19	5	0	5	12	11	14	.260	.534	.353
July	76	11	0	0	3	6	3	29	.145	.263	.188
August	71	19	1	0	5	13	5	17	.268	.493	.325
Sept./Oct.	81	21	3	2	3	9	17	19	.259	.457	.400
Leading Off Inn.	82	23	4	1	5	5	6	24	.280	.537	.330
Bases Empty	231	61	13	2	12	12	24	65	.264	.494	.341
Runners On	188	40	5	1	7	39	25	47	.213	.362	.309
Runners/Scor. Pos.	108	21	2	0	4	32	20	32	.194	.324	.315
Runners On/2 Out	68	17	1	1	4	19	11	15	.250	.471	.354
Scor. Pos./2 Out	46	10	1	0	2	14	8	11	.217	.370	.333
Late-Inning Pressure	78	24	5	0	4	9	11	17	.308	.526	.393
Leading Off	28	11	1	0	2	2	0	6	.393	.643	.393
Runners On	34	8	1	0	2	7	8	8	.235	.441	.381
Runners/Scor. Pos.	16	4	0	0	2	7	7	1	.250	.625	.478

RUNS BATTED IN	From 1B	From 2B	From 3B	Scoring Position
Totals	6/131	14/77	12/48	26/125
Percentage	4.6%	18.2%	25.0%	20.8%

Loves to face: Kelly Downs (3-for-3, 1 HR)
Bill Long (3-for-3, 1 2B, 1 3B, 1 HR)

Hates to face: Tom Browning (0-for-9)
Doug Drabek (.133, 2-for-15)

Miscellaneous statistics: Ground outs-to-air outs ratio: 1.61 last season, 1.56 for career. . . . Grounded into 8 double plays in 97 opportunities (one per 12.1). . . . Drove in 10 of 25 runners from third base with less than two outs (40%), 4th-lowest rate in N.L. . . . Direction of balls hit to the outfield: 33% to left field, 32% to center, 35% to right. . . . Base running: Advanced from first base to third on 10 of 19 outfield singles (53%); scored from second on 11 of 11. . . . Made 2.23 putouts per nine innings in right field.

Comments: Among N.L. rookies, only Todd Zeile (144) played more games than Walker (133). Walker qualified as a rookie last season despite having over a year of major league service, most of which he accumulated when he spent the entire 1988 season on the disabled list. Those days are ignored for purposes of rookie qualification—the so-called "Donnell Nixon rule." . . . At 23, Walker was the youngest National League player to appear in at least 100 games in right field. The youngest to play that many games at other positions in the N.L., along with their ages at the end of the 1990 season: 1B, Mark Grace (26); 2B, Delino DeShields (21); 3B, Matt Williams (24); SS, Jay Bell (24); LF, Barry Bonds (26); CF, Ron Gant (25); C, Craig Biggio (24). . . . Became the first rookie in franchise history to strike out more than 100 times in his rookie season. He also tied Andre Dawson's club record for most home runs by a rookie. . . . Walker was born in British Columbia in 1966, before the Expos were even a gleam in Charles Bronfman's eye; he is the fifth Canadian-born player in team history. . . . Had only one hit in 18 at-bats as a pinch hitter last season. . . . Career average of .203 in day games, .246 at night. . . . Career average of .429 (12-for-28, 3 HR) at Wrigley Field. . . . Comparable rookie seasons: Byron Browne (1966), Jesse Barfield (1982), and Mike Young (1984). A little less similar but of interest to optimistic Expos fans: George Foster (1971) and Ralph Kiner (1946).

Tim Wallach

Bats Right

Montreal Expos	AB	H	2B	3B	HR	RBI	BB	SO	BA	SA	OBA
Season	626	185	37	5	21	98	42	80	.296	.471	.339
vs. Left-Handers	204	59	12	2	6	29	21	23	.289	.456	.355
vs. Right-Handers	422	126	25	3	15	69	21	57	.299	.479	.331
vs. Ground-Ballers	347	111	23	4	13	54	22	35	.320	.522	.357
vs. Fly-Ballers	279	74	14	1	8	44	20	45	.265	.409	.317
Home Games	301	83	16	5	9	46	24	43	.276	.452	.328
Road Games	325	102	21	0	12	52	18	37	.314	.489	.350
Grass Fields	173	59	13	0	8	33	7	15	.341	.555	.365
Artificial Turf	453	126	24	5	13	65	35	65	.278	.439	.330
April	72	23	6	0	2	9	6	13	.319	.486	.375
May	105	34	10	1	9	25	7	12	.324	.695	.366
June	110	30	8	1	1	15	10	15	.273	.391	.339
July	101	27	4	2	5	19	10	15	.267	.495	.336
August	110	39	5	0	0	10	3	8	.355	.400	.365
Sept./Oct.	128	32	4	1	4	20	6	17	.250	.391	.277
Leading Off Inn.	171	50	13	0	6	6	9	18	.292	.474	.328
Bases Empty	354	101	20	2	10	10	20	43	.285	.438	.324
Runners On	272	84	17	3	11	88	22	37	.309	.515	.359
Runners/Scor. Pos.	174	49	9	2	8	76	20	26	.282	.494	.353
Runners On/2 Out	121	35	8	0	5	35	8	17	.289	.479	.338
Scor. Pos./2 Out	84	21	4	0	4	30	8	14	.250	.440	.323
Late-Inning Pressure	110	32	5	1	3	14	8	13	.291	.436	.350
Leading Off	22	5	0	0	0	0	1	2	.227	.227	.261
Runners On	48	15	4	0	2	13	5	5	.313	.521	.400
Runners/Scor. Pos.	30	7	1	0	2	11	4	1	.233	.467	.361

RUNS BATTED IN	From 1B	From 2B	From 3B	Scoring Position
Totals	18/183	33/132	26/75	59/207
Percentage	9.8%	25.0%	34.7%	28.5%

Loves to face: Joe Boever (.538, 7-for-13)
Mark Grant (.474, 9-for-19, 2 HR)
Bruce Ruffin (.500, 11-for-22, 2 HR)

Hates to face: Pat Combs (.063, 1-for-16)
Sid Fernandez (.167, 7-for-42, 0 BB)
Alejandro Pena (.133, 4-for-30, 1 HR)

Miscellaneous statistics: Ground outs-to-air outs ratio: 0.81 last season, 0.84 for career. . . . Grounded into 12 double plays in 115 opportunities (one per 9.6). . . . Drove in 20 of 38 runners from third base with less than two outs (53%). . . . Direction of balls hit to the outfield: 30% to left field, 36% to center, 34% to right. . . . Base running: Advanced from first base to third on 8 of 22 outfield singles (36%); scored from second on 8 of 12 (67%). . . . Made 1.95 assists per nine innings at third base.

Comments: Home runs and strikeouts usually rise and fall together. But Wallach is one of several players to increase his home runs and decrease his strikeouts in each of the last two seasons. (The others: Brook Jacoby, Ernest Riles, Luis Rivera, and Ryne Sandberg.) Wallach's HR/SO totals, year-by-year since 1988: 12/88, 13/81, 21/80. Only four players in major league history had streaks longer than two years: Sam Thompson (5 years, 1891–95), Charlie Gehringer (4, 1927–30), George Cutshaw (3, 1916–18), and Lou Gehrig (3, 1929–31). . . . Had two or more hits in 58 games last season, tying Eddie Murray for the National League lead. . . . Led the Expos with 46 hits to the opposite field (hardly to be expected from a player who, as a right-handed fly-ball hitter, closely matches the profile of poor opposite-field hitters as described in the Expos essay). . . . His streak of nine straight opening-day starts is one shy of the team record, shared by Gary Carter (1975–84) and Andre Dawson (1978–87). . . . Has batted above .300 vs. ground-ball pitchers in three of the last four seasons. . . . Leads the National League with 300 doubles over the last nine seasons. For his career, Wallach has averaged one double every 15 at-bats in home games, compared to one per 20 at-bats on the road, suggesting that he would hit 40 doubles if he played 162 games at Olympic Stadium, 31 doubles if he played a full season of road games. The bottom line: He can hit doubles anywhere.

Jerome Walton

Bats Right

Chicago Cubs	AB	H	2B	3B	HR	RBI	BB	SO	BA	SA	OBA
Season	392	103	16	2	2	21	50	70	.263	.329	.350
vs. Left-Handers	146	42	7	1	1	12	19	20	.288	.370	.369
vs. Right-Handers	246	61	9	1	1	9	31	50	.248	.305	.339
vs. Ground-Ballers	200	51	7	2	0	16	21	36	.255	.310	.330
vs. Fly-Ballers	192	52	9	0	2	5	29	34	.271	.349	.371
Home Games	200	58	5	2	2	8	24	32	.290	.365	.363
Road Games	192	45	11	0	0	13	26	38	.234	.292	.338
Grass Fields	268	77	8	2	2	12	35	43	.287	.354	.371
Artificial Turf	124	26	8	0	0	9	15	27	.210	.274	.305
April	70	20	2	0	0	2	8	13	.286	.314	.375
May	82	25	4	1	0	5	10	14	.305	.378	.376
June	63	13	4	0	0	6	11	12	.206	.270	.329
July	0	0	0	0	0	0	0	0	—	—	—
August	78	21	2	0	1	4	11	16	.269	.333	.367
Sept./Oct.	99	24	4	1	1	4	10	15	.242	.333	.312
Leading Off Inn.	163	45	9	1	2	2	18	24	.276	.380	.348
Bases Empty	265	68	11	1	2	2	29	47	.257	.328	.332
Runners On	127	35	5	1	0	19	21	23	.276	.331	.386
Runners/Scor. Pos.	73	17	1	1	0	19	16	16	.233	.274	.363
Runners On/2 Out	65	13	2	1	0	9	6	13	.200	.262	.268
Scor. Pos./2 Out	41	8	1	1	0	9	6	11	.195	.268	.298
Late-Inning Pressure	55	16	3	0	1	4	4	13	.291	.400	.339
Leading Off	14	4	1	0	1	1	1	2	.286	.571	.333
Runners On	19	8	1	0	0	3	2	3	.421	.474	.476
Runners/Scor. Pos.	10	4	0	0	0	3	2	2	.400	.400	.500

RUNS BATTED IN	From 1B	From 2B	From 3B	Scoring Position
Totals	1/79	6/52	12/38	18/90
Percentage	1.3%	11.5%	31.6%	20.0%

Loves to face: Alejandro Pena (.556, 5-for-9)
Dennis Rasmussen (.600, 6-for-10)
John Smiley (.471, 8-for-17, 2 HR, 5 SO)

Hates to face: Roger McDowell (0-for-8)
Bruce Ruffin (.167, 4-for-24)
Bryn Smith (.217, 5-for-23)

Miscellaneous statistics: Ground outs-to-air outs ratio: 1.19 last season, 1.45 for career. . . . Grounded into 4 double plays in 50 opportunities (one per 12.5). . . . Drove in 8 of 18 runners from third base with less than two outs (44%). . . . Direction of balls hit to the outfield: 34% to left field, 35% to center, 31% to right. . . . Base running: Advanced from first base to third on 14 of 35 outfield singles (40%); scored from second on 8 of 12 (67%). . . . Made 2.62 putouts per nine innings in center field.

Comments: Drove in only 21 runs, the fewest ever by an incumbent National League rookie of the year (pitchers excluded). Due to military service, Willie Mays played only 34 games in 1952, the year after he won the award; he still managed to drive in 23 runs. Joe Charboneau drove in only 27 more runs *over the remainder of his major league career* after winning the A.L. Rookie Award in 1980. . . . His batting average with runners in scoring position fell by more than 100 points, from .348 as a rookie. . . . Spent 45 days on the disabled list after a Ken Howell pitch fractured a bone in his left hand on June 17. . . . Offensive production declined from his rookie season in almost every category with the exception of walks. He averaged one walk every 19.1 plate appearances in 1989, compared to one every nine times to the plate last season. . . . He also improved on his 1989 batting average of .222 in Late-Inning Pressure Situations. . . . He was the Cubs' leadoff batter in all but one of his 97 starts. . . . Batted 78 points higher on grass fields (.287) than on artificial turf (.210) last season, the 5th-largest margin in the majors. Career figures: .297 at Wrigley Field, .291 on other grass fields, .245 artificial turf. . . . Has five hits, all singles, in 10 career at-bats with the bases loaded. . . . Has hit seven home runs in his career, all with the bases empty, six of them leading off innings.

Ernie Whitt

Bats Left

Atlanta Braves	AB	H	2B	3B	HR	RBI	BB	SO	BA	SA	OBA
Season	180	31	8	0	2	10	23	27	.172	.250	.265
vs. Left-Handers	17	2	0	0	0	2	1	5	.118	.118	.167
vs. Right-Handers	163	29	8	0	2	8	22	22	.178	.264	.274
vs. Ground-Ballers	91	16	3	0	2	5	13	15	.176	.275	.279
vs. Fly-Ballers	89	15	5	0	0	5	10	12	.169	.225	.250
Home Games	86	14	4	0	2	8	15	10	.163	.279	.284
Road Games	94	17	4	0	0	2	8	17	.181	.223	.245
Grass Fields	138	22	5	0	2	9	16	22	.159	.239	.245
Artificial Turf	42	9	3	0	0	1	7	5	.214	.286	.327
April	31	4	3	0	0	2	10	8	.129	.226	.341
May	39	8	2	0	2	4	3	5	.205	.410	.262
June	1	0	0	0	0	0	0	0	.000	.000	.000
July	8	0	0	0	0	0	0	1	.000	.000	.000
August	56	9	1	0	0	1	8	7	.161	.179	.262
Sept./Oct.	45	10	2	0	0	3	2	6	.222	.267	.255
Leading Off Inn.	41	9	5	0	0	0	5	7	.220	.341	.304
Bases Empty	109	20	6	0	2	2	11	18	.183	.294	.258
Runners On	71	11	2	0	0	8	12	9	.155	.183	.274
Runners/Scor. Pos.	37	5	2	0	0	8	9	7	.135	.189	.298
Runners On/2 Out	31	4	0	0	0	1	9	7	.129	.129	.325
Scor. Pos./2 Out	16	1	0	0	0	1	7	6	.063	.063	.348
Late-Inning Pressure	33	9	3	0	0	2	3	5	.273	.364	.333
Leading Off	9	3	2	0	0	0	1	1	.333	.556	.400
Runners On	8	2	1	0	0	2	1	0	.250	.375	.333
Runners/Scor. Pos.	6	1	1	0	0	2	1	0	.167	.333	.286

RUNS BATTED IN	From 1B	From 2B	From 3B	Scoring Position
Totals	1/49	2/31	5/13	7/44
Percentage	2.0%	6.5%	38.5%	15.9%

Loves to face: Charlie Hough (.305, 18-for-59, 4 HR)
Mike Moore (.302, 16-for-53, 7 2B, 2 HR)
Jeff Russell (.462, 6-for-13, 1 HR)

Hates to face: Gene Nelson (.133, 2-for-15)
Bobby Witt (.143, 2-for-14)
Nolan Ryan (0-for-7, 6 SO)

Miscellaneous statistics: Ground outs-to-air outs ratio: 1.11 last season, 0.94 for career.... Grounded into 6 double plays in 26 opportunities (one per 4.3).... Drove in 4 of 8 runners from third base with less than two outs (50%).... Direction of balls hit to the outfield: 32% to left field, 36% to center, 32% to right.... Base running: Advanced from first base to third on 1 of 11 outfield singles (9%), 3d-lowest rate in N.L.; scored from second on 1 of 4 (25%).... Opposing base stealers: 70-for-101 (69%).

Comments: Only four Braves players since 1900 had lower batting averages (minimum: 150 AB): Jody Davis (.169 in 1989), Bob Didier (.149 in 1970), Bob Uecker (.146 in 1967), and Frank O'Rourke (.122 in 1912).... Started 53 games against right-handed pitchers, but only one against a left-hander. In his 14 years in the majors, he has never batted as many as 100 times against left-handed pitchers in a season.... Only three players from the 1977 Toronto Blue Jays were active during the 1990 season: Whitt, Rick Cerone, and Jim Clancy. The 1977 Seattle Mariners had two survivors: Dave Collins and Rick Honeycutt. The final players to have remained active from each of baseball's previous eight expansion franchises: 1961 Angels, Jim Fregosi (last played for the Pirates in 1978); 1961 Senators, Ed Brinkman (Yankees, 1975) and Claude Osteen (White Sox, 1975); 1962 Colt .45s, Dave Giusti (Cubs, 1977); 1962 Mets, Ed Kranepool (Mets, 1979); 1969 Pilots, Fred Stanley (Athletics, 1982); 1969 Royals, Buck Martinez (Blue Jays, 1986); 1969 Expos, Rusty Staub (Mets, 1985); 1969 Padres, Joe Niekro (Twins, 1988).... An odd duck of a note: Whitt made 12 postseason starts in his career without a multi-hit game. Among others without a two-hit game in postseason, seven had more starts: Dal Maxvill (24), Whitey Ford (22), Johnny Roseboro (22), Travis Jackson (18), Gorman Thomas (17), Billy North (16), and Darrel Chaney (13). Alfredo Griffin also has 12.

Matt Williams

Bats Right

San Francisco Giants	AB	H	2B	3B	HR	RBI	BB	SO	BA	SA	OBA
Season	617	171	27	2	33	122	33	138	.277	.488	.319
vs. Left-Handers	208	59	9	0	12	48	13	40	.284	.500	.332
vs. Right-Handers	409	112	18	2	21	74	20	98	.274	.482	.312
vs. Ground-Ballers	270	75	13	1	12	58	14	61	.278	.467	.318
vs. Fly-Ballers	347	96	14	1	21	64	19	77	.277	.504	.319
Home Games	303	82	14	1	20	63	15	66	.271	.521	.312
Road Games	314	89	13	1	13	59	18	72	.283	.455	.325
Grass Fields	460	137	23	1	28	101	22	94	.298	.535	.334
Artificial Turf	157	34	4	1	5	21	11	44	.217	.350	.275
April	77	23	3	0	2	15	4	16	.299	.416	.329
May	105	28	4	0	7	18	6	22	.267	.505	.306
June	110	37	6	0	7	29	4	27	.336	.582	.359
July	106	26	5	2	4	21	5	26	.245	.443	.292
August	104	23	3	0	7	15	6	23	.221	.452	.277
Sept./Oct.	115	34	6	0	6	24	8	24	.296	.504	.346
Leading Off Inn.	147	31	2	1	7	7	7	37	.211	.381	.252
Bases Empty	344	81	9	2	17	17	13	86	.235	.422	.265
Runners On	273	90	18	0	16	105	20	52	.330	.571	.382
Runners/Scor. Pos.	156	52	8	0	11	90	17	34	.333	.596	.394
Runners On/2 Out	122	35	7	0	7	41	8	31	.287	.516	.346
Scor. Pos./2 Out	76	23	5	0	5	35	7	20	.303	.566	.361
Late-Inning Pressure	87	19	4	0	2	11	3	25	.218	.333	.253
Leading Off	18	1	0	0	0	0	2	6	.056	.056	.150
Runners On	40	13	4	0	1	10	1	9	.325	.500	.357
Runners/Scor. Pos.	19	6	1	0	1	8	1	6	.316	.526	.350

RUNS BATTED IN	From 1B	From 2B	From 3B	Scoring Position
Totals	22/214	31/120	36/69	67/189
Percentage	10.3%	25.8%	52.2%	35.4%

Loves to face: David Cone (.500, 8-for-16, 2 HR)
Mike Harkey (.556, 5-for-9, 2 HR)
Dennis Rasmussen (.533, 8-for-15, 2 2B, 3 HR)

Hates to face: Mark Portugal (.077, 2-for-26)
Jose Rijo (0-for-11, 1 BB, 6 SO)
Fernando Valenzuela (.115, 3-for-26, 2 2B, 1 HR, 3 BB)

Miscellaneous statistics: Ground outs-to-air outs ratio: 0.85 last season, 0.95 for career.... Grounded into 13 double plays in 129 opportunities (one per 9.9).... Drove in 25 of 35 runners from third base with less than two outs (71%).... Direction of balls hit to the outfield: 41% to left field, 34% to center, 25% to right.... Base running: Advanced from first base to third on 12 of 26 outfield singles (46%); scored from second on 16 of 19 (84%).... Made 2.01 assists per nine innings at third base.

Comments: Williams was the third different Giants player to lead the National League in RBIs in as many seasons, following Will Clark (1988) and Kevin Mitchell (1989). The only other team ever to do that in either league was the Yankees from 1925 through 1927. The RBI leaders were Bob Meusel, Babe Ruth, and Lou Gehrig.... Batted .333 from the sixth slot in the batting order, the highest average of any National League player with at least 100 at-bats from that spot.... Batted 81 points higher on grass fields (.298) than on artificial turf (.217) last season, the 2d-largest margin in the majors.... Tied Darrell Evans's club record of 159 games at third base, set in 1979.... His error rate at third base has incrased throughout his four-year career. Chances per error, year by year since 1987: 31.0, 30.5, 25.6, 24.5.... Career batting average of .183 in Late-Inning Pressure Situations, .243 in other at-bats.... Has hit 42 home runs at Candlestick, 25 on the road.... Has homered at every current National League ballpark except Busch Stadium (36 career AB).... Are Will Clark and Williams the best-ever first-round picks made by one club in consecutive years (1985–86)? You make the call. Other contenders: 1965–66 K.C. Athletics, Rick Monday and Reggie Jackson; 1976–77 Dodgers, Mike Scioscia and Bob Welch; 1981–82 Cubs, Joe Carter and Shawon Dunston; 1984–85 Athletics, Mark McGwire and Walt Weiss.

Glenn Wilson

Bats Right

Houston Astros	AB	H	2B	3B	HR	RBI	BB	SO	BA	SA	OBA
Season	368	90	14	0	10	55	26	64	.245	.364	.293
vs. Left-Handers	164	43	10	0	2	25	13	27	.262	.360	.311
vs. Right-Handers	204	47	4	0	8	30	13	37	.230	.368	.279
vs. Ground-Ballers	183	45	7	0	3	22	10	21	.246	.333	.284
vs. Fly-Ballers	185	45	7	0	7	33	16	43	.243	.395	.302
Home Games	174	45	10	0	5	33	13	28	.259	.402	.307
Road Games	194	45	4	0	5	22	13	36	.232	.330	.281
Grass Fields	106	22	0	0	4	13	8	22	.208	.321	.261
Artificial Turf	262	68	14	0	6	42	18	42	.260	.382	.306
April	64	14	1	0	2	5	4	8	.219	.328	.265
May	68	17	2	0	1	9	3	8	.250	.324	.274
June	82	21	2	0	4	17	6	18	.256	.427	.303
July	68	14	4	0	1	10	10	17	.206	.309	.316
August	85	24	5	0	2	13	3	13	.282	.412	.307
Sept./Oct.	1	0	0	0	0	1	0	0	.000	.000	.000
Leading Off Inn.	77	25	4	0	3	3	7	11	.325	.494	.381
Bases Empty	200	50	7	0	6	6	15	34	.250	.375	.302
Runners On	168	40	7	0	4	49	11	30	.238	.351	.283
Runners/Scor. Pos.	106	30	5	0	3	46	6	23	.283	.415	.316
Runners On/2 Out	70	17	2	0	2	19	6	12	.243	.357	.303
Scor. Pos./2 Out	47	14	2	0	2	19	2	10	.298	.468	.327
Late-Inning Pressure	61	14	0	0	1	11	5	11	.230	.279	.279
Leading Off	15	3	0	0	0	0	1	2	.200	.200	.250
Runners On	34	9	0	0	1	11	2	6	.265	.353	.289
Runners/Scor. Pos.	23	7	0	0	1	11	1	4	.304	.435	.308

RUNS BATTED IN	From 1B	From 2B	From 3B	Scoring Position
Totals	5/118	19/87	21/43	40/130
Percentage	4.2%	21.8%	48.8%	30.8%

Loves to face: Frank DiPino (.667, 8-for-12, 2 HR)
Ken Howell (.429, 6-for-14, 2 HR, 5 SO)
Zane Smith (.433, 13-for-30, 1 HR)

Hates to face: Paul Assenmacher (0-for-11)
Fernando Valenzuela (.171, 7-for-41)
Frank Viola (0-for-17)

Miscellaneous statistics: Ground outs-to-air outs ratio: 1.27 last season, 1.24 for career.... Grounded into 16 double plays in 71 opportunities (one per 4.4), 2d-worst rate in N.L.... Drove in 15 of 24 runners from third base with less than two outs (63%).... Direction of balls hit to the outfield: 25% to left field, 33% to center, 42% to right.... Base running: Advanced from first base to third on 5 of 15 outfield singles (33%); scored from second on 10 of 17 (59%).... Made 2.51 putouts per nine innings in right field, highest rate in N.L.

Comments: Has been the opening-day right fielder for a different club in each of the last four seasons: Phillies in 1987, Mariners in 1988, Pirates in 1989, Astros in 1990.... He has a career total of 108 outfield assists. Since Wilson made his major league debut in 1982, only Jesse Barfield (147) has more.... Accumulated at least 100 at-bats in each of three different batting order positions last season. He batted .308 as a cleanup hitter, .243 from the fifth slot, and .202 from the sixth slot.... Has stolen only one base in nine attempts over the last two seasons.... Hit five home runs to left field, two to center field, and three to the opposite field. Two of those three opposite-field shots were hit at the Astrodome.... Had batted between .250 and .275 in each of the six prevous seasons.... Never hit more than 15 home runs in one season. (Did that surprise you as much as it did us?)... Has hit for a higher average against ground-ball pitchers than against fly-ball pitchers in each of the last six seasons. Career averages: .274 vs. ground-ballers, .255 vs. fly-ballers.... The Tigers made Wilson the 18th pick in the first round of the 1980 draft. The sixth pick of that draft was Darnell Coles, one of the many players for whom Wilson has been traded in his nine-year career, spanning five organizations.

Marvell Wynne

Bats Left

Chicago Cubs	AB	H	2B	3B	HR	RBI	BB	SO	BA	SA	OBA
Season	186	38	8	2	4	19	14	25	.204	.333	.264
vs. Left-Handers	17	3	0	0	1	2	2	2	.176	.353	.263
vs. Right-Handers	169	35	8	2	3	17	12	23	.207	.331	.264
vs. Ground-Ballers	73	12	2	1	1	6	5	13	.164	.260	.228
vs. Fly-Ballers	113	26	6	1	3	13	9	12	.230	.381	.287
Home Games	103	24	6	1	2	10	5	13	.233	.369	.275
Road Games	83	14	2	1	2	9	9	12	.169	.289	.250
Grass Fields	152	36	7	2	3	17	11	19	.237	.368	.293
Artificial Turf	34	2	1	0	1	2	3	6	.059	.176	.135
April	24	2	0	1	0	4	2	5	.083	.167	.154
May	29	5	1	0	0	0	3	4	.172	.207	.250
June	56	12	2	1	3	7	4	6	.214	.446	.279
July	66	17	5	0	1	8	3	7	.258	.379	.290
August	9	2	0	0	0	0	1	2	.222	.222	.300
Sept./Oct.	2	0	0	0	0	0	1	1	.000	.000	.333
Leading Off Inn.	50	5	1	0	1	1	1	8	.100	.180	.135
Bases Empty	102	18	3	0	3	3	5	14	.176	.294	.222
Runners On	84	20	5	2	1	16	9	11	.238	.381	.312
Runners/Scor. Pos.	49	11	4	2	0	14	7	7	.224	.388	.321
Runners On/2 Out	42	8	2	1	1	10	2	7	.190	.357	.227
Scor. Pos./2 Out	32	6	2	1	0	8	2	5	.188	.313	.235
Late-Inning Pressure	46	9	2	0	0	2	5	8	.196	.239	.275
Leading Off	17	2	1	0	0	0	0	4	.118	.176	.118
Runners On	18	5	1	0	0	2	4	2	.278	.333	.409
Runners/Scor. Pos.	13	2	0	0	0	2	4	2	.154	.154	.353

RUNS BATTED IN	From 1B	From 2B	From 3B	Scoring Position
Totals	4/62	6/41	5/14	11/55
Percentage	6.5%	14.6%	35.7%	20.0%

Loves to face: Jose Rijo (.385, 5-for-13, 2 HR)
Rick Sutcliffe (.419, 13-for-31)
Fernando Valenzuela (.389, 7-for-18, 1 HR)

Hates to face: Tim Belcher (.097, 3-for-31, 1 HR, 0 BB)
Dwight Gooden (.071, 2-for-28, 0 BB)
Bryn Smith (.128, 5-for-39)

Miscellaneous statistics: Ground outs-to-air outs ratio: 0.83 last season, 1.13 for career.... Grounded into 4 double plays in 42 opportunities (one per 10.5).... Drove in 2 of 2 runners from third base with less than two outs.... Direction of balls hit to the outfield: 32% to left field, 33% to center, 35% to right.... Base running: Advanced from first base to third on 2 of 2 outfield singles; scored from second on 2 of 2.... Made 2.52 putouts per nine innings in center field.

Comments: Batted .371 in his first plate appearances of each start, only .165 thereafter.... Started 37 games vs. right-handed pitchers, but only one against a left-hander. His 20 plate appearances vs. left-handers last season were the fewest of his eight-year career.... Started three games in the Cubs' cleanup spot, and earned the distinction of being the only National Leaguer to be credited with a sacrifice bunt from that spot in the batting order last season. (Why did he bat cleanup? Only Zim knows.)... Didn't start a game for the Cubs after July 27.... Batted .154 in 26 at-bats as a pinch hitter last season, including a streak of 12 hitless at-bats, evoking memories of another futile Cubs pinch hitter, Paul Popovich. Popovich was 2-for-26 as a pinch hitter in 1970, and 2-for-30 in 1971.... Drew only one base on balls in the 52 innings that he led off.... Was not thrown out trying to advance an extra base on any batted ball last season.... Has driven in fewer than 20 percent of runners from scoring position in Late-Inning Pressure Situations in five of the last six seasons.... Completed his career with the Cubs with a .201 batting average, three points lower than Lynn McGlothen's career average with them.

Eric Yelding

Bats Right

Houston Astros	AB	H	2B	3B	HR	RBI	BB	SO	BA	SA	OBA
Season	511	130	9	5	1	28	39	87	.254	.297	.305
vs. Left-Handers	235	66	6	3	0	16	16	31	.281	.332	.324
vs. Right-Handers	276	64	3	2	1	12	23	56	.232	.268	.288
vs. Ground-Ballers	286	72	7	2	1	10	19	48	.252	.301	.298
vs. Fly-Ballers	225	58	2	3	0	18	20	39	.258	.293	.312
Home Games	245	62	1	4	0	13	23	38	.253	.290	.314
Road Games	266	68	8	1	1	15	16	49	.256	.305	.296
Grass Fields	166	48	7	1	0	11	15	26	.289	.343	.344
Artificial Turf	345	82	2	4	1	17	24	61	.238	.275	.285
April	36	10	0	1	0	6	1	5	.278	.333	.282
May	88	27	0	1	0	6	6	13	.307	.330	.351
June	79	17	0	1	0	1	10	14	.215	.241	.303
July	112	34	3	1	0	8	8	19	.304	.348	.344
August	94	17	3	0	0	3	4	14	.181	.213	.212
Sept./Oct.	102	25	3	1	1	4	10	22	.245	.324	.313
Leading Off Inn.	222	58	3	0	1	1	17	43	.261	.288	.314
Bases Empty	350	92	7	1	1	1	29	70	.263	.297	.319
Runners On	161	38	2	4	0	27	10	17	.236	.298	.273
Runners/Scor. Pos.	101	23	1	2	0	25	7	8	.228	.277	.265
Runners On/2 Out	67	14	0	1	0	10	4	6	.209	.239	.254
Scor. Pos./2 Out	56	12	0	1	0	10	3	5	.214	.250	.254
Late-Inning Pressure	69	16	0	0	0	1	8	12	.232	.232	.312
Leading Off	21	3	0	0	0	0	2	5	.143	.143	.217
Runners On	28	4	0	0	0	1	2	5	.143	.143	.200
Runners/Scor. Pos.	15	3	0	0	0	1	1	3	.200	.200	.250

RUNS BATTED IN	From 1B	From 2B	From 3B	Scoring Position
Totals	2/104	9/89	16/36	25/125
Percentage	1.9%	10.1%	44.4%	20.0%

Loves to face: Steve Avery (.571, 4-for-7, 3 2B)
Frank Viola (.583, 7-for-12)

Hates to face: Mark Gardner (.100, 1-for-10)
Jose Rijo (0-for-7)
Zane Smith (.167, 2-for-12)

Miscellaneous statistics: Ground outs-to-air outs ratio: 1.40 last season, 1.36 for career. . . . Grounded into 11 double plays in 80 opportunities (one per 7.3). . . . Drove in 13 of 19 runners from third base with less than two outs (68%). . . . Direction of balls hit to the outfield: 27% to left field, 42% to center, 31% to right. . . . Base running: Advanced from first base to third on 9 of 18 outfield singles (50%); scored from second on 16 of 18 (89%), 5th-highest rate in N.L. . . . Made 2.92 putouts per nine innings in center field, 2d-highest rate in N.L.

Comments: Among the 83 players with at least 500 major league at-bats last season, Yelding had the fewest extra-base hits (15). Since baseball's expansion era began in 1961, only five players had fewer than 15 XBH in seasons of at least 500 AB: Don Kessinger (11 in 1966), Sonny Jackson (14 in 1966), Horace Clarke (9 in 1968), Enzo Hernandez (12 in 1971, his infamous 12-RBI year), and Frank Taveras (14 in 1976). . . . Started at five different fielding positions, all before the season was even a month old (2B, SS, LF, CF, and RF). . . . Led the league in times caught stealing (25), in the great Houston tradition of Cesar Cedeno and Gerald Young. He ranked second in stolen bases (64), behind Vince Coleman (77). . . . The leadoff spot in Houston's batting order ranked last in the National League in batting average (.252) and scored only 81 runs, 19 fewer than the 2d-lowest total in the league. Yelding made 113 starts from the leadoff position, followed by Gerald Young (25) and Bill Doran (12). . . . Collected 23 infield hits, 2d most on the Astros to Craig Biggio's 31. . . . Drove in only one of 16 runners from scoring position in Late-Inning Pressure Situations.

Todd Zeile

Bats Right

St. Louis Cardinals	AB	H	2B	3B	HR	RBI	BB	SO	BA	SA	OBA
Season	495	121	25	3	15	57	67	77	.244	.398	.333
vs. Left-Handers	173	46	12	1	6	22	21	21	.266	.451	.347
vs. Right-Handers	322	75	13	2	9	35	46	56	.233	.370	.326
vs. Ground-Ballers	242	60	12	3	8	28	35	38	.248	.421	.341
vs. Fly-Ballers	253	61	13	0	7	29	32	39	.241	.375	.326
Home Games	233	61	11	2	8	26	34	31	.262	.429	.358
Road Games	262	60	14	1	7	31	33	46	.229	.370	.311
Grass Fields	133	27	8	0	3	12	15	31	.203	.331	.278
Artificial Turf	362	94	17	3	12	45	52	46	.260	.423	.353
April	66	17	4	1	2	8	9	12	.258	.439	.342
May	75	14	4	0	2	10	10	15	.187	.320	.279
June	92	22	2	1	4	10	14	13	.239	.413	.340
July	72	16	2	0	3	7	6	10	.222	.375	.278
August	102	33	3	1	2	11	8	14	.324	.431	.366
Sept./Oct.	88	19	10	0	2	11	20	13	.216	.398	.369
Leading Off Inn.	151	39	8	0	8	8	14	23	.258	.470	.321
Bases Empty	282	72	10	2	10	10	29	43	.255	.411	.327
Runners On	213	49	15	1	5	47	38	34	.230	.380	.341
Runners/Scor. Pos.	130	21	8	0	2	35	29	22	.162	.269	.307
Runners On/2 Out	105	20	6	0	2	17	19	15	.190	.305	.315
Scor. Pos./2 Out	71	11	4	0	1	13	15	8	.155	.254	.302
Late-Inning Pressure	83	16	3	0	1	6	15	18	.193	.265	.313
Leading Off	34	7	2	0	1	1	1	6	.206	.353	.229
Runners On	27	4	1	0	0	5	10	7	.148	.185	.368
Runners/Scor. Pos.	21	2	1	0	0	5	9	6	.095	.143	.355

RUNS BATTED IN	From 1B	From 2B	From 3B	Scoring Position
Totals	10/136	17/102	15/64	32/166
Percentage	7.4%	16.7%	23.4%	19.3%

Loves to face: Stan Belinda (2-for-2, 1 HR, 3 BB)
Dennis Cook (.750, 6-for-8)
Jose DeJesus (.750, 3-for-4, 1 HR, 1 SO)

Hates to face: Tom Browning (.091, 1-for-11)
Danny Darwin (0-for-8)
John Smoltz (.077, 1-for-13, 1 2B)

Miscellaneous statistics: Ground outs-to-air outs ratio: 0.99 last season, 0.99 for career. . . . Grounded into 11 double plays in 90 opportunities (one per 8.2). . . . Drove in 12 of 25 runners from third base with less than two outs (48%). . . . Direction of balls hit to the outfield: 35% to left field, 34% to center, 31% to right. . . . Base running: Advanced from first base to third on 7 of 22 outfield singles (32%); scored from second on 8 of 15 (53%). . . . Opposing base stealers: 93-for-136 (68%).

Comments: The most home runs by a Cardinals rookie since 1955, when Ken Boyer hit 18 and Bill Virdon hit 17. The team record for a rookie is 21, set in 1953 by Ray Jablonski. . . . Zeile was the fourth Cardinals rookie to catch as many as 100 games. The others: Bill Sarni (1954), Tim McCarver (1963), and Mike LaValliere (1986). . . . Started only two games behind the plate after August 18. . . . Started 24 of the Cardinals' last 27 games at third base. . . . Cardinals pitchers allowed 5.54 runs per nine innings with Zeile at third base, compared to 4.16 runs per nine innings with others there. . . . Batting average of .162 with runners in scoring position was the lowest in National League. Batted 112 points lower with runners in scoring position than in other at-bats (.274), the largest margin in the majors. . . . Career batting average of .180 in Late-Inning Pressure Situations, .260 in other at-bats. Has only two hits in 24 career at-bats with RISP in LIPS. . . . St. Louis picked Zeile in the 1986 draft as compensation for the Yankees' signing free agent Ivan DeJesus. DeJesus played only 16 games in the majors after leaving the Cardinals. . . . Comparable rookie seasons: Ron Cey (1973), Carmelo Martinez (1984), Craig Worthington (1989).

PITCHER SECTION

The Pitcher Section is an alphabetical listing of every pitcher who either faced 400 batters or finished 20 games in relief in the major leagues last season. Pitchers who pitched in both leagues are listed in the league where they finished the season.

Column Headings Information

Jim Abbott

California Angels	W-L	ERA	AB	H	HR	BB	SO	BA	SA	OBA

W-L	Won-Lost Record
ERA	Earned Run Average
AB	At-Bats
H	Hits
HR	Home Runs
BB	Bases on Balls
SO	Strikeouts
BA	Batting Average
SA	Slugging Average
OBA	On-Base Average

In addition to the traditional statistics used to evaluate pitchers—won-lost record, ERA, walks, and strikeouts—this section provides the batting performance of the league against each pitcher. This enables us to break down his performance into the same types of categories used to measure batters' performance. We can identify those pitchers with huge platoon differentials, or those who give up a lot of hits and home runs but can bear down with runners on base and avoid giving up the clutch run-scoring hit. (Bear in mind that overall batting average increases with runners on base, as a result of the altered defensive alignment and the effects of pitching out of the stretch position. This makes any pitcher who holds opponents to a lower average with runners on all the more impressive.)

Season Summary Information

Season	10-14	4.51	833	246	16	72	105	.295	.401	.353
vs. Left-Handers			110	35	3	15	20	.318	.436	.398
vs. Right-Handers			723	211	13	57	85	.292	.396	.345
vs. Ground-Ballers			410	114	8	35	54	.278	.366	.334
vs. Fly-Ballers			423	132	8	37	51	.312	.435	.370
Home Games	4-7	4.75	437	138	9	31	46	.316	.421	.362
Road Games	6-7	4.25	396	108	7	41	59	.273	.379	.343
Grass Fields	8-11	4.54	702	209	14	60	89	.298	.400	.354
Artificial Turf	2-3	4.32	131	37	2	12	16	.282	.405	.347
April	0-1	6.06	62	21	0	9	5	.339	.419	.425
May	2-3	5.01	163	47	3	18	22	.288	.393	.359
June	3-2	4.35	145	40	1	14	20	.276	.338	.340
July	2-3	2.63	143	37	4	8	16	.259	.371	.299
August	2-3	6.08	155	51	4	12	20	.329	.458	.375
Sept./Oct.	1-2	3.83	165	50	4	11	22	.303	.430	.354

Each pitcher's performance for the season is broken down into a variety of special categories. The first line given for each pitcher is his season total. This is followed by a breakdown of his performance against left- and right-handed hitters, against ground-ball and fly-ball hitters (defined by whether their ground outs-to-air outs ratio is above or below the league average), in home and road games, on grass fields and artificial turf, and by month (regular season October games are combined with September). For pitchers who pitched with more than one team, all totals are combined; the "home" totals for Bud Black, for example, include all games pitched in Cleveland while with the Indians, and in Toronto while with the Blue Jays.

Leading Off Inn.	206	61	6	19	20	.296	.442	.358
Bases Empty	474	139	10	35	53	.293	.407	.344
Runners On	359	107	6	37	52	.298	.393	.363
Runners/Scor. Pos.	182	52	1	29	29	.286	.352	.379
Runners On/2 Out	146	39	4	20	28	.267	.384	.363
Scor. Pos./2 Out	83	19	1	17	14	.229	.301	.366

Following these breakdowns, each pitcher's performance is divided into specific game situations. Totals are given for each pitcher against batters who lead off an inning (for relievers, this would not include the first batter faced if not leading off an inning), with bases empty and runners on base, with runners in scoring position (on second or third, or both), with runners on base and two out, and with runners in scoring position and two out.

Late-Inning Pressure	61	16	2	2	7	.262	.377	.286
Leading Off	19	4	1	0	3	.211	.368	.211
Runners On	12	5	0	1	1	.417	.417	.462
Runners/Scor. Pos.	7	3	0	1	1	.429	.429	.500

The next group shows the pitcher's performance in Late-Inning Pressure Situations (LIPS). These are the flip side of the batters' pressure situations: any at-bats in the seventh inning or later, with the score tied, or the pitcher's team leading by one, two, or three runs (or four if there are two or more runners on base).

The statistics for Late-Inning Pressure Situations are then broken down for each pitcher's performance when the hitter is leading off an inning, batting with runners on base, or with runners in scoring position.

First 9 Batters	268	81	4	24	36	.302	.410	.360
Second 9 Batters	264	72	3	22	32	.273	.348	.328
All Batters Thereafter	301	93	9	26	37	.309	.439	.368

The last set of breakdowns tracks a pitcher's performance through each appearance by listing the opponents' record in his first time through the batting order, his second time through, and all at-bats thereafter. This spotlights those pitchers who get stronger as the game progresses, as well as those who breeze through the first time around but falter on repeated viewing.

Following the statistics for each pitcher is a list of batters he "loves and hates to face." The stats listed for each match-up include all regular-season games since 1975 inclusive. Next are miscellaneous statistics given in text form; these include: the pitcher's ground outs-to-air outs ratio; the number of double-play grounders he induced and the number of opportunities he faced (runner on first, less than two out); the number of doubles and triples he allowed in his innings pitched; and the performance of opposing base-stealers, along with his totals of pickoffs and balks. In addition, for starting pitchers there are his totals of first-inning runs allowed, and the batting support per start given him by his team. For relievers, the number of inherited runners he stranded and allowed to score are given.

As with batters, for purposes of comparison the league totals in all these categories are listed in the introduction to the Team Section (see page 2).

Jim Abbott

Throws Left

California Angels	W-L	ERA	AB	H	HR	BB	SO	BA	SA	OBA
Season	10-14	4.51	833	246	16	72	105	.295	.401	.353
vs. Left-Handers			110	35	3	15	20	.318	.436	.398
vs. Right-Handers			723	211	13	57	85	.292	.396	.345
vs. Ground-Ballers			410	114	8	35	54	.278	.366	.334
vs. Fly-Ballers			423	132	8	37	51	.312	.435	.370
Home Games	4-7	4.75	437	138	9	31	46	.316	.421	.362
Road Games	6-7	4.25	396	108	7	41	59	.273	.379	.343
Grass Fields	8-11	4.54	702	209	14	60	89	.298	.400	.354
Artificial Turf	2-3	4.32	131	37	2	12	16	.282	.405	.347
April	0-1	6.06	62	21	0	9	5	.339	.419	.425
May	2-3	5.01	163	47	3	18	22	.288	.393	.359
June	3-2	4.35	145	40	1	14	20	.276	.338	.340
July	2-3	2.63	143	37	4	8	16	.259	.371	.299
August	2-3	6.08	155	51	4	12	20	.329	.458	.375
Sept./Oct.	1-2	3.83	165	50	4	11	22	.303	.430	.354
Leading Off Inn.			206	61	6	19	20	.296	.442	.358
Bases Empty			474	139	10	35	53	.293	.407	.344
Runners On			359	107	6	37	52	.298	.393	.363
Runners/Scor. Pos.			182	52	1	29	29	.286	.352	.379
Runners On/2 Out			146	39	4	20	28	.267	.384	.363
Scor. Pos./2 Out			83	19	1	17	14	.229	.301	.366
Late-Inning Pressure			61	16	2	2	7	.262	.377	.286
Leading Off			19	4	1	0	3	.211	.368	.211
Runners On			12	5	0	1	1	.417	.417	.462
Runners/Scor. Pos.			7	3	0	1	1	.429	.429	.500
First 9 Batters			268	81	4	24	36	.302	.410	.360
Second 9 Batters			264	72	3	22	32	.273	.348	.328
All Batters Thereafter			301	93	9	26	37	.309	.439	.368

Loves to face: Dwight Evans (.053, 1-for-19, 1 2B, 2 BB)
Scott Fletcher (.077, 1-for-13)
Kelly Gruber (.188, 3-for-16)

Hates to face: George Brett (.647, 11-for-17, 3 HR)
Alvin Davis (.800, 4-for-5, 4 BB)
Dave Henderson (.667, 8-for-12, 1 2B, 4 HR)

Miscellaneous statistics: Ground outs-to-air outs ratio: 1.72 last season, 1.72 for career. . . . Induced 27 double-play ground outs in 180 opportunities (one per 6.7). . . . Allowed 36 doubles, 2 triples in 211.2 innings. . . . Allowed 21 first-inning runs in 33 starts (4.64 ERA). . . . Batting support: 3.97 runs per start. . . . Opposing base stealers: 15-for-19 (79%); 1 pickoff, 3 balks.

Comments: No other pitcher in the majors had at least 20 decisions last season without either a three-game winning streak or a three-game losing streak. In fact, over two seasons and 48 decisions, Abbott has had a single three-game winning streak and has never lost more than two consecutive decisions. . . . Had identical 5–7 records before and after the All-Star break. . . . Completed four of his 33 starts, including three over a four-game period (June 29–July 18). During that time, he walked only two batters in 34⅓ innings. . . . Walked 4.09 batters per nine innings in his first 15 starts through June 23, but only 2.33 per nine innings thereafter. . . . His rate of walks allowed during the first inning was his highest in any inning. . . . Opposing left-handed batters have hit over .300 against this southpaw in both of his seasons in the majors. The last southpaw to allow consecutive .300-plus BAs to left-handed hitters was Neal Heaton (1984–85). Abbott's career figures: .322 by left-handers, .279 by right-handers. . . . Has faced 40 batters with the bases loaded in his career and walked in only one run. . . . Career records of 0–5 vs. the Royals and 0–3 vs. the Athletics. . . . Was the eighth pick in the June 1988 free-agent draft, which produced several of baseball's most promising pitchers. Other first-round pitchers already in the majors include Andy Benes (1st pick), Steve Avery (3d), Gregg Olson (4th), Pat Combs (11th), and Alex Fernandez (24th, but not signed by the Brewers).

Jim Acker

Throws Right

Toronto Blue Jays	W-L	ERA	AB	H	HR	BB	SO	BA	SA	OBA
Season	4-4	3.83	366	103	9	30	54	.281	.418	.340
vs. Left-Handers			149	43	2	14	13	.289	.409	.355
vs. Right-Handers			217	60	7	16	41	.276	.424	.329
vs. Ground-Ballers			171	41	3	11	29	.240	.351	.284
vs. Fly-Ballers			195	62	6	19	25	.318	.477	.387
Home Games	2-3	3.76	209	63	3	20	27	.301	.426	.368
Road Games	2-1	3.92	157	40	6	10	27	.255	.408	.302
Grass Fields	1-1	3.66	126	30	5	6	26	.238	.381	.276
Artificial Turf	3-3	3.92	240	73	4	24	28	.304	.438	.372
April	0-0	3.45	63	16	2	5	13	.254	.413	.319
May	1-1	0.45	67	14	0	5	9	.209	.299	.264
June	0-1	7.62	55	16	1	10	4	.291	.418	.400
July	1-0	3.38	66	21	2	5	11	.318	.485	.366
August	1-2	5.19	73	21	2	4	10	.288	.411	.329
Sept./Oct.	1-0	4.66	42	15	2	1	7	.357	.524	.386
Leading Off Inn.			83	24	1	5	6	.289	.386	.337
Bases Empty			194	54	3	14	28	.278	.392	.333
Runners On			172	49	6	16	26	.285	.448	.347
Runners/Scor. Pos.			109	29	5	11	17	.266	.459	.336
Runners On/2 Out			75	18	3	9	15	.240	.413	.321
Scor. Pos./2 Out			51	13	2	6	11	.255	.431	.333
Late-Inning Pressure			81	27	2	6	10	.333	.481	.379
Leading Off			22	5	1	1	2	.227	.409	.261
Runners On			33	15	1	1	4	.455	.606	.471
Runners/Scor. Pos.			19	8	0	0	3	.421	.474	.421
First 9 Batters			323	92	9	23	48	.285	.427	.335
Second 9 Batters			43	11	0	7	6	.256	.349	.373
All Batters Thereafter			0	0	0	0	0	—	—	—

Loves to face: Brian Downing (.077, 1-for-13, 2 BB)
Rickey Henderson (.182, 2-for-11)
Willie Wilson (.133, 2-for-15)

Hates to face: Tom Brunansky (.389, 7-for-18, 2 HR)
Alvin Davis (.667, 6-for-9, 1 HR)
Mitch Webster (.833, 5-for-6, 1 HR)

Miscellaneous statistics: Ground outs-to-air outs ratio: 1.35 last season, 1.83 for career. . . . Induced 6 double-play ground outs in 75 opportunities (one per 12.5). . . . Allowed 21 doubles, 1 triple in 91.2 innings. . . . Stranded 24 inherited runners, allowed 16 to score (60% success rate). . . . Opposing base stealers: 6-for-13 (46%), including only two of their last seven attempts; 0 pickoffs, 1 balk.

Comments: He's been to hell and back. Has a career record of 23–17 in two stints with the Blue Jays (1983–86, 1989–90), but only a 7–27 mark with the Braves in between. His .217 winning percentage with Atlanta is the lowest of any pitcher in franchise history (minimum: 30 decisions). . . . Faced an average 6.8 batters per appearance, facing a single batter in three games. His longest outing of the season was four innings (18 batters). . . . Had streaks of seven and ten consecutive inherited runners stranded, but twice entered bases-loaded situations and allowed all three runners to score. . . . Opponents have a career batting average of .310 with runners in scoring position in Late-Inning Pressure Situations. Over the last three seasons: .382 (21-for-55). . . . He last started a game in 1988 for the Braves. . . . His career record is 3–13 during April and May but nearly .500 from June through the end of the season (27–31). . . . The Braves had two first-round picks in the June 1980 free-agent draft: Ken Dayley and Acker, both of whom now pitch for Toronto. . . . Keep this in mind for October: Both Acker and Dayley rank among the active leaders in postseason ERA (minimum: 10 IP). The top five: Randy Myers, 0.00 (13⅓ IP); Dayley, 0.44; Mike Scott, 0.50; Andy Hawkins, 0.57; and Acker, 0.73.

Rick Aguilera

Throws Right

Minnesota Twins	W-L	ERA	AB	H	HR	BB	SO	BA	SA	OBA
Season	5-3	2.76	245	55	5	19	61	.224	.322	.291
vs. Left-Handers			114	25	0	12	29	.219	.237	.299
vs. Right-Handers			131	30	5	7	32	.229	.397	.284
vs. Ground-Ballers			102	27	0	7	17	.265	.304	.312
vs. Fly-Ballers			143	28	5	12	44	.196	.336	.277
Home Games	3-2	3.44	132	34	3	13	32	.258	.371	.338
Road Games	2-1	2.01	113	21	2	6	29	.186	.265	.233
Grass Fields	1-1	3.00	77	16	2	4	23	.208	.325	.256
Artificial Turf	4-2	2.64	168	39	3	15	38	.232	.321	.306
April	0-1	3.52	26	4	1	2	7	.154	.269	.214
May	1-0	1.17	55	11	1	1	16	.200	.255	.214
June	0-0	1.64	40	9	0	2	8	.225	.300	.279
July	2-2	4.26	51	11	2	5	16	.216	.392	.298
August	1-0	1.93	36	9	0	4	8	.250	.306	.341
Sept./Oct.	1-0	4.82	37	11	1	5	6	.297	.405	.395
Leading Off Inn.			48	13	2	1	12	.271	.458	.327
Bases Empty			112	28	2	4	32	.250	.339	.300
Runners On			133	27	3	15	29	.203	.308	.284
Runners/Scor. Pos.			78	18	3	13	20	.231	.372	.341
Runners On/2 Out			56	12	3	9	9	.214	.411	.323
Scor. Pos./2 Out			39	9	3	8	7	.231	.487	.362
Late-Inning Pressure			180	38	4	12	54	.211	.300	.268
Leading Off			36	10	2	0	11	.278	.500	.297
Runners On			97	18	2	10	26	.186	.268	.262
Runners/Scor. Pos.			58	11	2	8	18	.190	.293	.288
First 9 Batters			240	54	5	19	61	.225	.325	.293
Second 9 Batters			5	1	0	0	0	.200	.200	.200
All Batters Thereafter			0	0	0	0	0	—	—	—

Loves to face: Joe Orsulak (.208, 5-for-24)
Tim Raines (.148, 4-for-27)
Franklin Stubbs (0-for-12)

Hates to face: Chris James (.364, 4-for-11, 1 HR)
Mark McGwire (.500, 3-for-6, 1 2B, 2 HR)
Jeff Stone (3-for-3, 1 BB)

Miscellaneous statistics: Ground outs-to-air outs ratio: 0.76 last season, 1.16 for career. . . . Induced 8 double-play ground outs in 64 opportunities (one per 8.0). . . . Allowed 9 doubles, 0 triples in 65.1 innings. . . . Stranded 30 inherited runners, allowed 8 to score (79%). . . . Opposing base stealers: 3-for-3; 0 pickoffs, 0 balks.

Comments: Minnesota's acquisition of Steve Bedrosian could be Aguilera's return ticket to the starting rotation. Only one player in major league history has made as many as five starts following a 30-save season: Clay Carroll (37 SV in 1972, 5 GS in 1973). However, Wilbur Wood (1971), Terry Forster (1973), Goose Gossage (1976), Ted Power (1986), and Greg A. Harris (1987) all started at least 10 games following seasons of 20 to 29 saves. . . . Career record of 32–23 with a 3.75 ERA as a starter; 13–12, 2.68 ERA as a reliever. . . . Career record of 29–29 with a 3.61 ERA from April through the end of August, but he's 16–6 with a 2.99 ERA from September 1 on. . . . Made 56 appearances last season, all in relief, and was removed from only two. . . . Like Minnesota's starting pitchers, Aguilera was stingy with leadoff walks. During five seasons with the Mets, Aguilera walked 25 of 484 leadoff batters (one per 19). . . . Batting average by opposing left-handed hitters was the lowest of his career. . . . Hasn't allowed a home run to a left-handed batter since August 19, 1989 against Dave Parker. His career home-run rate is twice as high against right-handed batters (one per 35 at-bats) as against left-handers (one per 71 AB). . . . Opponents have only one hit in 22 career at-bats with two outs and the bases loaded (.045), the lowest average against any pitcher over the last 16 years (minimum: 20 AB). . . . Reardon, Aguilera, Bedrosian. We've heard of strange obsessions, but bearded closers?

Larry Andersen

Throws Right

Astros/Red Sox	W-L	ERA	AB	H	HR	BB	SO	BA	SA	OBA
Season	5-2	1.79	348	79	2	27	93	.227	.273	.283
vs. Left-Handers			166	46	2	17	26	.277	.349	.346
vs. Right-Handers			182	33	0	10	67	.181	.203	.222
vs. Ground-Ballers			166	42	1	14	48	.253	.289	.315
vs. Fly-Ballers			182	37	1	13	45	.203	.258	.254
Home Games	4-0	0.68	195	41	0	10	57	.210	.226	.256
Road Games	1-2	3.19	153	38	2	17	36	.248	.333	.314
Grass Fields	0-0	1.70	157	36	1	7	38	.229	.287	.263
Artificial Turf	5-2	1.86	191	43	1	20	55	.225	.262	.298
April	2-0	0.82	44	10	0	3	8	.227	.250	.277
May	0-1	2.00	60	12	0	9	12	.200	.283	.300
June	2-0	1.29	53	12	1	3	14	.226	.302	.268
July	1-1	5.40	46	12	1	4	16	.261	.348	.302
August	0-0	0.52	63	15	0	5	18	.238	.238	.300
Sept./Oct.	0-0	1.23	82	18	0	3	25	.220	.244	.256
Leading Off Inn.			77	21	0	7	24	.273	.273	.333
Bases Empty			174	46	1	12	46	.264	.282	.316
Runners On			174	33	1	15	47	.190	.264	.251
Runners/Scor. Pos.			109	26	1	10	33	.239	.339	.296
Runners On/2 Out			82	17	1	8	23	.207	.317	.278
Scor. Pos./2 Out			60	15	1	7	18	.250	.367	.328
Late-Inning Pressure			154	38	0	14	46	.247	.273	.308
Leading Off			36	11	0	3	14	.306	.306	.359
Runners On			77	16	0	9	22	.208	.260	.281
Runners/Scor. Pos.			54	13	0	6	18	.241	.315	.302
First 9 Batters			336	75	2	24	90	.223	.259	.275
Second 9 Batters			12	4	0	3	3	.333	.667	.467
All Batters Thereafter			0	0	0	0	0	—	—	—

Loves to face: Ryne Sandberg (.086, 3-for-35, 0 BB)
Benito Santiago (.077, 1-for-13)
Mike Scioscia (0-for-13)

Hates to face: John Kruk (.800, 4-for-5)
Dale Murphy (.360, 9-for-25, 3 HR)
Ozzie Smith (.500, 7-for-14, 8 BB)

Miscellaneous statistics: Ground outs-to-air outs ratio: 1.46 last season, 1.29 for career. . . . Induced 6 double-play ground outs in 84 opportunities (one per 14.0). . . . Allowed 8 doubles, 1 triple in 95.2 innings. . . . Stranded 33 inherited runners, allowed 20 to score (62%). . . . Opposing base stealers: 16-for-19 (84%); 0 pickoffs, 0 balks.

Comments: Earned seven saves last season, the highest total of his career. Has the fewest career saves (34) of any pitcher in major league history with at least 500 relief appearances. That's true even if you include unofficial save figures for years prior to 1969. The bottom five: Andersen, Bob Miller (52), Dale Murray (60), Paul Lindblad (64), and Johnny Klippstein (66). . . . Had a 1.95 ERA in 50 games with the Astros last season, and then improved to 1.23 in 15 games with the Red Sox. He was the first pitcher since 1968 with ERAs under 2.00 for each of two different clubs in the same season. In 1968, both Vicente Romo and Willie Smith did it. . . . In only his second appearance after joining Boston, he struck out a career-high six batters vs. Oakland (September 4). . . . The National League's top 10 hitters batted only .120 against him with no extra-base hits. No N.L. pitcher held that group of hitters to a lower batting average (minimum: 15 at-bats). . . . Total of 175 batters faced without allowing a home run in Late-Inning Pressure Situations was the 2d highest in the majors. Mark Eichhorn faced 179 batters in LIPS with no home runs. . . . Opponents batted 75 points higher with the bases empty (.264) than with runners on base (.190) last season, the 4th-largest margin in the majors. . . . Over the last two seasons, Andersen has an ERA of 1.67 in 183.1 innings pitched. . . . The last home run he allowed to a right-handed batter was hit by Dale Murphy, on June 17, 1988.

Allan Anderson

Throws Left

Minnesota Twins	W-L	ERA	AB	H	HR	BB	SO	BA	SA	OBA
Season	7-18	4.53	741	214	20	39	82	.289	.433	.325
vs. Left-Handers			109	28	2	7	11	.257	.330	.297
vs. Right-Handers			632	186	18	32	71	.294	.451	.330
vs. Ground-Ballers			328	97	5	8	34	.296	.405	.317
vs. Fly-Ballers			413	117	15	31	48	.283	.455	.332
Home Games	4-12	4.77	426	119	13	25	51	.279	.437	.322
Road Games	3-6	4.19	315	95	7	14	31	.302	.429	.329
Grass Fields	2-5	3.94	244	73	4	11	20	.299	.406	.328
Artificial Turf	5-13	4.80	497	141	16	28	62	.284	.447	.324
April	1-3	5.47	111	36	2	8	10	.324	.486	.367
May	1-3	4.86	124	34	6	10	12	.274	.516	.328
June	0-5	6.55	140	52	2	8	16	.371	.457	.404
July	2-3	3.95	159	43	4	4	19	.270	.390	.298
August	2-2	2.73	121	28	2	6	19	.231	.347	.266
Sept./Oct.	1-2	3.68	86	21	4	3	6	.244	.407	.270
Leading Off Inn.			194	56	4	2	15	.289	.433	.299
Bases Empty			435	120	14	22	48	.276	.434	.315
Runners On			306	94	6	17	34	.307	.431	.339
Runners/Scor. Pos.			171	56	2	14	17	.327	.439	.366
Runners On/2 Out			119	35	4	5	13	.294	.445	.328
Scor. Pos./2 Out			72	20	2	5	7	.278	.403	.325
Late-Inning Pressure			60	18	2	4	4	.300	.400	.344
Leading Off			17	4	0	1	0	.235	.235	.278
Runners On			22	6	1	1	0	.273	.409	.304
Runners/Scor. Pos.			3	1	0	0	0	.333	.333	.333
First 9 Batters			255	61	4	15	34	.239	.325	.285
Second 9 Batters			241	87	7	12	25	.361	.531	.389
All Batters Thereafter			245	66	9	12	23	.269	.449	.305

Loves to face: Jesse Barfield (.125, 2-for-16)
Mark McGwire (.083, 2-for-24)
Ruben Sierra (.067, 1-for-15)

Hates to face: Jeff Kunkel (.833, 5-for-6)
Chet Lemon (.452, 14-for-31, 2 HR)
Kevin Seitzer (.478, 11-for-23, 1 HR)

Miscellaneous statistics: Ground outs-to-air outs ratio: 1.25 last season, 1.17 for career. . . . Induced 19 double-play ground outs in 141 opportunities (one per 7.4). . . . Allowed 41 doubles (tied for 4th most in A.L.), 3 triples in 188.2 innings. . . . Allowed 15 first-inning runs in 31 starts (4.11 ERA). . . . Batting support: 3.19 runs per start (2d lowest in A.L.; minimum: 20 starts). . . . Opposing base stealers: 10-for-21 (48%); 8 pickoffs, 3 balks.

Comments: Finished the season with the worst winning percentage of any opening-day starting pitcher in the majors last season (.280). . . . His winning percentage was the lowest in Minnesota Twins history (minimum: 15 decisions). The last pitchers with marks that low during the franchise's Washington Senators era were Bob Wiesler (.200, 3–12) and Camilo Pascual (.250, 6–18) in 1956. . . . His winning percentage declined from .630 (17–10) in 1989, the largest single-season decrease since Dave McNally fell from .808 in 1971 (21–5) to .433 in 1972 (13–17). . . . ERA year by year since 1988: 2.45, 3.80, 4.53. The last pitcher whose ERA rose by at least 0.70 in consecutive seasons was Scott McGregor in 1983–85 (3.18, 3.94, 4.81). . . . Had the lowest average run support of any Twins starter last season, almost two runs per game lower than Scott Erickson's. . . . He had a lower ERA in his six no-decision starts (1.66) than in his seven victories (1.72). . . . Opponents batted 76 points lower on his first pass through the batting order (.239) than in subsequent at-bats (.315) last season, the 3d-largest margin in the majors. . . . Had the lowest walk rate of any pitcher in the American League (1.89 per nine innings). He started strong (2.53 per nine innings through the end of June) and finished with a flourish (1.22 thereafter). . . . Opponents have a career batting average of .294 with 124 extra-base hits at the Metrodome, .270 with 96 extra-base hits on the road. . . . Career record of 4–0 vs. the Yankees.

Kevin Appier

Throws Right

Kansas City Royals	W-L	ERA	AB	H	HR	BB	SO	BA	SA	OBA
Season	12-8	2.76	709	179	13	54	127	.252	.334	.307
vs. Left-Handers			311	81	7	35	50	.260	.363	.331
vs. Right-Handers			398	98	6	19	77	.246	.312	.287
vs. Ground-Ballers			335	78	1	26	54	.233	.269	.292
vs. Fly-Ballers			374	101	12	28	73	.270	.393	.321
Home Games	7-4	2.77	325	83	5	18	59	.255	.329	.297
Road Games	5-4	2.75	384	96	8	36	68	.250	.339	.315
Grass Fields	5-3	2.79	305	79	7	30	54	.259	.357	.327
Artificial Turf	7-5	2.74	404	100	6	24	73	.248	.317	.291
April	0-0	0.00	9	2	0	2	4	.222	.333	.364
May	1-0	3.75	100	33	4	8	12	.330	.480	.387
June	1-3	3.00	137	32	4	13	24	.234	.343	.296
July	4-1	3.02	170	38	1	12	36	.224	.265	.276
August	5-0	1.85	126	29	1	7	20	.230	.270	.276
Sept./Oct.	1-4	2.62	167	45	3	12	31	.269	.359	.319
Leading Off Inn.			180	42	5	11	35	.233	.344	.277
Bases Empty			417	103	9	33	79	.247	.333	.307
Runners On			292	76	4	21	48	.260	.336	.308
Runners/Scor. Pos.			154	32	1	16	28	.208	.273	.280
Runners On/2 Out			130	34	3	14	26	.262	.362	.338
Scor. Pos./2 Out			81	20	1	13	15	.247	.321	.358
Late-Inning Pressure			46	12	1	4	10	.261	.326	.320
Leading Off			11	2	1	2	4	.182	.455	.308
Runners On			22	5	0	0	4	.227	.227	.227
Runners/Scor. Pos.			10	3	0	0	2	.300	.300	.300
First 9 Batters			245	62	6	22	47	.253	.343	.313
Second 9 Batters			213	45	1	13	32	.211	.254	.263
All Batters Thereafter			251	72	6	19	48	.287	.394	.339

Loves to face: Gary Gaetti (0-for-7)
Mike Gallego (.143, 2-for-14)
Pete Incaviglia (0-for-8, 5 SO)

Hates to face: Carlton Fisk (.625, 5-for-8, 1 HR, 2 SO)
Rickey Henderson (.500, 6-for-12)
Luis Polonia (.750, 6-for-8)

Miscellaneous statistics: Ground outs-to-air outs ratio: 1.22 last season, 1.14 for career. . . . Induced 21 double-play ground outs in 148 opportunities (one per 7.0). . . . Allowed 17 doubles, 1 triple in 185.2 innings. . . . Allowed 8 first-inning runs in 24 starts (2.63 ERA). . . . Batting support: 4.21 runs per start. . . . Opposing base stealers: 13-for-14 (93%), 3d-highest rate in A.L.; 0 pickoffs, 1 balk.

Comments: Finished fourth in the American League in ERA. The last A.L. rookie to rank that high was Mike Boddicker, runner-up to Rick Honeycutt for the league ERA title in 1983. Prior to that, Britt Burns finished third in 1980. . . . Only four rookies pitched enough innings to qualify for their league's ERA title (162), with Appier having the lowest ERA among them. The other three qualifiers: Mike Harkey (3.26), John Burkett (3.79), and Pat Combs (4.07). . . . Threw three shutouts, tying him with Montreal's Mark Gardner for the major league lead among rookies. He and Mark Knudson were the only pitchers to shut out both A.L. division champions. . . . Made eight relief appearances, but none after June 5. From that point on, he had an 11–7 record with a 2.52 ERA in 21 starts. . . . Had an ERA of 2.30 through the first six innings of his starts, 4.03 in the seventh inning or later. . . . Opponents were hitless in 15 at-bats with the bases loaded last season. In the 16-year history of *The Player Analysis*, only two pitchers had better seasons: Bill Travers (0-for-17 in 1976) and Lindy McDaniel (0-for-16 in 1975). . . . Opposing base runners have attempted 19 steals over two seasons. Luis Polonia was caught stealing in the first and last of those attempts; but in between, only one runner was caught.

Brad Arnsberg

Throws Right

Texas Rangers	W-L	ERA	AB	H	HR	BB	SO	BA	SA	OBA
Season	6-1	2.15	238	56	4	33	44	.235	.332	.331
vs. Left-Handers			89	20	2	10	12	.225	.337	.310
vs. Right-Handers			149	36	2	23	32	.242	.329	.343
vs. Ground-Ballers			109	26	2	13	17	.239	.321	.323
vs. Fly-Ballers			129	30	2	20	27	.233	.341	.338
Home Games	4-0	2.02	132	32	2	14	25	.242	.326	.318
Road Games	2-1	2.33	106	24	2	19	19	.226	.340	.346
Grass Fields	5-1	2.29	209	50	4	29	38	.239	.335	.332
Artificial Turf	1-0	1.17	29	6	0	4	6	.207	.310	.324
April	0-0	—	0	0	0	0	0	—	—	—
May	0-0	2.25	15	3	0	2	5	.200	.200	.294
June	2-1	1.06	64	12	1	6	11	.188	.281	.260
July	2-0	1.29	51	10	0	11	12	.196	.235	.339
August	1-0	3.38	61	17	2	5	6	.279	.410	.333
Sept./Oct.	1-0	3.09	47	14	1	9	10	.298	.447	.421
Leading Off Inn.			54	9	1	6	9	.167	.278	.250
Bases Empty			128	32	1	18	20	.250	.352	.347
Runners On			110	24	3	15	24	.218	.309	.313
Runners/Scor. Pos.			67	15	2	10	15	.224	.328	.325
Runners On/2 Out			57	14	2	6	12	.246	.351	.317
Scor. Pos./2 Out			38	11	2	4	9	.289	.447	.357
Late-Inning Pressure			119	26	0	18	22	.218	.277	.321
Leading Off			32	5	0	4	5	.156	.219	.250
Runners On			45	8	0	9	13	.178	.200	.315
Runners/Scor. Pos.			24	4	0	6	8	.167	.208	.333
First 9 Batters			230	54	4	33	44	.235	.335	.333
Second 9 Batters			8	2	0	0	0	.250	.250	.250
All Batters Thereafter			0	0	0	0	0	—	—	—

Loves to face: Pat Tabler (0-for-5)
Greg Vaughn (0-for-5, 3 SO)

Hates to face: Wade Boggs (2-for-2, 1 3B, 1 HR, 1 BB)
Brook Jacoby (.571, 4-for-7, 2 2B, 2 HR)

Miscellaneous statistics: Ground outs-to-air outs ratio: 1.07 last season, 1.09 for career. . . . Induced 3 double-play ground outs in 50 opportunities (one per 16.7). . . . Allowed 11 doubles, 0 triples in 62.2 innings. . . . Stranded 26 inherited runners, allowed 18 to score (59%). . . . Opposing base stealers: 1-for-1; 2 pickoffs, 0 balks.

Comments: Received on-the-job training as a reliever last season. He had made 111 starts and only 11 relief appearances over six seasons in the minors. Current major-league totals: four starts, 73 relief appearances (including all 53 games in 1990). . . . Saved five games for the Rangers while Jeff Russell was on the disabled list, raising his career total to six. . . . Faced 13 batters in his first major league appearance of 1990 (May 26); that remained his high for the season. He pitched more than two innings in only four of his 53 appearances. . . . His ERA in parts of three previous seasons in the majors (4.42) was more than double last season's figure. . . . Didn't induce a double-play grounder in his first 37 opportunities. . . . Opponents have a career batting average of .277 with the bases empty, .230 with runners on base. . . . Left-handed hitters batted above .300 against him in each of his three previous seasons in the majors. . . . He has allowed only one home run in 134 career at-bats in Late-Inning Pressure Situations, compared to one per 27 at-bats at other times. . . . Roughly half the batters he faced last season were in Late-Inning Pressure Situations (138 of 277); in 1989, only eight of the 209 batters he faced were in LIPS. . . . As the Yankees search for Dave Righetti's successor, it's interesting to note that last season only two pitchers who made their major league debuts with New York had more than one save: Arnsberg and Oakland's Gene Nelson, who had five each.

Jeff Ballard

Throws Left

Baltimore Orioles	W-L	ERA	AB	H	HR	BB	SO	BA	SA	OBA
Season	2-11	4.93	525	152	22	42	50	.290	.480	.344
vs. Left-Handers			136	39	4	9	23	.287	.404	.336
vs. Right-Handers			389	113	18	33	27	.290	.506	.347
vs. Ground-Ballers			250	70	10	19	20	.280	.456	.330
vs. Fly-Ballers			275	82	12	23	30	.298	.502	.358
Home Games	1-5	4.52	261	71	10	17	29	.272	.441	.320
Road Games	1-6	5.35	264	81	12	25	21	.307	.519	.368
Grass Fields	2-9	4.94	460	133	19	36	46	.289	.474	.343
Artificial Turf	0-2	4.86	65	19	3	6	4	.292	.523	.352
April	0-3	3.91	97	23	5	3	7	.237	.464	.267
May	1-2	3.95	109	33	5	13	7	.303	.505	.379
June	0-4	7.34	143	49	6	11	16	.343	.559	.391
July	0-0	2.08	45	8	1	3	5	.178	.267	.229
August	0-1	6.52	78	25	2	9	8	.321	.449	.391
Sept./Oct.	1-1	3.21	53	14	3	3	7	.264	.472	.304
Leading Off Inn.			127	38	7	10	13	.299	.543	.350
Bases Empty			321	91	11	17	32	.283	.464	.324
Runners On			204	61	11	25	18	.299	.505	.375
Runners/Scor. Pos.			121	33	6	23	14	.273	.479	.384
Runners On/2 Out			84	26	2	15	8	.310	.452	.420
Scor. Pos./2 Out			60	19	2	14	5	.317	.517	.446
Late-Inning Pressure			36	12	0	3	5	.333	.417	.385
Leading Off			9	3	0	1	1	.333	.333	.400
Runners On			19	5	0	2	3	.263	.316	.333
Runners/Scor. Pos.			11	3	0	2	3	.273	.364	.385
First 9 Batters			254	63	10	23	29	.248	.409	.315
Second 9 Batters			164	56	8	8	8	.341	.585	.376
All Batters Thereafter			107	33	4	11	13	.308	.486	.367

Loves to face: Mike Gallego (0-for-12)
Tony Phillips (.071, 1-for-14, 2 BB)
Lou Whitaker (.071, 1-for-14)

Hates to face: Chili Davis (.429, 9-for-21, 1 HR)
Ken Griffey, Jr. (.636, 7-for-11)
Wally Joyner (.421, 8-for-19, 2 HR)

Miscellaneous statistics: Ground outs-to-air outs ratio: 0.98 last season, 1.08 for career. . . . Induced 15 double-play ground outs in 96 opportunities (one per 6.4). . . . Allowed 34 doubles, 0 triples in 133.1 innings. . . . Allowed 7 first-inning runs in 17 starts (3.71 ERA). . . . Batting support: 3.94 runs per start. . . . Record of 1-10, 5.09 ERA as a starter; 1-1, 4.50 ERA in 27 relief appearances. . . . Stranded 12 inherited runners, allowed 4 to score (75%). . . . Opposing base stealers: 8-for-14 (57%); 3 pickoffs, 1 balk.

Comments: Ballard's winning percentage (.154) was the lowest by an Orioles pitcher since Don Larsen posted a .125 mark (3–21) in 1954, the team's first year in Baltimore. . . . Won 16 fewer games last season than he did in 1989 while losing three more. That makes him minus-19 in baseball's version of everyone's favorite NHL category. The only pitcher with a lower rating last season: Bret Saberhagen (-21). . . . Started each of 89 appearances in the majors before Frank Robinson sent Ballard and his 1–9 record to the bullpen in early July. . . . Opponents batted 80 points lower on his first pass through the batting order (.248) than in subsequent at-bats (.328) last season, the largest margin in the majors. He had an ERA of 2.29 over the first three innings of his starts, but look out below: Ballard posted an 8.16 ERA in the fourth inning or later. . . . Career average of 2.83 strikeouts per nine innings is the lowest among active pitchers (minimum: 500 IP). That rate was typical of turn-of-the-century baseball; no fewer than 239 players in major league history with at least 500 innings pitched had rates lower than Ballard's. But the most recent of those pitchers was Bob Keegan, who retired in 1958. . . . With apologies to Deborah Norville's sidekick, baseball *is* a funny game: Ballard remains the only pitcher ever to strike out Don Mattingly three times in a single game. . . . Opponents have a career batting average of .322 leading off innings, the highest mark among active pitchers (minimum: 500 BFP). . . . Had a career record of 5–0 in April prior to last season.

Juan Berenguer

Throws Right

Minnesota Twins	W-L	ERA	AB	H	HR	BB	SO	BA	SA	OBA
Season	8-5	3.41	367	85	9	58	77	.232	.346	.338
vs. Left-Handers			159	42	3	23	34	.264	.390	.361
vs. Right-Handers			208	43	6	35	43	.207	.313	.321
vs. Ground-Ballers			179	39	1	29	32	.218	.274	.330
vs. Fly-Ballers			188	46	8	29	45	.245	.415	.345
Home Games	4-2	3.54	182	46	4	34	37	.253	.363	.372
Road Games	4-3	3.29	185	39	5	24	40	.211	.330	.303
Grass Fields	3-3	4.42	139	33	5	21	30	.237	.374	.340
Artificial Turf	5-2	2.77	228	52	4	37	47	.228	.329	.337
April	1-0	6.10	37	9	2	10	8	.243	.514	.404
May	3-0	3.57	66	16	2	8	12	.242	.333	.329
June	1-1	3.79	75	18	2	15	15	.240	.347	.363
July	2-2	2.60	66	18	1	7	16	.273	.379	.342
August	0-0	1.96	61	12	1	9	8	.197	.295	.300
Sept./Oct.	1-2	3.57	62	12	1	9	18	.194	.274	.306
Leading Off Inn.			80	14	0	14	16	.175	.225	.305
Bases Empty			187	43	5	32	35	.230	.353	.345
Runners On			180	42	4	26	42	.233	.339	.330
Runners/Scor. Pos.			108	22	1	17	22	.204	.278	.307
Runners On/2 Out			80	17	2	9	20	.213	.350	.300
Scor. Pos./2 Out			48	8	1	9	11	.167	.292	.298
Late-Inning Pressure			115	29	4	16	27	.252	.435	.344
Leading Off			32	5	0	2	8	.156	.219	.206
Runners On			45	11	0	6	12	.244	.311	.333
Runners/Scor. Pos.			30	7	0	3	9	.233	.333	.303
First 9 Batters			302	64	6	43	70	.212	.308	.313
Second 9 Batters			60	19	3	13	7	.317	.533	.432
All Batters Thereafter			5	2	0	2	0	.400	.400	.571

Loves to face: Ivan Calderon (.105, 2-for-19, 8 SO)
Mike Heath (.053, 1-for-19)
Don Slaught (.133, 2-for-15)

Hates to face: George Bell (.429, 6-for-14, 1 HR)
Tim Teufel (.667, 4-for-6, 1 2B, 1 HR)
Curtis Wilkerson (.45, 5-for-11)

Miscellaneous statistics: Ground outs-to-air outs ratio: 0.75 last season, 0.63 for career. . . . Induced 8 double-play ground outs in 89 opportunities (one per 11.1). . . . Allowed 11 doubles, 2 triples in 100.1 innings. . . . Stranded 26 inherited runners (including nine in a row to end the season), allowed 10 to score (72%). . . . Opposing base stealers: 12-for-18 (67%); 1 pickoff, 0 balks.

Comments: Career record of 26–35 (3.96 ERA) as a starter, 37–19 (3.81 ERA) as a reliever. . . . Of those 37 career victories in relief, 31 have come in his four seasons with the Twins. That's the 2d-highest total in Twins history, behind Al Worthington (37). But if we trace the franchise history back to the original Washington Senators, Berenguer's total ranks fourth behind Firpo Marberry (45), Walter Johnson (40), and Worthington. . . . His winning percentage over the past four seasons (.717, 33–13) is the highest in the majors (minimum: 40 decisions). The only other pitcher above .700 is Bob Welch (.704). Berenguer's is also the highest winning percentage in franchise history. . . . Faced 10 or more batters in 19 of his 51 games, a questionable strategy considering that opponents batted .323 after his first pass through the batting order. . . . Average of 5.20 walks allowed per nine innings was the highest among A.L. relievers (minimum: 75 IP). . . . Made the most relief appearances of any major league pitcher without a save last season (51). . . . Opponents have batted under .175 with two outs and runners in scoring position in each of the last three seasons. . . . Has never allowed a grand slam home run, but has walked 20 of 122 batters he has faced with the bags full, the highest rate of any pitcher over the last 16 years (minimum: 100 BFP).

Bud Black

Throws Left

Indians/Blue Jays	W-L	ERA	AB	H	HR	BB	SO	BA	SA	OBA
Season	13-11	3.57	778	181	19	61	106	.233	.350	.290
vs. Left-Handers			145	39	7	11	12	.269	.441	.314
vs. Right-Handers			633	142	12	50	94	.224	.329	.285
vs. Ground-Ballers			342	82	4	28	50	.240	.310	.297
vs. Fly-Ballers			436	99	15	33	56	.227	.381	.285
Home Games	8-5	3.13	392	94	11	27	53	.240	.349	.293
Road Games	5-6	4.02	386	87	8	34	53	.225	.350	.287
Grass Fields	11-9	3.73	671	161	17	52	97	.240	.358	.296
Artificial Turf	2-2	2.67	107	20	2	9	9	.187	.299	.254
April	2-0	2.73	96	21	2	6	11	.219	.313	.262
May	2-2	1.50	174	36	2	11	23	.207	.287	.261
June	2-2	6.88	137	38	7	21	15	.277	.474	.371
July	3-2	2.83	149	29	1	11	22	.195	.248	.258
August	1-2	6.52	86	28	3	8	17	.326	.477	.379
Sept./Oct.	3-3	3.11	136	29	4	4	18	.213	.360	.238
Leading Off Inn.			204	44	3	12	25	.216	.299	.259
Bases Empty			499	111	13	33	65	.222	.341	.275
Runners On			279	70	6	28	41	.251	.366	.316
Runners/Scor. Pos.			153	32	3	17	27	.209	.340	.285
Runners On/2 Out			116	21	2	13	22	.181	.250	.269
Scor. Pos./2 Out			71	11	2	7	15	.155	.268	.241
Late-Inning Pressure			74	16	1	7	12	.216	.270	.289
Leading Off			22	5	0	2	3	.227	.227	.292
Runners On			23	7	0	1	6	.304	.304	.320
Runners/Scor. Pos.			9	2	0	0	3	.222	.222	.200
First 9 Batters			262	69	7	20	35	.263	.397	.317
Second 9 Batters			247	57	4	17	31	.231	.336	.281
All Batters Thereafter			269	55	8	24	40	.204	.316	.273

Loves to face: Tony Fernandez (.204, 11-for-54)
Jim Presley (.148, 4-for-27, 1 HR)
Tim Teufel (0-for-10)

Hates to face: Alfredo Griffin (.571, 12-for-21)
Mike Heath (.323, 10-for-31)
Luis Salazar (.462, 6-for-13, 1 2B, 1 3B, 1 HR)

Miscellaneous statistics: Ground outs-to-air outs ratio: 1.04 last season, 1.09 for career. . . . Induced 9 double-play ground outs in 140 opportunities (one per 15.6), 5th-lowest rate in A.L. . . . Allowed 30 doubles, 2 triples in 206.2 innings. . . . Allowed 15 first-inning runs in 31 starts (4.35 ERA). . . . Batting support: 4.39 runs per start. . . . Opposing base stealers: 12-for-20 (60%); 5 pick-offs, 1 balk.

Comments: Last season was the first in which opposing left-handed batters outhit right-handed batters. The batting average by opposing right-handers was the lowest of his career. He had held left-handers under the .200 mark in each of the previous two seasons; he had never before allowed more than four home runs in one season to left-handers. . . . Opponents batted .305 during the first innings of his starts, .333 during the ninth innings, and .215 during the innings in between. He faced 25 batters in the ninth inning, and allowed three home runs. . . . Has held opponents to a lower batting average with runners in scoring position than in other at-bats in each of the last five seasons. . . . Has pitched five shutouts over the last two seasons after going three years without one. . . . Defeated Baltimore on the next to last day of the 1990 season, raising his career record above the .500 mark (83–82); incidentally, his teams have won exactly as many games as they have lost (739). . . . Has batted only once in his major league career: a strikeout against John Tudor in the fourth game of the 1985 World Series. Giants hitting coach Dusty Baker may have his hands full this spring with Black and Dave Righetti. . . . See the Giants essay for a detailed look at the success of left-handed pitchers moving from the American League to the National League.

Bert Blyleven

Throws Right

California Angels	W-L	ERA	AB	H	HR	BB	SO	BA	SA	OBA
Season	8-7	5.24	538	163	15	25	69	.303	.463	.339
vs. Left-Handers			270	84	8	14	27	.311	.470	.346
vs. Right-Handers			268	79	7	11	42	.295	.455	.331
vs. Ground-Ballers			242	73	3	14	29	.302	.426	.347
vs. Fly-Ballers			296	90	12	11	40	.304	.493	.331
Home Games	4-2	3.82	273	78	4	10	30	.286	.414	.311
Road Games	4-5	6.82	265	85	11	15	39	.321	.513	.366
Grass Fields	7-4	4.75	439	133	12	20	58	.303	.462	.337
Artificial Turf	1-3	7.50	99	30	3	5	11	.303	.465	.346
April	0-2	9.00	84	31	5	0	8	.369	.631	.376
May	3-1	2.50	151	37	1	7	29	.245	.338	.286
June	4-1	4.39	157	46	4	9	19	.293	.446	.333
July	1-3	8.58	125	45	5	8	10	.360	.560	.401
August	0-0	1.50	21	4	0	1	3	.190	.238	.227
Sept./Oct.	0-0	—	0	0	0	0	0	—	—	—
Leading Off Inn.			129	35	3	7	18	.271	.388	.324
Bases Empty			315	89	7	12	42	.283	.432	.315
Runners On			223	74	8	13	27	.332	.507	.370
Runners/Scor. Pos.			130	41	5	8	18	.315	.523	.354
Runners On/2 Out			85	28	4	7	9	.329	.529	.394
Scor. Pos./2 Out			57	20	4	5	5	.351	.649	.422
Late-Inning Pressure			10	3	0	2	1	.300	.300	.385
Leading Off			3	0	0	0	1	.000	.000	.000
Runners On			4	3	0	0	0	.750	.750	.600
Runners/Scor. Pos.			2	2	0	0	0	1.000	1.000	.667
First 9 Batters			193	59	9	8	24	.306	.497	.341
Second 9 Batters			193	45	2	7	28	.233	.326	.272
All Batters Thereafter			152	59	4	10	17	.388	.592	.418

Loves to face: Greg Briley (.071, 1-for-14)
Tom Brunansky (.111, 2-for-18)
Gary Pettis (.128, 5-for-39)

Hates to face: Jack Clark (.417, 10-for-24, 2 HR)
Ron Kittle (.318, 14-for-44, 1 2B, 9 HR)
Don Mattingly (.410, 16-for-39, 3 HR)

Miscellaneous statistics: Ground outs-to-air outs ratio: 1.22 last season, 1.21 for career.... Induced 10 double-play ground outs in 108 opportunities (one per 10.8).... Allowed 33 doubles, 4 triples in 134.0 innings.... Allowed 17 first-inning runs in 23 starts (6.65 ERA).... Batting support: 4.61 runs per start.... Opposing base stealers: 4-for-13 (31%), 3d-lowest rate in A.L., and best in the majors among right-handed pitchers; 1 pickoff, 0 balks.

Comments: Needs four more starts to crack the all-time top 10 by tying Warren Spahn at 665. He could also surpass the totals of Walter Johnson (666) and Pud Galvin (682) this season.... Earned that Century 21 endorsement by becoming the first pitcher in major league history to start at least 50 games for five different teams during his career; 16 other pitchers made 50 starts for four teams.... Blyleven was the youngest player in the majors when he debuted at age 19 on June 5, 1970. At that time, the oldest active players were Hoyt Wilhelm (46), Don McMahon (40), and Dick Hall (39). Bert replaced the injured Luis Tiant on Minnesota's roster, and made his first appearance against the Senators at RFK Stadium.... Among the players involved in trades with Blyleven: Bill Singer, Manny Sanguillen, and John Milner.... Has visited the disabled list four times in his career, once each in 1982, 1984, 1988, and 1990. What happened to 1986?... His ERA rose by more than two-and-a-half runs from 2.73 in 1989. Over the past 25 years, only three pitchers had larger single-season increases (minimum: 25 GS in each): Tom Seaver, 2.95 (2.54 in 1981, 5.50 in 1982); Danny Jackson, 2.87 (2.73 in 1988, 5.60 in 1989); Rich Gale, 2.56 (3.09 in 1978, 5.65 in 1979).... Had the highest average run support of any regular Angels starter last season.... Opposing base runners stole only one base in eight attempts against the battery of Blyleven and Parrish.... Enters 1991 needing 21 wins to reach the 300-mark. He has won exactly 20 games once (1973), but never more than that in a single season.

Mike Boddicker

Throws Right

Boston Red Sox	W-L	ERA	AB	H	HR	BB	SO	BA	SA	OBA
Season	17-8	3.36	873	225	16	69	143	.258	.368	.319
vs. Left-Handers			464	121	7	33	51	.261	.366	.317
vs. Right-Handers			409	104	9	36	92	.254	.369	.321
vs. Ground-Ballers			384	93	6	20	58	.242	.354	.289
vs. Fly-Ballers			489	132	10	49	85	.270	.378	.342
Home Games	11-5	2.97	519	138	5	36	83	.266	.343	.323
Road Games	6-3	3.93	354	87	11	33	60	.246	.404	.314
Grass Fields	16-8	3.44	787	205	14	63	129	.260	.368	.322
Artificial Turf	1-0	2.66	86	20	2	6	14	.233	.360	.290
April	2-3	4.85	105	29	1	5	14	.276	.390	.321
May	4-0	2.63	136	28	5	12	26	.206	.353	.275
June	4-0	2.87	178	43	1	11	27	.242	.309	.286
July	1-3	7.34	132	49	7	11	24	.371	.591	.428
August	2-2	1.11	151	33	1	12	25	.219	.285	.276
Sept./Oct.	4-0	2.93	171	43	1	18	27	.251	.327	.338
Leading Off Inn.			223	47	2	11	41	.211	.283	.251
Bases Empty			519	136	9	32	83	.262	.378	.309
Runners On			354	89	7	37	60	.251	.353	.333
Runners/Scor. Pos.			195	51	4	23	35	.262	.364	.350
Runners On/2 Out			139	31	3	21	35	.223	.324	.337
Scor. Pos./2 Out			88	21	2	16	21	.239	.318	.374
Late-Inning Pressure			81	16	0	9	17	.198	.222	.286
Leading Off			24	3	0	0	5	.125	.125	.125
Runners On			25	3	0	6	7	.120	.120	.313
Runners/Scor. Pos.			14	3	0	3	3	.214	.214	.389
First 9 Batters			280	75	9	21	50	.268	.418	.327
Second 9 Batters			272	71	5	21	45	.261	.379	.319
All Batters Thereafter			321	79	2	27	48	.246	.315	.313

Loves to face: Gary Pettis (.033, 1-for-30, 6 BB)
Tony Phillips (.107, 3-for-28)
Gary Ward (.136, 6-for-44)

Hates to face: Jay Buhner (.556, 5-for-9, 3 2B, 1 HR)
Carney Lansford (.423, 22-for-52, 4 HR)
Geno Petralli (.462, 12-for-26, 2 HR)

Miscellaneous statistics: Ground outs-to-air outs ratio: 1.09 last season, 1.33 for career.... Induced 21 double-play ground outs in 187 opportunities (one per 8.9).... Allowed 38 doubles, 5 triples in 228.0 innings.... Allowed 11 first-inning runs in 34 starts (2.91 ERA).... Batting support: 5.00 runs per start.... Opposing base stealers: 13-for-23 (57%); 1 pickoff, 0 balks.

Comments: During Boddicker's two-and-a-half seasons with the Red Sox, he had a higher winning percentage (.639, 39–22) than Roger Clemens (.630, 41–24). Blame it on Dave Stewart.... Had a five-game losing streak sandwiched between winning streaks of ten and five games last season.... Had the highest average batting support of any regular Red Sox starter.... Opposing fly-ball hitters have hit for a higher average than ground-ball hitters in each of the last five seasons.... Has held opponents to a lower average with runners on base than with the bases empty in each of the last four seasons.... Hasn't thrown a complete-game shutout in 47 starts, since July 25, 1989.... Opponents have batted under .200 in Late-Inning Pressure Situations in each of the last three seasons. His opponents' career average of .207 in LIPS is the 4th lowest among starting pitchers over the last 16 years (minimum: 500 BFP), behind J.R. Richard (.200), Nolan Ryan (.201), and Roger Clemens (.206). Opponents have a career average of only .177 with runners in scoring position in LIPS.... Has faced a career total of 101 batters with the bases loaded, but has allowed only two extra-base hits, both doubles.... He has a 5–1 record vs. his former mates in Baltimore.... Has won at least 10 games in all eight seasons starting with his rookie year of 1983. The last pitcher with that long a streak of double-figure winning seasons starting as a rookie: Ron Guidry (nine years, 1977–85).

Tom Bolton

Throws Left

Boston Red Sox	W-L	ERA	AB	H	HR	BB	SO	BA	SA	OBA
Season	10-5	3.38	443	111	6	47	65	.251	.339	.323
vs. Left-Handers			99	24	1	6	11	.242	.293	.283
vs. Right-Handers			344	87	5	41	54	.253	.352	.334
vs. Ground-Ballers			235	60	4	18	36	.255	.357	.311
vs. Fly-Ballers			208	51	2	29	29	.245	.317	.336
Home Games	6-1	1.99	193	42	2	16	32	.218	.290	.278
Road Games	4-4	4.55	250	69	4	31	33	.276	.376	.357
Grass Fields	9-4	3.13	351	87	5	37	51	.248	.330	.321
Artificial Turf	1-1	4.38	92	24	1	10	14	.261	.370	.333
April	0-0	—	0	0	0	0	.0	—	—	—
May	0-0	—	0	0	0	0	0	—	—	—
June	0-0	22.50	11	6	0	0	1	.545	.818	.500
July	4-1	1.04	119	21	1	16	20	.176	.244	.274
August	3-1	3.70	152	41	3	17	19	.270	.375	.349
Sept./Oct.	3-3	4.10	161	43	2	14	25	.267	.342	.324
Leading Off Inn.			113	26	3	12	13	.230	.336	.304
Bases Empty			253	55	4	29	42	.217	.300	.303
Runners On			190	56	2	18	23	.295	.389	.350
Runners/Scor. Pos.			101	32	2	13	14	.317	.446	.378
Runners On/2 Out			72	19	1	11	7	.264	.389	.361
Scor. Pos./2 Out			47	12	1	9	5	.255	.404	.375
Late-Inning Pressure			46	13	2	6	5	.283	.413	.365
Leading Off			13	5	1	2	1	.385	.615	.467
Runners On			20	7	1	1	1	.350	.500	.381
Runners/Scor. Pos.			6	4	1	1	0	.667	1.167	.714
First 9 Batters			154	36	2	22	28	.234	.299	.328
Second 9 Batters			131	31	0	11	17	.237	.305	.303
All Batters Thereafter			158	44	4	14	20	.278	.405	.335

Loves to face: Jesse Barfield (0-for-4, 3 SO)
Lloyd Moseby (.125, 1-for-8)
Willie Wilson (0-for-5, 4 SO)

Hates to face: Joe Carter (.429, 3-for-7, 2 HR)
Alvin Davis (.500, 4-for-8, 2 2B, 1 HR)
Ozzie Guillen (.538, 7-for-13)

Miscellaneous statistics: Ground outs-to-air outs ratio: 1.06 last season, 1.26 for career. . . . Induced 16 double-play ground outs in 107 opportunities (one per 6.7). . . . Allowed 19 doubles, 1 triple in 119.2 innings. . . . Allowed 3 first-inning runs in 16 starts (1.69 ERA). . . . Batting support: 4.38 runs per start. . . . Opposing base stealers: 7-for-12 (58%); 3 pickoffs, 1 balk.

Comments: Held a regular spot in the rotation from July 17 until the end of the season, but was passed by in the playoffs in favor of the three-man rotation of Clemens, Boddicker, and Kiecker. . . . Opponents batted 86 points higher with runners in scoring position (.317) than in other at-bats (.231) last season, the 3d-largest margin in the majors. . . . The only home run he allowed to a left-handed batter was hit by Ken Griffey, Jr. on August 12. . . . Has split time between Pawtucket and Boston in each of the last four seasons. His 10–5 record with Boston last season lifted his career major league record to .500 (12–12). . . . His average of one home run per 19.9 innings was the best by a Red Sox southpaw since Mickey McDermott allowed nine homers in 206⅓ innings in 1953 (one HR per 22.9 IP). . . . Has learned to cope with Fenway; opponents' batting averages there year by year since 1987: .373, .295, .258, .218. . . . Career record of 6–2 (3.79 ERA) at Fenway, 4–10 (4.76) on the road. . . . Opponents' career batting-average breakdown: .254 with the bases empty, .311 with runners on base, .307 with runners in scoring position. . . . Opponents have a career average of .347 with one home run every 25 at-bats in Late-Inning Pressure Situations, compared to a .275 average with one home run every 81 at-bats at other times.

Chris Bosio

Throws Right

Milwaukee Brewers	W-L	ERA	AB	H	HR	BB	SO	BA	SA	OBA
Season	4-9	4.00	508	131	15	38	76	.258	.411	.311
vs. Left-Handers			273	78	10	19	25	.286	.465	.336
vs. Right-Handers			235	53	5	19	51	.226	.349	.282
vs. Ground-Ballers			264	64	5	14	37	.242	.360	.281
vs. Fly-Ballers			244	67	10	24	39	.275	.467	.342
Home Games	2-7	5.11	315	87	9	25	46	.276	.448	.331
Road Games	2-2	2.26	193	44	6	13	30	.228	.352	.277
Grass Fields	4-8	4.11	475	120	14	38	71	.253	.408	.310
Artificial Turf	0-1	2.25	33	11	1	0	5	.333	.455	.333
April	3-0	1.39	117	22	0	8	17	.188	.239	.246
May	1-3	3.19	181	45	8	6	28	.249	.436	.274
June	0-3	8.07	127	43	4	12	17	.339	.488	.397
July	0-3	4.24	83	21	3	12	14	.253	.482	.344
August	0-0	—	0	0	0	0	0	—	—	—
Sept./Oct.	0-0	—	0	0	0	0	0	—	—	—
Leading Off Inn.			131	36	4	6	18	.275	.427	.307
Bases Empty			310	76	9	19	40	.245	.397	.293
Runners On			198	55	6	19	36	.278	.434	.338
Runners/Scor. Pos.			113	28	1	15	23	.248	.354	.331
Runners On/2 Out			86	28	3	7	17	.326	.523	.376
Scor. Pos./2 Out			57	17	1	6	14	.298	.474	.365
Late-Inning Pressure			14	2	0	1	1	.143	.143	.200
Leading Off			4	1	0	0	0	.250	.250	.250
Runners On			6	0	0	0	0	.000	.000	.000
Runners/Scor. Pos.			1	0	0	0	0	.000	.000	.000
First 9 Batters			168	38	6	9	28	.226	.375	.266
Second 9 Batters			159	48	8	14	23	.302	.503	.360
All Batters Thereafter			181	45	1	15	25	.249	.365	.308

Loves to face: Bob Boone (.071, 1-for-14)
Jim Eisenreich (.059, 1-for-17, 1 2B)
Willie Wilson (.045, 1-for-22)

Hates to face: Carlos Quintana (2-for-2, 1 HR, 1 BB)
Harold Reynolds (.692, 9-for-13)
Ernie Whitt (.526, 10-for-19)

Miscellaneous statistics: Ground outs-to-air outs ratio: 1.20 last season, 1.29 for career. . . . Induced 10 double-play ground outs in 92 opportunities (one per 9.2). . . . Allowed 23 doubles, 5 triples in 132.2 innings. . . . Allowed 8 first-inning runs in 20 starts (1.80 ERA, 5th lowest in A.L.; minimum: 20 starts). . . . Batting support: 3.80 runs per start. . . . Opposing base stealers: 7-for-11 (64%); 1 pickoff, 0 balks.

Comments: Ended the season with the fewest wins of any opening-day starter in the American League last season. Six of the 14 A.L. opening-day starters failed to win 10 games. . . . Bosio's two visits to the disabled list cost him a total of 78 days, and roughly 15 starts. . . . Had the lowest average run support of any regular starter on the Brewers last season. . . . Had a higher ERA in his seven no-decision starts (5.21) than in his nine defeats (4.55). . . . Opponents batted 81 points higher in night games (.287) than in day games (.207), the largest margin in the majors. He had a 2–3 record with a 1.92 ERA in day games, and a record of 2–6 (5.33 ERA) at night. . . . Posted an ERA of 2.84 with Charlie O'Brien as a batterymate last season; with B.J. Surhoff behind the plate, his ERA was 5.06. . . . Opponents' career batting average in Late-Inning Pressure Situations (.209) is 59 points lower than their average in other at-bats (.269). That's the 4th-largest margin in the majors over the last five seasons. . . . Opponents have hit for a higher average with runners on base than with the bases empty in each of the last five years. . . . Opponents' first inning batting average of .159 was the 2d lowest of any starting pitcher in the majors (minimum: 20 starts). Opponents batted .273 after the first inning. . . . Has lost his last five decisions vs. the Blue Jays. . . . Has a career record of 13–2 in April, 24–44 from May to October.

Kevin Brown

Throws Right

Texas Rangers	W-L	ERA	AB	H	HR	BB	SO	BA	SA	OBA
Season	12-10	3.60	685	175	13	60	88	.255	.365	.315
vs. Left-Handers			337	84	6	30	47	.249	.362	.309
vs. Right-Handers			348	91	7	30	41	.261	.368	.321
vs. Ground-Ballers			320	84	5	24	47	.262	.359	.311
vs. Fly-Ballers			365	91	8	36	41	.249	.370	.319
Home Games	6-4	2.58	321	78	9	28	44	.243	.361	.309
Road Games	6-6	4.56	364	97	4	32	44	.266	.368	.321
Grass Fields	9-8	3.46	531	135	11	51	67	.254	.363	.321
Artificial Turf	3-2	4.08	154	40	2	9	21	.260	.370	.295
April	4-0	3.58	108	30	2	9	15	.278	.380	.333
May	1-4	4.29	155	39	3	20	14	.252	.348	.341
June	4-1	1.50	151	27	1	5	19	.179	.245	.206
July	3-2	3.67	158	39	4	17	23	.247	.367	.318
August	0-2	5.40	91	31	1	8	13	.341	.473	.390
Sept./Oct.	0-1	7.20	22	9	2	1	4	.409	.773	.435
Leading Off Inn.			169	41	3	17	20	.243	.331	.316
Bases Empty			391	104	6	33	49	.266	.371	.326
Runners On			294	71	7	27	39	.241	.357	.301
Runners/Scor. Pos.			149	40	5	23	22	.268	.430	.356
Runners On/2 Out			130	36	3	15	12	.277	.392	.352
Scor. Pos./2 Out			77	24	3	12	8	.312	.481	.404
Late-Inning Pressure			94	25	5	8	6	.266	.521	.327
Leading Off			28	9	2	3	1	.321	.607	.387
Runners On			31	7	2	3	1	.226	.548	.286
Runners/Scor. Pos.			15	6	2	3	1	.400	1.067	.474
First 9 Batters			213	50	2	19	40	.235	.305	.299
Second 9 Batters			200	56	2	20	25	.280	.355	.345
All Batters Thereafter			272	69	9	21	23	.254	.419	.305

Loves to face: Alvaro Espinoza (.071, 1-for-14)
Mike Greenwell (.071, 1-for-14, 2 BB)
Ozzie Guillen (0-for-12)

Hates to face: Greg Briley (.714, 5-for-7)
Jerry Browne (.556, 5-for-9)
Lance Johnson (.833, 5-for-6)

Miscellaneous statistics: Ground outs-to-air outs ratio: 2.53 last season, highest rate in A.L.; 2.51 for career.... Induced 24 double-play ground outs in 126 opportunities (one per 5.3).... Allowed 34 doubles, 1 triple in 180.0 innings.... Allowed 9 first-inning runs in 26 starts (2.77 ERA).... Batting support: 4.65 runs per start.... Opposing base stealers: 7-for-11 (64%); 2 pickoffs, 2 balks.

Comments: The American League's premier ground-ball pitcher must be rolling his pitches up to the plate early in the game. His ground outs-to-air outs ratio was 6.12 during the first two innings last season, compared to 1.98 in the third inning or later. He induced 10 double-play grounders in only 40 opportunites during the first two frames.... Opponents have averaged one home run per 93 at-bats on Brown's first two passes through the batting order, compared to one every 39 at-bats after that.... How low will we go? Never underestimate our willingness to dig where no man has gone before. Brown has never allowed a triple on his first or second pass through the batting order.... Won each of his first five starts last season despite a 4.15 ERA during that time.... Only seven A.L. pitchers earned 10 wins faster than Brown. His 10th victory came on July 6, but he won only two games thereafter.... Threw his first career shutout in his 47th career start on June 15. Three starts later, he notched number two.... The first pitcher since Ted Higuera and Kirk McCaskill to complete at least six starts in both his rookie and sophomore seasons. McCaskill's streak ended at two; Higuera's continued for another two seasons.

Greg Cadaret

Throws Left

New York Yankees	W-L	ERA	AB	H	HR	BB	SO	BA	SA	OBA
Season	5-4	4.15	447	120	8	64	80	.268	.405	.359
vs. Left-Handers			119	30	3	15	17	.252	.370	.333
vs. Right-Handers			328	90	5	49	63	.274	.418	.367
vs. Ground-Ballers			222	71	5	27	35	.320	.505	.390
vs. Fly-Ballers			225	49	3	37	45	.218	.307	.328
Home Games	3-0	2.78	205	47	1	31	41	.229	.327	.328
Road Games	2-4	5.43	242	73	7	33	39	.302	.471	.385
Grass Fields	3-2	4.09	359	94	5	56	70	.262	.387	.360
Artificial Turf	2-2	4.43	88	26	3	8	10	.295	.477	.354
April	1-1	7.90	56	18	2	7	9	.321	.554	.391
May	0-3	4.24	83	22	3	9	13	.265	.422	.333
June	1-0	3.20	98	30	2	11	15	.306	.449	.376
July	1-0	1.93	83	20	0	10	9	.241	.325	.323
August	2-0	3.22	81	19	0	15	22	.235	.321	.354
Sept./Oct.	0-0	7.43	46	11	1	12	12	.239	.391	.397
Leading Off Inn.			99	23	1	13	18	.232	.333	.327
Bases Empty			232	63	6	33	41	.272	.435	.365
Runners On			215	57	2	31	39	.265	.372	.352
Runners/Scor. Pos.			136	34	1	25	29	.250	.331	.358
Runners On/2 Out			89	16	0	14	16	.180	.258	.291
Scor. Pos./2 Out			58	7	0	13	14	.121	.172	.282
Late-Inning Pressure			85	22	0	11	11	.259	.353	.344
Leading Off			21	8	0	2	1	.381	.429	.435
Runners On			44	7	0	5	8	.159	.250	.245
Runners/Scor. Pos.			21	2	0	4	5	.095	.190	.240
First 9 Batters			268	77	4	45	58	.287	.414	.387
Second 9 Batters			126	27	3	14	18	.214	.365	.293
All Batters Thereafter			53	16	1	5	4	.302	.453	.362

Loves to face: Kent Hrbek (0-for-10, 2 BB)
Mickey Tettleton (0-for-7, 4 SO)
Kenny Williams (0-for-8, 6 SO)

Hates to face: Jose Canseco (.500, 2-for-4, 1 HR, 2 SO)
Gary Gaetti (.714, 5-for-7)
Pete Incaviglia (.444, 4-for-9, 2 2B, 1 HR)

Miscellaneous statistics: Ground outs-to-air outs ratio: 1.37 last season, 1.09 for career.... Induced 10 double-play ground outs in 107 opportunities (one per 10.7).... Allowed 27 doubles, 5 triples in 121.1 innings.... Stranded 32 inherited runners, allowed 16 to score (67%).... Opposing base stealers: 6-for-23 (26%), 2d-lowest rate in A.L.; 10 pickoffs, 0 balks.

Comments: It took the Yankees almost a full year to discover what the Athletics knew all along: He's not a starting pitcher. He made 113 appearances, all in relief, during his two-plus seasons in Oakland, but he was the starting pitcher in 19 of his first 28 games in pinstripes. He became a full-time reliever for New York on May 13.... Career record of 5–8 (4.56 ERA) as a starter, 16–5 (3.61 ERA) as a reliever.... Didn't allow a home run over his last 64⅓ innings last season, the longest streak of his career.... Stranded 16 of the 18 runners he inherited before the All-Star break (89%); during the second half of the season he stranded only 16 of 30 inherited runners (53%).... Threw 14 wild pitches as a reliever, five more than any other reliever in the majors.... His total of 10 pickoffs was 2d highest in the majors, behind Mark Guthrie (13). Each of the 10 runners picked off by Cadaret was retired at the following base; in other words, all were badly fooled.... Has faced 313 batters in Late-Inning Pressure Situations during his career, but has allowed only one LIPS home run. In the 16 years we've kept track, there have been 408 pitchers who have faced at least 300 batters in LIPS, but only two of them had lower home-run rates than Cadaret: Paul Mirabella and Bill Landrum.... Right-handed opponents have outhit left-handers by at least 20 points in each of his four seasons in the majors. Career batting averages: left-handers, .234; right-handers, .275.

Tom Candiotti

Throws Right

Cleveland Indians	W-L	ERA	AB	H	HR	BB	SO	BA	SA	OBA
Season	15-11	3.65	788	207	23	55	128	.263	.388	.315
vs. Left-Handers			403	103	9	32	52	.256	.355	.311
vs. Right-Handers			385	104	14	23	76	.270	.423	.318
vs. Ground-Ballers			372	84	7	23	66	.226	.306	.275
vs. Fly-Ballers			416	123	16	32	62	.296	.462	.350
Home Games	7-6	4.10	437	112	15	38	74	.256	.398	.320
Road Games	8-5	3.10	351	95	8	17	54	.271	.376	.308
Grass Fields	12-11	3.68	717	189	22	49	110	.264	.396	.315
Artificial Turf	3-0	3.44	71	18	1	6	18	.254	.310	.312
April	3-0	4.91	71	17	2	4	14	.239	.338	.280
May	2-2	3.38	102	26	4	10	15	.255	.422	.321
June	4-1	3.00	164	42	5	14	19	.256	.378	.315
July	2-3	2.82	166	42	4	13	28	.253	.337	.307
August	2-3	4.39	164	44	6	9	36	.268	.451	.316
Sept./Oct.	2-2	4.30	121	36	2	5	16	.298	.388	.336
Leading Off Inn.			195	41	4	11	29	.210	.297	.256
Bases Empty			472	115	13	34	82	.244	.367	.300
Runners On			316	92	10	21	46	.291	.421	.336
Runners/Scor. Pos.			171	54	5	15	26	.316	.427	.372
Runners On/2 Out			148	45	1	13	20	.304	.378	.364
Scor. Pos./2 Out			93	31	1	11	13	.333	.409	.410
Late-Inning Pressure			50	15	2	2	7	.300	.460	.340
Leading Off			14	6	1	0	2	.429	.714	.429
Runners On			22	7	1	0	2	.318	.455	.348
Runners/Scor. Pos.			11	5	1	0	0	.455	.727	.500
First 9 Batters			254	62	7	20	42	.244	.354	.306
Second 9 Batters			243	65	7	25	38	.267	.395	.341
All Batters Thereafter			291	80	9	10	48	.275	.412	.299

Loves to face: Gary Sheffield (0-for-11)
Bill Spiers (.056, 1-for-18)
Willie Wilson (.156, 5-for-32)

Hates to face: Gary Gaetti (.382, 13-for-34, 2 HR)
Greg Gagne (.414, 12-for-29, 7 2B, 1 HR, 0 BB)
Wally Joyner (.423, 11-for-26, 1 HR, 0 SO)

Miscellaneous statistics: Ground outs-to-air outs ratio: 1.29 last season, 1.29 for career. . . . Induced 17 double-play ground outs in 139 opportunities (one per 8.2). . . . Allowed 30 doubles, 0 triples in 202.0 innings. . . . Allowed 15 first-inning runs in 29 starts (3.72 ERA). . . . Batting support: 4.70 runs per start. . . . Opposing base stealers: 18-for-25 (72%); 0 pickoffs, 3 balks.

Comments: Only 10 pitchers in major league history compiled records at least three games above .500 in three consecutive seasons while pitching for teams with losing records throughout that period—including current streaks by Candiotti and teammate Greg Swindell. The others: Jim Brosnan (1958–60), Al Mamaux (1914–16), Claude Passeau (1942–44), Dick Radatz (1962–64), Schoolboy Rowe (1943, 1946–47), Nolan Ryan (1972–74), Frank Tanana (1975–77), and Cy Young (1907–09). . . . Candiotti's winning percentage during that time (.591, 42–29) was 143 points higher than that of his Indians teammates (.448). . . . Completed 35 of 97 starts from 1986 to 1988, but has completed only seven of 60 over the last two seasons. . . . Became the 11th player in Indians history, and the first since Sam McDowell (1967–71), to pitch at least 200 innings in five consecutive seasons. The last Cleveland pitcher with a longer streak was Early Wynn (8 years, 1950–57). . . . Posted an ERA of 4.24 in 157.0 innings with Sandy Alomar behind the plate, but had a 1.60 ERA in 45.0 innings with Joel Skinner catching. . . . Career average of opposing ground-ball hitters (.239) is 32 points lower than that of opposing fly-ballers (.271). . . . Career breakdown: 44–30 in home games, 27–35 on the road. . . . Has a career record of 18–7 (2.69 ERA) during August, but only 11–19 (4.15 ERA) in September. . . . Has faced 57 batters leading off innings in Late-Inning Pressure Situations without walking one during the last three seasons.

Chuck Cary

Throws Left

New York Yankees	W-L	ERA	AB	H	HR	BB	SO	BA	SA	OBA
Season	6-12	4.19	597	155	21	55	134	.260	.437	.321
vs. Left-Handers			113	33	4	10	16	.292	.478	.344
vs. Right-Handers			484	122	17	45	118	.252	.428	.315
vs. Ground-Ballers			298	70	5	28	53	.235	.356	.299
vs. Fly-Ballers			299	85	16	27	81	.284	.518	.342
Home Games	4-3	3.04	338	76	10	26	82	.225	.370	.278
Road Games	2-9	5.82	259	79	11	29	52	.305	.525	.375
Grass Fields	5-11	3.66	526	130	17	50	123	.247	.403	.312
Artificial Turf	1-1	8.82	71	25	4	5	11	.352	.690	.390
April	0-0	—	0	0	0	0	0	—	—	—
May	2-1	4.05	101	24	2	9	27	.238	.366	.297
June	2-3	5.22	114	35	5	14	16	.307	.553	.380
July	0-3	3.18	128	34	4	12	25	.266	.438	.329
August	1-2	4.45	118	32	5	12	25	.271	.449	.338
Sept./Oct.	1-3	4.21	136	30	5	8	41	.221	.382	.262
Leading Off Inn.			152	37	3	13	34	.243	.375	.307
Bases Empty			369	92	13	37	79	.249	.431	.319
Runners On			228	63	8	18	55	.276	.447	.323
Runners/Scor. Pos.			121	39	6	14	32	.322	.562	.379
Runners On/2 Out			93	20	3	6	25	.215	.333	.263
Scor. Pos./2 Out			51	16	3	6	13	.314	.529	.386
Late-Inning Pressure			20	7	0	6	6	.350	.500	.500
Leading Off			5	0	0	4	1	.000	.000	.444
Runners On			7	2	0	2	5	.286	.286	.444
Runners/Scor. Pos.			5	1	0	2	4	.200	.200	.429
First 9 Batters			233	59	7	14	55	.253	.416	.292
Second 9 Batters			188	53	7	20	39	.282	.473	.351
All Batters Thereafter			176	43	7	21	40	.244	.426	.325

Loves to face: Mike Devereaux (.071, 1-for-14)
Gary Gaetti (.083, 1-for-12)
Luis Rivera (0-for-12)

Hates to face: Chili Davis (.500, 3-for-6, 1 HR)
Jody Reed (.385, 5-for-13)
Harold Reynolds (.600, 3-for-5, 2 2B)

Miscellaneous statistics: Ground outs-to-air outs ratio: 0.48 last season, lowest rate in A.L.; 0.57 for career. . . . Induced 7 double-play ground outs in 105 opportunities (one per 15.0). . . . Allowed 33 doubles, 5 triples in 156.2 innings. . . . Allowed 17 first-inning runs in 27 starts (5.40 ERA). . . . Batting support: 3.33 runs per start (3d lowest in A.L.) . . . Opposing base stealers: 14-for-24 (58%); 3 pickoffs, 2 balks.

Comments: His average of 7.70 strikeouts per nine innings was the fourth highest in Yankees history (minimum: 25 GS). The top three: Ron Guidry, 8.16 (1978); Dave Righetti, 8.02 (1982); and Al Downing, 8.00 (1964). . . . Matched his previous career total with six wins in 1990. Among the 87 pitchers who made at least 25 starts last season only two have career winning percentages lower than his .375 mark (12–20): Mike Morgan (.361) and Mark Gardner (.368). . . . Opponents batted 80 points higher in road games (.305) than in home games (.225) last season, the 5th-largest margin in the majors. . . . Opponents have hit for a higher average with runners on base than with the bases empty in each of his six years in the majors. Opponents' career breakdown: .270 with runners on base, .224 with the bases empty. . . . Opponents batted 59 points higher with runners in scoring position (.290) than in other at-bats (.232) over the last five seasons, the 3d-largest margin in the majors. . . . Left-handed batters have a higher career batting average (.256) against this southpaw than right-handers (.237). . . . Cary faced 10 batters with the bases loaded last season, and allowed only one of a possible 40 runs to those batters. . . . Faced Sid Fernandez of the Mets in the final preseason game—a matchup of each league's most extreme fly-ball pitchers. Someone forgot to tell Cary to duck; a line drive fractured his left hand, and Cary didn't make his regular-season debut until May 15.

John Cerutti

Throws Left

Toronto Blue Jays	W-L	ERA	AB	H	HR	BB	SO	BA	SA	OBA
Season	9-9	4.76	546	162	23	49	49	.297	.489	.356
vs. Left-Handers			111	30	3	6	7	.270	.432	.311
vs. Right-Handers			435	132	20	43	42	.303	.503	.367
vs. Ground-Ballers			255	81	6	16	19	.318	.467	.356
vs. Fly-Ballers			291	81	17	33	30	.278	.509	.356
Home Games	5-5	5.32	274	82	14	20	27	.299	.518	.352
Road Games	4-4	4.17	272	80	9	29	22	.294	.460	.360
Grass Fields	2-4	5.02	203	59	8	26	18	.291	.478	.370
Artificial Turf	7-5	4.60	343	103	15	23	31	.300	.496	.348
April	1-3	5.79	68	18	3	3	8	.265	.441	.292
May	1-2	3.69	125	35	5	12	11	.280	.408	.353
June	2-1	3.55	145	41	4	11	13	.283	.441	.331
July	3-1	6.51	112	39	7	13	13	.348	.634	.416
August	1-2	6.27	76	24	4	7	4	.316	.579	.373
Sept./Oct.	1-0	1.69	20	5	0	3	0	.250	.350	.360
Leading Off Inn.			137	48	7	10	6	.350	.591	.395
Bases Empty			310	98	12	30	23	.316	.506	.378
Runners On			236	64	11	19	26	.271	.466	.327
Runners/Scor. Pos.			108	29	4	11	14	.269	.454	.333
Runners On/2 Out			91	26	6	7	9	.286	.593	.343
Scor. Pos./2 Out			47	13	2	6	6	.277	.574	.370
Late-Inning Pressure			25	11	3	3	0	.440	.840	.483
Leading Off			8	5	1	0	0	.625	1.125	.625
Runners On			13	3	1	1	0	.231	.462	.267
Runners/Scor. Pos.			3	1	0	1	0	.333	.333	.400
First 9 Batters			207	62	8	23	15	.300	.493	.370
Second 9 Batters			191	57	8	9	22	.298	.497	.330
All Batters Thereafter			148	43	7	17	12	.291	.473	.367

Loves to face: Dan Gladden (.136, 3-for-22)
Rafael Palmeiro (.091, 1-for-11)
Cory Snyder (.067, 1-for-15, 8 SO)

Hates to face: Steve Buechele (.400, 10-for-25, 3 2B, 4 HR)
Jose Canseco (.429, 9-for-21, 4 HR)
Mark McGwire (.412, 7-for-17, 1 HR, 7 BB)

Miscellaneous statistics: Ground outs-to-air outs ratio: 1.23 last season, 1.00 for career. . . . Induced 21 double-play ground outs in 136 opportunities (one per 6.5). . . . Allowed 26 doubles, 5 triples in 140.0 innings. . . . Allowed 18 first-inning runs in 23 starts (7.15 ERA, 5th highest in A.L.) . . . Batting support: 4.87 runs per start. . . . Opposing base stealers: 6-for-9 (67%); 3 pickoffs, 1 balk.

Comments: His strikeout rate during the first inning (6 SO in 22.2 IP) was the lowest in the majors (minimum: 20 GS). . . . Made 23 starts without a complete game last season. . . . Posted a 3.89 ERA in 74 innings with Pat Borders catching, and a 5.65 ERA in 65.1 innings with Greg Myers behind the plate. . . . Opponents' batting average year by year since 1987: .251, .256, .273, .297. . . . Opponents have hit for a higher average on artificial turf than on grass fields in each of his five full seasons in the majors. . . . Opponents have hit for a higher average in Late-Inning Pressure Situations than they have in other at-bats in each of his six seasons. Opponents' career averages: .318 (one home run every 15 at-bats) in LIPS, .266 (one home run every 29 at-bats) at other times. . . . Has held opponents to a lower average with runners on base than he has with the bases empty in each of his five full seasons with Toronto. Opponents' career breakdown: .280 with the bases empty, .255 with runners on base, .240 with runners in scoring position. . . . Had a career regular-season record of 0–7 vs. the Athletics before beating them on July 20. . . . Although he turns 31 before the season is a month old, Cerutti would be the youngster in a rotation that could include Frank Tanana (37 in July), Bill Gullickson (32), Walt Terrell (33 in May), and Dan Petry (32).

Roger Clemens

Throws Right

Boston Red Sox	W-L	ERA	AB	H	HR	BB	SO	BA	SA	OBA
Season	21-6	1.93	847	193	7	54	209	.228	.306	.278
vs. Left-Handers			443	107	7	27	97	.242	.343	.288
vs. Right-Handers			404	86	0	27	112	.213	.265	.267
vs. Ground-Ballers			430	96	2	24	100	.223	.279	.269
vs. Fly-Ballers			417	97	5	30	109	.233	.333	.288
Home Games	11-2	1.53	414	95	3	31	95	.229	.314	.290
Road Games	10-4	2.31	433	98	4	23	114	.226	.298	.267
Grass Fields	19-4	2.00	707	164	6	44	183	.232	.308	.283
Artificial Turf	2-2	1.62	140	29	1	10	26	.207	.293	.257
April	4-1	3.09	129	26	1	9	34	.202	.264	.261
May	4-1	2.54	163	34	2	11	35	.209	.288	.264
June	4-1	2.38	163	43	3	12	43	.264	.368	.324
July	2-2	1.00	165	38	1	9	38	.230	.327	.270
August	6-0	1.09	186	43	0	5	48	.231	.274	.251
Sept./Oct.	1-1	1.59	41	9	0	8	11	.220	.317	.347
Leading Off Inn.			216	53	1	17	49	.245	.315	.303
Bases Empty			479	123	3	36	109	.257	.332	.313
Runners On			368	70	4	18	100	.190	.272	.233
Runners/Scor. Pos.			187	32	1	12	61	.171	.230	.216
Runners On/2 Out			153	26	1	7	40	.170	.242	.216
Scor. Pos./2 Out			88	15	0	6	25	.170	.227	.223
Late-Inning Pressure			136	24	2	10	28	.176	.243	.238
Leading Off			37	7	0	3	8	.189	.216	.250
Runners On			52	8	1	3	7	.154	.250	.200
Runners/Scor. Pos.			23	1	0	2	5	.043	.043	.120
First 9 Batters			255	64	1	17	67	.251	.341	.301
Second 9 Batters			260	53	0	11	77	.204	.250	.242
All Batters Thereafter			332	76	6	26	65	.229	.322	.288

Loves to face: Jim Gantner (.097, 3-for-31, 0 BB)
Ron Kittle (0-for-14, 1 BB, 10 SO)
Cory Snyder (.091, 2-for-22, 12 SO)

Hates to face: Alvin Davis (.364, 12-for-33, 3 HR)
Pete O'Brien (.455, 15-for-33)
Steve Sax (.500, 9-for-18, 1 HR)

Miscellaneous statistics: Ground outs-to-air outs ratio: 1.21 last season, 1.00 for career. . . . Induced 11 double-play ground outs in 167 opportunities (one per 15.2). . . . Allowed 35 doubles, 5 triples in 228.1 innings. . . . Allowed 6 first-inning runs in 31 starts (1.45 ERA, 3d lowest in A.L.) . . . Batting support: 4.23 runs per start. . . . Opposing base stealers: 14-for-28 (50%); 4 pickoffs, 0 balks.

Comments: Career record of 116–51 gives him the 2d-highest winning percentage in American League history (minimum: 100 wins). The top five: Spud Chandler (.717), Clemens (.695), Whitey Ford (.690), Vic Raschi (.689), Lefty Grove (.680). . . . First pitcher since Catfish Hunter (1970 to 1976) to win at least 17 games in five consecutive seasons. . . . Became only the second American League pitcher in the era of the designated hitter to post a season ERA under 2.00. The other was Ron Guidry (1.74 in 1978). . . . Had a total of 23 innings pitched in the eighth and ninth innings, allowing only two earned runs for an ERA of 0.78. . . . Had a 9–2 record with a 0.97 ERA after the All-Star break. . . . Opposing batters had eight hits in the last 81 at-bats against Clemens with runners in scoring position. . . . Hasn't allowed a first-inning home run or a home run to a right-handed batter since Jose Canseco homered off him on September 15, 1989. . . . Average of one home run allowed per 32 innings pitched was the best in the majors. . . . Has allowed more than one home run in a game only once in his last 48 starts. That was on June 28, when Fred McGriff hit a pair off of him at Fenway Park. McGriff, Eddie Murray (1986), and Carlton Fisk (1987) are the only players to homer off Clemens twice in one game. . . . Had the poorest run support of any regular Red Sox starter last season. . . . Career record of 3–9 vs. the Athletics during the regular season, 0–1 in the playoffs.

Chuck Crim

Throws Right

Milwaukee Brewers	W-L	ERA	AB	H	HR	BB	SO	BA	SA	OBA
Season	3-5	3.47	337	88	7	23	39	.261	.371	.309
vs. Left-Handers			131	33	1	7	16	.252	.321	.288
vs. Right-Handers			206	55	6	16	23	.267	.403	.322
vs. Ground-Ballers			152	40	1	6	19	.263	.336	.294
vs. Fly-Ballers			185	48	6	17	20	.259	.400	.320
Home Games	0-3	3.10	164	45	3	7	20	.274	.366	.308
Road Games	3-2	3.80	173	43	4	16	19	.249	.376	.309
Grass Fields	2-4	3.25	293	77	6	20	32	.263	.365	.311
Artificial Turf	1-1	4.91	44	11	1	3	7	.250	.409	.292
April	1-0	2.57	57	15	2	3	4	.263	.386	.317
May	1-1	5.06	43	12	0	3	6	.279	.302	.319
June	0-3	6.41	82	26	3	9	9	.317	.537	.380
July	0-0	0.00	41	6	0	2	9	.146	.171	.186
August	1-0	1.32	48	11	1	2	4	.229	.313	.255
Sept./Oct.	0-1	3.86	66	18	1	4	7	.273	.364	.314
Leading Off Inn.			78	21	0	4	12	.269	.359	.313
Bases Empty			189	44	4	10	25	.233	.360	.275
Runners On			148	44	3	13	14	.297	.385	.349
Runners/Scor. Pos.			83	26	3	9	7	.313	.458	.365
Runners On/2 Out			74	23	1	5	7	.311	.378	.354
Scor. Pos./2 Out			46	12	1	3	3	.261	.370	.306
Late-Inning Pressure			207	47	4	12	29	.227	.309	.267
Leading Off			49	12	0	3	11	.245	.306	.288
Runners On			89	25	1	4	9	.281	.337	.305
Runners/Scor. Pos.			49	13	1	2	5	.265	.367	.283
First 9 Batters			317	86	7	22	35	.271	.388	.320
Second 9 Batters			20	2	0	1	4	.100	.100	.136
All Batters Thereafter			0	0	0	0	0	—	—	—

Loves to face: George Brett (0-for-10, 1 BB)
Brian Harper (0-for-7)
Cory Snyder (.063, 1-for-16)

Hates to face: Jerry Browne (.600, 6-for-10, 1 HR)
Gary Gaetti (.462, 6-for-13, 1 HR)
Steve Lyons (.500, 4-for-8, 2 2B, 1 HR)

Miscellaneous statistics: Ground outs-to-air outs ratio: 1.49 last season, 1.48 for career. . . . Induced 7 double-play ground outs in 63 opportunities (one per 9.0). . . . Allowed 12 doubles, 2 triples in 85.2 innings. . . . Stranded 28 inherited runners, allowed 15 to score (65%). . . . Opposing base stealers: 5-for-5; 0 pickoffs, 1 balk.

Comments: Career total of 24 relief wins ranks second in Brewers franchise history, one behind Ed Rodriguez. . . . In an era of specialization, when even relief pitching is divided into various roles (set-up, closer, lefty vs. lefty), Crim is unusual: He has had between seven and 12 saves in each of his four seasons—a range within which only five other pitchers have ever fallen for four consecutive seasons. But if the range is expanded to include pitchers with between five and 15 saves in four straight seasons, it becomes apparent that during the 1980s, fewer relievers are being used as part-time closers. There were eight streaks of four years or more that began in the 1980s, compared to 18 in the 1970s. . . . Although he faced fewer batters than ever before, his total of 221 faced in Late-Inning Pressure Situations last season was a career high (due to Dan Plesac's off season). The percentage of batters facing Crim in LIPS year by year since 1987: 31.5, 43.1, 39.4, 60.2. . . . Only home run allowed to a left-handed batter last season was hit by Matt Nokes on June 26. . . . Opponents batted 88 points lower in Late-Inning Pressure Situations (.227) than in other at-bats (.315) last season, the 5th-largest margin in the majors. . . . Total of 85⅔ innings pitched was the lowest of his career; he had topped the 100-inning mark in each of his previous three seasons. . . . Since becoming a full-time reliever in 1988, opponents have batted .264 on his first pass through the order, but only .190 in subsequent at-bats. . . . Career record of 4–12 in June, 21–14 at other times.

Mark Davis

Throws Left

Kansas City Royals	W-L	ERA	AB	H	HR	BB	SO	BA	SA	OBA
Season	2-7	5.11	274	71	9	52	73	.259	.423	.383
vs. Left-Handers			55	10	0	11	19	.182	.236	.348
vs. Right-Handers			219	61	9	41	54	.279	.470	.392
vs. Ground-Ballers			125	24	2	22	36	.192	.304	.315
vs. Fly-Ballers			149	47	7	30	37	.315	.523	.437
Home Games	2-1	4.46	147	35	2	29	43	.238	.340	.369
Road Games	0-6	5.93	127	36	7	23	30	.283	.520	.399
Grass Fields	0-4	5.70	100	29	6	16	21	.290	.560	.390
Artificial Turf	2-3	4.80	174	42	3	36	52	.241	.345	.379
April	0-1	6.48	36	11	0	6	12	.306	.333	.405
May	1-1	6.23	58	18	2	10	15	.310	.517	.412
June	0-3	3.72	39	9	1	6	13	.231	.308	.362
July	0-1	8.03	49	14	4	16	7	.286	.633	.463
August	0-1	7.71	18	5	0	2	3	.278	.444	.364
Sept./Oct.	1-0	2.18	74	14	2	12	23	.189	.311	.302
Leading Off Inn.			56	8	1	9	21	.143	.232	.273
Bases Empty			129	30	4	20	37	.233	.395	.349
Runners On			145	41	5	32	36	.283	.448	.411
Runners/Scor. Pos.			96	27	3	18	23	.281	.438	.393
Runners On/2 Out			69	18	2	13	16	.261	.420	.386
Scor. Pos./2 Out			52	12	1	8	11	.231	.327	.344
Late-Inning Pressure			98	29	3	12	27	.296	.449	.384
Leading Off			23	2	0	0	9	.087	.087	.087
Runners On			46	17	2	9	11	.370	.543	.482
Runners/Scor. Pos.			29	9	1	6	7	.310	.448	.444
First 9 Batters			236	60	8	45	69	.254	.411	.379
Second 9 Batters			30	6	1	5	4	.200	.400	.333
All Batters Thereafter			8	5	0	2	0	.625	.875	.636

Loves to face: Dave Parker (.138, 4-for-29, 11 SO)
Tim Raines (.158, 3-for-19)
Glenn Wilson (.188, 3-for-16)

Hates to face: Keith Hernandez (.324, 11-for-34, 1 HR)
Tracy Jones (.571, 8-for-14, 4 BB)
Mike Marshall (.355, 11-for-31, 2 HR)

Miscellaneous statistics: Ground outs-to-air outs ratio: 0.81 last season, 1.00 for career. . . . Induced 5 double-play ground outs in 72 opportunities (one per 14.4). . . . Allowed 16 doubles, 1 triple in 68.2 innings. . . . Stranded 20 inherited runners, allowed 16 to score (56%). . . . Opposing base stealers: 15-for-15; 0 pickoffs, 0 balks.

Comments: Had 44 saves in 70 relief appearances in 1989, but a total of only 47 saves in 325 relief appearances in other seasons, before and since. . . . His ERA of 5.11 was the highest ever by a pitcher following a Cy Young season. He broke the "record" of Pete Vuckovich, who posted a 4.90 ERA in 1983, the year after he won the award. . . . Batting average by opposing left-handed batters was lower last season than in his Cy Young season (.239). But opposing right-handers had hit below .200 in each of the previous two seasons. . . . During a two-week period from June 28 through July 11, Kansas City used nine different starting pitchers in 13 games: Mark Gubicza, Davis, Tom Gordon, Bret Saberhagen, Steve Farr, Luis Aquino, Kevin Appier, Mark Davis, and Pete Filson. . . . Career record of 13–30 (5.21 ERA) as a starter, 29–42 (2.90 ERA) as a reliever. . . . Held the American League's top-ten batters to a .095 average (2-for-21), the lowest of any pitcher in the league (minimum: 15 at bats). . . . The silver lining: Davis had 20⅔ innings after returning from the disabled list on September 5; the figures above indicate that it was his best month of the season. . . . Lowest career winning percentages since 1960 (minimum: 100 decisions): Jesse Jefferson, .325 (39–81); Steve Arlin, .337 (34–67); Roger Craig, .355 (38–69); Mike Morgan, .361 (53–94); Pete Broberg, .366 (41–71); Davis, .368 (42–72).

Storm Davis

Throws Right

Kansas City Royals	W-L	ERA	AB	H	HR	BB	SO	BA	SA	OBA
Season	7-10	4.74	459	129	9	35	62	.281	.407	.330
vs. Left-Handers			235	69	4	22	32	.294	.421	.353
vs. Right-Handers			224	60	5	13	30	.268	.393	.305
vs. Ground-Ballers			217	60	6	16	22	.276	.424	.326
vs. Fly-Ballers			242	69	3	19	40	.285	.393	.333
Home Games	5-7	4.50	325	89	6	22	45	.274	.394	.317
Road Games	2-3	5.34	134	40	3	13	17	.299	.440	.361
Grass Fields	1-2	6.52	82	25	2	6	15	.305	.476	.352
Artificial Turf	6-8	4.37	377	104	7	29	47	.276	.393	.325
April	1-3	4.57	93	27	1	6	15	.290	.376	.333
May	0-2	6.17	95	26	2	9	17	.274	.421	.337
June	1-1	4.91	46	13	3	3	5	.283	.500	.327
July	2-1	5.79	56	20	1	6	4	.357	.500	.406
August	3-3	3.32	151	37	1	11	17	.245	.338	.294
Sept./Oct.	0-0	6.75	18	6	1	0	4	.333	.556	.333
Leading Off Inn.			110	32	3	8	12	.291	.464	.339
Bases Empty			246	71	5	18	27	.289	.435	.337
Runners On			213	58	4	17	35	.272	.376	.322
Runners/Scor. Pos.			125	36	2	9	16	.288	.384	.328
Runners On/2 Out			80	18	1	2	15	.225	.313	.244
Scor. Pos./2 Out			49	12	1	2	5	.245	.367	.275
Late-Inning Pressure			15	4	0	4	3	.267	.267	.421
Leading Off			5	1	0	0	1	.200	.200	.200
Runners On			6	2	0	2	0	.333	.333	.500
Runners/Scor. Pos.			1	1	0	1	0	1.000	1.000	1.000
First 9 Batters			173	54	2	15	27	.312	.416	.365
Second 9 Batters			170	43	4	8	22	.253	.382	.285
All Batters Thereafter			116	32	3	12	13	.276	.431	.341

Loves to face: Alvaro Espinoza (.071, 1-for-14)
Jack Howell (.071, 1-for-14, 3 BB, 8 SO)
Pete Incaviglia (.063, 1-for-16, 3 BB)

Hates to face: Ron Hassey (.500, 8-for-16, 1 HR)
Roberto Kelly (.500, 7-for-14, 1 HR)
Bill Schroeder (.571, 8-for-14)

Miscellaneous statistics: Ground outs-to-air outs ratio: 1.07 last season, 1.10 for career. . . . Induced 9 double-play ground outs in 115 opportunities (one per 12.8). . . . Allowed 27 doubles, 2 triples in 112.0 innings. . . . Allowed 15 first-inning runs in 20 starts (6.30 ERA). . . . Batting support: 4.65 runs per start. . . . Opposing base stealers: 3-for-3; 0 pickoffs, 1 balk.

Comments: One of five pitchers to throw at least 100 innings last season without hitting a batter. He has hit 13 right-handed batters over nine seasons, but plunked only one of the 3126 left-handers he's faced during that time. . . . Didn't complete any of his 20 starts in 1990, and has completed only two of 99 since leaving the Orioles after the 1986 season. . . . Hasn't allowed a first-inning home run in 41 starts since Cal Ripken nailed him in June 1989. . . . Has a career winning percentage of .500 or better vs. every American League club except the Red Sox (5–9) and the Yankees (5–8). . . . His career winning percentage of .579 (99–72) ranks 11th among active pitchers with at least 150 decisions. But he's played for some awfully good teams; his teammates have had a .537 percentage. The 1990 Royals were only the second losing team for which Davis finished a season. . . . Career record of 41–42 before the All-Star break, 58–30 during the second half. . . . Has held opponents to a lower batting average with runners on base than he has with the bases empty in each of the last four seasons. . . . One season short of his 30th birthday, Davis has already pitched 1431 innings. That total seems high now, but a quarter-century ago it was nothing—Don Drysdale, for example, pitched 2746 innings before turning 30. But before you make any snap judgments about post-30 injury rates, keep in mind the fact that Bert Blyleven pitched 2842 innings before turning 30, and nearly 2000 more since.

Dennis Eckersley

Throws Right

Oakland A's	W-L	ERA	AB	H	HR	BB	SO	BA	SA	OBA
Season	4-2	0.61	257	41	2	4	73	.160	.226	.172
vs. Left-Handers			119	20	1	2	22	.168	.244	.180
vs. Right-Handers			138	21	1	2	51	.152	.210	.164
vs. Ground-Ballers			114	18	1	2	28	.158	.219	.171
vs. Fly-Ballers			143	23	1	2	45	.161	.231	.172
Home Games	3-2	1.02	126	20	2	4	35	.159	.254	.183
Road Games	1-0	0.24	131	21	0	0	38	.160	.198	.160
Grass Fields	4-2	0.57	222	35	2	4	59	.158	.221	.172
Artificial Turf	0-0	0.90	35	6	0	0	14	.171	.257	.171
April	1-0	0.00	34	5	0	0	9	.147	.206	.143
May	1-0	0.77	41	7	0	0	15	.171	.220	.171
June	0-1	0.77	45	10	0	2	8	.222	.289	.255
July	0-1	1.64	34	2	1	1	12	.059	.147	.086
August	1-0	0.64	51	8	1	0	13	.157	.275	.157
Sept./Oct.	1-0	0.00	52	9	0	1	16	.173	.192	.189
Leading Off Inn.			60	8	0	0	18	.133	.183	.133
Bases Empty			160	26	1	1	50	.162	.237	.168
Runners On			97	15	1	3	23	.155	.206	.178
Runners/Scor. Pos.			49	11	0	2	9	.224	.245	.250
Runners On/2 Out			50	8	1	2	13	.160	.260	.192
Scor. Pos./2 Out			27	5	0	2	5	.185	.222	.241
Late-Inning Pressure			221	35	2	3	67	.158	.226	.169
Leading Off			50	5	0	0	16	.100	.140	.100
Runners On			85	13	1	2	21	.153	.212	.170
Runners/Scor. Pos.			43	10	0	1	9	.233	.256	.244
First 9 Batters			256	41	2	4	73	.160	.227	.172
Second 9 Batters			1	0	0	0	0	.000	.000	.000
All Batters Thereafter			0	0	0	0	0	—	—	—

Loves to face: Ellis Burks (.077, 1-for-13)
Rickey Henderson (.128, 5-for-39, 6 BB)
Gary Ward (.100, 2-for-20)

Hates to face: Ken Griffey, Sr. (.500, 7-for-14, 1 HR)
Kent Hrbek (.409, 9-for-22, 4 2B, 2 HR)
Dave Parker (.348, 8-for-23, 3 2B, 2 HR)

Miscellaneous statistics: Ground outs-to-air outs ratio: 0.65 last season, 0.71 for career. . . . Induced 3 double-play ground outs in 39 opportunities (one per 13.0). . . . Allowed 9 doubles, 1 triple in 73.1 innings. . . . Stranded 25 inherited runners, allowed 4 to score (86%), shared highest rate in A.L. . . . Opposing base stealers: 1-for-3 (33%); 0 pickoffs, 0 balks.

Comments: His 1990 ERA was the lowest in major league history *even if eligibility is granted for as few as 25 innings pitched*. . . . Nice comeback for the pitcher who compiled the highest ERA in the majors in 1983: 5.61 (minimum: 162 IP). . . . ERA year by year since 1986: 4.57, 3.03, 2.35, 1.56, 0.61. Blastoff! . . . His average of one walk per 18.3 innings last season was the 2d-best mark in major league history, *behind only his own 1989 average of one per 19.2 innings* (minimum: 50 IP). . . . Over the last two seasons, he has walked an average of one batter for every 67 faced. He has started 106 innings during that time without walking a leadoff batter. . . . Opponents batted 75 points lower in Late-Inning Pressure Situations (.188) than in other at-bats (.263) over the last five seasons, the 2d-largest margin in the majors. . . . Right-handed batters have hit below .200 against him in five of the last six seasons. . . . Has faced 136 batters with the bases loaded, walked two (one in 1975, the other in 1985). . . . The only pitcher in major league history with at least 100 complete games and 100 saves, even if you hypothecate saves prior to 1969. . . . Career ERA: 3.69 as a starter, 1.84 in relief. . . . Eckersley earned his first start in 1975 after pitching 14⅓ innings of scoreless relief over the first 10 appearances of his career. Who was it that said, "Leave well enough alone"? . . . Lowest career relief ERAs (minimum: 250 IP): Wilbur Cooper, 1.72; Eddie Cicotte, 1.74; Eckersley, 1.84; Ed Walsh, 1.85; Three Finger Brown, 1.88.

Mark Eichhorn

Throws Right

California Angels	W-L	ERA	AB	H	HR	BB	SO	BA	SA	OBA
Season	2-5	3.08	339	98	2	23	69	.289	.354	.341
vs. Left-Handers			155	45	1	10	29	.290	.348	.353
vs. Right-Handers			184	53	1	13	40	.288	.359	.332
vs. Ground-Ballers			140	39	1	13	27	.279	.364	.350
vs. Fly-Ballers			199	59	1	10	42	.296	.347	.335
Home Games	2-4	2.82	153	44	1	8	32	.288	.366	.323
Road Games	0-1	3.30	186	54	1	15	37	.290	.344	.356
Grass Fields	2-5	3.44	287	85	2	16	58	.296	.362	.340
Artificial Turf	0-0	1.29	52	13	0	7	11	.250	.308	.350
April	0-1	1.04	61	11	0	3	16	.180	.230	.219
May	0-2	1.83	73	17	1	5	15	.233	.315	.282
June	0-1	2.00	75	24	0	2	17	.320	.373	.350
July	1-0	14.54	49	23	1	5	7	.469	.612	.536
August	1-0	1.46	47	12	0	6	10	.255	.255	.345
Sept./Oct.	0-1	3.12	34	11	0	2	4	.324	.382	.359
Leading Off Inn.			63	21	1	2	13	.333	.492	.364
Bases Empty			135	42	1	7	26	.311	.400	.350
Runners On			204	56	1	16	43	.275	.324	.336
Runners/Scor. Pos.			153	38	1	11	33	.248	.294	.308
Runners On/2 Out			98	30	1	7	16	.306	.378	.376
Scor. Pos./2 Out			80	24	1	7	13	.300	.387	.385
Late-Inning Pressure			161	38	0	13	37	.236	.273	.299
Leading Off			33	10	0	2	9	.303	.455	.343
Runners On			87	19	0	8	19	.218	.230	.296
Runners/Scor. Pos.			67	14	0	4	16	.209	.224	.270
First 9 Batters			323	93	2	22	65	.288	.356	.339
Second 9 Batters			16	5	0	1	4	.313	.313	.389
All Batters Thereafter			0	0	0	0	0	—	—	—

Loves to face: Steve Buechele (.067, 1-for-15)
Randy Bush (.053, 1-for-19, 1 2B)
Brook Jacoby (.063, 1-for-16)

Hates to face: Tom Brunansky (.444, 8-for-18, 4 2B, 1 HR)
Ron Kittle (.750, 3-for-4, 1 HR)
Larry Sheets (.545, 6-for-11)

Miscellaneous statistics: Ground outs-to-air outs ratio: 1.73 last season, 1.67 for career. . . . Induced 5 double-play ground outs in 90 opportunities (one per 18.0). . . . Allowed 14 doubles, 1 triple in 84.2 innings. . . . Stranded 49 inherited runners (including first 13 of the season), allowed 20 to score (71%). . . . Opposing base stealers: 4-for-7 (57%); 2 pickoffs, 0 balks.

Comments: Submarine delivery gives him an enormous lefty/righty skew. Opposing left-handed batters have outhit right-handers by 57 points (.279 to .222), typical of bowlers. Other extreme right-handed sidearmers show similar career-long disparities: Dennis Eckersley, 51 points (.219 vs. RHB, .270 vs. LHB); Todd Frohwirth, 145 points (.206, .351); Terry Leach, 51 points (.238, .289); Kent Tekulve, 43 points (.226, .269); Frank Williams, 62 points (.215, .277). Stan Belinda could be an exception; right-handers have outhit lefties by 42 points (.257 to .215). . . . Debuted in the majors as a starting pitcher for the Blue Jays in 1982, then didn't resurface until 1986. Since then, he's appeared in 300 games, all as a reliever. . . . Collected his 13th save of the 1990 season on June 19. He appeared in 27 more games without a save after that. . . . Opponents batted 101 points lower in Late-Inning Pressure Situations (.236) than in other at-bats (.337) last season, the 4th-largest margin in the majors. Faced 179 batters in LIPS, the most of any pitcher who did not surrender an LIPS home run. . . . The American League's top 10 home run hitters had 33 at-bats against Eichhorn last season, but hit no home runs. But the league's top 10 hitters (i.e. ranked by batting average) batted .444 against him (12-for-27), their highest collective mark against any pitcher in the league (minimum: 15 AB).

Scott Erickson

Throws Right

Minnesota Twins	W-L	ERA	AB	H	HR	BB	SO	BA	SA	OBA
Season	8-4	2.87	422	108	9	51	53	.256	.367	.342
vs. Left-Handers			224	55	4	27	16	.246	.348	.329
vs. Right-Handers			198	53	5	24	37	.268	.389	.356
vs. Ground-Ballers			210	48	3	30	26	.229	.319	.329
vs. Fly-Ballers			212	60	6	21	27	.283	.415	.354
Home Games	7-2	3.45	305	83	7	24	44	.272	.393	.332
Road Games	1-2	1.56	117	25	2	27	9	.214	.299	.363
Grass Fields	1-1	0.35	80	13	1	21	8	.162	.237	.340
Artificial Turf	7-3	3.62	342	95	8	30	45	.278	.398	.342
April	0-0	—	0	0	0	0	0	—	—	—
May	0-0	—	0	0	0	0	0	—	—	—
June	1-1	2.92	46	9	0	8	9	.196	.217	.339
July	1-1	3.81	111	36	5	13	13	.324	.523	.400
August	1-2	4.56	107	36	2	9	10	.336	.458	.388
Sept./Oct.	5-0	1.35	158	27	2	21	21	.171	.241	.273
Leading Off Inn.			99	21	3	18	14	.212	.354	.345
Bases Empty			240	57	6	29	32	.237	.350	.325
Runners On			182	51	3	22	21	.280	.390	.364
Runners/Scor. Pos.			104	24	1	14	17	.231	.298	.317
Runners On/2 Out			68	20	2	14	10	.294	.397	.422
Scor. Pos./2 Out			46	11	0	9	10	.239	.239	.364
Late-Inning Pressure			21	4	1	6	2	.190	.333	.370
Leading Off			5	1	0	4	1	.200	.200	.556
Runners On			8	2	1	1	1	.250	.625	.333
Runners/Scor. Pos.			2	0	0	1	0	.000	.000	.333
First 9 Batters			150	32	3	14	21	.213	.287	.292
Second 9 Batters			132	38	1	22	16	.288	.394	.397
All Batters Thereafter			140	38	5	15	16	.271	.429	.340

Loves to face: Mike Greenwell (0-for-5)
Kevin Seitzer (0-for-5)

Hates to face: Wade Boggs (.600, 3-for-5)
Randy Milligan (.500, 3-for-6, 1 HR)

Miscellaneous statistics: Ground outs-to-air outs ratio: 1.85 last season, his first in the majors. . . . Induced 14 double-play ground outs in 99 opportunities (one per 7.1). . . . Allowed 16 doubles, 2 triples in 113.0 innings. . . . Allowed 2 first-inning runs in 17 starts (0.00 ERA). . . . Batting support: 5.12 runs per start. . . . Opposing base stealers: 6-for-9 (67%); 1 pickoff, 0 balks.

Comments: Had the lowest ERA by a Twins rookie since Doug Corbett's 1.99 mark in 1980 (minimum: 100 IP). . . . Twins rookies made a total of 59 starts last season, the highest total in the American League (Tapani, 28; Erickson, 17; Abbott, 7; Drummond, 4; Casian, 3). . . . He was the only starter on the Twins' staff with a run-support average greater than five runs per game. . . . Opponents batted 61 points higher in night games (.281) than in day games (.220) last season, the 5th-largest margin in the majors. That translated into wins and losses: 4–0 with a 1.68 ERA in day games; 4–4, 3.76 at night. . . . His average of 4.22 strikeouts per nine innings was the lowest of any rookie who pitched at least 100 innings; but his .667 winning percentage tied him for the top spot among rookies with at least 10 decisions. . . . Had the lowest ERA of any A.L. pitcher against the Rangers (0.66). . . . Was Minnesota's 4th-round pick in the 1989 June free-agent draft, from which just six other players have already appeared in the majors. Only two of those six made their debuts before Erickson's on June 25 (Ben McDonald and John Olerud). . . . As good as his numbers look, they could have been better; he had the misfortune to make 12 of his 17 starts at the Metrodome. Can anyone out there explain why he walked three times as many batters as he struck out in road games, while striking out almost twice as many batters as he walked in home games? (If so, try your hand at the Roberto Kelly comment, p. 148).

Steve Farr

Throws Right

Kansas City Royals	W-L	ERA	AB	H	HR	BB	SO	BA	SA	OBA
Season	13-7	1.98	451	99	6	48	94	.220	.295	.301
vs. Left-Handers			204	46	2	27	34	.225	.294	.319
vs. Right-Handers			247	53	4	21	60	.215	.296	.286
vs. Ground-Ballers			206	46	4	17	39	.223	.316	.289
vs. Fly-Ballers			245	53	2	31	55	.216	.278	.311
Home Games	9-2	1.37	231	45	2	23	45	.195	.251	.273
Road Games	4-5	2.64	220	54	4	25	49	.245	.341	.329
Grass Fields	2-5	3.43	164	44	4	22	40	.268	.390	.363
Artificial Turf	11-2	1.20	287	55	2	26	54	.192	.240	.263
April	1-0	3.27	39	9	1	2	8	.231	.333	.286
May	3-2	1.86	72	15	2	11	19	.208	.319	.313
June	1-1	2.08	62	12	0	6	13	.194	.242	.265
July	3-2	2.35	78	18	1	12	19	.231	.321	.344
August	2-0	1.35	91	21	0	3	17	.231	.286	.255
Sept./Oct.	3-2	1.82	109	24	2	14	18	.220	.284	.320
Leading Off Inn.			111	31	3	7	17	.279	.432	.328
Bases Empty			247	62	5	20	47	.251	.356	.312
Runners On			204	37	1	28	47	.181	.221	.288
Runners/Scor. Pos.			127	20	1	20	39	.157	.213	.285
Runners On/2 Out			91	18	0	15	17	.198	.231	.318
Scor. Pos./2 Out			64	11	0	11	15	.172	.219	.303
Late-Inning Pressure			121	30	2	17	30	.248	.322	.350
Leading Off			30	7	0	3	6	.233	.300	.324
Runners On			55	13	1	11	17	.236	.309	.364
Runners/Scor. Pos.			32	7	1	9	15	.219	.313	.390
First 9 Batters			332	76	5	38	75	.229	.301	.313
Second 9 Batters			76	13	0	9	15	.171	.237	.267
All Batters Thereafter			43	10	1	1	4	.233	.349	.267

Loves to face: Carlton Fisk (.105, 2-for-19, 1 HR, 10 SO)
Kelly Gruber (.091, 1-for-11)
Mickey Tettleton (.100, 1-for-10, 6 SO)

Hates to face: Bill Schroeder (.714, 5-for-7, 3 2B, 2 HR)
Larry Sheets (.545, 6-for-11, 3 2B, 1 HR)
Ruben Sierra (.571, 8-for-14, 1 HR, 5 SO)

Miscellaneous statistics: Ground outs-to-air outs ratio: 1.03 last season, 1.10 for career. . . . Induced 13 double-play ground outs in 105 opportunities (one per 8.1). . . . Allowed 12 doubles, 2 triples in 127.0 innings. . . . Stranded 36 inherited runners, allowed 9 to score (80%), shared 5th-highest rate in A.L. . . . Opposing base stealers: 8-for-11 (73%); 1 pickoff, 0 balks.

Comments: Among Royals pitchers with at least 500 career innings, only Dan Quisenberry (2.55) had a lower ERA than Farr (3.05). . . . Over the past 40 years, only one other pitcher won at least five games as a starter and reliever and compiled ERAs below 2.50 in both roles: Jose Rijo in 1988 (7–7, 2.47 as a starter; 6–1, 2.20 in relief). Several Hall of Famers did it roughly 75 years ago: Walter Johnson (3 times, 1912–13 and 1917), Chief Bender (1913), and Eddie Plank (1912). . . . Career record of 10–11 (3.77 ERA) as a starter, 27–24 (3.19 ERA) as a reliever. He started six games last season, and pitched to a decision in each of them, including his first career shutout. Farr and new teammate Mike Witt were the only American League pitchers with both a save and a shutout last season. . . . Pitched a career-high 127 innings last season, while establishing a new career low for ERA. . . . Farr's 70-point margin between opponents' batting average with bases empty (.251) and runners on base (.181) and his 86-point edge with runners in scoring position (.157) over other at-bats (.244) each ranked fifth in the majors last season. . . . Opponents batted 77 points higher on grass fields (.268) than on artificial turf (.192) last season, the 4th-largest margin in the majors. . . . Career records: 8–25 with a 4.23 ERA on grass fields; 29–10 record with a 2.61 ERA on artificial turf.

John Farrell

Throws Right

Cleveland Indians	W-L	ERA	AB	H	HR	BB	SO	BA	SA	OBA
Season	4-5	4.28	377	108	10	33	44	.286	.446	.344
vs. Left-Handers			205	57	4	19	19	.278	.400	.336
vs. Right-Handers			172	51	6	14	25	.297	.500	.353
vs. Ground-Ballers			190	47	3	17	17	.247	.347	.308
vs. Fly-Ballers			187	61	7	16	27	.326	.545	.380
Home Games	1-2	3.54	113	36	2	4	13	.319	.407	.342
Road Games	3-3	4.59	264	72	8	29	31	.273	.462	.345
Grass Fields	4-4	3.47	267	72	6	22	31	.270	.404	.325
Artificial Turf	0-1	6.41	110	36	4	11	13	.327	.545	.388
April	2-1	4.32	93	24	1	9	9	.258	.376	.324
May	1-1	4.29	140	45	4	14	16	.321	.493	.381
June	1-2	4.39	109	30	4	9	11	.275	.477	.333
July	0-0	—	0	0	0	0	0	—	—	—
August	0-0	—	0	0	0	0	0	—	—	—
Sept./Oct.	0-1	3.86	35	9	1	1	8	.257	.343	.278
Leading Off Inn.			92	27	2	11	10	.293	.467	.369
Bases Empty			226	62	6	19	27	.274	.429	.333
Runners On			151	46	4	14	17	.305	.470	.359
Runners/Scor. Pos.			87	23	2	8	11	.264	.425	.320
Runners On/2 Out			60	17	1	6	5	.283	.417	.348
Scor. Pos./2 Out			42	9	1	5	5	.214	.357	.298
Late-Inning Pressure			20	10	0	1	1	.500	.550	.524
Leading Off			6	2	0	0	1	.333	.333	.333
Runners On			6	4	0	1	0	.667	.833	.714
Runners/Scor. Pos.			2	1	0	0	0	.500	1.000	.500
First 9 Batters			145	29	2	7	23	.200	.317	.237
Second 9 Batters			133	43	1	12	14	.323	.436	.381
All Batters Thereafter			99	36	7	14	7	.364	.646	.439

Loves to face: Scott Fletcher (.083, 1-for-12)
Jeff Kunkel (0-for-10, 1 BB)
Danny Tartabull (.071, 1-for-14)

Hates to face: Ellis Burks (.412, 7-for-17, 1 HR)
Dan Gladden (.474, 9-for-19, 1 HR)
Edgar Martinez (.500, 6-for-12, 1 HR)

Miscellaneous statistics: Ground outs-to-air outs ratio: 1.01 last season, 0.90 for career. . . . Induced 10 double-play ground outs in 72 opportunities (one per 7.2). . . . Allowed 24 doubles, 3 triples in 96.2 innings. . . . Allowed 2 first-inning runs in 17 starts (1.06 ERA). . . . Batting support: 4.41 runs per start. . . . Opposing base stealers: 6-for-10 (60%); 0 pickoffs, 0 balks.

Comments: Spent 88 days on the disabled list last season, and will probably miss at least that much in 1991 while recovering from knee surgery. Spent time on the D.L. in both 1988 (August 28–September 20) and 1989 (March 19–April 16) as well. . . . Had an ERA of 1.06 over the first two innings of his starts, but from the 3d inning on he had a 6.03 ERA. Opponents' batting average of .150 during the first inning was his lowest of any inning. . . . Had the highest rate of no-decision starts in the American League last season (minimum: 10 GS). The top five: Farrell, 47.1% (8 of 17); Bill Krueger, 47.1% (8 of 17); Bob Milacki, 45.8% (11 of 24); Frank Tanana, 41.4% (12 of 29); David West, 40.7% (11 of 27). . . . Has a career average of one walk for every 13 batters faced, but has faced 34 batters with the bases loaded without walking in a run. . . . Right-handed opponents have averaged one home run per 37 at-bats, nearly double the rate of opposing left-handed hitters (one per 67 AB). Batting averages are similar (.264 and .259, respectively). . . . One of three players in major league history with records at least four games above .500 for teams with losing records in both his rookie and sophomore seasons (1987–88). The others: Ted Higuera (1985–86) and Erik Hanson (1989–90). . . . Won 19 of 30 decisions over his first two seasons, but only 13 of 32 in two seasons since. . . . Has a career record of 4–0 vs. the Rangers, 5–1 vs. the Brewers.

Chuck Finley

Throws Left

California Angels	W-L	ERA	AB	H	HR	BB	SO	BA	SA	OBA
Season	18-9	2.40	864	210	17	81	177	.243	.351	.308
vs. Left-Handers			121	31	0	14	15	.256	.273	.333
vs. Right-Handers			743	179	17	67	162	.241	.363	.304
vs. Ground-Ballers			376	88	5	36	71	.234	.309	.302
vs. Fly-Ballers			488	122	12	45	106	.250	.383	.313
Home Games	11-4	1.63	481	107	9	42	98	.222	.322	.286
Road Games	7-5	3.39	383	103	8	39	79	.269	.386	.336
Grass Fields	15-7	2.25	742	178	14	68	159	.240	.344	.303
Artificial Turf	3-2	3.34	122	32	3	13	18	.262	.393	.338
April	3-1	0.96	95	19	0	7	13	.200	.263	.262
May	4-1	3.41	129	30	2	10	24	.233	.357	.288
June	3-2	3.13	142	36	6	14	33	.254	.408	.321
July	4-0	1.69	193	49	4	13	39	.254	.347	.303
August	2-2	3.53	132	33	3	15	24	.250	.356	.324
Sept./Oct.	2-3	1.90	173	43	2	22	44	.249	.347	.332
Leading Off Inn.			230	54	6	16	40	.235	.357	.285
Bases Empty			516	131	15	49	100	.254	.382	.321
Runners On			348	79	2	32	77	.227	.305	.290
Runners/Scor. Pos.			182	43	2	25	38	.236	.335	.324
Runners On/2 Out			138	29	2	9	31	.210	.348	.259
Scor. Pos./2 Out			80	16	2	6	15	.200	.363	.256
Late-Inning Pressure			118	32	0	13	24	.271	.314	.344
Leading Off			31	10	0	5	7	.323	.387	.417
Runners On			59	15	0	2	9	.254	.305	.279
Runners/Scor. Pos.			33	7	0	2	6	.212	.273	.257
First 9 Batters			261	63	6	25	57	.241	.352	.308
Second 9 Batters			256	59	7	25	52	.230	.359	.298
All Batters Thereafter			347	88	4	31	68	.254	.343	.317

Loves to face: Jerry Browne (.050, 1-for-20, 1 2B)
Mike Devereaux (.053, 1-for-19)
Pete Incaviglia (.105, 2-for-19, 1 HR, 10 SO)

Hates to face: Brian Harper (.429, 9-for-21, 1 HR)
Chet Lemon (.421, 8-for-19, 2 HR, 7 SO)
Pat Tabler (.438, 7-for-16, 1 HR, 6 BB)

Miscellaneous statistics: Ground outs-to-air outs ratio: 1.07 last season, 1.08 for career. . . . Induced 22 double-play ground outs in 187 opportunities (one per 8.5). . . . Allowed 36 doubles, 3 triples in 236.0 innings. . . . Allowed 7 first-inning runs in 32 starts (1.41 ERA, 2d lowest in A.L.). . .Batting support: 4.50 runs per start. . . . Opposing base stealers: 15-for-33 (45%); 1 pickoff, 0 balks.

Comments: The first American League pitcher to win at least 15 games with an ERA below 2.60 in consecutive seasons since Frank Tanana (1976–77). . . . His 2.40 ERA was the 3d lowest in Angels history, behind Dean Chance (1.65 in 1964) and Nolan Ryan (2.28 in 1972). . . . His average of 7.38 innings pitched per start was 2d highest in the majors last season (minimum: 20 GS), behind only Dave Stewart (7.42). . . . Had an ERA of 2.94 during the first four innings of his starts, 1.79 in the fifth inning or later. . . . Finley was the only pitcher to throw a complete-game shutout against the Red Sox at Fenway Park last season. . . . Opponents stole five bases in their first six attempts, but only 10 in 27 tries after that (including none in their last six). . . . The total of 18 runners caught stealing with Finley on the mound was the highest of any pitcher in the majors last season. . . . Held opponents to one hit in 15 at-bats with nine strikeouts with the bases loaded last season. . . . Has faced 641 left-handed batters in his career, but has only allowed two home runs (to Fred Lynn in 1987 and George Brett in 1988). Opposing right-handers have a career average of one home run per 44 at-bats. Batting averages are nearly identical: .252 by left-handers, .250 by right-handers.

Willie Fraser

Throws Right

California Angels	W-L	ERA	AB	H	HR	BB	SO	BA	SA	OBA
Season	5-4	3.08	286	69	4	24	32	.241	.336	.297
vs. Left-Handers			121	25	1	14	16	.207	.273	.287
vs. Right-Handers			165	44	3	10	16	.267	.382	.305
vs. Ground-Ballers			124	29	2	9	16	.234	.331	.286
vs. Fly-Ballers			162	40	2	15	16	.247	.340	.306
Home Games	4-1	2.62	169	40	3	15	22	.237	.343	.299
Road Games	1-3	3.73	117	29	1	9	10	.248	.325	.295
Grass Fields	4-4	2.71	264	62	3	20	31	.235	.318	.288
Artificial Turf	1-0	7.11	22	7	1	4	1	.318	.545	.393
April	0-1	11.81	26	10	1	3	1	.385	.654	.433
May	2-1	3.86	39	14	0	3	2	.359	.462	.395
June	0-0	4.82	39	11	1	5	7	.282	.410	.364
July	0-0	1.47	64	9	1	3	7	.141	.234	.179
August	3-1	1.27	72	15	1	7	8	.208	.264	.275
Sept./Oct.	0-1	2.92	46	10	0	3	7	.217	.239	.265
Leading Off Inn.			69	12	1	3	8	.174	.261	.208
Bases Empty			165	35	1	12	19	.212	.273	.266
Runners On			121	34	3	12	13	.281	.421	.338
Runners/Scor. Pos.			69	22	2	8	8	.319	.435	.375
Runners On/2 Out			57	14	2	5	4	.246	.421	.306
Scor. Pos./2 Out			34	11	2	4	4	.324	.559	.395
Late-Inning Pressure			106	31	0	6	9	.292	.358	.327
Leading Off			25	5	0	2	2	.200	.280	.259
Runners On			52	18	0	1	4	.346	.442	.352
Runners/Scor. Pos.			29	12	0	1	2	.414	.448	.419
First 9 Batters			248	61	4	23	30	.246	.351	.307
Second 9 Batters			38	8	0	1	2	.211	.237	.231
All Batters Thereafter			0	0	0	0	0	—	—	—

Loves to face: Steve Balboni (0-for-15)
Pete O'Brien (.071, 1-for-14)
Billy Ripken (.077, 1-for-13)

Hates to face: Dave Bergman (.462, 6-for-13, 3 HR)
Mel Hall (.500, 7-for-14, 1 HR)
Don Mattingly (.389, 7-for-18, 3 HR)

Miscellaneous statistics: Ground outs-to-air outs ratio: 0.82 last season, 0.82 for career. . . . Induced 7 double-play ground outs in 60 opportunities (one per 8.6). . . . Allowed 13 doubles, 1 triple in 76.0 innings. . . . Stranded 22 inherited runners, allowed 14 to score (61%). . . . Opposing base stealers: 4-for-6 (67%); 0 pickoffs, 0 balks.

Comments: The only home run he allowed to a left-handed batter last season was hit by Rafael Palmeiro on June 8. That's quite an accomplishment for a pitcher who allowed 24 homers to left-handed batters only two years ago. Prior to 1990, Fraser had allowed an average of one home run every 22 at-bats to LHB. . . . Ground outs-to-air outs ratio has remained below 1.00 throughout that period; year by year since 1986: 0.65, 0.89, 0.96, 0.88. . . . Has appeared in 89 games over the last two seasons, all in relief, after starting 55 games for the Angels during 1987–88. Career breakdown: 18–22 (4.90 ERA) in 56 starts, 13–12 (3.19 ERA) in 105 relief appearances. . . . Opponents have had a higher batting average with runners on base than with the bases empty in each of his four full seasons in the majors. Opponents' career breakdown: .237 with the bases empty, .269 with runners on base, .279 with runners in scoring position. . . . Was the Angels' first-round pick in the June 1985 free-agent draft, selected three slots ahead of Joe Magrane, five ahead of Gregg Jefferies, and seven ahead of Rafael Palmeiro. . . . Born in New York City on May 26, 1964. What else happened in New York sports that day? Roger Maris, in his fifth season in pinstripes, hit his first opposite-field home run at Yankee Stadium.

Paul Gibson

Throws Left

Detroit Tigers	W-L	ERA	AB	H	HR	BB	SO	BA	SA	OBA
Season	5-4	3.05	368	99	10	44	56	.269	.427	.344
vs. Left-Handers			118	31	2	11	11	.263	.356	.321
vs. Right-Handers			250	68	8	33	45	.272	.460	.356
vs. Ground-Ballers			182	46	4	22	24	.253	.390	.329
vs. Fly-Ballers			186	53	6	22	32	.285	.462	.360
Home Games	4-2	2.58	199	48	2	26	35	.241	.347	.332
Road Games	1-2	3.60	169	51	8	18	21	.302	.521	.359
Grass Fields	5-3	2.90	308	81	6	36	49	.263	.393	.338
Artificial Turf	0-1	3.78	60	18	4	8	7	.300	.600	.377
April	0-0	5.40	36	15	1	8	4	.417	.583	.500
May	1-1	1.14	82	18	0	13	13	.220	.317	.327
June	1-1	1.46	50	15	0	5	9	.300	.460	.364
July	1-0	3.52	83	16	2	9	13	.193	.289	.272
August	0-2	5.51	70	22	6	4	8	.314	.643	.351
Sept./Oct.	2-0	2.25	47	13	1	5	9	.277	.383	.340
Leading Off Inn.			81	25	3	9	10	.309	.519	.385
Bases Empty			186	56	7	20	27	.301	.484	.372
Runners On			182	43	3	24	29	.236	.368	.318
Runners/Scor. Pos.			106	21	2	22	17	.198	.302	.323
Runners On/2 Out			77	12	1	14	15	.156	.247	.286
Scor. Pos./2 Out			55	8	1	13	10	.145	.255	.309
Late-Inning Pressure			105	28	3	12	21	.267	.419	.339
Leading Off			26	7	0	4	5	.269	.346	.367
Runners On			47	11	1	5	8	.234	.383	.302
Runners/Scor. Pos.			22	2	1	5	4	.091	.227	.250
First 9 Batters			294	75	9	38	54	.255	.412	.337
Second 9 Batters			72	23	1	6	2	.319	.472	.370
All Batters Thereafter			2	1	0	0	0	.500	1.000	.500

Loves to face: Wade Boggs (.200, 3-for-15)
Mike Felder (0-for-12, 1 BB)
Kelly Gruber (.067, 1-for-15)

Hates to face: Dante Bichette (.750, 3-for-4)
Ellis Burks (.545, 6-for-11)
Jim Gantner (.500, 8-for-16)

Miscellaneous statistics: Ground outs-to-air outs ratio: 0.86 last season, 0.83 for career.... Induced 7 double-play ground outs in 90 opportunities (one per 12.9).... Allowed 24 doubles, 2 triples in 97.1 innings.... Stranded 48 inherited runners, allowed 16 to score (75%).... Opposing base stealers: 7-for-10 (70%); 2 pickoffs, 1 balk.

Comments: Most games facing 10 or more batters in relief last season: Dennis Lamp, 23; Duane Ward, 20; Juan Berenguer, 19; Steve Crawford, 16; Gibson, 16; Edwin Nunez, 16. The National League leader was Mark Grant with 14.... His performance with runners on base in Late-Inning Pressure Situations (0-for-16) was the 2d-best in the 16-year history of *The Player Analysis*. Opponents were hitless in 19 such at bats against Greg A. Harris in 1985.... Opponents batted 100 points lower with runners in scoring position (.198) than in other at-bats (.298) last season, the 2d-largest margin in the majors.... Allowed only one home run over his first 48.2 innings, but surrendered nine homers in 48.2 innings thereafter (including five over a nine-inning span in early August).... Twelve of his 44 walks were intentional.... Opponents were hitless in eight at bats with the bases loaded last season, and have a career average of .056 (1-for-18) against him with two outs and the bags full.... Tiger Stadium is a hitters' ballpark? Don't tell that to anyone who has checked our Ballparks section or to Gibson. His career ERA in Detroit (3.10) is almost two runs lower than in road games (4.95). Opponents have hit .229 against him at Tiger Stadium, .288 elsewhere. Untypical of Tigers pitchers, he's also allowed half as many home runs in home games (9) as he has on the road (18).... Career record of only 1–6 in August, but 4–0 in September.

Jerry Don Gleaton

Throws Left

Detroit Tigers	W-L	ERA	AB	H	HR	BB	SO	BA	SA	OBA
Season	1-3	2.94	291	62	5	25	56	.213	.289	.279
vs. Left-Handers			91	22	1	3	13	.242	.297	.276
vs. Right-Handers			200	40	4	22	43	.200	.285	.280
vs. Ground-Ballers			142	32	1	13	23	.225	.282	.289
vs. Fly-Ballers			149	30	4	12	33	.201	.295	.268
Home Games	1-2	3.73	138	25	2	14	31	.181	.261	.256
Road Games	0-1	2.16	153	37	3	11	25	.242	.314	.299
Grass Fields	1-3	2.86	252	52	4	22	51	.206	.278	.272
Artificial Turf	0-0	3.48	39	10	1	3	5	.256	.359	.318
April	0-1	5.14	23	6	0	2	2	.261	.304	.345
May	0-0	1.98	45	8	2	4	11	.178	.311	.245
June	1-0	2.84	63	12	0	6	16	.190	.206	.271
July	0-1	3.63	62	11	0	6	7	.177	.258	.243
August	0-1	3.38	63	17	2	4	11	.270	.365	.313
Sept./Oct.	0-0	0.93	35	8	1	3	9	.229	.314	.289
Leading Off Inn.			59	15	1	8	13	.254	.322	.343
Bases Empty			137	34	3	15	24	.248	.328	.322
Runners On			154	28	2	10	32	.182	.253	.240
Runners/Scor. Pos.			81	17	2	5	14	.210	.309	.269
Runners On/2 Out			68	14	1	4	11	.206	.294	.250
Scor. Pos./2 Out			39	10	1	1	4	.256	.359	.275
Late-Inning Pressure			94	21	2	11	18	.223	.309	.311
Leading Off			17	3	1	5	5	.176	.353	.364
Runners On			47	11	1	5	9	.234	.340	.321
Runners/Scor. Pos.			28	7	1	3	4	.250	.393	.344
First 9 Batters			260	53	5	25	53	.204	.281	.278
Second 9 Batters			31	9	0	0	3	.290	.355	.281
All Batters Thereafter			0	0	0	0	0	—	—	—

Loves to face: Jesse Barfield (0-for-6, 4 SO)
Alvin Davis (.111, 1-for-9)
Jack Howell (0-for-5)

Hates to face: Willie Randolph (.545, 6-for-11)
Ruben Sierra (.500, 5-for-10, 1 HR)
Dave Winfield (.545, 6-for-11, 1 HR)

Miscellaneous statistics: Ground outs-to-air outs ratio: 1.19 last season, 1.04 for career.... Induced 9 double-play ground outs in 83 opportunities (one per 9.2).... Allowed 7 doubles, 0 triples in 82.2 innings.... Stranded 39 inherited runners, allowed 17 to score (70%).... Opposing base stealers: 3-for-7 (43%); 3 pickoffs, 1 balk.

Comments: His only victory last season (on June 15 vs. California) was his first since September 22, 1987—a winless span of 81 games—and finally boosted him past 10 wins in his 203d major league game. Other pitchers who failed to exceed 10 wins in their first 200 appearances: Larry Andersen (264), Steve Mingori (258), Dave Tomlin (251), Ray Searage (245), Ramon Hernandez (223), Mike Stanton (217), Pat Clements (213), Arnold Earley (211), and Juan Agosto (204). Some group. Three pitchers never passed the 10-win mark in 200 games: Bob Allen, Kevin Hickey (still trying), and Bill Scherrer.... Has pitched parts of 10 seasons in the majors, but has had a winning record only once, when he was 1-0 with the Chicago White Sox in 1985. Among active pitchers, only Pete Smith (18–37, .327) has a lower winning percentage than Gleaton's .344 (11–21) mark (minimum: 30 decisions).... His 13 saves last season surpassed his previous career total (11). He collected 11 of those 13 saves after the All-Star break, making him a no-brainer fantasy-league cheap choice for 1991.... Faced a single batter in 12 of his 57 appearances. Most one-batter appearances last season: Keith Comstock, 16; Kevin Hickey, 16; Gleaton, 12; Juan Agosto, 11; Rob Murphy, 11; Scott Radinsky, 11.... Started and lost the last game in the managerial career of Maury Wills (1981). Can he last long enough to do the same to Maury's son Bump?

Tom Gordon

Throws Right

Kansas City Royals	W-L	ERA	AB	H	HR	BB	SO	BA	SA	OBA
Season	12-11	3.73	745	192	17	99	175	.258	.387	.346
vs. Left-Handers			365	92	6	55	75	.252	.345	.352
vs. Right-Handers			380	100	11	44	100	.263	.426	.340
vs. Ground-Ballers			377	97	7	47	89	.257	.355	.340
vs. Fly-Ballers			368	95	10	52	86	.258	.418	.353
Home Games	7-5	3.10	352	83	4	45	90	.236	.335	.322
Road Games	5-6	4.31	393	109	13	54	85	.277	.433	.367
Grass Fields	1-5	5.25	233	75	11	32	51	.322	.524	.403
Artificial Turf	11-6	3.06	512	117	6	67	124	.229	.324	.320
April	1-0	1.59	65	15	2	6	25	.231	.338	.296
May	1-3	4.41	123	29	0	25	30	.236	.293	.369
June	3-1	2.78	119	27	3	12	32	.227	.395	.303
July	1-3	4.96	132	45	4	22	24	.341	.515	.435
August	3-2	3.00	166	40	6	15	37	.241	.361	.304
Sept./Oct.	3-2	4.79	140	36	2	19	27	.257	.393	.346
Leading Off Inn.			176	50	5	24	48	.284	.432	.373
Bases Empty			395	112	12	57	85	.284	.448	.375
Runners On			350	80	5	42	90	.229	.317	.313
Runners/Scor. Pos.			197	48	4	25	54	.244	.355	.332
Runners On/2 Out			156	40	3	16	40	.256	.385	.326
Scor. Pos./2 Out			100	28	3	8	27	.280	.450	.333
Late-Inning Pressure			25	6	0	1	4	.240	.280	.269
Leading Off			6	1	0	0	0	.167	.167	.167
Runners On			11	4	0	0	3	.364	.455	.364
Runners/Scor. Pos.			6	2	0	0	1	.333	.500	.333
First 9 Batters			236	58	4	48	69	.246	.335	.373
Second 9 Batters			244	58	7	27	64	.238	.373	.319
All Batters Thereafter			265	76	6	24	42	.287	.445	.346

Loves to face: Jeffrey Leonard (0-for-10, 2 BB, 7 SO)
Harold Reynolds (.067, 1-for-15, 4 BB)
Mookie Wilson (.143, 3-for-21)

Hates to face: Randy Bush (.455, 5-for-11, 1 HR)
Sam Horn (3-for-3, 1 HR, 2 BB)
Cal Ripken (.444, 4-for-9, 1 2B, 2 HR)

Miscellaneous statistics: Ground outs-to-air outs ratio: 1.02 last season, 1.17 for career. . . . Induced 19 double-play ground outs in 173 opportunities (one per 9.1). . . . Allowed 31 doubles, 7 triples in 195.1 innings. . . . Allowed 9 first-inning runs in 32 starts (2.25 ERA). . . . Batting support: 4.88 runs per start. . . . Opposing base stealers: 8-for-18 (44%); 1 pickoff, 0 balks.

Comments: Career average of 8.33 strikeouts per nine innings ranks 10th in major league history among pitchers with at least 50 starts. . . . The last pitcher smaller than five-foot-ten to pitch as many innings in a single season was Fredie Norman in 1979. . . . Gordon and teammate Kevin Appier were the two youngest American League pitchers to start at least 20 games last season. Gordon is less than one month older than Appier. . . . Had the highest average run support of any regular starter on the Royals last season. . . . Had a higher ERA in his 12 victories (2.18) than in his nine no-decision starts (2.10). . . . Had an ERA of 2.03 in 71 innings with Bob Boone behind the plate, 4.00 in 90 innings with Mike Macfarlane catching. . . . Has thrown 23 wild pitches over the last two seasons, already enough to rank fifth in franchise history, behind Mark Gubicza (67), Charlie Leibrandt (39), Bret Saberhagen (33), and Bud Black (28). . . . Opponents batted 93 points higher on grass fields (.322) than on artificial turf (.229) last season, the largest margin in the majors. . . . Career record: 4–10 on grass fields, 25–12 on artificial turf. . . . Career record by months is like a roller coaster ride: April, 5–0; May, 2–5; June, 7–1; July, 3–5; August, 8–3; September, 4–8. . . . Career record of 19–20 (3.95 ERA) as a starter, 10–2 (2.90 ERA) as a reliever. . . . Career record of 5–0 vs. the Blue Jays, 1–5 vs. the Tigers.

Jeff Gray

Throws Right

Boston Red Sox	W-L	ERA	AB	H	HR	BB	SO	BA	SA	OBA
Season	2-4	4.44	198	53	3	15	50	.268	.369	.321
vs. Left-Handers			98	27	2	8	26	.276	.388	.330
vs. Right-Handers			100	26	1	7	24	.260	.350	.312
vs. Ground-Ballers			100	25	1	6	25	.250	.340	.299
vs. Fly-Ballers			98	28	2	9	25	.286	.398	.343
Home Games	2-2	4.01	94	26	2	4	20	.277	.415	.303
Road Games	0-2	4.85	104	27	1	11	30	.260	.327	.336
Grass Fields	2-4	3.64	164	45	3	11	37	.274	.384	.322
Artificial Turf	0-0	8.31	34	8	0	4	13	.235	.294	.316
April	0-0	—	0	0	0	0	0	—	—	—
May	0-0	—	0	0	0	0	0	—	—	—
June	1-1	3.65	42	9	0	2	11	.214	.238	.267
July	0-2	7.94	52	21	1	4	7	.404	.596	.446
August	0-0	0.60	51	6	0	4	17	.118	.118	.182
Sept./Oct.	1-1	6.75	53	17	2	5	15	.321	.491	.373
Leading Off Inn.			45	14	0	2	9	.311	.378	.354
Bases Empty			102	28	1	6	24	.275	.343	.321
Runners On			96	25	2	9	26	.260	.396	.321
Runners/Scor. Pos.			60	17	0	7	19	.283	.367	.353
Runners On/2 Out			42	7	0	3	13	.167	.167	.222
Scor. Pos./2 Out			28	6	0	3	8	.214	.214	.290
Late-Inning Pressure			106	26	2	5	22	.245	.358	.279
Leading Off			28	10	0	0	6	.357	.393	.357
Runners On			41	9	2	3	9	.220	.463	.273
Runners/Scor. Pos.			20	3	0	1	7	.150	.250	.190
First 9 Batters			195	52	3	15	50	.267	.364	.321
Second 9 Batters			3	1	0	0	0	.333	.667	.333
All Batters Thereafter			0	0	0	0	0	—	—	—

Loves to face: Mookie Wilson (0-for-4)

Hates to face: Junior Felix (.667, 2-for-3, 1 HR)

Miscellaneous statistics: Ground outs-to-air outs ratio: 1.22 last season, 1.12 for career. . . . Induced 4 double-play ground outs in 44 opportunities (one per 11.0). . . . Allowed 7 doubles, 2 triples in 50.2 innings. . . . Stranded 20 inherited runners, allowed 6 to score (77%). . . . Opposing base stealers: 4-for-5 (80%); 0 pickoffs, 0 balks.

Comments: Led major league rookies with nine saves, and his average of 8.88 strikeouts per nine innings was the highest of any rookie who pitched at least 50 innings last season. . . . His nine saves came while Jeff Reardon was injured; but Gray blew his most important save opportunity after Reardon's return. With the Jays and Sox tied for first place with six games remaining, Gray took the mound with a one-run ninth-inning lead and a streak of seven saves in his last seven opportunities. He left two batters later with a one-run deficit, following a home run by Junior Felix. Reardon, bypassed in favor of Gray to start the inning, was the eventual winning pitcher in that game, thanks to pinch hitter Jeff Stone's only hit of the season. . . . Dick Radatz had 24 "unofficial" saves in 1962; the official record for saves by a Red Sox rookie (that is, since 1969) is 10 by Wes Gardner in 1987. . . . Gray was the only American League rookie who faced more batters in Late-Inning Pressure Situations than in "unpressured" situations. . . . Has pitched 296 minor league games and 46 in the majors, all in relief. He's played in the minor league systems of the Reds, Phillies, and Red Sox, and was the "unknown" who accompanied John Denny from the Phillies to the Reds in exchange for Gary Redus and Tom Hume.

Mark Gubicza

Throws Right

Kansas City Royals	W-L	ERA	AB	H	HR	BB	SO	BA	SA	OBA
Season	4-7	4.50	357	101	5	38	71	.283	.389	.355
vs. Left-Handers			158	42	3	24	30	.266	.367	.371
vs. Right-Handers			199	59	2	14	41	.296	.407	.341
vs. Ground-Ballers			144	37	1	15	21	.257	.333	.333
vs. Fly-Ballers			213	64	4	23	50	.300	.427	.369
Home Games	3-2	5.45	152	45	3	16	28	.296	.421	.363
Road Games	1-5	3.86	205	56	2	22	43	.273	.366	.349
Grass Fields	1-3	3.40	165	44	2	16	34	.267	.364	.337
Artificial Turf	3-4	5.51	192	57	3	22	37	.297	.411	.370
April	1-3	6.38	72	22	0	13	17	.306	.389	.414
May	1-2	4.76	149	43	4	16	24	.289	.416	.363
June	2-2	3.25	136	36	1	9	30	.265	.360	.311
July	0-0	—	0	0	0	0	0	—	—	—
August	0-0	—	0	0	0	0	0	—	—	—
Sept./Oct.	0-0	—	0	0	0	0	0	—	—	—
Leading Off Inn.			87	30	1	8	15	.345	.506	.412
Bases Empty			183	55	2	19	42	.301	.410	.373
Runners On			174	46	3	19	29	.264	.368	.337
Runners/Scor. Pos.			105	23	3	15	21	.219	.352	.306
Runners On/2 Out			69	23	2	9	9	.333	.449	.418
Scor. Pos./2 Out			48	13	2	8	7	.271	.417	.375
Late-Inning Pressure			14	4	0	2	3	.286	.357	.375
Leading Off			4	1	0	1	1	.250	.250	.400
Runners On			4	2	0	1	0	.500	.750	.600
Runners/Scor. Pos.			2	1	0	1	0	.500	.500	.667
First 9 Batters			120	38	1	16	25	.317	.400	.407
Second 9 Batters			117	32	0	9	18	.274	.325	.323
All Batters Thereafter			120	31	4	13	28	.258	.442	.331

Loves to face: Al Newman (.056, 1-for-18)
Geno Petralli (.053, 1-for-19, 2 BB)
Dick Schofield (0-for-25, 1 BB)

Hates to face: Wade Boggs (.364, 20-for-55, 1 HR, 17 BB)
Don Mattingly (.379, 22-for-58, 3 HR)
Lloyd Moseby (.423, 11-for-26, 2 HR)

Miscellaneous statistics: Ground outs-to-air outs ratio: 1.88 last season, 4th-highest rate in A.L.; 1.66 for career. . . . Induced 12 double-play ground outs in 77 opportunities (one per 6.4). . . . Allowed 19 doubles, 2 triples in 94.0 innings. . . . Allowed 8 first-inning runs in 16 starts (4.50 ERA). . . . Batting support: 4.13 runs per start. . . . Opposing base stealers: 11-for-13 (85%); 1 pickoff, 1 balk.

Comments: Gubicza was among seven pitchers who threw at least 240 innings in every season from 1987 to 1989. Three of those seven—Gubicza, Bret Saberhagen, and Orel Hershiser— spent a total of 309 days on the disabled list with arm problems last season. Another, Roger Clemens, had arm problems severe enough to keep him from taking his regular turn in the rotation during a pennant race. The remaining three—Mark Langston, Frank Viola, and Dave Stewart—all topped 200 innings again in 1990. Now what about 1991? . . . Gubicza had the lowest average run support of any regular starter on the Royals last season. . . . Opponents batted 90 points lower with runners in scoring position (.219) than in other at-bats (.310) last season, the 3d-largest margin in the majors. . . . Has held opponents to a lower average with runners on base than he has with the bases empty in each of the last four seasons. . . . Has not allowed a first-inning home run in 30 starts dating back to July 23, 1989. . . . Year after year, Gubicza has been one of the toughest pitchers to homer against, thanks in large part to Royals Stadium. He has allowed an average of one home run every 92 at-bats at home, compared to one every 50 at-bats in road games. . . . Career record of 6–15 (.286) in April, 82–59 (.582) in other months combined. . . . Has a career record of 12–3 vs. the Mariners, including wins in each of his last seven decisions against them.

Lee Guetterman

Throws Left

New York Yankees	W-L	ERA	AB	H	HR	BB	SO	BA	SA	OBA
Season	11-7	3.39	339	80	6	26	48	.236	.342	.288
vs. Left-Handers			99	24	1	9	21	.242	.354	.306
vs. Right-Handers			240	56	5	17	27	.233	.338	.281
vs. Ground-Ballers			161	34	4	10	26	.211	.311	.256
vs. Fly-Ballers			178	46	2	16	22	.258	.371	.316
Home Games	9-4	2.64	205	44	2	15	31	.215	.298	.267
Road Games	2-3	4.63	134	36	4	11	17	.269	.410	.320
Grass Fields	10-5	2.94	288	64	3	22	42	.222	.306	.276
Artificial Turf	1-2	6.07	51	16	3	4	6	.314	.549	.357
April	1-1	4.15	45	11	1	2	13	.244	.400	.277
May	1-1	0.63	52	11	0	4	7	.212	.269	.263
June	3-0	1.88	87	16	1	7	10	.184	.287	.245
July	1-2	5.91	41	13	3	4	3	.317	.561	.370
August	3-0	2.60	60	13	0	3	9	.217	.217	.250
Sept./Oct.	2-3	7.24	54	16	1	6	6	.296	.426	.367
Leading Off Inn.			75	20	1	2	8	.267	.307	.286
Bases Empty			188	46	2	9	24	.245	.335	.279
Runners On			151	34	4	17	24	.225	.351	.298
Runners/Scor. Pos.			102	21	4	15	18	.206	.382	.300
Runners On/2 Out			73	16	0	9	9	.219	.274	.305
Scor. Pos./2 Out			54	13	0	8	7	.241	.315	.339
Late-Inning Pressure			193	43	4	17	21	.223	.326	.286
Leading Off			45	10	0	2	3	.222	.222	.255
Runners On			81	20	3	9	12	.247	.407	.322
Runners/Scor. Pos.			52	9	3	8	9	.173	.404	.283
First 9 Batters			296	71	6	24	44	.240	.348	.294
Second 9 Batters			41	9	0	2	3	.220	.317	.256
All Batters Thereafter			2	0	0	0	1	.000	.000	.000

Loves to face: Mike Felder (.091, 1-for-11, 10 ground outs)
Wally Joyner (.188, 3-for-16)
Gary Pettis (0-for-9)

Hates to face: Jose Canseco (.714, 5-for-7, 1 HR)
Ozzie Guillen (.571, 8-for-14)
Lou Whitaker (.545, 6-for-11, 1 HR)

Miscellaneous statistics: Ground outs-to-air outs ratio: 2.03 last season, 1.69 for career. . . . Induced 11 double-play ground outs in 71 opportunities (one per 6.5). . . . Allowed 8 doubles, 5 triples in 93.0 innings. . . . Stranded 47 inherited runners, allowed 18 to score (72%). . . . Opposing base stealers: 8-for-10 (80%); 1 pickoff, 1 balk.

Comments: Guetterman is the first relief pitcher ever to lead the Yankees in wins. The Yankees have had different leaders in each of the last seven years: Phil Niekro in 1984, followed by Ron Guidry, Dennis Rasmussen, Rick Rhoden, John Candelaria, Andy Hawkins, and Guetterman. . . . He's been groomed for Dave Righetti's closer role over the last two seasons. From 1984 through 1988, he faced a total of 65 batters in Late-Inning Pressure Situations; that increased to 141 (of 412) in 1989, and jumped to 216 (of 376) last season. . . . Opponents had a career batting average of .291 through the 1989 season, 55 points higher than they batted in 1990. . . . Has allowed only four home runs in over 400 career at-bats by left-handed batters. The only home run he allowed to a lefty last season was hit by John Olerud on June 22. He joins Mike Greenwell (1989), Wade Boggs (1986), and Lou Whitaker (1986). . . . Opponents have a career batting average of .318 (with an average of one home run every 31 at-bats) leading off innings, .268 (one HR per 58 AB) in other at-bats. . . . Career record of 19–9 in home games, 9–13 on the road. . . . We warned you in the Cardinals essay about how low we'd stoop, and here it comes: Guetterman's strikeout average of 4.65 per nine innings, while a career high, ranked 11th among the 13 pitchers 6′6″ or taller (minimum: 50 IP). Strikeout averages by height for last season: 5′10″ or under, 6.30; 5′11″, 5.64; 6′, 5.25; 6′1″, 6.08; 6′2″, 5.67; 6′3″, 5.55; 6′4″, 5.70; 6′5″, 6.02; 6′6″ or over, 6.15.

Mark Guthrie

Throws Left

Minnesota Twins	W-L	ERA	AB	H	HR	BB	SO	BA	SA	OBA
Season	7-9	3.79	557	154	8	39	101	.276	.370	.325
vs. Left-Handers			99	34	1	3	13	.343	.414	.363
vs. Right-Handers			458	120	7	36	88	.262	.360	.317
vs. Ground-Ballers			280	79	5	13	45	.282	.382	.316
vs. Fly-Ballers			277	75	3	26	56	.271	.357	.333
Home Games	2-4	3.93	258	70	5	16	55	.271	.391	.314
Road Games	5-5	3.67	299	84	3	23	46	.281	.351	.334
Grass Fields	5-3	2.72	228	60	0	11	35	.263	.307	.300
Artificial Turf	2-6	4.55	329	94	8	28	66	.286	.413	.342
April	0-0	2.57	29	9	1	3	5	.310	.517	.375
May	2-0	4.50	60	15	0	5	12	.250	.300	.308
June	0-2	8.49	52	19	4	9	8	.365	.596	.459
July	1-1	2.42	83	20	1	4	17	.241	.325	.276
August	2-4	4.25	165	47	2	11	28	.285	.376	.333
Sept./Oct.	2-2	2.78	168	44	0	7	31	.262	.315	.291
Leading Off Inn.			143	34	1	8	35	.238	.308	.278
Bases Empty			331	89	3	26	62	.269	.350	.322
Runners On			226	65	5	13	39	.288	.398	.329
Runners/Scor. Pos.			125	37	1	8	26	.296	.360	.343
Runners On/2 Out			86	17	1	9	14	.198	.291	.281
Scor. Pos./2 Out			47	10	0	7	10	.213	.234	.327
Late-Inning Pressure			44	15	1	4	10	.341	.545	.396
Leading Off			12	1	0	0	5	.083	.083	.083
Runners On			16	7	0	2	4	.438	.688	.500
Runners/Scor. Pos.			8	4	0	2	3	.500	.750	.600
First 9 Batters			200	61	4	12	42	.305	.420	.344
Second 9 Batters			179	38	1	15	26	.212	.274	.277
All Batters Thereafter			178	55	3	12	33	.309	.410	.353

Loves to face: Henry Cotto (.091, 1-for-11)
Manny Lee (.100, 1-for-10)
Sammy Sosa (.214, 3-for-14)

Hates to face: Glenallen Hill (.500, 5-for-10, 1 HR, 3 SO)
Danny Tartabull (.667, 4-for-6, 2 HR)
Dave Valle (.500, 5-for-10, 1 HR)

Miscellaneous statistics: Ground outs-to-air outs ratio: 1.27 last season, 1.24 for career.... Induced 12 double-play ground outs in 100 opportunities (one per 8.3).... Allowed 28 doubles, 0 triples in 144.2 innings.... Allowed 6 first-inning runs in 21 starts (2.57 ERA).... Batting support: 4.19 runs per start.... Opposing base stealers: 17-for-29 (59%); 13 pickoffs, 0 balks.

Comments: Minnesota's 1990 rotation had an average age of 25.9 years, making it the Twins' youngest since 1982 (Brad Havens, Al Williams, Roberto Castillo, Frank Viola, Jack O'Connor, and Pete Redfern).... Led all major league pitchers with 13 pickoffs.... His average of 6.42 innings pitched per start was the highest on the Twins' staff last season.... The only home run he allowed to a left-handed batter was hit by Lou Whitaker on April 24.... Opponents have a career average of .370 in Late-Inning Pressure Situations, .274 in other at-bats.... Left-handed batters have a career average of .329 vs. Guthrie. No left-handed pitcher over the last 16 years has allowed a higher mark to left-handers (minimum: 150 BFPs).... Here's some trivia: Guthrie has never allowed a home run in a stadium with a grass field. Opponents are homerless in 280 at-bats at those stadiums, but have averaged one home run every 34 at-bats on fields with artificial surfaces.... A further complexity: Guthrie apparently keeps the ball down at the Metrodome to a greater degree than elsewhere. Ground outs-to-air outs ratios: 1.60 at home, 0.67 at other carpeted fields, 1.03 on grass fields.... If you have an explanation for the last two notes that doesn't use the words *random* or *coincidence*, don't send it to us; use it to start a chain letter.

Erik Hanson

Throws Right

Seattle Mariners	W-L	ERA	AB	H	HR	BB	SO	BA	SA	OBA
Season	18-9	3.24	883	205	15	68	211	.232	.332	.287
vs. Left-Handers			465	103	5	41	114	.222	.308	.283
vs. Right-Handers			418	102	10	27	97	.244	.359	.291
vs. Ground-Ballers			414	94	3	24	92	.227	.287	.270
vs. Fly-Ballers			469	111	12	44	119	.237	.371	.301
Home Games	7-6	3.56	421	103	8	32	94	.245	.359	.296
Road Games	11-3	2.96	462	102	7	36	117	.221	.307	.278
Grass Fields	9-2	2.82	370	76	6	33	99	.205	.289	.272
Artificial Turf	9-7	3.56	513	129	9	35	112	.251	.363	.298
April	2-0	3.13	89	22	0	9	25	.247	.315	.313
May	3-3	3.92	159	43	2	12	35	.270	.371	.322
June	3-3	5.05	157	41	7	15	38	.261	.439	.326
July	3-2	3.28	124	25	2	15	30	.202	.306	.282
August	1-1	2.28	172	37	1	9	40	.215	.256	.255
Sept./Oct.	6-0	2.16	182	37	3	8	43	.203	.302	.241
Leading Off Inn.			228	41	3	19	62	.180	.268	.243
Bases Empty			556	123	9	37	138	.221	.311	.271
Runners On			327	82	6	31	73	.251	.367	.312
Runners/Scor. Pos.			181	39	2	19	45	.215	.326	.285
Runners On/2 Out			134	25	1	10	38	.187	.224	.248
Scor. Pos./2 Out			84	14	1	8	23	.167	.214	.247
Late-Inning Pressure			105	20	1	3	32	.190	.267	.218
Leading Off			33	3	0	1	14	.091	.121	.118
Runners On			23	4	1	2	7	.174	.304	.259
Runners/Scor. Pos.			6	1	0	2	1	.167	.167	.400
First 9 Batters			273	52	3	20	61	.190	.264	.244
Second 9 Batters			269	67	6	27	63	.249	.368	.320
All Batters Thereafter			341	86	6	21	87	.252	.358	.294

Loves to face: Jerry Browne (.118, 2-for-17, 1 3B)
Rob Deer (0-for-16, 9 SO)
Ozzie Guillen (.071, 1-for-14)

Hates to face: Ellis Burks (.714, 10-for-14, 2 HR)
Paul Molitor (.474, 9-for-19, 1 HR)
Kevin Seitzer (.545, 6-for-11)

Miscellaneous statistics: Ground outs-to-air outs ratio: 1.19 last season, 1.24 for career.... Induced 17 double-play ground outs in 158 opportunities (one per 9.3).... Allowed 35 doubles, 4 triples in 236.0 innings.... Allowed 4 first-inning runs in 33 starts (1.09 ERA, lowest in A.L.)... Batting support: 4.09 runs per start.... Opposing base stealers: 18-for-26 (69%); 1 pickoff, 1 balk.

Comments: Has had records at least four games above .500 in both his rookie and sophomore seasons. See the John Farrell comment (p. 274).... Hanson's .630 winning percentage (29–17) is the highest in team history (minimum: 40 decisions). Others above the .500 mark: Scott Bankhead (.545, 30–25), Mark Langston (.525, 74–67), and Randy Johnson (.512, 21–20).... Opponents' batting average of .159 during the first inning was the lowest in the majors last season (minimum: 20 GS).... His total of 30 putouts was 2d highest among American League pitchers, behind Jack Morris (38).... Opponents' career average on artificial turf (.253) is 46 points higher than on grass fields (.207), the 3d-largest margin in the majors over the last five seasons.... Opponents' career batting average of .192 in Late-Inning Pressure Situations is 2d best among active starting pitchers (minimum: 150 BFP), behind Jim Deshaies (.192).... Mariners pitchers have had six seasons of 200 or more strikeouts in the franchise's 14-year history: Langston has done it four times, Hanson and Bankhead once apiece. That's twice as many 200-K seasons as the Brewers/Browns/Orioles have managed in their 89 years.

Pete Harnisch

Throws Right

Baltimore Orioles	W-L	ERA	AB	H	HR	BB	SO	BA	SA	OBA
Season	11-11	4.34	723	189	17	86	122	.261	.394	.339
vs. Left-Handers			435	125	10	49	59	.287	.439	.358
vs. Right-Handers			288	64	7	37	63	.222	.326	.310
vs. Ground-Ballers			348	95	5	39	56	.273	.394	.346
vs. Fly-Ballers			375	94	12	47	66	.251	.395	.332
Home Games	7-6	4.63	345	85	10	33	67	.246	.383	.311
Road Games	4-5	4.08	378	104	7	53	55	.275	.405	.363
Grass Fields	10-9	3.93	563	139	13	66	105	.247	.375	.325
Artificial Turf	1-2	5.90	160	50	4	20	17	.313	.463	.385
April	2-0	4.43	89	23	3	10	12	.258	.438	.333
May	3-2	3.57	150	37	1	16	20	.247	.347	.320
June	2-2	3.86	114	27	2	15	26	.237	.333	.326
July	2-1	5.45	141	39	5	13	26	.277	.447	.333
August	1-4	3.82	124	35	5	24	25	.282	.452	.396
Sept./Oct.	1-2	5.13	105	28	1	8	13	.267	.352	.319
Leading Off Inn.			180	41	4	23	31	.228	.339	.319
Bases Empty			417	101	8	52	72	.242	.360	.328
Runners On			306	88	9	34	50	.288	.441	.354
Runners/Scor. Pos.			164	42	5	25	26	.256	.415	.345
Runners On/2 Out			125	32	2	15	23	.256	.376	.336
Scor. Pos./2 Out			77	17	1	13	15	.221	.325	.333
Late-Inning Pressure			42	11	2	9	6	.262	.500	.392
Leading Off			15	3	0	1	3	.200	.200	.250
Runners On			14	5	1	2	3	.357	.714	.438
Runners/Scor. Pos.			8	2	1	2	2	.250	.875	.400
First 9 Batters			247	64	3	28	47	.259	.364	.331
Second 9 Batters			230	60	6	30	42	.261	.409	.346
All Batters Thereafter			246	65	8	28	33	.264	.411	.339

Loves to face: Jeffrey Leonard (.083, 1-for-12)
Fred McGriff (.111, 1-for-9)
Ruben Sierra (.067, 1-for-15)

Hates to face: Tony Fernandez (.400, 4-for-10, 2 2B)
Mike Heath (.571, 4-for-7)
Kent Hrbek (.556, 5-for-9, 2 2B, 2 HR)

Miscellaneous statistics: Ground outs-to-air outs ratio: 0.79 last season, 0.75 for career.... Induced 11 double-play ground outs in 156 opportunities (one per 14.2).... Allowed 33 doubles, 6 triples in 188.2 innings.... Allowed 13 first-inning runs in 31 starts (3.19 ERA).... Batting support: 4.81 runs per start.... Opposing base stealers: 18-for-28 (64%); 2 pickoffs, 2 balks.

Comments: Averaged 5.57 walks per nine innings in 1989, but improved that figure to 4.10 last season.... Opponents' stolen-base rate also declined from 1989, when all 14 runners who tried to steal against him were successful.... Had the highest batting support of any of the Orioles' regular starters.... Opponents batted 66 points higher on artificial turf (.313) than on grass fields (.247) last season, the 3d-largest margin in the majors. (Psst! Don't tell Art Howe.)... Hasn't allowed a first-inning home run in 45 starts since Robin Yount homered against him on July 7, 1989.... Opposing batters have hit .187 with two outs and runners in scoring position over the last three years.... Has faced 28 batters with the bases loaded without walking in a run. But he has allowed two grand-slam home runs.... He'll miss Memorial Stadium. He had a career record of 10–7 there, compared to a 6–15 mark in road games.... Here's the inverse of the surprising chart on page 72: Over the past 20 years, 11 pitchers made at least 10 starts for the Astros after finishing the previous season with other teams. Seven had better ERAs for Houston than for their old clubs, but only two won more games for the Astros (Mike Scott in 1983, Mark Portugal in 1989). Average records before and after: 11–11, 4.02 for the old teams; 8–8, 3.50 for Houston.... Was born the day after the Orioles clinched the 1966 American League pennant.

Greg A. Harris

Throws Right

Boston Red Sox	W-L	ERA	AB	H	HR	BB	SO	BA	SA	OBA
Season	13-9	4.00	703	186	13	77	117	.265	.381	.338
vs. Left-Handers			352	84	5	37	52	.239	.338	.312
vs. Right-Handers			351	102	8	40	65	.291	.425	.364
vs. Ground-Ballers			309	72	3	34	53	.233	.298	.313
vs. Fly-Ballers			394	114	10	43	64	.289	.447	.358
Home Games	8-5	4.45	342	91	9	37	66	.266	.401	.335
Road Games	5-4	3.59	361	95	4	40	51	.263	.363	.341
Grass Fields	11-9	4.25	635	169	13	68	103	.266	.387	.338
Artificial Turf	2-0	1.86	68	17	0	9	14	.250	.324	.346
April	2-0	0.90	34	7	0	5	6	.206	.324	.333
May	2-3	4.24	134	38	2	11	19	.284	.388	.338
June	3-0	2.63	138	28	1	10	23	.203	.290	.253
July	1-1	3.03	124	35	0	16	15	.282	.347	.362
August	4-1	3.43	155	34	5	19	33	.219	.368	.313
Sept./Oct.	1-4	8.68	118	44	5	16	21	.373	.551	.442
Leading Off Inn.			179	46	6	15	19	.257	.408	.318
Bases Empty			417	106	10	38	69	.254	.396	.319
Runners On			286	80	3	39	48	.280	.360	.364
Runners/Scor. Pos.			164	41	1	27	32	.250	.305	.353
Runners On/2 Out			117	25	1	20	20	.214	.291	.333
Scor. Pos./2 Out			78	13	0	17	15	.167	.218	.323
Late-Inning Pressure			49	11	0	5	8	.224	.327	.304
Leading Off			14	3	0	0	0	.214	.214	.267
Runners On			14	2	0	4	1	.143	.143	.316
Runners/Scor. Pos.			9	1	0	2	0	.111	.111	.250
First 9 Batters			254	67	6	28	54	.264	.409	.338
Second 9 Batters			237	52	2	21	35	.219	.278	.280
All Batters Thereafter			212	67	5	28	28	.316	.462	.401

Loves to face: Jose Canseco (0-for-13, 9 SO)
Darnell Coles (0-for-10)
Mookie Wilson (.063, 1-for-16)

Hates to face: Gary Gaetti (.625, 10-for-16, 1 HR, 6 SO)
Kirk Gibson (.444, 4-for-9, 1 HR, 6 BB)
Pat Tabler (.500, 9-for-18, 1 HR)

Miscellaneous statistics: Ground outs-to-air outs ratio: 1.52 last season, 1.33 for career.... Induced 17 double-play ground outs in 150 opportunities (one per 8.8).... Allowed 37 doubles, 3 triples in 184.1 innings.... Allowed 11 first-inning runs in 30 starts (2.70 ERA).... Batting support: 4.47 runs per start.... Opposing base stealers: 15-for-22 (68%); 3 pickoffs, 1 balk.

Comments: Started 25 games for the Mets and the Reds over his first two seasons in the majors, but only 20 more compared to 313 relief appearances from 1983 through 1989.... Started 30 games for the Sox last season despite opening the season in the bullpen. Career breakdown: 22–26 (4.51 ERA) as a starter, 26–28 (2.95 ERA) in relief. He has completed only two of 75 career starts, and both were less than nine innings: a rain-shortened seven-inning win in 1982 and an eight-inning complete-game loss last July. He has never pitched a complete-game shutout.... Last season, Harris averaged only 5.98 innings per start, and he reached the ninth inning just once.... Opponents batted 69 points higher in night games (.281) than in day games (.212) last season, the 3d-largest margin in the majors. He had a record of 6–0 in day games last season, after a previous career record of 6–14 under the sun.... His average of 3.1 fielding chances per nine innings was the highest among American League pitchers (minimum: 100 IP).... Opponents have a career batting average of .219 in Late-Inning Pressure Situations, .249 in other at-bats.... Has pitched for seven different major league clubs while accumulating fewer than 1000 innings pitched. The unofficial champ at that sort of thing is Jack Spring, who appeared with seven clubs while pitching a total of less than 200 innings during a major league career that lasted from 1955 through 1965.

Bryan Harvey

Throws Right

California Angels	W-L	ERA	AB	H	HR	BB	SO	BA	SA	OBA
Season	4-4	3.22	224	45	4	35	82	.201	.295	.304
vs. Left-Handers			106	22	1	21	42	.208	.292	.331
vs. Right-Handers			118	23	3	14	40	.195	.297	.278
vs. Ground-Ballers			110	27	0	12	40	.245	.309	.312
vs. Fly-Ballers			114	18	4	23	42	.158	.281	.297
Home Games	3-1	4.00	132	33	2	19	43	.250	.348	.342
Road Games	1-3	2.22	92	12	2	16	39	.130	.217	.252
Grass Fields	4-4	3.43	203	41	4	32	75	.202	.300	.308
Artificial Turf	0-0	1.35	21	4	0	3	7	.190	.238	.269
April	1-1	6.48	33	12	1	9	10	.364	.485	.488
May	1-0	2.20	54	9	0	3	14	.167	.222	.203
June	0-1	1.04	29	4	0	6	13	.138	.138	.286
July	1-0	1.35	25	6	0	5	12	.240	.360	.355
August	0-0	0.68	44	4	1	4	18	.091	.159	.167
Sept./Oct.	1-2	8.18	39	10	2	8	15	.256	.462	.383
Leading Off Inn.			43	6	0	8	19	.140	.140	.275
Bases Empty			115	22	2	12	46	.191	.252	.268
Runners On			109	23	2	23	36	.211	.339	.338
Runners/Scor. Pos.			60	13	1	18	19	.217	.367	.378
Runners On/2 Out			48	9	1	10	16	.188	.292	.328
Scor. Pos./2 Out			33	6	0	9	11	.182	.212	.357
Late-Inning Pressure			138	24	4	26	60	.174	.283	.298
Leading Off			26	3	0	6	14	.115	.115	.281
Runners On			72	13	2	16	28	.181	.306	.315
Runners/Scor. Pos.			38	7	1	12	13	.184	.316	.352
First 9 Batters			222	45	4	35	82	.203	.297	.307
Second 9 Batters			2	0	0	0	0	.000	.000	.000
All Batters Thereafter			0	0	0	0	0	—	—	—

Loves to face: Mike Greenwell (0-for-6)
Pete O'Brien (.100, 1-for-10, 1 HR, 5 SO)
Cal Ripken (0-for-6)

Hates to face: Jesse Barfield (.429, 3-for-7, 2 HR, 3 SO)
Nelson Liriano (.375, 3-for-8, 1 HR, 3 SO)
Paul Molitor (4-for-4, 1 BB)

Miscellaneous statistics: Ground outs-to-air outs ratio: 0.83 last season, 0.66 for career. . . . Induced 4 double-play ground outs in 65 opportunities (one per 16.3). . . . Allowed 7 doubles, 1 triple in 64.1 innings. . . . Stranded 22 inherited runners, allowed 6 to score (79%). . . . Opposing base stealers: 3-for-5 (60%); 2 pickoffs, 1 balk.

Comments: Believe it or not, Harvey is already the Angels' all-time leader in saves with 67, two more than Dave LaRoche. . . . He saved 17 games as a rookie in 1988, and 25 in each of the last two seasons. The only other pitchers with at least 17 saves in three consecutive seasons starting with their rookie years: Dick Radatz, Roger McDowell, and Todd Worrell. . . . The only home run he allowed to a left-handed batter last season was hit by Ken Griffey, Jr. on September 16. . . . Opponents' career batting average of .191 in Late-Inning Pressure Situations is 3d lowest in the history of *The Player Analysis* (minimum: 500 BFP), behind Randy Myers (.183) and Gregg Olson (.189). . . . In the grand-daddy of *Player Analysis* categories, two outs and runners in scoring position in Late-Inning Pressure Situations, Harvey has no equal. Opponents batted .182 in that situation last season, *raising* Harvey's career average to .082. In 1989, he held batters hitless in 27 such at-bats; they were 2-for-24 in 1988. . . . Allowed only one hit in 14 at-bats with the bases loaded last season, to lower his opponents' career average to .116 with the bags full. . . . Career ERA of 0.79 during August, 6.23 during September. . . . All-time career leaders in strikeouts per nine innings among pitchers with 200 innings: Rob Dibble, 11.80; Tom Henke, 10.38; Harvey, 10.33.

Andy Hawkins

Throws Right

New York Yankees	W-L	ERA	AB	H	HR	BB	SO	BA	SA	OBA
Season	5-12	5.37	599	156	20	82	74	.260	.421	.349
vs. Left-Handers			313	92	8	55	31	.294	.431	.398
vs. Right-Handers			286	64	12	27	43	.224	.409	.291
vs. Ground-Ballers			301	81	8	41	37	.269	.409	.354
vs. Fly-Ballers			298	75	12	41	37	.252	.433	.343
Home Games	2-8	5.44	341	87	12	49	41	.255	.402	.349
Road Games	3-4	5.27	258	69	8	33	33	.267	.446	.348
Grass Fields	5-11	5.03	524	128	18	70	68	.244	.397	.333
Artificial Turf	0-1	8.00	75	28	2	12	6	.373	.587	.456
April	0-2	7.88	67	21	1	10	8	.313	.448	.403
May	1-2	7.30	105	34	3	12	9	.324	.514	.398
June	0-0	4.94	101	27	7	15	17	.267	.505	.359
July	1-4	4.40	152	29	5	18	22	.191	.322	.277
August	3-2	3.18	141	34	1	20	14	.241	.319	.331
Sept./Oct.	0-2	12.86	33	11	3	7	4	.333	.697	.450
Leading Off Inn.			151	39	5	18	21	.258	.417	.337
Bases Empty			348	86	10	44	42	.247	.399	.333
Runners On			251	70	10	38	32	.279	.450	.369
Runners/Scor. Pos.			119	41	6	28	17	.345	.571	.458
Runners On/2 Out			99	32	4	13	12	.323	.515	.402
Scor. Pos./2 Out			56	19	2	9	10	.339	.554	.431
Late-Inning Pressure			65	8	1	11	8	.123	.169	.260
Leading Off			20	1	0	2	3	.050	.050	.136
Runners On			17	2	1	5	2	.118	.294	.318
Runners/Scor. Pos.			7	1	0	4	1	.143	.143	.455
First 9 Batters			216	60	9	26	31	.278	.468	.355
Second 9 Batters			188	47	8	25	25	.250	.431	.336
All Batters Thereafter			195	49	3	31	18	.251	.359	.354

Loves to face: Dan Gladden (.105, 2-for-19)
Kelly Gruber (.130, 3-for-23)
Mookie Wilson (.071, 2-for-28, 3 BB)

Hates to face: Darnell Coles (.583, 7-for-12, 1 HR)
Ron Hassey (.667, 8-for-12)
Lloyd Moseby (.417, 5-for-12, 2 HR)

Miscellaneous statistics: Ground outs-to-air outs ratio: 0.73 last season, 0.93 for career. . . . Induced 17 double-play ground outs in 143 opportunities (one per 8.4). . . . Allowed 30 doubles, 3 triples in 157.2 innings. . . . Allowed 14 first-inning runs in 26 starts (5.11 ERA). . . . Batting support: 3.77 runs per start. . . . Opposing base stealers: 11-for-19 (58%); 2 pickoffs, 1 balk.

Comments: Only one Yankees pitcher in the last 70 years had a lower winning percentage than Hawkins did last season (.294): Jim Bouton, who was 4–15 in 1965 (.211). . . . During his Yankees tenure, Hawkins has played under three managers: 13–11, 4.49 ERA under Dallas Green; 3–8, 7.23 ERA under Bucky Dent; 4–8, 4.24 ERA under Stump Merrill. . . . The American League's top 10 batters hit .429 (21-for-49) against Hawkins. . . . Opponents batted 105 points higher with runners in scoring position (.345) than in other at-bats (.240) last season, the largest margin in the majors. . . . Reduced the rate of extra-base hits by opposing left-handers by 41 percent from 1989 (one XBH per 7.6 AB) to 1990 (one per 13.0 AB). . . . It's time to play *Jeopardy!* We'll take "Humiliation" for one hundred, please. The answer is: One inning, 13 hits, six walks, 18 earned runs. The question: What are Hawkins's cumulative statistics in three career starts at Fenway Park? . . . OK, no more Hawkins jokes—the Yankees simply haven't found his niche. Hawkins happens to be one of the best postseason pitchers in baseball history. Opponents have only four hits in 45 at-bats for an .089 batting average—the 3d lowest ever, behind Bill James's .065 mark (he pitched, too?) and Bill Bevens's .083 (minimum: 10 IP). . . . Hawkins is also one of two pitchers in postseason history to have stranded eight inherited runners without allowing any to score. The other: Ramon Hernandez.

Tom Henke

Throws Right

Toronto Blue Jays	W-L	ERA	AB	H	HR	BB	SO	BA	SA	OBA
Season	2-4	2.17	272	58	8	19	75	.213	.342	.266
vs. Left-Handers			138	29	4	11	42	.210	.355	.267
vs. Right-Handers			134	29	4	8	33	.216	.328	.266
vs. Ground-Ballers			113	24	4	11	32	.212	.381	.280
vs. Fly-Ballers			159	34	4	8	43	.214	.314	.256
Home Games	2-0	2.39	143	31	6	11	40	.217	.392	.273
Road Games	0-4	1.95	129	27	2	8	35	.209	.287	.259
Grass Fields	0-4	2.32	110	24	2	8	29	.218	.309	.275
Artificial Turf	2-0	2.06	162	34	6	11	46	.210	.364	.260
April	0-0	2.89	40	11	2	2	8	.275	.475	.310
May	0-1	1.76	51	9	2	3	19	.176	.314	.236
June	0-0	0.73	40	4	0	1	13	.100	.125	.122
July	0-1	3.38	51	12	1	6	12	.235	.392	.316
August	1-0	0.75	46	12	1	1	12	.261	.370	.277
Sept./Oct.	1-2	3.65	44	10	2	6	11	.227	.364	.314
Leading Off Inn.			62	17	1	4	13	.274	.371	.318
Bases Empty			148	36	4	11	36	.243	.385	.296
Runners On			124	22	4	8	39	.177	.290	.231
Runners/Scor. Pos.			77	10	0	7	26	.130	.156	.209
Runners On/2 Out			57	12	3	4	17	.211	.386	.274
Scor. Pos./2 Out			40	5	0	3	13	.125	.150	.205
Late-Inning Pressure			182	43	6	16	54	.236	.385	.300
Leading Off			37	9	0	4	6	.243	.324	.317
Runners On			91	19	4	7	32	.209	.363	.270
Runners/Scor. Pos.			62	9	0	6	24	.145	.177	.229
First 9 Batters			267	56	8	18	75	.210	.337	.261
Second 9 Batters			5	2	0	1	0	.400	.600	.500
All Batters Thereafter			0	0	0	0	0	—	—	—

Loves to face: Dave Bergman (0-for-13)
Brian Downing (.056, 1-for-18)
Lou Whitaker (.042, 1-for-24)

Hates to face: Wally Joyner (.455, 5-for-11, 1 HR)
Don Mattingly (.389, 7-for-18, 2 HR)
Jody Reed (.667, 4-for-6)

Miscellaneous statistics: Ground outs-to-air outs ratio: 0.79 last season, 0.73 for career. . . . Induced 3 double-play ground outs in 52 opportunities (one per 17.3). . . . Allowed 9 doubles, 1 triple in 74.2 innings. . . . Stranded 26 inherited runners (including 19 of the first 20), allowed 6 to score (81%), 4th-highest rate in A.L. . . . Opposing base stealers: 5-for-5; 0 pickoffs, 0 balks.

Comments: Has a career rate of 10.38 strikeouts per nine innings, the highest in major league history among pitchers with 500 innings pitched. His average fell from 11.73 in 1989 to 9.08 in 1990. . . . Last season was the sixth in which Henke struck out at least one batter per inning. Only two pitchers have done that more often: Nolan Ryan (15) and Sandy Koufax (7). . . . Dave Smith saved 33 games while pitching only 56 innings in 1986—until 1988, that was the only 30-save season in fewer than 80 innings pitched. But over the last three years, 17 pitchers have done that, including Henke in 1990. Henke pitched more than one inning in nine of his first 11 saves, but in only four of his other 21 saves. . . . Henke blew four of his last 10 save opportunities, including two against the Red Sox during Toronto's late-season fold. (Maybe Jimy knew what he was doing after all.). . . Opponents' batting average with runners in scoring position was the lowest of his career, and the 4th-lowest single-season average in the last 16 years (minimum: 75 AB). The lowest mark was .118 against Tug McGraw in the Phillies' championship year of 1980. (But Henke's mark was not the lowest in the American League last season; Ben McDonald held opponents to a .127 average with RISP.). . . Career record of 18–7 in home games, 11–19 on the road.

Mike Henneman

Throws Right

Detroit Tigers	W-L	ERA	AB	H	HR	BB	SO	BA	SA	OBA
Season	8-6	3.05	356	90	4	33	50	.253	.334	.320
vs. Left-Handers			144	40	0	18	14	.278	.326	.364
vs. Right-Handers			212	50	4	15	36	.236	.340	.288
vs. Ground-Ballers			160	35	0	13	25	.219	.262	.282
vs. Fly-Ballers			196	55	4	20	25	.281	.393	.350
Home Games	5-3	3.72	180	43	3	12	26	.239	.333	.294
Road Games	3-3	2.35	176	47	1	21	24	.267	.335	.345
Grass Fields	7-5	3.17	315	83	4	28	44	.263	.352	.326
Artificial Turf	1-1	2.25	41	7	0	5	6	.171	.195	.277
April	0-1	1.46	45	13	0	4	4	.289	.311	.347
May	1-3	4.96	61	14	1	7	6	.230	.295	.319
June	3-0	1.02	68	13	0	7	13	.191	.250	.267
July	2-2	8.59	65	22	2	8	7	.338	.523	.411
August	1-0	1.50	62	16	1	4	8	.258	.339	.319
Sept./Oct.	1-0	1.17	55	12	0	3	12	.218	.273	.254
Leading Off Inn.			80	16	0	6	13	.200	.237	.264
Bases Empty			190	47	2	13	28	.247	.326	.306
Runners On			166	43	2	20	22	.259	.343	.335
Runners/Scor. Pos.			111	20	1	19	18	.180	.243	.295
Runners On/2 Out			72	12	0	10	10	.167	.208	.268
Scor. Pos./2 Out			50	5	0	9	9	.100	.140	.237
Late-Inning Pressure			203	50	3	23	32	.246	.325	.329
Leading Off			45	7	0	3	9	.156	.200	.224
Runners On			96	23	1	15	14	.240	.302	.342
Runners/Scor. Pos.			66	11	0	14	12	.167	.197	.313
First 9 Batters			340	86	4	32	48	.253	.338	.321
Second 9 Batters			16	4	0	1	2	.250	.250	.294
All Batters Thereafter			0	0	0	0	0	—	—	—

Loves to face: Steve Buechele (0-for-11)
Pete Incaviglia (.077, 1-for-13)
Bo Jackson (0-for-9, 3 SO)

Hates to face: Steve Balboni (.444, 4-for-9, 1 HR)
Carlton Fisk (.556, 5-for-9, 3 SO)
Devon White (.500, 4-for-8)

Miscellaneous statistics: Ground outs-to-air outs ratio: 1.41 last season, 1.33 for career. . . . Induced 13 double-play ground outs in 74 opportunities (one per 5.7). . . . Allowed 15 doubles, 1 triple in 94.1 innings. . . . Stranded 28 inherited runners, allowed 7 to score (80%), shared 5th-best rate in A.L. . . . Opposing base stealers: 7-for-9 (78%); 0 pickoff, 0 balks.

Comments: After only four years, he has accumulated 39 wins as a relief pitcher, 4th most in Tigers history, behind John Hiller (72), Aurelio Lopez (51), and Hooks Dauss (40). The last pitcher to win more relief games over four seasons was Mark Clear (44, 1979–82). The all-time four-year high: 52 by Mike Marshall (1972–75). . . . Henneman has a career winning percentage of .672 (39–19), the 3d highest among active pitchers (minimum: 50 decisions), behind Dwight Gooden (.721) and Roger Clemens (.695). . . . Henneman's winning percentage ranks sixth in major league history among pitchers with at least 50 decisions in relief, behind Doc Crandall (.725), Hugh Casey (.718), Bobby Bolin (.691), Ernie Johnson (.686), and Guy Bush (.683). . . . Held the American League's top 10 hitters to a .176 batting average last season (3-for-17, no XBH), and didn't allow a home run in 30 at-bats by the league's top 10 home run hitters. . . . A home run by Dan Pasqua in 1989 was the only one Henneman has allowed to a left-handed batter over the last two seasons. . . . Opponents batted 106 points lower with runners in scoring position (.180) than in other at-bats (.286) last season, the largest margin in the majors. . . . Opponents' career average in day games is 61 points higher than in night games (.221), the largest margin in the majors over the last five seasons. . . . Has a career record of 27–6 in Tiger Stadium, 12–13 elsewhere. . . . Has a career record of 7–0 vs. the Mariners.

Greg Hibbard

Throws Left

Chicago White Sox	W-L	ERA	AB	H	HR	BB	SO	BA	SA	OBA
Season	14-9	3.16	792	202	11	55	92	.255	.355	.305
vs. Left-Handers			91	19	0	8	10	.209	.275	.270
vs. Right-Handers			701	183	11	47	82	.261	.365	.309
vs. Ground-Ballers			346	89	2	24	37	.257	.347	.307
vs. Fly-Ballers			446	113	9	31	55	.253	.361	.303
Home Games	8-5	2.98	444	104	6	33	51	.234	.329	.287
Road Games	6-4	3.39	348	98	5	22	41	.282	.388	.327
Grass Fields	12-7	2.89	701	174	10	46	76	.248	.345	.296
Artificial Turf	2-2	5.48	91	28	1	9	16	.308	.429	.370
April	2-1	2.89	69	17	1	4	10	.246	.319	.280
May	2-2	2.21	153	33	2	10	18	.216	.294	.271
June	2-1	2.90	120	29	2	11	16	.242	.317	.311
July	2-1	3.68	148	42	3	4	14	.284	.419	.299
August	3-3	3.68	159	46	2	13	15	.289	.384	.341
Sept./Oct.	3-1	3.38	143	35	1	13	19	.245	.371	.312
Leading Off Inn.			212	43	4	10	24	.203	.316	.242
Bases Empty			498	122	8	32	64	.245	.345	.295
Runners On			294	80	3	23	28	.272	.371	.321
Runners/Scor. Pos.			147	37	0	16	13	.252	.347	.318
Runners On/2 Out			131	34	2	10	12	.260	.374	.317
Scor. Pos./2 Out			74	17	0	8	5	.230	.311	.313
Late-Inning Pressure			78	19	1	5	11	.244	.333	.298
Leading Off			26	7	1	0	2	.269	.423	.269
Runners On			22	5	0	4	5	.227	.318	.370
Runners/Scor. Pos.			8	2	0	4	2	.250	.375	.538
First 9 Batters			270	63	2	19	39	.233	.296	.281
Second 9 Batters			270	78	3	15	27	.289	.404	.329
All Batters Thereafter			252	61	6	21	26	.242	.365	.304

Loves to face: Felix Fermin (.077, 1-for-13, 2 BB)
Don Mattingly (.143, 2-for-14)
Gary Pettis (.125, 2-for-16)

Hates to face: Steve Balboni (.357, 5-for-14, 2 2B, 2 HR)
Dave Henderson (.750, 3-for-4, 1 HR)
Pat Tabler (.714, 5-for-7)

Miscellaneous statistics: Ground outs-to-air outs ratio: 1.25 last season, 1.33 for career. . . . Induced 25 double-play ground outs in 141 opportunities (one per 5.6), 4th-highest rate in A.L. . . . Allowed 34 doubles, 6 triples in 211.0 innings. . . . Allowed 10 first-inning runs in 33 starts (2.45 ERA). . . . Batting support: 3.58 runs per start (4th lowest in A.L.). . . Opposing base stealers: 11-for-19 (58%); 3 pickoffs, 1 balk.

Comments: Has allowed only 16 home runs in $348\frac{1}{3}$ innings over the last two seasons. His average of one homer per 21.8 innings is 3d best during that time (minimum: 50 GS), behind Joe Magrane (one HR per 29.2 IP) and Mark Gubicza (one per 23.3). . . . Hibbard has been particularly gopher-stingy against left-handed batters (184 batters faced, no HR) and with runners in scoring position (322 BFP, no HR). . . . Opponents' on-base percentage of .242 leading off innings was 2d lowest in the American League last season (minimum: 150 BFP). Only Nolan Ryan had a better mark (.230). . . . Posted an ERA of 3.50 with Carlton Fisk catching, 2.59 with Ron Karkovice calling the signals. . . . Lost consecutive starts only once last season; ditto for consecutive wins. . . . Had the poorest average run support of any regular White Sox starter last season. . . . Opponents have a career batting average of .239 at Comiskey Park, .272 on other grass fields, .313 on artificial turf. . . . Opponents' batting average of .212 during the first inning was their lowest in any inning against Hibbard. They batted .262 against him after the first frame. . . . Hibbard has played errorless ball over the first two years of his major league career. Frank Tanana is the only other pitcher in the majors to handle at least 30 chances without an error in each of the last two seasons.

Ted Higuera

Throws Left

Milwaukee Brewers	W-L	ERA	AB	H	HR	BB	SO	BA	SA	OBA
Season	11-10	3.76	653	167	16	50	129	.256	.378	.310
vs. Left-Handers			126	30	1	7	23	.238	.286	.284
vs. Right-Handers			527	137	15	43	106	.260	.400	.316
vs. Ground-Ballers			303	78	5	20	59	.257	.373	.301
vs. Fly-Ballers			350	89	11	30	70	.254	.383	.318
Home Games	7-4	3.36	369	89	12	24	79	.241	.382	.289
Road Games	4-6	4.28	284	78	4	26	50	.275	.373	.337
Grass Fields	8-9	3.78	552	143	15	42	106	.259	.386	.312
Artificial Turf	3-1	3.67	101	24	1	8	23	.238	.337	.300
April	2-0	0.00	70	9	0	9	16	.129	.143	.228
May	2-1	3.46	104	28	2	6	18	.269	.375	.309
June	1-1	3.77	54	13	1	4	9	.241	.352	.305
July	1-3	5.40	117	34	3	6	26	.291	.427	.328
August	2-1	2.78	113	22	4	6	24	.195	.345	.233
Sept./Oct.	3-4	5.18	195	61	6	19	36	.313	.462	.373
Leading Off Inn.			161	40	4	14	35	.248	.391	.309
Bases Empty			379	90	10	31	81	.237	.364	.300
Runners On			274	77	6	19	48	.281	.398	.323
Runners/Scor. Pos.			139	40	1	12	28	.288	.353	.335
Runners On/2 Out			108	29	3	8	19	.269	.407	.319
Scor. Pos./2 Out			57	16	1	6	12	.281	.386	.349
Late-Inning Pressure			69	17	1	8	15	.246	.362	.321
Leading Off			17	5	0	2	1	.294	.471	.368
Runners On			33	8	0	3	10	.242	.303	.297
Runners/Scor. Pos.			19	2	0	2	6	.105	.158	.182
First 9 Batters			215	57	5	17	41	.265	.391	.325
Second 9 Batters			210	45	4	15	50	.214	.319	.265
All Batters Thereafter			228	65	7	18	38	.285	.421	.336

Loves to face: Joe Carter (.143, 5-for-35, 1 HR)
Jack Clark (.083, 1-for-12, 9 SO)
Ruben Sierra (.059, 1-for-17)

Hates to face: Alvaro Espinoza (.714, 10-for-14)
Kirby Puckett (.353, 12-for-34, 2 HR)
John Shelby (.563, 9-for-16)

Miscellaneous statistics: Ground outs-to-air outs ratio: 0.72 last season, 0.77 for career. . . . Induced 14 double-play ground outs in 142 opportunities (one per 10.1). . . . Allowed 30 doubles, 1 triple in 170.0 innings. . . . Allowed 11 first-inning runs in 27 starts (3.08 ERA). . . . Batting support: 4.33 runs per start. . . . Opposing base stealers: 15-for-19 (79%); 0 pickoffs, 1 balk.

Comments: Needs 11 wins to become the third pitcher to win 100 games for the Brewers franchise. The others: Jim Slaton (117) and Mike Caldwell (102). . . . His winning percentage has declined slightly in every season since his rookie year: .652, .645, .643, .640, .600, .524. His streak of five consecutive declines is one short of the major league record, coheld by six pitchers (the most recent: Frank Tanana, 1977–82). . . . Nevertheless, Higuera is the first pitcher since Ron Guidry to make at least 20 starts and compile winning records in each of six consecutive seasons starting with his rookie year. . . . He was 5–1 with a 1.78 ERA when placed on the disabled list in June. After he returned to the active roster, he was 6–9 with a 4.72 ERA. . . . Pitched the most innings of any left-hander in the majors who didn't pick off at least one base runner. . . . Opponents batted 76 points higher in night games (.283) than in day games (.207) last season, the 2d-largest margin in the majors. . . . Opponents have hit for a higher average in road games than in home games in each of the last five seasons. Opponents' career averages: .227 at County Stadium (52–22 won-lost record), .247 on the road (37–32). . . . Has held opponents to a lower average during his first two passes through the batting order than in subsequent at-bats in each of his six years in the majors. Opponents' career averages: .221 in his first pass through the order, .219 in his second pass, .263 in subsequent at-bats. . . . Opponents' overall batting average was the highest of his career. . . . Career record of 7–0 vs. the Royals.

Brian Holman

Throws Right

Seattle Mariners	W-L	ERA	AB	H	HR	BB	SO	BA	SA	OBA
Season	11-11	4.03	724	188	17	66	121	.260	.383	.324
vs. Left-Handers			379	106	10	38	49	.280	.417	.346
vs. Right-Handers			345	82	7	28	72	.238	.345	.299
vs. Ground-Ballers			347	89	3	28	51	.256	.340	.312
vs. Fly-Ballers			377	99	14	38	70	.263	.422	.334
Home Games	4-6	4.04	407	114	7	44	59	.280	.386	.349
Road Games	7-5	4.02	317	74	10	22	62	.233	.379	.290
Grass Fields	5-3	4.75	206	50	9	16	39	.243	.413	.301
Artificial Turf	6-8	3.74	518	138	8	50	82	.266	.371	.333
April	3-2	3.86	108	25	3	10	23	.231	.352	.292
May	3-1	4.04	138	38	2	14	20	.275	.384	.355
June	2-3	4.68	134	41	3	9	22	.306	.455	.349
July	2-1	3.12	157	37	5	13	20	.236	.363	.297
August	1-3	4.23	164	40	4	16	34	.244	.348	.311
Sept./Oct.	0-1	6.00	23	7	0	4	2	.304	.478	.407
Leading Off Inn.			185	49	3	17	30	.265	.357	.327
Bases Empty			439	104	12	32	77	.237	.353	.292
Runners On			285	84	5	34	44	.295	.428	.370
Runners/Scor. Pos.			159	44	3	16	25	.277	.396	.341
Runners On/2 Out			100	20	1	16	24	.200	.260	.328
Scor. Pos./2 Out			66	12	1	6	16	.182	.258	.270
Late-Inning Pressure			56	17	1	3	9	.304	.375	.339
Leading Off			17	5	1	1	3	.294	.471	.333
Runners On			17	7	0	1	3	.412	.471	.444
Runners/Scor. Pos.			5	2	0	1	2	.400	.400	.500
First 9 Batters			230	54	5	19	35	.235	.370	.294
Second 9 Batters			216	53	4	27	34	.245	.347	.336
All Batters Thereafter			278	81	8	20	52	.291	.421	.339

Loves to face: Greg Brock (0-for-9)
Steve Sax (.130, 3-for-23)
Danny Tartabull (.160, 4-for-25)

Hates to face: Bo Jackson (.375, 6-for-16, 2 HR)
Kurt Stillwell (.400, 10-for-25)
Mookie Wilson (.500, 8-for-16, 1 HR)

Miscellaneous statistics: Ground outs-to-air outs ratio: 1.28 last season, 1.17 for career. . . . Induced 15 double-play ground outs in 155 opportunities (one per 10.3). . . . Allowed 34 doubles, 2 triples in 189.2 innings. . . . Allowed 15 first-inning runs in 28 starts (4.18 ERA). . . . Batting support: 3.79 runs per start. . . . Opposing base stealers: 8-for-16 (50%); 2 pickoffs, 2 balks.

Comments: Ken Phelps's pinch-hit home run with two outs in the ninth on April 20 spoiled what would have been the first perfect game ever thrown against a defending world champion. It was the third time in as many years that a pitcher lost a perfect game with one out to go. (Ron Robinson lost one in 1988 to Wallace Johnson; Dave Stieb lost his in 1989 to Roberto Kelly.) But Holman was the first pitcher in major league history to lose a perfecto with two outs in the ninth inning to a home run. . . . Holman would have become the first pitcher to throw a perfect game in a season in which he did not have a winning record since Catfish Hunter, 13–13 in 1968. Only one pitcher in major league history had a losing record in a season in which he pitched a perfect game: Charles Robertson, who was 14–15 in 1922. . . . He was Seattle's opening-day pitcher in 1990. Of the 26 opening-day starters, only nine finished the year with a winning record. . . . Although opponents have batted within a four-point range in his three seasons in the majors (.264, .263, .260), his ERA has increased by nearly a half-run in each of the last two; year-by-year since 1988: 3.23, 3.67, 4.03. . . . Has faced 36 batters with the bases loaded, allowing neither a home run nor a walk. . . . Has a career record of 3–11 in August, 21–20 in other months.

Charlie Hough

Throws Right

Texas Rangers	W-L	ERA	AB	H	HR	BB	SO	BA	SA	OBA
Season	12-12	4.07	807	190	24	119	114	.235	.369	.338
vs. Left-Handers			346	84	7	56	47	.243	.350	.349
vs. Right-Handers			461	106	17	63	67	.230	.384	.329
vs. Ground-Ballers			401	100	13	52	50	.249	.394	.338
vs. Fly-Ballers			406	90	11	67	64	.222	.345	.337
Home Games	5-8	4.47	362	91	11	53	48	.251	.387	.350
Road Games	7-4	3.76	445	99	13	66	66	.222	.355	.327
Grass Fields	12-9	4.04	691	160	21	100	92	.232	.365	.333
Artificial Turf	0-3	4.31	116	30	3	19	22	.259	.397	.368
April	1-1	4.44	89	21	4	14	15	.236	.404	.346
May	4-2	3.20	160	34	3	23	19	.213	.319	.323
June	2-2	5.26	143	31	7	20	25	.217	.413	.313
July	0-2	3.95	105	30	3	15	13	.286	.400	.369
August	3-2	3.46	152	35	2	27	25	.230	.322	.343
Sept./Oct.	2-3	4.43	158	39	5	20	17	.247	.386	.344
Leading Off Inn.			204	56	10	23	24	.275	.451	.351
Bases Empty			465	113	18	62	66	.243	.404	.336
Runners On			342	77	6	57	48	.225	.322	.340
Runners/Scor. Pos.			199	47	4	38	33	.236	.342	.356
Runners On/2 Out			149	34	2	30	24	.228	.329	.368
Scor. Pos./2 Out			102	25	1	21	16	.245	.314	.389
Late-Inning Pressure			42	9	0	11	6	.214	.238	.370
Leading Off			12	2	0	3	2	.167	.167	.333
Runners On			15	3	0	6	0	.200	.267	.409
Runners/Scor. Pos.			6	1	0	3	0	.167	.167	.400
First 9 Batters			242	67	9	39	38	.277	.434	.383
Second 9 Batters			239	54	7	37	38	.226	.360	.333
All Batters Thereafter			326	69	8	43	38	.212	.328	.306

Loves to face: Kelly Gruber (.100, 2-for-20)
Jack Howell (.045, 1-for-22, 5 BB)
Harold Reynolds (.200, 10-for-50)

Hates to face: Joe Carter (.361, 13-for-36, 6 HR)
Mark Salas (.433, 13-for-30, 3 HR)
Lou Whitaker (.350, 21-for-60, 3 HR)

Miscellaneous statistics: Ground outs-to-air outs ratio: 1.07 last season, 1.04 for career. . . . Induced 20 double-play ground outs in 174 opportunities (one per 8.7). . . . Allowed 28 doubles, 4 triples in 218.2 innings. . . . Allowed 21 first-inning runs in 32 starts (5.63 ERA). . . . Batting support: 4.41 runs per start. . . . Opposing base stealers: 33-for-39 (85%); 6 pickoffs, 0 balks.

Comments: Made his major league debut on August 12, 1970. Let's put that in perspective: (1) He was pitching for the Dodgers in relief of Pete Mikkelsen; (2) his catcher was current White Sox manager Jeff Torborg; (3) new teammate Alex Fernandez was one day short of his first birthday. . . . Hough's first manager in professional baseball (at Ogden of the Pioneer League in 1966) was a 38-year-old second-year skipper named Tommy Lasorda. . . . During the 1980s Chicago had four pitchers over the age of 40: Steve Carlton, Tom Seaver, Ron Reed, and Jerry Koosman. But Hough will become the oldest Chisox hurler since Hoyt Wilhelm pitched for them in 1968 at the age of 45. . . . Opponents batted 59 points higher on his first pass through the batting order (.277) than in subsequent at-bats (.218) last season, the 5th-largest margin in the majors. . . . One of only five players in major league history to pitch at least 300 games for two different ballclubs. The others: Hoyt Wilhelm, Cy Young, Tug McGraw, and Willie Hernandez. . . . One of three pitchers to make at least 300 starts and 300 relief appearances. The others: Jack Quinn and Woodie Fryman. . . . With the defection of Phil Bradley to Japan, only three players remain active with career batting averages of .300 or better against each of the four most recent knuckleballers (Hough, Tom Candiotti, and the Niekros): Wade Boggs, Pete O'Brien, and Mookie Wilson.

Mike Jackson

Throws Right

Seattle Mariners	W-L	ERA	AB	H	HR	BB	SO	BA	SA	OBA
Season	5-7	4.54	279	64	8	44	69	.229	.348	.333
vs. Left-Handers			105	27	5	21	9	.257	.438	.375
vs. Right-Handers			174	37	3	23	60	.213	.293	.307
vs. Ground-Ballers			116	29	3	17	17	.250	.345	.336
vs. Fly-Ballers			163	35	5	27	52	.215	.350	.332
Home Games	3-4	4.95	141	31	3	24	31	.220	.326	.337
Road Games	2-3	4.10	138	33	5	20	38	.239	.370	.329
Grass Fields	2-3	4.08	107	27	4	18	30	.252	.364	.352
Artificial Turf	3-4	4.81	172	37	4	26	39	.215	.337	.322
April	1-1	3.09	42	10	3	1	12	.238	.476	.267
May	0-2	4.86	61	12	3	9	17	.197	.361	.296
June	2-0	1.35	46	6	0	4	13	.130	.174	.216
July	1-0	9.00	44	11	1	9	8	.250	.386	.377
August	1-3	5.40	47	13	0	11	7	.277	.319	.407
Sept./Oct.	0-1	3.48	39	12	1	10	12	.308	.385	.431
Leading Off Inn.			56	14	4	6	12	.250	.464	.323
Bases Empty			129	29	6	19	30	.225	.372	.333
Runners On			150	35	2	25	39	.233	.327	.333
Runners/Scor. Pos.			96	25	2	22	22	.260	.406	.382
Runners On/2 Out			66	11	2	12	19	.167	.288	.295
Scor. Pos./2 Out			46	9	2	10	11	.196	.370	.339
Late-Inning Pressure			157	39	2	25	36	.248	.325	.348
Leading Off			30	7	0	4	4	.233	.233	.324
Runners On			91	24	1	14	21	.264	.352	.349
Runners/Scor. Pos.			58	16	1	12	12	.276	.414	.378
First 9 Batters			272	59	8	41	69	.217	.338	.319
Second 9 Batters			7	5	0	3	0	.714	.714	.800
All Batters Thereafter			0	0	0	0	0	—	—	—

Loves to face: Rob Deer (0-for-10, 7 SO)
Paul Molitor (0-for-9)
Cory Snyder (0-for-10, 2 BB)

Hates to face: Kent Hrbek (.571, 4-for-7, 1 2B, 2 HR)
Rafael Palmeiro (.714, 5-for-7, 1 HR)
Robin Yount (.455, 5-for-11, 1 HR)

Miscellaneous statistics: Ground outs-to-air outs ratio: 0.80 last season, 0.72 career.... Induced 5 double-play ground outs in 81 opportunities (one per 16.2).... Allowed 9 doubles, 0 triples in 77.1 innings.... Stranded 37 inherited runners, allowed 25 to score (60%).... Opposing base stealers: 12-for-14 (86%); 0 pickoffs, 2 balks.

Comments: Has won 15 games in relief during his three seasons with the Mariners, the 3d-highest total in franchise history, behind Shane Rawley (20), Enrique Romo (19), and Ed Vande Berg (16).... Has pitched exclusively in relief for Seattle. Has made 225 consecutive relief appearances since a seven-game tryout in the Phillies' rotation in 1987, during which he compiled a 1–4 record and a 6.30 ERA.... Among pitchers who worked at least 50 innings last season while holding opponents to a batting average under .230, only Jackson and Don Carman (4.15) had ERAs over 4.00.... Allowed an average of 5.12 walks per nine innings, 2d-highest rate among A.L. relievers (minimum: 75 IP), but 12 of his last 32 walks allowed were intentional.... Opposing ground-ball hitters have hit for a higher average than fly-ball hitters in each of his five seasons in the majors. Ground-ballers have a career average of .237 against him, 31 points higher than fly-ballers (.206).... In three seasons with Seattle, Jackson has allowed 17 home runs at the Kingdome, nine on the road.... Career record of 12–12 in home games, 6–16 on the road.... Opposing left-handed batters have a career batting average of .253, with an average of one walk for every 6.8 plate appearances against Jackson. Right-handers have batted only .195, averaging one walk every 10.7 times up.... Has a career record of 0–5 on or after September 1.

Mike Jeffcoat

Throws Left

Texas Rangers	W-L	ERA	AB	H	HR	BB	SO	BA	SA	OBA
Season	5-6	4.47	431	122	12	28	58	.283	.427	.328
vs. Left-Handers			90	21	0	2	13	.233	.267	.263
vs. Right-Handers			341	101	12	26	45	.296	.469	.345
vs. Ground-Ballers			181	53	4	13	24	.293	.414	.338
vs. Fly-Ballers			250	69	8	15	34	.276	.436	.321
Home Games	3-1	3.03	247	63	3	14	37	.255	.356	.294
Road Games	2-5	6.55	184	59	9	14	21	.321	.522	.373
Grass Fields	5-4	4.04	361	101	9	23	48	.280	.421	.325
Artificial Turf	0-2	6.88	70	21	3	5	10	.300	.457	.347
April	0-0	2.08	48	9	1	2	8	.188	.292	.220
May	0-1	3.81	98	28	3	9	10	.286	.459	.358
June	2-2	6.41	158	49	5	12	19	.310	.462	.355
July	1-2	6.35	48	17	3	3	6	.354	.646	.392
August	1-0	2.57	28	9	0	0	2	.321	.357	.321
Sept./Oct.	1-1	1.93	51	10	0	2	13	.196	.216	.226
Leading Off Inn.			110	25	3	5	19	.227	.318	.261
Bases Empty			274	67	6	13	44	.245	.358	.281
Runners On			157	55	6	15	14	.350	.548	.406
Runners/Scor. Pos.			84	28	4	10	6	.333	.524	.396
Runners On/2 Out			76	27	3	5	10	.355	.553	.395
Scor. Pos./2 Out			43	15	1	5	5	.349	.488	.417
Late-Inning Pressure			81	21	1	7	13	.259	.370	.315
Leading Off			24	6	0	0	5	.250	.250	.250
Runners On			24	7	0	6	2	.292	.417	.419
Runners/Scor. Pos.			17	5	0	5	1	.294	.353	.435
First 9 Batters			247	63	6	15	41	.255	.368	.300
Second 9 Batters			91	32	4	7	9	.352	.560	.400
All Batters Thereafter			93	27	2	6	8	.290	.452	.330

Loves to face: Dante Bichette (.077, 1-for-13)
Dick Schofield (.083, 1-for-12, 2 BB)
Lou Whitaker (.154, 2-for-13)

Hates to face: Darnell Coles (.600, 6-for-10)
Glenn Davis (3-for-3, 2 HR)
Brian Downing (.474, 9-for-19, 1 HR)

Miscellaneous statistics: Ground outs-to-air outs ratio: 1.04 last season, 1.12 for career.... Induced 11 double-play ground outs in 73 opportunities (one per 6.6).... Allowed 24 doubles, 1 triple in 110.2 innings.... Allowed 8 first-inning runs in 12 starts (6.00 ERA).... Batting support: 3.58 runs per start.... Record of 3–5, 5.91 ERA as a starter; 2–1, 2.27 ERA in 32 relief appearances.... Stranded 14 inherited runners, allowed 10 to score (58%).... Opposing base stealers: 0-for-6; 1 pickoff, 0 balks.

Comments: Jeffcoat's career winning percentage and ERA are nearly identical to those of his father, Hal, who pitched for the Cubs, Reds, and Cardinals in the 1950s. Hal had a .513 winning percentage (39–37) and a 4.22 ERA; Mike's figures: .476 (20–22), 4.14.... Hal also played the outfield for the first six years of his career, and as you might expect, he had a terrific arm; he had an average of one assist for every 8.7 games. Over the past 40 years, only one outfielder has a better average: Jesse Barfield (one per 8.6).... Had two saves in his first five appearances of 1990, after saving only one of his previous 101 career relief appearances.... Opponents batted .330 in his starts, but only .203 in his relief appearances.... One of four pitchers who pitched at least 50 innings last season and didn't allow a stolen base; the others were Bill Swift (128 IP), Jeff Pico (92), and Dave Righetti (53).... Hit Lloyd Moseby with pitches in consecutive plate appearances against him on May 23, but faced 464 other batters without hitting any.... Opponents batted 106 points higher with runners on base (.350) than with the bases empty (.245) last season, the 3d-largest margin in the majors.... Uncorked eight wild pitches in 75 innings pitched for the 1984 Cleveland Indians, but has thrown only two in 290 innings since then.... Only two things on this planet are said to be "uncorked": champagne and wild pitches.

Dave Johnson

Throws Right

Baltimore Orioles	W-L	ERA	AB	H	HR	BB	SO	BA	SA	OBA
Season	13-9	4.10	700	196	30	43	68	.280	.476	.321
vs. Left-Handers			347	103	15	24	24	.297	.522	.340
vs. Right-Handers			353	93	15	19	44	.263	.431	.303
vs. Ground-Ballers			322	88	8	18	30	.273	.422	.312
vs. Fly-Ballers			378	108	22	25	38	.286	.521	.329
Home Games	5-6	3.72	333	88	12	25	30	.264	.429	.316
Road Games	8-3	4.45	367	108	18	18	38	.294	.518	.327
Grass Fields	11-7	3.81	574	157	23	38	58	.274	.449	.318
Artificial Turf	2-2	5.52	126	39	7	5	10	.310	.595	.336
April	2-1	4.50	94	29	5	10	8	.309	.521	.375
May	1-2	4.18	134	40	5	5	16	.299	.448	.326
June	4-1	3.23	153	43	6	8	5	.281	.471	.315
July	3-2	5.20	135	33	7	7	20	.244	.467	.285
August	1-2	5.79	55	14	3	3	7	.255	.564	.288
Sept./Oct.	2-1	2.88	129	37	4	10	12	.287	.450	.336
Leading Off Inn.			184	52	7	8	14	.283	.484	.313
Bases Empty			441	130	20	27	44	.295	.515	.335
Runners On			259	66	10	16	24	.255	.409	.298
Runners/Scor. Pos.			131	31	3	10	13	.237	.359	.277
Runners On/2 Out			108	22	5	8	12	.204	.370	.271
Scor. Pos./2 Out			60	10	0	4	7	.167	.200	.219
Late-Inning Pressure			34	10	4	3	1	.294	.676	.351
Leading Off			11	2	1	1	0	.182	.545	.250
Runners On			6	2	0	0	0	.333	.333	.333
Runners/Scor. Pos.			1	1	0	0	0	1.000	1.000	1.000
First 9 Batters			242	70	9	15	34	.289	.463	.332
Second 9 Batters			235	62	9	12	19	.264	.447	.298
All Batters Thereafter			223	64	12	16	15	.287	.520	.335

Loves to face: Felix Fermin (0-for-7)
Greg Gagne (.091, 1-for-11)
Ozzie Guillen (0-for-8)

Hates to face: Scott Fletcher (.600, 6-for-10)
Kent Hrbek (.545, 6-for-11, 3 2B, 2 HR)
Dan Pasqua (.800, 4-for-5, 1 2B, 3 HR)

Miscellaneous statistics: Ground outs-to-air outs ratio: 0.70 last season, 4th-lowest rate in A.L.; 0.70 for career.... Induced 17 double-play ground outs in 120 opportunities (one per 7.1).... Allowed 43 doubles (most in A.L.), 2 triples in 180.0 innings.... Allowed 17 first-inning runs in 29 starts (5.28 ERA).... Batting support: 4.38 runs per start.... Opposing base stealers: 1-for-5 (20%); 1 pickoff, 2 balks.

Comments: Allowed seven first-inning home runs last season, tying him with Don Robinson, Detroit's Jeff Robinson, and Scott Sanderson for the most among major league pitchers. (We would have made some routine bad joke—about all four names ending in "-son"—but we were afraid ESPN's "Sportscenter" would take it seriously.)... Allowed an average of one home run every 6.0 innings, the worst rate in the majors (minimum: 100 IP). Allowed 75 extra-base hits, 2d most in the majors. The leader: Greg Swindell (76).... The last Orioles pitchers to allow at least 30 home runs in a season were Eric Bell and Ken Dixon in 1987.... Didn't allow a stolen base until stung by Alex Cole on September 27.... Opponents' career batting-average breakdown: .292 with the bases empty, .259 with runners on base, .239 with runners in scoring position, .170 with two outs and RISP.... A Johnson Primer: Of the 39 Johnsons to pitch in the majors, Walter, of course, has the most career wins (416). But only two others won as many as 100 games: Syl (112) and Si (101).... Dave W. is the third Dave Johnson to play for the Orioles in the last 20 years. Everybody remembers Davey, the second baseman; but another Dave Johnson pitched in 17 games for Baltimore in 1974–75.... Actually, he wasn't even the first Johnson to lead the Orioles in wins. Connie Johnson led the club with 14 victories in 1957. By the way, Connie lasted only one more season in the majors after that.

Randy Johnson

Throws Left

Seattle Mariners	W-L	ERA	AB	H	HR	BB	SO	BA	SA	OBA
Season	14-11	3.65	806	174	26	120	194	.216	.355	.319
vs. Left-Handers			82	16	0	7	23	.195	.232	.256
vs. Right-Handers			724	158	26	113	171	.218	.369	.326
vs. Ground-Ballers			383	89	9	67	88	.232	.350	.346
vs. Fly-Ballers			423	85	17	53	106	.201	.359	.294
Home Games	8-4	2.90	363	71	8	60	84	.196	.298	.310
Road Games	6-7	4.30	443	103	18	60	110	.233	.402	.327
Grass Fields	5-4	3.88	351	79	14	46	83	.225	.382	.317
Artificial Turf	9-7	3.47	455	95	12	74	111	.209	.334	.320
April	2-1	4.07	88	18	8	11	19	.205	.511	.293
May	1-2	5.19	129	29	4	22	32	.225	.364	.344
June	5-0	2.40	158	30	1	23	38	.190	.234	.295
July	1-4	3.34	129	29	5	20	34	.225	.395	.329
August	4-1	2.74	161	29	4	22	41	.180	.286	.276
Sept./Oct.	1-3	4.93	141	39	4	22	30	.277	.426	.378
Leading Off Inn.			196	49	7	39	42	.250	.429	.377
Bases Empty			464	101	20	73	93	.218	.392	.327
Runners On			342	73	6	47	101	.213	.304	.309
Runners/Scor. Pos.			191	35	2	28	63	.183	.257	.283
Runners On/2 Out			143	31	2	23	39	.217	.322	.325
Scor. Pos./2 Out			97	18	0	16	29	.186	.258	.301
Late-Inning Pressure			66	8	2	12	13	.121	.212	.256
Leading Off			21	3	1	5	5	.143	.286	.308
Runners On			16	3	0	3	4	.188	.188	.316
Runners/Scor. Pos.			7	0	0	1	1	.000	.000	.125
First 9 Batters			251	67	14	40	59	.267	.494	.369
Second 9 Batters			252	55	5	32	57	.218	.325	.309
All Batters Thereafter			303	52	7	48	78	.172	.264	.287

Loves to face: Rob Deer (.071, 1-for-14)
Brook Jacoby (0-for-12, 1 BB)
Rafael Palmeiro (.071, 1-for-14)

Hates to face: Jesse Barfield (.444, 4-for-9, 2 HR)
Chris James (.400, 4-for-10, 1 3B, 2 HR)
Carney Lansford (.417, 5-for-12)

Miscellaneous statistics: Ground outs-to-air outs ratio: 0.87 last season, 0.96 for career.... Induced 16 double-play ground outs in 182 opportunities (one per 11.4).... Allowed 26 doubles, 4 triples in 219.2 innings.... Allowed 9 first-inning runs in 33 starts (1.64 ERA, 4th lowest in A.L.)... Batting support: 4.15 runs per start.... Opposing base stealers: 28-for-36 (78%); 5 pickoffs, 2 balks.

Comments: Until 1990, the Mariners were the only team in the majors that had never been involved in a no-hit game. Mark Langston and Mike Witt took care of that by no-hitting the M's on April 11. Less than two months later, Johnson became the first Mariners pitcher to hurl a no-hitter.... Johnson, who pitched his no-hitter on June 2, has a career record of 7–0 with a 2.92 ERA in that month. Others months combined: 17–24, 4.24 ERA.... Opponents batted 74 points higher on his first pass through the batting order (.267) than in subsequent at-bats (.193) last season, the 3d-largest margin in the majors.... Walked 113 right-handed batters, the highest total in the past 16 years.... His career walk percentage is 75 percent higher vs. right-handers (one per 7.5 plate appearances) than vs. left-handed batters (one per 13.2 PA).... Most stolen bases against American League pitchers last season: Jack Morris, 45; Bobby Witt, 36; Charlie Hough, 33; Johnson, 28; Nolan Ryan, 25.... Is it easier to steal on a six-ten pitcher like Johnson than on a smaller pitcher with a more compact delivery? Nope! Stolen-base percentages by pitchers' heights: 5′10″ and under, 71%; 5′11″, 65%; 6′0″, 67%; 6′1″, 68%; 6′2″, 73%; 6′3″, 70%; 6′4″, 68%; 6′5″, 69%; 6′6″ and up, 64%. (All right, we'll accept that the conventional wisdom is wrong. *But a bell-shaped curve peaking at 6′2″?*)

Doug Jones

Throws Right

Cleveland Indians	W-L	ERA	AB	H	HR	BB	SO	BA	SA	OBA
Season	5-5	2.56	303	66	5	22	55	.218	.323	.274
vs. Left-Handers			165	33	3	11	26	.200	.315	.249
vs. Right-Handers			138	33	2	11	29	.239	.333	.303
vs. Ground-Ballers			140	24	1	8	27	.171	.243	.221
vs. Fly-Ballers			163	42	4	14	28	.258	.393	.317
Home Games	4-4	3.11	163	33	2	13	26	.202	.288	.260
Road Games	1-1	1.89	140	33	3	9	29	.236	.364	.289
Grass Fields	5-5	2.88	245	50	5	17	44	.204	.322	.258
Artificial Turf	0-0	1.15	58	16	0	5	11	.276	.328	.338
April	0-0	0.00	30	6	0	1	4	.200	.233	.226
May	0-1	1.42	64	13	2	6	11	.203	.328	.271
June	4-1	2.51	55	14	0	2	8	.255	.345	.281
July	0-0	0.00	36	6	0	1	7	.167	.194	.211
August	0-2	8.10	48	12	2	8	6	.250	.479	.362
Sept./Oct.	1-1	2.37	70	15	1	4	19	.214	.300	.253
Leading Off Inn.			61	16	2	5	6	.262	.443	.318
Bases Empty			148	32	2	9	22	.216	.318	.266
Runners On			155	34	3	13	33	.219	.329	.281
Runners/Scor. Pos.			101	24	2	10	25	.238	.347	.301
Runners On/2 Out			64	13	3	6	18	.203	.391	.282
Scor. Pos./2 Out			45	9	2	5	15	.200	.333	.280
Late-Inning Pressure			251	55	4	16	46	.219	.323	.270
Leading Off			51	15	2	4	6	.294	.510	.345
Runners On			131	27	2	9	28	.206	.298	.261
Runners/Scor. Pos.			90	17	1	7	24	.189	.256	.245
First 9 Batters			301	64	5	22	55	.213	.319	.269
Second 9 Batters			2	2	0	0	0	1.000	1.000	1.000
All Batters Thereafter			0	0	0	0	0	—	—	—

Loves to face: Pete Incaviglia (.071, 1-for-14)
Dan Pasqua (.077, 1-for-13)
Ruben Sierra (.083, 1-for-12)

Hates to face: Kent Hrbek (.500, 7-for-14, 2 HR)
Mark McGwire (.467, 7-for-15, 1 HR)
Cal Ripken (.563, 9-for-16, 1 HR)

Miscellaneous statistics: Ground outs-to-air outs ratio: 0.95 last season, 1.30 for career.... Induced 13 double-play ground outs in 75 opportunities (one per 5.8).... Allowed 13 doubles, 2 triples in 84.1 innings.... Stranded 35 inherited runners, allowed 13 to score (73%).... Opposing base stealers: 3-for-4 (75%); 0 pickoffs, 0 balks.

Comments: Saved a career-high 43 games (in 51 opportunities) last season. Only five other pitchers in Indians history had that many saves—official or not—in their *careers*: Ray Narleski (53), Jim Kern (46), Sid Monge (46), Gary Bell (45), and Ernie Camacho (44).... Twenty-four pitchers have saved at least 30 games for teams with losing records, but only Lee Smith (1985–87, 1990) and Jones (1988–90) have done it more than twice.... Most saves for a losing team: 45, by Dan Quisenberry for the 1983 Royals (79–83).... Pitched at least two innings in 14 of his 43 saves.... Hadn't allowed a home run to a right-handed batter since July 24, 1987, when he was tagged by righties Mark McGwire and Dante Bichette within two weeks last May.... But opposing right-handers have outhit left-handers in each of the last four seasons. Career averages: .232 by LHB, .260 by RHB.... Opponents' career batting-average breakdown: .257 at Cleveland Stadium, .239 on other grass fields, .218 on artificial surfaces.... Career average of 2.05 walks per nine innings is 3d lowest among active pitchers (minimum: 200 IP), behind Bret Saberhagen (1.76) and Bob Tewksbury (1.95).... Was named to the All-Star team last season, but didn't appear in the game. Had he pitched, he would have become the first Indians hurler to appear in three consecutive All-Star contests since Sam McDowell (1968–70).

Jimmy Key

Throws Left

Toronto Blue Jays	W-L	ERA	AB	H	HR	BB	SO	BA	SA	OBA
Season	13-7	4.25	602	169	20	22	88	.281	.439	.304
vs. Left-Handers			88	16	0	4	14	.182	.193	.213
vs. Right-Handers			514	153	20	18	74	.298	.481	.320
vs. Ground-Ballers			274	78	6	9	35	.285	.416	.306
vs. Fly-Ballers			328	91	14	13	53	.277	.457	.303
Home Games	7-3	4.47	350	97	13	13	52	.277	.437	.301
Road Games	6-4	3.95	252	72	7	9	36	.286	.440	.308
Grass Fields	3-4	5.48	184	60	7	8	24	.326	.516	.347
Artificial Turf	10-3	3.73	418	109	13	14	64	.261	.404	.285
April	2-1	5.21	77	25	3	0	10	.325	.558	.321
May	2-1	8.10	69	21	5	5	7	.304	.565	.347
June	0-1	7.84	49	19	1	2	5	.388	.531	.412
July	2-2	2.12	119	27	3	7	14	.227	.328	.266
August	3-1	3.38	147	41	4	1	24	.279	.422	.287
Sept./Oct.	4-1	3.86	141	36	4	7	28	.255	.390	.289
Leading Off Inn.			154	43	6	5	23	.279	.461	.306
Bases Empty			370	105	12	13	61	.284	.441	.310
Runners On			232	64	8	9	27	.276	.435	.296
Runners/Scor. Pos.			101	28	3	8	13	.277	.436	.313
Runners On/2 Out			99	28	4	5	11	.283	.444	.317
Scor. Pos./2 Out			53	16	2	4	8	.302	.472	.351
Late-Inning Pressure			18	4	0	0	4	.222	.278	.222
Leading Off			5	1	0	0	2	.200	.200	.200
Runners On			4	1	0	0	1	.250	.250	.250
Runners/Scor. Pos.			1	0	0	0	0	.000	.000	.000
First 9 Batters			231	64	5	8	36	.277	.398	.302
Second 9 Batters			215	65	6	10	27	.302	.456	.328
All Batters Thereafter			156	40	9	4	25	.256	.474	.275

Loves to face: Ellis Burks (0-for-16, 1 BB)
Darnell Coles (.077, 2-for-26)
Kirk Gibson (.083, 2-for-24, 4 BB)

Hates to face: Cecil Fielder (.538, 7-for-13, 1 2B, 4 HR)
Dave Henderson (.452, 19-for-42, 3 HR)
Pat Tabler (.385, 15-for-39, 3 HR)

Miscellaneous statistics: Ground outs-to-air outs ratio: 0.92 last season, 1.23 for career.... Induced 17 double-play ground outs in 106 opportunities (one per 6.2).... Allowed 31 doubles, 2 triples in 154.2 innings.... Allowed 16 first-inning runs in 27 starts (5.00 ERA).... Batting support: 4.93 runs per start.... Opposing base stealers: 6-for-10 (60%); 2 pickoffs, 1 balk.

Comments: One of only two pitchers to win 12 games or more in each of the last six seasons. The other: Frank Viola.... Didn't complete any of his 27 starts, and pitched into the ninth inning only once. His average of 5.73 innings pitched per start was the lowest among the Blue Jays' regular starters.... Posted an ERA of 5.33 in 76 innings with Pat Borders behind the plate, but 3.20 in 78.2 innings with Greg Myers catching.... Walked three of the last 15 leadoff batters he faced, after walking only two of 145 leadoff batters until then.... Opponents batted 77 points higher in day games (.322) than in night games (.245) last season, the largest margin in the majors. He had a 5–6 record (5.58 ERA) in day games, compared to 8–1 (3.16 ERA) at night.... Career record of 19–7 on or after September 1.... Has lost his last four regular season decisions to the Athletics, but is the only pitcher to defeat them in Championship Series play over the last three years.... Began his career in Toronto's bullpen in 1984, making 10 saves in 63 relief appearances without a start. He then won 13 games as a starter in 1985, making him one of two players in major league history with at least 10 saves as a rookie and 10 wins as a starter in his sophomore season. The other: Sammy Ellis (14 SV in 1964, 22 wins [20 as a starter] in 1965).

Dana Kiecker

Throws Right

Boston Red Sox	W-L	ERA	AB	H	HR	BB	SO	BA	SA	OBA
Season	8-9	3.97	572	145	7	54	93	.253	.355	.325
vs. Left-Handers			299	95	4	29	21	.318	.431	.375
vs. Right-Handers			273	50	3	25	72	.183	.271	.272
vs. Ground-Ballers			288	77	2	23	28	.267	.361	.322
vs. Fly-Ballers			284	68	5	31	65	.239	.349	.328
Home Games	3-5	6.50	252	79	5	24	30	.313	.444	.376
Road Games	5-4	2.14	320	66	2	30	63	.206	.284	.285
Grass Fields	5-7	5.23	395	107	6	36	64	.271	.385	.338
Artificial Turf	3-2	1.29	177	38	1	18	29	.215	.288	.296
April	0-0	8.38	39	11	1	6	6	.282	.487	.408
May	0-2	3.60	77	24	1	6	10	.312	.403	.369
June	2-1	3.69	120	31	2	5	24	.258	.392	.286
July	2-1	4.08	109	27	0	12	21	.248	.321	.344
August	2-2	2.86	107	25	1	12	20	.234	.308	.314
Sept./Oct.	2-3	4.01	120	27	2	13	12	.225	.317	.296
Leading Off Inn.			153	46	4	12	24	.301	.471	.352
Bases Empty			347	81	4	27	55	.233	.337	.294
Runners On			225	64	3	27	38	.284	.382	.369
Runners/Scor. Pos.			144	41	2	18	28	.285	.389	.368
Runners On/2 Out			82	12	1	14	15	.146	.220	.307
Scor. Pos./2 Out			63	9	1	10	12	.143	.238	.299
Late-Inning Pressure			38	9	0	0	3	.237	.342	.256
Leading Off			13	4	0	0	2	.308	.538	.308
Runners On			12	4	0	0	0	.333	.333	.385
Runners/Scor. Pos.			8	2	0	0	0	.250	.250	.333
First 9 Batters			237	62	5	24	39	.262	.388	.341
Second 9 Batters			196	45	2	19	36	.230	.316	.301
All Batters Thereafter			139	38	0	11	18	.273	.353	.331

Loves to face: Sandy Alomar (0-for-7, 3 SO)
Kelly Gruber (0-for-9)
Chris James (0-for-8)

Hates to face: Jack Daugherty (.800, 4-for-5)
Rafael Palmeiro (.800, 4-for-5)
Ruben Sierra (.750, 3-for-4)

Miscellaneous statistics: Ground outs-to-air outs ratio: 1.87 (5th-highest rate in A.L.) last season, his first in the majors.... Induced 16 double-play ground outs in 111 opportunities (one per 6.9).... Allowed 31 doubles, 3 triples in 152.0 innings.... Allowed 18 first-inning runs in 25 starts (6.46 ERA).... Batting support: 4.24 runs per start.... Opposing base stealers: 15-for-21 (71%); 1 pick-off, 1 balk.

Comments: The oldest pitcher to make at least 25 starts in his debut season since Billy Martin's old buddy Art Fowler made 29 starts for the Cincinnati Reds in 1954 at age 32.... Made the most starts by a Red Sox rookie pitcher since Mike Nagy started 28 games in 1969. Then he became the first Red Sox rookie pitcher to start a postseason game since Gary Waslewski started the sixth game of the 1967 World Series against the Cardinals.... Didn't complete a start, and pitched into the ninth inning in only two of his 25 starts.... Posted an ERA of 0.80 in his eight victories, 7.19 in his nine defeats.... Didn't allow more than one home run in any game.... Get him early, or not at all: He compiled a 7–3 record with a 2.81 ERA in games in which he didn't allow a first-inning run, compared to 1–6 with a 7.61 ERA in games in which he did.... Walked as many batters as he struck out in the first inning (14); struck out nearly twice as many as he walked thereafter (79 to 41).... Opponents batted 107 points higher in home games (.313) than in road games (.206) last season, the largest margin in the majors.... Opposing left-handers (.318) batted 135 points higher than right-handers (.183), also the largest margin in the majors.... At Fenway, left-handed batters (.397) outhit right-handers (.216) by a 181-point margin.... Opponents' batting average with two outs and runners on base was the lowest in the majors.

Eric King

Throws Right

Chicago White Sox	W-L	ERA	AB	H	HR	BB	SO	BA	SA	OBA
Season	12-4	3.28	570	135	10	40	70	.237	.333	.293
vs. Left-Handers			268	58	5	25	30	.216	.321	.286
vs. Right-Handers			302	77	5	15	40	.255	.344	.300
vs. Ground-Ballers			269	66	1	17	31	.245	.305	.298
vs. Fly-Ballers			301	69	9	23	39	.229	.359	.290
Home Games	5-3	3.93	293	74	8	18	26	.253	.386	.304
Road Games	7-1	2.63	277	61	2	22	44	.220	.278	.282
Grass Fields	9-4	3.51	498	120	9	35	63	.241	.341	.297
Artificial Turf	3-0	1.77	72	15	1	5	7	.208	.278	.269
April	1-0	3.15	76	18	0	7	14	.237	.289	.301
May	3-0	2.31	123	24	4	8	12	.195	.317	.254
June	4-1	1.50	134	30	1	7	24	.224	.284	.268
July	0-3	6.97	132	41	4	8	14	.311	.462	.355
August	0-0	—	0	0	0	0	0	—	—	—
Sept./Oct.	4-0	2.79	105	22	1	10	6	.210	.286	.291
Leading Off Inn.			150	32	2	11	17	.213	.260	.276
Bases Empty			357	80	4	25	47	.224	.291	.282
Runners On			213	55	6	15	23	.258	.404	.312
Runners/Scor. Pos.			110	25	2	8	12	.227	.345	.289
Runners On/2 Out			92	23	3	6	12	.250	.391	.303
Scor. Pos./2 Out			56	13	1	5	8	.232	.321	.306
Late-Inning Pressure			22	5	1	5	2	.227	.500	.370
Leading Off			5	1	0	5	0	.200	.200	.600
Runners On			10	3	1	0	1	.300	.900	.300
Runners/Scor. Pos.			4	1	0	0	1	.250	.750	.250
First 9 Batters			212	49	1	8	28	.231	.288	.268
Second 9 Batters			200	49	6	16	25	.245	.370	.311
All Batters Thereafter			158	37	3	16	17	.234	.348	.305

Loves to face: Gary Gaetti (.143, 3-for-21, 1 HR)
Dave Henderson (.100, 2-for-20)
Harold Reynolds (.080, 2-for-25)

Hates to face: Jesse Barfield (.368, 7-for-19, 2 2B, 3 HR)
Don Mattingly (.421, 8-for-19, 1 HR)
Dan Pasqua (.750, 3-for-4, 2 HR)

Miscellaneous statistics: Ground outs-to-air outs ratio: 1.11 last season, 1.20 for career.... Induced 12 double-play ground outs in 107 opportunities (one per 8.9).... Allowed 17 doubles, 4 triples in 151.0 innings.... Allowed 5 first-inning runs in 25 starts (1.80 ERA).... Batting support: 4.64 runs per start.... Opposing base stealers: 8-for-13 (62%); 0 pickoffs, 3 balks.

Comments: Last season, King compiled the sixth-highest single-season winning percentage in White Sox history (.750); teammate Barry Jones's .733 mark (11–4) was the 11th highest (minimum: 15 decisions). Both were traded after the season (to the Indians and Expos, respectively). Only one White Sox pitcher in the last 35 years had a winning percentage as high as either of those 1990 marks: Rich Dotson in 1983 (22–7, .759).... Had the highest average run support of any regular White Sox starter last season.... A proven second-half pitcher; career won-lost records: 22–20 before the All-Star break, 20–8 after the break (including 10–2 on or after September 1).... Has won all three of his career starts at Cleveland Stadium.... Opponents' career batting average is 41 points higher in day games than in night games, the 5th-largest margin in the majors over the last five seasons. Career breakdown: .266 (10–10, 4.92 ERA) in day games, .226 (32–18, 3.24 ERA) at night.... Appeared in 50 games, all as a starter, during his two seasons with the White Sox and pitched three complete games in two seasons with Chicago, all shutouts—a sign of the times. Shutouts accounted for nearly one-third of all complete games last season, the highest average in major league history (140 of 429). By comparison, complete-game shutouts represented less than one-seventh of all complete games in 1950 (139 of 997).

Mark Knudson

Throws Right

Milwaukee Brewers	W-L	ERA	AB	H	HR	BB	SO	BA	SA	OBA
Season	10-9	4.12	663	187	14	40	56	.282	.419	.322
vs. Left-Handers			340	95	6	23	29	.279	.406	.320
vs. Right-Handers			323	92	8	17	27	.285	.433	.324
vs. Ground-Ballers			335	96	7	19	23	.287	.418	.323
vs. Fly-Ballers			328	91	7	21	33	.277	.421	.320
Home Games	5-3	3.55	301	75	7	19	29	.249	.389	.293
Road Games	5-6	4.62	362	112	7	21	27	.309	.445	.345
Grass Fields	10-5	3.74	544	144	11	35	52	.265	.393	.310
Artificial Turf	0-4	6.15	119	43	3	5	4	.361	.538	.378
April	2-0	2.21	74	19	2	6	7	.257	.392	.309
May	1-2	4.28	147	44	5	5	8	.299	.463	.318
June	2-2	4.63	135	38	3	13	15	.281	.415	.342
July	3-0	2.19	136	36	2	6	14	.265	.368	.297
August	2-3	5.14	137	36	2	5	10	.263	.394	.292
Sept./Oct.	0-2	11.05	34	14	0	5	2	.412	.618	.487
Leading Off Inn.			167	47	2	9	18	.281	.425	.318
Bases Empty			388	123	10	20	30	.317	.497	.350
Runners On			275	64	4	20	26	.233	.309	.283
Runners/Scor. Pos.			151	38	1	17	16	.252	.318	.315
Runners On/2 Out			119	29	2	9	10	.244	.328	.302
Scor. Pos./2 Out			74	20	1	6	6	.270	.365	.325
Late-Inning Pressure			47	14	0	0	5	.298	.426	.313
Leading Off			14	4	0	0	3	.286	.357	.286
Runners On			15	3	0	0	1	.200	.333	.250
Runners/Scor. Pos.			7	1	0	0	1	.143	.429	.143
First 9 Batters			230	71	4	21	22	.309	.452	.365
Second 9 Batters			222	63	7	10	16	.284	.450	.311
All Batters Thereafter			211	53	3	9	18	.251	.351	.284

Loves to face: Alvin Davis (.059, 1-for-17, 2 BB)
Brian Downing (0-for-12)
Craig Worthington (.091, 1-for-11)

Hates to face: Chili Davis (.563, 9-for-16, 1 HR)
Ron Kittle (4-for-4, 1 HR, 1 HBP)
Kirby Puckett (.727, 8-for-11, 1 HR)

Miscellaneous statistics: Ground outs-to-air outs ratio: 1.01 last season, 0.98 for career.... Induced 16 double-play ground outs in 121 opportunities (one per 7.6).... Allowed 39 doubles, 5 triples in 168.1 innings.... Allowed 25 first-inning runs in 27 starts (7.76 ERA, 2d highest in A.L.) ... Batting support: 4.11 runs per start.... Opposing base stealers: 8-for-17 (47%); 0 pickoffs, 0 balks.

Comments: A week (and a half) to remember: Over an 11-day period last July, he threw shutouts against both eventual division champs, the Athletics and Red Sox, for the only two shutouts of his career. The only other pitcher to blank two division champs last season: Kansas City's Kevin Appier.... Incidentally, seven pitchers shut out the A's in Oakland last season: Knudson, Appier, Roger Clemens, Eric King, Melido Perez, Nolan Ryan, and Dave Stieb.... Induced only one double play grounder in his last 45 opportunities, after averaging one GIDP every five opportunities over the first three months of the season.... Started only 25 games over the first five years of his major league career (1985–89), 27 last season.... Opponents batted 84 points higher with the bases empty (.317) than with runners on base (.233) last season, the 3d-largest margin in the majors.... Career mark of 21–17 on grass fields, 2–9 on artificial turf.... Career records of 0–4 vs. the Twins and 4–0 against the Yankees.... His average of 2.99 strikeouts per nine innings was the lowest of any pitcher in the majors last season (minimum: 162 IP). As Knudson's record proves, a low strikeout rate is hardly the sign of a losing pitcher. Among 72 pitchers with rates of less than three SO per nine innings over the last 20 years (minimum: 20 GS), 39 had winning records, including three 20-game winners: Randy Jones (1976), Ross Grimsley (1978), and Tommy John (1982). The group's winning percentage was .516.

Bill Krueger

Throws Left

Milwaukee Brewers	W-L	ERA	AB	H	HR	BB	SO	BA	SA	OBA
Season	6-8	3.98	496	137	10	54	64	.276	.401	.345
vs. Left-Handers			93	22	1	4	14	.237	.323	.265
vs. Right-Handers			403	115	9	50	50	.285	.419	.361
vs. Ground-Ballers			254	75	4	27	28	.295	.409	.362
vs. Fly-Ballers			242	62	6	27	36	.256	.393	.327
Home Games	4-6	4.23	299	79	7	28	44	.264	.398	.327
Road Games	2-2	3.61	197	58	3	26	20	.294	.406	.370
Grass Fields	6-7	3.91	451	121	10	46	59	.268	.399	.335
Artificial Turf	0-1	4.63	45	16	0	8	5	.356	.422	.436
April	1-0	4.05	25	7	0	5	4	.280	.400	.400
May	1-1	3.68	76	18	1	14	12	.237	.316	.348
June	2-2	2.68	137	33	3	11	20	.241	.328	.296
July	1-3	4.09	132	38	5	12	17	.288	.462	.345
August	0-1	6.43	31	10	0	4	2	.323	.419	.378
Sept./Oct.	1-1	5.40	95	31	1	8	9	.326	.484	.383
Leading Off Inn.			119	35	1	9	8	.294	.387	.354
Bases Empty			265	72	7	24	28	.272	.404	.339
Runners On			231	65	3	30	36	.281	.398	.351
Runners/Scor. Pos.			132	34	2	22	22	.258	.356	.341
Runners On/2 Out			91	22	1	18	17	.242	.385	.367
Scor. Pos./2 Out			63	14	1	15	11	.222	.349	.372
Late-Inning Pressure			31	6	1	2	5	.194	.290	.235
Leading Off			11	1	0	0	0	.091	.091	.091
Runners On			7	1	0	0	2	.143	.143	.125
Runners/Scor. Pos.			4	0	0	0	1	.000	.000	.000
First 9 Batters			231	69	1	21	34	.299	.372	.358
Second 9 Batters			166	43	4	19	19	.259	.392	.328
All Batters Thereafter			99	25	5	14	11	.253	.485	.342

Loves to face: Wade Boggs (.185, 5-for-27)
Junior Felix (0-for-11)
Lou Whitaker (.083, 1-for-12, 3 BB)

Hates to face: Carmelo Castillo (.385, 5-for-13, 2 HR)
Greg Gagne (.533, 8-for-15, 1 HR)
Cory Snyder (.800, 4-for-5)

Miscellaneous statistics: Ground outs-to-air outs ratio: 0.98 last season, 1.10 for career.... Induced 13 double-play ground outs in 124 opportunities (one per 9.5).... Allowed 22 doubles, 5 triples in 129.0 innings.... Allowed 9 first-inning runs in 17 starts (4.76 ERA).... Batting support: 5.18 runs per start.... Opposing base stealers: 9-for-15 (60%); 4 pickoffs, 0 balks.

Comments: His average of 13.7 batters faced per relief appearance was the highest in the majors last season (minimum: 10 relief appearances). The top five long men: Krueger, Luis Aquino (11.5 BFP per relief appearance), Jimmy Jones (10.8), Mike Fetters (10.2), Tim Drummond (10.2).... Pitched to a decision in only nine of 17 starts, matching John Farrell for the lowest rate in the A.L. See the Farrell comments (p. 274) for a list of the bottom five.... Average of 5.18 innings pitched per start was the lowest on the Brewers' staff last season.... Has not pitched a complete game in his last 47 starts, dating back to April 1985.... Over the last four seasons, he has allowed 19 home runs: 18 to right-handed batters, one by Harold Baines. Before Baines spanked him last season, Krueger hadn't allowed a home run to a left-hander since Ernie Whitt and Lloyd Moseby took him deep in consecutive innings back in 1986.... Opponents have hit for a higher average with runners on base than they have with the bases empty in each of his eight years in the majors.... Opponents have a career average of .179 in Late-Inning Pressure Situations, .282 in other at-bats; but—and this is a *big* but—he has faced only 209 batters in LIPS in his entire career (compared to a total of 2972 BFP).... Krueger's career record of 36–41 may not look like much (.468), but his teammates have compiled a winning percentage only slightly higher (.470).

Dennis Lamp

Throws Right

Boston Red Sox	W-L	ERA	AB	H	HR	BB	SO	BA	SA	OBA
Season	3-5	4.68	408	114	10	30	49	.279	.422	.330
vs. Left-Handers			194	58	3	17	24	.299	.418	.354
vs. Right-Handers			214	56	7	13	25	.262	.425	.309
vs. Ground-Ballers			189	49	2	9	21	.259	.360	.292
vs. Fly-Ballers			219	65	8	21	28	.297	.475	.362
Home Games	2-2	4.40	227	65	4	17	28	.286	.396	.336
Road Games	1-3	5.03	181	49	6	13	21	.271	.453	.323
Grass Fields	2-5	4.71	389	109	10	30	48	.280	.424	.333
Artificial Turf	1-0	4.15	19	5	0	0	1	.263	.368	.263
April	0-0	3.24	60	16	1	3	7	.267	.367	.313
May	0-1	1.83	74	19	0	3	8	.257	.338	.291
June	1-1	3.12	73	22	3	7	10	.301	.521	.358
July	2-1	7.20	73	22	2	8	7	.301	.466	.361
August	0-1	7.15	47	15	2	3	6	.319	.489	.373
Sept./Oct.	0-1	6.10	81	20	2	6	11	.247	.370	.299
Leading Off Inn.			88	20	2	3	8	.227	.330	.269
Bases Empty			207	44	6	12	22	.213	.357	.266
Runners On			201	70	4	18	27	.348	.488	.395
Runners/Scor. Pos.			138	46	2	17	22	.333	.457	.396
Runners On/2 Out			96	38	3	7	10	.396	.563	.437
Scor. Pos./2 Out			74	30	2	7	8	.405	.568	.457
Late-Inning Pressure			66	20	4	4	12	.303	.561	.347
Leading Off			18	4	1	1	3	.222	.389	.300
Runners On			24	10	1	3	4	.417	.625	.464
Runners/Scor. Pos.			15	5	0	3	3	.333	.400	.421
First 9 Batters			304	80	5	26	35	.263	.382	.323
Second 9 Batters			98	32	5	3	12	.327	.541	.347
All Batters Thereafter			6	2	0	1	2	.333	.500	.429

Loves to face: Chet Lemon (.189, 7-for-37)
Mark McGwire (0-for-11, 1 BB)
Lance Parrish (.143, 6-for-42, 2 HR)

Hates to face: Dwight Evans (.474, 9-for-19)
Dave Parker (.441, 15-for-34)
Larry Sheets (.636, 7-for-11)

Miscellaneous statistics: Ground outs-to-air outs ratio: 1.59 last season, 2.24 for career. . . . Induced 10 double-play ground outs in 93 opportunities (one per 9.3). . . . Allowed 22 doubles, 3 triples in 105.2 innings. . . . Stranded 31 inherited runners, allowed 26 to score (54%), 5th-lowest rate in A.L. . . . Opposing base stealers: 12-for-16 (75%); 0 pickoffs, 0 balks.

Comments: Had pitched 11.1 scoreless innings in postseason play prior to 1990. But he allowed four runs (all earned) in one-third of an inning during last season's A.L.C.S. Red Sox relievers allowed 11 earned runs in only 12⅔ innings during that series. . . . More than doubled his ERA from 2.32 in 1989. The last A.L. pitcher to "double" was Goose Gossage in 1976 (minimum: 100 IP in both seasons). The White Sox used Goose as a starter that season, and his ERA rose from 1.84 to 3.94. . . . He averaged 9.4 batters faced per relief appearance, the highest average of any reliever who pitched in at least 40 games last season. He faced 10 or more batters in a game 23 times, the most of any reliever in baseball. . . . His starting assignment against the Brewers in September was his only start in three seasons with the Red Sox. . . . Career record of 48–59 (4.02 ERA) as a starter, 41–33 (3.66 ERA) as a reliever. . . . Had only two opportunities to record saves last season, and was the losing pitcher in both of those games. . . . Lost a game to the Tigers in July, his first loss in 12 decisions against them. . . . Opponents batted 136 points higher with runners on base (.348) than with the bases empty (.213) last season, the largest margin in the majors. . . . Opponents batted 61 points higher with runners in scoring position (.323) than in other at-bats (.262) over the last five seasons, the 2d-largest margin in the majors.

Mark Langston

Throws Left

California Angels	W-L	ERA	AB	H	HR	BB	SO	BA	SA	OBA
Season	10-17	4.40	829	215	13	104	195	.259	.374	.343
vs. Left-Handers			138	34	1	15	27	.246	.348	.318
vs. Right-Handers			691	181	12	89	168	.262	.379	.348
vs. Ground-Ballers			368	91	3	36	87	.247	.332	.316
vs. Fly-Ballers			461	124	10	68	108	.269	.408	.364
Home Games	3-11	4.55	437	108	9	52	104	.247	.352	.329
Road Games	7-6	4.23	392	107	4	52	91	.273	.398	.358
Grass Fields	8-14	4.14	707	177	12	92	174	.250	.352	.337
Artificial Turf	2-3	6.07	122	38	1	12	21	.311	.500	.377
April	2-1	2.16	88	18	2	12	19	.205	.352	.297
May	1-4	4.36	157	35	2	22	40	.223	.306	.317
June	1-3	2.37	139	36	2	14	41	.259	.403	.325
July	0-5	7.46	142	45	2	19	23	.317	.437	.405
August	4-3	5.76	174	51	4	22	41	.293	.425	.372
Sept./Oct.	2-1	3.47	129	30	1	15	31	.233	.302	.320
Leading Off Inn.			201	47	0	32	49	.234	.264	.339
Bases Empty			461	113	8	63	110	.245	.356	.338
Runners On			368	102	5	41	85	.277	.397	.349
Runners/Scor. Pos.			205	58	4	26	49	.283	.415	.354
Runners On/2 Out			148	42	4	25	33	.284	.426	.387
Scor. Pos./2 Out			101	34	3	17	23	.337	.495	.432
Late-Inning Pressure			43	12	2	5	9	.279	.488	.367
Leading Off			12	3	0	3	3	.250	.333	.400
Runners On			13	6	0	2	1	.462	.615	.563
Runners/Scor. Pos.			8	3	0	2	0	.375	.375	.500
First 9 Batters			260	63	2	34	69	.242	.312	.328
Second 9 Batters			254	66	4	35	59	.260	.362	.350
All Batters Thereafter			315	86	7	35	67	.273	.435	.350

Loves to face: Harold Baines (.139, 5-for-36, 1 HR, 0 BB)
Kelly Gruber (.053, 1-for-19)
Bo Jackson (.056, 1-for-18, 1 HR, 13 SO)

Hates to face: Jeff Conine (3-for-3, 1 BB)
Danny Tartabull (.412, 7-for-17, 4 2B, 6 BB)
Alan Trammell (.375, 18-for-48, 3 HR)

Miscellaneous statistics: Ground outs-to-air outs ratio: 1.04 last season, 1.04 for career. . . . Induced 20 double-play ground outs in 180 opportunities (one per 9.0). . . . Allowed 40 doubles, 8 triples in 223.0 innings. . . . Allowed 16 first-inning runs in 33 starts (4.36 ERA). . . . Batting support: 3.94 runs per start. . . . Opposing base stealers: 22-for-36 (61%); 9 pickoffs, 0 balks.

Comments: Career record now stands just three games above .500 (96–93), but his teammates have compiled a .450 winning percentage. By the method explained in the Rangers essay (p. 53), we estimate Langston's value to have been approximately 29 wins over seven seasons. . . . Combined with Mike Witt to throw a no-hit shutout against Seattle in his first appearance with the Angels. The most pitchers used in a no-hitter is four. That was on the last day of the 1975 season, when Alvin Dark—tuning up his staff for the playoffs—sent Vida Blue, Glenn Abbott, Paul Lindblad, and Rollie Fingers to the mound in a 5–0 blanking of the Angels. . . . Langston lost his next nine decisions at Anaheim Stadium after the combo no-hitter. . . . Walked 32 leadoff batters, 2d most in the majors to Randy Johnson (39). . . . The only home run he allowed to a left-handed batter was hit by Rafael Palmeiro on September 24. . . . Opponents' batting average was the highest of his career, but his home-run rate of one for every 64 at-bats was the best of his career. . . . Allowed only one home run to 271 batters during the first two innings of his starts last season. . . . Left-handed batters hit 62 points higher last season than they had over the previous four seasons (.184). . . . Once again, he topped the 200-inning mark, but his total has decreased in each of the last three seasons. Year by year since 1987: 272.0, 261.1, 250.0, 223.0.

Dave LaPoint

Throws Left

New York Yankees	W-L	ERA	AB	H	HR	BB	SO	BA	SA	OBA
Season	7-10	4.11	617	180	11	57	67	.292	.417	.347
vs. Left-Handers			95	27	2	9	7	.284	.400	.340
vs. Right-Handers			522	153	9	48	60	.293	.420	.348
vs. Ground-Ballers			280	82	3	23	25	.293	.368	.341
vs. Fly-Ballers			337	98	8	34	42	.291	.457	.352
Home Games	6-3	3.13	360	90	9	33	38	.250	.375	.311
Road Games	1-7	5.60	257	90	2	24	29	.350	.475	.397
Grass Fields	7-8	4.09	531	154	11	51	61	.290	.416	.349
Artificial Turf	0-2	4.22	86	26	0	6	6	.302	.419	.337
April	1-2	4.86	72	25	1	5	9	.347	.417	.380
May	2-2	3.81	109	31	3	10	11	.284	.459	.336
June	1-2	4.86	142	41	4	12	18	.289	.465	.335
July	2-1	3.21	130	34	1	12	15	.262	.338	.324
August	0-3	4.94	124	40	2	16	13	.323	.427	.399
Sept./Oct.	1-0	1.64	40	9	0	2	1	.225	.350	.262
Leading Off Inn.			161	50	3	11	12	.311	.447	.355
Bases Empty			353	111	8	32	32	.314	.462	.373
Runners On			264	69	3	25	35	.261	.356	.313
Runners/Scor. Pos.			139	39	2	13	20	.281	.381	.319
Runners On/2 Out			109	24	1	9	19	.220	.284	.280
Scor. Pos./2 Out			69	16	1	5	10	.232	.319	.284
Late-Inning Pressure			33	10	0	4	2	.303	.364	.378
Leading Off			11	3	0	0	1	.273	.364	.273
Runners On			11	3	0	2	0	.273	.273	.385
Runners/Scor. Pos.			7	2	0	2	0	.286	.286	.444
First 9 Batters			222	65	4	22	28	.293	.401	.347
Second 9 Batters			224	70	6	12	24	.313	.482	.346
All Batters Thereafter			171	45	1	23	15	.263	.351	.349

Loves to face: Lance Parrish (0-for-14, 2 BB)
Johnny Ray (.200, 11-for-55)
Tim Wallach (.154, 6-for-39)

Hates to face: George Brett (.600, 6-for-10)
Scott Fletcher (.483, 14-for-29)
Tim Raines (.459, 17-for-37, 2 HR)

Miscellaneous statistics: Ground outs-to-air outs ratio: 1.07 last season, 1.25 for career. . . . Induced 21 double-play ground outs in 139 opportunities (one per 6.6). . . . Allowed 32 doubles, 6 triples in 157.2 innings. . . . Allowed 14 first-inning runs in 27 starts (4.33 ERA). . . . Batting support: 3.85 runs per start. . . . Opposing base stealers: 10-for-19 (53%); 4 pickoffs, 0 balks.

Comments: What's a 5.62 ERA worth in New York these days? That was LaPoint's mark in 1989, and it earned him an opening-day start for the Yankees in 1990. He was the sixth different opening-day starter in a row for the Yankees. The last American League club with a different opening-day starter in seven straight seasons: the Indians (1977–83). . . . He'd be a winning pitcher without his annual June swoon. Career mark of 8–20 during that month, 72–65 in all other months combined. . . . Opposing ground-ball hitters have hit for a higher average than fly-ball hitters in each of the last five seasons. . . . Has lost at least one game to every current major league franchise, and has beaten every team except the Royals. . . . Compiled a 13–19 record with a 4.74 ERA in his first two seasons with the Yankees, during which time he spent 77 days on the disabled list. . . . Has now spent two consecutive complete seasons with the same club for the first time since his four-year stint with the Cardinals from 1981 through 1984. . . . LaPoint is the only active player to have pitched for eight different teams (in order: Brewers, Cardinals, Giants, Tigers, Padres, White Sox, Pirates, and Yankees). He has also started and won games for each of those teams. The only pitcher in major league history to win games for more than eight teams: Bob L. Miller (9, 1957–74). Two pitchers started for as many as 10 teams: Frank Foreman (1884–1902) and Gus Weyhing (1887–1901).

Terry Leach

Throws Right

Minnesota Twins	W-L	ERA	AB	H	HR	BB	SO	BA	SA	OBA
Season	2-5	3.20	313	84	2	21	46	.268	.364	.315
vs. Left-Handers			126	34	0	11	9	.270	.381	.331
vs. Right-Handers			187	50	2	10	37	.267	.353	.303
vs. Ground-Ballers			135	33	0	8	16	.244	.319	.290
vs. Fly-Ballers			178	51	2	13	30	.287	.399	.333
Home Games	0-0	3.53	167	45	1	13	27	.269	.377	.322
Road Games	2-5	2.82	146	39	1	8	19	.267	.349	.306
Grass Fields	1-4	2.20	107	28	0	8	15	.262	.290	.314
Artificial Turf	1-1	3.74	206	56	2	13	31	.272	.403	.315
April	1-0	0.00	39	5	0	2	8	.128	.128	.171
May	1-0	3.50	67	15	1	5	7	.224	.313	.274
June	0-1	4.02	64	21	0	2	10	.328	.453	.348
July	0-2	1.98	50	11	0	4	6	.220	.240	.278
August	0-2	4.76	48	17	1	1	5	.354	.563	.373
Sept./Oct.	0-0	5.06	45	15	0	7	10	.333	.444	.423
Leading Off Inn.			66	12	1	3	11	.182	.303	.217
Bases Empty			162	39	1	8	24	.241	.346	.276
Runners On			151	45	1	13	22	.298	.384	.353
Runners/Scor. Pos.			107	29	1	12	18	.271	.383	.344
Runners On/2 Out			76	19	1	6	9	.250	.355	.305
Scor. Pos./2 Out			55	13	1	6	9	.236	.364	.311
Late-Inning Pressure			90	30	1	8	8	.333	.444	.390
Leading Off			20	4	0	3	1	.200	.250	.304
Runners On			44	18	1	4	3	.409	.545	.460
Runners/Scor. Pos.			31	12	1	4	2	.387	.581	.459
First 9 Batters			285	76	2	18	41	.267	.368	.310
Second 9 Batters			28	8	0	3	5	.286	.321	.355
All Batters Thereafter			0	0	0	0	0	—	—	—

Loves to face: Dave Gallagher (0-for-9)
Candy Maldonado (.091, 1-for-11)
Steve Sax (.143, 3-for-21)

Hates to face: Harold Baines (.500, 5-for-10, 1 HR)
Jack Daugherty (.800, 4-for-5)
Tim Raines (.400, 10-for-25, 1 HR)

Miscellaneous statistics: Ground outs-to-air outs ratio: 1.51 last season, 1.53 for career. . . . Induced 4 double-play ground outs in 65 opportunities (one per 16.3). . . . Allowed 18 doubles, 3 triples in 81.2 innings. . . . Stranded 42 inherited runners, allowed 16 to score (72%). . . . Opposing base stealers: 6-for-7 (86%); 0 pickoffs, 1 balk.

Comments: Of the 14 players who pitched at least 20 innings for the Twins last season, eight had spent time in the New York Mets organization. Minnesota acquired five of those pitchers (Rick Aguilera, Tim Drummond, Kevin Tapani, Jack Savage, and David West) in exchange for Frank Viola. The other three former Mets on Minnesota's staff were signed as free agents (John Candelaria, Juan Berenguer, and Leach). . . . The last left-handed batter to homer against the right-handed Leach was Ruben Sierra on September 2, 1989. . . . Left-handed batters have a career average of .289 against him, 51 points higher than the career average of opposing right-handers (.238). See the Mark Eichhorn comment (p. 273) for more on lefty/righty skews against sidearm pitchers. . . . Opponents have collected 14 hits in 32 at-bats with the bases loaded over the last two years (.438), but he has never allowed a grand slam. Small consolation. . . . Had a record of 24–9 in seven seasons with the Mets, but is 7–11 in his two American League campaigns. . . . Won-lost record year by year since 1987: 11–1, 7–2, 5–6, 2–5. . . . His career record now stands at 25–7 in night games, after winning the first 20 night-game decisions of his career; he is 6–13 in day games. . . . His career record on artificial surfaces is 16–3, compared to 15–17 on grass fields. . . . He's never lost a game prior to June; he has one win in April and five in May.

Tim Leary

Throws Right

New York Yankees	W-L	ERA	AB	H	HR	BB	SO	BA	SA	OBA
Season	9-19	4.11	785	202	18	78	138	.257	.378	.328
vs. Left-Handers			408	106	10	46	61	.260	.392	.338
vs. Right-Handers			377	96	8	32	77	.255	.363	.318
vs. Ground-Ballers			349	96	9	34	55	.275	.410	.344
vs. Fly-Ballers			436	106	9	44	83	.243	.353	.316
Home Games	1-9	4.73	323	89	9	34	59	.276	.412	.346
Road Games	8-10	3.69	462	113	9	44	79	.245	.355	.316
Grass Fields	5-16	4.25	600	159	16	64	99	.265	.392	.340
Artificial Turf	4-3	3.65	185	43	2	14	39	.232	.335	.291
April	1-1	2.75	77	19	6	8	19	.247	.506	.318
May	2-4	2.44	173	40	5	11	36	.231	.347	.285
June	0-5	4.75	165	51	0	10	18	.309	.364	.354
July	2-3	6.75	131	43	0	15	16	.328	.412	.397
August	3-3	3.43	146	29	5	20	32	.199	.356	.299
Sept./Oct.	1-3	5.11	93	20	2	14	17	.215	.344	.318
Leading Off Inn.			197	52	6	19	32	.264	.406	.338
Bases Empty			461	117	10	40	82	.254	.371	.320
Runners On			324	85	8	38	56	.262	.389	.340
Runners/Scor. Pos.			178	40	6	26	39	.225	.365	.321
Runners On/2 Out			125	31	3	20	26	.248	.368	.356
Scor. Pos./2 Out			80	20	2	12	21	.250	.363	.355
Late-Inning Pressure			39	13	2	9	4	.333	.538	.458
Leading Off			10	5	1	4	1	.500	.900	.643
Runners On			18	5	0	3	1	.278	.333	.381
Runners/Scor. Pos.			9	3	0	2	1	.333	.444	.455
First 9 Batters			252	72	4	22	45	.286	.393	.344
Second 9 Batters			246	53	4	22	46	.215	.305	.289
All Batters Thereafter			287	77	10	34	47	.268	.429	.348

Loves to face: Gary Gaetti (.059, 1-for-17)
Candy Maldonado (.045, 1-for-22, 3 BB)
Edgar Martinez (0-for-9)

Hates to face: Jose Canseco (.444, 8-for-18, 3 HR)
John Marzano (4-for-4)
Cory Snyder (.667, 6-for-9, 2 HR)

Miscellaneous statistics: Ground outs-to-air outs ratio: 1.69 last season, 1.32 for career. . . . Induced 20 double-play ground outs in 161 opportunities (one per 8.1). . . . Allowed 39 doubles, 1 triple in 208.0 innings. . . . Allowed 17 first-inning runs in 31 starts (3.77 ERA). . . . Batting support: 3.06 runs per start (lowest in majors). . . . Opposing base stealers: 18-for-26 (69%); 6 pickoffs, 0 balks.

Comments: Has posted winning percentages below .400 in each of the last two seasons after compiling a 17–11 (.607) record for the Dodgers in 1988. The only other pitchers with consecutive sub-.400 seasons after a .600-plus year (with at least 30 starts in all three seasons): Clyde Wright (1973–74) and Jerry Koosman (1977–78). . . . Leary's eight-game losing streak (May 28–July 8) was only one short of the team record, shared by Thad Tillotson (1967) and Bill Hogg (1908). . . . Shared the major league lead for pickoffs by right-handed pitchers with Charlie Hough and Jose Rijo. . . . Had a streak of 90⅔ innings without allowing a home run (May 18–August 4), the longest of his career, immediately following a streak of allowing at least one home run in seven consecutive starts. . . . Had the lowest average run support of any regular Yankees starter last season, but got excellent support in the field. New York infielders committed only six errors in 576 chances with Leary on the mound, the 8th-best percentage (.990) in the majors last season (minimum: 162 IP). . . . Held the American League's top 10 hitters to a .191 batting average (13-for-68). . . . There hasn't been a 20-game loser in the majors since Brian Kingman in 1980. Since then, four pitchers have lost 19 games: Jose DeLeon (1985 and 1990), Matt Young (1985), Mike Moore (1987), and Leary (1990). Of them, only Moore was brave enough to take the mound after his 19th loss, winning twice to raise his record to 9–19.

Julio Machado

Throws Right

Mets/Brewers	W-L	ERA	AB	H	HR	BB	SO	BA	SA	OBA
Season	4-1	2.47	176	41	4	25	39	.233	.375	.330
vs. Left-Handers			76	15	1	13	19	.197	.329	.315
vs. Right-Handers			100	26	3	12	20	.260	.410	.342
vs. Ground-Ballers			80	16	1	11	19	.200	.287	.312
vs. Fly-Ballers			96	25	3	14	20	.260	.448	.345
Home Games	1-0	0.86	74	15	1	9	24	.203	.297	.282
Road Games	3-1	3.76	102	26	3	16	15	.255	.431	.364
Grass Fields	1-0	1.49	132	30	2	17	32	.227	.356	.309
Artificial Turf	3-1	5.73	44	11	2	8	7	.250	.432	.389
April	2-1	1.86	36	8	0	3	11	.222	.278	.293
May	0-0	2.25	14	3	1	0	2	.214	.429	.214
June	0-0	5.14	27	8	2	3	5	.296	.667	.367
July	1-0	9.00	13	4	1	2	3	.308	.538	.438
August	1-0	1.69	39	9	0	9	6	.231	.282	.367
Sept./Oct.	0-0	0.69	47	9	0	8	12	.191	.298	.304
Leading Off Inn.			37	12	3	3	8	.324	.649	.375
Bases Empty			83	20	3	11	21	.241	.398	.337
Runners On			93	21	1	14	18	.226	.355	.324
Runners/Scor. Pos.			55	13	1	10	8	.236	.382	.348
Runners On/2 Out			47	12	1	10	6	.255	.404	.397
Scor. Pos./2 Out			33	7	1	8	3	.212	.333	.381
Late-Inning Pressure			41	12	1	6	11	.293	.439	.396
Leading Off			8	4	1	2	2	.500	1.000	.600
Runners On			25	6	0	2	6	.240	.320	.321
Runners/Scor. Pos.			12	5	0	2	0	.417	.583	.533
First 9 Batters			165	39	4	24	37	.236	.388	.335
Second 9 Batters			11	2	0	1	2	.182	.182	.250
All Batters Thereafter			0	0	0	0	0	—	—	—

Loves to face: Jay Bell (0-for-6)

Hates to face: Dave Clark (.667, 2-for-3, 1 3B)
Ryne Sandberg (.667, 2-for-3, 1 HR)

Miscellaneous statistics: Ground outs-to-air outs ratio: 0.59 last season, 0.71 for career. . . . Induced 0 double-play ground outs in 44 opportunities. . . . Allowed 7 doubles, 3 triples in 47.1 innings. . . . Stranded 16 inherited runners, allowed 16 to score (50%). . . . Opposing base stealers: 5-for-8 (63%); 0 pickoffs, 0 balks.

Comments: Why all this fuss about Machado's penchant for eating iguana? According to *The Merriam-Webster Dictionary*, *iguana* is "a large edible tropical American lizard," whereas the word *edible* is not included in the definition of *cow, pig,* or *pizza*. . . . Ground outs-to-air outs ratio was the 10th lowest among pitchers who worked at least as many innings as Machado did last season. That's a contributing factor in his not inducing a double play grounder in 44 opportunities, the highest total by a pitcher who came up empty. . . . A strange twist: Machado got Barry Bonds to ground into a twin killing in Iguana-man's first career opportunity in 1989; he's 0-for-45 since then. . . . Allowed only one run in 13 innings after his acquisition by the Brewers. . . . Opponents have six hits in 12 career at-bats with the bases loaded. . . . Machado threw a total of 47⅓ innings last season to no fewer than seven different catchers—including six in only 34⅓ innings with the Mets. (And that doesn't even include Rob Dromerhauser, their bullpen catcher.) The roll call: B.J. Surhoff with the Brewers (13 innings); Mackey Sasser (17⅔), Barry Lyons (7⅔), Alex Trevino (6), Orlando Mercado (1⅔), Dave Liddell (1), and Todd Hundley (⅓) with the Mets. . . . Split his 1989 season among five teams in five different leagues; he restricted it to three teams last season.

Kirk McCaskill

Throws Right

California Angels	W-L	ERA	AB	H	HR	BB	SO	BA	SA	OBA
Season	12-11	3.25	660	161	9	72	78	.244	.332	.320
vs. Left-Handers			334	84	6	34	30	.251	.368	.322
vs. Right-Handers			326	77	3	38	48	.236	.294	.318
vs. Ground-Ballers			334	84	2	29	42	.251	.332	.311
vs. Fly-Ballers			326	77	7	43	36	.236	.331	.328
Home Games	7-3	2.77	308	74	5	31	37	.240	.328	.311
Road Games	5-8	3.68	352	87	4	41	41	.247	.335	.327
Grass Fields	11-8	2.91	557	134	7	59	67	.241	.323	.315
Artificial Turf	1-3	5.19	103	27	2	13	11	.262	.379	.345
April	2-0	1.07	91	22	1	13	13	.242	.297	.333
May	1-2	5.03	84	25	0	8	11	.298	.393	.359
June	3-2	1.78	110	24	1	13	9	.218	.291	.301
July	1-3	3.41	111	22	2	16	10	.198	.306	.305
August	3-2	3.76	144	38	2	14	19	.264	.326	.333
Sept./Oct.	2-2	4.55	120	30	3	8	16	.250	.383	.297
Leading Off Inn.			158	31	1	23	21	.196	.241	.306
Bases Empty			373	85	5	45	51	.228	.311	.314
Runners On			287	76	4	27	27	.265	.359	.327
Runners/Scor. Pos.			148	39	2	19	12	.264	.372	.345
Runners On/2 Out			119	30	1	13	15	.252	.336	.326
Scor. Pos./2 Out			70	18	1	10	7	.257	.357	.350
Late-Inning Pressure			31	8	0	4	5	.258	.355	.343
Leading Off			8	1	0	2	2	.125	.125	.300
Runners On			14	4	0	0	3	.286	.286	.286
Runners/Scor. Pos.			7	3	0	0	1	.429	.429	.429
First 9 Batters			244	59	4	15	35	.242	.311	.287
Second 9 Batters			230	54	3	29	23	.235	.326	.323
All Batters Thereafter			186	48	2	28	20	.258	.366	.355

Loves to face: Scott Fletcher (.107, 3-for-28)
Rance Mulliniks (.147, 5-for-34)
John Shelby (0-for-10)

Hates to face: George Brett (.647, 11-for-17)
Kirk Gibson (.563, 9-for-16, 4 HR, 4 SO)
Lance Parrish (.462, 6-for-13, 1 2B, 3 HR)

Miscellaneous statistics: Ground outs-to-air outs ratio: 1.36 last season, 1.12 for career.... Induced 19 double-play ground outs in 148 opportunities (one per 7.8).... Allowed 19 doubles, 6 triples in 174.1 innings.... Allowed 11 first-inning runs in 29 starts (3.10 ERA).... Batting support: 3.93 runs per start. ....Opposing base stealers: 6-for-16 (38%), shared 5th-lowest rate in A.L.; 4 pickoffs, 1 balk.

Comments: Career winning percentage of .553 (68–55) is the 3d highest in Angels history (minimum: 100 decisions), behind Frank Tanana (.567, 102–78) and Andy Messersmith (.557, 59–47).... Joins an impressive group of four other Angels pitchers who posted three consecutive winning seasons with at least 20 starts, including Andy Messersmith (3 years, 1969–71), Nolan Ryan (4, 1972–75), Frank Tanana (4, 1975–78), and Mike Witt (4, 1984–87).... Held opponents to less than two runs in each of his first four starts last season. The only Angels pitcher to do that in five straight starts was Tanana in 1977.... Allowed only one home run in his first 65⅓ innings last season; his average of one home run every 19.4 innings was the 2d-best rate in the American League (minimum: 162 IP).... Had the poorest average run support among the Angels' regular starters last season.... Opponents have hit for a higher average in road games than in home games in each of his six seasons in the majors. He has a career record of 36–22 (.621) at home, 32–33 (.492) on the road.... Which three American League pitchers have finished in the top 10 in ERA in each of the last two seasons? Not Clemens, Stewart, and Stieb, but Bob Welch, Chuck Finley, and McCaskill. McCaskill ranked tenth in 1990, fifth in 1989 (2.93).

Ben McDonald

Throws Right

Baltimore Orioles	W-L	ERA	AB	H	HR	BB	SO	BA	SA	OBA
Season	8-5	2.43	429	88	9	35	65	.205	.301	.262
vs. Left-Handers			216	39	2	17	38	.181	.236	.236
vs. Right-Handers			213	49	7	18	27	.230	.366	.289
vs. Ground-Ballers			205	38	1	18	35	.185	.239	.247
vs. Fly-Ballers			224	50	8	17	30	.223	.357	.277
Home Games	4-3	2.41	270	59	7	18	43	.219	.319	.265
Road Games	4-2	2.45	159	29	2	17	22	.182	.270	.258
Grass Fields	6-5	2.44	376	78	9	28	55	.207	.306	.260
Artificial Turf	2-0	2.35	53	10	0	7	10	.189	.264	.274
April	0-0	—	0	0	0	0	0	—	—	—
May	0-0	—	0	0	0	0	0	—	—	—
June	0-0	—	0	0	0	0	0	—	—	—
July	3-0	1.39	115	25	0	6	19	.217	.270	.252
August	2-3	4.22	121	28	5	11	15	.231	.397	.293
Sept./Oct.	3-2	1.99	193	35	4	18	31	.181	.259	.249
Leading Off Inn.			111	23	2	10	16	.207	.279	.273
Bases Empty			269	56	5	21	43	.208	.294	.266
Runners On			160	32	4	14	22	.200	.313	.257
Runners/Scor. Pos.			79	10	1	7	16	.127	.203	.187
Runners On/2 Out			59	7	0	7	10	.119	.153	.212
Scor. Pos./2 Out			36	4	0	3	7	.111	.167	.179
Late-Inning Pressure			67	12	3	5	7	.179	.343	.236
Leading Off			19	3	0	2	1	.158	.211	.238
Runners On			16	5	3	3	1	.313	.938	.421
Runners/Scor. Pos.			8	2	1	1	0	.250	.750	.333
First 9 Batters			154	33	2	13	27	.214	.286	.274
Second 9 Batters			121	24	2	10	20	.198	.289	.254
All Batters Thereafter			154	31	5	12	18	.201	.325	.257

Loves to face: Greg Brock (0-for-7)
Mike Macfarlane (0-for-3, 3 SO)
Luis Sojo (0-for-7)

Hates to face: Matt Nokes (.750, 3-for-4, 1 2B, 1 HR)
John Olerud (.375, 3-for-8, 1 HR)
Tony Pena (1-for-1, 1 2B, 3 BB)

Miscellaneous statistics: Ground outs-to-air outs ratio: 0.90 last season, 0.91 for career.... Induced 5 double-play ground outs in 88 opportunities (one per 17.6), 4th-lowest rate in A.L.... Allowed 14 doubles, 0 triples in 118.2 innings.... Allowed 2 first-inning runs in 15 starts (1.20 ERA).... Batting support: 3.20 runs per start.... Opposing base stealers: 10-for-12 (10-for-last-10; 83%); 2 pickoffs, 0 balks.

Comments: Threw a shutout against the White Sox in his first major league start, becoming the first Orioles pitcher to open with a whitewash since Tom Phoebus in 1966.... Had the lowest ERA of any rookie in 1990 (minimum: 50 IP).... The last rookie pitcher with a lower ERA in at least as many innings as McDonald pitched last season was Mark Fidrych, who posted a 2.34 ERA in 1976.... Started the season with 52 consecutive innings without allowing a home run, then allowed one per 7.4 innings for the rest of the season. That streak was apparently snapped by George Brett at 33 innings, but was raised from the dead when the game was rained out.... Faced a total of 56 batters in the first inning, allowing only one extra-base hit (a double).... Had the poorest batting support among the Orioles' regular starters, but his average of 7.26 innings pitched per start was more than an inning per game more than any other Orioles starter.... Has faced 505 batters in his career and never hit one with a pitch. Only two active pitchers have faced more batters with no HBPs: Bill Landrum (1013) and Keith Comstock (646).... Baltimore's starting rotation as of the end of August, before rosters expanded, had a total of 44 major league starts prior to the 1990 season. The starting five at that time included John Mitchell (20 pre-1990 starts), Pete Harnisch (19), Jose Mesa (5), Ben McDonald (0), and Anthony Telford (0).

Jack McDowell

Throws Right

Chicago White Sox	W-L	ERA	AB	H	HR	BB	SO	BA	SA	OBA
Season	14-9	3.82	776	189	20	77	165	.244	.380	.316
vs. Left-Handers			408	99	11	34	76	.243	.380	.302
vs. Right-Handers			368	90	9	43	89	.245	.380	.330
vs. Ground-Ballers			364	96	8	36	64	.264	.382	.335
vs. Fly-Ballers			412	93	12	41	101	.226	.379	.299
Home Games	9-4	3.30	475	108	10	45	108	.227	.337	.298
Road Games	5-5	4.70	301	81	10	32	57	.269	.449	.343
Grass Fields	12-7	3.77	649	158	15	65	149	.243	.376	.317
Artificial Turf	2-2	4.05	127	31	5	12	16	.244	.402	.307
April	1-1	5.74	59	14	3	7	15	.237	.424	.324
May	0-2	4.72	103	28	5	12	26	.272	.476	.350
June	4-1	2.21	153	33	2	16	35	.216	.307	.298
July	1-1	5.35	133	38	4	13	29	.286	.421	.354
August	5-1	2.63	185	36	3	13	30	.195	.319	.250
Sept./Oct.	3-3	4.38	143	40	3	16	30	.280	.413	.352
Leading Off Inn.			201	40	2	14	44	.199	.284	.258
Bases Empty			481	113	12	43	101	.235	.364	.303
Runners On			295	76	8	34	64	.258	.407	.335
Runners/Scor. Pos.			163	40	6	23	43	.245	.417	.330
Runners On/2 Out			122	27	4	15	23	.221	.361	.307
Scor. Pos./2 Out			77	17	3	13	16	.221	.390	.333
Late-Inning Pressure			53	11	0	4	13	.208	.302	.288
Leading Off			15	2	0	1	4	.133	.200	.235
Runners On			20	4	0	0	6	.200	.250	.200
Runners/Scor. Pos.			11	1	0	0	3	.091	.182	.091
First 9 Batters			265	79	5	24	56	.298	.423	.360
Second 9 Batters			250	57	7	27	62	.228	.356	.305
All Batters Thereafter			261	53	8	26	47	.203	.360	.280

Loves to face: Greg Gagne (.067, 1-for-15, 1 HR)
Mickey Tettleton (0-for-8, 7 SO)
Walt Weiss (.071, 1-for-14)

Hates to face: Don Mattingly (.500, 7-for-14, 1 HR)
Jody Reed (.583, 7-for-12)
Gary Sheffield (.833, 5-for-6)

Miscellaneous statistics: Ground outs-to-air outs ratio: 0.77 last season, 1.02 for career. . . . Induced 12 double-play ground outs in 144 opportunities (one per 12.0). . . . Allowed 32 doubles, 7 triples in 205.0 innings. . . . Allowed 15 first-inning runs in 33 starts (3.82 ERA). . . . Batting support: 4.39 runs per start. . . . Opposing base stealers: 23-for-34 (68%); 5 pickoffs, 1 balk.

Comments: Chicago's starting rotation last season was the youngest in the American League since that of the 1981 White Sox. (See page 16 for details and analysis.) The youngest ever was that of the 1914 Washington Senators, whose oldest member was 26-year-old Walter Johnson. . . . Opponents batted 83 points higher on his first pass through the batting order (.298) than in subsequent at-bats (.215) last season, the largest margin in the majors. . . . Opponents had a career batting average of .268 in road games, but only .220 at Comiskey Park. He posted a career record of 36–22 at Comiskey, but had a losing record in road games (32–33). . . . He's allowed only one home run in 119 career at-bats in Late-Inning Pressure Situations. . . . He has walked five of 31 career batters faced with the bases loaded, an average of one for every 6.2 batters, compared to a rate of one every 11.1 batters at other times. . . . Has a career record of 14–5 vs. western division clubs, 8–14 vs. the beasts from the east—numbers full of sound and fury, signifying nothing. There's no quality inherent in the teams from either division to explain such a difference, or to justify noting it on a regular basis, for that matter. If McDowell keeps it up for a few more years, we'll rack our brains; until then, we're treating it as an oddity—nothing more.

Bob Milacki

Throws Right

Baltimore Orioles	W-L	ERA	AB	H	HR	BB	SO	BA	SA	OBA
Season	5-8	4.46	523	143	18	61	60	.273	.434	.346
vs. Left-Handers			261	72	6	35	31	.276	.410	.358
vs. Right-Handers			262	71	12	26	29	.271	.458	.334
vs. Ground-Ballers			240	66	7	25	26	.275	.429	.341
vs. Fly-Ballers			283	77	11	36	34	.272	.438	.351
Home Games	1-3	5.29	200	57	8	24	23	.285	.480	.357
Road Games	4-5	3.98	323	86	10	37	37	.266	.406	.340
Grass Fields	3-8	4.81	430	121	17	55	49	.281	.463	.359
Artificial Turf	2-0	2.88	93	22	1	6	11	.237	.301	.283
April	1-0	2.84	111	22	2	19	13	.198	.279	.313
May	1-3	7.61	103	38	3	13	9	.369	.524	.432
June	2-1	3.63	151	41	6	12	20	.272	.457	.325
July	0-4	5.60	110	33	6	14	11	.300	.555	.373
August	0-0	—	0	0	0	0	0	—	—	—
Sept./Oct.	1-0	2.77	48	9	1	3	7	.188	.250	.235
Leading Off Inn.			130	33	6	16	11	.254	.438	.336
Bases Empty			304	80	9	39	40	.263	.411	.347
Runners On			219	63	9	22	20	.288	.466	.346
Runners/Scor. Pos.			117	32	2	16	10	.274	.376	.348
Runners On/2 Out			89	25	4	10	11	.281	.483	.354
Scor. Pos./2 Out			53	14	1	8	6	.264	.396	.361
Late-Inning Pressure			22	10	2	4	2	.455	.773	.538
Leading Off			9	4	1	2	1	.444	.778	.545
Runners On			3	1	0	2	0	.333	.333	.600
Runners/Scor. Pos.			1	0	0	2	0	.000	.000	.667
First 9 Batters			206	54	7	28	22	.262	.413	.347
Second 9 Batters			179	50	7	14	23	.279	.469	.327
All Batters Thereafter			138	39	4	19	15	.283	.420	.369

Loves to face: Tony Phillips (.083, 1-for-12, 2 BB)
Alan Trammell (.087, 2-for-23, 4 BB)
Lou Whitaker (.045, 1-for-22, 2 BB)

Hates to face: George Brett (.571, 8-for-14)
Carlos Martinez (.538, 7-for-13, 1 HR)
Rafael Palmeiro (.600, 6-for-10, 1 HR)

Miscellaneous statistics: Ground outs-to-air outs ratio: 0.95 last season, 1.04 for career. . . . Induced 13 double-play ground outs in 107 opportunities (one per 8.2). . . . Allowed 30 doubles, 0 triples in 135.1 innings. . . . Allowed 14 first-inning runs in 24 starts (5.01 ERA). . . . Batting support: 3.88 runs per start. . . . Opposing base stealers: 19-for-22 (86%); 0 pickoffs, 1 balk.

Comments: Pitched 243 innings in 1989, the highest total by an American League rookie since Roger Erickson in 1978. Since 1976, 10 pitchers have worked at least 225 innings in their rookie seasons. None equaled or surpassed his rookie total in his sophomore season; the group fell short by an average of 98 innings. . . . Milacki was one of eight pitchers to walk more batters than he struck out last season (minimum: 100 IP). All eight were American Leaguers: Charlie Hough, Mike Moore, Andy Hawkins, Dan Petry, Detroit's Jeff Robinson, John Cerutti, John Mitchell, and Milacki. They combined for a record of 70–80 with a 4.76 ERA; only two had winning records—Petry and Robinson, both 10–9. (By the way, this A.L. skew appears to be a coincidence; five N.L. pitchers had more walks than strikeouts in at least 100 innings in 1989). . . . Had an ERA of 5.29 through the first four innings of his starts last season, but posted a 2.64 mark from the fifth inning on. . . . Prior to 1990, opponents had batted .169 in Late-Inning Pressure Situations, including four hits in 36 at-bats with runners on base in LIPS. . . . Has a career record of 4–0 vs. the Yankees. . . . Has a career record of 8–1 in September, including a victory in his only start after returning from a 32-day visit to the disabled list last season.

John Mitchell

Throws Right

Baltimore Orioles	W-L	ERA	AB	H	HR	BB	SO	BA	SA	OBA
Season	6-6	4.64	444	133	7	48	43	.300	.423	.366
vs. Left-Handers			202	64	4	29	16	.317	.455	.397
vs. Right-Handers			242	69	3	19	27	.285	.397	.338
vs. Ground-Ballers			210	65	1	24	18	.310	.381	.380
vs. Fly-Ballers			234	68	6	24	25	.291	.462	.353
Home Games	2-2	4.47	196	62	2	26	17	.316	.423	.398
Road Games	4-4	4.78	248	71	5	22	26	.286	.423	.339
Grass Fields	5-6	5.04	404	126	7	46	39	.312	.441	.378
Artificial Turf	1-0	0.84	40	7	0	2	4	.175	.250	.233
April	0-0	3.00	32	8	0	4	2	.250	.313	.342
May	0-0	—	0	0	0	0	0	—	—	—
June	0-1	5.03	72	20	1	7	7	.278	.458	.341
July	3-2	3.89	135	33	3	16	17	.244	.378	.327
August	3-3	5.35	153	53	3	15	13	.346	.464	.398
Sept./Oct.	0-0	5.40	52	19	0	6	4	.365	.442	.424
Leading Off Inn.			110	33	1	8	10	.300	.427	.358
Bases Empty			246	72	4	21	21	.293	.431	.353
Runners On			198	61	3	27	22	.308	.414	.380
Runners/Scor. Pos.			121	34	2	17	18	.281	.397	.354
Runners On/2 Out			80	27	2	15	12	.338	.488	.442
Scor. Pos./2 Out			55	17	2	8	11	.309	.491	.397
Late-Inning Pressure			43	14	0	3	2	.326	.395	.370
Leading Off			15	4	0	0	1	.267	.333	.267
Runners On			8	5	0	3	0	.625	.750	.727
Runners/Scor. Pos.			4	2	0	2	0	.500	.750	.667
First 9 Batters			186	58	0	18	21	.312	.409	.370
Second 9 Batters			130	32	3	18	14	.246	.369	.333
All Batters Thereafter			128	43	4	12	8	.336	.500	.394

Loves to face: Rickey Henderson (0-for-7)
Candy Maldonado (.083, 1-for-12)
Sammy Sosa (0-for-6, 3 SO)

Hates to face: Brian Downing (2-for-2, 1 HR, 1 BB)
Dave Parker (.625, 5-for-8)
Mitch Webster (.556, 5-for-9, 3 2B)

Miscellaneous statistics: Ground outs-to-air outs ratio: 1.45 last season, 1.80 for career. . . . Induced 15 double-play ground outs in 97 opportunities (one per 6.5). . . . Allowed 34 doubles, 0 triples in 114.1 innings. . . . Allowed 10 first-inning runs in 17 starts (5.29 ERA). . . . Batting support: 4.65 runs per start. . . . Opposing base stealers: 1-for-3 (33%); 2 pickoffs, 0 balks.

Comments: There were 11 American League pitchers with at least 100 innings pitched and an average of fewer than four strikeouts per nine innings last season. Four of those 11 pitchers were on the Orioles staff: Bob Milacki (3.99), Dave Johnson (3.40), Jeff Ballard (3.38), and Mitchell (3.38). But Milwaukee actually had a lower team strikeout rate (4.80) than Baltimore (4.87) last season. . . . Didn't allow a first-inning home run in any of his 17 starts last season. . . . Hadn't started in the majors since 1987, when he made 17 starts for the Mets. (Incidentally, Mitchell allowed a first-inning home run in his final start that season for New York.) . . . Blame Mitchell for an early end to the A.L. West pennant race last season. He lost both of his decisions to the Athletics, but defeated the White Sox twice without a loss. . . . With Dave Johnson, Jeff Ballard, and Bob Milacki gone from the Orioles' rotation by late August, the 25-year-old Mitchell was Baltimore's veteran starter. (See the Ben McDonald comment for more.) . . . Mitchell should consider himself lucky to have escaped last season with a .500 record. Other A.L. starters with ERAs over 4.50 and opponents' batting averages above .300 combined for a 39–82 record, a .322 winning percentage.

Jeff Montgomery

Throws Right

Kansas City Royals	W-L	ERA	AB	H	HR	BB	SO	BA	SA	OBA
Season	6-5	2.39	356	81	6	34	94	.228	.331	.302
vs. Left-Handers			176	49	4	21	27	.278	.415	.357
vs. Right-Handers			180	32	2	13	67	.178	.250	.247
vs. Ground-Ballers			155	36	2	19	38	.232	.303	.322
vs. Fly-Ballers			201	45	4	15	56	.224	.353	.286
Home Games	3-1	1.20	199	44	1	14	57	.221	.291	.272
Road Games	3-4	3.89	157	37	5	20	37	.236	.382	.337
Grass Fields	3-3	4.05	123	27	4	16	31	.220	.366	.329
Artificial Turf	3-2	1.48	233	54	2	18	63	.232	.313	.287
April	1-1	2.40	58	16	0	3	14	.276	.345	.323
May	3-1	2.11	74	11	2	8	24	.149	.284	.238
June	0-0	2.38	42	10	1	3	14	.238	.357	.289
July	0-0	3.31	62	14	2	8	18	.226	.419	.319
August	1-1	1.29	56	14	0	5	14	.250	.286	.323
Sept./Oct.	1-2	2.76	64	16	1	7	10	.250	.313	.333
Leading Off Inn.			78	14	1	5	20	.179	.244	.256
Bases Empty			186	44	2	11	42	.237	.339	.294
Runners On			170	37	4	23	52	.218	.324	.311
Runners/Scor. Pos.			102	22	2	21	35	.216	.304	.349
Runners On/2 Out			77	19	3	8	22	.247	.403	.318
Scor. Pos./2 Out			51	14	2	7	16	.275	.431	.362
Late-Inning Pressure			222	54	3	26	56	.243	.347	.325
Leading Off			48	9	0	3	11	.188	.229	.250
Runners On			110	22	3	20	36	.200	.291	.323
Runners/Scor. Pos.			67	13	1	18	23	.194	.239	.364
First 9 Batters			342	78	6	33	91	.228	.336	.304
Second 9 Batters			14	3	0	1	3	.214	.214	.250
All Batters Thereafter			0	0	0	0	0	—	—	—

Loves to face: Jesse Barfield (0-for-8)
Mike Devereaux (0-for-6, 4 SO)
Pete Incaviglia (.091, 1-for-11, 2 BB)

Hates to face: Jose Canseco (.750, 3-for-4, 1 HR, 1 SO)
Kent Hrbek (.556, 5-for-9, 1 HR)
Kirby Puckett (.417, 5-for-12, 3 2B)

Miscellaneous statistics: Ground outs-to-air outs ratio: 0.99 last season, 1.12 for career. . . . Induced 2 double-play ground outs in 83 opportunities (one per 41.5). . . . Allowed 17 doubles, 1 triple in 94.1 innings. . . . Stranded 19 inherited runners, allowed 12 to score (61%). . . . Opposing base stealers: 14-for-17 (82%); 1 pickoff, 0 balks.

Comments: Montgomery's career average of 8.49 strikeouts per nine innings is 2d highest in Royals history (minimum: 200 IP), just ahead of Tom Gordon (8.33) and just behind Bob Johnson (8.66). . . . Over the last 16 years, only Rob Dibble has struck out a higher percentage of right-handed batters than Montgomery has (minimum: 150 SO). See page 402 for a deeper list. . . . Saved 24 games in 34 opportunities. His save percentage (71%) ranked only 12th of 14 American League pitchers with at least 20 save opportunities. But a look at his monthly breakdown indicates that his effectiveness increased as the season progressed: April, 0-for-2; May, 3-for-6; June, 4-for-5; July, 8-for-9; August, 4-for-6; September, 5-for-6. . . . Entered a game with runners on base in only four of 35 appearances after the All-Star break. . . . Held the top 10 American League batters to a .179 average last season (5-for-28). . . . Career record of 17–5 with an ERA of 1.79 in home games, 5–7 with a 3.45 ERA on the road. . . . With so many closers now entering games only when their teams have the lead, many compile losing records. For example, of the 24 pitchers with more than 15 saves last season, only nine had records above the .500 mark. A sign of Montgomery's effectiveness: he is one of four pitchers with at least 15 saves and winning records in both 1989 and 1990. The others: Dennis Eckersley, Gregg Olson, and Jeff Reardon.

Mike Moore

Throws Right

Oakland A's	W-L	ERA	AB	H	HR	BB	SO	BA	SA	OBA
Season	13-15	4.65	764	204	14	84	73	.267	.397	.339
vs. Left-Handers			404	105	5	47	34	.260	.374	.333
vs. Right-Handers			360	99	9	37	39	.275	.422	.346
vs. Ground-Ballers			375	93	5	45	35	.248	.349	.326
vs. Fly-Ballers			389	111	9	39	38	.285	.442	.352
Home Games	7-10	4.66	466	127	10	47	43	.273	.403	.339
Road Games	6-5	4.63	298	77	4	37	30	.258	.386	.339
Grass Fields	12-13	4.39	698	182	14	75	69	.261	.387	.332
Artificial Turf	1-2	7.80	66	22	0	9	4	.333	.500	.408
April	1-1	6.08	88	22	4	12	6	.250	.420	.343
May	3-3	3.24	156	33	2	10	12	.212	.314	.259
June	1-3	4.81	140	44	3	11	15	.314	.464	.362
July	4-3	3.69	173	44	0	25	14	.254	.347	.347
August	2-2	4.20	110	27	1	14	13	.245	.364	.333
Sept./Oct.	2-3	7.88	97	34	4	12	13	.351	.536	.418
Leading Off Inn.			194	52	1	15	26	.268	.356	.327
Bases Empty			435	113	9	39	52	.260	.384	.324
Runners On			329	91	5	45	21	.277	.413	.359
Runners/Scor. Pos.			201	57	3	35	14	.284	.433	.381
Runners On/2 Out			122	30	1	19	10	.246	.369	.352
Scor. Pos./2 Out			88	23	1	16	7	.261	.409	.381
Late-Inning Pressure			35	8	3	4	4	.229	.571	.300
Leading Off			13	4	1	1	3	.308	.692	.357
Runners On			7	0	0	2	1	.000	.000	.200
Runners/Scor. Pos.			7	0	0	2	1	.000	.000	.200
First 9 Batters			259	75	2	32	28	.290	.371	.367
Second 9 Batters			264	79	7	24	21	.299	.470	.360
All Batters Thereafter			241	50	5	28	24	.207	.344	.287

Loves to face: Brian Downing (.125, 6-for-48, 1 HR)
Paul Molitor (.146, 6-for-41)
Gary Pettis (.148, 9-for-61)

Hates to face: Darnell Coles (.444, 4-for-9, 1 3B, 3 HR)
Danny Tartabull (.462, 6-for-13, 3 2B, 1 HR)
Dave Winfield (.500, 13-for-26, 2 HR)

Miscellaneous statistics: Ground outs-to-air outs ratio: 1.35 last season, 1.25 for career.... Induced 23 double-play ground outs in 165 opportunities (one per 7.2).... Allowed 41 doubles (tied for 4th most in A.L.), 8 triples in 199.1 innings.... Allowed 25 first-inning runs in 33 starts (4.91 ERA).... Batting support: 3.79 runs per start.... Opposing base stealers: 17-for-23 (74%); 1 pick-off, 0 balks.

Comments: Became only the third pitcher since 1905 to lose as many as 15 games for a club that won 100 or more. The others: Ralph Terry (17–15 for the 1963 Yankees) and Dennis Martinez (15–16 for the 1979 Orioles).... His won-lost record dropped from 19–11 in 1989; his ERA rose more than two runs per game from 2.61.... His strikeout rate fell by 49 percent, from 6.41 per nine innings in 1989 to 3.30 last season, *the largest decrease in this century* (minimum: 30 GS in both seasons).... Walk/strikeout totals year by year since 1988: 63/182, 83/172, 84/73. Only two other pitchers have increased their walks and decreased their strikeouts in each of the last two seasons: Steve Bedrosian and Mike Scott. Only four pitchers in major league history had three-year streaks: Cliff Melton (1938–40), Joel Horlen (1966–68), Cal Koonce (1968–70), and Bill Laskey (1983–85).... Had the lowest average run support on the team, more than a full run per game less than his teammates received.... Opponents have hit for a higher average with runners on base than with the bases empty in each of his nine seasons, the longest current streak in the majors.... Has winning career records against only two teams: Milwaukee (11–9) and Texas (11–5).... Moore is one of two players in major league history with more RBIs in postseason play (2) than in regular-season play (0). The other: Mike Boddicker (1–0).

Jack Morris

Throws Right

Detroit Tigers	W-L	ERA	AB	H	HR	BB	SO	BA	SA	OBA
Season	15-18	4.51	953	231	26	97	162	.242	.375	.313
vs. Left-Handers			466	125	13	58	70	.268	.397	.350
vs. Right-Handers			487	106	13	39	92	.218	.353	.277
vs. Ground-Ballers			447	105	9	44	66	.235	.336	.305
vs. Fly-Ballers			506	126	17	53	96	.249	.409	.320
Home Games	8-8	4.06	430	109	9	30	71	.253	.372	.301
Road Games	7-10	4.87	523	122	17	67	91	.233	.377	.323
Grass Fields	13-16	4.14	831	198	20	86	144	.238	.357	.310
Artificial Turf	2-2	7.20	122	33	6	11	18	.270	.492	.333
April	2-2	5.34	120	36	1	12	23	.300	.450	.358
May	0-5	5.20	175	41	6	21	23	.234	.383	.315
June	4-2	5.86	144	45	7	12	27	.313	.507	.369
July	2-4	3.20	168	33	5	13	32	.196	.315	.259
August	3-2	5.79	143	37	2	19	17	.259	.343	.348
Sept./Oct.	4-3	2.86	203	39	5	20	40	.192	.300	.265
Leading Off Inn.			229	62	7	26	30	.271	.424	.348
Bases Empty			544	129	10	47	88	.237	.349	.303
Runners On			409	102	16	50	74	.249	.408	.327
Runners/Scor. Pos.			234	60	11	35	52	.256	.449	.345
Runners On/2 Out			157	34	7	19	32	.217	.389	.305
Scor. Pos./2 Out			105	22	5	14	26	.210	.400	.308
Late-Inning Pressure			85	27	2	6	10	.318	.412	.359
Leading Off			22	4	2	1	1	.182	.500	.217
Runners On			36	14	0	3	5	.389	.417	.425
Runners/Scor. Pos.			15	7	0	3	2	.467	.533	.526
First 9 Batters			279	68	7	35	44	.244	.376	.332
Second 9 Batters			290	71	10	27	56	.245	.400	.308
All Batters Thereafter			384	92	9	35	62	.240	.354	.303

Loves to face: George Brett (.338, 23-for-68—but 4-for-last-25, 0 XBH)
Ozzie Guillen (.143, 7-for-49, 1 HR)
Steve Sax (.125, 2-for-16)

Hates to face: Henry Cotto (.538, 7-for-13, 1 HR)
Ken Griffey, Jr. (.400, 4-for-10, 2 2B, 1 HR)
Mark McGwire (.308, 4-for-13, 3 HR, 5 SO)

Miscellaneous statistics: Ground outs-to-air outs ratio: 1.04 last season, 1.12 for career.... Induced 23 double-play ground outs in 209 opportunities (one per 9.1).... Allowed 42 doubles (tied for 2d most in A.L.), 3 triples in 249.2 innings.... Allowed 24 first-inning runs in 36 starts (5.50 ERA).... Batting support: 4.81 runs per start.... Opposing base stealers: 45-for-51 (88%); 1 pick-off, 2 balks.

Comments: One of only four of last season's opening-day starters to lead their teams in victories.... Has drawn 11 consecutive opening-day assignments, one shy of the modern record for pitchers, shared by Tom Seaver (1968–79) and Robin Roberts (1950–61).... Leaves the Tigers 5th on their career victories list with 198, behind Hooks Dauss (221), George Mullin (209), Mickey Lolich (207), and Hal Newhouser (200).... The "Winningest Pitcher of the 1980s" currently ranks 15th in the 1990s.... Shared A.L. lead in complete games with Dave Stewart (11). It was the lowest total ever to lead the American League.... Allowed an average of 10.34 hits per nine innings over his first 16 starts, but only 6.92 in 20 starts thereafter. His walk rate fell (3.77 per nine innings to 3.31), his home-run rate fell (one HR per 7.3 IP to one per 12.3) and his strikeout rate rose (5.65 per nine innings to 5.94) during that later segment as well.... The Tigers committed 31 errors with Morris on the mound, the most of any team behind any pitcher in the majors.... Has a career record of 27–9 vs. the Indians, his best against any club.... Has made 396 consecutive starts since his last relief appearance.... After signing with the Twins, Morris said that the Metrodome would pose no problem after pitching in "a great hitter's park" like Tiger Stadium. Jack, check out the "effect on runs" chart on page 416. You ain't seen nothing yet!

Jamie Moyer

Throws Left

Texas Rangers	W-L	ERA	AB	H	HR	BB	SO	BA	SA	OBA
Season	2-6	4.66	396	115	6	39	58	.290	.434	.354
vs. Left-Handers			81	18	1	4	9	.222	.333	.267
vs. Right-Handers			315	97	5	35	49	.308	.460	.376
vs. Ground-Ballers			180	53	4	12	24	.294	.439	.333
vs. Fly-Ballers			216	62	2	27	34	.287	.431	.371
Home Games	2-2	3.77	224	61	1	22	44	.272	.384	.339
Road Games	0-4	5.91	172	54	5	17	14	.314	.500	.375
Grass Fields	2-5	4.30	312	88	3	29	50	.282	.404	.342
Artificial Turf	0-1	6.10	84	27	3	10	8	.321	.548	.400
April	0-3	4.08	69	21	2	6	5	.304	.449	.377
May	0-0	3.55	44	10	0	6	11	.227	.364	.308
June	0-0	5.11	52	19	2	2	10	.365	.596	.400
July	0-0	6.63	75	22	2	10	14	.293	.467	.376
August	1-3	4.00	135	35	0	13	14	.259	.356	.316
Sept./Oct.	1-0	5.79	21	8	0	2	4	.381	.524	.440
Leading Off Inn.			100	35	3	10	10	.350	.600	.420
Bases Empty			220	63	5	20	30	.286	.459	.354
Runners On			176	52	1	19	28	.295	.403	.355
Runners/Scor. Pos.			109	32	1	14	18	.294	.394	.359
Runners On/2 Out			70	20	0	6	11	.286	.357	.342
Scor. Pos./2 Out			51	14	0	4	8	.275	.314	.327
Late-Inning Pressure			21	4	0	2	3	.190	.286	.261
Leading Off			8	2	0	0	2	.250	.500	.250
Runners On			5	1	0	1	1	.200	.200	.333
Runners/Scor. Pos.			4	1	0	1	1	.250	.250	.400
First 9 Batters			205	53	3	26	34	.259	.395	.345
Second 9 Batters			112	35	1	9	15	.313	.438	.354
All Batters Thereafter			79	27	2	4	9	.342	.532	.381

Loves to face: Al Newman (.077, 1-for-13)
Luis Rivera (.048, 1-for-21)
Glenn Wilson (.120, 3-for-25)

Hates to face: Darnell Coles (.375, 6-for-16, 1 2B, 3 HR)
Lance Parrish (.360, 9-for-25, 4 HR)
Tim Raines (.474, 9-for-19, 1 HR)

Miscellaneous statistics: Ground outs-to-air outs ratio: 1.16 last season, 1.39 for career. . . . Induced 15 double-play ground outs in 81 opportunities (one per 5.4), 2d-highest rate in A.L. . . . Allowed 33 doubles, 3 triples in 102.1 innings. . . . Allowed 9 first-inning runs in 10 starts (5.40 ERA). . . . Batting support: 4.10 runs per start. . . . Record of 1–5, 4.72 ERA as a starter; 1–1, 4.60 ERA in 23 relief appearances. . . . Stranded 17 inherited runners, allowed 6 to score (74%). . . . Opposing base stealers: 9-for-16 (56%); 6 pickoffs, 0 balks.

Comments: Allowed only two home runs in 55⅓ innings pitched as a starter last season. . . . Walked eight batters in the first innings of his 10 starts. . . . Opponents' on-base percentage of .420 leading off innings was the worst in the majors last season (minimum: 100 BFP). . . . Opposing left-handed batters have a career batting average of .231; right-handers have hit .290 against him. . . . Career breakdown of opponents' batting: .258 on his first pass through the order, .274 on his second time through, .317 thereafter. . . . Has pitched a total of 178⅓ innings in his two seasons with the Rangers, after hurling over 200 innings in each of the previous two seasons with the Cubs. . . . Hasn't committed a balk in 461 innings since July 21, 1987—that includes 1988, the "year of the balk". . . . Winning percentages year by year, starting with his rookie season of 1986: .636 (7–4), .444 (12–15), .375 (9–15), .308 (4–9), .250 (2–6). Moyer's and Brian Fisher's winning percentages have declined by at least 50 points for four consecutive seasons—just about the point of no return. Among 34 other pitchers in major league history to do that, 22 were never even given a chance to snap their streaks. To paraphrase Mel Allen, they're going, going, gone.

Rob Murphy

Throws Left

Boston Red Sox	W-L	ERA	AB	H	HR	BB	SO	BA	SA	OBA
Season	0-6	6.32	244	85	10	32	54	.348	.545	.420
vs. Left-Handers			83	20	0	12	19	.241	.289	.340
vs. Right-Handers			161	65	10	20	35	.404	.677	.462
vs. Ground-Ballers			103	34	2	14	24	.330	.456	.415
vs. Fly-Ballers			141	51	8	18	30	.362	.610	.423
Home Games	0-2	5.10	127	41	4	11	33	.323	.480	.371
Road Games	0-4	7.67	117	44	6	21	21	.376	.615	.468
Grass Fields	0-4	6.26	200	72	8	26	47	.360	.540	.429
Artificial Turf	0-2	6.55	44	13	2	6	7	.295	.568	.380
April	0-1	3.86	65	18	2	5	19	.277	.431	.329
May	0-1	6.55	46	16	5	6	7	.348	.717	.415
June	0-2	6.75	43	16	1	4	14	.372	.512	.408
July	0-2	9.95	34	14	0	5	6	.412	.588	.500
August	0-0	7.36	31	12	2	9	6	.387	.581	.512
Sept./Oct.	0-0	6.75	25	9	0	3	2	.360	.480	.429
Leading Off Inn.			49	21	3	5	10	.429	.694	.481
Bases Empty			106	39	8	13	22	.368	.651	.437
Runners On			138	46	2	19	32	.333	.464	.407
Runners/Scor. Pos.			89	30	2	10	21	.337	.461	.394
Runners On/2 Out			57	17	0	9	17	.298	.368	.394
Scor. Pos./2 Out			38	12	0	4	11	.316	.316	.381
Late-Inning Pressure			118	40	4	17	28	.339	.517	.416
Leading Off			25	12	1	3	4	.480	.640	.536
Runners On			69	21	1	11	15	.304	.449	.390
Runners/Scor. Pos.			45	12	1	6	11	.267	.422	.340
First 9 Batters			239	85	10	31	51	.356	.556	.425
Second 9 Batters			5	0	0	1	3	.000	.000	.167
All Batters Thereafter			0	0	0	0	0	—	—	—

Loves to face: Henry Cotto (.125, 1-for-8, 3 SO)
Dion James (.182, 2-for-11)
Lou Whitaker (0-for-8)

Hates to face: Greg Brock (.556, 5-for-9)
Mark McGwire (.750, 3-for-4, 1 2B, 2 HR, 1 SO)
Kirby Puckett (.667, 4-for-6, 1 HR)

Miscellaneous statistics: Ground outs-to-air outs ratio: 1.07 last season, 1.20 for career. . . . Induced 5 double-play ground outs in 70 opportunities (one per 14.0). . . . Allowed 16 doubles, 1 triple in 57.0 innings. . . . Stranded 32 inherited runners, allowed 19 to score (63%). . . . Opposing base stealers: 5-for-8 (63%); 0 pickoffs, 0 balks.

Comments: Forget the 40/40 club. Murphy is the first player in major league history to appear in over 60 games in a season with an ERA over 6.00. . . . He also became the first player ever to lose as many as six games in a winless season more than once. He was also 0–6 in 1988. . . . Won the first eight decisions of his career, but has lost 24 of 35 since then. . . . Prior to 1990, he had a career average of one home run for every 19 innings pitched. But in a season when the Red Sox staff allowed the fewest home runs in the majors, Murphy allowed them at a rate of one every 5.7 innings, worst on the club. . . . Remained as effective as ever against left-handed hitters; he has faced 494 in his career, and they've batted .224 with no triples and three home runs. But over the last 16 years, no other pitcher who faced as many right-handed batters as Murphy did last season (186) was rattled by them for so high a batting or slugging average. . . . Opponents batted 51 points higher on grass fields (.273) than on artificial turf (.223) over the last five seasons, the 3d-largest margin in the majors. . . . Ranked sixth among American League pitchers with 68 games, even though his total of appearances has decreased in every year since 1987: 87, 76, 74, 68. . . . Has a career record of 5–15 before the All-Star break, but he's 14–9 during the second half of the season. . . . Oh, yes. Just to put an appropriate punctuation mark on the end of a lost season, Murphy threw away a grounder on September 5 and was charged with the first error of his major league career. His 332 errorless games at the start of a career was an all-time record, regardless of position.

Jaime Navarro

Throws Right

Milwaukee Brewers	W-L	ERA	AB	H	HR	BB	SO	BA	SA	OBA
Season	8-7	4.46	600	176	11	41	75	.293	.403	.340
vs. Left-Handers			321	96	4	25	37	.299	.374	.348
vs. Right-Handers			279	80	7	16	38	.287	.437	.330
vs. Ground-Ballers			286	88	3	25	36	.308	.402	.363
vs. Fly-Ballers			314	88	8	16	39	.280	.404	.318
Home Games	4-4	4.09	285	79	5	26	33	.277	.372	.339
Road Games	4-3	4.81	315	97	6	15	42	.308	.432	.341
Grass Fields	5-5	4.00	468	132	9	34	53	.282	.385	.335
Artificial Turf	3-2	6.12	132	44	2	7	22	.333	.470	.357
April	0-0	5.21	81	27	2	8	8	.333	.444	.407
May	1-1	8.82	75	30	3	4	6	.400	.627	.420
June	1-1	5.79	33	8	0	9	4	.242	.303	.405
July	0-0	1.59	83	17	1	4	14	.205	.265	.241
August	3-3	5.06	149	45	2	8	26	.302	.403	.335
Sept./Oct.	3-2	3.22	179	49	3	8	17	.274	.374	.309
Leading Off Inn.			145	35	1	11	14	.241	.297	.299
Bases Empty			325	92	6	22	39	.283	.388	.334
Runners On			275	84	5	19	36	.305	.422	.347
Runners/Scor. Pos.			153	42	2	13	24	.275	.353	.326
Runners On/2 Out			106	30	2	6	21	.283	.406	.321
Scor. Pos./2 Out			72	19	1	5	13	.264	.333	.312
Late-Inning Pressure			47	19	1	2	5	.404	.553	.420
Leading Off			10	3	0	1	0	.300	.300	.364
Runners On			25	11	1	1	3	.440	.560	.444
Runners/Scor. Pos.			15	7	0	0	2	.467	.467	.438
First 9 Batters			242	61	1	20	32	.252	.298	.309
Second 9 Batters			196	58	4	12	28	.296	.418	.343
All Batters Thereafter			162	57	6	9	15	.352	.543	.383

Loves to face: Roberto Kelly (.083, 1-for-12)
Cal Ripken (0-for-9, 2 BB)
Mickey Tettleton (.100, 1-for-10)

Hates to face: Wade Boggs (.714, 5-for-7)
Mike Devereaux (.714, 5-for-7, 1 HR)
Jeff Manto (3-for-3, 1 HR)

Miscellaneous statistics: Ground outs-to-air outs ratio: 1.14 last season, 1.14 for career. . . . Induced 14 double-play ground outs in 139 opportunities (one per 9.9). . . . Allowed 25 doubles, 4 triples in 149.1 innings. . . . Allowed 9 first-inning runs in 22 starts (3.27 ERA). . . . Batting support: 5.27 runs per start (3d highest in A.L.) . . . Opposing base stealers: 11-for-15 (73%); 0 pickoffs, 5 balks.

Comments: Completed three of his last eight starts, after only one complete game in his previous 31 starts. . . . Had a record of 8–7 with a 4.99 ERA as a starting pitcher. Last season, only three other major league pitchers, all American Leaguers, had winning records while posting an ERA as high as Navarro's: Jeff Robinson (Det.), Bert Blyleven, and Frank Tanana (minimum: 20 GS). . . . Stranded seven of the eight runners he inherited in his 10 relief appearances. . . . Led the American League with five balks. . . . Hasn't allowed a first-inning home run in 29 starts dating back to a Joe Carter shot in August 1989. . . . Opponents have a career average of .249 in Navarro's first pass through the batting order, .281 in his second pass through the order, .341 thereafter. One more pass and he'll need CPR. . . . Is he starting to sound like an ideal reliever to you? Don't get carried away with that idea. Opposing batters have hit .441 in Late-Inning Pressure Situations (30-for-68), the highest mark over the last 16 years (minimum: 50 AB). . . . Gap of 32 points between the career batting averages of opposing ground-ball hitters (.303) and fly-ball hitters (.271) is considerably larger than the six-pointer between those of opposing left-handed (.289) and right-handed (.283) batters. (We're warning you, managers. You better start paying attention to this stuff.)

Gregg Olson

Throws Right

Baltimore Orioles	W-L	ERA	AB	H	HR	BB	SO	BA	SA	OBA
Season	6-5	2.42	268	57	3	31	74	.213	.276	.299
vs. Left-Handers			145	29	1	19	34	.200	.248	.298
vs. Right-Handers			123	28	2	12	40	.228	.309	.301
vs. Ground-Ballers			125	25	1	14	34	.200	.248	.284
vs. Fly-Ballers			143	32	2	17	40	.224	.301	.313
Home Games	5-0	2.93	113	24	2	11	35	.212	.301	.286
Road Games	1-5	2.06	155	33	1	20	39	.213	.258	.309
Grass Fields	6-3	2.37	214	43	3	25	65	.201	.280	.291
Artificial Turf	0-2	2.63	54	14	0	6	9	.259	.259	.333
April	1-0	0.00	40	5	0	3	7	.125	.150	.205
May	1-0	0.60	48	6	0	6	19	.125	.125	.218
June	2-2	2.84	47	12	1	4	12	.255	.362	.314
July	1-1	0.68	47	8	0	8	17	.170	.191	.304
August	0-1	8.38	39	11	2	7	8	.282	.487	.404
Sept./Oct.	1-1	3.97	47	15	0	3	11	.319	.362	.353
Leading Off Inn.			55	7	1	7	15	.127	.182	.250
Bases Empty			140	28	1	15	37	.200	.257	.287
Runners On			128	29	2	16	37	.227	.297	.313
Runners/Scor. Pos.			81	17	1	12	27	.210	.272	.305
Runners On/2 Out			62	13	1	10	20	.210	.258	.329
Scor. Pos./2 Out			45	10	1	8	15	.222	.289	.340
Late-Inning Pressure			225	49	3	27	64	.218	.289	.302
Leading Off			46	6	1	6	13	.130	.196	.245
Runners On			107	24	2	15	31	.224	.299	.315
Runners/Scor. Pos.			71	14	1	11	24	.197	.254	.298
First 9 Batters			265	57	3	30	73	.215	.279	.300
Second 9 Batters			3	0	0	1	1	.000	.000	.250
All Batters Thereafter			0	0	0	0	0	—	—	—

Loves to face: Dave Henderson (0-for-4, 3 SO)
Pete Incaviglia (0-for-5, 5 SO)
Pete O'Brien (0-for-6)

Hates to face: Steve Balboni (.400, 2-for-5, 1 HR)
Scott Bradley (.600, 3-for-5, 1 BB)
Mark McGwire (.400, 2-for-5, 1 HR, 2 SO)

Miscellaneous statistics: Ground outs-to-air outs ratio: 0.87 last season, 0.91 for career. . . . Induced 6 double-play ground outs in 55 opportunities (one per 9.2). . . . Allowed 8 doubles, 0 triples in 74.1 innings. . . . Stranded 27 inherited runners, allowed 10 to score (73%). . . . Opposing base stealers: 11-for-13 (85%); 0 pickoffs, 0 balks.

Comments: Was the youngest player on the American League All-Star squad last season. . . . Although he didn't turn 24 until after the 1990 season ended, he has already saved 64 games. Only five other pitchers in history had half as many saves by age 24, including the leader, Terry Forster (74). The others: Billy McCool (50), Neil Allen (48), Victor Cruz (32), and Mitch Williams (32). . . . Now needs only 42 saves to break Tippy Martinez's franchise record. . . . Ended the 1989 season with 26⅔ consecutive scoreless innings, and extended that streak to 41 innings before allowing his first run of 1990 on May 7. . . . The Orioles didn't commit an error while Olson was on the mound last season. Baltimore fielders have played 85⅔ consecutive errorless innings in support of Olson dating back to September 5, 1989. . . . Opponents' career batting average of .189 in Late-Inning Pressure Situations is 2d lowest over the last 16 years (minimum: 500 BFP), behind Randy Myers (.183). . . . Opponents' career breakdown: .176 at Memorial Stadium, .181 on other grass fields, .290 on artificial surfaces. Olson is undefeated at Memorial Stadium (8–0), but has a 4–8 record in road games. . . . Hasn't allowed a triple in 170⅓ innings over three seasons. . . . New teammate Dwight Evans is the only player with more than one career home run off of Olson (3-for-5, 2 HR). If you can't beat him. . .

Jesse Orosco

Throws Left

Cleveland Indians	W-L	ERA	AB	H	HR	BB	SO	BA	SA	OBA
Season	5-4	3.90	243	58	9	38	55	.239	.407	.338
vs. Left-Handers			67	15	2	12	16	.224	.358	.338
vs. Right-Handers			176	43	7	26	39	.244	.426	.338
vs. Ground-Ballers			120	27	3	18	25	.225	.325	.324
vs. Fly-Ballers			123	31	6	20	30	.252	.488	.352
Home Games	3-3	3.00	143	34	6	17	35	.238	.413	.313
Road Games	2-1	5.26	100	24	3	21	20	.240	.400	.372
Grass Fields	4-4	3.88	207	49	8	29	45	.237	.406	.326
Artificial Turf	1-0	4.00	36	9	1	9	10	.250	.417	.400
April	0-1	1.59	17	2	0	6	4	.118	.176	.348
May	3-1	5.79	36	10	2	4	4	.278	.472	.341
June	0-1	5.52	56	12	2	7	13	.214	.375	.302
July	0-1	2.51	52	12	0	13	13	.231	.327	.385
August	1-0	2.08	51	13	2	6	9	.255	.412	.322
Sept./Oct.	1-0	5.87	31	9	3	2	12	.290	.645	.333
Leading Off Inn.			48	11	2	8	12	.229	.396	.339
Bases Empty			119	32	6	16	27	.269	.479	.356
Runners On			124	26	3	22	28	.210	.339	.322
Runners/Scor. Pos.			80	17	0	18	20	.213	.287	.347
Runners On/2 Out			65	16	2	10	14	.246	.415	.347
Scor. Pos./2 Out			47	12	0	7	11	.255	.362	.352
Late-Inning Pressure			63	13	2	11	13	.206	.333	.324
Leading Off			14	1	0	4	5	.071	.071	.278
Runners On			27	6	1	4	5	.222	.370	.323
Runners/Scor. Pos.			13	2	0	3	3	.154	.154	.313
First 9 Batters			228	53	9	37	54	.232	.412	.337
Second 9 Batters			14	5	0	1	1	.357	.357	.375
All Batters Thereafter			1	0	0	0	0	.000	.000	.000

Loves to face: Ozzie Guillen (0-for-5)
Dave Parker (.105, 2-for-19)
Steve Sax (.125, 2-for-16)

Hates to face: Ellis Burks (.667, 2-for-3, 1 HR)
Chili Davis (.400, 8-for-20, 1 HR)
Jeffrey Leonard (.294, 5-for-17, 2 HR)

Miscellaneous statistics: Ground outs-to-air outs ratio: 0.88 last season, 0.88 for career. . . . Induced 5 double-play ground outs in 56 opportunities (one per 11.2). . . . Allowed 10 doubles, 2 triples in 64.2 innings. . . . Stranded 36 inherited runners, allowed 13 to score (73%). . . . Opposing base stealers: 3-for-4 (75%); 0 pickoffs, 0 balks.

Comments: Has the 5th lowest career ERA among pitchers active in 1990 (minimum: 500 IP). The top five: Tim Burke, 2.48; John Franco, 2.49; Dave Smith, 2.53; Orel Hershiser, 2.71; and Orosco, 2.76. . . . Has held opponents to a lower batting average with runners on base than he has with the bases empty in each of the last 10 seasons, the longest streak in the 16-year history of *The Player Analysis*. . . . Opponents have batted 68 points lower with runners in scoring position (.181) than in other at-bats (.249) over the last five seasons, the largest margin in the majors. . . . Opposing fly-ball hitters have hit for a higher average than ground-ball hitters in each of the last six seasons. . . . Although Bryan Harvey is the new bases-loaded champ (see p. 408), Orosco continues to excel with the bags full. He has held opposing batters below the .200 mark in eight of his 11 seasons, including each of the past two. During 1989–90, opponents were 3-for-26 with the bases loaded. . . . Hasn't committed a balk in his last 372 appearances. . . . Saves year by year since 1984: 31, 17, 21, 16, 9, 3, 2. . . . Both Orosco and Lee Smith have appeared in at least 50 games in each of the last nine seasons. Ron Perranoski is the only pitcher in history to appear in 50 games in 10 straight seasons (1961–70). Others with streaks of nine years: Roy Face (1956–64) and Rollie Fingers (1972–80).

Melido Perez

Throws Right

Chicago White Sox	W-L	ERA	AB	H	HR	BB	SO	BA	SA	OBA
Season	13-14	4.61	735	177	14	86	161	.241	.367	.320
vs. Left-Handers			380	95	6	42	81	.250	.374	.322
vs. Right-Handers			355	82	8	44	80	.231	.361	.318
vs. Ground-Ballers			357	82	6	41	75	.230	.350	.306
vs. Fly-Ballers			378	95	8	45	86	.251	.384	.333
Home Games	5-6	5.11	314	79	6	32	62	.252	.379	.321
Road Game	8-8	4.27	421	98	8	54	99	.233	.359	.319
Grass Fields	12-11	4.08	625	143	13	69	137	.229	.357	.306
Artificial Turf	1-3	7.90	110	34	1	17	24	.309	.427	.395
April	1-2	4.50	82	18	2	7	20	.220	.341	.281
May	3-2	4.28	120	22	2	18	35	.183	.300	.293
June	2-3	3.66	149	35	2	12	22	.235	.302	.292
July	3-1	3.29	99	18	5	11	24	.182	.414	.268
August	2-4	6.57	146	46	1	18	28	.315	.425	.386
Sept./Oct.	2-2	5.02	139	38	2	20	32	.273	.417	.360
Leading Off Inn.			192	57	4	20	28	.297	.427	.365
Bases Empty			438	99	11	52	94	.226	.356	.310
Runners On			297	78	3	34	67	.263	.384	.334
Runners/Scor. Pos.			155	46	2	18	34	.297	.439	.358
Runners On/2 Out			114	28	2	12	28	.246	.404	.323
Scor. Pos./2 Out			68	18	2	7	17	.265	.471	.333
Late-Inning Pressure			43	10	1	7	6	.233	.395	.340
Leading Off			14	5	1	1	0	.357	.643	.400
Runners On			13	3	0	2	1	.231	.308	.333
Runners/Scor. Pos.			4	1	0	1	1	.250	.500	.400
First 9 Batters			274	74	5	34	53	.270	.394	.348
Second 9 Batters			249	61	7	24	61	.245	.394	.310
All Batters Thereafter			212	42	2	28	47	.198	.302	.293

Loves to face: Dan Gladden (.120, 3-for-25)
Dave Parker (.148, 4-for-27)
Terry Steinbach (.125, 2-for-16)

Hates to face: Jose Canseco (.500, 9-for-18, 2 HR)
Kirby Puckett (.577, 15-for-26, 1 HR, 0 SO)
B.J. Surhoff (.375, 6-for-16)

Miscellaneous statistics: Ground outs-to-air outs ratio: 0.96 last season, 0.85 for career. . . . Induced 20 double-play ground outs in 159 opportunities (one per 8.0). . . . Allowed 31 doubles, 10 triples (2d most in A.L.) in 197.0 innings. . . . Allowed 28 first-inning runs in 35 starts (6.23 ERA). . . . Batting support: 4.31 runs per start. . . . Opposing base stealers: 12-for-23 (52%); 1 pickoff, 4 balks.

Comments: There have been four rain-shortened no-hitters in baseball's expansion era: two by the Perez brothers, and two by the rest of the world. Here's the list: Dean Chance (1967), David Palmer (1984), Pascual Perez (1988), and Melido Perez (1990). (Nice comeback by the Perezes, don't you think?). . .The White Sox have used a different opening-day starting pitcher in every season since 1986: Tom Seaver, Rich Dotson, Ricky Horton, Jerry Reuss, and Perez. . . . He completed only three of 35 starts last season; all three were shutouts. . . . Ranked second in the A.L. with an average of 6.8 hits per nine innings through August 2, but fell from the top 10 by allowing 10.56 per nine innings thereafter. . . . His home-run rate improved during the second half. He allowed 11 in his first 22 starts, only three in his final 13 starts. . . . Posted an ERA of 1.32 in his 13 victories, 9.57 in his 14 defeats. . . . Prior to 1990, he had a career average of one home run allowed every 7.7 innings pitched. Last season, he allowed one every 14.1 innings. . . . Rate of strikeouts (per nine innings) has increased by roughly half-a-K in each of the past two seasons. Year by year since 1988: 6.30, 6.92, 7.35. . . . Check out the up-and-down career record by months: April, 3–5; May, 9–5; June, 5–11; July, 9–3; August, 3–9; Sept./Oct., 8–6. . . . And before you write off brother Pascual, we'd like to remind you that his 2.75 ERA since 1987 is the third best in the majors (minimum: 400 IP), behind Orel Hershiser (2.60) and John Tudor (2.69). (Are you thinking what we're thinking?)

Dan Petry

Throws Right

Detroit Tigers	W-L	ERA	AB	H	HR	BB	SO	BA	SA	OBA
Season	10-9	4.45	563	148	14	77	73	.263	.403	.349
vs. Left-Handers			245	61	3	37	32	.249	.351	.345
vs. Right-Handers			318	87	11	40	41	.274	.443	.353
vs. Ground-Ballers			277	72	4	39	31	.260	.375	.351
vs. Fly-Ballers			286	76	10	38	42	.266	.430	.348
Home Games	4-5	5.49	243	65	9	37	28	.267	.428	.365
Road Games	6-4	3.71	320	83	5	40	45	.259	.384	.337
Grass Fields	9-8	4.58	490	129	14	71	66	.263	.410	.355
Artificial Turf	1-1	3.60	73	19	0	6	7	.260	.356	.309
April	1-1	3.20	73	18	2	13	11	.247	.397	.360
May	3-1	2.47	141	33	0	17	26	.234	.291	.313
June	1-3	5.16	115	31	4	21	12	.270	.435	.382
July	3-2	5.40	119	31	4	12	12	.261	.445	.319
August	2-2	6.38	99	30	4	10	11	.303	.485	.367
Sept./Oct.	0-0	5.79	16	5	0	4	1	.313	.375	.476
Leading Off Inn.			146	45	6	14	17	.308	.521	.369
Bases Empty			324	86	10	40	43	.265	.429	.346
Runners On			239	62	4	37	30	.259	.368	.353
Runners/Scor. Pos.			154	37	2	23	22	.240	.331	.332
Runners On/2 Out			102	26	1	16	14	.255	.353	.356
Scor. Pos./2 Out			74	20	0	13	11	.270	.338	.379
Late-Inning Pressure			31	11	1	5	2	.355	.548	.444
Leading Off			9	2	0	1	1	.222	.222	.300
Runners On			13	5	1	1	1	.385	.692	.429
Runners/Scor. Pos.			7	3	1	0	1	.429	1.000	.429
First 9 Batters			221	54	2	30	35	.244	.339	.335
Second 9 Batters			189	54	7	23	19	.286	.460	.360
All Batters Thereafter			153	40	5	24	19	.261	.425	.358

Loves to face: Ozzie Guillen (.143, 4-for-28, 0 SO)
Donnie Hill (.118, 2-for-17)
Kurt Stillwell (.077, 1-for-13)

Hates to face: George Brett (.345, 20-for-58, 5 2B, 2 3B, 6 HR)
Alvin Davis (.567, 17-for-30, 2 HR)
Don Mattingly (.457, 21-for-46, 6 2B, 1 3B, 3 HR)

Miscellaneous statistics: Ground outs-to-air outs ratio: 1.34 last season, 1.45 for career.... Induced 13 double-play ground outs in 109 opportunities (one per 8.4).... Allowed 31 doubles, 3 triples in 149.2 innings.... Allowed 9 first-inning runs in 23 starts (3.52 ERA).... Batting support: 4.17 runs per start.... Opposing base stealers: 13-for-19 (0-for-5, then 13-for-last-14; 68%); 2 pickoffs, 0 balks.

Comments: His career winning percentage of .565 (117–90) with the Tigers is only slightly lower than Jack Morris's (.569, 198–150).... Has a career record of 7–0 as a reliever. Only two other pitchers in major league history had seven relief wins without a loss: Charlie Buffinton and Slick Castleman.... Didn't allow a first-inning home run in 23 starts last season.... Total of innings pitched was his highest in any season since 1985, the last of his four consecutive 200-inning seasons.... Had the lowest average run support of any regular starter on the Tigers last season.... His only complete game over the last two seasons was a loss in which he pitched only eight innings.... Has held opponents to a lower batting average with runners in scoring position than he has in other at-bats in each of the last five seasons.... Walked more batters than he struck out in each of the last two seasons, after not having done that in any of his previous 10 seasons.... Lance Parrish had never batted against Petry before 1990, although he had probably seen more of his pitches than any player in the majors, having been Petry's batterymate for eight seasons in Detroit (1979–86) and another one in California (1989). So it shouldn't come as a surprise that Parrish hit the second pitch he saw from Petry for a home run. (You might want to check our study in the 1986 *Analyst* of the success of catchers batting against their former teammates, pp. 77–78.)

Dan Plesac

Throws Left

Milwaukee Brewers	W-L	ERA	AB	H	HR	BB	SO	BA	SA	OBA
Season	3-7	4.43	261	67	5	31	65	.257	.372	.340
vs. Left-Handers			62	10	0	6	18	.161	.226	.254
vs. Right-Handers			199	57	5	25	47	.286	.417	.367
vs. Ground-Ballers			124	32	1	13	32	.258	.323	.340
vs. Fly-Ballers			137	35	4	18	33	.255	.416	.340
Home Games	2-3	6.03	117	33	2	15	28	.282	.410	.368
Road Games	1-4	3.11	144	34	3	16	37	.236	.340	.317
Grass Fields	3-6	5.08	218	59	5	25	55	.271	.399	.351
Artificial Turf	0-1	1.46	43	8	0	6	10	.186	.233	.286
April	0-1	2.00	30	6	0	3	6	.200	.233	.273
May	0-1	7.84	44	16	1	3	12	.364	.523	.396
June	0-1	7.59	43	13	2	8	8	.302	.512	.404
July	2-1	2.25	58	13	0	6	18	.224	.293	.328
August	1-2	3.21	49	7	2	7	14	.143	.286	.250
Sept./Oct.	0-1	5.00	37	12	0	4	7	.324	.378	.390
Leading Off Inn.			53	15	2	5	13	.283	.434	.367
Bases Empty			123	27	3	15	35	.220	.325	.314
Runners On			138	40	2	16	30	.290	.413	.363
Runners/Scor. Pos.			82	25	1	13	20	.305	.439	.398
Runners On/2 Out			64	16	0	7	16	.250	.344	.324
Scor. Pos./2 Out			44	10	0	5	13	.227	.341	.306
Late-Inning Pressure			171	51	4	19	44	.298	.433	.376
Leading Off			35	12	1	4	9	.343	.486	.439
Runners On			94	31	2	10	23	.330	.479	.396
Runners/Scor. Pos.			55	20	1	8	14	.364	.527	.446
First 9 Batters			248	63	5	29	61	.254	.367	.337
Second 9 Batters			13	4	0	2	4	.308	.462	.400
All Batters Thereafter			0	0	0	0	0	—	—	—

Loves to face: Steve Balboni (.083, 1-for-12, 8 SO)
Cal Ripken (.071, 1-for-14)
Ruben Sierra (.067, 1-for-15)

Hates to face: Alvin Davis (.455, 5-for-11, 1 HR)
Brian Harper (.556, 5-for-9, 2 HR)
Cory Snyder (.500, 4-for-8, 1 2B, 2 HR)

Miscellaneous statistics: Ground outs-to-air outs ratio: 1.01 last season, 0.86 for career.... Induced 8 double-play ground outs in 72 opportunities (one per 9.0).... Allowed 13 doubles, 1 triple in 69.0 innings.... Stranded 32 inherited runners, allowed 15 to score (68%).... Opposing base stealers: 8-for-9 (89%); 1 pickoff, 0 balks.

Comments: Had compiled ERAs below 3.00 in each of his four previous seasons.... Walked an average of 4.04 batters per nine innings last season, a 57 percent increase over his previous career rate of 2.57.... The worst two months of his career obviously affected Plesac's normally gentle demeanor. After going 146 games without hitting a batter with a pitch (a streak dating back to September 1987), he hit three in three games over a five-day period in late July.... Collected only 24 saves in 36 opportunities, the 2d-lowest percentage (.667) in the American League (minimum: 20 opportunities).... Opponents batted 120 points higher in Late-Inning Pressure Situations (.298) than in other at-bats (.178) last season, the largest margin in the majors, the fifth straight season in which they've hit better in LIPS than otherwise. Not exactly strong resume material for a closer. ... And there's more bad stuff. Opponents' career batting-average breakdown: .218 with the bases empty, .245 with runners on base, .260 with runners in scoring position.... Nevertheless, his total of 110 saves over the last four seasons is ninth highest in the majors.... Has allowed 26 home runs in his career, but only four to left-handed batters. The only left-hander to homer against him over the last three seasons was Don Mattingly in 1989.... Has a career ERA of 3.27 on grass fields, 1.46 on artificial turf.

Jeff Reardon

Throws Right

Boston Red Sox	W-L	ERA	AB	H	HR	BB	SO	BA	SA	OBA
Season	5-3	3.16	189	39	5	19	33	.206	.344	.282
vs. Left-Handers			91	13	1	12	12	.143	.209	.243
vs. Right-Handers			98	26	4	7	21	.265	.469	.321
vs. Ground-Ballers			89	16	2	9	12	.180	.292	.255
vs. Fly-Ballers			100	23	3	10	21	.230	.390	.306
Home Games	5-1	2.03	97	17	2	8	19	.175	.289	.245
Road Games	0-2	4.38	92	22	3	11	14	.239	.402	.320
Grass Fields	5-1	1.93	165	28	4	15	32	.170	.291	.243
Artificial Turf	0-2	15.43	24	11	1	4	1	.458	.708	.536
April	1-0	0.00	25	1	0	3	6	.040	.040	.143
May	0-1	3.75	43	9	1	3	7	.209	.302	.261
June	2-1	4.20	56	12	3	7	11	.214	.446	.302
July	0-1	4.32	34	10	1	4	2	.294	.441	.368
August	0-0	—	0	0	0	0	0	—	—	—
Sept./Oct.	2-0	2.35	31	7	0	2	7	.226	.355	.294
Leading Off Inn.			39	6	1	2	9	.154	.308	.195
Bases Empty			110	17	3	9	20	.155	.282	.218
Runners On			79	22	2	10	13	.278	.430	.367
Runners/Scor. Pos.			58	18	2	10	11	.310	.500	.412
Runners On/2 Out			38	9	1	7	6	.237	.395	.370
Scor. Pos./2 Out			28	6	1	7	5	.214	.393	.371
Late-Inning Pressure			138	31	5	15	24	.225	.391	.305
Leading Off			27	5	1	1	7	.185	.370	.214
Runners On			62	16	2	8	10	.258	.419	.352
Runners/Scor. Pos.			48	14	2	8	9	.292	.500	.393
First 9 Batters			185	38	4	18	33	.205	.330	.279
Second 9 Batters			4	1	1	1	0	.250	1.000	.400
All Batters Thereafter			0	0	0	0	0	—	—	—

Loves to face: Brook Jacoby (.091, 1-for-11)
Jeffrey Leonard (.111, 2-for-18)
Cory Snyder (.083, 1-for-12, 6 SO)

Hates to face: Carlton Fisk (.400, 4-for-10, 2 2B, 2 HR)
Chet Lemon (.750, 3-for-4, 1 2B, 1 HR, 2 BB)
Harold Reynolds (.833, 5-for-6, 2 2B)

Miscellaneous statistics: Ground outs-to-air outs ratio: 0.54 last season, 0.54 for career. . . . Induced 2 double-play ground outs in 26 opportunities (one per 13.0). . . . Allowed 11 doubles, 0 triples in 51.1 innings. . . . Stranded 13 inherited runners, allowed 8 to score (62%). . . . Opposing base stealers: 8-for-9 (89%); 0 pickoffs, 0 balks.

Comments: A save against the Twins on July 4 made Reardon only the third pitcher to collect at least one save against each of the current 26 teams. The others: Goose Gossage and Mike Marshall. . . . Career total of 694 appearances is the most of any active pitcher who has never started a game. Kent Tekulve made 1050 relief appearances, the most ever by a pitcher who never started. Incidentally, no one has ever started after making his first 500 appearances in relief. . . . Entered the 1990 season with a streak of eight consecutive seasons of at least 60 games, tying him with Pedro Borbon and Lee Smith for the longest streak ever by a pitcher. Smith extended his streak to nine seasons, but Reardon fell 13 games short after spending 44 days on the disabled list. . . . But he did equal Bruce Sutter's all-time record with a ninth consecutive 20-save season. Reardon is running one season ahead of Smith, whose eight-year streak survived last season as well. . . . Reardon had a peculiar breakdown last season. His opponents' batting average with the bases empty was the lowest of his career, but their average with runners on base was the highest of his career. . . . Has not allowed a triple in 277⅔ innings over the last four seasons. . . . The heat is gone. Strikeouts per nine innings, year by year since 1987: 9.30, 6.90, 5.67, 5.79.

Dave Righetti

Throws Left

New York Yankees	W-L	ERA	AB	H	HR	BB	SO	BA	SA	OBA
Season	1-1	3.57	205	48	8	26	43	.234	.400	.325
vs. Left-Handers			41	10	2	2	10	.244	.415	.295
vs. Right-Handers			164	38	6	24	33	.232	.396	.332
vs. Ground-Ballers			98	21	2	13	20	.214	.337	.304
vs. Fly-Ballers			107	27	6	13	23	.252	.458	.344
Home Games	1-1	2.60	105	23	2	13	26	.219	.314	.311
Road Games	0-0	4.62	100	25	6	13	17	.250	.490	.339
Grass Fields	1-1	3.86	160	36	6	21	36	.225	.394	.319
Artificial Turf	0-0	2.45	45	12	2	5	7	.267	.422	.346
April	0-0	4.05	25	6	2	2	4	.240	.480	.296
May	0-0	4.50	27	8	0	4	6	.296	.333	.387
June	1-0	4.35	39	9	3	5	8	.231	.513	.318
July	0-0	3.86	45	11	1	6	9	.244	.422	.340
August	0-1	4.22	43	12	2	5	12	.279	.419	.367
Sept./Oct.	0-0	0.00	26	2	0	4	4	.077	.154	.200
Leading Off Inn.			43	8	2	5	7	.186	.349	.286
Bases Empty			96	22	3	16	16	.229	.365	.351
Runners On			109	26	5	10	27	.239	.431	.300
Runners/Scor. Pos.			57	8	2	7	13	.140	.263	.231
Runners On/2 Out			47	12	4	6	10	.255	.574	.340
Scor. Pos./2 Out			29	4	1	4	5	.138	.276	.242
Late-Inning Pressure			165	35	6	19	34	.212	.358	.301
Leading Off			36	8	2	2	5	.222	.417	.282
Runners On			87	16	3	9	21	.184	.310	.260
Runners/Scor. Pos.			47	4	1	6	12	.085	.149	.189
First 9 Batters			198	47	7	26	41	.237	.394	.330
Second 9 Batters			7	1	1	0	2	.143	.571	.143
All Batters Thereafter			0	0	0	0	0	—	—	—

Loves to face: Mike Heath (.136, 3-for-22, 3 BB)
Oddibe McDowell (0-for-8)
Don Slaught (0-for-12, 1 BB)

Hates to face: George Bell (.385, 10-for-26, 2 2B, 2 3B, 3 HR, 0 BB)
Alfredo Griffin (.500, 9-for-18)
Gary Redus (.600, 3-for-5, 1 HR)

Miscellaneous statistics: Ground outs-to-air outs ratio: 0.85 last season, 1.03 for career. . . . Induced 4 double-play ground outs in 54 opportunities (one per 13.5). . . . Allowed 6 doubles, 2 triples in 53.0 innings. . . . Stranded 11 inherited runners, allowed 4 to score (73%). . . . Opposing base stealers: 0-for-0; 0 pickoffs, 0 balks.

Comments: Ended his career in pinstripes as the Yankees' all-time leader in games pitched (522) and saves (224). . . . Saved 36 games in 39 opportunities, the 2d-highest percentage among major league relievers with at least 20 opportunities last season. . . . He tied the record for most saves for a last place club, set in 1987 by Lee Smith of the Chicago Cubs. . . . His total of innings pitched has decreased in every season since 1985, his second year in the bullpen: 107, 106.2, 95, 87, 69, 53. Of course, New York's need for a closer has steadily diminished during that time as well. (See p. 39.) . . . Saved 54 percent of the Yankees' victories in 1990—a higher percentage than in 1986, when he saved 46 of their 90 wins (51%). . . . Became the first pitcher with as few as two decisions in a 30-save season. Both of his decisions were against the Brewers. . . . Allowed as many home runs in 53 innings last season as in 156 innings over the previous two seasons combined. . . . The only pitcher to work more than 25 innings last season without a stolen base attempted. . . . Opponents batted 113 points lower in Late-Inning Pressure Situations (.212) than in other at-bats (.325), the 2d-largest margin in the majors. . . . Memo to all Bay Area talk-show hosts: His career record is 33–23 with a 3.32 ERA as a starter, 41–38 with a 2.94 ERA as a reliever. Commit those figures to memory; you'll need them.

Jeff M. Robinson

Throws Right

Detroit Tigers	W-L	ERA	AB	H	HR	BB	SO	BA	SA	OBA
Season	10-9	5.96	551	141	23	88	76	.256	.457	.362
vs. Left-Handers			254	62	10	39	35	.244	.437	.348
vs. Right-Handers			297	79	13	49	41	.266	.475	.373
vs. Ground-Ballers			277	71	10	44	34	.256	.440	.363
vs. Fly-Ballers			274	70	13	44	42	.255	.474	.360
Home Games	6-4	5.63	329	80	13	54	45	.243	.426	.351
Road Games	4-5	6.44	222	61	10	34	31	.275	.505	.378
Grass Fields	8-6	5.89	434	112	18	69	63	.258	.454	.361
Artificial Turf	2-3	6.19	117	29	5	19	13	.248	.470	.364
April	1-2	5.83	118	33	4	12	15	.280	.483	.344
May	3-2	6.35	110	30	7	16	21	.273	.555	.372
June	2-2	3.72	130	29	5	26	13	.223	.377	.348
July	2-2	5.68	93	22	3	20	17	.237	.409	.377
August	2-1	9.12	100	27	4	14	10	.270	.470	.373
Sept./Oct.	0-0	—	0	0	0	0	0	—	—	—
Leading Off Inn.			142	30	7	14	19	.211	.415	.287
Bases Empty			321	77	16	52	45	.240	.464	.351
Runners On			230	64	7	36	31	.278	.448	.376
Runners/Scor. Pos.			143	40	5	26	21	.280	.455	.383
Runners On/2 Out			89	19	4	15	8	.213	.382	.333
Scor. Pos./2 Out			57	11	2	11	5	.193	.316	.333
Late-Inning Pressure			18	7	1	2	2	.389	.667	.450
Leading Off			7	3	0	0	1	.429	.714	.429
Runners On			5	3	1	1	0	.600	1.200	.667
Runners/Scor. Pos.			3	2	1	1	0	.667	1.667	.750
First 9 Batters			193	44	9	42	30	.228	.456	.372
Second 9 Batters			185	52	7	30	19	.281	.470	.386
All Batters Thereafter			173	45	7	16	27	.260	.445	.319

Loves to face: Scott Bradley (.158, 3-for-19)
Joe Carter (.133, 2-for-15)
Danny Tartabull (.150, 3-for-20)

Hates to face: George Brett (.286, 4-for-14, 3 HR, 8 BB)
Kent Hrbek (.294, 5-for-17, 4 HR, 6 BB)
Ron Karkovice (.800, 4-for-5, 1 HR)

Miscellaneous statistics: Ground outs-to-air outs ratio: 1.09 last season, 1.03 for career.... Induced 13 double-play ground outs in 105 opportunities (one per 8.1).... Allowed 34 doubles, 4 triples in 145.0 innings.... Allowed 25 first-inning runs in 27 starts (8.65 ERA, highest in A.L.) ... Batting support: 5.37 runs per start (2d highest in A.L.) ... Opposing base stealers: 10-for-19 (53%); 1 pickoff, 1 balk.

Comments: Robinson's ERA was the highest in Tigers history among pitchers with at least 140 innings.... Starting pitchers with ERAs of 5.00 or higher had a combined .288 winning percentage last season. But *two* Tigers starters—Robinson and Frank Tanana—had winning records despite five-plus ERAs.... Since 1900, only three pitchers have posted winning records with ERAs higher than Robinson's (minimum: 15 decisions): Wes Ferrell, 15–10 with a 6.28 ERA in 1938; Guy Bush, 15–10 with a 6.20 ERA in 1930; and Mike Smithson, 9–6 with a 5.97 ERA in 1988.... Walked 25 of the 128 batters faced during the first inning, the worst rate in the majors (minimum: 20 GS). Translated into walks per nine innings, he averaged 8.65 in the first frame, 4.77 thereafter.... Had the highest average run support of any regular Tigers starter last season.... Has held opponents to one hit in 18 at-bats with the bases loaded over the last three seasons.... Opponents have a career batting average of .213 at Tiger Stadium, .271 on the road. As a result, he's 21–10 at home, 15–16 on the road.... ERAs year by year since 1987: 5.37, 2.98, 4.73, 5.96. Despite a career ERA of 4.65, his winning percentage is .581 (36–26). Only one pitcher in major league history has a higher winning percentage with an ERA above 4.50 (minimum: 50 decisions): Erv Brame, .584 (52–37, 4.77).

Ron Robinson

Throws Right

Reds/Brewers	W-L	ERA	AB	H	HR	BB	SO	BA	SA	OBA
Season	14-7	3.26	696	194	7	51	71	.279	.364	.330
vs. Left-Handers			368	98	4	30	30	.266	.348	.322
vs. Right-Handers			328	96	3	21	41	.293	.381	.340
vs. Ground-Ballers			358	103	4	26	26	.288	.380	.340
vs. Fly-Ballers			338	91	3	25	45	.269	.346	.320
Home Games	6-3	2.40	328	85	2	21	33	.259	.311	.304
Road Games	8-4	4.05	368	109	5	30	38	.296	.410	.353
Grass Fields	10-6	3.67	503	147	5	29	50	.292	.374	.334
Artificial Turf	4-1	2.25	193	47	2	22	21	.244	.337	.321
April	0-1	3.86	16	3	0	3	1	.188	.188	.316
May	2-0	2.74	85	23	2	10	12	.271	.435	.347
June	1-2	4.44	109	34	2	11	11	.312	.413	.377
July	3-1	4.88	115	41	1	6	12	.357	.478	.385
August	4-1	2.82	198	51	2	10	18	.258	.313	.300
Sept./Oct.	4-2	2.30	173	42	0	11	17	.243	.295	.291
Leading Off Inn.			174	50	1	11	21	.287	.362	.330
Bases Empty			385	108	6	31	40	.281	.379	.340
Runners On			311	86	1	20	31	.277	.344	.318
Runners/Scor. Pos.			168	44	1	8	19	.262	.345	.288
Runners On/2 Out			130	34	0	12	17	.262	.315	.329
Scor. Pos./2 Out			81	19	0	5	12	.235	.284	.279
Late-Inning Pressure			46	7	1	6	3	.152	.217	.250
Leading Off			15	0	0	1	2	.000	.000	.063
Runners On			8	3	1	2	0	.375	.750	.500
Runners/Scor. Pos.			4	1	1	2	0	.250	1.000	.500
First 9 Batters			224	74	2	23	24	.330	.446	.396
Second 9 Batters			239	66	2	6	24	.276	.339	.300
All Batters Thereafter			233	54	3	22	23	.232	.309	.296

Loves to face: Joe Orsulak (0-for-13)
Mickey Tettleton (0-for-7, 3 SO)

Hates to face: Cecil Fielder (3-for-3, 1 HR)
Keith Hernandez (.500, 5-for-10, 1 HR)
John Shelby (.440, 11-for-25)
Steve Sax (.436, 17-for-39)

Miscellaneous statistics: Ground outs-to-air outs ratio: 0.81 last season, 0.94 for career.... Induced 14 double-play ground outs in 158 opportunities (one per 11.3).... Allowed 36 doubles, 1 triple in 179.2 innings.... Allowed 21 first-inning runs in 27 starts (6.67 ERA).... Batting support: 5.59 runs per start (5.37 with Brewers, 2d highest in A.L.) ... Opposing base stealers: 15-for-26 (58%); 1 pickoff, 0 balks.

Comments: Had completed only one of 71 career starts before his midseason trade to the Brewers, then completed seven of 22 starts for Milwaukee, including the only two shutouts of his career. The DH rule strikes again!... Averaged 6.74 innings per start with the Brewers, the highest of any starter on the club. He had an average of only 5.33 in five starts with Cincinnati.... Over his last 12 starts with Milwaukee, he had a record of 8–2 with a 2.22 ERA.... Had the highest average run support of any Brewers starter last season, almost two runs more per game than Chris Bosio.... Opponents batted 76 points higher on his first pass through the batting order (.330) than in subsequent at-bats (.254) last season, the 2d-largest margin in the majors.... Career record of 33–27 (3.69 ERA) as a starter, 14–7 (3.09 ERA) as a reliever.... Opposing right-handers had hit for a higher average than left-handers in each of his previous five seasons. His previous high against right-handers was .238 as a rookie in 1984. Career averages: .286 by left-handers, .239 by right-handers.... Opponents have batted over .300 against him in day games in each of the last three seasons.... One of only eight pitchers with winning percentages above .600 in each of the past two seasons (minimum: 15 decisions in each). The others: Roger Clemens, Chuck Finley, Dwight Gooden, Erik Hanson, Dave Stewart, Dave Stieb, and Bob Welch.

Kenny Rogers

Throws Left

Texas Rangers	W-L	ERA	AB	H	HR	BB	SO	BA	SA	OBA
Season	10-6	3.13	374	93	6	42	74	.249	.372	.323
vs. Left-Handers			96	21	1	6	19	.219	.333	.272
vs. Right-Handers			278	72	5	36	55	.259	.385	.340
vs. Ground-Ballers			172	44	2	22	26	.256	.395	.338
vs. Fly-Ballers			202	49	4	20	48	.243	.351	.310
Home Games	9-1	2.01	206	50	1	18	37	.243	.345	.303
Road Games	1-5	4.50	168	43	5	24	37	.256	.405	.347
Grass Fields	10-4	2.41	311	74	4	33	62	.238	.347	.310
Artificial Turf	0-2	6.89	63	19	2	9	12	.302	.492	.384
April	1-1	4.76	49	15	1	5	5	.306	.469	.370
May	1-0	5.40	76	19	2	5	12	.250	.434	.298
June	0-2	2.70	65	19	0	9	16	.292	.369	.368
July	2-2	2.03	48	9	1	7	17	.188	.271	.291
August	1-0	2.31	44	11	1	6	6	.250	.432	.340
Sept./Oct.	5-1	1.82	92	20	1	10	18	.217	.293	.294
Leading Off Inn.			73	16	1	5	15	.219	.315	.269
Bases Empty			170	46	3	13	32	.271	.394	.326
Runners On			204	47	3	29	42	.230	.353	.321
Runners/Scor. Pos.			142	32	2	19	36	.225	.345	.309
Runners On/2 Out			97	19	2	16	21	.196	.299	.310
Scor. Pos./2 Out			73	15	2	11	19	.205	.315	.310
Late-Inning Pressure			184	45	2	20	41	.245	.348	.314
Leading Off			36	6	1	1	9	.167	.306	.189
Runners On			100	23	0	17	22	.230	.280	.333
Runners/Scor. Pos.			77	17	0	12	20	.221	.286	.315
First 9 Batters			320	77	5	36	64	.241	.359	.316
Second 9 Batters			40	13	1	6	8	.325	.525	.413
All Batters Thereafter			14	3	0	0	2	.214	.214	.214

Loves to face: Jesse Barfield (0-for-8, 1 BB, 6 SO)
Ozzie Guillen (.091, 1-for-11)
Pete O'Brien (0-for-9, 1 BB)

Hates to face: Wade Boggs (.400, 4-for-10)
Kevin Romine (3-for-3, 1 HR)
Robin Yount (4-for-4, 2 BB)

Miscellaneous statistics: Ground outs-to-air outs ratio: 0.96 last season, 0.97 for career.... Induced 5 double-play ground outs in 86 opportunities (one per 17.2).... Allowed 22 doubles, 3 triples in 97.2 innings.... Stranded 33 inherited runners, allowed 18 to score (65%).... Opposing base stealers: 6-for-7 (86%); 1 pickoff, 0 balks.

Comments: Started three games (including his last two games of the season) after pitching exclusively as a reliever in 1989 (73 games).... Completed only five of 58 starts over five seasons in the minors.... Saved 15 games last season, but only 13 games in 22 opportunities while Jeff Russell was on the disabled list (May 29–September 10).... His ERA stood at 7.40 on May 18, but he compiled a 1.99 mark in 55 appearances after that.... Saved his best for last. Only one pitcher in either league won more games from September 1 on: Erik Hanson (6). Rogers shared the runner-up spot in the American League with Scott Erickson, Dave Stewart, and Bob Welch.... Walked 11 of 56 leadoff batters as a rookie in 1989, but overcame that problem last season, particularly in Late-Inning Pressure Situations (see figures above).... A home run by Alvin Davis last September 18 was the only one he has allowed to a left-handed batter in his two seasons in the majors.... Opponents' career batting averages: left-handers, .196; right-handers, .260.... Has allowed only two career home runs at Arlington Stadium, six elsewhere. Career records: 12–4 at home, 1–6 on the road.... Has a career record of 3–0 vs. the White Sox.

Jeff Russell

Throws Right

Texas Rangers	W-L	ERA	AB	H	HR	BB	SO	BA	SA	OBA
Season	1-5	4.26	91	23	1	16	16	.253	.363	.361
vs. Left-Handers			39	5	1	4	7	.128	.231	.209
vs. Right-Handers			52	18	0	12	9	.346	.462	.462
vs. Ground-Ballers			42	12	0	5	6	.286	.357	.354
vs. Fly-Ballers			49	11	1	11	10	.224	.367	.367
Home Games	0-4	5.54	46	11	1	10	9	.239	.370	.375
Road Games	1-1	2.92	45	12	0	6	7	.267	.356	.346
Grass Fields	0-5	3.91	83	21	1	15	15	.253	.373	.364
Artificial Turf	1-0	7.71	8	2	0	1	1	.250	.250	.333
April	1-1	3.18	36	8	1	6	9	.222	.333	.326
May	0-4	6.52	40	13	0	7	6	.325	.450	.426
June	0-0	—	0	0	0	0	0	—	—	—
July	0-0	—	0	0	0	0	0	—	—	—
August	0-0	—	0	0	0	0	0	—	—	—
Sept./Oct.	0-0	2.08	15	2	0	3	1	.133	.200	.278
Leading Off Inn.			13	2	0	4	2	.154	.231	.353
Bases Empty			37	6	0	7	7	.162	.216	.295
Runners On			54	17	1	9	9	.315	.463	.406
Runners/Scor. Pos.			42	11	0	8	9	.262	.357	.373
Runners On/2 Out			27	7	0	4	6	.259	.407	.355
Scor. Pos./2 Out			21	4	0	3	6	.190	.333	.292
Late-Inning Pressure			57	18	1	11	11	.316	.491	.426
Leading Off			8	2	0	3	1	.250	.375	.455
Runners On			36	12	1	7	7	.333	.556	.442
Runners/Scor. Pos.			29	8	0	7	7	.276	.414	.417
First 9 Batters			89	23	1	14	14	.258	.371	.356
Second 9 Batters			2	0	0	2	2	.000	.000	.500
All Batters Thereafter			0	0	0	0	0	—	—	—

Loves to face: Gary Gaetti (.063, 1-for-16)
Dan Gladden (.148, 4-for-27, 0 BB)
Paul Molitor (.158, 3-for-19)

Hates to face: Ellis Burks (.533, 8-for-15, 2 HR)
Don Mattingly (.500, 8-for-16, 1 HR)
Dave Winfield (.700, 7-for-10, 2 SO)

Miscellaneous statistics: Ground outs-to-air outs ratio: 1.11 last season, 1.21 for career.... Induced 3 double-play ground outs in 22 opportunities (one per 7.3).... Allowed 7 doubles, 0 triples in 25.1 innings.... Stranded 17 inherited runners (including 16 of the last 18), allowed 5 to score (77%).... Opposing base stealers: 5-for-5; 0 pickoffs, 0 balks.

Comments: Spent 108 days on the disabled list from May 29 to September 10, but returned to pitch in seven games at the end of the season. He converted save opportunities in each of his last two appearances.... On the day that Russell was placed on the D.L. (May 29), the Rangers were already in last place (18–27), 13 games behind Oakland. By the time he returned, Texas was in third place with a 73–67 record, having lost only 3½ games to Oakland in the interim.... Had his most ineffective year in Late-Inning Pressure Situations, but his opponents' career average in LIPS (.238) is still 25 points lower than in other at-bats (.263).... Among the 35 pitchers active in 1990 with at least 50 career saves, only Jim Gott (4.07) and Russell (4.03) have career ERAs above 4.00. For the record, both marks are tainted with more than twice as many innings as starting pitchers than they have as relievers, and in both cases their relief ERAs are well below their marks as starters. Russell's career breakdown: 22–39, 4.47 ERA in 79 starts; 18–14, 3.28 ERA in 198 relief appearances.... Russell's career strikeout rate is more than one per inning higher as a reliever (6.30) than as a starter (5.03).... Owns impressive career won-lost records against several clubs: 4–0 against the Athletics and Indians, 3–0 vs. the Angels and the Yankees.... Opponents have a career average of only .205 with the bases loaded, but have hit five grand slams in 83 at-bats.

Nolan Ryan

Throws Right

Texas Rangers	W-L	ERA	AB	H	HR	BB	SO	BA	SA	OBA
Season	13-9	3.44	729	137	18	74	232	.188	.322	.267
vs. Left-Handers			362	79	8	43	92	.218	.356	.305
vs. Right-Handers			367	58	10	31	140	.158	.289	.230
vs. Ground-Ballers			332	63	4	42	93	.190	.283	.281
vs. Fly-Ballers			397	74	14	32	139	.186	.355	.256
Home Games	8-5	3.32	456	78	15	43	158	.171	.327	.249
Road Games	5-4	3.65	273	59	3	31	74	.216	.315	.299
Grass Fields	12-8	3.33	662	118	17	66	218	.178	.316	.258
Artificial Turf	1-1	4.58	67	19	1	8	14	.284	.388	.355
April	4-0	2.25	92	14	2	8	33	.152	.250	.225
May	0-2	10.47	63	16	3	13	21	.254	.524	.390
June	3-2	2.16	116	19	3	11	43	.164	.259	.234
July	4-0	3.61	159	34	4	19	46	.214	.365	.296
August	1-3	3.23	143	29	3	7	38	.203	.350	.253
Sept./Oct.	1-2	2.60	156	25	3	16	51	.160	.263	.246
Leading Off Inn.			191	30	4	17	61	.157	.257	.230
Bases Empty			492	89	12	43	178	.181	.309	.251
Runners On			237	48	6	31	54	.203	.350	.300
Runners/Scor. Pos.			141	22	3	25	38	.156	.234	.291
Runners On/2 Out			105	17	3	12	19	.162	.333	.254
Scor. Pos./2 Out			63	10	1	10	12	.159	.238	.284
Late-Inning Pressure			60	8	1	4	24	.133	.200	.188
Leading Off			17	1	0	1	6	.059	.059	.111
Runners On			17	3	1	1	2	.176	.412	.222
Runners/Scor. Pos.			12	2	1	1	2	.167	.417	.231
First 9 Batters			240	52	10	28	80	.217	.429	.304
Second 9 Batters			238	38	5	18	78	.160	.273	.226
All Batters Thereafter			251	47	3	28	74	.187	.267	.271

Loves to face: Jesse Barfield (0-for-9, 8 SO)
Chet Lemon (.122, 5-for-41, 5 BB)
Devon White (.045, 1-for-22)

Hates to face: Harold Baines (.429, 3-for-7, 2 HR)
Roberto Kelly (.556, 5-for-9, 1 HR)
Larry Sheets (.467, 7-for-15, 2 HR)

Miscellaneous statistics: Ground outs-to-air outs ratio: 0.71 last season, 5th-lowest rate in A.L.; 1.04 for career. . . . Induced 5 double-play ground outs in 102 opportunities (one per 20.4), 2d-lowest rate in A.L. . . . Allowed 20 doubles, 12 triples (most in majors) in 204.0 innings. . . . Allowed 25 first-inning runs in 30 starts (7.58 ERA, 3d highest in A.L.) . . . Batting support: 4.27 runs per start. . . . Opposing base stealers: 25-for-34 (74%); 0 pickoffs, 1 balk.

Comments: Has averaged at least a strikeout an inning in 15 seasons, more than twice as many as runner-up Sandy Koufax (7). As it should be; his career of 24 seasons is twice as long as Koufax's. . . . Has appeared in at least one major league game in 32 different ballparks. In 1991, he can add both the Skydome and the new Comiskey to that list. He is the only active player to have played at Forbes Field, Connie Mack Stadium, or Crosley Field. . . . Has pitched a total of 10 seasons in the American League, and led the league in strikeouts nine times. . . . His .604 winning percentage as a member of the Rangers tops his marks with the Mets (.433), Angels (.533), and Astros (.530). . . . Has pitched four shutouts in his two seasons with the Rangers, after hurling only one in his previous four seasons with Houston. . . . He has allowed 26 home runs at Arlington Stadium over the last two years, which equals his total of homers allowed at the Astrodome over the previous six seasons. . . . Had his first perfect season in the field since 1966, when he played two errorless games in his debut season for the Mets. He committed at least one error in each of the next 22 seasons, until breaking the streak last year. . . . Has lost nine decisions against the Orioles since last defeating them on April 20, 1976. Ryan hurled a three-hitter on that day, with the only Baltimore hits coming from Brooks Robinson (1) and Mark Belanger (2).

Bret Saberhagen

Throws Right

Kansas City Royals	W-L	ERA	AB	H	HR	BB	SO	BA	SA	OBA
Season	5-9	3.27	524	146	9	28	87	.279	.387	.314
vs. Left-Handers			222	61	5	16	42	.275	.405	.318
vs. Right-Handers			302	85	4	12	45	.281	.374	.311
vs. Ground-Ballers			215	60	2	7	34	.279	.372	.302
vs. Fly-Ballers			309	86	7	21	53	.278	.398	.322
Home Games	3-5	3.42	293	88	6	14	52	.300	.416	.331
Road Games	2-4	3.08	231	58	3	14	35	.251	.351	.293
Grass Fields	2-2	2.06	160	36	1	8	26	.225	.294	.257
Artificial Turf	3-7	3.84	364	110	8	20	61	.302	.429	.339
April	1-2	3.55	96	25	3	4	15	.260	.396	.287
May	3-1	2.53	172	41	3	10	29	.238	.326	.277
June	1-4	3.07	170	47	1	8	33	.276	.376	.313
July	0-0	4.82	43	19	2	3	0	.442	.628	.478
August	0-0	—	0	0	0	0	0	—	—	—
Sept./Oct.	0-2	5.40	43	14	0	3	10	.326	.419	.362
Leading Off Inn.			130	38	3	9	20	.292	.462	.338
Bases Empty			307	85	4	17	54	.277	.378	.315
Runners On			217	61	5	11	33	.281	.401	.313
Runners/Scor. Pos.			110	28	4	7	18	.255	.418	.295
Runners On/2 Out			89	23	2	3	13	.258	.393	.290
Scor. Pos./2 Out			48	11	1	2	9	.229	.375	.275
Late-Inning Pressure			47	12	2	1	7	.255	.447	.280
Leading Off			13	3	1	0	2	.231	.538	.231
Runners On			11	3	0	1	1	.273	.455	.357
Runners/Scor. Pos.			6	2	0	0	0	.333	.667	.375
First 9 Batters			165	44	4	13	22	.267	.400	.318
Second 9 Batters			169	47	1	7	25	.278	.367	.303
All Batters Thereafter			190	55	4	8	40	.289	.395	.320

Loves to face: Brook Jacoby (.159, 7-for-44)
Chet Lemon (.146, 7-for-48)
Devon White (.121, 4-for-33, 0 BB)

Hates to face: Wade Boggs (.476, 20-for-42, 1 HR)
Steve Buechele (.500, 10-for-20, 1 HR)
Mark McGwire (.394, 13-for-33)

Miscellaneous statistics: Ground outs-to-air outs ratio: 1.13 last season, 1.11 for career. . . . Induced 10 double-play ground outs in 111 opportunities (one per 11.1). . . . Allowed 20 doubles, 5 triples in 135.0 innings. . . . Allowed 9 first-inning runs in 20 starts (3.60 ERA). . . . Batting support: 4.60 runs per start. . . . Opposing base stealers: 2-for-7 (29%); 3 pickoffs, 0 balks.

Comments: Has allowed a career average of 1.76 walks per nine innings. Since the dawn of the live-ball era in 1920, only four pitchers with as many starts as Saberhagen (198) had lower marks: Grover Cleveland Alexander, 1.31; pinch hitter deluxe Red Lucas, 1.61; Fritz Peterson, 1.73; and Robin Roberts, 1.73. . . . Needs three victories to become the fourth pitcher to win 100 games for the Royals. The others: Paul Splittorff (166), Dennis Leonard (144), and Larry Gura (111). . . . He's been around so long that it's easy to overlook how young he still is. So keep this in mind: Saberhagen is eight weeks younger than Kevin Tapani. . . . Career breakdown: 17–20, 3.76 ERA in day games; 80–50, 3.07 ERA at night. . . . All right, now let's talk about this odd- and even-numbered years thing. Sabe's career record is 61–22 (.735) in odd-numbered years, but only 36–48 (.429) in even-numbered ones. But let's not get carried away; things like this happen. Saberhagen has crossed over the .500 line in each of the last six seasons; big deal—Turk Lown, Lindy McDaniel, and Dave Wickersham went him one better. Check Gaylord Perry's record; over his first seven seasons, he was 52–35 in even years, 24–35 in odd years. How about John Denny, whose ERAs bounced from two-point-something to four-point-something, and back and forth again from 1976 through 1979 (mimicking Ernie Broglio, 1959–62)? Denny's pattern, as we recall, came to an end just about the time it was noticed.

Scott Sanderson

Throws Right

Oakland A's	W-L	ERA	AB	H	HR	BB	SO	BA	SA	OBA
Season	17-11	3.88	803	205	27	66	128	.255	.422	.312
vs. Left-Handers			402	94	13	39	54	.234	.391	.300
vs. Right-Handers			401	111	14	27	74	.277	.454	.325
vs. Ground-Ballers			346	92	11	28	49	.266	.428	.324
vs. Fly-Ballers			457	113	16	38	79	.247	.418	.303
Home Games	6-7	3.17	363	81	13	30	60	.223	.388	.281
Road Games	11-4	4.51	440	124	14	36	68	.282	.450	.337
Grass Fields	13-11	3.90	690	175	24	58	112	.254	.417	.311
Artificial Turf	4-0	3.77	113	30	3	8	16	.265	.451	.320
April	2-1	3.97	89	24	4	10	7	.270	.483	.340
May	3-1	2.35	117	29	1	9	21	.248	.316	.299
June	4-2	4.21	145	40	5	11	16	.276	.421	.327
July	2-2	3.20	192	43	7	8	38	.224	.411	.256
August	2-3	4.54	135	38	5	16	24	.281	.459	.359
Sept./Oct.	4-2	5.29	125	31	5	12	22	.248	.456	.317
Leading Off Inn.			206	51	4	9	27	.248	.374	.282
Bases Empty			492	119	15	37	77	.242	.394	.298
Runners On			311	86	12	29	51	.277	.466	.334
Runners/Scor. Pos.			169	42	3	23	30	.249	.367	.328
Runners On/2 Out			143	37	4	14	24	.259	.406	.325
Scor. Pos./2 Out			85	18	0	12	16	.212	.271	.309
Late-Inning Pressure			26	5	0	3	9	.192	.192	.276
Leading Off			9	0	0	1	4	.000	.000	.100
Runners On			5	2	0	0	0	.400	.400	.400
Runners/Scor. Pos.			1	0	0	0	0	.000	.000	.000
First 9 Batters			270	68	10	29	53	.252	.441	.328
Second 9 Batters			285	74	9	14	38	.260	.411	.290
All Batters Thereafter			248	63	8	23	37	.254	.415	.319

Loves to face: Greg Briley (0-for-11)
Cory Snyder (0-for-10)
Glenn Wilson (.158, 3-for-19)

Hates to face: Joe Orsulak (.375, 6-for-16, 2 2B, 2 HR)
Kirby Puckett (3-for-3, 2 2B)
Dave Winfield (.571, 8-for-14, 1 HR)

Miscellaneous statistics: Ground outs-to-air outs ratio: 0.67 last season, 3d-lowest rate in A.L.; 0.79 for career. . . . Induced 6 double-play ground outs in 134 opportunities (one per 22.3), lowest rate in A.L. . . . Allowed 39 doubles, 7 triples in 206.1 innings. . . . Allowed 24 first-inning runs in 34 starts (5.29 ERA). . . . Batting support: 4.41 runs per start. . . . Opposing base stealers: 13-for-18 (72%); 0 pick-offs, 1 balk.

Comments: It's unfair to discredit Sanderson and his 17–11 record simply because he played for the A's during one season of a 13-year career. But his .535 *career* winning percentage (115–100) is lower than that of his teammates as well (.544). By the method described on page 53, we estimate his career-long value over a typical "replacement pitcher" to be roughly 20 wins, which ranks 28th among the 32 active pitchers with at least 100 career victories. . . . Allowed an average of one home run per 7.6 innings last season, the 3d-worst rate in the American League. . . . Has held opponents to a lower batting average on his first pass through the batting order than he has in subsequent at-bats in each of the last 10 seasons, the longest streak in the majors over the last 16 years. . . . So it's not surprising that his ERA is lower in 57 relief appearances (3.12) than in 286 starts (3.61). . . . His career record for April and May is 46–25, but only 69–75 from June through October. . . . He has been on a championship series roster in four of the last 10 years, but has pitched in only two of them, with the Cubs in 1984 and 1989. Both the Expos (1981) and A's (1990) kept him seated through the L.C.S. . . . Small blessings: career record of 2–0 (1.29 ERA) at Yankee Stadium. Of course, that was against the 1990 Yankees. . . . His losing record in home games resulted from poor support: only 37 runs in 15 starts at the Coliseum. Welcome to the Yankees, Mr. Sanderson.

Mike Schooler

Throws Right

Seattle Mariners	W-L	ERA	AB	H	HR	BB	SO	BA	SA	OBA
Season	1-4	2.25	207	47	5	16	45	.227	.357	.283
vs. Left-Handers			110	23	2	13	19	.209	.327	.294
vs. Right-Handers			97	24	3	3	26	.247	.392	.270
vs. Ground-Ballers			94	19	1	9	16	.202	.298	.269
vs. Fly-Ballers			113	28	4	7	29	.248	.407	.295
Home Games	0-3	1.72	115	27	2	10	24	.235	.357	.297
Road Games	1-1	2.92	92	20	3	6	21	.217	.359	.265
Grass Fields	1-1	3.10	77	18	3	5	17	.234	.390	.280
Artificial Turf	0-3	1.77	130	29	2	11	28	.223	.338	.285
April	0-0	3.00	35	8	1	4	8	.229	.400	.308
May	1-0	0.57	53	8	1	5	14	.151	.226	.237
June	0-0	2.70	35	6	1	1	9	.171	.314	.194
July	0-1	3.09	41	10	0	4	7	.244	.317	.304
August	0-3	2.79	43	15	2	2	7	.349	.558	.370
Sept./Oct.	0-0	—	0	0	0	0	0	—	—	—
Leading Off Inn.			47	8	0	2	10	.170	.213	.204
Bases Empty			124	26	2	8	26	.210	.306	.258
Runners On			83	21	3	8	19	.253	.434	.319
Runners/Scor. Pos.			43	10	2	6	7	.233	.395	.314
Runners On/2 Out			42	11	3	5	8	.262	.548	.340
Scor. Pos./2 Out			23	6	2	3	4	.261	.565	.346
Late-Inning Pressure			171	37	3	11	40	.216	.322	.261
Leading Off			41	8	0	1	10	.195	.244	.214
Runners On			61	16	1	6	14	.262	.410	.319
Runners/Scor. Pos.			31	7	1	4	4	.226	.355	.297
First 9 Batters			192	41	2	16	43	.214	.307	.276
Second 9 Batters			15	6	3	0	2	.400	1.000	.375
All Batters Thereafter			0	0	0	0	0	—	—	—

Loves to face: Rob Deer (0-for-5, 3 SO)
Geno Petralli (0-for-6, 3 SO)
Cory Snyder (0-for-6, 3 SO)

Hates to face: Harold Baines (.667, 4-for-6, 1 HR)
Darryl Hamilton (2-for-2, 1 BB)
Lou Whitaker (.444, 4-for-9)

Miscellaneous statistics: Ground outs-to-air outs ratio: 0.94 last season, 1.03 for career. . . . Induced 2 double-play ground outs in 37 opportunities (one per 18.5; none is his last 24). . . . Allowed 8 doubles, 2 triples in 56.0 innings. . . . Stranded 8 inherited runners, allowed 3 to score (73%). . . . Opposing base stealers: 5-for-6 (83%); 0 pick-offs, 0 balks.

Comments: Recorded 30 saves in 34 opportunities, the 3d-highest percentage (.882) in the majors (minimum: 20 opportunities), behind Dennis Eckersley (.960) and Dave Righetti (.923). . . . Collected his 50th career save in the 110th game of his career. Only Todd Worrell (109 games) reached 50 saves in fewer games than Schooler. . . . Last season, opponents batted .333 in day games, .163 at night. Career averages: .295 in day games, .231 in night games. . . . Opponents have a career average of .223 with the bases empty, .275 with runners on base. . . . Has never saved a game against the Athletics, but has at least two career saves against every other American League club. . . . A reliever for the '90s: After pitching exclusively as a starter in his first three minor league seasons, he was made a full-time reliever at Calgary in 1988, and has been nothing but since, including 156 relief appearances without a start over three seasons in the majors. He has pitched an average of 1.16 innings per game; among 914 pitchers in major league history with at least 100 innings as relievers, only 13 had lower averages (and eight of those 13 were active in 1990). He has been removed from only 18 of his 156 career appearances (12 percent), the lowest average of any active pitcher (minimum: 100 games). He has saved 78 games, pitching one inning or less in 52 of them (24 of 30 last season). And his career winning percentage (.269, 7–19) reflects the fact that he rarely enters a game without the lead.

Roy Smith

Throws Right

Minnesota Twins	W-L	ERA	AB	H	HR	BB	SO	BA	SA	OBA
Season	5-10	4.81	611	191	20	47	87	.313	.480	.356
vs. Left-Handers			287	106	9	31	36	.369	.554	.423
vs. Right-Handers			324	85	11	16	51	.262	.414	.293
vs. Ground-Ballers			284	86	6	19	37	.303	.437	.344
vs. Fly-Ballers			327	105	14	28	50	.321	.517	.365
Home Games	4-5	4.30	290	85	10	17	44	.293	.459	.329
Road Games	1-5	5.29	321	106	10	30	43	.330	.498	.379
Grass Fields	1-4	5.23	251	83	9	19	33	.331	.502	.370
Artificial Turf	4-6	4.53	360	108	11	28	54	.300	.464	.346
April	0-3	6.26	94	33	3	6	13	.351	.553	.371
May	4-1	3.69	152	42	3	5	23	.276	.355	.297
June	0-2	4.84	89	27	5	8	17	.303	.607	.361
July	1-2	2.93	119	31	6	10	21	.261	.454	.318
August	0-2	8.25	97	37	1	16	10	.381	.515	.449
Sept./Oct.	0-0	3.77	60	21	2	2	3	.350	.483	.371
Leading Off Inn.			151	48	6	7	24	.318	.477	.348
Bases Empty			356	109	13	24	56	.306	.458	.350
Runners On			255	82	7	23	31	.322	.510	.363
Runners/Scor. Pos.			134	42	2	20	18	.313	.478	.376
Runners On/2 Out			114	40	5	11	15	.351	.605	.408
Scor. Pos./2 Out			67	23	1	10	10	.343	.507	.429
Late-Inning Pressure			13	8	1	0	2	.615	.846	.615
Leading Off			5	4	1	0	0	.800	1.400	.800
Runners On			4	1	0	0	1	.250	.250	.250
Runners/Scor. Pos.			2	1	0	0	0	.500	.500	.500
First 9 Batters			249	72	4	22	49	.289	.390	.338
Second 9 Batters			226	75	10	12	28	.332	.544	.363
All Batters Thereafter			136	44	6	13	10	.324	.537	.377

Loves to face: Rob Deer (.083, 1-for-12)
Bo Jackson (0-for-11)
Carney Lansford (.211, 4-for-19)

Hates to face: Ken Griffey, Jr. (.600, 6-for-10)
Lance Parrish (.353, 6-for-17, 3 HR)
Danny Tartabull (.455, 5-for-11, 1 2B, 3 HR)

Miscellaneous statistics: Ground outs-to-air outs ratio: 0.63 last season, 2d-lowest rate in A.L.; 0.60 career. . . . Induced 11 double-play ground outs in 120 opportunities (one per 10.9). . . . Allowed 34 doubles, 4 triples in 153.1 innings. . . . Allowed 13 first-inning runs in 23 starts (3.52 ERA). . . . Batting support: 4.78 runs per start. . . . Opposing base stealers: 15-for-28 (54%); 0 pickoffs, 0 balks.

Comments: Opposing left-handers (.369) batted 107 points higher than right-handers (.262) last season, the 4th-largest margin in the majors. . . . Pitched the most innings (153⅓) of any American League pitcher who didn't hit a batter with a pitch last season. He hit five in 1989. . . . More runners were caught stealing with Smith on the mound (13) than with any other Twins pitcher last season. Smith's total was 2d highest among American League right-handers. Only Roger Clemens (14) had a higher one. . . . Threw 10 wild pitches, equaling his previous career total. . . . Stranded four inherited runners, allowed five to score in nine relief appearances. . . . Opponents batted .289 with one home run every 62 at-bats during his first pass through the batting order. But in subsequent at-bats, opponents hit .329 with one home run every 22 AB. . . . Faced 617 batters, but only 15 in Late-Inning Pressure Situations, the lowest percentage in the majors (minimum: 400 BFP). . . . Compare the career statistics of Smith (25–27, 4.45 ERA) to those of Melido Perez (37–39, 4.52 ERA). And keep in mind that Perez has played for better teams than Smith has; Melido's teammates have a .490 winning percentage, Smith's only a .467 mark. It's simply incongruous that two players can have such similar numbers, considering that one's star is obviously on the rise while the other's is apparently burning out.

Dave Stewart

Throws Right

Oakland A's	W-L	ERA	AB	H	HR	BB	SO	BA	SA	OBA
Season	22-11	2.56	980	226	16	83	166	.231	.326	.291
vs. Left-Handers			478	99	8	48	80	.207	.305	.280
vs. Right-Handers			502	127	8	35	86	.253	.345	.303
vs. Ground-Ballers			421	109	7	38	67	.259	.354	.317
vs. Fly-Ballers			559	117	9	45	99	.209	.304	.272
Home Games	11-4	1.74	519	111	5	39	86	.214	.285	.270
Road Games	11-7	3.54	461	115	11	44	80	.249	.371	.315
Grass Fields	18-9	2.45	826	196	13	68	140	.237	.331	.295
Artificial Turf	4-2	3.14	154	30	3	15	26	.195	.299	.269
April	5-0	1.32	125	26	2	12	14	.208	.296	.283
May	3-2	2.18	154	36	1	7	28	.234	.292	.277
June	2-4	3.72	169	37	3	18	37	.219	.320	.291
July	3-2	3.86	153	43	5	13	19	.281	.418	.333
August	4-2	2.63	201	43	5	17	40	.214	.348	.274
Sept./Oct.	5-1	1.47	178	41	0	16	28	.230	.275	.292
Leading Off Inn.			250	59	6	23	45	.236	.348	.300
Bases Empty			577	134	8	51	102	.232	.315	.299
Runners On			403	92	8	32	64	.228	.340	.280
Runners/Scor. Pos.			210	43	4	19	32	.205	.324	.259
Runners On/2 Out			175	37	4	14	25	.211	.326	.274
Scor. Pos./2 Out			107	20	2	9	18	.187	.308	.250
Late-Inning Pressure			92	20	2	9	18	.217	.304	.287
Leading Off			25	5	1	4	5	.200	.320	.310
Runners On			38	6	1	1	7	.158	.237	.179
Runners/Scor. Pos.			12	2	0	0	1	.167	.167	.167
First 9 Batters			287	70	6	32	43	.244	.352	.318
Second 9 Batters			291	58	4	23	58	.199	.275	.260
All Batters Thereafter			402	98	6	28	65	.244	.343	.294

Loves to face: Steve Lyons (.043, 1-for-23, 1 2B, 2 BB)
Rance Mulliniks (.040, 1-for-25, 3 BB)
Harold Reynolds (.087, 4-for-46, 5 BB)

Hates to face: Cecil Fielder (.571, 4-for-7, 2 HR)
Ken Griffey, Jr. (.467, 7-for-15, 4 2B)
Danny Tartabull (.478, 11-for-23, 2 HR)

Miscellaneous statistics: Ground outs-to-air outs ratio: 0.82 last season, 0.85 for career. . . . Induced 23 double-play ground outs in 193 opportunities (one per 8.4). . . . Allowed 39 doubles, 3 triples in 267.0 innings. . . . Allowed 15 first-inning runs in 36 starts (3.50 ERA). . . . Batting support: 4.64 runs per start. . . . Opposing base stealers: 13-for-19 (68%); 0 pickoffs, 0 balks.

Comments: Came within one win of one of baseball's most prestigious postseason records: Bob Gibson's seven consecutive wins. Stewart lost the Series opener to snap his streak at six. . . . His total of seven postseason wins is tied for fourth, behind Whitey Ford (10), Catfish Hunter (9), and Jim Palmer (8). . . . Has played in four League Championship Series, with his team advancing to the World Series each time. Gary Nolan is the only other pitcher to have done that. . . . Has been Oakland's opening-day starting pitcher in each of the last three seasons, matching the franchise record for consecutive years, shared by Rick Langford (1978–80) and Scott Perry (1919–21). . . . First pitcher to lead the American League in games started for three consecutive seasons since Wilbur Wood did it for four straight years (1972–75). . . . Tied Jack Morris for the A.L. lead with 11 complete games last season; his ERA from the 7th inning on was 0.95. . . . His four shutouts tied Roger Clemens for the A.L. lead, and equaled his own previous career total. . . . Opponents have hit for a higher average in road games than in home games in each of his five seasons with the Athletics. . . . Has held opponents to a lower batting average with runners in scoring position than he has in other at-bats in each of the last eight seasons, the longest streak over the last 16 years. . . . Has a 14–0 record vs. the Mariners since being acquired by the Athletics. . . . Has won his last 14 April decisions, immediately following a streak of 12 consecutive April losses.

Dave Stieb

Throws Right

Toronto Blue Jays	W-L	ERA	AB	H	HR	BB	SO	BA	SA	OBA
Season	18-6	2.93	778	179	11	64	125	.230	.320	.296
vs. Left-Handers			403	102	8	40	47	.253	.357	.326
vs. Right-Handers			375	77	3	24	78	.205	.280	.263
vs. Ground-Ballers			389	100	1	34	54	.257	.311	.321
vs. Fly-Ballers			389	79	10	30	71	.203	.329	.271
Home Games	9-5	3.15	399	102	6	35	64	.256	.358	.321
Road Games	9-1	2.73	379	77	5	29	61	.203	.280	.269
Grass Fields	6-1	3.01	306	61	4	28	50	.199	.278	.278
Artificial Turf	12-5	2.88	472	118	7	36	75	.250	.347	.308
April	3-1	2.35	92	22	2	6	13	.239	.315	.293
May	3-1	2.47	143	30	3	9	20	.210	.308	.260
June	4-1	5.40	122	36	2	11	18	.295	.434	.360
July	3-0	0.94	98	16	0	13	17	.163	.194	.268
August	3-2	3.86	148	34	2	11	22	.230	.318	.294
Sept./Oct.	2-1	2.47	175	41	2	14	35	.234	.326	.298
Leading Off Inn.			197	34	3	16	30	.173	.244	.245
Bases Empty			480	103	9	38	75	.215	.315	.283
Runners On			298	76	2	26	50	.255	.329	.316
Runners/Scor. Pos.			170	43	0	15	29	.253	.324	.316
Runners On/2 Out			139	32	1	6	27	.230	.288	.267
Scor. Pos./2 Out			82	18	0	2	14	.220	.256	.247
Late-Inning Pressure			77	15	0	5	9	.195	.247	.271
Leading Off			20	4	0	2	3	.200	.200	.304
Runners On			30	6	0	1	5	.200	.300	.250
Runners/Scor. Pos.			14	2	0	0	3	.143	.214	.200
First 9 Batters			261	58	4	32	49	.222	.318	.308
Second 9 Batters			259	50	3	14	46	.193	.270	.245
All Batters Thereafter			258	71	4	18	30	.275	.372	.333

Loves to face: Brady Anderson (0-for-14, 1 BB)
Rob Deer (.045, 1-for-22, 3 BB)
Steve Lyons (.045, 1-for-22, 1 2B)

Hates to face: Jack Howell (.440, 11-for-25, 3 HR)
Wally Joyner (.368, 14-for-38, 4 HR)
Geno Petralli (.444, 8-for-18)

Miscellaneous statistics: Ground outs-to-air outs ratio: 1.11 last season, 1.14 for career. . . . Induced 7 double-play ground outs in 137 opportunities (one per 19.6), 3d-lowest rate in A.L. . . . Allowed 31 doubles, 3 triples in 208.2 innings. . . . Allowed 15 first-inning runs in 33 starts (4.22 ERA). . . . Batting support: 4.52 runs per start. . . . Opposing base stealers: 6-for-14 (43%); 2 pickoffs, 0 balks.

Comments: The most amazing turnaround of 1990: Stieb went 5–0 with a 1.41 ERA over a six-start period from May 23 through June 20, and took the mound at Fenway on June 25 ready to wrest a half-game lead away from the Sox. During that period, his slider had been untouchable; opposing right-handers had only 12 hits in 79 at-bats. He failed to retire a batter in Boston; in fact, in that start and his next combined, Stieb faced 18 batters, allowing seven hits, seven walks, and 12 earned runs. That bit of nastiness out of the way, Stieb went 3–0 with a 1.82 ERA over his next five starts. . . . Made his seventh All-Star appearance, tying the American League record for pitchers held by Early Wynn. . . . The A.L.'s top 10 home run hitters had 38 at-bats against Stieb last season, the most against a pitcher who didn't allow them a home run. . . . Has equaled or surpassed his career-high winning percentage in each of the last three seasons; starting with 1988: .667 (16–8), .680 (17–8), .750 (18–6). (See the Bob Welch comments (p. 312) re: seasons of 15 or more wins and less than 10 losses.) . . . Opponents batted 43 points higher in day games (.268) than in night games (.226) over the last five seasons, the 3d-largest margin in the majors. Career records of 53–47 (3.78 ERA) by day, 113–76 (3.10 ERA) under cover of darkness. . . . Opponents have hit for a higher average with runners in scoring position than in other at-bats in each of the last five years.

Todd Stottlemyre

Throws Right

Toronto Blue Jays	W-L	ERA	AB	H	HR	BB	SO	BA	SA	OBA
Season	13-17	4.34	781	214	18	69	115	.274	.410	.337
vs. Left-Handers			393	118	8	37	42	.300	.443	.365
vs. Right-Handers			388	96	10	32	73	.247	.376	.309
vs. Ground-Ballers			373	98	4	29	57	.263	.362	.319
vs. Fly-Ballers			408	116	14	40	58	.284	.453	.354
Home Games	7-8	4.28	405	112	9	35	62	.277	.405	.339
Road Games	6-9	4.41	376	102	9	34	53	.271	.415	.335
Grass Fields	5-6	3.67	288	70	8	20	44	.243	.396	.298
Artificial Turf	8-11	4.75	493	144	10	49	71	.292	.418	.359
April	3-2	4.67	100	25	2	11	13	.250	.430	.333
May	1-3	5.04	116	31	4	13	17	.267	.422	.344
June	4-2	3.13	172	47	3	11	15	.273	.366	.324
July	2-4	5.86	118	39	2	11	20	.331	.458	.389
August	1-3	3.31	131	29	2	9	26	.221	.328	.271
Sept./Oct.	2-3	4.91	144	43	5	14	24	.299	.472	.365
Leading Off Inn.			198	59	4	10	30	.298	.424	.335
Bases Empty			460	124	7	34	69	.270	.380	.325
Runners On			321	90	11	35	46	.280	.452	.353
Runners/Scor. Pos.			183	56	5	22	18	.306	.464	.380
Runners On/2 Out			133	33	1	17	19	.248	.368	.342
Scor. Pos./2 Out			84	20	0	11	10	.238	.321	.333
Late-Inning Pressure			32	5	0	3	7	.156	.156	.229
Leading Off			9	1	0	1	1	.111	.111	.200
Runners On			9	1	0	0	4	.111	.111	.111
Runners/Scor. Pos.			3	1	0	0	1	.333	.333	.333
First 9 Batters			269	68	9	22	54	.253	.431	.307
Second 9 Batters			255	72	4	27	31	.282	.408	.359
All Batters Thereafter			257	74	5	20	30	.288	.389	.346

Loves to face: Scott Fletcher (.056, 1-for-18)
Pete Incaviglia (.067, 1-for-15, 8 SO)
Cory Snyder (.063, 1-for-16)

Hates to face: Mel Hall (.524, 11-for-21)
Roberto Kelly (.438, 7-for-16)
Matt Nokes (.519, 14-for-27, 3 HR)

Miscellaneous statistics: Ground outs-to-air outs ratio: 0.95 last season, 0.96 for career. . . . Induced 13 double-play ground outs in 152 opportunities (one per 11.7). . . . Allowed 36 doubles, 8 triples in 203.0 innings. . . . Allowed 18 first-inning runs in 33 starts (4.91 ERA). . . . Batting support: 5.03 runs per start. . . . Opposing base stealers: 23-for-36 (64%); 2 pickoffs, 1 balk.

Comments: Has made 88 career appearances (67 as a starter, 21 in relief), the highest total among active pitchers with neither a shutout nor a save. . . . Enjoyed the highest run support among the Blue Jays' regular starters last season, but it didn't stop there. He also enjoyed some great defensive support. (Actually, we assume he "enjoyed" it; but for all we know, he wasn't even aware of it.) Toronto infielders committed only four errors behind Stottlemyre, registering the 2d-best fielding percentage in support of any A.L. pitcher (minimum: 162 IP). . . . Had an ERA of 3.78 with Greg Myers catching, 3.31 with Pat Borders behind the plate. Jimmy Key and Dave Stieb also had lower ERAs with Myers than with Borders. . . . Pitched to a decision in 28 of 31 starts (91%). Only three A.L. pitchers had a higher decision rate: Bob Welch, Dave Stewart, and Jack Morris (minimum: 10 GS). . . . Opponents' career batting average of .324 leading off innings is the worst of any pitcher over the last 16 years (minimum: 400 AB). . . . Opposing left-handers have a career average of .321, 84 points higher than right-handers (.237), the 3d-largest margin in the majors over the last five seasons. . . . Todd was the opening day starter for the Blue Jays last season, making him and his dad only the second father-son combination in major league history to have both taken the mound as starters on opening day. The other duo: Dizzy and Steve Trout.

Bill Swift

Throws Right

Seattle Mariners	W-L	ERA	AB	H	HR	BB	SO	BA	SA	OBA
Season	6-4	2.39	496	135	4	21	42	.272	.351	.309
vs. Left-Handers			216	62	4	8	15	.287	.398	.317
vs. Right-Handers			280	73	0	13	27	.261	.314	.302
vs. Ground-Ballers			219	50	2	6	26	.228	.279	.261
vs. Fly-Ballers			277	85	2	15	16	.307	.408	.346
Home Games	3-1	1.34	197	49	2	8	12	.249	.325	.278
Road Games	3-3	3.15	299	86	2	13	30	.288	.368	.329
Grass Fields	2-3	3.67	229	68	2	12	27	.297	.380	.344
Artificial Turf	4-1	1.38	267	67	2	9	15	.251	.326	.278
April	0-0	2.08	57	19	0	4	5	.333	.368	.365
May	2-2	3.18	68	20	1	2	7	.294	.412	.324
June	0-0	0.50	65	14	0	2	6	.215	.246	.246
July	3-0	2.02	137	35	1	5	10	.255	.328	.292
August	0-2	2.77	97	25	2	3	6	.258	.381	.298
Sept./Oct.	1-0	3.93	72	22	0	5	8	.306	.375	.351
Leading Off Inn.			116	28	0	1	10	.241	.276	.261
Bases Empty			267	69	2	7	27	.258	.330	.288
Runners On			229	66	2	14	15	.288	.376	.332
Runners/Scor. Pos.			136	34	0	13	9	.250	.301	.321
Runners On/2 Out			93	24	0	9	5	.258	.301	.343
Scor. Pos./2 Out			66	17	0	8	2	.258	.303	.364
Late-Inning Pressure			104	29	2	9	7	.279	.375	.348
Leading Off			28	8	0	0	1	.286	.321	.310
Runners On			45	12	1	6	2	.267	.356	.365
Runners/Scor. Pos.			27	4	0	6	1	.148	.148	.324
First 9 Batters			325	87	1	15	31	.268	.332	.303
Second 9 Batters			106	36	2	3	5	.340	.434	.366
All Batters Thereafter			65	12	1	3	6	.185	.308	.243

Loves to face: Steve Buechele (0-for-10, 1 BB)
Jack Clark (0-for-10)
Dan Gladden (.071, 1-for-14)

Hates to face: Harold Baines (.452, 14-for-31, 2 HR, 0 SO)
George Brett (.435, 10-for-23)
Kent Hrbek (.500, 13-for-26, 1 HR)

Miscellaneous statistics: Ground outs-to-air outs ratio: 2.67 last season, highest rate in majors; 2.73 for career.... Induced 17 double-play ground outs in 107 opportunities (one per 6.3).... Allowed 27 doubles, 0 triples in 128.0 innings.... Stranded 32 inherited runners, allowed 21 to score (60%).... Opposing base stealers: 0-for-2; 0 pickoffs, 3 balks.

Comments: Career record of 20–35 (4.99 ERA) as a starter, 9–3 (2.62 ERA) as a reliever.... Swift has worked as both a starter and a reliever in each of his five seasons in the majors, but over the last three years his bullpen innings have increased; year by year since 1988: $28\frac{1}{3}$, $44\frac{2}{3}$, $76\frac{2}{3}$.... Cut down his rate of walks last season to 1.48 per nine innings, compared to a previous career average of 3.43 per nine. He was the only relief pitcher in the majors with at least 75 innings pitched and fewer than two walks allowed per nine innings.... Had an ERA of 1.59 in 51 innings with Scott Bradley behind the plate, 3.18 in 68 innings with Dave Valle catching.... Pitched the most innings of any pitcher in the majors who was not on the mound for a stolen base.... Hasn't allowed a first-inning home run in his last 32 starts. But his average of one homer per 16 innings as a starter is far worse than his relief rate of one per 47 innings.... Hasn't allowed a home run to a right-handed batter since Dwight Evans hit one on September 2, 1989.... Last season's batting average by opposing left-handers was the lowest of his career. Career averages: .321 by left-handers, .257 by right-handers.... Has walked only one of 75 career batters faced with the bases loaded, and he hasn't allowed a grand slam in 68 at-bats with the bags full.... Career record of 17–17 before the All-Star break, 12–21 thereafter.

Greg Swindell

Throws Left

Cleveland Indians	W-L	ERA	AB	H	HR	BB	SO	BA	SA	OBA
Season	12-9	4.40	850	245	27	47	135	.288	.451	.324
vs. Left-Handers			126	36	4	6	18	.286	.421	.318
vs. Right-Handers			724	209	23	41	117	.289	.456	.325
vs. Ground-Ballers			365	106	1	17	45	.290	.359	.322
vs. Fly-Ballers			485	139	26	30	90	.287	.520	.326
Home Games	7-4	4.67	449	128	15	23	63	.285	.452	.319
Road Games	5-5	4.10	401	117	12	24	72	.292	.449	.330
Grass Fields	11-7	4.28	741	209	25	38	123	.282	.445	.315
Artificial Turf	1-2	5.27	109	36	2	9	12	.330	.486	.383
April	2-2	4.79	82	21	2	7	12	.256	.463	.319
May	0-2	6.18	109	36	6	8	10	.330	.596	.376
June	0-1	4.54	141	40	7	11	31	.284	.511	.336
July	4-1	2.49	171	39	3	8	27	.228	.304	.258
August	4-2	4.37	200	61	5	9	36	.305	.430	.335
Sept./Oct.	2-1	5.20	147	48	4	4	19	.327	.476	.340
Leading Off Inn.			217	65	11	10	35	.300	.553	.333
Bases Empty			514	136	20	29	87	.265	.453	.305
Runners On			336	109	7	18	48	.324	.446	.353
Runners/Scor. Pos.			189	60	5	13	33	.317	.460	.351
Runners On/2 Out			132	39	3	7	20	.295	.402	.331
Scor. Pos./2 Out			82	26	3	6	12	.317	.488	.364
Late-Inning Pressure			42	15	1	4	6	.357	.476	.413
Leading Off			15	5	0	1	3	.333	.467	.375
Runners On			13	4	0	3	2	.308	.308	.438
Runners/Scor. Pos.			3	2	0	3	0	.667	.667	.833
First 9 Batters			286	75	9	16	51	.262	.423	.302
Second 9 Batters			273	75	9	15	41	.275	.440	.311
All Batters Thereafter			291	95	9	16	43	.326	.488	.358

Loves to face: Pete Incaviglia (0-for-22, 3 BB, 12 SO)
Chet Lemon (.080, 2-for-25, 1 3B, 1 HR)
Mike Macfarlane (.067, 1-for-15)

Hates to face: Tim Hulett (.600, 9-for-15)
Edgar Martinez (.833, 5-for-6, 1 HR)
Dave Valle (.389, 7-for-18, 4 2B, 1 HR)

Miscellaneous statistics: Ground outs-to-air outs ratio: 0.76 last season, 0.76 for career.... Induced 14 double-play ground outs in 160 opportunities (one per 11.4).... Allowed 41 doubles (tied for 4th most in A.L.), 8 triples in 214.2 innings.... Allowed 18 first-inning runs in 34 starts (4.76 ERA).... Batting support: 5.24 runs per start (4th highest in A.L.) ... Opposing base stealers: 3-for-15 (20%), lowest rate in majors; 5 pickoffs, 2 balks.

Comments: Cleveland had a record of 20–14 with Swindell starting last season, and a 39–37 mark with their other three top starters (Bud Black, Tom Candiotti, and John Farrell). But the Indians were doomed by an 18–34 record behind their other nine pretenders.... Swindell's .567 career winning percentage (51–39) is 120 points higher than that of his teammates during that time (.447). Only three active pitchers with at least 50 career wins have higher differentials: Roger Clemens (194), Dwight Gooden (153), and Ted Higuera (148).... Allowed the most extra-base hits (76) of any pitcher in the majors last season.... The three opposing runners to steal bases are all excellent stealers: Rickey Henderson, Roberto Kelly, and Jim Gantner.... Opponents' overall batting average was the highest of his career.... Opponents have hit for a higher average with runners on base than with the bases empty in each of his five years in the majors.... Opponents' career breakdown: .236 on his first pass through the batting order, .266 the second time though, .286 in subsequent at bats.... Career records: 47–29 (3.66 ERA) on grass fields, 4–10 (5.22 ERA) on artificial turf.... Career record of 34–16 (.680) vs. western division clubs, 17–23 (.425) vs. eastern division clubs. (See Jack McDowell, p. 294.)

Frank Tanana

Throws Left

Detroit Tigers	W-L	ERA	AB	H	HR	BB	SO	BA	SA	OBA
Season	9-8	5.31	678	190	25	66	114	.280	.453	.349
vs. Left-Handers			113	26	1	7	15	.230	.292	.290
vs. Right-Handers			565	164	24	59	99	.290	.485	.360
vs. Ground-Ballers			315	82	7	30	52	.260	.387	.328
vs. Fly-Ballers			363	108	18	36	62	.298	.510	.367
Home Games	4-6	6.00	385	112	16	37	70	.291	.481	.357
Road Games	5-2	4.42	293	78	9	29	44	.266	.416	.337
Grass Fields	7-8	6.02	556	164	25	54	100	.295	.493	.362
Artificial Turf	2-0	2.36	122	26	0	12	14	.213	.270	.287
April	2-1	6.29	96	32	3	5	11	.333	.479	.381
May	1-2	4.17	155	39	6	10	22	.252	.400	.305
June	2-2	6.75	112	35	7	10	21	.313	.589	.363
July	0-2	9.38	102	34	0	14	18	.333	.480	.415
August	1-0	6.05	74	21	4	11	11	.284	.500	.371
Sept./Oct.	3-1	2.04	139	29	5	16	31	.209	.338	.299
Leading Off Inn.			171	49	5	11	33	.287	.444	.330
Bases Empty			415	112	14	26	71	.270	.434	.322
Runners On			263	78	11	40	43	.297	.483	.387
Runners/Scor. Pos.			134	44	7	30	27	.328	.545	.439
Runners On/2 Out			113	38	5	23	18	.336	.504	.449
Scor. Pos./2 Out			66	22	5	17	12	.333	.591	.470
Late-Inning Pressure			47	11	2	9	3	.234	.404	.362
Leading Off			15	5	1	1	2	.333	.667	.375
Runners On			17	4	0	3	0	.235	.235	.333
Runners/Scor. Pos.			5	1	0	2	0	.200	.200	.375
First 9 Batters			251	68	7	30	48	.271	.426	.352
Second 9 Batters			236	68	13	16	37	.288	.496	.339
All Batters Thereafter			191	54	5	20	29	.283	.435	.356

Loves to face: Jim Gantner (.132, 5-for-38)
Minnie Minoso (0-for-4—yes, really)
Cory Snyder (.111, 3-for-27)

Hates to face: Rickey Henderson (.372, 29-for-78, 7 HR)
Paul Molitor (.406, 26-for-64, 2 HR)
Rafael Palmeiro (.467, 7-for-15, 1 HR)

Miscellaneous statistics: Ground outs-to-air outs ratio: 0.90 last season, 0.99 for career. . . . Induced 14 double-play ground outs in 134 opportunities (one per 9.6). . . . Allowed 40 doubles, 1 triple in 176.1 innings. . . . Allowed 23 first-inning runs in 29 starts (7.31 ERA, 4th highest in A.L.) . . . Batting support: 5.14 runs per start (5th highest in A.L.) . . . Opposing base stealers: 9-for-24 (38%), shared 5th-lowest rate in A.L.; 9 pickoffs, 1 balk.

Comments: Do older men take longer to get warmed up? Well, you can either ask Pia Zadora, or take a look at the first-inning ERAs of the American League's four most ancient starters: Hough, 5.63; Ryan, 7.58; Blyleven, 6.65; Tanana, 7.31. Hough, Ryan, and Tanana all had higher ERAs in the first inning than in any other. . . . But you *can* teach an old dog new tricks. (Can we get confirmation from Pia on this one, too?) Tanana earned the first save of his career on August 2 last season in his 530th career appearance. No player in major league history took as long to make his first such score. Jim Clancy notched his first in game number 336 in 1988. And if we accept the *Baseball Encyclopedia* saves prior to 1969, Tim Keefe and Pud Galvin took longer than Clancy, but not as long as Tanana. . . . The Tigers made only five errors behind Tanana, an average of one every 35 innings. Tigers infielders made only three in 438 chances, the best rate behind any A.L. pitcher. . . . Tanana has pitched in the majors for 18 seasons, all in the American League. Which pitchers played the most seasons all in one league? Warren Spahn and Eppa Rixey (21 years each in the N.L.), and Early Wynn (23 in the A.L.) . . . Career total of 196 losses is 9th most in American League history. Eighth place on the list belongs to Bobo Newsom (209). . . . An odd coincidence: Tanana was the pitcher Minnie Minoso faced when he made his *decade*nt plate appearances in both 1976 and 1980.

Kevin Tapani

Throws Right

Minnesota Twins	W-L	ERA	AB	H	HR	BB	SO	BA	SA	OBA
Season	12-8	4.07	621	164	12	29	101	.264	.393	.297
vs. Left-Handers			317	90	6	21	53	.284	.435	.328
vs. Right-Handers			304	74	6	8	48	.243	.349	.263
vs. Ground-Ballers			288	80	1	12	46	.278	.385	.305
vs. Fly-Ballers			333	84	11	17	55	.252	.399	.291
Home Games	8-2	3.38	293	78	1	16	44	.266	.362	.304
Road Games	4-6	4.68	328	86	11	13	57	.262	.421	.292
Grass Fields	3-5	4.66	264	69	8	11	48	.261	.402	.293
Artificial Turf	9-3	3.63	357	95	4	18	53	.266	.387	.300
April	2-2	2.86	84	20	0	5	15	.238	.310	.286
May	4-1	4.03	152	42	4	7	31	.276	.414	.308
June	2-2	4.82	146	40	3	5	24	.274	.438	.292
July	3-0	3.10	110	27	1	3	17	.245	.327	.265
August	0-1	5.63	28	7	1	4	3	.250	.464	.344
Sept./Oct.	1-2	4.68	101	28	3	5	11	.277	.416	.318
Leading Off Inn.			166	38	4	3	33	.229	.404	.243
Bases Empty			403	94	7	16	69	.233	.360	.263
Runners On			218	70	5	13	32	.321	.454	.359
Runners/Scor. Pos.			128	40	3	9	20	.313	.438	.348
Runners On/2 Out			99	32	2	6	17	.323	.444	.368
Scor. Pos./2 Out			62	19	1	4	12	.306	.419	.348
Late-Inning Pressure			46	16	0	1	6	.348	.500	.362
Leading Off			14	5	0	0	2	.357	.571	.357
Runners On			18	7	0	1	2	.389	.611	.421
Runners/Scor. Pos.			11	5	0	1	2	.455	.818	.500
First 9 Batters			227	57	5	14	45	.251	.392	.294
Second 9 Batters			220	61	6	8	29	.277	.427	.301
All Batters Thereafter			174	46	1	7	27	.264	.351	.297

Loves to face: Scott Bradley (.091, 1-for-11)
Brian Downing (0-for-8)
Omar Vizquel (.111, 1-for-9)

Hates to face: Harold Baines (.500, 3-for-6, 1 HR)
Chili Davis (.667, 6-for-9)
Edgar Diaz (.667, 4-for-6)

Miscellaneous statistics: Ground outs-to-air outs ratio: 0.98 last season, 0.99 for career. . . . Induced 9 double-play ground outs in 83 opportunities (one per 9.2). . . . Allowed 28 doubles, 8 triples in 159.1 innings. . . . Allowed 15 first-inning runs in 28 starts (5.00 ERA). . . . Batting support: 4.11 runs per start. . . . Opposing base stealers: 9-for-18 (50%); 0 pickoffs, 0 balks.

Comments: His average of 1.64 walks per nine innings was the lowest by a rookie since Atlee Hammaker's 1.44 mark in 1982 (minimum: 25 GS). Over the past 100 years, only two other rookies had rates as low as Tapani's: Watty Lee (1.55 in 1901) and Dave Rozema (1.40 in 1977). . . . Didn't walk more than three batters in any game. . . . Led A.L. rookie pitchers with 28 games started. . . . Of the 19 rookies who won at least five games last season, only four are older than Tapani, who turned 27 in February: Dana Kiecker, Mike Hartley, Mark Gardner, and Bill Sampen. . . . Opponents batted 88 points higher with runners on base (.321) than with the bases empty (.233), the 5th-largest margin in the majors. . . . Opponents batted 64 points higher in night games (.282) than in day games (.218), the 4th-largest margin in the majors. He had a 4–1 record (2.38) in day games, 8–7 (4.74 ERA) at night. . . . Faced 149 batters in the sixth inning or later without allowing a home run. . . . Since joining the Twins, he has allowed only two home runs in 93 innings at the Metrodome, compared to 12 homers in 99 innings in road games. Thanks, Kevin, for another blow against the "Homerdome" boobs. (See pp. 36–37.) . . . Has walked only three leadoff batters in 211 innings in his career (one per 70), the lowest rate over the last 16 years (minimum: 200 BFP).

Walt Terrell

Throws Right

Pirates/Tigers	W-L	ERA	AB	H	HR	BB	SO	BA	SA	OBA
Season	8-11	5.24	629	184	20	57	64	.293	.458	.361
vs. Left-Handers			342	110	16	37	35	.322	.532	.389
vs. Right-Handers			287	74	4	20	29	.258	.369	.327
vs. Ground-Ballers			297	84	6	24	40	.283	.404	.347
vs. Fly-Ballers			332	100	14	33	24	.301	.506	.374
Home Games	5-4	4.58	306	85	7	25	31	.278	.422	.348
Road Games	3-7	5.90	323	99	13	32	33	.307	.492	.373
Grass Fields	5-7	4.74	399	116	11	30	39	.291	.439	.350
Artificial Turf	3-4	6.12	230	68	9	27	25	.296	.491	.379
April	0-0	4.08	64	18	1	6	5	.281	.438	.333
May	2-4	5.64	123	38	5	11	16	.309	.512	.375
June	0-2	6.59	114	32	5	13	11	.281	.465	.364
July	0-1	8.68	41	14	2	3	2	.341	.634	.386
August	3-2	5.71	144	44	4	12	14	.306	.438	.367
Sept./Oct.	3-2	3.26	143	38	3	12	16	.266	.385	.346
Leading Off Inn.			154	45	4	13	17	.292	.429	.355
Bases Empty			351	102	11	29	40	.291	.439	.355
Runners On			278	82	9	28	24	.295	.482	.368
Runners/Scor. Pos.			171	47	8	22	19	.275	.474	.368
Runners On/2 Out			112	34	4	14	7	.304	.500	.400
Scor. Pos./2 Out			81	23	4	11	7	.284	.506	.396
Late-Inning Pressure			36	11	1	5	6	.306	.472	.390
Leading Off			12	2	1	2	2	.167	.500	.286
Runners On			11	3	0	2	2	.273	.364	.385
Runners/Scor. Pos.			7	1	0	2	2	.143	.143	.333
First 9 Batters			233	62	9	20	32	.266	.442	.335
Second 9 Batters			214	70	6	18	12	.327	.486	.387
All Batters Thereafter			182	52	5	19	20	.286	.445	.364

Loves to face: Greg Gagne (.118, 4-for-34, 4 BB)
Dan Pasqua (.077, 2-for-26, 1 HR, 4 BB)
Cory Snyder (.059, 1-for-17)

Hates to face: Steve Balboni (.424, 14-for-33, 4 HR)
Nelson Liriano (.750, 6-for-8)
Paul Molitor (.485, 16-for-33, 2 HR)

Miscellaneous statistics: Ground outs-to-air outs ratio: 1.45 last season, 1.41 for career.... Induced 21 double-play ground outs in 132 opportunities (one per 6.3).... Allowed 36 doubles, 4 triples in 158.0 innings.... Allowed 17 first-inning runs in 28 starts (5.46 ERA).... Batting support: 4.71 runs per start.... Opposing base stealers: 10-for-16 (63%); 0 pickoffs, 2 balks.

Comments: He has a career record of 66–57 as an American Leaguer (.537), with winning records in five of his six A.L. campaigns (including each of the last two seasons, with the Yankees and Tigers, respectively). His career record in the N.L. is 26–43 (.377), with his best single-season record an 8–8 mark for the Mets in 1983.... Interesting trivia: Only five pitchers had career records at least 10 games above .500 in the A.L. and 10 below in the N.L.: Hal Brown (77–66, 8–26), Mike Caldwell (102–80, 35–50), Dave Goltz (104–90, 9–19), Cal McLish (56–40, 36–52), and Frank Sullivan (94–82, 3–18).... Last season, Terrell followed his career-long pattern: He had a 2–7 record with a 5.88 ERA in 16 games with the Pirates, followed by a 6–4 record (4.54 ERA) in 13 games for the Tigers.... Career record of 39–14 with a 3.07 ERA at Tiger Stadium; only 53–86 with a 4.53 ERA elsewhere.... Didn't allow a home run in 78 at-bats by right-handed hitters at Tiger Stadium last season. Then again, he didn't have to face Cecil Fielder.... Opponents' overall batting average was the highest of his career.... He has pitched in both the American and National Leagues in each of the last two seasons. Only three men have played in both leagues for three straight years: Dave LaPoint (1986–88), Dal Maxvill (1972–74), and Sal Maglie (four years, 1955–58).

Bobby Thigpen

Throws Right

Chicago White Sox	W-L	ERA	AB	H	HR	BB	SO	BA	SA	OBA
Season	4-6	1.83	307	60	5	32	70	.195	.283	.271
vs. Left-Handers			158	34	3	18	35	.215	.310	.294
vs. Right-Handers			149	26	2	14	35	.174	.255	.247
vs. Ground-Ballers			135	30	2	16	25	.222	.319	.301
vs. Fly-Ballers			172	30	3	16	45	.174	.256	.247
Home Games	3-3	1.94	168	40	2	17	39	.238	.310	.308
Road Games	1-3	1.70	139	20	3	15	31	.144	.252	.228
Grass Fields	4-5	1.89	263	53	5	29	60	.202	.293	.281
Artificial Turf	0-1	1.42	44	7	0	3	10	.159	.227	.208
April	1-1	2.53	36	6	2	3	8	.167	.333	.231
May	1-1	1.76	51	7	1	5	10	.137	.294	.211
June	1-0	1.35	46	8	1	7	15	.174	.239	.283
July	1-2	2.40	55	14	0	7	14	.255	.309	.344
August	0-2	2.55	63	14	1	5	15	.222	.302	.279
Sept./Oct.	0-0	0.54	56	11	0	5	8	.196	.232	.258
Leading Off Inn.			65	8	1	10	16	.123	.185	.240
Bases Empty			161	33	1	23	36	.205	.292	.304
Runners On			146	27	4	9	34	.185	.274	.233
Runners/Scor. Pos.			75	13	2	6	18	.173	.267	.235
Runners On/2 Out			74	18	2	3	16	.243	.338	.282
Scor. Pos./2 Out			46	10	2	3	9	.217	.370	.280
Late-Inning Pressure			276	53	5	31	67	.192	.286	.273
Leading Off			59	7	1	10	15	.119	.186	.246
Runners On			128	24	4	9	32	.188	.289	.241
Runners/Scor. Pos.			63	12	2	6	16	.190	.302	.260
First 9 Batters			301	58	5	32	70	.193	.279	.270
Second 9 Batters			6	2	0	0	0	.333	.500	.333
All Batters Thereafter			0	0	0	0	0	—	—	—

Loves to face: George Brett (.077, 1-for-13, 2 BB)
Sam Horn (0-for-7, 4 SO)
Devon White (.071, 1-for-14)

Hates to face: Randy Bush (.800, 4-for-5, 1 HR)
Rickey Henderson (.400, 4-for-10, 1 HR)
Alan Trammell (.667, 6-for-9)

Miscellaneous statistics: Ground outs-to-air outs ratio: 0.98 last season, 0.89 for career.... Induced 12 double-play ground outs in 72 opportunities (one per 6.0).... Allowed 8 doubles, 2 triples in 88.2 innings.... Stranded 28 inherited runners, allowed 6 to score (82%), 3d-highest rate in A.L.... Opposing base stealers: 3-for-3; 0 pickoffs, 0 balks.

Comments: Set a major league record with 57 saves, breaking Dave Righetti's previous mark of 46 on September 3.... His save percentage of .877 (57 saves in 65 opportunities) ranked only fifth among A.L. relievers (minimum: 20 opportunities), but he converted 29 of 31 chances in August and September. He had 14 more save opportunities than any other pitcher in the majors.... Was credited with either a win or a save in 65 percent of the White Sox's victories (61 of 94), the highest percentage in this century, surpassing Dan Quisenberry's 63 percent mark in 1983. But let's not ignore four pitchers who accounted for all of their teams' wins more than 100 years ago: George Bradley (1876), Will White (1879), and Jim Devlin *twice* (1876–77). We're serious: Thigpen's accomplishment, awesome as it was, is no less a product of baseball in the 1990s than was Devlin's a result of the 19th-century game.... His ERA was the lowest by an American League pitcher with a losing record since 1917, when Eddie Plank compiled a 1.79 ERA with a 5–6 record (minimum: 10 decisions). It goes with the territory.... Over 90 percent of the batters he faced last season were in Late-Inning Pressure Situations, the highest percentage in the majors over the last 16 years (minimum: 100 BFP). The previous *Player Analysis* record was 88 percent by Dennis Eckersley in 1989.... Has held opponents to a lower average with runners on base than with the bases empty in each of his three full seasons.

Sergio Valdez

Throws Right

Braves/Indians	W-L	ERA	AB	H	HR	BB	SO	BA	SA	OBA
Season	6-6	4.85	417	115	17	38	66	.276	.468	.334
vs. Left-Handers			192	40	6	21	29	.208	.365	.284
vs. Right-Handers			225	75	11	17	37	.333	.556	.379
vs. Ground-Ballers			197	57	4	15	25	.289	.406	.338
vs. Fly-Ballers			220	58	13	23	41	.264	.523	.331
Home Games	3-2	3.49	210	56	7	14	34	.267	.424	.308
Road Games	3-4	6.35	207	59	10	24	32	.285	.512	.359
Grass Fields	4-6	5.26	336	94	16	30	57	.280	.485	.338
Artificial Turf	2-0	3.10	81	21	1	8	9	.259	.395	.319
April	0-0	6.75	22	6	0	3	3	.273	.318	.360
May	1-1	4.29	81	22	2	6	14	.272	.395	.318
June	1-3	6.91	109	30	7	12	21	.275	.514	.347
July	0-1	19.29	12	5	4	0	1	.417	1.417	.417
August	0-0	2.53	48	16	1	5	4	.333	.458	.396
Sept./Oct.	4-1	3.18	145	36	3	12	23	.248	.421	.302
Leading Off Inn.			101	28	4	8	12	.277	.465	.336
Bases Empty			236	67	10	22	37	.284	.475	.347
Runners On			181	48	7	16	29	.265	.459	.317
Runners/Scor. Pos.			89	17	1	12	18	.191	.281	.274
Runners On/2 Out			83	26	5	10	17	.313	.578	.387
Scor. Pos./2 Out			49	10	0	7	12	.204	.265	.304
Late-Inning Pressure			33	12	1	2	3	.364	.545	.400
Leading Off			7	1	0	1	0	.143	.143	.250
Runners On			16	7	1	1	1	.438	.688	.471
Runners/Scor. Pos.			8	2	1	1	1	.250	.625	.333
First 9 Batters			185	50	6	23	37	.270	.427	.351
Second 9 Batters			123	34	7	11	20	.276	.504	.331
All Batters Thereafter			109	31	4	4	9	.284	.495	.307

Loves to face: Darryl Strawberry (0-for-6)
Lou Whitaker (0-for-5)

Hates to face: Tom Foley (1-for-1, 1 HR, 1 BB)
Keith Hernandez (.750, 3-for-4, 1 HR)

Miscellaneous statistics: Ground outs-to-air outs ratio: 1.10 last season, 1.28 for career. . . . Induced 10 double-play ground outs in 82 opportunities (one per 8.2). . . . Allowed 27 doubles, 1 triple in 107.2 innings. . . . Allowed 7 first-inning runs in 13 starts (4.85 ERA). . . . Batting support: 5.31 runs per start. . . . Record of 5–5, 4.97 ERA as a starter; 1–1, 4.55 ERA in 17 relief appearances. . . . Stranded 15 inherited runners, allowed 5 to score (75%). . . . Opposing base stealers: 6-for-10 (60%); 1 pick-off, 0 balks.

Comments: Has played only 54 games in his career, but has already graced three home cities on his whirlwind tour of the continent. He played five games with the Expos, 25 with the Braves, and 24 with the Indians. . . . Made 13 starts for the Indians last season after starting only once in 25 appearances for the Braves. He's a starter by trade, having been used in relief in only 13 of his 137 career games in the minor leagues. . . . Struck out 5.52 batters per nine innings last season, compared to a 7.18 mark in two previous seasons. . . . Career ERA of 5.39 is 2d highest among active pitchers with at least 150 innings pitched. Only David West has a higher mark (5.54). . . . Opposing right-handers (.333) batted 125 points higher than left-handers (.208) last season, the largest margin in the majors. . . . Opposing batters have a career average of .538 (7-for-13, 1 BB) with the bases loaded. . . . Opponents have a career batting average of .326 in day games (one home run per 18 at-bats); at night: .274 (one HR per 31 AB). . . . The birds of Baltimore defeated Valdez twice last season, hardly suitable retribution for the thousands of feathered friends taken out in 1989 by the friendly Exxon tanker bearing Sergio's name. . . . We'll be honest—it's not easy to find a lot to say about Sergio Valdez. But it could have been worse; at least Efrain and Rafael Valdez didn't pitch enough to get in the book.

Duane Ward

Throws Right

Toronto Blue Jays	W-L	ERA	AB	H	HR	BB	SO	BA	SA	OBA
Season	2-8	3.45	457	101	9	42	112	.221	.322	.287
vs. Left-Handers			189	49	5	33	49	.259	.386	.372
vs. Right-Handers			268	52	4	9	63	.194	.276	.219
vs. Ground-Ballers			208	46	4	21	50	.221	.303	.293
vs. Fly-Ballers			249	55	5	21	62	.221	.337	.282
Home Games	0-4	3.02	236	48	4	14	53	.203	.292	.251
Road Games	2-4	3.92	221	53	5	28	59	.240	.353	.323
Grass Fields	2-3	5.18	152	37	5	21	40	.243	.382	.331
Artificial Turf	0-5	2.62	305	64	4	21	72	.210	.292	.263
April	0-0	1.08	55	10	0	4	18	.182	.218	.237
May	1-2	4.57	81	21	1	14	22	.259	.370	.375
June	0-1	5.09	88	27	1	9	15	.307	.409	.364
July	0-3	3.15	71	15	4	4	16	.211	.394	.253
August	1-1	1.52	83	14	0	2	22	.169	.205	.188
Sept./Oct.	0-1	4.76	79	14	3	9	19	.177	.304	.261
Leading Off Inn.			113	17	0	10	39	.150	.168	.220
Bases Empty			289	54	4	19	76	.187	.260	.239
Runners On			168	47	5	23	36	.280	.429	.363
Runners/Scor. Pos.			103	30	4	14	26	.291	.447	.370
Runners On/2 Out			66	16	0	10	14	.242	.318	.342
Scor. Pos./2 Out			45	12	0	7	11	.267	.333	.365
Late-Inning Pressure			193	45	3	18	51	.233	.347	.296
Leading Off			54	10	0	3	19	.185	.204	.228
Runners On			67	20	2	10	15	.299	.493	.380
Runners/Scor. Pos.			36	11	1	7	10	.306	.444	.400
First 9 Batters			419	95	7	39	106	.227	.320	.293
Second 9 Batters			38	6	2	3	6	.158	.342	.220
All Batters Thereafter			0	0	0	0	0	—	—	—

Loves to face: Carlos Quintana (0-for-7, 5 SO)
Jody Reed (0-for-9)
Harold Reynolds (.091, 1-for-11)

Hates to face: Brian Downing (.500, 2-for-4, 2 HR)
Rickey Henderson (.500, 7-for-14)
Alan Trammell (.714, 5-for-7)

Miscellaneous statistics: Ground outs-to-air outs ratio: 1.76 last season, 1.99 for career. . . . Induced 14 double-play ground outs in 83 opportunities (one per 5.9). . . . Allowed 13 doubles, 3 triples in 127.2 innings. . . . Stranded 19 inherited runners, allowed 12 to score (61%). . . . Opposing base stealers: 12-for-18 (67%); 0 pick-offs, 0 balks.

Comments: Ward is the only player in the majors to pitch at least 100 innings in relief in each of the last three seasons. The last pitcher with a streak longer than three years was Dan Quisenberry (4 years, 1982–85). The longest streak ever was seven years, by Rollie Fingers (1972–78). . . . Opponents batted 91 points higher with runners in scoring position (.291) than in other at-bats (.201) last season, the 2d-largest margin in the majors. . . . Opponents' on-base percentage of .220 leading off innings was the lowest in the American League (minimum: 100 BFP). . . . Opponents had four hits in seven at-bats with the bases loaded. Over the last two seasons, Ward has given up grand slams to Sam Horn, Kent Hrbek, and Terry Steinbach. . . . Opponents' overall batting average has decreased in each of his seasons in the majors. Starting with 1986: .342, .326, .245, .230, .221. . . . One of four A.L. pitchers to hold the league's top 10 home run hitters homerless in at least 30 at-bats last season. Now he has to learn to handle Brian Downing, who homered both times he faced Ward in 1990. . . . Actually, it's not just Downing but all the Angels who give Ward fits. He has a record of 0–6 against California over the last two seasons. . . . Has thrown 28 wild pitches over the past three seasons. Only three other pitchers have thrown even 20 in relief: Mark Davis (23), Greg Cadaret (21), and Greg A. Harris (20).

Bob Welch

Throws Right

Oakland A's	W-L	ERA	AB	H	HR	BB	SO	BA	SA	OBA
Season	27-6	2.95	886	214	26	77	127	.242	.391	.304
vs. Left-Handers			465	120	12	43	55	.258	.404	.325
vs. Right-Handers			421	94	14	34	72	.223	.375	.281
vs. Ground-Ballers			427	98	13	33	58	.230	.384	.285
vs. Fly-Ballers			459	116	13	44	69	.253	.397	.322
Home Games	14-2	1.92	426	94	7	39	69	.221	.336	.290
Road Games	13-4	3.94	460	120	19	38	58	.261	.441	.317
Grass Fields	22-4	2.58	715	165	19	62	102	.231	.373	.294
Artificial Turf	5-2	4.64	171	49	7	15	25	.287	.462	.346
April	3-1	1.06	118	23	2	7	13	.195	.305	.246
May	4-1	2.84	164	40	5	16	23	.244	.390	.309
June	6-0	3.83	158	41	5	15	21	.259	.437	.322
July	3-2	4.78	104	31	4	14	20	.298	.471	.387
August	6-1	3.47	176	43	6	16	31	.244	.392	.311
Sept./Oct.	5-1	2.03	166	36	4	9	19	.217	.355	.260
Leading Off Inn.			238	61	8	10	23	.256	.412	.286
Bases Empty			564	138	16	41	71	.245	.397	.299
Runners On			322	76	10	36	56	.236	.379	.312
Runners/Scor. Pos.			180	44	7	22	39	.244	.433	.325
Runners On/2 Out			150	39	6	17	27	.260	.447	.339
Scor. Pos./2 Out			93	27	6	11	23	.290	.581	.371
Late-Inning Pressure			74	13	1	8	18	.176	.243	.256
Leading Off			25	6	1	2	5	.240	.400	.296
Runners On			20	5	0	1	2	.250	.250	.286
Runners/Scor. Pos.			10	1	0	1	1	.100	.100	.182
First 9 Batters			290	69	9	21	50	.238	.397	.289
Second 9 Batters			274	70	6	32	37	.255	.391	.334
All Batters Thereafter			322	75	11	24	40	.233	.385	.291

Loves to face: Brady Anderson (0-for-13)
Wade Boggs (0-for-18)
Pete Incaviglia (0-for-12)

Hates to face: Glenn Davis (.467, 14-for-30, 2 HR)
Sam Horn (.538, 7-for-13, 1 HR)
Tony Phillips (.556, 5-for-9, 1 HR)

Miscellaneous statistics: Ground outs-to-air outs ratio: 1.09 last season, 0.94 for career. . . . Induced 25 double-play ground outs in 138 opportunities (one per 5.5), 3d-highest rate in A.L. . . . Allowed 42 doubles (tied for 2d most in A.L.), 6 triples in 238.0 innings. . . . Allowed 17 first-inning runs in 35 starts (3.60 ERA). . . . Batting support: 5.03 runs per start. . . . Opposing base stealers: 10-for-17 (59%); 0 pickoffs, 2 balks.

Comments: Had a 15–9 record (.625) with the Dodgers in 1987. That seems like it would be hard to improve on, but Welch has steadily increased his winning percentage in *every* season since then: 17–9 (.653) in 1988, 17–8 (.680) in 1989, and 27–6 (.818) last season. . . . He is now one of six pitchers in major league history with four consecutive seasons of at least 15 wins and fewer than 10 losses. The others: Three Finger Brown (1906–09), Whitey Ford (1953–56 and 1961–64), Dwight Gooden (1984–88), Lefty Grove (1928–31), and Sandy Koufax (1963–66). Gooden's was the only five-year streak, and the only one to start as a rookie. Koufax's streak ended his career. (And our judges have ruled that should Koufax join Jim Palmer in a comeback, his streak continues.) . . . Welch's career winning percentage of .726 in the American League (61–23) is the highest in league history among pitchers with at least 50 wins. . . . Combined with Dave Stewart for 49 victories last season, the most by teammates since Koufax and Don Drysdale combined for 49 for the Dodgers in 1965. . . . His only two complete games were both shutouts. He had the fewest complete games ever by a 20-game winner. . . . Walked only one of the last 81 leadoff batters he faced. . . . Opposing fly-ball hitters have outhit ground-ball hitters in each of the last eight seasons, the longest current streak. . . . Has allowed an average of 15.7 base runners per nine innings in postseason play, the 2d highest rate in history (minimum: 25 IP). The leader: Roger Craig (16.1).

David Wells

Throws Left

Toronto Blue Jays	W-L	ERA	AB	H	HR	BB	SO	BA	SA	OBA
Season	11-6	3.14	701	165	14	45	115	.235	.371	.283
vs. Left-Handers			110	29	2	8	12	.264	.436	.319
vs. Right-Handers			591	136	12	37	103	.230	.359	.276
vs. Ground-Ballers			318	80	5	24	39	.252	.387	.303
vs. Fly-Ballers			383	85	9	21	76	.222	.358	.265
Home Games	3-2	2.61	302	71	9	20	48	.235	.387	.284
Road Games	8-4	3.55	399	94	5	25	67	.236	.358	.282
Grass Fields	6-4	4.26	316	80	4	22	59	.253	.380	.303
Artificial Turf	5-2	2.28	385	85	10	23	56	.221	.364	.266
April	0-0	0.93	31	3	1	1	8	.097	.194	.125
May	2-0	3.86	78	16	2	4	19	.205	.333	.253
June	3-2	4.41	130	33	4	13	27	.254	.438	.322
July	2-0	1.82	144	34	1	7	20	.236	.326	.270
August	2-2	3.89	152	41	1	13	16	.270	.401	.331
Sept./Oct.	2-2	2.82	166	38	5	7	25	.229	.380	.259
Leading Off Inn.			173	40	6	14	26	.231	.387	.289
Bases Empty			424	100	7	30	78	.236	.351	.286
Runners On			277	65	7	15	37	.235	.401	.277
Runners/Scor. Pos.			146	34	1	13	20	.233	.370	.296
Runners On/2 Out			126	34	4	8	16	.270	.468	.319
Scor. Pos./2 Out			74	15	1	7	10	.203	.338	.272
Late-Inning Pressure			75	16	2	3	12	.213	.360	.244
Leading Off			21	7	2	0	2	.333	.667	.333
Runners On			25	4	0	1	4	.160	.280	.192
Runners/Scor. Pos.			15	2	0	1	3	.133	.267	.188
First 9 Batters			286	66	6	11	60	.231	.371	.260
Second 9 Batters			201	41	1	18	29	.204	.284	.269
All Batters Thereafter			214	58	7	16	26	.271	.453	.325

Loves to face: Henry Cotto (.091, 1-for-11)
Lance Parrish (0-for-8, 5 SO)
Luis Rivera (0-for-10)

Hates to face: Chili Davis (.438, 7-for-16, 2 HR)
Dwight Evans (.412, 7-for-17, 2 HR)
Cal Ripken (.500, 6-for-12, 2 2B, 2 HR)

Miscellaneous statistics: Ground outs-to-air outs ratio: 0.72 last season, 0.94 for career. . . . Induced 9 double-play ground outs in 116 opportunities (one per 12.9). . . . Allowed 39 doubles, 7 triples in 189.0 innings. . . . Allowed 6 first-inning runs in 25 starts (2.16 ERA). . . . Batting support: 4.76 runs per start. . . . Record of 10–5, 3.11 ERA as a starter; 1–1, 3.38 ERA in 18 relief appearances. . . . Stranded 10 inherited runners, allowed 2 to score (83%). . . . Opposing base stealers: 11-for-22 (50%); 8 pickoffs, 1 balk.

Comments: Ranked seventh in the league in ERA last season, behind a dream staff of Roger Clemens, Chuck Finley, Dave Stewart, Kevin Appier, Dave Stieb, and Bob Welch. He also compiled a fine ERA in 1989 as well (2.40). . . . Made 25 starts without a complete game, but his average of 6.71 innings per start was the highest on the team. Toronto's total of six complete games was the lowest in major league history. . . . Did anyone notice that Toronto's road-game ERA was fractionally better than Oakland's? . . . Walked only one of 97 batters faced during the first inning, the lowest rate in the majors. . . . Has held opponents to a lower average with runners on base than with the bases empty in each of his four seasons in the majors. . . . Opponents have a career batting average of .218 with runners in scoring position, .249 in other at-bats. Last season's mark with RISP was a career high. . . . Opposing left-handers have outhit right-handers by 28 points over his three seasons (.263 to .235). But the home-run rate by right-handers (one per 39 at-bats) is more than double that of lefties (3 HR in 300 AB). . . . Career breakdown: 10–7 (3.49 ERA) in 27 starts, 15–11 (3.12 ERA) in 129 relief appearances. . . . Lost his major league debut to the Yankees in 1987, but has a record of 6–0 against them since then.

David West

Throws Left

Minnesota Twins	W-L	ERA	AB	H	HR	BB	SO	BA	SA	OBA
Season	7-9	5.10	554	142	21	78	92	.256	.451	.350
vs. Left-Handers			90	22	1	12	14	.244	.356	.333
vs. Right-Handers			464	120	20	66	78	.259	.470	.353
vs. Ground-Ballers			255	66	8	41	41	.259	.420	.361
vs. Fly-Ballers			299	76	13	37	51	.254	.478	.340
Home Games	2-4	6.03	240	62	10	33	46	.258	.471	.354
Road Games	5-5	4.41	314	80	11	45	46	.255	.436	.347
Grass Fields	4-3	4.35	237	63	9	35	37	.266	.464	.361
Artificial Turf	3-6	5.66	317	79	12	43	55	.249	.442	.342
April	1-3	3.52	86	20	5	11	12	.233	.419	.333
May	1-0	6.56	89	21	5	16	12	.236	.528	.355
June	1-3	4.88	126	35	2	12	29	.278	.421	.341
July	2-1	5.93	121	37	5	18	19	.306	.521	.396
August	2-2	5.00	126	29	4	19	20	.230	.405	.329
Sept./Oct.	0-0	0.00	6	0	0	2	0	.000	.000	.250
Leading Off Inn.			144	32	5	11	20	.222	.396	.282
Bases Empty			338	76	7	46	54	.225	.367	.321
Runners On			216	66	14	32	38	.306	.583	.394
Runners/Scor. Pos.			118	36	6	20	19	.305	.551	.399
Runners On/2 Out			106	36	5	17	15	.340	.585	.440
Scor. Pos./2 Out			63	23	3	11	7	.365	.619	.467
Late-Inning Pressure			14	8	0	2	0	.571	.786	.625
Leading Off			5	3	0	0	0	.600	1.000	.600
Runners On			8	4	0	1	0	.500	.625	.556
Runners/Scor. Pos.			6	2	0	1	0	.333	.500	.429
First 9 Batters			216	55	11	32	40	.255	.486	.354
Second 9 Batters			184	46	7	27	31	.250	.446	.346
All Batters Thereafter			154	41	3	19	21	.266	.409	.349

Loves to face: Pat Borders (.100, 1-for-10, 1 2B)
Darnell Coles (0-for-7)
Manny Lee (.125, 1-for-8)

Hates to face: Jose Canseco (2-for-2, 2 HR)
Luis Quinones (.750, 3-for-4, 2 HR)
Sammy Sosa (.556, 5-for-9, 2 2B, 1 3B, 1 HR)

Miscellaneous statistics: Ground outs-to-air outs ratio: 0.86 last season, 0.77 for career. . . . Induced 16 double-play ground outs in 93 opportunities (one per 5.8), 5th-highest rate in A.L. (1-for-41 to start the season, 15-for-52 thereafter). . . . Allowed 35 doubles, 5 triples in 146.1 innings. . . . Allowed 20 first-inning runs in 27 starts (6.67 ERA). . . . Batting support: 4.44 runs per start. . . . Opposing base stealers: 5-for-10 (50%); 1 pickoff, 1 balk.

Comments: His career ERA of 5.54 is the highest of any active pitcher with at least 200 innings pitched. In fact, only three pitchers have compiled higher ERAs than West's since 1960: Mike Brown (5.75), Jerry Stephenson (5.70), and Keith Creel (5.60). . . . It's hard to believe that this is the same pitcher who looked unhittable in his brief trial with the Mets (1988–89). Take away those 20⅓ innings and his career ERA (that is, his ERA with the Twins) is 5.93. . . . Fewest innings pitched per start in the American League last season (minimum: 20 GS): Curt Young, 5.21; West, 5.30; Jeff Robinson (Det.), 5.37; Bob Milacki, 5.39; Storm Davis, 5.40. . . . His streak of six consecutive starts without a decision (May 8–June 8) was the longest in the majors last season. No other American League pitcher had more than four consecutive no-decision starts. . . . A home run by Ken Griffey, Jr., last April 16 is the only one West has allowed in 139 career at-bats by opposing left-handed batters. Career batting-average breakdown: left-handers, .209; right-handers, .278. . . . Other breakdowns: .242 with the bases empty, .299 with runners on base; .306 with runners in scoring position (compared to .243 in other at-bats), .365 with two outs and RISP. . . . Allowed only one stolen base in 63⅓ innings in 1989.

Frank Wills

Throws Right

Toronto Blue Jays	W-L	ERA	AB	H	HR	BB	SO	BA	SA	OBA
Season	6-4	4.73	380	101	13	38	72	.266	.424	.333
vs. Left-Handers			172	42	4	17	18	.244	.372	.314
vs. Right-Handers			208	59	9	21	54	.284	.466	.349
vs. Ground-Ballers			182	52	6	15	31	.286	.445	.343
vs. Fly-Ballers			198	49	7	23	41	.247	.404	.324
Home Games	3-4	4.50	234	60	10	16	40	.256	.423	.304
Road Games	3-0	5.11	146	41	3	22	32	.281	.425	.376
Grass Fields	1-0	5.34	113	30	3	20	28	.265	.434	.376
Artificial Turf	5-4	4.48	267	71	10	18	44	.266	.419	.314
April	1-1	8.74	47	17	3	4	11	.362	.596	.412
May	3-1	5.59	74	20	3	10	10	.270	.405	.357
June	1-0	3.86	53	12	1	4	12	.226	.358	.281
July	0-1	3.00	55	13	3	4	11	.236	.473	.288
August	0-0	2.37	69	14	1	6	11	.203	.304	.267
Sept./Oct.	1-1	5.75	82	25	2	10	17	.305	.451	.383
Leading Off Inn.			86	26	5	9	22	.302	.570	.375
Bases Empty			205	50	7	20	45	.244	.410	.314
Runners On			175	51	6	18	27	.291	.440	.356
Runners/Scor. Pos.			98	33	4	12	19	.337	.510	.405
Runners On/2 Out			63	16	2	11	14	.254	.413	.365
Scor. Pos./2 Out			42	11	2	8	12	.262	.452	.380
Late-Inning Pressure			62	16	3	3	11	.258	.419	.292
Leading Off			17	3	1	3	3	.176	.353	.300
Runners On			20	7	1	0	3	.350	.550	.350
Runners/Scor. Pos.			8	2	0	0	2	.250	.250	.250
First 9 Batters			285	77	9	30	60	.270	.414	.340
Second 9 Batters			81	19	3	7	11	.235	.420	.300
All Batters Thereafter			14	5	1	1	1	.357	.643	.400

Loves to face: Steve Buechele (0-for-12, 1 BB)
Mike Devereaux (0-for-10)
Kent Hrbek (.125, 2-for-16, 1 HR)

Hates to face: George Brett (.500, 5-for-10, 2 HR)
Lloyd Moseby (.500, 6-for-12, 1 HR)
Kirby Puckett (.533, 8-for-15, 1 HR)

Miscellaneous statistics: Ground outs-to-air outs ratio: 1.24 last season, 1.06 for career. . . . Induced 14 double-play ground outs in 94 opportunities (one per 6.7). . . . Allowed 19 doubles, 1 triple in 99.0 innings. . . . Stranded 22 inherited runners, allowed 6 to score (79%). . . . Opposing base stealers: 8-for-12 (67%); 0 pickoffs, 0 balks.

Comments: Wills is one of four Blue Jays players selected in the first round of the June 1980 free-agent draft. And that doesn't even include Tom Henke, who was the first-round choice of Texas in the secondary phase of that draft. Ken Dayley was chosen third by the Braves; Kelly Gruber was selected 10th by the Indians; Wills was the 16th pick, selected by the Royals; and Jim Acker went 21st, also to the Braves. So who did the Blue Jays select with their own first-round pick, the second choice overall? Well, after the Mets chose Darryl Strawberry with the first selection, Toronto chose a high-school shortstop named Garry Harris, who retired after batting .224 and committing 20 errors at second base for Knoxville of the Class AA Southern League in 1983. . . . Now don't get us started on Augie Schmidt. . . . Wills—remember him?—took a regular turn in the Jays' rotation for three weeks late in the season. He started four games, and failed to pitch into the seventh inning in any of them. He has completed only one of 35 career starts. . . . Has a career record of 9–16 (5.64 ERA) as a starter, 13–9 (4.41 ERA) as a reliever. . . . Had never allowed a grand slam home run until last season, when he gave up two in a six-day span to a pair of noted sluggers, Jose Canseco and Brian Giles. (Think that's bad? Lance McCullers allowed a pair of salamis over a *four*-day period in June.)

Bobby Witt

Throws Right

Texas Rangers	W-L	ERA	AB	H	HR	BB	SO	BA	SA	OBA
Season	17-10	3.36	829	197	12	110	221	.238	.326	.328
vs. Left-Handers			396	92	5	54	98	.232	.321	.323
vs. Right-Handers			433	105	7	56	123	.242	.330	.332
vs. Ground-Ballers			389	85	1	52	105	.219	.267	.312
vs. Fly-Ballers			440	112	11	58	116	.255	.377	.341
Home Games	7-5	3.40	383	104	6	46	93	.272	.363	.350
Road Games	10-5	3.34	446	93	6	64	128	.209	.294	.309
Grass Fields	13-9	3.64	674	165	11	91	180	.245	.341	.335
Artificial Turf	4-1	2.16	155	32	1	19	41	.206	.258	.297
April	0-3	5.12	77	21	3	12	16	.273	.468	.374
May	2-3	4.96	123	32	2	17	31	.260	.358	.359
June	2-2	4.23	156	42	1	20	40	.269	.321	.356
July	5-0	1.99	163	36	5	24	49	.221	.337	.317
August	4-0	2.31	139	29	1	11	35	.209	.281	.265
Sept./Oct.	4-2	3.04	171	37	0	26	50	.216	.269	.317
Leading Off Inn.			210	45	4	17	51	.214	.300	.276
Bases Empty			473	107	8	63	123	.226	.315	.321
Runners On			356	90	4	47	98	.253	.340	.337
Runners/Scor. Pos.			200	49	0	32	60	.245	.300	.343
Runners On/2 Out			158	36	0	27	45	.228	.291	.344
Scor. Pos./2 Out			103	25	0	20	30	.243	.330	.371
Late-Inning Pressure			85	17	0	14	17	.200	.282	.313
Leading Off			21	0	0	4	5	.000	.000	.160
Runners On			34	10	0	4	5	.294	.441	.368
Runners/Scor. Pos.			15	4	0	2	3	.267	.467	.353
First 9 Batters			253	58	4	41	75	.229	.308	.337
Second 9 Batters			266	60	2	27	75	.226	.293	.300
All Batters Thereafter			310	79	6	42	71	.255	.368	.344

Loves to face: Gary Gaetti (.125, 3-for-24)
Greg Gagne (.148, 4-for-27, 1 HR)
Dan Gladden (.080, 2-for-25, 3 BB)

Hates to face: Rickey Henderson (.370, 10-for-27, 1 HR)
Randy Milligan (.583, 7-for-12, 1 HR, 6 BB)
B.J. Surhoff (.382, 13-for-34, 2 HR)

Miscellaneous statistics: Ground outs-to-air outs ratio: 0.94 last season, 0.95 for career.... Induced 18 double-play ground outs in 168 opportunities (one per 9.3).... Allowed 31 doubles, 3 triples in 222.0 innings.... Allowed 21 first-inning runs in 32 starts (4.78 ERA).... Batting support: 4.28 runs per start.... Opposing base stealers: 36-for-43 (84%); 1 pickoff, 2 balks.

Comments: Won 12 consecutive decisions over a span of 14 starts (June 28–September 6), during which time he compiled a 1.97 ERA. (If that's impressive, how good was Roger Clemens, whose ERA for the season was 1.93?)...Allowed an average of 4.46 walks per nine innings last season, more than two walks per game lower than his average coming into the season (6.69). But he still managed to walk 100 batters for the fifth straight season, four years short of Nolan Ryan's record streak (1971–79).... Strikeout rate of 8.96 per nine innings was his highest since 1986 when he averaged 9.93 as a rookie, but walked 143 batters in 157⅔ innings.... Allowed one home run every 18.5 innings, the 5th-best rate in the American League (minimum: 162 IP).... Opposing base runners stole 36 bases, 2d most against any American League pitcher. (Jack Morris allowed 45.)... Opponents batted 63 points higher in home games (.272) than in road games (.209) last season, the 4th-largest margin in the majors.... Opponents have hit for a higher average with runners on base than with the bases empty in each of his five years in the majors. Opponents' career averages: .248 with runners on base, .216 with the bases empty.... Completed only one of his first 57 starts, but has completed 25 of 84 since then.... Career record of 20–34 (5.29 ERA) before the All-Star break, 36–18 (3.83 ERA) during the second half of the season.... Career ERA of 4.48 is the highest in franchise history (minimum: 500 IP).

Mike Witt

Throws Right

Angels/Yankees	W-L	ERA	AB	H	HR	BB	SO	BA	SA	OBA
Season	5-9	4.00	439	106	9	47	74	.241	.360	.318
vs. Left-Handers			217	58	3	23	29	.267	.364	.339
vs. Right-Handers			222	48	6	24	45	.216	.356	.298
vs. Ground-Ballers			202	49	1	22	33	.243	.312	.317
vs. Fly-Ballers			237	57	8	25	41	.241	.401	.319
Home Games	2-5	3.29	195	46	5	15	34	.236	.344	.294
Road Games	3-4	4.57	244	60	4	32	40	.246	.373	.336
Grass Fields	4-9	4.35	354	90	8	34	64	.254	.379	.322
Artificial Turf	1-0	2.63	85	16	1	13	10	.188	.282	.300
April	0-3	3.00	47	11	1	8	8	.234	.319	.351
May	0-0	2.63	102	27	1	10	22	.265	.353	.336
June	0-1	4.00	35	8	1	2	8	.229	.371	.270
July	0-0	—	0	0	0	0	0	—	—	—
August	3-2	4.66	108	27	4	11	15	.250	.407	.328
Sept./Oct.	2-3	4.76	147	33	2	16	21	.224	.340	.298
Leading Off Inn.			116	32	2	4	18	.276	.388	.311
Bases Empty			261	60	4	22	41	.230	.322	.295
Runners On			178	46	5	25	33	.258	.416	.349
Runners/Scor. Pos.			107	23	3	13	25	.215	.364	.302
Runners On/2 Out			60	9	1	7	11	.150	.250	.250
Scor. Pos./2 Out			36	2	0	5	7	.056	.056	.190
Late-Inning Pressure			55	15	3	4	8	.273	.473	.311
Leading Off			16	4	1	0	2	.250	.438	.250
Runners On			19	7	2	2	1	.368	.789	.391
Runners/Scor. Pos.			10	3	0	0	1	.300	.400	.250
First 9 Batters			194	53	4	19	42	.273	.376	.340
Second 9 Batters			122	27	1	15	19	.221	.311	.315
All Batters Thereafter			123	26	4	13	13	.211	.382	.288

Loves to face: Gary Gaetti (.174, 8-for-46, 1 HR)
Bo Jackson (.071, 1-for-14, 8 SO)
Jamie Quirk (.125, 3-for-24)

Hates to face: Glenn Braggs (.423, 11-for-26, 3 HR)
Jerry Browne (.429, 9-for-21, 1 HR)
Carney Lansford (.385, 25-for-65, 2 HR)

Miscellaneous statistics: Ground outs-to-air outs ratio: 1.73 last season, 1.41 for career.... Induced 12 double-play ground outs in 101 opportunities (one per 8.4).... Allowed 19 doubles, 3 triples in 117.0 innings.... Allowed 15 first-inning runs in 16 starts (7.88 ERA).... Batting support: 3.81 runs per start.... Opposing base stealers: 7-for-11 (64%); 0 pickoffs, 0 balks.

Comments: Has a record of 27–40 over the past three seasons. But during the four years before that (1984–87), he ranked sixth among all major league pitchers with 64 wins, behind only Jack Morris (74), Dwight Gooden (73), Frank Viola (69), Bert Blyleven (68), and Charlie Hough (65).... The only other pitcher with ERAs of 4.00 or higher in at least 100 innings in each of the last four seasons is Bruce Ruffin.... He's another pitcher who spent time on the disabled list last season (59 days, June 9–August 7) with arm trouble after a long streak of 200-inning seasons (1984–89).... Games won year by year since 1986: 18, 16, 13, 9, 5.... Inherited six runners and stranded them all in 10 relief appearances (all for California).... Opponents' batting average with runners in scoring position was the lowest of his career.... Opponents have hit for a higher average in road games than in home games in each of the last five seasons.... Left California as the Angels' all-time leader in pitching appearances with 314. The only other pitcher in club history with more than 300 games is Dave LaRoche (304).... According to the *Baseball Encyclopedia*, Lee Guetterman at 6'8" is the tallest player in Yankees history. Big Mac lists Mike Witt and six other Yankees at 6'7"; the others: Rich Bordi (1985–87), John Candelaria (1988–89), Edward ("Slim") Love (1916–18), Dennis Rasmussen (1984–87), Tim Stoddard (1986–88), and Stefan Wever (1982).

Curt Young

Throws Left

Oakland A's	W-L	ERA	AB	H	HR	BB	SO	BA	SA	OBA
Season	9-6	4.85	466	124	17	53	56	.266	.418	.342
vs. Left-Handers			96	25	1	6	13	.260	.333	.311
vs. Right-Handers			370	99	16	47	43	.268	.441	.350
vs. Ground-Ballers			213	50	7	20	26	.235	.380	.300
vs. Fly-Ballers			253	74	10	33	30	.292	.451	.376
Home Games	5-2	3.18	253	56	6	36	40	.221	.324	.320
Road Games	4-4	7.04	213	68	11	17	16	.319	.531	.371
Grass Fields	7-5	4.05	377	94	13	49	51	.249	.390	.338
Artificial Turf	2-1	8.59	89	30	4	4	5	.337	.539	.362
April	0-1	11.08	53	19	3	3	1	.358	.604	.404
May	2-0	3.60	87	20	6	10	11	.230	.483	.306
June	1-1	2.45	64	9	1	11	12	.141	.219	.267
July	3-2	3.97	129	38	3	10	19	.295	.395	.345
August	1-0	3.55	47	12	3	7	4	.255	.447	.364
Sept./Oct.	2-2	6.75	86	26	1	12	9	.302	.407	.384
Leading Off Inn.			122	35	3	11	19	.287	.393	.346
Bases Empty			280	69	10	33	37	.246	.393	.330
Runners On			186	55	7	20	19	.296	.457	.361
Runners/Scor. Pos.			96	28	6	14	12	.292	.521	.375
Runners On/2 Out			67	17	0	9	7	.254	.299	.342
Scor. Pos./2 Out			40	11	0	9	5	.275	.325	.408
Late-Inning Pressure			18	3	0	3	6	.167	.167	.286
Leading Off			6	1	0	1	2	.167	.167	.286
Runners On			3	0	0	1	0	.000	.000	.250
Runners/Scor. Pos.			0	0	0	0	0	—	—	—
First 9 Batters			211	57	8	19	28	.270	.431	.336
Second 9 Batters			171	51	7	20	19	.298	.456	.368
All Batters Thereafter			84	16	2	14	9	.190	.310	.306

Loves to face: Steve Buechele (.056, 1-for-18, 1 2B, 2 BB)
Carlton Fisk (.077, 2-for-26)
Ozzie Guillen (.154, 4-for-26, 0 BB)

Hates to face: Brian Downing (.393, 11-for-28, 3 HR)
Dwight Evans (.400, 10-for-25, 3 HR)
Kirby Puckett (.441, 15-for-34, 2 HR)

Miscellaneous statistics: Ground outs-to-air outs ratio: 1.08 last season, 0.86 for career.... Induced 12 double-play ground outs in 97 opportunities (one per 8.1).... Allowed 20 doubles, 0 triples in 124.1 innings.... Allowed 16 first-inning runs in 21 starts (6.86 ERA).... Batting support: 4.90 runs per start.... Opposing base stealers: 9-for-20 (45%); 4 pickoffs, 0 balks.

Comments: Although Young has started at least 20 games for the Athletics in each of the last three seasons, he has pitched a total of only 3⅓ innings in Oakland's 26 post-season games during that time.... His record of 25–23 over the last three seasons may not look like much considering the success of his team, but he went 35–25 over five previous seasons during which time Oakland never had a winning record.... How things have changed. When Young first joined the A's rotation in 1984, his mates included Ray Burris, Steve McCatty, Bill Krueger, and Lary Sorensen.... Young and Carney Lansford are the only players to appear in a game for the Athletics in each of the last eight seasons.... Young's average of 5.21 innings pitched per start was the lowest in the American League last season (minimum: 20 GS).... Opponents have hit for a higher average with runners in scoring position than in other at-bats in each of his six full years in the majors.... The only home run he allowed to a left-handed batter over the last two seasons was hit by Wade Boggs on April 28, 1990.... Has never allowed a triple to a left-handed batter (712 AB).... Hasn't pitched a complete-game shutout since his final appearance of the 1986 season. He has started 67 games since then.... Career record of 29–31 (4.62 ERA) before the All-Star break, 31–17 (3.95) during the second half of the season.

Matt Young

Throws Left

Seattle Mariners	W-L	ERA	AB	H	HR	BB	SO	BA	SA	OBA
Season	8-18	3.51	836	198	15	107	176	.237	.328	.325
vs. Left-Handers			101	15	0	7	27	.149	.158	.209
vs. Right-Handers			735	183	15	100	149	.249	.351	.340
vs. Ground-Ballers			386	86	4	46	80	.223	.282	.307
vs. Fly-Ballers			450	112	11	61	96	.249	.367	.340
Home Games	4-10	2.69	492	107	10	62	101	.217	.309	.308
Road Games	4-8	4.73	344	91	5	45	75	.265	.355	.350
Grass Fields	2-8	5.56	261	74	4	36	57	.284	.387	.371
Artificial Turf	6-10	2.63	575	124	11	71	119	.216	.301	.304
April	0-3	5.03	77	19	1	13	11	.247	.299	.356
May	1-2	4.68	124	34	3	15	25	.274	.403	.352
June	1-3	2.84	141	30	2	14	39	.213	.277	.298
July	3-3	3.27	156	30	2	26	28	.192	.263	.304
August	1-3	2.47	170	39	4	16	33	.229	.347	.294
Sept./Oct.	2-4	3.92	168	46	3	23	40	.274	.369	.365
Leading Off Inn.			208	41	2	30	49	.197	.264	.301
Bases Empty			479	113	8	62	104	.236	.330	.327
Runners On			357	85	7	45	72	.238	.325	.323
Runners/Scor. Pos.			201	46	6	28	47	.229	.348	.322
Runners On/2 Out			142	35	3	14	32	.246	.338	.318
Scor. Pos./2 Out			92	23	3	8	26	.250	.380	.317
Late-Inning Pressure			59	19	3	9	13	.322	.559	.412
Leading Off			20	7	0	1	5	.350	.450	.381
Runners On			18	7	1	6	4	.389	.667	.542
Runners/Scor. Pos.			10	4	1	5	2	.400	.700	.600
First 9 Batters			266	71	3	34	61	.267	.346	.352
Second 9 Batters			258	53	5	30	49	.205	.279	.294
All Batters Thereafter			312	74	7	43	66	.237	.353	.329

Loves to face: Wade Boggs (.080, 2-for-25, 3 BB)
Ozzie Guillen (0-for-17)
Ron Karkovice (0-for-9, 5 SO)

Hates to face: Chet Lemon (.571, 12-for-21, 4 HR)
Alan Trammell (.393, 11-for-28, 1 HR)
Dave Winfield (.281, 9-for-32, 2 2B, 5 HR)

Miscellaneous statistics: Ground outs-to-air outs ratio: 1.92 last season, 3d-highest rate in A.L.; 1.76 for career.... Induced 27 double-play ground outs in 192 opportunities (one per 7.1).... Allowed 25 doubles, 3 triples in 225.1 innings.... Allowed 22 first-inning runs in 33 starts (5.18 ERA).... Batting support: 3.70 runs per start (5th lowest in A.L.)... Opposing base stealers: 20-for-34 (59%); 4 pickoffs, 0 balks.

Comments: Interesting: Danny Darwin and Young have a combined career winning percentage of .606 as relievers, but only .412 as starters. Neither has ever won more than 12 starts in a season. But Darwin won the N.L. ERA title last season at age 35, and not-so-Young established career highs in innings and strikeouts at age 32.... Young's first-inning strikeout rate (33 SO in 33 IP) was the 2d highest in the American League, behind Nolan Ryan (10.92 SO per nine first innings).... Held the American League's top 10 hitters to an average of .186 last season (8-for-43).... Was one of two pitchers to walk at least 100 right-handed batters last season. The other: Randy Johnson (113).... Opponents batted 45 points higher on his first pass through the batting order (.278) than in subsequent at-bats (.232) over the last five seasons, the 2d-largest margin in the majors.... The last left-handed batter to homer against him was Jose Cruz on April 8, 1987.... The Red Sox will be his fourth club in his last four years in the majors.... Career winning percentage of .395 (51–78) is 3d lowest among active pitchers (minimum: 100 decisions).... Career record of 39–65 (4.25 ERA) as a starter, 12–13 (4.30 ERA) as a reliever.... So why did Boston *really* sign this guy? Was it because he had the lowest ERA against the Red Sox last season (0.48)? Or was it to improve Wade Boggs's chances of batting .400 this season? (See "Loves to Face" above.)

Juan Agosto

Throws Left

Houston Astros	W-L	ERA	AB	H	HR	BB	SO	BA	SA	OBA
Season	9-8	4.29	349	91	4	39	50	.261	.350	.345
vs. Left-Handers			110	25	1	7	24	.227	.282	.303
vs. Right-Handers			239	66	3	32	26	.276	.381	.364
vs. Ground-Ballers			159	40	3	18	24	.252	.365	.346
vs. Fly-Ballers			190	51	1	21	26	.268	.337	.344
Home Games	6-4	2.47	149	27	1	22	30	.181	.235	.299
Road Games	3-4	5.92	200	64	3	17	20	.320	.435	.381
Grass Fields	2-3	7.66	106	37	2	10	8	.349	.453	.408
Artificial Turf	7-5	3.06	243	54	2	29	42	.222	.305	.318
April	1-1	0.82	40	7	0	6	10	.175	.200	.283
May	3-0	1.59	76	14	0	4	8	.184	.250	.241
June	0-0	4.70	62	20	0	9	9	.323	.371	.411
July	1-5	7.52	80	24	2	8	10	.300	.438	.371
August	1-1	5.59	40	13	0	4	6	.325	.425	.400
Sept./Oct.	3-1	5.40	51	13	2	8	7	.255	.392	.377
Leading Off Inn.			84	22	0	5	14	.262	.321	.311
Bases Empty			183	50	0	18	22	.273	.339	.342
Runners On			166	41	4	21	28	.247	.361	.349
Runners/Scor. Pos.			95	25	3	17	16	.263	.389	.390
Runners On/2 Out			67	13	2	12	13	.194	.284	.341
Scor. Pos./2 Out			46	10	2	9	10	.217	.348	.379
Late-Inning Pressure			168	45	2	21	21	.268	.339	.363
Leading Off			43	13	0	4	7	.302	.326	.362
Runners On			77	19	2	10	9	.247	.351	.363
Runners/Scor. Pos.			42	12	1	10	4	.286	.381	.444
First 9 Batters			336	89	4	37	46	.265	.357	.346
Second 9 Batters			13	2	0	2	4	.154	.154	.313
All Batters Thereafter			0	0	0	0	0	—	—	—

Loves to face: Barry Bonds (.118, 2-for-17)
Brett Butler (.182, 4-for-22)
Mike Scioscia (.067, 1-for-15)

Hates to face: Eric Davis (.625, 5-for-8, 1 HR, 3 SO)
Otis Nixon (.500, 5-for-10)
Spike Owen (.500, 5-for-10, 1 HR)

Miscellaneous statistics: Ground outs-to-air outs ratio: 1.78 last season, 5th-highest rate in N.L.; 2.29 for career.... Induced 5 double-play ground outs in 87 opportunities (one per 17.4).... Allowed 15 doubles, 2 triples in 92.1 innings.... Stranded 38 inherited runners, allowed 10 to score (79%), 3d-best rate in N.L.... Opposing base stealers: 5-for-6 (83%); 0 pickoffs, 0 balks.

Comments: Joins Cardinals after four years with Astros, during which he was much more effective in the Astrodome than anywhere else. At the Dome, he owned a 15–6 record and 1.90 ERA; opponents batted .215, with two home runs in 559 at-bats. In road games, his record was 9–10 with a 4.49 ERA; he allowed a .283 batting average, with 12 homers in 538 at-bats.... In four years with Houston he never allowed a home run to a left-handed batter in the Astrodome.... Allowed only one home run to a left-handed batter last season (Dave Justice).... Allowed an average of one home run every 23.1 innings pitched, the 3d-best rate among National League pitchers last season (minimum: 90 innings). Moving from the Astrodome to Busch Stadium shouldn't have much of an effect on that.... It's amazing that Whitey (Lefty/Righty/Lefty/Righty) Herzog never had this guy; a look at the career batting average breakdown against him (right-handed batters .292, left-handers .209) suggests he would have been a Rat favorite.... Art Howe used him to face a single batter 11 times last season, the most one-batter outings for any reliever in the National League last season.... A 3–0 record against the Pirates last season raised his career mark to 5–1 against them. It was the first time in his career that he ever defeated a club three times in one season.... No more Mr. Nice Guy: he drilled seven batters with pitches last season, after hitting only seven over the previous five years.

Jack Armstrong

Throws Right

Cincinnati Reds	W-L	ERA	AB	H	HR	BB	SO	BA	SA	OBA
Season	12-9	3.42	625	151	9	59	110	.242	.352	.311
vs. Left-Handers			387	100	6	40	51	.258	.380	.329
vs. Right-Handers			238	51	3	19	59	.214	.307	.281
vs. Ground-Ballers			290	65	1	24	53	.224	.310	.293
vs. Fly-Ballers			335	86	8	35	57	.257	.388	.326
Home Games	6-4	3.93	275	68	4	29	46	.247	.345	.320
Road Games	6-5	3.03	350	83	5	30	64	.237	.357	.303
Grass Fields	2-3	3.83	193	49	3	18	31	.254	.378	.323
Artificial Turf	10-6	3.23	432	102	6	41	79	.236	.340	.305
April	4-0	1.40	97	21	0	5	20	.216	.289	.260
May	4-1	1.64	156	32	0	12	22	.205	.250	.267
June	2-2	3.79	149	37	4	13	31	.248	.423	.307
July	1-4	6.21	118	35	3	8	19	.297	.441	.352
August	1-2	5.47	91	26	2	20	12	.286	.418	.416
Sept./Oct.	0-0	0.00	14	0	0	1	6	.000	.000	.067
Leading Off Inn.			159	33	1	10	34	.208	.296	.263
Bases Empty			369	80	3	34	73	.217	.312	.288
Runners On			256	71	6	25	37	.277	.410	.343
Runners/Scor. Pos.			162	42	3	19	28	.259	.383	.335
Runners On/2 Out			106	26	2	13	17	.245	.349	.339
Scor. Pos./2 Out			72	18	2	12	13	.250	.389	.365
Late-Inning Pressure			43	8	0	1	5	.186	.256	.222
Leading Off			12	2	0	0	3	.167	.167	.231
Runners On			16	2	0	0	1	.125	.250	.125
Runners/Scor. Pos.			8	2	0	0	0	.250	.500	.250
First 9 Batters			219	56	5	22	44	.256	.393	.322
Second 9 Batters			196	38	2	23	36	.194	.286	.288
All Batters Thereafter			210	57	2	14	30	.271	.371	.320

Loves to face: Craig Biggio (.143, 2-for-14)
Ken Caminiti (0-for-9)
Robby Thompson (.176, 3-for-17, 8 SO)

Hates to face: Bobby Bonilla (.500, 4-for-8, 1 HR)
Howard Johnson (.357, 5-for-14, 2 HR)
Kevin Mitchell (.429, 3-for-7, 2 2B, 1 HR)

Miscellaneous statistics: Ground outs-to-air outs ratio: 0.91 last season, 0.83 for career.... Induced 9 double-play ground outs in 120 opportunities (one per 13.3).... Allowed 30 doubles, 6 triples in 166.0 innings.... Allowed 21 first-inning runs in 27 starts (6.75 ERA, 5th highest in N.L.)... Batting support: 4.22 runs per start.... Opposing base stealers: 14-for-20 (70%); 0 pickoffs, 5 balks.

Comments: The streak continues! No starting pitcher for the National League in the All-Star Game has gone on to win 20 or more games in that season since Randy Jones did it in 1976. Only Jones and Andy Messersmith in 1974 have done it in the last 24 years. Armstrong's 12 victories were the fewest by an All-Star starter in either league since the J. R. Richard tragedy limited him to only 10 wins in 1980. Before that, you have to go back to 1962 to find a pitcher with fewer than 12 wins in a season in which he started an All-Star game. (And you were wondering how we would get Dave Stenhouse's name into the book!)... Armstrong was 11–3 at the break, but had a record of 1–6 during the second half, and spent 15 days on the disabled list. Over the last seven years, the N.L.'s All-Star starter has posted a winning record during the second half of the season only twice (Dwight Gooden in both 1986 and 1988). Since 1977, the National League's All-Star starters have compiled a .704 winning percentage during the first half of the season, but only a .534 mark after the break.... The only Reds pitcher who didn't see action in the Championship Series, but he tossed three shutout innings in Game Two of the World Series.... Has a career record of 0–4 vs. San Diego.... Has limited batters to a .227 career batting average with the bases empty, but opponents have hit .272 with runners on base.... Has started 48 games in his career, but has allowed more than one home run in a game only once.... Had a 2.97 ERA with Joe Oliver catching last season, 4.63 with Jeff Reed behind the plate.

Paul Assenmacher

Throws Left

Chicago Cubs	W-L	ERA	AB	H	HR	BB	SO	BA	SA	OBA
Season	7-2	2.80	376	90	10	36	95	.239	.351	.305
vs. Left-Handers			121	27	1	6	30	.223	.281	.262
vs. Right-Handers			255	63	9	30	65	.247	.384	.325
vs. Ground-Ballers			158	30	3	13	41	.190	.272	.250
vs. Fly-Ballers			218	60	7	23	54	.275	.408	.344
Home Games	6-1	3.46	201	51	6	18	50	.254	.388	.315
Road Games	1-1	2.12	175	39	4	18	45	.223	.309	.294
Grass Fields	7-2	2.71	303	71	8	29	78	.234	.343	.301
Artificial Turf	0-0	3.15	73	19	2	7	17	.260	.384	.325
April	1-0	0.54	52	4	1	5	16	.077	.135	.158
May	0-1	3.10	77	19	3	7	14	.247	.390	.318
June	1-0	6.75	71	27	2	9	13	.380	.535	.444
July	1-1	3.86	34	10	0	7	9	.294	.353	.405
August	1-0	2.29	67	12	2	3	19	.179	.313	.214
Sept./Oct.	3-0	1.29	75	18	2	5	24	.240	.320	.284
Leading Off Inn.			82	20	3	6	18	.244	.366	.295
Bases Empty			203	53	5	15	40	.261	.360	.312
Runners On			173	37	5	21	55	.214	.341	.298
Runners/Scor. Pos.			104	20	2	18	33	.192	.260	.304
Runners On/2 Out			77	13	1	12	28	.169	.247	.281
Scor. Pos./2 Out			52	8	1	11	19	.154	.212	.302
Late-Inning Pressure			179	42	5	20	50	.235	.335	.310
Leading Off			40	9	2	3	12	.225	.375	.279
Runners On			83	17	2	13	25	.205	.289	.309
Runners/Scor. Pos.			50	10	1	11	14	.200	.260	.339
First 9 Batters			342	83	8	35	88	.243	.348	.312
Second 9 Batters			33	7	2	1	7	.212	.394	.235
All Batters Thereafter			1	0	0	0	0	.000	.000	.000

Loves to face: Barry Bonds (.063, 1-for-16, 2 BB)
Keith Miller (.111, 1-for-9, 7 SO)
Glenn Wilson (0-for-11)

Hates to face: Eric Davis (.833, 5-for-6, 2 HR)
Barry Larkin (.750, 3-for-4, 1 HR, 1 SO)
Robby Thompson (.750, 6-for-8)

Miscellaneous statistics: Ground outs-to-air outs ratio: 1.29 last season, 1.30 for career. . . . Induced 9 double-play ground outs in 90 opportunities (one per 10.0). . . . Allowed 8 doubles, 2 triples in 103.0 innings. . . . Stranded 28 inherited runners, allowed 16 to score (64%). . . . Opposing base stealers: 6-for-10 (60%); 2 pickoffs, 0 balks.

Comments: Let's start with some fielding and batting notes. Assenmacher has the lowest career batting average of any active player with at least 25 at-bats. His .038 (1-for-26) average is the worst we've seen since Andy Hassler retired with an 0-for-29 streak intact. Assenmacher's only hit was a double off Larry Andersen in 1988. . . . However, he starts the 1991 season just 19 games away from an all-time fielding record. He has pitched in 314 major-league games and has never committed an error. The all-time record for most errorless games to start a career (at any position) is 332 by Rob Murphy; that streak came to an end in 1990. . . . Has allowed only one home run to a left-handed batter in 206 at-bats over the last two seasons; Kal Daniels hit it last May 23. In his career, lefties have batted .238 against him, with only five homers in 458 at-bats. . . . In three of his seven victories last year, he entered the game with the Cubs leading and subsequently allowed the opponents to tie the score. . . . Had a 3–0 record against the Mets last season. . . . He started against the Pirates on June 5, the only start of his career, and if his performance was any guide it's likely to remain so. He pitched only one inning, during which four runs scored before he retired a batter. The Cubs eventually tied the score, taking Assenmacher off the hook, and keeping intact his perfect career record against the Bucs (4–0).

Steve Avery

Throws Left

Atlanta Braves	W-L	ERA	AB	H	HR	BB	SO	BA	SA	OBA
Season	3-11	5.64	401	121	7	45	75	.302	.431	.372
vs. Left-Handers			61	16	0	5	19	.262	.311	.318
vs. Right-Handers			340	105	7	40	56	.309	.453	.381
vs. Ground-Ballers			188	56	4	26	37	.298	.457	.381
vs. Fly-Ballers			213	65	3	19	38	.305	.408	.363
Home Games	3-4	4.25	231	65	4	27	43	.281	.377	.356
Road Games	0-7	7.71	170	56	3	18	32	.329	.506	.393
Grass Fields	3-6	4.63	316	92	4	32	56	.291	.389	.356
Artificial Turf	0-5	9.78	85	29	3	13	19	.341	.588	.426
April	0-0	—	0	0	0	0	0	—	—	—
May	0-0	—	0	0	0	0	0	—	—	—
June	1-1	6.43	59	18	0	10	10	.305	.390	.406
July	0-4	4.63	134	38	1	16	18	.284	.381	.358
August	2-3	4.36	125	34	2	13	33	.272	.384	.338
Sept./Oct.	0-3	9.53	83	31	4	6	14	.373	.614	.422
Leading Off Inn.			91	26	0	16	15	.286	.407	.398
Bases Empty			195	53	1	28	34	.272	.369	.369
Runners On			206	68	6	17	41	.330	.490	.374
Runners/Scor. Pos.			136	42	2	13	30	.309	.404	.359
Runners On/2 Out			84	24	3	8	18	.286	.452	.348
Scor. Pos./2 Out			64	18	1	6	15	.281	.375	.343
Late-Inning Pressure			31	9	0	2	6	.290	.387	.333
Leading Off			8	0	0	0	1	.000	.000	.000
Runners On			15	4	0	1	4	.267	.467	.313
Runners/Scor. Pos.			5	2	0	0	1	.400	.600	.400
First 9 Batters			167	51	2	17	32	.305	.419	.370
Second 9 Batters			139	44	3	14	28	.317	.475	.380
All Batters Thereafter			95	26	2	14	15	.274	.389	.364

Loves to face: Andre Dawson (0-for-7)
Luis Salazar (0-for-7)

Hates to face: Glenn Braggs (.500, 4-for-8, 1 3B, 2 HR)
Tim Wallach (.600, 3-for-5, 1 HR)

Miscellaneous statistics: Ground outs-to-air outs ratio: 1.30 last season, his first in the majors. . . . Induced 5 double-play ground outs in 98 opportunities (one per 19.6). . . . Allowed 25 doubles, 3 triples in 99.0 innings. . . . Allowed 13 first-inning runs in 20 starts (4.95 ERA). . . . Batting support: 4.10 runs per start. . . . Opposing base stealers: 20-for-28 (71%); 3 pickoffs, 1 balk.

Comments: Had the highest ERA of any rookie who pitched more than 55 innings last season, and was the only rookie pitcher in the National League against whom opponents batted .300 or higher. His .214 winning percentage was the lowest by any rookie with at least 10 decisions last season, and the worst by a Braves rookie since Frank LaCorte's 3–12 baptism in 1976. . . . When he was good, he was very good; he had an ERA of 0.78 in his three wins. Two of those wins were achieved against the Dodgers. . . . He also had the National League's best ERA (1.20) against the Cubs last season. . . . Threw a six-hit shutout vs. Chicago on August 19 to become the youngest Braves pitcher to throw a shutout since 18-year old Joey Jay blanked the team then known as the Redlegs at the height of the Red Scare in 1953. (Jay's game was halted by darkness after six-and-one-half innings.) . . . Avery was the youngest player to appear in a National League game last season. Five players active in 1990 had already made their major league debuts when Avery was born on April 14, 1970: Nolan Ryan, Carlton Fisk, Jerry Reuss, Rick Dempsey, and Bill Buckner. Rich Garces, a 19-year-old who relieved in five games with the Twins, was the only player younger than Avery to appear in a major league box score last season. . . . Opponents' on-base average leading off innings was 2d highest among National League pitchers who faced at least 100 leadoff batters last season. . . . The only pitcher in the majors to start at least 20 games and average fewer than five innings per start. He averaged 4.85 innings. . . . Career minor league record: 24–13, 2.34 ERA.

Steve Bedrosian

Throws Right

San Francisco Giants	W-L	ERA	AB	H	HR	BB	SO	BA	SA	OBA
Season	9-9	4.20	299	72	6	44	43	.241	.341	.341
vs. Left-Handers			165	44	4	26	23	.267	.388	.373
vs. Right-Handers			134	28	2	18	20	.209	.284	.301
vs. Ground-Ballers			132	28	1	15	21	.212	.273	.297
vs. Fly-Ballers			167	44	5	29	22	.263	.395	.374
Home Games	8-4	3.54	177	40	3	19	28	.226	.322	.301
Road Games	1-5	5.23	122	32	3	25	15	.262	.369	.393
Grass Fields	8-5	3.13	218	48	3	23	35	.220	.298	.299
Artificial Turf	1-4	7.58	81	24	3	21	8	.296	.457	.441
April	0-2	9.00	31	10	2	5	4	.323	.548	.417
May	0-1	2.77	47	9	1	8	5	.191	.277	.304
June	3-2	3.50	67	16	1	6	16	.239	.358	.320
July	2-1	4.15	49	12	1	11	7	.245	.347	.383
August	1-2	6.00	62	18	1	9	4	.290	.371	.380
Sept./Oct.	3-1	1.46	43	7	0	5	7	.163	.186	.250
Leading Off Inn.			65	16	2	9	8	.246	.400	.338
Bases Empty			146	33	3	21	21	.226	.336	.323
Runners On			153	39	3	23	22	.255	.346	.358
Runners/Scor. Pos.			101	24	2	20	15	.238	.317	.366
Runners On/2 Out			66	18	0	11	7	.273	.273	.377
Scor. Pos./2 Out			46	12	0	10	5	.261	.261	.393
Late-Inning Pressure			151	35	3	28	20	.232	.344	.356
Leading Off			33	6	1	7	6	.182	.364	.325
Runners On			79	20	1	14	10	.253	.342	.372
Runners/Scor. Pos.			54	13	1	13	7	.241	.333	.397
First 9 Batters			290	69	6	38	41	.238	.341	.329
Second 9 Batters			9	3	0	6	2	.333	.333	.600
All Batters Thereafter			0	0	0	0	0	—	—	—

Loves to face: Rafael Palmeiro (0-for-9)
Tony Pena (.160, 4-for-25)
Max Venable (.100, 1-for-10)

Hates to face: Glenn Davis (.412, 7-for-17, 1 HR)
Kirk Gibson (3-for-3, 1 HR, 1 BB)
Franklin Stubbs (.417, 5-for-12, 2 2B, 2 HR)

Miscellaneous statistics: Ground outs-to-air outs ratio: 0.84 last season, 0.79 for career. . . . Induced 9 double-play ground outs in 67 opportunities (one per 7.4). . . . Allowed 10 doubles, 1 triple in 79.1 innings. . . . Stranded 24 inherited runners, allowed 7 to score (77%). . . . Opposing base stealers: 14-for-15 (93%), shared 2d-highest rate in N.L.; 0 pickoffs, 0 balks.

Comments: Has held opponents to a career .202 batting average with runners in scoring position. That's over a span of 10 years and includes more than 1000 at-bats in those situations. . . . Saved 178 games in 10 seasons (including 1985, when he was a starter) in the National League. That's the 8th-highest N.L. total since the save rule was established in 1969. . . . He'll be playing an American tune for the first time in 1991, after 552 games in the senior circuit. Among active pitchers who have spent their entire careers in one league, only Dave Smith has appeared in more games (563). . . . Over the last four seasons, has limited right-handed batters to a .205 average, while left-handers have batted .251. . . . Tied the Yankees' Lee Guetterman for the most decisions (18) by a reliever last season. Bedrosian led major league relievers with nine losses. . . . Had six of those decisions (3–3) against the Astros, the most by any pitcher against a particular opponent in either of the last two years. . . . Aside from posting a better won-lost record at home than he did on the road, he also registered 11 of his 17 saves at Candlestick. . . . Has made 326 consecutive relief appearances since starting 37 games for Atlanta in 1985. . . . Had his highest ERA since 1981, when he pitched just 24 innings for the Braves in his major league debut. Last year was also the first time since '81 that he walked more batters than he struck out.

Tim Belcher

Throws Right

Los Angeles Dodgers	W-L	ERA	AB	H	HR	BB	SO	BA	SA	OBA
Season	9-9	4.00	566	136	17	48	102	.240	.382	.299
vs. Left-Handers			299	68	8	31	55	.227	.358	.296
vs. Right-Handers			267	68	9	17	47	.255	.408	.302
vs. Ground-Ballers			248	65	5	24	47	.262	.367	.326
vs. Fly-Ballers			318	71	12	24	55	.223	.393	.277
Home Games	6-3	2.77	271	62	6	22	45	.229	.339	.282
Road Games	3-6	5.17	295	74	11	26	57	.251	420	.315
Grass Fields	8-6	3.62	443	111	12	36	70	.251	.391	.304
Artificial Turf	1-3	5.25	123	25	5	12	32	.203	.350	.283
April	1-2	4.45	103	26	4	5	20	.252	.379	.284
May	3-1	2.50	129	27	3	9	27	.209	.333	.264
June	1-3	6.12	130	39	7	12	23	.300	.508	.364
July	4-2	2.05	152	28	1	16	21	.184	.257	.256
August	0-1	8.76	52	16	2	6	11	.308	.558	.379
Sept./Oct.	0-0	—	0	0	0	0	0	—	—	—
Leading Off Inn.			145	33	6	12	22	.228	.414	.291
Bases Empty			367	81	10	27	67	.221	.351	.276
Runners On			199	55	7	21	35	.276	.437	.339
Runners/Scor. Pos.			105	27	3	13	26	.257	.400	.328
Runners On/2 Out			81	17	1	10	18	.210	.272	.297
Scor. Pos./2 Out			49	9	0	9	15	.184	.204	.310
Late-Inning Pressure			51	11	0	3	3	.216	.235	.250
Leading Off			13	2	0	1	0	.154	.154	.214
Runners On			20	3	0	1	2	.150	.150	.174
Runners/Scor. Pos.			6	0	0	1	2	.000	.000	.111
First 9 Batters			197	43	7	17	41	.218	.381	.280
Second 9 Batters			183	54	4	17	31	.295	.432	.353
All Batters Thereafter			186	39	6	14	30	.210	.333	.265

Loves to face: Craig Biggio (.125, 3-for-24)
Ken Caminiti (.087, 2-for-23)
Shawon Dunston (.133, 2-for-15)

Hates to face: Vince Coleman (.600, 6-for-10)
Andre Dawson (.435, 10-for-23, 2 HR)
Barry Larkin (.393, 11-for-28, 1 HR)

Miscellaneous statistics: Ground outs-to-air outs ratio: 0.73 last season, 0.74 for career. . . . Induced 11 double-play ground outs in 104 opportunities (one per 9.5). . . . Allowed 19 doubles, 5 triples in 153.0 innings. . . . Allowed 11 first-inning runs in 24 starts (4.13 ERA). . . . Batting support: 3.79 runs per start. . . . Opposing base stealers: 11-for-18 (61%); 2 pickoffs, 1 balk.

Comments: Did not have a winning streak or a losing streak of more than two games last season. . . . Had the lowest average run support of any pitcher on the Dodgers' staff last season. . . . Led National League pitchers with a 1.03 ERA against the Pirates last season; he's 6–1 lifetime against them. . . . Picked a runner off base in each of his first two starts of the season, but didn't do it again for the remainder of the year. . . . Spent the last 47 days of the season on the disabled list with a shoulder problem, after an 0–2 record with an ERA of 6.52 ERA over his last four starts. . . . Pitched 153 innings last season without walking a batter intentionally (unless he hid his intentions very well). No other National League pitcher threw more than 60 innings without at least one IBB. . . . He had a winning record and an ERA under 3.00 in each of his previous three seasons in the majors. . . . He has held opponents to a career batting average of .199 during his first pass through the batting order, but they've hit .240 against him in subsequent at-bats. . . . Career won-lost records: 26–11 (2.47) in home games, 14–18 (3.80) on the road. . . . His complete-game shutout in his first start of the season reinforced the belief that the proposed lockout-settlement exception to Rule 10.19(a), which would have allowed starting pitchers to be credited with a win despite pitching fewer than five innings, was no more than an ill-conceived and frivolous consideration that someone actually thought important at the time. You'd forgotten all about it? Good.

Andy Benes

Throws Right

San Diego Padres	W-L	ERA	AB	H	HR	BB	SO	BA	SA	OBA
Season	10-11	3.60	730	177	18	69	140	.242	.374	.306
vs. Left-Handers			437	107	9	40	73	.245	.371	.307
vs. Right-Handers			293	70	9	29	67	.239	.379	.306
vs. Ground-Ballers			339	89	6	27	73	.263	.383	.314
vs. Fly-Ballers			391	88	12	42	67	.225	.366	.300
Home Games	6-4	3.93	338	78	8	33	74	.231	.376	.298
Road Games	4-7	3.32	392	99	10	36	66	.253	.372	.314
Grass Fields	8-8	3.24	609	142	14	52	118	.233	.365	.292
Artificial Turf	2-3	5.46	121	35	4	17	22	.289	.421	.376
April	2-2	4.35	80	20	2	10	20	.250	.363	.333
May	3-2	3.89	146	30	6	13	25	.205	.349	.270
June	1-2	3.00	137	27	2	16	33	.197	.285	.274
July	1-1	3.04	95	25	2	8	20	.263	.411	.327
August	3-1	3.38	121	32	2	13	13	.264	.388	.333
Sept./Oct.	0-3	4.06	151	43	4	9	29	.285	.450	.323
Leading Off Inn.			190	50	10	13	33	.263	.468	.310
Bases Empty			449	109	14	32	81	.243	.394	.295
Runners On			281	68	4	37	59	.242	.342	.324
Runners/Scor. Pos.			173	36	2	20	42	.208	.301	.281
Runners On/2 Out			120	25	3	16	25	.208	.342	.301
Scor. Pos./2 Out			81	14	1	11	21	.173	.272	.272
Late-Inning Pressure			48	16	3	1	5	.333	.604	.347
Leading Off			16	8	3	0	1	.500	1.188	.500
Runners On			16	5	0	1	2	.313	.438	.353
Runners/Scor. Pos.			9	5	0	1	1	.556	.778	.600
First 9 Batters			259	59	2	24	65	.228	.324	.295
Second 9 Batters			246	52	5	27	40	.211	.309	.286
All Batters Thereafter			225	66	11	18	35	.293	.502	.343

Loves to face: Andres Galarraga (.100, 1-for-10)
Tom Herr (0-for-12, 2 BB)
Mike Scioscia (0-for-14, 2 BB)

Hates to face: Tommy Gregg (.545, 6-for-11)
Gregg Jefferies (.556, 5-for-9, 1 HR)
Jeff Treadway (.500, 7-for-14)

Miscellaneous statistics: Ground outs-to-air outs ratio: 0.78 last season, 0.77 for career.... Induced 14 double-play ground outs in 134 opportunities (one per 9.6).... Allowed 24 doubles, 9 triples (tied for most in N.L.) in 192.1 innings.... Allowed 8 first-inning runs in 31 starts (2.32 ERA).... Batting support: 3.90 runs per start.... Opposing base stealers: 23-for-28 (82%); 0 pickoffs, 5 balks.

Comments: His earned run average was lower in his 10 no-decision starts (2.20) than it was in his 10 victories (2.36).... Won three starts in a row, August 7–24, to lift his record to 10–8, but followed that streak with four no-decisions and three losses to end up below .500.... Like most fly-ball pitchers, he held fly-ball hitters to a much lower batting average (.225) than ground-ball hitters (.263).... He's 5–0 lifetime against the Phillies, 11–14 against everyone else.... The third time is definitely *not* the charm for Benes: opponents own a .202 career batting average in his first two passes through the lineup, but they've hit .306 against him after that.... He won't turn 24 until this August. Only five pitchers younger than he started 20 or more games last season: Steve Avery, Ramon Martinez, Kevin Appier, Tom Gordon, and Jim Abbott.... Committed five balks last season, tying him with four other pitchers for the most in the league.... Has held opponents to three hits in 16 at-bats with the bases loaded, and 0-for-8 with the bases loaded and two outs.... Has completed only two of 41 career starts, and in one of those complete games he pitched only eight innings in a losing effort.... As a hitter, he went 6-for-24 with a home run as a rookie in 1989; but forewarned is forearmed, and opposing pitchers held him to 6-for-60 last season.

Mike Bielecki

Throws Right

Chicago Cubs	W-L	ERA	AB	H	HR	BB	SO	BA	SA	OBA
Season	8-11	4.93	654	188	13	70	103	.287	.428	.359
vs. Left-Handers			399	109	8	45	62	.273	.409	.347
vs. Right-Handers			255	79	5	25	41	.310	.459	.377
vs. Ground-Ballers			315	85	5	24	61	.270	.416	.321
vs. Fly-Ballers			339	103	8	46	42	.304	.440	.392
Home Games	2-7	4.88	284	77	6	31	54	.271	.426	.346
Road Games	6-4	4.97	370	111	7	39	49	.300	.430	.369
Grass Fields	4-9	5.33	399	115	10	47	68	.288	.439	.365
Artificial Turf	4-2	4.29	255	73	3	23	35	.286	.412	.349
April	0-2	4.09	83	22	4	9	10	.265	.458	.344
May	3-1	3.44	144	42	1	15	22	.292	.354	.364
June	0-4	8.07	116	38	2	16	21	.328	.500	.403
July	1-1	8.14	89	29	4	5	10	.326	.539	.368
August	2-1	4.76	111	27	1	12	20	.243	.360	.315
Sept./Oct.	2-2	2.32	111	30	1	13	20	.270	.405	.352
Leading Off Inn.			164	49	4	15	22	.299	.433	.361
Bases Empty			372	106	7	33	56	.285	.425	.346
Runners On			282	82	6	37	47	.291	.433	.374
Runners/Scor. Pos.			164	49	3	31	26	.299	.445	.408
Runners On/2 Out			120	29	2	20	19	.242	.367	.350
Scor. Pos./2 Out			78	20	1	17	12	.256	.385	.389
Late-Inning Pressure			34	7	1	3	13	.206	.353	.270
Leading Off			10	2	0	2	3	.200	.200	.333
Runners On			11	3	1	0	4	.273	.636	.273
Runners/Scor. Pos.			8	2	0	0	3	.250	.375	.250
First 9 Batters			267	74	7	32	48	.277	.431	.360
Second 9 Batters			210	67	4	24	32	.319	.476	.388
All Batters Thereafter			177	47	2	14	23	.266	.367	.321

Loves to face: Todd Benzinger (0-for-12)
Barry Bonds (.040, 1-for-25, 1 2B, 5 BB)
Spike Owen (0-for-15, 1 BB)

Hates to face: Jay Bell (.667, 8-for-12)
Len Dykstra (.371, 13-for-35, 5 2B, 2 HR)
Juan Samuel (.438, 7-for-16, 1 HR)

Miscellaneous statistics: Ground outs-to-air outs ratio: 1.20 last season, 1.14 for career.... Induced 11 double-play ground outs in 137 opportunities (one per 12.5).... Allowed 35 doubles, 9 triples (tied for most in N.L.) in 168.0 innings.... Allowed 19 first-inning runs in 29 starts (5.72 ERA).... Batting support: 4.31 runs per start.... Opposing base stealers: 17-for-26 (65%); 3 pickoffs, 0 balks.

Comments: Averaged 5.21 innings pitched per start, the 2d-lowest rate among National League pitchers with at least 20 starts last season. He failed to last two innings in four starts.... Started 29 games last season without completing any, breaking the club record set in 1979 by Mike Krukow, who went 0-for-28. (Bielecki came close, pitching 10 shutout innings against the Reds in May, but no cee-gar.) The all-time record of 37 starts without a complete game was set by Steve Bedrosian in 1985.... Bielecki enters 1991 with a streak of 33 consecutive starts without a complete game. Of his four CG's in 1989, three were shutouts.... His 18–7 year in 1989 was the only "plus" season of his major league career, but it was good enough to keep his career record above the .500 mark (38–37).... Opposing base runners were successful in 11 of their last 12 stolen base attempts.... He induced double play grounders in only four of his first 111 opportunities, but got a DP grounder seven times in 26 chances after that.... It was not a kinder, gentler Bielecki that we saw in 1990. He hit five batters with pitches last season after not hitting anyone over the previous two seasons.... The National League's top 10 hitters batted .457 (16-for-38) against him last season.... As a hitter, batted a career-high .163. That lifted his career batting average to .076, with no extra-base hits in 197 at-bats. Among active players with at least 150 at-bats, only Don Carman (.059) ranks below him.

Joe Boever

Throws Right

Braves/Phillies	W-L	ERA	AB	H	HR	BB	SO	BA	SA	OBA
Season	3-6	3.36	331	77	6	51	75	.233	.347	.333
vs. Left-Handers			174	32	1	34	41	.184	.241	.317
vs. Right-Handers			157	45	5	17	34	.287	.465	.352
vs. Ground-Ballers			157	36	1	20	29	.229	.312	.313
vs. Fly-Ballers			174	41	5	31	46	.236	.379	.351
Home Games	2-3	4.10	199	51	4	32	45	.256	.387	.356
Road Games	1-3	2.27	132	26	2	19	30	.197	.288	.298
Grass Fields	2-2	5.12	150	42	6	27	31	.280	.460	.385
Artificial Turf	1-4	1.99	181	35	0	24	44	.193	.254	.288
April	0-1	3.38	37	8	2	7	8	.216	.405	.326
May	1-1	2.70	40	9	2	8	10	.225	.425	.354
June	0-1	6.46	58	15	2	15	16	.259	.466	.411
July	0-0	4.50	37	11	0	6	3	.297	.405	.395
August	1-2	3.15	79	20	0	9	17	.253	.304	.330
Sept./Oct.	1-1	1.21	80	14	0	6	21	.175	.213	.233
Leading Off Inn.			73	18	2	8	13	.247	.384	.321
Bases Empty			168	40	5	20	34	.238	.381	.319
Runners On			163	37	1	31	41	.227	.313	.347
Runners/Scor. Pos.			101	21	1	27	23	.208	.297	.369
Runners On/2 Out			76	19	0	17	23	.250	.329	.387
Scor. Pos./2 Out			51	11	0	16	15	.216	.294	.403
Late-Inning Pressure			174	38	2	31	44	.218	.322	.335
Leading Off			40	8	1	6	10	.200	.325	.304
Runners On			85	19	0	17	25	.224	.306	.350
Runners/Scor. Pos.			50	9	0	17	13	.180	.240	.382
First 9 Batters			311	70	6	49	69	.225	.338	.330
Second 9 Batters			20	7	0	2	6	.350	.500	.391
All Batters Thereafter			0	0	0	0	0	—	—	—

Loves to face: Kevin Bass (0-for-8, 2 BB)
Ken Caminiti (.111, 1-for-9)
Tom Foley (.111, 1-for-9)

Hates to face: Andres Galarraga (.500, 8-for-16, 2 HR, 5 SO)
Mike Scioscia (.750, 3-for-4, 3 BB)
Tim Wallach (.538, 7-for-13)

Miscellaneous statistics: Ground outs-to-air outs ratio: 0.82 last season, 0.84 for career. . . . Induced 4 double-play ground outs in 69 opportunities (one per 17.3). . . . Allowed 20 doubles, 0 triples in 88.1 innings. . . . Stranded 21 inherited runners, allowed 14 to score (60%). . . . Opposing base stealers: 12-for-15 (80%); 0 pickoffs, 2 balks.

Comments: Suffers from Dennis Martinez Syndrome: a right-handed pitcher who has far more trouble with right-handed batters than with lefties. Last year, right-handers hit 103 points higher than left-handers, the 2d-largest margin in the majors. For his career, right-handers have hit .270 with one home run every 25 at-bats; left-handers have hit .230 with one home run every 120 at-bats. . . . Only one lefty poled a homer off him last year; Will Clark did it on June 8. . . . The battery combination of Boever and Darren Daulton played 38⅓ innings last season, 3d most among National League batteries that did not surrender a home run. The top two: Andersen-Biggio (45⅓ innings) and Smith-LaValliere (43⅓ innings). . . . Allowed six home runs through his first 30 innings last season, but ended the year with a streak of 58 consecutive innings without allowing a homer, including all 46 innings he pitched after being acquired by Philadelphia. . . . Opponents batted 87 points higher on grass fields (.280) than on artificial turf (.193) last season, the 3d-largest margin in the majors. . . . Has a career total of 187 major league games, all in relief. In fact, he has never started a game at any level of professional ball (514 total games, major and minors). . . . Career won-lost breakdown: 7–9 (3.21 ERA) through July 31, 1–11 (4.35 ERA) on or after August 1.

Shawn Boskie

Throws Right

Chicago Cubs	W-L	ERA	AB	H	HR	BB	SO	BA	SA	OBA
Season	5-6	3.69	373	99	8	31	49	.265	.397	.322
vs. Left-Handers			214	59	2	28	23	.276	.393	.357
vs. Right-Handers			159	40	6	3	26	.252	.403	.270
vs. Ground-Ballers			183	52	1	15	23	.284	.388	.337
vs. Fly-Ballers			190	47	7	16	26	.247	.405	.308
Home Games	2-5	4.07	229	64	7	16	27	.279	.428	.324
Road Games	3-1	3.08	144	35	1	15	22	.243	.347	.319
Grass Fields	3-5	4.10	262	74	7	26	31	.282	.435	.347
Artificial Turf	2-1	2.73	111	25	1	5	18	.225	.306	.259
April	0-0	—	0	0	0	0	0	—	—	—
May	1-2	3.38	91	23	3	5	11	.253	.374	.292
June	1-2	4.82	112	29	2	13	21	.259	.393	.341
July	2-2	3.40	146	40	3	12	16	.274	.425	.325
August	1-0	1.50	24	7	0	1	1	.292	.333	.320
Sept./Oct.	0-0	—	0	0	0	0	0	—	—	—
Leading Off Inn.			99	27	1	5	16	.273	.374	.308
Bases Empty			230	61	3	17	36	.265	.365	.316
Runners On			143	38	5	14	13	.266	.448	.331
Runners/Scor. Pos.			81	20	2	9	11	.247	.444	.315
Runners On/2 Out			64	16	0	7	5	.250	.328	.324
Scor. Pos./2 Out			40	8	0	4	4	.200	.325	.273
Late-Inning Pressure			31	8	0	5	5	.258	.323	.361
Leading Off			8	3	0	3	2	.375	.500	.545
Runners On			15	3	0	2	2	.200	.267	.294
Runners/Scor. Pos.			10	3	0	0	1	.300	.400	.300
First 9 Batters			121	26	3	11	22	.215	.331	.278
Second 9 Batters			118	40	4	7	14	.339	.517	.381
All Batters Thereafter			134	33	1	13	13	.246	.351	.311

Loves to face: Ken Caminiti (0-for-7)
Will Clark (0-for-8, 2 BB)
Jose Uribe (0-for-8)

Hates to face: Wally Backman (.667, 4-for-6)
Terry Kennedy (.600, 6-for-10)
Larry Walker (.667, 4-for-6)

Miscellaneous statistics: Ground outs-to-air outs ratio: 1.09 last season, his first in the majors. . . . Induced 7 double-play ground outs in 63 opportunities (one per 9.0). . . . Allowed 21 doubles, 2 triples in 97.2 innings. . . . Allowed 2 first-inning runs in 15 starts (1.20 ERA). . . . Batting support: 3.73 runs per start. . . . Opposing base stealers: 6-for-12 (50%), 5th-lowest rate in N.L.; 2 pickoffs, 2 balks.

Comments: Started 15 games in his rookie season, a total not to be sneezed at. Only six other rookie pitchers in the National League started at least 15 games last season. The Cubs used rookies to start 47 of their 162 games last season; only two teams in the league used more rookie starters: Philadelphia (71) and Montreal (52). . . . His ERA was lower in the first inning (1.20) than in any other. Remember, on a league-wide basis, more runs are scored in the first inning than in any other. . . . He didn't allow a home run in the first inning in any of his 15 starts. In addition, he surrendered no more than one home run in any game he pitched. . . . Pitched his only complete game of the season in his major league debut on May 20. Boskie also collected two hits off Mike Scott in that game. Boskie has three hits, including two doubles, in five career at-bats against Scott. . . . He had balks called against him in each of his first two appearances, but none thereafter. . . . As the season went on, he achieved an increasing percentage of his outs on grounders. Ground outs-to-air outs ratio: 0.79 in his first eight starts, 1.38 in his last seven. . . . Held opponents to a lower batting average in his no-decision starts (.220) than he did in his five victories (.227). . . . Pitched his final game on August 4, then went on the disabled list with a sore elbow.

Oil Can Boyd

Throws Right

Montreal Expos	W-L	ERA	AB	H	HR	BB	SO	BA	SA	OBA
Season	10-6	2.93	702	164	19	52	113	.234	.376	.288
vs. Left-Handers			429	96	9	35	67	.224	.340	.285
vs. Right-Handers			273	68	10	17	46	.249	.432	.292
vs. Ground-Ballers			304	70	4	24	50	.230	.322	.289
vs. Fly-Ballers			398	94	15	28	63	.236	.417	.287
Home Games	6-3	2.91	336	77	9	19	61	.229	.366	.276
Road Games	4-3	2.94	366	87	10	33	52	.238	.385	.299
Grass Fields	2-2	2.60	241	62	5	18	31	.257	.402	.307
Artificial Turf	8-4	3.10	461	102	14	34	82	.221	.362	.278
April	1-2	7.06	89	27	6	5	13	.303	.584	.337
May	2-0	0.55	117	26	0	9	24	.222	.299	.278
June	0-1	4.03	110	28	3	5	17	.255	.409	.291
July	3-0	2.08	137	27	4	10	20	.197	.314	.257
August	1-2	4.03	109	30	3	9	12	.275	.431	.331
Sept./Oct.	3-1	1.85	140	26	3	14	27	.186	.300	.260
Leading Off Inn.			181	56	5	13	29	.309	.470	.359
Bases Empty			421	109	12	27	64	.259	.409	.308
Runners On			281	55	7	25	49	.196	.327	.258
Runners/Scor. Pos.			174	29	4	22	33	.167	.276	.255
Runners On/2 Out			113	18	2	13	26	.159	.248	.246
Scor. Pos./2 Out			77	11	1	12	17	.143	.195	.258
Late-Inning Pressure			16	2	0	3	1	.125	.125	.263
Leading Off			4	0	0	2	1	.000	.000	.333
Runners On			5	0	0	1	0	.000	.000	.167
Runners/Scor. Pos.			1	0	0	1	0	.000	.000	.500
First 9 Batters			255	53	4	18	47	.208	.325	.264
Second 9 Batters			252	63	6	10	43	.250	.393	.279
All Batters Thereafter			195	48	9	24	23	.246	.421	.327

Loves to face: Ron Gant (0-for-8)
Alfredo Griffin (.136, 3-for-22)
Dave Justice (0-for-7)

Hates to face: Brett Butler (.455, 15-for-33)
Andre Dawson (.625, 5-for-8, 1 HR)
Len Dykstra (.500, 5-for-10, 2 HR)

Miscellaneous statistics: Ground outs-to-air outs ratio: 0.76 last season, 0.97 for career. . . . Induced 9 double-play ground outs in 115 opportunities (one per 12.8). . . . Allowed 39 doubles, 2 triples in 190.2 innings. . . . Allowed 7 first-inning runs in 31 starts (2.03 ERA, 5th lowest in N.L.) . . . Batting support: 4.48 runs per start. . . . Opposing base stealers: 25-for-31 (81%); 0 pickoffs, 3 balks.

Comments: Montreal's infielders committed only two errors in 414 chances with Boyd on the mound last season, the best fielding percentage (.995) for any infield behind any pitcher in the majors last season. During his 190⅔ innings pitched, Boyd was charged with more errors (three) than his infielders and outfielders *combined* (two)! . . . Opponents batted 89 points lower with runners in scoring position (.167) than in other at-bats (.256) last season, the 4th-largest margin in the majors. . . . He tossed three complete games last season, all shutouts. They were the only three games all season in which he pitched more than seven innings. He had gone 97 consecutive starts without a shutout before blanking the Padres twice within a 10-day period. Only two other pitchers threw two shutouts against one team last season: Mike Morgan vs. St. Louis, and Dave Stewart vs. Kansas City. . . . Opponents have only three hits in 37 career at-bats (.081) with the bases loaded. . . . Opponents' overall batting average and his overall ERA were both career-low figures. . . . Opponents' batting average at Olympic Stadium (.229) was a far cry from their career mark of .284 at Fenway Park. . . . Pitched to a decision in only 16 of his 31 starts, 2d-lowest rate among pitchers who started at least 15 games last season. The Expos had a 9–6 record in his 15 no-decision starts.

Jeff Brantley

Throws Right

San Francisco Giants	W-L	ERA	AB	H	HR	BB	SO	BA	SA	OBA
Season	5-3	1.56	321	77	3	33	61	.240	.293	.315
vs. Left-Handers			186	51	1	20	27	.274	.328	.341
vs. Right-Handers			135	26	2	13	34	.193	.244	.278
vs. Ground-Ballers			134	29	0	12	24	.216	.231	.277
vs. Fly-Ballers			187	48	3	21	37	.257	.337	.341
Home Games	4-1	1.77	150	35	3	17	31	.233	.327	.310
Road Games	1-2	1.37	171	42	0	16	30	.246	.263	.319
Grass Fields	4-3	2.01	236	61	3	25	43	.258	.326	.335
Artificial Turf	1-0	0.38	85	16	0	8	18	.188	.200	.258
April	0-1	2.76	61	14	0	7	14	.230	.246	.304
May	1-0	0.00	69	15	0	5	9	.217	.217	.270
June	1-0	1.82	91	21	3	5	14	.231	.352	.278
July	2-2	1.88	51	12	0	5	13	.235	.294	.322
August	1-0	0.93	38	11	0	9	9	.289	.316	.426
Sept./Oct.	0-0	3.38	11	4	0	2	2	.364	.455	.462
Leading Off Inn.			69	20	2	6	12	.290	.391	.347
Bases Empty			154	39	3	15	29	.253	.338	.324
Runners On			167	38	0	18	32	.228	.251	.307
Runners/Scor. Pos.			97	15	0	13	25	.155	.155	.263
Runners On/2 Out			78	18	0	9	11	.231	.244	.318
Scor. Pos./2 Out			54	9	0	7	11	.167	.167	.274
Late-Inning Pressure			211	52	2	23	36	.246	.303	.328
Leading Off			47	14	1	3	8	.298	.362	.340
Runners On			109	23	0	14	18	.211	.248	.310
Runners/Scor. Pos.			64	7	0	10	14	.109	.109	.247
First 9 Batters			301	74	3	32	57	.246	.302	.323
Second 9 Batters			20	3	0	1	4	.150	.150	.182
All Batters Thereafter			0	0	0	0	0	—	—	—

Loves to face: Jack Clark (0-for-7)
Mariano Duncan (.100, 1-for-10)

Hates to face: Ron Gant (.571, 4-for-7, 1 2B, 2 HR)
Tony Gwynn (.727, 8-for-11)
Herm Winningham (3-for-3, 3 2B, 1 BB)

Miscellaneous statistics: Ground outs-to-air outs ratio: 1.01 last season, 1.28 for career. . . . Induced 8 double-play ground outs in 81 opportunities (one per 10.1). . . . Allowed 8 doubles, 0 triples in 86.2 innings. . . . Stranded 32 inherited runners, allowed 9 to score (78%), 4th-best rate in N.L. . . . Opposing base stealers: 7-for-11 (64%); 1 pickoff, 3 balks.

Comments: Over the last 70 years, only one Giants pitcher had a lower single-season ERA than Brantley's 1.56 (minimum: 75 innings pitched). That pitcher, however, did it twice: Frank Linzy posted ERAs of 1.43 in 1965 and 1.51 two years later. . . . Allowed only one home run to a left-handed batter last season; Fred Lynn hit it on June 18. . . . Opponents went hitless in 14 at-bats with the bases loaded last season, the most bases-loaded at-bats without a hit against any National League pitcher. Kevin Appier, against whom batters went 0-for-15, led the majors. . . . Had only one save in 66 career relief appearances prior to 1990, when he saved 19 games to rank 9th among N.L. relievers. . . . Allowed one home run every 28.9 innings last season, a dramatic improvement over his previous career rate of one every 9.8 innings. . . . Opponents batting average with runners in scoring position was 2d lowest among pitchers who faced at least 100 batters in those situations last season. Only Randy Myers (.143) stood ahead of him. . . . Opponents have a career batting average of .252 at Candlestick Park, .294 on other grass fields, .232 on artificial surfaces. . . . Brantley was the losing pitcher in the All-Star Game at Wrigley Field last July (remember "Rescue 911"?); he returned there about a week later with the Giants, only to be charged with losses in consecutive games. . . . Career breakdown: 7–1 before the All-Star Break, 5–4 after the Break (and 0–1 during the Break).

Tom Browning

Throws Left

Cincinnati Reds	W-L	ERA	AB	H	HR	BB	SO	BA	SA	OBA
Season	15-9	3.80	882	235	24	52	99	.266	.412	.309
vs. Left-Handers			162	41	5	13	30	.253	.395	.309
vs. Right-Handers			720	194	19	39	69	.269	.415	.309
vs. Ground-Ballers			391	87	4	17	51	.223	.299	.256
vs. Fly-Ballers			491	148	20	35	48	.301	.501	.350
Home Games	8-8	4.64	505	141	18	30	52	.279	.455	.319
Road Games	7-1	2.71	377	94	6	22	47	.249	.353	.297
Grass Fields	5-1	3.22	258	71	6	12	29	.275	.407	.311
Artificial Turf	10-8	4.02	624	164	18	40	70	.263	.413	.308
April	2-1	3.34	115	32	3	6	17	.278	.400	.325
May	2-3	1.97	165	31	3	10	16	.188	.309	.234
June	3-1	3.73	158	47	3	9	18	.297	.430	.341
July	3-0	2.28	161	38	4	6	20	.236	.360	.262
August	2-2	5.52	125	37	5	9	11	.296	.464	.336
Sept./Oct.	3-2	6.81	158	50	6	12	17	.316	.519	.368
Leading Off Inn.			228	63	7	7	13	.276	.412	.307
Bases Empty			544	144	18	22	60	.265	.410	.298
Runners On			338	91	6	30	39	.269	.414	.326
Runners/Scor. Pos.			169	40	2	26	28	.237	.379	.333
Runners On/2 Out			154	40	3	14	24	.260	.416	.321
Scor. Pos./2 Out			90	20	2	13	20	.222	.400	.320
Late-Inning Pressure			106	30	2	8	11	.283	.415	.333
Leading Off			34	9	2	1	2	.265	.471	.286
Runners On			29	8	0	5	4	.276	.414	.382
Runners/Scor. Pos.			15	4	0	5	2	.267	.400	.450
First 9 Batters			289	75	9	17	35	.260	.408	.307
Second 9 Batters			289	74	5	15	40	.256	.381	.295
All Batters Thereafter			304	86	10	20	24	.283	.444	.324

Loves to face: Vince Coleman (.040, 1-for-25, 1 2B, 5 BB)
Jeff Hamilton (.091, 2-for-22)
Howard Johnson (.067, 2-for-30, 1 HR)

Hates to face: Barry Bonds (.400, 10-for-25, 4 HR, 10 BB)
Bobby Bonilla (.387, 12-for-31, 4 2B, 5 HR, 0 BB)
Tim Teufel (.459, 17-for-37, 4 HR)

Miscellaneous statistics: Ground outs-to-air outs ratio: 0.62 last season, 0.64 for career. . . . Induced 6 double-play ground outs in 161 opportunities (one per 26.8), 3d-worst rate in N.L. . . . Allowed 44 doubles (4th most in N.L.), 6 triples in 227.2 innings. . . . Allowed 15 first-inning runs in 35 starts (3.60 ERA). . . . Batting support: 4.09 runs per start. . . . Opposing base stealers: 12-for-22 (55%); 2 pickoffs, 1 balk.

Comments: Has led National League pitchers in starts four times in past five years. Only three other N.L. pitchers since 1900 have led league in starts four times: Robin Roberts (six), Don Drysdale, and Phil Niekro. . . . Because he rarely throws double-play balls, the running game is not as imperative against Browning as it would be against a pitcher more adept at inducing double plays. . . . Opponents' on-base average leading off innings (.307) was the lowest in the majors last season (minimum: 100 leadoff batters faced), but it was higher than his career mark in that category (.300). . . . He's a sub-.500 pitcher (20–26) during April and May, but 73–35 on or after June 1. . . . Browning has a .604 winning percentage (93–61); Reds have played .514 ball in games in which he hasn't had a decision. . . . His career winning percentage is 7th highest in Reds history (minimum: 100 decisions): Don Gullett (91–44, .674), Jim Maloney (134–81, .623), Clay Carroll (71–43, .623), Gary Nolan (110–67, .621), Tom Seaver (75–46, .620), Hod Eller (61–40, .604), Browning. . . . With 93 career wins, Browning will likely become the 16th pitcher in Reds history to reach 100 wins. Historical note: Eppa Rixey's club record of 179 wins is the lowest win total by the record-holder on any of baseball's 16 pre-expansion teams. All but one of the other 15 teams have had a 200-game winner; Cy Young holds the Red Sox record with 193.

Tim Burke

Throws Right

Montreal Expos	W-L	ERA	AB	H	HR	BB	SO	BA	SA	OBA
Season	3-3	2.52	287	71	6	21	47	.247	.345	.300
vs. Left-Handers			144	41	3	10	19	.285	.403	.331
vs. Right-Handers			143	30	3	11	28	.210	.287	.270
vs. Ground-Ballers			96	28	0	7	12	.292	.344	.336
vs. Fly-Ballers			191	43	6	14	35	.225	.346	.282
Home Games	2-2	2.87	122	31	5	11	19	.254	.418	.316
Road Games	1-1	2.27	165	40	1	10	28	.242	.291	.289
Grass Fields	1-1	1.93	76	18	1	4	16	.237	.276	.284
Artificial Turf	2-2	2.72	211	53	5	17	31	.251	.370	.306
April	0-0	5.06	45	16	1	3	6	.356	.533	.388
May	0-1	3.65	49	13	2	5	9	.265	.408	.333
June	0-0	—	0	0	0	0	0	—	—	—
July	1-1	2.13	51	15	1	5	7	.294	.392	.351
August	0-1	3.31	65	18	2	4	11	.277	.385	.338
Sept./Oct.	2-0	0.39	77	9	0	4	14	.117	.130	.159
Leading Off Inn.			59	14	0	3	10	.237	.288	.274
Bases Empty			142	33	2	8	21	.232	.310	.283
Runners On			145	38	4	13	26	.262	.379	.317
Runners/Scor. Pos.			93	25	2	10	16	.269	.376	.330
Runners On/2 Out			69	16	3	11	17	.232	.391	.338
Scor. Pos./2 Out			49	12	1	8	11	.245	.347	.351
Late-Inning Pressure			206	48	4	14	34	.233	.320	.287
Leading Off			44	9	0	1	8	.205	.227	.222
Runners On			98	25	2	8	19	.255	.347	.308
Runners/Scor. Pos.			64	16	1	7	11	.250	.328	.319
First 9 Batters			271	69	6	19	44	.255	.351	.305
Second 9 Batters			16	2	0	2	3	.125	.250	.222
All Batters Thereafter			0	0	0	0	0	—	—	—

Loves to face: Len Dykstra (.077, 1-for-13, 2 BB)
Kevin McReynolds (.148, 4-for-27)
Rob Thompson (.071, 1-for-14)

Hates to face: Bobby Bonilla (.571, 4-for-7, 2 HR)
Pedro Guerrero (.462, 6-for-13, 1 HR)
Jose Uribe (.429, 6-for-14, 1 HR)

Miscellaneous statistics: Ground outs-to-air outs ratio: 1.39 last season, 1.49 for career. . . . Induced 7 double-play ground outs in 60 opportunities (one per 8.6). . . . Allowed 8 doubles, 1 triple in 75.0 innings. . . . Stranded 32 inherited runners, allowed 13 to score (71%). . . . Opposing base stealers: 4-for-5 (80%); 0 pickoffs, 1 balk.

Comments: Top career winning percentages among active pitchers (minimum: 50 decisions): Dwight Gooden (119–46, .721), Roger Clemens (116–51, .695), Mike Henneman (39–19, .672), David Cone (53–27, .663), Burke (40–22, .645). . . . Opponents have hit for a higher average on artificial surfaces than they have on grass fields in each of the last six seasons, matching Gene Nelson and Curt Young for the longest current streak of its kind. Career breakdown: .244 on artificial turf, .207 on grass fields. . . . After August 9, he stranded 21 inherited runners while allowing only four to score. . . . Opponents' batting average stood over .300 as late as August 10, but he held opposing batters to a .158 mark thereafter. He was charged with only one run in his last 23 innings pitched. . . . Stood second in the National League with 11 saves when he went on the disabled list at the end of May. . . . Opponents' career breakdown: .267 by left-handed batters, .200 by right-handed batters. Among active pitchers who have faced at least 1000 right-handed batters in their careers, only Jose DeLeon (.185) has held them to a lower average than Burke. . . . Over the last three seasons Burke has allowed 15 home runs at Olympic Stadium, but only four in road games. . . . Career fielding percentage (.986, one error per 72 chances) is the best among active National League pitchers with at least 100 fielding chances.

John Burkett

Throws Right

San Francisco Giants	W-L	ERA	AB	H	HR	BB	SO	BA	SA	OBA
Season	14-7	3.79	781	201	18	61	118	.257	.374	.313
vs. Left-Handers			454	117	11	36	63	.258	.377	.312
vs. Right-Handers			327	84	7	25	55	.257	.370	.314
vs. Ground-Ballers			372	95	8	26	59	.255	.363	.307
vs. Fly-Ballers			409	106	10	35	59	.259	.384	.318
Home Games	6-2	3.98	399	102	12	33	67	.256	.396	.319
Road Games	8-5	3.60	382	99	6	28	51	.259	.351	.306
Grass Fields	10-4	3.54	581	145	15	47	92	.250	.372	.310
Artificial Turf	4-3	4.53	200	56	3	14	26	.280	.380	.321
April	1-0	2.57	27	7	0	1	3	.259	.259	.286
May	3-1	4.86	131	37	3	16	14	.282	.382	.356
June	3-1	2.68	162	34	3	12	31	.210	.296	.273
July	2-1	3.65	140	39	2	8	23	.279	.386	.320
August	2-2	3.96	136	34	4	11	19	.250	.382	.302
Sept./Oct.	3-2	4.24	185	50	6	13	28	.270	.438	.322
Leading Off Inn.			202	56	3	10	28	.277	.371	.311
Bases Empty			466	118	10	31	75	.253	.361	.303
Runners On			315	83	8	30	43	.263	.394	.327
Runners/Scor. Pos.			170	41	5	23	24	.241	.359	.330
Runners On/2 Out			134	37	4	17	18	.276	.433	.366
Scor. Pos./2 Out			77	20	3	15	11	.260	.403	.394
Late-Inning Pressure			63	20	0	4	5	.317	.397	.358
Leading Off			17	6	0	1	1	.353	.412	.389
Runners On			22	8	0	2	4	.364	.500	.417
Runners/Scor. Pos.			11	2	0	1	2	.182	.182	.250
First 9 Batters			272	61	7	20	51	.224	.324	.276
Second 9 Batters			251	64	6	24	32	.255	.375	.320
All Batters Thereafter			258	76	5	17	35	.295	.426	.343

Loves to face: Mariano Duncan (.091, 1-for-11)
Joe Oliver (0-for-9)
Jeff Treadway (.143, 2-for-14)

Hates to face: Lonnie Smith (.545, 6-for-11, 2 2B, 1 3B, 1 HR)
Larry Walker (.600, 3-for-5, 2 HR)

Miscellaneous statistics: Ground outs-to-air outs ratio: 1.45 last season, 1.43 for career. . . . Induced 14 double-play ground outs in 140 opportunities (one per 10.0). . . . Allowed 33 doubles, 2 triples in 204.0 innings. . . . Allowed 13 first-inning runs in 32 starts (3.66 ERA). . . . Batting support: 5.19 runs per start (3d highest in N.L.) . . . Opposing base stealers: 18-for-25 (72%); 2 pickoffs, 3 balks.

Comments: Led major league rookie pitchers in wins, games started (32) and innings (204); stood third in strikeouts behind Mark Gardner (135) and Kevin Appier (127). . . . First National League rookie to pitch 200 innings since Tom Browning in 1985. Burkett was one of 42 pitchers to reach the 200-inning plateau last year, but he was the only one among them who started the season in the minor leagues. . . . Burkett, Scott Erickson, and Mike Harkey shared the major league lead among rookies with .667 winning percentages. That's the highest winning percentage by a Giants rookie (minimum: 15 decisions) since Hoyt Wilhelm broke into the majors with a 15–3 mark for New York in 1952. . . . Giants had a record of 4–7 in Burkett's no-decision starts. . . . Averaged 6.28 innings pitched per start, the highest by any of the 14 pitchers who started for the Giants last season. . . . Had a record of 8–2 with a 3.25 ERA in day games, 6–5 with an ERA of 4.38 at night. . . . Had a 9–2 record at the All-Star break. . . . Coming into 1991, has allowed 13 consecutive stolen bases. . . . Opponents were hitless in eight at-bats with two outs and the bases loaded. . . . Pitched three innings of hitless ball and recorded a save in his only relief appearance of the season. . . . Burkett is only 12 days younger than Dwight Gooden, who has pitched in the majors since 1984.

Norm Charlton

Throws Left

Cincinnati Reds	W-L	ERA	AB	H	HR	BB	SO	BA	SA	OBA
Season	12-9	2.74	567	131	10	70	117	.231	.326	.319
vs. Left-Handers			116	26	4	17	25	.224	.379	.338
vs. Right-Handers			451	105	6	53	92	.233	.313	.314
vs. Ground-Ballers			244	58	1	29	41	.238	.295	.325
vs. Fly-Ballers			323	73	9	41	76	.226	.350	.314
Home Games	6-4	3.09	280	65	7	36	53	.232	.343	.325
Road Games	6-5	2.40	287	66	3	34	64	.230	.310	.313
Grass Fields	4-4	3.47	137	35	3	17	21	.255	.380	.340
Artificial Turf	8-5	2.52	430	96	7	53	96	.223	.309	.312
April	0-0	3.38	39	9	0	9	19	.231	.282	.388
May	3-1	3.24	63	17	2	8	19	.270	.413	.352
June	3-0	2.65	66	17	0	4	13	.258	.288	.296
July	2-5	2.37	111	25	2	10	19	.225	.333	.289
August	2-1	1.22	155	30	0	18	25	.194	.245	.276
Sept./Oct.	2-2	4.58	133	33	6	21	22	.248	.406	.363
Leading Off Inn.			142	33	3	14	25	.232	.380	.301
Bases Empty			318	70	8	37	65	.220	.355	.307
Runners On			249	61	2	33	52	.245	.289	.333
Runners/Scor. Pos.			153	34	1	25	37	.222	.255	.331
Runners On/2 Out			104	26	1	12	19	.250	.288	.328
Scor. Pos./2 Out			67	18	0	10	12	.269	.269	.364
Late-Inning Pressure			102	21	2	13	28	.206	.324	.302
Leading Off			27	8	1	2	7	.296	.556	.345
Runners On			47	7	0	7	13	.149	.170	.259
Runners/Scor. Pos.			28	4	0	6	8	.143	.143	.294
First 9 Batters			302	71	3	38	64	.235	.305	.325
Second 9 Batters			140	26	4	16	34	.186	.314	.266
All Batters Thereafter			125	34	3	16	19	.272	.392	.364

Loves to face: Kevin Bass (0-for-12)
Ken Caminiti (0-for-15)
Carmelo Martinez (0-for-11)

Hates to face: Jose Oquendo (.571, 4-for-7, 1 HR)
Lonnie Smith (.385, 5-for-13, 1 2B, 1 3B, 2 HR)
Matt Williams (.400, 4-for-10, 1 HR)

Miscellaneous statistics: Ground outs-to-air outs ratio: 1.43 last season, 1.34 for career. . . . Induced 19 double-play ground outs in 114 opportunities (one per 6.0), 2d-best rate in N.L. . . . Allowed 20 doubles, 2 triples in 154.1 innings. . . . Allowed 8 first-inning runs in 16 starts (3.38 ERA). . . . Batting support: 3.38 runs per start. . . . Record of 6–5, 2.60 ERA as a starter; 6–4, 3.02 ERA in 40 relief appearances. . . . Stranded 16 inherited runners, allowed 5 to score (76%). . . . Opposing base stealers: 17-for-21 (81%); 4 pickoffs, 1 balk.

Comments: Had made 108 consecutive relief appearances before moving into the starting rotation on July 15. He then made 16 starts before returning to the bullpen for postseason play. . . . A victim of poor run support last season; the Reds averaged two runs per game less in Charlton's starts than they did in Rick Mahler's. . . . Career breakdown: 10–10 (3.11 ERA) in 26 starts, 14–7 (2.96 ERA) in 109 relief appearances. . . . Opponents' career batting breakdown: .214 with the bases empty, .243 with runners on base. . . . Has yielded 15 career home runs at Riverfront Stadium, only six in road games. . . . In 109 career relief appearances, Charlton has had only two saves. Among active pitchers with at least 100 relief appearances, only Tim Birtsas has a lower ratio of saves (one) to games (108). . . . Opponents' career breakdown: .191 by left-handed batters, .235 by right-handed batters. But left-handed batters don't fare any better against Randy Myers (.173) or Rob Dibble (.192). . . . Nasty Boys, relievers that they are, don't step up to the plate all too often. But Charlton had to stand in there quite often after he was moved to the starting rotation last season, and it seems that he received payback for some past nastiness. He was one of four pitchers to be hit by a pitch twice last season. The others: Jack Armstrong, Tim Belcher, and Doc Gooden.

Marty Clary

Throws Right

Atlanta Braves	W-L	ERA	AB	H	HR	BB	SO	BA	SA	OBA
Season	1-10	5.67	416	128	9	39	44	.308	.442	.364
vs. Left-Handers			236	77	7	22	19	.326	.483	.381
vs. Right-Handers			180	51	2	17	25	.283	.389	.343
vs. Ground-Ballers			192	50	4	16	24	.260	.370	.321
vs. Fly-Ballers			224	78	5	23	20	.348	.504	.401
Home Games	0-5	5.01	198	65	5	13	19	.328	.460	.371
Road Games	1-5	6.22	218	63	4	26	25	.289	.427	.359
Grass Fields	0-7	6.29	289	92	9	22	34	.318	.478	.364
Artificial Turf	1-3	4.36	127	36	0	17	10	.283	.362	.366
April	0-1	3.65	46	11	1	7	10	.239	.391	.340
May	1-2	6.08	99	34	2	10	8	.343	.515	.404
June	0-0	3.86	64	26	2	1	6	.406	.563	.409
July	0-5	5.45	136	35	3	12	13	.257	.375	.311
August	0-2	12.60	48	19	1	7	5	.396	.521	.474
Sept./Oct.	0-0	2.57	23	3	0	2	2	.130	.130	.200
Leading Off Inn.			104	35	4	3	10	.337	.510	.361
Bases Empty			220	62	5	21	23	.282	.423	.347
Runners On			196	66	4	18	21	.337	.464	.384
Runners/Scor. Pos.			123	32	4	14	14	.260	.398	.324
Runners On/2 Out			86	25	2	12	9	.291	.430	.378
Scor. Pos./2 Out			66	16	2	9	7	.242	.364	.333
Late-Inning Pressure			20	8	1	1	3	.400	.550	.455
Leading Off			5	3	0	0	0	.600	.600	.667
Runners On			9	4	1	1	1	.444	.778	.500
Runners/Scor. Pos.			6	2	1	1	1	.333	.833	.429
First 9 Batters			214	66	5	20	27	.308	.435	.366
Second 9 Batters			120	37	3	7	12	.308	.467	.344
All Batters Thereafter			82	25	1	12	5	.305	.427	.389

Loves to face: Vince Coleman (.167, 2-for-12)
Charlie Hayes (.083, 1-for-12, 2 BB)
John Kruk (.100, 1-for-10)

Hates to face: Will Clark (.500, 4-for-8, 2 2B, 1 HR)
Eddie Murray (.667, 4-for-6, 1 HR)
Darryl Strawberry (.455, 5-for-11, 2 HR)

Miscellaneous statistics: Ground outs-to-air outs ratio: 1.62 last season, 1.33 for career. . . . Induced 8 double-play ground outs in 81 opportunities (one per 10.1). . . . Allowed 21 doubles, 4 triples in 101.2 innings. . . . Allowed 13 first-inning runs in 14 starts (5.79 ERA). . . . Batting support: 3.64 runs per start. . . . Record of 1–9, 5.88 ERA as a starter; 0–1, 5.06 ERA in 19 relief appearances. . . . Stranded 3 inherited runners, allowed 5 to score (38%). . . . Opposing base stealers: 11-for-14 (79%); 0 pickoffs, 1 balk.

Comments: He had a record of 0–10 on American soil (and good old American synthetics) last season, gaining his only victory at Olympic Stadium. . . . Clary's 1990 ERA was the 2d highest by any Braves pitcher (minimum: 100 innings) since the Milwaukee move. That's not the move *from* Milwaukee, but the move *to* Milwaukee from Boston in 1953. The one higher: Mickey Mahler, who posted a 5.85 ERA in exactly 100 innings in 1979. . . . Lost five consecutive starts, July 3–26; that's the bad news. The good news: he finished off the month with a no-decision at San Diego. . . . As bad as his performance on the mound was last season, he was even less effective at the plate; sort of the negative image of Babe Ruth. His 28 at-bats were the most by any player without a hit last year. Others with at least 10 hitless at-bats: Chris Nabholz (21), Kelly Downs (13), and Jose Nunez (11). The last player to have more at-bats than Clary in a hitless season was Don Carman, in his infamous 0-for-31 season of 1986. . . . Despite everything written here, if history repeats itself, Clary should be a millionaire very soon. The last two Braves pitchers with lower single-season winning percentages than Clary are both making big bucks today: Pascual Perez had a 1–13 record for Atlanta in 1985, and Zane Smith was 1–12 for the Braves in 1989.

Pat Combs

Throws Left

Philadelphia Phillies	W-L	ERA	AB	H	HR	BB	SO	BA	SA	OBA
Season	10-10	4.07	696	179	12	86	108	.257	.375	.339
vs. Left-Handers			138	35	5	17	26	.254	.399	.340
vs. Right-Handers			558	144	7	69	82	.258	.369	.339
vs. Ground-Ballers			294	90	3	34	44	.306	.422	.379
vs. Fly-Ballers			402	89	9	52	64	.221	.341	.310
Home Games	4-2	3.05	305	72	6	33	47	.236	.364	.313
Road Games	6-8	4.92	391	107	6	53	61	.274	.384	.359
Grass Fields	1-6	5.40	171	48	5	25	22	.281	.409	.374
Artificial Turf	9-4	3.66	525	131	7	61	86	.250	.364	.328
April	1-2	4.29	78	19	2	9	13	.244	.385	.318
May	1-3	4.81	103	36	3	13	17	.350	.505	.427
June	2-1	3.28	127	29	2	20	20	.228	.339	.336
July	2-2	4.45	125	34	2	15	22	.272	.360	.343
August	0-1	4.40	110	29	0	15	17	.264	.336	.357
Sept./Oct.	4-1	3.70	153	32	3	14	19	.209	.353	.275
Leading Off Inn.			165	42	0	28	28	.255	.321	.369
Bases Empty			394	94	3	48	64	.239	.332	.326
Runners On			302	85	9	38	44	.281	.430	.356
Runners/Scor. Pos.			172	47	3	21	28	.273	.390	.343
Runners On/2 Out			129	33	1	17	21	.256	.349	.342
Scor. Pos./2 Out			81	22	1	14	14	.272	.407	.379
Late-Inning Pressure			46	9	1	2	5	.196	.261	.229
Leading Off			15	2	0	0	2	.133	.133	.133
Runners On			8	3	1	0	0	.375	.750	.375
Runners/Scor. Pos.			0	0	0	0	0	—	—	—
First 9 Batters			244	63	3	31	44	.258	.381	.342
Second 9 Batters			231	61	3	33	32	.264	.372	.357
All Batters Thereafter			221	55	6	22	32	.249	.371	.317

Loves to face: Gregg Jefferies (.100, 2-for-20)
Kevin McReynolds (.105, 2-for-19)
Tim Wallach (.063, 1-for-16, 2 BB)

Hates to face: Hubie Brooks (.500, 6-for-12, 2 2B, 2 HR, 4 SO)
Kal Daniels (.600, 3-for-5, 1 HR)

Miscellaneous statistics: Ground outs-to-air outs ratio: 1.06 last season, 1.13 for career. . . . Induced 14 double-play ground outs in 154 opportunities (one per 11.0). . . . Allowed 36 doubles, 5 triples in 183.1 innings. . . . Allowed 9 first-inning runs in 31 starts (2.61 ERA). . . . Batting support: 3.90 runs per start. . . . Opposing base stealers: 11-for-21 (52%); 1 pickoff, 1 balk.

Comments: Phillies' first-round choice in the 1988 amateur draft. Five of the first six pitchers chosen in that draft have already logged considerable major league time. The others: Andy Benes, Steve Avery, Gregg Olson, and Jim Abbott. . . . Opponents' career breakdown: .230 at Veterans Stadium, .267 on other artificial surfaces, .289 on grass fields. . . . In 37 career starts, he has never allowed more than one home run in a game. . . . Has completed four of his 37 career starts, three of them for shutouts. . . . Combs and Sid Fernandez were the only pitchers to throw shutouts against the Expos last season. . . . Threw nine wild pitches last season, but none after July 14. . . . Pitched the most innings (183⅓) of any Phillies rookie since Tom Underwood (219) in 1975. . . . Combs's form chart shows only a one-point difference between the career batting averages of opposing left-handed (.255) and right-handed (.256) batters; however, there's a 70-point difference between the career averages of opposing ground-ball (.296) and fly-ball (.226) hitters. Open suggestion to National League managers: Instead of employing the knee-jerk platoon pattern of loading your lineup with right-handed hitters, why not live a little and load them with ground-ball hitters? A free *1992 Analyst* to the first 500 managers who do so.

David Cone

Throws Right

New York Mets	W-L	ERA	AB	H	HR	BB	SO	BA	SA	OBA
Season	14-10	3.23	784	177	21	65	233	.226	.364	.284
vs. Left-Handers			467	100	14	38	124	.214	.377	.274
vs. Right-Handers			317	77	7	27	109	.243	.344	.299
vs. Ground-Ballers			399	78	6	33	127	.195	.308	.257
vs. Fly-Ballers			385	99	15	32	106	.257	.421	.311
Home Games	7-6	3.85	404	98	11	35	114	.243	.391	.303
Road Games	7-4	2.60	380	79	10	30	119	.208	.334	.263
Grass Fields	10-9	3.77	573	139	18	46	165	.243	.396	.298
Artificial Turf	4-1	1.83	211	38	3	19	68	.180	.275	.247
April	0-2	6.65	90	27	3	12	29	.300	.478	.379
May	1-1	5.59	72	17	4	2	16	.236	.472	.253
June	3-1	2.63	141	33	2	8	41	.234	.355	.272
July	3-1	2.70	131	26	6	11	46	.198	.389	.264
August	3-2	2.27	173	36	3	12	47	.208	.306	.259
Sept./Oct.	4-3	2.59	177	38	3	20	54	.215	.305	.293
Leading Off Inn.			202	55	10	16	45	.272	.480	.326
Bases Empty			488	108	13	41	146	.221	.352	.282
Runners On			296	69	8	24	87	.233	.382	.287
Runners/Scor. Pos.			186	34	5	18	66	.183	.296	.251
Runners On/2 Out			120	27	4	12	39	.225	.392	.295
Scor. Pos./2 Out			85	17	3	10	31	.200	.353	.284
Late-Inning Pressure			62	14	2	4	16	.226	.419	.269
Leading Off			19	7	2	0	2	.368	.789	.368
Runners On			21	4	0	3	7	.190	.333	.280
Runners/Scor. Pos.			17	3	0	1	7	.176	.235	.211
First 9 Batters			252	62	5	19	81	.246	.369	.300
Second 9 Batters			241	49	8	26	75	.203	.353	.281
All Batters Thereafter			291	66	8	20	77	.227	.368	.272

Loves to face: Jay Bell (.067, 1-for-15, 3 BB)
Chris James (0-for-19)
Rafael Ramirez (.067, 1-for-15)

Hates to face: John Morris (.474, 9-for-19, 1 HR)
Milt Thompson (.424, 14-for-33, 1 HR)
Matt Williams (.500, 8-for-16, 2 HR)

Miscellaneous statistics: Ground outs-to-air outs ratio: 0.80 last season, 0.83 for career. . . . Induced 9 double-play ground outs in 123 opportunities (one per 13.7). . . . Allowed 31 doubles, 7 triples in 211.2 innings. . . . Allowed 17 first-inning runs in 30 starts (4.80 ERA). . . . Batting support: 4.93 runs per start. . . . Opposing base stealers: 23-for-32 (72%); 3 pickoffs, 4 balks.

Comments: As a transition from the last comment on Pat Combs, we note that fly-ball hitters have hit Cone for a higher average than have ground-ball hitters in each of his five seasons in the majors. . . . Yearly averages by opposing right-handed batters since 1988: .165, .209, .243; meanwhile, opposing left-handed batters are falling: .257, .234, .214. . . . Struck out 37 batters during the first inning of his 30 starts, the highest first-inning strikeout rate by any pitcher in the majors last season. He averaged 11.1 strikeouts per nine innings in the first inning, 9.7 strikeouts per nine innings thereafter. But opponents batted .289 against Cone in the first inning, .215 thereafter. . . . Averaged 7.02 innings pitched per start, 4th-highest rate among National League pitchers with at least 20 starts last season. . . . Owns a 6–0 career record against the Pirates, including three wins last year. Mets were 7–8 in their 15 other games vs. Pittsburgh. . . . The Mets have had a rich history of developing pitching talent within their organization, but of their six primary starters over last couple of seasons, only Doc Gooden is a home-grown talent. Cone, Ron Darling, Sid Fernandez, Bob Ojeda, and Frank Viola were all acquired from other clubs. Maybe their reputation should no longer be for developing such talent, but rather recognizing it.

Dennis Cook

Throws Left

Phillies/Dodgers	W-L	ERA	AB	H	HR	BB	SO	BA	SA	OBA
Season	9-4	3.92	591	155	20	56	64	.262	.413	.325
vs. Left-Handers			135	40	4	16	15	.296	.474	.373
vs. Right-Handers			456	115	16	40	49	.252	.395	.310
vs. Ground-Ballers			275	73	5	23	35	.265	.375	.323
vs. Fly-Ballers			316	82	15	33	29	.259	.446	.326
Home Games	5-3	3.65	368	92	16	30	46	.250	.421	.306
Road Games	4-1	4.40	223	63	4	26	18	.283	.399	.354
Grass Fields	3-2	4.86	148	41	8	15	16	.277	.480	.343
Artificial Turf	6-2	3.63	443	114	12	41	48	.257	.391	.318
April	3-0	0.66	91	15	1	6	6	.165	.242	.222
May	2-0	4.31	122	31	5	7	11	.254	.393	.295
June	0-2	5.04	114	34	3	15	18	.298	.447	.371
July	2-0	2.25	73	15	0	6	8	.205	.219	.272
August	1-1	5.14	87	28	2	17	8	.322	.437	.433
Sept./Oct.	1-1	5.88	104	32	9	5	13	.308	.663	.333
Leading Off Inn.			150	31	5	9	12	.207	.353	.252
Bases Empty			371	96	13	22	40	.259	.407	.302
Runners On			220	59	7	34	24	.268	.423	.359
Runners/Scor. Pos.			124	34	5	24	11	.274	.460	.378
Runners On/2 Out			91	19	2	19	8	.209	.319	.351
Scor. Pos./2 Out			55	12	2	17	5	.218	.382	.411
Late-Inning Pressure			48	15	0	5	3	.313	.333	.377
Leading Off			11	0	0	2	0	.000	.000	.154
Runners On			18	5	0	3	1	.278	.278	.381
Runners/Scor. Pos.			8	3	0	1	0	.375	.375	.444
First 9 Batters			311	78	7	32	36	.251	.370	.320
Second 9 Batters			162	45	9	18	18	.278	.494	.348
All Batters Thereafter			118	32	4	6	10	.271	.415	.304

Loves to face: Bobby Bonilla (0-for-10)
Will Clark (.067, 1-for-15)
Andres Galarraga (0-for-9, 1 BB)

Hates to face: Greg Litton (.615, 8-for-13, 1 HR)
Lonnie Smith (.412, 7-for-17, 3 HR)
Todd Zeile (.750, 6-for-8)

Miscellaneous statistics: Ground outs-to-air outs ratio: 0.78 last season, 0.73 for career. . . . Induced 10 double-play ground outs in 115 opportunities (one per 11.5). . . . Allowed 23 doubles, 3 triples in 156.0 innings. . . . Allowed 5 first-inning runs in 16 starts (2.81 ERA). . . . Batting support: 5.31 runs per start. . . . Record of 6–3, 4.03 ERA as a starter; 3–1, 3.75 ERA in 31 relief appearances. . . . Stranded 17 inherited runners, allowed 17 to score (50%), 3d-worst rate in N.L. . . . Opposing base stealers: 16-for-20 (80%); 3 pickoffs, 3 balks.

Comments: Opponents' career batting average breakdown shows an alarming tendency: .235 with the bases empty, .265 with runners on base, .281 with runners in scoring position, .368 (7-for-19) with the bases loaded. . . . Opponents have a career average of .283 in road games, but only .219 in home games. That margin of 64 points is the 4th-largest margin in the majors over the last five years. What makes the margin particularly unusual is that Cook's called three different ballparks home in the last three seasons. . . . Familiarity seems to breed success for opposing batters. They have a career average of .230 in Cook's first pass through the batting order, .252 in his second time through, and .270 in all subsequent at bats. . . . Has allowed an average of one home run every 29 at-bats during his career, but has never allowed a home run in a total of 87 opponents' at-bats in Late-Inning Pressure Situations. Opponents have a career batting average of .207 in LIPS, .249 in other at-bats. . . . Had the highest batting average (.306) by any pitcher in the majors last season (minimum: 20 at-bats). Homered off Fernando Valenzuela in May, and was his teammate come September. . . . Struck out only four times in 53 plate appearances, making him the 2d-toughest pitcher in the league to strike out last season. Pete Smith held the top spot, with one whiff in 28 times up.

Tim Crews

Throws Right

Los Angeles Dodgers	W-L	ERA	AB	H	HR	BB	SO	BA	SA	OBA
Season	4-5	2.77	411	98	9	24	76	.238	.358	.280
vs. Left-Handers			218	57	3	11	32	.261	.376	.296
vs. Right-Handers			193	41	6	13	44	.212	.337	.263
vs. Ground-Ballers			179	46	3	6	37	.257	.374	.281
vs. Fly-Ballers			232	52	6	18	39	.224	.345	.280
Home Games	0-4	3.04	200	55	6	7	40	.275	.405	.297
Road Games	4-1	2.53	211	43	3	17	36	.204	.313	.265
Grass Fields	2-5	2.62	306	79	6	17	52	.258	.353	.297
Artificial Turf	2-0	3.18	105	19	3	7	24	.181	.371	.232
April	0-0	2.25	51	15	2	2	9	.294	.471	.321
May	1-1	4.91	80	26	1	9	17	.325	.475	.389
June	0-1	1.80	54	10	0	3	8	.185	.204	.228
July	0-1	1.69	76	16	3	4	16	.211	.368	.250
August	0-1	2.60	63	12	1	2	12	.190	.286	.224
Sept./Oct.	3-1	3.09	87	19	2	4	14	.218	.322	.250
Leading Off Inn.			101	18	1	1	23	.178	.248	.186
Bases Empty			259	61	6	6	50	.236	.351	.253
Runners On			152	37	3	18	26	.243	.368	.322
Runners/Scor. Pos.			91	18	2	17	14	.198	.341	.315
Runners On/2 Out			73	14	0	10	9	.192	.301	.289
Scor. Pos./2 Out			48	6	0	9	5	.125	.250	.263
Late-Inning Pressure			91	25	3	6	16	.275	.407	.323
Leading Off			20	2	0	0	5	.100	.150	.100
Runners On			37	13	2	6	6	.351	.568	.444
Runners/Scor. Pos.			28	9	2	6	5	.321	.536	.429
First 9 Batters			361	86	9	21	70	.238	.366	.280
Second 9 Batters			45	8	0	3	6	.178	.222	.229
All Batters Thereafter			5	4	0	0	0	.800	1.000	.800

Loves to face: Eric Davis (.133, 2-for-15, 7 SO)
Barry Larkin (.143, 2-for-14)
Jose Uribe (0-for-12)

Hates to face: Kevin Bass (.625, 5-for-8)
Kevin Mitchell (.467, 7-for-15, 2 HR)
Ozzie Smith (.625, 5-for-8, 1 HR)

Miscellaneous statistics: Ground outs-to-air outs ratio: 1.19 last season, 1.14 for career. . . . Induced 6 double-play ground outs in 70 opportunities (one per 11.7). . . . Allowed 16 doubles, 3 triples in 107.1 innings. . . . Stranded 25 inherited runners, allowed 13 to score (66%). . . . Opposing base stealers: 8-for-11 (73%); 1 pickoff, 0 balks.

Comments: Last season, opponents batted 71 points higher in home games than in road games, the 3d-largest margin in the majors. On a career basis, the gap is 56 points (.289 in home games, .233 in road games), the 2d-largest margin in the majors over the last five years. That's unusual since Dodger Stadium is a pronounced pitcher's park that does reduce batting average, though not to the degree to which it depresses runs and home runs. . . . Opponents' on-base average leading off innings (.186) was the 3d lowest of any pitcher in the last 16 years. The two lowest single-season averages both belong to guys named Greg Harris. Leadoff batters had a .175 on-base average against Greg A. Harris (the fellow with Boston last season) in 1985, and a .180 on-base average against Greg W. Harris (of the Padres) in 1989. . . . In the same vein, Crews has walked only one of 61 leadoff batters faced during Late-Inning Pressure Situations during his career. That one came in his rookie year (1987). . . . Margin of 49 points between the 1990 batting averages of opposing left- and right-handed batters is not indicative of his previous performance. In fact, there's a difference of only two points between the career averages of left-handers (.264) and right-handers (.262).

Ron Darling

Throws Right

New York Mets	W-L	ERA	AB	H	HR	BB	SO	BA	SA	OBA
Season	7-9	4.50	495	135	20	44	99	.273	.451	.336
vs. Left-Handers			283	73	10	30	56	.258	.403	.333
vs. Right-Handers			212	62	10	14	43	.292	.514	.341
vs. Ground-Ballers			269	78	9	25	58	.290	.442	.351
vs. Fly-Ballers			226	57	11	19	41	.252	.460	.319
Home Games	4-2	3.52	203	49	7	19	41	.241	.414	.314
Road Games	3-7	5.23	292	86	13	25	58	.295	.476	.352
Grass Fields	6-6	4.78	332	86	17	29	70	.259	.467	.325
Artificial Turf	1-3	3.92	163	49	3	15	29	.301	.417	.359
April	1-2	3.00	45	12	2	4	17	.267	.467	.333
May	0-2	8.35	71	19	7	10	13	.268	.592	.366
June	1-0	2.79	74	21	1	7	12	.284	.392	.337
July	2-1	2.51	110	26	3	6	26	.236	.373	.288
August	1-4	6.51	119	38	4	9	21	.319	.513	.372
Sept./Oct.	2-0	3.60	76	19	3	8	10	.250	.382	.321
Leading Off Inn.			120	34	7	6	23	.283	.475	.323
Bases Empty			299	81	14	18	55	.271	.455	.317
Runners On			196	54	6	26	44	.276	.444	.364
Runners/Scor. Pos.			125	28	3	19	35	.224	.360	.329
Runners On/2 Out			83	15	0	14	20	.181	.229	.299
Scor. Pos./2 Out			56	7	0	10	17	.125	.143	.258
Late-Inning Pressure			36	6	1	5	8	.167	.306	.286
Leading Off			9	1	0	1	1	.111	.111	.200
Runners On			14	2	0	3	4	.143	.143	.333
Runners/Scor. Pos.			13	2	0	3	4	.154	.154	.313
First 9 Batters			237	70	9	18	46	.295	.468	.352
Second 9 Batters			158	46	6	13	31	.291	.475	.343
All Batters Thereafter			100	19	5	13	22	.190	.370	.289

Loves to face: Tom Browning (0-for-11)
Casey Candaele (.167, 4-for-24)
Jose DeLeon (.056, 1-for-18, 11 SO)

Hates to face: Pedro Guerrero (.385, 15-for-39, 2 HR)
Tony Gwynn (.472, 25-for-53)
Derek Lilliquist (2-for-2, 2 HR)

Miscellaneous statistics: Ground outs-to-air outs ratio: 1.21 last season, 1.08 for career. . . . Induced 3 double-play ground outs in 91 opportunities (one per 30.3), 2d-worst rate in N.L. . . . Allowed 18 doubles, 5 triples in 126.0 innings. . . . Allowed 17 first-inning runs in 18 starts (6.00 ERA). . . . Batting support: 4.39 runs per start. . . . Record of 6–7, 4.66 ERA as a starter; 1–2, 3.99 ERA in 15 relief appearances. . . . Stranded 6 inherited runners, allowed 4 to score (60%). . . . Opposing base stealers: 24-for-28 (86%); 5 pickoffs, 1 balk.

Comments: Needs six more wins to join Tom Seaver (198), Jerry Koosman (140), and Doc Gooden (119) in the Mets' 100-win club. That would give the Mets four 100-game winners in 30 years; their National League neighbors, the Phillies, now in their 109th season, have had only five. Houston, born in '62 like the Mets, already has six. . . . Had a 73–41 record through the 1988 season, but he's 21–23 since losing Game Seven of the '88 Championship Series. . . . Career breakdown: 56–25, 2.93 ERA at Shea Stadium; 38–39, 4.08 ERA elsewhere. . . . Allowed a home run every 6.3 innings, the worst rate by any National League pitcher who threw at least 90 innings last year. . . . Before last season, right-handed hitters had a .234 career batting average against Darling and had never hit .250 against him in any season. . . . Has a career record of 8–9 vs. Chicago, the only team to have a leg up on him. . . . With the Mets in a pennant race, Darling did not start a game from August 21 to September 22 while "Who?-lio" Valera started three. Darling eventually was granted a couple of starts in the final 11 days of the season, and he won both of them. . . . In his 18 starts, Darling had an ERA of 6.88 over the first two innings, 3.38 thereafter. . . . Still a master at getting that third out in tough situations. Active career leaders in lowest opponents' batting average with two outs and runners in scoring position (minimum: 500 at bats): Lee Smith, .178; Darling, .188; Gooden, .189; Dave Stewart, .192.

Danny Darwin

Throws Right

Houston Astros	W-L	ERA	AB	H	HR	BB	SO	BA	SA	OBA
Season	11-4	2.21	605	136	11	31	109	.225	.331	.266
vs. Left-Handers			364	96	7	23	68	.264	.382	.311
vs. Right-Handers			241	40	4	8	41	.166	.253	.198
vs. Ground-Ballers			293	67	3	13	58	.229	.311	.264
vs. Fly-Ballers			312	69	8	18	51	.221	.349	.269
Home Games	6-2	2.42	297	72	4	16	59	.242	.337	.282
Road Games	5-2	2.02	308	64	7	15	50	.208	.325	.252
Grass Fields	3-2	2.82	166	39	4	10	32	.235	.337	.287
Artificial Turf	8-2	1.98	439	97	7	21	77	.221	.328	.259
April	1-0	1.80	35	7	2	1	9	.200	.371	.222
May	0-0	0.95	69	14	1	3	14	.203	.319	.253
June	1-1	4.50	64	17	2	4	12	.266	.391	.309
July	4-0	1.04	154	28	2	7	28	.182	.273	.222
August	4-0	2.25	136	31	1	7	21	.228	.301	.264
Sept./Oct.	1-3	3.29	147	39	3	9	25	.265	.388	.312
Leading Off Inn.			155	36	3	4	32	.232	.355	.252
Bases Empty			375	87	8	15	68	.232	.347	.263
Runners On			230	49	3	16	41	.213	.304	.271
Runners/Scor. Pos.			140	28	3	12	27	.200	.329	.265
Runners On/2 Out			104	20	1	11	18	.192	.288	.288
Scor. Pos./2 Out			70	13	1	7	12	.186	.300	.269
Late-Inning Pressure			111	27	3	5	21	.243	.378	.276
Leading Off			28	5	1	1	8	.179	.357	.207
Runners On			39	6	0	3	9	.154	.179	.214
Runners/Scor. Pos.			19	2	0	2	2	.105	.105	.190
First 9 Batters			308	69	7	12	64	.224	.344	.258
Second 9 Batters			148	30	2	8	24	.203	.277	.248
All Batters Thereafter			149	37	2	11	21	.248	.356	.300

Loves to face: Tony Phillips (.063, 1-for-16)
Kirby Puckett (.125, 3-for-24)
Dick Schofield (0-for-15, 2 BB)

Hates to face: Alvin Davis (.421, 8-for-19, 2 HR)
Ron Hassey (.636, 7-for-11)
Rance Mulliniks (.433, 13-for-30, 1 HR)

Miscellaneous statistics: Ground outs-to-air outs ratio: 0.57 last season, 2d-lowest rate in N.L.; 0.83 for career.... Induced 8 double-play ground outs in 83 opportunities (one per 10.4).... Allowed 31 doubles, 0 triples in 162.2 innings.... Allowed 4 first-inning runs in 17 starts (2.12 ERA).... Batting support: 4.00 runs per start.... Record of 9–3, 2.14 ERA as a starter; 2–1, 2.40 ERA in 31 relief appearances.... Stranded 16 inherited runners, allowed 4 to score (80%).... Opposing base stealers: 17-for-23 (74%); 1 pickoff, 2 balks.

Comments: Pitched in 31 games from April through June, all in relief; pitched in 17 games, July through September, all as a starter. Qualified as National League ERA leader with less than an inning to spare; impressively, his ERA as a starter (2.14) was lower than his ERA in relief (2.40).... Career breakdown: 66–85, 3.61 ERA as a starter; 45–24, 2.52 ERA as a reliever.... Averaged 1.72 walks per nine innings, lowest rate in majors last season (minimum: 162 innings).... Held the National League's top 10 home run hitters homerless in 51 at-bats last season.... There have been only 15 players to appear in at least one game for both Texas teams; Darwin is the only one to play at least 200 games for each. The other players with at least 100 games for both: Leon Roberts and Rusty Staub. The only others to have pitched for both clubs: Joe Hoerner, Mike Marshall, and Nolan Ryan.... Career numbers at Fenway Park: 6–2 record, but a 5.68 ERA in 52⅓ career innings.... Darwin's evolution: 53–50 with a 3.58 ERA from 1978–84 with Texas; 14–26 with a 3.70 ERA in 1985–86 with Milwaukee; 44–33 with a 3.05 ERA since 1986 with Houston.... Became a free agent at a propitious time, with his stock rising, and received an eight-figure contract from the Red Sox. Remember this basic difference between salary-arbitration contracts and free-agency contracts: the former are based on what you have done, the latter on what some team thinks you will do.

Jose DeJesus

Throws Right

Philadelphia Phillies	W-L	ERA	AB	H	HR	BB	SO	BA	SA	OBA
Season	7-8	3.74	460	97	10	73	87	.211	.320	.321
vs. Left-Handers			298	57	4	53	57	.191	.275	.315
vs. Right-Handers			162	40	6	20	30	.247	.401	.333
vs. Ground-Ballers			187	40	5	36	39	.214	.321	.344
vs. Fly-Ballers			273	57	5	37	48	.209	.319	.305
Home Games	2-5	3.68	256	57	7	34	49	.223	.348	.316
Road Games	5-3	3.81	204	40	3	39	38	.196	.284	.328
Grass Fields	3-1	2.87	129	23	0	19	23	.178	.209	.289
Artificial Turf	4-7	4.09	331	74	10	54	64	.224	.363	.334
April	0-0	—	0	0	0	0	0	—	—	—
May	0-0	—	0	0	0	0	0	—	—	—
June	0-1	2.65	55	13	0	14	8	.236	.273	.391
July	2-1	3.94	119	29	3	17	25	.244	.378	.338
August	2-3	3.07	141	25	4	16	29	.177	.277	.266
Sept./Oct.	3-3	4.72	145	30	3	26	25	.207	.331	.331
Leading Off Inn.			110	26	3	26	26	.236	.382	.382
Bases Empty			253	55	6	45	50	.217	.344	.338
Runners On			207	42	4	28	37	.203	.290	.301
Runners/Scor. Pos.			123	30	2	15	24	.244	.317	.331
Runners On/2 Out			74	14	1	8	17	.189	.270	.277
Scor. Pos./2 Out			51	11	0	7	11	.216	.255	.322
Late-Inning Pressure			43	8	0	4	9	.186	.233	.255
Leading Off			12	2	0	2	4	.167	.167	.286
Runners On			15	2	0	1	2	.133	.133	.188
Runners/Scor. Pos.			8	1	0	0	0	.125	.125	.125
First 9 Batters			158	36	3	33	34	.228	.329	.361
Second 9 Batters			147	25	4	25	24	.170	.286	.291
All Batters Thereafter			155	36	3	15	29	.232	.342	.308

Loves to face: Lenny Harris (0-for-7)
Howard Johnson (0-for-10, 1 BB)
Kevin McReynolds (.200, 2-for-10)

Hates to face: Doug Dascenzo (2-for-2, 1 3B, 1 BB)
Dave Martinez (.625, 5-for-8, 2 HR)

Miscellaneous statistics: Ground outs-to-air outs ratio: 1.19 last season, 1.17 for career.... Induced 14 double-play ground outs in 121 opportunities (one per 8.6).... Allowed 16 doubles, 2 triples in 130.0 innings.... Allowed 20 first-inning runs in 22 starts (7.06 ERA, 4th highest in N.L.)... Batting support: 3.73 runs per start.... Opposing base stealers: 10-for-16 (63%); 0 pickoffs, 0 balks.

Comments: A hard-throwing right-handed rookie who handcuffed left-handed batters. Right-handers (.247) batted 56 points higher than left-handers (.191) last season, the 4th-largest such difference in the majors.... Lowest opponents' batting averages by rookie pitchers (minimum: 50 innings pitched): Chris Nabholz, Mtl. (.176); Mike Hartley, L.A. (.200); Ben McDonald, Balt. (.205); DeJesus (.211); Randy Tomlin, Pitt. (.221).... Rate of 5.05 walks per nine innings was the highest among the 10 rookie pitchers who threw least 100 innings last season. His walk rate was especially high early in the game: he walked 20 of 102 batters faced during the first inning, the highest rate by any N.L. pitcher last season (minimum: 20 starts).... Defeated the Mets three times without a loss last season, all within a six-week span; he was the only visiting pitcher to win two games at Shea Stadium last season. He and Nabholz were the only pitchers to shut the Mets out at Shea.... Lowest opponents' batting averages among starting pitchers with losing records in 1990 (minimum: 10 decisions): Sid Fernandez (.200, 9–14); DeJesus (.211, 7–8); Dennis Martinez (.228, 10–11); Mark Gardner (.230, 7–8); Matt Young (.235, 8–18).

Jose DeLeon

Throws Right

St. Louis Cardinals	W-L	ERA	AB	H	HR	BB	SO	BA	SA	OBA
Season	7-19	4.43	683	168	15	86	164	.246	.370	.331
vs. Left-Handers			404	115	8	58	69	.285	.423	.373
vs. Right-Handers			279	53	7	28	95	.190	.294	.268
vs. Ground-Ballers			329	75	3	49	78	.228	.322	.332
vs. Fly-Ballers			354	93	12	37	86	.263	.415	.330
Home Games	3-9	5.55	324	87	8	43	74	.269	.414	.359
Road Games	4-10	3.48	359	81	7	43	90	.226	.331	.306
Grass Fields	2-6	3.70	244	60	6	22	65	.246	.357	.305
Artificial Turf	5-13	4.85	439	108	9	64	99	.246	.378	.345
April	2-0	2.95	70	17	1	6	16	.243	.329	.299
May	2-3	4.50	140	35	3	11	36	.250	.364	.318
June	2-3	3.49	137	34	3	24	37	.248	.358	.356
July	0-5	4.85	110	26	3	15	22	.236	.400	.331
August	1-3	4.58	128	27	1	15	37	.211	.289	.290
Sept./Oct.	0-5	6.20	98	29	4	15	16	.296	.500	.388
Leading Off Inn.			167	37	2	23	32	.222	.329	.319
Bases Empty			389	88	8	48	87	.226	.352	.316
Runners On			294	80	7	38	77	.272	.395	.351
Runners/Scor. Pos.			175	49	1	29	47	.280	.360	.371
Runners On/2 Out			119	24	3	17	40	.202	.336	.307
Scor. Pos./2 Out			76	16	1	14	22	.211	.329	.333
Late-Inning Pressure			40	10	1	4	10	.250	.475	.326
Leading Off			14	7	1	1	4	.500	1.071	.533
Runners On			11	3	0	3	2	.273	.364	.400
Runners/Scor. Pos.			7	1	0	2	1	.143	.143	.300
First 9 Batters			238	55	3	35	53	.231	.328	.337
Second 9 Batters			230	54	4	26	65	.235	.348	.309
All Batters Thereafter			215	59	8	25	46	.274	.442	.348

Loves to face: Doug Dascenzo (0-for-14)
Shawon Dunston (.135, 5-for-37, 0 BB)
Andres Galarraga (.040, 1-for-25, 3 BB)

Hates to face: Brett Butler (.440, 11-for-25, 3 2B, 3 3B, 1 HR)
Eddie Murray (.524, 11-for-21, 4 HR)
Terry Pendleton (.563, 9-for-16)

Miscellaneous statistics: Ground outs-to-air outs ratio: 0.63 last season, 5th-lowest rate in N.L.; 0.78 for career. . . . Induced 8 double-play ground outs in 151 opportunities (one per 18.9). . . . Allowed 30 doubles, 5 triples in 182.2 innings. . . . Allowed 22 first-inning runs in 32 starts (5.97 ERA). . . . Batting support: 3.13 runs per start (tied for 2d lowest in N.L.) . . . Opposing base stealers: 20-for-32 (63%); 0 pickoffs, 0 balks.

Comments: Has held right-handed hitters to a .185 career batting average, the lowest among pitchers who have faced at least 1000 right-handed hitters since 1975. Only twice in eight seasons have righties hit .200 or better against him, with .213 in 1988 standing as the high-water mark. . . . Lefties have a .253 career average against him. . . . Has allowed 12 hits, including one home run, in 25 at-bats with the bases loaded over the past two years. . . . Did not complete any of his 32 starts last year. Only three pitchers in history have had more starts in a season without completing one: Steve Bedrosian (37 in 1985), Nolan Ryan (34 in 1987), and Milt Wilcox (33 in 1984). . . . Had a 1–14 record over his last 17 starts, losing his last seven, to tie Tim Leary for the major league lead in losses. He's the first pitcher since Phil Niekro to lead the majors in losses at least twice; since 1900, only Pedro Ramos has led the majors in losses three times. . . . Over the last 50 years, only one Cardinals pitcher had a lower single-season winning percentage (minimum: 15 decisions): Nelson Briles went 4–15 (.211) in 1966. . . . Lowest career winning percentages, active pitchers with at least 100 decisions: Mike Morgan (.361, 53–94), Mark Davis (.368, 42–72), Matt Young (.395, 51–78), DeLeon (.415, 68–96). His 1–14 span last year, coupled with his 2–19 record in 1985, have served as an albatross for DeLeon's career statistics, if not for his income.

Jim Deshaies

Throws Left

Houston Astros	W-L	ERA	AB	H	HR	BB	SO	BA	SA	OBA
Season	7-12	3.78	760	186	21	84	119	.245	.386	.322
vs. Left-Handers			115	35	1	23	20	.304	.426	.429
vs. Right-Handers			645	151	20	61	99	.234	.378	.301
vs. Ground-Ballers			381	96	13	27	63	.252	.420	.306
vs. Fly-Ballers			379	90	8	57	56	.237	.351	.336
Home Games	4-3	2.75	349	79	8	32	51	.226	.344	.295
Road Games	3-9	4.70	411	107	13	52	68	.260	.421	.344
Grass Fields	3-2	3.84	226	58	3	21	36	.257	.358	.320
Artificial Turf	4-10	3.76	534	128	18	63	83	.240	.397	.322
April	1-0	1.99	105	22	1	13	14	.210	.305	.311
May	2-2	4.63	128	31	2	13	15	.242	.367	.310
June	1-3	6.75	101	31	6	11	10	.307	.535	.381
July	0-4	4.59	127	33	5	18	21	.260	.441	.351
August	2-2	4.50	127	33	5	8	22	.260	.449	.304
Sept./Oct.	1-1	1.93	172	36	2	21	37	.209	.273	.293
Leading Off Inn.			202	53	7	14	27	.262	.441	.313
Bases Empty			467	115	17	40	68	.246	.418	.311
Runners On			293	71	4	44	51	.242	.334	.337
Runners/Scor. Pos.			180	46	3	33	34	.256	.361	.357
Runners On/2 Out			121	21	0	20	31	.174	.240	.301
Scor. Pos./2 Out			83	15	0	14	22	.181	.253	.306
Late-Inning Pressure			53	7	1	5	15	.132	.226	.207
Leading Off			18	2	1	0	5	.111	.278	.111
Runners On			10	1	0	1	5	.100	.100	.182
Runners/Scor. Pos.			8	0	0	1	4	.000	.000	.111
First 9 Batters			266	66	4	24	40	.248	.338	.306
Second 9 Batters			258	56	7	34	43	.217	.341	.315
All Batters Thereafter			236	64	10	26	36	.271	.487	.346

Loves to face: Howard Johnson (.056, 1-for-18)
Luis Quinones (0-for-16, 1 BB)
Andres Thomas (.121, 4-for-33, 0 BB)

Hates to face: Eric Davis (.324, 12-for-37, 5 HR)
Von Hayes (.583, 7-for-12, 6 BB)
Chris Sabo (.417, 10-for-24, 2 HR)

Miscellaneous statistics: Ground outs-to-air outs ratio: 0.63 last season, 4th-lowest rate in N.L.; 0.63 for career. . . . Induced 8 double-play ground outs in 155 opportunities (one per 19.4). . . . Allowed 34 doubles, 5 triples in 209.1 innings. . . . Allowed 16 first-inning runs in 34 starts (3.71 ERA). . . . Batting support: 3.91 runs per start. . . . Opposing base stealers: 21-for-30 (70%); 8 pickoffs, 3 balks.

Comments: One of four left-handed starters in majors last season against whom lefty batters hit .300 or better; the others: Dennis Rasmussen (.330), Jim Abbott (.318) and Fernando Valenzuela (.315). But Deshaies has allowed only one homer to a left-handed batter over the last two years; Larry Walker hit it last July 7. During that time, he's yielded 35 to right-handed batters. . . . Hasn't allowed a first-inning home run in his last 39 starts, since Roberto Alomar nailed him in September 1989. . . . Held the National League's top 10 home run hitters homerless in 53 at-bats last season, and he's never allowed a grand-slam. . . . He had a 2.09 ERA in his seven wins, 7.89 in his 12 losses. . . . Pitched to a decision in only 19 of 34 starts, 3d-lowest rate among National League pitchers with at least 15 starts last season. . . . Career record of 31–18, 2.99 ERA at the Astrodome; 25–30, 4.06 ERA elsewhere. . . . What goes around, comes around: he's 9–3 lifetime against the Dodgers, 3–9 against the Padres. . . . Deshaies, one of the world's worst hitters, has struck out in nearly half (45.5 percent) of his career plate appearances. Among players with at least 300 times up since 1975, only Joaquin Andujar has gone down on strikes at a greater rate (45.7 percent). . . . Deshaies's career batting statistics with the bases loaded: 0-for-18, two walks and 15 strikeouts. Shame on Davids Palmer and Cone, who walked Deshaies to force in runs in 1987.

Rob Dibble

Throws Right

Cincinnati Reds	W-L	ERA	AB	H	HR	BB	SO	BA	SA	OBA
Season	8-3	1.74	339	62	3	34	136	.183	.254	.255
vs. Left-Handers			173	32	1	24	69	.185	.254	.282
vs. Right-Handers			166	30	2	10	67	.181	.253	.225
vs. Ground-Ballers			144	32	1	10	56	.222	.299	.274
vs. Fly-Ballers			195	30	2	24	80	.154	.221	.242
Home Games	4-1	2.15	160	32	1	20	61	.200	.244	.288
Road Games	4-2	1.38	179	30	2	14	75	.168	.263	.224
Grass Fields	1-2	1.47	101	18	1	6	45	.178	.297	.218
Artificial Turf	7-1	1.87	238	44	2	28	91	.185	.235	.270
April	1-0	0.00	50	9	0	5	23	.180	.200	.255
May	2-0	2.92	46	12	0	7	19	.261	.326	.364
June	1-2	2.00	61	8	1	5	27	.131	.213	.197
July	0-0	2.70	50	8	1	10	19	.160	.240	.290
August	2-1	1.83	70	13	0	4	24	.186	.243	.230
Sept./Oct.	2-0	1.02	62	12	1	3	24	.194	.306	.221
Leading Off Inn.			80	16	2	8	28	.200	.313	.273
Bases Empty			187	32	3	19	82	.171	.251	.248
Runners On			152	30	0	15	54	.197	.257	.264
Runners/Scor. Pos.			107	19	0	10	42	.178	.252	.242
Runners On/2 Out			60	5	0	6	27	.083	.100	.167
Scor. Pos./2 Out			51	5	0	3	24	.098	.118	.148
Late-Inning Pressure			210	47	1	18	76	.224	.295	.284
Leading Off			48	11	0	3	14	.229	.271	.275
Runners On			101	23	0	7	32	.228	.297	.275
Runners/Scor. Pos.			68	15	0	4	24	.221	.309	.260
First 9 Batters			331	61	3	34	131	.184	.251	.258
Second 9 Batters			8	1	0	0	5	.125	.375	.125
All Batters Thereafter			0	0	0	0	0	—	—	—

Loves to face: Andres Galarraga (0-for-6, 6 SO)
Ryne Sandberg (0-for-9, 1 BB, 6 SO)
Matt Williams (0-for-7, 5 SO)

Hates to face: Pedro Guerrero (.444, 4-for-9)
Jose Lind (.833, 5-for-6)
Willie McGee (.625, 5-for-8)

Miscellaneous statistics: Ground outs-to-air outs ratio: 1.09 last season, 0.95 for career. . . . Induced 8 double-play ground outs in 73 opportunities (one per 9.1). . . . Allowed 13 doubles, 1 triple in 98.0 innings. . . . Stranded 33 inherited runners, allowed 18 to score (65%). . . . Opposing base stealers: 20-for-23 (87%); 0 pickoffs, 1 balk.

Comments: Averaged 12.5 strikeouts per nine innings last season, the 2d-highest single-season rate in major league history (minimum: 100 strikeouts). The highest? Dibble's average of 12.8 strikeouts per nine innings in 1989. . . . Home run rate (allowed one every 32.7 innings) was the best by any National League pitcher last season (minimum: 90 innings). . . . Vultured five wins in games in which he entered with the Reds leading, and subsequently allowed the opposing team to tie the score. . . . Opposing base stealers were successful in 17 of their last 18 attempts. . . . Pitches better as a set-up man than as a closer. How do we know? A look at opponents' career batting average in Late-Inning Pressure Situations compared with other at-bats: .220 in LIPS, .146 in other at-bats. That 74-point difference is the widest by any pitcher in the majors over the last five seasons. Of course, that .146 average pretty much guarantees an unfavorable comparison. . . . Opponents have only one hit in 19 career at-bats with two outs and the bases loaded. . . . Which leads us to his best category, opponents' batting average with two outs and runners in scoring position. Dibble held opponents to an .098 average (5-for-51) in such situations last year, lowering their already infinitesimal career batting average in those situations to .104. That's by far the lowest among all pitchers since we started tracking this category in 1975; Bob Apodaca ranks second at .165, with 20 pitchers bunched between .165 and .189.

Frank DiPino

Throws Left

St. Louis Cardinals	W-L	ERA	AB	H	HR	BB	SO	BA	SA	OBA
Season	5-2	4.56	313	92	8	31	49	.294	.447	.352
vs. Left-Handers			133	39	2	12	18	.293	.391	.349
vs. Right-Handers			180	53	6	19	31	.294	.489	.354
vs. Ground-Ballers			134	42	4	11	24	.313	.485	.365
vs. Fly-Ballers			179	50	4	20	25	.279	.419	.343
Home Games	3-2	3.92	159	46	5	15	26	.289	.447	.346
Road Games	2-0	5.22	154	46	3	16	23	.299	.448	.358
Grass Fields	2-0	5.16	96	32	1	9	11	.333	.490	.387
Artificial Turf	3-2	4.32	217	60	7	22	38	.276	.429	.337
April	0-0	1.80	43	14	1	1	0	.326	.488	.333
May	1-0	7.71	35	16	2	2	7	.457	.629	.486
June	2-1	6.75	60	19	2	10	12	.317	.500	.403
July	1-0	2.50	64	15	0	5	12	.234	.328	.286
August	1-1	4.60	58	16	1	6	6	.276	.397	.343
Sept./Oct.	0-0	5.02	53	12	2	7	12	.226	.434	.311
Leading Off Inn.			70	22	1	4	11	.314	.429	.351
Bases Empty			158	44	2	14	26	.278	.367	.337
Runners On			155	48	6	17	23	.310	.529	.367
Runners/Scor. Pos.			96	29	3	15	12	.302	.479	.373
Runners On/2 Out			70	21	3	9	14	.300	.529	.380
Scor. Pos./2 Out			48	16	2	8	9	.333	.563	.429
Late-Inning Pressure			42	13	0	5	5	.310	.357	.360
Leading Off			10	2	0	1	1	.200	.200	.273
Runners On			22	7	0	3	4	.318	.409	.357
Runners/Scor. Pos.			11	5	0	3	1	.455	.455	.471
First 9 Batters			280	86	8	29	45	.307	.475	.366
Second 9 Batters			33	6	0	2	4	.182	.212	.229
All Batters Thereafter			0	0	0	0	0	—	—	—

Loves to face: Tony Gwynn (.053, 1-for-19)
John Kruk (.111, 2-for-18, 9 SO)
Mike LaValliere (.111, 2-for-18)

Hates to face: Bobby Bonilla (.455, 10-for-22, 1 HR)
Tom Herr (.480, 12-for-25)
Howard Johnson (.350, 7-for-20, 4 HR)

Miscellaneous statistics: Ground outs-to-air outs ratio: 1.16 last season, 1.27 for career. . . . Induced 5 double-play ground outs in 78 opportunities (one per 15.6). . . . Allowed 18 doubles, 3 triples in 81.0 innings. . . . Stranded 16 inherited runners, allowed 21 to score (43%), worst rate in N.L. . . . Opposing base stealers: 4-for-6 (67%); 0 pickoffs, 1 balk.

Comments: Career total of 486 National League appearances in relief ranks 20th in league history. He should become the 17th N.L. pitcher to relieve in 500 games, passing Randy Moffitt (488), Tom Hume (488), and Elias ("Baseball Analyst") Sosa (492) along the way. . . . Has pitched only 644⅓ innings in 488 career relief appearances (including two with Brewers in 1981); in other words, he has averaged fewer than four outs per appearance. . . . Consistent workload: he has faced between 325 and 400 batters in each of the past seven seasons. Last year, 41 percent were left-handed batters, a career high. Danger sign: lefties hit .293 against him last year, after hitting .204 over previous four years. . . . Opponents have hit for a higher average in road games than they have in home games in each of the last six seasons. Career breakdown: 23–19 in home games, 11–18 on the road. . . . Has a record of 14–2 (.875) in two seasons with St. Louis after accumulating a 20–35 mark (.364) over eight previous seasons. . . . Entered two games in bases-loaded situations last season, and stranded all six of those inherited runners. . . . Starting with their rookie season in 1983, both DiPino and Craig Lefferts have made at least 50 relief appearances in eight consecutive seasons. Only two relievers in major league history have had longer streaks, starting with their rookie seasons: Ron Perranoski (10 years, 1961–70) and Willie Hernandez (nine years, 1977–86).

Doug Drabek

Throws Right

Pittsburgh Pirates	W-L	ERA	AB	H	HR	BB	SO	BA	SA	OBA
Season	22-6	2.76	846	190	15	56	131	.225	.331	.274
vs. Left-Handers			532	130	10	35	69	.244	.370	.290
vs. Right-Handers			314	60	5	21	62	.191	.264	.248
vs. Ground-Ballers			420	100	2	25	73	.238	.314	.283
vs. Fly-Ballers			426	90	13	31	58	.211	.347	.265
Home Games	11-3	3.00	438	96	11	28	72	.219	.347	.268
Road Games	11-3	2.51	408	94	4	28	59	.230	.314	.281
Grass Fields	6-1	3.35	181	43	3	11	27	.238	.337	.285
Artificial Turf	16-5	2.61	665	147	12	45	104	.221	.329	.271
April	4-1	2.37	111	26	2	9	16	.234	.297	.295
May	3-0	2.93	108	22	4	7	16	.204	.352	.250
June	1-3	4.29	143	44	4	13	16	.308	.503	.369
July	5-0	2.23	163	33	1	13	29	.202	.294	.261
August	4-1	2.23	162	34	2	6	30	.210	.296	.241
Sept./Oct.	5-1	2.74	159	31	2	8	24	.195	.258	.234
Leading Off Inn.			228	48	5	10	32	.211	.338	.244
Bases Empty			555	120	11	32	92	.216	.326	.260
Runners On			291	70	4	24	39	.241	.340	.300
Runners/Scor. Pos.			168	37	2	16	25	.220	.310	.287
Runners On/2 Out			127	25	1	12	19	.197	.276	.266
Scor. Pos./2 Out			81	15	1	9	14	.185	.296	.267
Late-Inning Pressure			74	12	2	6	13	.162	.257	.225
Leading Off			24	4	1	0	3	.167	.333	.167
Runners On			17	3	0	2	2	.176	.176	.263
Runners/Scor. Pos.			7	1	0	1	2	.143	.143	.250
First 9 Batters			278	57	6	12	46	.205	.302	.236
Second 9 Batters			271	64	3	23	44	.236	.328	.298
All Batters Thereafter			297	69	6	21	41	.232	.360	.287

Loves to face: Ron Gant (.125, 2-for-16, 7 SO)
Ricky Jordan (0-for-13)
Jose Uribe (.067, 1-for-15)

Hates to face: Kal Daniels (.389, 7-for-18, 1 HR)
Mark Grace (.471, 16-for-34, 1 HR)
Tony Gwynn (.400, 10-for-25)

Miscellaneous statistics: Ground outs-to-air outs ratio: 1.42 last season, 1.06 for career. . . . Induced 11 double-play ground outs in 24 opportunities (one per 11.3). . . . Allowed 37 doubles, 4 triples in 231.1 innings. . . . Allowed 9 first-inning runs in 33 starts (2.45 ERA). . . . Batting support: 5.36 runs per start (2d highest in N.L.) . . . Opposing base stealers: 18-for-27 (67%); 4 pickoffs, 0 balks.

Comments: Finished 16 games over .500, most by a Pittsburgh starter since Howard Camnitz went 25–6 in 1909. (Roy Face went 18–1 in relief in 1959.) . . . Last Pirates pitcher with consecutive 20-win seasons was Rip Sewell in 1943–44. No other team has ever gone so long without one of its pitchers winning 20 two years in a row. The old record: the Browns/Orioles went 45 years between repeat 20-game winners (Urban Shocker, 1922–23; Dave McNally, 1968–69). . . . How low can you go, limbo fans? Drabek has pitched in the majors for five years and has lowered his ERA every year (four improvements). Among pitchers who made 20 or more starts each year, the all-time record for consecutive ERA improvements is six by Sandy Koufax (1959–64). After that, Koufax's ERA was so low that despite its rise in '65, he won the major league Cy Young Award that year and the next!. . .Drabek has also lowered his opponents' batting average every year in the majors, but they've also hit for a higher average with runners on base than with bases empty in all five seasons. . . . Walked only three of 122 batters faced during the first inning last season, the best rate in the National League (minimum: 20 starts). Opponents' batting average during first innings (.186) was his lowest in any inning. . . . Career breakdown: 23–25 before the All-Star break, 46–20 after. . . . Breakdown of 1990 ERA by batterymate: 2.06 in 109⅓ innings with Don Slaught, 4.01 in 92 innings with Mike LaValliere; 1.50 in 30 innings with Dann Bilardello.

Sid Fernandez

Throws Left

New York Mets	W-L	ERA	AB	H	HR	BB	SO	BA	SA	OBA
Season	9-14	3.46	650	130	18	67	181	.200	.340	.277
vs. Left-Handers			126	28	3	16	44	.222	.357	.317
vs. Right-Handers			524	102	15	51	137	.195	.336	.268
vs. Ground-Ballers			310	58	3	37	97	.187	.284	.277
vs. Fly-Ballers			340	72	15	30	84	.212	.391	.278
Home Games	8-5	2.41	359	55	10	34	99	.153	.273	.229
Road Games	1-9	4.94	291	75	8	33	82	.258	.423	.335
Grass Fields	8-7	2.83	481	81	16	44	136	.168	.306	.241
Artificial Turf	1-7	5.48	169	49	2	23	45	.290	.438	.378
April	1-2	4.44	84	14	2	14	15	.167	.321	.287
May	2-2	1.41	119	24	3	8	25	.202	.319	.258
June	2-1	6.05	80	23	5	8	20	.287	.525	.352
July	2-2	3.45	106	23	3	13	37	.217	.396	.300
August	2-3	2.95	140	25	3	8	44	.179	.293	.230
Sept./Oct.	0-4	3.82	121	21	2	16	40	.174	.256	.273
Leading Off Inn.			167	43	8	17	46	.257	.467	.330
Bases Empty			409	79	9	40	123	.193	.313	.273
Runners On			241	51	9	27	58	.212	.386	.285
Runners/Scor. Pos.			127	28	4	19	31	.220	.386	.309
Runners On/2 Out			95	16	3	11	27	.168	.316	.255
Scor. Pos./2 Out			57	8	1	11	16	.140	.246	.279
Late-Inning Pressure			21	9	1	0	2	.429	.667	.429
Leading Off			5	2	1	0	1	.400	1.000	.400
Runners On			9	3	0	0	1	.333	.444	.333
Runners/Scor. Pos.			6	2	0	0	0	.333	.500	.333
First 9 Batters			241	37	4	23	87	.154	.245	.228
Second 9 Batters			216	48	7	29	56	.222	.394	.320
All Batters Thereafter			193	45	7	15	38	.233	.399	.288

Loves to face: Juan Samuel (.120, 6-for-50, 3 2B, 1 HR)
Benito Santiago (.080, 2-for-25, 0 BB, 12 SO)
Ozzie Smith (.130, 6-for-46, 5 BB)

Hates to face: Mariano Duncan (.440, 11-for-25)
Mike Fitzgerald (.400, 6-for-15, 2 2B, 2 HR)
Jeff Hamilton (.462, 6-for-13, 1 HR)

Miscellaneous statistics: Ground outs-to-air outs ratio: 0.48 last season, lowest rate in majors; 0.46 for career. . . . Induced 4 double-play ground outs in 132 opportunities (one per 33.0), worst rate in N.L. . . . Allowed 25 doubles, 6 triples in 179.1 innings. . . . Allowed 9 first-inning runs in 30 starts (2.70 ERA). . . . Batting support: 4.20 runs per start. . . . Opposing base stealers: 20-for-26 (77%); 1 pickoff, 0 balks.

Comments: All-time major league leaders in fewest hits allowed per nine innings (minimum: 1000 innings): Nolan Ryan, 6.54; Fernandez, 6.64; Sandy Koufax, 6.79; J. R. Richard, 6.88; Andy Messersmith, 6.94; six through 10 on the list: Hoyt Wilhelm, Sam McDowell, Ed Walsh, Joe Wood, and Babe Ruth. . . . Third pitcher over the last 10 years to post a losing record (minimum: 15 decisions) while holding opponents to a batting average of .200 or lower. The others: Mark Davis (.199, 5–10) in 1988, and Nolan Ryan (.200, 8–16) in 1987. One reason: poorest batting support for any Mets starter; team scored 1.5 fewer runs per game for Fernandez than for Gooden. . . . Opponents batted .154 on his first pass through the batting order, the lowest against any pitcher in the majors last season (minimum: 150 BFP), but not low enough to beat Sid's personal best (.134 on the first pass in 1985). . . . Opponents batted 105 points higher in road games (.258) than in home games (.153) last season, the largest margin in the majors. Opponents' career averages: .181 at Shea Stadium, .229 elsewhere. Ripple effect: 48–24, 2.54 ERA at Shea, 30–35, 4.08 ERA at other venues. . . . Lost his last four decisions last season, and was winless in his last six starts, one start shy of the longest winless span of his career. . . . Induced two of his season's total of four double-play grounders in the same game. . . . When was the last time Sid covered first base for a putout? August 15, 1989, when he beat Tony Gywnn to the bag. His only putout of 1990 came on a pop up.

John Franco

Throws Left

New York Mets	W-L	ERA	AB	H	HR	BB	SO	BA	SA	OBA
Season	5-3	2.53	262	66	4	21	56	.252	.347	.306
vs. Left-Handers			57	13	0	8	16	.228	.298	.323
vs. Right-Handers			205	53	4	13	40	.259	.361	.301
vs. Ground-Ballers			116	31	1	9	22	.267	.353	.317
vs. Fly-Ballers			146	35	3	12	34	.240	.342	.297
Home Games	4-2	2.82	156	45	0	13	38	.288	.346	.341
Road Games	1-1	2.15	106	21	4	8	18	.198	.349	.254
Grass Fields	5-2	2.85	188	51	3	18	45	.271	.367	.333
Artificial Turf	0-1	1.77	74	15	1	3	11	.203	.297	.234
April	0-0	1.08	30	6	0	1	8	.200	.233	.226
May	1-0	5.14	26	7	1	4	6	.269	.462	.367
June	2-0	0.55	61	13	1	2	13	.213	.262	.238
July	1-0	2.51	53	11	1	4	14	.208	.377	.263
August	0-0	1.64	41	11	1	4	4	.268	.366	.333
Sept./Oct.	1-3	5.91	51	18	0	6	11	.353	.412	.414
Leading Off Inn.			53	16	2	3	10	.302	.509	.339
Bases Empty			126	34	4	9	29	.270	.413	.319
Runners On			136	32	0	12	27	.235	.287	.295
Runners/Scor. Pos.			92	20	0	9	18	.217	.283	.284
Runners On/2 Out			65	12	0	4	14	.185	.215	.232
Scor. Pos./2 Out			45	6	0	3	11	.133	.178	.188
Late-Inning Pressure			211	52	4	18	44	.246	.332	.304
Leading Off			42	13	2	3	9	.310	.524	.356
Runners On			110	26	0	10	20	.236	.264	.298
Runners/Scor. Pos.			75	14	0	7	14	.187	.213	.253
First 9 Batters			254	66	4	21	56	.260	.358	.315
Second 9 Batters			8	0	0	0	0	.000	.000	.000
All Batters Thereafter			0	0	0	0	0	—	—	—

Loves to face: Barry Bonds (.125, 2-for-16)
Carmelo Martinez (.136, 3-for-22, 4 BB)
Ken Oberkfell (.118, 2-for-17)

Hates to face: Mariano Duncan (.538, 7-for-13)
Kevin Mitchell (.364, 4-for-11, 1 HR, 4 BB)
Terry Pendleton (.500, 6-for-12)

Miscellaneous statistics: Ground outs-to-air outs ratio: 1.66 last season, 1.84 for career.... Induced 5 double-play ground outs in 55 opportunities (one per 11.0).... Allowed 11 doubles, 1 triple in 67.2 innings.... Stranded 19 inherited runners, allowed 10 to score (66%).... Opposing base stealers: 6-for-7 (86%); 1 pickoff, 2 balks.

Comments: Needs 19 saves to reach 200 for career. Only two pitchers have had 200 National League saves (Bruce Sutter 300, Lee Smith 207), with Dave Smith (199) on the verge.... Became first Mets pitcher to lead the league in saves, leaving only the Giants and the Astros without a league leader in that category.... He had the best saves percentage in the National League, converting 33 of 39 opportunities (including 17 in a row at one point), but converted only two of five chances after September 1, and lost another game to the Pirates. He allowed nine runs in nine innings over his last nine appearances.... In 1989, he blew six of his last 15 chances, after converting 23 of his first 25.... Opponents batted .349 against him in 17 appearances after August 3.... Has not hit a batter with a pitch in the last four seasons.... He's allowed only three home runs to left-handed batters in 441 at bats. The only lefties to have taken him deep: Ken Landreaux (1984) and Darryl Strawberry (1985 and 1988, both game-winners).... The Mets stated at the time of the Myers-for-Franco deal that Franco was more effective against right-handed batters. Say what? Here's the breakdown by opposing right-handed batters. Franco: .259 in 1990, .250 career; Myers .197 in 1990, .215 career. Well, at least Franco gets along better with Gregg Jefferies.

Steve Frey

Throws Left

Montreal Expos	W-L	ERA	AB	H	HR	BB	SO	BA	SA	OBA
Season	8-2	2.10	201	44	4	29	29	.219	.318	.318
vs. Left-Handers			62	16	2	9	11	.258	.387	.347
vs. Right-Handers			139	28	2	20	18	.201	.288	.304
vs. Ground-Ballers			79	18	1	6	12	.228	.304	.282
vs. Fly-Ballers			122	26	3	23	17	.213	.328	.338
Home Games	4-0	0.59	105	20	1	15	17	.190	.276	.293
Road Games	4-2	3.91	96	24	3	14	12	.250	.365	.345
Grass Fields	1-2	6.17	47	14	1	10	2	.298	.383	.421
Artificial Turf	7-0	1.02	154	30	3	19	27	.195	.299	.284
April	1-0	3.00	40	6	2	5	9	.150	.350	.261
May	1-1	11.25	18	9	1	5	2	.500	.778	.583
June	1-0	3.86	9	3	0	0	1	.333	.444	.333
July	1-0	0.00	36	6	0	3	3	.167	.167	.231
August	2-1	1.23	53	13	1	10	3	.245	.340	.359
Sept./Oct.	2-0	0.69	45	7	0	6	11	.156	.178	.255
Leading Off Inn.			47	10	1	6	8	.213	.319	.315
Bases Empty			108	23	3	16	17	.213	.352	.320
Runners On			93	21	1	13	12	.226	.280	.315
Runners/Scor. Pos.			59	10	0	11	9	.169	.186	.292
Runners On/2 Out			39	8	0	10	5	.205	.205	.367
Scor. Pos./2 Out			29	4	0	8	3	.138	.138	.324
Late-Inning Pressure			130	26	3	17	21	.200	.300	.295
Leading Off			33	4	0	2	7	.121	.152	.194
Runners On			53	12	1	7	8	.226	.283	.311
Runners/Scor. Pos.			32	3	0	6	5	.094	.094	.231
First 9 Batters			197	44	4	28	28	.223	.325	.320
Second 9 Batters			4	0	0	1	1	.000	.000	.200
All Batters Thereafter			0	0	0	0	0	—	—	—

Loves to face: Sil Campusano (0-for-2, 2 SO)
Garry Templeton (.143, 1-for-7)
Andy Van Slyke (0-for-3, 2 SO)

Hates to face: Howard Johnson (.500, 3-for-6, 1 HR)
Kevin McReynolds (.400, 2-for-5, 1 HR)
Juan Samuel (.667, 2-for-3, 1 HR)

Miscellaneous statistics: Ground outs-to-air outs ratio: 0.83 last season, 0.81 for career.... Induced 4 double-play ground outs in 40 opportunities (one per 10.0).... Allowed 8 doubles, 0 triples in 55.2 innings.... Stranded 17 inherited runners, allowed 4 to score (81%).... Opposing base stealers: 7-for-8 (88%); 1 pickoff, 0 balks.

Comments: When he went onto the disabled list on May 25, he took with him a 5.06 ERA and a .259 opponents' batting average. After his return to the active roster on June 15, he compiled a 0.91 ERA while opponents batted .203. He must have spent those three weeks in Lourdes.... He achieved that turnaround despite a remarkable lack of strikeouts; he fanned only one of 61 batters he faced from July 24 to August 26. His season rate of strikeouts was 4.69 per nine innings, about a full strikeout below the overall National League rate (5.78).... Although he never played a game for either New York team, he toiled in the minor league systems of both the Mets and the Yankees.... He has started only one game in his professional career (with Tidewater in 1988), while appearing 371 times out of the bullpen.... Expos relievers had the lowest ground outs-to-air outs ratio (0.93) in the National League last season; Frey did his part with a G/A ratio of 0.83.... Opponents' career breakdown: .214 at Olympic Stadium, .235 on other artificially turfed fields, .333 on grass fields.... Among National League relievers who inherited at least 20 base runners last season, only Randy Myers, Lee Smith, and Bill Long stranded a greater percentage.... Opponents are hitless in nine career at-bats with the bases loaded.... Allowed seven home runs over the first 37 innings of his career, but has allowed only one in 40 innings since then.

Mark Gardner

Throws Right

Montreal Expos	W-L	ERA	AB	H	HR	BB	SO	BA	SA	OBA
Season	7-9	3.42	561	129	13	61	135	.230	.351	.312
vs. Left-Handers			318	73	8	47	70	.230	.362	.327
vs. Right-Handers			243	56	5	14	65	.230	.337	.291
vs. Ground-Ballers			262	61	7	27	65	.233	.370	.306
vs. Fly-Ballers			299	68	6	34	70	.227	.334	.317
Home Games	5-3	1.91	288	60	4	28	79	.208	.299	.290
Road Games	2-6	5.08	273	69	9	33	56	.253	.407	.334
Grass Fields	2-3	5.11	193	51	6	22	42	.264	.415	.339
Artificial Turf	5-6	2.61	368	78	7	39	93	.212	.318	.298
April	0-2	3.18	40	12	1	5	8	.300	.425	.404
May	2-0	2.03	144	31	2	13	36	.215	.299	.290
June	2-2	3.57	129	29	4	16	23	.225	.341	.306
July	2-1	1.35	131	19	1	11	40	.145	.198	.219
August	1-2	6.85	99	29	2	12	25	.293	.475	.375
Sept./Oct.	0-2	19.64	18	9	3	4	3	.500	1.111	.583
Leading Off Inn.			148	26	3	8	35	.176	.264	.218
Bases Empty			355	65	8	34	97	.183	.296	.260
Runners On			206	64	5	27	38	.311	.447	.394
Runners/Scor. Pos.			127	33	2	21	25	.260	.378	.373
Runners On/2 Out			98	30	1	15	23	.306	.408	.409
Scor. Pos./2 Out			65	17	0	13	16	.262	.338	.400
Late-Inning Pressure			46	9	0	4	11	.196	.196	.260
Leading Off			13	0	0	1	4	.000	.000	.071
Runners On			11	7	0	1	0	.636	.636	.667
Runners/Scor. Pos.			8	5	0	0	0	.625	.625	.625
First 9 Batters			202	55	4	27	65	.272	.386	.357
Second 9 Batters			186	40	6	22	38	.215	.371	.313
All Batters Thereafter			173	34	3	12	32	.197	.289	.253

Loves to face: Will Clark (.111, 1-for-9)
Juan Samuel (0-for-6)
Eric Yelding (.100, 1-for-10)

Hates to face: Kal Daniels (.500, 3-for-6, 1 3B, 2 HR)
Pedro Guerrero (.444, 4-for-9, 1 HR)
Lenny Harris (.500, 3-for-6, 1 HR)

Miscellaneous statistics: Ground outs-to-air outs ratio: 0.99 last season, 0.90 for career. . . . Induced 10 double-play ground outs in 96 opportunities (one per 9.6). . . . Allowed 21 doubles, 4 triples in 152.2 innings. . . . Allowed 21 first-inning runs in 26 starts (6.31 ERA). . . . Batting support: 3.77 runs per start. . . . Opposing base stealers: 16-for-22 (73%); 1 pickoff, 4 balks.

Comments: Threw three shutouts last season, tying Kevin Appier for the major league lead among rookies. Gardner also pitched nine shutout innings in another game in which the Expos lost, 2–0 in ten innings. . . . One of four pitchers to throw shutouts in consecutive starts last season. His consecutive shutouts were separated by the All-Star break. But in his 10 starts after those shutouts, he had a 1–5 record and 5.81 ERA. . . . Opponents batted 128 points higher with runners on base (.311) than with the bases empty (.183) last season, the 2d-largest difference in the majors. . . . Opponents batted 66 points higher on his first pass through the batting order (.272) than in subsequent at-bats (.206) last season, the 4th-largest margin in the majors. . . . Averaged 7.96 strikeouts per nine innings, the highest rate by any rookie with at least 100 innings last season. He struck out 27 batters during the first innings of his 26 starts, the 2d-highest rate (to David Cone) among National League pitchers (minimum: 20 starts). . . . Posted an ERA of 0.99 in his seven victories, 10.86 in his eight losses as a starter. . . . His only relief appearance was his first game of the season. . . . Had 2.02 ERA in $80\frac{1}{3}$ innings with Nelson Santovenia catching, 4.98 ERA in $72\frac{1}{3}$ innings with Mike Fitzgerald or Jerry Goff catching. Opponents stole seven bases in 12 attempts with Santovenia catching, nine bases in 10 attempts with the other guys.

Scott Garrelts

Throws Right

San Francisco Giants	W-L	ERA	AB	H	HR	BB	SO	BA	SA	OBA
Season	12-11	4.15	698	190	16	70	80	.272	.404	.339
vs. Left-Handers			391	115	8	41	33	.294	.425	.363
vs. Right-Handers			307	75	8	29	47	.244	.378	.308
vs. Ground-Ballers			322	85	8	34	39	.264	.416	.336
vs. Fly-Ballers			376	105	8	36	41	.279	.394	.341
Home Games	6-7	3.83	396	106	8	42	54	.268	.386	.339
Road Games	6-4	4.58	302	84	8	28	26	.278	.427	.339
Grass Fields	8-7	3.70	475	127	11	47	60	.267	.396	.334
Artificial Turf	4-4	5.12	223	63	5	23	20	.283	.422	.349
April	0-2	4.29	79	22	2	11	5	.278	.405	.363
May	1-4	8.54	145	54	3	16	11	.372	.517	.432
June	4-0	1.45	131	26	3	9	17	.198	.321	.248
July	4-1	2.68	183	39	4	13	21	.213	.322	.265
August	1-3	6.08	96	32	3	12	14	.333	.500	.420
Sept./Oct.	2-1	3.18	64	17	1	9	12	.266	.406	.351
Leading Off Inn.			182	54	5	12	11	.297	.456	.340
Bases Empty			410	110	7	36	41	.268	.393	.329
Runners On			288	80	9	34	39	.278	.420	.353
Runners/Scor. Pos.			158	42	5	26	28	.266	.418	.363
Runners On/2 Out			127	34	6	17	24	.268	.449	.354
Scor. Pos./2 Out			84	19	3	16	18	.226	.369	.350
Late-Inning Pressure			66	18	2	5	5	.273	.409	.324
Leading Off			18	5	0	2	1	.278	.278	.350
Runners On			25	7	2	1	2	.280	.600	.308
Runners/Scor. Pos.			11	3	1	0	1	.273	.636	.273
First 9 Batters			251	68	5	19	30	.271	.378	.321
Second 9 Batters			229	62	5	32	27	.271	.397	.364
All Batters Thereafter			218	60	6	19	23	.275	.440	.332

Loves to face: Jeff Blauser (.100, 2-for-20)
Tom Foley (0-for-12, 2 BB)
Tom Herr (.087, 2-for-23)

Hates to face: Barry Bonds (.412, 7-for-17, 1 HR)
Mark Grace (.579, 11-for-19, 1 HR)
Gerald Perry (.385, 5-for-13, 3 HR)

Miscellaneous statistics: Ground outs-to-air outs ratio: 1.07 last season, 1.19 for career. . . . Induced 22 double-play ground outs in 147 opportunities (one per 6.7), 3d-best rate in N.L. . . . Allowed 34 doubles, 5 triples in 182.0 innings. . . . Allowed 13 first-inning runs in 31 starts (3.48 ERA). . . . Batting support: 3.81 runs per start. . . . Opposing base stealers: 18-for-23 (78%); 1 pickoff, 0 balks.

Comments: Opponents batted .272 last season, compared with .214 over the five previous seasons. . . . Averaged only 3.96 strikeouts per nine innings last season, the 4th-lowest rate in the National League, after averaging 7.31 per nine innings previously, in a career split between the rotation and the bullpen. "Helped" by Garrelts, the Giants' starting pitchers had the fewest strikeouts (501) and the lowest rate (4.69) in the league last season. . . . Garrelts seemed to pace himself last season: he fanned only 11 batters in the first innings of his 31 starts, the 2d-lowest rate in the league (minimum: 20 starts). . . . Career breakdowns: 33–25, 3.39 ERA in 86 starts, 35–27, 3.01 ERA in 160 relief appearances; 35–19 in day games, 33–33 at night; 30–31 before the All-Star break, 38–21 after the break. . . . Lost his first decision against the Mets in 1985, but he's 7–0 against them since then. . . . Before last season, right-handed batters had a career average of only .208 against him; last year's .244 was the highest he's ever allowed to righties. . . . Pinch-ran 11 times last season, the most by any pitcher in the majors. Next-highest totals: four apiece by Danny Darwin and John Smoltz. . . . Had a no-hit bid spoiled with two outs in the ninth inning by Paul O'Neill. Doug Drabek and Brian Holman also came within one out of no-hitters last season. The last Giants pitcher to lose a no-hitter after $8\frac{2}{3}$ innings was Jeff Tesreau in 1914.

Tom Glavine

Throws Left

Atlanta Braves	W-L	ERA	AB	H	HR	BB	SO	BA	SA	OBA
Season	10-12	4.28	827	232	18	78	129	.281	.410	.343
vs. Left-Handers			154	34	2	20	34	.221	.279	.310
vs. Right-Handers			673	198	16	58	95	.294	.440	.350
vs. Ground-Ballers			406	121	6	40	71	.298	.404	.359
vs. Fly-Ballers			421	111	12	38	58	.264	.416	.326
Home Games	5-8	4.86	405	115	12	31	65	.284	.447	.334
Road Games	5-4	3.74	422	117	6	47	64	.277	.374	.350
Grass Fields	5-9	4.94	556	166	14	51	93	.299	.446	.357
Artificial Turf	5-3	3.04	271	66	4	27	36	.244	.336	.313
April	1-2	3.62	103	29	3	3	11	.282	.476	.302
May	1-1	2.72	141	32	4	18	33	.227	.340	.317
June	2-2	5.67	137	43	4	14	24	.314	.460	.377
July	2-1	4.32	127	34	2	12	13	.268	.370	.331
August	0-5	6.30	169	58	3	14	24	.343	.479	.391
Sept./Oct.	4-1	3.10	150	36	2	17	24	.240	.340	.317
Leading Off Inn.			206	60	2	14	22	.291	.393	.339
Bases Empty			486	132	15	30	72	.272	.416	.315
Runners On			341	100	3	48	57	.293	.402	.379
Runners/Scor. Pos.			209	57	3	41	40	.273	.397	.389
Runners On/2 Out			148	41	1	24	27	.277	.365	.378
Scor. Pos./2 Out			102	30	1	21	19	.294	.412	.415
Late-Inning Pressure			73	30	3	4	8	.411	.630	.442
Leading Off			21	10	1	1	2	.476	.810	.500
Runners On			28	12	1	3	2	.429	.536	.484
Runners/Scor. Pos.			14	6	1	3	1	.429	.643	.529
First 9 Batters			261	64	5	28	50	.245	.352	.318
Second 9 Batters			265	73	8	26	39	.275	.445	.342
All Batters Thereafter			301	95	5	24	40	.316	.429	.364

Loves to face: Paul O'Neill (.059, 1-for-17)
Spike Owen (.063, 1-for-16)
Darryl Strawberry (.067, 1-for-15, 1 HR)

Hates to face: Bill Doran (.563, 9-for-16)
Charlie Hayes (.500, 6-for-12, 1 HR)
Robby Thompson (.467, 7-for-15, 3 2B, 1 3B, 1 HR)

Miscellaneous statistics: Ground outs-to-air outs ratio: 1.44 last season, 1.30 for career.... Induced 22 double-play ground outs in 168 opportunities (one per 7.6).... Allowed 45 doubles (tied for 2d most in N.L.), 4 triples in 214.1 innings.... Allowed 26 first-inning runs in 33 starts (5.45 ERA).... Batting support: 4.18 runs per start.... Opposing base stealers: 22-for-31 (71%); 4 pick-offs, 1 balk.

Comments: Impressive: Glavine was the only pitcher to defeat the Reds four times last season; they beat him only once. More impressive: his 3–0 record at Riverfront Stadium made him the only pitcher in the majors to win three games in any enemy stadium. Most impressive: No starter had defeated the world champions-to-be at their own stadium three times in one season since Mike Flanagan went 3–0 at Yankee Stadium in 1978.... But baseball is a funny game; he's 0–6 lifetime against the Astros.... Opposing right-handers (.294) batted 73 points higher than left-handers (.221) last season, the 3d-largest margin in the majors. Career breakdown: .274 by right-handers, .226 by left-handers.... Walked 22 of 156 batters faced during the first inning, the 2d-highest rate among N.L. pitchers who started at least 20 games.... Opponents legged out 38 infield hits, the most against any pitcher in the majors last season.... Completed only one of 33 starts in 1990, after completing six games, four of them shutouts, the previous year.... Over his four seasons with the Braves, he has allowed almost twice as many home runs in home games (36) as he has on the road (19).... Has a career total of 105 pitching appearances, all as a starter. Only one pitcher in baseball history had more starts without ever entering a game in relief. That would be Jim Devlin, who made 129 starts for the Louisville Grays in 1876–77, then was kicked out of the league following the 1887 season for allegedly throwing games.

Dwight Gooden

Throws Right

New York Mets	W-L	ERA	AB	H	HR	BB	SO	BA	SA	OBA
Season	19-7	3.83	888	229	10	70	223	.258	.345	.315
vs. Left-Handers			523	135	6	44	132	.258	.354	.315
vs. Right-Handers			365	94	4	26	91	.258	.332	.314
vs. Ground-Ballers			443	105	2	35	119	.237	.280	.300
vs. Fly-Ballers			445	124	8	35	104	.279	.409	.330
Home Games	9-3	3.56	475	117	5	31	119	.246	.333	.296
Road Games	10-4	4.15	413	112	5	39	104	.271	.358	.336
Grass Fields	14-3	3.70	632	155	7	51	160	.245	.328	.306
Artificial Turf	5-4	4.15	256	74	3	19	63	.289	.387	.336
April	1-2	3.82	115	27	1	10	32	.235	.322	.302
May	2-2	4.59	132	32	2	12	38	.242	.326	.308
June	4-1	4.15	169	46	1	13	33	.272	.367	.326
July	4-0	2.45	132	34	1	10	32	.258	.333	.303
August	3-1	5.50	149	40	3	11	39	.268	.376	.331
Sept./Oct.	5-1	2.82	191	50	2	14	49	.262	.335	.312
Leading Off Inn.			210	57	0	26	41	.271	.333	.357
Bases Empty			486	127	2	51	120	.261	.331	.336
Runners On			402	102	8	19	103	.254	.361	.288
Runners/Scor. Pos.			254	61	3	15	71	.240	.331	.281
Runners On/2 Out			165	33	2	10	41	.200	.285	.250
Scor. Pos./2 Out			112	23	0	7	32	.205	.277	.252
Late-Inning Pressure			80	16	1	7	24	.200	.275	.261
Leading Off			22	5	0	2	4	.227	.273	.292
Runners On			30	9	1	3	7	.300	.400	.353
Runners/Scor. Pos.			23	5	1	3	7	.217	.348	.296
First 9 Batters			282	69	1	18	72	.245	.333	.296
Second 9 Batters			273	75	2	20	65	.275	.341	.329
All Batters Thereafter			333	85	7	32	86	.255	.357	.319

Loves to face: Shawon Dunston (.143, 6-for-42, 3 2B, 1 HR)
Juan Samuel (.179, 12-for-67)
Mike Scott (0-for-14, 9 SO)

Hates to face: John Kruk (.375, 9-for-24, 1 HR)
Luis Quinones (.571, 4-for-7, 3 2B)
Chris Sabo (.429, 6-for-14)

Miscellaneous statistics: Ground outs-to-air outs ratio: 1.27 last season, 1.26 for career.... Induced 12 double-play ground outs in 161 opportunities (one per 13.4).... Allowed 33 doubles, 7 triples in 232.2 innings.... Allowed 12 first-inning runs in 34 starts (2.91 ERA).... Batting support: 5.88 runs per start (highest in majors).... Opposing base stealers: 60-for-76 (79%); 4 pickoffs, 3 balks.

Comments: Just to complete the thought on Glavine: Gooden started the first 175 games of his career before pitching in relief late in the 1989 season. That's the modern major league record for consecutive pitching appearances, none in relief, from the start of a career.... Doc's 1990 opening-day loss to the Pirates marked the first time his won-lost record had dipped below the .500 mark in any season of his career. Over the last 75 years, no other pitcher had made as many career starts without ever falling below .500 in any season.... Opponents have hit for a higher average in day games than they have at night in each of seven seasons in the majors, matching Mike Scott for the longest such streak over the last 16 years. Career breakdown: .252 in day games, .215 at night.... Walked only six of 135 batters faced in the first inning last season, 2d-best rate among N.L. pitchers (minimum: 20 starts).... Allowed one home run every 23.3 innings pitched, the best rate among National League starters last season. He held the league's top 10 home run hitters homerless in 65 at-bats.... His ERA in his eight no-decision starts (2.72) was lower than his ERA in his 19 wins (3.06).... Opponents had five hits in nine at-bats with the bases full last season; Ernest Riles's grand slam was the first ever allowed by Doc.... Gooden and Roger Clemens have both started their careers with seven consecutive winning seasons. The last pitcher to post a winning record in his first eight seasons was Jim Palmer.

Jim Gott

Throws Right

Los Angeles Dodgers	W-L	ERA	AB	H	HR	BB	SO	BA	SA	OBA
Season	3-5	2.90	230	59	5	34	44	.257	.370	.347
vs. Left-Handers			132	38	1	20	22	.288	.379	.379
vs. Right-Handers			98	21	4	14	22	.214	.357	.304
vs. Ground-Ballers			95	31	2	12	12	.326	.442	.398
vs. Fly-Ballers			135	28	3	22	32	.207	.319	.313
Home Games	2-3	2.88	120	26	3	21	25	.217	.333	.324
Road Games	1-2	2.93	110	33	2	13	19	.300	.409	.374
Grass Fields	2-5	2.88	185	47	4	30	35	.254	.373	.352
Artificial Turf	1-0	3.00	45	12	1	4	9	.267	.356	.327
April	0-0	—	0	0	0	0	0	—	—	—
May	0-0	10.80	7	3	0	0	0	.429	.429	.429
June	0-2	5.68	55	18	4	7	12	.327	.600	.403
July	0-0	0.73	39	9	0	9	4	.231	.231	.360
August	2-1	0.49	61	9	1	6	13	.148	.230	.224
Sept./Oct.	1-2	4.24	68	20	0	12	15	.294	.382	.390
Leading Off Inn.			54	13	0	4	8	.241	.352	.293
Bases Empty			126	31	2	14	24	.246	.365	.321
Runners On			104	28	3	20	20	.269	.375	.375
Runners/Scor. Pos.			67	15	2	16	17	.224	.313	.356
Runners On/2 Out			46	9	0	13	10	.196	.196	.373
Scor. Pos./2 Out			30	5	0	11	8	.167	.167	.390
Late-Inning Pressure			80	14	2	13	17	.175	.287	.290
Leading Off			21	2	0	2	2	.095	.143	.174
Runners On			30	7	1	7	6	.233	.367	.378
Runners/Scor. Pos.			21	4	1	7	6	.190	.333	.393
First 9 Batters			224	56	5	34	44	.250	.362	.345
Second 9 Batters			6	3	0	0	0	.500	.667	.429
All Batters Thereafter			0	0	0	0	0	—	—	—

Loves to face: Rick Cerone (0-for-7)
Kevin Mitchell (0-for-9, 1 BB)
Tom Herr (.100, 1-for-10)

Hates to face: Eric Davis (.385, 5-for-13, 2 2B, 2 HR, 5 SO)
Tony Gwynn (.533, 8-for-15)
Rafael Ramirez (.462, 6-for-13)

Miscellaneous statistics: Ground outs-to-air outs ratio: 1.00 last season, 1.31 for career. . . . Induced 5 double-play ground outs in 47 opportunities (one per 9.4). . . . Allowed 9 doubles, 1 triple in 62.0 innings. . . . Stranded 16 inherited runners, allowed 6 to score (73%). . . . Opposing base stealers: 2-for-4 (50%); 0 pickoffs, 0 balks.

Comments: He was tough when it counted: opponents batted 125 points lower in Late-Inning Pressure Situations (.175) than in other at-bats (.300) last season, the largest margin in the majors. . . . Despite having pitched for three different teams since 1986, opponents have batted 69 points higher in road games (.284) than in home games (.214) over the last five seasons, the 2d-largest margin in the majors. One big reason: all three of those home stadiums have a negative effect on batting averages; see page 417 for details. End result: 25–24 record, 3.57 ERA in home games; 13–29, 4.66 ERA in road games. . . . Allowed only one home run to a left-handed batter last season; Franklin Stubbs hit it on June 13. . . . Bases-loaded numbers: has allowed only one walk in 69 batters faced; has never allowed a grand-slam home run. . . . Made 1990 season debut on May 27 and gott off to a poor start: a 9.82 ERA and four home runs allowed in his first seven games. From then on, he gott better: 1.98 ERA and only one home run over the remainder of the season. . . . Has held opponents to a .193 career batting average with two outs and runners in scoring position. . . . Has pitched in the major leagues for nine years, but has never had a winning record in any season; two of those seasons were without any decisions. . . . Four of his 11 career hits are home runs, including two in the same game in 1985. Only three active pitchers have more career homers: Don Robinson (13), Fernando Valenzuela (8), and Dan Schatzeder (5).

Mark Grant

Throws Right

Padres/Braves	W-L	ERA	AB	H	HR	BB	SO	BA	SA	OBA
Season	2-3	4.73	362	108	9	37	69	.298	.450	.360
vs. Left-Handers			197	60	4	21	42	.305	.477	.372
vs. Right-Handers			165	48	5	16	27	.291	.418	.348
vs. Ground-Ballers			187	50	2	14	41	.267	.358	.320
vs. Fly-Ballers			175	58	7	23	28	.331	.549	.401
Home Games	1-0	5.70	186	54	7	24	41	.290	.468	.369
Road Games	1-3	3.68	176	54	2	13	28	.307	.432	.351
Grass Fields	1-2	5.40	274	81	8	30	57	.296	.456	.362
Artificial Turf	1-1	2.74	88	27	1	7	12	.307	.432	.354
April	0-0	8.76	49	17	3	8	9	.347	.612	.439
May	1-0	2.61	40	13	1	2	4	.325	.475	.349
June	0-1	3.09	50	14	1	4	11	.280	.400	.333
July	0-1	9.00	70	27	2	11	15	.386	.586	.458
August	0-0	5.17	60	18	1	9	11	.300	.450	.391
Sept./Oct.	1-1	1.71	93	19	1	3	19	.204	.280	.232
Leading Off Inn.			77	21	2	5	13	.273	.429	.317
Bases Empty			179	51	3	14	30	.285	.402	.337
Runners On			183	57	6	23	39	.311	.497	.382
Runners/Scor. Pos.			121	37	3	20	27	.306	.471	.390
Runners On/2 Out			84	26	3	17	21	.310	.476	.426
Scor. Pos./2 Out			63	18	1	14	18	.286	.397	.416
Late-Inning Pressure			43	17	1	6	10	.395	.558	.480
Leading Off			10	4	0	0	2	.400	.600	.400
Runners On			27	9	1	4	7	.333	.519	.438
Runners/Scor. Pos.			20	6	0	3	6	.300	.350	.391
First 9 Batters			312	95	8	29	61	.304	.455	.359
Second 9 Batters			49	13	1	8	7	.265	.429	.373
All Batters Thereafter			1	0	0	0	1	.000	.000	.000

Loves to face: Ken Oberkfell (.077, 1-for-13, 1 3B, 3 BB)
Rafael Ramirez (.083, 1-for-12)
Ozzie Smith (.105, 2-for-19, 3 BB)

Hates to face: Eric Davis (.450, 9-for-20, 4 HR)
Andre Dawson (.571, 12-for-21, 3 HR)
Eddie Murray (.500, 4-for-8, 2 HR)

Miscellaneous statistics: Ground outs-to-air outs ratio: 1.15 last season, 1.26 for career. . . . Induced 8 double-play ground outs in 82 opportunities (one per 10.3). . . . Allowed 22 doubles, 3 triples in 91.1 innings. . . . Stranded 27 inherited runners, allowed 24 to score (53%), 4th-worst rate in N.L. . . . Opposing base stealers: 12-for-15 (80%); 0 pickoffs, 1 balk.

Comments: Braves relievers finished last in the majors in both ERA (5.01) and hits allowed per nine innings (10.28). Grant was in there doin' his share, with a 4.64 ERA and a 10.49 hits rate after coming to Atlanta from San Diego. . . . But he took a licking and kept on ticking: he faced 10 or more batters in 14 games last season, the most such appearances by any National League reliever. . . . Saved three games after his acquisition by the Braves. Before the trade, he had accumulated only four saves in 110 career relief appearances with the Giants and Padres. . . . Opponents own a career batting average of .303 in Late-Inning Pressure Situations, .265 in other at-bats. . . . There is only a 12-point difference between the career batting averages of opposing left-handed (.263) and right-handed batters (.275), but there is a much greater margin (27 points) between the career averages of opposing ground-ball hitters (.255) and fly-ball hitters (.282). . . . Has a career batting average of .017 (1-for-60) in road games. That is not a typo. He's 0-for-30 on artificial surfaces.

Kevin Gross

Throws Right

Montreal Expos	W-L	ERA	AB	H	HR	BB	SO	BA	SA	OBA
Season	9-12	4.57	628	171	9	65	111	.272	.368	.340
vs. Left-Handers			369	109	7	48	73	.295	.415	.373
vs. Right-Handers			259	62	2	17	38	.239	.301	.291
vs. Ground-Ballers			308	84	2	30	55	.273	.347	.333
vs. Fly-Ballers			320	87	7	35	56	.272	.387	.346
Home Games	3-5	4.43	264	72	4	27	40	.273	.379	.340
Road Games	6-7	4.67	364	99	5	38	71	.272	.360	.340
Grass Fields	2-6	6.57	198	61	5	19	32	.308	.429	.366
Artificial Turf	7-6	3.71	430	110	4	46	79	.256	.340	.328
April	2-1	2.84	96	23	0	17	13	.240	.271	.354
May	4-2	4.74	141	36	3	10	25	.255	.397	.299
June	2-2	3.07	155	39	2	12	34	.252	.342	.308
July	0-3	6.17	43	9	1	9	6	.209	.349	.352
August	0-2	7.56	108	41	2	10	18	.380	.481	.423
Sept./Oct.	1-2	4.84	85	23	1	7	15	.271	.341	.333
Leading Off Inn.			156	47	3	14	28	.301	.404	.363
Bases Empty			358	97	6	27	62	.271	.366	.326
Runners On			270	74	3	38	49	.274	.370	.357
Runners/Scor. Pos.			170	44	2	31	34	.259	.359	.363
Runners On/2 Out			108	21	1	17	26	.194	.269	.310
Scor. Pos./2 Out			77	14	1	14	17	.182	.260	.315
Late-Inning Pressure			40	10	1	1	10	.250	.350	.262
Leading Off			10	2	0	0	3	.200	.200	.200
Runners On			15	4	0	1	3	.267	.333	.294
Runners/Scor. Pos.			8	0	0	1	2	.000	.000	.100
First 9 Batters			241	56	2	25	46	.232	.295	.309
Second 9 Batters			204	60	3	21	37	.294	.397	.355
All Batters Thereafter			183	55	4	19	28	.301	.432	.364

Loves to face: Craig Biggio (0-for-14)
Doug Drabek (0-for-12)
Jose Uribe (.184, 7-for-38)

Hates to face: Eric Davis (.417, 10-for-24, 3 HR)
Ron Oester (.538, 14-for-26)
Lonnie Smith (.500, 8-for-16, 2 HR)

Miscellaneous statistics: Ground outs-to-air outs ratio: 0.84 last season, 0.96 for career.... Induced 8 double-play ground outs in 133 opportunities (one per 16.6).... Allowed 29 doubles, 2 triples in 163.1 innings.... Allowed 9 first-inning runs in 26 starts (3.16 ERA).... Batting support: 3.65 runs per start.... Opposing base stealers: 31-for-36 (86%); 0 pickoffs, 1 balk.

Comments: Hit a home run off, and allowed a home run to, Fernando Valenzuela in the third inning of a game at Dodger Stadium last May 14. (Don't think that didn't set off a nice little flurry of phone calls to the old ESB.) Research results: it was the first instance of pitchers hitting home runs off each other in the same inning since May 12, 1961, when Eli Grba (L.A. Angels) and Pedro Ramos (Twins) did it. Twice since then, pitchers have hit homers off one another in the same game, but not the same inning: Tony Cloninger and Ray Sadecki exchanged pleasantries on July 3, 1966, and that old vaudeville team of Buster Narum and Earl Wilson took each other deep on April 14, 1965.... Career breakdown: 73–88, 4.11 ERA as a starter, 7–2, 2.44 ERA as a reliever.... He'd be a .500 pitcher if he never pitched in July. He has a career record of 9–19 in that month, 71–71 in all other months combined.... Has a 5–5 career record with a 3.05 ERA at Dodger Stadium, but his ERA is 1.67 over his last seven starts there.... Can the Dodgers' infielders give Gross the type of defensive support to which he's grown accustomed? Last season, the Expos' infielders committed only four errors in 163⅓ innings behind Gross. Their fielding percentage with Gross on the mound (.990) was the 2d best by any infield behind any pitcher in the league last season (minimum: 162 innings). Number one: the Expos behind Oil Can Boyd (.995).

Bill Gullickson

Throws Right

Houston Astros	W-L	ERA	AB	H	HR	BB	SO	BA	SA	OBA
Season	10-14	3.82	769	221	21	61	73	.287	.441	.338
vs. Left-Handers			467	146	11	43	29	.313	.452	.370
vs. Right-Handers			302	75	10	18	44	.248	.424	.287
vs. Ground-Ballers			360	94	3	26	35	.261	.336	.308
vs. Fly-Ballers			409	127	18	35	38	.311	.533	.364
Home Games	8-7	3.94	451	127	12	31	45	.282	.448	.327
Road Games	2-7	3.65	318	94	9	30	28	.296	.431	.354
Grass Fields	1-3	3.48	179	52	6	14	17	.291	.436	.340
Artificial Turf	9-11	3.92	590	169	15	47	56	.286	.442	.337
April	1-1	4.97	53	16	0	3	8	.302	.453	.328
May	2-2	3.63	135	40	1	15	16	.296	.400	.362
June	2-3	2.42	173	46	3	12	23	.266	.387	.309
July	1-2	6.26	115	40	6	8	6	.348	.574	.395
August	2-4	4.00	145	37	5	10	11	.255	.421	.306
Sept./Oct.	2-2	3.32	148	42	6	13	9	.284	.453	.342
Leading Off Inn.			188	51	7	14	21	.271	.436	.325
Bases Empty			439	128	14	32	45	.292	.453	.342
Runners On			330	93	7	29	28	.282	.424	.332
Runners/Scor. Pos.			192	49	5	22	20	.255	.406	.320
Runners On/2 Out			132	34	3	13	15	.258	.386	.324
Scor. Pos./2 Out			87	22	3	9	11	.253	.414	.323
Late-Inning Pressure			35	13	2	1	5	.371	.571	.378
Leading Off			10	3	0	0	2	.300	.400	.300
Runners On			12	4	0	1	2	.333	.333	.357
Runners/Scor. Pos.			7	1	0	1	2	.143	.143	.222
First 9 Batters			263	81	6	19	30	.308	.479	.354
Second 9 Batters			252	67	6	22	23	.266	.409	.321
All Batters Thereafter			254	73	9	20	20	.287	.433	.338

Loves to face: Chili Davis (.149, 7-for-47, 2 HR)
Danny Heep (.083, 2-for-24)
Mike Marshall (.167, 5-for-30, 0 BB)

Hates to face: Ken Griffey, Sr. (.450, 9-for-20, 4 HR)
Franklin Stubbs (.368, 7-for-19, 1 HR)
Dale Sveum (.800, 4-for-5, 2 HR)

Miscellaneous statistics: Ground outs-to-air outs ratio: 0.94 last season, 0.91 for career.... Induced 18 double-play ground outs in 151 opportunities (one per 8.4).... Allowed 37 doubles, 9 triples (tied for most in N.L.) in 193.1 innings.... Allowed 23 first-inning runs in 32 starts (6.19 ERA).... Batting support: 3.66 runs per start.... Opposing base stealers: 23-for-32 (72%); 0 pickoffs, 2 balks.

Comments: Averaged only 3.40 strikeouts per nine innings last season, making him low man among the 36 National League pitchers who qualified for the ERA title. In his pre-Japan days in the majors, Gullickson averaged 5.02 strikeouts per nine innings. He still holds the rookie record of 18 strikeouts in a game, set while pitching for the Expos in 1980. Does sushi sap arm strength? ... His total of 61 walks was inflated by 14 of the intentional variety, the highest total in the majors. When you pitch for a losing team, you have to adopt losers' strategies.... Had allowed only three home runs over his first 14 starts, but then surrendered dingers in each of his next eight appearances, the first Houston pitcher to do that in the team's 29-year history. Guess he was just getting warmed up for Tiger Stadium.... Tigers starting pitchers had a 5.00 ERA last season, worst in the majors.... His shutout over the Braves in his final start of the season gave him his seventh consecutive season in double figures in wins. Only four other pitchers have current streaks at least that long: Charlie Hough, nine years; Mike Boddicker and Bruce Hurst, eight years; Frank Viola, seven years.... In the last five of those seasons, Gully has more hits allowed than innings pitched.... Career record of 71–40 in home games, 40–60 on the road. How many players have started home games in the United States, Canada, and Japan?

Mike Harkey

Throws Right

Chicago Cubs	W-L	ERA	AB	H	HR	BB	SO	BA	SA	OBA
Season	12-6	3.26	653	153	14	59	94	.234	.358	.303
vs. Left-Handers			404	96	7	37	56	.238	.351	.302
vs. Right-Handers			249	57	7	22	38	.229	.369	.304
vs. Ground-Ballers			330	75	3	31	48	.227	.309	.297
vs. Fly-Ballers			323	78	11	28	46	.241	.409	.309
Home Games	5-2	2.43	323	79	6	28	46	.245	.337	.310
Road Games	7-4	4.08	330	74	8	31	48	.224	.379	.296
Grass Fields	9-3	2.62	485	109	13	39	73	.225	.351	.288
Artificial Turf	3-3	5.23	168	44	1	20	21	.262	.381	.346
April	2-1	2.60	57	9	1	7	11	.158	.246	.265
May	3-0	5.35	140	43	5	13	20	.307	.443	.366
June	0-2	2.79	107	23	2	9	14	.215	.364	.295
July	4-2	3.82	147	39	1	10	17	.265	.361	.312
August	3-1	2.42	183	38	5	16	28	.208	.350	.275
Sept./Oct.	0-0	0.00	19	1	0	4	4	.053	.105	.217
Leading Off Inn.			170	33	4	10	30	.194	.318	.247
Bases Empty			411	94	11	26	62	.229	.377	.280
Runners On			242	59	3	33	32	.244	.326	.339
Runners/Scor. Pos.			141	33	1	26	17	.234	.305	.353
Runners On/2 Out			105	22	2	15	17	.210	.286	.320
Scor. Pos./2 Out			69	13	1	14	9	.188	.261	.333
Late-Inning Pressure			59	16	1	8	2	.271	.407	.358
Leading Off			16	1	1	3	0	.063	.250	.211
Runners On			20	7	0	4	1	.350	.400	.458
Runners/Scor. Pos.			12	3	0	2	0	.250	.333	.357
First 9 Batters			221	54	6	16	37	.244	.362	.306
Second 9 Batters			207	44	2	22	36	.213	.309	.292
All Batters Thereafter			225	55	6	21	21	.244	.400	.310

Loves to face: Will Clark (0-for-9, 1 BB)
Kal Daniels (0-for-9)
Jose DeLeon (0-for-10, 1 BB)

Hates to face: Billy Hatcher (.571, 4-for-7, 3 2B, 1 HR)
Matt Williams (.556, 5-for-9, 2 HR)

Miscellaneous statistics: Ground outs-to-air outs ratio: 1.20 last season, 1.28 for career. . . . Induced 10 double-play ground outs in 120 opportunities (one per 12.0). . . . Allowed 29 doubles, 5 triples in 173.2 innings. . . . Allowed 19 first-inning runs in 27 starts (5.81 ERA). . . . Batting support: 4.41 runs per start. . . . Opposing base stealers: 8-for-14 (57%); 1 pickoff, 1 balk.

Comments: Four times during the 1980s, the Cubs had one of the top four picks in baseball's amateur draft. They came away with pretty good value: Joe Carter (2d pick in 1981), Shawon Dunston (1st in 1982), Drew Hall (3d in 1984) and Harkey (4th in 1987). . . . One of only four rookie pitchers in the majors to pitch at least 162 innings last season. . . . Harkey's .667 winning percentage was the highest by a Cubs' rookie (minimum: 15 decisions) since Roy Henshaw's 13–5 record in 1935. The bad news for Harkey is that Henshaw posted a career record of 18–34 after his rookie season. . . . His 3.26 ERA stood out on a team that had the worst ERA in the league by its starting pitchers (4.48); the collective ERA for Harkey's rotation-mates was 4.64. . . . Has hit nine batters with pitches in 208⅓ innings in the majors, or one every 23.1 innings; Don Drysdale's career numbers: 154 HBPs in 3432 innings, or one every 22.3 innings. . . . Put up excellent situational numbers during his brief stint with the Cubs in 1988. His opponents' career breakdown is quite impressive: .244 with the bases empty, .225 with runners on base, .216 with runners in scoring position, .196 with two outs and runners in scoring position. . . . Worked all but six innings last season with Joe Girardi as a batterymate. . . . Has held opponents to a .243 career batting average at Wrigley Field, while batting .286 there himself.

Greg W. Harris

Throws Right

San Diego Padres	W-L	ERA	AB	H	HR	BB	SO	BA	SA	OBA
Season	8-8	2.30	419	92	6	49	97	.220	.310	.303
vs. Left-Handers			220	61	2	27	36	.277	.364	.355
vs. Right-Handers			199	31	4	22	61	.156	.251	.246
vs. Ground-Ballers			191	42	1	20	49	.220	.293	.291
vs. Fly-Ballers			228	50	5	29	48	.219	.325	.312
Home Games	4-4	2.10	202	49	3	21	52	.243	.347	.314
Road Games	4-4	2.48	217	43	3	28	45	.198	.276	.292
Grass Fields	6-5	1.89	307	71	4	31	73	.231	.326	.303
Artificial Turf	2-3	3.41	112	21	2	18	24	.188	.268	.301
April	2-0	1.20	52	9	1	3	13	.173	.231	.218
May	1-0	2.05	80	16	1	12	22	.200	.287	.309
June	1-2	2.84	69	16	2	12	14	.232	.406	.349
July	1-3	4.43	76	18	0	8	11	.237	.329	.302
August	2-1	1.62	58	13	0	9	16	.224	.259	.338
Sept./Oct.	1-2	1.21	84	20	2	5	21	.238	.321	.278
Leading Off Inn.			94	21	1	11	18	.223	.298	.318
Bases Empty			223	47	5	21	52	.211	.309	.287
Runners On			196	45	1	28	45	.230	.311	.319
Runners/Scor. Pos.			114	22	0	24	29	.193	.272	.317
Runners On/2 Out			78	17	1	12	22	.218	.333	.322
Scor. Pos./2 Out			50	9	0	10	16	.180	.300	.317
Late-Inning Pressure			203	46	2	35	47	.227	.315	.341
Leading Off			53	13	0	7	10	.245	.302	.344
Runners On			86	23	0	19	19	.267	.360	.387
Runners/Scor. Pos.			49	12	0	18	14	.245	.327	.417
First 9 Batters			393	86	6	48	92	.219	.310	.306
Second 9 Batters			26	6	0	1	5	.231	.308	.250
All Batters Thereafter			0	0	0	0	0	—	—	—

Loves to face: Todd Benzinger (.063, 1-for-16)
Juan Samuel (0-for-11)
Matt Williams (0-for-10)

Hates to face: Kevin Mitchell (.444, 4-for-9, 3 2B)
Tom Pagnozzi (3-for-3, 2 2B)
Glenn Wilson (.500, 3-for-6, 2 HR)

Miscellaneous statistics: Ground outs-to-air outs ratio: 1.21 last season, 1.18 for career. . . . Induced 6 double-play ground outs in 109 opportunities (one per 18.2). . . . Allowed 16 doubles, 2 triples in 117.1 innings. . . . Stranded 19 inherited runners, allowed 21 to score (48%), 2d-worst rate in N.L. . . . Opposing base stealers: 8-for-10 (80%); 0 pickoffs, 3 balks.

Comments: Among active relief pitchers with at least 200 career innings out of the bullpen, only two have lower figures than Harris in both ERA (2.19) and opponents' batting average (.213). They are Rob Dibble and Dennis Eckersley. . . . Batting average by opposing right-handed batters was the 5th-lowest allowed by any National League pitcher over the last 16 years (minimum: 175 BFP). Trouble was, left-handers hit .277 against him, and 52 percent of the batters he faced hit from that side. The lefty/righty disparity of 121 points was the second largest in the majors last season. . . . Pitching coaches who preach against letting the leadoff hitter reach base would love Harris. In his career, opponents have a .244 on-base average when leading off an inning. Only one pitcher in the majors over the past 16 years has done better (Erik Hanson, .235). . . . Harris has a career rate of one home run allowed every 70 at bats, but he has allowed only one home run in 349 career at-bats during day games. . . . Only three of 14 career home runs allowed have been hit with runners on base. . . . He's been 2–0 against the Astros in each of his three seasons in the majors. . . . From August 31 through September 22, he stranded only one inherited runner, while allowing 10 to score. For you fans of relief pitchers' ERAs, let us point out that he lowered his ERA from 2.59 to 2.40 during that period.

Neal Heaton

Throws Left

Pittsburgh Pirates	W-L	ERA	AB	H	HR	BB	SO	BA	SA	OBA
Season	12-9	3.45	543	143	17	38	68	.263	.413	.311
vs. Left-Handers			90	28	4	10	13	.311	.522	.376
vs. Right-Handers			453	115	13	28	55	.254	.391	.297
vs. Ground-Ballers			234	61	5	13	28	.261	.385	.301
vs. Fly-Ballers			309	82	12	25	40	.265	.434	.318
Home Games	6-5	3.02	287	73	8	27	40	.254	.397	.316
Road Games	6-4	3.97	256	70	9	11	28	.273	.430	.305
Grass Fields	3-3	4.34	156	47	5	6	18	.301	.436	.331
Artificial Turf	9-6	3.15	387	96	12	32	50	.248	.403	.303
April	4-0	2.59	92	22	2	4	14	.239	.326	.268
May	4-1	3.16	112	28	2	10	14	.250	.384	.306
June	2-2	4.01	128	36	6	7	10	.281	.469	.316
July	0-4	6.75	73	21	4	6	12	.288	.507	.341
August	1-1	1.73	93	24	1	10	11	.258	.355	.337
Sept./Oct.	1-1	3.00	45	12	2	1	7	.267	.467	.283
Leading Off Inn.			144	44	7	9	17	.306	.500	.346
Bases Empty			345	92	11	23	43	.267	.414	.314
Runners On			198	51	6	15	25	.258	.409	.305
Runners/Scor. Pos.			107	28	3	11	10	.262	.402	.320
Runners On/2 Out			87	27	4	10	9	.310	.529	.388
Scor. Pos./2 Out			57	19	3	8	3	.333	.561	.424
Late-Inning Pressure			31	12	1	1	2	.387	.581	.394
Leading Off			10	5	0	0	0	.500	.600	.500
Runners On			11	4	1	0	1	.364	.727	.333
Runners/Scor. Pos.			6	2	1	0	1	.333	.833	.286
First 9 Batters			227	56	5	19	36	.247	.366	.304
Second 9 Batters			187	45	7	13	20	.241	.401	.292
All Batters Thereafter			129	42	5	6	12	.326	.512	.350

Loves to face: Kevin McReynolds (.125, 2-for-16)
Rafael Ramirez (.118, 2-for-17)
Garry Templeton (.136, 3-for-22)

Hates to face: George Bell (.409, 9-for-22, 3 2B, 3 HR)
Mark Carreon (.714, 5-for-7, 2 HR)
Luis Quinones (.750, 3-for-4, 2 HR, 1 SO)

Miscellaneous statistics: Ground outs-to-air outs ratio: 1.24 last season, 0.97 for career. . . . Induced 10 double-play ground outs in 87 opportunities (one per 8.7). . . . Allowed 26 doubles, 2 triples in 146.0 innings. . . . Allowed 14 first-inning runs in 24 starts (4.56 ERA). . . . Batting support: 4.29 runs per start. . . . Opposing base stealers: 15-for-28 (54%); 6 pickoffs, 1 balk.

Comments: The Pirates' only representative on last year's National League All-Star pitching staff, he had a poor second half and was unused in the Championship Series. . . . Won eight of his first nine starts, including each of his first six, and had posted a 10–2 record by June 24. He then lost his next six decisions to become the only pitcher in the majors last season with both a winning streak and a losing streak of at least six games. . . . His only start after August 20 came against New York on September 5 during the Mets' "We'll-never-hit-another-lefty" campaign. Heaton lasted five innings and won, 3–1. . . . If he's not choosy about his catcher, maybe he should be: Heaton had a 2.94 ERA in 67⅓ innings pitching to Mike LaValliere, but a 4.55 ERA in 59⅓ innings pitching to Don Slaught. In 1989, he had a 1.41 ERA in 38⅓ innings with LaValliere. . . . Has a career record of 5–0 against the Cardinals. He defeated both the Braves and Mets last season, leaving Cleveland as the only major league club he has never defeated. . . . Did not pitch into the ninth inning in any of his 24 starts last season, and has completed only one of 53 starts over the last three years. . . . Left-handed batters hit .311 against him last season, a year after Heaton limited lefties to a .132 average, the lowest single-season average by lefties against any pitcher since 1975 (minimum: 125 plate appearances).

Jay Howell

Throws Right

Los Angeles Dodgers	W-L	ERA	AB	H	HR	BB	SO	BA	SA	OBA
Season	5-5	2.18	244	59	5	20	59	.242	.344	.315
vs. Left-Handers			149	36	3	10	41	.242	.349	.307
vs. Right-Handers			95	23	2	10	18	.242	.337	.327
vs. Ground-Ballers			98	24	2	6	26	.245	.347	.302
vs. Fly-Ballers			146	35	3	14	33	.240	.342	.323
Home Games	1-3	2.91	124	29	3	9	29	.234	.347	.296
Road Games	4-2	1.41	120	30	2	11	30	.250	.342	.333
Grass Fields	2-4	2.57	181	43	4	13	42	.238	.343	.307
Artificial Turf	3-1	1.06	63	16	1	7	17	.254	.349	.338
April	1-1	4.50	14	4	0	2	2	.286	.357	.375
May	0-2	4.05	30	12	0	2	4	.400	.467	.455
June	2-1	2.65	62	15	2	7	17	.242	.371	.338
July	0-0	0.82	36	5	1	2	11	.139	.250	.205
August	1-1	1.10	60	12	2	4	13	.200	.333	.262
Sept./Oct.	1-0	2.45	42	11	0	3	12	.262	.310	.326
Leading Off Inn.			57	16	4	2	13	.281	.526	.328
Bases Empty			136	32	5	7	37	.235	.375	.293
Runners On			108	27	0	13	22	.250	.306	.341
Runners/Scor. Pos.			68	17	0	9	12	.250	.309	.354
Runners On/2 Out			44	8	0	7	9	.182	.250	.308
Scor. Pos./2 Out			31	5	0	5	5	.161	.258	.297
Late-Inning Pressure			179	48	5	16	43	.268	.402	.348
Leading Off			41	12	4	2	8	.293	.610	.356
Runners On			80	23	0	11	16	.287	.363	.387
Runners/Scor. Pos.			52	15	0	7	9	.288	.365	.393
First 9 Batters			234	55	5	18	59	.235	.325	.306
Second 9 Batters			10	4	0	2	0	.400	.800	.500
All Batters Thereafter			0	0	0	0	0	—	—	—

Loves to face: Ken Caminiti (0-for-8, 5 SO)
Rob Thompson (.091, 1-for-11, 6 SO)
Glenn Wilson (0-for-8)

Hates to face: George Bell (.833, 5-for-6, 1 HR, 1 SO)
Paul O'Neill (.714, 5-for-7, 1 HR)

Miscellaneous statistics: Ground outs-to-air outs ratio: 0.76 last season, 1.03 for career. . . . Induced 6 double-play ground outs in 51 opportunities (one per 8.5). . . . Allowed 8 doubles, 1 triple in 66.0 innings. . . . Stranded 6 inherited runners, allowed 9 to score (40%). . . . Opposing base stealers: 10-for-11 (91%), shared 5th-highest rate in N.L.; 1 pickoff, 1 balk.

Comments: Has played under Tommy Lasorda for three straight years after playing for nine different managers in his first seven seasons in majors. . . . With the Dodgers leading their league in complete games once again—they've done it seven years in a row, an all-time major league record—Howell doesn't pile up saves like some other closers. Dodgers remain the only team that has never had a pitcher save 30 games in a season. . . . His 1.92 ERA in his three years with the Dodgers is the lowest in team history among pitchers who have pitched at least 200 innings in the Blue. . . . Opponents batted 99 points higher in Late-Inning Pressure Situations (.268) than in other at-bats (.169) last season, a breakdown that stands in contrast with his earlier career. Career numbers through 1990: .240 in LIPS, .261 in other at-bats. . . . Allowed only one run in 25⅓ innings with Rick Dempsey as his catcher last season: a solo home run by Dave Justice. . . . Limited the National League's top 10 hitters to a .125 mark (2-for-16 with no extra-base hits) last season. . . . Opponents have averaged one home run every 63 at-bats against Howell during his career but have never hit a grand-slam against him in a total of 61 at-bats with the bases loaded. Does that mean that the second batter to face him with the bases loaded this season will hit a home run? What if it's Jim Deshaies?

Ken Howell

Throws Right

Philadelphia Phillies	W-L	ERA	AB	H	HR	BB	SO	BA	SA	OBA
Season	8-7	4.64	408	106	12	49	70	.260	.422	.343
vs. Left-Handers			254	76	7	36	33	.299	.469	.385
vs. Right-Handers			154	30	5	13	37	.195	.344	.271
vs. Ground-Ballers			231	60	4	23	42	.260	.372	.331
vs. Fly-Ballers			177	46	8	26	28	.260	.486	.358
Home Games	4-4	5.43	243	69	9	29	32	.284	.481	.364
Road Games	4-3	3.57	165	37	3	20	38	.224	.333	.312
Grass Fields	3-1	3.33	84	18	2	10	19	.214	.321	.298
Artificial Turf	5-6	5.03	324	88	10	39	51	.272	.448	.354
April	2-2	3.28	91	22	1	14	18	.242	.341	.352
May	3-1	4.31	113	25	4	13	18	.221	.407	.302
June	3-2	3.98	156	42	4	13	27	.269	.417	.329
July	0-2	13.50	31	11	3	5	4	.355	.677	.444
August	0-0	9.00	17	6	0	4	3	.353	.529	.476
Sept./Oct.	0-0	—	0	0	0	0	0	—	—	—
Leading Off Inn.			97	21	1	14	16	.216	.289	.315
Bases Empty			231	64	5	28	36	.277	.407	.355
Runners On			177	42	7	21	34	.237	.441	.327
Runners/Scor. Pos.			97	23	4	12	17	.237	.443	.318
Runners On/2 Out			75	18	2	14	14	.240	.427	.360
Scor. Pos./2 Out			50	13	2	8	9	.260	.520	.362
Late-Inning Pressure			29	6	1	2	5	.207	.414	.258
Leading Off			7	1	0	2	2	.143	.143	.333
Runners On			10	1	0	0	1	.100	.200	.100
Runners/Scor. Pos.			5	1	0	0	0	.200	.400	.200
First 9 Batters			145	37	7	14	24	.255	.441	.321
Second 9 Batters			130	38	1	18	23	.292	.400	.387
All Batters Thereafter			133	31	4	17	23	.233	.421	.322

Loves to face: Andres Galarraga (0-for-10, 2 BB, 8 SO)
Rafael Ramirez (0-for-12)
Andy Van Slyke (.143, 3-for-21)

Hates to face: Bobby Bonilla (.412, 7-for-17, 1 HR)
Mackey Sasser (.600, 6-for-10)
Mike Scioscia (.500, 5-for-10, 1 HR)

Miscellaneous statistics: Ground outs-to-air outs ratio: 1.82 last season, 4th-highest rate in N.L.; 1.41 for career. . . . Induced 6 double-play ground outs in 87 opportunities (one per 14.5). . . . Allowed 26 doubles, 2 triples in 106.2 innings. . . . Allowed 16 first-inning runs in 18 starts (6.00 ERA). . . . Batting support: 3.94 runs per start. . . . Opposing base stealers: 11-for-15 (73%); 0 pickoffs, 0 balks.

Comments: Posted a winning record for the first time in his seven-year career, but he did it the hard way. His 4.64 ERA was the highest among the 39 National League pitchers who had winning records covering at least 10 decisions. . . . In six previous seasons, he was 30–41 with a 3.80 ERA. . . . Owns a career rate of 8.06 strikeouts per nine innings. That stands ninth among active pitchers with 500 or more innings. . . . His career ground outs-to-air outs ratio (1.41) is somewhat unusual in that strikeout pitchers generally tend to be fly-ball pitchers. Last season, for instance, the 11 major league pitchers who pitched at least 100 innings and averaged at least eight strikeouts per nine innings had a composite G/A ratio of 0.90. . . . Won eight of 11 decisions through June 22, but the rest of the year was a disaster: four losses, a no-decision, and a 10.53 ERA in five starts sandwiched around two trips onto the disabled list. . . . Opponents' career breakdown: .233 with the bases empty, .243 with runners on base, .264 with runners in scoring position. . . . Opponents batted 60 points higher in home games (.284) than in road games (.224) last season, the 5th-largest difference in the majors. . . . Opposing left-handers (.299) hit 104 points higher than right-handers (.195) last season, also the 5th-largest spread in the majors. . . . Howell has held right-handed batters below .200 in each of the last three seasons (.188 composite over those three years).

Bruce Hurst

Throws Left

San Diego Padres	W-L	ERA	AB	H	HR	BB	SO	BA	SA	OBA
Season	11-9	3.14	823	188	21	63	162	.228	.357	.284
vs. Left-Handers			165	38	7	17	43	.230	.400	.302
vs. Right-Handers			658	150	14	46	119	.228	.347	.279
vs. Ground-Ballers			404	87	8	24	86	.215	.309	.261
vs. Fly-Ballers			419	101	13	39	76	.241	.403	.305
Home Games	7-3	2.66	436	94	11	33	97	.216	.335	.270
Road Games	4-6	3.72	387	94	10	30	65	.243	.382	.299
Grass Fields	9-4	2.96	547	119	14	45	115	.218	.344	.278
Artificial Turf	2-5	3.52	276	69	7	18	47	.250	.384	.296
April	0-3	4.55	102	22	3	8	14	.216	.363	.273
May	3-2	3.63	149	39	4	10	35	.262	.389	.308
June	1-2	6.21	116	33	4	13	24	.284	.466	.359
July	2-1	2.79	151	29	6	10	27	.192	.338	.242
August	2-1	1.89	139	30	3	14	29	.216	.338	.288
Sept./Oct.	3-0	1.33	166	35	1	8	33	.211	.283	.247
Leading Off Inn.			206	46	7	24	39	.223	.379	.307
Bases Empty			508	118	14	37	104	.232	.356	.286
Runners On			315	70	7	26	58	.222	.359	.281
Runners/Scor. Pos.			175	39	5	17	38	.223	.377	.290
Runners On/2 Out			139	37	6	11	25	.266	.468	.320
Scor. Pos./2 Out			92	25	5	9	16	.272	.500	.337
Late-Inning Pressure			93	27	4	8	12	.290	.462	.347
Leading Off			24	7	1	3	1	.292	.458	.370
Runners On			37	10	2	4	8	.270	.486	.341
Runners/Scor. Pos.			30	8	2	1	7	.267	.533	.290
First 9 Batters			268	53	6	21	69	.198	.321	.258
Second 9 Batters			272	58	6	16	59	.213	.338	.257
All Batters Thereafter			283	77	9	26	34	.272	.410	.333

Loves to face: Todd Benzinger (.059, 1-for-17)
Jeff Hamilton (0-for-17)
Ozzie Smith (.105, 2-for-19)

Hates to face: Barry Bonds (.476, 10-for-21, 2 HR)
Will Clark (.435, 10-for-23, 2 HR)
Kevin Mitchell (.313, 5-for-16, 3 HR)

Miscellaneous statistics: Ground outs-to-air outs ratio: 1.39 last season, 1.16 for career. . . . Induced 21 double-play ground outs in 148 opportunities (one per 7.0), 5th-best rate in N.L. . . . Allowed 35 doubles, 4 triples in 223.2 innings. . . . Allowed 16 first-inning runs in 33 starts (3.55 ERA). . . . Batting support: 3.79 runs per start. . . . Opposing base stealers: 19-for-26 (73%); 4 pickoffs, 1 balk.

Comments: One of only four opening-day starters in the National League to finish the season with a winning record. The others: Doug Drabek, Dwight Gooden, and Tom Browning. . . . Opponents' overall batting average was the lowest of his career. . . . Threw four shutouts last season to tie Dave Stewart, Roger Clemens, and Mike Morgan for the major league lead. Hurst's first shutout wasn't until July 24; he salvaged a winning season with a 6–1 record and a 0.89 ERA over his last 13 starts. . . . Left-handed batters hit him hard early in the season: their average had climbed to .319 by July 14. But Hurst got even, allowing lefties only one hit (a double by Paul O'Neill) in their last 29 at-bats against him. . . . He's pitched over 200 innings in seven of the last eight years. Only Frank Viola has topped 200 innings in each of the last eight. . . . Career breakdown: 72–42 in home games, 42–51 on the road. . . . In nine seasons with the Red Sox, opponents batted .278 at Fenway Park; in two seasons with San Diego, opponents have hit .221 at Jack Murphy Stadium. . . . We know that his home stadium is a strikeout-enhancing environment, but Hurst is taking things to an extreme with 90 strikeouts in 165 career plate appearances. That's the highest rate among active National League pitchers who have had at least 100 trips to the plate. He has 15 sacrifices and 13 walks but only 11 hits.

Danny Jackson

Throws Left

Cincinnati Reds	W-L	ERA	AB	H	HR	BB	SO	BA	SA	OBA
Season	6-6	3.61	448	119	11	40	76	.266	.386	.325
vs. Left-Handers			85	20	2	11	16	.235	.365	.330
vs. Right-Handers			363	99	9	29	60	.273	.391	.324
vs. Ground-Ballers			189	48	3	11	35	.254	.328	.291
vs. Fly-Ballers			259	71	8	29	41	.274	.429	.349
Home Games	2-3	3.83	203	50	6	17	36	.246	.379	.306
Road Games	4-3	3.41	245	69	5	23	40	.282	.392	.341
Grass Fields	3-2	3.61	182	50	3	15	33	.275	.368	.327
Artificial Turf	3-4	3.60	266	69	8	25	43	.259	.398	.324
April	0-0	10.80	17	7	1	1	2	.412	.588	.444
May	0-1	2.13	48	13	0	4	2	.271	.333	.321
June	2-1	3.60	124	33	3	16	19	.266	.411	.345
July	2-0	1.33	74	14	2	9	15	.189	.284	.286
August	1-0	5.14	30	9	0	1	5	.300	.433	.323
Sept./Oct.	1-4	4.38	155	43	5	9	33	.277	.400	.317
Leading Off Inn.			113	28	1	11	19	.248	.319	.315
Bases Empty			269	73	4	21	44	.271	.375	.324
Runners On			179	46	7	19	32	.257	.402	.327
Runners/Scor. Pos.			112	28	1	12	23	.250	.286	.321
Runners On/2 Out			73	18	3	5	14	.247	.384	.304
Scor. Pos./2 Out			51	12	0	4	10	.235	.235	.304
Late-Inning Pressure			36	10	2	1	8	.278	.444	.289
Leading Off			12	3	1	0	3	.250	.500	.250
Runners On			7	2	0	0	1	.286	.286	.250
Runners/Scor. Pos.			3	1	0	0	0	.333	.333	.250
First 9 Batters			173	45	3	15	31	.260	.364	.319
Second 9 Batters			150	41	2	13	24	.273	.387	.329
All Batters Thereafter			125	33	6	12	21	.264	.416	.329

Loves to face: Gary Redus (0-for-17, 4 BB)
Darryl Strawberry (.071, 1-for-14, 2 BB)
Dickie Thon (0-for-11)

Hates to face: Kevin Bass (.500, 5-for-10)
Craig Biggio (.667, 6-for-9)
Ken Caminiti (.455, 5-for-11, 1 HR)

Miscellaneous statistics: Ground outs-to-air outs ratio: 1.58 last season, 1.69 for career. . . . Induced 11 double-play ground outs in 86 opportunities (one per 7.8). . . . Allowed 13 doubles, 4 triples in 117.1 innings. . . . Allowed 4 first-inning runs in 21 starts (1.77 ERA, 3d lowest in N.L.) . . . Batting support: 3.91 runs per start. . . . Opposing base stealers: 15-for-18 (83%); 2 pickoffs, 1 balk.

Comments: One of two players to be placed on the disabled list three separate times last season. The other: "Hamstrings" Hernandez. . . . The only pitcher on last year's Reds World Series roster who had previously experienced the Fall Classic. Now the same can be said of his position on the Cubs' staff. . . . Wrigley Warning: he's 15–25 with a 4.38 ERA lifetime in day games, 57–49, 3.38 at night. Cubs played 83 day games last season, 20 more than the nearest total (Giants and A's). . . . He has pitched 19 innings at Wrigley Field without allowing a home run there. . . . Averaged 5.49 innings per start last season, 5th-lowest rate among National League pitchers (minimum: 20 starts). . . . No left-handed pitcher has shut out the Pirates in their home cove since Jackson did it on August 22, 1988. . . . Jackson never allowed a grand-slam home run until 1989; he's allowed three in the past two years. Opponents have a .359 career batting average with bases loaded. . . . Has not thrown a complete-game victory in 42 starts since September 1988. . . . A brief review: Jackson was 23–8 in 1988, but he's 72–74 for his career. Only seven other pitchers in major league history have ever had a "plus-15" (or better) season in a sub-.500 career. Three of them were pre-1900; the others are George McConnell (25–10 in 1915, 41–51 career), Larry Benton (25–9 in 1928, 127–128 career), Bobo Newsom (21–5 in 1940, 211–222 career), and Rich Dotson (22–7 in 1983, 111–113 career).

Les Lancaster

Throws Right

Chicago Cubs	W-L	ERA	AB	H	HR	BB	SO	BA	SA	OBA
Season	9-5	4.62	427	121	11	40	65	.283	.412	.342
vs. Left-Handers			228	65	4	30	30	.285	.390	.367
vs. Right-Handers			199	56	7	10	35	.281	.437	.313
vs. Ground-Ballers			180	44	1	18	33	.244	.317	.310
vs. Fly-Ballers			247	77	10	22	32	.312	.482	.366
Home Games	4-3	5.37	225	65	6	19	36	.289	.431	.343
Road Games	5-2	3.81	202	56	5	21	29	.277	.391	.342
Grass Fields	6-4	4.92	324	92	9	29	51	.284	.429	.342
Artificial Turf	3-1	3.71	103	29	2	11	14	.282	.359	.345
April	1-1	2.13	48	12	1	5	7	.250	.333	.315
May	2-1	4.91	121	39	3	11	16	.322	.471	.383
June	3-2	6.75	96	31	3	14	17	.323	.458	.398
July	1-1	6.75	69	21	1	6	10	.304	.391	.360
August	0-0	2.45	16	6	0	0	3	.375	.563	.375
Sept./Oct.	2-0	2.05	77	12	3	4	12	.156	.299	.195
Leading Off Inn.			100	28	2	3	18	.280	.400	.301
Bases Empty			228	59	7	17	40	.259	.404	.313
Runners On			199	62	4	23	25	.312	.422	.374
Runners/Scor. Pos.			122	34	4	17	17	.279	.443	.354
Runners On/2 Out			95	29	1	13	10	.305	.400	.389
Scor. Pos./2 Out			62	14	1	10	7	.226	.339	.333
Late-Inning Pressure			128	38	2	13	18	.297	.383	.362
Leading Off			31	10	1	1	3	.323	.516	.344
Runners On			63	19	1	8	8	.302	.349	.380
Runners/Scor. Pos.			41	10	1	6	6	.244	.317	.340
First 9 Batters			292	85	7	29	53	.291	.414	.352
Second 9 Batters			107	26	3	10	11	.243	.393	.308
All Batters Thereafter			28	10	1	1	1	.357	.464	.379

Loves to face: Billy Hatcher (0-for-9)
Dickie Thon (.083, 1-for-12)
Jose Uribe (0-for-10, 3 BB)

Hates to face: Howard Johnson (.357, 10-for-28, 3 HR)
Darryl Strawberry (.450, 9-for-20, 2 HR)
Milt Thompson (.444, 8-for-18)

Miscellaneous statistics: Ground outs-to-air outs ratio: 1.18 last season, 1.01 for career. . . . Induced 7 double-play ground outs in 94 opportunities (one per 13.4). . . . Allowed 20 doubles, 1 triple in 109.0 innings. . . . Stranded 27 inherited runners, allowed 17 to score (61%). . . . Opposing base stealers: 4-for-7 (57%); 1 pickoff, 0 balks.

Comments: Remember when Lancaster stood the National League on its ear in the summer of '89? A 1.36 ERA with eight saves, a .205 opponents' batting average with runners on base, and a .162 opponents' average with runners in scoring position? All of it receded to a distant memory in 1990. . . . He had his most trouble at the time of the team's greatest need, when Mitch Williams was on the disabled list (June 12–July 12). During that 30-day span, Lancaster allowed 20 earned runs and 28 hits in 17⅓ innings. . . . At least he could count on the Braves to help him out; he had the lowest ERA in the league vs. Atlanta (0.73). . . . Which National League pitchers were most often used in long relief last season? Here are the N.L. relievers who most often faced 10 or more batters in a game: Mark Grant (14 times), Lancaster (13), Don Carman (12), Paul Assenmacher (11), Xavier Hernandez (11). . . . One of eight National League pitchers with both a shutout and a save last season. . . . One of three National League pitchers who registered winning records with ERAs over 4.50 last season (minimum: 10 decisions). . . . As a batter, he's not exactly Rickey Henderson: he's 0-for-22 when leading off innings, with no walks and 15 strikeouts. . . . Has the highest career total of fielding chances (90) among active pitchers who have never committed an error. Maybe that's what inspired Zimmer to put him in the outfield one day last summer.

Bill Landrum

Throws Right

Pittsburgh Pirates	W-L	ERA	AB	H	HR	BB	SO	BA	SA	OBA
Season	7-3	2.13	263	69	4	21	39	.262	.342	.314
vs. Left-Handers			137	37	2	13	16	.270	.350	.329
vs. Right-Handers			126	32	2	8	23	.254	.333	.296
vs. Ground-Ballers			105	29	2	8	19	.276	.371	.322
vs. Fly-Ballers			158	40	2	13	20	.253	.323	.308
Home Games	4-2	1.93	136	37	1	9	20	.272	.316	.315
Road Games	3-1	2.36	127	32	3	12	19	.252	.370	.312
Grass Fields	1-0	2.20	60	13	3	4	10	.217	.417	.262
Artificial Turf	6-3	2.11	203	56	1	17	29	.276	.320	.329
April	0-0	0.87	37	7	1	1	9	.189	.297	.205
May	1-0	1.20	52	11	1	2	5	.212	.327	.232
June	1-1	3.09	44	14	0	7	8	.318	.341	.412
July	1-1	2.35	57	16	0	4	9	.281	.316	.328
August	1-1	5.40	41	16	2	5	4	.390	.585	.457
Sept./Oct.	3-0	0.00	32	5	0	2	4	.156	.156	.206
Leading Off Inn.			59	21	2	4	6	.356	.492	.397
Bases Empty			132	39	3	11	15	.295	.417	.350
Runners On			131	30	1	10	24	.229	.267	.278
Runners/Scor. Pos.			83	21	0	7	11	.253	.277	.301
Runners On/2 Out			52	10	0	6	9	.192	.212	.276
Scor. Pos./2 Out			36	7	0	5	6	.194	.222	.293
Late-Inning Pressure			117	33	0	16	17	.282	.342	.363
Leading Off			24	10	0	3	2	.417	.500	.481
Runners On			70	16	0	8	11	.229	.257	.300
Runners/Scor. Pos.			55	12	0	6	7	.218	.255	.286
First 9 Batters			256	65	4	21	38	.254	.332	.307
Second 9 Batters			7	4	0	0	1	.571	.714	.571
All Batters Thereafter			0	0	0	0	0	—	—	—

Loves to face: Kevin Bass (0-for-10, 1 BB)
Darren Daulton (0-for-9)
Jose Oquendo (0-for-9)

Hates to face: Billy Hatcher (.643, 9-for-14)
Kevin McReynolds (.636, 7-for-11)
Juan Samuel (.429, 6-for-14)

Miscellaneous statistics: Ground outs-to-air outs ratio: 1.77 last season, 1.35 for career. . . . Induced 9 double-play ground outs in 66 opportunities (one per 7.3). . . . Allowed 3 doubles, 3 triples in 71.2 innings. . . . Stranded 20 inherited runners, allowed 10 to score (67%). . . . Opposing base stealers: 8-for-10 (80%); 0 pickoffs, 1 balk.

Comments: Dig in, boys: Landrum has faced 1013 batters in the majors but has never hit one with a pitch. That's the most batters faced by any active pacifist. . . . But he gets tough at the right times: Opponents have a .208 career batting average in Late-Inning Pressure Situations, compared to a .307 mark at other times. That 99-point difference is the largest in the majors by any pitcher over the last five seasons. . . . Last year's .282 average in LIPS was by far the highest of his career. . . . Recorded his 12th save of the season on July 1, but would save only one game in 26 relief appearances after that. . . . Has allowed only 10 home runs in 243⅓ career innings; no player has dinged him twice. . . . Opponents have a .419 career batting average in 31 at-bats with the bases loaded. . . . Opponents have a .327 career average when leading off innings, 2d highest among active pitchers who have faced at least 200 leadoff batters. Dennis Powell (.335) has the highest. . . . National League managers, now hear this: This right-handed pitcher is much tougher on left-handed batters (.239 career batting average) than on right-handers (.292). Use your pinch hitters accordingly. . . . Born on August 17, 1958, a day on which the Pirates dropped a doubleheader at Cincinnati, with the Reds scoring winning runs in their last at-bat in each game. Little Bill determined then and there that he would be the Pirates' closer.

Craig Lefferts

Throws Left

San Diego Padres	W-L	ERA	AB	H	HR	BB	SO	BA	SA	OBA
Season	7-5	2.52	298	68	10	22	60	.228	.352	.283
vs. Left-Handers			87	18	1	8	18	.207	.241	.281
vs. Right-Handers			211	50	9	14	42	.237	.398	.283
vs. Ground-Ballers			121	32	1	6	24	.264	.314	.299
vs. Fly-Ballers			177	36	9	16	36	.203	.379	.272
Home Games	4-2	2.39	139	32	5	8	33	.230	.345	.270
Road Games	3-3	2.63	159	36	5	14	27	.226	.358	.293
Grass Fields	7-5	3.02	243	57	9	19	49	.235	.362	.289
Artificial Turf	0-0	0.56	55	11	1	3	11	.200	.309	.254
April	1-0	1.17	28	4	1	0	8	.143	.286	.143
May	1-1	1.84	49	6	2	5	11	.122	.265	.204
June	3-1	3.09	89	19	3	9	17	.213	.337	.286
July	1-2	4.15	52	16	1	3	11	.308	.365	.351
August	0-0	1.46	45	12	2	2	4	.267	.467	.298
Sept./Oct.	1-1	2.35	35	11	1	3	9	.314	.400	.368
Leading Off Inn.			62	12	2	3	12	.194	.306	.242
Bases Empty			157	34	7	9	34	.217	.389	.263
Runners On			141	34	3	13	26	.241	.312	.303
Runners/Scor. Pos.			88	21	3	11	16	.239	.341	.320
Runners On/2 Out			70	15	2	6	13	.214	.314	.276
Scor. Pos./2 Out			48	10	2	5	8	.208	.333	.283
Late-Inning Pressure			231	57	8	17	38	.247	.377	.300
Leading Off			46	10	2	1	6	.217	.370	.250
Runners On			116	31	3	11	18	.267	.353	.328
Runners/Scor. Pos.			79	20	3	10	13	.253	.367	.333
First 9 Batters			281	61	9	21	58	.217	.338	.273
Second 9 Batters			17	7	1	1	2	.412	.588	.444
All Batters Thereafter			0	0	0	0	0	—	—	—

Loves to face: Mark Carreon (0-for-9, 5 SO)
Len Dykstra (.071, 1-for-14, 1 2B)
Ozzie Smith (.087, 2-for-23)

Hates to face: Bill Doran (.483, 14-for-29)
Howard Johnson (.500, 6-for-12, 6 BB, 4 SO)
R. J. Reynolds (.769, 10-for-13)

Miscellaneous statistics: Ground outs-to-air outs ratio: 0.80 last season, 0.83 for career. . . . Induced 4 double-play ground outs in 66 opportunities (one per 16.5). . . . Allowed 7 doubles, 0 triples in 78.2 innings. . . . Stranded 33 inherited runners, allowed 10 to score (77%). . . . Opposing base stealers: 3-for-5 (60%); 0 pickoffs, 0 balks.

Comments: Has pitched in 50 or more games in each of his first eight seasons in the majors. The major league record for consecutive seasons pitching in at least 50 games is 10, set by Ron Perranoski, 1961–70. Perranoski's streak, like Lefferts's, grew from the start of his career. Jesse Orosco and Lee Smith currently have 50-game streaks of nine years, but their streaks did not start with their rookie seasons. . . . Established a new single-season high in saves for the third successive year. . . . Has lowered his ERA in each of those three years as well: 3.83 in 1987, followed by 2.92, 2.69, 2.52. . . . Opponents have hit for a higher average in night games than they have in day games in each of his eight seasons in the majors, the longest streak of its kind by any pitcher over the last 16 years. Opponents' career averages: .217 in day games, .251 at night. . . . Other career breakdowns show him to be a pitcher who gets tougher as the situation does: .248 with the bases empty, .225 with runners on base, .208 with runners in scoring position, .174 with two outs and RISP. . . . Needs 16 games to break Eric Show's team record of 309 games by a pitcher. . . . What a difference a May makes: Lefferts has a 38–29 career record in other months, but is 1–15 in May. . . . Has a career record of 0–7 vs. the Mets. . . . Yep, five of those losses to the Mets came in May.

Charlie Leibrandt

Throws Left

Atlanta Braves	W-L	ERA	AB	H	HR	BB	SO	BA	SA	OBA
Season	9-11	3.16	628	164	9	35	76	.261	.374	.302
vs. Left-Handers			105	22	3	6	14	.210	.314	.263
vs. Right-Handers			523	142	6	29	62	.272	.386	.309
vs. Ground-Ballers			302	84	4	14	45	.278	.391	.313
vs. Fly-Ballers			326	80	5	21	31	.245	.359	.292
Home Games	6-5	2.59	340	90	4	17	33	.265	.353	.298
Road Games	3-6	3.82	288	74	5	18	43	.257	.399	.305
Grass Fields	8-8	2.66	505	126	6	27	61	.250	.345	.289
Artificial Turf	1-3	5.34	123	38	3	8	15	.309	.496	.351
April	0-0	—	0	0	0	0	0	—	—	—
May	0-0	—	0	0	0	0	0	—	—	—
June	3-1	2.72	181	48	1	6	16	.265	.348	.293
July	1-3	5.13	126	34	4	12	26	.270	.421	.331
August	2-4	3.60	138	38	2	7	13	.275	.413	.313
Sept./Oct.	3-3	1.89	183	44	2	10	21	.240	.339	.281
Leading Off Inn.			158	39	3	5	19	.247	.361	.274
Bases Empty			371	96	4	11	47	.259	.369	.282
Runners On			257	68	5	24	29	.265	.381	.328
Runners/Scor. Pos.			161	44	4	15	19	.273	.391	.328
Runners On/2 Out			113	31	1	13	15	.274	.345	.359
Scor. Pos./2 Out			81	24	1	8	10	.296	.370	.360
Late-Inning Pressure			59	13	0	1	6	.220	.237	.233
Leading Off			15	3	0	1	2	.200	.267	.250
Runners On			24	1	0	0	3	.042	.042	.042
Runners/Scor. Pos.			9	0	0	0	2	.000	.000	.000
First 9 Batters			197	58	3	11	26	.294	.416	.333
Second 9 Batters			200	51	4	13	28	.255	.405	.302
All Batters Thereafter			231	55	2	11	22	.238	.312	.273

Loves to face: Hubie Brooks (.071, 1-for-14)
Alfredo Griffin (.175, 7-for-40)
Howard Johnson (.100, 1-for-10)

Hates to face: Daryl Boston (.400, 4-for-10, 2 3B)
Gary Redus (.444, 8-for-18)
Mike Sharperson (.357, 5-for-14, 2 2B)

Miscellaneous statistics: Ground outs-to-air outs ratio: 0.98 last season, 1.16 for career. . . . Induced 10 double-play ground outs in 112 opportunities (one per 11.2). . . . Allowed 38 doubles, 3 triples in 162.1 innings. . . . Allowed 21 first-inning runs in 24 starts (4.50 ERA). . . . Batting support: 4.17 runs per start. . . . Opposing base stealers: 21-for-24 (88%); 3 pickoffs, 3 balks.

Comments: His 3.16 ERA stood out among the Braves like Sinead O'Connor in the cast of *Hair*. Atlanta had the worst ERA (4.58) in the majors. . . . His 9–11 season in 1990 was a far cry from his 5–11 experience with Kansas City the previous season. With the Braves, his record was really a reflection of his team. Other National League starters who had ERAs within 15 points of Leibrandt's combined for a .583 winning percentage. Typical was Bruce Hurst, who had an 11–9 record with an ERA just 0.02 lower than Leibrandt's. . . . Averaged just 1.94 walks per nine innings, the 4th-lowest rate in the majors (minimum: 162 innings), behind Danny Darwin (1.72), Ed Whitson (1.85), and Allan Anderson (1.86). Prior to 1990, Leibrandt had a career rate of 2.74 walks per nine. . . . Made his season debut on June 3 after spending the first 55 days of the season on the disabled list. . . . ERA in the first inning of his 24 starts was 4.50; opponents hit .314 and slugged .431. All those figures are highs against Leibrandt in any inning. . . . Traded from one of baseball's worst home-run parks, Royals Stadium, to one of the best, The Lauching Pad, but cut his home run yield from 13 (in 161 innings in 1989) to nine (in 162⅓ innings in 1990). . . . Brings into 1991 a streak of 52⅔ consecutive innings at Atlanta Stadium without allowing a home run; the last round-tripper he allowed there was hit by Mike Fitzgerald on July 14.

Derek Lilliquist

Throws Left

Braves/Padres	W-L	ERA	AB	H	HR	BB	SO	BA	SA	OBA
Season	5-11	5.31	478	136	16	42	63	.285	.437	.343
vs. Left-Handers			92	30	3	9	23	.326	.478	.392
vs. Right-Handers			386	106	13	33	40	.275	.427	.331
vs. Ground-Ballers			232	71	7	15	31	.306	.453	.349
vs. Fly-Ballers			246	65	9	27	32	.264	.423	.337
Home Games	2-6	4.71	223	58	9	18	38	.260	.426	.316
Road Games	3-5	5.85	255	78	7	24	25	.306	.447	.366
Grass Fields	3-9	6.07	322	94	12	28	47	.292	.457	.347
Artificial Turf	2-2	3.86	156	42	4	14	16	.269	.397	.333
April	0-3	7.98	63	22	3	4	11	.349	.556	.388
May	2-3	3.66	146	34	5	11	19	.233	.397	.281
June	0-2	16.43	40	19	2	4	4	.475	.675	.522
July	0-0	5.84	49	15	3	5	4	.306	.510	.364
August	1-0	2.95	65	15	1	8	7	.231	.323	.315
Sept./Oct.	2-3	4.55	115	31	2	10	18	.270	.374	.339
Leading Off Inn.			117	35	5	9	17	.299	.479	.359
Bases Empty			272	77	8	21	39	.283	.426	.341
Runners On			206	59	8	21	24	.286	.451	.345
Runners/Scor. Pos.			113	30	5	18	17	.265	.451	.353
Runners On/2 Out			84	17	3	8	13	.202	.333	.272
Scor. Pos./2 Out			52	12	2	8	8	.231	.385	.333
Late-Inning Pressure			23	5	1	4	5	.217	.348	.333
Leading Off			8	4	1	1	0	.500	.875	.556
Runners On			9	1	0	1	2	.111	.111	.200
Runners/Scor. Pos.			2	0	0	1	0	.000	.000	.333
First 9 Batters			222	64	8	20	33	.288	.432	.350
Second 9 Batters			143	46	4	12	20	.322	.462	.369
All Batters Thereafter			113	26	4	10	10	.230	.416	.296

Loves to face: Jose Lind (.100, 1-for-10)
Kevin McReynolds (0-for-9)
Paul O'Neill (0-for-9)

Hates to face: Todd Benzinger (.688, 11-for-16)
Will Clark (.526, 10-for-19, 2 HR)
Bip Roberts (.750, 6-for-8, 1 HR)

Miscellaneous statistics: Ground outs-to-air outs ratio: 0.74 last season, 0.77 for career. . . . Induced 9 double-play ground outs in 105 opportunities (one per 11.7). . . . Allowed 25 doubles, 0 triples in 122.0 innings. . . . Allowed 9 first-inning runs in 18 starts (4.50 ERA). . . . Batting support: 3.61 runs per start. . . . Opposing base stealers: 12-for-15 (80%); 1 pickoff, 3 balks.

Comments: The sixth selection of the first round in the 1987 amateur draft; selected just behind Jack McDowell, but ahead of Kevin Appier, Delino DeShields, Jack Armstrong, and Craig Biggio. . . . Has allowed 16 home runs in each of his two seasons in the majors. In each case, 13 were hit by right-handed batters and three by lefties. . . . Became the first pitcher to hit two home runs in a game since Jim Gott did it on May 12, 1985. He was, technically, the only pitcher to hit two home runs last season; Don Robinson connected twice but once as a pinch hitter. . . . We don't have much else to say about Lilliquist, so let's put this space to better use by sharing some of our favorite fun facts on the subject of good-hitting pitchers: In 1925, at the age of 37, Walter Johnson batted .433 (42-for-97), the single-season record for pitchers with 75 or more at-bats. . . . Years ago, pitchers who were out of the lineup were among the most frequent pinch hitters. Red Lucas won 157 games in his 16-year career in the majors (1923–38, mostly with Reds and Pirates), and he set a major league record of 114 pinch-hits that stood until Smoky Burgess broke it in 1965. . . . Red Ruffing had 273 career RBIs; no pitcher in history had more. That total exactly equalled his total of career victories. . . . Johnny Sain struck out only 20 times in 770 career at bats; in 1946, he came to bat 104 times without a strikeout or a walk! (Mickey Tettleton he ain't.)

Bill Long

Throws Right

White Sox/Cubs	W-L	ERA	AB	H	HR	BB	SO	BA	SA	OBA
Season	6-2	4.55	242	72	10	23	34	.298	.471	.361
vs. Left-Handers			122	40	5	14	17	.328	.533	.397
vs. Right-Handers			120	32	5	9	17	.267	.408	.323
vs. Ground-Ballers			113	32	3	11	18	.283	.416	.352
vs. Fly-Ballers			129	40	7	12	16	.310	.519	.369
Home Games	4-2	6.41	111	40	6	12	10	.360	.595	.427
Road Games	2-0	3.12	131	32	4	11	24	.244	.366	.303
Grass Fields	5-2	6.00	166	58	9	14	21	.349	.560	.403
Artificial Turf	1-0	2.01	76	14	1	9	13	.184	.276	.271
April	0-1	6.35	23	6	2	2	2	.261	.565	.320
May	2-0	4.00	69	23	2	5	13	.333	.464	.387
June	1-0	2.53	38	9	1	4	4	.237	.395	.310
July	1-0	2.89	35	8	1	4	7	.229	.314	.308
August	2-0	3.00	24	6	2	1	0	.250	.542	.280
Sept./Oct.	0-1	8.49	53	20	2	7	8	.377	.566	.450
Leading Off Inn.			56	20	1	5	8	.357	.464	.410
Bases Empty			127	40	3	11	17	.315	.425	.374
Runners On			115	32	7	12	17	.278	.522	.346
Runners/Scor. Pos.			64	11	2	11	13	.172	.281	.293
Runners On/2 Out			55	16	1	5	8	.291	.436	.350
Scor. Pos./2 Out			36	5	1	5	8	.139	.222	.244
Late-Inning Pressure			75	18	2	7	11	.240	.360	.305
Leading Off			20	7	1	0	3	.350	.650	.350
Runners On			33	6	1	6	4	.182	.273	.308
Runners/Scor. Pos.			20	2	0	6	2	.100	.100	.308
First 9 Batters			217	66	9	20	30	.304	.479	.366
Second 9 Batters			23	6	1	3	3	.261	.435	.346
All Batters Thereafter			2	0	0	0	1	.000	.000	.000

Loves to face: Gary Pettis (.071, 1-for-14)
Jim Presley (.083, 1-for-12, 6 SO)
Willie Randolph (.167, 3-for-18)

Hates to face: Wade Boggs (.588, 10-for-17, 3 2B, 2 3B)
Alvin Davis (.471, 8-for-17, 1 HR)
Larry Walker (3-for-3, 1 2B, 1 3B, 1 HR)

Miscellaneous statistics: Ground outs-to-air outs ratio: 1.00 last season, 1.13 for career. . . . Induced 6 double-play ground outs in 53 opportunities (one per 8.8). . . . Allowed 8 doubles, 2 triples in 61.1 innings. . . . Stranded 20 inherited runners, allowed 8 to score (71%). . . . Opposing base stealers: 11-for-16 (69%); 2 pickoffs, 0 balks.

Comments: Appropriately named pitcher has allowed 63 home runs in 517 innings, or one every 32 at-bats; that's approximately equal to the career home-run rate of Steve Garvey. Last year, he allowed a round-tripper every 24 at bats, which is up in Don Baylor territory. . . . Career breakdown: 16–22, 4.92 ERA as a starter; 11–5, 3.45 ERA as a reliever. . . . Stranded 82 percent of inherited runners (18-of-22) while with the Cubs. Among N.L. pitchers who inherited at least 20 runners, only Randy Myers and Lee Smith stranded a greater percentage. . . . Became the first player since Lynn McGlothen in 1981 to play for both the Cubs and White Sox in the same season. Five other pitchers have done that: Emmett O'Neill (1946), Turk Lown (1958), Bob Miller (1970), Phil Regan (1972), and Steve Renko (1977). Four nonpitchers have played for both Chicago clubs in the same season: Sammy Strang (1902), Lloyd Merriman (1955), Earl Averill, Jr. (1960), and Jimmy Stewart (1967). . . . Outside of Illinois, he has held opponents to a .263 career batting average; but he's been hit hard at both Comiskey Park (.291) and Wrigley Field (.374). . . . A .297 career batting average by opposing left-handed hitters will not look good on his resume. . . . Then again, maybe he can hook on with the Giants. Al Rosen's always looking for pitchers, and Rosen and Long share a common bond: They are two of the eight leap-year day babies in major league history. Rosen was born in 1924, Long in 1960. (And if Rosen's desperate enough, Steve Mingori's only 47.)

Greg Maddux

Throws Right

Chicago Cubs	W-L	ERA	AB	H	HR	BB	SO	BA	SA	OBA
Season	15-15	3.46	913	242	11	71	144	.265	.354	.319
vs. Left-Handers			564	164	6	53	81	.291	.376	.351
vs. Right-Handers			349	78	5	18	63	.223	.318	.267
vs. Ground-Ballers			406	99	3	26	75	.244	.305	.293
vs. Fly-Ballers			507	143	8	45	69	.282	.393	.340
Home Games	8-6	3.58	443	127	4	40	66	.287	.363	.344
Road Games	7-9	3.34	470	115	7	31	78	.245	.345	.295
Grass Fields	10-11	3.96	646	182	9	59	96	.282	.385	.342
Artificial Turf	5-4	2.28	267	60	2	12	48	.225	.277	.261
April	3-1	1.95	99	20	1	5	13	.202	.293	.245
May	1-3	5.12	125	37	0	6	18	.296	.376	.326
June	0-4	5.03	139	40	2	11	22	.288	.374	.340
July	3-1	3.86	147	38	5	14	23	.259	.401	.327
August	5-2	1.91	210	50	1	18	36	.238	.295	.299
Sept./Oct.	3-4	3.61	193	57	2	17	32	.295	.383	.354
Leading Off Inn.			224	59	4	20	39	.263	.344	.327
Bases Empty			533	130	5	37	94	.244	.310	.294
Runners On			380	112	6	34	50	.295	.416	.353
Runners/Scor. Pos.			209	59	5	27	35	.282	.416	.362
Runners On/2 Out			169	49	2	20	30	.290	.408	.375
Scor. Pos./2 Out			111	36	2	15	21	.324	.477	.414
Late-Inning Pressure			94	29	1	9	8	.309	.372	.375
Leading Off			23	10	0	3	1	.435	.478	.519
Runners On			47	13	0	3	3	.277	.277	.320
Runners/Scor. Pos.			26	9	0	3	2	.346	.346	.414
First 9 Batters			291	72	3	20	60	.247	.316	.295
Second 9 Batters			278	63	3	21	45	.227	.306	.280
All Batters Thereafter			344	107	5	30	39	.311	.424	.370

Loves to face: Charlie Hayes (.063, 1-for-16)
Dale Murphy (.111, 2-for-18)
Robby Thompson (.136, 3-for-22)

Hates to face: Pedro Guerrero (.469, 15-for-32, 2 HR)
Tony Gwynn (.542, 13-for-24, 0 SO)
Tim Teufel (.583, 7-for-12, 1 HR)

Miscellaneous statistics: Ground outs-to-air outs ratio: 2.07 last season, 2d-highest rate in N.L.; 1.94 for career. . . . Induced 27 double-play ground outs in 186 opportunities (one per 6.9), 4th-best rate in N.L. . . . Allowed 42 doubles (5th most in N.L.), 3 triples in 237.0 innings. . . . Allowed 24 first-inning runs in 35 starts (4.93 ERA). . . . Batting support: 3.86 runs per start. . . . Opposing base stealers: 13-for-17 (76%); 3 pickoffs, 3 balks.

Comments: Pitched 237 innings last season, his *lowest* total since 1987. Only Maddux, Dave Stewart, and Frank Viola have pitched at least that many innings in each of the last three seasons. . . . Allowed an average of one home run every 21.5 innings, 2d-best rate among National League starters last season, a remarkable feat for someone pitching half his games in Wrigley. . . . Has won 60 games before his 25th birthday; no Cubs pitcher had done that since Ken Holtzman, who won 65. . . . Opponents' stolen base rate was a surprise, considering that in 1989 base runners stole only 11 times in 23 attempts against him. . . . Opponents batted 70 points higher in day games (.305) than in night games (.235) last season, which is nothing new to Maddux. Their average has been higher by day in each of his five seasons in the majors. Opponents' career averages: .279 in day games, .243 at night. . . . The National League's top 10 hitters batted .463 (25-for-54) against him last season. . . . He was the only pitcher to shut out the Dodgers in Los Angeles last season. . . . Led major league pitchers in total fielding chances, and did not commit an error in the process. The last pitcher with a 1.000 fielding percentage to lead the league in total chances was Randy Jones in 1979. . . . Too bad that didn't rub off on his teammates, who committed 27 errors behind him, tied for the most behind any pitcher in the majors. Not only that, but his teammates provided him with the worst run support of any Cubs pitcher. Hope he reacted to all that better than Dave Stieb!

Joe Magrane

Throws Left

St. Louis Cardinals	W-L	ERA	AB	H	HR	BB	SO	BA	SA	OBA
Season	10-17	3.59	773	204	10	59	100	.264	.373	.320
vs. Left-Handers			153	43	1	16	26	.281	.373	.357
vs. Right-Handers			620	161	9	43	74	.260	.373	.311
vs. Ground-Ballers			341	88	3	24	50	.258	.334	.312
vs. Fly-Ballers			432	116	7	35	50	.269	.403	.327
Home Games	4-10	4.27	442	122	7	28	49	.276	.403	.325
Road Games	6-7	2.68	331	82	3	31	51	.248	.332	.314
Grass Fields	2-4	3.44	141	35	1	14	27	.248	.305	.318
Artificial Turf	8-13	3.62	632	169	9	45	73	.267	.388	.321
April	0-4	5.54	102	31	0	9	13	.304	.382	.365
May	2-4	3.35	164	42	2	8	17	.256	.366	.299
June	2-2	4.06	145	39	1	14	23	.269	.372	.340
July	2-2	3.28	138	39	1	8	22	.283	.370	.327
August	2-3	2.65	135	31	4	11	14	.230	.385	.293
Sept./Oct.	2-2	3.04	89	22	2	9	11	.247	.360	.307
Leading Off Inn.			195	59	3	15	28	.303	.415	.352
Bases Empty			444	121	6	34	61	.273	.376	.330
Runners On			329	83	4	25	39	.252	.368	.308
Runners/Scor. Pos.			185	41	1	21	20	.222	.286	.296
Runners On/2 Out			128	21	2	11	14	.164	.227	.246
Scor. Pos./2 Out			77	11	1	10	9	.143	.208	.250
Late-Inning Pressure			54	19	1	2	7	.352	.537	.379
Leading Off			16	4	0	1	7	.250	.313	.294
Runners On			20	9	1	1	0	.450	.850	.455
Runners/Scor. Pos.			9	6	0	1	0	.667	1.222	.636
First 9 Batters			259	69	2	15	41	.266	.351	.308
Second 9 Batters			241	63	2	23	31	.261	.349	.331
All Batters Thereafter			273	72	6	21	28	.264	.414	.322

Loves to face: Len Dykstra (.087, 2-for-23)
Billy Hatcher (.100, 3-for-30)
Joe Oliver (.083, 1-for-12)

Hates to face: Mickey Hatcher (.524, 11-for-21)
Gary Redus (.389, 7-for-18, 3 2B, 2 3B)
Tim Wallach (.385, 15-for-39, 5 2B, 2 3B, 1 HR)

Miscellaneous statistics: Ground outs-to-air outs ratio: 1.15 last season, 1.69 for career. . . . Induced 15 double-play ground outs in 151 opportunities (one per 10.1). . . . Allowed 36 doubles, 9 triples (tied for most in N.L.) in 203.1 innings. . . . Allowed 10 first-inning runs in 31 starts (2.32 ERA). . . . Batting support: 3.13 runs per start (4th lowest in N.L.) . . . Opposing base stealers: 21-for-37 (57%); 6 pickoffs, 1 balk.

Comments: His career rate of home runs allowed—one every 96.5 at-bats—is 3d best among pitchers active in 1990 (minimum: 1000 at-bats). Only Dave Smith (one every 100.1 at-bats) and Greg Minton (97.6) stand ahead of him. And don't make the mistake of ascribing that ranking exclusively to Magrane's pitching in spacious Busch Stadium: his home-run rate on the road (one every 113.5 at-bats) is even better than it is at Busch (one every 85.2). . . . Magrane has allowed only one homer to a left-handed batter over the last two seasons (Barry Bonds hit it last August 11), and he hasn't allowed a first-inning home run in his last 35 starts (since Ryne Sandberg connected on September 8, 1989). . . . After first seven starts of 1990 season, he stood 0–6 with a 6.45 ERA. . . . He'll come inside: He's hit 26 batters over the past four seasons; Kevin Gross (31) is the only National League pitcher with more hides on his wall over that span. . . . Despite a career ERA of 3.07, he's just a .500 pitcher (42–42) after four years. Only three other active pitchers (minimum: 100 starts) have career ERAs as low as Joe, and those three pitchers—Dwight Gooden, Roger Clemens, and Orel Hershiser—have a combined record of 334–162, a .673 winning percentage. But as bad as a fella's luck can be, there's always a guy who has worse: Consider Farmer Bell, who pitched for the Dodgers from 1907 to 1911. Career ERA: 2.85. Won-lost record: 43–79, for a percentage of .352. Now *that's* a hard-luck pitcher!

Rick Mahler

Throws Right

Cincinnati Reds	W-L	ERA	AB	H	HR	BB	SO	BA	SA	OBA
Season	7-6	4.28	514	134	16	39	68	.261	.403	.314
vs. Left-Handers			301	82	9	22	37	.272	.415	.323
vs. Right-Handers			213	52	7	17	31	.244	.385	.302
vs. Ground-Ballers			228	57	5	13	28	.250	.360	.294
vs. Fly-Ballers			286	77	11	26	40	.269	.437	.330
Home Games	3-1	4.45	215	58	9	18	33	.270	.437	.328
Road Games	4-5	4.15	299	76	7	21	35	.254	.378	.305
Grass Fields	1-4	5.04	175	47	5	9	20	.269	.429	.305
Artificial Turf	6-2	3.90	339	87	11	30	48	.257	.389	.319
April	1-0	5.68	47	11	1	3	4	.234	.340	.288
May	0-0	5.14	29	7	0	3	3	.241	.310	.333
June	1-3	4.30	114	33	4	12	17	.289	.430	.357
July	2-1	3.58	107	29	3	7	15	.271	.402	.316
August	2-1	4.50	114	30	4	9	16	.263	.395	.317
Sept./Oct.	1-1	3.86	103	24	4	5	13	.233	.437	.266
Leading Off Inn.			130	36	5	7	11	.277	.431	.314
Bases Empty			324	78	12	18	43	.241	.395	.281
Runners On			190	56	4	21	25	.295	.416	.367
Runners/Scor. Pos.			111	30	4	16	21	.270	.441	.361
Runners On/2 Out			86	25	3	14	15	.291	.465	.408
Scor. Pos./2 Out			60	17	3	13	13	.283	.517	.427
Late-Inning Pressure			25	6	1	4	2	.240	.440	.345
Leading Off			5	1	0	2	1	.200	.200	.429
Runners On			9	3	1	2	0	.333	.778	.455
Runners/Scor. Pos.			5	2	1	2	0	.400	1.000	.571
First 9 Batters			261	58	8	18	32	.222	.349	.277
Second 9 Batters			143	47	5	15	21	.329	.510	.390
All Batters Thereafter			110	29	3	6	15	.264	.391	.302

Loves to face: Barry Bonds (.133, 4-for-30)
Jose Oquendo (.120, 3-for-25, 0 BB)
Luis Quinones (0-for-12)

Hates to face: Kevin Mitchell (.419, 13-for-31, 3 HR)
Darryl Strawberry (.457, 21-for-46, 5 HR)
Andy Van Slyke (.500, 24-for-48, 3 HR)

Miscellaneous statistics: Ground outs-to-air outs ratio: 1.18 last season, 1.53 for career. . . . Induced 11 double-play ground outs in 94 opportunities (one per 8.5). . . . Allowed 21 doubles, 2 triples in 134.2 innings. . . . Allowed 11 first-inning runs in 16 starts (5.06 ERA). . . . Batting support: 5.44 runs per start. . . . Record of 6–5, 4.22 ERA as a starter; 1–1, 4.40 ERA in 19 relief appearances. . . . Stranded 12 inherited runners, allowed 0 to score (100%). . . . Opposing base stealers: 9-for-13 (69%); 1 pick-off, 2 balks.

Comments: After two consecutive seasons in which he kept his ERA below 4.00 but wound up with a losing record, Mahler wised up. His ERA went up to 4.28 and he was 7–6. . . . Did a good job out of the bullpen last season, stranding all 12 runners he inherited; that's the most inherited runners stranded by any pitcher who didn't allow any to score last season. . . . Owns a 7–2 record and 3.23 ERA in 89 career relief appearances. . . . Long man: He averaged 9.53 batters faced per relief outing, the highest among National League pitchers who relieved at least 10 times last season. . . . Opponents batted 78 points lower on his first pass through the lineup (.222) than in subsequent at-bats (.300), the 2d-biggest difference in the majors. . . . Opponents have hit for a higher average with runners on base than they have with the bases empty in each of the last seven years, and they've hit better with runners in scoring position than in other at-bats in each of the last five. . . . Has lost 10 straight decisions to the Mets since last defeating them in 1982. . . . The next hit he allows will be the 2000th of his career. Will they stop the game, put it on the scoreboard, and give him the ball? In post-game interviews, Mahler can thank Tony Gwynn (32), Wally Backman (24), Hubie Brooks (24), and Andy Van Slyke (24), who had the most, as well as the little people like Gary Krug, Phil Ouellette, and Gene Walter, who had one apiece. (Don't think he doesn't remember these guys; last we heard, he rolled some pretty mean dice around the Strat-O-Matic table.)

Dennis Martinez

Throws Right

Montreal Expos	W-L	ERA	AB	H	HR	BB	SO	BA	SA	OBA
Season	10-11	2.95	839	191	16	49	156	.228	.335	.274
vs. Left-Handers			507	113	9	28	95	.223	.321	.263
vs. Right-Handers			332	78	7	21	61	.235	.355	.292
vs. Ground-Ballers			392	83	4	18	85	.212	.283	.252
vs. Fly-Ballers			447	108	12	31	71	.242	.380	.293
Home Games	6-10	3.41	500	117	12	26	84	.234	.358	.277
Road Games	4-1	2.27	339	74	4	23	72	.218	.301	.270
Grass Fields	2-1	2.00	140	32	2	10	33	.229	.300	.278
Artificial Turf	8-10	3.13	699	159	14	39	123	.227	.342	.273
April	2-1	2.31	128	30	2	12	21	.234	.320	.301
May	1-3	2.84	144	33	4	8	30	.229	.354	.273
June	2-2	2.79	148	32	2	11	25	.216	.331	.275
July	2-1	3.70	161	38	1	6	33	.236	.304	.272
August	3-2	2.85	176	39	4	6	33	.222	.347	.251
Sept./Oct.	0-2	3.22	82	19	3	6	14	.232	.366	.284
Leading Off Inn.			218	51	4	9	35	.234	.330	.268
Bases Empty			523	122	9	20	99	.233	.331	.264
Runners On			316	69	7	29	57	.218	.342	.290
Runners/Scor. Pos.			191	40	3	23	37	.209	.298	.300
Runners On/2 Out			141	33	3	11	26	.234	.355	.289
Scor. Pos./2 Out			93	22	1	9	17	.237	.312	.304
Late-Inning Pressure			67	20	5	5	9	.299	.537	.356
Leading Off			17	8	2	0	2	.471	.824	.471
Runners On			27	8	2	5	4	.296	.556	.424
Runners/Scor. Pos.			21	5	2	5	4	.238	.571	.407
First 9 Batters			258	56	3	12	59	.217	.298	.253
Second 9 Batters			260	53	2	15	44	.204	.265	.249
All Batters Thereafter			321	82	11	22	53	.255	.421	.311

Loves to face: Gary Carter (.080, 2-for-25)
Rick Cerone (.059, 1-for-17)
Billy Hatcher (.067, 1-for-15)

Hates to face: Gregg Jefferies (.421, 8-for-19)
Ryne Sandberg (.370, 17-for-46, 4 HR)
Don Slaught (.500, 7-for-14)

Miscellaneous statistics: Ground outs-to-air outs ratio: 1.60 last season, 1.20 for career.... Induced 13 double-play ground outs in 136 opportunities (one per 10.5).... Allowed 30 doubles, 6 triples in 226.0 innings.... Allowed 8 first-inning runs in 32 starts (2.01 ERA, 4th lowest in N.L.).... Batting support: 4.31 runs per start.... Opposing base stealers: 19-for-28 (68%); 0 pickoffs, 1 balk.

Comments: Had the lowest ERA of any starting pitcher with a losing record last season (minimum: 10 decisions). That's the second straight year that a Montreal pitcher has had that hard-luck distinction; in 1989 it was Bryn Smith.... Posted a higher ERA in his 11 no-decision starts (3.90) than he did in his 11 defeats (3.66).... Opponents stole only five bases in 11 attempts (45%) against the Martinez-Fitzgerald battery, but were successful in 14 of 17 tries (82%) when Martinez was paired with other catchers. Flip side: Martinez's ERA was considerably higher with Fitzgerald (3.76) than with Jeff Goff (2.40) or Nelson Santovenia (1.93).... His career ERA with the Expos is 3.1731, just a shade higher than the 3.1729 ERA compiled by Steve Rogers in his 13 years with Montreal. If he retires the first batter this year, he'll take over first place among pitchers with at least 800 innings in the funny caps.... Opponents have hit for a higher average on grass fields than on artificial surfaces in each of the last seven seasons, the longest current streak of its kind by any pitcher in the majors. Doug Bird and Len Barker were the last pitchers to have streaks that long.... He's two days older than Jack Morris and five days older than Ed Whitson. May of 1955 was a good month for pitchers. Then again, it also produced Ray Searage.

Ramon Martinez

Throws Right

Los Angeles Dodgers	W-L	ERA	AB	H	HR	BB	SO	BA	SA	OBA
Season	20-6	2.92	866	191	22	67	223	.221	.357	.278
vs. Left-Handers			509	125	13	53	118	.246	.389	.319
vs. Right-Handers			357	66	9	14	105	.185	.311	.217
vs. Ground-Ballers			391	82	3	30	98	.210	.286	.264
vs. Fly-Ballers			475	109	19	37	125	.229	.415	.290
Home Games	12-2	2.71	472	96	14	39	134	.203	.341	.265
Road Games	8-4	3.18	394	95	8	28	89	.241	.376	.294
Grass Fields	15-3	2.84	646	137	18	51	169	.212	.353	.271
Artificial Turf	5-3	3.16	220	54	4	16	54	.245	.368	.298
April	2-0	2.25	102	20	2	5	28	.196	.284	.234
May	3-3	4.76	129	34	4	13	41	.264	.442	.331
June	4-0	1.76	168	36	2	15	56	.214	.315	.283
July	4-1	2.72	132	26	5	8	34	.197	.356	.236
August	3-2	3.71	161	40	4	15	31	.248	.373	.315
Sept./Oct.	4-0	2.53	174	35	5	11	33	.201	.362	.257
Leading Off Inn.			222	50	9	13	54	.225	.414	.277
Bases Empty			538	117	16	43	144	.217	.364	.279
Runners On			328	74	6	24	79	.226	.345	.277
Runners/Scor. Pos.			179	39	4	17	52	.218	.346	.282
Runners On/2 Out			144	31	3	13	43	.215	.326	.280
Scor. Pos./2 Out			87	17	2	12	30	.195	.287	.293
Late-Inning Pressure			117	25	3	7	26	.214	.342	.258
Leading Off			33	6	1	0	5	.182	.273	.182
Runners On			42	7	1	1	11	.167	.286	.186
Runners/Scor. Pos.			22	3	1	0	8	.136	.318	.136
First 9 Batters			268	48	6	23	83	.179	.306	.248
Second 9 Batters			271	65	8	18	70	.240	.384	.288
All Batters Thereafter			327	78	8	26	70	.239	.376	.295

Loves to face: Dennis Martinez (0-for-8, 6 SO)
Ryne Sandberg (0-for-11)
Darryl Strawberry (.083, 1-for-12)

Hates to face: Bobby Bonilla (.444, 4-for-9, 1 3B, 2 HR)
Sid Bream (.750, 3-for-4, 1 2B, 2 HR)
Ricky Jordan (.462, 6-for-13, 1 HR)

Miscellaneous statistics: Ground outs-to-air outs ratio: 0.73 last season, 0.81 for career.... Induced 11 double-play ground outs in 146 opportunities (one per 13.3).... Allowed 38 doubles, 7 triples in 234.1 innings.... Allowed 14 first-inning runs in 33 starts (3.00 ERA).... Batting support: 4.94 runs per start (5th highest in N.L.).... Opposing base stealers: 22-for-35 (63%); 3 pickoffs, 3 balks.

Comments: Most recent addition to a seemingly endless line of top-quality pitchers produced by the Dodgers organization. Over the last 25 years, 11 pitchers who played for the Dodgers as rookies went on to win at least 100 games. (Hershiser, with 99 wins, will be next.) The list includes many players who made their marks with other teams after they were unable to crack the Dodgers' always formidable starting rotation: Don Sutton (debuted with L.A. in 1966), Bill Singer (1967), Jack Billingham (1968), Doyle Alexander (1971), Charlie Hough (1973), Geoff Zahn (1974), Rick Rhoden (1975), Bob Welch (1978), Rick Sutcliffe (1979), Fernando Valenzuela (1981), and Dave Stewart (1981). Over the past 25 years, no other organization has spawned as many future 100-game winners; surprise—the next-highest total (nine) belongs to the Cubs.... The Dodgers infielders fielded only .963 (one error every 44 chances) behind Martinez last season, the worst fielding percentage by any infield in "support" of any National League pitcher last season.... Averaged 7.10 innings pitched per start last season, 3d highest among National League pitchers (minimum: 20 starts).... The only pitcher to shut out the Reds at Riverfront Stadium last season.... Has 0–3 career record vs. New York, 27–10 against the rest of the league.... Opponents' career breakdown: .199 at Dodger Stadium, .238 on other grass fields, .250 on artificial surfaces.

Roger McDowell

Throws Right

Philadelphia Phillies	W-L	ERA	AB	H	HR	BB	SO	BA	SA	OBA
Season	6-8	3.86	322	92	2	35	39	.286	.363	.355
vs. Left-Handers			183	60	2	28	16	.328	.415	.414
vs. Right-Handers			139	32	0	7	23	.230	.295	.270
vs. Ground-Ballers			153	43	1	14	21	.281	.320	.343
vs. Fly-Ballers			169	49	1	21	18	.290	.402	.366
Home Games	3-4	5.40	140	41	1	14	17	.293	.414	.353
Road Games	3-4	2.72	182	51	1	21	22	.280	.324	.357
Grass Fields	2-2	1.71	92	24	0	13	13	.261	.283	.352
Artificial Turf	4-6	4.80	230	68	2	22	26	.296	.396	.357
April	1-0	7.56	31	7	0	6	2	.226	.258	.351
May	1-0	4.32	61	21	0	6	6	.344	.393	.397
June	0-3	7.71	52	19	1	5	11	.365	.481	.431
July	1-1	2.30	58	13	1	10	10	.224	.362	.338
August	3-2	1.71	69	15	0	7	5	.217	.275	.286
Sept./Oct.	0-2	2.77	51	17	0	1	5	.333	.392	.345
Leading Off Inn.			65	17	0	6	9	.262	.292	.324
Bases Empty			142	35	1	15	19	.246	.331	.318
Runners On			180	57	1	20	20	.317	.389	.383
Runners/Scor. Pos.			115	37	1	15	13	.322	.409	.393
Runners On/2 Out			71	20	0	8	11	.282	.310	.370
Scor. Pos./2 Out			49	13	0	7	9	.265	.286	.368
Late-Inning Pressure			187	62	1	19	21	.332	.412	.392
Leading Off			34	12	0	5	3	.353	.382	.436
Runners On			112	40	1	13	11	.357	.446	.422
Runners/Scor. Pos.			75	26	1	8	6	.347	.453	.407
First 9 Batters			312	89	2	33	38	.285	.365	.353
Second 9 Batters			10	3	0	2	1	.300	.300	.417
All Batters Thereafter			0	0	0	0	0	—	—	—

Loves to face: Andres Galarraga (.111, 2-for-18)
Gerald Perry (.077, 1-for-13)
Juan Samuel (.091, 2-for-22)

Hates to face: Bill Doran (.455, 5-for-11, 1 HR)
Milt Thompson (.500, 10-for-20)
Andy Van Slyke (.444, 8-for-18, 2 HR)

Miscellaneous statistics: Ground outs-to-air outs ratio: 2.95 last season, 3.05 for career (highest among active pitchers). . . . Induced 16 double-play ground outs in 103 opportunities (one per 6.4). . . . Allowed 15 doubles, 2 triples in 86.1 innings. . . . Stranded 27 inherited runners, allowed 16 to score (63%). . . . Opposing base stealers: 7-for-9 (78%); 0 pickoffs, 1 balk.

Comments: They call it the Summer Game, but Roger did his best work in the spring and the fall: He had 13 saves before June 21 and three more after September 21, but had only six in the three months between the solstice and equinox. . . . Has a career record of 8–0 during April. . . . Opponents batted 109 points higher in Late-Inning Pressure Situations (.332) than in other at-bats (.222) last season, the 2d-largest difference in the majors. . . . Maintained his steady mastery of right-handed batters last season, but lefties killed him. In five previous seasons in the majors, left-handers had never before hit higher than .265 against him. . . . His career strikeout/walk ratio indicates that he goes after right-handed batters, but backs away from lefties: 2.5 strikeouts for every walk by righties, but 0.85 by lefty swingers. . . . Has held right-handed batters without a home run in their last 458 at-bats against him; Bo Diaz was the last right-hander to take him deep, on April 29, 1988. . . . Committed five errors last season, the most by any pitcher in the National League. Other Phillies pitchers also did their fair share; the team's total of 21 errors by pitchers was the highest in the league. . . . Opposing fly-ball hitters have had a higher batting average than ground-ball hitters in each of his six seasons in the majors. That fits the general rule for ground-ball pitchers, of which McDowell is the prototype. Opponents' career breakdown: .230 by ground-ballers, .261 by fly-ballers.

Kent Mercker

Throws Left

Atlanta Braves	W-L	ERA	AB	H	HR	BB	SO	BA	SA	OBA
Season	4-7	3.17	182	43	6	24	39	.236	.374	.329
vs. Left-Handers			48	12	1	8	11	.250	.354	.351
vs. Right-Handers			134	31	5	16	28	.231	.381	.320
vs. Ground-Ballers			84	21	3	7	21	.250	.429	.319
vs. Fly-Ballers			98	22	3	17	18	.224	.327	.336
Home Games	3-2	2.53	81	20	2	8	16	.247	.346	.319
Road Games	1-5	3.67	101	23	4	16	23	.228	.396	.336
Grass Fields	4-5	2.97	136	32	4	20	24	.235	.353	.333
Artificial Turf	0-2	3.75	46	11	2	4	15	.239	.435	.314
April	0-0	—	0	0	0	0	0	—	—	—
May	0-0	—	0	0	0	0	0	—	—	—
June	0-0	—	1	1	0	0	0	1.000	2.000	1.000
July	4-1	1.77	76	16	2	12	19	.211	.303	.315
August	0-2	2.93	57	12	2	3	17	.211	.351	.274
Sept./Oct.	0-4	5.68	48	14	2	9	3	.292	.479	.397
Leading Off Inn.			39	5	1	7	8	.128	.282	.261
Bases Empty			103	22	5	11	19	.214	.398	.296
Runners On			79	21	1	13	20	.266	.342	.368
Runners/Scor. Pos.			47	10	0	11	16	.213	.255	.361
Runners On/2 Out			38	9	1	7	14	.237	.342	.356
Scor. Pos./2 Out			26	5	0	7	12	.192	.231	.364
Late-Inning Pressure			112	27	5	18	20	.241	.411	.348
Leading Off			25	3	1	5	5	.120	.320	.267
Runners On			48	15	1	10	11	.313	.417	.424
Runners/Scor. Pos.			29	6	0	8	8	.207	.241	.368
First 9 Batters			175	41	5	22	37	.234	.360	.325
Second 9 Batters			7	2	1	2	2	.286	.714	.400
All Batters Thereafter			0	0	0	0	0	—	—	—

Loves to face: Tony Gwynn (0-for-5)
Kevin McReynolds (0-for-4)

Hates to face: Kal Daniels (.500, 1-for-2, 2 BB)
Tom Herr (.500, 1-for-2, 1 HR)

Miscellaneous statistics: Ground outs-to-air outs ratio: 0.76 last season, 0.75 for career. . . . Induced 1 double-play ground out in 38 opportunities (one per 38.0). . . . Allowed 5 doubles, 1 triple in 48.1 innings. . . . Stranded 10 inherited runners, allowed 4 to score (71%). . . . Opposing base stealers: 5-for-9 (56%); 0 pickoffs, 0 balks.

Comments: Held opponents to .236 batting average in 1990; they hit .296 against Mercker's bullpenmates. ERA breakdown: Mercker 3.17, other Atlanta relievers 5.23. . . . Braves weren't afraid to use this rookie with the game on the line: 63 percent of the batters he faced last season were in Late-Inning Pressure Situations, the highest percentage by any rookie in the majors. Only two other rookies in the majors had rates above 50 percent, and they were both on division winners: Jeff Gray (51.6%) and Stan Belinda (55.5%). . . . Has walked the leadoff batter in nine of 51 innings he has started, a rate that he'll have to lower if he's to be successful. National League average for 1990: one leadoff walk every 13.5 innings. . . . Andy Van Slyke is the only left-handed batter to hit a home run off Mercker. . . . Two of his four victories came against the Mets. That should come as no surprise—he's left-handed, isn't he? . . . The sixth selection in the first round of the 1986 amateur draft, picked before Gary Sheffield, Erik Hanson, and Bo Jackson, to name a few. . . . For a team with as much experience with early selections in the June draft, the Braves' top draft choices during the 1980s can pretty fairly be called disappointing. Here they are, chronologically, starting with 1980: Ken Dayley, Jay Roberts, Duane Ward, Marty Clary, Drew Denson, Tommy Greene, Mercker, Derek Lilliquist, Steve Avery, and Tyler Houston.

Mike Morgan

Throws Right

Los Angeles Dodgers	W-L	ERA	AB	H	HR	BB	SO	BA	SA	OBA
Season	11-15	3.75	811	216	19	60	106	.266	.392	.319
vs. Left-Handers			455	132	9	34	53	.290	.418	.341
vs. Right-Handers			356	84	10	26	53	.236	.360	.292
vs. Ground-Ballers			370	81	3	26	51	.219	.292	.276
vs. Fly-Ballers			441	135	16	34	55	.306	.476	.356
Home Games	5-6	3.77	408	111	16	24	56	.272	.436	.313
Road Games	6-9	3.74	403	105	3	36	50	.261	.347	.325
Grass Fields	8-10	3.59	593	159	17	42	79	.268	.403	.319
Artificial Turf	3-5	4.20	218	57	2	18	27	.261	.362	.321
April	3-1	1.82	110	27	1	2	13	.245	.318	.265
May	3-2	4.02	147	35	4	14	24	.238	.361	.313
June	1-3	3.53	144	38	4	8	17	.264	.438	.301
July	2-3	4.14	142	34	1	14	17	.239	.331	.308
August	1-3	2.92	150	41	1	10	20	.273	.327	.319
Sept./Oct.	1-3	6.35	118	41	8	12	15	.347	.602	.409
Leading Off Inn.			203	50	4	15	28	.246	.350	.308
Bases Empty			493	125	12	31	72	.254	.375	.302
Runners On			318	91	7	29	34	.286	.418	.346
Runners/Scor. Pos.			186	44	4	19	24	.237	.376	.305
Runners On/2 Out			137	35	1	8	21	.255	.350	.297
Scor. Pos./2 Out			89	16	1	7	15	.180	.292	.240
Late-Inning Pressure			85	24	2	7	11	.282	.388	.344
Leading Off			25	9	0	1	3	.360	.360	.385
Runners On			30	7	1	5	2	.233	.367	.361
Runners/Scor. Pos.			17	3	1	2	2	.176	.353	.263
First 9 Batters			262	57	5	19	38	.218	.324	.276
Second 9 Batters			263	76	7	18	41	.289	.426	.335
All Batters Thereafter			286	83	7	23	27	.290	.423	.345

Loves to face: Jay Bell (.071, 1-for-14, 1 2B)
Vince Coleman (.077, 1-for-13)
Gerald Young (0-for-10)

Hates to face: Bobby Bonilla (.500, 8-for-16, 1 HR)
Daryl Boston (.375, 6-for-16, 2 HR)
Jeff Treadway (.471, 8-for-17)

Miscellaneous statistics: Ground outs-to-air outs ratio: 2.35 last season, highest rate in N.L.; 1.78 for career.... Induced 19 double-play ground outs in 154 opportunities (one per 8.1).... Allowed 37 doubles, 4 triples in 211.0 innings.... Allowed 17 first-inning runs in 33 starts (4.73 ERA).... Batting support: 3.94 runs per start.... Opposing base stealers: 16-for-29 (55%); 1 pickoff, 1 balk.

Comments: Lasorda might bleed Dodger blue, but Morgan was born to be a Dodger. He was born on October 8, 1959, the day the Dodgers beat the White Sox in Game Six of the World Series to take their first world championship representing Los Angeles.... Morgan has had a losing record in all but one of his 10 years in the majors. His 1–1 record with the Mariners in 1985 saved him from tying the all-time record of 10 consecutive seasons with a losing record, shared by Bill Bailey and Ron Kline. As it is, he and Al Nipper have had losing records in each of the last five seasons, the 2d-longest current streak among active pitchers. Mark Thurmond is in a six-year spin.... Morgan's career winning percentage (.361, 53–94) is the lowest among active pitchers with at least 100 decisions. Coldwater Jim Hughey holds the all-time worst record (.266, 29–80).... Opponents batted 72 points lower on his first pass through the lineup (.218) than in later at-bats (.290) last season, the 5th-largest margin in the majors.... He was the only pitcher to throw two complete games against St. Louis last season; both of them were shutouts.... Four of his 11 victories were shutouts. Bob Ojeda had five shutouts among 10 wins in 1988.... Batting breakdown for ground-ball and fly-ball hitters is in accord with the usual rule. We'll keep repeating it until we're sure everyone understands: ground-ball pitchers are hit harder by fly-ball hitters than they are by ground-ball hitters. And it's vice versa for fly-ball pitchers. Got it?

Terry Mulholland

Throws Left

Philadelphia Phillies	W-L	ERA	AB	H	HR	BB	SO	BA	SA	OBA
Season	9-10	3.34	683	172	15	42	75	.252	.388	.292
vs. Left-Handers			101	28	2	3	13	.277	.366	.299
vs. Right-Handers			582	144	13	39	62	.247	.392	.291
vs. Ground-Ballers			352	78	4	22	47	.222	.327	.265
vs. Fly-Ballers			331	94	11	20	28	.284	.453	.320
Home Games	3-4	2.66	261	59	5	13	33	.226	.364	.261
Road Games	6-6	3.78	422	113	10	29	42	.268	.403	.312
Grass Fields	4-4	3.72	220	59	5	17	24	.268	.386	.322
Artificial Turf	5-6	3.17	463	113	10	25	51	.244	.389	.278
April	1-0	4.66	73	24	2	6	5	.329	.466	.366
May	2-2	2.77	100	27	2	8	7	.270	.400	.321
June	0-1	10.24	41	14	1	4	3	.341	.512	.391
July	2-1	2.05	119	29	2	4	11	.244	.378	.268
August	2-4	3.75	187	48	4	11	31	.257	.380	.295
Sept./Oct.	2-2	2.11	163	30	4	9	18	.184	.331	.227
Leading Off Inn.			173	52	7	13	15	.301	.503	.349
Bases Empty			412	101	12	23	47	.245	.410	.287
Runners On			271	71	3	19	28	.262	.354	.300
Runners/Scor. Pos.			159	34	2	14	18	.214	.296	.263
Runners On/2 Out			108	26	1	11	15	.241	.306	.317
Scor. Pos./2 Out			71	15	1	10	10	.211	.282	.317
Late-Inning Pressure			36	10	2	0	8	.278	.611	.297
Leading Off			12	3	0	0	2	.250	.417	.250
Runners On			9	1	0	0	3	.111	.222	.200
Runners/Scor. Pos.			5	1	0	0	1	.200	.400	.333
First 9 Batters			237	62	3	20	30	.262	.363	.314
Second 9 Batters			218	46	5	14	29	.211	.317	.253
All Batters Thereafter			228	64	7	8	16	.281	.482	.307

Loves to face: Todd Benzinger (.100, 1-for-10)
Will Clark (.063, 1-for-16, 1 2B)
Rex Hudler (.071, 1-for-14)

Hates to face: Tony Gwynn (.462, 6-for-13)
Gary Redus (.429, 6-for-14, 4 2B, 2 HR)
Ryne Sandberg (.381, 8-for-21, 3 HR)

Miscellaneous statistics: Ground outs-to-air outs ratio: 1.10 last season, 1.28 for career.... Induced 17 double-play ground outs in 135 opportunities (one per 7.9), worst rate in N.L. ... Allowed 40 doubles, 4 triples in 180.2 innings.... Allowed 17 first-inning runs in 26 starts (5.54 ERA).... Batting support: 3.65 runs per start.... Opposing base stealers: 3-for-6 (50%); 2 pickoffs, 2 balks.

Comments: Did not have a winning streak or a losing streak of more than two games last season; his 19 decisions were the most by any National League pitcher who didn't have a streak of three games in either direction.... His no-hitter was sandwiched between a couple of two-game losing streaks. The last pitcher with losing streaks of two or more games surrounding a no-hitter: Jim Colborn in 1977.... There have been 168 pitchers who have thrown complete-game no-hitters of nine or more innings since 1900. Of that total, 41 pitchers finished their no-hit season with a losing record, and nine others finished at .500. (Pitchers who threw two no-hitters in a season are counted only once in this tally, but let's give special recognition to Virgil Trucks, who threw two no-hitters and a one-hitter for the Tigers in 1952 but finished the season 5–19.) ... Mulholland's career fielding percentage (.884, one error every 8.6 chances) is the lowest among active National League pitchers; no-hit classmate Randy Johnson (.831, one error every 5.9 chances) has the lowest among active American League pitchers (minimum: 50 fielding chances).... One of four National League pitchers to average fewer than four strikeouts per nine innings last season (minimum: 162 innings): Bill Gullickson (3.40), Mulholland (3.74), Tom Browning (3.91), and Scott Garrelts (3.96).... The Expos stole three bases off him in his second appearance of the season, but no one stole a base against him after that.

Randy Myers

Throws Left

Cincinnati Reds	W-L	ERA	AB	H	HR	BB	SO	BA	SA	OBA
Season	4-6	2.08	306	59	6	38	98	.193	.281	.287
vs. Left-Handers			72	13	2	12	32	.181	.264	.294
vs. Right-Handers			234	46	4	26	66	.197	.286	.284
vs. Ground-Ballers			140	27	2	14	44	.193	.257	.271
vs. Fly-Ballers			166	32	4	24	54	.193	.301	.299
Home Games	2-2	0.62	154	30	1	17	43	.195	.227	.273
Road Games	2-4	3.53	152	29	5	21	55	.191	.336	.299
Grass Fields	1-2	2.96	100	21	4	12	37	.210	.390	.295
Artificial Turf	3-4	1.67	206	38	2	26	61	.184	.228	.283
April	1-0	4.66	36	10	0	7	14	.278	.333	.400
May	0-0	0.64	45	5	1	2	20	.111	.178	.149
June	2-2	2.33	67	12	2	11	18	.179	.299	.295
July	0-1	0.66	51	9	1	4	14	.176	.255	.250
August	0-1	2.35	55	14	1	4	12	.255	.327	.300
Sept./Oct.	1-2	2.45	52	9	1	10	20	.173	.288	.317
Leading Off Inn.			69	16	3	5	23	.232	.406	.284
Bases Empty			169	35	4	17	53	.207	.314	.280
Runners On			137	24	2	21	45	.175	.241	.294
Runners/Scor. Pos.			84	12	2	16	35	.143	.250	.282
Runners On/2 Out			68	14	2	14	21	.206	.338	.349
Scor. Pos./2 Out			46	9	2	11	17	.196	.391	.362
Late-Inning Pressure			210	37	5	22	71	.176	.267	.260
Leading Off			47	11	2	2	18	.234	.383	.265
Runners On			94	17	2	12	30	.181	.255	.284
Runners/Scor. Pos.			61	9	2	10	23	.148	.262	.274
First 9 Batters			303	58	5	37	97	.191	.271	.284
Second 9 Batters			3	1	1	1	1	.333	1.333	.500
All Batters Thereafter			0	0	0	0	0	—	—	—

Loves to face: Hubie Brooks (.083, 1-for-12)
Jose Lind (.067, 1-for-15, 3 BB)
Robby Thompson (0-for-8, 6 SO)

Hates to face: Andres Galarraga (.308, 4-for-13, 2 HR, 4 BB)
Mark Grace (.444, 4-for-9, 2 3B, 1 HR)
Juan Samuel (.455, 5-for-11)

Miscellaneous statistics: Ground outs-to-air outs ratio: 0.64 last season, 0.65 for career. . . . Induced 4 double-play ground outs in 65 opportunities (one per 16.3). . . . Allowed 7 doubles, 1 triple in 86.2 innings. . . . Stranded 28 inherited runners, allowed 3 to score (90%), best rate in majors. . . . Opposing base stealers: 2-for-6 (33%); 3 pickoffs, 1 balk.

Comments: We started keeping track of all these situational numbers in 1975. Since then, Myers owns the lowest opponents' batting average with runners on base (.186) among pitchers who have faced at least 500 batters in such situations. In addition, he has allowed a .166 batting average with runners in scoring position, second over that span to nastymate Rob Dibble (.164); the minimum there is 300 batters faced with RISP. . . . Opponents' annual averages with RISP since 1986: .154, .203, .160, .167, .143. . . . There's more: Myers also is the career leader in lowest opponents' batting average (.189) in Late-Inning Pressure Situations. . . . We're not through. He's the only pitcher who, over the last 16 seasons, has struck out more than one-third (actually 34.5 percent) of the left-handed batters he has faced. Lefties have a .173 career batting average against him, which is especially significant because only the best left-handed batters remain in the game after Randall K. struts in. Left-handed batters hit .181 against Myers last season, the *highest* they've ever hit against him. Yearly averages by left-handers since 1986: .111, .175, .180, .164, .181. . . . What do Myers, Will McEnaney, Paul Derringer and Hod Eller have in common? They're the pitchers who got the final outs in each of the Reds' World Series clinching victories. (McEnaney did it in both 1975 and 1976.)

Bob Ojeda

Throws Left

New York Mets	W-L	ERA	AB	H	HR	BB	SO	BA	SA	OBA
Season	7-6	3.66	452	123	10	40	62	.272	.414	.332
vs. Left-Handers			113	19	1	7	20	.168	.257	.230
vs. Right-Handers			339	104	9	33	42	.307	.466	.365
vs. Ground-Ballers			240	61	5	19	35	.254	.387	.310
vs. Fly-Ballers			212	62	5	21	27	.292	.443	.356
Home Games	4-2	3.50	244	67	4	20	38	.275	.398	.330
Road Games	3-4	3.86	208	56	6	20	24	.269	.433	.335
Grass Fields	5-3	3.51	313	84	4	25	46	.268	.380	.322
Artificial Turf	2-3	4.00	139	39	6	15	16	.281	.489	.355
April	0-0	1.64	40	7	1	4	9	.175	.325	.267
May	1-3	2.60	102	18	4	5	15	.176	.324	.215
June	3-0	4.59	133	43	3	11	19	.323	.459	.372
July	0-2	4.50	73	24	0	6	12	.329	.479	.370
August	3-0	2.89	62	15	0	8	5	.242	.323	.329
Sept./Oct.	0-1	5.79	42	16	2	6	2	.381	.595	.469
Leading Off Inn.			108	32	3	11	8	.296	.491	.367
Bases Empty			251	78	7	24	36	.311	.490	.375
Runners On			201	45	3	16	26	.224	.318	.277
Runners/Scor. Pos.			113	25	2	10	16	.221	.319	.278
Runners On/2 Out			83	19	2	6	10	.229	.325	.281
Scor. Pos./2 Out			53	10	1	3	6	.189	.283	.232
Late-Inning Pressure			63	12	0	9	9	.190	.254	.292
Leading Off			16	4	0	4	0	.250	.375	.400
Runners On			27	5	0	2	5	.185	.259	.241
Runners/Scor. Pos.			13	3	0	2	3	.231	.385	.333
First 9 Batters			263	68	5	22	39	.259	.392	.318
Second 9 Batters			111	31	3	9	15	.279	.441	.333
All Batters Thereafter			78	24	2	9	8	.308	.449	.375

Loves to face: Sid Bream (.172, 5-for-29)
Von Hayes (.125, 4-for-32)
Andres Thomas (.125, 3-for-24)

Hates to face: Willie McGee (.393, 11-for-28, 5 2B, 1 3B, 2 HR, 0 BB)
Dale Murphy (.632, 12-for-19, 1 HR)
Ryne Sandberg (.458, 11-for-24, 3 HR)

Miscellaneous statistics: Ground outs-to-air outs ratio: 1.56 last season, 1.08 for career. . . . Induced 11 double-play ground outs in 85 opportunities (one per 7.7). . . . Allowed 26 doubles, 4 triples in 118.0 innings. . . . Allowed 11 first-inning runs in 12 starts (8.25 ERA). . . . Batting support: 4.50 runs per start. . . . Record of 4–5, 4.72 ERA as a starter; 3–1, 2.19 ERA in 26 relief appearances. . . . Stranded 4 inherited runners, allowed 1 to score (80%). . . . Opposing base stealers: 14-for-25 (56%); 8 pickoffs, 3 balks.

Comments: Pitched five years with the Mets: 18–5 in first season, 33–35 thereafter. . . . But you can see why the Dodgers were impressed: a career record of 5–0 against L.A., including a 3–0 mark with a 2.57 ERA in 28 career innings at Dodger Stadium. . . . Opponents batted 87 points higher with the bases empty (.311) than with runners on base (.224) last season, the largest margin in the majors. . . . Over five years in the National League, right-handed batters have hit .253, left-handers .190; that's the 3d-largest such difference in the majors over that span. Right-handed batters really roughed him up last season; their .307 batting avarage was the highest that Bobby O. has ever allowed them in a full season. . . . The National League's top ten hitters batted only .143 (3-for-21) against him last season (and five of the ten bat right-handed—at least against him). . . . Allowed 11 earned runs and 16 hits in the first innings of his 12 starts last season. . . . Has allowed only three hits in 31 at-bats with the bases loaded since coming to the N.L., the lowest bases-loaded average allowed by any pitcher in the majors over that span (minimum: 25 at-bats). . . . No left-handed pitcher has shut out the Phillies at Veterans Stadium since Ojeda did it in August of 1989. . . . After spending most of last season as the sixth man in a five-man starting rotation, he'll now seek to fit into a staff that includes Ramon Martinez, Orel Hershiser, Fernando Valenzuela, Tim Belcher, Kevin Gross, and Mike Morgan.

Jeff Parrett

Throws Right

Phillies/Braves	W-L	ERA	AB	H	HR	BB	SO	BA	SA	OBA
Season	5-10	4.64	410	119	11	55	86	.290	.441	.373
vs. Left-Handers			207	57	7	39	36	.275	.454	.390
vs. Right-Handers			203	62	4	16	50	.305	.429	.354
vs. Ground-Ballers			176	56	2	31	34	.318	.432	.421
vs. Fly-Ballers			234	63	9	24	52	.269	.449	.335
Home Games	2-5	5.06	222	62	8	32	44	.279	.464	.372
Road Games	3-5	4.14	188	57	3	23	42	.303	.415	.374
Grass Fields	2-3	4.76	129	41	3	23	23	.318	.419	.417
Artificial Turf	3-7	4.58	281	78	8	32	63	.278	.452	.351
April	1-2	4.50	70	24	2	5	13	.343	.486	.387
May	1-1	7.02	63	18	1	12	14	.286	.349	.400
June	0-3	4.80	56	14	3	5	13	.250	.500	.323
July	2-3	4.50	108	30	3	13	21	.278	.472	.352
August	0-0	4.26	70	22	2	13	16	.314	.457	.407
Sept./Oct.	1-1	2.25	43	11	0	7	9	.256	.326	.365
Leading Off Inn.			92	31	3	11	21	.337	.500	.413
Bases Empty			197	62	6	29	39	.315	.467	.405
Runners On			213	57	5	26	47	.268	.418	.343
Runners/Scor. Pos.			123	32	1	23	26	.260	.374	.368
Runners On/2 Out			88	26	1	11	22	.295	.443	.374
Scor. Pos./2 Out			58	19	0	11	15	.328	.466	.435
Late-Inning Pressure			128	41	2	17	25	.320	.422	.403
Leading Off			33	13	1	5	7	.394	.485	.487
Runners On			62	18	1	8	12	.290	.435	.370
Runners/Scor. Pos.			25	12	0	7	4	.480	.680	.571
First 9 Batters			336	90	9	42	75	.268	.405	.349
Second 9 Batters			54	22	2	8	8	.407	.611	.476
All Batters Thereafter			20	7	0	5	3	.350	.600	.480

Loves to face: Ken Oberkfell (0-for-10)
Paul O'Neill (0-for-15, 1 BB)
Garry Templeton (0-for-11)

Hates to face: Kevin McReynolds (.429, 9-for-21, 3 HR)
Gerald Perry (.800, 4-for-5, 3 BB)
Andy Van Slyke (.294, 5-for-17, 1 2B, 1 3B, 3 HR)

Miscellaneous statistics: Ground outs-to-air outs ratio: 0.89 last season, 0.88 for career. . . . Induced 10 double-play ground outs in 107 opportunities (one per 10.7). . . . Allowed 17 doubles, 6 triples in 108.2 innings. . . . Stranded 18 inherited runners, allowed 14 to score (56%). . . . Opposing base stealers: 8-for-15 (53%); 3 pickoffs, 1 balk.

Comments: Much like the Dodgers' acquisition of Bob Ojeda, the Braves traded for Parrett after he had compiled outstanding numbers against them: 6–1 record, 1.41 ERA for his career; 3–0, 0.82 in 11 innings last season. . . . After two years of high-flying won-lost records (12–4 in 1988, 12–6 in 1989), he crashed (5–10) in 1990. . . . His problems were the direct result of letting the leadoff batter reach base more frequently than any other pitcher in the National League last season. Opponents had a .413 on-base average when leading off innings (minimum: 100 leadoff batters faced). . . . He had been the first reliever since Bill Campbell in 1976–77 with 12 or more wins in consecutive seasons. Still is, come to think of it. . . . Opponents batted .320 in Late-Inning Pressure Situations last season, more than 100 points higher than they had in each of the previous two seasons. . . . Allowed seven home runs to left-handed batters last season after holding them homerless since 1987. . . . Opponents have hit for a higher average in road games than in home games in each of his five years in the majors. Opponents' career averages: .219 at home, .274 on the road; .282 on grass fields, .232 on artificial surfaces. Before coming to Atlanta, he'd pitched all his home games on artificial turf. . . . Ran his career record at Veterans Stadium to 10–0 before finally dropping a decision there on May 28.

Alejandro Pena

Throws Right

New York Mets	W-L	ERA	AB	H	HR	BB	SO	BA	SA	OBA
Season	3-3	3.20	290	71	4	22	76	.245	.338	.295
vs. Left-Handers			131	33	1	14	39	.252	.321	.322
vs. Right-Handers			159	38	3	8	37	.239	.352	.272
vs. Ground-Ballers			149	36	1	7	41	.242	.309	.275
vs. Fly-Ballers			141	35	3	15	35	.248	.369	.314
Home Games	1-0	3.19	115	25	3	13	27	.217	.330	.295
Road Games	2-3	3.20	175	46	1	9	49	.263	.343	.294
Grass Fields	1-2	3.81	201	50	4	17	45	.249	.363	.305
Artificial Turf	2-1	1.88	89	21	0	5	31	.236	.281	.271
April	0-0	5.00	37	12	0	1	9	.324	.405	.325
May	1-1	2.31	42	9	1	5	13	.214	.357	.292
June	1-1	6.92	52	15	1	5	11	.288	.404	.339
July	0-1	2.19	45	8	0	3	15	.178	.222	.229
August	0-0	3.46	52	16	2	7	8	.308	.442	.393
Sept./Oct.	1-0	0.53	62	11	0	1	20	.177	.226	.190
Leading Off Inn.			69	13	1	4	17	.188	.275	.233
Bases Empty			164	37	3	10	44	.226	.335	.270
Runners On			126	34	1	12	32	.270	.341	.324
Runners/Scor. Pos.			79	20	0	10	23	.253	.316	.316
Runners On/2 Out			60	17	0	8	14	.283	.350	.368
Scor. Pos./2 Out			44	13	0	7	12	.295	.386	.392
Late-Inning Pressure			75	16	1	5	20	.213	.293	.256
Leading Off			16	4	0	3	2	.250	.313	.368
Runners On			35	9	0	1	9	.257	.314	.263
Runners/Scor. Pos.			25	5	0	0	8	.200	.240	.185
First 9 Batters			263	63	3	21	69	.240	.323	.292
Second 9 Batters			27	8	1	1	7	.296	.481	.321
All Batters Thereafter			0	0	0	0	0	—	—	—

Loves to face: Ron Gant (0-for-10)
Terry Kennedy (.043, 1-for-23, 1 HR, 2 BB)
Gary Redus (.063, 1-for-16)

Hates to face: Ken Caminiti (.500, 4-for-8)
Billy Hatcher (.438, 7-for-16, 1 HR, 5 SO)
Jerome Walton (.556, 5-for-9)

Miscellaneous statistics: Ground outs-to-air outs ratio: 0.70 last season, 1.02 for career. . . . Induced 3 double-play ground outs in 56 opportunities (one per 18.7). . . . Allowed 11 doubles, 2 triples in 76.0 innings. . . . Stranded 13 inherited runners, allowed 7 to score (65%). . . . Opposing base stealers: 11-for-11; 0 pickoffs, 0 balks.

Comments: His 3–3 record last year leaves him 41–41 for his major league career. That breaks down as follows: 19–19 at home, 21–21 on the road; 29–30 on grass fields, 11–10 on artificial surfaces; 11–10 in day games, 29–30 in night games. He's also 1–1 in postseason play. You can't get much more consistent than that. . . . But, of course, we'll try. Compare Pena's numbers for the Dodgers in 1989 with his statistics with the Mets last season. In 1989: 53 games, 4–3 record, five saves, 76 innings, 75 strikeouts. In 1990: 52 games, 3–3 record, five saves, 76 innings, 76 strikeouts. . . . One of five active pitchers with at least 800 innings and a career ERA below 3.00. Pena's never been an All-Star, but he's in company with four: Orel Hershiser (2.71), Dwight Gooden (2.82), Lee Smith (2.88), and Roger Clemens (2.89), then Pena (2.95). . . . Allowed only one run in 23⅓ innings over the last seven weeks of the season, and issued only one walk—an intentional one, at that—to the last 66 batters he faced. . . . At the age of 31, he finished the 1990 season with 76 strikeouts in 76 innings, the first time in his career that he has averaged a strikeout an inning. That's reminiscent of the career of Harvey Haddix, who never struck out a batter per inning until he did it in consecutive seasons (70 strikeouts in 70 innings in 1963 and 90-in-90 in 1964) during which he turned 38 and 39 years of age.

Jeff Pico

Throws Right

Chicago Cubs	W-L	ERA	AB	H	HR	BB	SO	BA	SA	OBA
Season	4-4	4.79	374	120	7	37	37	.321	.455	.382
vs. Left-Handers			198	74	3	25	13	.374	.495	.442
vs. Right-Handers			176	46	4	12	24	.261	.409	.309
vs. Ground-Ballers			168	52	2	14	18	.310	.411	.364
vs. Fly-Ballers			206	68	5	23	19	.330	.490	.396
Home Games	2-1	5.37	222	76	5	22	22	.342	.486	.400
Road Games	2-3	3.99	152	44	2	15	15	.289	.408	.355
Grass Fields	3-3	5.06	309	102	6	33	29	.330	.463	.394
Artificial Turf	1-1	3.63	65	18	1	4	8	.277	.415	.324
April	0-0	10.13	37	14	1	8	3	.378	.595	.489
May	1-0	4.76	43	13	1	4	3	.302	.372	.362
June	3-0	3.66	123	35	2	11	16	.285	.390	.341
July	0-2	3.32	87	28	2	5	7	.322	.448	.362
August	0-2	6.88	77	29	1	7	6	.377	.558	.429
Sept./Oct.	0-0	0.00	7	1	0	2	2	.143	.286	.333
Leading Off Inn.			82	25	4	5	4	.305	.524	.345
Bases Empty			182	56	4	17	19	.308	.434	.367
Runners On			192	64	3	20	18	.333	.474	.395
Runners/Scor. Pos.			115	39	3	18	11	.339	.513	.426
Runners On/2 Out			78	21	1	10	7	.269	.397	.360
Scor. Pos./2 Out			51	14	1	9	6	.275	.451	.393
Late-Inning Pressure			30	10	2	1	1	.333	.600	.355
Leading Off			10	4	2	0	0	.400	1.200	.400
Runners On			8	1	0	1	0	.125	.125	.222
Runners/Scor. Pos.			2	1	0	1	0	.500	.500	.667
First 9 Batters			195	73	3	26	21	.374	.523	.446
Second 9 Batters			100	28	2	9	14	.280	.410	.339
All Batters Thereafter			79	19	2	2	2	.241	.342	.259

Loves to face: Kevin Elster (.143, 2-for-14)
Barry Larkin (.071, 1-for-14)
Lonnie Smith (.100, 1-for-10, 5 SO)

Hates to face: Kal Daniels (.615, 8-for-13)
John Kruk (.714, 5-for-7, 1 HR)
Andy Van Slyke (.545, 6-for-11, 2 HR)

Miscellaneous statistics: Ground outs-to-air outs ratio: 1.39 last season, 1.36 for career.... Induced 11 double-play ground outs in 98 opportunities (one per 8.9).... Allowed 19 doubles, 5 triples in 92.0 innings.... Stranded 11 inherited runners, allowed 10 to score (52%).... Opposing base stealers: 0-for-4; 0 pickoffs, 1 balk.

Comments: A virtual Welcome Wagon for left-handed batters, who smacked him for a .374 batting average last year. That's the highest batting average by lefties against any National League pitcher (minimum: 200 lefty batters faced) since we've been keeping track, beating the tar out of the old record of .349 that lefties hit against then-Cub Dick Ruthven in 1984. Ruthven, in turn, had broken the mark of then-Cub Dennis Lamp, who let lefties hit .348 in 1980, so the Cubs own the Gold, Silver, and Bronze in this category.... On a career basis, left-handers have hit .327 vs. Pico, the highest among active pitchers in either league (minimum: 500 lefty batters faced).... Opponents' career breakdown: .258 with the bases empty, .311 with runners on base, .314 with runners in scoring position.... Opponents have a .308 career average on his first pass through the lineup compared to .248 in subsequent at-bats, the largest disparity in the majors over the last five years.... Posted a 5.77 ERA in 64 innings with Joe Girardi catching, 2.57 in 28 innings with Hector Villanueva or Rick Wrona catching.... On the positive side (it's about time!), he was the only National League pitcher with at least 30 innings last season who didn't allow a stolen base.... Leading hitters among pitchers with at least 20 at-bats last season: Dennis Cook (.318 as pitcher, .306 overall), Fernando Valenzuela (.284 as pitcher, .304 overall), Dennis Rasmussen (.279 as pitcher, .290 overall), Pico (.273 on 6-for-22).

Mark Portugal

Throws Right

Houston Astros	W-L	ERA	AB	H	HR	BB	SO	BA	SA	OBA
Season	11-10	3.62	747	187	21	67	136	.250	.375	.313
vs. Left-Handers			428	97	10	44	90	.227	.329	.301
vs. Right-Handers			319	90	11	23	46	.282	.436	.330
vs. Ground-Ballers			354	80	5	36	69	.226	.311	.303
vs. Fly-Ballers			393	107	16	31	67	.272	.433	.322
Home Games	8-2	1.78	366	78	4	31	74	.213	.284	.276
Road Games	3-8	5.57	381	109	17	36	62	.286	.462	.348
Grass Fields	2-6	6.31	279	85	13	18	42	.305	.484	.346
Artificial Turf	9-4	2.22	468	102	8	49	94	.218	.310	.294
April	1-3	3.68	90	27	1	4	14	.300	.411	.330
May	0-2	5.02	115	32	4	11	14	.278	.426	.346
June	1-2	3.40	139	30	6	12	28	.216	.381	.281
July	2-2	4.24	132	36	6	12	27	.273	.439	.329
August	4-0	1.27	134	33	0	12	29	.246	.299	.306
Sept./Oct.	3-1	4.38	137	29	4	16	24	.212	.314	.299
Leading Off Inn.			182	48	5	24	32	.264	.401	.356
Bases Empty			438	111	10	35	76	.253	.370	.312
Runners On			309	76	11	32	60	.246	.382	.315
Runners/Scor. Pos.			161	40	6	23	35	.248	.398	.339
Runners On/2 Out			118	23	2	15	28	.195	.263	.291
Scor. Pos./2 Out			73	13	0	12	18	.178	.192	.302
Late-Inning Pressure			44	13	1	7	6	.295	.386	.392
Leading Off			14	5	0	2	2	.357	.357	.438
Runners On			14	3	1	4	2	.214	.429	.389
Runners/Scor. Pos.			5	0	0	2	1	.000	.000	.286
First 9 Batters			253	57	4	26	54	.225	.316	.298
Second 9 Batters			265	66	8	15	47	.249	.381	.291
All Batters Thereafter			229	64	9	26	35	.279	.432	.354

Loves to face: Howard Johnson (.077, 1-for-13)
Jose Uribe (.067, 1-for-15, 2 BB)
Matt Williams (.077, 2-for-26)

Hates to face: Kal Daniels (.625, 5-for-8, 2 HR)
Ron Gant (.750, 6-for-8, 1 HR)
Darryl Strawberry (.500, 5-for-10, 2 HR, 4 SO)

Miscellaneous statistics: Ground outs-to-air outs ratio: 1.31 last season, 1.29 for career.... Induced 16 double-play ground outs in 163 opportunities (one per 10.2).... Allowed 28 doubles, 1 triple in 196.2 innings.... Allowed 19 first-inning runs in 32 starts (4.50 ERA).... Batting support: 3.44 runs per start (5th lowest in N.L.) ... Opposing base stealers: 23-for-32 (72%); 1 pickoff, 0 balks.

Comments: Owns 18–11 record in two years with Houston after compiling 11–19 mark in four years with Minnesota.... He must spend All-Star breaks reading *Dr. Jekyll and Mr. Hyde*. His career breakdown: 6–21, 5.44 ERA during the first half of the season; 23–9, 3.03 ERA after the break. Last season he was 8–2 in the second half.... His streak of 11 consecutive starts without a victory was two shy of the team record shared by the unlikely combination of Bob Bruce (1966) and Nolan Ryan (1985).... Opponents batted 87 points higher on grass fields (.305) than on artificial turf (.218) last season, the 2d-largest gap of that type in the majors.... Opposing right-handers (.282) batted 55 points higher than left-handers (.227) last season, the 5th-largest margin in the majors.... Has held opponents to a lower batting average with runners in scoring position than he has in other at-bats in each of his six seasons in the majors. Opponents' career breakdown: .224 with RISP, .271 in other at-bats. Opponents have batted under .200 with two outs and RISP in four of the last five seasons.... National League's top 10 home-run hitters combined to hit seven shots against Portugal. Only Pete Smith did as much to help give that list its shape.... Had a 2.88 ERA in 121⅔ innings with Craig Biggio behind the plate, but a 4.80 ERA in 75 innings when teamed with other catchers.

Ted Power

Throws Right

Pittsburgh Pirates	W-L	ERA	AB	H	HR	BB	SO	BA	SA	OBA
Season	1-3	3.66	196	50	5	17	42	.255	.378	.312
vs. Left-Handers			78	20	2	14	18	.256	.372	.366
vs. Right-Handers			118	30	3	3	24	.254	.381	.270
vs. Ground-Ballers			80	18	1	8	21	.225	.338	.295
vs. Fly-Ballers			116	32	4	9	21	.276	.405	.323
Home Games	1-1	4.88	101	27	2	11	23	.267	.396	.333
Road Games	0-2	2.25	95	23	3	6	19	.242	.358	.287
Grass Fields	0-0	2.08	57	15	2	3	11	.263	.386	.300
Artificial Turf	1-3	4.19	139	35	3	14	31	.252	.374	.316
April	0-0	0.00	37	6	0	2	6	.162	.162	.205
May	0-2	5.73	47	13	3	1	13	.277	.532	.286
June	0-0	0.00	9	2	0	2	3	.222	.222	.333
July	1-0	3.18	40	9	0	5	8	.225	.275	.311
August	0-0	1.23	25	6	1	4	4	.240	.440	.345
Sept./Oct.	0-1	9.35	38	14	1	3	8	.368	.500	.415
Leading Off Inn.			46	13	2	0	13	.283	.457	.283
Bases Empty			109	24	3	5	26	.220	.349	.254
Runners On			87	26	2	12	16	.299	.414	.376
Runners/Scor. Pos.			54	17	2	9	10	.315	.500	.400
Runners On/2 Out			40	10	0	7	8	.250	.300	.362
Scor. Pos./2 Out			29	8	0	5	5	.276	.345	.382
Late-Inning Pressure			67	16	2	6	14	.239	.388	.301
Leading Off			18	6	0	0	6	.333	.444	.333
Runners On			26	7	1	3	3	.269	.462	.345
Runners/Scor. Pos.			13	6	1	3	1	.462	.846	.563
First 9 Batters			184	47	5	17	39	.255	.375	.315
Second 9 Batters			10	3	0	0	3	.300	.500	.300
All Batters Thereafter			2	0	0	0	0	.000	.000	.000

Loves to face: Rafael Ramirez (.120, 3-for-25)
Benito Santiago (.067, 1-for-15)
Andres Thomas (.067, 1-for-15)

Hates to face: Will Clark (.500, 6-for-12, 2 HR)
John Kruk (.588, 10-for-17)
Willie McGee (.438, 7-for-16)

Miscellaneous statistics: Ground outs-to-air outs ratio: 0.79 last season, 0.86 for career. . . . Induced 4 double-play ground outs in 39 opportunities (one per 9.8). . . . Allowed 7 doubles, 1 triple in 51.2 innings. . . . Stranded 15 inherited runners, allowed 8 to score (65%). . . . Opposing base stealers: 4-for-6 (67%); 0 pickoffs, 0 balks.

Comments: Started Game Six of 1990 Championship Series in strategic gambit by Jim Leyland, after not starting a game all season. There have been 725 postseason games in major league history (meaning 1450 starting pitchers); only one other pitcher has ever started a postseason game after not starting any games during the regular season. That was Jim Konstanty of the 1950 Phillies, who opened the World Series against the Yankees. He went eight innings and lost 1–0 on a scoring fly ball by Jerry Coleman. . . . Career breakdown: 26–32, 4.52 ERA as a starter, 32–27, 3.68 ERA as a reliever. . . . As a hitter, he's 0-for-31 in his career with two outs and runners in scoring position. . . . Has played on clubs with winning records in each of the last six seasons, but has not played two consecutive years for any club since 1986–87 with Cincinnati. He is one of eight players who have appeared with at least five different clubs over the last four years. Two of them, Jerry Reuss and Orlando Mercado, appeared with six clubs over that span. . . . He'll become the 15th pitcher to have had two separate tours of duty with the Cincinnati Reds. The most famous: Joe Nuxhall. Like Power, Nuxie missed out on a Reds pennant winner in the interim: the Ol' Left-Hander was sent to Kansas City before the 1961 season, then returned to the Rhineland the next year.

Dennis Rasmussen

Throws Left

San Diego Padres	W-L	ERA	AB	H	HR	BB	SO	BA	SA	OBA
Season	11-15	4.51	742	217	28	62	86	.292	.451	.348
vs. Left-Handers			109	36	5	7	13	.330	.532	.381
vs. Right-Handers			633	181	23	55	73	.286	.438	.342
vs. Ground-Ballers			321	84	11	31	39	.262	.399	.330
vs. Fly-Ballers			421	133	17	31	47	.316	.492	.362
Home Games	5-9	4.37	399	119	16	31	45	.298	.461	.352
Road Games	6-6	4.67	343	98	12	31	41	.286	.440	.343
Grass Fields	8-13	4.81	578	172	25	42	65	.298	.471	.346
Artificial Turf	3-2	3.50	164	45	3	20	21	.274	.384	.353
April	1-1	5.12	77	23	3	8	7	.299	.455	.365
May	4-1	2.61	145	37	4	9	22	.255	.372	.297
June	2-2	3.46	100	28	3	8	10	.280	.410	.330
July	0-5	6.34	142	50	3	12	12	.352	.472	.404
August	1-4	4.63	130	35	4	14	16	.269	.415	.345
Sept./Oct.	3-2	5.15	148	44	11	11	19	.297	.568	.348
Leading Off Inn.			179	52	9	15	19	.291	.503	.349
Bases Empty			437	130	19	32	50	.297	.476	.348
Runners On			305	87	9	30	36	.285	.416	.347
Runners/Scor. Pos.			166	47	5	22	28	.283	.428	.363
Runners On/2 Out			133	34	4	19	22	.256	.376	.353
Scor. Pos./2 Out			86	20	4	12	19	.233	.407	.333
Late-Inning Pressure			18	8	1	2	1	.444	.611	.500
Leading Off			6	2	1	1	1	.333	.833	.429
Runners On			8	4	0	1	0	.500	.500	.556
Runners/Scor. Pos.			4	3	0	1	0	.750	.750	.800
First 9 Batters			258	69	9	24	43	.267	.407	.327
Second 9 Batters			237	72	10	20	19	.304	.511	.364
All Batters Thereafter			247	76	9	18	24	.308	.441	.353

Loves to face: Vince Coleman (.083, 1-for-12, 5 SO)
Alfredo Griffin (.156, 5-for-32)
Spike Owen (.069, 2-for-29, 3 BB)

Hates to face: Pedro Guerrero (.733, 11-for-15)
Gerald Perry (.467, 7-for-15, 2 HR)
Matt Williams (.533, 8-for-15, 2 2B, 3 HR)

Miscellaneous statistics: Ground outs-to-air outs ratio: 0.85 last season, 0.78 for career. . . . Induced 13 double-play ground outs in 148 opportunities (one per 11.4). . . . Allowed 30 doubles, 2 triples in 187.2 innings. . . . Allowed 23 first-inning runs in 32 starts (4.78 ERA). . . . Batting support: 4.66 runs per start. . . . Opposing base stealers: 21-for-37 (57%); 8 pickoffs, 1 balk.

Comments: He's now 80–60 in 200 career starts and 10 relief appearances, despite a lofty 4.13 ERA. There are 45 other active pitchers with career ERAs between 4.00 and 4.25; those pitchers have a collective won-lost record of 1250–1437 (.465). . . . You can win a friendly brew with this one: Rasmussen had a plus-12 year (18–6) with the Yankees in 1986; he and Ron Guidry are the only Yankees pitchers with a plus-10 (or better) season over the past 10 years. . . . One of 12 pitchers with at least 30 starts in each of the past five seasons. . . . Led the National League in home runs allowed; his rate of one home run allowed every 6.7 innings was 3d-worst among N.L. pitchers (minimum: 90 innings). . . . Opponents' batting average has increased in each year since 1986, as he has set new career highs in that category in each of the last three years: .217, .253, .256, .270, .292. . . . His .290 batting average in 1990 raised his career mark to .205. Season's highlight had to be a three-run pinch-hit double off Joe Boever in 10th inning on June 24 (even though the Braves came back to win with three in the 10th and one in the 12th). No pitcher has hit a pinch-hit grand-slam home run since 1953, when White Sox manager Paul Richards used Tommy Byrne to pinch-hit for third baseman Vern Stephens (who hit 247 career home runs) against Yankees sidewheeler Ewell Blackwell. Byrne's grand slam won the game for the Sox. . . . Yankees reacquired Byrne that winter, after which he went 0-for-31 as a pinch-hitter for Casey Stengel.

Jose Rijo

Throws Right

Cincinnati Reds	W-L	ERA	AB	H	HR	BB	SO	BA	SA	OBA
Season	14-8	2.70	712	151	10	78	152	.212	.313	.291
vs. Left-Handers			409	89	7	58	83	.218	.318	.316
vs. Right-Handers			303	62	3	20	69	.205	.307	.255
vs. Ground-Ballers			328	78	5	32	66	.238	.341	.307
vs. Fly-Ballers			384	73	5	46	86	.190	.289	.278
Home Games	8-4	2.24	380	71	4	45	93	.187	.279	.276
Road Games	6-4	3.25	332	80	6	33	59	.241	.352	.309
Grass Fields	4-3	3.00	213	49	3	20	33	.230	.324	.295
Artificial Turf	10-5	2.57	499	102	7	58	119	.204	.309	.290
April	1-1	3.94	61	17	1	6	14	.279	.377	.343
May	2-0	3.10	105	26	2	15	25	.248	.390	.342
June	2-2	3.73	147	27	2	14	28	.184	.299	.259
July	2-1	3.10	82	22	2	5	13	.268	.378	.310
August	3-2	2.67	117	24	2	19	21	.205	.316	.321
Sept./Oct.	4-2	1.26	200	35	1	19	51	.175	.235	.245
Leading Off Inn.			180	32	4	22	36	.178	.289	.267
Bases Empty			446	88	7	46	93	.197	.303	.272
Runners On			266	63	3	32	59	.237	.331	.322
Runners/Scor. Pos.			161	38	1	23	37	.236	.311	.333
Runners On/2 Out			125	27	1	14	27	.216	.296	.305
Scor. Pos./2 Out			83	20	1	11	19	.241	.337	.337
Late-Inning Pressure			49	11	0	4	11	.224	.265	.283
Leading Off			14	3	0	1	2	.214	.286	.267
Runners On			15	6	0	1	2	.400	.467	.438
Runners/Scor. Pos.			6	2	0	0	0	.333	.333	.333
First 9 Batters			228	50	1	27	53	.219	.285	.304
Second 9 Batters			227	54	5	30	51	.238	.374	.329
All Batters Thereafter			257	47	4	21	48	.183	.284	.245

Loves to face: Doug Dascenzo (0-for-10)
Fred Lynn (0-for-14)
Rafael Ramirez (.105, 2-for-19)

Hates to face: George Bell (.636, 7-for-11, 1 HR)
Mark Grace (.462, 6-for-13, 1 HR)
Darryl Strawberry (.429, 6-for-14, 2 HR)

Miscellaneous statistics: Ground outs-to-air outs ratio: 1.10 last season, 1.16 for career.... Induced 10 double-play ground outs in 110 opportunities (one per 11.0).... Allowed 34 doubles, 4 triples in 197.0 innings.... Allowed 12 first-inning runs in 29 starts (3.41 ERA).... Batting support: 4.38 runs per start.... Opposing base stealers: 19-for-23 (83%); 6 pickoffs (led N.L. right-handers), 5 balks.

Comments: Held opposing batters to .313 slugging average, lowest among N.L. pitchers (minimum: 162 innings).... Rate of 10 home runs allowed in 197 innings was 4th lowest among the same group; he has not yielded two homers in a game since June 14, 1989.... Opponents have hit for a higher average in Late-Inning Pressure Situations than they have in other at-bats in each of the last five seasons.... A veteran at the age of 25, Rijo is actually younger than many of last season's most prominent rookies, including Kevin Maas, John Burkett, Felix Jose, and teammate Hal Morris. He's also younger than teammate Jack Armstrong, who completed his first full season in the majors last year.... Career record of 27–34 before the All-Star break, 26–18 after.... Had 3.46 ERA in 88⅓ innings with Joe Oliver as a batterymate; with Jeff Reed catching he had a 2.10 ERA in 98⅔ innings.... In three seasons in the National League, Rijo has compiled a 2.62 ERA. That's lower than the career ERAs of Orel Hershiser (2.71) or Dwight Gooden (2.82).... Pitchers have won the World Series MVP award in each of the last four Series, after only one pitcher (Bret Saberhagen) won it in the previous 12 years. Pitchers won the award in 11 of the first 12 years of its existence, starting with Johnny Podres in 1955.

Don Robinson

Throws Right

San Francisco Giants	W-L	ERA	AB	H	HR	BB	SO	BA	SA	OBA
Season	10-7	4.57	618	173	18	41	78	.280	.432	.324
vs. Left-Handers			365	104	12	32	39	.285	.455	.343
vs. Right-Handers			253	69	6	9	39	.273	.399	.295
vs. Ground-Ballers			299	70	1	17	48	.234	.301	.274
vs. Fly-Ballers			319	103	17	24	30	.323	.555	.371
Home Games	4-1	5.04	247	77	9	10	37	.312	.510	.336
Road Games	6-6	4.27	371	96	9	31	41	.259	.380	.317
Grass Fields	7-2	4.54	400	117	12	18	55	.293	.457	.322
Artificial Turf	3-5	4.61	218	56	6	23	23	.257	.385	.328
April	0-0	—	0	0	0	0	0	—	—	—
May	1-0	2.84	47	12	0	7	4	.255	.319	.352
June	2-1	4.40	121	33	6	5	13	.273	.471	.307
July	4-0	3.33	175	41	3	9	23	.234	.354	.270
August	3-3	3.80	176	44	7	11	27	.250	.409	.293
Sept./Oct.	0-3	10.29	99	43	2	9	11	.434	.616	.477
Leading Off Inn.			155	41	5	8	18	.265	.413	.301
Bases Empty			382	99	9	21	47	.259	.393	.300
Runners On			236	74	9	20	31	.314	.496	.363
Runners/Scor. Pos.			142	44	6	16	23	.310	.465	.373
Runners On/2 Out			111	35	6	8	16	.315	.541	.361
Scor. Pos./2 Out			76	24	4	7	13	.316	.500	.373
Late-Inning Pressure			76	21	1	5	10	.276	.395	.321
Leading Off			22	6	0	1	1	.273	.318	.304
Runners On			22	8	0	4	2	.364	.500	.462
Runners/Scor. Pos.			12	5	0	3	1	.417	.417	.533
First 9 Batters			215	67	10	14	26	.312	.521	.354
Second 9 Batters			187	44	2	15	26	.235	.305	.294
All Batters Thereafter			216	62	6	12	26	.287	.454	.322

Loves to face: Ken Caminiti (.103, 3-for-29, 2 2B)
Alfredo Griffin (.050, 1-for-20)
Howard Johnson (.125, 3-for-24)

Hates to face: Paul O'Neill (.313, 10-for-32, 5 HR)
Darryl Strawberry (.481, 13-for-27, 2 HR)
Jeff Treadway (.467, 7-for-15, 1 HR)

Miscellaneous statistics: Ground outs-to-air outs ratio: 0.84 last season, 0.86 for career.... Induced 6 double-play ground outs in 100 opportunities (one per 16.7).... Allowed 36 doubles, 2 triples in 157.2 innings.... Allowed 29 first-inning runs in 25 starts (10.44 ERA, highest in majors).... Batting support: 4.16 runs per start.... Opposing base stealers: 19-for-27 (70%); 2 pickoffs, 0 balks.

Comments: First-inning ERA was the highest among pitchers who started at least 15 games last season. He allowed a .360 batting average in that inning, and led National League pitchers with seven first-inning home runs allowed.... His pinch-hit home run against the Padres in June was the first by a pitcher since 1971, when Gary Peters homered in two consecutive pinch-hit at-bats for the Red Sox. No National League pitcher had hit a pinch-hit homer since Johnny Lindell of the Pirates, who hit two in 1953. But Lindell was really a position-player in disguise, since he had previously been an outfielder with the Yankees, and returned to the majors as a pitcher and pinch hitter in 1953. Except for Robinson and Lindell you'd have to go back to Schoolboy Rowe of the 1943 Phillies to find the last N.L. pitcher to hit a pinch-hit homer.... Robinson is the only active pitcher who has ever been intentionally walked in a major league game. It happened against Bill Campbell in 1984. O.K., we'll come clean. It was one of those sudden-death, load-up-the-bases-for-a-force-at-any-base type of intentional walks, and he was pinch hitting at the time, but what the hey. Before that, the last pitcher to be walked intentionally was Jim Kaat in 1970.... Highest ERAs by National League pitchers with winning records last season (minimum: 10 decisions): Ken Howell, 4.64; Les Lancaster, 4.62; Robinson, 4.57.... Career batting averages of opposing left- and right-handed batters are virtually the same (.2529 and .2535, respectively).

Bruce Ruffin

Throws Left

Philadelphia Phillies	W-L	ERA	AB	H	HR	BB	SO	BA	SA	OBA
Season	6-13	5.38	599	178	14	62	79	.297	.456	.361
vs. Left-Handers			120	35	0	12	19	.292	.358	.351
vs. Right-Handers			479	143	14	50	60	.299	.480	.363
vs. Ground-Ballers			272	73	5	32	41	.268	.386	.344
vs. Fly-Ballers			327	105	9	30	38	.321	.514	.375
Home Games	5-7	5.40	314	91	5	40	41	.290	.433	.369
Road Games	1-6	5.35	285	87	9	22	38	.305	.481	.352
Grass Fields	0-3	7.64	141	49	7	8	16	.348	.589	.377
Artificial Turf	6-10	4.73	458	129	7	54	63	.282	.415	.356
April	1-2	3.80	94	30	1	7	10	.319	.404	.363
May	2-3	5.93	125	39	4	14	9	.312	.512	.383
June	2-2	2.84	138	30	3	10	24	.217	.341	.267
July	1-3	6.84	110	35	6	14	14	.318	.573	.395
August	0-1	8.44	72	25	0	8	10	.347	.458	.407
Sept./Oct.	0-2	7.36	60	19	0	9	12	.317	.467	.400
Leading Off Inn.			143	37	4	16	19	.259	.413	.333
Bases Empty			330	86	8	34	44	.261	.412	.330
Runners On			269	92	6	28	35	.342	.509	.398
Runners/Scor. Pos.			153	55	4	19	19	.359	.549	.419
Runners On/2 Out			116	42	2	8	14	.362	.474	.403
Scor. Pos./2 Out			73	27	2	7	10	.370	.534	.425
Late-Inning Pressure			20	7	0	7	1	.350	.450	.519
Leading Off			6	1	0	3	0	.167	.167	.444
Runners On			7	2	0	3	0	.286	.286	.500
Runners/Scor. Pos.			3	1	0	2	0	.333	.333	.600
First 9 Batters			250	69	6	26	43	.276	.424	.342
Second 9 Batters			213	68	6	21	26	.319	.502	.379
All Batters Thereafter			136	41	2	15	10	.301	.441	.368

Loves to face: Barry Larkin (.071, 1-for-14, 2 BB)
Rafael Ramirez (.174, 4-for-23)
Jerome Walton (.167, 4-for-24)

Hates to face: Eric Davis (.500, 9-for-18, 1 HR)
Andres Galarraga (.478, 11-for-23, 1 HR)
Tim Wallach (.500, 11-for-22, 2 HR)

Miscellaneous statistics: Ground outs-to-air outs ratio: 1.08 last season, 2.08 for career.... Induced 10 double-play ground outs in 133 opportunities (one per 13.3).... Allowed 45 doubles (tied for 2d most in N.L.), 4 triples in 149.0 innings.... Allowed 17 first-inning runs in 25 starts (6.12 ERA).... Batting support: 4.24 runs per start.... Opposing base stealers: 3-for-7 (43%); 0 pickoffs, 2 balks.

Comments: He's good news to any hitter with RBIs on his mind. Ruffin's .359 opponents' batting average with runners in scoring position was the highest against any pitcher in the majors last season (minimum: 100 RISP at-bats). That was the third year in the last four in which he has allowed a scoring-position batting average above .300; it was .299 in the other year (1989).... A ground-ball pitcher despite last season, he has been hit for a higher average by fly-ball hitters than by ground-ball hitters in each of his five seasons in the majors. Opponents' career statistics: Fly-ball hitters .318, ground-ball hitters .253.... Finished last season with the highest ERA of any opening-day starter in the majors, and had the lowest winning percentage of any opening-day starter in the National League.... Has allowed only one home run to a left-handed batter over the last three seasons. Will Clark hit it on August 18, 1989.... His career record at Veterans Stadium is a winning one (25–24), but he's 13–27 in road games despite similar career ERAs (4.23 at home, 4.21 on road).... Had an ERA of 6.11 in 98.2 innings with Darren Daulton as his batterymate, 3.93 in 50.1 innings with either Steve Lake or Tom Nieto catching.... His ERA has increased in every season since his 1986 debut: 2.46, 4.35, 4.43, 4.44, 5.38. He's running out of major league room!

Bill Sampen

Throws Right

Montreal Expos	W-L	ERA	AB	H	HR	BB	SO	BA	SA	OBA
Season	12-7	2.99	351	94	7	33	69	.268	.362	.332
vs. Left-Handers			175	44	1	18	26	.251	.303	.318
vs. Right-Handers			176	50	6	15	43	.284	.420	.345
vs. Ground-Ballers			136	23	1	11	33	.169	.206	.235
vs. Fly-Ballers			215	71	6	22	36	.330	.460	.392
Home Games	7-4	2.96	181	53	3	12	35	.293	.376	.340
Road Games	5-3	3.02	170	41	4	21	34	.241	.347	.323
Grass Fields	3-1	3.20	98	24	3	9	22	.245	.378	.308
Artificial Turf	9-6	2.91	253	70	4	24	47	.277	.356	.340
April	0-0	0.00	25	3	0	2	5	.120	.120	.179
May	2-0	2.89	72	19	2	3	18	.264	.389	.303
June	4-1	1.89	69	17	2	8	16	.246	.362	.325
July	2-2	5.71	73	25	0	13	13	.342	.397	.438
August	2-2	2.57	52	11	2	5	12	.212	.346	.281
Sept./Oct.	2-2	3.21	60	19	1	2	5	.317	.400	.339
Leading Off Inn.			83	27	4	7	19	.325	.506	.385
Bases Empty			190	51	5	17	45	.268	.384	.332
Runners On			161	43	2	16	24	.267	.335	.331
Runners/Scor. Pos.			104	27	1	11	17	.260	.327	.328
Runners On/2 Out			70	15	0	9	14	.214	.229	.304
Scor. Pos./2 Out			50	7	0	6	9	.140	.160	.232
Late-Inning Pressure			95	20	2	16	18	.211	.295	.321
Leading Off			25	6	1	3	4	.240	.360	.321
Runners On			37	8	0	8	5	.216	.243	.348
Runners/Scor. Pos.			23	7	0	5	3	.304	.348	.414
First 9 Batters			299	80	6	28	60	.268	.365	.331
Second 9 Batters			51	14	1	5	8	.275	.353	.339
All Batters Thereafter			1	0	0	0	1	.000	.000	.000

Loves to face: Joe Girardi (0-for-5)
Dale Murphy (0-for-7)

Hates to face: Jim Presley (3-for-3, 2 2B, 1 BB)
Ryne Sandberg (.500, 3-for-6, 2 HR, 2 SO)

Miscellaneous statistics: Ground outs-to-air outs ratio: 0.86 last season, his first in the majors.... Induced 3 double-play ground outs in 73 opportunities (one per 24.3).... Allowed 12 doubles, 0 triples in 90.1 innings.... Stranded 17 inherited runners, allowed 10 to score (63%).... Opposing base stealers: 15-for-18 (83%); 0 pickoffs, 0 balks.

Comments: Tied Lee Guetterman and Barry Jones for major league lead with 11 wins in relief; the Expos' 36 bullpen wins were also a major league high, seven more than the next-highest team, the White Sox.... All 11 wins out of the bullpen were legit. That is, he was not credited with any cheap wins by entering a game with a lead and subsequently allowing the opposition to tie the game.... He had a 4–0 record against the Pirates last season. The only other National League pitcher to post a 4–0 record against any club was Dwight Gooden, who did it against both the Cubs and the Dodgers.... Allowed only one home run to a left-handed batter last season; Dave Justice hit it on May 30.... Had *never* pitched a game above the Double A level of the minors, and had *never* relieved in more than five games in any season at any level of minor league ball.... Nevertheless, he jumped to the majors last year and finished among National League rookie leaders in ERA (minimum: 70 innings): Randy Tomlin (2.55), Scott Ruskin (2.75), Chris Nabholz (2.83), Mike Hartley (2.95), Sampen (2.99).... (Our favorite "nevertheless" story: At the Madison Square Garden fights years ago, ring announcer Johnny Addie intoned, "Ladies and gentlemen, our national anthem will be played by Miss Gladys Goodding." From the darkened balcony a voice barked, "Gladys Goodding is a @#$?%*#&." Addie, unruffled, replied, *"Nevertheless, our national anthem!"*)

Calvin Schiraldi

Throws Right

San Diego Padres	W-L	ERA	AB	H	HR	BB	SO	BA	SA	OBA
Season	3-8	4.41	397	105	11	60	74	.264	.423	.360
vs. Left-Handers			201	52	7	40	32	.259	.428	.380
vs. Right-Handers			196	53	4	20	42	.270	.418	.338
vs. Ground-Ballers			175	48	4	21	36	.274	.411	.350
vs. Fly-Ballers			222	57	7	39	38	.257	.432	.367
Home Games	2-5	4.24	248	65	6	32	45	.262	.431	.348
Road Games	1-3	4.69	149	40	5	28	29	.268	.409	.380
Grass Fields	3-6	4.48	312	84	9	43	55	.269	.439	.358
Artificial Turf	0-2	4.18	85	21	2	17	19	.247	.365	.369
April	1-0	3.29	54	15	1	4	11	.278	.333	.328
May	0-0	9.00	40	12	2	14	6	.300	.525	.473
June	1-0	1.72	53	8	2	10	16	.151	.302	.286
July	1-3	2.75	73	21	1	8	16	.288	.466	.361
August	0-4	5.20	110	31	4	16	18	.282	.473	.370
Sept./Oct.	0-1	5.71	67	18	1	8	7	.269	.403	.347
Leading Off Inn.			89	26	4	14	14	.292	.506	.388
Bases Empty			199	54	6	34	38	.271	.442	.378
Runners On			198	51	5	26	36	.258	.404	.342
Runners/Scor. Pos.			119	35	2	19	24	.294	.445	.387
Runners On/2 Out			89	27	2	11	9	.303	.472	.386
Scor. Pos./2 Out			59	20	1	6	7	.339	.542	.409
Late-Inning Pressure			45	13	1	9	12	.289	.422	.407
Leading Off			12	5	1	3	5	.417	.750	.533
Runners On			20	4	0	5	4	.200	.300	.360
Runners/Scor. Pos.			14	4	0	4	4	.286	.429	.444
First 9 Batters			245	64	7	42	51	.261	.408	.369
Second 9 Batters			100	27	3	12	16	.270	.450	.348
All Batters Thereafter			52	14	1	6	7	.269	.442	.339

Loves to face: Sid Bream (0-for-11, 4 BB)
Alfredo Griffin (.067, 1-for-15, 2 BB)
Ricky Jordan (0-for-10)

Hates to face: Mike Aldrete (.800, 4-for-5, 1 SO)
Terry Kennedy (.600, 6-for-10, 1 HR)
Ozzie Smith (.636, 7-for-11)

Miscellaneous statistics: Ground outs-to-air outs ratio: 0.77 last season, 0.78 for career. . . . Induced 6 double-play ground outs in 89 opportunities (one per 14.8). . . . Allowed 18 doubles, 6 triples in 104.0 innings. . . . Stranded 3 inherited runners, allowed 16 to score (16%). . . . Opposing base stealers: 15-for-22 (68%); 1 pickoff, 1 balk.

Comments: At one end of the relief pitchers spectrum there is the Fireman of the Year Award. At the other end stands the Mrs. O'Leary's Cow Award. Meet the cow. Schiraldi stranded the first three runners he inherited last season, but then, incredibly, he let every inherited runner score for the rest of the season, a total of 16 runners. That includes three occasions on which he entered a game with the bases loaded and let all three men score. You can't make this stuff up. . . . Started eight games late in the season (undoubtedly after Greg Riddock realized that starting pitchers can't inherit any runners) but had a 1–5 record with two no-decisions. Career breakdown: 15–21, 4.64 ERA as a starter; 17–17, 3.83 ERA in relief. . . . Predictably, left-handed ground-ball hitters give this right-handed fly-ball pitcher the most trouble. Career breakdowns: Ground-ball hitters .271, fly-ball hitters .231; left-handers .264, right-handers .231. . . . Gives up homers at bad times—and no, we're not talking about the 1986 World Series. Has allowed 37 homers in 955 at-bats with runners on base, compared to 22 in 1128 with the bases empty. We'll save you the math: his rate of runners-on-base homers allowed is about twice his bases-empty rate. . . . Schiraldi and Don Robinson are the only pitchers who have hit home runs in each of the last two seasons. Bill Gullickson has homered in each of *his* last two seasons (1987 and 1990), while spending '88 and '89 in another hemisphere.

Dave Schmidt

Throws Right

Montreal Expos	W-L	ERA	AB	H	HR	BB	SO	BA	SA	OBA
Season	3-3	4.31	194	58	3	13	22	.299	.423	.341
vs. Left-Handers			109	33	2	9	10	.303	.450	.353
vs. Right-Handers			85	25	1	4	12	.294	.388	.326
vs. Ground-Ballers			93	27	1	5	10	.290	.419	.323
vs. Fly-Ballers			101	31	2	8	12	.307	.426	.358
Home Games	0-0	3.52	94	26	0	8	13	.277	.351	.333
Road Games	3-3	5.04	100	32	3	5	9	.320	.490	.349
Grass Fields	2-1	6.59	57	18	2	3	6	.316	.491	.350
Artificial Turf	1-2	3.41	137	40	1	10	16	.292	.394	.338
April	0-0	—	0	0	0	0	0	—	—	—
May	1-0	4.50	66	19	0	7	13	.288	.394	.356
June	2-0	2.37	71	18	1	3	4	.254	.352	.280
July	0-3	6.92	57	21	2	3	5	.368	.544	.400
August	0-0	—	0	0	0	0	0	—	—	—
Sept./Oct.	0-0	—	0	0	0	0	0	—	—	—
Leading Off Inn.			44	14	1	2	5	.318	.523	.348
Bases Empty			102	33	2	3	9	.324	.490	.343
Runners On			92	25	1	10	13	.272	.348	.340
Runners/Scor. Pos.			59	19	1	9	9	.322	.441	.406
Runners On/2 Out			44	14	0	7	6	.318	.386	.412
Scor. Pos./2 Out			33	12	0	6	3	.364	.455	.462
Late-Inning Pressure			127	42	3	6	10	.331	.465	.358
Leading Off			30	11	1	2	3	.367	.567	.406
Runners On			57	18	1	4	5	.316	.404	.355
Runners/Scor. Pos.			33	13	1	4	3	.394	.545	.447
First 9 Batters			184	54	3	13	22	.293	.413	.338
Second 9 Batters			10	4	0	0	0	.400	.600	.400
All Batters Thereafter			0	0	0	0	0	—	—	—

Loves to face: Stan Javier (0-for-9)
Mike Pagliarulo (.118, 2-for-17)
Lonnie Smith (0-for-8)

Hates to face: Fred Lynn (.500, 5-for-10, 2 HR)
Spike Owen (.500, 9-for-18, 1 HR)
Jim Presley (.480, 12-for-25)

Miscellaneous statistics: Ground outs-to-air outs ratio: 1.07 last season, 1.32 for career. . . . Induced 5 double-play ground outs in 34 opportunities (one per 6.8). . . . Allowed 9 doubles, 3 triples in 48.0 innings. . . . Stranded 7 inherited runners, allowed 4 to score (64%). . . . Opposing base stealers: 7-for-8 (88%); 0 pickoffs, 0 balks.

Comments: Filled in admirably as the Expos' replacement closer when Tim Burke was disabled, May 31 to July 12. Schmidt saved 13 games, a career high, all between June 3 and July 15. That was the highest total of saves by any pitcher in the National League during that 43-day stretch. . . . Looking at the opposition batting average with runners in scoring position and in Late-Inning Pressure Situations, it's hard to understand how he did it. . . . Schmidt himself spent the first 23 days and the final 69 days of the season on the disabled list. . . . Career breakdown: 33–22, 3.42 ERA before the All-Star break; 21–31, 4.35 ERA during the second half. . . . Did not surrender a home run at Olympic Stadium last season. Two of the three home runs he gave up were hit in Atlanta. . . . Allowed an average of one home run every 64.7 at-bats last season with the Expos, after allowing one every 26.3 at-bats in 1989 with the Orioles. . . . Has allowed a batting average of .300 or higher to batters leading off an inning in each of the past three seasons. . . . Opponents have hit for a higher average in LIPS than they have in other at-bats in each of the last five seasons. . . . Has faced 78 batters with the bases loaded, but has never allowed a grand-slam home run. . . . Texas's 26th-round selection in the 1979 amateur draft. Three other pitchers chosen later in that draft were still pitching in the majors last season: Kevin Gross, Mike Maddux, and Kelly Downs.

Mike Scott

Throws Right

Houston Astros	W-L	ERA	AB	H	HR	BB	SO	BA	SA	OBA
Season	9-13	3.81	789	194	27	66	121	.246	.403	.302
vs. Left-Handers			445	106	10	43	54	.238	.366	.302
vs. Right-Handers			344	88	17	23	67	.256	.451	.302
vs. Ground-Ballers			383	105	10	38	54	.274	.413	.336
vs. Fly-Ballers			406	89	17	28	67	.219	.394	.269
Home Games	5-4	2.42	472	100	11	38	81	.212	.326	.267
Road Games	4-9	6.19	317	94	16	28	40	.297	.517	.353
Grass Fields	3-6	5.30	228	63	14	18	26	.276	.531	.329
Artificial Turf	6-7	3.25	561	131	13	48	95	.234	.351	.291
April	0-2	5.74	100	24	5	16	12	.240	.430	.342
May	2-3	4.54	161	51	5	11	19	.317	.472	.358
June	4-2	3.03	144	28	5	11	31	.194	.326	.250
July	2-3	4.01	128	30	5	12	25	.234	.391	.298
August	1-2	3.43	162	40	5	9	22	.247	.414	.285
Sept./Oct.	0-1	2.33	94	21	2	7	12	.223	.372	.275
Leading Off Inn.			195	41	6	12	31	.210	.354	.256
Bases Empty			484	119	17	39	75	.246	.411	.302
Runners On			305	75	10	27	46	.246	.390	.302
Runners/Scor. Pos.			192	44	5	25	34	.229	.339	.307
Runners On/2 Out			152	40	3	18	21	.263	.368	.341
Scor. Pos./2 Out			104	24	1	17	17	.231	.288	.339
Late-Inning Pressure			59	9	1	5	2	.153	.237	.219
Leading Off			14	0	0	3	1	.000	.000	.176
Runners On			14	3	0	1	0	.214	.214	.267
Runners/Scor. Pos.			6	1	0	1	0	.167	.167	.286
First 9 Batters			262	67	10	23	55	.256	.435	.316
Second 9 Batters			262	55	8	18	41	.210	.359	.258
All Batters Thereafter			265	72	9	25	25	.272	.415	.332

Loves to face: Garry Templeton (.171, 13-for-76)
Fernando Valenzuela (.080, 2-for-25, 0 BB)
Andy Van Slyke (.026, 1-for-38, 3 BB)

Hates to face: Mike Aldrete (.357, 10-for-28, 2 HR)
Willie McGee (.548, 23-for-42)
Dickie Thon (.500, 7-for-14, 2 HR)

Miscellaneous statistics: Ground outs-to-air outs ratio: 0.92 last season, 1.10 for career. . . . Induced 9 double-play ground outs in 98 opportunities (one per 10.9). . . . Allowed 33 doubles, 5 triples in 205.2 innings. . . . Allowed 15 first-inning runs in 32 starts (4.22 ERA). . . . Batting support: 3.13 runs per start (tied for 2d lowest in N.L.) . . . Opposing base stealers: 53-for-60 (88%); 0 pickoffs, 3 balks.

Comments: Averaged better than 10 strikeouts per nine innings when he won the Cy Young Award in 1986, but his strikeout rate has declined steadily in every season since then: 8.47, 7.82, 6.76, 5.29. Only one pitcher in major league history has had a longer series of strikeout declines in 30-start seasons: Mickey Lolich, whose strikeout rate declined six years in a row from 1970 to 1975. But even in six declines, Lolich's rate only fell from 8.69 (in 1969) to 5.19 (in 1975), a total loss of 3.5 strikeouts per nine innings; Scott has already exceeded that loss by more than a full strikeout per nine innings. . . . By the way, Nolan Ryan's rate fell for four consecutive 30-start seasons, 1977 through 1980; at the time, people thought he was through. . . . Still, Scott for Danny Heep, even-up, strikes us as a pretty decent deal for the Astros. . . . Only Dwight Gooden (60) allowed more stolen bases last year than Scott (53). . . . ERA breakdown: 1.97 in his nine victories, 2.15 in 10 no-decision starts, 7.17 in his 13 defeats. Started nine games without winning after August 3. . . . Allowed 27 home runs last season, the 2d most in franchise history, behind Larry Dierker's total of 31 in 1970. Allowed an average of one homer every 7.6 innings, the 4th-worst rate among National League pitchers (minimum: 90 innings pitched). . . . Has thrown at least two shutouts in each of the last six seasons. The last pitcher with a longer streak was Ryan, who did it for 13 years in succession, 1972–84.

Eric Show

Throws Right

San Diego Padres	W-L	ERA	AB	H	HR	BB	SO	BA	SA	OBA
Season	6-8	5.76	428	131	16	41	55	.306	.472	.369
vs. Left-Handers			232	72	8	31	25	.310	.474	.389
vs. Right-Handers			196	59	8	10	30	.301	.469	.344
vs. Ground-Ballers			221	62	3	19	31	.281	.357	.339
vs. Fly-Ballers			207	69	13	22	24	.333	.594	.400
Home Games	3-5	6.22	203	64	9	22	28	.315	.507	.382
Road Games	3-3	5.34	225	67	7	19	27	.298	.440	.357
Grass Fields	5-6	5.58	355	107	15	32	46	.301	.479	.361
Artificial Turf	1-2	6.62	73	24	1	9	9	.329	.438	.405
April	0-3	4.87	83	26	5	4	7	.313	.578	.345
May	0-2	14.09	40	17	2	4	9	.425	.625	.478
June	0-1	8.77	56	15	3	8	7	.268	.482	.359
July	2-2	3.77	112	36	2	12	12	.321	.438	.386
August	2-0	3.29	49	12	3	5	8	.245	.429	.315
Sept./Oct.	2-0	5.96	88	25	1	8	12	.284	.364	.354
Leading Off Inn.			104	34	6	3	17	.327	.538	.346
Bases Empty			252	74	9	15	31	.294	.464	.333
Runners On			176	57	7	26	24	.324	.483	.414
Runners/Scor. Pos.			117	38	4	22	15	.325	.462	.424
Runners On/2 Out			78	21	2	11	7	.269	.397	.367
Scor. Pos./2 Out			55	16	2	10	2	.291	.436	.400
Late-Inning Pressure			20	1	1	0	1	.050	.200	.095
Leading Off			7	1	1	0	1	.143	.571	.143
Runners On			1	0	0	0	0	.000	.000	.500
Runners/Scor. Pos.			1	0	0	0	0	.000	.000	.000
First 9 Batters			254	77	9	21	34	.303	.476	.361
Second 9 Batters			116	28	3	12	19	.241	.353	.310
All Batters Thereafter			58	26	4	8	2	.448	.690	.515

Loves to face: Kirk Gibson (.154, 2-for-13, 5 SO)
Dan Gladden (.154, 4-for-26)
Steve Sax (.208, 10-for-48)

Hates to face: Mike Marshall (.275, 11-for-40, 4 HR)
Dave Parker (.362, 17-for-47, 5 HR)
Tim Raines (.364, 16-for-44, 2 HR, 11 BB)

Miscellaneous statistics: Ground outs-to-air outs ratio: 1.00 last season, 1.00 for career. . . . Induced 7 double-play ground outs in 88 opportunities (one per 12.6). . . . Allowed 15 doubles, 4 triples in 106.1 innings. . . . Allowed 13 first-inning runs in 12 starts (9.75 ERA). . . . Batting support: 4.08 runs per start. . . . Record of 3–7, 6.36 ERA as a starter; 3–1, 5.03 ERA in 27 relief appearances. . . . Stranded 7 inherited runners, allowed 6 to score (54%). . . . Opposing base stealers: 15-for-23 (65%); 1 pickoff, 3 balks.

Comments: Succeeds Storm Davis and Scott Sanderson as the A's continue to play rent-a-pitcher with the four-spot in their rotation. . . . Oakland acquired Davis from San Diego in 1987, after Davis had compiled a 2–7 record and 6.18 ERA; he then went 36–15 in two-plus years with the A's. Show's numbers last year as a starter have Sandy Alderson hoping that lightning will strike twice. . . . With Oakland, Show won't have the Braves to kick around anymore. Lifetime won-lost record: 18–3 vs. Atlanta, 82–84 against everybody else. . . . Compiled the 2d-highest single-season ERA in the Padres' 22-year history among pitchers with at least 100 innings pitched. Who out there remembers Rick Sawyer, who had a 5.84 ERA in 1977? . . . His victory in the Padres' season finale came in his first starting assignment since August 7. It gave him the distinction of becoming the first pitcher in club history to win 100 games. . . . He was, at one time, one of the most effective pitchers in baseball against right-handed batters. Through the first eight years of his career, right-handers hit only .208 against him. But in 1989 and 1990, they've hit .281 and .301. . . . Allowed an average of one home run every 6.6 innings last season, the 2d-worst rate among National League pitchers with at least 90 innings pitched. . . . One of four National League pitchers with both winning streaks and losing streaks of at least five games last season. The others: Neal Heaton, Greg Maddux, and Jack Armstong.

John Smiley

Throws Left

Pittsburgh Pirates	W-L	ERA	AB	H	HR	BB	SO	BA	SA	OBA
Season	9-10	4.64	585	161	15	36	86	.275	.426	.317
vs. Left-Handers			93	28	3	7	9	.301	.484	.350
vs. Right-Handers			492	133	12	29	77	.270	.415	.311
vs. Ground-Ballers			312	93	5	14	52	.298	.423	.328
vs. Fly-Ballers			273	68	10	22	34	.249	.429	.305
Home Games	3-4	3.80	247	63	7	20	43	.255	.413	.312
Road Games	6-6	5.27	338	98	8	16	43	.290	.435	.321
Grass Fields	4-5	4.76	228	65	4	8	29	.285	.412	.309
Artificial Turf	5-5	4.56	357	96	11	28	57	.269	.434	.322
April	2-2	3.33	99	21	1	4	18	.212	.303	.243
May	1-1	3.38	71	20	1	1	11	.282	.394	.292
June	0-0	—	0	0	0	0	0	—	—	—
July	1-2	5.17	152	40	6	14	21	.263	.441	.325
August	3-2	4.58	144	45	3	8	20	.313	.444	.351
Sept./Oct.	2-3	6.00	119	35	4	9	16	.294	.504	.341
Leading Off Inn.			150	45	6	8	17	.300	.473	.340
Bases Empty			350	90	9	23	46	.257	.400	.307
Runners On			235	71	6	13	40	.302	.464	.333
Runners/Scor. Pos.			129	41	5	9	23	.318	.519	.352
Runners On/2 Out			97	26	2	9	20	.268	.381	.330
Scor. Pos./2 Out			60	15	1	7	11	.250	.367	.328
Late-Inning Pressure			34	8	2	3	7	.235	.441	.289
Leading Off			8	2	0	2	1	.250	.375	.400
Runners On			13	2	1	0	4	.154	.385	.143
Runners/Scor. Pos.			6	2	1	0	1	.333	.833	.286
First 9 Batters			212	63	7	14	32	.297	.453	.344
Second 9 Batters			203	44	5	7	36	.217	.355	.246
All Batters Thereafter			170	54	3	15	18	.318	.476	.365

Loves to face: Howard Johnson (.069, 2-for-29, 0 BB)
Jose Uribe (.167, 4-for-24)
Glenn Wilson (.091, 1-for-11)

Hates to face: Kevin Bass (.458, 11-for-24)
Andre Dawson (.533, 16-for-30, 4 HR, 0 BB)
Jerome Walton (.471, 8-for-17, 2 HR, 5 SO)

Miscellaneous statistics: Ground outs-to-air outs ratio: 0.88 last season, 0.87 for career. . . . Induced 9 double-play ground outs in 100 opportunities (one per 11.1). . . . Allowed 29 doubles, 7 triples in 149.1 innings. . . . Allowed 25 first-inning runs in 25 starts (8.88 ERA, 2d highest in N.L.) . . . Batting support: 3.72 runs per start. . . . Opposing base stealers: 13-for-19 (68%); 2 pickoffs, 2 balks.

Comments: Opponents have hit for a higher average in day games than they have in night games, and for a higher average in road games than they have in home games, and for a higher average with runners in scoring position than they have in other at-bats, in each of his five seasons in the majors. Have you got all that? His opponents' career batting averages: .269 in day games, .231 at night; .262 on the road, .222 at Three Rivers Stadium; .276 with runners in scoring position, .233 in other at-bats. . . . Opponents' first-inning batting average (.383) was the highest against any major league pitcher who made at least 20 starts last season. As you might expect, Smiley's first-inning ERA was 8.88, also the 2d highest among that same group of pitchers. . . . Career breakdown: 23–12, 3.20 ERA before the All-Star break; 21–31, 4.35 ERA during the second half. Last season, he had a 3.35 ERA before he broke his hand, 5.21 after he came back. . . . Had limited left-handed batters to .197 career batting average before they belted a .301 tune against him last season. . . . Got better results in 65 innings with other batterymates (Dann Bilardello, Tom Prince, Don Slaught) last season (3.32 ERA) than he did in 84⅓ innings with Pittsburgh's number-one catcher, Mike LaValliere (5.66).

Bryn Smith

Throws Right

St. Louis Cardinals	W-L	ERA	AB	H	HR	BB	SO	BA	SA	OBA
Season	9-8	4.27	559	160	11	30	78	.286	.401	.324
vs. Left-Handers			339	102	3	18	35	.301	.392	.339
vs. Right-Handers			220	58	8	12	43	.264	.414	.302
vs. Ground-Ballers			271	69	2	14	43	.255	.339	.295
vs. Fly-Ballers			288	91	9	16	35	.316	.458	.352
Home Games	6-4	3.84	330	90	4	21	50	.273	.379	.319
Road Games	3-4	4.89	229	70	7	9	28	.306	.432	.332
Grass Fields	2-2	4.23	151	43	6	5	20	.285	.437	.308
Artificial Turf	7-6	4.28	408	117	5	25	58	.287	.387	.330
April	2-2	2.67	106	30	1	4	8	.283	.377	.313
May	3-2	3.72	150	38	5	9	26	.253	.413	.298
June	1-2	7.04	95	30	3	7	18	.316	.474	.365
July	1-2	5.33	102	32	1	5	14	.314	.382	.349
August	0-0	—	0	0	0	0	0	—	—	—
Sept./Oct.	2-0	3.29	106	30	1	5	12	.283	.358	.313
Leading Off Inn.			139	34	2	7	14	.245	.353	.281
Bases Empty			323	84	8	18	40	.260	.381	.301
Runners On			236	76	3	12	38	.322	.428	.355
Runners/Scor. Pos.			146	45	2	9	29	.308	.425	.350
Runners On/2 Out			95	27	0	5	15	.284	.379	.320
Scor. Pos./2 Out			63	15	0	5	12	.238	.333	.294
Late-Inning Pressure			30	7	0	3	5	.233	.233	.303
Leading Off			9	0	0	0	1	.000	.000	.000
Runners On			8	2	0	0	1	.250	.250	.250
Runners/Scor. Pos.			4	0	0	0	1	.000	.000	.000
First 9 Batters			205	59	2	13	29	.288	.371	.335
Second 9 Batters			197	54	5	10	27	.274	.396	.308
All Batters Thereafter			157	47	4	7	22	.299	.446	.331

Loves to face: Ron Gant (0-for-18, 1 BB)
Terry Pendleton (.132, 5-for-38)
Dickie Thon (.121, 4-for-33, 1 HR, 0 BB)

Hates to face: Danny Heep (.516, 16-for-31)
Randy Ready (.471, 8-for-17, 1 HR)
Tim Wallach (.600, 6-for-10)

Miscellaneous statistics: Ground outs-to-air outs ratio: 1.28 last season, 1.65 for career. . . . Induced 13 double-play ground outs in 109 opportunities (one per 8.4). . . . Allowed 23 doubles, 4 triples in 141.1 innings. . . . Allowed 24 first-inning runs in 25 starts (8.14 ERA, 3d highest in N.L.) . . . Batting support: 4.12 runs per start. . . . Opposing base stealers: 21-for-25 (84%); 0 pickoffs, 0 balks.

Comments: The type of guy you want sitting next to you while undergoing turbulence at 30,000 feet. He allowed 10.19 hits per nine innings, but escaped with a 9–8 record. (Allan Anderson of the Twins allowed 10.21 hits per nine innings, and finished 7–18.) Smith was the only National League pitcher (minimum: 100 innings) who had a winning record despite allowing 10 or more hits per nine innings. There were three such lucky ones in the American League: Bert Blyleven, Jamie Navarro, and Greg Swindell. . . . Opponents have hit for a higher average with runners on base than they have with the bases empty in each of the last six seasons. . . . Not only did he not complete any of his 25 starts last season, he never even pitched into the ninth inning of any of those games. . . . Opponents' first-inning batting average (.359) was the 3d highest among major league pitchers who made at least 20 starts last season. . . . Led National League pitchers with a 0.93 ERA against the Dodgers last season. . . . Opponents' overall batting average was the highest of his career. . . . Averaged 5.64 innings per start, the lowest rate among the five Cardinals' primary starting pitchers. . . . Smith agrees with Thomas Wolfe. Last June 8, in his first appearance back in Olympic Stadium as a visiting player, he experienced the earliest knockout of his career; he retired only one batter while allowing six runs, all earned.

Dave Smith

Throws Right

Houston Astros	W-L	ERA	AB	H	HR	BB	SO	BA	SA	OBA
Season	6-6	2.39	214	45	4	20	50	.210	.308	.277
vs. Left-Handers			111	26	1	10	21	.234	.288	.298
vs. Right-Handers			103	19	3	10	29	.184	.330	.254
vs. Ground-Ballers			102	24	0	9	24	.235	.284	.297
vs. Fly-Ballers			112	21	4	11	26	.188	.330	.258
Home Games	3-4	2.25	112	23	2	10	31	.205	.295	.268
Road Games	3-2	2.54	102	22	2	10	19	.216	.324	.286
Grass Fields	1-2	4.02	61	15	2	5	12	.246	.393	.303
Artificial Turf	5-4	1.81	153	30	2	15	38	.196	.275	.266
April	0-1	0.73	45	9	0	3	16	.200	.222	.250
May	2-1	4.82	34	6	1	3	6	.176	.324	.243
June	0-0	3.12	29	7	1	2	7	.241	.379	.290
July	0-1	2.00	34	7	2	2	10	.206	.382	.250
August	2-2	2.31	41	11	0	5	3	.268	.341	.340
Sept./Oct.	2-1	1.93	31	5	0	5	8	.161	.226	.278
Leading Off Inn.			50	13	0	3	7	.260	.260	.302
Bases Empty			114	24	1	12	27	.211	.263	.286
Runners On			100	21	3	8	23	.210	.360	.266
Runners/Scor. Pos.			58	12	3	8	13	.207	.414	.299
Runners On/2 Out			45	7	2	4	8	.156	.311	.224
Scor. Pos./2 Out			31	4	2	4	6	.129	.355	.229
Late-Inning Pressure			155	33	4	19	36	.213	.342	.299
Leading Off			37	10	0	3	6	.270	.270	.325
Runners On			74	16	3	8	16	.216	.419	.293
Runners/Scor. Pos.			44	8	3	8	9	.182	.455	.308
First 9 Batters			211	44	4	20	49	.209	.308	.276
Second 9 Batters			3	1	0	0	1	.333	.333	.333
All Batters Thereafter			0	0	0	0	0	—	—	—

Loves to face: Gary Carter (.059, 1-for-17)
Von Hayes (0-for-12)
Ken Oberkfell (.077, 2-for-26, 3 BB)

Hates to face: Len Dykstra (.667, 4-for-6)
Tony Gwynn (.571, 8-for-14)
Kevin McReynolds (.389, 7-for-18, 3 HR)

Miscellaneous statistics: Ground outs-to-air outs ratio: 0.86 last season, 1.40 for career. . . . Induced 4 double-play ground outs in 46 opportunities (one per 11.5). . . . Allowed 5 doubles, 2 triples in 60.1 innings. . . . Stranded 16 inherited runners, allowed 5 to score (76%). . . . Opposing base stealers: 4-for-12 (33%), 2d-lowest rate in N.L.; 0 pickoffs, 5 balks.

Comments: Has allowed 28 home runs in 2803 career at-bats, a rate of one home run allowed for every 100.1 at-bats, the best among active pitchers (minimum: 1000 at-bats). That rate will undergo a severe challenge as he shifts his base of operations from the Astrodome to Wrigley Field. Smith has allowed one homer every 122 at-bats at the Astrodome, and one every 84 at-bats on the road, but he has never allowed a home run in 103 at-bats at Wrigley Field!. . .Kevin McReynolds is the only player who has tagged Smith for three home runs (in only 18 at-bats); Jack Clark, Andre Dawson, and Dale Murphy have each hit two. Two players have homered in their only at-bat vs. Smith: Fred Lynn (in 1990) and Tom Seaver (in 1981). . . . Had a winning record in each of his first six seasons in the majors, but has not had a winning record in any of five seasons since. . . . Concluded his Houston career as the all-time club leader in games pitched (563), relief wins (53), and saves (199). His 2.53 ERA ranks second in team history (minimum: 500 innings) behind Joe Sambito (2.42). . . . His saves total puts him third in National League history behind Bruce Sutter (300) and Lee Smith (207), and his total of games pitched is the highest among active pitchers who have spent their entire career in a single league. . . . Has had six straight 20-save seasons; three pitchers currently own longer streaks: Jeff Reardon (nine years), Lee Smith (eight), and Dave Righetti (seven).

Lee Smith

Throws Right

Red Sox/Cardinals	W-L	ERA	AB	H	HR	BB	SO	BA	SA	OBA
Season	5-5	2.06	310	71	3	29	87	.229	.316	.292
vs. Left-Handers			178	41	3	24	54	.230	.337	.319
vs. Right-Handers			132	30	0	5	33	.227	.288	.254
vs. Ground-Ballers			130	27	0	13	38	.208	.262	.276
vs. Fly-Ballers			180	44	3	16	49	.244	.356	.305
Home Games	3-3	2.49	180	47	2	16	48	.261	.378	.318
Road Games	2-2	1.50	130	24	1	13	39	.185	.231	.257
Grass Fields	3-2	2.08	112	24	1	16	32	.214	.286	.310
Artificial Turf	2-3	2.05	198	47	2	13	55	.237	.333	.282
April	2-1	2.03	52	13	0	9	16	.250	.308	.361
May	1-0	2.04	60	10	0	2	18	.167	.250	.194
June	0-2	2.93	60	15	1	6	17	.250	.383	.313
July	2-0	0.00	58	11	0	4	20	.190	.207	.242
August	0-1	3.65	50	16	1	2	10	.320	.420	.340
Sept./Oct.	0-1	2.25	30	6	1	6	6	.200	.367	.324
Leading Off Inn.			66	12	1	6	20	.182	.303	.250
Bases Empty			161	36	1	13	40	.224	.317	.282
Runners On			149	35	2	16	47	.235	.315	.304
Runners/Scor. Pos.			95	19	0	15	32	.200	.211	.301
Runners On/2 Out			78	17	0	9	24	.218	.256	.299
Scor. Pos./2 Out			58	12	0	8	17	.207	.207	.303
Late-Inning Pressure			245	60	3	24	70	.245	.331	.309
Leading Off			53	9	1	5	17	.170	.283	.241
Runners On			119	31	2	12	37	.261	.353	.321
Runners/Scor. Pos.			74	17	0	11	25	.230	.243	.318
First 9 Batters			301	70	2	28	86	.233	.312	.295
Second 9 Batters			9	1	1	1	1	.111	.444	.200
All Batters Thereafter			0	0	0	0	0	—	—	—

Loves to face: Terry Pendleton (.083, 1-for-12)
Andy Van Slyke (.043, 1-for-23, 1 HR, 4 BB)
Herm Winningham (.083, 1-for-12, 1 2B, 7 SO)

Hates to face: Ron Jones (3-for-3, 1 HR)
Mike Scioscia (.429, 6-for-14, 1 HR)
Garry Templeton (.333, 7-for-21, 1 HR)

Miscellaneous statistics: Ground outs-to-air outs ratio: 0.71 last season, 1.09 for career. . . . Induced 2 double-play ground outs in 62 opportunities (one per 31.0). . . . Allowed 16 doubles, 1 triple in 83.0 innings. . . . Stranded 28 inherited runners, allowed 6 to score (82%), shared 4th-best rate in majors. . . . Opposing base stealers: 14-for-19 (74%); 0 pickoffs, 0 balks.

Comments: Extended his record streak to eight consecutive years of at least 25 saves; Dave Righetti kept pace in 1990, and remains a year behind. . . . Pitched in exactly 64 games for the third straight season, extending his streak of consecutive seasons with at least 60 games to nine, a major league record. Jeff Reardon's streak, which had run concurrent with Smith's, was snapped last season. The only other pitcher in history to achieve a seven-year streak was Pedro Borbon (1972–79). . . . Faced 280 batters after being acquired by the Cardinals last season, and 82 percent of those were during Late-Inning Pressure Situations. That was the highest percentage of LIPS use (wouldn't Mick Jagger love this category?) by any pitcher in the National League last season (minimum: 100 total batters faced). . . . Three of his four defeats with the Cardinals came at the hands of the Mets. . . . Opponents had only one hit in 14 at-bats with the bases loaded last season. . . . Thank goodness he's a gentle giant: Smith has hit only seven batters in his 11-year career, only one in the last five years. . . . How would an eight-man pitching staff of all the Smiths active in 1990, fare? The rotation includes Zane, Bryn, Pete, and Roy. The bullpen would have Lee, Dave, Daryl, Mike. (Sorry, Dave Schmidt, you can't play.) Last year's totals for those eight: 42–45 record with 54 saves. How you can get 54 saves on a staff that produces only 42 wins beats us.

Zane Smith

Throws Left

Expos/Pirates	W-L	ERA	AB	H	HR	BB	SO	BA	SA	OBA
Season	12-9	2.55	801	196	15	50	130	.245	.350	.291
vs. Left-Handers			116	19	1	10	28	.164	.233	.230
vs. Right-Handers			685	177	14	40	102	.258	.369	.301
vs. Ground-Ballers			372	91	6	22	61	.245	.344	.286
vs. Fly-Ballers			429	105	9	28	69	.245	.354	.294
Home Games	9-3	2.05	442	105	5	27	83	.238	.312	.284
Road Games	3-6	3.15	359	91	10	23	47	.253	.396	.299
Grass Fields	1-1	2.70	72	14	1	7	8	.194	.264	.266
Artificial Turf	11-8	2.53	729	182	14	43	122	.250	.358	.293
April	2-1	1.61	102	22	1	6	18	.216	.294	.259
May	0-2	4.94	96	34	1	13	9	.354	.438	.427
June	2-2	3.44	139	35	5	12	20	.252	.403	.320
July	2-2	3.08	143	38	4	10	25	.266	.385	.318
August	3-0	2.72	160	37	3	4	25	.231	.375	.248
Sept./Oct.	3-2	0.59	161	30	1	5	33	.186	.230	.210
Leading Off Inn.			212	52	4	9	35	.245	.368	.279
Bases Empty			510	122	10	29	82	.239	.347	.281
Runners On			291	74	5	21	48	.254	.354	.306
Runners/Scor. Pos.			154	41	5	14	32	.266	.403	.329
Runners On/2 Out			115	25	2	13	26	.217	.304	.302
Scor. Pos./2 Out			70	13	2	9	17	.186	.314	.287
Late-Inning Pressure			94	20	1	3	13	.213	.255	.235
Leading Off			28	8	0	1	6	.286	.286	.310
Runners On			34	9	0	0	1	.265	.294	.257
Runners/Scor. Pos.			15	5	0	0	1	.333	.400	.313
First 9 Batters			267	58	5	18	50	.217	.315	.272
Second 9 Batters			254	63	3	22	46	.248	.358	.306
All Batters Thereafter			280	75	7	10	34	.268	.375	.295

Loves to face: Tom Herr (.171, 6-for-35)
Darryl Strawberry (.175, 7-for-40, 1 HR)
Tim Teufel (.111, 4-for-36, 5 BB)

Hates to face: Andres Galarraga (.450, 9-for-20, 1 HR)
Barry Larkin (.433, 13-for-30, 3 HR)
Glenn Wilson (.433, 13-for-30, 1 HR)

Miscellaneous statistics: Ground outs-to-air outs ratio: 1.89 last season, 3d-highest rate in N.L.; 2.00 for career.... Induced 34 double-play ground outs in 141 opportunities (one per 4.1), best rate in majors.... Allowed 25 doubles, 7 triples in 215.1 innings.... Allowed 5 first-inning runs in 31 starts (0.87 ERA, lowest in majors).... Batting support: 3.10 runs per start (lowest in N.L.) ... Opposing base stealers: 27-for-31 (87%), 4th-highest success rate in N.L.; 2 pickoffs, 0 balks.

Comments: His 0.59 ERA from September 1 to the end of the season was the lowest in majors.... Did not walk a leadoff batter in his last 102 regular-season innings; the last one came on July 21, while he was still with Montreal.... The only left-handed batter to hit a home run off him last year was future teammate Barry Bonds, June 23. In 656 career at-bats, opposing left-handed batters have hit only four home runs (Bonds 2, Greg Brock, and Darryl Strawberry).... Hasn't allowed a first-inning home run in his last 53 starts, since Chris James homered against him on July 19, 1988.... Opposing right-handed batters (.277) have hit 78 points higher than left-handers (.199) over the last five seasons, the largest difference of that kind in the majors.... Opponents have hit for a higher average with runners in scoring position than they have in other at-bats in each of the last five seasons.... Led National League pitchers with a 0.97 ERA against the Mets last season.... While he was with Montreal, opposing base runners stole 26 bases and were caught only twice; while with Pittsburgh, opponents stole only one base in three attempts. In fact, the 43⅓ innings that Smith pitched to Mike LaValliere were the most innings for any N.L. battery to allow no stolen bases. They didn't allow a home run, either.... Still, because of his ability to induce double-play balls (see above), a running strategy is important against Smith.

John Smoltz

Throws Right

Atlanta Braves	W-L	ERA	AB	H	HR	BB	SO	BA	SA	OBA
Season	14-11	3.85	858	206	20	90	170	.240	.358	.310
vs. Left-Handers			506	136	10	63	76	.269	.383	.347
vs. Right-Handers			352	70	10	27	94	.199	.321	.255
vs. Ground-Ballers			407	102	7	46	84	.251	.346	.325
vs. Fly-Ballers			451	104	13	44	86	.231	.368	.297
Home Games	9-4	2.76	444	97	7	48	104	.218	.309	.294
Road Games	5-7	5.11	414	109	13	42	66	.263	.411	.328
Grass Fields	11-6	3.73	664	157	16	68	137	.236	.354	.305
Artificial Turf	3-5	4.29	194	49	4	22	33	.253	.371	.327
April	1-2	7.40	88	27	3	9	15	.307	.500	.371
May	2-2	3.15	122	24	1	12	29	.197	.262	.269
June	2-2	5.17	152	44	3	12	31	.289	.395	.339
July	2-1	2.93	158	29	3	20	34	.184	.291	.272
August	5-2	2.03	198	44	6	16	39	.222	.343	.280
Sept./Oct.	2-2	4.89	140	38	4	21	22	.271	.407	.360
Leading Off Inn.			223	48	4	15	40	.215	.305	.265
Bases Empty			527	122	9	49	107	.231	.326	.297
Runners On			331	84	11	41	63	.254	.408	.331
Runners/Scor. Pos.			180	49	5	29	43	.272	.428	.359
Runners On/2 Out			157	43	4	19	37	.274	.427	.352
Scor. Pos./2 Out			101	30	3	16	24	.297	.475	.393
Late-Inning Pressure			71	16	2	8	19	.225	.352	.300
Leading Off			20	2	1	0	5	.100	.250	.100
Runners On			22	7	0	4	8	.318	.455	.407
Runners/Scor. Pos.			9	3	0	4	4	.333	.556	.500
First 9 Batters			267	62	4	30	59	.232	.318	.306
Second 9 Batters			262	65	3	31	50	.248	.340	.325
All Batters Thereafter			329	79	13	29	61	.240	.404	.302

Loves to face: Darren Daulton (0-for-18, 1 BB)
Andre Dawson (.059, 1-for-17)
Garry Templeton (.105, 2-for-19)

Hates to face: Eric Davis (.643, 9-for-14, 2 2B, 4 HR)
Tony Gwynn (.481, 13-for-27, 1 HR)
Bip Roberts (.455, 5-for-11, 6 BB)

Miscellaneous statistics: Ground outs-to-air outs ratio: 0.83 last season, 0.77 for career.... Induced 16 double-play ground outs in 157 opportunities (one per 9.8).... Allowed 31 doubles, 5 triples in 231.1 innings.... Allowed 20 first-inning runs in 34 starts (4.24 ERA).... Batting support: 4.56 runs per start.... Opposing base stealers: 31-for-41 (76%); 2 pickoffs, 3 balks.

Comments: His 14 wins were the most by any pitcher on any of the four last-place teams last season. He has had a winning record for last-place teams for two straight seasons, becoming the first pitcher to do that since Mario Soto for the Reds in 1982–83.... First Atlanta pitcher with winning records in consecutive seasons (minimum: 15 decisions in each) since Rick Mahler in 1985–86.... Has not allowed a first-inning home run in his last 52 starts, since Ryne Sandberg connected on May 31, 1989.... Career won-lost breakdown: 17–12 before the All-Star break, 11–17 after the break.... Some strange lefty/righty numbers. He has limited right-handed hitters to a .208 career average, compared to .253 by lefties. His strikeout rate against right-handers over the past two years (one every 4.02 plate appearances) ranks fourth among National League pitchers over the past two years (minimum: 400 RHB faced). So far, so good. But left-handed hitters have averaged one home run every 55.8 at-bats, while righties have homered once every 30.3 at-bats.... Opponents' career at-bat total is divided equally: 937 at Atlanta, 937 on the road. Opponents have more hits on the road (237–203), but more home runs in Atlanta (25–20).... Owns 8–3 career record in day games, during which opponents have hit a collective .198.... Opponents had six hits in 12 at-bats with the bases loaded last season.... Among major league pitchers, only Randy Johnson (12) has made more errors than Smoltz (10) over the last two years.

Scott Terry

Throws Right

St. Louis Cardinals	W-L	ERA	AB	H	HR	BB	SO	BA	SA	OBA
Season	2-6	4.75	284	75	7	27	35	.264	.415	.331
vs. Left-Handers			127	33	4	15	21	.260	.433	.336
vs. Right-Handers			157	42	3	12	14	.268	.401	.328
vs. Ground-Ballers			122	27	0	16	18	.221	.279	.322
vs. Fly-Ballers			162	48	7	11	17	.296	.519	.339
Home Games	1-3	4.04	136	33	2	15	15	.243	.338	.316
Road Games	1-3	5.45	148	42	5	12	20	.284	.486	.345
Grass Fields	0-2	4.26	79	23	2	4	11	.291	.456	.337
Artificial Turf	2-4	4.92	205	52	5	23	24	.254	.400	.329
April	0-1	9.82	16	5	0	4	2	.313	.375	.450
May	0-2	7.62	57	19	1	6	7	.333	.509	.385
June	0-2	5.84	52	18	1	5	4	.346	.500	.400
July	1-0	3.18	46	12	0	1	6	.261	.326	.292
August	1-1	3.44	67	13	3	4	9	.194	.388	.250
Sept./Oct.	0-0	2.70	46	8	2	7	7	.174	.348	.291
Leading Off Inn.			62	16	0	6	8	.258	.323	.324
Bases Empty			155	31	2	12	21	.200	.310	.262
Runners On			129	44	5	15	14	.341	.543	.408
Runners/Scor. Pos.			89	29	3	15	9	.326	.551	.420
Runners On/2 Out			54	15	0	5	8	.278	.352	.371
Scor. Pos./2 Out			42	12	0	5	5	.286	.381	.400
Late-Inning Pressure			36	11	1	5	6	.306	.472	.395
Leading Off			9	3	0	0	0	.333	.444	.333
Runners On			18	6	1	5	4	.333	.556	.480
Runners/Scor. Pos.			15	4	0	5	3	.267	.333	.455
First 9 Batters			247	65	6	23	31	.263	.413	.330
Second 9 Batters			34	7	1	4	4	.206	.324	.289
All Batters Thereafter			3	3	0	0	0	1.000	1.667	1.000

Loves to face: Jose Gonzalez (0-for-7, 4 SO)
Ron Jones (0-for-7)
Ricky Jordan (.143, 2-for-14)

Hates to face: Shawon Dunston (.375, 6-for-16, 2 HR)
Von Hayes (.429, 6-for-14, 2 HR)
Ryne Sandberg (.360, 9-for-25, 2 2B, 5 HR)

Miscellaneous statistics: Ground outs-to-air outs ratio: 1.77 last season, 1.98 for career. . . . Induced 1 double-play ground out in 63 opportunities (one per 63.0). . . . Allowed 20 doubles, 1 triple in 72.0 innings. . . . Stranded 18 inherited runners, allowed 13 to score (58%). . . . Opposing base stealers: 7-for-10 (70%); 0 pickoffs, 0 balks.

Comments: Ground-ball pitcher who, not surprisingly, is hit harder by fly-ball hitters (.279 career) than by ground-ball hitters (.239 career). That's a larger disparity than is exhibited in the lefty/righty averages (.272/.249) against him. . . . Opponents' career batting average with runners on base (.298) is 67 points higher than with the bases empty (.231), the 3d-largest margin in the majors over the last five seasons. . . . Opponents' career average in day games (.296) is 52 points higher than in night games (.244), the 2d-largest margin in the majors over the last five seasons. . . . Career breakdown: 8–17, 4.79 ERA before the All-Star break; 12–7, 3.00 ERA after the break. . . . So, Joe Torre, pick your spots with this guy. Use him against ground-ball hitters with the bases empty in night games after the All-Star break. Or any combination thereof. . . . Failed to induce a double play grounder in any of his first 58 chances to do so. The only opponent to ground into a twin killing against him was Tim Wallach on September 5. What makes Terry's inability to induce double-play grounders strange is his high ratio of ground outs-to-air outs (1.77). Other major league pitchers with a G/A Ratio between 1.75 and 2.00 induce an average of one GIDP every 8.1 opportunities, almost eight times greater than the rate against Terry last season. Bill Landrum, who had a G/A ratio identical to Terry's, induced nine double-play grounders in 66 opportunities.

Bob Tewksbury

Throws Right

St. Louis Cardinals	W-L	ERA	AB	H	HR	BB	SO	BA	SA	OBA
Season	10-9	3.47	565	151	7	15	50	.267	.379	.286
vs. Left-Handers			334	93	4	13	22	.278	.383	.302
vs. Right-Handers			231	58	3	2	28	.251	.372	.263
vs. Ground-Ballers			270	67	1	9	24	.248	.341	.274
vs. Fly-Ballers			295	84	6	6	26	.285	.414	.298
Home Games	4-5	3.66	256	64	3	5	22	.250	.367	.264
Road Games	6-4	3.30	309	87	4	10	28	.282	.388	.305
Grass Fields	3-2	3.53	171	47	2	8	17	.275	.374	.302
Artificial Turf	7-7	3.44	394	104	5	7	33	.264	.381	.279
April	0-0	6.35	49	19	0	4	2	.388	.469	.426
May	0-0	3.00	11	2	0	0	2	.182	.182	.182
June	3-0	2.91	82	18	2	2	7	.220	.415	.235
July	2-3	2.25	126	33	0	5	13	.262	.310	.288
August	4-1	1.60	165	38	1	2	12	.230	.309	.243
Sept./Oct.	1-5	6.68	132	41	4	2	14	.311	.492	.324
Leading Off Inn.			150	36	1	1	15	.240	.320	.245
Bases Empty			356	84	3	7	31	.236	.337	.255
Runners On			209	67	4	8	19	.321	.450	.338
Runners/Scor. Pos.			132	43	4	7	12	.326	.492	.347
Runners On/2 Out			90	24	2	5	9	.267	.422	.305
Scor. Pos./2 Out			63	18	2	4	7	.286	.460	.328
Late-Inning Pressure			29	5	0	1	3	.172	.241	.200
Leading Off			9	2	0	0	1	.222	.222	.222
Runners On			7	0	0	0	1	.000	.000	.000
Runners/Scor. Pos.			3	0	0	0	0	.000	.000	.000
First 9 Batters			221	56	1	7	18	.253	.326	.276
Second 9 Batters			180	49	2	5	18	.272	.372	.293
All Batters Thereafter			164	46	4	3	14	.280	.457	.294

Loves to face: Barry Bonds (.176, 3-for-17)
Andres Galarraga (0-for-10)
Joe Girardi (.100, 1-for-10)

Hates to face: Gregg Jefferies (.600, 3-for-5, 1 HR)
Ryne Sandberg (.571, 4-for-7, 2 2B, 1 HR)

Miscellaneous statistics: Ground outs-to-air outs ratio: 1.36 last season, 1.55 for career. . . . Induced 9 double-play ground outs in 86 opportunities (one per 9.6). . . . Allowed 36 doubles, 3 triples in 145.1 innings. . . . Allowed 11 first-inning runs in 20 starts (4.95 ERA). . . . Batting support: 3.55 runs per start. . . . Opposing base stealers: 8-for-13 (62%); 0 pickoffs, 0 balks.

Comments: Pitched to a decision in 19 of his 20 starts, the highest percentage by any pitcher who started more than six games last season. The top five: Tewksbury (95%), Bob Welch (94%), Jack Morris (92%), Dave Stewart (92%), and Frank Viola (91%). Tewks will never find himself in more select company. . . . One of four pitchers to hurl shutouts in consecutive starts last season. The others: Bruce Hurst, Mark Gardner, and Roger Clemens. That company's good, but we'll still take the first group. . . . Opponents' career breakdown is ominous: .267 with the bases empty, .314 with runners on base, .310 with runners in scoring position. . . . Posted 2.69 ERA in 97 innings with Todd Zeile catching, but had 5.03 in 48⅓ innings with Tom Pagnozzi behind the plate. . . . Did not pitch the 162 innings necessary to qualify for the official title, but he was the only pitcher in the majors last season to average less than one walk per nine innings while pitching at least 100 innings. His rate of 0.93 walks per nine innings was the lowest in Cardinals' history by a pitcher with 100 or more innings, besting Cy Young's rate of 1.01 walks per nine innings in 1900, when Cy threw 321 innings. . . . Damned if Tewksbury *didn't* manage to get himself into better company. . . . Reminds us of JFK's line as he addressed an assemblage of Nobel Prize winners: "I think this is the most extraordinary collection of talent, of human knowledge, that has been gathered together at the White House, with the possible exception of when Thomas Jefferson dined alone."

John Tudor

Throws Left

St. Louis Cardinals	W-L	ERA	AB	H	HR	BB	SO	BA	SA	OBA
Season	12-4	2.40	534	120	10	30	63	.225	.331	.268
vs. Left-Handers			131	28	2	5	24	.214	.298	.243
vs. Right-Handers			403	92	8	25	39	.228	.342	.276
vs. Ground-Ballers			211	41	1	10	30	.194	.237	.238
vs. Fly-Ballers			323	79	9	20	33	.245	.393	.288
Home Games	4-1	2.52	278	62	5	17	32	.223	.342	.273
Road Games	8-3	2.27	256	58	5	13	31	.227	.320	.263
Grass Fields	4-2	3.44	126	32	4	7	11	.254	.389	.291
Artificial Turf	8-2	2.08	408	88	6	23	52	.216	.314	.261
April	4-0	0.96	95	19	0	7	8	.200	.242	.262
May	1-2	4.67	103	30	2	4	10	.291	.456	.318
June	1-1	3.19	124	36	4	7	14	.290	.444	.331
July	4-0	1.98	128	21	4	9	16	.164	.273	.219
August	1-0	0.00	35	5	0	1	10	.143	.143	.167
Sept./Oct.	1-1	1.93	49	9	0	2	5	.184	.245	.216
Leading Off Inn.			143	31	4	7	13	.217	.350	.258
Bases Empty			349	79	8	18	39	.226	.344	.268
Runners On			185	41	2	12	24	.222	.308	.268
Runners/Scor. Pos.			91	24	1	9	15	.264	.385	.327
Runners On/2 Out			81	15	1	7	15	.185	.272	.250
Scor. Pos./2 Out			44	10	0	7	8	.227	.318	.333
Late-Inning Pressure			49	12	1	6	3	.245	.327	.327
Leading Off			13	2	1	1	0	.154	.385	.214
Runners On			18	4	0	2	1	.222	.222	.300
Runners/Scor. Pos.			5	2	0	0	1	.400	.400	.400
First 9 Batters			200	42	3	10	24	.210	.315	.254
Second 9 Batters			178	42	6	8	22	.236	.371	.269
All Batters Thereafter			156	36	1	12	17	.231	.308	.286

Loved to face: Eric Davis (.059, 1-for-17)
Rick Dempsey (.111, 3-for-27)
Von Hayes (.136, 6-for-44)

Hated to face: Rickey Henderson (.538, 7-for-13)
Kevin Mitchell (.619, 13-for-21, 3 HR)
Eddie Murray (.462, 12-for-26, 1 HR)

Miscellaneous statistics: Ground outs-to-air outs ratio: 0.99 last season, 0.93 for career. . . . Induced 7 double-play ground outs in 83 opportunities (one per 11.9). . . . Allowed 25 doubles, 1 triple in 146.1 innings. . . . Allowed 7 first-inning runs in 22 starts (2.45 ERA). . . . Batting support: 4.68 runs per start. . . . Opposing base stealers: 8-for-17 (47%), 4th-lowest rate in N.L.; 5 pickoffs, 0 balks.

Comments: Finished his career with a lifetime record of 117–72 (.619). Only four others who pitched into the expansion era had better career winning percentages with at least as many decisions as Tudor: Sandy Koufax (.655), Ron Guidry (.651), Jim Palmer (.638), and Juan Marichal (.631). . . . Guidry and Tudor for the Hall of Fame? You'll hear comparisons with Dizzy Dean, who had a 150–83 (.644) career record while pitching in 20 or more games in only six seasons. Our first hunch, mostly on instinct: Guidry *si*, Tudor *no*. . . . Not including years of 0–0 records, no pitcher has had a streak longer than Tudor's 10 consecutive winning seasons since Bob Gibson put together 13 winning seasons in a row, 1961–73. . . . Last season's .750 winning percentage was the highest ever by a pitcher on a last-place ballclub (minimum: 15 decisions). He might have preferred going out as the tail of a lion (does his role with the '88 Dodgers come to mind?) rather than as the head of a mouse. . . . Tudor, Bob Tewksbury, and Bryn Smith all posted winning records for the last-place Cardinals in 1990. Only seven other last-place teams in major league history had at least three pitchers with winning records in 15-plus decisions. The last one: the 1984 Pirates, who had a league-leading team ERA and winning records from four regular hurlers: Rick Rhoden (14–9), Larry McWilliams (12–11), John Candelaria (12–11)—and Tudor (12–11), who obviously has experience at this kind of thing.

Fernando Valenzuela

Throws Left

Los Angeles Dodgers	W-L	ERA	AB	H	HR	BB	SO	BA	SA	OBA
Season	13-13	4.59	808	223	19	77	115	.276	.412	.337
vs. Left-Handers			130	41	4	15	19	.315	.454	.381
vs. Right-Handers			678	182	15	62	96	.268	.404	.329
vs. Ground-Ballers			402	114	10	26	69	.284	.418	.326
vs. Fly-Ballers			406	109	9	51	46	.268	.406	.348
Home Games	8-5	3.75	453	117	7	44	61	.258	.353	.323
Road Games	5-8	5.73	355	106	12	33	54	.299	.487	.356
Grass Fields	10-9	4.46	615	166	14	57	96	.270	.397	.331
Artificial Turf	3-4	4.99	193	57	5	20	19	.295	.461	.358
April	1-2	3.12	97	23	2	7	17	.237	.351	.286
May	3-2	4.79	144	39	4	16	17	.271	.444	.342
June	2-2	3.21	156	35	4	17	31	.224	.340	.301
July	2-2	4.73	129	39	2	9	17	.302	.465	.348
August	4-2	3.79	148	39	5	14	21	.264	.419	.327
Sept./Oct.	1-3	8.40	134	48	2	14	12	.358	.448	.413
Leading Off Inn.			196	56	1	14	32	.286	.347	.333
Bases Empty			440	114	8	39	67	.259	.373	.319
Runners On			368	109	11	38	48	.296	.459	.359
Runners/Scor. Pos.			210	58	5	25	30	.276	.410	.347
Runners On/2 Out			154	42	6	19	30	.273	.435	.353
Scor. Pos./2 Out			99	21	3	16	21	.212	.343	.322
Late-Inning Pressure			53	12	0	7	4	.226	.283	.317
Leading Off			12	2	0	4	1	.167	.167	.375
Runners On			25	5	0	2	3	.200	.280	.259
Runners/Scor. Pos.			12	3	0	0	1	.250	.333	.250
First 9 Batters			263	60	5	26	40	.228	.342	.296
Second 9 Batters			266	78	5	26	32	.293	.414	.355
All Batters Thereafter			279	85	9	25	43	.305	.477	.361

Loves to face: Vince Coleman (.133, 8-for-60)
Ron Oester (.111, 6-for-54, 5 BB)
Luis Salazar (.114, 8-for-70, 1 HR)

Hates to face: Casey Candaele (.476, 10-for-21, 2 HR)
Pedro Guerrero (.467, 7-for-15)
Dale Murphy (.318, 35-for-110, 8 HR)

Miscellaneous statistics: Ground outs-to-air outs ratio: 0.99 last season, 1.25 for career. . . . Induced 9 double-play ground outs in 177 opportunities (one per 19.7). . . . Allowed 51 doubles (most in majors), 1 triple in 204.0 innings. . . . Allowed 18 first-inning runs in 33 starts (4.64 ERA). . . . Batting support: 5.03 runs per start (4th highest in N.L.) . . . Opposing base stealers: 19-for-26 (73%); 5 pickoffs, 1 balk.

Comments: If he starts 16 games this season, the little round man will move into third place in Dodgers history in what Ralph Kiner for some reason calls "game starts," behind Don Sutton and Don Drysdale. . . . Has held opponents to a lower average during his first pass through the lineup than he has in subsequent at-bats in each of the last eight seasons. . . . Opponents' overall batting average was the highest of his career. . . . Here come a couple of real screwball numbers: Left-handed batters have hit this southpaw for a higher average than right-handers in each of the last three seasons. Career averages: .254 by lefties, .237 by right-handers. . . . Had the highest average run support of any pitcher on the Dodgers' staff last season, but what his teammates giveth, his teammates taketh away. The Dodgers committed 27 errors behind Fernando, tying the Cubs' Greg Maddux for the worst fielding support in the league. . . . Five pitchers, including two current teammates, have homered against Fernando in his career: Rick Behenna, Steve Carlton, Dennis Cook, Kevin Gross, and Calvin Schiraldi. . . . Batted .304 in 69 at-bats last season, becoming first pitcher since Don Robinson in 1984 to bat over .300 in a season of 50 or more at-bats. . . . Believe it or not, Fernando's eight career at-bats without a strikeout against Nolan Ryan are the most among all active players who have never gone down on strikes against the whiff king. Yes, that includes *real* players, not just pitchers.

Frank Viola

Throws Left

New York Mets	W-L	ERA	AB	H	HR	BB	SO	BA	SA	OBA
Season	20-12	2.67	938	227	15	60	182	.242	.333	.288
vs. Left-Handers			183	47	1	14	47	.257	.328	.317
vs. Right-Handers			755	180	14	46	135	.238	.334	.281
vs. Ground-Ballers			453	104	3	20	85	.230	.287	.261
vs. Fly-Ballers			485	123	12	40	97	.254	.375	.313
Home Games	12-5	2.44	477	115	7	22	104	.241	.323	.273
Road Games	8-7	2.90	461	112	8	38	78	.243	.343	.303
Grass Fields	15-9	2.65	685	172	12	33	140	.251	.342	.285
Artificial Turf	5-3	2.73	253	55	3	27	42	.217	.308	.295
April	4-0	1.32	97	18	1	2	29	.186	.247	.202
May	3-2	2.78	139	34	2	7	30	.245	.302	.284
June	4-1	2.91	167	46	2	11	24	.275	.353	.318
July	3-2	2.11	146	29	1	19	24	.199	.267	.289
August	3-4	3.83	196	54	4	8	37	.276	.388	.304
Sept./Oct.	3-3	2.45	193	46	5	13	38	.238	.373	.290
Leading Off Inn.			240	59	5	15	36	.246	.354	.290
Bases Empty			564	139	11	35	97	.246	.348	.292
Runners On			374	88	4	25	85	.235	.310	.283
Runners/Scor. Pos.			204	43	4	16	47	.211	.309	.268
Runners On/2 Out			155	28	1	9	30	.181	.245	.226
Scor. Pos./2 Out			98	18	1	7	16	.184	.245	.238
Late-Inning Pressure			70	14	1	6	10	.200	.300	.263
Leading Off			19	3	1	2	4	.158	.368	.238
Runners On			25	3	0	1	4	.120	.120	.154
Runners/Scor. Pos.			10	1	0	1	1	.100	.100	.182
First 9 Batters			288	66	4	16	69	.229	.306	.270
Second 9 Batters			287	72	2	21	56	.251	.317	.301
All Batters Thereafter			363	89	9	23	57	.245	.366	.292

Loves to face: Todd Benzinger (.059, 1-for-17)
Don Slaught (.147, 5-for-34)
Glenn Wilson (0-for-17)

Hates to face: Mark Grace (.474, 9-for-19, 1 HR)
Mike LaValliere (3-for-3, 2 BB)
Kevin Mitchell (.364, 4-for-11, 2 HR)

Miscellaneous statistics: Ground outs-to-air outs ratio: 1.37 last season, 0.88 for career. . . . Induced 17 double-play ground outs in 190 opportunities (one per 11.2). . . . Allowed 36 doubles, 2 triples in 249.2 innings. . . . Allowed 6 first-inning runs in 35 starts (1.54 ERA, 2d lowest in N.L.) . . . Batting support: 4.31 runs per start. . . . Opposing base stealers: 25-for-40 (63%); 1 pickoff, 0 balks.

Comments: Led the National League with 249⅔ innings, the lowest total to lead the league in any of its 115 seasons except for the '81 strike season. . . . The only major leaguer to accumulate at least 200 innings pitched in each of the last eight seasons. No pitcher has had a streak of that length since that old streak-killer, the 1981 strike season itself, interrupted no fewer than eight such streaks (including 15-year jobs by both Gaylord Perry and Don Sutton). . . . Has held opponents to a lower batting average with runners on base than he has with the bases empty in each of the last five seasons. . . . Allowed only one home run to a left-handed batter last season; Mark Grace hit it on August 12. . . . Held opponents to a .175 batting average during the first inning, the 2d-lowest average against any National League pitcher (minimum: 20 starts) last season. . . . Averaged 7.13 innings pitched per start, 2d highest among the same group. . . . His 92 plate appearances were the most by any player in the majors who did not draw a walk last season. . . . Received a decision in 32 of his 35 starts, 2d-highest percentage among National League pitchers who started at least 10 games last season. . . . Career won-lost breakdown: 77–46 (.626) before the All-Star break, 60–64 (.484) after the break. Lost three important starts in late September before getting 20th win in meaningless season finale at Pittsburgh.

Bob Walk

Throws Right

Pittsburgh Pirates	W-L	ERA	AB	H	HR	BB	SO	BA	SA	OBA
Season	7-5	3.75	503	136	17	36	73	.270	.419	.322
vs. Left-Handers			297	78	9	26	36	.263	.394	.326
vs. Right-Handers			206	58	8	10	37	.282	.456	.317
vs. Ground-Ballers			242	64	5	16	36	.264	.364	.314
vs. Fly-Ballers			261	72	12	20	37	.276	.471	.330
Home Games	3-3	3.90	228	63	7	17	31	.276	.434	.328
Road Games	4-2	3.62	275	73	10	19	42	.265	.407	.318
Grass Fields	3-1	3.12	103	26	6	6	15	.252	.447	.300
Artificial Turf	4-4	3.91	400	110	11	30	58	.275	.412	.328
April	1-3	3.92	85	27	5	6	11	.318	.529	.359
May	3-0	2.43	112	29	0	8	21	.259	.304	.317
June	0-1	4.71	84	24	5	8	12	.286	.512	.348
July	1-0	4.34	69	17	3	5	7	.246	.391	.293
August	0-0	3.21	53	13	0	3	7	.245	.321	.298
Sept./Oct.	2-1	4.21	100	26	4	6	15	.260	.450	.308
Leading Off Inn.			128	37	4	7	15	.289	.438	.331
Bases Empty			303	86	8	20	43	.284	.422	.334
Runners On			200	50	9	16	30	.250	.415	.305
Runners/Scor. Pos.			118	26	4	9	21	.220	.347	.275
Runners On/2 Out			90	24	4	6	15	.267	.411	.320
Scor. Pos./2 Out			62	17	2	5	12	.274	.387	.338
Late-Inning Pressure			26	5	0	1	5	.192	.231	.222
Leading Off			6	2	0	1	1	.333	.333	.429
Runners On			7	1	0	0	1	.143	.143	.143
Runners/Scor. Pos.			2	1	0	0	0	.500	.500	.500
First 9 Batters			203	54	3	13	30	.266	.360	.306
Second 9 Batters			177	50	5	11	31	.282	.429	.328
All Batters Thereafter			123	32	9	12	12	.260	.504	.341

Loves to face: Vince Coleman (.207, 12-for-58, 1 HR)
Dickie Thon (.100, 2-for-20, 1 HR)
Tim Wallach (.180, 9-for-50, 1 HR)

Hates to face: Ron Jones (4-for-4, 1 HR)
John Kruk (.500, 12-for-24, 1 HR)
Lonnie Smith (.625, 10-for-16, 2 HR)

Miscellaneous statistics: Ground outs-to-air outs ratio: 1.14 last season, 1.26 for career. . . . Induced 6 double-play ground outs in 87 opportunities (one per 14.5). . . . Allowed 22 doubles, 1 triple in 129.2 innings. . . . Allowed 13 first-inning runs in 24 starts (4.50 ERA). . . . Batting support: 4.92 runs per start. . . . Opposing base stealers: 13-for-22 (59%); 1 pickoff, 3 balks.

Comments: Pirates' surprise starter in Game One of the 1990 Championship Series, just as he was the Phillies' surprise starter in Game One of the 1980 World Series. He won both games, the only postseason victories of his career. . . . One of only 10 pitchers in the majors with at least 10 decisions and a winning record in each of the past four seasons. Dwight Gooden and Don Robinson are the only other National League pitchers among them. Walk is 40–27 over that span. . . . Received a decision in only 12 of his 24 starts last season, the lowest percentage by any pitcher in the majors who started at least 15 games last season. He earned a decision in each of his first seven starts, but in only five of 17 thereafter. . . . His only complete game of the season was a shutout in his final regular-season start. He averaged 5.31 innings pitched per start, the 4th lowest among National League pitchers who started at least 20 games last season. . . . Opponents' batting average (.297) and rate of walks (3.75 per nine innings) were higher in the first inning than in any other inning. . . . Last season, right-handed batters hit slightly better against him, both for average and for power, than did left-handers. In each of the previous seven seasons, lefties had hit for a higher average than righties. . . . Most career at-bats among active players who have never homered: Jeff Huson (512), Tom Browning (469), Orel Hershiser (456), Bert Blyleven (451), Bob Walk (370).

Ed Whitson

Throws Right

San Diego Padres	W-L	ERA	AB	H	HR	BB	SO	BA	SA	OBA
Season	14-9	2.60	855	215	13	47	127	.251	.347	.289
vs. Left-Handers			522	141	6	30	72	.270	.358	.309
vs. Right-Handers			333	74	7	17	55	.222	.330	.259
vs. Ground-Ballers			428	116	3	22	66	.271	.339	.307
vs. Fly-Ballers			427	99	10	25	61	.232	.356	.272
Home Games	5-6	2.65	462	110	7	21	77	.238	.333	.270
Road Games	9-3	2.53	393	105	6	26	50	.267	.364	.311
Grass Fields	8-7	2.74	597	143	11	26	93	.240	.348	.271
Artificial Turf	6-2	2.25	258	72	2	21	34	.279	.345	.331
April	2-0	1.50	87	22	0	3	9	.253	.299	.278
May	2-3	3.95	159	38	7	10	25	.239	.409	.287
June	2-2	2.61	155	33	4	10	25	.213	.348	.261
July	2-2	2.49	157	38	0	4	21	.242	.306	.256
August	3-0	0.86	157	41	1	6	24	.261	.312	.287
Sept./Oct.	3-2	3.89	140	43	1	14	23	.307	.393	.368
Leading Off Inn.			224	52	2	8	32	.232	.326	.259
Bases Empty			530	130	9	27	82	.245	.349	.283
Runners On			325	85	4	20	45	.262	.345	.299
Runners/Scor. Pos.			173	45	3	15	23	.260	.370	.309
Runners On/2 Out			143	37	2	13	22	.259	.357	.321
Scor. Pos./2 Out			83	23	2	10	9	.277	.422	.355
Late-Inning Pressure			80	25	1	6	5	.313	.438	.352
Leading Off			22	9	0	1	2	.409	.545	.435
Runners On			36	10	0	3	2	.278	.333	.317
Runners/Scor. Pos.			16	3	0	3	2	.188	.188	.286
First 9 Batters			272	58	3	13	54	.213	.276	.248
Second 9 Batters			269	73	4	13	42	.271	.375	.306
All Batters Thereafter			314	84	6	21	31	.268	.385	.310

Loves to face: Craig Biggio (.100, 2-for-20)
Darren Daulton (0-for-13)
Jose Uribe (.091, 3-for-33, 0 BB)

Hates to face: Pedro Guerrero (.368, 21-for-57, 6 HR)
Eddie Murray (.417, 10-for-24, 3 HR)
Mackey Sasser (.579, 11-for-19, 1 HR, 8 fly outs)

Miscellaneous statistics: Ground outs-to-air outs ratio: 0.96 last season, 1.01 for career.... Induced 16 double-play ground outs in 143 opportunities (one per 8.9).... Allowed 41 doubles, 1 triple in 228.2 innings.... Allowed 10 first-inning runs in 32 starts (2.53 ERA).... Batting support: 4.44 runs per start.... Opposing base stealers: 12-for-19 (63%); 0 pickoffs, 0 balks.

Comments: Since being re-acquired by the Padres in 1986, his ERA and winning percentage have improved in every season: 1–7, 5.59 in 1986; then 10–13, 4.73; 13–11, 3.77; 16–11, 2.66; 14–9, 2.60. If that doesn't look hard, try it sometime. *No other pitcher in major-league history ever had a streak of four years of improvement*, starting at least 30 games in each. Among the 11 who fell by the wayside after three seasons: Christy Mathewson (1910), Mudcat Grant (1966), Jim Kaat (1967), and Joe Bush *twice* (1919 and 1923).... Career record now stands at 122–117; plus-five is the best that he has ever stood at any point of his career.... Stands third on the Padres' all-time win list with 73; Randy Jones (92) and Eric Show (100) are the leaders in the clubhouse.... Averaged 7.15 innings per start last season, the highest rate in the National League (minimum: 20 GS).... A homebody: Opponents have hit for a higher average in road games than they have in home games in each of the last seven seasons, the longest current streak.... Allowed 11 home runs over his first 13 starts (one per 8.6 IP), but only two in his last 19 (one per 67.2 IP).... Whitson has won his last eight decisions against the Pirates, his original major league team.... Hit the only home run of his career on April 25, in his 491st career at-bat. At the time, he had the most career at-bats of any active pitcher who had never homered.

Mitch Williams

Throws Left

Chicago Cubs	W-L	ERA	AB	H	HR	BB	SO	BA	SA	OBA
Season	1-8	3.93	251	60	4	50	55	.239	.390	.364
vs. Left-Handers			66	15	2	16	18	.227	.424	.369
vs. Right-Handers			185	45	2	34	37	.243	.378	.362
vs. Ground-Ballers			110	22	0	30	24	.200	.282	.376
vs. Fly-Ballers			141	38	4	20	31	.270	.475	.354
Home Games	1-1	3.78	128	32	3	25	25	.250	.406	.370
Road Games	0-7	4.09	123	28	1	25	30	.228	.374	.358
Grass Fields	1-4	3.77	168	43	3	32	35	.256	.405	.373
Artificial Turf	0-4	4.24	83	17	1	18	20	.205	.361	.346
April	0-1	0.00	41	6	0	8	12	.146	.195	.286
May	0-3	4.11	59	13	3	9	12	.220	.458	.324
June	1-1	1.69	17	5	0	6	6	.294	.353	.440
July	0-1	3.00	23	5	0	4	7	.217	.304	.333
August	0-1	3.86	43	11	0	12	6	.256	.326	.418
Sept./Oct.	0-1	7.88	68	20	1	11	12	.294	.529	.395
Leading Off Inn.			44	7	0	10	5	.159	.205	.315
Bases Empty			106	21	0	23	20	.198	.274	.341
Runners On			145	39	4	27	35	.269	.476	.381
Runners/Scor. Pos.			93	24	2	20	21	.258	.452	.379
Runners On/2 Out			73	22	2	9	19	.301	.548	.386
Scor. Pos./2 Out			52	17	2	8	12	.327	.615	.417
Late-Inning Pressure			106	24	1	24	30	.226	.340	.371
Leading Off			16	3	0	6	3	.188	.250	.409
Runners On			64	15	1	13	20	.234	.391	.367
Runners/Scor. Pos.			39	7	0	11	14	.179	.282	.353
First 9 Batters			231	51	4	46	51	.221	.364	.349
Second 9 Batters			19	9	0	3	3	.474	.737	.545
All Batters Thereafter			1	0	0	1	1	.000	.000	.500

Loves to face: Todd Benzinger (.100, 1-for-10)
Howard Johnson (.125, 1-for-8)
Milt Thompson (0-for-6, 4 SO)

Hates to face: Pedro Guerrero (.600, 3-for-5, 2 2B, 1 HR)
Jim Presley (.455, 5-for-11, 1 HR, 5 BB)
Ozzie Smith (.571, 4-for-7)

Miscellaneous statistics: Ground outs-to-air outs ratio: 0.58 last season, 0.68 for career.... Induced 3 double-play ground outs in 68 opportunities (one per 22.7).... Allowed 20 doubles, 3 triples in 66.1 innings.... Stranded 20 inherited runners, allowed 14 to score (59%).... Opposing base stealers: 6-for-6; 1 pickoff, 2 balks.

Comments: Career rate of 6.86 walks per nine innings is the highest in major league history among pitchers who have hurled at least 400 innings. Second on that list: Tommy Byrne, whose career average (6.85) is so close that if Mitch records his first two outs of the 1991 season before he walks a batter, he will drop below Byrne on the all-time list.... Since the 1986 season, Williams's first in the majors, he has forced home the most runs by virtue of bases-loaded walks (17). Others with 10 or more since 1986: Charlie Hough (13), Steve Farr (11), Eric Plunk (11), Mark Davis (10).... National Leaguers have a two-year batting average of .239 against him; American Leaguers, in three years, batted .192.... Has held left-handed batters to a .196 career average. Among active National League pitchers, only Rob Dibble (.192) stands above him (minimum: 400 LHB faced).... Only win of 1990 came against Mets on June 11, but he hurt his knee and was out for 30 days. Still, it helped him avoid breaking Dick Drott's 1960 team record of six losses without a win.... Owns 1–11 career record (with 5.96 ERA) on or after September 1. He has a pre-September record of 22–20 (with 3.05 ERA).... Had not allowed a home run to a left-handed batter in 1988 or 1989, but both Paul O'Neill and Andy Van Slyke raked him last season.... One of 14 players in major league history whose only career hit is a home run. He's 1-for-10, with a long one off Don Aase in 1989.

Steve Wilson

Throws Left

Chicago Cubs	W-L	ERA	AB	H	HR	BB	SO	BA	SA	OBA
Season	4-9	4.79	540	140	17	43	95	.259	.419	.315
vs. Left-Handers			140	31	3	8	34	.221	.343	.268
vs. Right-Handers			400	109	14	35	61	.272	.445	.330
vs. Ground-Ballers			237	58	3	18	46	.245	.350	.298
vs. Fly-Ballers			303	82	14	25	49	.271	.472	.327
Home Games	2-5	5.40	287	81	11	23	51	.282	.470	.334
Road Games	2-4	4.14	253	59	6	20	44	.233	.360	.292
Grass Fields	4-5	4.64	413	110	13	32	72	.266	.431	.320
Artificial Turf	0-4	5.24	127	30	4	11	23	.236	.378	.297
April	0-3	5.85	85	27	2	7	8	.318	.412	.366
May	0-1	7.36	61	19	5	6	8	.311	.607	.368
June	2-1	2.91	126	25	4	12	18	.198	.333	.268
July	1-1	3.96	95	23	2	7	23	.242	.389	.301
August	1-1	4.35	78	20	2	2	18	.256	.410	.275
Sept./Oct.	0-2	6.20	95	26	2	9	20	.274	.453	.340
Leading Off Inn.			134	37	3	8	18	.276	.388	.317
Bases Empty			317	76	12	24	55	.240	.391	.293
Runners On			223	64	5	19	40	.287	.457	.344
Runners/Scor. Pos.			128	41	1	12	25	.320	.469	.375
Runners On/2 Out			102	31	1	11	16	.304	.412	.377
Scor. Pos./2 Out			63	20	1	8	13	.317	.413	.394
Late-Inning Pressure			53	17	0	3	13	.321	.396	.368
Leading Off			18	8	0	0	2	.444	.556	.444
Runners On			20	6	0	2	6	.300	.300	.391
Runners/Scor. Pos.			16	6	0	1	4	.375	.375	.412
First 9 Batters			276	72	9	25	58	.261	.420	.324
Second 9 Batters			152	35	4	11	24	.230	.362	.282
All Batters Thereafter			112	33	4	7	13	.295	.491	.336

Loves to face: Barry Bonds (.091, 1-for-11)
Brett Butler (0-for-8, 2 BB)
Dave Magadan (.100, 1-for-10)

Hates to face: Len Dykstra (.438, 7-for-16, 1 HR)
Greg Olson (3-for-3, 1 HR, 1 BB)
Andy Van Slyke (.500, 6-for-12, 1 HR)

Miscellaneous statistics: Ground outs-to-air outs ratio: 0.63 last season, 0.70 for career. . . . Induced 5 double-play ground outs in 100 opportunities (one per 20.0). . . . Allowed 23 doubles, 6 triples in 139.0 innings. . . . Allowed 11 first-inning runs in 15 starts (6.60 ERA). . . . Batting support: 4.40 runs per start. . . . Record of 2–7, 5.67 ERA as a starter; 2–2, 3.62 ERA in 30 relief appearances. . . . Stranded 19 inherited runners, allowed 6 to score (76%). . . . Opposing base stealers: 6-for-14 (43%), 3d-lowest rate in N.L.; 7 pickoffs, 1 balk.

Comments: Has allowed 20 home runs in 650 at-bats by right-handed batters, compared to only four in 240 at-bats by left-handers. Two-thirds of the home runs allowed by this extreme fly-ball pitcher have been hit at Wrigley Field. . . . Cubs and Expos were the only National League teams last season whose relief pitchers had collective ground outs-to-air outs ratios under 1.00. It would seem that you could get away with something like that more easily within The Big Owe than you could within The Friendly Confines. . . . Opponents batted .320 with runners in scoring position after hitting only .238 in those situations in 1989. That's sort of the story of the Cubs' pitching staff; team numbers in that category: opponents hit .239 in 1989, .276 in 1990. . . . Allowed only one of the last 16 runners he inherited to score. . . . Has held opponents to only two hits in 16 career at-bats with the bases loaded. And, perhaps to counterbalance the efforts of teammate Mitch Williams, he has never walked in a run. . . . Career numbers: 5–9, 5.50 ERA as a starter, 5–4, 3.77 ERA as a reliever. . . . Opponents have hit considerably better in Late-Inning Pressure Situations (.310) than at other times (.251). . . . Opponents' career breakdown: .246 in Wilson's first pass through the lineup, .260 during his second pass, .305 in subsequent at-bats. . . . The last previous Canadian-born pitcher to play for the Cubs was elected to the Hall of Fame in January.

Trevor Wilson

Throws Left

San Francisco Giants	W-L	ERA	AB	H	HR	BB	SO	BA	SA	OBA
Season	8-7	4.00	399	87	11	49	66	.218	.333	.304
vs. Left-Handers			64	14	1	5	12	.219	.313	.275
vs. Right-Handers			335	73	10	44	54	.218	.337	.309
vs. Ground-Ballers			182	35	5	23	29	.192	.297	.283
vs. Fly-Ballers			217	52	6	26	37	.240	.364	.321
Home Games	5-3	2.88	242	48	5	33	37	.198	.289	.295
Road Games	3-4	5.83	157	39	6	16	29	.248	.401	.318
Grass Fields	7-4	3.51	304	63	9	35	50	.207	.322	.289
Artificial Turf	1-3	5.61	95	24	2	14	16	.253	.368	.349
April	0-0	—	0	0	0	0	0	—	—	—
May	0-0	—	0	0	0	0	0	—	—	—
June	4-0	2.12	116	19	2	13	24	.164	.224	.248
July	2-3	4.58	148	35	4	20	18	.236	.338	.327
August	2-3	6.45	81	20	2	11	13	.247	.395	.337
Sept./Oct.	0-1	3.07	54	13	3	5	11	.241	.463	.305
Leading Off Inn.			100	20	1	15	14	.200	.250	.304
Bases Empty			247	47	5	35	45	.190	.271	.291
Runners On			152	40	6	14	21	.263	.434	.325
Runners/Scor. Pos.			71	24	5	8	10	.338	.606	.402
Runners On/2 Out			68	20	2	9	9	.294	.441	.377
Scor. Pos./2 Out			35	13	2	6	4	.371	.571	.463
Late-Inning Pressure			50	7	0	7	10	.140	.160	.246
Leading Off			14	2	0	2	2	.143	.143	.250
Runners On			20	2	0	1	5	.100	.100	.143
Runners/Scor. Pos.			6	1	0	1	2	.167	.167	.286
First 9 Batters			178	37	6	21	26	.208	.331	.290
Second 9 Batters			122	34	4	15	20	.279	.443	.362
All Batters Thereafter			99	16	1	13	20	.162	.202	.257

Loves to face: Roberto Alomar (.091, 1-for-11)
Milt Thompson (0-for-8)

Hates to face: Rafael Ramirez (.333, 5-for-15, 1 HR)
Juan Samuel (2-for-2, 1 HR, 1 BB)

Miscellaneous statistics: Ground outs-to-air outs ratio: 1.51 last season, 1.57 for career. . . . Induced 10 double-play ground outs in 75 opportunities (one per 7.5). . . . Allowed 13 doubles, 0 triples in 110.1 innings. . . . Allowed 6 first-inning runs in 17 starts (3.18 ERA). . . . Batting support: 3.59 runs per start. . . . Opposing base stealers: 3-for-11 (27%), lowest rate in N.L.; 6 pickoffs, 2 balks.

Comments: Joined Giants in June, and immediately rejuvenated the pitching staff. Giants had a 4.57 team ERA in April (11th in N.L.) and 4.59 in May (last in N.L.), and had a 19–31 record coming into June. With Wilson in the rotation, Giants went 19–8 in June, with a 3.05 ERA that was the lowest in the league. . . . Wilson got off to a 6–0 start with two shutouts and a 2.03 ERA in nine appearances before the All-Star break. But he was broken by the break, and went 2–7 with a 5.55 ERA in the second half. . . . On June 13, he became the first of two Giants pitchers to lose a no-hitter in the ninth inning, as Mike Pagliarulo led off the ninth with a single. Less than three weeks later, it happened to teammate Scott Garrelts. In all, five major league pitchers had no-hit bids foiled in the ninth inning last season. . . . He was the only left-handed pitcher to shut out San Diego last season, and enters the 1991 season with a streak of 19⅓ scoreless innings against them. . . . Needs to toughen up when under fire: opponents have a .333 career batting average in 120 at-bats with runners in scoring position. At other times, he's held batters to a .201 average. . . . At first glance, the two young Wilsons, Steve and Trevor, look similar: both drafted in 1985, both left-handed, each has done some starting and some relieving in the majors. Difference: Steve is a devout fly-ball pitcher; Trevor receives hate mail from burrowing animals.

RANKINGS SECTION

The Rankings Section consists of a series of lists ranking players in a wide variety of batting and pitching categories. Players are ranked in 21 batting and 18 pitching categories. In each category, American and National League rankings appear on facing pages.

The exact number of plate appearances needed to qualify for each category varies with the category. The number of eligible players is determined by the number of players in each league who had 400 plate appearances or who faced 400 batters for the season. In the American League, the 101 batters and 82 pitchers with the most plate appearances or batters faced in a given category are listed; in the National League, the top 84 batters and 70 pitchers are included. (If there is a tie for the final qualifying position that would necessitate listing more, all tied players are eliminated.)

The categories in this section are generally based on those used in the Batter and Pitcher sections. If any of the breakdowns are unfamiliar, detailed descriptions can be found in the introductions to those sections (pages 107 and 259, respectively).

American League

Batting Average vs. Left-Handed Pitchers

1.	Alomar, Cle.	.376
2.	Fielder, Det.	.371
3.	Mack, Min.	.370
4.	D. Henderson, Oak.	.353
5.	Quintana, Bos.	.352
6.	Downing, Cal.	.345
7.	Lansford, Oak.	.345
8.	Palmeiro, Tex.	.339
9.	Maldonado, Cle.	.331
10.	Sierra, Tex.	.324
11.	Johnson, Chi.	.321
12.	Jacoby, Cle.	.316
13.	Brett, K.C.	.316
14.	Fisk, Chi.	.315
15.	Harper, Min.	.315
16.	B. Ripken, Bal.	.314
17.	R. Henderson, Oak.	.313
18.	Leonard, Sea.	.309
19.	E. Martinez, Sea.	.308
20.	Brunansky, Bos.	.307
21.	Griffey Jr., Sea.	.306
22.	Parrish, Cal.	.304
23.	Kelly, NY	.304
24.	C. James, Cle.	.302
25.	Jo. Reed, Bos.	.299
26.	Puckett, Min.	.299
27.	Gagne, Min.	.298
28.	Burks, Bos.	.298
29.	Franco, Tex.	.296
30.	Gruber, Tor.	.295
31.	Calderon, Chi.	.295
32.	Deer, Mil.	.293
33.	Webster, Cle.	.292
34.	Pena, Bos.	.290
35.	Trammell, Det.	.289
36.	Winfield, NY-Cal.	.288
37.	Hrbek, Min.	.287
38.	Reynolds, Sea.	.285
39.	Borders, Tor.	.285
40.	Fletcher, Chi.	.283
41.	Lemon, Det.	.283
42.	Browne, Cle.	.281
43.	Seitzer, K.C.	.278
44.	Stanley, Tex.	.277
45.	J. Canseco, Oak.	.276
46.	Melvin, Bal.	.276
47.	Sheffield, Mil.	.274
48.	Bichette, Cal.	.274
49.	Boggs, Bos.	.274
50.	Jackson, K.C.	.273
51.	Gladden, Min.	.270
52.	Yount, Mil.	.269
53.	Guillen, Chi.	.267
54.	Evans, Bos.	.265
55.	C. Ripken, Bal.	.264
56.	Mattingly, NY	.262
57.	Sosa, Chi.	.262
58.	Fermin, Cle.	.262
59.	Cotto, Sea.	.260
60.	Parker, Mil.	.259
61.	Barfield, NY	.259
62.	McGwire, Oak.	.258
63.	Greenwell, Bos.	.257
64.	McGriff, Tor.	.257
65.	Ward, Det.	.257
66.	Davis, Sea.	.256
67.	Davis, Cal.	.254
68.	Worthington, Bal.	.254
69.	Newman, Min.	.252
70.	Espinoza, NY	.250
71.	Sax, NY	.249
72.	Incaviglia, Tex.	.249
73.	Bell, Tor.	.248
74.	Larkin, Min.	.248
75.	Phillips, Det.	.248
76.	White, Cal.	.246
77.	MacFarlane, K.C.	.245
78.	Wilson, Tor.	.245
79.	Lee, Tor.	.242
80.	Fernandez, Tor.	.238
81.	Bradley, Bal.-Chi.	.236
82.	Tettleton, Bal.	.234
83.	Devereaux, Bal.	.231
84.	Heath, Det.	.228
85.	Kittle, Chi.-Bal.	.225
86.	Eisenreich, K.C.	.224
87.	Hill, Tor.	.224
88.	Gaetti, Min.	.223
89.	Snyder, Cle.	.222
90.	Martinez, Chi.	.221
91.	Ventura, Chi.	.221
92.	Pettis, Tex.	.217
93.	Coles, Sea.-Det.	.215
94.	Balboni, NY	.211
95.	Stillwell, K.C.	.211
96.	Felix, Tor.	.211
97.	Perry, K.C.	.209
98.	O'Brien, Sea.	.200
99.	Vaughn, Mil.	.197
100.	Moseby, Det.	.182
101.	Gallego, Oak.	.180

Slugging Average vs. Left-Handed Pitchers

1.	Fielder, Det.	.854
2.	Deer, Mil.	.671
3.	D. Henderson, Oak.	.654
4.	J. Canseco, Oak.	.610
5.	R. Henderson, Oak.	.604
6.	Downing, Cal.	.555
7.	Gruber, Tor.	.554
8.	Borders, Tor.	.554
9.	Mack, Min.	.548
10.	Barfield, NY	.543
11.	Maldonado, Cle.	.543
12.	Harper, Min.	.541
13.	Fisk, Chi.	.539
14.	McGwire, Oak.	.530
15.	Brunansky, Bos.	.527
16.	Kittle, Chi.-Bal.	.523
17.	Jackson, K.C.	.510
18.	Sosa, Chi.	.502
19.	Balboni, NY	.497
20.	Webster, Cle.	.495
21.	Parrish, Cal.	.488
22.	E. Martinez, Sea.	.487
23.	Brett, K.C.	.487
24.	Trammell, Det.	.486
25.	Gagne, Min.	.484
26.	Palmeiro, Tex.	.476
27.	Calderon, Chi.	.476
28.	C. Ripken, Bal.	.473
29.	Alomar, Cle.	.470
30.	Winfield, NY-Cal.	.468
31.	Quintana, Bos.	.467
32.	Leonard, Sea.	.463
33.	Seitzer, K.C.	.455
34.	Felix, Tor.	.454
35.	Burks, Bos.	.452
36.	Puckett, Min.	.451
37.	Griffey Jr., Sea.	.447
38.	Bichette, Cal.	.445
39.	Sheffield, Mil.	.444
40.	Incaviglia, Tex.	.444
41.	Kelly, NY	.442
42.	Sierra, Tex.	.440
43.	C. James, Cle.	.432
44.	Lansford, Oak.	.429
45.	Evans, Bos.	.422
46.	B. Ripken, Bal.	.421
47.	Ward, Det.	.421
48.	Lemon, Det.	.420
49.	Tettleton, Bal.	.414
50.	Pena, Bos.	.413
51.	Jacoby, Cle.	.411
52.	McGriff, Tor.	.411
53.	Yount, Mil.	.410
54.	Lee, Tor.	.410
55.	Melvin, Bal.	.408
56.	Devereaux, Bal.	.406
57.	Hill, Tor.	.406
58.	Davis, Sea.	.405
59.	Franco, Tex.	.397
60.	Reynolds, Sea.	.391
61.	Bell, Tor.	.389
62.	Parker, Mil.	.389
63.	Davis, Cal.	.389
64.	Browne, Cle.	.388
65.	Jo. Reed, Bos.	.386
66.	Vaughn, Mil.	.386
67.	MacFarlane, K.C.	.381
68.	Stanley, Tex.	.380
69.	Johnson, Chi.	.378
70.	Snyder, Cle.	.370
71.	Boggs, Bos.	.365
72.	Gaetti, Min.	.361
73.	Greenwell, Bos.	.361
74.	Worthington, Bal.	.357
75.	Hrbek, Min.	.357
76.	Gladden, Min.	.356
77.	White, Cal.	.354
78.	Phillips, Det.	.351
79.	Wilson, Tor.	.351
80.	Cotto, Sea.	.349
81.	Bradley, Bal.-Chi.	.342
82.	Larkin, Min.	.331
83.	Heath, Det.	.329
84.	Eisenreich, K.C.	.327
85.	Fletcher, Chi.	.324
86.	Guillen, Chi.	.316
87.	Stillwell, K.C.	.313
88.	Mattingly, NY	.310
89.	Martinez, Chi.	.307
90.	Fernandez, Tor.	.302
91.	Newman, Min.	.301
92.	Sax, NY	.299
93.	Espinoza, NY	.299
94.	Pettis, Tex.	.296
95.	Coles, Sea.-Det.	.289
96.	Fermin, Cle.	.285
97.	Perry, K.C.	.269
98.	Ventura, Chi.	.247
99.	Moseby, Det.	.242
100.	Gallego, Oak.	.242
101.	O'Brien, Sea.	.238

On-Base Average vs. Left-Handed Pitchers

1.	Fielder, Det.	.479
2.	Downing, Cal.	.466
3.	Mack, Min.	.439
4.	Lansford, Oak.	.439
5.	R. Henderson, Oak.	.421
6.	E. Martinez, Sea.	.412
7.	Quintana, Bos.	.407
8.	Alomar, Cle.	.403
9.	D. Henderson, Oak.	.400
10.	Deer, Mil.	.399
11.	Franco, Tex.	.398
12.	Fisk, Chi.	.397
13.	Barfield, NY	.394
14.	Browne, Cle.	.392
15.	Worthington, Bal.	.387
16.	McGwire, Oak.	.387
17.	Maldonado, Cle.	.387
18.	Stanley, Tex.	.385
19.	Jacoby, Cle.	.383
20.	Puckett, Min.	.382
21.	Hrbek, Min.	.377
22.	Jo. Reed, Bos.	.376
23.	Evans, Bos.	.375
24.	Lemon, Det.	.375
25.	B. Ripken, Bal.	.370
26.	Parrish, Cal.	.370
27.	Trammell, Det.	.367
28.	Brett, K.C.	.366
29.	Fletcher, Chi.	.365
30.	Burks, Bos.	.365
31.	Winfield, NY-Cal.	.365
32.	C. Ripken, Bal.	.363
33.	J. Canseco, Oak.	.362
34.	C. James, Cle.	.361
35.	Palmeiro, Tex.	.361
36.	Leonard, Sea.	.361
37.	Sierra, Tex.	.361
38.	Davis, Sea.	.360
39.	Griffey Jr., Sea.	.357
40.	Harper, Min.	.357
41.	Yount, Mil.	.356
42.	Johnson, Chi.	.353
43.	Calderon, Chi.	.353
44.	Gagne, Min.	.353
45.	Kelly, NY	.352
46.	Tettleton, Bal.	.351
47.	Gruber, Tor.	.349
48.	Jackson, K.C.	.348
49.	Brunansky, Bos.	.347
50.	Incaviglia, Tex.	.347
51.	Davis, Cal.	.345
52.	Seitzer, K.C.	.345
53.	Pena, Bos.	.341
54.	Phillips, Det.	.341
55.	Fernandez, Tor.	.340
56.	Balboni, NY	.340
57.	Bradley, Bal.-Chi.	.339
58.	Sheffield, Mil.	.338
59.	Borders, Tor.	.337
60.	Reynolds, Sea.	.335
61.	Newman, Min.	.333
62.	Boggs, Bos.	.332
63.	Greenwell, Bos.	.326
64.	Sax, NY	.325
65.	McGriff, Tor.	.324
66.	Webster, Cle.	.320
67.	Pettis, Tex.	.320
68.	Sosa, Chi.	.316
69.	Bell, Tor.	.315
70.	Ward, Det.	.315
71.	White, Cal.	.315
72.	Ventura, Chi.	.315
73.	Bichette, Cal.	.312
74.	Cotto, Sea.	.308
75.	Larkin, Min.	.303
76.	Fermin, Cle.	.303
77.	Stillwell, K.C.	.302
78.	Mattingly, NY	.301
79.	MacFarlane, K.C.	.300
80.	Melvin, Bal.	.298
81.	Gladden, Min.	.297
82.	Espinoza, NY	.294
83.	Wilson, Tor.	.294
84.	Snyder, Cle.	.291
85.	Kittle, Chi.-Bal.	.291
86.	O'Brien, Sea.	.291
87.	Guillen, Chi.	.288
88.	Coles, Sea.-Det.	.287
89.	Gaetti, Min.	.283
90.	Felix, Tor.	.282
91.	Parker, Mil.	.282
92.	Hill, Tor.	.275
93.	Devereaux, Bal.	.273
94.	Eisenreich, K.C.	.268
95.	Lee, Tor.	.265
96.	Heath, Det.	.264
97.	Moseby, Det.	.264
98.	Vaughn, Mil.	.254
99.	Perry, K.C.	.252
100.	Martinez, Chi.	.248
101.	Gallego, Oak.	.234

National League

Batting Average vs. Left-Handed Pitchers

1.	Duncan, Cin.	.410
2.	Ja. Clark, S.D.	.377
3.	Justice, Atl.	.366
4.	McGee, St.L.	.335
5.	Sabo, Cin.	.327
6.	Sharperson, L.A.	.322
7.	Clark, S.F.	.317
8.	Slaught, Pit.	.317
9.	Murray, L.A.	.316
10.	Olson, Atl.	.312
11.	Murphy, Atl.-Phi.	.311
12.	Grace, Chi.	.308
13.	Mitchell, S.F.	.306
14.	Bonds, Pit.	.304
15.	Butler, S.F.	.302
16.	Gant, Atl.	.299
17.	Dawson, Chi.	.298
18.	C. Hayes, Phi.	.295
19.	L. Smith, Atl.	.294
20.	Blauser, Atl.	.294
21.	Roberts, S.D.	.294
22.	Salazar, Chi.	.293
23.	Dykstra, Phi.	.290
24.	Wallach, Mon.	.289
25.	Raines, Mon.	.289
26.	Samuel, L.A.	.289
27.	Miller, NY	.289
28.	O. Smith, St.L	.289
29.	Walton, Chi.	.288
30.	Dunston, Chi.	.287
31.	Davis, Cin.	.287
32.	Benzinger, Cin.	.285
33.	Daniels, L.A.	.285
34.	Williams, S.F.	.284
35.	Oliver, Cin.	.283
36.	Uribe, S.F.	.282
37.	Yelding, Hou.	.281
38.	Gwynn, S.D.	.281
39.	Dascenzo, Chi.	.279
40.	Bell, Pit.	.275
41.	Guerrero, St.L	.274
42.	V. Hayes, Phi.	.274
43.	Thompson, S.F.	.273
44.	Doran, Hou.-Cin.	.268
45.	Presley, Atl.	.267
46.	Larkin, Cin.	.266
47.	Zeile, St.L	.266
48.	Jefferies, NY	.266
49.	Herr, Phi.-NY	.264
50.	DeShields, Mon.	.264
51.	King, Pit.	.264
52.	Redus, Pit.	.262
53.	Thon, Phi.	.262
54.	Wilson, Hou.	.262
55.	Coleman, St.L	.262
56.	Bonilla, Pit.	.261
57.	Van Slyke, Pit.	.261
58.	Ramirez, Hou.	.260
59.	Alomar, S.D.	.260
60.	O'Neill, Cin.	.259
61.	Owen, Mon.	.259
62.	Stubbs, Hou.	.258
63.	Magadan, NY	.256
64.	Templeton, S.D.	.254
65.	Sandberg, Chi.	.252
66.	Davis, Hou.	.252
67.	Ready, Phi.	.250
68.	Hatcher, Cin.	.246
69.	Caminiti, Hou.	.246
70.	Strawberry, NY	.244
71.	Grissom, Mon.	.243
72.	Brooks, L.A.	.240
73.	Nixon, Mon.	.238
74.	Hudler, Mon.-St.L	.234
75.	McReynolds, NY	.232
76.	Lind, Pit.	.231
77.	Biggio, Hou.	.229
78.	Galarraga, Mon.	.226
79.	Fitzgerald, Mon.	.225
80.	Oquendo, St.L	.220
81.	Pendleton, St.L	.209
82.	Johnson, NY	.208
83.	Griffin, L.A.	.207
84.	Carter, S.D.	.197

Slugging Average vs. Left-Handed Pitchers

1.	Ja. Clark, S.D.	.667
2.	Justice, Atl.	.656
3.	Murphy, Atl.-Phi.	.617
4.	Duncan, Cin.	.606
5.	Bonds, Pit.	.592
6.	Sabo, Cin.	.589
7.	Davis, Hou.	.569
8.	Mitchell, S.F.	.547
9.	Samuel, L.A.	.524
10.	Davis, Cin.	.520
11.	Gant, Atl.	.520
12.	Dawson, Chi.	.508
13.	Dunston, Chi.	.505
14.	Williams, S.F.	.500
15.	Bonilla, Pit.	.493
16.	L. Smith, Atl.	.487
17.	Clark, S.F.	.486
18.	Olson, Atl.	.481
19.	Thompson, S.F.	.475
20.	Murray, L.A.	.466
21.	Stubbs, Hou.	.465
22.	Salazar, Chi.	.465
23.	Blauser, Atl.	.463
24.	Slaught, Pit.	.457
25.	Wallach, Mon.	.456
26.	Redus, Pit.	.455
27.	Sandberg, Chi.	.453
28.	Zeile, St.L	.451
29.	Coleman, St.L	.450
30.	Presley, Atl.	.450
31.	Guerrero, St.L	.446
32.	King, Pit.	.446
33.	Daniels, L.A.	.444
34.	McGee, St.L.	.442
35.	Oliver, Cin.	.439
36.	Roberts, S.D.	.425
37.	C. Hayes, Phi.	.425
38.	Grace, Chi.	.422
39.	Brooks, L.A.	.419
40.	V. Hayes, Phi.	.419
41.	Jefferies, NY	.419
42.	Doran, Hou.-Cin.	.408
43.	O'Neill, Cin.	.406
44.	Strawberry, NY	.406
45.	Larkin, Cin.	.404
46.	Owen, Mon.	.403
47.	Hudler, Mon.-St.L	.394
48.	Galarraga, Mon.	.392
49.	Thon, Phi.	.391
50.	Sharperson, L.A.	.385
51.	Bell, Pit.	.382
52.	Van Slyke, Pit.	.378
53.	Alomar, S.D.	.377
54.	O. Smith, St.L	.373
55.	DeShields, Mon.	.373
56.	Gwynn, S.D.	.373
57.	Templeton, S.D.	.370
58.	Walton, Chi.	.370
59.	Dascenzo, Chi.	.368
60.	Fitzgerald, Mon.	.362
61.	Raines, Mon.	.361
62.	Pendleton, St.L	.361
63.	Benzinger, Cin.	.360
64.	Wilson, Hou.	.360
65.	Grissom, Mon.	.359
66.	Butler, S.F.	.355
67.	Ready, Phi.	.352
68.	Magadan, NY	.351
69.	McReynolds, NY	.351
70.	Dykstra, Phi.	.345
71.	Johnson, NY	.344
72.	Miller, NY	.336
73.	Carter, S.D.	.335
74.	Ramirez, Hou.	.333
75.	Yelding, Hou.	.332
76.	Lind, Pit.	.329
77.	Herr, Phi.-NY	.327
78.	Uribe, S.F.	.324
79.	Hatcher, Cin.	.319
80.	Caminiti, Hou.	.317
81.	Nixon, Mon.	.305
82.	Biggio, Hou.	.294
83.	Oquendo, St.L	.287
84.	Griffin, L.A.	.237

On-Base Average vs. Left-Handed Pitchers

1.	Ja. Clark, S.D.	.541
2.	Justice, Atl.	.443
3.	Duncan, Cin.	.437
4.	Murphy, Atl.-Phi.	.410
5.	Sabo, Cin.	.408
6.	Doran, Hou.-Cin.	.408
7.	Sharperson, L.A.	.396
8.	Mitchell, S.F.	.395
9.	Daniels, L.A.	.393
10.	Slaught, Pit.	.393
11.	Butler, S.F.	.389
12.	Murray, L.A.	.387
13.	Bonds, Pit.	.386
14.	Dykstra, Phi.	.385
15.	Davis, Hou.	.378
16.	Grace, Chi.	.378
17.	Olson, Atl.	.374
18.	Blauser, Atl.	.373
19.	Clark, S.F.	.372
20.	Walton, Chi.	.369
21.	V. Hayes, Phi.	.365
22.	L. Smith, Atl.	.365
23.	Davis, Cin.	.365
24.	McGee, St.L.	.362
25.	Gant, Atl.	.361
26.	Bell, Pit.	.359
27.	Fitzgerald, Mon.	.359
28.	McReynolds, NY	.358
29.	Raines, Mon.	.357
30.	DeShields, Mon.	.356
31.	Wallach, Mon.	.355
32.	Oliver, Cin.	.350
33.	Roberts, S.D.	.350
34.	O. Smith, St.L.	.350
35.	Samuel, L.A.	.350
36.	Van Slyke, Pit.	.349
37.	Zeile, St.L	.347
38.	Redus, Pit.	.345
39.	Larkin, Cin.	.344
40.	Dawson, Chi.	.343
41.	Miller, NY	.340
42.	Ready, Phi.	.336
43.	Magadan, NY	.335
44.	Presley, Atl.	.333
45.	Williams, S.F.	.332
46.	Alomar, S.D.	.330
47.	Owen, Mon.	.330
48.	Herr, Phi.-NY	.329
49.	Thompson, S.F.	.325
50.	Uribe, S.F.	.325
51.	Yelding, Hou.	.324
52.	C. Hayes, Phi.	.324
53.	Dascenzo, Chi.	.322
54.	Oquendo, St.L	.319
55.	Sandberg, Chi.	.319
56.	Salazar, Chi.	.319
57.	Guerrero, St.L	.319
58.	Grissom, Mon.	.317
59.	Biggio, Hou.	.316
60.	Wilson, Hou.	.311
61.	Thon, Phi.	.310
62.	O'Neill, Cin.	.310
63.	Jefferies, NY	.308
64.	Nixon, Mon.	.307
65.	Gwynn, S.D.	.307
66.	Ramirez, Hou.	.306
67.	Benzinger, Cin.	.306
68.	Bonilla, Pit.	.303
69.	King, Pit.	.303
70.	Stubbs, Hou.	.300
71.	Strawberry, NY	.300
72.	Hatcher, Cin.	.299
73.	Coleman, St.L	.297
74.	Johnson, NY	.296
75.	Dunston, Chi.	.295
76.	Brooks, L.A.	.294
77.	Templeton, S.D.	.286
78.	Lind, Pit.	.285
79.	Hudler, Mon.-St.L	.281
80.	Caminiti, Hou.	.280
81.	Galarraga, Mon.	.260
82.	Carter, S.D.	.258
83.	Griffin, L.A.	.257
84.	Pendleton, St.L	.235

American League

Batting Average vs. Right-Handed Pitchers

1.	Polonia, NY-Cal.	.341
2.	Brett, K.C.	.336
3.	R. Henderson, Oak.	.330
4.	McGriff, Tor.	.324
5.	Boggs, Bos.	.319
6.	Greenwell, Bos.	.316
7.	Trammell, Det.	.311
8.	Palmeiro, Tex.	.311
9.	Eisenreich, K.C.	.306
10.	Parker, Mil.	.301
11.	Sheffield, Mil.	.301
12.	E. Martinez, Sea.	.299
13.	C. James, Cle.	.298
14.	Davis, Sea.	.298
15.	Puckett, Min.	.297
16.	Griffey Jr., Sea.	.296
17.	Franco, Tex.	.295
18.	Burks, Bos.	.295
19.	Fernandez, Tor.	.293
20.	Baines, Tex.-Oak.	.293
21.	Felix, Tor.	.289
22.	Guillen, Chi.	.287
23.	Hrbek, Min.	.287
24.	Harper, Min.	.285
25.	Jo. Reed, Bos.	.285
26.	Jacoby, Cle.	.284
27.	Pasqua, Chi.	.282
28.	Larkin, Min.	.279
29.	Kelly, NY	.278
30.	B. Ripken, Bal.	.278
31.	Gladden, Min.	.278
32.	Moseby, Det.	.278
33.	Finley, Bal.	.277
34.	Wilson, Tor.	.275
35.	Molitor, Mil.	.275
36.	J. Canseco, Oak.	.274
37.	Seitzer, K.C.	.274
38.	Orsulak, Bal.	.273
39.	Perry, K.C.	.272
40.	Bell, Tor.	.271
41.	Jackson, K.C.	.271
42.	Johnson, Chi.	.270
43.	Davis, Cal.	.269
44.	Fisk, Chi.	.268
45.	Hall, NY	.268
46.	Bradley, Bal.-Chi.	.268
47.	Ray, Cal.	.268
48.	Weiss, Oak.	.267
49.	Gruber, Tor.	.265
50.	Surhoff, Mil.	.265
51.	Sax, NY	.265
52.	Ventura, Chi.	.263
53.	Sheets, Det.	.262
54.	Browne, Cle.	.262
55.	Stillwell, K.C.	.262
56.	Calderon, Chi.	.261
57.	Brock, Mil.	.260
58.	Alomar, Cle.	.259
59.	Whitaker, Det.	.257
60.	Winfield, NY-Cal.	.257
61.	Sierra, Tex.	.255
62.	Parrish, Cal.	.255
63.	Fermin, Cle.	.254
64.	Phillips, Det.	.253
65.	Petralli, Tex.	.252
66.	Nokes, Det.-NY	.252
67.	Jose, Oak.	.252
68.	Quintana, Bos.	.252
69.	Pettis, Tex.	.251
70.	Briley, Sea.	.250
71.	Pena, Bos.	.250
72.	Maldonado, Cle.	.248
73.	Brunansky, Bos.	.248
74.	Olerud, Tor.	.246
75.	Lansford, Oak.	.245
76.	Spiers, Mil.	.245
77.	C. Ripken, Bal.	.244
78.	Liriano, Tor.-Min.	.243
79.	Evans, Bos.	.242
80.	Milligan, Bal.	.240
81.	Howell, Cal.	.240
82.	Yount, Mil.	.239
83.	Barfield, NY	.239
84.	Snyder, Cle.	.238
85.	Huson, Tex.	.237
86.	Reynolds, Sea.	.237
87.	D. Henderson, Oak.	.237
88.	Fielder, Det.	.235
89.	Gaetti, Min.	.231
90.	McGwire, Oak.	.228
91.	Incaviglia, Tex.	.225
92.	Fletcher, Chi.	.220
93.	Gallego, Oak.	.218
94.	Tettleton, Bal.	.218
95.	Leonard, Sea.	.218
96.	Worthington, Bal.	.214
97.	Espinoza, NY	.211
98.	Sosa, Chi.	.211
99.	White, Cal.	.204
100.	Deer, Mil.	.170

Slugging Average vs. Right-Handed Pitchers

1.	McGriff, Tor.	.597
2.	R. Henderson, Oak.	.566
3.	Jackson, K.C.	.531
4.	Brett, K.C.	.529
5.	J. Canseco, Oak.	.520
6.	Pasqua, Chi.	.517
7.	Hrbek, Min.	.515
8.	Burks, Bos.	.503
9.	Griffey Jr., Sea.	.500
10.	Gruber, Tor.	.495
11.	Moseby, Det.	.478
12.	Parker, Mil.	.478
13.	McGwire, Oak.	.476
14.	Fielder, Det.	.473
15.	Greenwell, Bos.	.471
16.	Palmeiro, Tex.	.465
17.	Hall, NY	.457
18.	Baines, Tex.-Oak.	.457
19.	Boggs, Bos.	.450
20.	C. James, Cle.	.448
21.	Whitaker, Det.	.448
22.	Winfield, NY-Cal.	.445
23.	Puckett, Min.	.444
24.	Davis, Sea.	.442
25.	Parrish, Cal.	.438
26.	Felix, Tor.	.434
27.	Bell, Tor.	.433
28.	Jacoby, Cle.	.433
29.	Trammell, Det.	.433
30.	Fernandez, Tor.	.432
31.	Eisenreich, K.C.	.429
32.	Molitor, Mil.	.428
33.	Orsulak, Bal.	.422
34.	Milligan, Bal.	.420
35.	Snyder, Cle.	.419
36.	Sierra, Tex.	.418
37.	Larkin, Min.	.418
38.	Polonia, NY-Cal.	.418
39.	Sheffield, Mil.	.412
40.	Sheets, Det.	.411
41.	Barfield, NY	.411
42.	Howell, Cal.	.409
43.	Kelly, NY	.409
44.	Incaviglia, Tex.	.408
45.	E. Martinez, Sea.	.408
46.	Maldonado, Cle.	.405
47.	Franco, Tex.	.404
48.	Olerud, Tor.	.404
49.	Davis, Cal.	.402
50.	Fisk, Chi.	.401
51.	Alomar, Cle.	.399
52.	Perry, K.C.	.399
53.	Brunansky, Bos.	.395
54.	Jo. Reed, Bos.	.391
55.	C. Ripken, Bal.	.390
56.	Calderon, Chi.	.389
57.	D. Henderson, Oak.	.388
58.	Gladden, Min.	.385
59.	Harper, Min.	.384
60.	Ray, Cal.	.384
61.	Nokes, Det.-NY	.383
62.	Gaetti, Min.	.382
63.	Brock, Mil.	.377
64.	Evans, Bos.	.376
65.	Yount, Mil.	.369
66.	Briley, Sea.	.368
67.	B. Ripken, Bal.	.368
68.	Tettleton, Bal.	.367
69.	Browne, Cle.	.366
70.	Stillwell, K.C.	.365
71.	Jose, Oak.	.360
72.	Surhoff, Mil.	.359
73.	Guillen, Chi.	.358
74.	Pettis, Tex.	.358
75.	Wilson, Tor.	.357
76.	Finley, Bal.	.357
77.	Ventura, Chi.	.351
78.	Phillips, Det.	.350
79.	Johnson, Chi.	.348
80.	White, Cal.	.339
81.	Quintana, Bos.	.336
82.	Sax, NY	.336
83.	Liriano, Tor.-Min.	.333
84.	Sosa, Chi.	.328
85.	Weiss, Oak.	.327
86.	Seitzer, K.C.	.327
87.	Reynolds, Sea.	.326
88.	Spiers, Mil.	.323
89.	Deer, Mil.	.320
90.	Pena, Bos.	.318
91.	Bradley, Bal.-Chi.	.318
92.	Fermin, Cle.	.313
93.	Worthington, Bal.	.308
94.	Fletcher, Chi.	.307
95.	Petralli, Tex.	.302
96.	Leonard, Sea.	.294
97.	Gallego, Oak.	.287
98.	Lansford, Oak.	.286
99.	Huson, Tex.	.280
100.	Espinoza, NY	.262

On-Base Average vs. Right-Handed Pitchers

1.	R. Henderson, Oak.	.446
2.	McGriff, Tor.	.440
3.	Boggs, Bos.	.415
4.	Davis, Sea.	.401
5.	Brett, K.C.	.398
6.	Baines, Tex.-Oak.	.392
7.	E. Martinez, Sea.	.390
8.	Greenwell, Bos.	.386
9.	Tettleton, Bal.	.385
10.	Milligan, Bal.	.382
11.	Trammell, Det.	.382
12.	Phillips, Det.	.377
13.	Hrbek, Min.	.376
14.	Franco, Tex.	.376
15.	Polonia, NY-Cal.	.376
16.	J. Canseco, Oak.	.374
17.	Griffey Jr., Sea.	.371
18.	Jo. Reed, Bos.	.368
19.	Fisk, Chi.	.367
20.	Eisenreich, K.C.	.365
21.	McGwire, Oak.	.364
22.	Davis, Cal.	.363
23.	Palmeiro, Tex.	.360
24.	Larkin, Min.	.359
25.	Moseby, Det.	.358
26.	Jacoby, Cle.	.358
27.	Fernandez, Tor.	.358
28.	Puckett, Min.	.357
29.	Bradley, Bal.-Chi.	.356
30.	Pasqua, Chi.	.355
31.	Sheffield, Mil.	.355
32.	Whitaker, Det.	.353
33.	Felix, Tor.	.351
34.	Parker, Mil.	.350
35.	Seitzer, K.C.	.347
36.	Weiss, Oak.	.347
37.	Petralli, Tex.	.347
38.	Orsulak, Bal.	.346
39.	Olerud, Tor.	.342
40.	Burks, Bos.	.341
41.	Barfield, NY	.341
42.	Brunansky, Bos.	.340
43.	Pettis, Tex.	.340
44.	Jackson, K.C.	.339
45.	Browne, Cle.	.337
46.	Reynolds, Sea.	.337
47.	Brock, Mil.	.336
48.	Perry, K.C.	.336
49.	Finley, Bal.	.336
50.	Molitor, Mil.	.335
51.	Evans, Bos.	.335
52.	Howell, Cal.	.334
53.	C. Ripken, Bal.	.332
54.	C. James, Cle.	.332
55.	Yount, Mil.	.331
56.	Fielder, Det.	.330
57.	Ventura, Chi.	.329
58.	Guillen, Chi.	.327
59.	Parrish, Cal.	.327
60.	B. Ripken, Bal.	.326
61.	Quintana, Bos.	.325
62.	Surhoff, Mil.	.324
63.	Winfield, NY-Cal.	.324
64.	Gruber, Tor.	.322
65.	Briley, Sea.	.322
66.	Gladden, Min.	.322
67.	Huson, Tex.	.319
68.	Harper, Min.	.315
69.	Sierra, Tex.	.314
70.	Johnson, Chi.	.313
71.	Pena, Bos.	.313
72.	Sax, NY	.312
73.	Calderon, Chi.	.311
74.	Kelly, NY	.311
75.	Nokes, Det.-NY	.311
76.	Sheets, Det.	.309
77.	Liriano, Tor.-Min.	.308
78.	Maldonado, Cle.	.306
79.	Stillwell, K.C.	.305
80.	Ray, Cal.	.304
81.	Wilson, Tor.	.303
82.	D. Henderson, Oak.	.302
83.	Worthington, Bal.	.301
84.	Alomar, Cle.	.298
85.	Lansford, Oak.	.298
86.	Bell, Tor.	.298
87.	Gallego, Oak.	.297
88.	Fermin, Cle.	.294
89.	Jose, Oak.	.293
90.	Hall, NY	.285
91.	White, Cal.	.280
92.	Incaviglia, Tex.	.279
93.	Spiers, Mil.	.273
94.	Leonard, Sea.	.272
95.	Fletcher, Chi.	.271
96.	Deer, Mil.	.271
97.	Gaetti, Min.	.270
98.	Snyder, Cle.	.256
99.	Sosa, Chi.	.255
100.	Espinoza, NY	.240

National League

Batting Average vs. Right-Handed Pitchers

1. Magadan, NY .371
2. Dykstra, Phi .344
3. Murray, L.A. .338
4. McGee, St.L .336
5. Sandberg, Chi. .334
6. Gwynn, S.D. .328
7. Roberts, S.D. .319
8. Larkin, Cin. .319
9. Doran, Hou.-Cin .318
10. Dawson, Chi. .316
11. Kruk, Phi. .316
12. Butler, S.F. .313
13. L. Smith, Atl. .312
14. Harris, L.A. .311
15. Coleman, St.L .310
16. Grace, Chi. .309
17. Biggio, Hou. .306
18. Gant, Atl. .305
19. DeShields, Mon. .304
20. Backman, Pit. .303
21. Alomar, S.D. .301
22. Daniels, L.A. .301
23. Wallach, Mon. .299
24. Strawberry, NY .298
25. Van Slyke, Pit. .298
26. Bonds, Pit. .297
27. Hatcher, Cin. .296
28. Bonilla, Pit. .296
29. Jefferies, NY .293
30. McReynolds, NY .291
31. Kennedy, S.F. .288
32. Da. Martinez, Mon. .288
33. Raines, Mon. .285
34. Guerrero, St.L .285
35. Mitchell, S.F. .282
36. Brooks, L.A. .282
37. Lind, Pit. .282
38. Clark, S.F. .279
39. Boston, NY .278
40. Treadway, Atl. .276
41. Scioscia, L.A. .275
42. O'Neill, Cin. .275
43. Williams, S.F. .274
44. Galarraga, Mon. .273
45. Bream, Pit. .273
46. Daulton, Phi. .272
47. Oquendo, St.L .269
48. D. Smith, Chi. .268
49. Johnson, NY .266
50. McDowell, Atl. .263
51. Stubbs, Hou. .263
52. Ramirez, Hou. .261
53. Herr, Phi.-NY .260
54. Blauser, Atl. .256
55. Pagliarulo, S.D. .256
56. Walker, Mon. .254
57. V. Hayes, Phi. .253
58. Thon, Phi. .251
59. Dunston, Chi. .249
60. Carter, S.D. .248
61. Walton, Chi. .248
62. Davis, Cin. .248
63. Justice, Atl. .247
64. Templeton, S.D. .244
65. Pendleton, St.L .242
66. Girardi, Chi. .241
67. Caminiti, Hou. .239
68. C. Hayes, Phi. .239
69. Bell, Pit. .238
70. Sabo, Cin. .235
71. Thompson, St.L. .235
72. Zeile, St.L. .233
73. Yelding, Hou. .232
74. O. Smith, St.L. .232
75. Uribe, S.F. .231
76. Presley, Atl. .230
77. Salazar, Chi. .229
78. Thompson, S.F. .229
79. Duncan, Cin. .227
80. Owen, Mon. .214
81. Murphy, Atl.-Phi. .214
82. Samuel, L.A. .213
83. Griffin, L.A. .212
84. Ja. Clark, S.D. .209

Slugging Average vs. Right-Handed Pitchers

1. Sandberg, Chi. .616
2. Strawberry, NY .594
3. Daniels, L.A. .575
4. Murray, L.A. .551
5. Gant, Atl. .550
6. Dawson, Chi. .549
7. Mitchell, S.F. .542
8. Bonds, Pit. .541
9. Bonilla, Pit. .539
10. Magadan, NY .519
11. Van Slyke, Pit. .518
12. McReynolds, NY .517
13. Dykstra, Phi. .490
14. Johnson, NY .488
15. Justice, Atl. .484
16. Williams, S.F. .482
17. Stubbs, Hou. .481
18. Wallach, Mon. .479
19. Boston, NY .471
20. Kruk, Phi. .469
21. Davis, Cin. .469
22. Bream, Pit. .464
23. Ja. Clark, S.D. .464
24. Da. Martinez, Mon. .450
25. Doran, Hou.-Cin. .448
26. Gwynn, S.D. .443
27. Jefferies, NY .442
28. Walker, Mon. .442
29. Roberts, S.D. .439
30. L. Smith, Atl. .439
31. Daulton, Phi. .436
32. McGee, St.L. .434
33. Scioscia, L.A. .434
34. O'Neill, Cin. .428
35. Brooks, L.A. .427
36. Hatcher, Cin. .424
37. Clark, S.F. .422
38. Galarraga, Mon. .420
39. Carter, S.D. .418
40. Backman, Pit. .415
41. Guerrero, St.L. .415
42. Raines, Mon. .412
43. V. Hayes, Phi. .410
44. Grace, Chi. .408
45. Sabo, Cin. .408
46. DeShields, Mon. .405
47. Butler, S.F. .403
48. Presley, Atl. .396
49. McDowell, Atl. .395
50. Larkin, Cin. .392
51. Treadway, Atl. .389
52. Kennedy, S.F. .387
53. Dunston, Chi. .384
54. Harris, L.A. .383
55. Biggio, Hou. .383
56. Alomar, S.D. .382
57. Blauser, Atl. .380
58. D. Smith, Chi. .378
59. Duncan, Cin. .377
60. Zeile, St.L. .370
61. Coleman, St.L .369
62. Pagliarulo, S.D. .367
63. Thompson, St.L. .366
64. Herr, Phi.-NY .360
65. Templeton, S.D. .358
66. Lind, Pit. .349
67. Bell, Pit. .346
68. Thompson, S.F. .343
69. Salazar, Chi. .340
70. Oquendo, St.L .331
71. Ramirez, Hou. .328
72. Thon, Phi. .326
73. Murphy, Atl.-Phi. .324
74. C. Hayes, Phi. .307
75. Walton, Chi. .305
76. Pendleton, St.L .304
77. Caminiti, Hou. .302
78. Samuel, L.A. .295
79. Owen, Mon. .294
80. Uribe, S.F. .293
81. Girardi, Chi. .281
82. Yelding, Hou. .268
83. Griffin, L.A. .264
84. O. Smith, St.L. .260

On-Base Average vs. Right-Handed Pitchers

1. Magadan, NY .462
2. Dykstra, Phi. .434
3. Murray, L.A. .429
4. Bonds, Pit. .422
5. Kruk, Phi. .415
6. Doran, Hou.-Cin. .412
7. Butler, S.F. .403
8. Strawberry, NY .398
9. L. Smith, Atl. .397
10. McGee, St.L. .394
11. Raines, Mon. .393
12. Roberts, S.D. .391
13. Gwynn, S.D. .388
14. Daniels, L.A. .387
15. DeShields, Mon. .387
16. Ja. Clark, S.D. .386
17. V. Hayes, Phi. .381
18. Van Slyke, Pit. .378
19. Backman, Pit. .376
20. Sandberg, Chi. .373
21. Grace, Chi. .369
22. Scioscia, L.A. .367
23. Oquendo, St.L .367
24. Coleman, St.L .366
25. Dawson, Chi. .366
26. Larkin, Cin. .365
27. Daulton, Phi. .363
28. Bream, Pit. .362
29. Biggio, Hou. .359
30. Gant, Atl. .355
31. Harris, L.A. .353
32. Jefferies, NY .353
33. Kennedy, S.F. .352
34. Stubbs, Hou. .352
35. O'Neill, Cin. .351
36. McReynolds, NY .350
37. Walker, Mon. .349
38. Hatcher, Cin. .347
39. Clark, S.F. .347
40. Alomar, S.D. .345
41. Justice, Atl. .344
42. Mitchell, S.F. .342
43. Guerrero, St.L .341
44. Walton, Chi. .339
45. Davis, Cin. .339
46. D. Smith, Chi. .338
47. Bonilla, Pit. .338
48. Owen, Mon. .336
49. Johnson, NY .333
50. Galarraga, Mon. .332
51. Wallach, Mon. .331
52. Boston, NY .328
53. Zeile, St.L. .326
54. Herr, Phi.-NY .322
55. Lind, Pit. .321
56. Blauser, Atl. .319
57. Caminiti, Hou. .318
58. O. Smith, St.L. .318
59. Thompson, St.L. .317
60. Da. Martinez, Mon. .317
61. Brooks, L.A. .316
62. Williams, S.F. .312
63. Pagliarulo, S.D. .311
64. Treadway, Atl. .307
65. McDowell, Atl. .306
66. Bell, Pit. .305
67. Carter, S.D. .305
68. Sabo, Cin. .303
69. Thon, Phi. .302
70. Pendleton, St.L .299
71. Samuel, L.A. .297
72. Ramirez, Hou. .294
73. Yelding, Hou. .288
74. Thompson, S.F. .284
75. Uribe, S.F. .283
76. Girardi, Chi. .283
77. C. Hayes, Phi. .277
78. Salazar, Chi. .277
79. Dunston, Chi. .277
80. Duncan, Cin. .276
81. Templeton, S.D. .275
82. Murphy, Atl.-Phi. .271
83. Griffin, L.A. .259
84. Presley, Atl. .255

American League

Batting Average, Home Games

1.	Boggs, Bos.	.359
2.	Polonia, NY-Cal.	.353
3.	Puckett, Min.	.344
4.	Brunansky, Bos.	.340
5.	Trammell, Det.	.339
6.	Brett, K.C.	.319
7.	Franco, Tex.	.317
8.	Seitzer, K.C.	.312
9.	Greenwell, Bos.	.310
10.	Fernandez, Tor.	.308
11.	Jackson, K.C.	.307
12.	Burks, Bos.	.306
13.	Surhoff, Mil.	.306
14.	Calderon, Chi.	.306
15.	Davis, Cal.	.306
16.	Kelly, NY	.305
17.	R. Henderson, Oak.	.305
18.	Johnson, Chi.	.302
19.	D. Henderson, Oak.	.302
20.	Gladden, Min.	.300
21.	Alomar, Cle.	.300
22.	E. Martinez, Sea.	.299
23.	Quintana, Bos.	.299
24.	Lansford, Oak.	.298
25.	Jo. Reed, Bos.	.293
26.	Griffey Jr., Sea.	.292
27.	Gruber, Tor.	.292
28.	Palmeiro, Tex.	.288
29.	Fisk, Chi.	.288
30.	Jacoby, Cle.	.287
31.	Molitor, Mil.	.286
32.	Larkin, Min.	.286
33.	C. James, Cle.	.286
34.	Perry, K.C.	.286
35.	Harper, Min.	.283
36.	Fielder, Det.	.280
37.	Baines, Tex.-Oak.	.280
38.	Guillen, Chi.	.279
39.	Hrbek, Min.	.279
40.	Fermin, Cle.	.278
41.	Davis, Sea.	.278
42.	B. Ripken, Bal.	.278
43.	Parrish, Cal.	.277
44.	McGriff, Tor.	.277
45.	Pena, Bos.	.275
46.	Ventura, Chi.	.273
47.	Parker, Mil.	.273
48.	Olerud, Tor.	.273
49.	Orsulak, Bal.	.272
50.	Browne, Cle.	.272
51.	Sheffield, Mil.	.272
52.	Ray, Cal.	.271
53.	Maldonado, Cle.	.268
54.	Stillwell, K.C.	.268
55.	Sierra, Tex.	.266
56.	Milligan, Bal.	.265
57.	Petralli, Tex.	.265
58.	Lee, Tor.	.263
59.	O'Brien, Sea.	.262
60.	Newman, Min.	.261
61.	Winfield, NY-Cal.	.261
62.	Sax, NY	.259
63.	Eisenreich, K.C.	.258
64.	J. Canseco, Oak.	.258
65.	MacFarlane, K.C.	.257
66.	Sosa, Chi.	.256
67.	Bell, Tor.	.255
68.	Pettis, Tex.	.253
69.	Liriano, Tor.-Min.	.253
70.	Reynolds, Sea.	.253
71.	Evans, Bos.	.252
72.	Steinbach, Oak.	.249
73.	Gagne, Min.	.247
74.	Wilson, Tor.	.247
75.	Incaviglia, Tex.	.247
76.	Weiss, Oak.	.247
77.	Webster, Cle.	.247
78.	Felix, Tor.	.246
79.	Fletcher, Chi.	.242
80.	Phillips, Det.	.241
81.	Moseby, Det.	.240
82.	Brock, Mil.	.239
83.	Gaetti, Min.	.238
84.	Tettleton, Bal.	.237
85.	Bradley, Bal.-Chi.	.237
86.	Snyder, Cle.	.235
87.	Worthington, Bal.	.234
88.	Finley, Bal.	.231
89.	McGwire, Oak.	.224
90.	Leonard, Sea.	.222
91.	Yount, Mil.	.222
92.	Huson, Tex.	.220
93.	Vaughn, Mil.	.218
94.	Barfield, NY	.218
95.	Espinoza, NY	.215
96.	Whitaker, Det.	.215
97.	White, Cal.	.215
98.	Gallego, Oak.	.214
99.	C. Ripken, Bal.	.213
100.	Deer, Mil.	.187

Batting Average, Road Games

1.	Palmeiro, Tex.	.350
2.	R. Henderson, Oak.	.342
3.	Brett, K.C.	.340
4.	McGriff, Tor.	.321
5.	Polonia, NY-Cal.	.316
6.	Sheffield, Mil.	.315
7.	C. James, Cle.	.310
8.	Griffey Jr., Sea.	.308
9.	Harper, Min.	.305
10.	E. Martinez, Sea.	.305
11.	B. Ripken, Bal.	.303
12.	Parker, Mil.	.303
13.	Eisenreich, K.C.	.300
14.	Jacoby, Cle.	.298
15.	Hrbek, Min.	.294
16.	Sierra, Tex.	.293
17.	Davis, Sea.	.289
18.	Baines, Tex.-Oak.	.288
19.	J. Canseco, Oak.	.288
20.	C. Ripken, Bal.	.287
21.	Finley, Bal.	.286
22.	Jo. Reed, Bos.	.286
23.	Weiss, Oak.	.286
24.	Burks, Bos.	.285
25.	Fisk, Chi.	.283
26.	Molitor, Mil.	.283
27.	Greenwell, Bos.	.283
28.	Felix, Tor.	.282
29.	Wilson, Tor.	.281
30.	Alomar, Cle.	.280
31.	Guillen, Chi.	.279
32.	Leonard, Sea.	.279
33.	Maldonado, Cle.	.277
34.	Quintana, Bos.	.276
35.	Fielder, Det.	.275
36.	Bell, Tor.	.274
37.	Barfield, NY	.274
38.	Winfield, NY-Cal.	.274
39.	Franco, Tex.	.272
40.	Yount, Mil.	.272
41.	Bradley, Bal.-Chi.	.272
42.	Trammell, Det.	.271
43.	Heath, Det.	.269
44.	Johnson, Chi.	.268
45.	Kelly, NY	.267
46.	Mattingly, NY	.265
47.	Orsulak, Bal.	.265
48.	Milligan, Bal.	.265
49.	Browne, Cle.	.262
50.	Sax, NY	.262
51.	Phillips, Det.	.261
52.	Parrish, Cal.	.260
53.	Lemon, Det.	.259
54.	Huson, Tex.	.259
55.	Webster, Cle.	.257
56.	Moseby, Det.	.257
57.	Whitaker, Det.	.257
58.	Brock, Mil.	.257
59.	Gruber, Tor.	.254
60.	MacFarlane, K.C.	.254
61.	Steinbach, Oak.	.253
62.	Larkin, Min.	.252
63.	Reynolds, Sea.	.252
64.	Puckett, Min.	.252
65.	Gladden, Min.	.251
66.	Pena, Bos.	.250
67.	Surhoff, Mil.	.247
68.	Evans, Bos.	.247
69.	Lansford, Oak.	.247
70.	Boggs, Bos.	.245
71.	McGwire, Oak.	.245
72.	Calderon, Chi.	.245
73.	Devereaux, Bal.	.244
74.	Nokes, Det.-NY	.242
75.	Fernandez, Tor.	.242
76.	Fletcher, Chi.	.242
77.	D. Henderson, Oak.	.241
78.	Jackson, K.C.	.239
79.	Seitzer, K.C.	.239
80.	Fermin, Cle.	.234
81.	Espinoza, NY	.233
82.	Snyder, Cle.	.231
83.	Stillwell, K.C.	.230
84.	Deer, Mil.	.230
85.	Ventura, Chi.	.227
86.	Lee, Tor.	.224
87.	Gagne, Min.	.223
88.	Pettis, Tex.	.223
89.	Vaughn, Mil.	.222
90.	Perry, K.C.	.220
91.	Gaetti, Min.	.220
92.	Incaviglia, Tex.	.220
93.	Davis, Cal.	.219
94.	White, Cal.	.219
95.	Worthington, Bal.	.218
96.	Sosa, Chi.	.211
97.	Tettleton, Bal.	.210
98.	Gallego, Oak.	.198
99.	O'Brien, Sea.	.191
100.	Brunansky, Bos.	.190

Batting Average, Grass Surfaces

1.	Polonia, NY-Cal.	.339
2.	McGriff, Tor.	.330
3.	Griffey Jr., Sea.	.323
4.	Palmeiro, Tex.	.318
5.	Quintana, Bos.	.313
6.	Boggs, Bos.	.309
7.	Trammell, Det.	.309
8.	C. James, Cle.	.307
9.	Greenwell, Bos.	.307
10.	R. Henderson, Oak.	.304
11.	Alomar, Cle.	.303
12.	Sheffield, Mil.	.301
13.	Jacoby, Cle.	.301
14.	Franco, Tex.	.299
15.	Burks, Bos.	.297
16.	Fisk, Chi.	.296
17.	Calderon, Chi.	.295
18.	Daugherty, Tex.	.290
19.	Jo. Reed, Bos.	.289
20.	Baines, Tex.-Oak.	.284
21.	Kelly, NY	.284
22.	Johnson, Chi.	.284
23.	Browne, Cle.	.282
24.	Brunansky, Bos.	.282
25.	Ray, Cal.	.281
26.	D. Henderson, Oak.	.279
27.	Pasqua, Chi.	.278
28.	Parker, Mil.	.278
29.	Parrish, Cal.	.277
30.	B. Ripken, Bal.	.276
31.	Wilson, Tor.	.273
32.	Guillen, Chi.	.273
33.	Pena, Bos.	.273
34.	Gantner, Mil.	.272
35.	Maldonado, Cle.	.272
36.	Baerga, Cle.	.271
37.	Surhoff, Mil.	.271
38.	Fielder, Det.	.271
39.	Orsulak, Bal.	.270
40.	Downing, Cal.	.269
41.	Jose, Oak.	.269
42.	Heath, Det.	.268
43.	Molitor, Mil.	.268
44.	Milligan, Bal.	.267
45.	J. Canseco, Oak.	.267
46.	Davis, Cal.	.265
47.	Weiss, Oak.	.264
48.	Lansford, Oak.	.263
49.	Bichette, Cal.	.262
50.	Schofield, Cal.	.260
51.	Hill, Cal.	.260
52.	Sheets, Det.	.260
53.	Sierra, Tex.	.259
54.	Winfield, NY-Cal.	.258
55.	Reynolds, Sea.	.257
56.	Mattingly, NY	.257
57.	Finley, Bal.	.257
58.	Randolph, Oak.	.256
59.	Sax, NY	.255
60.	Steinbach, Oak.	.254
61.	Ventura, Chi.	.253
62.	Leyritz, NY	.253
63.	Brock, Mil.	.252
64.	Petralli, Tex.	.252
65.	Joyner, Cal.	.251
66.	Bradley, Bal.-Chi.	.251
67.	Devereaux, Bal.	.250
68.	Yount, Mil.	.248
69.	Ward, Det.	.248
70.	Evans, Bos.	.247
71.	Phillips, Det.	.247
72.	Spiers, Mil.	.247
73.	Webster, Cle.	.247
74.	Fermin, Cle.	.245
75.	Hall, NY	.244
76.	Fletcher, Chi.	.242
77.	Moseby, Det.	.241
78.	Lemon, Det.	.241
79.	C. Ripken, Bal.	.241
80.	Fernandez, Tor.	.241
81.	Gruber, Tor.	.240
82.	Huson, Tex.	.239
83.	Pettis, Tex.	.236
84.	Kittle, Chi.-Bal.	.235
85.	Barfield, NY	.234
86.	Worthington, Bal.	.233
87.	Nokes, Det.-NY	.233
88.	Whitaker, Det.	.233
89.	Seitzer, K.C.	.232
90.	McGwire, Oak.	.232
91.	Tettleton, Bal.	.230
92.	Sosa, Chi.	.229
93.	Rivera, Bos.	.229
94.	Snyder, Cle.	.228
95.	Incaviglia, Tex.	.228
96.	White, Cal.	.223
97.	Vaughn, Mil.	.222
98.	Howell, Cal.	.218
99.	Gallego, Oak.	.216
100.	Deer, Mil.	.214
101.	Espinoza, NY	.208

National League

Batting Average, Home Games

1. Sandberg, Chi. .357
2. McGee, St.L. .348
3. Murray, L.A. .343
4. Dykstra, Phi. .339
5. Butler, S.F. .337
6. Doran, Hou.-Cin. .332
7. Grace, Chi. .331
8. Justice, Atl. .320
9. Jefferies, NY .318
10. Kruk, Phi. .318
11. Clark, S.F. .318
12. Dawson, Chi. .316
13. DeShields, Mon. .314
14. Gant, Atl. .313
15. L. Smith, Atl. .312
16. Gwynn, S.D. .310
17. Duncan, Cin. .309
18. Sharperson, L.A. .308
19. Raines, Mon. .307
20. Treadway, Atl. .301
21. Coleman, St.L .297
22. Blauser, Atl. .297
23. Salazar, Chi. .294
24. O'Neill, Cin. .290
25. Daniels, L.A. .290
26. Walton, Chi. .290
27. Caminiti, Hou. .288
28. Van Slyke, Pit. .288
29. Santiago, S.D. .286
30. Alomar, S.D. .285
31. Roberts, S.D. .282
32. Sabo, Cin. .280
33. Scioscia, L.A. .279
34. Magadan, NY .278
35. Mitchell, S.F. .278
36. Harris, L.A. .276
37. Bream, Pit. .276
38. Bonds, Pit. .276
39. Guerrero, St.L. .276
40. V. Hayes, Phi. .276
41. Wallach, Mon. .276
42. Da. Martinez, Mon. .275
43. Biggio, Hou. .274
44. Larkin, Cin. .273
45. Girardi, Chi. .272
46. Herr, Phi.-NY .272
47. Williams, S.F. .271
48. Boston, NY .270
49. Ramirez, Hou. .267
50. Thompson, S.F. .266
51. Galarraga, Mon. .266
52. O. Smith, St.L. .266
53. Hatcher, Cin. .264
54. Zeile, St.L. .262
55. Bell, Pit. .261
56. Bonilla, Pit. .261
57. Lind, Pit. .261
58. Presley, Atl. .260
59. McReynolds, NY .258
60. Benzinger, Cin. .258
61. Ja. Clark, S.D. .256
62. Walker, Mon. .255
63. Strawberry, NY .254
64. Stubbs, Hou. .253
65. Yelding, Hou. .253
66. Brooks, L.A. .251
67. Daulton, Phi. .250
68. Dunston, Chi. .250
69. Thon, Phi. .248
70. Templeton, S.D. .247
71. Samuel, L.A. .246
72. C. Hayes, Phi. .245
73. Pendleton, St.L .243
74. Oquendo, St.L .239
75. Johnson, NY .234
76. Davis, Cin. .233
77. Murphy, Atl.-Phi. .229
78. Owen, Mon. .228
79. Uribe, S.F. .223
80. Oliver, Cin. .221
81. Carter, S.D. .220
82. Griffin, L.A. .220
83. Davis, Hou. .217
84. Thompson, St.L. .213

Batting Average, Road Games

1. Magadan, NY .372
2. Roberts, S.D. .338
3. Harris, L.A. .332
4. Larkin, Cin. .326
5. Bonds, Pit. .321
6. McGee, St.L. .320
7. Murray, L.A. .317
8. Wallach, Mon. .314
9. Dykstra, Phi. .313
10. Gwynn, S.D. .307
11. Dawson, Chi. .304
12. Duncan, Cin. .302
13. Daniels, L.A. .301
14. Mitchell, S.F. .300
15. Strawberry, NY .299
16. Bonilla, Pit. .298
17. L. Smith, Atl. .298
18. Gant, Atl. .293
19. Alomar, S.D. .288
20. Guerrero, St.L. .287
21. Hatcher, Cin. .287
22. Coleman, St.L .286
23. Daulton, Phi. .285
24. Grace, Chi. .285
25. Williams, S.F. .283
26. Da. Martinez, Mon. .283
27. Van Slyke, Pit. .281
28. Davis, Cin. .281
29. Butler, S.F. .281
30. Brooks, L.A. .280
31. Ja. Clark, S.D. .278
32. McReynolds, NY .278
33. Biggio, Hou. .277
34. Dunston, Chi. .274
35. Clark, S.F. .273
36. C. Hayes, Phi. .272
37. Uribe, S.F. .271
38. Raines, Mon. .271
39. Doran, Hou.-Cin. .270
40. Stubbs, Hou. .269
41. DeShields, Mon. .267
42. Girardi, Chi. .267
43. Treadway, Atl. .267
44. Kruk, Phi. .265
45. Bream, Pit. .264
46. Oquendo, St.L .264
47. Thon, Phi. .262
48. Murphy, Atl.-Phi. .261
49. Sabo, Cin. .260
50. Lind, Pit. .260
51. Yelding, Hou. .256
52. Ramirez, Hou. .255
53. Sandberg, Chi. .255
54. Johnson, NY .254
55. O'Neill, Cin. .252
56. Herr, Phi.-NY .252
57. Scioscia, L.A. .251
58. V. Hayes, Phi. .250
59. Templeton, S.D. .248
60. Blauser, Atl. .248
61. Benzinger, Cin. .247
62. Bell, Pit. .247
63. Galarraga, Mon. .246
64. Jefferies, NY .246
65. Carter, S.D. .244
66. Justice, Atl. .243
67. O. Smith, St.L. .242
68. Fitzgerald, Mon. .240
69. Pagliarulo, S.D. .240
70. Oliver, Cin. .240
71. Owen, Mon. .239
72. Samuel, L.A. .239
73. Walton, Chi. .234
74. Wilson, Hou. .232
75. Zeile, St.L. .229
76. Walker, Mon. .229
77. Thompson, S.F. .224
78. Thompson, St.L. .223
79. Presley, Atl. .221
80. King, Pit. .219
81. Pendleton, St.L .214
82. Salazar, Chi. .208
83. Griffin, L.A. .202
84. Caminiti, Hou. .191

Batting Average, Grass Surfaces

1. Bonds, Pit. .349
2. Wallach, Mon. .341
3. Murray, L.A. .339
4. Bonilla, Pit. .333
5. Larkin, Cin. .330
6. Sandberg, Chi. .329
7. Van Slyke, Pit. .327
8. Butler, S.F. .323
9. Kingery, S.F. .318
10. Sharperson, L.A. .318
11. L. Smith, Atl. .315
12. Doran, Hou.-Cin. .312
13. Harris, L.A. .311
14. Grace, Chi. .311
15. Magadan, NY .308
16. Clark, S.F. .308
17. Gwynn, S.D. .306
18. Jefferies, NY .305
19. Gant, Atl. .305
20. Leach, S.F. .305
21. Kennedy, S.F. .305
22. Dawson, Chi. .303
23. Biggio, Hou. .301
24. Dykstra, Phi. .301
25. Daniels, L.A. .299
26. Carter, S.F. .298
27. Williams, S.F. .298
28. Treadway, Atl. .294
29. Davis, Cin. .292
30. Justice, Atl. .292
31. Mitchell, S.F. .290
32. Alomar, S.D. .289
33. Yelding, Hou. .289
34. Raines, Mon. .289
35. Walton, Chi. .287
36. Girardi, Chi. .285
37. D. Smith, Chi. .284
38. Santiago, S.D. .279
39. Roberts, S.D. .278
40. Dascenzo, Chi. .277
41. Boston, NY .277
42. Gregg, Atl. .276
43. McReynolds, NY .276
44. Scioscia, L.A. .275
45. Sasser, NY .275
46. Herr, Phi.-NY .270
47. Pagliarulo, S.D. .270
48. Ramos, Chi. .269
49. Strawberry, NY .268
50. Salazar, Chi. .267
51. Hatcher, Cin. .267
52. Lynn, S.D. .267
53. Blauser, Atl. .264
54. Thompson, S.F. .263
55. Thon, Phi. .261
56. Ja. Clark, S.D. .260
57. Dunston, Chi. .260
58. Sabo, Cin. .260
59. Templeton, S.D. .259
60. Javier, L.A. .257
61. Olson, Atl. .257
62. O'Neill, Cin. .257
63. Samuel, L.A. .252
64. O. Smith, St.L. .252
65. Brooks, L.A. .251
66. Johnson, NY .249
67. Murphy, Atl.-Phi. .249
68. McDowell, Atl. .248
69. Uribe, S.F. .246
70. Presley, Atl. .246
71. Lemke, Atl. .246
72. Litton, S.F. .243
73. Gibson, L.A. .243
74. Bell, Pit. .242
75. Miller, NY .241
76. V. Hayes, Phi. .241
77. Wynne, Chi. .237
78. Bass, S.F. .231
79. Carter, S.D. .224
80. Galarraga, Mon. .218
81. Thomas, Atl. .217
82. Elster, NY .206
83. Griffin, L.A. .203
84. Caminiti, Hou. .195

American League

Batting Average, Artificial Surfaces

1. R. Henderson, Oak. .... .432
2. Sierra, Tex. .377
3. Ortiz, Min. .370
4. Molitor, Mil. .344
5. Parker, Mil. .344
6. Mack, Min. .341
7. Brett, K.C. .331
8. Puckett, Min. .330
9. Palmeiro, Tex. .330
10. J. Canseco, Oak. .319
11. Fielder, Det. .315
12. Wilson, K.C. .314
13. Guillen, Chi. .310
14. Barfield, NY .307
15. Jones, Det.-Sea. .306
16. C. Ripken, Bal. .303
17. E. Martinez, Sea. .303
18. McRae, K.C. .302
19. Seitzer, K.C. .301
20. Davis, Sea. .298
21. Gladden, Min. .297
22. Bush, Min. .297
23. Fernandez, Tor. .296
24. Gruber, Tor. .295
25. Kelly, NY .293
26. Harper, Min. .293
27. Jo. Reed, Bos. .291
28. Burks, Bos. .289
29. Jackson, K.C. .289
30. Johnson, Chi. .289
31. Griffey Jr., Sea. .285
32. Boone, K.C. .284
33. Baines, Tex.-Oak. .284
34. Hrbek, Min. .283
35. Sax, NY .282
36. Larkin, Min. .281
37. Manrique, Min. .281
38. Trammell, Det. .281
39. Borders, Tor. .279
40. Franco, Tex. .278
41. Maldonado, Cle. .278
42. McGriff, Tor. .278
43. Phillips, Det. .274
44. Bradley, Bal.-Chi. .273
45. Perry, K.C. .271
46. Weiss, Oak. .269
47. Stillwell, K.C. .268
48. Eisenreich, K.C. .267
49. Lee, Tor. .265
50. Bell, Tor. .265
51. Felix, Tor. .265
52. Cotto, Sea. .262
53. Whitaker, Det. .260
54. Wilson, Tor. .259
55. Boggs, Bos. .258
56. Sosa, Chi. .256
57. Olerud, Tor. .256
58. Incaviglia, Tex. .255
59. MacFarlane, K.C. .254
60. Pettis, Tex. .254
61. C. James, Cle. .253
62. Mattingly, NY .253
63. McGwire, Oak. .253
64. O'Brien, Sea. .251
65. Briley, Sea. .249
66. Reynolds, Sea. .249
67. Buhner, Sea. .247
68. Jacoby, Cle. .247
69. Huson, Tex. .246
70. Tartabull, K.C. .246
71. Tabler, K.C. .242
72. Newman, Min. .242
73. Yount, Mil. .239
74. Vizquel, Sea. .239
75. Fletcher, Chi. .239
76. Liriano, Tor.-Min. .237
77. Bradley, Sea. .236
78. Brumley, Sea. .235
79. Greenwell, Bos. .235
80. Moses, Min. .235
81. Pecota, K.C. .233
82. Gagne, Min. .231
83. Hill, Tor. .230
84. Fisk, Chi. .230
85. Leonard, Sea. .228
86. Myers, Tor. .227
87. Ventura, Chi. .227
88. Gaetti, Min. .227
89. Alomar, Cle. .227
90. Castillo, Min. .225
91. White, K.C. .220
92. Coles, Sea.-Det. .202
93. Valle, Sea. .201
94. Brunansky, Bos. .198
95. Browne, Cle. .193
96. Worthington, Bal. .192
97. Tettleton, Bal. .190
98. White, Cal. .183
99. Jeltz, K.C. .169
100. Calderon, Chi. .162
101. Quintana, Bos. .150

Batting Average, Day Games

1. Puckett, Min. .358
2. Griffey Jr., Sea. .349
3. Eisenreich, K.C. .345
4. B. Ripken, Bal. .344
5. Maldonado, Cle. .343
6. Greenwell, Bos. .343
7. Trammell, Det. .333
8. Jo. Reed, Bos. .328
9. C. James, Cle. .324
10. Gladden, Min. .323
11. Sax, NY .322
12. Boggs, Bos. .319
13. Mattingly, NY .316
14. Palmeiro, Tex. .315
15. Bell, Tor. .311
16. Kelly, NY .309
17. Perry, K.C. .308
18. Brett, K.C. .307
19. Borders, Tor. .307
20. Stillwell, K.C. .306
21. Harper, Min. .306
22. Johnson, Chi. .299
23. Fermin, Cle. .298
24. Devereaux, Bal. .297
25. Newman, Min. .297
26. Brunansky, Bos. .296
27. Burks, Bos. .296
28. Quintana, Bos. .296
29. McGriff, Tor. .294
30. Milligan, Bal. .293
31. R. Henderson, Oak. .293
32. Fernandez, Tor. .292
33. Guillen, Chi. .291
34. Ward, Det. .287
35. Baines, Tex.-Oak. .286
36. J. Canseco, Oak. .285
37. Evans, Bos. .285
38. Brock, Mil. .285
39. Alomar, Cle. .284
40. Molitor, Mil. .283
41. Hill, Cal. .283
42. Hrbek, Min. .282
43. Bradley, Bal.-Chi. .279
44. Parker, Mil. .279
45. Sheffield, Mil. .277
46. Jackson, K.C. .276
47. Weiss, Oak. .276
48. C. Ripken, Bal. .275
49. Lee, Tor. .272
50. E. Martinez, Sea. .272
51. Nokes, Det.-NY .272
52. Calderon, Chi. .272
53. Snyder, Cle. .271
54. Jacoby, Cle. .269
55. Davis, Sea. .268
56. Randolph, Oak. .268
57. Franco, Tex. .266
58. Fletcher, Chi. .264
59. D. Henderson, Oak. .263
60. Felix, Tor. .261
61. Lansford, Oak. .260
62. Sierra, Tex. .259
63. Surhoff, Mil. .253
64. Leonard, Sea. .252
65. Browne, Cle. .252
66. Baerga, Cle. .248
67. Steinbach, Oak. .247
68. Pena, Bos. .246
69. Jose, Oak. .245
70. Seitzer, K.C. .245
71. Downing, Cal. .243
72. Orsulak, Bal. .243
73. Barfield, NY .238
74. Ventura, Chi. .238
75. Davis, Cal. .237
76. Phillips, Det. .236
77. Gruber, Tor. .236
78. Kittle, Chi.-Bal. .236
79. Reynolds, Sea. .234
80. Winfield, NY-Cal. .233
81. Larkin, Min. .232
82. Worthington, Bal. .232
83. Spiers, Mil. .231
84. Wilson, Tor. .231
85. Webster, Cle. .224
86. Whitaker, Det. .221
87. McGwire, Oak. .221
88. Fielder, Det. .213
89. Tettleton, Bal. .213
90. Gagne, Min. .212
91. Rivera, Bos. .212
92. Gaetti, Min. .210
93. Moseby, Det. .209
94. Finley, Bal. .208
95. Gallego, Oak. .201
96. Yount, Mil. .201
97. Espinoza, NY .190
98. Sosa, Chi. .186
99. Olerud, Tor. .177
100. Deer, Mil. .152

Batting Average, Night Games

1. R. Henderson, Oak. .342
2. Brett, K.C. .337
3. Polonia, NY-Cal. .332
4. Palmeiro, Tex. .320
5. E. Martinez, Sea. .311
6. McGriff, Tor. .303
7. Jacoby, Cle. .302
8. Sheffield, Mil. .302
9. Fielder, Det. .301
10. Franco, Tex. .301
11. Olerud, Tor. .298
12. Burks, Bos. .296
13. Boggs, Bos. .294
14. Parker, Mil. .293
15. Trammell, Det. .292
16. Alomar, Cle. .292
17. Harper, Min. .291
18. C. James, Cle. .290
19. Fisk, Chi. .290
20. Gruber, Tor. .290
21. Hrbek, Min. .288
22. Davis, Sea. .288
23. Surhoff, Mil. .287
24. Molitor, Mil. .285
25. Sierra, Tex. .284
26. Seitzer, K.C. .284
27. Baines, Tex.-Oak. .284
28. Larkin, Min. .284
29. Griffey Jr., Sea. .283
30. Quintana, Bos. .283
31. Winfield, NY-Cal. .280
32. Johnson, Chi. .280
33. Wilson, Tor. .279
34. Parrish, Cal. .279
35. Orsulak, Bal. .277
36. Greenwell, Bos. .277
37. Kelly, NY .277
38. D. Henderson, Oak. .277
39. Heath, Det. .275
40. Guillen, Chi. .275
41. Puckett, Min. .275
42. B. Ripken, Bal. .274
43. Calderon, Chi. .274
44. Finley, Bal. .273
45. Browne, Cle. .273
46. Jo. Reed, Bos. .273
47. Davis, Cal. .273
48. Lansford, Oak. .272
49. Schofield, Cal. .270
50. Jackson, K.C. .270
51. J. Canseco, Oak. .269
52. Pena, Bos. .269
53. Fernandez, Tor. .268
54. Yount, Mil. .268
55. Ray, Cal. .268
56. Felix, Tor. .265
57. Webster, Cle. .263
58. Moseby, Det. .263
59. Eisenreich, K.C. .261
60. Gladden, Min. .260
61. Reynolds, Sea. .258
62. Weiss, Oak. .258
63. Phillips, Det. .257
64. Milligan, Bal. .256
65. Brunansky, Bos. .255
66. Ventura, Chi. .253
67. MacFarlane, K.C. .251
68. Leonard, Sea. .251
69. Sosa, Chi. .248
70. Barfield, NY .248
71. Bradley, Bal.-Chi. .248
72. Petralli, Tex. .247
73. Bell, Tor. .247
74. Incaviglia, Tex. .247
75. Maldonado, Cle. .245
76. McGwire, Oak. .244
77. Gagne, Min. .244
78. Whitaker, Det. .243
79. C. Ripken, Bal. .242
80. Fermin, Cle. .240
81. Huson, Tex. .237
82. Perry, K.C. .236
83. Sax, NY .235
84. O'Brien, Sea. .235
85. Gaetti, Min. .235
86. Fletcher, Chi. .234
87. Espinoza, NY .234
88. Deer, Mil. .234
89. Evans, Bos. .233
90. Mattingly, NY .232
91. Lee, Tor. .229
92. Stillwell, K.C. .228
93. Liriano, Tor.-Min. .227
94. Tettleton, Bal. .227
95. Vaughn, Mil. .226
96. Pettis, Tex. .224
97. Worthington, Bal. .224
98. Newman, Min. .219
99. Devereaux, Bal. .218
100. Snyder, Cle. .216
101. White, Cal. .213

National League

Batting Average, Artificial Surfaces

1.	Roberts, S.D.	.401
2.	Magadan, NY	.370
3.	Morris, Cin.	.360
4.	McGee, St.L	.338
5.	Dykstra, Phi	.334
6.	Dawson, Chi.	.327
7.	Gwynn, S.D.	.318
8.	Braggs, Cin.	.317
9.	Duncan, Cin.	.311
10.	DeShields, Mon.	.306
11.	Reynolds, Pit.	.306
12.	Brooks, L.A.	.305
13.	Grace, Chi.	.304
14.	Murray, L.A.	.304
15.	Strawberry, NY	.301
16.	Coleman, St.L	.299
17.	Pagnozzi, St.L	.297
18.	Da. Martinez, Mon.	.296
19.	Kruk, Phi.	.295
20.	Gant, Atl.	.295
21.	Doran, Hou.-Cin.	.294
22.	Mitchell, S.F.	.291
23.	Larkin, Cin.	.288
24.	Bream, Pit.	.286
25.	Raines, Mon.	.286
26.	Bonds, Pit.	.282
27.	Hatcher, Cin.	.280
28.	Alomar, S.D.	.280
29.	Slaught, Pit.	.279
30.	Guerrero, St.L	.279
31.	Wallach, Mon.	.278
32.	O'Neill, Cin.	.276
33.	Lind, Pit.	.275
34.	Stubbs, Hou.	.274
35.	Sabo, Cin.	.274
36.	LaValliere, Pit.	.271
37.	V. Hayes, Phi.	.270
38.	Galarraga, Mon.	.269
39.	Grissom, Mon.	.267
40.	Butler, S.F.	.266
41.	Van Slyke, Pit.	.265
42.	Biggio, Hou.	.265
43.	Backman, Pit.	.263
44.	Benzinger, Cin.	.263
45.	Candaele, Hou.	.262
46.	Caminiti, Hou.	.262
47.	Clark, S.F.	.261
48.	Daulton, Phi.	.261
49.	Bonilla, Pit.	.260
50.	Zeile, St.L	.260
51.	Wilson, Hou.	.260
52.	Bell, Pit.	.258
53.	King, Pit.	.257
54.	Treadway, Atl.	.257
55.	Herr, Phi.-NY	.257
56.	Ready, Phi.	.256
57.	O. Smith, St.L	.255
58.	Thon, Phi.	.253
59.	McReynolds, NY	.253
60.	Carter, S.D.	.253
61.	Ramirez, Hou.	.252
62.	Sandberg, Chi.	.250
63.	C. Hayes, Phi.	.246
64.	Hudler, Mon.-St.L	.243
65.	Nixon, Mon.	.243
66.	Davis, Cin.	.241
67.	Murphy, Atl.-Phi.	.239
68.	Oliver, Cin.	.239
69.	Fitzgerald, Mon.	.239
70.	Yelding, Hou.	.238
71.	Redus, Pit.	.237
72.	Owen, Mon.	.236
73.	Pendleton, St.L	.234
74.	Jordan, Phi.	.231
75.	Johnson, NY	.230
76.	Oquendo, St.L	.229
77.	Martinez, Phi.-Pit.	.228
78.	Walker, Mon.	.226
79.	Davis, Hou.	.226
80.	Thompson, St.L	.225
81.	Jefferies, NY	.222
82.	Samuel, L.A.	.217
83.	Williams, S.F.	.217
84.	Anthony, Hou.	.212

Batting Average, Day Games

1.	McGee, St.L	.385
2.	Biggio, Hou.	.374
3.	Dykstra, Phi.	.370
4.	Doran, Hou.-Cin.	.361
5.	Wallach, Mon.	.335
6.	Dawson, Chi.	.326
7.	Alomar, S.D.	.325
8.	L. Smith, Atl.	.325
9.	Guerrero, St.L	.321
10.	Jefferies, NY	.321
11.	Grace, Chi.	.320
12.	Sandberg, Chi.	.320
13.	Fitzgerald, Mon.	.313
14.	Magadan, NY	.310
15.	Lind, Pit.	.307
16.	Ramos, Chi.	.304
17.	McReynolds, NY	.303
18.	Strawberry, NY	.301
19.	Mitchell, S.F.	.300
20.	Daulton, Phi.	.299
21.	Gant, Atl.	.299
22.	Kruk, Phi.	.296
23.	Brooks, L.A.	.296
24.	Murray, L.A.	.295
25.	Davis, Cin.	.295
26.	Butler, S.F.	.294
27.	V. Hayes, Phi.	.292
28.	Larkin, Cin.	.292
29.	Bonilla, Pit.	.289
30.	Williams, S.F.	.287
31.	Kennedy, S.F.	.287
32.	Coleman, St.L	.285
33.	DeShields, Mon.	.284
34.	Roberts, S.D.	.283
35.	Bonds, Pit.	.283
36.	Bell, Pit.	.281
37.	Duncan, Cin.	.281
38.	Benzinger, Cin.	.280
39.	Van Slyke, Pit.	.277
40.	Bream, Pit.	.275
41.	Dunston, Chi.	.274
42.	Pendleton, St.L	.273
43.	Raines, Mon.	.273
44.	Walton, Chi.	.271
45.	Templeton, S.D.	.269
46.	Johnson, NY	.264
47.	D. Smith, Chi.	.263
48.	Clark, S.F.	.263
49.	Salazar, Chi.	.263
50.	Boston, NY	.262
51.	Girardi, Chi.	.260
52.	King, Pit.	.259
53.	Yelding, Hou.	.255
54.	Zeile, St.L	.255
55.	Gwynn, S.D.	.255
56.	Ramirez, Hou.	.254
57.	Dascenzo, Chi.	.252
58.	Caminiti, Hou.	.250
59.	O'Neill, Cin.	.250
60.	Thompson, S.F.	.250
61.	Samuel, L.A.	.248
62.	Herr, Phi.-NY	.245
63.	Owen, Mon.	.242
64.	Presley, Atl.	.239
65.	Pagliarulo, S.D.	.237
66.	O. Smith, St.L	.236
67.	Ja. Clark, S.D.	.235
68.	Hatcher, Cin.	.235
69.	Thompson, St.L	.232
70.	Wynne, Chi.	.231
71.	Sabo, Cin.	.231
72.	Stubbs, Hou.	.227
73.	Walker, Mon.	.216
74.	Galarraga, Mon.	.207
75.	C. Hayes, Phi.	.204
76.	Carter, S.D.	.202
77.	Murphy, Atl.-Phi.	.202
78.	Oquendo, St.L	.201
79.	Uribe, S.F.	.196
80.	Thon, Phi.	.185
81.	Griffin, L.A.	.179
82.	Elster, NY	.132

Batting Average, Night Games

1.	Murray, L.A.	.340
2.	Magadan, NY	.337
3.	Gwynn, S.D.	.331
4.	Roberts, S.D.	.319
5.	Butler, S.F.	.318
6.	McGee, St.L	.318
7.	Duncan, Cin.	.315
8.	Clark, S.F.	.315
9.	Dykstra, Phi.	.312
10.	Bonds, Pit.	.307
11.	Harris, L.A.	.305
12.	Larkin, Cin.	.305
13.	Gant, Atl.	.304
14.	Daniels, L.A.	.303
15.	L. Smith, Atl.	.298
16.	Grace, Chi.	.296
17.	Justice, Atl.	.295
18.	Coleman, St.L	.294
19.	Dawson, Chi.	.294
20.	Raines, Mon.	.292
21.	Da. Martinez, Mon.	.292
22.	Sandberg, Chi.	.291
23.	DeShields, Mon.	.290
24.	Kruk, Phi.	.290
25.	Hatcher, Cin.	.288
26.	Van Slyke, Pit.	.287
27.	Mitchell, S.F.	.284
28.	Treadway, Atl.	.283
29.	Sabo, Cin.	.282
30.	Uribe, S.F.	.282
31.	Wallach, Mon.	.280
32.	O'Neill, Cin.	.279
33.	Thon, Phi.	.278
34.	Ja. Clark, S.D.	.277
35.	Sharperson, L.A.	.277
36.	C. Hayes, Phi.	.277
37.	Bonilla, Pit.	.277
38.	Galarraga, Mon.	.275
39.	Doran, Hou.-Cin.	.274
40.	Oquendo, St.L	.274
41.	Stubbs, Hou.	.274
42.	Blauser, Atl.	.272
43.	Alomar, S.D.	.272
44.	Williams, S.F.	.270
45.	Bream, Pit.	.268
46.	Herr, Phi.-NY	.267
47.	Guerrero, St.L	.265
48.	Strawberry, NY	.265
49.	Ramirez, Hou.	.263
50.	Jefferies, NY	.263
51.	O. Smith, St.L	.262
52.	Pagliarulo, S.D.	.261
53.	Daulton, Phi.	.259
54.	Murphy, Atl.-Phi.	.257
55.	Brooks, L.A.	.257
56.	Scioscia, L.A.	.254
57.	Yelding, Hou.	.254
58.	McReynolds, NY	.251
59.	V. Hayes, Phi.	.251
60.	Walker, Mon.	.251
61.	Dunston, Chi.	.250
62.	Santiago, S.D.	.249
63.	Davis, Cin.	.248
64.	Lind, Pit.	.245
65.	Bell, Pit.	.244
66.	Carter, S.D.	.244
67.	Presley, Atl.	.243
68.	Davis, Hou.	.243
69.	Biggio, Hou.	.243
70.	Zeile, St.L	.242
71.	Benzinger, Cin.	.242
72.	Thompson, S.F.	.241
73.	Templeton, S.D.	.241
74.	Samuel, L.A.	.240
75.	Caminiti, Hou.	.240
76.	King, Pit.	.239
77.	Johnson, NY	.232
78.	Owen, Mon.	.231
79.	Wilson, Hou.	.229
80.	Griffin, L.A.	.221
81.	Pendleton, St.L	.213
82.	Thompson, St.L	.211
83.	Oliver, Cin.	.201

American League

On-Base Average Leading Off Innings

1. Fisk, Chi. .450
2. O'Brien, Sea. .436
3. Petralli, Tex. .414
4. Hrbek, Min. .402
5. Cole, Cle. .400
6. R. Henderson, Oak. .400
7. Worthington, Bal. .398
8. Polonia, NY-Cal. .398
9. McGwire, Oak. .396
10. Milligan, Bal. .391
11. Boggs, Bos. .389
12. Puckett, Min. .379
13. Bradley, Bal.-Chi. .378
14. McGriff, Tor. .376
15. Winfield, NY-Cal. .373
16. Davis, Cal. .363
17. Fernandez, Tor. .358
18. E. Martinez, Sea. .357
19. Baines, Tex.-Oak. .353
20. Pena, Bos. .350
21. Calderon, Chi. .350
22. Davis, Sea. .350
23. Evans, Bos. .348
24. Jo. Reed, Bos. .348
25. Reynolds, Sea. .348
26. Webster, Cle. .347
27. Moseby, Det. .347
28. Fielder, Det. .347
29. Alomar, Cle. .346
30. Phillips, Det. .345
31. Larkin, Min. .344
32. Kelly, NY .344
33. Jacoby, Cle. .341
34. Sierra, Tex. .341
35. Harper, Min. .339
36. Molitor, Mil. .337
37. C. Ripken, Bal. .336
38. Seitzer, K.C. .336
39. Parker, Mil. .335
40. Burks, Bos. .333
41. Eisenreich, K.C. .333
42. Gladden, Min. .333
43. Brett, K.C. .330
44. Sheffield, Mil. .330
45. Lansford, Oak. .330
46. Felix, Tor. .329
47. Perry, K.C. .328
48. Downing, Cal. .327
49. Schofield, Cal. .327
50. Brunansky, Bos. .324
51. Newman, Min. .324
52. Franco, Tex. .321
53. Palmeiro, Tex. .320
54. Maldonado, Cle. .320
55. C. James, Cle. .318
56. Yount, Mil. .318
57. Parrish, Cal. .318
58. J. Canseco, Oak. .315
59. Tettleton, Bal. .314
60. Devereaux, Bal. .313
61. Whitaker, Det. .313
62. Johnson, Chi. .311
63. Gruber, Tor. .309
64. D. Henderson, Oak. .307
65. Huson, Tex. .307
66. Guillen, Chi. .304
67. Ventura, Chi. .303
68. Nokes, Det.-NY .301
69. Lee, Tor. .301
70. Quintana, Bos. .301
71. Deer, Mil. .301
72. Surhoff, Mil. .300
73. Weiss, Oak. .298
74. Griffey Jr., Sea. .296
75. Browne, Cle. .295
76. Incaviglia, Tex. .292
77. Sax, NY .292
78. Barfield, NY .291
79. Pasqua, Chi. .291
80. Pettis, Tex. .286
81. Wilson, Tor. .284
82. Liriano, Tor.-Min. .283
83. Greenwell, Bos. .282
84. Jackson, K.C. .282
85. Bell, Tor. .281
86. Trammell, Det. .279
87. Sosa, Chi. .269
88. Gaetti, Min. .267
89. Hall, NY .261
90. MacFarlane, K.C. .258
91. Spiers, Mil. .257
92. Stillwell, K.C. .255
93. Finley, Bal. .253
94. Leonard, Sea. .252
95. Espinoza, NY .250
96. Fermin, Cle. .247
97. Snyder, Cle. .247
98. Gallego, Oak. .245
99. White, Cal. .242
100. Vaughn, Mil. .222
101. Fletcher, Chi. .216

Batting Average with Runners On Base

1. Brett, K.C. .367
2. Palmeiro, Tex. .362
3. Sheffield, Mil. .359
4. Puckett, Min. .343
5. Franco, Tex. .336
6. B. Ripken, Bal. .335
7. Trammell, Det. .335
8. C. James, Cle. .324
9. Fletcher, Chi. .323
10. Boggs, Bos. .320
11. Johnson, Chi. .318
12. Jacoby, Cle. .314
13. Fernandez, Tor. .309
14. R. Henderson, Oak. .307
15. Hrbek, Min. .307
16. Guillen, Chi. .305
17. Jo. Reed, Bos. .304
18. Ventura, Chi. .303
19. Alomar, Cle. .303
20. Davis, Sea. .301
21. Mattingly, NY .299
22. Quintana, Bos. .298
23. Greenwell, Bos. .298
24. Griffey Jr., Sea. .298
25. Harper, Min. .297
26. Olerud, Tor. .295
27. Seitzer, K.C. .293
28. Parrish, Cal. .292
29. Sierra, Tex. .290
30. Gruber, Tor. .289
31. Parker, Mil. .289
32. Surhoff, Mil. .288
33. Calderon, Chi. .287
34. Milligan, Bal. .287
35. Weiss, Oak. .287
36. Burks, Bos. .286
37. J. Canseco, Oak. .286
38. Pena, Bos. .285
39. Fielder, Det. .284
40. Stillwell, K.C. .284
41. Maldonado, Cle. .283
42. Phillips, Det. .282
43. Kelly, NY .282
44. Perry, K.C. .282
45. Webster, Cle. .282
46. Browne, Cle. .280
47. Tartabull, K.C. .276
48. MacFarlane, K.C. .276
49. Cotto, Sea. .274
50. Reynolds, Sea. .274
51. Felix, Tor. .274
52. Fermin, Cle. .273
53. Gladden, Min. .273
54. Hill, Cal. .273
55. Lansford, Oak. .272
56. McGriff, Tor. .270
57. Barfield, NY .270
58. Leonard, Sea. .270
59. Steinbach, Oak. .270
60. Wilson, Tor. .268
61. D. Henderson, Oak. .268
62. Eisenreich, K.C. .268
63. E. Martinez, Sea. .268
64. Brock, Mil. .267
65. Finley, Bal. .266
66. Jackson, K.C. .264
67. Ray, Cal. .264
68. Winfield, NY-Cal. .263
69. Yount, Mil. .263
70. Baines, Tex.-Oak. .263
71. Gallego, Oak. .258
72. Brunansky, Bos. .257
73. Vaughn, Mil. .256
74. Bell, Tor. .255
75. Orsulak, Bal. .253
76. Sheets, Det. .251
77. Snyder, Cle. .251
78. Davis, Cal. .250
79. Gaetti, Min. .250
80. Devereaux, Bal. .249
81. Rivera, Bos. .248
82. Fisk, Chi. .247
83. Incaviglia, Tex. .245
84. Sax, NY .242
85. Evans, Bos. .241
86. Sosa, Chi. .240
87. Larkin, Min. .240
88. C. Ripken, Bal. .238
89. Espinoza, NY .235
90. Whitaker, Det. .231
91. Newman, Min. .230
92. Deer, Mil. .229
93. Moseby, Det. .225
94. McGwire, Oak. .224
95. Tettleton, Bal. .223
96. Bichette, Cal. .222
97. Gagne, Min. .220
98. White, Cal. .215
99. Worthington, Bal. .204
100. O'Brien, Sea. .157

Batting Average with Runners in Scoring Position

1. Trammell, Det. .379
2. Brett, K.C. .360
3. Johnson, Chi. .345
4. Sheffield, Mil. .339
5. Boggs, Bos. .338
6. Puckett, Min. .336
7. Guillen, Chi. .331
8. Calderon, Chi. .328
9. Palmeiro, Tex. .324
10. C. James, Cle. .324
11. Sierra, Tex. .321
12. Gruber, Tor. .315
13. Griffey Jr., Sea. .311
14. Quintana, Bos. .310
15. B. Ripken, Bal. .310
16. Fernandez, Tor. .309
17. Alomar, Cle. .307
18. Leonard, Sea. .306
19. Burks, Bos. .306
20. Harper, Min. .303
21. Reynolds, Sea. .301
22. Orsulak, Bal. .300
23. Ventura, Chi. .300
24. Pena, Bos. .299
25. Franco, Tex. .299
26. Steinbach, Oak. .297
27. Wilson, K.C. .297
28. Felix, Tor. .295
29. Olerud, Tor. .294
30. Jacoby, Cle. .293
31. Mattingly, NY .292
32. Ray, Cal. .290
33. Vaughn, Mil. .283
34. Gladden, Min. .282
35. Phillips, Det. .281
36. Davis, Sea. .280
37. Pasqua, Chi. .280
38. Jo. Reed, Bos. .277
39. Sheets, Det. .277
40. Hrbek, Min. .276
41. Bell, Tor. .275
42. Surhoff, Mil. .275
43. R. Henderson, Oak. .271
44. Fletcher, Chi. .270
45. Evans, Bos. .268
46. Maldonado, Cle. .268
47. Lansford, Oak. .268
48. Seitzer, K.C. .268
49. Webster, Cle. .266
50. Fielder, Det. .265
51. Barfield, NY .264
52. McGriff, Tor. .264
53. Gaetti, Min. .263
54. Parker, Mil. .263
55. J. Canseco, Oak. .262
56. Browne, Cle. .260
57. Tartabull, K.C. .260
58. Wilson, Tor. .257
59. Perry, K.C. .256
60. Finley, Bal. .255
61. MacFarlane, K.C. .254
62. Baines, Tex.-Oak. .254
63. Milligan, Bal. .253
64. Fermin, Cle. .252
65. D. Henderson, Oak. .252
66. Parrish, Cal. .252
67. McGwire, Oak. .248
68. Winfield, NY-Cal. .248
69. Larkin, Min. .248
70. Rivera, Bos. .248
71. Lee, Tor. .248
72. Brock, Mil. .247
73. Kelly, NY .246
74. E. Martinez, Sea. .246
75. Stillwell, K.C. .244
76. Sosa, Chi. .241
77. Eisenreich, K.C. .241
78. Jackson, K.C. .239
79. Sax, NY .239
80. Incaviglia, Tex. .230
81. Greenwell, Bos. .228
82. Yount, Mil. .228
83. Snyder, Cle. .227
84. Cotto, Sea. .226
85. Weiss, Oak. .224
86. Fisk, Chi. .221
87. Brunansky, Bos. .220
88. Whitaker, Det. .219
89. Davis, Cal. .219
90. Newman, Min. .218
91. Deer, Mil. .214
92. Heath, Det. .210
93. C. Ripken, Bal. .204
94. Gallego, Oak. .202
95. Moseby, Det. .202
96. White, Cal. .198
97. Worthington, Bal. .198
98. O'Brien, Sea. .156
99. Tettleton, Bal. .155

National League

On-Base Average Leading Off Innings

1.	Doran, Hou.-Cin.	.477
2.	Magadan, NY	.446
3.	Bonds, Pit.	.421
4.	Mitchell, S.F.	.407
5.	Gant, Atl.	.400
6.	Butler, S.F.	.399
7.	Dykstra, Phi	.393
8.	Bell, Pit.	.389
9.	Ja. Clark, S.D.	.385
10.	Miller, NY	.385
11.	Murray, L.A.	.384
12.	Grace, Chi.	.383
13.	DeShields, Mon.	.378
14.	Clark, S.F.	.372
15.	L. Smith, Atl.	.369
16.	Redus, Pit.	.366
17.	Salazar, Chi	.365
18.	McGee, St.L.	.362
19.	Roberts, S.D.	.361
20.	V. Hayes, Phi.	.360
21.	Stubbs, Hou.	.360
22.	Boston, NY	.359
23.	Blauser, Atl.	.358
24.	Davis, Cin.	.358
25.	Strawberry, NY	.358
26.	Duncan, Cin.	.352
27.	Alomar, S.D.	.352
28.	Backman, Pit.	.352
29.	Caminiti, Hou.	.348
30.	Walton, Chi.	.348
31.	Samuel, L.A.	.348
32.	Da. Martinez, Mon.	.344
33.	Sharperson, L.A.	.343
34.	Thon, Phi	.340
35.	Galarraga, Mon	.336
36.	Larkin, Cin.	.336
37.	Harris, L.A.	.335
38.	Sabo, Cin.	.332
39.	O'Neill, Cin.	.331
40.	Coleman, St.L	.330
41.	Wallach, Mon.	.328
42.	Hatcher, Cin.	.328
43.	Ramirez, Hou.	.324
44.	Scioscia, L.A.	.323
45.	Justice, Atl.	.322
46.	Zeile, St.L.	.321
47.	McReynolds, NY	.320
48.	Sandberg, Chi.	.320
49.	Guerrero, St.L.	.317
50.	Yelding, Hou.	.314
51.	Dunston, Chi.	.313
52.	McDowell, Atl.	.311
53.	Pagliarulo, S.D.	.310
54.	Bonilla, Pit.	.305
55.	Herr, Phi.-NY	.304
56.	O. Smith, St.L.	.304
57.	Dawson, Chi.	.302
58.	Oquendo, St.L	.302
59.	Owen, Mon.	.300
60.	Thompson, S.F.	.299
61.	Johnson, NY	.299
62.	Brooks, L.A.	.297
63.	Kruk, Phi.	.294
64.	Biggio, Hou.	.291
65.	Jefferies, NY	.289
66.	C. Hayes, Phi.	.288
67.	Girardi, Chi.	.284
68.	Templeton, S.D.	.283
69.	Raines, Mon.	.283
70.	Santiago, S.D.	.283
71.	Griffin, L.A.	.280
72.	Daulton, Phi.	.277
73.	Lind, Pit.	.272
74.	Uribe, S.F.	.270
75.	D. Smith, Chi.	.269
76.	Davis, Hou.	.269
77.	Thompson, St.L.	.267
78.	Carter, S.D.	.265
79.	Presley, Atl.	.260
80.	Pendleton, St.L	.257
81.	Williams, S.F.	.252
82.	Gwynn, S.D.	.245
83.	Murphy, Atl.-Phi.	.197

Batting Average with Runners On Base

1.	Dykstra, Phi	.418
2.	Magadan, NY	.406
3.	Sandberg, Chi.	.367
4.	Justice, Atl.	.351
5.	Gwynn, S.D.	.347
6.	Bonds, Pit.	.344
7.	Sharperson, L.A.	.336
8.	Murray, L.A.	.335
9.	Roberts, S.D.	.333
10.	Williams, S.F.	.330
11.	Treadway, Atl.	.325
12.	McGee, St.L.	.323
13.	Raines, Mon.	.323
14.	Kruk, Phi.	.321
15.	Dawson, Chi.	.321
16.	Butler, S.F.	.320
17.	Ramirez, Hou.	.319
18.	Larkin, Cin.	.316
19.	Daniels, L.A.	.312
20.	Alomar, S.D.	.311
21.	Daulton, Phi	.310
22.	V. Hayes, Phi.	.310
23.	Wallach, Mon.	.309
24.	Murphy, Atl.-Phi.	.309
25.	Clark, S.F.	.308
26.	Grace, Chi.	.293
27.	Herr, Phi.-NY	.293
28.	Bell, Pit.	.292
29.	Biggio, Hou.	.291
30.	Doran, Hou.-Cin.	.291
31.	Girardi, Chi.	.289
32.	Van Slyke, Pit.	.289
33.	McReynolds, NY	.286
34.	Ja. Clark, S.D.	.286
35.	Templeton, S.D.	.284
36.	Oquendo, St.L	.282
37.	Jefferies, NY	.282
38.	L. Smith, Atl.	.281
39.	Brooks, L.A.	.280
40.	Duncan, Cin.	.277
41.	Bream, Pit.	.277
42.	Lind, Pit.	.275
43.	O'Neill, Cin.	.274
44.	Blauser, Atl.	.272
45.	Pagliarulo, S.D.	.272
46.	Johnson, NY	.272
47.	Oliver, Cin.	.272
48.	Strawberry, NY	.271
49.	Coleman, St.L	.269
50.	Gant, Atl.	.269
51.	DeShields, Mon.	.267
52.	Galarraga, Mon	.266
53.	Benzinger, Cin.	.266
54.	Guerrero, St.L.	.266
55.	Scioscia, L.A.	.265
56.	Bonilla, Pit.	.258
57.	Hatcher, Cin.	.258
58.	O. Smith, St.L.	.258
59.	Uribe, S.F.	.258
60.	Sabo, Cin.	.257
61.	Thompson, S.F.	.256
62.	Presley, Atl.	.253
63.	Carter, S.D.	.252
64.	Davis, Hou	.248
65.	C. Hayes, Phi.	.247
66.	Davis, Cin.	.244
67.	Thompson, St.L.	.244
68.	Caminiti, Hou.	.243
69.	Jordan, Phi	.242
70.	Thon, Phi	.242
71.	Mitchell, S.F.	.241
72.	Stubbs, Hou.	.240
73.	Dunston, Chi.	.240
74.	Wilson, Hou.	.238
75.	Yelding, Hou.	.236
76.	Salazar, Chi	.232
77.	Zeile, St.L.	.230
78.	Griffin, L.A.	.229
79.	Pendleton, St.L	.229
80.	King, Pit.	.222
81.	Samuel, L.A.	.219
82.	Walker, Mon.	.213
83.	Owen, Mon.	.206

Batting Average with Runners in Scoring Position

1.	Dykstra, Phi	.423
2.	Magadan, NY	.382
3.	Bonds, Pit.	.377
4.	Treadway, Atl.	.341
5.	Alomar, S.D.	.338
6.	Williams, S.F.	.333
7.	Grace, Chi.	.329
8.	Murray, L.A.	.327
9.	Justice, Atl.	.319
10.	McGee, St.L.	.318
11.	Larkin, Cin.	.314
12.	Ramirez, Hou.	.314
13.	Raines, Mon.	.312
14.	Scioscia, L.A.	.311
15.	Gwynn, S.D.	.305
16.	Strawberry, NY	.304
17.	Johnson, NY	.302
18.	Sandberg, Chi.	.298
19.	Kruk, Phi.	.298
20.	Biggio, Hou.	.297
21.	Dawson, Chi.	.297
22.	McReynolds, NY	.295
23.	Van Slyke, Pit.	.293
24.	Daniels, L.A.	.292
25.	Murphy, Atl.-Phi.	.292
26.	O'Neill, Cin.	.292
27.	Clark, S.F.	.291
28.	Bream, Pit.	.291
29.	Templeton, S.D.	.287
30.	Lind, Pit.	.285
31.	DeShields, Mon.	.283
32.	Wilson, Hou.	.283
33.	Daulton, Phi	.282
34.	Bonilla, Pit.	.282
35.	Wallach, Mon.	.282
36.	Butler, S.F.	.282
37.	Bell, Pit.	.281
38.	Fitzgerald, Mon.	.280
39.	Roberts, S.D.	.280
40.	Ja. Clark, S.D.	.278
41.	Girardi, Chi.	.276
42.	Boston, NY	.276
43.	Oliver, Cin.	.274
44.	Sharperson, L.A.	.273
45.	Jefferies, NY	.271
46.	Carter, S.D.	.267
47.	Brooks, L.A.	.267
48.	Galarraga, Mon	.266
49.	Oquendo, St.L	.263
50.	Davis, Hou	.263
51.	Caminiti, Hou.	.261
52.	Coleman, St.L	.259
53.	Duncan, Cin.	.257
54.	Gant, Atl.	.257
55.	V. Hayes, Phi.	.254
56.	Davis, Cin.	.252
57.	Guerrero, St.L.	.252
58.	Benzinger, Cin.	.250
59.	Thompson, S.F.	.248
60.	Thon, Phi	.245
61.	Salazar, Chi	.243
62.	Sabo, Cin.	.243
63.	Santiago, S.D.	.242
64.	O. Smith, St.L.	.240
65.	Herr, Phi.-NY	.235
66.	C. Hayes, Phi.	.234
67.	L. Smith, Atl.	.233
68.	Pendleton, St.L	.233
69.	King, Pit.	.232
70.	Dunston, Chi.	.230
71.	Yelding, Hou.	.228
72.	Doran, Hou.-Cin.	.226
73.	Pagliarulo, S.D.	.223
74.	Mitchell, S.F.	.222
75.	Jordan, Phi	.221
76.	Stubbs, Hou.	.220
77.	Uribe, S.F.	.214
78.	Presley, Atl.	.213
79.	Griffin, L.A.	.213
80.	Samuel, L.A.	.206
81.	Hatcher, Cin.	.198
82.	Walker, Mon.	.194
83.	Owen, Mon.	.168
84.	Zeile, St.L.	.162

American League

Batting Average in Pressure Situations

1.	R. Henderson, Oak.	.447
2.	Weiss, Oak.	.441
3.	Sheffield, Mil.	.364
4.	Franco, Tex.	.360
5.	E. Martinez, Sea.	.354
6.	Pena, Bos.	.348
7.	Baines, Tex.-Oak.	.346
8.	Fernandez, Tor.	.333
9.	Trammell, Det.	.333
10.	Bichette, Cal.	.327
11.	B. Ripken, Bal.	.327
12.	Gruber, Tor.	.326
13.	Reynolds, Sea.	.322
14.	Palmeiro, Tex.	.320
15.	MacFarlane, K.C.	.313
16.	Polonia, NY-Cal.	.310
17.	Davis, Cal.	.309
18.	Harper, Min.	.306
19.	Hrbek, Min.	.304
20.	Quintana, Bos.	.304
21.	Evans, Bos.	.304
22.	Sax, NY	.303
23.	Olerud, Tor.	.303
24.	Boggs, Bos.	.302
25.	Huson, Tex.	.302
26.	Stillwell, K.C.	.301
27.	Alomar, Cle.	.298
28.	Burks, Bos.	.293
29.	Phillips, Det.	.288
30.	Wilson, Tor.	.287
31.	Guillen, Chi.	.286
32.	Jo. Reed, Bos.	.286
33.	Davis, Sea.	.284
34.	Winfield, NY-Cal.	.282
35.	Sierra, Tex.	.279
36.	Devereaux, Bal.	.276
37.	Worthington, Bal.	.273
38.	Maldonado, Cle.	.268
39.	Brett, K.C.	.267
40.	Deer, Mil.	.267
41.	Fisk, Chi.	.267
42.	C. Ripken, Bal.	.264
43.	Jacoby, Cle.	.261
44.	Browne, Cle.	.261
45.	Johnson, Chi.	.260
46.	McGriff, Tor.	.259
47.	Perry, K.C.	.258
48.	Ray, Cal.	.256
49.	Kelly, NY	.255
50.	Hall, NY	.250
51.	Parrish, Cal.	.250
52.	Pettis, Tex.	.250
53.	Spiers, Mil.	.250
54.	Greenwell, Bos.	.247
55.	Moseby, Det.	.246
56.	Cotto, Sea.	.245
57.	Eisenreich, K.C.	.244
58.	Baerga, Cle.	.242
59.	Brunansky, Bos.	.242
60.	Jackson, K.C.	.242
61.	Ventura, Chi.	.242
62.	McGwire, Oak.	.240
63.	Milligan, Bal.	.237
64.	Steinbach, Oak.	.237
65.	Yount, Mil.	.232
66.	Bradley, Bal.-Chi.	.222
67.	Tettleton, Bal.	.222
68.	Finley, Bal.	.221
69.	Petralli, Tex.	.218
70.	Puckett, Min.	.218
71.	Webster, Cle.	.215
72.	Mattingly, NY	.214
73.	Borders, Tor.	.213
74.	Barfield, NY	.212
75.	Griffey Jr., Sea.	.212
76.	Downing, Cal.	.210
77.	Orsulak, Bal.	.210
78.	Surhoff, Mil.	.210
79.	C. James, Cle.	.208
80.	Incaviglia, Tex.	.207
81.	Calderon, Chi.	.206
82.	Gaetti, Min.	.205
83.	Fletcher, Chi.	.203
84.	Fielder, Det.	.200
85.	Lee, Tor.	.200
86.	Seitzer, K.C.	.198
87.	Gladden, Min.	.197
88.	Balboni, NY	.197
89.	Snyder, Cle.	.194
90.	Parker, Mil.	.194
91.	Newman, Min.	.186
92.	O'Brien, Sea.	.186
93.	White, Cal.	.185
94.	Larkin, Min.	.182
95.	Sosa, Chi.	.174
96.	Bell, Tor.	.173
97.	Felix, Tor.	.153
98.	Whitaker, Det.	.133
99.	Leonard, Sea.	.074

Batting Average with Two Outs and Runners On Base

1.	Wilson, K.C.	.368
2.	Sheffield, Mil.	.355
3.	Palmeiro, Tex.	.354
4.	Jacoby, Cle.	.353
5.	Fernandez, Tor.	.340
6.	Boggs, Bos.	.333
7.	Molitor, Mil.	.328
8.	Quintana, Bos.	.324
9.	Seitzer, K.C.	.321
10.	Olerud, Tor.	.317
11.	Trammell, Det.	.316
12.	Pena, Bos.	.312
13.	Reynolds, Sea.	.311
14.	Brett, K.C.	.310
15.	C. James, Cle.	.306
16.	Gaetti, Min.	.301
17.	Barfield, NY	.300
18.	Franco, Tex.	.300
19.	Eisenreich, K.C.	.298
20.	Alomar, Cle.	.296
21.	Hall, NY	.295
22.	Melvin, Bal.	.293
23.	Phillips, Det.	.292
24.	Jo. Reed, Bos.	.290
25.	Johnson, Chi.	.289
26.	Kelly, NY	.289
27.	Fielder, Det.	.287
28.	Burks, Bos.	.287
29.	Ventura, Chi.	.282
30.	MacFarlane, K.C.	.281
31.	Perry, K.C.	.281
32.	Gruber, Tor.	.280
33.	Calderon, Chi.	.279
34.	Sierra, Tex.	.278
35.	Parrish, Cal.	.278
36.	Sosa, Chi.	.278
37.	B. Ripken, Bal.	.276
38.	J. Canseco, Oak.	.273
39.	Gladden, Min.	.272
40.	Guillen, Chi.	.271
41.	Harper, Min.	.271
42.	D. Henderson, Oak.	.270
43.	Jackson, K.C.	.268
44.	Pettis, Tex.	.268
45.	Weiss, Oak.	.267
46.	Felix, Tor.	.265
47.	Maldonado, Cle.	.265
48.	Larkin, Min.	.264
49.	Stillwell, K.C.	.264
50.	Rivera, Bos.	.263
51.	Puckett, Min.	.262
52.	Bell, Tor.	.262
53.	Fermin, Cle.	.261
54.	Fletcher, Chi.	.260
55.	Pasqua, Chi.	.258
56.	Evans, Bos.	.256
57.	Deer, Mil.	.256
58.	Gallego, Oak.	.253
59.	Orsulak, Bal.	.253
60.	Leonard, Sea.	.252
61.	R. Henderson, Oak.	.250
62.	Parker, Mil.	.250
63.	Steinbach, Oak.	.250
64.	Tartabull, K.C.	.250
65.	Brunansky, Bos.	.248
66.	McGriff, Tor.	.248
67.	Wilson, Tor.	.247
68.	Surhoff, Mil.	.247
69.	Fisk, Chi.	.245
70.	Greenwell, Bos.	.243
71.	Baines, Tex.-Oak.	.241
72.	Incaviglia, Tex.	.240
73.	Brock, Mil.	.239
74.	Griffey Jr., Sea.	.239
75.	Lansford, Oak.	.238
76.	Gagne, Min.	.236
77.	Milligan, Bal.	.236
78.	McGwire, Oak.	.234
79.	Sax, NY	.233
80.	Sheets, Det.	.232
81.	Whitaker, Det.	.229
82.	Davis, Cal.	.227
83.	Howell, Cal.	.225
84.	Snyder, Cle.	.224
85.	E. Martinez, Sea.	.223
86.	Worthington, Bal.	.223
87.	Davis, Sea.	.222
88.	C. Ripken, Bal.	.220
89.	Winfield, NY-Cal.	.216
90.	Hrbek, Min.	.216
91.	Browne, Cle.	.212
92.	Nokes, Det.-NY	.211
93.	Tettleton, Bal.	.202
94.	Ray, Cal.	.200
95.	White, Cal.	.198
96.	Yount, Mil.	.196
97.	Newman, Min.	.188
98.	Vaughn, Mil.	.186
99.	Schofield, Cal.	.169
100.	Moseby, Det.	.149
101.	O'Brien, Sea.	.113

Batting Average with Two Outs and Runners in Scoring Position

1.	Jacoby, Cle.	.359
2.	Fernandez, Tor.	.343
3.	Burks, Bos.	.341
4.	Molitor, Mil.	.341
5.	Alomar, Cle.	.338
6.	Wilson, K.C.	.333
7.	Johnson, Chi.	.327
8.	Boggs, Bos.	.324
9.	Gaetti, Min.	.319
10.	Palmeiro, Tex.	.319
11.	Quintana, Bos.	.319
12.	Trammell, Det.	.316
13.	Ventura, Chi.	.311
14.	Barfield, NY	.309
15.	Phillips, Det.	.309
16.	Felix, Tor.	.308
17.	Sheets, Det.	.306
18.	Sheffield, Mil.	.305
19.	C. James, Cle.	.303
20.	Reynolds, Sea.	.303
21.	Melvin, Bal.	.298
22.	Pena, Bos.	.298
23.	Puckett, Min.	.294
24.	Brett, K.C.	.293
25.	Harper, Min.	.293
26.	Jo. Reed, Bos.	.293
27.	Hall, NY	.292
28.	Eisenreich, K.C.	.291
29.	Deer, Mil.	.288
30.	Gruber, Tor.	.279
31.	Kelly, NY	.278
32.	Gladden, Min.	.275
33.	Larkin, Min.	.271
34.	Calderon, Chi.	.271
35.	Finley, Bal.	.271
36.	Jackson, K.C.	.271
37.	Maldonado, Cle.	.270
38.	Sierra, Tex.	.270
39.	Perry, K.C.	.270
40.	Sosa, Chi.	.270
41.	Incaviglia, Tex.	.269
42.	Borders, Tor.	.267
43.	Orsulak, Bal.	.267
44.	Steinbach, Oak.	.263
45.	Leonard, Sea.	.261
46.	Whitaker, Det.	.261
47.	Bell, Tor.	.260
48.	Evans, Bos.	.259
49.	Franco, Tex.	.258
50.	MacFarlane, K.C.	.254
51.	McGwire, Oak.	.254
52.	Davis, Sea.	.250
53.	Davis, Cal.	.250
54.	Guillen, Chi.	.250
55.	E. Martinez, Sea.	.250
56.	McGriff, Tor.	.250
57.	Nokes, Det.-NY	.250
58.	Seitzer, K.C.	.250
59.	Fermin, Cle.	.246
60.	Lansford, Oak.	.246
61.	Rivera, Bos.	.245
62.	Ray, Cal.	.245
63.	Parrish, Cal.	.242
64.	D. Henderson, Oak.	.241
65.	Sax, NY	.241
66.	Snyder, Cle.	.240
67.	Stillwell, K.C.	.238
68.	Wilson, Tor.	.235
69.	Griffey Jr., Sea.	.234
70.	B. Ripken, Bal.	.231
71.	Baines, Tex.-Oak.	.228
72.	Parker, Mil.	.227
73.	Pasqua, Chi.	.227
74.	Surhoff, Mil.	.224
75.	Fielder, Det.	.224
76.	Fisk, Chi.	.224
77.	Fletcher, Chi.	.220
78.	J. Canseco, Oak.	.217
79.	Spiers, Mil.	.213
80.	Weiss, Oak.	.213
81.	Brock, Mil.	.212
82.	Worthington, Bal.	.210
83.	Gallego, Oak.	.209
84.	Brunansky, Bos.	.209
85.	Cotto, Sea.	.208
86.	Milligan, Bal.	.208
87.	Hrbek, Min.	.200
88.	C. Ripken, Bal.	.198
89.	White, Cal.	.192
90.	Yount, Mil.	.189
91.	Newman, Min.	.183
92.	Browne, Cle.	.182
93.	Moseby, Det.	.182
94.	Howell, Cal.	.179
95.	Greenwell, Bos.	.176
96.	Winfield, NY-Cal.	.167
97.	Tartabull, K.C.	.154
98.	R. Henderson, Oak.	.150
99.	Tettleton, Bal.	.123
100.	O'Brien, Sea.	.093

National League

Batting Average in Pressure Situations

1.	Magadan, NY	.415
2.	Santiago, S.D.	.403
3.	Stubbs, Hou.	.384
4.	McGee, St.L	.366
5.	Ready, Phi.	.362
6.	Mitchell, S.F.	.351
7.	Murray, L.A.	.338
8.	Dykstra, Phi	.337
9.	Girardi, Chi	.333
10.	Nixon, Mon	.333
11.	Bell, Pit.	.328
12.	Coleman, St.L	.324
13.	Thon, Phi	.322
14.	Lind, Pit.	.321
15.	Walker, Mon	.308
16.	Grace, Chi.	.307
17.	Raines, Mon.	.304
18.	Bream, Pit	.302
19.	Larkin, Cin.	.300
20.	Grissom, Mon.	.298
21.	Butler, S.F.	.294
22.	Salazar, Chi	.293
23.	V. Hayes, Phi.	.292
24.	Wallach, Mon.	.291
25.	Justice, Atl	.290
26.	L. Smith, Atl.	.290
27.	Brooks, L.A.	.290
28.	McReynolds, NY	.287
29.	Johnson, NY	.287
30.	Gwynn, S.D.	.284
31.	Duncan, Cin.	.283
32.	Samuel, L.A.	.281
33.	D. Smith, Chi.	.281
34.	Dunston, Chi.	.279
35.	Galarraga, Mon	.279
36.	Caminiti, Hou.	.278
37.	Sandberg, Chi.	.278
38.	Roberts, S.D.	.277
39.	Dawson, Chi	.275
40.	C. Hayes, Phi.	.275
41.	Jefferies, NY	.275
42.	Kruk, Phi.	.274
43.	Treadway, Atl.	.270
44.	Oquendo, St.L	.269
45.	Bonds, Pit.	.268
46.	O'Neill, Cin.	.268
47.	Sabo, Cin.	.263
48.	Clark, S.F.	.259
49.	Ramirez, Hou.	.256
50.	Gant, Atl.	.250
51.	Van Slyke, Pit	.250
52.	Carter, S.D.	.243
53.	Bonilla, Pit.	.243
54.	Guerrero, St.L	.243
55.	Davis, Hou	.237
56.	Ja. Clark, S.D.	.236
57.	Hatcher, Cin.	.235
58.	Owen, Mon.	.234
59.	Yelding, Hou.	.232
60.	Daulton, Phi	.231
61.	Wilson, Hou	.230
62.	Strawberry, NY	.229
63.	Thompson, St.L	.229
64.	Templeton, S.D.	.221
65.	Griffin, L.A.	.220
66.	Doran, Hou.-Cin.	.220
67.	Williams, S.F.	.218
68.	Candaele, Hou	.213
69.	Alomar, S.D.	.213
70.	Biggio, Hou.	.210
71.	Pendleton, St.L	.210
72.	Davis, Cin.	.209
73.	Pagliarulo, S.D.	.206
74.	Blauser, Atl.	.194
75.	Zeile, St.L.	.193
76.	DeShields, Mon.	.190
77.	Scioscia, L.A.	.185
78.	Thompson, S.F.	.182
79.	Presley, Atl.	.181
80.	O. Smith, St.L	.178
81.	Fitzgerald, Mon	.176
82.	Murphy, Atl.-Phi.	.174
83.	Herr, Phi.-NY	.173
84.	King, Pit.	.123

Batting Average with Two Outs and Runners On Base

1.	Dykstra, Phi	.446
2.	Magadan, NY	.406
3.	Clark, S.F.	.371
4.	Butler, S.F.	.365
5.	Murphy, Atl.-Phi.	.345
6.	Bonds, Pit.	.333
7.	Gwynn, S.D.	.333
8.	Templeton, S.D.	.324
9.	Treadway, Atl.	.319
10.	Alomar, S.D.	.318
11.	Larkin, Cin.	.312
12.	Sandberg, Chi.	.311
13.	Boston, NY	.304
14.	Santiago, S.D.	.304
15.	Raines, Mon.	.303
16.	Presley, Atl.	.299
17.	Daniels, L.A.	.299
18.	Bell, Pit.	.298
19.	Dawson, Chi.	.298
20.	Roberts, S.D.	.297
21.	Kruk, Phi.	.292
22.	O'Neill, Cin.	.292
23.	Daulton, Phi	.291
24.	Justice, Atl.	.291
25.	Wallach, Mon.	.289
26.	Williams, S.F.	.287
27.	Dunston, Chi.	.286
28.	Sharperson, L.A.	.279
29.	Van Slyke, Pit	.275
30.	Strawberry, NY	.274
31.	Thompson, S.F.	.274
32.	Ramirez, Hou.	.271
33.	Biggio, Hou.	.270
34.	Brooks, L.A.	.268
35.	Murray, L.A.	.266
36.	Ja. Clark, S.D.	.262
37.	Jefferies, NY	.262
38.	McReynolds, NY	.262
39.	Girardi, Chi	.260
40.	Duncan, Cin.	.260
41.	Guerrero, St.L	.256
42.	Herr, Phi.-NY	.255
43.	Thon, Phi	.254
44.	King, Pit	.254
45.	Pagliarulo, S.D.	.253
46.	Uribe, S.F.	.253
47.	Coleman, St.L	.250
48.	Oliver, Cin	.250
49.	Walker, Mon	.250
50.	C. Hayes, Phi.	.248
51.	Sabo, Cin.	.248
52.	Grace, Chi.	.247
53.	Jordan, Phi	.247
54.	Pendleton, St.L	.244
55.	Johnson, NY	.243
56.	Wilson, Hou	.243
57.	Lind, Pit.	.243
58.	McGee, St.L	.237
59.	O. Smith, St.L	.236
60.	Hatcher, Cin.	.235
61.	Galarraga, Mon	.232
62.	Stubbs, Hou	.231
63.	Oquendo, St.L	.229
64.	Scioscia, L.A.	.229
65.	L. Smith, Atl	.228
66.	V. Hayes, Phi.	.228
67.	DeShields, Mon.	.224
68.	Bream, Pit.	.224
69.	Griffin, L.A.	.222
70.	Mitchell, S.F.	.222
71.	Davis, Hou	.212
72.	Blauser, Atl.	.211
73.	Carter, S.D.	.208
74.	Caminiti, Hou.	.208
75.	Davis, Cin.	.206
76.	Doran, Hou.-Cin.	.203
77.	Walton, Chi.	.200
78.	Gant, Atl.	.198
79.	Samuel, L.A.	.196
80.	Bonilla, Pit.	.194
81.	Zeile, St.L	.190
82.	Benzinger, Cin.	.189
83.	Salazar, Chi	.141
84.	Owen, Mon.	.136

Batting Average with Two Outs and Runners in Scoring Position

1.	Dykstra, Phi	.415
2.	Magadan, NY	.370
3.	Clark, S.F.	.362
4.	Bonds, Pit.	.350
5.	Butler, S.F.	.340
6.	Raines, Mon.	.339
7.	Boston, NY	.326
8.	Alomar, S.D	.316
9.	Murphy, Atl.-Phi.	.312
10.	Treadway, Atl.	.311
11.	Van Slyke, Pit	.311
12.	Larkin, Cin.	.311
13.	Kruk, Phi.	.308
14.	Santiago, S.D.	.306
15.	Scioscia, L.A.	.306
16.	Biggio, Hou.	.305
17.	Gwynn, S.D.	.304
18.	Templeton, S.D.	.303
19.	Williams, S.F.	.303
20.	Daniels, L.A.	.295
21.	Dawson, Chi.	.294
22.	Dunston, Chi.	.294
23.	O'Neill, Cin.	.290
24.	Strawberry, NY	.290
25.	Sandberg, Chi.	.289
26.	Thompson, S.F.	.288
27.	Roberts, S.D.	.286
28.	Grace, Chi.	.281
29.	McGee, St.L	.279
30.	Oliver, Cin	.275
31.	Girardi, Chi	.273
32.	Duncan, Cin.	.271
33.	Bell, Pit.	.267
34.	Martinez, Phi.-Pit	.267
35.	King, Pit	.264
36.	Griffin, L.A.	.259
37.	Pendleton, St.L	.258
38.	Jefferies, NY	.257
39.	Thon, Phi	.257
40.	Ja. Clark, S.D.	.256
41.	Daulton, Phi	.254
42.	Johnson, NY	.254
43.	Sabo, Cin.	.253
44.	Brooks, L.A.	.250
45.	McReynolds, NY	.250
46.	Murray, L.A.	.250
47.	Wallach, Mon.	.250
48.	Lind, Pit.	.246
49.	Justice, Atl.	.237
50.	Presley, Atl.	.237
51.	Sharperson, L.A.	.235
52.	Coleman, St.L	.230
53.	Pagliarulo, S.D.	.230
54.	Davis, Cin.	.228
55.	Uribe, S.F.	.224
56.	Caminiti, Hou.	.224
57.	Blauser, Atl.	.222
58.	Ramirez, Hou.	.222
59.	O. Smith, St.L	.222
60.	Herr, Phi.-NY	.221
61.	Walker, Mon	.217
62.	Oquendo, St.L	.217
63.	Galarraga, Mon	.216
64.	DeShields, Mon.	.214
65.	Yelding, Hou.	.214
66.	Stubbs, Hou	.213
67.	Carter, S.D.	.213
68.	C. Hayes, Phi.	.212
69.	Bonilla, Pit.	.210
70.	Guerrero, St.L	.208
71.	Davis, Hou	.208
72.	Gant, Atl.	.203
73.	Samuel, L.A.	.197
74.	Da. Martinez, Mon	.188
75.	Bream, Pit	.186
76.	Jordan, Phi	.184
77.	Hatcher, Cin.	.175
78.	Mitchell, S.F.	.173
79.	V. Hayes, Phi.	.160
80.	Doran, Hou.-Cin.	.156
81.	Zeile, St.L	.155
82.	Salazar, Chi	.143
83.	Benzinger, Cin.	.140
84.	Owen, Mon.	.089

American League

% of Runners Driven in from Third with Less than Two Out

1.	Brock, Mil.	81.8
2.	Alomar, Cle.	74.1
3.	Lansford, Oak.	74.1
4.	Davis, Sea.	73.1
5.	Brett, K.C.	72.7
6.	Griffey Jr., Sea.	72.0
7.	Newman, Min.	72.0
8.	Stillwell, K.C.	72.0
9.	Hill, Cal.	70.0
10.	Surhoff, Mil.	70.0
11.	Puckett, Min.	69.4
12.	Guillen, Chi.	68.8
13.	Sheffield, Mil.	68.8
14.	Gruber, Tor.	66.7
15.	Webster, Cle.	66.7
16.	Polonia, NY-Cal.	65.0
17.	Trammell, Det.	65.0
18.	Boggs, Bos.	64.5
19.	Palmeiro, Tex.	64.5
20.	Parker, Mil.	64.4
21.	Baines, Tex.-Oak.	64.3
22.	Jo. Reed, Bos.	64.0
23.	Tartabull, K.C.	64.0
24.	Yount, Mil.	63.9
25.	Hrbek, Min.	63.2
26.	Franco, Tex.	63.0
27.	Phillips, Det.	63.0
28.	Finley, Bal.	62.5
29.	Browne, Cle.	62.1
30.	Fisk, Chi.	61.9
31.	Rivera, Bos.	61.9
32.	C. Ripken, Bal.	61.4
33.	Gaetti, Min.	61.0
34.	Sheets, Det.	60.9
35.	Ventura, Chi.	60.7
36.	Bell, Tor.	60.5
37.	Spiers, Mil.	60.0
38.	Winfield, NY-Cal.	59.5
39.	Wilson, Tor.	59.4
40.	Felix, Tor.	59.3
41.	Perry, K.C.	59.3
42.	Sierra, Tex.	59.1
43.	Brunansky, Bos.	58.3
44.	Maldonado, Cle.	58.3
45.	Ray, Cal.	58.3
46.	Steinbach, Oak.	58.3
47.	Fernandez, Tor.	58.1
48.	Reynolds, Sea.	57.7
49.	Bergman, Det.	57.1
50.	Gallego, Oak.	57.1
51.	Sax, NY	57.1
52.	Calderon, Chi.	56.8
53.	Leonard, Sea.	56.4
54.	Fletcher, Chi.	56.3
55.	Pena, Bos.	56.3
56.	Barfield, NY	56.0
57.	Lee, Tor.	56.0
58.	Mattingly, NY	55.6
59.	R. Henderson, Oak.	54.5
60.	Worthington, Bal.	54.5
61.	Davis, Cal.	54.3
62.	C. James, Cle.	54.3
63.	McGwire, Oak.	54.1
64.	Bichette, Cal.	53.8
65.	Tettleton, Bal.	53.6
66.	Johnson, Chi.	53.1
67.	Orsulak, Bal.	52.4
68.	E. Martinez, Sea.	52.0
69.	Pasqua, Chi.	52.0
70.	Eisenreich, K.C.	51.9
71.	Heath, Det.	51.9
72.	Jackson, K.C.	51.9
73.	Harper, Min.	51.6
74.	Vaughn, Mil.	51.6
75.	Greenwell, Bos.	51.2
76.	Downing, Cal.	50.0
77.	Evans, Bos.	50.0
78.	Joyner, Cal.	50.0
79.	MacFarlane, K.C.	50.0
80.	McGriff, Tor.	50.0
81.	Wilson, K.C.	50.0
82.	Jacoby, Cle.	48.6
83.	Sosa, Chi.	48.3
84.	Kelly, NY	48.1
85.	Fielder, Det.	45.5
86.	White, Cal.	44.4
87.	Fermin, Cle.	44.0
88.	J. Canseco, Oak.	43.9
89.	Incaviglia, Tex.	43.6
90.	D. Henderson, Oak.	42.3
91.	O'Brien, Sea.	41.4
92.	Quintana, Bos.	40.7
93.	Snyder, Cle.	40.0
94.	Gladden, Min.	39.3
95.	Moseby, Det.	39.3
96.	Melvin, Bal.	39.1
97.	Burks, Bos.	36.7
98.	Whitaker, Det.	32.3
99.	Deer, Mil.	31.8

% of Runners Driven in from Scoring Position

1.	Brett, K.C.	37.3
2.	Trammell, Det.	36.5
3.	Ward, Det.	36.2
4.	Gruber, Tor.	36.1
5.	Mack, Min.	36.0
6.	Sierra, Tex.	34.8
7.	Puckett, Min.	34.2
8.	Sheffield, Mil.	33.3
9.	Johnson, Chi.	33.1
10.	Palmeiro, Tex.	33.0
11.	Guillen, Chi.	32.5
12.	Steinbach, Oak.	32.1
13.	Calderon, Chi.	31.6
14.	Felix, Tor.	31.5
15.	Jacoby, Cle.	31.5
16.	Leonard, Sea.	31.5
17.	Alomar, Cle.	31.4
18.	Daugherty, Tex.	31.3
19.	Browne, Cle.	31.0
20.	Phillips, Det.	30.9
21.	Quintana, Bos.	30.8
22.	Vaughn, Mil.	30.8
23.	J. Canseco, Oak.	30.7
24.	Boggs, Bos.	30.6
25.	Ray, Cal.	30.5
26.	Brock, Mil.	30.5
27.	Maldonado, Cle.	30.4
28.	Webster, Cle.	30.4
29.	Parker, Mil.	30.4
30.	Hrbek, Min.	30.3
31.	Pasqua, Chi.	30.3
32.	Bell, Tor.	30.1
33.	C. James, Cle.	29.9
34.	Wilson, K.C.	29.7
35.	Joyner, Cal.	29.6
36.	Polonia, NY-Cal.	29.5
37.	Pena, Bos.	29.5
38.	Fielder, Det.	29.4
39.	Franco, Tex.	29.3
40.	Gaetti, Min.	29.3
41.	Surhoff, Mil.	29.2
42.	Orsulak, Bal.	29.2
43.	Perry, K.C.	29.0
44.	Downing, Cal.	29.0
45.	Barfield, NY	29.0
46.	Fernandez, Tor.	29.0
47.	Ventura, Chi.	28.9
48.	Davis, Sea.	28.8
49.	Baerga, Cle.	28.8
50.	Mattingly, NY	28.8
51.	Baines, Tex.-Oak.	28.8
52.	Tartabull, K.C.	28.7
53.	Lansford, Oak.	28.7
54.	Burks, Bos.	28.5
55.	McGwire, Oak.	28.5
56.	Winfield, NY-Cal.	28.0
57.	Griffey Jr., Sea.	28.0
58.	MacFarlane, K.C.	27.9
59.	Sheets, Det.	27.8
60.	Davis, Cal.	27.6
61.	Eisenreich, K.C.	27.6
62.	B. Ripken, Bal.	27.6
63.	Bichette, Cal.	27.5
64.	Fletcher, Chi.	27.5
65.	Harper, Min.	27.2
66.	Rivera, Bos.	27.2
67.	Reynolds, Sea.	27.2
68.	Milligan, Bal.	27.1
69.	Jo. Reed, Bos.	27.1
70.	Lee, Tor.	27.0
71.	Stillwell, K.C.	26.8
72.	Spiers, Mil.	26.7
73.	Weiss, Oak.	26.7
74.	Wilson, Tor.	26.2
75.	Finley, Bal.	26.2
76.	Fisk, Chi.	26.1
77.	McGriff, Tor.	26.1
78.	Kelly, NY	26.0
79.	Larkin, Min.	26.0
80.	Devereaux, Bal.	25.9
81.	Evans, Bos.	25.8
82.	Jackson, K.C.	25.7
83.	Sosa, Chi.	25.6
84.	Yount, Mil.	25.4
85.	Brunansky, Bos.	25.3
86.	Worthington, Bal.	24.8
87.	Fermin, Cle.	24.6
88.	Incaviglia, Tex.	24.3
89.	Deer, Mil.	24.2
90.	C. Ripken, Bal.	23.7
91.	Parrish, Cal.	23.6
92.	Greenwell, Bos.	23.4
93.	D. Henderson, Oak.	23.4
94.	Snyder, Cle.	22.3
95.	Gladden, Min.	21.8
96.	Newman, Min.	21.8
97.	E. Martinez, Sea.	21.6
98.	Whitaker, Det.	21.4
99.	Moseby, Det.	20.6
100.	Sax, NY	19.8

% of Runners Driven in from Scoring Position in Pressure Situations

1.	Thomas, Chi.	55.6
2.	Anderson, Bal.	54.5
3.	Mulliniks, Tor.	53.3
4.	Milligan, Bal.	50.0
5.	Gruber, Tor.	47.1
6.	Weiss, Oak.	46.7
7.	Olerud, Tor.	45.8
8.	Guillen, Chi.	43.3
9.	Harper, Min.	42.9
10.	Ward, Det.	42.1
11.	Horn, Bal.	41.7
12.	Jose, Oak.	41.7
13.	Reynolds, Sea.	41.0
14.	Yount, Mil.	40.7
15.	Hamilton, Mil.	40.0
16.	Mack, Min.	40.0
17.	Sheets, Det.	40.0
18.	Huson, Tex.	38.5
19.	Sierra, Tex.	38.5
20.	Bradley, Sea.	37.5
21.	Bradley, Bal.-Chi.	36.4
22.	Eisenreich, K.C.	36.4
23.	Trammell, Det.	36.0
24.	Davis, Cal.	35.7
25.	Hrbek, Min.	35.3
26.	Webster, Cle.	35.0
27.	Baerga, Cle.	34.6
28.	Baines, Tex.-Oak.	33.3
29.	Felder, Mil.	33.3
30.	Gallego, Oak.	33.3
31.	Incaviglia, Tex.	33.3
32.	Lemon, Det.	33.3
33.	MacFarlane, K.C.	33.3
34.	Steinbach, Oak.	33.3
35.	Maldonado, Cle.	32.1
36.	Bichette, Cal.	31.8
37.	Deer, Mil.	31.8
38.	Fisk, Chi.	31.8
39.	Evans, Bos.	31.0
40.	Ray, Cal.	31.0
41.	Browne, Cle.	30.8
42.	Devereaux, Bal.	30.8
43.	Pena, Bos.	30.4
44.	Alomar, Cle.	30.3
45.	C. Ripken, Bal.	30.0
46.	Spiers, Mil.	30.0
47.	Tabler, K.C.	29.4
48.	Brookens, Cle.	28.6
49.	D. Henderson, Oak.	28.6
50.	Johnson, Chi.	28.6
51.	Lansford, Oak.	28.6
52.	E. Martinez, Sea.	28.6
53.	Wilson, Tor.	28.6
54.	Perry, K.C.	27.8
55.	Sheffield, Mil.	27.8
56.	Jacoby, Cle.	27.3
57.	Jo. Reed, Bos.	26.9
58.	Borders, Tor.	26.7
59.	Melvin, Bal.	26.7
60.	Leyritz, NY	26.3
61.	Ventura, Chi.	26.1
62.	McGriff, Tor.	25.0
63.	Polonia, NY-Cal.	25.0
64.	Quintana, Bos.	25.0
65.	Reimer, Tex.	25.0
66.	Burks, Bos.	24.0
67.	Barfield, NY	23.8
68.	Hall, NY	23.8
69.	Leonard, Sea.	23.8
70.	Surhoff, Mil.	23.8
71.	Cotto, Sea.	23.5
72.	Fletcher, Chi.	22.7
73.	Griffey Jr., Sea.	22.7
74.	Franco, Tex.	22.2
75.	Gaetti, Min.	22.2
76.	Mattingly, NY	22.2
77.	Pasqua, Chi.	22.2
78.	Greenwell, Bos.	21.7
79.	Felix, Tor.	21.1
80.	Bell, Tor.	19.2
81.	Winfield, NY-Cal.	19.2
82.	Fernandez, Tor.	19.0
83.	Sax, NY	18.9
84.	Boggs, Bos.	18.5
85.	Kelly, NY	17.9
86.	Moseby, Det.	17.9
87.	Parrish, Cal.	16.7
88.	Balboni, NY	15.4
89.	Palmeiro, Tex.	15.4
90.	Jackson, K.C.	14.8
91.	Gladden, Min.	12.5
92.	Fielder, Det.	11.8

National League

% of Runners Driven in from Third with Less than Two Out

1. L. Smith, Atl. 81.0
2. Benzinger, Cin. 80.6
3. Raines, Mon. 80.6
4. Dykstra, Phi 72.7
5. Dawson, Chi. 72.2
6. Williams, S.F. 71.4
7. O. Smith, St.L 70.7
8. Elster, NY 70.0
9. Justice, Atl. 70.0
10. Grace, Chi. 68.9
11. Yelding, Hou. 68.4
12. Brooks, L.A. 67.5
13. Bonds, Pit. 66.7
14. Butler, S.F. 66.7
15. Magadan, NY 66.7
16. Santovenia, Mon. 66.7
17. Sharperson, L.A. 66.7
18. V. Hayes, Phi. 65.7
19. Pendleton, St.L 65.5
20. Duncan, Cin. 65.4
21. Lind, Pit. 65.4
22. Bream, Pit. 65.0
23. McReynolds, NY 64.0
24. Murray, L.A. 63.9
25. Sandberg, Chi. 63.3
26. Bonilla, Pit. 63.2
27. DeShields, Mon. 62.5
28. Johnson, NY 62.5
29. Wilson, Hou. 62.5
30. Templeton, S.D. 61.9
31. Gwynn, S.D. 61.8
32. Galarraga, Mon. 61.1
33. Carter, S.D. 60.9
34. Treadway, Atl. 60.9
35. McGee, St.L 60.7
36. Caminiti, Hou. 60.0
37. Kruk, Phi. 60.0
38. Scioscia, L.A. 59.4
39. Van Slyke, Pit. 59.4
40. Oquendo, St.L 58.3
41. Harris, L.A. 57.9
42. Jefferies, NY 57.7
43. Owen, Mon. 56.7
44. Daniels, L.A. 56.3
45. Bell, Pit. 56.0
46. Mitchell, S.F. 55.6
47. Thompson, S.F. 55.2
48. Strawberry, NY 54.8
49. Sabo, Cin. 53.6
50. Grissom, Mon. 52.6
51. Wallach, Mon. 52.6
52. Guerrero, St.L 52.3
53. Alomar, S.D. 52.2
54. Salazar, Chi. 52.2
55. Dunston, Chi. 52.0
56. Jordan, Phi. 52.0
57. Gant, Atl. 51.5
58. Davis, Cin. 51.4
59. Clark, S.F. 51.2
60. Girardi, Chi. 50.0
61. Griffin, L.A. 50.0
62. Larkin, Cin. 50.0
63. Presley, Atl. 50.0
64. Samuel, L.A. 50.0
65. Santiago, S.D. 50.0
66. Herr, Phi.-NY 48.5
67. Daulton, Phi 48.1
68. Stubbs, Hou. 48.0
69. Zeile, St.L 48.0
70. C. Hayes, Phi. 47.5
71. O'Neill, Cin. 45.0
72. Biggio, Hou. 44.8
73. Murphy, Atl.-Phi. 44.4
74. Morris, Cin. 44.0
75. King, Pit. 43.3
76. Thon, Phi. 41.4
77. Walker, Mon. 40.0
78. Fitzgerald, Mon. 36.8
79. Ja. Clark, S.D. 33.3

% of Runners Driven in from Scoring Position

1. Magadan, NY 42.1
2. Bonds, Pit. 37.1
3. Williams, S.F. 35.4
4. Murray, L.A. 34.7
5. Dawson, Chi. 33.5
6. Grace, Chi. 33.5
7. Dykstra, Phi 33.1
8. Clark, S.F. 32.5
9. Scioscia, L.A. 32.5
10. Gwynn, S.D. 32.4
11. Brooks, L.A. 32.3
12. Strawberry, NY 32.0
13. Daniels, L.A. 31.1
14. O'Neill, Cin. 31.0
15. Johnson, NY 31.0
16. McGee, St.L 31.0
17. Wilson, Hou. 30.8
18. Carter, S.D. 30.7
19. Kruk, Phi. 30.6
20. Sasser, NY 30.4
21. Raines, Mon. 30.2
22. Bonilla, Pit. 29.8
23. Bream, Pit. 29.7
24. Alomar, S.D. 29.6
25. Davis, Cin. 29.5
26. McReynolds, NY 29.5
27. Larkin, Cin. 29.5
28. Santiago, S.D. 29.4
29. DeShields, Mon. 29.4
30. Justice, Atl. 29.3
31. Guerrero, St.L 29.2
32. Treadway, Atl. 29.2
33. Elster, NY 28.8
34. Duncan, Cin. 28.7
35. Pendleton, St.L 28.7
36. Van Slyke, Pit. 28.7
37. Wallach, Mon. 28.5
38. Oliver, Cin. 27.7
39. Fitzgerald, Mon. 27.7
40. O. Smith, St.L 27.6
41. Sandberg, Chi. 27.2
42. Templeton, S.D. 27.1
43. Butler, S.F. 27.1
44. Lind, Pit. 26.9
45. Galarraga, Mon. 26.8
46. Ramirez, Hou. 26.8
47. V. Hayes, Phi. 26.7
48. Bell, Pit. 26.6
49. Sharperson, L.A. 26.5
50. Jefferies, NY 26.4
51. Ja. Clark, S.D. 26.4
52. Davis, Hou. 26.3
53. Girardi, Chi. 26.2
54. Benzinger, Cin. 25.9
55. Jordan, Phi. 25.6
56. Dunston, Chi. 25.5
57. L. Smith, Atl. 25.5
58. Daulton, Phi 25.4
59. Murphy, Atl.-Phi. 25.2
60. Herr, Phi.-NY 24.9
61. Presley, Atl. 24.6
62. Sabo, Cin. 24.5
63. Mitchell, S.F. 24.3
64. Caminiti, Hou. 24.3
65. Stubbs, Hou. 24.1
66. Gant, Atl. 24.1
67. Roberts, S.D. 24.0
68. Pagliarulo, S.D. 23.9
69. C. Hayes, Phi. 23.6
70. Oquendo, St.L 23.6
71. Coleman, St.L 23.4
72. Boston, NY 22.9
73. King, Pit. 22.3
74. Owen, Mon. 22.1
75. Griffin, L.A. 21.9
76. Thompson, S.F. 21.9
77. Salazar, Chi. 21.8
78. Biggio, Hou. 21.4
79. Walker, Mon. 20.8
80. Samuel, L.A. 20.4
81. Thon, Phi. 20.1
82. Zeile, St.L 19.3

% of Runners Driven in from Scoring Position in Pressure Situations

1. Kingery, S.F. 77.8
2. Bathe, S.F. 55.6
3. Marshall, NY 53.8
4. Litton, S.F. 46.2
5. Dykstra, Phi 41.9
6. Olson, Atl. 41.7
7. Jefferies, NY 40.0
8. Thompson, St.L 40.0
9. Treadway, Atl. 40.0
10. Murray, L.A. 38.9
11. Davis, Hou. 37.5
12. Da. Martinez, Mon. 37.5
13. McReynolds, NY 37.0
14. Carter, S.D. 36.1
15. Bream, Pit. 35.7
16. McGee, St.L 35.5
17. Bell, Pit. 35.0
18. Brooks, L.A. 35.0
19. Reynolds, Pit. 35.0
20. Van Slyke, Pit. 34.8
21. Raines, Mon. 34.6
22. Gibson, L.A. 33.3
23. Wilson, Hou. 33.3
24. Bonilla, Pit. 31.8
25. Benzinger, Cin. 31.6
26. Clark, Chi. 31.3
27. Kruk, Phi. 31.3
28. Larkin, Cin. 31.3
29. Daniels, L.A. 30.0
30. Sharperson, L.A. 30.0
31. Stubbs, Hou. 30.0
32. Magadan, NY 29.4
33. Oquendo, St.L 29.4
34. Lind, Pit. 29.2
35. Dunston, Chi. 28.6
36. Williams, S.F. 28.6
37. Dawson, Chi. 28.0
38. Roberts, S.D. 28.0
39. Galarraga, Mon. 27.9
40. Girardi, Chi. 27.8
41. Javier, L.A. 27.8
42. Salazar, Chi. 27.8
43. Templeton, S.D. 27.8
44. Butler, S.F. 27.3
45. Davis, Cin. 27.3
46. Jordan, Phi. 27.3
47. Fitzgerald, Mon. 26.9
48. Alomar, S.D. 26.7
49. Sandberg, Chi. 26.5
50. D. Smith, Chi. 26.3
51. Grissom, Mon. 26.1
52. Guerrero, St.L 26.1
53. Grace, Chi. 25.9
54. Gwynn, S.D. 25.0
55. Owen, Mon. 25.0
56. Presley, Atl. 25.0
57. Pendleton, St.L 24.1
58. Thompson, S.F. 24.0
59. Ramirez, Hou. 23.8
60. Wallach, Mon. 23.5
61. V. Hayes, Phi. 22.7
62. Caminiti, Hou. 22.6
63. Samuel, L.A. 22.2
64. Sasser, NY 21.7
65. Biggio, Hou. 20.8
66. O. Smith, St.L 20.7
67. Clark, S.F. 20.6
68. Zeile, St.L 19.2
69. Ready, Phi. 18.5
70. Mitchell, S.F. 16.1
71. Daulton, Phi 14.7

American League

Opponents' Batting Average, Left-Handed Batters

1. McDonald, Bal. .181
2. Jones, Cle. .200
3. Olson, Bal. .200
4. S. Valdez, Cle. .207
5. Stewart, Oak. .207
6. Henke, Tor. .210
7. Thigpen, Chi. .215
8. King, Chi. .216
9. Ryan, Tex. .218
10. Robinson, NY .221
11. Hanson, Sea. .222
12. Williamson, Bal. .223
13. Farr, K.C. .225
14. Witt, Tex. .232
15. Sanderson, Oak. .234
16. Harris, Bos. .239
17. Aquino, K.C. .241
18. Clemens, Bos. .242
19. McDowell, Chi. .243
20. Hough, Tex. .243
21. Robinson, Det. .244
22. Wills, Tor. .244
23. Erickson, Min. .246
24. Blair, Tor. .246
25. Langston, Cal. .246
26. Petry, Det. .249
27. Brown, Tex. .249
28. Perez, Chi. .250
29. Walker, Cle. .250
30. McCaskill, Cal. .251
31. Crim, Mil. .252
32. Gordon, K.C. .252
33. Cadaret, NY .252
34. Stieb, Tor. .253
35. Candiotti, Cle. .256
36. Welch, Oak. .258
37. Ward, Tor. .259
38. McGaffigan, K.C. .259
39. Leary, NY .260
40. Moore, Oak. .260
41. Robinson, Mil. .260
42. Appier, K.C. .260
43. Boddicker, Bos. .261
44. Berenguer, Min. .264
45. Gubicza, K.C. .266
46. Witt, Cal.-NY .267
47. Burns, Oak. .268
48. Morris, Det. .268
49. Black, Cle.-Tor. .269
50. Leach, Min. .270
51. Fernandez, Chi. .273
52. Edens, Mil. .275
53. Saberhagen, K.C. .275
54. Milacki, Bal. .276
55. Henneman, Det. .278
56. Farrell, Cle. .278
57. Montgomery, K.C. .278
58. Knudson, Mil. .279
59. Holman, Sea. .280
60. Gardner, Bos. .282
61. Tapani, Min. .284
62. Bosio, Mil. .286
63. Ballard, Bal. .287
64. Swift, Sea. .287
65. Harnisch, Bal. .287
66. Acker, Tor. .289
67. Eichhorn, Cal. .290
68. S. Davis, K.C. .294
69. Hawkins, NY .294
70. Johnson, Bal. .297
71. Lamp, Bos. .299
72. Navarro, Mil. .299
73. Olin, Cle. .300
74. Stottlemyre, Tor. .300
75. Drummond, Min. .302
76. Blyleven, Cal. .311
77. Terrell, Det. .314
78. Mitchell, Bal. .317
79. Kiecker, Bos. .318
80. Crawford, K.C. .347
81. Peterson, Chi. .354
82. Smith, Min. .369

Opponents' Slugging Average, Left-Handed Batters

1. McDonald, Bal. .236
2. Olson, Bal. .248
3. Farr, K.C. .294
4. Stewart, Oak. .305
5. Hanson, Sea. .308
6. Thigpen, Chi. .310
7. Robinson, NY .314
8. Jones, Cle. .315
9. Crim, Mil. .321
10. Witt, Tex. .321
11. King, Chi. .321
12. Robinson, Mil. .324
13. Henneman, Det. .326
14. Harris, Bos. .338
15. Clemens, Bos. .343
16. Gordon, K.C. .345
17. Langston, Cal. .348
18. Erickson, Min. .348
19. Eichhorn, Cal. .348
20. Gardner, Bos. .349
21. Hough, Tex. .350
22. Petry, Det. .351
23. Candiotti, Cle. .355
24. Henke, Tor. .355
25. Ryan, Tex. .356
26. Stieb, Tor. .357
27. Edens, Mil. .359
28. Brown, Tex. .362
29. Appier, K.C. .363
30. Witt, Cal.-NY .364
31. Boddicker, Bos. .366
32. Gubicza, K.C. .367
33. McCaskill, Cal. .368
34. S. Valdez, Cle. .369
35. Fernandez, Chi. .369
36. Cadaret, NY .370
37. Olin, Cle. .371
38. Walker, Cle. .371
39. Wills, Tor. .372
40. Blair, Tor. .373
41. Perez, Chi. .374
42. Moore, Oak. .374
43. Navarro, Mil. .374
44. Aquino, K.C. .379
45. McDowell, Chi. .380
46. Leach, Min. .381
47. Ward, Tor. .386
48. Berenguer, Min. .390
49. Sanderson, Oak. .391
50. Leary, NY .392
51. Morris, Det. .397
52. Swift, Sea. .398
53. Farrell, Cle. .400
54. Welch, Oak. .404
55. Ballard, Bal. .404
56. McGaffigan, K.C. .405
57. Saberhagen, K.C. .405
58. Knudson, Mil. .406
59. Acker, Tor. .409
60. Milacki, Bal. .410
61. Williamson, Bal. .410
62. Montgomery, K.C. .415
63. Holman, Sea. .417
64. Lamp, Bos. .418
65. S. Davis, K.C. .421
66. Hawkins, NY .431
67. Kiecker, Bos. .431
68. Tapani, Min. .435
69. Robinson, Det. .437
70. Harnisch, Bal. .439
71. Black, Cle.-Tor. .441
72. Stottlemyre, Tor. .443
73. Burns, Oak. .449
74. Mitchell, Bal. .455
75. Bosio, Mil. .465
76. Blyleven, Cal. .470
77. Terrell, Det. .471
78. Drummond, Min. .477
79. Johnson, Bal. .522
80. Crawford, K.C. .524
81. Smith, Min. .554
82. Peterson, Chi. .565

Opponents' On-Base Average, Left-Handed Batters

1. McDonald, Bal. .236
2. Jones, Cle. .249
3. Williamson, Bal. .257
4. Henke, Tor. .267
5. Robinson, NY .273
6. Stewart, Oak. .280
7. S. Valdez, Cle. .281
8. Hanson, Sea. .283
9. King, Chi. .286
10. Crim, Mil. .288
11. Clemens, Bos. .288
12. Thigpen, Chi. .294
13. Olson, Bal. .298
14. Sanderson, Oak. .300
15. McDowell, Chi. .302
16. Ryan, Tex. .305
17. Brown, Tex. .309
18. Robinson, Mil. .309
19. Candiotti, Cle. .311
20. Harris, Bos. .312
21. Wills, Tor. .314
22. Black, Cle.-Tor. .314
23. Blair, Tor. .317
24. Swift, Sea. .317
25. Boddicker, Bos. .317
26. Langston, Cal. .318
27. Saberhagen, K.C. .318
28. Farr, K.C. .319
29. Knudson, Mil. .320
30. Perez, Chi. .322
31. McCaskill, Cal. .322
32. Witt, Tex. .323
33. McGaffigan, K.C. .324
34. Welch, Oak. .325
35. Stieb, Tor. .326
36. Tapani, Min. .328
37. Erickson, Min. .329
38. Leach, Min. .331
39. Appier, K.C. .331
40. Cadaret, NY .333
41. Moore, Oak. .333
42. Bosio, Mil. .336
43. Ballard, Bal. .336
44. Farrell, Cle. .336
45. Edens, Mil. .338
46. Leary, NY .338
47. Witt, Cal.-NY .339
48. Fernandez, Chi. .340
49. Johnson, Bal. .340
50. Petry, Det. .345
51. Aquino, K.C. .346
52. Holman, Sea. .346
53. Blyleven, Cal. .346
54. Robinson, Det. .348
55. Navarro, Mil. .348
56. Hough, Tex. .349
57. Walker, Cle. .350
58. Morris, Det. .350
59. Gordon, K.C. .352
60. Eichhorn, Cal. .353
61. S. Davis, K.C. .353
62. Lamp, Bos. .354
63. Burns, Oak. .354
64. Acker, Tor. .355
65. Drummond, Min. .355
66. Montgomery, K.C. .357
67. Olin, Cle. .357
68. Milacki, Bal. .358
69. Harnisch, Bal. .358
70. Berenguer, Min. .361
71. Henneman, Det. .364
72. Stottlemyre, Tor. .365
73. Gardner, Bos. .366
74. Terrell, Det. .369
75. Gubicza, K.C. .371
76. Ward, Tor. .372
77. Kiecker, Bos. .375
78. Peterson, Chi. .383
79. Mitchell, Bal. .397
80. Hawkins, NY .398
81. Crawford, K.C. .407
82. Smith, Min. .423

National League

Opponents' Batting Average, Left-Handed Batters

1. Boever, Atl.-Phi. .184
2. Dibble, Cin. .185
3. DeJesus, Phi .191
4. Akerfelds, Phi. .200
5. Hartley, L.A. .213
6. Cone, NY .214
7. Rijo, Cin. .218
8. Glavine, Atl. .221
9. De. Martinez, Mon. .223
10. Boyd, Mon. .224
11. Portugal, Hou .227
12. Belcher, L.A. .227
13. Gardner, Mon. .230
14. Hurst, S.D. .230
15. Downs, S.F. .233
16. L. Smith, St.L .237
17. Harkey, Chi .238
18. Scott, Hou .238
19. LaCoss, S.F. .239
20. Howell, L.A. .242
21. Drabek, Pit .244
22. Benes, S.D. .245
23. Martinez, L.A. .246
24. Sampen, Mon. .251
25. Browning, Cin. .253
26. Combs, Phi. .254
27. Layana, Cin. .256
28. Viola, NY .257
29. Burkett, S.F. .258
30. Darling, NY .258
31. Gooden, NY .258
32. Armstrong, Cin. .258
33. Schiraldi, S.D. .259
34. Hill, St.L .261
35. Crews, L.A. .261
36. Walk, Pit. .263
37. Darwin, Hou .264
38. Bedrosian, S.F. .267
39. Nunez, Chi. .267
40. Smoltz, Atl. .269
41. Whitson, S.D. .270
42. Mahler, Cin. .272
43. Bielecki, Chi. .273
44. Brantley, S.F. .274
45. Parrett, Phi.-Atl. .275
46. Boskie, Chi. .276
47. Harris, S.D. .277
48. Tewksbury, St.L. .278
49. Magrane, St.L .281
50. Neidlinger, L.A. .283
51. DeLeon, St.L .285
52. Robinson, S.F. .285
53. Lancaster, Chi. .285
54. Morgan, L.A. .290
55. Maddux, Chi. .291
56. Garrelts, S.F. .294
57. P. Smith, Atl. .295
58. Gross, Mon. .295
59. Scudder, Cin. .297
60. Howell, Phi. .299
61. B. Smith, St.L .301
62. Grant, S.D.-Atl. .305
63. Show, S.D. .310
64. Gullickson, Hou. .313
65. Reuschel, S.F. .325
66. Clary, Atl. .326
67. McDowell, Phi. .328
68. Terrell, Pit. .328
69. Clancy, Hou .366
70. Pico, Chi. .374

Opponents' Slugging Average, Left-Handed Batters

1. Boever, Atl.-Phi. .241
2. Dibble, Cin. .254
3. DeJesus, Phi .275
4. Glavine, Atl. .279
5. Sampen, Mon. .303
6. Hartley, L.A. .316
7. Rijo, Cin. .318
8. Downs, S.F. .320
9. De. Martinez, Mon. .321
10. LaCoss, S.F. .328
11. Viola, NY .328
12. Brantley, S.F. .328
13. Portugal, Hou .329
14. Neidlinger, L.A. .331
15. Boyd, Mon. .340
16. L. Smith, St.L .349
17. Howell, L.A. .349
18. Harkey, Chi .351
19. Gooden, NY .354
20. Belcher, L.A. .358
21. Whitson, S.D. .358
22. Gardner, Mon. .362
23. Harris, S.D. .364
24. Scott, Hou .366
25. Drabek, Pit .370
26. Benes, S.D. .371
27. Magrane, St.L .373
28. Maddux, Chi .376
29. Crews, L.A. .376
30. Burkett, S.F. .377
31. Cone, NY .377
32. Armstrong, Cin. .380
33. Darwin, Hou .382
34. Tewksbury, St.L. .383
35. Smoltz, Atl. .383
36. Bedrosian, S.F. .388
37. Martinez, L.A. .389
38. Lancaster, Chi .390
39. B. Smith, St.L .392
40. Boskie, Chi. .393
41. Nunez, Chi. .393
42. Akerfelds, Phi. .394
43. Walk, Pit. .394
44. Browning, Cin. .395
45. Hill, St.L .397
46. Combs, Phi. .399
47. Hurst, S.D. .400
48. Darling, NY .403
49. Bielecki, Chi. .409
50. Layana, Cin. .414
51. Gross, Mon. .415
52. Mahler, Cin. .415
53. McDowell, Phi .415
54. P. Smith, Atl. .416
55. Morgan, L.A. .418
56. DeLeon, St.L .423
57. Garrelts, S.F. .425
58. Schiraldi, S.D. .428
59. Gullickson, Hou. .452
60. Parrett, Phi.-Atl. .454
61. Robinson, S.F. .455
62. Scudder, Cin. .468
63. Howell, Phi. .469
64. Show, S.D. .474
65. Grant, S.D.-Atl. .477
66. Clary, Atl. .483
67. Clancy, Hou. .488
68. Pico, Chi. .495
69. Reuschel, S.F. .505
70. Terrell, Pit. .582

Opponents' On-Base Average, Left-Handed Batters

1. De. Martinez, Mon. .263
2. Cone, NY .274
3. Dibble, Cin. .282
4. Boyd, Mon. .285
5. Downs, S.F. .288
6. Drabek, Pit. .290
7. Crews, L.A. .296
8. Belcher, L.A. .296
9. Portugal, Hou .301
10. Scott, Hou .302
11. Harkey, Chi .302
12. Hurst, S.D. .302
13. Tewksbury, St.L. .302
14. L. Smith, St.L .306
15. Akerfelds, Phi. .306
16. Howell, L.A. .307
17. Benes, S.D. .307
18. Browning, Cin. .309
19. Whitson, S.D. .309
20. Glavine, Atl. .310
21. Darwin, Hou .311
22. Burkett, S.F. .312
23. Gooden, NY .315
24. DeJesus, Phi .315
25. Rijo, Cin. .316
26. Viola, NY .317
27. Boever, Atl.-Phi. .317
28. Sampen, Mon. .318
29. Martinez, L.A. .319
30. Hartley, L.A. .322
31. Mahler, Cin. .323
32. Neidlinger, L.A. .324
33. Walk, Pit. .326
34. Gardner, Mon. .327
35. Armstrong, Cin. .329
36. Darling, NY .333
37. B. Smith, St.L .339
38. Combs, Phi. .340
39. LaCoss, S.F. .340
40. Morgan, L.A. .341
41. Brantley, S.F. .341
42. Robinson, S.F. .343
43. Hill, St.L .344
44. Smoltz, Atl. .347
45. Bielecki, Chi. .347
46. Maddux, Chi .351
47. Nunez, Chi. .354
48. Harris, S.D. .355
49. Boskie, Chi. .357
50. Magrane, St.L .357
51. P. Smith, Atl. .357
52. Garrelts, S.F. .363
53. Lancaster, Chi .367
54. Scudder, Cin. .369
55. Gullickson, Hou. .370
56. Grant, S.D.-Atl. .372
57. Gross, Mon. .373
58. Bedrosian, S.F. .373
59. DeLeon, St.L .373
60. Layana, Cin. .375
61. Schiraldi, S.D. .380
62. Clary, Atl. .381
63. Reuschel, S.F. .384
64. Howell, Phi .385
65. Show, S.D. .389
66. Parrett, Phi.-Atl. .390
67. Terrell, Pit. .405
68. McDowell, Phi. .414
69. Clancy, Hou. .436
70. Pico, Chi. .442

American League

Opponents' Batting Average, Right-Handed Batters

1. Ryan, Tex. .158
2. Kiecker, Bos. .183
3. Ward, Tor. .194
4. Stieb, Tor. .205
5. Berenguer, Min. .207
6. Clemens, Bos. .213
7. Farr, K.C. .215
8. Witt, Cal.-NY .216
9. Morris, Det. .218
10. Johnson, Sea. .218
11. Harnisch, Bal. .222
12. Welch, Oak. .223
13. Hawkins, NY .224
14. Black, Cle.-Tor. .224
15. Bosio, Mil. .226
16. Hough, Tex. .230
17. Wells, Tor. .230
18. Perez, Chi. .231
19. Guetterman, NY .233
20. McCaskill, Cal. .236
21. Holman, Sea. .238
22. Finley, Cal. .241
23. Witt, Tex. .242
24. Tapani, Min. .243
25. Hanson, Sea. .244
26. McDowell, Chi. .245
27. Appier, K.C. .246
28. Stottlemyre, Tor. .247
29. Young, Sea. .249
30. Olin, Cle. .251
31. Cary, NY .252
32. Bolton, Bos. .253
33. Edwards, Chi. .253
34. Stewart, Oak. .253
35. Boddicker, Bos. .254
36. Leary, NY .255
37. King, Chi. .255
38. Searcy, Det. .258
39. West, Min. .259
40. Rogers, Tex. .259
41. Higuera, Mil. .260
42. Swift, Sea. .261
43. Hibbard, Chi. .261
44. Brown, Tex. .261
45. Lamp, Bos. .262
46. Langston, Cal. .262
47. Guthrie, Min. .262
48. Smith, Min. .262
49. Gordon, K.C. .263
50. Johnson, Bal. .263
51. Robinson, Det. .266
52. Young, Oak. .268
53. S. Davis, K.C. .268
54. Candiotti, Cle. .270
55. Milacki, Bal. .271
56. Gibson, Det. .272
57. Petry, Det. .274
58. Cadaret, NY .274
59. Moore, Oak. .275
60. Acker, Tor. .276
61. Sanderson, Oak. .277
62. M. Davis, K.C. .279
63. Saberhagen, K.C. .281
64. Candelaria, Min.-Tor. .284
65. Knudson, Mil. .285
66. Mitchell, Bal. .285
67. Krueger, Mil. .285
68. Navarro, Mil. .287
69. Swindell, Cle. .289
70. Tanana, Det. .290
71. Ballard, Bal. .290
72. Harris, Bos. .291
73. Robinson, Mil. .291
74. Abbott, Cal. .292
75. LaPoint, NY .293
76. Anderson, Min. .294
77. Blyleven, Cal. .295
78. Jeffcoat, Tex. .296
79. Key, Tor. .298
80. Cerutti, Tor. .303
81. Moyer, Tex. .308
82. S. Valdez, Cle. .333

Opponents' Slugging Average, Right-Handed Batters

1. Clemens, Bos. .265
2. Kiecker, Bos. .271
3. Ward, Tor. .276
4. Stieb, Tor. .280
5. Ryan, Tex. .289
6. McCaskill, Cal. .294
7. Farr, K.C. .296
8. Appier, K.C. .312
9. Berenguer, Min. .313
10. Swift, Sea. .314
11. Olin, Cle. .316
12. Harnisch, Bal. .326
13. Black, Cle.-Tor. .329
14. Witt, Tex. .330
15. Guetterman, NY .338
16. King, Chi. .344
17. Stewart, Oak. .345
18. Holman, Sea. .345
19. Tapani, Min. .349
20. Bosio, Mil. .349
21. Young, Sea. .351
22. Bolton, Bos. .352
23. Morris, Det. .353
24. Witt, Cal.-NY .356
25. Wells, Tor. .359
26. Hanson, Sea. .359
27. Guthrie, Min. .360
28. Perez, Chi. .361
29. Finley, Cal. .363
30. Leary, NY .363
31. Edwards, Chi. .364
32. Hibbard, Chi. .365
33. Brown, Tex. .368
34. Johnson, Sea. .369
35. Boddicker, Bos. .369
36. Saberhagen, K.C. .374
37. Welch, Oak. .375
38. Stottlemyre, Tor. .376
39. Langston, Cal. .379
40. McDowell, Chi. .380
41. Robinson, Mil. .381
42. Hough, Tex. .384
43. Rogers, Tex. .385
44. S. Davis, K.C. .393
45. Abbott, Cal. .396
46. Mitchell, Bal. .397
47. Higuera, Mil. .400
48. Hawkins, NY .409
49. Searcy, Det. .411
50. Smith, Min. .414
51. Cadaret, NY .418
52. Krueger, Mil. .419
53. LaPoint, NY .420
54. Moore, Oak. .422
55. Candiotti, Cle. .423
56. Acker, Tor. .424
57. Harris, Bos. .425
58. Lamp, Bos. .425
59. Gordon, K.C. .426
60. Cary, NY .428
61. Johnson, Bal. .431
62. Knudson, Mil. .433
63. Navarro, Mil. .437
64. Young, Oak. .441
65. Petry, Det. .443
66. Anderson, Min. .451
67. Sanderson, Oak. .454
68. Blyleven, Cal. .455
69. Swindell, Cle. .456
70. Milacki, Bal. .458
71. Gibson, Det. .460
72. Moyer, Tex. .460
73. Jeffcoat, Tex. .469
74. West, Min. .470
75. M. Davis, K.C. .470
76. Robinson, Det. .475
77. Key, Tor. .481
78. Tanana, Det. .485
79. Candelaria, Min.-Tor. .496
80. Cerutti, Tor. .503
81. Ballard, Bal. .506
82. S. Valdez, Cle. .565

Opponents' On-Base Average, Right-Handed Batters

1. Ward, Tor. .219
2. Ryan, Tex. .230
3. Stieb, Tor. .263
4. Tapani, Min. .263
5. Clemens, Bos. .267
6. Kiecker, Bos. .272
7. Wells, Tor. .276
8. Morris, Det. .277
9. Guetterman, NY .281
10. Welch, Oak. .281
11. Bosio, Mil. .282
12. Black, Cle.-Tor. .285
13. Farr, K.C. .286
14. Appier, K.C. .287
15. Hanson, Sea. .291
16. Hawkins, NY .291
17. Smith, Min. .293
18. Witt, Cal.-NY .298
19. Holman, Sea. .299
20. King, Chi. .300
21. Swift, Sea. .302
22. Johnson, Bal. .303
23. Stewart, Oak. .303
24. Finley, Cal. .304
25. S. Davis, K.C. .305
26. Lamp, Bos. .309
27. Stottlemyre, Tor. .309
28. Hibbard, Chi. .309
29. Harnisch, Bal. .310
30. Olin, Cle. .311
31. Saberhagen, K.C. .311
32. Cary, NY .315
33. Higuera, Mil. .316
34. Guthrie, Min. .317
35. Perez, Chi. .318
36. McCaskill, Cal. .318
37. Candiotti, Cle. .318
38. Leary, NY .318
39. Key, Tor. .320
40. Boddicker, Bos. .321
41. Berenguer, Min. .321
42. Brown, Tex. .321
43. Knudson, Mil. .324
44. Sanderson, Oak. .325
45. Swindell, Cle. .325
46. Johnson, Sea. .326
47. Hough, Tex. .329
48. Acker, Tor. .329
49. Navarro, Mil. .330
50. McDowell, Chi. .330
51. Anderson, Min. .330
52. Edwards, Chi. .331
53. Blyleven, Cal. .331
54. Witt, Tex. .332
55. Candelaria, Min.-Tor. .332
56. Bolton, Bos. .334
57. Milacki, Bal. .334
58. Robinson, Mil. .336
59. Mitchell, Bal. .338
60. Rogers, Tex. .340
61. Gordon, K.C. .340
62. Young, Sea. .340
63. Jeffcoat, Tex. .345
64. Abbott, Cal. .345
65. Moore, Oak. .346
66. Ballard, Bal. .347
67. Langston, Cal. .348
68. LaPoint, NY .348
69. Young, Oak. .350
70. Petry, Det. .353
71. West, Min. .353
72. Gibson, Det. .356
73. Tanana, Det. .360
74. Krueger, Mil. .361
75. Harris, Bos. .364
76. Cerutti, Tor. .367
77. Cadaret, NY .367
78. Searcy, Det. .368
79. Robinson, Det. .373
80. Moyer, Tex. .376
81. S. Valdez, Cle. .378
82. M. Davis, K.C. .392

National League

Opponents' Batting Average, Right-Handed Batters

1. Harris, S.D. .156
2. Darwin, Hou .166
3. Martinez, L.A. .185
4. Nabholz, Mon. .188
5. DeLeon, St.L .190
6. Drabek, Pit. .191
7. Fernandez, NY .195
8. Myers, Cin. .197
9. Smoltz, Atl. .199
10. Rijo, Cin. .205
11. Tomlin, Pit. .213
12. Armstrong, Cin. .214
13. Wilson, S.F. .218
14. Whitson, S.D. .222
15. Maddux, Chi. .223
16. Hurst, S.D. .228
17. Tudor, St.L .228
18. Harkey, Chi. .229
19. Gardner, Mon. .230
20. Charlton, Cin. .233
21. Deshaies, Hou. .234
22. De. Martinez, Mon. .235
23. Morgan, L.A. .236
24. Lefferts, S.D. .237
25. Viola, NY .238
26. Benes, S.D. .239
27. Gross, Mon. .239
28. Carman, Phi. .239
29. Cone, NY .243
30. Williams, Chi. .243
31. Mahler, Cin. .244
32. Garrelts, S.F. .244
33. Assenmacher, Chi. .247
34. Mulholland, Phi. .247
35. Gullickson, Hou. .248
36. Boyd, Mon. .249
37. Tewksbury, St.L .251
38. Cook, Phi.-L.A. .252
39. Heaton, Pit. .254
40. Belcher, L.A. .255
41. Scott, Hou. .256
42. Burkett, S.F. .257
43. Gooden, NY .258
44. Combs, Phi. .258
45. Smith, Mon.-Pit. .258
46. Franco, NY .259
47. Magrane, St.L .260
48. B. Smith, St.L .264
49. Patterson, Pit. .267
50. Valenzuela, L.A. .268
51. Browning, Cin. .269
52. Smiley, Pit. .270
53. Schiraldi, S.D. .270
54. Leibrandt, Atl. .272
55. Wilson, Chi. .272
56. Jackson, Cin. .273
57. Robinson, S.F. .273
58. Lilliquist, Atl.-S.D. .275
59. Agosto, Hou. .276
60. Hammaker, S.F.-S.D. .278
61. Portugal, Hou. .282
62. Rasmussen, S.D. .286
63. Darling, NY .292
64. Glavine, Atl. .294
65. Ruffin, Phi. .299
66. Parrett, Phi.-Atl. .305
67. Ojeda, NY .307
68. Avery, Atl. .309
69. Bielecki, Chi. .310
70. Castillo, Atl. .310

Opponents' Slugging Average, Right-Handed Batters

1. Harris, S.D. .251
2. Darwin, Hou .253
3. Drabek, Pit. .264
4. Myers, Cin. .286
5. DeLeon, St.L .294
6. Gross, Mon. .301
7. Armstrong, Cin. .307
8. Rijo, Cin. .307
9. Martinez, L.A. .311
10. Charlton, Cin. .313
11. Nabholz, Mon. .317
12. Maddux, Chi. .318
13. Smoltz, Atl. .321
14. Tomlin, Pit. .323
15. Whitson, S.D. .330
16. Gooden, NY .332
17. Viola, NY .334
18. Fernandez, NY .336
19. Wilson, S.F. .337
20. Gardner, Mon. .337
21. Tudor, St.L .342
22. Cone, NY .344
23. Hurst, S.D. .347
24. De. Martinez, Mon. .355
25. Morgan, L.A. .360
26. Franco, NY .361
27. Combs, Phi. .369
28. Smith, Mon.-Pit. .369
29. Harkey, Chi. .369
30. Burkett, S.F. .370
31. Tewksbury, St.L. .372
32. Magrane, St.L .373
33. Garrelts, S.F. .378
34. Deshaies, Hou. .378
35. Williams, Chi. .378
36. Benes, S.D. .379
37. Agosto, Hou. .381
38. Assenmacher, Chi. .384
39. Mahler, Cin. .385
40. Leibrandt, Atl. .386
41. Carman, Phi. .390
42. Heaton, Pit. .391
43. Jackson, Cin. .391
44. Mulholland, Phi. .392
45. Cook, Phi.-L.A. .395
46. Hammaker, S.F.-S.D. .398
47. Lefferts, S.D. .398
48. Robinson, S.F. .399
49. Valenzuela, L.A. .404
50. Belcher, L.A. .408
51. Castillo, Atl. .413
52. B. Smith, St.L .414
53. Patterson, Pit. .414
54. Smiley, Pit. .415
55. Browning, Cin. .415
56. Schiraldi, S.D. .418
57. Gullickson, Hou. .424
58. Lilliquist, Atl.-S.D. .427
59. Parrett, Phi.-Atl. .429
60. Boyd, Mon. .432
61. Portugal, Hou. .436
62. Rasmussen, S.D. .438
63. Glavine, Atl. .440
64. Wilson, Chi. .445
65. Scott, Hou. .451
66. Avery, Atl. .453
67. Bielecki, Chi. .459
68. Ojeda, NY .466
69. Ruffin, Phi. .480
70. Darling, NY .514

Opponents' On-Base Average, Right-Handed Batters

1. Darwin, Hou .198
2. Martinez, L.A. .217
3. Harris, S.D. .246
4. Drabek, Pit. .248
5. Tomlin, Pit. .249
6. Smoltz, Atl. .255
7. Rijo, Cin. .255
8. Whitson, S.D. .259
9. Tewksbury, St.L. .263
10. Maddux, Chi. .267
11. Fernandez, NY .268
12. DeLeon, St.L .268
13. Nabholz, Mon. .272
14. Tudor, St.L .276
15. Hurst, S.D. .279
16. Viola, NY .281
17. Armstrong, Cin. .281
18. Lefferts, S.D. .283
19. Myers, Cin. .284
20. Gullickson, Hou. .287
21. Gross, Mon. .291
22. Gardner, Mon. .291
23. Mulholland, Phi. .291
24. De. Martinez, Mon. .292
25. Morgan, L.A. .292
26. Boyd, Mon. .292
27. Robinson, S.F. .295
28. Heaton, Pit. .297
29. Cone, NY .299
30. Smith, Mon.-Pit. .301
31. Deshaies, Hou. .301
32. Franco, NY .301
33. Mahler, Cin. .302
34. Belcher, L.A. .302
35. B. Smith, St.L .302
36. Scott, Hou. .302
37. Harkey, Chi. .304
38. Benes, S.D. .306
39. Garrelts, S.F. .308
40. Wilson, S.F. .309
41. Leibrandt, Atl. .309
42. Browning, Cin. .309
43. Cook, Phi.-L.A. .310
44. Magrane, St.L .311
45. Patterson, Pit. .311
46. Smiley, Pit. .311
47. Burkett, S.F. .314
48. Charlton, Cin. .314
49. Gooden, NY .314
50. Jackson, Cin. .324
51. Assenmacher, Chi. .325
52. Hammaker, S.F.-S.D. .326
53. Valenzuela, L.A. .329
54. Wilson, Chi. .330
55. Portugal, Hou. .330
56. Lilliquist, Atl.-S.D. .331
57. Carman, Phi. .333
58. Schiraldi, S.D. .338
59. Combs, Phi. .339
60. Darling, NY .341
61. Rasmussen, S.D. .342
62. Castillo, Atl. .348
63. Glavine, Atl. .350
64. Parrett, Phi.-Atl. .354
65. Williams, Chi. .362
66. Ruffin, Phi. .363
67. Agosto, Hou. .364
68. Ojeda, NY .365
69. Bielecki, Chi. .377
70. Avery, Atl. .381

American League

Opponents' Batting Average, Home Games

1. Ryan, Tex. .171
2. Farr, K.C. .195
3. Johnson, Sea. .196
4. Ward, Tor. .203
5. Stewart, Oak. .214
6. Guetterman, NY .215
7. Young, Sea. .217
8. Bolton, Bos. .218
9. McDonald, Bal. .219
10. Welch, Oak. .221
11. Montgomery, K.C. .221
12. Young, Oak. .221
13. Finley, Cal. .222
14. Sanderson, Oak. .223
15. Cary, NY .225
16. McDowell, Chi. .227
17. Crawford, K.C. .228
18. Cadaret, NY .229
19. Clemens, Bos. .229
20. Hibbard, Chi. .234
21. Wells, Tor. .235
22. Gordon, K.C. .236
23. Witt, Cal.-NY .236
24. Black, Cle.-Tor. .240
25. McCaskill, Cal. .240
26. Higuera, Mil. .241
27. Gibson, Det. .241
28. Rogers, Tex. .243
29. Brown, Tex. .243
30. Robinson, Det. .243
31. Hanson, Sea. .245
32. Harnisch, Bal. .246
33. Langston, Cal. .247
34. Swift, Sea. .249
35. Knudson, Mil. .249
36. LaPoint, NY .250
37. Hough, Tex. .251
38. Perez, Chi. .252
39. King, Chi. .253
40. Berenguer, Min. .253
41. Morris, Det. .253
42. Jeffcoat, Tex. .255
43. Hawkins, NY .255
44. Appier, K.C. .255
45. Stieb, Tor. .256
46. Candiotti, Cle. .256
47. Wills, Tor. .256
48. West, Min. .258
49. Robinson, Mil. .259
50. S. Valdez, Cle. .260
51. Krueger, Mil. .264
52. Johnson, Bal. .264
53. Boddicker, Bos. .266
54. Harris, Bos. .266
55. Tapani, Min. .266
56. Petry, Det. .267
57. Guthrie, Min. .271
58. Witt, Tex. .272
59. Ballard, Bal. .272
60. Erickson, Min. .272
61. Moyer, Tex. .272
62. Moore, Oak. .273
63. S. Davis, K.C. .274
64. Leary, NY .276
65. Bosio, Mil. .276
66. Stottlemyre, Tor. .277
67. Key, Tor. .277
68. Navarro, Mil. .277
69. Anderson, Min. .279
70. Holman, Sea. .280
71. Milacki, Bal. .285
72. Swindell, Cle. .285
73. Blyleven, Cal. .286
74. Lamp, Bos. .286
75. Tanana, Det. .291
76. Smith, Min. .293
77. Cerutti, Tor. .299
78. Saberhagen, K.C. .300
79. Acker, Tor. .301
80. Kiecker, Bos. .313
81. Abbott, Cal. .316
82. Mitchell, Bal. .316

Opponents' Batting Average, Road Games

1. Stieb, Tor. .203
2. Kiecker, Bos. .206
3. Witt, Tex. .209
4. Berenguer, Min. .211
5. Ryan, Tex. .216
6. Edens, Mil. .216
7. King, Chi. .220
8. Hanson, Sea. .221
9. Hough, Tex. .222
10. Black, Cle.-Tor. .225
11. Clemens, Bos. .226
12. Bosio, Mil. .228
13. Johnson, Sea. .233
14. Perez, Chi. .233
15. Morris, Det. .233
16. Holman, Sea. .233
17. Wells, Tor. .236
18. McGaffigan, K.C. .236
19. Ward, Tor. .240
20. Leary, NY .245
21. Farr, K.C. .245
22. Boddicker, Bos. .246
23. Witt, Cal.-NY .246
24. Olin, Cle. .246
25. McCaskill, Cal. .247
26. Stewart, Oak. .249
27. Appier, K.C. .250
28. Saberhagen, K.C. .251
29. Edwards, Chi. .251
30. West, Min. .255
31. Moore, Oak. .258
32. Petry, Det. .259
33. Fernandez, Chi. .260
34. Welch, Oak. .261
35. Tapani, Min. .262
36. Harris, Bos. .263
37. Young, Sea. .265
38. Tanana, Det. .266
39. Milacki, Bal. .266
40. Brown, Tex. .266
41. Henneman, Det. .267
42. Hawkins, NY .267
43. Finley, Cal. .269
44. McDowell, Chi. .269
45. Candiotti, Cle. .271
46. Lamp, Bos. .271
47. Stottlemyre, Tor. .271
48. Abbott, Cal. .273
49. Farrell, Cle. .273
50. Langston, Cal. .273
51. Gubicza, K.C. .273
52. Drummond, Min. .274
53. Higuera, Mil. .275
54. Robinson, Det. .275
55. Harnisch, Bal. .275
56. Bolton, Bos. .276
57. Gordon, K.C. .277
58. Guthrie, Min. .281
59. Hibbard, Chi. .282
60. Sanderson, Oak. .282
61. Key, Tor. .286
62. Peterson, Chi. .286
63. Mitchell, Bal. .286
64. Swift, Sea. .288
65. Robinson, Mil. .289
66. Eichhorn, Cal. .290
67. Swindell, Cle. .292
68. S. Valdez, Cle. .292
69. Cerutti, Tor. .294
70. Johnson, Bal. .294
71. Krueger, Mil. .294
72. Anderson, Min. .302
73. Cadaret, NY .302
74. Cary, NY .305
75. Ballard, Bal. .307
76. Navarro, Mil. .308
77. Knudson, Mil. .309
78. Young, Oak. .319
79. Jeffcoat, Tex. .321
80. Blyleven, Cal. .321
81. Smith, Min. .330
82. LaPoint, NY .350

Opponents' Batting Average, Grass Surfaces

1. Ryan, Tex. .178
2. Williamson, Bal. .197
3. Stieb, Tor. .199
4. Thigpen, Chi. .202
5. Hanson, Sea. .205
6. Gleaton, Det. .206
7. McDonald, Bal. .207
8. Guetterman, NY .222
9. Jones, Chi. .222
10. Johnson, Sea. .225
11. Nunez, Det. .228
12. Perez, Chi. .229
13. Welch, Oak. .231
14. Hough, Tex. .232
15. Clemens, Bos. .232
16. Parker, NY-Det. .234
17. Fraser, Cal. .235
18. Edwards, Chi. .237
19. Stewart, Oak. .237
20. Rogers, Tex. .238
21. Morris, Det. .238
22. Robinson, NY .239
23. Finley, Cal. .240
24. Black, Cle.-Tor. .240
25. McCaskill, Cal. .241
26. King, Chi. .241
27. Stottlemyre, Tor. .243
28. Burns, Oak. .243
29. McDowell, Chi. .243
30. Hawkins, NY .244
31. Witt, Tex. .245
32. Harnisch, Bal. .247
33. Cary, NY .247
34. Bolton, Bos. .248
35. Hibbard, Chi. .248
36. Young, Oak. .249
37. Langston, Cal. .250
38. Bosio, Mil. .253
39. Wells, Tor. .253
40. Sanderson, Oak. .254
41. Brown, Tex. .254
42. Witt, Cal.-NY .254
43. Robinson, Det. .258
44. Appier, K.C. .259
45. Higuera, Mil. .259
46. Peterson, Chi. .259
47. Boddicker, Bos. .260
48. Walker, Cle. .261
49. Moore, Oak. .261
50. Cadaret, NY .262
51. Crim, Mil. .263
52. Gibson, Det. .263
53. Petry, Det. .263
54. Henneman, Det. .263
55. Candiotti, Cle. .264
56. Knudson, Mil. .265
57. Leary, NY .265
58. Olin, Cle. .266
59. Harris, Bos. .266
60. Krueger, Mil. .268
61. Searcy, Det. .270
62. Farrell, Cle. .270
63. Kiecker, Bos. .271
64. Edens, Mil. .272
65. Johnson, Bal. .274
66. S. Valdez, Cle. .276
67. Jeffcoat, Tex. .280
68. Lamp, Bos. .280
69. Milacki, Bal. .281
70. Moyer, Tex. .282
71. Navarro, Mil. .282
72. Swindell, Cle. .282
73. Young, Sea. .284
74. Robinson, Mil. .284
75. Ballard, Bal. .289
76. LaPoint, NY .290
77. Tanana, Det. .295
78. Eichhorn, Cal. .296
79. Abbott, Cal. .298
80. Blyleven, Cal. .303
81. Mitchell, Bal. .312

National League

Opponents' Batting Average, Home Games

1. Fernandez, NY .153
2. Rijo, Cin. .187
3. Akerfelds, Phi. .192
4. Wilson, S.F. .198
5. Martinez, L.A. .203
6. Gardner, Mon. .208
7. Scott, Hou. .212
8. Portugal, Hou. .213
9. Hurst, S.D. .216
10. Smoltz, Atl. .218
11. Drabek, Pit. .219
12. DeJesus, Phi. .223
13. Tudor, St.L .223
14. Mulholland, Phi. .226
15. Deshaies, Hou. .226
16. Belcher, L.A. .229
17. Boyd, Mon. .229
18. Benes, S.D. .231
19. Charlton, Cin. .232
20. De. Martinez, Mon. .234
21. Combs, Phi. .236
22. Smith, Mon.-Pit. .238
23. Whitson, S.D. .238
24. Viola, NY .241
25. Darling, NY .241
26. Darwin, Hou. .242
27. Cone, NY .243
28. Harris, S.D. .243
29. Harkey, Chi. .245
30. Jackson, Cin. .246
31. Gooden, NY .246
32. Armstrong, Cin. .247
33. Cook, Phi.-L.A. .250
34. Tewksbury, St.L. .250
35. Assenmacher, Chi. .254
36. Heaton, Pit. .254
37. Smiley, Pit. .255
38. Burkett, S.F. .256
39. Boever, Atl.-Phi. .256
40. Valenzuela, L.A. .258
41. Lilliquist, Atl.-S.D. .260
42. Schiraldi, S.D. .262
43. Leibrandt, Atl. .265
44. Garrelts, S.F. .268
45. DeLeon, St.L .269
46. Mahler, Cin. .270
47. Bielecki, Chi. .271
48. Morgan, L.A. .272
49. Gross, Mon. .273
50. B. Smith, St.L .273
51. Ojeda, NY .275
52. Magrane, St.L .276
53. Walk, Pit. .276
54. Browning, Cin. .279
55. Parrett, Phi.-Atl. .279
56. Boskie, Chi. .279
57. Avery, Atl. .281
58. Gullickson, Hou. .282
59. Wilson, Chi. .282
60. Glavine, Atl. .284
61. Howell, Phi. .284
62. Maddux, Chi. .287
63. Lancaster, Chi. .289
64. Ruffin, Phi. .290
65. Grant, S.D.-Atl. .290
66. Rasmussen, S.D. .298
67. Robinson, S.F. .312
68. Show, S.D. .315
69. Clary, Atl. .328
70. Pico, Chi. .342

Opponents' Batting Average, Road Games

1. Dibble, Cin. .168
2. DeJesus, Phi. .196
3. Harris, S.D. .198
4. Crews, L.A. .204
5. Darwin, Hou. .208
6. Cone, NY .208
7. De. Martinez, Mon. .218
8. Assenmacher, Chi. .223
9. Harkey, Chi. .224
10. DeLeon, St.L .226
11. Tudor, St.L .227
12. Hill, St.L .229
13. Charlton, Cin. .230
14. Drabek, Pit. .230
15. Wilson, Chi. .233
16. Armstrong, Cin. .237
17. Boyd, Mon. .238
18. LaCoss, S.F. .239
19. Rijo, Cin. .241
20. Martinez, L.A. .241
21. Hurst, S.D. .243
22. Viola, NY .243
23. Maddux, Chi. .245
24. Magrane, St.L .248
25. Browning, Cin. .249
26. Belcher, L.A. .251
27. Benes, S.D. .253
28. Gardner, Mon. .253
29. Smith, Mon.-Pit. .253
30. Mahler, Cin. .254
31. Leibrandt, Atl. .257
32. Fernandez, NY .258
33. Robinson, S.F. .259
34. Burkett, S.F. .259
35. Deshaies, Hou. .260
36. Morgan, L.A. .261
37. Smoltz, Atl. .263
38. Walk, Pit. .265
39. Whitson, S.D. .267
40. Mulholland, Phi. .268
41. Ojeda, NY .269
42. Gooden, NY .271
43. Reuschel, S.F. .272
44. Gross, Mon. .272
45. Heaton, Pit. .273
46. Combs, Phi. .274
47. Lancaster, Chi. .277
48. Glavine, Atl. .277
49. Garrelts, S.F. .278
50. McDowell, Phi. .280
51. Tewksbury, St.L. .282
52. Jackson, Cin. .282
53. Cook, Phi.-L.A. .283
54. Rasmussen, S.D. .286
55. Portugal, Hou. .286
56. Terrell, Pit. .289
57. Clary, Atl. .289
58. Smiley, Pit. .290
59. Darling, NY .295
60. Gullickson, Hou. .296
61. Scott, Hou. .297
62. Show, S.D. .298
63. Valenzuela, L.A. .299
64. Bielecki, Chi. .300
65. Parrett, Phi.-Atl. .303
66. Ruffin, Phi. .305
67. B. Smith, St.L .306
68. Lilliquist, Atl.-S.D. .306
69. Clancy, Hou. .306
70. Agosto, Hou. .320

Opponents' Batting Average, Grass Surfaces

1. Hartley, L.A. .161
2. Fernandez, NY .168
3. Wilson, S.F. .207
4. Downs, S.F. .210
5. Martinez, L.A. .212
6. Hurst, S.D. .218
7. Bedrosian, S.F. .220
8. Harkey, Chi. .225
9. Rijo, Cin. .230
10. Harris, S.D. .231
11. Benes, S.D. .233
12. Assenmacher, Chi. .234
13. Lefferts, S.D. .235
14. Smoltz, Atl. .236
15. Drabek, Pit. .238
16. Howell, L.A. .238
17. Whitson, S.D. .240
18. Cone, NY .243
19. Gooden, NY .245
20. DeLeon, St.L .246
21. Pena, NY .249
22. Leibrandt, Atl. .250
23. Burkett, S.F. .250
24. Belcher, L.A. .251
25. Viola, NY .251
26. Neidlinger, L.A. .252
27. Armstrong, Cin. .254
28. Gott, L.A. .254
29. Williams, Chi. .256
30. Deshaies, Hou. .257
31. Boyd, Mon. .257
32. Hammaker, S.F.-S.D. .258
33. Crews, L.A. .258
34. Brantley, S.F. .258
35. Darling, NY .259
36. P. Smith, Atl. .263
37. Gardner, Mon. .264
38. Wilson, Chi. .266
39. Garrelts, S.F. .267
40. Morgan, L.A. .268
41. Mulholland, Phi. .268
42. Ojeda, NY .268
43. LaCoss, S.F. .269
44. Schiraldi, S.D. .269
45. Valenzuela, L.A. .270
46. Franco, NY .271
47. Nunez, Chi. .273
48. Jackson, Cin. .275
49. Browning, Cin. .275
50. Scott, Hou. .276
51. Combs, Phi. .281
52. Maddux, Chi. .282
53. Boskie, Chi. .282
54. Reuschel, S.F. .283
55. Lancaster, Chi. .284
56. Smiley, Pit. .285
57. Bielecki, Chi. .288
58. Gullickson, Hou. .291
59. Avery, Atl. .291
60. Lilliquist, Atl.-S.D. .292
61. Robinson, S.F. .293
62. Grant, S.D.-Atl. .296
63. Rasmussen, S.D. .298
64. Glavine, Atl. .299
65. Show, S.D. .301
66. Portugal, Hou. .305
67. Gross, Mon. .308
68. Clary, Atl. .318
69. Pico, Chi. .330
70. Castillo, Atl. .335

American League

Opponents' Batting Average, Artificial Surfaces

1. Black, Cle.-Tor. .187
2. Witt, Cal.-NY .188
3. Farr, K.C. .192
4. Comstock, Sea. .193
5. Stewart, Oak. .195
6. Witt, Tex. .206
7. Clemens, Bos. .207
8. Johnson, Sea. .209
9. Ward, Tor. .210
10. Henke, Tor. .210
11. Tanana, Det. .213
12. Kiecker, Bos. .215
13. Jackson, Sea. .215
14. Young, Sea. .216
15. Wells, Tor. .221
16. Schooler, Sea. .223
17. Berenguer, Min. .228
18. Robinson, Mil. .228
19. Gordon, K.C. .229
20. Aquino, K.C. .230
21. Montgomery, K.C. .232
22. Aguilera, Min. .232
23. Blair, Tor. .232
24. Leary, NY .232
25. Milacki, Bal. .237
26. Higuera, Mil. .238
27. Crawford, K.C. .240
28. Harris, Sea. .241
29. M. Davis, K.C. .241
30. McDowell, Chi. .244
31. Appier, K.C. .248
32. Robinson, Det. .248
33. West, Min. .249
34. Stieb, Tor. .250
35. Swift, Sea. .251
36. Hanson, Sea. .251
37. McGaffigan, K.C. .257
38. Hough, Tex. .259
39. Brown, Tex. .260
40. Key, Tor. .261
41. Bolton, Bos. .261
42. McCaskill, Cal. .262
43. Finley, Cal. .262
44. Sanderson, Oak. .265
45. Wills, Tor. .266
46. Tapani, Min. .266
47. Holman, Sea. .266
48. Morris, Det. .270
49. Candelaria, Min.-Tor. .271
50. Leach, Min. .272
51. S. Davis, K.C. .276
52. Erickson, Min. .278
53. Swan, Sea. .280
54. Abbott, Cal. .282
55. Anderson, Min. .284
56. Fernandez, Chi. .286
57. Guthrie, Min. .286
58. Welch, Oak. .287
59. Stottlemyre, Tor. .292
60. Cadaret, NY .295
61. Gubicza, K.C. .297
62. Smith, Min. .300
63. Cerutti, Tor. .300
64. Saberhagen, K.C. .302
65. LaPoint, NY .302
66. Blyleven, Cal. .303
67. Acker, Tor. .304
68. Hibbard, Chi. .308
69. Perez, Chi. .309
70. Johnson, Bal. .310
71. Drummond, Min. .311
72. Langston, Cal. .311
73. Harnisch, Bal. .313
74. Moyer, Tex. .321
75. Farrell, Cle. .327
76. Swindell, Cle. .330
77. Navarro, Mil. .333
78. Young, Oak. .337
79. Knackert, Sea. .355
80. Knudson, Mil. .361

Opponents' Batting Average, Day Games

1. Eckersley, Oak. .148
2. Honeycutt, Oak. .190
3. Ward, Tor. .198
4. Bosio, Mil. .207
5. Higuera, Mil. .207
6. Witt, Tex. .208
7. McCullers, NY-Det. .209
8. Edens, Mil. .210
9. Clemens, Bos. .211
10. Harris, Bos. .212
11. Berenguer, Min. .212
12. Black, Cle.-Tor. .214
13. Stewart, Oak. .215
14. Tapani, Min. .218
15. Erickson, Min. .220
16. Hough, Tex. .220
17. Young, Sea. .220
18. Johnson, Sea. .221
19. Welch, Oak. .223
20. Burns, Oak. .223
21. Hanson, Sea. .224
22. Searcy, Det. .227
23. Gubicza, K.C. .230
24. Farr, K.C. .233
25. Witt, Cal.-NY .235
26. Stieb, Tor. .235
27. Sanderson, Oak. .241
28. Swift, Sea. .241
29. Bolton, Bos. .241
30. Perez, Chi. .242
31. McDowell, Chi. .244
32. M. Davis, K.C. .245
33. Morris, Det. .247
34. Holman, Sea. .248
35. Abbott, Cal. .248
36. Wells, Tor. .248
37. Candiotti, Cle. .250
38. Boddicker, Bos. .252
39. Hibbard, Chi. .254
40. Plesac, Mil. .255
41. Finley, Cal. .256
42. Cadaret, NY .256
43. Saberhagen, K.C. .257
44. Leary, NY .262
45. Young, Oak. .262
46. Milacki, Bal. .262
47. West, Min. .264
48. Gordon, K.C. .266
49. Petry, Det. .267
50. Appier, K.C. .269
51. Johnson, Bal. .269
52. Farrell, Cle. .269
53. Blair, Tor. .273
54. King, Chi. .274
55. Brown, Tex. .276
56. Stottlemyre, Tor. .277
57. Moore, Oak. .278
58. Guthrie, Min. .279
59. Tanana, Det. .279
60. LaPoint, NY .281
61. Hawkins, NY .281
62. Ballard, Bal. .281
63. Aguilera, Min. .282
64. Mirabella, Mil. .283
65. Cerutti, Tor. .285
66. Kiecker, Bos. .286
67. Swindell, Cle. .286
68. Acker, Tor. .289
69. Navarro, Mil. .289
70. Krueger, Mil. .296
71. Knudson, Mil. .297
72. Mitchell, Bal. .299
73. Eichhorn, Cal. .304
74. Langston, Cal. .305
75. Lamp, Bos. .307
76. Wills, Tor. .314
77. Anderson, Min. .316
78. Key, Tor. .322
79. Henneman, Det. .342
80. Olin, Cle. .345
81. Robinson, Mil. .360
82. Smith, Min. .366

Opponents' Batting Average, Night Games

1. Ryan, Tex. .181
2. McDonald, Bal. .203
3. Farr, K.C. .212
4. Johnson, Sea. .214
5. King, Chi. .223
6. Stieb, Tor. .227
7. Ward, Tor. .228
8. Wells, Tor. .231
9. Finley, Cal. .233
10. Hanson, Sea. .234
11. Montgomery, K.C. .235
12. Edwards, Chi. .236
13. Kiecker, Bos. .237
14. Black, Cle.-Tor. .238
15. Clemens, Bos. .238
16. Hough, Tex. .239
17. Berenguer, Min. .240
18. Morris, Det. .240
19. Perez, Chi. .241
20. Stewart, Oak. .241
21. Robinson, Det. .241
22. McDowell, Chi. .243
23. Rogers, Tex. .244
24. Witt, Cal.-NY .244
25. Young, Sea. .245
26. Witt, Tex. .245
27. Key, Tor. .245
28. Langston, Cal. .247
29. Brown, Tex. .247
30. Wills, Tor. .248
31. Appier, K.C. .250
32. Welch, Oak. .251
33. McCaskill, Cal. .252
34. West, Min. .254
35. Bolton, Bos. .254
36. Cary, NY .254
37. Hawkins, NY .255
38. Hibbard, Chi. .255
39. Gordon, K.C. .256
40. Leary, NY .256
41. Robinson, Mil. .257
42. Moore, Oak. .259
43. Boddicker, Bos. .260
44. S. Valdez, Cle. .260
45. Petry, Det. .261
46. Sanderson, Oak. .262
47. Holman, Sea. .263
48. Candiotti, Cle. .267
49. Harnisch, Bal. .268
50. Robinson, NY .268
51. Krueger, Mil. .270
52. Gibson, Det. .272
53. Stottlemyre, Tor. .273
54. Knudson, Mil. .273
55. Jeffcoat, Tex. .275
56. Guthrie, Min. .276
57. Anderson, Min. .279
58. Moyer, Tex. .279
59. Milacki, Bal. .279
60. Tanana, Det. .281
61. Harris, Bos. .281
62. Erickson, Min. .281
63. S. Davis, K.C. .281
64. Tapani, Min. .282
65. Higuera, Mil. .283
66. Swift, Sea. .284
67. Johnson, Bal. .286
68. Bosio, Mil. .287
69. Blyleven, Cal. .288
70. Swindell, Cle. .289
71. Saberhagen, K.C. .290
72. Ballard, Bal. .292
73. Farrell, Cle. .295
74. Navarro, Mil. .295
75. LaPoint, NY .296
76. Smith, Min. .299
77. Mitchell, Bal. .300
78. Cerutti, Tor. .300
79. Drummond, Min. .302
80. Abbott, Cal. .306

National League

Opponents' Batting Average, Artificial Surfaces

1. Cone, NY .180
2. Myers, Cin. .184
3. Dibble, Cin. .185
4. Carman, Phi .194
5. Akerfelds, Phi. .196
6. Rijo, Cin. .204
7. Grimsley, Phi. .207
8. Gardner, Mon. .212
9. Tudor, St.L .216
10. Viola, NY .217
11. Portugal, Hou .218
12. Darwin, Hou .221
13. Drabek, Pit. .221
14. Boyd, Mon. .221
15. Tomlin, Pit. .221
16. Agosto, Hou. .222
17. Charlton, Cin. .223
18. DeJesus, Phi .224
19. Maddux, Chi .225
20. Andersen, Hou. .225
21. De. Martinez, Mon. .227
22. Dayley, St.L .227
23. Layana, Cin. .233
24. Scott, Hou. .234
25. Armstrong, Cin. .236
26. L. Smith, St.L .237
27. Patterson, Pit. .239
28. Deshaies, Hou. .240
29. Glavine, Atl. .244
30. Mulholland, Phi. .244
31. Martinez, L.A. .245
32. DeLeon, St.L .246
33. Heaton, Pit. .248
34. Combs, Phi. .250
35. Smith, Mon.-Pit. .250
36. Hurst, S.D. .250
37. Burke, Mon. .251
38. Smoltz, Atl. .253
39. Terry, St.L. .254
40. Gross, Mon. .256
41. Mahler, Cin. .257
42. Robinson, S.F. .257
43. Cook, Phi.-L.A. .257
44. Jackson, Cin. .259
45. Ruskin, Pit.-Mon. .260
46. Morgan, L.A. .261
47. Browning, Cin. .263
48. Tewksbury, St.L. .264
49. Niedenfuer, St.L .266
50. Magrane, St.L .267
51. Smiley, Pit. .269
52. Howell, Phi. .272
53. Walk, Pit. .275
54. Landrum, Pit. .276
55. DiPino, St.L .276
56. Sampen, Mon. .277
57. Parrett, Phi.-Atl. .278
58. Whitson, S.D. .279
59. Burkett, S.F. .280
60. Ruffin, Phi. .282
61. Garrelts, S.F. .283
62. Bielecki, Chi. .286
63. Gullickson, Hou. .286
64. B. Smith, St.L .287
65. Scudder, Cin. .287
66. Gooden, NY .289
67. Hill, St.L .292
68. Valenzuela, L.A. .295
69. McDowell, Phi. .296
70. Clancy, Hou. .354

Opponents' Batting Average, Day Games

1. Smoltz, Atl. .197
2. Drabek, Pit. .198
3. Mahler, Cin. .200
4. Scudder, Cin. .202
5. Martinez, L.A. .207
6. Rijo, Cin. .219
7. Charlton, Cin. .223
8. Harkey, Chi. .223
9. Combs, Phi. .227
10. Viola, NY .230
11. Assenmacher, Chi. .231
12. Ojeda, NY .233
13. Magrane, St.L .236
14. Harris, S.D. .236
15. Brantley, S.F. .238
16. Fernandez, NY .239
17. Jackson, Cin. .245
18. Williams, Chi. .246
19. Tewksbury, St.L. .246
20. Benes, S.D. .247
21. Garrelts, S.F. .249
22. Boyd, Mon. .249
23. Hurst, S.D. .249
24. Burkett, S.F. .250
25. Cone, NY .250
26. Heaton, Pit. .252
27. Hammaker, S.F.-S.D. .256
28. DeJesus, Phi. .257
29. DeLeon, St.L .257
30. Boskie, Chi. .257
31. Cook, Phi.-L.A. .258
32. Whitson, S.D. .259
33. De. Martinez, Mon. .260
34. Deshaies, Hou. .260
35. Gullickson, Hou. .260
36. Gooden, NY .261
37. Bedrosian, S.F. .261
38. Gross, Mon. .264
39. Armstrong, Cin. .264
40. Portugal, Hou. .265
41. Mulholland, Phi. .265
42. Darwin, Hou. .266
43. Morgan, L.A. .268
44. Walk, Pit. .271
45. Leibrandt, Atl. .271
46. Crews, L.A. .271
47. Hill, St.L .273
48. Bielecki, Chi. .273
49. Carman, Phi. .275
50. Wilson, Chi. .277
51. B. Smith, St.L .278
52. Lilliquist, Atl.-S.D. .279
53. Schiraldi, S.D. .283
54. Browning, Cin. .285
55. Darling, NY .287
56. Ruffin, Phi. .287
57. Rasmussen, S.D. .288
58. Lancaster, Chi. .288
59. Smiley, Pit. .288
60. Belcher, L.A. .289
61. Scott, Hou. .292
62. Nunez, Chi. .294
63. Maddux, Chi. .305
64. Gardner, Mon. .308
65. Glavine, Atl. .309
66. Reuschel, S.F. .323
67. Robinson, S.F. .325
68. Parrett, Phi.-Atl. .327
69. Pico, Chi. .330
70. Avery, Atl. .336

Opponents' Batting Average, Night Games

1. Fernandez, NY .174
2. DeJesus, Phi. .197
3. Akerfelds, Phi. .201
4. Gardner, Mon. .202
5. Darwin, Hou. .207
6. Rijo, Cin. .210
7. Harris, S.D. .212
8. De. Martinez, Mon. .213
9. Cone, NY .216
10. Wilson, S.F. .218
11. Hurst, S.D. .220
12. Crews, L.A. .223
13. Boyd, Mon. .225
14. Martinez, L.A. .226
15. Belcher, L.A. .227
16. Scott, Hou. .227
17. Armstrong, Cin. .234
18. Charlton, Cin. .234
19. Maddux, Chi. .235
20. Drabek, Pit. .236
21. Tudor, St.L .240
22. Deshaies, Hou. .240
23. Benes, S.D. .241
24. DeLeon, St.L .242
25. Smith, Mon.-Pit. .242
26. Portugal, Hou. .242
27. Mulholland, Phi. .248
28. Smoltz, Atl. .248
29. Whitson, S.D. .248
30. Robinson, S.F. .249
31. Viola, NY .250
32. Agosto, Hou. .252
33. Sampen, Mon. .256
34. Gooden, NY .256
35. Schiraldi, S.D. .257
36. Leibrandt, Atl. .258
37. Browning, Cin. .260
38. Patterson, Pit. .262
39. Cook, Phi.-L.A. .263
40. Burkett, S.F. .265
41. Morgan, L.A. .266
42. Darling, NY .266
43. Combs, Phi. .267
44. Heaton, Pit. .268
45. Glavine, Atl. .270
46. Walk, Pit. .270
47. Smiley, Pit. .270
48. Howell, Phi. .272
49. Magrane, St.L .272
50. Valenzuela, L.A. .273
51. Gross, Mon. .276
52. Jackson, Cin. .277
53. Parrett, Phi.-Atl. .277
54. Tewksbury, St.L. .278
55. Garrelts, S.F. .284
56. Mahler, Cin. .285
57. Ojeda, NY .286
58. Lilliquist, Atl.-S.D. .286
59. Avery, Atl. .286
60. B. Smith, St.L .290
61. Terrell, Pit. .292
62. Rasmussen, S.D. .294
63. Gullickson, Hou. .296
64. Castillo, Atl. .297
65. Bielecki, Chi. .297
66. Ruffin, Phi. .301
67. Grant, S.D.-Atl. .307
68. Clary, Atl. .316
69. Show, S.D. .317
70. Clancy, Hou. .333

American League

Opponents' On-Base Average Leading Off the Inning

1. Ward, Tor. .220
2. Ryan, Tex. .230
3. Hibbard, Chi. .242
4. Tapani, Min. .243
5. Hanson, Sea. .243
6. Stieb, Tor. .245
7. Boddicker, Bos. .251
8. Candiotti, Cle. .256
9. McDowell, Chi. .258
10. Black, Cle.-Tor. .259
11. Swift, Sea. .261
12. Jeffcoat, Tex. .261
13. Lamp, Bos. .269
14. McDonald, Bal. .273
15. King, Chi. .276
16. Witt, Tex. .276
17. Appier, K.C. .277
18. Guthrie, Min. .278
19. West, Min. .282
20. Sanderson, Oak. .282
21. Finley, Cal. .285
22. Welch, Oak. .286
23. Robinson, Det. .287
24. Wells, Tor. .289
25. Navarro, Mil. .299
26. Anderson, Min. .299
27. Stewart, Oak. .300
28. Young, Sea. .301
29. Clemens, Bos. .303
30. Bolton, Bos. .304
31. Berenguer, Min. .305
32. McCaskill, Cal. .306
33. Key, Tor. .306
34. Bosio, Mil. .307
35. Cary, NY .307
36. Higuera, Mil. .309
37. Witt, Cal.-NY .311
38. Johnson, Bal. .313
39. Brown, Tex. .316
40. Harris, Bos. .318
41. Knudson, Mil. .318
42. Harnisch, Bal. .319
43. Fernandez, Chi. .322
44. Blyleven, Cal. .324
45. Holman, Sea. .327
46. Moore, Oak. .327
47. Cadaret, NY .327
48. Farr, K.C. .328
49. Robinson, Mil. .329
50. Tanana, Det. .330
51. Swindell, Cle. .333
52. Stottlemyre, Tor. .335
53. Milacki, Bal. .336
54. Acker, Tor. .337
55. Hawkins, NY .337
56. Leary, NY .338
57. Saberhagen, K.C. .338
58. S. Davis, K.C. .339
59. Langston, Cal. .339
60. S. Valdez, Cle. .340
61. Erickson, Min. .345
62. Young, Oak. .346
63. Morris, Det. .348
64. Smith, Min. .348
65. Ballard, Bal. .350
66. Hough, Tex. .351
67. Kiecker, Bos. .352
68. Krueger, Mil. .354
69. LaPoint, NY .355
70. Mitchell, Bal. .358
71. Abbott, Cal. .358
72. Perez, Chi. .366
73. Petry, Det. .369
74. Farrell, Cle. .369
75. Gordon, K.C. .373
76. Wills, Tor. .375
77. Johnson, Sea. .377
78. Peterson, Chi. .378
79. Gibson, Det. .385
80. Cerutti, Tor. .395
81. Gubicza, K.C. .412
82. Moyer, Tex. .420

Opponents' Batting Average with Runners On Base

1. Farr, K.C. .181
2. Clemens, Bos. .190
3. Ryan, Tex. .203
4. Johnson, Sea. .213
5. Montgomery, K.C. .218
6. Hough, Tex. .225
7. Finley, Cal. .227
8. Stewart, Oak. .228
9. Gordon, K.C. .229
10. Rogers, Tex. .230
11. Knudson, Mil. .233
12. Berenguer, Min. .233
13. Wells, Tor. .235
14. Welch, Oak. .236
15. Gibson, Det. .236
16. Young, Sea. .238
17. Brown, Tex. .241
18. Morris, Det. .249
19. Hanson, Sea. .251
20. Black, Cle.-Tor. .251
21. Boddicker, Bos. .251
22. Drummond, Min. .253
23. Witt, Tex. .253
24. Johnson, Bal. .255
25. Stieb, Tor. .255
26. McDowell, Chi. .258
27. King, Chi. .258
28. Witt, Cal.-NY .258
29. Henneman, Det. .259
30. Petry, Det. .259
31. Appier, K.C. .260
32. LaPoint, NY .261
33. Leary, NY .262
34. Perez, Chi. .263
35. Gubicza, K.C. .264
36. McCaskill, Cal. .265
37. Cadaret, NY .265
38. Cerutti, Tor. .271
39. Hibbard, Chi. .272
40. S. Davis, K.C. .272
41. Eichhorn, Cal. .275
42. Robinson, Mil. .275
43. Key, Tor. .276
44. Cary, NY .276
45. Sanderson, Oak. .277
46. Moore, Oak. .277
47. Langston, Cal. .277
48. Bosio, Mil. .278
49. Robinson, Det. .278
50. Hawkins, NY .279
51. Harris, Bos. .280
52. Ward, Tor. .280
53. Erickson, Min. .280
54. Stottlemyre, Tor. .280
55. Higuera, Mil. .281
56. Saberhagen, K.C. .281
57. Krueger, Mil. .281
58. Olin, Cle. .282
59. Kiecker, Bos. .284
60. Acker, Tor. .285
61. Harnisch, Bal. .288
62. Guthrie, Min. .288
63. Milacki, Bal. .288
64. Swift, Sea. .288
65. Candiotti, Cle. .291
66. Wills, Tor. .291
67. Bolton, Bos. .295
68. Holman, Sea. .295
69. Moyer, Tex. .295
70. Young, Oak. .296
71. Tanana, Det. .297
72. Abbott, Cal. .298
73. Ballard, Bal. .299
74. Navarro, Mil. .305
75. West, Min. .306
76. Anderson, Min. .307
77. Mitchell, Bal. .308
78. Tapani, Min. .321
79. Smith, Min. .322
80. Swindell, Cle. .324
81. Blyleven, Cal. .332
82. Lamp, Bos. .348

Opponents' Batting Average with Runners in Scoring Position

1. Ryan, Tex. .156
2. Farr, K.C. .157
3. Clemens, Bos. .171
4. Henneman, Det. .180
5. Johnson, Sea. .183
6. Gibson, Det. .198
7. Berenguer, Min. .204
8. Stewart, Oak. .205
9. Guetterman, NY .206
10. Appier, K.C. .208
11. Black, Cle.-Tor. .209
12. Witt, Cal.-NY .215
13. Hanson, Sea. .215
14. Montgomery, K.C. .216
15. Gubicza, K.C. .219
16. Leary, NY .225
17. Rogers, Tex. .225
18. King, Chi. .227
19. Young, Sea. .229
20. Erickson, Min. .231
21. Wells, Tor. .233
22. Hough, Tex. .236
23. Finley, Cal. .236
24. Johnson, Bal. .237
25. Petry, Det. .240
26. Gordon, K.C. .244
27. Welch, Oak. .244
28. Witt, Tex. .245
29. McDowell, Chi. .245
30. Bosio, Mil. .248
31. Eichhorn, Cal. .248
32. Sanderson, Oak. .249
33. Cadaret, NY .250
34. Drummond, Min. .250
35. Harris, Bos. .250
36. Swift, Sea. .250
37. Knudson, Mil. .252
38. Hibbard, Chi. .252
39. Stieb, Tor. .253
40. Saberhagen, K.C. .255
41. Harnisch, Bal. .256
42. Morris, Det. .256
43. Krueger, Mil. .258
44. Jackson, Sea. .260
45. Boddicker, Bos. .262
46. Robinson, Mil. .262
47. McCaskill, Cal. .264
48. Acker, Tor. .266
49. Brown, Tex. .268
50. Cerutti, Tor. .269
51. Leach, Min. .271
52. Ballard, Bal. .273
53. Milacki, Bal. .274
54. Navarro, Mil. .275
55. Holman, Sea. .277
56. Robinson, Det. .280
57. LaPoint, NY .281
58. Mitchell, Bal. .281
59. Langston, Cal. .283
60. Moore, Oak. .284
61. Kiecker, Bos. .285
62. Abbott, Cal. .286
63. Higuera, Mil. .288
64. S. Davis, K.C. .288
65. Ward, Tor. .291
66. Moyer, Tex. .294
67. Guthrie, Min. .296
68. Olin, Cle. .297
69. Perez, Chi. .297
70. West, Min. .305
71. Stottlemyre, Tor. .306
72. Tapani, Min. .313
73. Smith, Min. .313
74. Blyleven, Cal. .315
75. Candiotti, Cle. .316
76. Bolton, Bos. .317
77. Swindell, Cle. .317
78. Cary, NY .322
79. Anderson, Min. .327
80. Tanana, Det. .328
81. Lamp, Bos. .333
82. Hawkins, NY .345

National League

Opponents' On-Base Average Leading Off the Inning

1. Crews, L.A. .186
2. Gardner, Mon. .218
3. Hammaker, S.F.-S.D. .233
4. Drabek, Pit. .244
5. Tewksbury, St.L .245
6. Harkey, Chi. .247
7. Cook, Phi.-L.A. .252
8. Darwin, Hou. .252
9. Scott, Hou. .256
10. Tudor, St.L .258
11. Whitson, S.D. .259
12. Armstrong, Cin. .263
13. Smoltz, Atl. .265
14. Rijo, Cin. .267
15. De. Martinez, Mon. .268
16. Leibrandt, Atl. .274
17. Martinez, L.A. .277
18. Smith, Mon.-Pit. .279
19. B. Smith, St.L .281
20. Viola, NY .290
21. Belcher, L.A. .291
22. Robinson, S.F. .301
23. Lancaster, Chi. .301
24. Charlton, Cin. .301
25. Wilson, S.F. .304
26. Browning, Cin. .307
27. Hurst, S.D. .307
28. Boskie, Chi. .308
29. Morgan, L.A. .308
30. Benes, S.D. .310
31. Agosto, Hou. .311
32. Burkett, S.F. .311
33. Patterson, Pit. .312
34. Deshaies, Hou. .313
35. Mahler, Cin. .314
36. Jackson, Cin. .315
37. Howell, Phi. .315
38. Wilson, Chi. .317
39. Harris, S.D. .318
40. DeLeon, St.L .319
41. Darling, NY .323
42. Gullickson, Hou. .325
43. Cone, NY .326
44. Maddux, Chi. .327
45. Fernandez, NY .330
46. Walk, Pit. .331
47. Ruffin, Phi. .333
48. Valenzuela, L.A. .333
49. Glavine, Atl. .339
50. Smiley, Pit. .340
51. Garrelts, S.F. .340
52. Show, S.D. .346
53. Heaton, Pit. .346
54. Rasmussen, S.D. .349
55. Mulholland, Phi. .349
56. Magrane, St.L .352
57. Portugal, Hou. .356
58. Gooden, NY .357
59. Boyd, Mon. .359
60. Lilliquist, Atl.-S.D. .359
61. Bielecki, Chi. .361
62. Clary, Atl. .361
63. Gross, Mon. .363
64. Ojeda, NY .367
65. Combs, Phi. .369
66. DeJesus, Phi. .382
67. Sampen, Mon. .385
68. Schiraldi, S.D. .388
69. Avery, Atl. .398
70. Parrett, Phi.-Atl. .413

Opponents' Batting Average with Runners On Base

1. Akerfelds, Phi. .183
2. Boyd, Mon. .196
3. DeJesus, Phi. .203
4. Fernandez, NY .212
5. Darwin, Hou. .213
6. Assenmacher, Chi. .214
7. De. Martinez, Mon. .218
8. Tudor, St.L .222
9. Hurst, S.D. .222
10. Ojeda, NY .224
11. Martinez, L.A. .226
12. Boever, Atl.-Phi. .227
13. Harris, S.D. .230
14. Cone, NY .233
15. Viola, NY .235
16. Rijo, Cin. .237
17. Howell, Phi. .237
18. Drabek, Pit. .241
19. Benes, S.D. .242
20. Deshaies, Hou. .242
21. Harkey, Chi. .244
22. Charlton, Cin. .245
23. Scott, Hou. .246
24. Portugal, Hou. .246
25. Agosto, Hou. .247
26. Walk, Pit. .250
27. Magrane, St.L .252
28. Gooden, NY .254
29. Smoltz, Atl. .254
30. Smith, Mon.-Pit. .254
31. Jackson, Cin. .257
32. Heaton, Pit. .258
33. Schiraldi, S.D. .258
34. Whitson, S.D. .262
35. Mulholland, Phi. .262
36. Burkett, S.F. .263
37. Leibrandt, Atl. .265
38. Parrett, Phi.-Atl. .268
39. Cook, Phi.-L.A. .268
40. Browning, Cin. .269
41. DeLeon, St.L .272
42. Gross, Mon. .274
43. Darling, NY .276
44. Belcher, L.A. .276
45. Armstrong, Cin. .277
46. Garrelts, S.F. .278
47. Combs, Phi. .281
48. Gullickson, Hou. .282
49. Rasmussen, S.D. .285
50. Morgan, L.A. .286
51. Lilliquist, Atl.-S.D. .286
52. Wilson, Chi. .287
53. Bielecki, Chi. .291
54. Glavine, Atl. .293
55. Maddux, Chi. .295
56. Mahler, Cin. .295
57. Valenzuela, L.A. .296
58. Smiley, Pit. .302
59. Gardner, Mon. .311
60. Grant, S.D.-Atl. .311
61. Lancaster, Chi. .312
62. Robinson, S.F. .314
63. McDowell, Phi. .317
64. Tewksbury, St.L. .321
65. B. Smith, St.L .322
66. Show, S.D. .324
67. Avery, Atl. .330
68. Pico, Chi. .333
69. Clary, Atl. .337
70. Ruffin, Phi. .342

Opponents' Batting Average with Runners in Scoring Position

1. Boyd, Mon. .167
2. Akerfelds, Phi. .171
3. Dibble, Cin. .178
4. Cone, NY .183
5. Assenmacher, Chi. .192
6. Harris, S.D. .193
7. Darwin, Hou. .200
8. Boever, Atl.-Phi. .208
9. Benes, S.D. .208
10. De. Martinez, Mon. .209
11. Viola, NY .211
12. Mulholland, Phi. .214
13. Martinez, L.A. .218
14. Drabek, Pit. .220
15. Walk, Pit. .220
16. Fernandez, NY .220
17. Ojeda, NY .221
18. Magrane, St.L .222
19. Charlton, Cin. .222
20. Hurst, S.D. .223
21. Darling, NY .224
22. Scott, Hou. .229
23. Harkey, Chi. .234
24. Rijo, Cin. .236
25. Morgan, L.A. .237
26. Browning, Cin. .237
27. Bedrosian, S.F. .238
28. Gooden, NY .240
29. Burkett, S.F. .241
30. DeJesus, Phi. .244
31. Portugal, Hou. .248
32. Jackson, Cin. .250
33. Gullickson, Hou. .255
34. Deshaies, Hou. .256
35. Belcher, L.A. .257
36. Gross, Mon. .259
37. Armstrong, Cin. .259
38. Gardner, Mon. .260
39. Whitson, S.D. .260
40. Clary, Atl. .260
41. Parrett, Phi.-Atl. .260
42. Heaton, Pit. .262
43. Lilliquist, Atl.-S.D. .265
44. Garrelts, S.F. .266
45. Smith, Mon.-Pit. .266
46. Mahler, Cin. .270
47. Smoltz, Atl. .272
48. Glavine, Atl. .273
49. Combs, Phi. .273
50. Leibrandt, Atl. .273
51. Cook, Phi.-L.A. .274
52. Valenzuela, L.A. .276
53. Lancaster, Chi. .279
54. DeLeon, St.L .280
55. Maddux, Chi. .282
56. Rasmussen, S.D. .283
57. Schiraldi, S.D. .294
58. Bielecki, Chi. .299
59. Grant, S.D.-Atl. .306
60. B. Smith, St.L .308
61. Avery, Atl. .309
62. Robinson, S.F. .310
63. Smiley, Pit. .318
64. Wilson, Chi. .320
65. McDowell, Phi. .322
66. Show, S.D. .325
67. Tewksbury, St.L. .326
68. Pico, Chi. .339
69. Ruffin, Phi. .359

American League

Opponents' Batting Average in Pressure Situations

1. Johnson, Sea. .121
2. Hawkins, NY .123
3. Ryan, Tex. .133
4. Eckersley, Oak. .158
5. Honeycutt, Oak. .161
6. Harvey, Cal. .174
7. Welch, Oak. .176
8. Clemens, Bos. .176
9. Radinsky, Chi. .176
10. McDonald, Bal. .179
11. Hanson, Sea. .190
12. Thigpen, Chi. .192
13. Stieb, Tor. .195
14. Boddicker, Bos. .198
15. Witt, Tex. .200
16. Orosco, Cle. .206
17. McDowell, Chi. .208
18. Aguilera, Min. .211
19. Righetti, NY .212
20. Wells, Tor. .213
21. Hough, Tex. .214
22. Black, Cle.-Tor. .216
23. Schooler, Sea. .216
24. Stewart, Oak. .217
25. Olson, Bal. .218
26. Arnsberg, Tex. .218
27. Jones, Cle. .219
28. Williamson, Bal. .219
29. Guetterman, NY .223
30. Gleaton, Det. .223
31. Harris, Bos. .224
32. Reardon, Bos. .225
33. Crim, Mil. .227
34. Ward, Tor. .233
35. Tanana, Det. .234
36. Eichhorn, Cal. .236
37. Jones, Chi. .236
38. Henke, Tor. .236
39. Montgomery, K.C. .243
40. Hibbard, Chi. .244
41. Rogers, Tex. .245
42. Gray, Bos. .245
43. Henneman, Det. .246
44. Higuera, Mil. .246
45. Farr, K.C. .248
46. Jackson, Sea. .248
47. Berenguer, Min. .252
48. Burns, Oak. .254
49. Robinson, NY .254
50. Nunez, Det. .254
51. Wills, Tor. .258
52. Cadaret, NY .259
53. Jeffcoat, Tex. .259
54. Nelson, Oak. .261
55. Harnisch, Bal. .262
56. Abbott, Cal. .262
57. Candelaria, Min.-Tor. .262
58. Brown, Tex. .266
59. Gibson, Det. .267
60. Finley, Cal. .271
61. Witt, Cal.-NY .273
62. Swift, Sea. .279
63. Bolton, Bos. .283
64. Fraser, Cal. .292
65. Pall, Chi. .295
66. M. Davis, K.C. .296
67. Plesac, Mil. .298
68. Anderson, Min. .300
69. Candiotti, Cle. .300
70. Lamp, Bos. .303
71. Holman, Sea. .304
72. Crawford, K.C. .308
73. Je. Russell, Tex. .316
74. Morris, Det. .318
75. Young, Sea. .322
76. Comstock, Sea. .328
77. Acker, Tor. .333
78. Leach, Min. .333
79. Plunk, NY .333
80. Murphy, Bos. .339
81. Navarro, Mil. .404

Opponents' Batting Average with Two Outs and Runners On Base

1. Kiecker, Bos. .146
2. Gibson, Det. .156
3. Ryan, Tex. .162
4. Henneman, Det. .167
5. Clemens, Bos. .170
6. Cadaret, NY .180
7. Black, Cle.-Tor. .181
8. Hanson, Sea. .187
9. Nunez, Det. .188
10. Rogers, Tex. .196
11. Guthrie, Min. .198
12. Farr, K.C. .198
13. Holman, Sea. .200
14. Johnson, Bal. .204
15. Finley, Cal. .210
16. Stewart, Oak. .211
17. Berenguer, Min. .213
18. Robinson, Det. .213
19. Harris, Bos. .214
20. Cary, NY .215
21. Morris, Det. .217
22. Johnson, Sea. .217
23. Guetterman, NY .219
24. LaPoint, NY .220
25. McDowell, Chi. .221
26. Boddicker, Bos. .223
27. S. Davis, K.C. .225
28. Witt, Tex. .228
29. Hough, Tex. .228
30. Stieb, Tor. .230
31. Acker, Tor. .240
32. Krueger, Mil. .242
33. Knudson, Mil. .244
34. Perez, Chi. .246
35. Moore, Oak. .246
36. Young, Sea. .246
37. Montgomery, K.C. .247
38. Robinson, Mil. .248
39. Leary, NY .248
40. Stottlemyre, Tor. .248
41. King, Chi. .250
42. Leach, Min. .250
43. McCaskill, Cal. .252
44. Petry, Det. .255
45. Harnisch, Bal. .256
46. Gordon, K.C. .256
47. Edens, Mil. .257
48. Swift, Sea. .258
49. Saberhagen, K.C. .258
50. Sanderson, Oak. .259
51. Hibbard, Chi. .260
52. Welch, Oak. .260
53. M. Davis, K.C. .261
54. Appier, K.C. .262
55. Bolton, Bos. .264
56. Abbott, Cal. .267
57. Higuera, Mil. .269
58. Wells, Tor. .270
59. Brown, Tex. .277
60. Milacki, Bal. .281
61. Key, Tor. .283
62. Navarro, Mil. .283
63. Langston, Cal. .284
64. Cerutti, Tor. .286
65. Anderson, Min. .294
66. Erickson, Min. .294
67. Swindell, Cle. .295
68. Candiotti, Cle. .304
69. Eichhorn, Cal. .306
70. Ballard, Bal. .310
71. S. Valdez, Cle. .320
72. Hawkins, NY .323
73. Tapani, Min. .323
74. Bosio, Mil. .326
75. Blyleven, Cal. .329
76. Tanana, Det. .336
77. Mitchell, Bal. .338
78. West, Min. .340
79. Smith, Min. .351
80. Jeffcoat, Tex. .355
81. Lamp, Bos. .396

Opponents' Batting Average with Two Outs and Runners in Scoring Position

1. Henneman, Det. .100
2. Cadaret, NY .121
3. Kiecker, Bos. .143
4. Gibson, Det. .145
5. Black, Cle.-Tor. .155
6. Ryan, Tex. .159
7. Berenguer, Min. .167
8. Hanson, Sea. .167
9. Harris, Bos. .167
10. Johnson, Bal. .167
11. Clemens, Bos. .170
12. Farr, K.C. .172
13. Nunez, Det. .176
14. Holman, Sea. .182
15. Johnson, Sea. .186
16. Stewart, Oak. .187
17. Robinson, Det. .193
18. Jackson, Sea. .196
19. Finley, Cal. .200
20. Wells, Tor. .203
21. Rogers, Tex. .205
22. Morris, Det. .210
23. Sanderson, Oak. .212
24. Guthrie, Min. .213
25. Stieb, Tor. .220
26. Harnisch, Bal. .221
27. McDowell, Chi. .221
28. Krueger, Mil. .222
29. Robinson, NY .222
30. Abbott, Cal. .229
31. Robinson, Mil. .230
32. Hibbard, Chi. .230
33. M. Davis, K.C. .231
34. LaPoint, NY .232
35. King, Chi. .232
36. Leach, Min. .236
37. Stottlemyre, Tor. .238
38. Boddicker, Bos. .239
39. Crawford, K.C. .239
40. Erickson, Min. .239
41. Olin, Cle. .240
42. Guetterman, NY .241
43. Witt, Tex. .243
44. Hough, Tex. .245
45. Appier, K.C. .247
46. Leary, NY .250
47. Young, Sea. .250
48. Acker, Tor. .255
49. Bolton, Bos. .255
50. McCaskill, Cal. .257
51. Swift, Sea. .258
52. Moore, Oak. .261
53. Navarro, Mil. .264
54. Milacki, Bal. .264
55. Perez, Chi. .265
56. Knudson, Mil. .270
57. Petry, Det. .270
58. Gubicza, K.C. .271
59. Montgomery, K.C. .275
60. Moyer, Tex. .275
61. Plunk, NY .277
62. Anderson, Min. .278
63. Gordon, K.C. .280
64. Higuera, Mil. .281
65. Welch, Oak. .290
66. Bosio, Mil. .298
67. Eichhorn, Cal. .300
68. Key, Tor. .302
69. Tapani, Min. .306
70. Mitchell, Bal. .309
71. Brown, Tex. .312
72. Cary, NY .314
73. Ballard, Bal. .317
74. Swindell, Cle. .317
75. Candiotti, Cle. .333
76. Tanana, Det. .333
77. Langston, Cal. .337
78. Hawkins, NY .339
79. Smith, Min. .343
80. Blyleven, Cal. .351
81. West, Min. .365
82. Lamp, Bos. .405

National League

Opponents' Batting Average in Pressure Situations

1. Deshaies, Hou. .132
2. Carman, Phi .137
3. Wilson, S.F. .140
4. Akerfelds, Phi. .150
5. Scott, Hou. .153
6. Drabek, Pit .162
7. Gott, L.A. .175
8. Myers, Cin. .176
9. Ojeda, NY .190
10. Frey, Mon. .200
11. Gooden, NY .200
12. Viola, NY .200
13. Charlton, Cin. .206
14. Sampen, Mon. .211
15. Smith, Mon.-Pit. .213
16. Smith, Hou. .213
17. Pena, NY .213
18. Belinda, Pit. .214
19. Martinez, L.A. .214
20. Boever, Atl.-Phi. .218
21. Leibrandt, Atl. .220
22. Dibble, Cin. .224
23. Smoltz, Atl. .225
24. Patterson, Pit. .225
25. Cone, NY .226
26. Valenzuela, L.A. .226
27. Williams, Chi. .226
28. Harris, S.D. .227
29. Thurmond, S.F. .229
30. Bedrosian, S.F. .232
31. Burke, Mon. .233
32. Assenmacher, Chi. .235
33. Power, Pit. .239
34. Long, Chi. .240
35. Andersen, Hou. .241
36. Mercker, Atl. .241
37. L. Smith, St.L .242
38. Darwin, Hou .243
39. Brantley, S.F. .246
40. Franco, NY .246
41. Lefferts, S.D. .247
42. Meyer, Hou. .255
43. Hall, Mon. .263
44. Agosto, Hou. .268
45. Howell, L.A. .268
46. Hammaker, S.F.-S.D. .271
47. Harkey, Chi. .271
48. Dayley, St.L .272
49. Garrelts, S.F. .273
50. Crews, L.A. .275
51. Robinson, S.F. .276
52. Landrum, Pit. .282
53. Morgan, L.A. .282
54. Browning, Cin. .283
55. Schiraldi, S.D. .289
56. Hurst, S.D. .290
57. Lancaster, Chi. .297
58. De. Martinez, Mon. .299
59. Maddux, Chi. .309
60. Ruskin, Pit.-Mon. .309
61. Whitson, S.D. .313
62. Niedenfuer, St.L .314
63. Burkett, S.F. .317
64. Parrett, Phi.-Atl. .320
65. Wilson, Chi. .321
66. Kerfeld, Hou.-Atl. .327
67. Schmidt, Mon. .331
68. McDowell, Phi. .332
69. Magrane, St.L .352
70. Glavine, Atl. .411

Opponents' Batting Average with Two Outs and Runners on Base

1. Boyd, Mon. .159
2. Magrane, St.L .164
3. Fernandez, NY .168
4. Assenmacher, Chi. .169
5. Deshaies, Hou. .174
6. Viola, NY .181
7. Darling, NY .181
8. Tudor, St.L .185
9. DeJesus, Phi. .189
10. Crews, L.A. .192
11. Darwin, Hou. .192
12. Gross, Mon. .194
13. Portugal, Hou. .195
14. Drabek, Pit. .197
15. Gooden, NY .200
16. DeLeon, St.L .202
17. Lilliquist, Atl.-S.D. .202
18. Myers, Cin. .206
19. Benes, S.D. .208
20. Cook, Phi.-L.A. .209
21. Harkey, Chi. .210
22. Belcher, L.A. .210
23. Martinez, L.A. .215
24. Rijo, Cin. .216
25. Smith, Mon.-Pit. .217
26. Harris, S.D. .218
27. Cone, NY .225
28. Ojeda, NY .229
29. Brantley, S.F. .231
30. De. Martinez, Mon. .234
31. Howell, Phi. .240
32. Mulholland, Phi. .241
33. Bielecki, Chi. .242
34. Armstrong, Cin. .245
35. Boever, Atl.-Phi. .250
36. Charlton, Cin. .250
37. Morgan, L.A. .255
38. Rasmussen, S.D. .256
39. Combs, Phi. .256
40. Gullickson, Hou. .258
41. Whitson, S.D. .259
42. Browning, Cin. .260
43. Scott, Hou. .263
44. Hurst, S.D. .266
45. Tewksbury, St.L. .267
46. Walk, Pit. .267
47. Garrelts, S.F. .268
48. Smiley, Pit. .268
49. Pico, Chi. .269
50. Show, S.D. .269
51. Valenzuela, L.A. .273
52. Smoltz, Atl. .274
53. Leibrandt, Atl. .274
54. Burkett, S.F. .276
55. Glavine, Atl. .277
56. B. Smith, St.L .284
57. Avery, Atl. .286
58. Maddux, Chi. .290
59. Clary, Atl. .291
60. Mahler, Cin. .291
61. Parrett, Phi.-Atl. .295
62. Williams, Chi. .301
63. Schiraldi, S.D. .303
64. Wilson, Chi. .304
65. Lancaster, Chi. .305
66. Gardner, Mon. .306
67. Grant, S.D.-Atl. .310
68. Heaton, Pit. .310
69. Robinson, S.F. .315
70. Ruffin, Phi. .362

Opponents' Batting Average with Two Outs and Runners in Scoring Position

1. Darling, NY .125
2. Fernandez, NY .140
3. Boyd, Mon. .143
4. Magrane, St.L .143
5. Assenmacher, Chi. .154
6. Brantley, S.F. .167
7. Benes, S.D. .173
8. Portugal, Hou. .178
9. Morgan, L.A. .180
10. Harris, S.D. .180
11. Deshaies, Hou. .181
12. Gross, Mon. .182
13. Akerfelds, Phi. .184
14. Viola, NY .184
15. Drabek, Pit. .185
16. Darwin, Hou. .186
17. Smith, Mon.-Pit. .186
18. Harkey, Chi. .188
19. Martinez, L.A. .195
20. Cone, NY .200
21. Gooden, NY .205
22. DeLeon, St.L .211
23. Mulholland, Phi. .211
24. Valenzuela, L.A. .212
25. Boever, Atl.-Phi. .216
26. DeJesus, Phi. .216
27. Cook, Phi.-L.A. .218
28. Browning, Cin. .222
29. Lancaster, Chi. .226
30. Garrelts, S.F. .226
31. Ruskin, Pit.-Mon. .229
32. Lilliquist, Atl.-S.D. .231
33. Scott, Hou. .231
34. Rasmussen, S.D. .233
35. De. Martinez, Mon. .237
36. B. Smith, St.L .238
37. Rijo, Cin. .241
38. Clary, Atl. .242
39. Carman, Phi. .244
40. Armstrong, Cin. .250
41. Smiley, Pit. .250
42. Gullickson, Hou. .253
43. Bielecki, Chi. .256
44. Burkett, S.F. .260
45. Gardner, Mon. .262
46. Charlton, Cin. .269
47. Combs, Phi. .272
48. Hurst, S.D. .272
49. Walk, Pit. .274
50. Pico, Chi. .275
51. Whitson, S.D. .277
52. Avery, Atl. .281
53. Layana, Cin. .283
54. Mahler, Cin. .283
55. Grant, S.D.-Atl. .286
56. Tewksbury, St.L. .286
57. Show, S.D. .291
58. Glavine, Atl. .294
59. Leibrandt, Atl. .296
60. Smoltz, Atl. .297
61. Robinson, S.F. .316
62. Wilson, Chi. .317
63. Maddux, Chi. .324
64. Williams, Chi. .327
65. Parrett, Phi.-Atl. .328
66. Heaton, Pit. .333
67. Schiraldi, S.D. .339
68. Ruffin, Phi. .370

SINGLE SEASON AND CAREER LEADERS

The Single Season and Career Leaders section lists, for a variety of batting and pitching categories, the top 25 performers since we began *The Player Analysis* in 1975.

When we began our analysis of play-by-play data from every game, we had a dual purpose: We recognized the value of the information for immediate use, and we knew that we were accumulating and building a valuable resource for future study. This section is our annual chance to take stock of the results from those files, representing nearly two and a half million plate appearances.

The categories for this section were chosen both for significance and for general interest, however quirky. The single season bests provide an important context for evaluating the performances listed throughout this book. The career lists do considerably more: They provide the definitive look at situational statistics since 1975.

Minimum qualifiers for most batting categories are expressed in hits rather than in the equivalent number of plate appearances. This avoids penalizing those exceptional hitters whose performances would rank among the leaders even if all the at-bats between their current level and the qualifying level resulted in outs. In general, the hits qualifier is about one-third of the equivalent at-bats qualifier, if you're more comfortable with that as a measure.

In the pitching categories, it should not be too surprising that relievers dominate. They allow consistently lower batting averages than starters for a variety of reasons, not only in traditional statistics but in these situational statistics as well. We have tried to set qualifying levels that are meaningful for both starters and relievers; the levels are the equivalent of about one and a half seasons as a full-time starter, or three as a primary reliever.

In a few categories, several pitchers are tied with a rate of 0.00 (for example, lowest career walk percentage with bases loaded, on page 408). For these pitchers, we have also listed the number of batters faced in the situation. (In the example category, Steve Crawford's 0/85 indicates that he has not issued a walk to any of the 85 batters he's faced with the bases loaded.)

Bear in mind that *The Player Analysis* began in 1975. For the vast majority of active players, this poses no obstacle to calling these "career" statistics; in the case of George Brett, for example, we are missing fewer than 500 of his more than 8500 career at-bats. For retired players, however, this is more of a problem. We are obviously missing a substantial portion of the careers of Rod Carew and Johnny Bench, to name players listed in the first two categories. We'd love to be able to fill in the gaps; for now, we take comfort in the significance of what is included without dwelling too harshly on what isn't.

Career Batting Average vs. Left-Handed Pitchers
Min. 150 Hits

Kirby Puckett	.334
Tracy Jones	.318
Bob Watson	.318
Pat Tabler	.317
Julio Franco	.316
Jim Rice	.313
Barry Larkin	.312
Paul Molitor	.311
Tony Gwynn	.311
Rod Carew	.310
Mariano Duncan	.310
Rickey Henderson	.309
Don Mattingly	.309
Ron LeFlore	.309
Wade Boggs	.308
Ellis Burks	.308
Gene Larkin	.308
Ellis Valentine	.307
John Castino	.307
Hal McRae	.305
Bill Madlock	.305
Gary Matthews	.305
Will Clark	.305
Pedro Guerrero	.305
Carney Lansford	.304

Career Slugging Average vs. Left-Handed Pitchers
Min. 200 Total Bases

Cecil Fielder	.603
Jose Canseco	.578
Mike Schmidt	.573
Ellis Valentine	.562
Eric Davis	.558
Kevin Mitchell	.547
Rob Deer	.539
Jack Clark	.539
Dave Winfield	.535
Mark McGwire	.533
Johnny Bench	.531
George Foster	.530
Pete Incaviglia	.526
Jim Rice	.524
Ron Cey	.523
Dwight Evans	.521
Danny Tartabull	.521
Dale Murphy	.520
Cliff Johnson	.518
Dave Kingman	.518
Bill Robinson	.513
George Bell	.512
Andre Dawson	.512
Glenn Davis	.511
Hal McRae	.511

Career Home Run Pct. vs. Left-Handed Pitchers
Min. 20 Home Runs

Cecil Fielder	8.72
Rob Deer	7.61
Dave Kingman	7.58
Mark McGwire	7.41
Eric Davis	7.40
Jose Canseco	7.14
Matt Williams	7.03
Ron Kittle	6.86
Mike Schmidt	6.74
Ron Cey	6.56
Glenn Davis	6.49
Bill Schroeder	6.42
Steve Balboni	6.12
Gorman Thomas	6.12
Pete Incaviglia	6.11
Mike Diaz	6.10
Ellis Valentine	6.07
Bo Jackson	6.06
Kevin Mitchell	6.03
Johnny Bench	6.03
George Foster	5.93
Gene Tenace	5.90
John Wockenfuss	5.85
Dale Murphy	5.75
Jack Clark	5.59

Career Strikeout Pct. vs. Left-Handed Pitchers
Min. 500 PA

Ted Sizemore	2.90
Dave Cash	3.05
Tim Foli	3.08
Marty Barrett	3.22
Bob Bailor	3.41
Manny Sanguillen	3.48
Felix Millan	3.49
Barry Larkin	3.98
Doug Flynn	4.69
Rennie Stennett	4.72
Rich Dauer	4.96
Bob Boone	5.07
Bucky Dent	5.09
Pete Rose	5.21
Don Kessinger	5.30
Bill Russell	5.34
Mario Guerrero	5.46
Rob Andrews	5.48
Jerry Terrell	5.54
Steve Nicosia	5.71
Mickey Hatcher	5.72
Willie Randolph	5.73
Tony Gwynn	5.79
Bill Buckner	5.84
Bruce Benedict	5.95

Career Batting Average vs. Right-Handed Pitchers
Min. 250 Hits

Wade Boggs	.364
Rod Carew	.341
Tony Gwynn	.339
George Brett	.328
Al Oliver	.326
Lyman Bostock	.325
Mike Greenwell	.324
Don Mattingly	.322
Kal Daniels	.320
Mark Grace	.315
Kirby Puckett	.315
Dave Magadan	.314
Luis Polonia	.311
John Kruk	.308
Mike Easler	.307
Thurman Munson	.306
Bake McBride	.306
Cecil Cooper	.305
Pedro Guerrero	.305
Mickey Rivers	.305
Jerry Mumphrey	.303
Jose Cruz	.303
Bill Madlock	.302
Ken Griffey Sr.	.302
Willie McGee	.301

Career Slugging Average vs. Right-Handed Pitchers
Min. 300 Total Bases

Fred McGriff	.593
Kal Daniels	.572
Darryl Strawberry	.561
George Brett	.543
Reggie Smith	.539
Willie Stargell	.532
Mike Greenwell	.529
Kent Hrbek	.525
Mike Schmidt	.523
Will Clark	.522
Fred Lynn	.517
Don Mattingly	.515
Eddie Murray	.505
Eric Davis	.504
Reggie Jackson	.503
Mark McGwire	.503
Wade Boggs	.503
Kevin Mitchell	.500
Oscar Gamble	.498
Leon Durham	.497
Bob Horner	.497
Alvin Davis	.496
Cecil Cooper	.496
Jim Rice	.496
Bobby Bonilla	.495

Career Home Run Pct. vs. Right-Handed Pitchers
Min. 40 Home Runs

Fred McGriff	7.82
Mark McGwire	7.09
Ken Phelps	7.05
Darryl Strawberry	7.01
Mike Schmidt	6.66
Dave Kingman	6.35
Ron Kittle	6.31
Willie Stargell	6.19
Reggie Jackson	6.10
Reggie Smith	5.99
Eric Davis	5.98
Jose Canseco	5.89
Bo Jackson	5.88
Bob Horner	5.87
Gorman Thomas	5.80
Kal Daniels	5.77
Oscar Gamble	5.67
Steve Balboni	5.62
Dan Pasqua	5.59
Kevin Mitchell	5.48
Kent Hrbek	5.39
Tony Armas	5.33
Graig Nettles	5.32
Jason Thompson	5.29
Rob Deer	5.11

Career Strikeout Pct. vs. Right-Handed Pitchers
Min. 750 PA

Felix Millan	3.29
Bill Buckner	3.97
Dave Cash	4.30
Tony Gwynn	4.53
Don Mattingly	4.91
Larry Bowa	5.04
Jack Brohamer	5.17
Mike Squires	5.17
Greg Gross	5.22
Rich Dauer	5.31
Johnny Ray	5.33
Ken Oberkfell	5.35
Al Oliver	5.37
Scott Bradley	5.37
Mike Scioscia	5.37
Ozzie Smith	5.39
Rusty Staub	5.40
Wade Boggs	5.41
Tom Poquette	5.72
Pete Rose	5.83
Dan Meyer	5.95
Bob Bailor	5.98
Duane Kuiper	5.99
Mario Guerrero	6.01
Terry Francona	6.06

Single-Season Batting Average vs. Left-Handed Pitchers
Min. 40 Hits

Rennie Stennett, 1977	.435
Sixto Lezcano, 1979	.411
Mariano Duncan, 1990	.410
Kirby Puckett, 1988	.398
Tim Raines, 1987	.396
Steve Henderson, 1979	.395
Mike Vail, 1979	.395
Ken Griffey Sr., 1976	.393
Gerald Young, 1987	.390
Carney Lansford, 1989	.389
Bill Buckner, 1978	.389
Paul Molitor, 1979	.387
Brian Downing, 1979	.386
Andres Galarraga, 1989	.385
Chet Lemon, 1984	.384
Julio Franco, 1988	.383
Alvaro Espinoza, 1989	.383
Keith Moreland, 1983	.382
Buddy Bell, 1977	.382
Steve Sax, 1989	.381
Rico Carty, 1975	.381
Don Baylor, 1975	.380
Jack Clark, 1980	.380
Jeffrey Leonard, 1984	.380
Jose Cardenal, 1975	.379

Single-Season Batting Average vs. Right-Handed Pitchers
Min. 75 Hits

George Brett, 1980	.437
Wade Boggs, 1983	.398
Rod Carew, 1977	.398
Wade Boggs, 1988	.381
Rod Carew, 1975	.379
Hal Morris, 1990	.378
Wade Boggs, 1985	.377
Wade Boggs, 1987	.377
Tony Gwynn, 1987	.376
Tony Gwynn, 1984	.371
Dave Magadan, 1990	.371
Oscar Gamble, 1979	.370
Kal Daniels, 1987	.370
Cecil Cooper, 1980	.365
Fred Lynn, 1979	.364
Paul Molitor, 1987	.363
Willie Wilson, 1982	.360
Wade Boggs, 1986	.359
Rod Carew, 1983	.358
Bill Madlock, 1975	.357
Mike Easler, 1980	.357
Wade Boggs, 1982	.356
Wade Boggs, 1984	.356
Willie McGee, 1985	.356
Rod Carew, 1982	.355

Single-Season Batting Average in Home Games
Min. 75 Hits

Wade Boggs, 1985	.418
Wade Boggs, 1987	.411
Kirby Puckett, 1988	.406
Rod Carew, 1977	.401
Juan Beniquez, 1984	.399
Wade Boggs, 1983	.397
Paul Molitor, 1987	.394
George Brett, 1980	.391
Kirby Puckett, 1989	.390
Tony Gwynn, 1987	.390
Rod Carew, 1975	.387
Fred Lynn, 1979	.386
Al Oliver, 1980	.385
Wade Boggs, 1988	.382
Hal McRae, 1976	.382
Miguel Dilone, 1980	.378
Wade Boggs, 1989	.377
Tony Gwynn, 1984	.376
Dion James, 1987	.376
Mike Easler, 1984	.375
George Brett, 1979	.373
Bill Buckner, 1977	.372
Jim Rice, 1979	.369
Fred Lynn, 1975	.368
George Brett, 1985	.368

Single-Season Batting Average in Road Games
Min. 75 Hits

George Brett, 1980	.388
Cecil Cooper, 1980	.386
Rod Carew, 1977	.374
Dave Magadan, 1990	.372
Johnny Ray, 1984	.370
Rod Carew, 1983	.369
Don Mattingly, 1986	.367
Don Mattingly, 1984	.364
Kirby Puckett, 1987	.362
Carney Lansford, 1989	.360
Brian Downing, 1979	.360
Bob Watson, 1975	.358
Mickey Rivers, 1977	.358
Bill Madlock, 1975	.357
Wade Boggs, 1986	.356
Ken Singleton, 1977	.354
Ben Oglivie, 1980	.353
Willie McGee, 1985	.353
Pedro Guerrero, 1987	.352
Tony Gwynn, 1987	.352
Steve Sax, 1986	.352
Wade Boggs, 1988	.351
Keith Hernandez, 1979	.350
Rafael Palmeiro, 1990	.350
Dion James, 1989	.349

Career Home Run Pct. in Home Games
Min. 25 Home Runs

Cecil Fielder	8.53
Ken Phelps	7.51
Bob Horner	7.47
Mike Schmidt	6.66
Darryl Strawberry	6.57
Dave Kingman	6.52
Eric Davis	6.44
Matt Williams	6.40
Oscar Gamble	6.31
Willie Stargell	6.26
Greg Luzinski	6.25
Ron Kittle	6.24
Fred McGriff	6.15
Jose Canseco	6.07
Rob Deer	5.95
Gorman Thomas	5.87
Reggie Jackson	5.80
Dale Murphy	5.77
Mark McGwire	5.74
George Foster	5.71
Pete Incaviglia	5.70
Rick Monday	5.48
Gary Alexander	5.46
Bo Jackson	5.38
Jesse Barfield	5.38

Career Home Run Pct. in Road Games
Min. 25 Home Runs

Mark McGwire	8.52
Dave Kingman	6.90
Ron Kittle	6.83
Cecil Fielder	6.78
Mike Schmidt	6.69
Fred McGriff	6.69
Steve Balboni	6.49
Eric Davis	6.46
Bo Jackson	6.46
Jose Canseco	6.40
Darryl Strawberry	6.35
Glenn Davis	6.24
Bill Schroeder	6.15
Kevin Mitchell	6.08
Gorman Thomas	5.93
Rob Deer	5.78
Ken Phelps	5.73
Reggie Jackson	5.51
Jack Clark	5.43
Willie Stargell	5.35
Franklin Stubbs	5.30
Willie Aikens	5.29
Cory Snyder	5.25
Tony Armas	5.11
Pedro Guerrero	5.09

Career Batting Average in Home Games
Min. 200 Hits

Wade Boggs	.380
Kirby Puckett	.352
Tony Gwynn	.334
Rod Carew	.334
George Brett	.331
Al Oliver	.326
Luis Polonia	.325
Kevin Seitzer	.325
Mike Greenwell	.325
Mark Grace	.322
Jim Rice	.320
Julio Franco	.319
Lyman Bostock	.318
Don Mattingly	.317
Will Clark	.316
Paul Molitor	.312
Thurman Munson	.311
Dave Magadan	.310
Ellis Burks	.309
Ryne Sandberg	.309
Mike Easler	.308
Lonnie Smith	.307
Lou Brock	.306
Dave Parker	.306
Hal McRae	.306

Career Batting Average in Road Games
Min. 200 Hits

Rod Carew	.328
Tony Gwynn	.324
Don Mattingly	.317
Wade Boggs	.313
Pedro Guerrero	.309
Mickey Rivers	.308
Rafael Palmeiro	.307
Lyman Bostock	.305
Bob Watson	.305
Manny Sanguillen	.303
Mike Greenwell	.302
Cecil Cooper	.301
Bill Madlock	.301
Dave Magadan	.299
Barry Larkin	.299
Tim Raines	.298
Wally Joyner	.298
Thurman Munson	.297
Gene Richards	.297
George Brett	.297
Kal Daniels	.297
Rickey Henderson	.297
Ken Singleton	.296
Ken Griffey Sr.	.296
Dave Winfield	.295

Career Batting Average vs. Ground-Ball Pitchers
Min. 200 Hits

Wade Boggs .362
Tony Gwynn .331
Mike Greenwell .326
George Brett .325
Don Mattingly .324

Al Oliver .321
Lonnie Smith .320
Rod Carew .317
Lyman Bostock .317
Kirby Puckett .315

Reggie Smith .315
Kal Daniels .314
Cecil Cooper .314
Hal McRae .311
Bob Watson .309

Ron LeFlore .309
Pedro Guerrero .308
Jim Rice .307
Lee Lacy .307
Kevin Seitzer .307

Jerry Browne .306
Alvin Davis .305
Tim Raines .305
Harold Baines .304
Keith Hernandez .304

Career Slugging Average vs. Ground-Ball Pitchers
Min. 300 Total Bases

Fred McGriff .560
Mike Schmidt .547
Reggie Smith .539
Kal Daniels .526
Mark McGwire .517

Bo Jackson .517
George Brett .516
Jose Canseco .513
Eric Davis .513
Kevin Mitchell .512

Willie Stargell .511
Bobby Bonds .504
Darryl Strawberry .503
Ken Phelps .502
Mike Greenwell .501

Fred Lynn .500
Cecil Cooper .500
Reggie Jackson .498
Don Mattingly .498
Bob Horner .496

Jim Rice .495
Kent Hrbek .493
Greg Luzinski .491
Larry Hisle .489
Leon Durham .489

Single-Season Batting Average vs. Ground-Ball Pitchers
Min. 60 Hits

Wade Boggs, 1985 .394
Hal McRae, 1976 .391
Hubie Brooks, 1986 .390
Keith Hernandez, 1979 .389
Rod Carew, 1975 .386

Wade Boggs, 1990 .385
Wade Boggs, 1983 .383
Al Oliver, 1978 .382
Ron LeFlore, 1976 .381
Don Mattingly, 1986 .379

Wade Boggs, 1987 .378
Mike Hargrove, 1977 .376
George Brett, 1985 .376
George Brett, 1980 .372
Robin Yount, 1987 .371

Don Mattingly, 1984 .369
George Brett, 1990 .369
Tony Gwynn, 1984 .369
Cecil Cooper, 1982 .369
Mickey Rivers, 1976 .365

Cecil Cooper, 1980 .365
Bill Madlock, 1975 .365
Bill Madlock, 1976 .365
Bill Buckner, 1980 .364
Dwight Smith, 1989 .364

Single-Season Slugging Average vs. Ground-Ball Pitchers
Min. 100 Total Bases

Mike Schmidt, 1981 .739
Mark McGwire, 1987 .690
George Bell, 1987 672
Brian Downing, 1983 .647
Mike Greenwell, 1987 .647

Ron Gant, 1990 .647
Howard Johnson, 1989 .641
David Justice, 1990 .634
Dave Kingman, 1979 .634
George Brett, 1985 .633

Mike Schmidt, 1977 .629
Cecil Cooper, 1982 .627
Barry Bonds, 1990 .625
Hubie Brooks, 1986 .622
Greg Luzinski, 1977 .622

Andres Galarraga, 1988 .621
Reggie Jackson, 1977 .618
Dwight Evans, 1987 .616
Ben Oglivie, 1980 .615
Frank White, 1986 .613

Dave Winfield, 1982 .608
Don Mattingly, 1986 .608
George Brett, 1983 .607
Ken Phelps, 1987 .606
Richie Zisk, 1977 .605

Career Batting Average vs. Fly-Ball Pitchers
Min. 200 Hits

Rod Carew .342
Wade Boggs .335
Tony Gwynn .327
Kirby Puckett .324
Luis Polonia .322

Dave Magadan .320
Thurman Munson .315
Mark Grace .314
Don Mattingly .312
Will Clark .312

Jose Morales .307
Lyman Bostock .307
George Brett .305
Pete Rose .305
John Kruk .305

Dion James .304
Rafael Palmeiro .304
Mike Greenwell .303
Manny Sanguillen .303
Bill Madlock .303

Julio Franco .303
Jody Reed .302
Rico Carty .302
Paul Molitor .302
Barry Larkin .302

Career Slugging Average vs. Fly-Ball Pitchers
Min. 300 Total Bases

Cecil Fielder .589
Will Clark .560
Darryl Strawberry .538
Eric Davis .533
Andre Dawson .524

Danny Tartabull .523
Kevin Mitchell .522
Mike Schmidt .522
Willie Stargell .514
George Foster .514

Pedro Guerrero .513
Jack Clark .511
Jim Rice .510
Don Mattingly .509
Fred McGriff .508

George Brett .508
Jose Canseco .507
Mark McGwire .507
Ellis Burks .506
Dale Murphy .505

Dave Winfield .503
Bob Horner .502
George Bell .502
Kal Daniels .501
Bill Robinson .501

Single-Season Batting Average vs. Fly-Ball Pitchers
Min. 60 Hits

Rod Carew, 1977 .424
George Brett, 1980 .405
Tony Gwynn, 1987 .401
Willie McGee, 1985 .375
Rod Carew, 1979 .375

Hal Morris, 1990 .375
Len Dykstra, 1990 .374
Wade Boggs, 1988 .372
Tony Gwynn, 1986 .368
Luis Polonia, 1990 .368

Von Joshua, 1975 .368
Wade Boggs, 1982 .367
Paul Molitor, 1987 .365
Wade Boggs, 1986 .364
Rennie Stennett, 1977 .364

Manny Sanguillen, 1975 .364
Dion James, 1987 .363
Ted Simmons, 1975 .363
Mike Easler, 1980 .363
Kirby Puckett, 1988 .362

Pedro Guerrero, 1987 .359
Larry Biittner, 1975 .357
Will Clark, 1989 .356
Ken Griffey Sr., 1976 .355
George Brett, 1976 .353

Single-Season Slugging Average vs. Fly-Ball Pitchers
Min. 100 Total Bases

George Foster, 1977 .749
Will Clark, 1987 .726
George Brett, 1980 .715
Jack Clark, 1987 .712
Cecil Fielder, 1990 .696

Fred Lynn, 1979 .690
Darryl Strawberry, 1985 .686
Mike Schmidt, 1980 .675
Mike Easler, 1980 .672
Willie Stargell, 1978 .670

Chris James, 1987 .665
Kevin Mitchell, 1989 .664
Rod Carew, 1977 .661
Andre Dawson, 1990 .658
Mike Schmidt, 1987 .653

Don Money, 1982 .645
Larry Parrish, 1979 .637
Tony Armas, 1985 .636
Cecil Cooper, 1975 .635
Andre Dawson, 1987 .635

Pedro Guerrero, 1987 .634
Pedro Guerrero, 1982 .633
Kal Daniels, 1987 .632
Dale Murphy, 1987 .632
Larry Hisle, 1978 .628

Career Batting Average with Runners on Base

Min. 200 Hits

Wade Boggs	.353
Rod Carew	.348
Dave Magadan	.346
Tony Gwynn	.343
Kirby Puckett	.333
Lyman Bostock	.326
George Brett	.326
Don Mattingly	.322
Thurman Munson	.321
Barry Larkin	.320
Pete Rose	.319
Mark Grace	.319
Mike Greenwell	.319
Al Oliver	.316
Dave Parker	.316
Cecil Cooper	.315
Keith Hernandez	.313
Bill Madlock	.313
Tim Raines	.313
Pedro Guerrero	.312
Pat Tabler	.310
Will Clark	.310
Mike Easler	.307
Manny Sanguillen	.307
Bill Buckner	.307

Single-Season Batting Average with Runners on Base

Min. 75 Hits

Rod Carew, 1977	.422
Lonnie Smith, 1989	.407
Tony Gwynn, 1984	.406
George Brett, 1980	.400
Garry Templeton, 1979	.388
Wade Boggs, 1985	.387
Fred Lynn, 1979	.387
Keith Hernandez, 1979	.383
Dave Parker, 1978	.383
Tony Gwynn, 1988	.382
Wade Boggs, 1986	.379
Garry Templeton, 1977	.378
Rod Carew, 1975	.377
Robin Yount, 1987	.376
Mickey Rivers, 1977	.373
Bill Madlock, 1975	.370
Manny Sanguillen, 1975	.370
Bill Madlock, 1976	.368
Hal McRae, 1976	.368
George Brett, 1990	.367
Ryne Sandberg, 1990	.367
George Brett, 1985	.367
Hal McRae, 1982	.366
Pete Rose, 1975	.366
Fred Lynn, 1975	.365

Career Batting Average with Runners in Scoring Position

Min. 100 Hits

Wade Boggs	.352
Rod Carew	.345
Tony Gwynn	.329
Thurman Munson	.329
Dave Magadan	.327
Kirby Puckett	.325
Lyman Bostock	.324
Pete Rose	.323
Al Oliver	.323
Pat Tabler	.322
George Brett	.321
Don Mattingly	.320
Broderick Perkins	.318
Rennie Stennett	.315
Cecil Cooper	.315
Lou Piniella	.314
Bill Madlock	.314
Dane Iorg	.313
Lamar Johnson	.312
Luis Polonia	.312
Mark Grace	.312
Tim Raines	.310
Paul Molitor	.310
Jim Rice	.310
Julio Franco	.309

Single-Season Batting Average with Runners in Scoring Position

Min. 50 Hits

George Brett, 1980	.466
Cecil Cooper, 1980	.421
Tony Gwynn, 1984	.418
Bill Madlock, 1976	.414
Ken Griffey Sr., 1976	.412
Pete Rose, 1975	.412
Julio Franco, 1989	.407
Don Mattingly, 1984	.405
Pedro Guerrero, 1989	.405
Fred Lynn, 1975	.400
Mickey Rivers, 1977	.400
Kent Hrbek, 1982	.398
Wade Boggs, 1985	.392
Robin Yount, 1982	.392
Joe Morgan, 1976	.391
Willie McGee, 1985	.391
Will Clark, 1989	.389
Hal McRae, 1982	.383
Pat Tabler, 1987	.383
Rod Carew, 1977	.382
Bake McBride, 1980	.380
Bill Robinson, 1977	.380
Alan Trammell, 1990	.379
Garry Templeton, 1977	.379
Barry Bonds, 1990	.377

Career Batting Average with 2 Outs and Runners on Base

Min. 75 Hits

Wade Boggs	.333
Larry Hisle	.321
Kirby Puckett	.321
Milt Thompson	.321
Thurman Munson	.320
Will Clark	.318
Al Oliver	.311
John Kruk	.311
Barry Larkin	.309
Tony Gwynn	.307
Larry Biittner	.307
Cecil Cooper	.305
Jose Cardenal	.304
Rico Carty	.303
Bill Madlock	.302
Rod Carew	.301
Gene Richards	.301
Lyman Bostock	.301
Dave Valle	.300
Kevin Seitzer	.299
Pete Rose	.298
Tony Fernandez	.297
Oscar Gamble	.297
Don Mattingly	.296
Alan Trammell	.296

Single-Season Batting Average with 2 Outs and Runners on Base

Min. 30 Hits

Len Dykstra, 1990	.446
Barry Bonnell, 1977	.437
Lee Lacy, 1984	.432
Lonnie Smith, 1989	.429
Al Oliver, 1980	.424
Bruce Bochte, 1982	.418
Dave Parker, 1986	.412
Pat Tabler, 1987	.407
Will Clark, 1989	.405
Ted Simmons, 1983	.404
Sixto Lezcano, 1979	.402
Garry Templeton, 1979	.400
Ray Knight, 1986	.400
Rod Carew, 1977	.398
Harold Baines, 1985	.391
Greg Gross, 1975	.390
Lee Mazzilli, 1979	.390
Larry Parrish, 1979	.388
Rod Carew, 1975	.387
Joe Rudi, 1976	.386
Frank Taveras, 1978	.386
Rennie Stennett, 1975	.383
Larry Hisle, 1978	.379
Steve Garvey, 1979	.377
Rod Carew, 1978	.376

Career Batting Average with 2 Outs & Runners in Scoring Position

Min. 50 Hits

Larry Hisle	.332
Wade Boggs	.328
Luis Polonia	.327
Thurman Munson	.325
Will Clark	.324
Al Oliver	.320
John Kruk	.317
Kirby Puckett	.314
Tony Fernandez	.309
Lamar Johnson	.307
Lyman Bostock	.304
Gene Richards	.303
Pete Rose	.303
Lou Piniella	.303
John Castino	.302
Dane Iorg	.302
Terry Harper	.302
Bill Madlock	.302
Chris Brown	.302
Eric Davis	.302
Jose Morales	.301
Dave Valle	.299
Rod Carew	.299
Kevin Bass	.298
Dale Sveum	.298

Single-Season Batting Average with 2 Outs & Runners in Scoring Position

Min. 20 Hits

Kent Hrbek, 1982	.466
Bruce Bochte, 1982	.457
Al Oliver, 1980	.446
Rod Carew, 1975	.440
Pat Tabler, 1987	.440
Ted Simmons, 1983	.437
Will Clark, 1989	.435
George Foster, 1981	.426
Chris Speier, 1978	.426
Pedro Guerrero, 1989	.424
Dave Parker, 1986	.419
Steve Sax, 1988	.419
Len Dykstra, 1990	.415
Rod Carew, 1978	.414
Cecil Cooper, 1980	.414
Rod Carew, 1977	.412
Lee Mazzilli, 1978	.412
Joe Rudi, 1976	.410
Lyman Bostock, 1978	.407
Dave Winfield, 1979	.407
Mike Ivie, 1979	.404
Tony Fernandez, 1986	.404
Larry Hisle, 1978	.403
Lee Lacy, 1984	.400
Paul Molitor, 1986	.400

Career Batting Average in Late-Inning Pressure Situations

Min. 50 Hits

Tim Raines	.339
Tony Gwynn	.336
Mark Grace	.333
Tony Fernandez	.326
Benito Santiago	.325
Joe Lefebvre	.320
Wade Boggs	.319
Luis Polonia	.319
Steve Sax	.319
Cecil Cooper	.318
Rickey Henderson	.317
George Brett	.315
Kirby Puckett	.314
Ron LeFlore	.312
Barry Larkin	.311
Mike Greenwell	.311
Tom Paciorek	.309
Thurman Munson	.309
Mickey Rivers	.309
Jose Cardenal	.309
Ken Griffey Sr.	.309
Mike Ivie	.308
Alan Trammell	.308
Milt Thompson	.307
Mike Easler	.305

Single-Season Batting Average in Late-Inning Pressure Situations

Min. 25 Hits

Manny Trillo, 1981	.466
Bill Madlock, 1975	.464
Walt Weiss, 1990	.441
Mickey Rivers, 1977	.439
Wade Boggs, 1986	.433
George Brett, 1976	.433
Alan Trammell, 1987	.431
Steve Kemp, 1979	.429
Ken Griffey Sr., 1975	.423
Tom Paciorek, 1976	.419
Mike Easler, 1984	.416
Dave Magadan, 1990	.415
Mike Greenwell, 1989	.413
Scot Thompson, 1979	.413
Cecil Cooper, 1982	.412
Lloyd Moseby, 1983	.410
Luis Salazar, 1981	.408
Benito Santiago, 1990	.403
Bill Buckner, 1984	.403
Chris Chambliss, 1981	.403
Alan Trammell, 1988	.403
Rick Manning, 1983	.402
Ken Griffey Sr., 1986	.402
Cal Ripken, 1984	.398

Career Home Run Pct. in Late-Inning Pressure Situations

Min. 10 Home Runs

Gary Alexander	7.80
Ken Phelps	7.22
Steve Balboni	7.10
Mark McGwire	7.04
Dave Kingman	6.90
Craig Kusick	6.78
Tony Armas	6.03
Andre Thornton	6.01
Eric Davis	5.76
Kevin Mitchell	5.73
Eddie Murray	5.70
Darryl Strawberry	5.70
Mike Schmidt	5.60
Oscar Gamble	5.57
Reggie Smith	5.56
Graig Nettles	5.51
Bernie Carbo	5.41
Richie Zisk	5.32
Jack Clark	5.26
Willie Stargell	5.25
Cliff Johnson	5.24
Reggie Jackson	5.19
Howard Johnson	5.17
Pat Putnam	5.14
Dwight Evans	5.08

Career Batting Avg. in Late-Inning Pressure Situations with Runners in Scoring Position

Min. 25 Hits

Eric Soderholm	.429
Jose Canseco	.398
Kelly Gruber	.369
Kevin Seitzer	.369
Tim Raines	.368
Luis Salazar	.365
Willie Montanez	.355
Lee May	.352
Milt Thompson	.348
Don Mattingly	.347
Pete Rose	.346
Eddie Murray	.345
Oscar Gamble	.343
Thurman Munson	.341
Steve Lyons	.338
Bruce Bochte	.337
Dickie Thon	.336
Dave Chalk	.333
Garth Iorg	.333
Mike Ivie	.333
John Kruk	.333
Reggie Smith	.333
Rickey Henderson	.332
Will Clark	.330
Cesar Geronimo	.330

Career Batting Average in Late-Inning Pressure Situations with Runners on Base

Min. 25 Hits

Mike Ivie	.370
Tim Raines	.366
Eric Soderholm	.348
Scott Bradley	.347
Jeff Treadway	.344
Garth Iorg	.342
Manny Mota	.342
Bill Buckner	.339
Kelly Gruber	.338
Dale Sveum	.337
Tony Gwynn	.336
Eddie Murray	.335
Jose Cardenal	.335
Alan Trammell	.334
Dave Rader	.333
Reggie Smith	.333
Pete Rose	.332
Thurman Munson	.331
John Kruk	.331
U.L. Washington	.329
Joe Torre	.329
Wade Boggs	.329
Rickey Henderson	.328
Kevin Seitzer	.328
H. Pat Kelly	.326

Single-Season Batting Average in Late-Inning Pressure Situations with Runners on Base

Min. 10 Hits

Rance Mulliniks, 1984	.684
Eddie Murray, 1985	.567
Bill Buckner, 1984	.563
Rey Quinones, 1987	.538
Rowland Office, 1975	.536
Rusty Staub, 1981	.536
Jack Clark, 1984	.526
Ron Oester, 1981	.524
Carmelo Castillo, 1989	.524
Pedro Guerrero, 1980	.520
Manny Trillo, 1981	.520
17 players tied with	.500

Career Batting Average in Late-Inning Pressure Situations with 2 Outs and Runners on Base

Min. 15 Hits

Garth Iorg	.446
Eric Soderholm	.429
Scott Bradley	.409
Tim Raines	.407
Marty Perez	.405
Mike Ivie	.387
Milt Thompson	.386
Dave Rader	.383
Mike LaValliere	.381
Benito Santiago	.381
Jose Canseco	.368
Thurman Munson	.365
Oscar Gamble	.355
Hubie Brooks	.355
John Kruk	.354
Steve Henderson	.352
Harold Reynolds	.348
Glenn Adams	.345
H. Pat Kelly	.344
Ed Ott	.343
Will Clark	.343
Manny Sanguillen	.341
Wade Boggs	.339
U.L. Washington	.338

Career Batting Avg. in Late-Inning Pressure Situations with 2 Outs and Runners in Scoring Position

Min. 10 Hits

Eric Soderholm	.444
Garth Iorg	.441
Marty Perez	.435
Jim Norris	.417
Jose Canseco	.409
Rusty Staub	.405
Scott Bradley	.394
Milt Thompson	.394
Wallace Johnson	.393
Cesar Geronimo	.391
Thurman Munson	.387
Benito Santiago	.385
Oscar Gamble	.381
Vance Law	.380
Kelly Gruber	.378
Tim Raines	.374
Willie Horton	.373
Pete Rose	.372
Jose Cruz	.355
Lee May	.352
John Kruk	.351
Will Clark	.350
Mike Ivie	.349
Don Mattingly	.348
Gary Pettis	.348

Highest Career Ratio of Ground Outs to Air Outs
Min. 1,000 PA

Felix Fermin	2.46
Wally Backman	2.41
Milt Thompson	2.34
Willie McGee	2.26
Steve Jeltz	2.22
Rick Reuschel	2.11
Juan Bonilla	2.10
Gary Pettis	2.07
Steve Henderson	2.04
Rafael Belliard	2.02
Duane Kuiper	2.02
Billy North	2.02
Bob Forsch	2.01
Joel Skinner	2.00
Steve Carlton	1.99
Steve Sax	1.98
Domingo Ramos	1.93
Gene Richards	1.91
Rod Carew	1.89
Junior Ortiz	1.88
Alan Wiggins	1.84
Ron LeFlore	1.82
Miguel Dilone	1.82
Jackie Gutierrez	1.79
Pete Rose	1.79

Lowest Career Ratio of Ground Outs to Air Outs
Min. 1,000 PA

Rob Deer	0.58
Howard Johnson	0.59
Mark McGwire	0.61
Gene Tenace	0.63
Joe Morgan	0.65
Andre Thornton	0.65
Darrell Evans	0.66
Ken Phelps	0.66
Joe Carter	0.66
Jim Dwyer	0.67
Gary Redus	0.67
Don Baylor	0.67
Franklin Stubbs	0.68
Steve Balboni	0.69
Tom Brunansky	0.69
Ron Kittle	0.69
Mark Salas	0.70
Richie Hebner	0.70
Buck Martinez	0.71
Mike Schmidt	0.71
Dave Revering	0.72
Ron Gant	0.72
Bobby Murcer	0.73
Jerry White	0.74
Chris Sabo	0.74

Career Batting Average in Day Games
Min. 100 Hits

Rod Carew	.347
Wade Boggs	.341
Don Mattingly	.330
Mike Greenwell	.330
Willie McGee	.323
Jim Eisenreich	.322
Kirby Puckett	.321
Tony Gwynn	.320
George Brett	.318
Randy Ready	.318
Bake McBride	.316
Paul Molitor	.316
Bip Roberts	.315
Al Oliver	.315
Lyman Bostock	.313
Ken Griffey Sr.	.313
Jerry Grote	.312
Wayne Krenchicki	.312
Thurman Munson	.311
Jose Morales	.311
Mark Grace	.310
Reggie Smith	.310
Tim Raines	.310
Will Clark	.309
Gene Richards	.309

Career Batting Average in Night Games
Min. 100 Hits

Wade Boggs	.349
Tony Gwynn	.333
Rod Carew	.324
Kirby Puckett	.320
George Brett	.313
Don Mattingly	.311
Lyman Bostock	.310
Mickey Rivers	.309
Pedro Guerrero	.308
Al Oliver	.306
Mike Greenwell	.305
Dave Magadan	.304
Kal Daniels	.304
Cecil Cooper	.304
Manny Sanguillen	.303
Luis Polonia	.302
Mark Grace	.302
Bill Madlock	.302
Julio Franco	.301
Mike Easler	.301
Rick Peters	.301
Jim Rice	.300
Thurman Munson	.300
Edgar Martinez	.299
Rafael Palmeiro	.298

Career Batting Average on Grass Surfaces
Min. 150 Hits

Wade Boggs	.350
Rod Carew	.331
Tony Gwynn	.329
Al Oliver	.318
Mike Greenwell	.315
Don Mattingly	.315
Lyman Bostock	.313
Mark Grace	.312
Pedro Guerrero	.311
Will Clark	.311
Thurman Munson	.306
Luis Polonia	.306
Julio Franco	.305
Bob Watson	.305
Dave Magadan	.305
Bobby Bonilla	.305
Barry Larkin	.304
Jim Rice	.303
Bill Madlock	.303
Keith Hernandez	.301
Steve Garvey	.301
Cecil Cooper	.301
Gregg Jefferies	.300
Jose Cardenal	.300
Reggie Smith	.300

Career Batting Average on Artificial Turf
Min. 150 Hits

Kirby Puckett	.337
Rod Carew	.333
Don Mattingly	.331
Tony Gwynn	.330
George Brett	.330
Wade Boggs	.324
Kevin Seitzer	.316
Al Bumbry	.314
Tracy Jones	.312
Mickey Rivers	.312
Von Joshua	.311
John Kruk	.308
Lee Lacy	.308
Alan Trammell	.306
Mike Easler	.306
Rickey Henderson	.305
Kal Daniels	.305
Mickey Hatcher	.305
Rick Leach	.304
Bill Madlock	.304
Chris Chambliss	.303
Cal Ripken	.303
Dave Parker	.303
Hal McRae	.302
Tim Raines	.302

Single-Season Batting Average on Grass Surfaces
Min. 60 Hits

George Brett, 1980	.396
Rod Carew, 1977	.393
Paul Molitor, 1987	.376
Tony Gwynn, 1987	.374
Pete Rose, 1979	.373
Ray Knight, 1983	.370
Wade Boggs, 1987	.369
Ken Griffey Sr., 1976	.368
Rod Carew, 1975	.367
Keith Hernandez, 1979	.366
Gary Gaetti, 1986	.364
Wade Boggs, 1983	.364
Wade Boggs, 1985	.363
Wade Boggs, 1988	.363
Cecil Cooper, 1980	.363
Oscar Gamble, 1979	.362
Pat Sheridan, 1984	.358
Dan Gladden, 1984	.357
Dwight Smith, 1989	.354
Wade Boggs, 1982	.354
Wade Boggs, 1986	.352
Juan Beniquez, 1984	.352
Alan Trammell, 1987	.352
Bill Buckner, 1978	.351
Fred Lynn, 1979	.350

Single-Season Batting Average on Artificial Turf
Min. 60 Hits

Bill Madlock, 1975	.398
Steve Sax, 1986	.387
George Brett, 1980	.386
Hal McRae, 1976	.382
Kirby Puckett, 1989	.372
Kirby Puckett, 1988	.370
George Brett, 1979	.369
George Brett, 1976	.367
Keith Hernandez, 1985	.364
Hal Morris, 1990	.360
George Brett, 1978	.357
Lee Lacy, 1980	.356
Willie McGee, 1985	.356
George Brett, 1981	.356
Greg Gross, 1983	.356
Pete Rose, 1976	.354
Bake McBride, 1976	.354
Barry Larkin, 1989	.353
George Brett, 1975	.352
Bill Madlock, 1981	.352
Kirby Puckett, 1986	.352
George Brett, 1985	.352
Mike Easler, 1980	.349
Kent Hrbek, 1984	.349
Willie Wilson, 1982	.349

Career On-Base Average Leading Off Innings

Min. 200 PA

Wade Boggs	.434
Fred McGriff	.402
Mark Grace	.401
Kal Daniels	.400
Rickey Henderson	.397
Rod Carew	.392
Pepe Mangual	.384
Tony Gwynn	.384
Mike Hargrove	.382
Willie Randolph	.382
Tony Solaita	.382
Mike Schmidt	.378
Delino DeShields	.378
Bob Stinson	.377
Greg Gross	.377
Bobby Grich	.377
Jack Clark	.376
Alvin Davis	.376
Gene Tenace	.375
Otto Velez	.375
Phil Bradley	.375
Bernie Carbo	.374
Bobby Bonds	.374
Tim Raines	.373
Joe Morgan	.372

Single-Season On-Base Average Leading Off Innings

Min. 100 PA

Rod Carew, 1982	.523
Andre Thornton, 1975	.519
Carlton Fisk, 1977	.504
Wade Boggs, 1983	.494
Toby Harrah, 1981	.491
Bill Doran, 1990	.477
Wade Boggs, 1988	.476
Joe Morgan, 1975	.470
Ozzie Smith, 1987	.469
Wade Boggs, 1985	.468
Ken Griffey Sr., 1977	.466
Phil Bradley, 1987	.463
Kirby Puckett, 1987	.462
Fred McGriff, 1988	.460
Willie Randolph, 1980	.457
Wade Boggs, 1987	.457
Hal McRae, 1977	.456
Kirby Puckett, 1988	.453
Mike Hargrove, 1977	.453
Mitchell Page, 1977	.452
Cal Ripken, 1984	.452
Alvin Davis, 1989	.451
Kal Daniels, 1987	.450
Carlton Fisk, 1990	.450
Willie Randolph, 1985	.448

Career Walk Pct. Leading Off Innings

Min. 25 Walks

Jim Wynn	19.71
Randy Milligan	19.70
Gene Tenace	15.78
Joe Morgan	15.34
Bernie Carbo	15.05
Pepe Mangual	14.76
Otto Velez	14.55
Glenn Borgmann	14.35
Rickey Henderson	14.24
Jerry Hairston	14.15
Dwayne Murphy	14.03
Tommy Hutton	14.00
Jack Clark	13.87
Joe Ferguson	13.84
Mike Hargrove	13.67
Billy North	13.62
Steve Jeltz	13.60
Bud Harrelson	13.56
Willie Randolph	13.55
Lee Mazzilli	13.46
Ken Phelps	13.45
Mark McGwire	13.37
Merv Rettenmund	13.27
Toby Harrah	13.17
Tony Solaita	13.16

Single-Season Walk Pct. Leading Off Innings

Min. 15 Walks

John Cangelosi, 1987	24.77
Jim Wynn, 1975	23.85
Jack Clark, 1987	23.39
Dwayne Murphy, 1987	23.08
Lee Mazzilli, 1982	22.97
Randy Milligan, 1990	22.83
Lee Mazzilli, 1983	22.50
Joe Morgan, 1975	22.00
Gene Tenace, 1977	21.43
Dwayne Murphy, 1981	21.43
Andre Thornton, 1975	21.30
Carlton Fisk, 1977	21.17
Bernie Carbo, 1975	21.05
Mike R. Fitzgerald, 1990	20.93
Jerry Hairston, 1984	20.55
Mike Scioscia, 1985	20.54
Jack Clark, 1989	20.45
Jack Clark, 1990	20.19
Gary Matthews, 1984	19.82
Toby Harrah, 1981	19.81
Steve Kemp, 1981	19.74
Toby Harrah, 1985	19.71
Johnny Briggs, 1975	19.15
Gene Tenace, 1979	19.05
Mike Hargrove, 1977	18.95

Career Batting Average with Bases Loaded

Min. 15 Hits

Pat Tabler	.500
Rudy Law	.469
Terry Steinbach	.462
Miguel Dilone	.436
Biff Pocoroba	.435
Rick Bosetti	.429
Steve Lyons	.429
Lou Brock	.423
Tony Gwynn	.422
Ken Singleton	.417
Ellis Valentine	.417
Bill Madlock	.411
Eddie Murray	.407
Rico Carty	.404
Lee May	.402
Jay Johnstone	.400
Oscar Gamble	.392
B.J. Surhoff	.390
Larry Hisle	.389
Rod Carew	.388
Dale Berra	.383
Richie Zisk	.382
Alan Trammell	.381
Johnny Grubb	.379

Career RBI Ratio (per PA) with Bases Loaded

Min. 30 RBI

Kal Daniels	1.20
Matt Williams	1.15
Darryl Motley	1.13
John Milner	1.10
Tracy Jones	1.09
Eddie Murray	1.07
Biff Pocoroba	1.06
Terry Crowley	1.05
Mike Cubbage	1.04
Pat Tabler	1.03
Dane Iorg	1.03
Rico Carty	1.00
Lee Stanton	1.00
Roy Howell	0.99
Oscar Gamble	0.99
Jose Cruz	0.98
H. Pat Kelly	0.98
Dale Berra	0.98
Terry Steinbach	0.98
Steve Garvey	0.98
Alvin Davis	0.98
Joe Rudi	0.98
Mark Grace	0.97
Greg Walker	0.97
Wally Joyner	0.96

Career Walk Pct. with Bases Loaded

Min. 10 Walks

Jerry Browne	28.95
Mickey Tettleton	21.74
Oscar Gamble	17.65
Mike Hargrove	17.48
Sixto Lezcano	17.12
Gene Tenace	16.09
Gary Roenicke	15.91
Pete Rose	15.57
Leon Durham	15.49
Darrell Porter	15.32
Joe Morgan	14.55
Dwight Evans	13.85
Alvin Davis	13.13
Terry Puhl	13.10
Rickey Henderson	12.98
Jeff Burroughs	12.90
Lonnie Smith	12.82
Jack Clark	12.42
Dan Driessen	12.40
Carl Yastrzemski	12.15
Ken Oberkfell	12.12
Dave Winfield	11.59
Bobby Murcer	11.58
Ken Singleton	11.48
Darrell Evans	11.36

Career Strikeout Pct. with Bases Loaded

Min. 50 PA

Rico Carty	1.43
Jim Spencer	1.89
Biff Pocoroba	1.92
Craig Reynolds	1.98
Jerry Morales	2.02
Dave Cash	3.03
Ozzie Smith	3.25
Bruce Benedict	3.53
Bill Buckner	3.57
Lyman Bostock	3.92
Jose Cardenal	4.00
Ellis Valentine	4.00
Brett Butler	4.04
Doug Flynn	4.08
Rich Dauer	4.35
Pete O'Brien	4.44
Bill Madlock	4.46
Tim Raines	4.55
Lenny Randle	4.62
Frank Taveras	4.62
Rafael Ramirez	4.69
Jose Cruz	4.72
Larry Bowa	4.81
Mike Scioscia	4.90
George Bell	5.06

Career Pct. of Runs Batted in from Scoring Position

Min. 100 RBI

Don Mattingly	.360
Thurman Munson	.352
Dane Iorg	.352
George Brett	.351
Broderick Perkins	.349
Al Oliver	.349
Rusty Staub	.349
Cecil Cooper	.347
Rod Carew	.346
Lou Piniella	.341
Ted Simmons	.340
Dave Magadan	.340
Rico Carty	.340
Mike Hargrove	.340
Wade Boggs	.339
Larry Hisle	.338
Pedro Guerrero	.337
Dave Winfield	.336
Wally Joyner	.336
Bill Madlock	.335
Hal McRae	.335
Kent Hrbek	.334
Lyman Bostock	.334
Keith Hernandez	.334
Kirby Puckett	.333

Single-Season Pct. of Runs Batted in from Scoring Position

Min. 50 RBI

George Brett, 1980	.507
Bill Buckner, 1981	.476
Cecil Cooper, 1980	.470
Bill Madlock, 1976	.448
Pedro Guerrero, 1989	.447
Dave Parker, 1976	.430
Eddie Murray, 1985	.428
Bill Buckner, 1978	.427
Richie Hebner, 1980	.422
Dave Magadan, 1990	.421
Lonnie Smith, 1989	.420
Cecil Cooper, 1976	.420
Bake McBride, 1980	.419
Buddy Bell, 1984	.418
Larry Parrish, 1986	.415
John Milner, 1976	.412
Harold Baines, 1987	.412
Rod Carew, 1977	.411
Tony Gwynn, 1988	.410
Ted Simmons, 1983	.410
Tom Herr, 1985	.409
Rod Carew, 1975	.408
Joe Morgan, 1978	.408
Joe Morgan, 1976	.408
Pat Tabler, 1985	.407

Career Pct. of Runs Batted in from Scoring Position in Late-Inning Pressure Situations

Min. 20 RBI

Eric Soderholm	.427
Jim Essian	.403
Jim Norris	.392
Eddie Murray	.388
Pedro Guerrero	.386
Jose Canseco	.385
Pete LaCock	.379
Lenn Sakata	.377
Kelly Gruber	.376
Don Mattingly	.373
Mike Hargrove	.369
Eddie Milner	.367
Rico Carty	.364
Bill Melton	.361
Rusty Staub	.357
Reggie Smith	.354
Ellis Valentine	.352
Oscar Gamble	.349
Larry Sheets	.349
Tony Gwynn	.346
Garth Iorg	.346
Matt Nokes	.345
Ken Singleton	.345
Tommy Hutton	.344
Jason Thompson	.344

Single-Season RBI Opportunities from Scoring Position

Tony Perez, 1975	268
Willie McGee, 1987	260
Don Baylor, 1979	257
Jim Rice, 1986	250
Tim Wallach, 1987	247
Johnny Bench, 1975	246
George Foster, 1976	245
Julio Franco, 1985	244
Joe Carter, 1990	244
George Foster, 1977	243
Bill Buckner, 1986	242
Bobby Bonilla, 1990	242
Keith Moreland, 1985	238
Jerry Morales, 1975	236
Bob Watson, 1976	236
Lance Parrish, 1983	235
Ruben Sierra, 1987	233
Tom Herr, 1985	232
Joe Carter, 1987	232
Greg Luzinski, 1975	230
Thurman Munson, 1976	229
Cecil Cooper, 1983	229
Mike Greenwell, 1988	229
Jim Rice, 1975	228
Jim Rice, 1984	228

Career Pct. of Runs Batted in from 3d Base with Less than 2 Outs

Min. 40 RBI

Broderick Perkins	.753
Rico Carty	.722
Ed Kranepool	.720
Tony Solaita	.719
Rod Carew	.719
Mark Grace	.706
Jerry Hairston	.699
Wade Boggs	.697
Manny Sanguillen	.695
Tony Gwynn	.694
Al Newman	.693
Al Oliver	.692
George Brett	.690
Don Mattingly	.690
Mike Hargrove	.689
Rusty Staub	.686
Jeff Treadway	.683
Mike Felder	.682
Wayne Krenchicki	.682
Bill Madlock	.680
Rick Leach	.679
Pete Rose	.677
Hal McRae	.675
Toby Harrah	.674
John Moses	.672

Single-Season Pct. of Runs Batted in from 3d Base with Less than 2 Outs

Min. 15 RBI

Ben Oglivie, 1986	.913
Rod Carew, 1983	.900
Toby Harrah, 1981	.889
Bill Madlock, 1986	.880
Elliott Maddox, 1978	.875
Rickey Henderson, 1988	.870
Bill Madlock, 1976	.868
Tony Fernandez, 1989	.867
Charlie Hayes, 1989	.864
Dave Revering, 1979	.857
Kevin McReynolds, 1984	.852
Robin Yount, 1989	.848
Al Oliver, 1983	.846
Jerry Mumphrey, 1985	.846
Sid Bream, 1986	.846
Paul Molitor, 1978	.842
Dave Bergman, 1984	.842
Tom Foley, 1988	.842
Al Newman, 1989	.842
Carlos Baerga, 1990	.842
Pat Tabler, 1985	.840
George Brett, 1980	.838

Career Pct. of Runs Batted in from 1st Base

Min. 30 RBI

Willie Stargell	.110
Eric Davis	.109
Jose Canseco	.101
Glenn Davis	.099
Mark McGwire	.098
Darryl Strawberry	.098
Mike Schmidt	.096
Greg Luzinski	.092
Larry Hisle	.091
Dave Kingman	.091
Matt Williams	.090
Hal McRae	.089
Danny Tartabull	.089
Cecil Fielder	.087
Reggie Jackson	.087
Oscar Gamble	.086
Alvin Davis	.086
Dale Murphy	.086
Bill Robinson	.086
Dave Parker	.085
Steve Balboni	.085
Ron Kittle	.085
Ken Phelps	.084
George Brett	.083
Kal Daniels	.083

Single-Season Runs Batted in from 1st Base

Hal McRae, 1982	36
George Foster, 1977	31
Jim Rice, 1978	29
Don Mattingly, 1985	29
Greg Luzinski, 1977	28
Alvin Davis, 1984	28
Keith Hernandez, 1979	27
Joe Carter, 1986	26
Jim Rice, 1983	25
Kevin Mitchell, 1989	25
Steve Garvey, 1979	24
Fred Lynn, 1979	24
Dave Kingman, 1984	24
Jose Canseco, 1986	24
Mike Greenwell, 1988	24
Jeff Burroughs, 1977	23
Ron Cey, 1977	23
Jim Rice, 1979	23
Tony Armas, 1980	23
Tony Perez, 1980	23
Mike Schmidt, 1983	23
Eddie Murray, 1985	23
Darryl Strawberry, 1987	23
Cecil Fielder, 1990	23

Career Opp. Batting Average vs. Left-Handed Batters
Min. 400 PA

Bryan Harvey	.175
Jesse Orosco	.188
Rob Dibble	.192
Mitch Williams	.196
Mark Langston	.197
Pat Underwood	.201
Bob Lacey	.201
Mark Davis	.202
Dave Dravecky	.203
Atlee Hammaker	.204
John Franco	.204
Rod Scurry	.206
Nolan Ryan	.207
Zane Smith	.209
Juan Agosto	.209
John Candelaria	.209
Sid Fernandez	.209
Willie Hernandez	.210
Bill Scherrer	.210
Matt Young	.215
Al Holland	.215
Craig Lefferts	.215
Mike Norris	.216
Bob McClure	.216
John Fulgham	.216

Career Opp. Home Run Pct. vs. Left-Handed Batters
Min. 400 PA

Chuck Finley	0.35
Mickey Lolich	0.46
Bob Kipper	0.47
Doug Sisk	0.47
Paul Mirabella	0.49
Bert Roberge	0.51
Dave Smith	0.61
Zane Smith	0.61
Jim Crawford	0.64
Rob Murphy	0.67
John Franco	0.68
Rob Dibble	0.68
Bruce Berenyi	0.69
Joe Sambito	0.69
Ricky Horton	0.73
Greg W. Harris	0.74
Juan Agosto	0.76
Greg Minton	0.79
Jeff Lahti	0.80
Joe Magrane	0.82
Gary Lavelle	0.82
Joe Boever	0.84
Matt Young	0.88
Bill Landrum	0.90
Lee Guetterman	0.92

Career Opp. Walk Pct. vs. Left-Handed Batters
Min. 400 PA

Steve Howe	3.06
Gary Nolan	3.23
Scott McGregor	4.16
Greg Swindell	4.57
Dick Bosman	4.75
Tom Burgmeier	4.80
Curt Young	4.92
Jim Kaat	5.13
Jon Matlack	5.14
Ted Higuera	5.14
John Tudor	5.16
Bob Tewksbury	5.17
Dave Tomlin	5.37
Will McEnaney	5.42
Dan Quisenberry	5.43
John Candelaria	5.49
Jimmy Key	5.52
Charlie Leibrandt	5.63
Randy Jones	5.63
Bob Knepper	5.64
Jose Bautista	5.66
Pedro Borbon	5.69
Ron Guidry	5.72
Frank Tanana	5.72
Mike Jeffcoat	5.79

Career Opp. Strikeout Pct. vs. Left-Handed Batters
Min. 100 Strikeouts

Randy Myers	34.55
Rob Dibble	33.14
Bryan Harvey	29.01
Tom Henke	28.14
Sid Fernandez	27.31
Mitch Williams	25.63
Mark Davis	25.62
Nolan Ryan	24.84
John Candelaria	24.23
Jesse Orosco	24.17
Al Holland	23.35
Mark Langston	23.28
Joe Sambito	23.22
Paul Assenmacher	23.05
Dave Righetti	22.93
John Tudor	22.80
Zane Smith	22.54
Rob Murphy	22.47
Matt Young	22.25
Rod Scurry	22.12
Joe Hesketh	21.87
Lee Smith	21.86
Tippy Martinez	21.48
Steve Carlton	21.31
Todd Worrell	21.22

Career Opp. Batting Average vs. Right-Handed Batters
Min. 600 PA

Ramon Martinez	.184
Jose DeLeon	.185
J.R. Richard	.190
Mike Jackson	.195
Tim Burke	.200
Floyd Youmans	.201
Mark Littell	.202
Sid Fernandez	.203
Rich Gossage	.203
Luis DeLeon	.204
Victor Cruz	.206
Tom Henke	.207
Mario Soto	.207
Nolan Ryan	.208
Pat Perry	.208
John Smoltz	.208
David Cone	.209
Andy Messersmith	.209
Juan Berenguer	.210
Ken Howell	.211
Eric Plunk	.212
Roger Clemens	.212
Orel Hershiser	.213
Skip Lockwood	.213
Dan Warthen	.213

Career Opp. Home Run Pct. vs. Right-Handed Batters
Min. 600 PA

Mark Fidrych	0.63
Rick Lysander	0.70
Doug Jones	0.78
Steve Howe	0.80
Randy Niemann	0.93
Doug Sisk	0.95
J.R. Richard	0.98
Duane Ward	0.99
Bill Swift	0.99
Dave Heaverlo	1.00
Kent Tekulve	1.02
Roger McDowell	1.06
Joe Magrane	1.08
Dave Frost	1.09
Mike Barlow	1.14
Greg Minton	1.21
Pablo Torrealba	1.24
Ed Farmer	1.24
Mark Littell	1.26
Terry Forster	1.27
Jim Kern	1.28
Pat Combs	1.30
Dale Murray	1.31
Dan Quisenberry	1.32
Mark Gubicza	1.33

Career Opp. Walk Pct. vs. Right-Handed Batters
Min. 600 PA

Dan Quisenberry	2.23
LaMarr Hoyt	3.49
Gary Nolan	3.51
Bret Saberhagen	3.63
Bob Stanley	4.24
Lary Sorensen	4.43
Ferguson Jenkins	4.52
Dick Bosman	4.65
Jim Barr	4.73
Luis DeLeon	4.77
Fernando Arroyo	4.84
Larry Andersen	4.87
Dennis Leonard	4.95
Bob Tewksbury	4.95
Tom Hausman	4.96
Doug Jones	5.06
Bill Gullickson	5.06
Roger Erickson	5.08
Moose Haas	5.10
Rick Reuschel	5.11
Rick Wise	5.12
Dennis Eckersley	5.15
Mark Knudson	5.17
Ed Lynch	5.19
Mike Caldwell	5.19

Career Opp. Strikeout Pct. vs. Right-Handed Batters
Min. 150 Strikeouts

Rob Dibble	32.74
Jeff Montgomery	29.78
Tom Henke	28.71
David Cone	28.07
Jose DeLeon	27.42
Lee Smith	26.72
Ken Howell	26.63
Mike Jackson	26.51
Roger Clemens	26.37
J.R. Richard	26.06
Ramon Martinez	26.03
Nolan Ryan	25.66
Tom Gordon	25.38
Dwight Gooden	24.72
Calvin Schiraldi	24.69
Skip Lockwood	24.68
Randy Myers	24.63
Victor Cruz	24.38
Bobby Witt	24.24
Cecilio Guante	24.17
Jeff Reardon	24.13
Mark Clear	24.02
Mark Huismann	23.97
John Smoltz	23.51
Lance McCullers	23.14

Single-Season Opp. Batting Avg. vs. Left-Handed Batters

Min. 125 PA

Neal Heaton, 1989	.132
Gregg Olson, 1989	.135
Zane Smith, 1989	.139
Mark Langston, 1989	.142
Bill Dawley, 1983	.142
Bob Lacey, 1977	.146
Mitch Williams, 1987	.146
Bryan Harvey, 1988	.147
Mark Clear, 1984	.147
Dave Smith, 1984	.152
Nolan Ryan, 1981	.153
Lance McCullers, 1988	.153
Ron Guidry, 1978	.156
Bob Shirley, 1978	.156
Larry McWilliams, 1983	.156
Matt Young, 1983	.158
Gary Lavelle, 1984	.158
Bill Scherrer, 1983	.158
Bud Black, 1989	.158
Rich Wortham, 1979	.159
Larry Gura, 1983	.159
John Smiley, 1988	.159
Tom Burgmeier, 1980	.159
Mike Caldwell, 1978	.160
Sid Monge, 1979	.161

Single-Season Opp. Batting Avg. vs. Right-Handed Batters

Min. 175 PA

J.R. Richard, 1980	.124
Mark Eichhorn, 1986	.135
Dave LaRoche, 1976	.139
Rich Gossage, 1977	.140
Jose DeLeon, 1989	.146
Mario Soto, 1980	.147
Lance McCullers, 1986	.154
Greg W. Harris, 1990	.156
Hank Webb, 1975	.156
Mike Scott, 1986	.156
Mark Clear, 1979	.157
Nolan Ryan, 1990	.158
Don Carman, 1985	.161
Jim Kern, 1979	.161
Jeff Reardon, 1984	.161
Aurelio Lopez, 1983	.162
Tom Niedenfuer, 1983	.162
Luis DeLeon, 1982	.163
Sid Monge, 1978	.164
Frank Williams, 1985	.164
David Cone, 1988	.165
Frank Williams, 1984	.166
Tim Burke, 1985	.166
Cecilio Guante, 1985	.166
Danny Darwin, 1990	.166

Career Opp. Batting Average in Home Games

Min. 500 PA

Randy Myers	.182
Sid Fernandez	.182
Rob Dibble	.190
Nolan Ryan	.195
J.R. Richard	.197
Ramon Martinez	.199
Mike Jackson	.208
Tom Henke	.208
Bert Roberge	.212
Randy D. Johnson	.212
Jeff M. Robinson	.213
Dwight Gooden	.213
Lance McCullers	.213
Mike Armstrong	.215
Joe Cowley	.215
Jeff Montgomery	.215
Mike Henneman	.215
Mario Soto	.216
Todd Worrell	.216
Skip Lockwood	.217
John Smoltz	.217
Jose DeLeon	.217
Al Holland	.218
David Cone	.218
Jeff Parrett	.219

Career Opp. Batting Average in Road Games

Min. 500 PA

Rob Dibble	.182
Mitch Williams	.190
Pat Perry	.194
Mark Littell	.203
John Fulgham	.208
Bobby Thigpen	.212
Jesse Orosco	.213
Greg W. Harris	.213
Erik Hanson	.216
Floyd Youmans	.216
Bruce Sutter	.219
Lee Smith	.219
Rich Gossage	.219
Eric Plunk	.220
Nolan Ryan	.221
Tom Henke	.221
John Martin	.222
J.R. Richard	.223
Barry Jones	.223
Dan Warthen	.224
Mario Soto	.224
Steve Bedrosian	.225
Roger Clemens	.225
Jose DeLeon	.225
Andy Messersmith	.226

Career Opp. Batting Average on Grass Surfaces

Min. 500 PA

Gregg Olson	.178
Randy Myers	.190
Sid Fernandez	.195
J.R. Richard	.195
Danny Frisella	.199
Bryan Harvey	.202
Tim Burke	.207
Erik Hanson	.207
Nolan Ryan	.208
Ramon Martinez	.210
Mark Littell	.211
Barry Jones	.212
Greg W. Harris	.213
Dan Warthen	.213
Mitch Williams	.213
Tom Henke	.219
Rod Scurry	.221
Trevor Wilson	.221
Andy Messersmith	.221
Rich Gossage	.222
Bill Laxton	.222
Jeff Reardon	.222
Dwight Gooden	.223
DeWayne Buice	.223
Joe Cowley	.223

Career Opp. Batting Average on Artificial Turf

Min. 500 PA

Rob Dibble	.182
Jesse Orosco	.196
Mike Norris	.197
Roger Clemens	.202
Nolan Ryan	.206
Mike Jackson	.208
Tom Henke	.211
Craig McMurtry	.211
Mark Littell	.212
Floyd Youmans	.212
Rich Gossage	.213
Jose DeLeon	.214
Tim Belcher	.215
J.R. Richard	.215
Jim Kern	.216
Tom Gordon	.216
Bobby Witt	.218
Mark Clear	.218
Todd Worrell	.218
Pat Perry	.218
Mario Soto	.219
Al Holland	.220
Frank LaCorte	.222
Rob Murphy	.224
Joe Sambito	.224

Career Opp. Batting Average in Day Games

Min. 500 PA

Nolan Ryan	.201
Eric Plunk	.204
Bob Kipper	.208
Steve Ontiveros	.209
Sid Fernandez	.211
Tim Burke	.212
Mark Littell	.214
Roger Clemens	.214
Joe Cowley	.214
Mario Soto	.216
Al Hrabosky	.216
Craig Lefferts	.217
Scott Garrelts	.218
Bob James	.218
Andy Messersmith	.221
Kelly Downs	.221
Rollie Fingers	.222
Steve Busby	.222
Dan Plesac	.222
Steve Bedrosian	.223
Bruce Berenyi	.223
Randy D. Johnson	.224
Ted Higuera	.224
Dave Smith	.224
Rich Gossage	.224

Career Opp. Batting Average in Night Games

Min. 500 PA

Rob Dibble	.190
Bryan Harvey	.195
Mitch Williams	.197
Randy Myers	.199
Sid Fernandez	.200
J.R. Richard	.205
Gregg Olson	.206
Nolan Ryan	.209
Mark Littell	.210
Tom Henke	.211
Jesse Orosco	.212
Floyd Youmans	.213
Tim Belcher	.214
Jose DeLeon	.215
Mark Gardner	.215
Dwight Gooden	.215
Jeff Lahti	.215
Rich Gossage	.217
Pat Perry	.217
Mike Norris	.218
Greg W. Harris	.218
David Cone	.219
Ramon Martinez	.220
Mike Henneman	.221
Luis DeLeon	.222

Career Opp. Batting Average vs. Ground-Ball Hitters
Min. 500 PA

Jesse Orosco	.200
Floyd Youmans	.202
Sid Fernandez	.203
J.R. Richard	.206
Nolan Ryan	.207
Jeff Montgomery	.208
David Cone	.208
Doug Corbett	.209
Ramon Martinez	.212
Randy Myers	.215
Rod Scurry	.216
Clay Carroll	.216
Jeff Lahti	.218
Dwight Gooden	.219
Pat Perry	.219
John Dopson	.220
Larry Demery	.220
Bobby Thigpen	.221
Orel Hershiser	.221
Andy McGaffigan	.222
Andy Messersmith	.222
Mark Littell	.223
Paul Assenmacher	.224
Tom Seaver	.225
Tim Belcher	.225

Single-Season Opp. Batting Avg. vs. Ground-Ball Hitters
Min. 150 PA

Jesse Orosco, 1983	.144
Floyd Youmans, 1986	.156
Gregg Olson, 1989	.158
Juan Nieves, 1988	.160
Tom Henke, 1986	.160
Tippy Martinez, 1983	.165
Jeff Lahti, 1984	.165
Andy McGaffigan, 1986	.165
Aurelio Lopez, 1978	.165
Sid Fernandez, 1985	.166
Mike Scott, 1988	.166
Bill Caudill, 1982	.168
Bill Sampen, 1990	.169
Mike Madden, 1983	.170
Andy McGaffigan, 1988	.170
Tom Griffin, 1980	.171
Nolan Ryan, 1976	.171
Joe Sambito, 1980	.172
Don Carman, 1985	.173
Rich Gossage, 1977	.173
Charlie Hough, 1978	.173
David Palmer, 1982	.174
Bruce Sutter, 1977	.176
Dave LaRoche, 1976	.178
John Dopson, 1988	.178

Career Opp. Batting Average vs. Fly-Ball Hitters
Min. 500 PA

Rob Dibble	.166
Mitch Williams	.195
Randy Myers	.195
Mark Littell	.201
Tom Henke	.201
Sid Fernandez	.204
Mike Jackson	.206
Nolan Ryan	.207
Greg W. Harris	.209
Mario Soto	.210
Todd Burns	.210
Jose DeLeon	.211
J.R. Richard	.213
Lance McCullers	.214
Rich Gossage	.214
Jeff A. Jones	.216
Buddy Schultz	.217
Randy D. Johnson	.218
Al Holland	.218
Todd Worrell	.218
Dan Warthen	.218
Andy Benes	.219
Norm Charlton	.220
Tom Niedenfuer	.220
Mark Clear	.221

Single-Season Opp. Batting Avg. vs. Fly-Ball Hitters
Min. 150 PA

Grant Jackson, 1976	.129
Tom Henke, 1989	.131
Tom Niedenfuer, 1983	.133
Mitch Williams, 1987	.144
Tom Hausman, 1979	.147
Rogelio Moret, 1977	.147
Mark Littell, 1976	.149
J.R. Richard, 1980	.152
Bob Stoddard, 1982	.152
Rob Dibble, 1989	.152
Tom Henke, 1987	.154
Rob Dibble, 1990	.154
Bob Kipper, 1989	.154
John D'Acquisto, 1978	.160
Steve Ontiveros, 1985	.161
Ron Reed, 1976	.162
Lee Smith, 1983	.162
Sid Monge, 1979	.163
Jose Rijo, 1988	.164
Steve Bedrosian, 1989	.164
Ron Davis, 1981	.164
Bruce Sutter, 1981	.167
Cecilio Guante, 1985	.167
Rich Gossage, 1977	.167
Jose DeLeon, 1989	.167

Career Opp. Batting Average on First Pass Through Batting Order
Min. 500 PA

Sid Fernandez	.179
Ramon Martinez	.181
Rob Dibble	.184
Floyd Youmans	.194
J.R. Richard	.194
Tim Belcher	.199
Nolan Ryan	.204
Bryan Harvey	.205
Randy Myers	.205
Gregg Olson	.205
Mark Littell	.205
Dwight Gooden	.206
Greg W. Harris	.207
Mitch Williams	.207
Jose DeLeon	.208
Bob Kipper	.210
Mario Soto	.211
Rod Scurry	.212
Mike Jackson	.212
Dan Warthen	.213
Rich Gossage	.214
Tom Henke	.215
Jeff Calhoun	.215
Jesse Orosco	.215
Roger Clemens	.216

Single-Season Opp. Batting Average on First Pass Through Batting Order
Min. 150 PA

Rich Gossage, 1981	.133
Sid Fernandez, 1985	.134
Danny Darwin, 1979	.137
Nolan Ryan, 1983	.143
Nolan Ryan, 1986	.147
Atlee Hammaker, 1983	.149
Scott Bankhead, 1988	.149
Sid Fernandez, 1990	.154
J.R. Richard, 1980	.156
Rob Murphy, 1986	.156
Kevin Saucier, 1981	.156
Jose Guzman, 1988	.158
Dave LaRoche, 1976	.158
Dennis Eckersley, 1990	.160
Rich Gossage, 1977	.160
Frank Viola, 1987	.161
Roger Clemens, 1986	.161
Juan Berenguer, 1983	.161
John D'Acquisto, 1978	.161
Dennis Eckersley, 1989	.162
Sid Fernandez, 1989	.163
Dennis Eckersley, 1975	.164
Bill Gullickson, 1981	.165
Jose DeLeon, 1986	.167
Tom Browning, 1988	.168

Career Opp. Strikeout Pct. on First Pass Through Batting Order
Min. 100 SO

Rob Dibble	32.93
Tom Henke	28.87
Sid Fernandez	27.89
Bryan Harvey	27.84
Randy Myers	27.50
Roger Clemens	27.02
J.R. Richard	26.92
Tim Belcher	26.40
Nolan Ryan	26.13
Tom Gordon	26.12
Ramon Martinez	25.49
Bobby Witt	25.49
Lee Smith	24.74
Gregg Olson	24.31
Floyd Youmans	24.19
Mark Langston	24.04
Dwight Gooden	24.01
Mark Davis	23.65
Dan Plesac	23.56
David Cone	23.40
Jose Rijo	23.23
Jose DeLeon	23.16
Bill Caudill	23.14
Ken Howell	23.13
Ken Dixon	23.04

Single-Season Opp. Strikeout Pct. on First Pass Through Batting Order
Min. 30 SO

Tom Henke, 1987	36.47
Rob Dibble, 1989	35.61
Rob Dibble, 1990	34.84
Andy Benes, 1989	34.44
J.R. Richard, 1980	34.44
Nolan Ryan, 1989	33.33
Skip Lockwood, 1975	33.13
Frank Tanana, 1975	33.11
Lee Smith, 1989	32.87
Tom Henke, 1989	32.74
Tom Henke, 1986	32.64
Bruce Sutter, 1977	32.53
J.R. Richard, 1979	32.46
Bruce Hurst, 1986	32.44
Dwight Gooden, 1984	32.26
Sid Fernandez, 1990	32.22
Jose DeLeon, 1983	31.85
Bryan Harvey, 1989	31.84
Bill Caudill, 1979	31.51
J.R. Richard, 1978	31.48
Mario Soto, 1982	31.43
Nolan Ryan, 1987	31.05
Joe Price, 1987	31.03
Bobby Witt, 1987	31.00
Len Barker, 1977	31.00

Career Opp. Batting Average in Late-Inning Pressure Situations

Min. 400 PA

Randy Myers	.183
Gregg Olson	.189
Bryan Harvey	.191
J.R. Richard	.200
Nolan Ryan	.201
Ross Grimsley	.202
Roger Clemens	.206
Mike Boddicker	.207
Bill Landrum	.208
Tug McGraw	.209
Mitch Williams	.210
Mark Littell	.210
Skip Lockwood	.210
Mario Soto	.211
Tom Henke	.211
Rich Gossage	.214
Don Carman	.215
Mark Clear	.216
Dennis Eckersley	.217
Gene Nelson	.218
Jose DeLeon	.219
Greg A. Harris	.219
Rob Dibble	.220
Aurelio Lopez	.221
Bill Caudill	.221

Single-Season Opp. Batting Average in Late-Inning Pressure Situations

Min. 150 PA

Mark Clear, 1986	.131
Tug McGraw, 1977	.141
Gregg Olson, 1989	.152
Dennis Eckersley, 1989	.153
Randy Myers, 1988	.155
Tug McGraw, 1975	.155
Dennis Eckersley, 1990	.158
Steve Carlton, 1982	.159
Rick Honeycutt, 1990	.161
Mitch Williams, 1987	.162
Ed Farmer, 1979	.162
Tom Niedenfuer, 1983	.162
Willie Hernandez, 1984	.163
Aurelio Lopez, 1979	.163
F. Valenzuela, 1985	.164
Nolan Ryan, 1976	.165
Bill Dawley, 1983	.165
Bill Caudill, 1982	.167
Jay Howell, 1988	.168
Tug McGraw, 1980	.169
Greg Maddux, 1988	.170
Steve Bedrosian, 1982	.171
Bill Landrum, 1989	.172
Rich Gossage, 1977	.172
Dave LaRoche, 1976	.173

Career Opp. Home Run Pct. in Late-Inning Pressure Situations

Min. 400 PA

Bill Landrum	0.27
Jim Todd	0.51
Dave Giusti	0.52
Steve Comer	0.71
Frank Williams	0.75
Greg W. Harris	0.84
Doug Jones	0.85
Doug Sisk	0.85
Fernando Valenzuela	0.88
Dale Murray	0.90
Gregg Olson	0.90
Andy McGaffigan	0.92
Don Carman	0.98
Dickie Noles	1.00
Dave A. Roberts	1.00
Pat Zachry	1.02
Rob Dibble	1.04
Don Stanhouse	1.05
Kent Tekulve	1.06
Warren Brusstar	1.08
Tommy John	1.10
Greg Minton	1.10
Greg Maddux	1.10
Zane Smith	1.11
Steve Howe	1.12

Career Opp. Strikeout Pct. in Late-Inning Pressure Situations

Min. 100 Strikeouts

Rob Dibble	32.90
Tom Henke	30.83
Bryan Harvey	29.45
Randy Myers	27.08
Nolan Ryan	26.05
Ken Howell	25.18
Roger Clemens	25.07
Lee Smith	24.75
Gregg Olson	24.56
Duane Ward	24.51
Mark Davis	24.21
Rick Aguilera	23.97
Bill Caudill	23.88
Dwight Gooden	23.62
Rich Gossage	23.61
Mike Schooler	23.54
Skip Lockwood	23.47
Jeff Montgomery	23.24
Mitch Williams	23.03
Scott Garrelts	22.86
Rob Murphy	22.82
Mark Clear	22.55
Paul Assenmacher	22.35
Dan Plesac	22.30
Rod Scurry	22.19

Career Opp. Batting Average in Late-Inning Pressure Situations with Runners on Base

Min. 150 PA

Mike Boddicker	.160
Gregg Olson	.173
Dave Tobik	.176
Steve Ontiveros	.178
Randy Myers	.178
J.R. Richard	.179
Roger Clemens	.183
Bryan Harvey	.192
Pat Zachry	.194
Steve McCatty	.196
Bill Caudill	.200
Charlie Leibrandt	.203
Jeff Brantley	.203
Cecilio Guante	.204
David Wells	.205
Joe Hesketh	.206
Bill Landrum	.207
Rob Dibble	.207
Sid Monge	.208
Byron McLaughlin	.208
Al Holland	.209
Jim Palmer	.209
Frank Pastore	.209
Jesse Orosco	.210
Doug Bair	.210

Single-Season Opp. Batting Avg. in Late-Inning Pressure Situations with Runners on Base

Min. 60 PA

Mark Clear, 1986	.085
Steve Ontiveros, 1985	.091
F. Valenzuela, 1981	.115
Gregg Olson, 1989	.118
Randy Myers, 1988	.124
Bud Black, 1986	.127
Craig Lefferts, 1984	.133
Gary Lavelle, 1975	.135
Jim Kern, 1976	.135
Bruce Sutter, 1976	.138
Doug Sisk, 1984	.139
Norm Charlton, 1989	.140
Frank Tanana, 1976	.140
Cecilio Guante, 1983	.140
Dave Tobik, 1982	.141
Tim Burke, 1987	.141
Steve Bedrosian, 1982	.141
Tug McGraw, 1975	.143
Mike Krukow, 1986	.143
Mitch Williams, 1987	.145
Nolan Ryan, 1976	.148
Aurelio Lopez, 1979	.148
Willie Hernandez, 1984	.149
Steve Carlton, 1982	.149

Career Opp. Home Run Pct. in Late-Inning Pressure Situations with Runners on Base

Min. 150 PA

Alejandro Pena	0/347
Jim Todd	0/213
Steve Comer	0/204
Greg W. Harris	0/177
Paul Hartzell	0/168
Jeff Brantley	0/167
Pat Clements	0/160
Dave Tomlin	0.20
Steve Howe	0.24
Orel Hershiser	0.35
Jim Kaat	0.43
Charlie Leibrandt	0.45
Don Carman	0.46
Andy McGaffigan	0.47
Pat Zachry	0.47
Barry Jones	0.48
Jerry Reuss	0.49
Dave A. Roberts	0.49
Mike Boddicker	0.53
Dave Giusti	0.55
Mike Proly	0.56
Ron Darling	0.56

Career Opp. Strikeout Pct. in Late-Inning Pressure Situations with Runners on Base

Min. 40 Strikeouts

Tom Henke	29.06
Rob Dibble	28.46
Bryan Harvey	27.45
Mitch Williams	25.20
Gregg Olson	24.81
Nolan Ryan	24.73
Randy Myers	24.69
Bill Caudill	24.68
Roger Clemens	24.34
Jeff Montgomery	24.34
Mark Clear	23.93
Lee Smith	23.45
Juan Berenguer	23.15
Dwight Gooden	23.05
Skip Lockwood	22.92
Calvin Schiraldi	22.78
Mike Schooler	22.70
Scott Garrelts	22.65
Paul Assenmacher	22.58
Duane Ward	22.45
Mark Davis	22.45
Mark Littell	22.28
Rob Murphy	22.22
Doug Bair	22.15
Lance McCullers	21.99

Career Opp. Batting Average with Runners on Base

Min. 500 PA

Randy Myers	.186
Jesse Orosco	.201
Todd Worrell	.207
Sid Fernandez	.214
Tom Henke	.215
Mitch Williams	.219
Mike Jackson	.222
Eric Plunk	.222
Rod Scurry	.222
Roger Clemens	.222
Jeff Montgomery	.222
Bill Caudill	.223
Bobby Thigpen	.223
Mark Clear	.223
J.R. Richard	.224
Nolan Ryan	.225
Craig Lefferts	.225
Mark Littell	.225
Dwight Gooden	.226
Jim Deshaies	.226
Jeff Reardon	.227
Mario Soto	.228
Victor Cruz	.228
Lee Smith	.228
Lance McCullers	.228

Single-Season Opp. Batting Average with Runners on Base

Min. 175 PA

John D'Acquisto, 1978	.155
Gene Garber, 1978	.160
Gregg Olson, 1989	.164
Jesse Orosco, 1984	.167
Rob Dibble, 1989	.167
Bill Caudill, 1980	.173
Mark Davis, 1989	.174
Jesse Orosco, 1983	.175
Jeff M. Robinson, 1988	.175
Jose DeLeon, 1986	.175
Rich Gossage, 1977	.175
Willie Hernandez, 1984	.176
Al Holland, 1983	.177
Charlie Hough, 1976	.177
Lee Smith, 1983	.178
Mike Jackson, 1988	.179
Jim Deshaies, 1986	.180
Dwight Gooden, 1985	.180
Mitch Williams, 1987	.180
Doug Bair, 1978	.181
Mike Scott, 1986	.181
Tippy Martinez, 1983	.181
Steve Farr, 1990	.181
Sid Monge, 1979	.182
Bruce Sutter, 1977	.182

Career Opp. Batting Average with Runners in Scoring Position

Min. 300 PA

Rob Dibble	.164
Randy Myers	.166
Jesse Orosco	.191
Mike Henneman	.196
Todd Worrell	.199
Bob Apodaca	.199
Cecilio Guante	.201
Steve Bedrosian	.202
David Cone	.205
Mitch Williams	.205
Steve Busby	.206
Sid Fernandez	.207
Floyd Youmans	.208
Craig Lefferts	.208
Lee Smith	.208
Roger Clemens	.210
Orel Hershiser	.210
Jeff Lahti	.212
Ramon Martinez	.213
Stan Thomas	.213
Joe Cowley	.214
Nolan Ryan	.214
Dwight Gooden	.214
Rich Gossage	.215
Jim Deshaies	.215

Single-Season Opp. Batting Average with Runners in Scoring Position

Min. 125 PA

Mark Davis, 1989	.123
Jim Deshaies, 1986	.140
Rich Gossage, 1978	.143
Dwight Gooden, 1985	.144
Eric Show, 1986	.145
Tim Burke, 1985	.147
Joe Cowley, 1985	.148
Tom Hilgendorf, 1975	.149
John Candelaria, 1977	.149
Cecilio Guante, 1983	.151
Lance McCullers, 1988	.153
Don Sutton, 1980	.153
Gene Garber, 1982	.156
Nolan Ryan, 1990	.156
Bob Lacey, 1977	.157
Sid Fernandez, 1988	.157
Steve Farr, 1990	.157
Tom Hausman, 1975	.159
Rich Gossage, 1977	.159
Mike Scott, 1986	.159
Steve McCatty, 1981	.161
Joe Magrane, 1988	.161
Jeff D. Robinson, 1987	.161
Craig Lefferts, 1989	.161
Gregg Olson, 1989	.162

Career Opp. Batting Average with 2 Outs and Runners on Base

Min. 250 PA

Todd Worrell	.186
Bill Caudill	.186
Victor Cruz	.190
Dave Smith	.190
Pete Ladd	.190
Paul Gibson	.191
Jack McDowell	.191
Dwight Gooden	.192
Randy Myers	.192
Jesse Orosco	.193
Craig Lefferts	.194
Sid Fernandez	.196
Mike Jackson	.196
Pat Dobson	.196
Joe Magrane	.197
Jim Deshaies	.201
Tim Belcher	.201
Cecilio Guante	.201
Paul Assenmacher	.201
Ron Darling	.202
Bruce Sutter	.202
Mark Portugal	.202
Bobby Thigpen	.202
J.R. Richard	.202
Lance McCullers	.203

Single-Season Opp. Batting Average with 2 Outs and Runners on Base

Min. 100 PA

Bill Caudill, 1980	.103
Mike Scott, 1986	.109
Pat Dobson, 1976	.115
Jerry Ujdur, 1982	.122
Joe Magrane, 1988	.133
Jeff M. Robinson, 1988	.133
Eric Show, 1986	.138
Jose Rijo, 1988	.141
John Tudor, 1984	.143
Ed Whitson, 1984	.143
Ron Darling, 1986	.143
Jose DeLeon, 1985	.144
Bob Forsch, 1978	.147
Lance McCullers, 1986	.148
Eduardo Rodriguez, 1976	.149
Sparky Lyle, 1978	.149
Dan Warthen, 1975	.149
Bill Campbell, 1977	.149
Ron Darling, 1988	.150
Frank Tanana, 1977	.150
Fred Norman, 1978	.152
Scott Garrelts, 1985	.152
Tom Seaver, 1981	.153
Scott Sanderson, 1980	.154
Luis Tiant, 1978	.155

Career Opp. Batting Average with 2 Outs and Runners in Scoring Position

Min. 150 PA

Rob Dibble	.104
Bob Apodaca	.165
Todd Worrell	.167
Ramon Martinez	.172
Craig Lefferts	.174
Victor Cruz	.175
Cecilio Guante	.175
Mike Henneman	.176
Lee Smith	.178
Pete Ladd	.181
Jack McDowell	.181
Paul Gibson	.182
Dave Smith	.184
Barry Jones	.184
J.R. Richard	.185
Jesse Orosco	.185
Steve Busby	.186
Doug Jones	.186
Pete Harnisch	.187
Randy Myers	.187
Ron Darling	.188
Tippy Martinez	.189
Dwight Gooden	.189
Sid Fernandez	.190
Joe Magrane	.190

Single-Season Opp. Batting Average with 2 Outs and Runners in Scoring Position

Min. 75 PA

Jack Morris, 1987	.082
Joe Magrane, 1988	.097
Dan Warthen, 1975	.100
John Tudor, 1984	.110
Bobby Witt, 1987	.111
Luis Tiant, 1978	.113
Gregg Olson, 1989	.113
Bill Gullickson, 1982	.118
Mike Scott, 1986	.119
Rich Gossage, 1978	.119
Ed Whitson, 1984	.119
Mike Krukow, 1986	.123
Brian Fisher, 1987	.125
Doug Corbett, 1980	.127
Ron Darling, 1986	.129
Mark Langston, 1988	.129
Frank Tanana, 1977	.130
Fred Norman, 1978	.130
Dwight Gooden, 1985	.133
Pat Dobson, 1976	.133
Chris Bosio, 1989	.134
Tim Burke, 1985	.134
John Smoltz, 1989	.135
Frank Tanana, 1976	.135
Bill Campbell, 1977	.136

Single-Season Doubles Allowed

Dennis Leonard, 1978	62
Bruce Hurst, 1984	60
Rick Sutcliffe, 1983	58
Dennis Eckersley, 1986	58
Jim Barr, 1977	57
Jim Clancy, 1983	57
Bill Gullickson, 1983	56
Shane Rawley, 1987	56
Andy Hawkins, 1989	56
Scott McGregor, 1983	55
John Montefusco, 1975	54
Dennis Leonard, 1980	54
Steve Rogers, 1983	54
Doyle Alexander, 1986	54
Mike Moore, 1987	54
Jimmy Key, 1989	54
Wilbur Wood, 1975	53
Ron Guidry, 1983	53
Mike Torrez, 1983	53
Doyle Alexander, 1984	53
Bob Knepper, 1985	53
Charlie Leibrandt, 1986	53

Single-Season Triples Allowed

Larry Christenson, 1976	17
P. Thormodsgard, 1977	16
Bret Saberhagen, 1988	16
Jim Barr, 1975	14
Jim Barr, 1977	14
Dave Goltz, 1977	14
Jim Kaat, 1977	14
Randy Jones, 1979	14
Craig Swan, 1979	14
Rick Sutcliffe, 1984	14
Ray Burris, 1976	13
Rick Reuschel, 1976	13
Luis Tiant, 1979	13
Steve Carlton, 1980	13
Dick Ruthven, 1980	13
Rich Gale, 1982	13
Tommy John, 1982	13
Mike Smithson, 1983	13

Single-Season Extra-Base Hits Allowed

Bert Blyleven, 1986	100
Phil Niekro, 1979	97
Dennis Leonard, 1978	94
Dennis Leonard, 1980	92
Rick Sutcliffe, 1983	92
Bert Blyleven, 1987	92
LaMarr Hoyt, 1984	91
Mike Witt, 1987	91
Doyle Alexander, 1988	91
Jerry Garvin, 1977	90
Mike Moore, 1987	90
Wilbur Wood, 1975	89
Jim Barr, 1977	89
Dan Petry, 1983	89
Mark Langston, 1986	89
Jim Clancy, 1983	88
Bill Gullickson, 1987	88
Ferguson Jenkins, 1979	87
Frank Viola, 1986	87
Willie Fraser, 1988	87

Career Opp. Extra-Base Hit Pct. (per 100 AB)

Min. 1,000 PA

Steve Howe	4.04
John Franco	4.66
Doug Sisk	4.82
Greg Minton	4.88
Roger McDowell	4.91
Bobby Thigpen	5.12
Greg W. Harris	5.12
Doug Jones	5.12
Mark Fidrych	5.13
Rob Dibble	5.23
Gary Lavelle	5.24
J.R. Richard	5.28
Alejandro Pena	5.31
Jim Kern	5.35
Dave Smith	5.39
Dwight Gooden	5.39
Mark Littell	5.40
Randy Myers	5.41
Orel Hershiser	5.41
Nolan Ryan	5.55
Clay Carroll	5.56
Bill Landrum	5.56
Frank Williams	5.61
Rich Gossage	5.61

Highest Career Ratio of Ground Outs to Air Outs

Min. 1,000 PA

Roger McDowell	3.05
Doug Corbett	2.96
Doug Sisk	2.79
Bill Swift	2.73
Tommy John	2.55
Ray Fontenot	2.53
Kevin Brown	2.51
Jeff Dedmon	2.42
Jim Todd	2.39
Greg Minton	2.38
Jaime Cocanower	2.34
Dan Quisenberry	2.31
Juan Agosto	2.29
Dennis Lamp	2.24
Kent Tekulve	2.23
John Denny	2.21
Bob Stanley	2.18
Bill Castro	2.17
Gene Garber	2.17
Randy Jones	2.13
Orel Hershiser	2.12
Jim Winn	2.11
Steve Trout	2.09
Bruce Ruffin	2.08
Terry Forster	2.06

Lowest Career Ratio of Ground Outs to Air Outs

Min. 1,000 PA

Sid Fernandez	0.46
Jeff Reardon	0.54
Mike Armstrong	0.55
Keith Atherton	0.56
Tom Niedenfuer	0.57
Chuck Cary	0.57
Victor Cruz	0.59
Don Carman	0.59
Pete Ladd	0.60
Roy Smith	0.60
Bill Caudill	0.60
Dave LaRoche	0.61
Chris Knapp	0.62
Cecilio Guante	0.62
Jim Deshaies	0.63
Juan Berenguer	0.63
Al Hrabosky	0.63
Tom Browning	0.64
Al Holland	0.65
Randy Myers	0.65
Skip Lockwood	0.66
Aurelio Lopez	0.67
Tim Conroy	0.67
Bob Kipper	0.67
Luis Tiant	0.67

Career Ground Out Pct. (per 100 PA)

Min. 1,000 PA

Roger McDowell	42.7
Dan Quisenberry	42.4
Randy Jones	41.3
Tommy John	41.3
Bill Swift	40.6
Doug Sisk	40.3
Bill Castro	40.0
Doug Corbett	39.9
Kevin Brown	39.5
Greg Minton	39.2
Ray Fontenot	39.2
Jim Todd	38.6
Kent Tekulve	38.5
Bob Stanley	38.4
Dennis Lamp	38.3
Paul Hartzell	38.2
Fernando Arroyo	38.0
Rob Dressler	37.8
Clay Carroll	37.5
Juan Agosto	37.5
Jaime Cocanower	37.4
Rick Matula	37.3
Jeff Dedmon	37.2
Dave Rozema	37.2
Mike Proly	37.1

Career Air Out Pct. (per 100 PA)

Min. 1,000 PA

Dave W. Johnson	36.1
Gary Nolan	36.0
Catfish Hunter	35.8
Tom Browning	35.7
Keith Atherton	35.3
John Martin	35.2
Mike Armstrong	34.8
Luis Tiant	34.3
Manny Sarmiento	34.2
Jeff Reardon	34.2
Roy Smith	34.2
Don Carman	34.1
Dennis Cook	34.1
Scott McGregor	34.1
Tom Niedenfuer	33.8
Sid Fernandez	33.8
Jim Deshaies	33.6
Larry Gura	33.6
Jose Bautista	33.5
Chris Knapp	33.3
Pete Ladd	33.3
Grant Jackson	33.2
Steve McCatty	33.1
Pete Filson	33.0
Brian Kingman	32.9

Career Opp. On-Base Average Leading Off Innings

Min. 250 PA

Erik Hanson	.235
Greg W. Harris	.244
Tim Crews	.249
Dan Quisenberry	.251
Mike Armstrong	.252
Greg Hibbard	.253
Mark Williamson	.258
John Martin	.261
Brad Havens	.262
Dave Tobik	.262
Rich Gossage	.264
Steve Howe	.266
Dennis Cook	.266
Tom Henke	.267
Chuck Cary	.268
Tug McGraw	.269
Mike Henneman	.271
Gary Nolan	.272
Jeff Reardon	.272
Darold Knowles	.273
Jose Bautista	.278
Gene Garber	.279
Marty Pattin	.279
Ken Dayley	.279
Pete Filson	.279

Single-Season Opp. On-Base Average Leading Off Innings

Min. 100 PA

Greg A. Harris, 1985	.175
Greg W. Harris, 1989	.180
Tim Crews, 1990	.186
Dan Quisenberry, 1984	.188
Sid Fernandez, 1989	.190
Vern Ruhle, 1983	.191
Randy Martz, 1981	.202
Jeff D. Robinson, 1988	.211
Jeff D. Robinson, 1986	.212
Joe Price, 1983	.212
Dan Quisenberry, 1983	.215
Curt Young, 1989	.217
Dave J. Schmidt, 1982	.217
John Tudor, 1985	.217
Mark Gardner, 1990	.218
Rich Gossage, 1978	.219
Duane Ward, 1990	.220
Mike Armstrong, 1982	.220
Chuck Cary, 1989	.220
Erik Hanson, 1989	.220
Dan Schatzeder, 1984	.221
Don Sutton, 1975	.221
Dwight Gooden, 1989	.221
Dennis Eckersley, 1977	.223
Pat Underwood, 1982	.223

Career Opp. Walk Pct. Leading Off Innings

Min. 250 PA

Tim Crews	1.56
Dan Quisenberry	2.27
Gene Garber	2.48
Gary Nolan	2.49
Kevin Kobel	3.02
Brian Holton	3.13
Bob Tewksbury	3.15
Ron Reed	3.54
Mark Fidrych	3.55
Steve Howe	3.58
Atlee Hammaker	3.61
Gary Lucas	3.78
Dave J. Schmidt	3.87
Gary Ross	3.88
Pedro Borbon	3.95
Dave Rozema	4.04
Jimmy Key	4.05
Jim Barr	4.05
Tommy John	4.06
Dennis Eckersley	4.06
Rick Reuschel	4.07
Bret Saberhagen	4.14
Roger Erickson	4.16
Scott Sanderson	4.24
LaMarr Hoyt	4.25

Single-Season Opp. Walk Pct. Leading Off Innings

Min. 100 PA

Dan Quisenberry, 1983	0/121
Gene Garber, 1982	0/108
Dan Quisenberry, 1985	0/105
Rick Langford, 1982	0.41
John Candelaria, 1988	0.62
Bob Tewksbury, 1990	0.66
Jim Barr, 1982	0.78
Tom Hausman, 1980	0.82
Bill Swift, 1990	0.84
Bob Forsch, 1980	0.89
Dave J. Schmidt, 1982	0.94
Dennis Eckersley, 1987	0.94
Dennis Martinez, 1986	0.95
Jeff D. Robinson, 1986	0.96
Tim Crews, 1990	0.98
Ron Reed, 1978	1.00
Allan Anderson, 1990	1.02
Mike Smithson, 1983	1.29
Gaylord Perry, 1981	1.29
Bryn Smith, 1987	1.29
Ferguson Jenkins, 1976	1.38
Glenn Abbott, 1983	1.45
Roger Clemens, 1984	1.45
Neal Heaton, 1987	1.48
Ron Guidry, 1981	1.49

Career Opp. Batting Average with Bases Loaded

Min. 50 PA

Bryan Harvey	.116
Jesse Orosco	.141
Ed Figueroa	.147
Doug Rau	.152
Don Carman	.154
Dave LaRoche	.159
Charlie Lea	.159
Dave Lemanczyk	.167
Ken Schrom	.175
Tom House	.179
Jim Deshaies	.180
Eric Show	.181
Jeff Dedmon	.182
Chuck Finley	.182
Jimmy Key	.182
Tippy Martinez	.183
Bruce Berenyi	.185
Ed Halicki	.185
Orel Hershiser	.186
Butch Metzger	.188
Tom Griffin	.188
Mark Gubicza	.188
Craig Swan	.189
Mike Smithson	.189
Greg Maddux	.190

Career Most Batters Faced with Bases Loaded Without Allowing a Grand-Slam Home Run

Joaquin Andujar	158
Jim Kern	148
Mike Krukow	148
Pat Zachry	128
Juan Berenguer	122
Eric Show	109
Gene Nelson	107
Joe Price	106
Jim Palmer	105
Mike Boddicker	101
Al Hrabosky	96
Andy Hassler	93
Jesse Jefferson	91
Steve Crawford	85
Bruce Berenyi	84
Bill Krueger	83
Ed Figueroa	82
Doug Corbett	80
Craig McMurtry	79
Dave J. Schmidt	78
Jay Howell	76
Bill Swift	75
Roy Thomas	75
Don Hood	74

Career Opp. Walk Pct. with Bases Loaded

Min. 50 PA

Steve Crawford	0/85
Rob Murphy	0/55
Todd Worrell	0/55
Dave Heaverlo	0.81
Vern Ruhle	1.01
Steve McCatty	1.10
Ed Vande Berg	1.20
Bill Swift	1.33
Ed Lynch	1.39
Dave Tobik	1.43
Jim Gott	1.45
Dennis Eckersley	1.47
Joe Magrane	1.52
Ted Higuera	1.64
Mike G. Marshall	1.64
Jay Tibbs	1.64
John Cerutti	1.67
Tom Glavine	1.69
Fred Breining	1.72
Calvin Schiraldi	1.72
John Butcher	1.75
Larry Christenson	1.79
Dave Dravecky	1.79

Career Opp. Strikeout Pct. with Bases Loaded

Min. 15 Strikeouts

Tim Birtsas	37.50
Paul Assenmacher	34.78
Rob Dibble	34.09
Bobby Witt	33.68
Tom Henke	29.11
Greg Cadaret	28.85
John Hiller	28.13
David Cone	27.78
Nolan Ryan	27.44
Bruce Berenyi	27.38
Kirk McCaskill	27.27
Mitch Williams	26.55
Mark Littell	26.51
Roger Clemens	25.35
Dave LaRoche	25.20
Bill Caudill	25.00
Lance McCullers	24.72
Dave Smith	24.71
Sid Fernandez	24.66
Al Holland	24.14
Steve Carlton	24.11
Lee Smith	23.97
Ron Guidry	23.76
Sammy Stewart	23.61
Mario Soto	23.53

BALLPARKS

The Ballparks section lists, for all 26 parks in use last season, a variety of statistics about the games played there over the past several years.

The effect of each ballpark on performance has become an almost obsessively discussed topic in the last decade. Even the simplest conversation about an off-season trade these days is likely to touch on such factors as the relative dimensions of the two parks involved, whether they have natural or artificial turf, the size of their foul territory, and how far they are above sea level. Without going into the sometimes sticky question of the reasons for such differences, we present here the facts of those differences, park by park.

For each stadium, a box contains the basic statistics for the games played there, as contrasted with that home team's games played on the road. The totals listed are the complete statistics *for both teams* in those games. Totals and percentage differences are listed for the 1990 season, and for the five-year period from 1986 through 1990. (The differences, in many cases, don't reflect the change between the actual raw totals printed, but rather between related per-game averages. For instance, we print the number of runs scored in home and road games, but compute the difference between the average number of runs *per game.*) Since the statistics represent performances by roughly the same set of players, the differences can be attributed to the peculiarities of the park. (The one case where this assumption does not hold is Toronto's Skydome, which opened during the 1989 season. Excluded from the home totals for 1989 are the following games that were played at Exhibition Stadium: three each against Kansas City, New York, Texas, Seattle, California, Minnesota, Cleveland, and Chicago; and two against Oakland. This may create a skew in the statistics; we are confident that this is not a major problem, and it will shrink in significance as the years progress. If you prefer, ignore the 1989–90 statistics and concentrate on those from 1990 alone.)

Following the pages of ballpark data are tables that rank the stadiums according to their effects on various elements of play. To illustrate, let's say that you find that the Oakland Coliseum reduced scoring by 13.9 percent over the past five seasons. You won't have to look through twenty-five other boxes to see where this ranks; the table marked "Ranked by Effect on Runs" will show that it stands dead last, with a negative percentage more than twice that of the next-lowest American League park.

In addition to scoring, we've ranked the parks in seven other categories. The fields with artificial playing surfaces are marked with an asterisk, giving you a quick read on what kind of impact they have had on the category in question. While the effect on batting average is open to question, the effects on such categories as extra-base hit percentage, stolen-base percentage, and errors are unmistakable.

BALTIMORE ORIOLES · MEMORIAL STADIUM

	1990 SEASON Home Games	Road Games	Pct. Diff.	1986–1990 Home Games	Road Games	Pct. Diff.
G	80	81	−1.2	402	406	−1.0
AB	5398	5491	−1.7	27401	27601	−0.7
1B	902	1023	−10.3	4902	5053	−2.3
2B	246	272	−8.0	1183	1271	−6.2
3B	15	22	−30.6	92	179	−48.2
HR	156	137	15.8	853	776	10.7
R	657	710	−6.3	3499	3678	−3.9
BA	.244	.265	−7.7	.257	.264	−2.7
SLG	.382	.397	−3.8	.400	.407	−1.8
XB%	.224	.223	0.5	.206	.223	−7.4
E	104	119	−11.5	558	570	−1.1
SHO	6	6	1.2	44	45	−1.2

CHICAGO WHITE SOX · COMISKEY PARK

	1990 SEASON Home Games	Road Games	Pct. Diff.	1986–1990 Home Games	Road Games	Pct. Diff.
G	80	82	−2.4	403	405	−0.5
AB	5360	5430	−1.3	27213	27432	−0.8
1B	987	961	4.0	5003	4887	3.2
2B	224	229	−0.9	1175	1210	−2.1
3B	53	40	34.2	243	160	53.1
HR	94	118	−19.3	583	763	−23.0
R	660	655	3.3	3494	3489	0.6
BA	.253	.248	2.1	.257	.256	0.6
SLG	.368	.370	−0.8	.383	.395	−3.1
XB%	.219	.219	0.2	.221	.219	0.9
E	114	122	−4.2	621	649	−3.8
SHO	5	12	−57.3	35	48	−26.7

BOSTON RED SOX · FENWAY PARK

	1990 SEASON Home Games	Road Games	Pct. Diff.	1986–1990 Home Games	Road Games	Pct. Diff.
G	81	81	0.0	404	405	−0.2
AB	5548	5485	1.1	27836	27644	0.7
1B	1092	1024	5.4	5365	5156	3.3
2B	313	254	21.8	1611	1242	28.8
3B	27	33	−19.1	140	146	−4.8
HR	105	93	11.6	669	710	−6.4
R	712	651	9.4	3879	3652	6.5
BA	.277	.256	8.2	.280	.262	6.6
SLG	.400	.365	9.5	.420	.395	6.3
XB%	.237	.219	8.5	.246	.212	16.0
E	129	118	9.3	614	606	1.6
SHO	12	17	−29.4	55	53	4.0

CLEVELAND INDIANS · CLEVELAND STADIUM

	1990 SEASON Home Games	Road Games	Pct. Diff.	1986–1990 Home Games	Road Games	Pct. Diff.
G	81	81	0.0	405	406	−0.2
AB	5486	5525	−0.7	27927	27744	0.7
1B	1064	1017	5.4	5405	5100	5.3
2B	260	271	−3.4	1234	1303	−5.9
3B	27	44	−38.2	154	178	−14.1
HR	138	135	2.9	731	760	−4.4
R	736	733	0.4	3809	3686	3.6
BA	.271	.266	2.2	.269	.265	1.8
SLG	.404	.404	0.1	.403	.407	−0.8
XB%	.212	.236	−10.2	.204	.225	−9.2
E	118	129	−8.5	651	645	1.2
SHO	11	9	22.2	49	43	14.2

CALIFORNIA ANGELS · ANAHEIM STADIUM

	1990 SEASON Home Games	Road Games	Pct. Diff.	1986–1990 Home Games	Road Games	Pct. Diff.
G	81	81	0.0	406	404	0.5
AB	5577	5541	0.6	27633	27729	−0.3
1B	1099	1045	4.5	5059	5132	−1.1
2B	223	249	−11.0	1085	1271	−14.3
3B	26	35	−26.2	129	177	−26.9
HR	144	109	31.3	797	677	18.1
R	714	682	4.7	3505	3666	−4.9
BA	.268	.260	3.1	.256	.262	−2.2
SLG	.394	.376	4.8	.391	.394	−0.7
XB%	.185	.214	−13.6	.194	.220	−12.1
E	134	133	0.8	610	640	−5.2
SHO	12	7	71.4	61	46	32.0

DETROIT TIGERS · TIGER STADIUM

	1990 SEASON Home Games	Road Games	Pct. Diff.	1986–1990 Home Games	Road Games	Pct. Diff.
G	81	81	0.0	405	405	0.0
AB	5366	5522	−2.8	27181	27807	−2.3
1B	931	992	−3.4	4626	5136	−7.9
2B	242	274	−9.1	1107	1313	−13.7
3B	28	26	10.8	134	166	−17.4
HR	167	159	8.1	882	789	14.4
R	771	733	5.2	3605	3836	−6.0
BA	.255	.263	−3.0	.248	.266	−6.7
SLG	.404	.408	−1.1	.396	.411	−3.5
XB%	.225	.232	−3.2	.212	.224	−5.4
E	131	126	4.0	643	603	6.6
SHO	9	10	−10.0	51	36	41.7

KANSAS CITY ROYALS · ROYALS STADIUM

	1990 SEASON Home Games	Road Games	Pct. Diff.	1986–1990 Home Games	Road Games	Pct. Diff.
G	81	80	1.2	404	404	0.0
AB	5553	5427	2.3	27519	27372	0.5
1B	1049	1002	2.3	5085	5014	0.9
2B	306	263	13.7	1420	1161	21.7
3B	46	32	40.5	256	158	61.2
HR	88	128	−32.8	480	700	−31.8
R	712	704	−0.1	3407	3419	−0.4
BA	.268	.263	2.1	.263	.257	2.4
SLG	.387	.394	−1.6	.386	.388	−0.5
XB%	.251	.227	10.5	.248	.208	19.0
E	138	119	14.5	609	592	2.9
SHO	6	11	−46.1	60	65	−7.7

NEW YORK YANKEES · YANKEE STADIUM

	1990 SEASON Home Games	Road Games	Pct. Diff.	1986–1990 Home Games	Road Games	Pct. Diff.
G	81	81	0.0	403	405	−0.5
AB	5537	5421	2.1	27623	27755	−0.5
1B	958	964	−2.7	5142	5070	1.9
2B	242	234	1.3	1244	1308	−4.4
3B	28	35	−21.7	114	154	−25.6
HR	142	149	−6.7	821	793	4.0
R	657	695	−5.5	3699	3744	−0.7
BA	.247	.255	−2.9	.265	.264	0.4
SLG	.378	.393	−3.9	.407	.408	−0.1
XB%	.220	.218	0.8	.209	.224	−6.7
E	120	104	15.4	608	572	6.8
SHO	11	10	10.0	43	46	−6.1

MILWAUKEE BREWERS · COUNTY STADIUM

	1990 SEASON Home Games	Road Games	Pct. Diff.	1986–1990 Home Games	Road Games	Pct. Diff.
G	81	81	0.0	404	405	−0.2
AB	5530	5636	−1.9	27726	27722	0.0
1B	1034	1098	−4.0	5244	5207	0.7
2B	243	270	−8.3	1213	1239	−2.1
3B	33	39	−13.8	158	159	−0.6
HR	119	130	−6.7	660	699	−5.6
R	730	762	−4.2	3632	3624	0.5
BA	.258	.273	−5.2	.262	.263	−0.4
SLG	.379	.404	−6.1	.389	.395	−1.6
XB%	.211	.220	−4.1	.207	.212	−2.1
E	134	147	−8.8	688	638	8.1
SHO	13	5	160.0	49	39	26.0

OAKLAND A'S · OAKLAND–ALAMEDA COUNTY COLISEUM

	1990 SEASON Home Games	Road Games	Pct. Diff.	1986–1990 Home Games	Road Games	Pct. Diff.
G	81	81	0.0	407	403	1.0
AB	5535	5507	−3.1	27144	27612	−1.7
1B	918	960	−1.3	4820	4873	0.6
2B	190	257	−23.7	1015	1305	−20.9
3B	22	32	−29.0	114	175	−33.7
HR	121	166	−24.8	670	823	−17.2
R	565	738	−23.4	3301	3796	−13.9
BA	.234	.257	−8.7	.244	.260	−6.2
SLG	.346	.406	−14.6	.364	.409	−11.1
XB%	.188	.231	−18.9	.190	.233	−18.5
E	113	111	1.8	625	640	−3.3
SHO	18	10	80.0	62	37	65.9

MINNESOTA TWINS · METRODOME

	1990 SEASON Home Games	Road Games	Pct. Diff.	1986–1990 Home Games	Road Games	Pct. Diff.
G	81	81	0.0	405	405	0.0
AB	5532	5498	0.6	27943	27308	2.3
1B	1065	1034	2.4	5152	5035	−0.0
2B	313	248	25.4	1507	1275	15.5
3B	47	26	79.7	191	132	41.4
HR	115	119	−4.0	819	770	3.9
R	753	642	17.3	3924	3552	10.5
BA	.278	.260	7.3	.274	.264	3.9
SLG	.414	.379	9.3	.430	.405	6.2
XB%	.253	.209	20.6	.248	.218	13.5
E	103	124	−16.9	553	590	−6.3
SHO	13	14	−7.1	35	55	−36.4

SEATTLE MARINERS · KINGDOME

	1990 SEASON Home Games	Road Games	Pct. Diff.	1986–1990 Home Games	Road Games	Pct. Diff.
G	81	81	0.0	406	403	0.7
AB	5444	5450	−0.1	27741	27154	2.2
1B	975	1015	−3.8	4889	5059	−5.4
2B	248	222	11.8	1380	1224	10.4
3B	23	28	−17.8	175	160	7.1
HR	109	118	−7.5	836	620	32.0
R	651	669	−2.7	3797	3467	8.7
BA	.249	.254	−1.9	.262	.260	0.9
SLG	.363	.370	−1.8	.415	.385	7.7
XB%	.217	.198	10.1	.241	.215	12.3
E	108	103	4.9	619	605	1.6
SHO	11	11	0.0	48	55	−13.4

TEXAS RANGERS · ARLINGTON STADIUM

	1990 SEASON Home Games	Road Games	Pct. Diff.	1986–1990 Home Games	Road Games	Pct. Diff.
G	82	80	2.5	406	403	0.7
AB	5520	5368	2.8	27406	27189	0.8
1B	1008	960	2.1	4980	4702	5.1
2B	248	255	−5.4	1175	1268	−8.1
3B	39	26	45.9	158	150	4.5
HR	123	100	19.6	738	689	6.3
R	702	670	2.2	3719	3620	2.0
BA	.257	.250	2.8	.257	.250	2.7
SLG	.383	.363	5.5	.392	.384	2.2
XB%	.222	.226	−2.1	.211	.232	−8.9
E	123	103	16.5	630	615	1.7
SHO	9	11	−20.2	31	45	−31.6

TORONTO BLUE JAYS · SKYDOME

	1990 SEASON Home Games	Road Games	Pct. Diff.	1989–1990 Home Games	Road Games	Pct. Diff.
G	81	81	0.0	136	162	−16.0
AB	5614	5499	2.1	9327	11144	−16.3
1B	1003	990	−0.8	1630	2051	−5.0
2B	261	261	−2.0	437	536	−2.6
3B	46	42	7.3	77	77	19.5
HR	175	135	27.0	259	262	18.1
R	726	702	3.4	1137	1446	−6.3
BA	.265	.260	1.9	.258	.263	−1.9
SLG	.421	.396	6.3	.404	.395	2.4
XB%	.234	.234	0.0	.240	.230	4.2
E	95	106	−10.4	170	246	−17.7
SHO	8	11	−27.3	16	19	0.3

ATLANTA BRAVES · ATLANTA–FULTON COUNTY STADIUM

	1990 Season			1986–1990		
	Home Games	Road Games	Pct. Diff.	Home Games	Road Games	Pct. Diff.
G	81	81	0.0	401	404	−0.7
AB	5613	5441	3.2	27698	27020	2.5
1B	1077	951	9.8	5206	4827	5.2
2B	269	260	0.3	1268	1197	3.3
3B	21	35	−41.8	130	141	−10.1
HR	155	135	11.3	701	605	13.0
R	779	724	7.6	3670	3303	11.9
BA	.271	.254	6.8	.264	.251	5.3
SLG	.409	.389	5.3	.395	.372	6.0
XB%	.212	.237	−10.4	.212	.217	−2.5
E	150	136	10.3	718	661	9.4
SHO	12	10	20.0	41	50	−17.4

HOUSTON ASTROS · ASTRODOME

	1990 Season			1986–1990		
	Home Games	Road Games	Pct. Diff.	Home Games	Road Games	Pct. Diff.
G	81	81	0.0	406	404	0.5
AB	5414	5446	−0.6	27333	27354	−0.1
1B	970	989	−1.3	4870	4709	3.5
2B	221	225	−1.2	1138	1192	−4.5
3B	41	27	52.7	173	178	−2.7
HR	82	142	−41.9	459	690	−33.4
R	569	660	−13.8	3046	3296	−8.0
BA	.243	.254	−4.4	.243	.247	−1.8
SLG	.344	.383	−10.2	.348	.380	−8.5
XB%	.213	.203	4.7	.212	.225	−5.9
E	117	122	−4.1	617	673	−8.8
SHO	13	9	44.4	68	51	32.7

CHICAGO CUBS · WRIGLEY FIELD

	1990 Season			1986–1990		
	Home Games	Road Games	Pct. Diff.	Home Games	Road Games	Pct. Diff.
G	81	81	0.0	404	404	0.0
AB	5703	5465	4.4	28196	27457	2.7
1B	1167	967	15.6	5473	4916	8.4
2B	273	237	10.4	1264	1301	−5.4
3B	42	41	−1.8	197	188	2.0
HR	148	109	30.1	774	607	24.2
R	809	655	23.5	3806	3319	14.7
BA	.286	.248	15.4	.273	.255	7.0
SLG	.426	.366	16.5	.415	.383	8.3
XB%	.213	.223	−4.8	.211	.232	−9.4
E	146	134	9.0	738	609	21.2
SHO	5	11	−54.5	44	45	−2.2

LOS ANGELES DODGERS · DODGER STADIUM

	1990 Season			1986–1990		
	Home Games	Road Games	Pct. Diff.	Home Games	Road Games	Pct. Diff.
G	81	81	0.0	405	403	0.5
AB	5499	5469	0.5	27289	27515	−0.8
1B	1037	985	4.7	5151	4809	8.0
2B	193	262	−26.7	973	1323	−25.8
3B	25	32	−22.3	99	145	−31.2
HR	127	139	−9.1	508	625	−18.0
R	674	739	−8.8	2986	3316	−10.4
BA	.251	.259	−3.1	.247	.251	−1.7
SLG	.365	.395	−7.7	.345	.378	−8.5
XB%	.174	.230	−24.4	.172	.234	−26.3
E	159	113	40.7	720	692	3.5
SHO	8	12	−33.3	75	67	11.4

CINCINNATI REDS · RIVERFRONT STADIUM

	1990 Season			1986–1990		
	Home Games	Road Games	Pct. Diff.	Home Games	Road Games	Pct. Diff.
G	81	81	0.0	404	405	−0.2
AB	5418	5556	−2.5	27541	27488	0.2
1B	951	1009	−3.3	4860	4888	−0.8
2B	248	276	−7.9	1348	1212	11.0
3B	28	43	−33.2	151	162	−7.0
HR	143	106	38.3	767	620	23.5
R	646	644	0.3	3530	3304	7.1
BA	.253	.258	−2.0	.259	.250	3.3
SLG	.388	.380	2.0	.402	.374	7.6
XB%	.225	.240	−6.4	.236	.219	7.4
E	101	128	−21.1	581	680	−14.3
SHO	9	11	−18.2	39	60	−34.8

MONTREAL EXPOS · OLYMPIC STADIUM

	1990 Season			1986–1990		
	Home Games	Road Games	Pct. Diff.	Home Games	Road Games	Pct. Diff.
G	81	81	0.0	404	406	−0.5
AB	5400	5559	−2.9	27520	27568	−0.2
1B	943	1002	−3.1	4789	4894	−2.0
2B	234	221	9.0	1322	1181	12.1
3B	36	35	5.9	212	183	16.0
HR	110	131	−13.6	570	614	−7.0
R	596	664	−10.2	3300	3228	2.7
BA	.245	.250	−1.9	.250	.249	0.5
SLG	.363	.373	−2.7	.376	.372	1.0
XB%	.223	.203	9.4	.243	.218	11.3
E	125	125	0.0	673	643	5.2
SHO	10	8	25.0	46	63	−26.6

NEW YORK METS · SHEA STADIUM

	1990 Season			1986–1990		
	Home Games	Road Games	Pct. Diff.	Home Games	Road Games	Pct. Diff.
G	81	81	0.0	404	404	0.0
AB	5399	5548	−2.7	26994	27840	−3.0
1B	905	1003	−7.3	4623	4940	−3.5
2B	238	254	−3.7	1144	1305	−9.6
3B	25	33	−22.2	134	165	−16.2
HR	138	153	−7.3	653	708	−4.9
R	677	711	−4.8	3188	3595	−11.3
BA	.242	.260	−7.0	.243	.256	−5.0
SLG	.372	.401	−7.1	.368	.391	−5.9
XB%	.225	.222	1.2	.217	.229	−5.6
E	141	126	11.9	673	680	−1.0
SHO	14	8	75.0	55	43	27.9

ST. LOUIS CARDINALS · BUSCH STADIUM

	1990 Season			1986–1990		
	Home Games	Road Games	Pct. Diff.	Home Games	Road Games	Pct. Diff.
G	81	81	0.0	407	404	0.7
AB	5553	5397	2.9	27619	27235	1.4
1B	1020	1022	−3.0	4990	4967	−0.9
2B	285	250	10.8	1379	1234	10.2
3B	51	31	59.9	252	177	40.4
HR	90	81	8.0	413	493	−17.4
R	685	612	11.9	3294	3157	3.6
BA	.260	.256	1.5	.255	.252	0.9
SLG	.379	.359	5.4	.368	.365	0.8
XB%	.248	.216	14.9	.246	.221	11.3
E	116	121	−4.1	628	638	−2.3
SHO	10	18	−44.4	44	69	−36.7

PHILADELPHIA PHILLIES · VETERANS STADIUM

	1990 Season			1986–1990		
	Home Games	Road Games	Pct. Diff.	Home Games	Road Games	Pct. Diff.
G	81	81	0.0	404	406	−0.5
AB	5486	5500	−0.3	27387	27407	−0.1
1B	959	1032	−6.8	4750	4979	−4.5
2B	271	242	12.3	1386	1180	17.5
3B	33	27	22.5	203	147	38.2
HR	114	113	1.1	661	660	0.2
R	678	697	−2.7	3578	3395	5.9
BA	.251	.257	−2.4	.256	.254	0.6
SLG	.375	.373	0.6	.393	.380	3.5
XB%	.241	.207	16.4	.251	.210	19.1
E	94	128	−26.6	579	665	−12.5
SHO	13	5	160.0	57	39	46.9

SAN DIEGO PADRES · SAN DIEGO/JACK MURPHY STADIUM

	1990 Season			1986–1990		
	Home Games	Road Games	Pct. Diff.	Home Games	Road Games	Pct. Diff.
G	81	81	0.0	405	404	0.2
AB	5570	5550	0.4	27190	27484	−1.1
1B	1019	1035	−1.9	4810	5166	−5.9
2B	224	253	−11.8	1077	1232	−11.6
3B	41	24	70.2	166	157	6.9
HR	141	129	8.9	716	587	23.3
R	690	656	5.2	3249	3352	−3.3
BA	.256	.260	−1.5	.249	.260	−4.2
SLG	.387	.384	0.8	.380	.380	−0.1
XB%	.206	.211	−2.2	.205	.212	−3.1
E	135	137	−1.5	677	693	−2.6
SHO	9	9	0.0	54	45	19.7

PITTSBURGH PIRATES · THREE RIVERS STADIUM

	1990 Season			1986–1990		
	Home Games	Road Games	Pct. Diff.	Home Games	Road Games	Pct. Diff.
G	81	81	0.0	405	405	0.0
AB	5322	5514	−3.5	27340	27339	0.0
1B	902	988	−5.4	4638	4879	−4.9
2B	269	256	8.9	1337	1263	5.9
3B	36	38	−1.8	195	207	−5.8
HR	122	151	−16.3	614	637	−3.6
R	650	702	−7.4	3338	3428	−2.6
BA	.250	.260	−3.9	.248	.256	−2.9
SLG	.383	.402	−4.9	.379	.387	−2.1
XB%	.253	.229	10.2	.248	.232	7.2
E	109	133	−18.0	663	646	2.6
SHO	8	8	0.0	48	46	4.3

SAN FRANCISCO GIANTS · CANDLESTICK PARK

	1990 Season			1986–1990		
	Home Games	Road Games	Pct. Diff.	Home Games	Road Games	Pct. Diff.
G	81	81	0.0	405	405	0.0
AB	5591	5523	1.2	27247	27647	−1.4
1B	1074	1041	1.9	4787	4973	−2.3
2B	242	231	3.5	1179	1195	0.1
3B	26	39	−34.1	141	203	−29.5
HR	151	132	13.0	676	666	3.0
R	720	709	1.6	3250	3542	−8.2
BA	.267	.261	2.2	.249	.255	−2.2
SLG	.401	.389	3.0	.377	.385	−2.0
XB%	.200	.206	−3.0	.216	.219	−1.5
E	123	113	8.8	673	660	2.0
SHO	5	7	−28.6	54	47	14.9

RANKED BY EFFECT ON RUNS

	1990 SEASON			1986–1990		
	Home Games	Road Games	Pct. Diff.	Home Games	Road Games	Pct. Diff.
Wrigley Field	809	655	23.5	3806	3319	14.7
Atlanta Stadium	779	724	7.6	3670	3303	11.9
*Metrodome	753	642	17.3	3924	3552	10.5
*Kingdome	651	669	−2.7	3797	3467	8.7
*Riverfront Stadium	646	644	0.3	3530	3304	7.1
Fenway Park	712	651	9.4	3879	3652	6.5
*Veterans Stadium	678	697	−2.7	3578	3395	5.9
Cleveland Stadium	736	733	0.4	3809	3686	3.6
*Busch Stadium	685	612	11.9	3294	3157	3.6
*Olympic Stadium	596	664	−10.2	3300	3228	2.7
Arlington Stadium	702	670	2.2	3719	3620	2.0
Comiskey Park	660	655	3.3	3494	3489	0.6
County Stadium	730	762	−4.2	3632	3624	0.5
*Royals Stadium	712	704	−0.1	3407	3419	−0.4
Yankee Stadium	657	695	−5.5	3699	3744	−0.7
*Three Rivers Stadium	650	702	−7.4	3338	3428	−2.6
San Diego Stadium	690	656	5.2	3249	3352	−3.3
Memorial Stadium	657	710	−6.3	3499	3678	−3.9
Anaheim Stadium	714	682	4.7	3505	3666	−4.9
Tiger Stadium	771	733	5.2	3605	3836	−6.0
*Skydome	726	702	3.4	1137	1446	−6.3
*Astrodome	569	660	−13.8	3046	3296	−8.0
Candlestick Park	720	709	1.6	3250	3542	−8.2
Dodger Stadium	674	739	−8.8	2986	3316	−10.4
Shea Stadium	677	711	−4.8	3188	3595	−11.3
Oakland Coliseum	565	738	−23.4	3301	3796	−13.9

RANKED BY EFFECT ON HOME RUNS

	1990 SEASON			1986–1990		
	Home Games	Road Games	Pct. Diff.	Home Games	Road Games	Pct. Diff.
*Kingdome	109	118	−7.5	836	620	32.0
Wrigley Field	148	109	30.1	774	607	24.2
*Riverfront Stadium	143	106	38.3	767	620	23.5
San Diego Stadium	141	129	8.9	716	587	23.3
Anaheim Stadium	144	109	31.3	797	677	18.1
*Skydome	175	135	27.0	259	262	18.1
Tiger Stadium	167	159	8.1	882	789	14.4
Atlanta Stadium	155	135	11.3	701	605	13.0
Memorial Stadium	156	137	15.8	853	776	10.7
Arlington Stadium	123	100	19.6	738	689	6.3
Yankee Stadium	142	149	−6.7	821	793	4.0
*Metrodome	115	119	−4.0	819	770	3.9
Candlestick Park	151	132	13.0	676	666	3.0
*Veterans Stadium	114	113	1.1	661	660	0.2
*Three Rivers Stadium	122	151	−16.3	614	637	−3.6
Cleveland Stadium	138	135	2.9	731	760	−4.4
Shea Stadium	138	153	−7.3	653	708	−4.9
County Stadium	119	130	−6.7	660	699	−5.6
Fenway Park	105	93	11.6	669	710	−6.4
*Olympic Stadium	110	131	−13.6	570	614	−7.0
Oakland Coliseum	121	166	−24.8	670	823	−17.2
*Busch Stadium	90	81	8.0	413	493	−17.4
Dodger Stadium	127	139	−9.1	508	625	−18.0
Comiskey Park	94	118	−19.3	583	763	−23.0
*Royals Stadium	88	128	−32.8	480	700	−31.8
*Astrodome	82	142	−41.9	459	690	−33.4

RANKED BY EFFECT ON BATTING AVERAGE

	1990 SEASON			1986–1990		
	Home Games	Road Games	Pct. Diff.	Home Games	Road Games	Pct. Diff.
Wrigley Field	.286	.248	15.4	.273	.255	7.0
Fenway Park	.277	.256	8.2	.280	.262	6.6
Atlanta Stadium	.271	.254	6.8	.264	.251	5.3
*Metrodome	.278	.260	7.3	.274	.264	3.9
*Riverfront Stadium	.253	.258	−2.0	.259	.250	3.3
Arlington Stadium	.257	.250	2.8	.257	.250	2.7
*Royals Stadium	.268	.263	2.1	.263	.257	2.4
Cleveland Stadium	.271	.266	2.2	.269	.265	1.8
*Busch Stadium	.260	.256	1.5	.255	.252	0.9
*Kingdome	.249	.254	−1.9	.262	.260	0.9
Comiskey Park	.253	.248	2.1	.257	.256	0.6
*Veterans Stadium	.251	.257	−2.4	.256	.254	0.6
*Olympic Stadium	.245	.250	−1.9	.250	.249	0.5
Yankee Stadium	.247	.255	−2.9	.265	.264	0.4
County Stadium	.258	.273	−5.2	.262	.263	−0.4
Dodger Stadium	.251	.259	−3.1	.247	.251	−1.7
*Astrodome	.243	.254	−4.4	.243	.247	−1.8
*Skydome	.265	.260	1.9	.258	.263	−1.9
Candlestick Park	.267	.261	2.2	.249	.255	−2.2
Anaheim Stadium	.268	.260	3.1	.256	.262	−2.2
Memorial Stadium	.244	.265	−7.7	.257	.264	−2.7
*Three Rivers Stadium	.250	.260	−3.9	.248	.256	−2.9
San Diego Stadium	.256	.260	−1.5	.249	.260	−4.2
Shea Stadium	.242	.260	−7.0	.243	.256	−5.0
Oakland Coliseum	.234	.257	−8.7	.244	.260	−6.2
Tiger Stadium	.255	.263	−3.0	.248	.266	−6.7

RANKED BY EFFECT ON SLUGGING PERCENTAGE

	1990 SEASON			1986–1990		
	Home Games	Road Games	Pct. Diff.	Home Games	Road Games	Pct. Diff.
Wrigley Field	.426	.366	16.5	.415	.383	8.3
*Kingdome	.363	.370	−1.8	.415	.385	7.7
*Riverfront Stadium	.388	.380	2.0	.402	.374	7.6
Fenway Park	.400	.365	9.5	.420	.395	6.3
*Metrodome	.414	.379	9.3	.430	.405	6.2
Atlanta Stadium	.409	.389	5.3	.395	.372	6.0
*Veterans Stadium	.375	.373	0.6	.393	.380	3.5
*Skydome	.421	.396	6.3	.404	.395	2.4
Arlington Stadium	.383	.363	5.5	.392	.384	2.2
*Olympic Stadium	.363	.373	−2.7	.376	.372	1.0
*Busch Stadium	.379	.359	5.4	.368	.365	0.8
Yankee Stadium	.378	.393	−3.9	.407	.408	−0.1
San Diego Stadium	.387	.384	0.8	.380	.380	−0.1
*Royals Stadium	.387	.394	−1.6	.386	.388	−0.5
Anaheim Stadium	.394	.376	4.8	.391	.394	−0.7
Cleveland Stadium	.404	.404	0.1	.403	.407	−0.8
County Stadium	.379	.404	−6.1	.389	.395	−1.6
Memorial Stadium	.382	.397	−3.8	.400	.407	−1.8
Candlestick Park	.401	.389	3.0	.377	.385	−2.0
*Three Rivers Stadium	.383	.402	−4.9	.379	.387	−2.1
Comiskey Park	.368	.370	−0.8	.383	.395	−3.1
Tiger Stadium	.404	.408	−1.1	.396	.411	−3.5
Shea Stadium	.372	.401	−7.1	.368	.391	−5.9
*Astrodome	.344	.383	−10.2	.348	.380	8.5
Dodger Stadium	.365	.395	−7.7	.345	.378	−8.5
Oakland Coliseum	.346	.406	−14.6	.364	.409	−11.1

RANKED BY EFFECT ON EXTRA–BASE HIT PERCENTAGE

	1990 SEASON			1986–1990		
	Home Games	Road Games	Pct. Diff.	Home Games	Road Games	Pct. Diff.
*Veterans Stadium	.241	.207	16.4	.251	.210	19.1
*Royals Stadium	.251	.227	10.5	.248	.208	19.0
Fenway Park	.237	.219	8.5	.246	.212	16.0
*Metrodome	.253	.209	20.6	.248	.218	13.5
*Kingdome	.217	.198	10.1	.241	.215	12.3
*Busch Stadium	.248	.216	14.9	.246	.221	11.3
*Olympic Stadium	.223	.203	9.4	.243	.218	11.3
*Riverfront Stadium	.225	.240	−6.4	.236	.219	7.4
*Three Rivers Stadium	.253	.229	10.2	.248	.232	7.2
*Skydome	.234	.234	0.0	.240	.230	4.2
Comiskey Park	.219	.219	0.2	.221	.219	0.9
Candlestick Park	.200	.206	−3.0	.216	.219	−1.5
County Stadium	.211	.220	−4.1	.207	.212	−2.1
Atlanta Stadium	.212	.237	−10.4	.212	.217	−2.5
San Diego Stadium	.206	.211	−2.2	.205	.212	−3.1
Tiger Stadium	.225	.232	−3.2	.212	.224	−5.4
Shea Stadium	.225	.222	1.2	.217	.229	−5.6
*Astrodome	.213	.203	4.7	.212	.225	−5.9
Yankee Stadium	.220	.218	0.8	.209	.224	−6.7
Memorial Stadium	.224	.223	0.5	.206	.223	−7.4
Arlington Stadium	.222	.226	−2.1	.211	.232	−8.9
Cleveland Stadium	.212	.236	−10.2	.204	.225	−9.2
Wrigley Field	.213	.223	−4.8	.211	.232	−9.4
Anaheim Stadium	.185	.214	−13.6	.194	.220	−12.1
Oakland Coliseum	.188	.231	−18.9	.190	.233	−18.5
Dodger Stadium	.174	.230	−24.4	.172	.234	−26.3

RANKED BY EFFECT ON STRIKEOUT PERCENTAGE

	1990 SEASON			1986–1990		
	Home Games	Road Games	Pct. Diff.	Home Games	Road Games	Pct. Diff.
San Diego Stadium	.155	.140	10.5	.160	.143	11.7
Tiger Stadium	.149	.142	4.7	.148	.139	6.8
Oakland Coliseum	.151	.147	2.5	.159	.150	5.9
Shea Stadium	.170	.169	0.7	.169	.161	5.3
Memorial Stadium	.149	.133	12.2	.142	.136	4.8
*Astrodome	.156	.147	6.8	.162	.155	4.6
*Metrodome	.131	.134	−1.6	.145	.139	4.0
*Olympic Stadium	.164	.162	1.6	.164	.160	2.3
Arlington Stadium	.172	.160	7.4	.169	.166	1.7
County Stadium	.130	.126	2.9	.146	.144	1.5
Anaheim Stadium	.151	.160	−5.4	.149	.147	1.3
*Veterans Stadium	.142	.138	3.0	.153	.151	0.7
Candlestick Park	.144	.139	3.4	.159	.158	0.6
Wrigley Field	.135	.146	−7.5	.152	.151	0.4
Fenway Park	.146	.143	2.6	.144	.145	−0.5
*Kingdome	.140	.153	−8.5	.149	.150	−0.7
Yankee Stadium	.156	.159	−1.8	.144	.145	−0.8
*Three Rivers Stadium	.147	.143	2.5	.144	.146	−1.8
Dodger Stadium	.162	.160	0.8	.160	.165	−3.0
Comiskey Park	.149	.151	−1.8	.140	.146	−3.9
*Skydome	.149	,153	−2.9	.144	.150	−4.6
*Riverfront Stadium	.154	,162	−5.1	.150	.158	−4.6
Cleveland Stadium	.136	.141	−3.5	.136	.144	−5.4
*Bush Stadium	.128	.146	−11.9	.134	.144	−7.1
Atlanta Stadium	.155	.159	−2.3	.141	.154	−8.1
*Royals Stadium	.149	.158	−5.4	.143	.163	−12.4

RANKED BY EFFECT ON STOLEN BASE PERCENTAGE

	1990 SEASON			1986–1990		
	Home Games	Road Games	Pct. Diff.	Home Games	Road Games	Pct. Diff.
*Astrodome	.751	.672	11.7	.782	.712	9.8
*Kingdome	.724	.627	15.6	.673	.637	5.6
*Metrodome	.606	.661	−8.2	.693	.657	5.5
*Busch Stadium	.739	.677	9.2	.742	.710	4.6
*Veterans Stadium	.743	.665	11.7	.728	.697	4.4
Comiskey Park	.632	.571	10.7	.673	.647	3.9
*Olympic Stadium	.781	.718	8.9	.741	.720	3.0
*Royals Stadium	.679	.737	−7.9	.694	.684	1.4
Oakland Coliseum	.680	.694	−2.1	.695	.686	1.3
County Stadium	.721	.681	6.0	.694	.686	1.1
*Riverfront Stadium	.704	.705	−0.1	.710	.704	0.9
Memorial Stadium	.662	.683	−3.1	.679	.675	0.5
Tiger Stadium	.659	.646	2.0	.676	.673	0.4
San Diego Stadium	.690	.698	−1.1	.673	.671	0.3
*Skydome	.603	.661	−8.8	.659	.663	−0.6
Cleveland Stadium	.675	.642	5.3	.677	.690	−1.8
*Three Rivers Stadium	.663	.726	−8.7	.676	.691	−2.1
Candlestick Park	.705	.697	1.2	.624	.645	−3.4
Atlanta Stadium	.686	.713	−3.7	.648	.672	−3.6
Yankee Stadium	.665	.615	8.2	.671	.708	−5.2
Anaheim Stadium	.517	.641	−19.3	.621	662	−6.2
Shea Stadium	.728	.772	−5.8	.722	.772	−6.5
Arlington Stadium	.694	.732	−5.2	.680	.729	−6.6
Wrigley Field	.652	.741	−12.0	.648	.694	−6.6
Dodger Stadium	.636	.751	−15.4	.640	.686	−6.7
Fenway Park	.612	.627	−2.4	.614	.664	−7.6

RANKED BY EFFECT ON ERRORS

	1990 SEASON			1986–1990		
	Home Games	Road Games	Pct. Diff.	Home Games	Road Games	Pct. Diff.
Wrigley Field	146	134	9.0	738	609	21.2
Atlanta Stadium	150	136	10.3	718	661	9.4
County Stadium	134	147	−8.8	688	638	8.1
Yankee Stadium	120	104	15.4	608	572	6.8
Tiger Stadium	131	126	4.0	643	603	6.6
*Olympic Stadium	125	125	0.0	673	643	5.2
Dodger Stadium	159	113	40.7	720	692	3.5
*Royals Stadium	138	119	14.5	609	592	2.9
*Three Rivers Stadium	109	133	−18.0	663	646	2.6
Candlestick Park	123	113	8.8	673	660	2.0
Arlington Stadium	123	103	16.5	630	615	1.7
Fenway Park	129	118	9.3	614	606	1.6
*Kingdome	108	103	4.9	619	605	1.6
Cleveland Stadium	118	129	−8.5	651	645	1.2
Shea Stadium	141	126	11.9	673	680	−1.0
Memorial Stadium	104	119	−11.5	558	570	−1.1
*Busch Stadium	116	121	−4.1	628	638	−2.3
San Diego Stadium	135	137	−1.5	677	693	−2.6
Oakland Coliseum	113	111	1.8	625	640	−3.3
Comiskey Park	114	122	−4.2	621	649	−3.8
Anaheim Stadium	134	133	0.8	610	640	−5.2
*Metrodome	103	124	−16.9	553	590	−6.3
*Astrodome	117	122	−4.1	617	673	−8.8
*Veterans Stadium	94	128	−26.6	579	665	−12.5
*Riverfront Stadium	101	128	−21.1	581	680	−14.3
*Skydome	95	106	−10.4	170	246	−17.7

THE 1961 YANKEES

Two years ago we took a look back at the 1969 Mets, using all the analytical tools currently at our disposal that were not available to sportswriters and fans at the time. (Not that they—or we—would have known what to make of them then anyway.) This year, we are proud to take a similar look back at baseball's most powerful team, the 1961 Yankees, and of the signature accomplishment of that season, Roger Maris's successful pursuit of Babe Ruth's home-run record.

The material presented is a reflection of what *The 1962 Elias Baseball Analyst* might have contained, though with the added virtue of hindsight. A team essay, dealing in detail with issues raised by Maris's 61 home runs, is followed by the Won-Lost Record by Starting Position chart, and team total grids for batting and pitching. The batter and pitcher "sections" that follow list everyone who would have qualified under our current standards: 200 plate appearances for batters, 400 batters faced (or 300 with a Bullet) or 20 games finished in relief for pitchers; 10 batters and 8 pitchers met these criteria. (The "loved to face" and "hated to face" listed for each player reflect the 1961 season only. As a result, it was difficult to find qualifiers for certain combinations; hardly anyone hated to face Hector Lopez in 1961, and no one particularly loved to face Luis Arroyo.) For all pitchers, we have made the contemporary adjustment of using actual innings pitched to calculate earned run average, instead of rounding off partial innings as was the custom until 1982 (the year after the Steve McCatty–Sammy Stewart controversy).

This section is meant as both a fond tribute to this great team and a serious contribution to the analysis of baseball history. And, even if nothing else came of all the work involved in putting it together, we feel the final Hector Lopez batter comment alone makes the effort worthwhile.

THE 1961 YANKEES

"Ease his pain."

"Did you hear that?"

"Yeah, we all heard it, buddy. Now shut up and let the rest of us enjoy the movie."

If only it were that simple. Since the winter of 1961, the unspoken rule at the Elias Sports Bureau has been: "Ignore the voice. Tell no one." We'd even hoped it might be a long-running practical joke. But to be honest, 25 years is a little long even for some of the jokers we deal with. Now there could be no avoiding the issue: This was the real deal. Aren't things like this supposed to happen only, you know, in the movies?

The next evening, as the night crew at our office was shutting down, they heard it again.

"Ease his pain."

"Whose pain?" they called out.

"Well, it's about time! Thought you'd never ask. Roger Maris's, of course."

"Roger Maris? He's dead, you boob. What pain?"

Same whisper, new message: *"Go the distance."* Then, in a louder voice: "And don't call me a boob."

This was getting weird. "What distance?"

"Now you're catching on," came the reply. "Take the A train."

"This got something to do with Duke Ellington?" we asked.

"And you called me a boob? You guys do sports, right? Take the A train. Six miles, due north. To 161st Street. Yankee Stadium. You've heard of it, I assume. You'll enjoy the crosstown stroll." Just what we needed—a ghost with an attitude. "Anyway, I'm outta here."

"No, wait!"

When we arrived, we found a package addressed to Elias Sports Bureau, New York City, Planet Earth. Plain brown wrapper, no return address. Inside was a play-by-play record of the Yankees' 1961 season. Every game, every batter, every detail. The whole magilla. In our business, that's like finding the Holy Grail. Our mission was becoming clearer.

Thirty years ago, Roger Maris broke perhaps the most glorified of all baseball records: Babe Ruth's 60 home runs in a season. The sport could have treated the Rajah as a conquering hero—someone to forge a path into baseball's new era of expansion, just as Ruth had blazed the trail from the depths of the Black Sox scandal into the glory days of the live-ball era. Instead, the baseball public took its cue from Commissioner Ford Frick and the collectively resentful old-guard media, which repeatedly disparaged Maris and his signature achievement. It was Frick who polled the crusty writers and capitulated to them when they recommended that the record be recognized only if accomplished over the first 154 games of the season.

That was only the opening salvo. The routinely cited objections to legitimizing Maris's record were many and passionate: Baseball's first-ever expansion had diluted the talent, and Maris was exploiting patsies who belonged in the bush leagues. Maris had a swing tailor-made for a home ballpark that made even moderately powerful left-handed hitters look like, well, like Ruth himself. Maris played nine games at a stadium (Wrigley Field in Los Angeles) that turned would-be fly balls into home runs. Maris benefited from batting with Mickey Mantle on deck, and so received a steady diet of belt-high fastballs. The deck was clearly stacked against Roger. The commissioner stood by as the baseball media treated Maris's assault on 60 as an unwanted stepchild. And the public fell right in step.

The effect of all this journalistic trash took its toll on more than Maris's emotional well-being (making his accomplishment all the more impressive, at least to some open-minded mavericks of the day). The calculated flow of propaganda also vented its misguided fury at the box office. Perhaps no single fact that we uncovered during the months of research on this project was as extraordinary as this: When the Yankees played their final series of the season, a three-game weekender in ideal late-summer New York weather against their old antagonists, the Boston Red Sox, they drew 63,700 fans hoping to see the most hallowed page in the baseball record book rewritten. That's not 63,700 for the first game, but for all three combined. Or, to put it in terms that would stand a ticket scalper's hair on end: 49,000 empty seats per game. But, of course, that wouldn't have come as a surprise had we noted that two days earlier, with Maris's record-tying 60th home run commanding banner headlines on every newspaper in the city, fewer than 8,000 fans found their way to the Stadium to see Roger, after a wildly invigorating summer-long pursuit, take his first honest-to-goodness crack at breaking the mark. (There's a photo of Maris following through on number 60 in Tony Kubek's book, *Sixty-One*. The stands look like those of Cleveland Stadium on day two of any recent season.)

"Ease his pain."

So that was our mysterious mandate: to analyze the circumstances surrounding Maris's record. With the emotions of the moment all but erased by the passage of time, to take a fresh look at one of baseball's greatest, but at the same time most discredited, individual performances.

Let's start with the most basic indictment handed down against Maris. The American League schedule was lengthened to 162 games for the 1961 season, in conjuction with an expansion from eight teams to 10. The 154-game schedule had been standard since

1904. For the sake of argument, let's forgive the baseball writers for their lack of vision; many failed to anticipate that the schedule would never return to 154 games, and that the shorter schedule would inevitably erode as a standard of measure. Thirty years later, the 162-game schedule has become as comfortable and traditional to contemporary baseball fans as the once-beloved 154-game season had been to fans of an earlier generation.

But did anyone bother to point out that when Ruth set a universally accepted major-league record of 29 home runs in 1919, he broke the mark of Ned Williamson, who hit 27 for the 1884 Chicago White Stockings (the National League forerunner of the Cubs) over a schedule of just 112 games? Ruth's total after the first 112 games of the 1919 season: 23 home runs. He didn't break Williamson's record until Boston's 134th game. The recognition of the Babe's 29-home-run mark over Williamson's should have constituted an irrefutable precedent. But 42 years later, with Ruth the incumbent and his buddy Frick the commissioner, a ruling was made against the challenger, Maris. How pathetic.

A slightly more involved issue: Did Maris hit 61 home runs off a representative group of major-league pitchers? Or did he exploit a group of meatballs who should have been pitching in places like Amarillo, Savannah, and Keokuk? The expansion of 1961 undeniably afforded major-league roster spots to many pitchers who otherwise would have been riding buses. But nothing in Maris's record indicates that he would have hit fewer than 61 home runs against a more experienced or more talented set of pitchers.

A compelling example: Maris had 166 at-bats against pitchers who made 25 starts or saved 10 games in the previous, preexpansion season. He batted .343 against them, compared to .241 against the other, less accomplished throwers. Maris hit 23 home runs, or one for every 7.2 at-bats, against the pitchers who had good seasons a year earlier. Had he hit home runs at the same rate against all pitchers, Maris would have accumulated 82 for the season.

The following table shows how Maris hit in 1961 against various groups of pitchers. No matter what classifications we devised, none supported the theory that Maris exploited inferior pitching made available to him only by expansion. Contrast Maris's performance against the subsets of elite pitchers to his performance against other, presumably inferior pitchers. "Rate" below refers to at-bats per home run:

	Against Subset			Against Others		
Opposing Pitchers	**BA**	**HR**	**Rate**	**BA**	**HR**	**Rate**
25 GS or 10 SV in 1960	.343	23	7.2	.241	38	11.2
10 wins in 1960	.314	22	8.7	.248	39	10.2
25 GS or 10 SV in 1961	.282	36	9.3	.253	25	10.3
10 wins, .500+ in 1961	.272	12	14.1	.268	49	8.6
75 innings pitched in 1961	.272	51	9.9	.253	10	8.7

Only when the elite group was limited to pitchers with at least 10 wins and a winning record in 1961 did Maris hit with significantly more power against lesser pitchers. But remember, the question isn't whether Maris handled the best pitchers as well as he hit against the rest. The pertinent question is: Did Maris hit disproportionately better against the worst pitchers (that is, those who would have been in the minors were it not for expansion) than he did against a more established group? The answer to the first question—that Maris hit better against superior pitchers than he did against inferior ones—pretty much answers the second as well.

The numbers above indicate overwhelmingly that Maris did not exploit lesser pitchers. Note in particular the final line of the table: Against pitchers who worked fewer than 75 innings in 1961—the group that most closely approximates those who wouldn't have pitched in the majors in an eight-team league—Maris hit slightly worse than he did against others.

So if it wasn't the pitchers, then how about the stadiums? The legitimacy of Maris's record was also discounted by the argument that Roger was a custom-crafted Yankee Stadium hitter. There existed widespread sentiment that Maris's home park was in large part responsible for his impressive home-run total. After all, Roger had averaged only 19 home runs in three seasons with the Indians and Athletics before joining the Yankees, and then hit 39 and 61 in his first two seasons with New York. But even in 1961, when he broke Ruth's record, Maris hit more home runs on the road (31) than he did at Yankee Stadium (30). And the margin was even greater for his seven seasons with the team: 94 at home, 109 on the road.

Surprised? Don't be. Lou Gehrig hit only nine more home runs at Yankee Stadium than he hit on the road (251 to 242). And even Ruth hit only four more in "the house that he built" than he hit elsewhere during his tenure with the Yankees (259 to 255).

Think about that for a moment: Yankee Stadium, prior to its reconstruction in the mid-1970s, was considered a great home-run park for left-handed hitters. But during their years with the team, Maris, Ruth, and Gehrig combined for more home runs on the road (606) than at home (604). Something's wrong here. A more detailed examination of Yankee Stadium's home-run tendencies illustrates that those three left-handed sluggers weren't exceptional; actually, they typify the park's effect on home-runs.

Throughout its first 50 years, Yankee Stadium was thought to diminish greatly the home-run potential of right-handed hitters while increasing that of left-handers, and to a somewhat equal degree. The stadium's distant fences in left-center field created the infamous "Death Valley," which time and again turned would-be home runs by right-handers like Tony Lazzeri, Joe DiMaggio, Joe Gordon, and Moose Skowron (to name a few) into long fly outs. But the stadium was thought to pad the home-run totals of left-handed hitters by equal number. That simply wasn't the case.

Sure, the power of right-handed hitters was severely compromised by the distant fences of an earlier time. The following table compares the home-run rates of left- and right-handed hitters in all Yankees games from the 1961 season, at Yankee Stadium and elsewhere:

	Yankee Stadium			Other Stadiums			
Batters	AB	HR	Rate	AB	HR	Rate	Diff.
Left-Handers	1986	100	19.9	2057	103	20.0	+0.6%
Right-Handers	3337	71	47.0	3528	103	34.3	−37.2%

Right-handed hitters were 37 percent less likely to hit home runs at Yankee Stadium than at the other A.L. ballparks. But left-handed hitters experienced no advantage at all, hitting home runs at almost exactly the same rate there as on the road. The four-foot-high fence that ran from the right-field foul pole (only 296 feet from home plate) to the bullpen occasionally turned a sharp line drive or a mediocre fly ball down the line into a home run. But if a lefty didn't pull the ball, he was hitting into a right-center field nearly as spacious as Death Valley across the way; and if he was a straightaway or opposite-field hitter, he was as disadvantaged as a right-handed pull hitter. Clearly, those two features canceled each other out, creating a balanced home-run effect for left-handed hitters. But the extreme to which right-handed hitters were penalized made the stadium seem downright hospitable to lefties—that and a 40-year stream of left-handed sluggers (Ruth, Gehrig, and Maris as well as Yogi Berra, Bill Dickey, Tommy Henrich, Charlie Keller, and switch-hitting Mickey Mantle) whose power would have made even the Astrodome appear to be a home-run park. But it was an illusion nonetheless.

And there's more. When the stadium reopened in 1976 after two years of reconstruction, it was expected that right-handed hitters would no longer be placed at such a great disadvantage. Not only was that expectation exaggerated, but the Yankee Stadium of today, while still suppressing the home-run potential of right-handers (though to a lesser degree than before) has become the home-run haven for left-handers that was wrongly presumed to exist before the changes.

You want numbers, we'll give you numbers. For the past two seasons, Yankee Stadium has diminished home runs by right-handed hitters by 23 percent—down somewhat from the levels of Ruth's and Maris's days, but still daunting. On the other hand, a typical left-handed hitter now has nearly a 50 percent better chance of hitting a home run at Yankee Stadium than he does at other American League stadiums. (And no cracks, please, about the current state of the Yankees' pitching staff.) Don't believe us? Ask Don Mattingly, whose career home run rate is a cool 61 percent higher at Yankee Stadium (one home run per 21 at-bats) than elsewhere (one per 34 AB).

One other pertinent item you might find interesting: Remember Ned Williamson's feat of 27 home runs that we mentioned earlier, which stood as the major-league record from 1884 until 1919? That mark, which appropriately received official sanction, was nonetheless the product of gerrymandered playing rules at Lake Front Park in Chicago, where the foul-line distances were—prepare yourself—180 feet to left field and 196 to right. The White Stockings used the field for only two seasons. In the first, 1883, balls hit over the fence were ground-rule doubles. But for 1884 the rule was changed, and balls clearing the fence were considered home runs. Williamson set an individual record for home runs in a single season (nearly doubling the previous mark), and the White Stockings set a team mark of 142—all but 11 of them at home.

An outraged *Boston Herald* wrote: "That over-the-fence rule is a perfect sham and burlesque." (Took the words right out of our mouths!) Was it fair? Certainly. The fences were equally distant for both the White Stockings and their opponents, weren't they? Should the records be sanctioned? Absolutely. Record-keeping is a method of describing historical events free of value judgments. If Williamson hit 27 balls over the fence—any fence—then he hit 27 home runs, plain and simple, unless the ground rules state otherwise. In Maris's case, the advantage was illusory. But even had it been real and substantial, the Williamson mark was accepted despite a bias that was far more extreme.

The expansion of 1961 also added two new ballparks to the American League mix: Metropolitan Stadium, home of the Minnesota Twins (formerly the Washington Senators), and Wrigley Field, home of the Los Angeles Angels. Both new parks were home-run producers. But Wrigley Field, an extreme example of a good home-run park, rightfully drew the most attention.

With fences only slightly farther from home plate in the power alleys (345 feet) than down the lines (340 feet in left, 338 in right), it's only natural that the total of 248 home runs hit at Wrigley in 1961 (its only season of major-league play) is still an all-time major-league high. It was a no-brainer choice as the site for "Home Run Derby," the syndicated television series of the early 1960s still seen occasionally on ESPN. (Think about it: If you're a producer, and you have to shoot "Home Run Derby" locally, where else would you go? The Coliseum?) A comparison of the home runs hit there to those hit in Angels road games suggests that Wrigley Field doubled the home-run potential of the typical major-league player. Home runs in each team's home and road games in 1961 follow. The differences represent the approximate effects of the teams' home fields:

Team	Home Field	Home Games	Road Games	Diff.
Los Angeles	Wrigley Field	248	121	+105%
Boston	Fenway Park	154	125	+23%
Minnesota	Metropolitan Stadium	181	149	+21%
Detroit	Tiger Stadium	185	165	+12%
Cleveland	Cleveland Stadium	172	156	+10%
Chicago	Comiskey Park	135	161	−16%
New York	Yankee Stadium	171	206	−17%
Baltimore	Memorial Stadium	107	151	−29%
Kansas City	Municipal Stadium	94	137	−31%
Washington	Griffith Stadium	87	163	−47%

Granted: Had Maris hit eight or 10 home runs at Wrigley Field, and another four or five at Metropolitan Stadium, the objection that he played in small ballparks might have had some merit. But Maris hit only three home runs at those two stadiums combined. Maris's home runs by stadium: Yankee Stadium, 30; Comiskey Park, 5; Cleveland Stadium, 5; Tiger Stadium, 5; Fenway Park, 4; Municipal Stadium, 4; Griffith Stadium, 4; Wrigley Field, 2; Memorial Stadium, 1; and Metropolitan Stadium, 1. Considering that a former home-run-record holder played half his games at a stadium that would have made Wrigley Field in L.A. look like Yosemite, Maris's perceived advantage should never have become an issue. Still, Wrigley Field became another symbol for those anxious to discredit Maris.

Frankly, the discussion of Wrigley Field points us toward a somewhat less focused issue that has arisen in recent times. Contemporary players bemoan the big plastic stadiums of today that they say don't produce as many home runs as the venerable green cathedrals of days gone by. To a degree, that attitude continues to tarnish Maris's record (along with the achievements of many great home-run hitters of the past). And it does so unfairly. Our exhibit: Tiger Stadium.

The configuration of Tiger Stadium has undergone little change over the past 30 years. (The height of the left-field fence was reduced from 11 feet to nine feet in 1962, and the distance to the fence in right-center was increased from 370 to 375 feet twenty years later.) Had stadiums grown collectively tougher for home-run hitters during that time, the influence of Tiger Stadium on home runs, relative to other parks, would have increased markedly. But that simply hasn't happened.

During the five-year period from 1959 through 1963, Tiger Stadium increased home runs by approximately 18 percent in relation to the other A.L. stadiums. Fast forward to the present: From 1985 through 1989, Tiger Stadium increased home runs by 20 percent compared to contemporary American League ballparks. The fact that (a) Tiger Stadium itself has remained basically unchanged and (b) its relative standing in the league with regard to home runs is roughly the same suggests that the landscape itself has remained equivalent as well. That is, A.L. ballparks of today, taken as a whole, have about the same effect on home runs as another somewhat different set had 30 years ago. Or, to put it another way, 61 home runs in the stadiums of 1961 are equivalent to 61 home runs in the stadiums of 1991. No more, no less.

We'll be honest: Unable for years to resolve the issue adequately, we've questioned the value of batting with a feared slugger on deck. So Maris's performance with Mickey Mantle on deck in 1961 shocked us. Many of you know, of course, that Maris didn't receive a single intentional pass all season—not only the ultimate statement of the respect opposing pitchers had for Mantle, but also a clue that Maris saw more than his share of fat pitches, especially with runners on base. But even that didn't prepare us for this breakdown of Maris's 1961 statistics, divided according to the on-deck hitter:

On Deck	AB	H	2B	3B	HR	RBI	BB	SO	BA	SA	OBA	HR Rate
Mantle	475	139	15	4	54	130	72	51	.293	.682	.392	8.8
Others	115	20	1	0	7	12	22	16	.174	.365	.312	16.4

Gulp. Or, as Erlichman said to Haldeman, "H.R. (Bob), I think we may have a teeny little problem explaining this one." Could it be that without Mantle, Maris would have been little more than Dave Kingman in pinstripes? As it happens, there is little with which to reason away the disparity in those figures.

Maris spent the first six weeks of the 1961 season batting seventh in the lineup when the Yankees faced left-handers (with Tony Kubek, Clete Boyer, or Deron Johnson on deck). As a result, the 139 plate appearances with players other than Mantle in the on-deck circle include a disproportionately large number of at-bats against left-handed pitchers, drawn from Maris's worst period of the season. The figures below divide Maris's plate appearances into those against left- and right-handers. Even at this level, it's clear that Mickey's presence had a significant impact on both Roger's batting average and his home-run potential:

	On Deck	AB	H	2B	3B	HR	RBI	BB	SO	BA	SA	HR Rate
Vs. LHP	Mantle	138	34	6	0	11	31	20	23	.246	.529	12.5
Vs. LHP	Others	39	7	1	0	1	4	10	7	.179	.282	39.0
Vs. RHP	Mantle	337	105	9	4	43	99	52	28	.312	.745	7.8
Vs. RHP	Others	76	13	0	0	6	8	12	9	.171	.407	12.7

Let's play around with those numbers a little. Let's assume Mantle decided to take early retirement after the 1960 season. As a result, Maris spent most of the 1961 season batting with Yogi Berra or Moose Skowron on deck. We'll take both Others lines from the table above, prorate them for the number of times Maris faced left- and right-handers, and construct a new Totals line for the 1961 season. (Hey, this ain't science.) Here are the somewhat startling results:

	AB	H	2B	3B	HR	RBI	BB	SO	BA	SA	HR Rate
Vs. LHP	166	30	4	0	4	17	43	30	.181	.277	41.5
Vs. RHP	414	71	0	0	33	44	65	49	.171	.411	12.5
Totals	580	101	4	0	37	61	108	79	.174	.372	15.7

Does such a profile make any sense in the real world? After all, no player has ever batted below .200 while hitting as many as 37 home runs. (Kingman came close, at .204 with 37 homers in 1982. But the second-lowest mark was a much more respectable .235 and 39 homers by Mark McGwire in 1990.) Conversely, no player with a batting average as low as .174 has ever hit more than the 13 home runs than Deron Johnson hit in 1974, when he batted .171 for three different teams. So let's be clear about one thing: The totals above do not—repeat, *do not*—represent a best guess as to what Maris would have done in 1961 without Mantle to support him. But if we think of those figures as a caricature—an exaggerated, grotesquely misshapen representation of Roger without the Mick—it bears a reasonable resemblence to Maris's sophomore season of 1958 (as well as to that previously mentioned Kingman season):

	AB	H	2B	3B	HR	RBI	BB	SO	BA	SA	HR Rate
1958 Maris	583	140	19	4	28	80	45	85	.240	.431	20.8
1961 Caricature	580	101	4	0	37	61	108	79	.174	.372	15.7
1982 Kingman	535	109	9	1	37	99	59	156	.204	.432	14.5

The profile now comes more clearly into focus. Start with a developing young star, Maris circa 1958, who suddenly exceeds his potential, and does it to an unprecedented degree. Opposing pitchers now put the ball over the plate only when absolutely necessary. They know the rule: Make a mistake, take a shower. (Note the walk total in the 1961 caricature.) His batting average plummets, but he retains that long-ball potential. (Did someone mention Mark McGwire?) Hanging curves, flat sliders, and fat fastballs are lost in a hurry. All of a sudden, those numbers don't look as bizarre as they once seemed.

So could Maris have hit 61 without Mantle? Don't forget, he did manage home runs 59 and 61 under enormous pressure with Mantle on the bench nursing an infected hip. But based on the numbers above, it's doubtful Maris could have achieved such season-long success. So what? We did a little checking and found that Ruth himself had a pretty fair hitter batting behind him—for most of his career. How many great home-run hitters bat in front of .230-hitting shortstops? Great hitters bat in the middle of the order, surrounded by the best of their teammates. Only Maris hit 61 home runs.

That wraps up our analysis of the challenges to the legitimacy of Maris's home-run record. Any suggestion that Maris set the record primarily because he benefited from ideal conditions is purely in the eye of a blind beholder. Few records are ever set under adverse conditions. The best example is that of Hack Wilson, who drove in 190 runs in 1930, when National League teams scored an average of 11.4 runs per game, the highest mark of the century in either league. Maris knocked out 61 home runs in a season in which home runs increased by about 8 percent, batting in front of perhaps the only hitter American League pitchers feared as much as they feared Roger himself. Big deal! The effect of the ballparks was a wash. The effect of season length, which might have seemed an obstacle to common sense in 1961, has been rendered moot by the passage of time. Thirty years later, Maris's record should be accorded the same respect given those of Wilson and other great players of the past and present. But now there's an entirely new generation of baseball fans who don't remember when Ruth held the record and who bear no prejudice toward Maris on Ruth's account. Maybe they're wondering what all this fuss is about in the first place.

Although 30 years have erased the prejudices of an earlier era, the question of Maris's greatness remains unresolved. Roger's absence from the Baseball Hall of Fame is not only the most compelling illustration of that question, but also the most visible and damning evidence against him.

Was the failure of the Baseball Writers Association of America to enshrine Maris in the Hall of Fame a monumental injustice, or a coldly objective assessment of his achievements? We're certainly not about to get into a dogmatic treatise on the merits of the electorate or the voting process. God knows, there's enough of that every January. But one thing is certain: An awful lot of fairly informed baseball fans, who also happen to write about the sport for a living, voiced their opinion by refusing to write Maris's name on their annual Cooperstown ballots.

And although the members of the Elias Sports Bureau who voted during the period of Maris's eligibility all voted for his induction, neither are we about to proselytize on his behalf. On the other hand, we're probably not the only ones who sense that many of the voters failed to cast ballots for Maris because they considered only career-long performance, thereby discounting the value of his most significant achievement. So we decided to look into the question of how much value that single feat was accorded by the electorate. And what we found may surprise you (it certainly did us): The voters may have failed to give that mark recognition proportional to its significance, but to say that the record was discounted is erroneous.

Compare Maris's career totals to those of three players with comparable statistics:

Player	G	AB	R	H	2B	3B	HR	RBI	BA
Roger Maris	1463	5101	826	1325	195	42	275	851	.260
Bob Allison	1541	5032	811	1281	216	53	256	796	.255
John Mayberry	1620	5447	733	1379	211	19	255	879	.253
Hank Sauer	1399	4796	709	1278	200	19	288	876	.266

The other three players listed above had a composite career batting average of .258, with averages of 266 home runs and 850 runs batted in. They scored fewer runs than Maris, but they also had slightly longer careers, with more walks and extra-base hits. Nevertheless, those players, so similar to Maris on a career basis, were all but ignored in Hall of Fame voting. Sauer received four votes in 1966—not many, but four more than the combined total for Allison and Mayberry. For all intents, we can conclude that nearly every vote ever cast for Maris was cast on the basis of his 61-home-run season (and, perhaps to a lesser degree, his consecutive MVP seasons of 1960 and 1961, of which the 61 homers were an integral part).

For the record, Maris was named on more than 40 percent of the ballots in the years after his death prompted voters to reevaluate his achievements. That was far below the level needed to earn a Cooperstown plaque, and far below what we at Elias felt was deserved. But that's what makes a horse race (or at least a pari-mutuel system): different voters, different perspectives.

No, Maris wasn't kept out of Cooperstown by the voters. It was a fateful series of injuries that denied Roger what would certainly have been his place at baseball's mecca. By the mid-1960s, injuries to hand, wrist, and leg had robbed Maris of his power and transformed him into a capable hitter who gave only occasional glimpses of what he'd been a few years earlier. How might Maris's career have progressed had his talent not been compromised by injury? Our computers tried to answer that question.

Readers of past *Analyst*s may be familiar with our technique of projecting a player's future based on the careers of players from the past with the most similar statistical profiles. Technical stock-market analysts base their buy and sell recommendations on a similar process. For example, if Canadian Allied Petroleum added 10 percent to its share price on three consecutive days with increasing volume, an analyst might find that of the past 50 stocks to match those criteria, 40 fell over the near term but rose to even higher levels within two months. The recommendation: Hold the shares you've got, buy more only after a decline.

Our baseball version works like this: Through a series of algebraic deductions, we find players who (a) at some point in their careers had career statistics that most closely matched the player in question; and (b) were coming off seasons most similar to the most recent season of the player in question. In last year's *Analyst,* we used that method to show that Keith Hernandez had little left to offer the Indians in return for his two-year, $3.5 million contract. We also forecast that Dale Murphy had, at most, one or two solid years left, suggesting that Atlanta get what they could for him.

To project Maris's career without the injuries that derailed it, we identified the players whose profiles most closely matched that of Maris following the 1962 season (his last injury-free year). (For those who want to see for themselves, in detail, how this works, the five players who matched most closely were: Gil Hodges, through 1952; Rocky Colavito, through 1962; Jesse Barfield, through 1987; Bob Horner, through 1985; and Larry Doby, through 1953. The computer actually used a much deeper list.) The average of their performances a year later (in proportion to their similarity to Maris) was used to estimate what a healthy Rajah would have accomplished in 1963. Maris's adjusted figures for 1963 were then used to recompute his new adjusted career statistics to that point—are you still with us? The process was repeated to forecast his 1964 season; and so on, and so on, until a point was reached at which we guessed Maris would have retired—five years later than he was actually forced to give it up. The following figures represent Maris's reconstructed career totals, which far exceed his actual figures:

	G	AB	R	H	2B	3B	HR	RBI	BB	SO	SB	BA
Actual	1463	5101	826	1325	195	42	275	851	652	723	31	.260
Projected	2112	7371	1143	1944	299	49	408	1283	953	1160	45	.264

On a career basis, those adjusted figures put Maris in the company of players like Gil Hodges, Dale Murphy, Norm Cash, and George Foster—still somewhat short of certain Hall of Fame status. But combined with the single-event value of hitting 61 home runs (which, as we've seen, was alone worth roughly half the votes needed for induction), they would have been plenty.

WON-LOST RECORD BY STARTING POSITION

New York Yankees	C	1B	2B	3B	SS	LF	CF	RF	DH	P	Leadoff	Cleanup	Starts vs. LH	Starts vs. RH	Total Starts
Luis Arroyo	–	–	–	–	–	–	–	–	–	–	–	–	–	–	–
Yogi Berra	7-8	–	–	–	–	54-24	–	4-1	–	–	–	6-1	3	95	65-33
Johnny Blanchard	29-13	–	–	–	–	6-1	–	5-0	–	–	–	0-1	–	54	40-14
Clete Boyer	–	–	–	92-45	6-2	–	–	–	–	–	19-7	–	44	101	98-47
Bob Cerv	–	2-1	–	–	–	18-6	–	–	–	–	–	–	21	6	20-7
Tex Clevenger	–	–	–	–	–	–	–	–	–	–	–	–	–	–	–
Jim Coates	–	–	–	–	–	–	–	–	–	6-4	–	–	4	6	6-4
Bud Daley	–	–	–	–	–	–	–	–	–	9-8	–	–	5	12	9-8
Joe DeMaestri	–	–	–	–	5-4	–	–	–	–	–	–	–	4	5	5-4
Art Ditmar	–	–	–	–	–	–	–	–	–	5-3	–	–	2	6	5-3
Al Downing	–	–	–	–	–	–	–	–	–	0-1	–	–	–	1	0-1
Ryne Duren	–	–	–	–	–	–	–	–	–	–	–	–	–	–	–
Whitey Ford	–	–	–	–	–	–	–	–	–	34-5	–	–	13	26	34-5
Billy Gardner	–	–	1-2	15-7	–	–	–	–	–	–	1-1	–	7	18	16-9
Jesse Gonder	–	–	–	–	–	–	–	–	–	–	–	–	–	–	–
Bob Hale	–	0-1	–	–	–	–	–	–	–	–	–	–	–	1	0-1
Elston Howard	73-32	7-2	–	–	–	–	–	–	–	–	–	1-2	51	63	80-34
Johnny James	–	–	–	–	–	–	–	–	–	–	–	–	–	–	–
Deron Johnson	–	–	–	2-1	–	–	–	–	–	–	–	–	2	1	2-1
Tony Kubek	–	–	–	–	98-46	–	–	–	–	–	10-8	–	46	98	98-46
Hector Lopez	–	–	–	–	–	31-22	–	2-2	–	–	–	–	32	25	33-24
Duke Maas	–	–	–	–	–	–	–	–	–	–	–	–	–	–	–
Mickey Mantle	–	–	–	–	–	–	99-49	–	–	–	–	99-49	48	100	99-49
Roger Maris	–	–	–	–	–	–	10-1	98-50	–	–	–	3-0	49	110	108-50
Danny McDevitt	–	–	–	–	–	–	–	–	–	0-2	–	–	1	1	0-2
Jack Reed	–	–	–	–	–	–	0-3	–	–	–	–	–	2	1	0-3
Hal Reniff	–	–	–	–	–	–	–	–	–	–	–	–	–	–	–
Bobby Richardson	–	–	108-51	–	–	–	–	–	–	–	79-37	–	50	109	108-51
Rollie Sheldon	–	–	–	–	–	–	–	–	–	14-7	–	–	7	14	14-7
Bill Skowron	–	98-48	–	–	–	–	–	–	–	–	–	–	49	97	98-48
Bill Stafford	–	–	–	–	–	–	–	–	–	18-7	–	–	12	13	18-7
Ralph Terry	–	–	–	–	–	–	–	–	–	20-7	–	–	6	21	20-7
Lee Thomas	–	–	–	–	–	–	–	–	–	–	–	–	–	–	–
Earl Torgeson	–	2-1	–	–	–	–	–	–	–	–	–	–	–	3	2-1
Tom Tresh	–	–	–	–	0-1	–	–	–	–	–	–	–	–	1	0-1
Bob Turley	–	–	–	–	–	–	–	–	–	3-9	–	–	1	11	3-9

TEAM TOTALS: BATTING

	AB	H	2B	3B	HR	RBI	BB	SO	BA	SA	OBA
Season	5559	1461	194	40	240	782	543	786	.263	.442	.330
vs. Left-Handers	1626	446	69	16	53	222	171	232	.274	.434	.342
vs. Right-Handers	3933	1015	125	24	187	560	372	554	.258	.445	.325
Home Games	2654	712	93	23	112	387	287	354	.268	.447	.340
Road Games	2905	749	101	17	128	395	256	432	.258	.436	.320
Day Games	3062	823	101	24	140	438	306	398	.269	.455	.337
Night Games	2497	638	93	16	100	344	237	388	.256	.426	.321
April	488	127	14	1	12	58	45	54	.260	.367	.322
May	896	236	29	5	40	133	104	133	.263	.441	.344
June	1130	298	44	6	53	173	97	166	.264	.454	.322
July	984	280	37	7	51	156	106	112	.285	.492	.353
August	1085	277	43	9	39	131	103	170	.255	.419	.324
Sept./Oct.	947	238	27	12	44	130	87	146	.251	.445	.315
Leading Off Inn.	1320	327	52	13	53	53	110	180	.248	.427	.308
Bases Empty	3164	822	117	28	134	134	296	452	.260	.442	.327
Runners On	2395	639	77	12	106	648	247	334	.267	.442	.334
Runners/Scor. Pos.	1240	339	42	4	59	537	151	171	.273	.456	.346
Runners On/2 Out	1020	261	26	8	46	260	104	152	.256	.432	.327
Scor. Pos./2 Out	594	158	17	3	26	211	76	85	.266	.436	.350
Late-Inning Pressure	739	201	28	7	35	113	86	102	.272	.471	.347
Leading Off	191	50	8	1	9	9	13	20	.262	.455	.309
Runners On	315	90	11	3	19	97	44	47	.286	.521	.368
Runners/Scor. Pos.	176	47	5	1	11	79	30	22	.267	.494	.364

RUNS BATTED IN	From 1B	From 2B	From 3B	Scoring Position
Totals	103/1871	205/978	234/533	439/1511
Percentage	5.5%	21.0%	43.9%	29.1%

TEAM TOTALS: PITCHING

	W-L	ERA	AB	H	HR	BB	SO	BA	SA	OBA
Season	109-53	3.46	5387	1288	137	542	868	.239	.370	.311
vs. Left-Handers			1647	403	48	183	289	.245	.391	.321
vs. Right-Handers			3740	885	89	359	579	.237	.360	.306
Home Games	65-16	2.77	2683	588	59	248	452	.219	.334	.288
Road Games	44-37	4.18	2704	700	78	294	416	.259	.405	.333
Day Games	63-26	3.61	2990	731	85	314	474	.244	.384	.318
Night Games	46-27	3.28	2397	557	52	228	394	.232	.352	.301
April	9-5	3.54	471	116	12	50	84	.246	.391	.325
May	14-12	4.29	857	207	28	106	134	.242	.405	.327
June	22-10	3.60	1047	234	31	93	178	.223	.374	.288
July	20-9	3.64	982	244	22	107	151	.248	.363	.324
August	22-9	3.10	1053	252	22	99	154	.239	.349	.304
Sept./Oct.	21-8	2.87	947	231	22	86	159	.244	.357	.311
Leading Off Inn.			1341	317	35	107	215	.236	.371	.296
Bases Empty			3151	748	81	301	543	.237	.371	.307
Runners On			2236	540	56	241	325	.242	.368	.315
Runners/Scor. Pos.			1146	281	28	147	167	.245	.372	.327
Runners On/2 Out			920	185	22	109	147	.201	.314	.288
Scor. Pos./2 Out			518	99	12	66	74	.191	.301	.286
Late-Inning Pressure			896	205	22	94	157	.229	.360	.305
Leading Off			233	60	5	18	39	.258	.386	.311
Runners On			372	83	9	42	59	.223	.333	.309
Runners/Scor. Pos.			180	49	3	25	24	.272	.378	.370
First 9 Batters			2401	561	58	269	439	.234	.358	.313
Second 9 Batters			1452	338	37	152	217	.233	.360	.308
All Batters Thereafter			1534	389	42	121	212	.254	.397	.310

Yogi Berra

Bats Left

New York Yankees	AB	H	2B	3B	HR	RBI	BB	SO	BA	SA	OBA
Season	395	107	11	0	22	61	35	28	.271	.466	.330
vs. Left-Handers	55	15	0	0	3	12	6	2	.273	.436	.339
vs. Right-Handers	340	92	11	0	19	49	29	26	.271	.471	.328
Home Games	176	51	4	0	12	29	12	12	.290	.517	.332
Road Games	219	56	7	0	10	32	23	16	.256	.425	.328
Day Games	218	56	4	0	13	35	22	11	.257	.454	.327
Night Games	177	51	7	0	9	26	13	17	.288	.480	.333
April	34	9	0	0	1	4	2	1	.265	.353	.306
May	70	23	3	0	5	16	6	5	.329	.586	.377
June	86	22	2	0	5	11	5	8	.256	.453	.293
July	64	17	3	0	2	9	9	3	.266	.406	.351
August	82	20	2	0	5	14	6	3	.244	.451	.308
Sept./Oct.	57	16	1	0	4	7	7	8	.281	.509	.354
Leading Off Inn.	75	18	1	0	6	6	4	6	.240	.493	.278
Bases Empty	207	59	7	0	14	14	15	15	.285	.522	.336
Runners On	188	48	4	0	8	47	20	13	.255	.404	.322
Runners/Scor. Pos.	104	27	1	0	3	37	11	7	.260	.356	.317
Runners On/2 Out	90	21	0	0	5	20	11	6	.233	.400	.317
Scor. Pos./2 Out	58	11	0	0	1	12	7	5	.190	.241	.277
Late-Inning Pressure	60	14	0	0	4	11	3	5	.233	.433	.266
Leading Off	18	3	0	0	2	2	0	1	.167	.500	.167
Runners On	33	10	0	0	2	9	3	4	.303	.485	.351
Runners/Scor. Pos.	19	4	0	0	0	5	3	3	.211	.211	.304

RUNS BATTED IN	From 1B	From 2B	From 3B	Scoring Position
Totals	7/167	17/84	15/46	32/130
Percentage	4.2%	20.2%	32.6%	24.6%

Loved to face: Jack Fisher (.600, 6-for-10, 1 HR, 3 SO)
Ken McBride (.333, 5-for-15, 4 HR)
Jim Perry (.700, 7-for-10, 2 HR)

Hated to face: Dick Donovan (.154, 2-for-13)
Ray Herbert (.083, 1-for-12)
Frank Lary (.091, 2-for-22)

Miscellaneous statistics: Ground outs-to-air outs ratio: 0.62. . . . Grounded into 7 double plays in 101 opportunities . . . . Drove in 13 of 20 runners from third base with less than two outs (65%). . . . Direction of balls hit to the outfield: 20% to left field, 30% to center, 51% to right. . . . Base running: Advanced from first base to third on 6 of 24 outfield singles (25%); scored from second on 12 of 15 (80%). . . . Made 2.0 putouts per nine innings in left field. . . . Opposing base stealers: 6-for-12 (50%).

Comments: Played more games in the outfield in 1961 (87) than he did behind the plate (15) for the only time in his 19-year career. . . . The Yankees won league titles in 14 of his 17 full seasons. . . . Played in more World Series games than anyone else in history (75), but in only 7 of the 16 from 1961 through 1963. He should hold that record forever—or at least until the World Series is expanded to a best-of-21 format. The leaders among active players: Ozzie Smith and Tommy Herr (21). . . . Had George Steinbrenner owned the team in the late 1940s, he might have labeled Yogi "Mr. May": Berra batted only .140 (7-for-50) over his first three Series (1947, 1949, and 1950). . . . Holds the A.L. record for hits in a season as a catcher: 191, set in 1950. Ted Simmons set the N.L. record in 1975 with 188, one more than he had two years earlier. . . . Three players in A.L. history drove in 100 runs in consecutive seasons in which they caught at least 100 games. All were Yankees, and all had streaks of at least three seasons: Berra (1953–56), Bill Dickey (1936–39), and Thurman Munson (1975–77). . . . Had only 415 career strikeouts compared to 358 home runs, 3d-best ratio in major-league history (minimum: 100 HR). Only Joe DiMaggio (361 HR, 369 SO) and Lefty O'Doul (113 HR, 122 SO) scored better. . . . Berra had more home runs than strikeouts in six different seasons, second only to DiMaggio's seven seasons. Sure, that includes a season of seven games (2 HR, 1 SO in 1946). But Berra also had several near misses in full seasons (by one in 1957, by five in 1949 and 1953). . . . Made his major-league debut in 1946. The only other member of the 1961 Yankees whose career began in the 1940s was Earl Torgeson (who debuted in 1947).

Johnny Blanchard

Bats Left

New York Yankees	AB	H	2B	3B	HR	RBI	BB	SO	BA	SA	OBA
Season	243	74	10	1	21	54	27	28	.305	.613	.382
vs. Left-Handers	23	4	2	0	2	5	4	5	.174	.522	.296
vs. Right-Handers	220	70	8	1	19	49	23	23	.318	.623	.391
Home Games	134	45	5	0	14	35	16	11	.336	.687	.414
Road Games	109	29	5	1	7	19	11	17	.266	.523	.341
Day Games	147	48	7	1	15	34	18	16	.327	.694	.405
Night Games	96	26	3	0	6	20	9	12	.271	.490	.346
April	3	0	0	0	0	0	0	1	.000	.000	.000
May	46	10	1	0	3	8	7	3	.217	.435	.321
June	39	14	2	0	5	12	4	6	.359	.795	.422
July	39	16	1	0	5	10	6	1	.410	.821	.489
August	48	10	1	1	2	8	5	10	.208	.396	.296
Sept./Oct.	65	24	5	0	6	16	5	7	.369	.723	.431
Leading Off Inn.	51	14	3	0	5	5	3	9	.275	.627	.315
Bases Empty	139	42	6	1	13	13	10	22	.302	.640	.366
Runners On	104	32	4	0	8	41	17	6	.308	.577	.402
Runners/Scor. Pos.	51	19	3	0	4	33	14	4	.373	.667	.500
Runners On/2 Out	38	9	1	0	3	13	7	2	.237	.500	.356
Scor. Pos./2 Out	21	7	1	0	2	11	7	1	.333	.667	.500
Late-Inning Pressure	49	18	2	0	8	21	9	3	.367	.898	.475
Leading Off	6	2	0	0	1	1	2	0	.333	.833	.500
Runners On	24	9	1	0	4	17	5	0	.375	.917	.483
Runners/Scor. Pos.	15	6	1	0	3	15	5	0	.400	1.067	.550

RUNS BATTED IN	From 1B	From 2B	From 3B	Scoring Position
Totals	8/91	9/38	16/23	25/61
Percentage	8.8%	23.7%	69.6%	41.0%

Loved to face: Bill Monbouquette (.667, 4-for-6, 1 HR)
Ray Herbert (.556, 5-for-9, 2 2B, 2 HR)

Hated to face: Jack Fisher (.182, 2-for-11)
Jim Bunning (0-for-7, 1 BB)

Miscellaneous statistics: Ground outs-to-air outs ratio: 0.59. . . . Grounded into 6 double plays in 63 opportunities. . . . Drove in 11 of 16 runners from third base with less than two outs (69%). . . . Direction of balls hit to the outfield: 9% to left field, 29% to center, 62% to right. . . . Base running: Advanced from first base to third on 3 of 14 outfield singles (21%); scored from second on 1 of 3 (33%). . . . Opposing base stealers: 17-for-24 (71%); 0-for-first-6, 17-for-18 after that.

Comments: The first player ever to hit 20 or more home runs in a season of less than 250 at-bats. Two National League players did it subsequently: Willie McCovey (1962) and Art Shamsky (1966). . . . Blanchard also hit 16 home runs in 218 at-bats in 1963. No other player in major-league history hit 15+ HRs in less than 250 ABs on two separate occasions. . . . Shares another distinction with Shamsky: Of the 12 players to hit home runs in four consecutive at-bats, they are the only ones to hit fewer than 100 career home runs (Blanchard hit 67, Shamsky 68). . . . Career average of one home run per 17.9 at-bats is highest in major-league history among retired players with between 50 and 150 HRs. Players with closest averages: Duke Snider, Norm Cash, and Johnny Mize (minimum: 50 HR). . . . Career high in at-bats was 246 in 1962. . . . Career-high batting average of .305 in 1961 was 50 points higher than his 2d-highest single-season mark (.255 in 1964). . . . Led the Yankees with 8 home runs and 21 RBIs in Late-Inning Pressure Situations. . . . Hit all 21 home runs to right or right-center field. . . . Drove in 41% of runners from scoring position, to rank a close second to team leader Mickey Mantle (42%). . . . Made his pro debut in 1951 at age 18, hit 112 home runs in six seasons in minors (losing two others to military service), but was still a rookie in 1960 . . . . Mets fans should note the similarity of Blanchard's career statistics to those of Marv Throneberry.

Clete Boyer

Bats Right

New York Yankees	AB	H	2B	3B	HR	RBI	BB	SO	BA	SA	OBA
Season	504	113	19	5	11	55	64	82	.224	.347	.310
vs. Left-Handers	134	26	7	2	3	12	25	22	.194	.343	.317
vs. Right-Handers	370	87	12	3	8	43	39	60	.235	.349	.307
Home Games	242	46	9	2	5	23	36	37	.190	.306	.294
Road Games	262	67	10	3	6	32	28	45	.256	.385	.324
Day Games	271	59	9	3	5	23	33	45	.218	.328	.300
Night Games	233	54	10	2	6	32	31	37	.232	.369	.321
April	35	6	0	0	0	2	4	7	.171	.171	.256
May	91	27	5	1	2	10	15	15	.297	.440	.407
June	104	19	3	0	1	12	12	14	.183	.240	.263
July	90	20	3	1	4	13	7	15	.222	.411	.270
August	96	22	5	1	1	4	12	18	.229	.333	.315
Sept./Oct.	86	19	3	2	3	14	13	13	.221	.407	.314
Leading Off Inn.	137	30	7	3	2	2	11	19	.219	.358	.282
Bases Empty	290	72	14	5	6	6	40	45	.248	.393	.343
Runners On	214	41	5	0	5	49	24	37	.192	.285	.264
Runners/Scor. Pos.	123	25	5	0	2	43	18	16	.203	.293	.289
Runners On/2 Out	95	18	1	0	2	16	13	20	.189	.263	.287
Scor. Pos./2 Out	58	11	1	0	1	14	13	11	.190	.259	.338
Late-Inning Pressure	58	19	4	0	1	7	6	7	.328	.448	.379
Leading Off	19	5	2	0	0	0	1	2	.263	.368	.300
Runners On	23	8	1	0	1	7	1	4	.348	.522	.346
Runners/Scor. Pos.	12	4	1	0	0	5	1	1	.333	.417	.333

RUNS BATTED IN	From 1B	From 2B	From 3B	Scoring Position
Totals	4/172	15/99	25/57	40/156
Percentage	2.3%	15.2%	43.9%	25.6%

Loved to face: Pete Burnside (.333, 2-for-6, 1 HR, 3 BB)
Ray Herbert (.417, 5-for-12, 1 HR)
Juan Pizarro (.429, 3-for-7, 1 HR, 5 BB)

Hated to face: Steve Barber (.118, 2-for-17, 3 BB)
Gary Bell (.077, 1-for-13)
Bill Monbouquette (.059, 1-for-17, 1 2B)

Miscellaneous statistics: Ground outs-to-air outs ratio: 0.93. . . . Grounded into 14 double plays in 108 opportunities. . . . Drove in 17 of 33 runners from third base with less than two outs (52%). . . . Direction of balls hit to the outfield: 44% to left field, 31% to center, 25% to right. . . . Base running: Advanced from first base to third on 15 of 26 outfield singles (58%); scored from second on 15 of 15. . . . Made 2.7 assists per nine innings at third base.

Comments: Yankees allowed 3.62 runs per nine innings with Boyer at third base, 4.66 with others there. . . . Started 35 double plays, compared to 24 by Yankees' opposing third basemen. . . . Committed only 1 error in 76 chances at third base in Late-Inning Pressure Situations (.987). . . . Career average of 2.36 assists per game ranks 3d among A.L. third basemen, behind Lee Tannehill (2.43) and Buddy Bell (2.38). Graig Nettles ranks 4th (2.32), Brooks Robinson 9th (2.16). . . . Was thrown out on the bases on batted balls 8 times, twice as often as any teammate. . . . One of four players in team history to bat below .225 in 500 or more at-bats. Boyer did it twice (1961 and 1964), as did Roger Peckinpaugh (1914 and 1915). Frank Crosetti (1940) and Tom Tresh (1968) were the others. . . . Raised his batting average to a career-high .272 in 1962, the only season in which he hit better than .251. . . . Only 3 hits in 38 career at-bats as a pinch hitter (1-for-26 for the Yankees). . . . One of three players on the 1961 Yankees who later played in a League Championship Series (1969 with Atlanta). The others: Al Downing (1974 with Los Angeles) and Deron Johnson (1973 with Oakland). . . . Everyone knows his brother Ken, an eight-time All-Star third baseman. But in 1955, 18-year-old Clete made his major-league debut for the Kansas City Athletics as a teammate of eldest brother Cloyd, in his final season in majors.

Elston Howard

Bats Right

New York Yankees	AB	H	2B	3B	HR	RBI	BB	SO	BA	SA	OBA
Season	446	155	17	5	21	77	28	64	.348	.549	.387
vs. Left-Handers	163	69	7	3	8	35	12	20	.423	.650	.466
vs. Right-Handers	283	86	10	2	13	42	16	44	.304	.491	.340
Home Games	211	77	9	3	10	38	17	24	.365	.578	.416
Road Games	235	78	8	2	11	39	11	40	.332	.523	.360
Day Games	222	74	10	1	12	44	14	25	.333	.550	.372
Night Games	224	81	7	4	9	33	14	39	.362	.549	.402
April	27	10	3	0	0	1	0	2	.370	.481	.379
May	42	17	1	0	0	6	1	5	.405	.429	.432
June	92	29	3	1	3	14	7	15	.315	.467	.364
July	87	31	1	2	7	19	5	10	.356	.655	.387
August	102	36	7	1	4	17	7	17	.353	.559	.396
Sept./Oct.	94	32	2	1	7	20	8	15	.340	.606	.388
Leading Off Inn.	112	42	3	2	4	4	4	13	.375	.545	.397
Bases Empty	248	89	6	3	13	13	12	33	.359	.565	.388
Runners On	198	66	11	2	8	64	16	31	.333	.530	.385
Runners/Scor. Pos.	109	36	6	2	5	56	11	21	.330	.560	.384
Runners On/2 Out	77	23	6	2	3	29	7	11	.299	.545	.365
Scor. Pos./2 Out	50	17	4	2	3	29	4	7	.340	.680	.389
Late-Inning Pressure	70	23	1	0	4	12	3	13	.329	.514	.356
Leading Off	20	7	0	0	0	0	0	3	.350	.350	.350
Runners On	29	10	1	0	3	11	2	4	.345	.690	.387
Runners/Scor. Pos.	17	6	0	0	2	9	2	2	.353	.706	.421

RUNS BATTED IN	From 1B	From 2B	From 3B	Scoring Position
Totals	13/154	27/95	16/34	43/129
Percentage	8.4%	28.4%	47.1%	33.3%

Loved to face: Pete Burnside (.667, 6-for-9, 1 HR)
Mudcat Grant (.444, 4-for-9, 2 HR)
Chuck Stobbs (4-for-4, 1 HR)

Hated to face: Ted Bowsfield (.182, 2-for-11)
Dick Donovan (0-for-8)
Jack Fisher (0-for-8)

Miscellaneous statistics: Ground outs-to-air outs ratio: 1.21. . . . Grounded into 5 double plays in 106 opportunities (2 for his last 88). . . . Drove in 8 of 17 runners from third base with less than two outs (47%). . . . Direction of balls hit to the outfield: 25% to left field, 41% to center, 34% to right. . . . Base running: Advanced from first base to third on 4 of 23 outfield singles (17%); scored from second on 5 of 7 (71%). . . . Opposing base stealers: 18-for-39 (46%).

Comments: Ranks 3d in major-league history with 54 World Series appearances, behind only Berra (75) and Mantle (65). The top seven on that list—including Bauer (53), McDougald (53), Rizzuto (52), and DiMaggio (51)—appeared only for the Yankees. Most Series games among players who never wore Yankee pinstripes: Frankie Frisch (50), who played four Series each for the Giants and Cardinals. . . . Made major-league debut at age 26 in 1955. Teamed briefly five years earlier with Satchel Paige on Kansas City Monarchs. . . . For seven seasons from 1958 through 1964, he batted .297, 3d-highest mark in A.L., behind Al Kaline (.308) and Mickey Mantle (.300) (minimum: 2500 AB). . . . Batting average in 1961 was the highest of the past 50 years by a player who caught at least 100 games. The all-time high: .362, by Bill Dickey in 1936. . . . Was batting .367 as late as Sept. 14, but had only 10 hits in his final 51 at-bats. . . . Yankees catchers combined for a .323 batting average in 1961, with 30 home runs and 102 RBI. Corresponding figures for opposing catchers: .242, 21 HR, 73 RBI. (Ask Darren Daulton what a season like that would be worth in today's market.) . . . Hit 7 of his 21 home runs to the opposite field. . . . Played 86 more games in the outfield during his first five seasons (263) than he caught (177). . . . Made only 2 errors in 146 games behind the plate in 1964. No other player in major-league history caught as many as 140 games and made less than 3 errors.

Tony Kubek

Bats Left

New York Yankees	AB	H	2B	3B	HR	RBI	BB	SO	BA	SA	OBA
Season	617	170	38	6	8	46	26	60	.276	.395	.304
vs. Left-Handers	185	49	8	1	1	11	8	17	.265	.335	.294
vs. Right-Handers	432	121	30	5	7	35	18	43	.280	.421	.309
Home Games	293	86	19	1	4	26	16	28	.294	.406	.329
Road Games	324	84	19	5	4	20	10	32	.259	.386	.282
Day Games	330	91	19	3	3	24	19	25	.276	.379	.315
Night Games	287	79	19	3	5	22	7	35	.275	.415	.292
April	56	18	4	0	1	2	6	4	.321	.446	.387
May	110	32	5	2	2	11	7	14	.291	.427	.336
June	135	40	10	0	1	9	2	13	.296	.393	.302
July	120	31	13	0	1	9	3	12	.258	.392	.276
August	95	23	3	2	1	6	2	8	.242	.347	.258
Sept./Oct.	97	24	3	2	2	9	6	8	.247	.381	.291
Leading Off Inn.	145	38	11	0	3	3	3	13	.262	.400	.277
Bases Empty	377	100	21	4	5	5	13	35	.265	.382	.290
Runners On	240	70	17	2	3	41	13	25	.292	.417	.327
Runners/Scor. Pos.	106	28	6	0	1	34	8	13	.264	.349	.314
Runners On/2 Out	101	27	4	0	0	17	5	10	.267	.307	.302
Scor. Pos./2 Out	61	15	2	0	0	16	4	8	.246	.279	.292
Late-Inning Pressure	77	26	10	1	1	5	6	5	.338	.532	.386
Leading Off	28	9	3	0	0	0	1	1	.321	.429	.345
Runners On	26	8	4	0	0	4	4	2	.308	.462	.400
Runners/Scor. Pos.	13	5	1	0	0	4	2	1	.385	.462	.467

RUNS BATTED IN	From 1B	From 2B	From 3B	Scoring Position
Totals	5/183	17/85	16/44	33/129
Percentage	2.7%	20.0%	36.4%	25.6%

Loved to face: Johnny Antonelli (.800, 4-for-5)
Gary Bell (.500, 7-for-14, 1 HR)
Billy Muffett (.750, 3-for-4, 1 HR)

Hated to face: Bennie Daniels (.091, 1-for-11)
Jim Kaat (0-for-5)
Ron Kline (0-for-8)

Miscellaneous statistics: Ground outs-to-air outs ratio: 0.82. . . . Grounded into 7 double plays in 127 opportunities . . . . Drove in 9 of 16 runners from third base with less than two outs (56%). . . . Direction of balls hit to the outfield: 30% to left field, 35% to center, 35% to right. . . . Base running: Advanced from first base to third on 21 of 36 outfield singles (58%); scored from second on 18 of 19 (95%). . . . Made 3.3 assists per nine innings at shortstop.

Comments: Only player on team to play every inning of every game in both April and May. . . . Led team in doubles, with 15 more than the runner-up, Moose Skowron. . . . Started the season with an 0-for-15 streak, then went 20-for-46 over his next 11 games. (Only two teammates had hitless streaks as long as 20 at-bats in 1961: Jim Coates went 0-for-his-last-30, and Joe DeMaestri went 0-for-the-last-20-at-bats-of-his-career.) . . . His 19-game hitting streak (May 22 through June 9) was the team's longest of the season. . . . Least selective Yankee batter in 1961, averaging 1 walk per 25.3 plate appearances. Led off 148 innings, drew only 3 walks. . . . The Yankees allowed 3.91 runs per nine innings with Kubek at short, 3.06 runs per nine innings with other shortstops. . . . Committed career-high 30 errors, and didn't have an errorless streak longer than 12 games. . . . Career took southbound turn after he spent most of the 1962 season in military service (during which time he suffered a broken neck that went undiagnosed until 1965 and healed improperly). First five seasons: 139 games per year, .277 batting average; last five seasons: 117 games per year, .238 BA. . . . Played his final major-league game at age 28 (with a home run off Dick Radatz in his final at-bat). Only three others reached the 1000-game mark but never played beyond their 29th birthdays: Buddy Kerr, Cass Michaels, and Bill Sweeney. Michaels retired in 1954, after he suffered a fractured skull when hit by a pitch from Marion Fricano.

Hector Lopez

Bats Right

New York Yankees	AB	H	2B	3B	HR	RBI	BB	SO	BA	SA	OBA
Season	243	54	7	2	3	22	24	38	.222	.305	.292
vs. Left-Handers	104	25	2	1	1	10	12	14	.240	.308	.314
vs. Right-Handers	139	29	5	1	2	12	12	24	.209	.302	.275
Home Games	123	29	5	2	1	10	14	21	.236	.333	.314
Road Games	120	25	2	0	2	12	10	17	.208	.275	.267
Day Games	142	37	5	1	1	13	14	19	.261	.331	.325
Night Games	101	17	2	1	2	9	10	19	.168	.267	.246
April	59	13	1	0	0	4	4	8	.220	.237	.266
May	60	10	1	0	2	5	10	10	.167	.283	.286
June	20	4	2	0	0	4	1	4	.200	.300	.261
July	30	8	0	1	0	3	2	5	.267	.333	.303
August	37	10	1	0	1	5	4	5	.270	.378	.341
Sept./Oct.	36	9	2	1	0	1	3	6	.250	.361	.308
Leading Off Inn.	45	9	3	1	0	0	8	4	.200	.311	.321
Bases Empty	134	28	5	2	1	1	19	21	.209	.299	.312
Runners On	109	26	2	0	2	21	5	17	.239	.312	.265
Runners/Scor. Pos.	61	15	1	0	2	20	4	11	.246	.361	.279
Runners On/2 Out	54	16	1	0	2	13	1	8	.296	.426	.309
Scor. Pos./2 Out	31	11	0	0	2	12	1	5	.355	.548	.375
Late-Inning Pressure	42	9	1	1	0	4	5	7	.214	.286	.292
Leading Off	10	3	1	1	0	0	1	0	.300	.600	.364
Runners On	24	5	0	0	0	4	2	4	.208	.208	.259
Runners/Scor. Pos.	16	4	0	0	0	4	2	3	.250	.250	.316

RUNS BATTED IN	From 1B	From 2B	From 3B	Scoring Position
Totals	1/81	7/48	11/25	18/73
Percentage	1.2%	14.6%	44.0%	24.7%

Loved to face:

Hated to face: Jim Archer (.100, 1-for-10)
Hal Brown (0-for-5)
Jack Fisher (.091, 1-for-11, 2 BB)

Miscellaneous statistics: Ground outs-to-air outs ratio: 1.67. . . . Grounded into 7 double plays in 43 opportunities. . . . Drove in 7 of 15 runners from third base with less than two outs (47%). . . . Direction of balls hit to the outfield: 24% to left field, 34% to center, 42% to right. . . . Base running: Advanced from first base to third on 4 of 12 outfield singles (33%); scored from second on 5 of 6 (83%). . . . Made 2.0 putouts per nine innings in left field.

Comments: Nobody pitched around Hector, despite his reputation as a clutch hitter. He drew only 1 walk in 55 plate appearances with two outs and runners on base, while batting 95 points higher in those situations than otherwise. . . . Drove in 7 runs in 4 games against Cincinnati in the 1961 Series, none in 11 other World Series games. . . . Started each of the Yankees' first 24 games (all in left field), but made only 33 more starts for the rest of the season. . . . Played 628 games in the outfield in eight seasons with the Yankees, 79 at third base. But he was used almost exclusively as an infielder in five seasons with Kansas City (380 games at third base, 177 at second, 5 at shortstop, 24 in the outfield). . . . Think about this: 38 different players appeared for both the Yankees and the A's in just a five-year period from 1956 through 1960. That's two more than the number of players who split time between New York and its Triple-A affiliates (Denver and Richmond) during the same period. The roll call: Hank Bauer, Zeke Bella, Clete Boyer, Andy Carey, Tommy Carroll, Bob Cerv, Rip Coleman, Joe DeMaestri, Murry Dickson, Art Ditmar, Ryne Duren, Mark Freeman, Bob Grim, Kent Hadley, Woodie Held, Billy Hunter, Johnny Kucks, Don Larsen, Hector Lopez, Jerry Lumpe, Duke Maas, Roger Maris, Billy Martin, Mickey McDermott, Tom Morgan, Irv Noren, Jim Pisoni, Eddie Robinson, Bobby Shantz, Norm Siebern, Harry Simpson, Lou Skizas, Enos Slaughter, Tom Sturdivant, Ralph Terry, Marv Throneberry, Virgil Trucks, and Elmer Valo.

Mickey Mantle

Bats Left and Right

New York Yankees	AB	H	2B	3B	HR	RBI	BB	SO	BA	SA	OBA
Season	514	163	16	6	54	128	126	112	.317	.687	.448
vs. Left-Handers	167	62	10	4	11	34	33	33	.371	.677	.468
vs. Right-Handers	347	101	6	2	43	94	93	79	.291	.692	.439
Home Games	230	76	8	6	24	59	66	44	.330	.730	.477
Road Games	284	87	8	0	30	69	60	68	.306	.651	.424
Day Games	281	96	7	6	29	76	76	55	.342	.719	.479
Night Games	233	67	9	0	25	52	50	57	.288	.648	.409
April	52	17	1	1	7	17	9	6	.327	.788	.419
May	80	25	4	0	7	16	19	15	.313	.625	.444
June	115	35	4	1	11	31	26	28	.304	.643	.430
July	96	36	2	1	14	28	27	16	.375	.854	.508
August	111	34	3	2	9	22	27	27	.306	.613	.439
Sept./Oct.	60	16	2	1	6	14	18	20	.267	.633	.430
Leading Off Inn.	127	39	5	2	12	12	27	25	.307	.661	.429
Bases Empty	272	80	11	2	27	27	69	56	.294	.647	.437
Runners On	242	83	5	4	27	101	57	56	.343	.731	.461
Runners/Scor. Pos.	105	39	2	1	18	80	31	23	.371	.924	.496
Runners On/2 Out	115	39	0	3	16	45	26	30	.339	.809	.461
Scor. Pos./2 Out	45	16	0	1	9	29	16	12	.356	1.000	.525
Late-Inning Pressure	58	20	4	2	7	16	21	14	.345	.845	.519
Leading Off	14	5	1	0	2	2	3	0	.357	.857	.471
Runners On	28	11	2	2	3	12	11	11	.393	.929	.564
Runners/Scor. Pos.	13	4	1	1	2	9	6	7	.308	1.000	.526

RUNS BATTED IN	From 1B	From 2B	From 3B	Scoring Position
Totals	20/196	23/76	31/52	54/128
Percentage	10.2%	30.3%	59.6%	42.2%

Loved to face: Steve Barber (.429, 6-for-14, 3 2B, 2 HR)
Jack Kralick (.538, 7-for-13, 1 HR)
Joe McClain (.556, 5-for-9, 3 HR)
Don Schwall (.571, 4-for-7, 1 HR, 4 BB)

Hated to face: Don Lee (0-for-5)
Ron Moeller (0-for-5)

Miscellaneous statistics: Ground outs-to-air outs ratio: 0.74. . . . Grounded into 2 double plays in 130 opportunities. . . . Drove in 24 of 34 runners from third base with less than two outs (71%). . . . Direction of balls hit to the outfield: 15% to left field, 25% to center, 60% to right batting left-handed; 51% to left, 26% to center, 23% to right batting right-handed. . . . Base running: Advanced from first base to third on 27 of 46 outfield singles (59%); scored from second on 11 of 14 (79%). . . . Made 2.4 putouts per nine innings in center field.

Comments: Average of 1 home run for every 9.5 at-bats was the 4th-highest single-season mark in major-league history, and the best by anyone other than the Bambino. . . . Led the American League in slugging average with a mark unsurpassed in the 30 years since. . . . Equaled his personal high with 132 runs scored, the last of his nine consecutive seasons in triple figures. The record: 13 straight seasons, by Lou Gehrig (1926–38) and Hank Aaron (1955–67). . . . Despite his team-high strikeout total, led the club by driving in more than 70% of runners from third base with less than two outs. . . . What made Mickey run? Of his 14 stolen base attempts, 9 came from first base with two outs and no one else on base, 13 were against right-handed pitchers, and 8 came in the sixth inning or later. . . . Led team with 12 steals, but ranked only 12th in A.L., ending streak of six straight seasons in top 10s in both home runs and stolen bases. . . . Hit 13 home runs in 96 games as a rookie in 1951, then hit 15 or more in each of the next 17 seasons, a streak ended by his retirement in 1968. The only other A.L. player ever to hit 15 or more homers in 17 consecutive seasons: Graig Nettles (1970–86). . . . Hit 37 doubles in 1952, his first full season in majors, but never reached the 30 mark thereafter. . . . Hit 18 postseason home runs, tied with Reggie Jackson for all-time lead. Mantle didn't have the advantage of playing in LCS, of course. But actually, Reggie played in only 12 more postseason games than Mantle.

Roger Maris

Bats Left

New York Yankees	AB	H	2B	3B	HR	RBI	BB	SO	BA	SA	OBA
Season	590	159	16	4	61	142	94	67	.269	.620	.372
vs. Left-Handers	177	41	7	0	12	35	30	30	.232	.475	.347
vs. Right-Handers	413	118	9	4	49	107	64	37	.286	.683	.384
Home Games	280	80	6	0	30	74	39	31	.286	.629	.372
Road Games	310	79	10	4	31	68	55	36	.255	.613	.373
Day Games	322	92	9	2	36	79	50	36	.286	.661	.384
Night Games	268	67	7	2	25	63	44	31	.250	.571	.358
April	49	10	1	0	1	4	10	4	.204	.286	.328
May	90	24	1	0	11	26	17	14	.267	.644	.387
June	123	34	6	1	15	35	18	9	.276	.707	.375
July	106	35	4	1	13	32	13	10	.330	.755	.403
August	115	28	3	1	11	24	21	16	.243	.574	.371
Sept./Oct.	103	27	1	1	9	20	15	13	.262	.553	.353
Leading Off Inn.	88	21	2	1	9	9	20	8	.239	.591	.396
Bases Empty	316	76	6	2	33	33	56	37	.241	.585	.362
Runners On	274	83	10	2	28	109	38	30	.303	.661	.385
Runners/Scor. Pos.	128	42	5	0	15	77	19	9	.328	.719	.408
Runners On/2 Out	87	29	4	2	8	32	8	8	.333	.701	.389
Scor. Pos./2 Out	50	14	2	0	5	23	6	3	.280	.620	.357
Late-Inning Pressure	76	18	2	1	6	17	15	7	.237	.526	.359
Leading Off	15	4	0	0	1	1	2	0	.267	.467	.353
Runners On	33	10	1	1	5	16	5	3	.303	.848	.385
Runners/Scor. Pos.	21	6	1	0	3	11	3	0	.286	.762	.360

RUNS BATTED IN	From 1B	From 2B	From 3B	Scoring Position
Totals	25/201	26/98	30/58	56/156
Percentage	12.4%	26.5%	51.7%	35.9%

Loved to face: Frank Lary (.389, 7-for-18, 3 HR)
Bill Monbouquette (.385, 5-for-13, 2 HR, 6 BB)
Billy Pierce (.833, 5-for-6, 2 HR, 1 SO)

Hated to face: Steve Barber (0-for-10, 4 BB)
Joe McClain (.091, 1-for-11)
Phil Regan (0-for-8)

Miscellaneous statistics: Ground outs-to-air outs ratio: 0.71. . . . Grounded into 18 double plays in 165 opportunities. . . . Drove in 23 of 34 runners from third base with less than two outs (68%). . . . Direction of balls hit to the outfield: 12% to left field, 25% to center, 63% to right. . . . Base running: Advanced from first base to third on 17 of 29 outfield singles (59%); scored from second on 15 of 19 (79%). . . . Made 1.7 putouts per nine innings in right field.

Comments: Faced Tracy Stallard only once prior to 1961 (and never again after home run number 61). That came on Oct. 1, 1960—a year to the day before his 61st homer. Maris struck out. . . . Hit 57 of his 61 home runs to right or right-center field, 3 to center, and 1 to the opposite field. . . . Here's a curiosity: Maris batted only twice during the entire 1961 season with the bases loaded (a pair of RBI ground outs). Four Yankees pitchers (Daley, Stafford, Turley, and Ford) combined for 5 hits in 6 AB (with 10 RBIs) with the bags full. . . . Advanced from first to second on 6 of 23 outfield fly outs, twice as many advances as any of his teammates. . . . Breakthrough season was 1959, when he led the A.L. in batting average as late as July 28. But he hit only .164 from that point on, to drop his season average from .344 to .273. . . . Other than his MVP seasons of 1960 and 1961, he never ranked among the top 10 home-run hitters in the majors. . . . Batted .219 in seven World Series. Among the 33 players with at least 100 Series at-bats, only Frank Crosetti (.174) and Jim Gilliam (.211) had lower marks. . . . When talk comes around to the topic of debuts under a national spotlight, how about John Powell, who became better known by his nickname, Boog? Powell made his major-league debut on Sept. 26, 1961, in the game in which Maris hit his 60th home run. He batted for Dick Williams and struck out.

Bobby Richardson

Bats Right

New York Yankees	AB	H	2B	3B	HR	RBI	BB	SO	BA	SA	OBA
Season	662	173	17	5	3	49	28	23	.261	.316	.293
vs. Left-Handers	195	57	7	1	1	16	11	6	.292	.354	.327
vs. Right-Handers	467	116	10	4	2	33	17	17	.248	.300	.278
Home Games	309	77	8	4	2	27	19	8	.249	.320	.293
Road Games	353	96	9	1	1	22	9	15	.272	.312	.292
Day Games	369	92	6	3	2	26	14	9	.249	.298	.280
Night Games	293	81	11	2	1	23	14	14	.276	.338	.308
April	59	13	0	0	0	5	1	1	.220	.220	.246
May	102	21	1	1	0	5	4	1	.206	.235	.236
June	126	37	4	2	1	8	3	9	.294	.381	.308
July	120	33	4	1	1	15	10	0	.275	.350	.328
August	139	42	5	0	1	10	6	8	.302	.360	.331
Sept./Oct.	112	27	3	1	0	6	4	4	.241	.286	.274
Leading Off Inn.	241	54	6	2	1	1	13	11	.224	.278	.267
Bases Empty	442	109	12	4	1	1	17	15	.247	.299	.278
Runners On	220	64	5	1	2	48	11	8	.291	.350	.322
Runners/Scor. Pos.	124	42	4	1	2	48	7	6	.339	.435	.368
Runners On/2 Out	94	25	2	0	2	24	7	3	.266	.351	.317
Scor. Pos./2 Out	58	20	2	0	2	24	5	2	.345	.483	.397
Late-Inning Pressure	73	14	0	0	0	4	3	5	.192	.192	.224
Leading Off	14	2	0	0	0	0	0	1	.143	.143	.143
Runners On	31	4	0	0	0	4	2	3	.129	.129	.182
Runners/Scor. Pos.	21	3	0	0	0	4	0	2	.143	.143	.143

RUNS BATTED IN	From 1B	From 2B	From 3B	Scoring Position
Totals	2/151	24/102	20/44	44/146
Percentage	1.3%	23.5%	45.5%	30.1%

Loved to face: Jim Archer (.529, 9-for-17)
Frank Baumann (.538, 7-for-13)
Dave Hillman (.800, 4-for-5)

Hated to face: Steve Barber (.150, 3-for-20)
Ryne Duren (0-for-7)
Eli Grba (.071, 1-for-14)

Miscellaneous statistics: Ground outs-to-air outs ratio: 1.31.... Grounded into 16 double plays in 101 opportunities.... Drove in 14 of 25 runners from third base with less than two outs (56%).... Direction of balls hit to the outfield: 36% to left field, 39% to center, 26% to right.... Base running: Advanced from first base to third on 20 of 28 outfield singles (71%); scored from second on 10 of 11 (91%).... Made 2.4 assists per nine innings at second base.

Comments: Led the American League in singles in 1961, 1962, and 1964. Since then, only three Yankees have led the league: Richardson's replacement, Horace Clarke (1967 and 1969); Thurman Munson (1975); and Steve Sax (1989). Some related topics: Sax also led the National League (in 1988); the only other player to lead both leagues: Willie Keeler. Nellie Fox led the A.L. 8 times, the highest total in either league. Munson was the only catcher ever to lead either league.... Had 36 infield hits, more than twice as many as team runners-up Tony Kubek and Moose Skowron, who had 15 apiece.... Average of 1 strikeout per 31 plate appearances was the best on the club—unless you include pitcher Bud Daley, who made 48 trips to the plate and struck out only once.... Hit his first major-league home run on July 25, 1959, in the 740th at-bat of his career. Fritz Brickell hit his only big-league homer in that game.... Batted .301 in 1959 and .302 in 1962, his only seasons of .270 or better. Composite batting average for the rest of his career was only .256.... Set a record that still stands with 12 RBIs in the 1960 World Series. Drove in only 26 runs in 150 regular-season games that year, and didn't drive in a run in the next three Series combined (16 games).... Played every inning of 26 consecutive World Series games from Oct. 12, 1960, (game 5) through the completion of the 1964 Series.

Bill Skowron

Bats Right

New York Yankees	AB	H	2B	3B	HR	RBI	BB	SO	BA	SA	OBA
Season	561	150	23	4	28	89	36	107	.267	.472	.319
vs. Left-Handers	169	51	9	3	6	28	12	24	.302	.497	.350
vs. Right-Handers	392	99	14	1	22	61	24	83	.253	.462	.306
Home Games	263	66	12	3	7	30	22	56	.251	.399	.313
Road Games	298	84	11	1	21	59	14	51	.282	.537	.325
Day Games	305	86	13	3	18	48	20	59	.282	.521	.334
Night Games	256	64	10	1	10	41	16	48	.250	.414	.301
April	55	17	3	0	2	9	4	6	.309	.473	.367
May	103	28	4	1	6	18	7	21	.272	.505	.324
June	130	32	4	1	8	25	5	26	.246	.477	.277
July	74	22	2	0	3	8	9	11	.297	.446	.395
August	99	29	6	1	4	13	6	18	.293	.495	.330
Sept./Oct.	98	22	4	1	5	16	5	23	.224	.439	.274
Leading Off Inn.	122	37	7	1	9	9	5	20	.303	.598	.331
Bases Empty	292	86	15	3	16	16	15	59	.295	.531	.338
Runners On	269	64	8	1	12	73	21	48	.238	.409	.300
Runners/Scor. Pos.	146	33	6	0	6	60	14	25	.226	.390	.301
Runners On/2 Out	108	24	4	1	4	25	11	22	.222	.389	.294
Scor. Pos./2 Out	67	15	3	0	1	18	7	12	.224	.313	.297
Late-Inning Pressure	76	22	1	1	3	9	5	17	.289	.447	.329
Leading Off	22	8	0	0	2	2	2	5	.364	.636	.417
Runners On	27	6	1	0	1	7	3	7	.222	.370	.290
Runners/Scor. Pos.	15	3	0	0	1	7	3	2	.200	.400	.316

RUNS BATTED IN	From 1B	From 2B	From 3B	Scoring Position
Totals	13/213	19/106	29/70	48/176
Percentage	6.1%	17.9%	41.4%	27.3%

Loved to face: Bill Kunkel (.625, 5-for-8, 1 HR)
Don Mossi (.412, 7-for-17, 2 HR)
Joe Nuxhall (.500, 5-for-10)

Hated to face: Dick Hall (0-for-6, 1 BB, 4 SO)
Juan Pizarro (.200, 2-for-10, 5 SO)
Bob Shaw (.143, 2-for-14)

Miscellaneous statistics: Ground outs-to-air outs ratio: 1.36.... Grounded into 23 double plays (team high) in 142 opportunities.... Drove in 23 of 38 runners from third base with less than two outs (58%).... Direction of balls hit to the outfield: 44% to left field, 30% to center, 26% to right.... Base running: Advanced from first base to third on 9 of 27 outfield singles (33%); scored from second on 12 of 15 (80%).... Made 0.7 assists per nine innings at first base.

Comments: Batted fifth, sixth, or seventh in all 146 starts.... Hit a career-high 28 home runs in 1961. Nine were to the opposite field.... Batted only 215 times as a rookie in 1954, but ranked 6th in the American League with 9 triples.... Ranked 7th in the A.L. with a .304 batting average over his first seven seasons (1954–60), behind only Ted Williams (.337), Harvey Kuenn (.314), Mickey Mantle (.312), Minnie Minoso (.307), Al Kaline (.307), and Nellie Fox (.305). But he batted only .261 thereafter.... Career statistics were strikingly similar to those of Elston Howard.... Only four players hit more career home runs than Skowron but, like the Moose, never led their teams outright in a season: Brooks Robinson, Roy Campanella, Tony Oliva, and Al Oliver.... One of six players to appear for both the Yankees and Dodgers in World Series competition. The others: Johnny Allen, Al Downing, Tommy John, Jay Johnstone, and Stan Williams (for whom Skowron was traded to Los Angeles).... Skowron is one of 13 players to hit home runs for two different teams in the World Series. No one has done it for three teams. Active contenders for that feat: Kirk Gibson and Dave Henderson.... Played football at Purdue in 1949 and 1950. The most famous of his fellow Boilermakers was Ample Abe Gibron, who played 10 years in NFL and was head coach of the Chicago Bears for three seasons (1972–74).

Luis Arroyo

Throws Left

New York Yankees	W-L	ERA	AB	H	HR	BB	SO	BA	SA	OBA
Season	15-5	2.19	417	83	5	49	87	.199	.276	.284
vs. Left-Handers			108	19	1	15	27	.176	.231	.288
vs. Right-Handers			309	64	4	34	60	.207	.291	.283
Home Games	8-1	1.44	211	39	1	26	41	.185	.232	.275
Road Games	7-4	3.04	206	44	4	23	46	.214	.320	.294
Day Games	8-3	1.93	247	50	2	28	57	.202	.271	.283
Night Games	7-2	2.57	170	33	3	21	30	.194	.282	.286
April	1-0	0.00	27	2	0	1	7	.074	.111	.103
May	0-2	5.19	64	17	1	13	10	.266	.375	.380
June	1-1	0.90	65	10	1	3	15	.154	.246	.200
July	5-0	0.88	107	18	0	13	21	.168	.206	.262
August	4-0	2.08	78	16	3	10	17	.205	.346	.300
Sept./Oct.	4-2	4.42	69	19	0	9	16	.275	.319	.359
Leading Off Inn.			86	19	0	7	21	.221	.256	.287
Bases Empty			198	39	3	21	51	.197	.288	.281
Runners On			219	44	2	28	36	.201	.265	.287
Runners/Scor. Pos.			127	32	2	20	16	.252	.354	.344
Runners On/2 Out			88	12	0	11	16	.136	.148	.232
Scor. Pos./2 Out			56	11	0	6	6	.196	.214	.274
Late-Inning Pressure			272	60	3	37	61	.221	.301	.314
Leading Off			56	14	0	6	13	.250	.304	.323
Runners On			148	34	2	18	30	.230	.304	.314
Runners/Scor. Pos.			79	26	2	12	11	.329	.468	.415
First 9 Batters			341	67	5	42	72	.196	.279	.286
Second 9 Batters			64	12	0	6	12	.188	.234	.257
All Batters Thereafter			12	4	0	1	3	.333	.417	.385

Loved to face: Luis Aparicio (0-for-8)
Norm Cash (.143, 1-for-7, 5 SO)

Hated to face:

Miscellaneous statistics: Ground outs-to-air outs ratio: 1.25. . . . Induced 17 double-play ground outs in 135 opportunities. . . . Allowed 15 doubles, 1 triple in 119.0 innings. . . . Stranded 33 inherited runners, allowed 32 to score (51%). . . . Opposing base stealers: 0-for-0; 2 pickoffs, no balks.

Comments: Why all the ballyhoo? This was hardly a great season: He saved 22 games (according to the current saves rule) in 28 opportunities, a good but not great average (79%), though reputation was enhanced by going 7-for-8 with Whitey Ford the pitcher of record. An excellent ERA masked the fact that he stranded only one more inherited runner than he allowed to score, a dreadful record. And his won-lost record was bolstered by batting support of 6.1 runs per nine innings while he was pitcher of decision. . . . Another myth: Screwball notwithstanding, he was not more effective against right-handers than left-handers (in 1961, at least). . . . No opposing runner even tried to steal a base in 1961. . . . Started 24 games as a 28-year-old rookie for the Cardinals in 1955. . . . Career breakdown: 11–15, 4.33 ERA in 36 starts; 29–17, 3.66 ERA in 208 relief appearances. . . . Was one of many past and future major-leaguers on powerhouse Havana team in International League that fled to Jersey City in July 1960. Among his teammates: Cookie Rojas, Leo Cardenas, Jose Azcue, Mike Cuellar, Brooks Lawrence, and Orlando Pena. . . . Why was he called "Yo-Yo"? According to 1957 *Baseball Register,* it was a bastardization of his last name by fans in Greensboro, N.C., (where he pitched in late 1940s) who, they report, "couldn't pronounce his name." In the immortal words of Dick Enberg: Oh, my!

Jim Coates

Throws Right

New York Yankees	W-L	ERA	AB	H	HR	BB	SO	BA	SA	OBA
Season	11-5	3.44	526	128	15	53	80	.243	.388	.318
vs. Left-Handers			174	44	4	19	27	.253	.408	.327
vs. Right-Handers			352	84	11	34	53	.239	.378	.314
Home Games	9-1	2.68	286	61	7	24	45	.213	.329	.278
Road Games	2-4	4.45	240	67	8	29	35	.279	.458	.364
Day Games	8-1	2.81	328	74	6	35	50	.226	.338	.307
Night Games	3-4	4.53	198	54	9	18	30	.273	.470	.336
April	0-0	5.14	28	9	2	1	2	.321	.571	.355
May	5-2	1.84	101	17	1	11	19	.168	.267	.270
June	1-1	5.70	91	25	5	7	15	.275	.484	.327
July	0-0	9.00	60	22	4	7	7	.367	.617	.426
August	3-2	2.97	136	32	2	18	18	.235	.346	.327
Sept./Oct.	2-0	0.87	110	23	1	9	19	.209	.300	.275
Leading Off Inn.			127	36	5	7	15	.283	.425	.331
Bases Empty			288	75	7	28	43	.260	.375	.339
Runners On			238	53	8	25	37	.223	.403	.294
Runners/Scor. Pos.			121	23	4	9	14	.190	.364	.243
Runners On/2 Out			96	19	4	10	12	.198	.396	.280
Scor. Pos./2 Out			54	10	2	6	5	.185	.389	.279
Late-Inning Pressure			110	19	2	11	22	.173	.291	.254
Leading Off			33	9	2	1	4	.273	.455	.294
Runners On			38	4	0	5	7	.105	.132	.227
Runners/Scor. Pos.			14	1	0	1	2	.071	.143	.188
First 9 Batters			280	75	11	29	50	.268	.454	.345
Second 9 Batters			143	29	1	13	14	.203	.273	.275
All Batters Thereafter			103	24	3	11	16	.233	.369	.304

Loved to face: Earl Battey (0-for-9, 1 BB)
Bob Johnson (0-for-9)
Marty Keough (0-for-7)

Hated to face: Dale Long (.714, 5-for-7, 1 HR)
Bubba Phillips (.667, 2-for-3, 2 HR)

Miscellaneous statistics: Ground outs-to-air outs ratio: 0.92. . . . Induced 16 double-play ground outs in 133 opportunities. . . . Allowed 21 doubles, 5 triples in 141.1 innings. . . . Allowed 15 first-inning runs (all earned) in 11 starts. Earned run average of 3.71 as a starter: 12.27 in first inning, 2.12 thereafter. . . . Batting support: 4.36 runs per start. . . . Opposing base stealers: 10-for-13 (77%); 2 pickoffs, no balks.

Comments: Career record of 37–15 for the Yankees, a .712 winning percentage. Only three other Yankees pitchers topped the .700 mark over careers of at least 50 decisions: Johnny Allen, .725 (50–19); Spud Chandler, .717 (109–43); and Vic Raschi, .706 (120–50). . . . Won 28 of his first 35 decisions, but only 15 of 30 thereafter. . . . Career average of 6.75 strikeouts per nine innings as a reliever was nearly double his mark as a starter (3.53). But ERAs were nearly the same (4.06 and 3.95, respectively). . . . Made only 80 appearances in majors (spread over four seasons and five years for three different teams) after leaving the Yankees in 1963. . . . Allowed the two-out, go-ahead home run to Hal Smith in the eighth inning of the seventh game of the 1960 World Series. Ralph Terry carries the stigma of allowing Mazeroski's game-winner an inning later. . . . Had a memorable, two-game cup o' Joe in 1956. Made his major-league debut on Sept. 21, in a game in which the Yankees broke the A.L. record for home runs in a season and set a record that still stands by leaving 20 men on base in a nine-inning game. Nine days later, Mickey Mantle pinch-hit for Coates in the season finale and drove in an insurance run in his battle with Al Kaline for the A.L. RBI lead—and with it, the Triple Crown.

Bud Daley

Throws Left

New York Yankees	W-L	ERA	AB	H	HR	BB	SO	BA	SA	OBA
Season	8-9	3.96	495	127	17	51	83	.257	.416	.330
vs. Left-Handers			112	31	2	15	25	.277	.393	.367
vs. Right-Handers			383	96	15	36	58	.251	.423	.319
Home Games	5-3	2.88	249	60	6	26	41	.241	.373	.320
Road Games	3-6	5.06	246	67	11	25	42	.272	.459	.341
Day Games	4-3	3.75	185	45	6	21	31	.243	.411	.330
Night Games	4-6	4.08	310	82	11	30	52	.265	.419	.330
April	0-0	—	0	0	0	0	0	—	—	—
May	0-0	—	0	0	0	0	0	—	—	—
June	1-2	9.00	64	22	3	8	9	.344	.531	.411
July	3-4	4.31	181	50	7	19	26	.276	.459	.345
August	1-2	2.49	98	23	1	9	17	.235	.337	.299
Sept./Oct.	3-1	2.61	152	32	6	15	31	.211	.368	.298
Leading Off Inn.			124	31	4	10	22	.250	.403	.306
Bases Empty			278	74	11	33	49	.266	.442	.348
Runners On			217	53	6	18	34	.244	.382	.307
Runners/Scor. Pos.			111	27	3	12	20	.243	.387	.325
Runners On/2 Out			93	21	4	7	17	.226	.376	.294
Scor. Pos./2 Out			51	8	2	6	9	.157	.275	.271
Late-Inning Pressure			62	14	0	8	7	.226	.274	.314
Leading Off			17	3	0	1	4	.176	.176	.222
Runners On			27	8	0	2	1	.296	.370	.345
Runners/Scor. Pos.			15	3	0	2	1	.200	.267	.294
First 9 Batters			169	43	7	18	31	.254	.444	.328
Second 9 Batters			148	36	4	11	26	.243	.365	.296
All Batters Thereafter			178	48	6	22	26	.270	.433	.360

Loved to face: Jerry Adair (.111, 1-for-9)
Chico Fernandez (0-for-5, 3 SO)
Willie Tasby (.083, 1-for-12, 2 BB)

Hated to face: Tito Francona (.750, 3-for-4, 1 HR)
Pumpsie Green (3-for-3)

Miscellaneous statistics: Ground outs-to-air outs ratio: 0.99. . . . Induced 17 double-play ground outs in 105 opportunities. . . . Allowed 24 doubles, 2 triples in 129.2 innings. . . . Allowed 16 first-inning runs (12 earned) in 17 starts. . . . Batting support: 5.00 runs per start. . . . Opposing base stealers: 1-for-3 (33%); 4 pickoffs, 1 balk.

Comments: Statisics above are with the Yankees only. . . . A teammate of Roger Maris's with Cleveland in 1957 and Kansas City in 1958 before rejoining him on the Yankees in 1961. . . . Won 16 games for the 1960 Kansas City Athletics, whose record was 59–96 (.377). From 1951, when Ned Garver won 20 games for the St. Louis Browns, to the present, no other American League pitcher won as many as 16 games for a team with a record as bad as Daley's 1960 A's. . . . Ranked 8th in the American League with a 3.16 ERA in 1958, the 4th consecutive season in which he lowered his mark. But he compiled a 4.28 mark in nine other seasons. Incidentally, Claude Osteen (1960–65) and Sandy Koufax (1959–64) were the only pitchers who reduced their ERAs in each of six straight seasons during the nearly 80 years the statistic has been compiled. . . . Pitched mainly in relief during his first four seasons in the majors. Then completed 34 of 91 games from 1959 through 1961, but made only 9 starts over his three remaining seasons, compared to 48 relief appearances. . . . Pitched 982 innings in five seasons in the minors, including nearly 400 prior to his 20th birthday, before making his major-league debut in 1955. Once you know that, his arm-induced retirement nine years later at age 32 no longer seems premature.

Whitey Ford

Throws Left

New York Yankees	W-L	ERA	AB	H	HR	BB	SO	BA	SA	OBA
Season	25-4	3.21	1056	242	23	92	210	.229	.346	.291
vs. Left-Handers			237	43	5	13	68	.181	.274	.224
vs. Right-Handers			819	199	18	79	142	.243	.366	.309
Home Games	12-2	2.65	548	119	12	39	116	.217	.327	.269
Road Games	13-2	3.84	508	123	11	53	94	.242	.366	.314
Day Games	14-1	3.30	550	128	16	37	103	.233	.362	.281
Night Games	11-3	3.12	506	114	7	55	107	.225	.328	.301
April	3-1	3.19	137	30	2	12	23	.219	.307	.282
May	3-1	3.27	156	31	3	15	30	.199	.314	.273
June	8-0	2.94	231	43	7	21	55	.186	.316	.253
July	5-0	3.43	175	42	2	15	40	.240	.314	.298
August	3-1	4.26	195	52	7	16	27	.267	.446	.321
Sept./Oct.	3-1	2.11	162	44	2	13	35	.272	.364	.326
Leading Off Inn.			278	57	7	15	59	.205	.342	.246
Bases Empty			683	146	15	50	153	.214	.335	.267
Runners On			373	96	8	42	57	.257	.365	.332
Runners/Scor. Pos.			185	44	4	27	29	.238	.341	.330
Runners On/2 Out			169	39	2	22	30	.231	.308	.319
Scor. Pos./2 Out			88	18	1	14	15	.205	.284	.314
Late-Inning Pressure			134	39	5	5	25	.291	.478	.321
Leading Off			39	11	1	1	10	.282	.487	.300
Runners On			43	12	1	4	8	.279	.349	.354
Runners/Scor. Pos.			23	5	0	3	6	.217	.217	.308
First 9 Batters			320	81	7	29	72	.253	.378	.314
Second 9 Batters			304	63	8	39	57	.207	.332	.297
All Batters Thereafter			432	98	8	24	81	.227	.331	.268

Loved to face: Norm Cash (.167, 3-for-18, 8 SO)
Jim Gentile (0-for-12, 1 BB, 7 SO)
Jake Wood (.100, 2-for-20)

Hated to face: Jackie Jensen (.615, 8-for-13, 3 HR)
Al Kaline (.421, 8-for-19)
Johnny Romano (.600, 6-for-10, 1 HR)

Miscellaneous statistics: Ground outs-to-air outs ratio: 1.38. . . . Induced 28 double-play ground outs in 178 opportunities. . . . Allowed 38 doubles, 8 triples in 283.0 innings. . . . Allowed 12 first-inning runs (11 earned) in 39 starts. . . . Batting support: 5.67 runs per start. . . . Opposing base stealers: 0-for-3; 6 pickoffs, no balks.

Comments: Pitched a complete game for his only major-league win—oh, sorry, that was Wenty Ford, not Whitey. . . . We wonder how many others in major-league history pitched as many as 283 innings in a season without allowing a stolen base. . . . Starting pitcher in 22 World Series games, twice as many as runners-up Christy Mathewson and Waite Hoyt. . . . Fifth-highest winning percentage in major-league history among pitchers with at least 100 wins. The list: Dwight Gooden (.721), Spud Chandler (.717), Roger Clemens (.695), Bob Caruthers (.692), and Ford (.690). Among those pitchers, only Caruthers and Ford have more than 200 wins—so far. . . . Won at least 6 games more than he lost in each of his first eight seasons. Only three pitchers in major-league history had streaks that long at any time during their careers: Christy Mathewson, 12 (1903–14); John Clarkson, 9 (1884–92); and Kid Nichols, his first nine seasons (1890–98). . . . Another streak: Winning records in 14 consecutive seasons of at least 10 decisions (1950, 1953–65), the 2d longest in major-league history. Cy Young had a 15-season streak (1890–1904). . . . During his 13 seasons as a full-time starter (1953–65), he pitched 147 complete games. Only Bob Friend had more over that span (152). . . . According to *The Baseball Encyclopedia,* Ford was 36 when he won 24 games in 1963. No other pitcher that old has won as many games since 1915, when George McConnell (38 by the end of the season) won 25 for the Federal League champions, the Chicago Whales.

Rollie Sheldon

Throws Right

New York Yankees	W-L	ERA	AB	H	HR	BB	SO	BA	SA	OBA
Season	11-5	3.60	606	149	17	55	84	.246	.384	.310
vs. Left-Handers			221	57	6	26	40	.258	.403	.336
vs. Right-Handers			385	92	11	29	44	.239	.374	.294
Home Games	8-1	2.33	343	76	6	36	47	.222	.318	.297
Road Games	3-4	5.45	263	73	11	19	37	.278	.471	.327
Day Games	7-4	3.92	415	108	13	45	54	.260	.405	.333
Night Games	4-1	2.92	191	41	4	10	30	.215	.340	.256
April	0-1	2.00	32	7	0	3	10	.219	.281	.286
May	1-1	3.79	71	19	2	10	10	.268	.423	.358
June	3-0	2.86	127	25	5	11	16	.197	.409	.261
July	3-1	3.10	181	44	1	14	24	.243	.304	.299
August	2-1	4.15	118	33	4	10	11	.280	.415	.333
Sept./Oct.	2-1	5.75	77	21	5	7	13	.273	.494	.341
Leading Off Inn.			156	38	6	14	29	.244	.442	.310
Bases Empty			367	92	11	33	59	.251	.398	.314
Runners On			239	57	6	22	25	.238	.364	.303
Runners/Scor. Pos.			110	33	5	12	10	.300	.491	.363
Runners On/2 Out			93	16	2	12	9	.172	.290	.267
Scor. Pos./2 Out			47	9	2	7	4	.191	.362	.296
Late-Inning Pressure			96	24	3	4	13	.250	.417	.280
Leading Off			26	9	1	1	4	.346	.615	.370
Runners On			37	8	1	3	2	.216	.351	.275
Runners/Scor. Pos.			22	5	1	3	1	.227	.364	.320
First 9 Batters			255	62	6	26	42	.243	.353	.313
Second 9 Batters			167	40	5	16	20	.240	.371	.312
All Batters Thereafter			184	47	6	13	22	.255	.440	.303

Loved to face: Gary Geiger (0-for-9)
Zoilo Versalles (0-for-12, 1 BB)
Carl Yastrzemski (.100, 1-for-10)
Hated to face: Earl Battey (3-for-3, 1 BB)
Jim Landis (.714, 5-for-7, 3 HR)

Miscellaneous statistics: Ground outs-to-air outs ratio: 0.94. . . . Induced 18 double-play ground outs in 121 opportunities. . . . Allowed 21 doubles, 6 triples in 162.2 innings. . . . Allowed 5 first-inning runs (all earned) in 21 starts. . . . Batting support: 4.71 runs per start. . . . Opposing base stealers: 7-for-11 (64%); no pickoffs, no balks.

Comments: Was promoted to the Yankees directly from Auburn of the Class D New York–Penn. League after compiling a 15–1 record in 1960, his first season in pro ball. . . . Won consecutive complete-game shutouts over Cleveland and Boston in July. Pitched only two other shutouts during a career in which he started 101 games. . . . Earned a decision in only 66 of 101 career starts (65.3%). Among the 998 pitchers in major-league history who started at least 100 games, only four had lower rates: Wayne Simpson (67 decisions in 107 starts, 62.6%), Lou Kretlow (67-for-104, 64.4%), Bill McGee (66-for-102, 64.7%), and Fred Talbot (66-for-101, 65.3%). Jim Hannan had figures identical to Sheldon's. . . . Had 209 career at-bats without an extra-base hit. Only seven players had no extra-base hits in more at-bats. The most: Virgil Barnes (371). The active leader: Jim Deshaies (297). Incidentally, Jim Hannan (again!) had the same number of at-bats—and no extra-base hits. (Does anyone have a photo of these two together?) . . . Won 10 games for the Kansas City Athletics in 1965 to share the team lead with Fred Talbot. That staff included two future Hall of Famers: Catfish Hunter and Satchel Paige.

Bill Stafford

Throws Right

New York Yankees	W-L	ERA	AB	H	HR	BB	SO	BA	SA	OBA
Season	14-9	2.68	724	168	13	59	101	.232	.329	.294
vs. Left-Handers			267	73	8	22	31	.273	.442	.328
vs. Right-Handers			457	95	5	37	70	.208	.263	.274
Home Games	7-4	2.26	386	85	5	22	53	.220	.293	.267
Road Games	7-5	3.15	338	83	8	37	48	.246	.370	.323
Day Games	6-5	3.05	348	83	7	34	47	.239	.339	.311
Night Games	8-4	2.32	376	85	6	25	54	.226	.319	.277
April	0-0	4.66	32	8	1	6	7	.250	.344	.400
May	1-2	2.84	47	12	0	2	7	.255	.298	.275
June	5-1	2.05	181	41	2	15	22	.227	.326	.289
July	3-2	2.60	126	27	5	10	13	.214	.365	.277
August	3-2	2.79	182	41	2	12	29	.225	.297	.273
Sept./Oct.	1-2	3.31	136	36	3	13	17	.265	.360	.333
Leading Off Inn.			187	42	3	11	22	.225	.299	.268
Bases Empty			435	103	6	33	56	.237	.329	.294
Runners On			289	65	7	26	45	.225	.329	.294
Runners/Scor. Pos.			125	31	4	16	20	.248	.376	.338
Runners On/2 Out			123	23	3	13	24	.187	.293	.265
Scor. Pos./2 Out			64	13	2	10	12	.203	.313	.311
Late-Inning Pressure			61	16	2	10	7	.262	.426	.384
Leading Off			16	5	0	4	0	.313	.313	.450
Runners On			27	7	2	4	5	.259	.556	.394
Runners/Scor. Pos.			8	4	0	2	2	.500	.625	.667
First 9 Batters			269	56	5	22	48	.208	.297	.275
Second 9 Batters			206	47	5	17	28	.228	.345	.292
All Batters Thereafter			249	65	3	20	25	.261	.349	.316

Loved to face: Earl Battey (.100, 1-for-10)
Jim Landis (0-for-16, 1 BB)
Joe Pignatano (0-for-9, 1 BB)
Hated to face: Norm Cash (.667, 6-for-9, 1 HR)
Russ Snyder (.700, 7-for-10, 1 HR)

Miscellaneous statistics: Ground outs-to-air outs ratio: 1.18. . . . Induced 23 double-play ground outs in 156 opportunities. . . . Allowed 19 doubles, 6 triples in 195.0 innings. . . . Allowed 11 first-inning runs (9 earned) in 25 starts. . . . Batting support: 5.04 runs per start. . . . Opposing base stealers: 3-for-9 (33%); no pickoffs, no balks.

Comments: Ranked second in the American League in ERA. Lost the lead on Sept. 24, when Washington's Dick Donovan pitched a one-hitter against the Twins and boosted his innings total above the 162 needed to qualify. Donovan got belted in his next and last start, but his ERA rose only to 2.40, good enough for the title. . . . Claims in Kubek's book *Sixty-One* that Luis Arroyo cost him a shot at 20 wins. In fact, Arroyo, who saved three of Stafford's wins, blew only three of his leads . . . . Pitched more than 400 innings during 1961 and 1962 seasons, only 317.1 after that. . . . Compiled a 29–31 record over seven other seasons in the majors (17–10 before, 12–21 after). Four other pitchers had winning records for the 1961 Yankees and losing records for the remainder of their careers: Luis Arroyo (15–5 in 1961, 25–27 in other seasons), Hal Reniff (2–0, 19–23), Rollie Sheldon (11–5, 27–31), and Ralph Terry (16–3, 91–96). . . . Came within one out of a complete-game shutout in game 3 of the 1962 World Series. But Ed Bailey narrowed New York's lead to 3–2 with a two-run home run before Stafford retired Jim Davenport for the final out. . . . Born in Catskill, New York. (Wife says to her husband, "For our vacation, I want to go somewhere I've never been before." Husband says, "Great! How about the kitchen?" Bah-da-bump.)

Ralph Terry

Throws Right

New York Yankees	W-L	ERA	AB	H	HR	BB	SO	BA	SA	OBA
Season	16-3	3.15	697	162	19	42	87	.232	.366	.275
vs. Left-Handers			259	57	8	19	37	.220	.340	.274
vs. Right-Handers			438	105	11	23	50	.240	.381	.276
Home Games	10-1	2.79	304	63	10	19	45	.207	.355	.255
Road Games	6-2	3.45	393	99	9	23	42	.252	.374	.291
Day Games	9-2	3.54	400	98	14	28	50	.245	.415	.293
Night Games	7-1	2.64	297	64	5	14	37	.215	.300	.251
April	1-0	4.05	53	17	3	7	4	.321	.623	.400
May	1-0	5.63	123	29	6	15	19	.236	.472	.317
June	3-0	2.00	125	21	2	5	20	.168	.272	.200
July	1-1	2.76	62	17	2	9	9	.274	.403	.370
August	5-1	2.45	158	37	2	2	14	.234	.291	.239
Sept./Oct.	5-1	2.89	176	41	4	4	21	.233	.335	.250
Leading Off Inn.			185	38	2	10	20	.205	.286	.246
Bases Empty			464	97	10	28	63	.209	.317	.256
Runners On			233	65	9	14	24	.279	.464	.313
Runners/Scor. Pos.			101	24	2	10	13	.238	.356	.293
Runners On/2 Out			102	24	3	8	13	.235	.373	.291
Scor. Pos./2 Out			51	10	1	4	6	.196	.275	.255
Late-Inning Pressure			87	15	3	4	12	.172	.299	.209
Leading Off			26	4	0	1	2	.154	.192	.185
Runners On			22	3	1	1	4	.136	.273	.174
Runners/Scor. Pos.			7	1	0	0	1	.143	.143	.143
First 9 Batters			254	47	7	14	34	.185	.303	.230
Second 9 Batters			216	53	3	16	32	.245	.347	.295
All Batters Thereafter			227	62	9	12	21	.273	.454	.307

Loved to face: Willie Kirkland (.053, 1-for-19)
Jim Landis (0-for-11, 1 BB)
Johnny Temple (.133, 2-for-15)

Hated to face: Rocky Colavito (.500, 4-for-8, 2 HR)
Norm Siebern (.500, 5-for-10, 2 HR)
Dick Williams (1-for-1, 1 3B, 2 BB)

Miscellaneous statistics: Ground outs-to-air outs ratio: 0.87. . . . Induced 14 double-play ground outs in 107 opportunities. . . . Allowed 24 doubles, 6 triples (none after June 7) in 188.1 innings. . . . Allowed 7 first-inning runs (4 earned) in 27 starts. . . . Batting support: 5.33 runs per start. . . . Opposing base stealers: 8-for-14 (57%); no pickoffs, no balks.

Comments: Losing pitcher in four of the Yankees' eight World Series losses from 1960 through 1962. Would have been 5-for-9 had Bobby Richardson not caught Willie McCovey's would-be game-winner that ended the 1962 Series. . . . Led the American League in wins in 1962 (23), and shared the lead in complete games with Camilo Pascual the next season (18). . . . Only two A.L. pitchers won more games than Terry during his first four full seasons with New York (1960–63). The top three: Whitey Ford, 78; Pascual, 68; Terry, 66. . . . Allowed 40 home runs in 1962, at the time the 2d-highest total in American League history. (Pedro Ramos allowed 43 in 1957.) Strange that Terry led the league in home runs and wins in the same season? No A.L. pitcher since Mike Cuellar in 1970 has done that. But Denny McLain allowed a major-league-high 42 homers when he won 31 games in 1968. . . . Allowed 13 home runs in first 84.2 innings in 1961, only six HRs in 103.2 innings thereafter. . . . Walked only 6 batters over his last 12 starts. . . . Shared league lead with 9 wins through July 4 in 1965, his first season with Cleveland. But he won only twice in 10 more starts that season, and only once more in two remaining seasons in the majors. . . . Struck out three batters over two perfect innings in his final appearance in the majors to reach the 1000-K mark.

Bob Turley

Throws Right

New York Yankees	W-L	ERA	AB	H	HR	BB	SO	BA	SA	OBA
Season	3-5	5.75	275	74	11	51	48	.269	.462	.390
vs. Left-Handers			83	26	6	22	13	.313	.627	.457
vs. Right-Handers			192	48	5	29	35	.250	.391	.358
Home Games	2-1	4.91	107	24	5	24	26	.224	.430	.376
Road Games	1-4	6.33	168	50	6	27	22	.298	.482	.399
Day Games	3-3	5.54	192	48	9	40	39	.250	.458	.386
Night Games	0-2	6.30	83	26	2	11	9	.313	.470	.400
April	2-1	4.05	73	18	2	16	17	.247	.438	.396
May	1-1	5.87	116	31	6	18	16	.267	.448	.372
June	0-3	7.56	69	22	3	11	11	.319	.565	.412
July	0-0	2.45	13	2	0	4	3	.154	.154	.353
August	0-0	—	0	0	0	0	0	—	—	—
Sept./Oct.	0-0	18.00	4	1	0	2	1	.250	.500	.500
Leading Off Inn.			64	17	3	12	11	.266	.500	.390
Bases Empty			143	38	6	29	21	.266	.483	.393
Runners On			132	36	5	22	27	.273	.439	.386
Runners/Scor. Pos.			79	22	2	11	20	.278	.430	.363
Runners On/2 Out			51	14	2	15	12	.275	.490	.448
Scor. Pos./2 Out			37	11	1	9	9	.297	.514	.435
Late-Inning Pressure			13	4	1	3	2	.308	.769	.438
Leading Off			3	1	0	1	1	.333	1.000	.500
Runners On			6	2	1	1	0	.333	1.000	.429
Runners/Scor. Pos.			3	1	0	0	0	.333	.667	.333
First 9 Batters			98	23	1	25	20	.235	.337	.387
Second 9 Batters			81	25	5	12	15	.309	.531	.404
All Batters Thereafter			96	26	5	14	13	.271	.531	.381

Loved to face: Fritzie Brickell (0-for-6, 1 BB)
Leon Wagner (.100, 1-for-10, 1 HR)

Hated to face: Norm Cash (2-for-2, 1 HR, 8 BB)
Rocky Colavito (.556, 5-for-9, 1 HR)
Ted Kluszewski (.714, 5-for-7)
Albie Pearson (.600, 3-for-5, 2 HR)

Miscellaneous statistics: Ground outs-to-air outs ratio: 0.71. . . . Induced 7 double-play ground outs in 75 opportunities. . . . Allowed 14 doubles, 3 triples in 72.0 innings. . . . Allowed 8 first-inning runs (all earned) in 12 starts. . . . Batting support: 4.33 runs per start. . . . Opposing base stealers: 2-for-6 (33%); no pickoffs, no balks.

Comments: Career average of 5.61 walks per nine innings, by far the highest in major-league history among pitchers who started at least 200 games. Runner-up Johnny Vander Meer walked 4.84 per nine. (Turley ranks 7th if the minimum is 100 starts.) . . . Allowed the fewest hits per nine innings in the American League in four of five seasons from 1954 through 1958. (Herb Score led the league in 1956.) Only two pitchers led the league as often as Turley: Nolan Ryan (6 times) and Walter Johnson (5). . . . Made his major-league debut in 1951, and lost in his only appearance of that season. Returned to the majors two years later, and posted these records in succession: 2–6, 14–15, 17–13, 8–4, 13–6, and 21–7 in 1958—a streak of six consecutive seasons in which Bullet Bob improved his winning percentage. The only other pitchers with streaks that long: Lefty Grove (1926–31) and Shufflin' Phil Douglas, who started his career with an 0–1 record in 1912 and improved in each of his eight other seasons until he retired after posting an 11–4 mark in 1922. . . . Joined the Yankees in 1955 as part of a 17-player deal with the Baltimore Orioles that boiled down to Gus Triandos, Hal Smith, Gene Woodling, and Willie Miranda for Turley and Don Larsen. You might say the Yankees overpaid, but a piece of history doesn't come cheaply.